CONDITION[...]
ARE VERY I[...] [...]ORTANT

Check the date on the title page carefully. If the entry herein does not have the date in parentheses, the date must be on the title page. Compare your book's condition with the conditions listed below. All prices in this volume are for books in the following condition:

Books published before 1800: Rebound in the nineteenth century unless otherwise stated. Copies in original bindings (even extensively repaired) or contemporary bindings would have a much higher value.

Books published from 1800 to 1839: Rebound at some early date after the date of publication unless otherwise stated. Binding is clean and intact. The original binding would greatly increase the value.

Books published from 1840 to 1919: In original leather, cloth (cloth-covered boards), boards (paper-covered boards), or wraps unless otherwise stated. Books published from 1840 to 1879 are in good to very good condition with only minor edge wear or loss and still tight and clean. Books published from 1880 to 1919 are clean and bright with no loss or tears on the edges. Copies in fine to very fine condition would bring much more.

Books published from 1920 to 1949: Must be in very good to fine condition with only minimal (if any) soiling. In original dust-wrapper (unless in wraps or in limited-edition slipcase) that is clean, with only minimal soiling or fading, and only a few *small* chips and closed tears. If the dustwrapper is missing, the value is greatly reduced (75 percent on fiction and 20 percent or more on nonfiction).

Books published after 1950: Those published from 1950 to 1975 must be in fine condition, in original dustwrapper that shows only very minor wear, fading, or soiling and that may or may not be price-clipped. Those published from 1975 until the present must, like their dustwrapper, look new, and the dustwrapper must not be price-clipped.

COLLECTED BOOKS

COLLECTED BOOKS

THE GUIDE TO VALUES
2002 EDITION

ALLEN AND
PATRICIA AHEARN

G. P. PUTNAM'S SONS

New York

G. P. Putnam's Sons
Publishers Since 1838
a member of
Penguin Putnam Inc.
375 Hudson Street
New York, NY 10014

Library of Congress Cataloging-in-Publication Data

Ahearn, Allen.
Collected books : the guide to values / Allen and Patricia Ahearn.
2002 ed.
p.   cm.
Includes bibliographical references.
ISBN 0-399-14781-0
1. First Editions—Prices—United States.   2. English imprints—
Prices—United States.   3. Rare books—Prices—United States.
I. Ahearn, Patricia.   II. Title.
Z1033.F53 A39   2001   2001019518
002'.075—dc21

Printed in the United States of America
1   3   5   7   9   10   8   6   4   2

This book is printed on acid-free paper. ∞

Book design by Marysarah Quinn

ACKNOWLEDGMENTS

First and foremost we want to thank the dealers who looked over some of the titles that we had questions about and suggested changes and additions to books in their fields. We do want the users of this volume to understand that we researched and priced all the books and then sent these dealers only those titles we were unsure of. So if there are horrendous errors herein, they most assuredly will be on the books the dealers did not see. These dealers are specialists in the finest sense of the word. They are: Lloyd Currey (L. W. Currey, Inc.), Robert Fleck (Oak Knoll Books), Mike Ginsberg (Michael Ginsberg Books), and Terry Halliday (Wm. Reese Co.).

In addition to the above dealers, we want to acknowledge the following people who took time to answer a number of our questions on certain titles or authors: Todd Amelio (Australian), Sarah Baldwin (nineteenth-century women writers), Lee Biondi (Dickens), Lew Buckingham and Nelson Freck (detective), Andy Cahan (photography), Larry Dingman (Westerns), Joyce Hanrahan (Sendak), Donald Mott (golf), Jo Ann Reisler (children's), Lin Respess (Americana), Richard Shuh (Canadian authors), and Dave Zullo (Civil War). Carl Hahn and Suzanne Regan helped with the research of this volume. And to our proofreaders: Elizabeth Ahearn, Sharon Cramer, Suzanne Regan, and Dyanne Ryan.

We would also like to express our gratitude to all the individuals who have furnished us with specific changes, corrections, additions, clarifications, or assistance over the years since the last edition. First, those who have taken the time to send us many changes: Alan Abrams, Steve Blackmer, Nelson Bond, Greg Brumfield, Richard Coffey, Joe Dermont, Jack

Hanrahan, Aaron Hanson, James Jaffe, Norman and Gary Kane, David Lilburne, Bill Loesser, Jon Meyers, Al Newgarden, Tom Nicely, Joel Sattler, Don Stine, Steve Temple, and Decherd Turner. And the others: Dan and Etta Adams, Don Albright, Tony and Nora Aldridge, Paul Appel, David Aronowitz, Bart Auerbach, Jack Bales, John Ballinger, Daniel Baranow, Pete Baughman, Natalie and David Bauman, Steve Bernard, George Bixby, Mike Van Blaricum, David Brass, Chris Bready, Andreas Brown, P. Scott Brown, Jackson Bryer, Bill Burton, Nigel Burwood, John Campbell, Julie Clem, Tom Congalton, Allan Covici, John Crichton, Jim Dawson, Barry Eigen, Mary Flanders, James Flechtner, Jack Freas, Paul and Beth Garon, Aaron Gobel, Chan and Megan Gordon, Charles Gould, Peter Gould, Craig and Patty Graham, Oscar Graham, Cliff Graubart, Steven Hahn, Bob Harrison, Bob Hicks, Kenneth Hooker, George Houle, Peter Howard, Don and Terry Johanson, Russ Johanson, Helen Kelly, Jeff Klaess, Gerry Kleier, George Koppelman, Richard Lackritz, Daniel Lauffer, Drew Lebby, Ann Lehr, Robert Liska, Ken Lopez, T. N. Luther, Jeff Marks, Dave Meeker, Edmund Miller, Larry Moskowitz, Andy Moursand, Ed and Judy Myers, Frannie Ness, Maurice Neville, Martin O'Connell, Gary Olsen, Al Palanker, Otto Penzler, A. E. Reiff, Lyman Rhodes, Ken Sanders, Harvey Sarner, Dick Scarafoni, Steve Schwartz, Ralph Sipper, Robin and Kathryn Smiley, Dan Spiegelman, R. Starnes, Peter Stern, Bill Swing, Dick Sykes, David Szewczyk, Vic Tavistock, Frederic Taylor, James Taylor, Jan Tonnesen, Jim Visbeck, Tom Wall, Martin Weinkle, Lou Weinstein, Marshall White, David Williams, Dick Wilson, John Windle, Gene Winn, John Wronosky, and Helen Younger.

A special thanks, of course, to the dealers who keep us on their mailing lists, which is the only way we can try (a vain attempt) to keep current on prices: About Books; Nick Adams & Co.; Charles Agvent; Alder Books; Aldredge Book Shop; Alphabet Bookshop; American Dust Co.; The Americanist; Am Here Books; Ampersand Books; Anacapa Books; Annex Books; Hugh Anson-Cartwright; Antic Hay Rare Books; Antipodean Books Maps & Prints; Any Amount of Books; Argosy Book Store; Ash Rare Books; Ashlar Books; The Associates; Attic Books; Authors of the West; Bert Babcock; Baltimore Book Company; Bartleby's Books; Bay Side Books; Beasley Books; Gordon Beckhorn; Bell, Book & Radmall; Steven C. Bernard; Between the Covers; Biblioctopus; Bishop of Books; Black-Bird Books; Black Sun Books; Blackwell's Rare Books; Bolerium Books; Nelson Bond; Book Block; Bookpress; The Book Shelf; Books & Autographs; The Bookshop; Books West Southwest; The Book Treasury; Boston Book Company & Book Annex; Bowie & Company; Marilyn Braiterman; The Brick Row Bookshop; Bromer Booksellers; Brunswick Press; Buckingham Books; Buddenbrooks; Burke's Book

Store; Harold M. Burnstein & Co.; Nicholas and Helen Burrows; John R. Butterworth; By the Way Books; Caliban Book Shop; Joel and Shelley Caney; The Captain's Book Shelf; Nicholas Certo; Bev Channey, Jr.; Chapel Hill Rare Books; Chloe's Books; Christie's; Christie's East; Clearwater Books; Clover Hill Books; Colophon Book Shop; Conundrum; Country Lane Books; N. A. Cournoyer Books; William Cowan Books; Cultured Oyster Books; James Cummins; L. W. Currey; Robert Dagg; William & Victoria Dailey; Dalian Books; D & D Galleries; Tom Davidson; Decline and Fall; Joseph A. Dermont; Detering Book Gallery; Dinkytown Antiquarian Bookstore; Thomas Dorn; James M. Dourgarian; Duga's Books; Dunn and Powell; I. D. Edrich; Francis Edwards; Else Fine Books; Ergo Books; Estates of Mind; Euclid Books; The Fine Book Co.; First Editions; First Editions Books; First Folio; First Impressions; Forest Books; Robert Gavora; R. A. Gekoski; Thomas A. Goldwasser; Gotham Book Mart; Gravesend Books; Great Northwest Bookstore; Paulette Greene; Gregor Books; J & J Hanrahan; Hawthorn Books; Heirloom Bookstore; Susan Heller; Heritage Bookshop; The Hermitage Bookshop; Willis E. Herr; Historicana; Richard L. Hoffman; David Holloway; David J. Holmes; Glenn Horowitz; George Houle; John Hudak; In Our Time; James S. Jaffe; Janus Books; Jarndyce Antiquarian Books; Joseph and Provider Books; The Jumping Frog; Priscilla Juvelis; Kane Antiquarian Auction; Kenneth Karmiole; Katonah Book Scout; Key West Island Bookstore; Gerry Kleier; Susan Klein; John W. Knott, Jr.; Ralph Kristiansen; Kugleman & Bent; Lame Duck Books; Larsen Books; James & Mary Laurie; Leaves of Grass; John Le Bow; Barry R. Levin; Ken Lopez; Robert Loren Link; Stephen Lupack; MacDonnell Rare Books; Ian McKelvie; George S. MacManus Co.; Robert A. Madle; Maggs Brothers ltd.; Magnum Opus; Maple Ridge Books; David Mason; David Mayou; McClintock Books; McGowan Book Company; Ming Books; George Robert Minkoff; Monroe Books; Hartley Moorhouse Books; Mordida Books; S. M. Mossberg; Howard S. Mott, Inc.; J. B. Muns; Mysterious Bookshop; Julian Nangle; Nineteenth Century Shop; Nouveau; Oak Knoll Books; Old New York Book Shop; John Oliveri; James F. O'Neil; Orpheus Books; James Pepper; Diane Peterson; R. & A. Petrilla; Pettler & Liberman; Phoenix Bookshop South; James M. Pickard; Philip J. Pirages; Polyanthos Books; Nicholas Pounder's Bookshop; John William Pye; Bernard Quaritch, Ltd.; Randall House; Paul Rassam; David Rees; William Reese Company; L & T Respess Books; Revere Books; Alice Robbins; Robert Frost Books; Bertram Rota; The Rue Morgue; Rulon-Miller Books, Rykken and Scull; Schoyer's Books; Bud Schweska; Andrew Sclanders; Second Life Books; Second Story Books; Peter Selley; Charles Seluzicki; Serendipity Books; Sherwood Fine Books; Skyline

Books; Ed Smith; Sotheby Parke Bernet, Inc.; Monroe Stahr Books; Christopher P. Stephens; Peter Stern; Summer & Stillman; Sylvester & Orphanos; Tamerlane Books; Taugher Books; Tavistock Books; Robert Temple; Steven Temple Books; Jeffrey Thomas; Michael Thompson; Michael R. Thompson; TLC Books; Henry E. Turlington; Turtle Island Booksellers; Ulysses Bookshop; Len Unger Rare Books; Vagabond Books; Versetility Books; Virgo Books; Waiting for Godot Books; Rob Warren; Watermark West; Water Row Books; Waverly Auctions; Waverly Books; Wessel & Liebermann; E. Wharton & Co.; Jett W. Whitehead; Nigel Williams; John Windle; J. Howard Woolmer; Robert Wright Books; Wrigley-Cross Books; Herb Yellin; and Yesterday's Books.

If we have inadvertently left anyone out, we sincerely apologize; we appreciate and use all of the feedback we get on our work.

CONTENTS

INTRODUCTION   *1*

USING THIS GUIDE   *3*

COLLECTED BOOKS AND THEIR VALUES   7

APPENDIX A. SELECTED BIBLIOGRAPHY
OF WORKS CONSULTED   *729*

APPENDIX B. FIRST-EDITION IDENTIFICATION
BY PUBLISHER   *772*

INTRODUCTION

This is the third edition of this book. We initiated the series in 1991 as a continuation of Van Allen Bradley's highly regarded *Handbook of Values.* We had been issuing price guides since 1975, when we self-published the *Book of First Books,* a price guide to authors' first books. We updated it in 1978, 1983, and 1986, and Putnam published an expanded edition in 1989 as *Book Collecting: A Comprehensive Guide.* In 1984, we started self-publishing our Author Price Guide series, which now counts 174 authors. We have tried to make our work bibliographically correct, so that a user can identify and price a book in hand. The Internet has become the pricer of first resort since it reached critical mass in 2000, with entries for at least 20 million books on-line. We are constantly reminded, however, that the points necessary to identify first printings and first states or issues are not always given on the Internet. In many cases, in fact, the information is incorrect or misleading, and thus there is a strong justification for this guide for people interested in buying or selling scarce and rare first editions and being assured their offerings or purchases are bibliographically correct.

Prices have risen drastically for first editions of important works in the last decade, and there seems no end in sight. When we compiled the first *Book of First Books* in 1975, J. D. Salinger's *The Catcher in the Rye* was priced at $75, and Harper Lee's *To Kill a Mockingbird* at $25. At a Christie's East auction in April 2001, unsigned first editions of these titles sold for $33,000 each (including the buyer's premium). This was a sharp increase over what we had thought was the going price, half the actual amounts at best. Like most other dealers and collectors, we are constantly surprised by the ever-escalating prices.

These rapidly increasing prices on highly prized titles represent only a small part of the overall collected-books market. The advent of Internet search engines, with ABE.com in the forefront at present, has shown a much more accurate picture of the availability or scarcity of individual titles. Books we thought were relatively scarce a few years ago are in reality relatively common, with 30 to 100 copies indicated on the Web. As a result, retail prices for those books, which might have been in the $50-to-$150 range, have dropped to $15 to $50. Conversely, titles that we knew were very scarce, if not rare, are not shown on the Web, or if they do turn up, they are priced higher and higher. The law of supply and demand, which drives the prices in this market as in other markets, has been affected by the much more accurate picture of true supply (about which we all made guesses before we relied on the Web).

We believe this book will prove useful by taking a snapshot in time of the values for a selection of the collected books. The bibliographic information for identifying first editions is, of course, necessary; but we sense that over the next few years, the Internet may not be as useful a price guide as it has been, because the comparable books will not be listed there. Already we find, in looking for certain titles, that where fifty copies were indicated on-line a year ago, with probably ten in collectible condition, now there may be only ten copies indicated, and none in collectible condition. The search on-line for copies comparable with or similar to yours, then, may not be as fruitful. And since condition is so important to price, with a fine copy in hand, does it really help to know there are five copies in poor condition available on-line for low prices?

We hope that the information presented here is accurate, and we encourage correspondence on errors or confusing entries. We believe the prices represent current retail, but with a total of 20,000 or so, it is unlikely that all the prices are right. We advise you to take everything with a grain of salt and consult other sources before making a final decision on pricing or buying an expensive book.

In addition to our own experience buying and selling, we have used auction, Internet, and catalogue prices, or projections from these prices, to estimate ours. Remember that a guide such as this may underprice scarce or rare books, and that truly scarce titles may be priced far above the estimates when and if they do appear on the market. This is only reasonable, for estimates on the scarce books are based on very few and, in some cases, relatively old appearances at auction or in catalogues.

Have fun and enjoy the chase. There are plenty of good books—and good people—to meet out there.

USING THIS GUIDE

All books listed herein are first editions/first printings of the individual titles unless otherwise stated. Each of the entries includes sufficient information to allow the reader to identify first editions of a book in hand. The prices are current (2001) rather than projections. What we have tried to do is outline how a publisher identifies first editions (see below) and then note exceptions. In other words, if Random House in the 1950s stated "first edition" and a Random House title herein does not state first, the entry will include "first edition not stated."

The estimated values are believed to be accurate plus or minus 20 percent. Remember, we are not trying to tell you if a book is $50 or $60, or $500 or $600; we are trying to tell you if it is a $50 book or a $500 book. The more expensive it is, the more research you should do before buying or selling.

Estimated prices at retail are based on:

Books published before 1800: Rebound in the nineteenth century unless otherwise stated. Copies in original bindings (even extensively repaired) or contemporary bindings would have a much higher value.

Books published from 1800 to 1839: Rebound at some early date after the date of publication unless otherwise stated. Binding is clean and intact. The original binding would greatly increase the value.

Books published after 1840 to 1919: In original leather, cloth (cloth-covered boards), boards (paper-covered boards), or wraps unless otherwise stated. From 1840 to 1879 the book is good to very good condition with only minor edge wear or loss but still tight and clean. From 1880 to 1919 the book is clean and bright with no loss or tears on the edges. Fine to very fine copies would bring much more.

Books published from 1920 to 1949: Must be very good to fine with only minimal (if any) soiling. In original dustwrapper (unless in wraps or a limited edition in slipcase) that is clean with only minimal soiling or fading and only a few *small* chips and closed tears. If the dustwrapper is missing the value is greatly reduced (75 percent on fiction and 20 percent or more on non-fiction).

Books published after 1950: A book from 1950 to 1975 must be fine in original dustwrapper that shows only very minor wear, fading or soiling and may or may not be price-clipped. From 1975 until the present the book and dustwrapper must look like new and the dustwrapper not be price-clipped.

NOTE:

Persons interested in offering books listed in this book for sale to book dealers must understand that the prices herein represent the estimated retail price one might expect to pay to a book dealer to purchase a particular book when the book is in the condition noted above. Lesser copies are worth less. Exceptional copies of notable rarities are worth more. Book dealers are classic examples of small independent businesses, and they cannot be expected to pay the full estimated value for copies of books listed. The percentage of value one can expect from a dealer will vary, but one should not anticipate more than 40 to 50 percent of estimated value for other than prime items from a dealer and lesser amounts on books with long shelf lives. One alternative to consider is a trade value for your books that can be used on books the dealer owns. The percentage of return on trade will normally be higher than a straight sale, but this will depend on what you are offering and what you wish to swap for. Most dealers are not interested in accepting several lower-value books in exchange for a higher-value title. They will usually be happy to accept them for similarly priced books. Understand further that even though you may own books listed in this volume, that is no guarantee that a dealer will automatically be interested in buying or trading for them. Most dealers specialize in particular areas and are not interested in less-than-prime titles outside their fields. On the other hand, most responsible dealers would be glad to try to suggest dealers in other fields for books that they have no interest in purchasing. This is usually a courtesy and not a payable service.

The entries are composed of:

Author, title, place of publication, date of publication, and only that additional information needed to identify the issue, the state or edition, and the value.

All entries are first editions (first printings) unless otherwise stated. "Trade" is used to indicate the first general edition available for public sale after a limited edition has been issued. Usually the same sheets are used for both the limited and trade editions.

If the author's name does not appear on the title page, the entry will start with the title. If the author used a pseudonym, the pseudonym will appear first and the entry will include the author's name in parentheses.

Occasionally, the entry will reference VAB (Van Allen Bradley's *Handbook of Values,* 1982–1983) if there were points in VAB that could not be found in any other reference work and we thought they should not be left out. In addition, some entries include reference to specific bibliographies, such as *Bibliography of American Literature* (BAL) and *Modern First Editions,* by Merle Johnson (Johnson). Full titles of these and other bibliographies used to develop this guide can be found at the end of this book.

If the place of publication or date does not appear on the title page, this information will be in parentheses. This is *particularly significant* because the presence of a date on the title page may be the only way to differentiate between first and later printings.

If the place of publication or date does not appear in the book at all but is known by the compilers, it will appear in brackets, i.e. [1969].

If there is no date on the title page, checking to see if the publisher is one of the following reprint publishers would immediately tell you the book is not a first edition (with a few exceptions specifically noted in the entries): Blakiston, A. L. Burt, Grosset & Dunlap, Hurst, Modern Library, Sun Dial, or Tower Books (World).

If the entry states a quantity of copies, such as **"One of 500 copies,"** this means the edition is numbered 1 to 500 or states somewhere in the book that it is one of 500 copies. If the entry states **"One of 26 copies,"** it means 26 copies were lettered A to Z. If the entry includes a quantity in parentheses **"(200 copies),"** it means it is known that there were 200 copies printed, but there is no indication in the book itself of this fact.

It should be noted that most Book-of-the-Month Club editions look exactly like true first editions and may actually state "First Edition," but until the 1970s had a small black circle or a blindstamp (in a circular, square, or maple-leaf pattern) on the lower right corner of the back cover. Since the 1970s, they have become difficult to identify, as the only difference is that the book-club edition dustwrappers do not bear a price. These books are not first editions.

COLLECTED BOOKS
AND THEIR VALUES

ALL books listed herein are
FIRST EDITIONS/FIRST PRINTINGS
OF THE INDIVIDUAL TITLES
unless otherwise stated.

A

A. *Strayed Reveller (The), and Other Poems.* London, 1849. By A. (Matthew Arnold.) Dark-green cloth. One of 500 copies, most withdrawn soon after publication. $750.

A., T.B. *The Bells: A Collection of Chimes.* By T.B.A. New York, 1855. (By Thomas Bailey Aldrich.) Author's first book. $350.

ABBEY, Edward. *Abbey's Road.* E. P. Dutton, 1979. Contains "The Right to Arms," The Winnebago Tribe," and "The Sorrows of Travel." $400.

ABBEY, Edward. *Appalachian Wilderness.* New York, 1970. With photographs by Eliot Porter. $200.

ABBEY, Edward. *The Brave Cowboy.* New York (1956). $7,500. London, 1957. $1,250. Santa Barbara/Salt Lake City, 1993. One of 500 copies signed by Kirk Douglas. $150.

ABBEY, Edward. *Desert Solitaire.* New York (1968). $750.

ABBEY, Edward. *Fire on the Mountain.* New York, 1962. $1,000. London, 1963. $500.

ABBEY, Edward. *Jonathan Troy.* New York, 1954. Author's first book. $1,750.

ABBEY, Edward. *The Monkey Wrench Gang.* Philadelphia (1975). $350. Edinburgh (1978). $175. Salt Lake City, 1985. One of 15 copies signed and lettered ("A" through "O") copies designated "Publisher's Presentation Copy," with signed print by Crumb laid in. In slipcase. $1,500. One of 250 signed copies with signed and numbered print by Crumb laid in. In slipcase. Tenth Anniversary Edition. $1,000. [There was an earlier version of the limited edition that was destroyed with very few surviving copies. Bound in black cloth with a red buckram slipcase.] Salt Lake City, 1985. Trade edition with added chapter. $125.

ABBEY, J. R. *Life in England in Aquatint and Lithography, 1770–1860.* London, 1953. One of 400 copies. $850.

ABBEY, J. R. *Scenery of Great Britain and Ireland in Aquatint and Lithography, 1770–1860 . . .* London, 1952. One of 500 copies. In dustwrapper. $1,000.

ABBEY, J. R. *Travel in Aquatint and Lithography, 1770–1860.* London, 1956. 2 vols. One of 400 copies. $1,000.

ABBEY, James. *California: A Trip Across the Plains in the Spring of 1850.* New Albany, Ind., 1850. 64 pages, printed wraps. $7,500.

ABBOT, Anthony. *About the Murder of Geraldine Foster.* New York, 1930. (By Charles Fulton Oursler.) Author's first book. $350.

ABBOTSFORD, *and Newstead Abbey.* London, 1835. By the Author of "The Sketch-Book" (Washington Irving.) $300. Philadelphia, 1835. With copyright notices on both pages (2) and (4). $200.

ABBOTT, Berenice. *Changing New York.* New York, 1939. $1,000.

ABBOTT, Berenice. *Greenwich Village, Today and Yesterday.* New York (1949). $300.

ABBOTT, Berenice. *The World of Atget.* New York, 1964. $200.

ABBOTT, Charles D. *Howard Pyle: A Chronicle.* New York, 1925. $350.

ABBOTT, E. C. (Teddy Blue), and SMITH, Helena Huntington. *We Pointed Them North.* New York (1939). $400.

ABBOTT, Edward Abott. See *A Square.*

ABBOTT, John S(tevens) C(abot). *The Mother at Home.* Boston, 1833. Blue cloth spine, tan boards. $250.

ABE, Kobo. *The Woman in the Dunes.* New York, 1964. (First U.S. edition). $175. London, 1965. $50.

A'BECKETT, Gilbert Abbott. *The Comic History of England.* London, 1846–48. Illustrated in color by John Leech. 20 parts in 19, blue wraps. $1,250. London, 1847–48. 2 vols. First edition in book form. $600.

A'BECKETT, Gilbert Abbott. *The Comic History of Rome.* London [1852]. $600. 10 parts in 9. Green wraps. $1,250.

ABERCROMBIE, John. *The British Fruit-Gardner; and Art of Pruning . . .* London, 1779. $600.

ABERCROMBIE, John. *The Hot-House Gardener on the General Culture of the Pineapple . . .* London, 1789. 5 hand-colored plates. $1,500.

ABERCROMBIE, Capt. W. R. *Cooper River Exploring Expedition.* Washington, D.C., 1900. Folding map. $750.

ABISH, Walter. *Duel Site.* New York, 1970. Author's first book. Wraps. One of 300 copies. $200.

ABRAHAMS, Peter. *A Blackman Speaks of Freedom.* Durban, 1938. Author's first book. Wraps. $400.

ABRAHAMS, Peter. *Dark Testament.* London, 1942. $300.

AB-SA-RA-KA, Home of the Crows. Philadelphia, 1868. (By Mrs. Henry B. Carrington.) Folding map. Cloth. $600.

ABSE, Dannie. *After Every Green Thing.* London, 1949. Author's first book. $100.

ABSTRACT of Land Claims Compiled from the Records of the General Land Office of the State of Texas . . . Galveston, 1852. By John Burlage and J. P. Hollingsworth. Third edition. $1,750. The first, 1838, is virtually unobtainable, while the second, 1841, is only slightly less rare.

ABSTRACT or The Leavves of Nevvy Englnd, as They Are Novv Established. London, 1641. This is the first Anglo-American law code. $10,000.

ACCUM, Frederick. *A Practical Treatise on Gas-Light.* London, 1815. 7 hand-colored plates, 2 folding. $1,250.

ACELDAMA, a Place to Bury Strangers In. London, 1898. By a Gentleman of the University of Cambridge. (Aleister Crowley.) Wraps. Author's first book. $1,250.

ACHEBE, Chinua. *Things Fall Apart.* London, 1958. Author's first book. $250. New York, 1958. $150.

ACKERLEY, J. R. *Poems by Four Authors.* London, 1923. Author's first book. $250.

ACKERLEY, J. R. *The Prisoners of War.* London, 1925. Wraps. $350.

ACKERMANN, Rudolph. *A History of Eton College.* 10 colored plates. $1,500.

ACKERMANN, Rudolph. *The History of the Abbey Church of St. Peter's . . .* London, 1812. 2 vols. Portrait. First plate in volume by MacKenzie. $3,500. With plate by Pugin. $3,500.

ACKERMANN, Rudolph. *The History of the Colleges of Winchester, Eton, and Westminster.* Ackermann, 1816. 48 hand-colored aquatints, uncolored extra plate. First issue of "Westminster School Room" has the masters bareheaded. $7,500. Second issue of Charter House plate has washerwomen but with slip pasted over original "school" title. $6,000. Third issue with the plate "Charter House from the Playground." $5,000.

ACKERMANN, Rudolph. *The Microcosm of London.* London, (1808–10). 3 vols. 104 colored aquatint plates by Pugin and Rowlandson. $12,500. London, 1904. 3 vols. Parchment and boards. $600.

ACKERMANN, Rudolph (publisher). *A History of the University of Cambridge.* London, 1815. 2 vols. Illustrated with color plates. $7,500.

ACKERMANN, Rudolph (publisher). *A History of the University of Oxford.* London, 1814. Illustrated with colored plates (check further, we have noted copies with 82 to 119 hand-colored plates). 2 vols. $7,500.

ACKLEY, Mary E. *Crossing the Plains and Early Days in California.* San Francisco, 1928. Illustrated. Boards, printed label on spine. $350.

ACKROYD, Peter. *London Lickpenny.* London, 1973. One of 26 signed copies. Wraps. $300. One of 474 copies. $75.

ACKROYD, Peter. *Ouch.* London, 1971. Author's first book. One of about 200 copies. Entire issue of *The Curiously Strong,* vol. 4, no. 2 (October 31, 1971). Wraps. $350.

ACORN, Milton. *In Love and Anger.* Montreal, 1956. Author's first book. Wraps. $750.

ACOSTA, Oscar "Zeta." *The Autobiography of a Brown Buffalo.* (San Francisco, 1972.) Hardcover and wraps. First printing stated. $100.

ACTON, Harold. *Aquarium.* London, 1923. Author's first book. Plain dustwrapper. $600.

ACTON, Harold. *The Last of the Medici.* Florence, Italy, 1930. Introduction by Norman Douglas. Portrait. Boards. One of 365 signed copies. $500.

ADAIR, James. *The History of the American Indians; Particularly Those Nations Adjoining to the Mississippi, East and West Florida, Georgia, South and North Carolina, and Virginia . . . Also an Appen-*

dix Containing a Description of the Floridas, and the Mississippi Lands . . . London, 1775. Folding map. $3,500.

ADAM, G. M. (editor). *Sandow's System of Physical Training.* New York, 1894. 8½ by 10 inches. $300.

ADAM, Helen (Douglas). *The Elfin Pedlar 7 Tales Told by Pixie Pool.* London, 1923. Author's first book. $200

ADAM, R. B. *The R. B. Adam Library Relating to Dr. Samuel Johnson.* London/New York, 1929, 1930. 4 vols. (the fourth was issued separately in 1930 without dustwrapper). The first three volumes were limited to 500 copies, the fourth volume was limited to 225 copies. The four together. $1,000.

ADAMS, Alice. *Careless Love.* New York, 1966. Author's first book. $300.

ADAMS, Andy. *The Log of a Cowboy.* Boston, 1903. Author's first book. Map, 6 plates. Brown pictorial cloth. First issue, with map at page 28 not in list of illustrations. $300.

ADAMS, Andy. *The Ranch on the Beaver.* Boston, 1927. With illustrations by Edward Borein. $300.

ADAMS, Andy. *Texas Matchmaker.* Boston, 1904. $100.

ADAMS, Ansel. See Austin, Mary.

ADAMS, Ansel (photographer). *Images: 1923–1974.* New York, 1974. $250. One of 1,000 copies, with original signed print. $2,500. Also for Time-Life subscribers with tipped-in signed page. $450.

ADAMS, Ansel (photographer). *Making a Photograph.* London (1935). $350.

ADAMS, Ansel (photographer). *My Camera in Yosemite Valley.* Yosemite and Boston, 1949. Wraps. $600.

ADAMS, Ansel (photographer). *Portfolio Four* . . . San Francisco, 1963. One of 250 copies. Portfolio includes 15 signed photographs. $25,000 at auction in 1998.

ADAMS, Ansel (photographer). *Portfolio Three* . . . San Francisco, 1960. One of 200 copies. Portfolio includes 16 signed photographs. $44,000 at auction in 1999.

ADAMS, Ansel (photographer). *Sierra Nevada* . . . Berkeley, 1938. One of 500 signed copies. Issued in dustwrapper. $3,000.

ADAMS, Ansel (photographer). *Taos Pueblo.* San Francisco: Grabhorn Press, 1930. Written with Mary Austin. Author's first book. One of 108 copies signed by both. Folio. $40,000. Boston, 1977. One of 950 copies signed by Adams. $1,500.

ADAMS, Charles F., Jr., and ADAMS, Henry. *Chapters of Erie, and Other Essays.* Boston, 1871. $350.

ADAMS, Edward C. L. *Congaree Sketches* . . . Chapel Hill, 1927. Author's first book. One of 200 signed copies. $300. Trade edition. $150.

ADAMS, Frederick Upham. *President John Smith* . . . Chicago, 1897. Wraps. $150.

ADAMS, Hannah. *An Alphabetical Compendium* . . . Boston, 1784. $1,250.

ADAMS, Hannah. *A Summary History of New England* . . . Dedham (1799). $250.

ADAMS, Henry. See Adams, Charles F., Jr. See also *Democracy; Mont Saint Michel and Chartres.*

ADAMS, Henry. *Civil Service Reform.* Boston, 1869. Author's first book. Wraps. $2,250.

ADAMS, Henry. *The Education of Henry Adams.* Washington, 1907. Blue cloth, leather spine label. One of 100 copies. $6,000. Boston, 1918. Revised and edited by Henry Cabot Lodge. First trade edition. In dustwrapper. $750. Without. $100. Limited Editions Club, New York, 1942. Etchings by Samuel Chamberlain. In slipcase. $125.

ADAMS, Henry. *A Letter to American Teachers of History.* Washington, 1910. $250.

ADAMS, J. C. *Life of J. C. Adams.* (Cover title.) (New York, 1860.) 29 pages, printed wraps. $2,000. Lacking covers, and with caption title only: *The Hair-Breadth Escapes and Adventures of "Grizzly Adams."* $1,500.

ADAMS, James Truslow. *Memorials of Old Bridgehampton.* 1916. Author's first book. $250.

ADAMS, John Quincy. *Oration on the Life and Character of Gilbert Motier de Lafayette.* Washington, 1835. Original wraps. $250. One of a few on thick paper, specially bound in morocco. $1,000.

ADAMS, Leonie. *High Falcon and Other Poems.* New York (1929). First binding in cloth and boards. $200. Second binding in brown cloth. $150.

ADAMS, Leonie. *Those Not Elect.* New York, 1925. Author's first book. One of 10 signed copies. $750. Trade. $250.

ADAMS, Ramon F. *Cowboy Lingo.* Boston, 1936. Author's first book. $250.

ADAMS, Ramon. *The Rampaging Herd.* Norman, Okla., 1959. $150.

ADAMS, Ramon F., and BRITZMAN, Homer E. *Charles M. Russell, The Cowboy Artist: A Biography* with *Charles M. Russell, The Cowboy Artist: A Bibliography.* By Karl Yost with a note by Homer E. Britzman and Frederic G. Renner. Pasadena (1948). 2 vols. In slipcase. (1,600 copies.) $400.

ADAMS, Richard. *Watership Down.* London, 1972. Author's first book. $1,500. New York, 1974. $175. London, 1976. One of 250 signed copies. In slipcase. $2,250.

ADAMS, Robert. *The New West.* (Boulder): 1974. $600.

ADAMS, Thomas. *Typographia: Or the Printer's Instructor* . . . Philadelphia, 1837. $500. Later editions with numerous emendations and additions are in the $200-to-$300 range.

ADAMS, Will. *Errata: or, The Works of Will Adams.* New York, 1823. (By John Neal.) 2 vols. $200.

ADAMS, William Taylor. See Ashton, Warren T.; Optic, Oliver.

ADDAMS, Charles. *Drawn and Quartered.* New York, 1942. Author's first book. $400.

ADDISON, Lancelot. *The Present State of the Jews.* London, 1675. $1,500.

ADDISON, Lancelot. *West Barbary . . .* Oxford, 1671. Title page, dedication, preface, and an index of Moorish words at end. $1,500.

ADE, George. *Artie.* Chicago, 1896. Author's first regularly published book. Cloth. $75.

ADE, George. *Circus Day.* Chicago, 1896. Author's first book. (5 previous anonymous offprints from Chicago quarterly.) $750.

ADE, George. *One Afternoon with Mark Twain.* (Chicago) 1939. One of 350 copies. Stiff wraps. $175.

ADE, George. *Revived Remarks on Mark Twain.* Chicago, 1936. 36 pages, wraps. One of 500 signed copies. $200. Also, one of 500 copies unsigned. $100.

ADE, George. *The Strenuous Lad's Library.* Phoenix, 1903–4. 3 vols. Wraps. $1,500.

ADELER, Max. *Out of the Hurly-Burly.* Illustrated by A. B. Frost and others. Philadelphia, 1874. (By Charles Heber Clark.) Author's first book and first book illustrated by Frost. Decorated cloth. $200.

ADVENTURES of a Brownie (The), as Told to My Child. London, 1872. By the Author of *"John Halifax, Gentleman."* (Dinah M. Craik.) $600.

ADVENTURES of a Post Captain . . . (The). London (1817). By a Naval Officer (Alfred Thornton.) Engraved title and 24 colored plates. First issued printed by J. and T. Agg. $1,000. Second issue printed by W. Lewis. $600.

ADVENTURES of a Younger Son (The). London, 1831. (By Edward John Trelawny.) 3 vols. Author's first book. $350.

ADVENTURES of David Simple (The). London, 1744. (By Sarah Fielding.) 2 vols. Author's first book. $1,250. Second, revised and corrected. $600.

ADVENTURES of Harry Franco (The). New York, 1839. (By Charles Frederick Briggs.) 2 vols. Author's first book. $350.

ADVENTURES of Hunters and Travellers, and Narratives of Border Warfare. Philadelphia, 1852. By "An Old Hunter." $350.

ADVENTURES of Peregrine Pickle (The). (London, 1751.) (By Tobias Smollett.) 4 vols. Blank leaf at end of volumes 2 and 3. $1,000. Limited Editions Club, Oxford, 1935. 2 vols. $100.

ADVENTURES of Robin Day (The). Philadelphia, 1839. (By Robert Montgomery Bird.) 2 vols. $450.

ADVENTURES of Roderick Random, The. London, 1748. (By Smollett, Tobias.) Author's first book. 2 vols. $1,500.

ADVENTURES of Timothy Peacock, Esquire (The). Middlebury, Vt., 1835. By a Member of the Vermont Bar. (Daniel Pierce Thompson.) Author's first novel. $750.

ADVENTURES of Ulysses (The). London, 1808. (By Charles Lamb.) Frontispiece, engraved title page. $750.

AESCHYLUS. *Agamemnon: A Tragedy.* (London, 1865.) Translated by Edward FitzGerald. Wraps. $1,250. London, 1876. Half leather. One of 250 copies. $500.

AESOP. *Fables.* [Auction price records for the past 20 years show that the earliest editions to appear on the market were from 1479 (which sold in 1993 for $19,240) and 1485 (with prices in 1988 of $121,550 and $168,000.)] London, 1651. Translated by John Ogilby. Frontispiece of Aesop among the animals and 80 engraved full-page plates. $7,500. London, 1793. 2 vols. 112 plates. $2,000. London, 1912. V. S. Vernon Jones translation. Illustrated by Arthur Rackham. 1,450 copies signed by Rackham. $2,500. Harrison of Paris: New York (1931). L'Estrange translation, with 50 drawings by Alexander Calder. One of 50 copies with an original signed ink drawing by Calder. $7,500. One of 495 copies. $1,250. London, 1936. Sir Roger L'Estrange translation. Illustrated by Stephen Gooden. Vellum. One of 525 copies signed by Gooden. In slipcase. $1,250. Limited Editions Club, New York, 1933. Samuel Croxall translation. Illustrated by Bruce Rogers. Boards and vellum. In slipcase. $300.

AGASSIZ, Louis. *Lake Superior.* Boston, 1850. 16 plates. $550.

AGATE, James. *L. of C. (Lines of Communication).* London, 1917. Author's first book. $100.

AGATE, James. *A Shorter Ego: The Autobiography of James Agate.* London (1945). 2 vols. half morocco. One of 100 signed copies. $175.

AGEE, G. W. *Rube Burrows, King of Outlaws.* (Cincinnati, 1890.) 194 pages, wraps. $350.

AGEE, James. *A Death in the Family.* New York (1957). Blue cloth. First issue, with title page printed in blue, "walking" for "waking" on page 80. $300. Second issue, "waking." $75.

AGEE, James. *Four Early Stories.* West Branch, Iowa, 1964. One of 285 copies. In handmade paper dustwrapper. $350.

AGEE, James. *Let Us Now Praise Famous Men.* Boston, 1941. Walker Evans photographs. Black cloth. $2,500. Boston (1960). $100. London, 1965. $75.

AGEE, James. *The Morning Watch.* Rome, 1950. Wraps. (Offprint from Botteghe Oscure.) $1,250. Boston, 1951. $250. London, 1952. $125.

AGEE, James. *Permit Me Voyage.* New Haven, 1934. Author's first book. $750.

Age of Bronze (The). London, 1823. (By George Gordon Noel, Lord Byron.) $450.

AGNER, Dwight. *The Books of WAD: A Bibliography of the Books Designed by W.A. Dwiggins.* Baton Rouge, 1974. One of 206 copies. 190 in cloth and boards. $250. One of 16 copies on large paper, half morocco. $600.

AGNES De Castro. London, 1696. (By Catherine Trotter Cockburn.) Author's first book. $750.

AGRICOLA, Georgius. See Hoover, Herbert C., and Henry, Lou.

AICKMAN, Robert. *Dark Entries.* London, 1964. $600.

AICKMAN, Robert. *Powers of Darkness.* London, 1966. $600.

AIKEN, Conrad. *Blue Voyage.* New York, 1927. $200. One of 125 signed copies. Issued in slipcase. $450. Trade edition. $150.

AIKEN, Conrad. *The Coming Forth by Day of Osiris Jones.* New York, 1931. Bluish-green cloth. With Scribner "A" on copyright page and "THE MUSIC" in capital letters on page 37. $250. With "The music." $200.

AIKEN, Conrad. *Costumes by Eros.* New York, 1928. $250.

AIKEN, Conrad. *Earth Triumphant and Other Tales in Verse.* New York, 1914. Author's first book. $250.

AIKEN, Conrad. *Great Circle.* New York, 1933. $175.

AIKEN, Conrad. *A Heart for the Gods of Mexico.* London, 1939. $350.

AIKEN, Conrad. *The Jig of Forslin: A Symphony.* Boston, 1916. Possible first issue with "r" missing in "warm" on page 117 line 1. $150.

AIKEN, Conrad. *King Coffin.* New York, 1935. Vivid-greenish cloth, lettered in purple-blue. One of few copies. $500. Grayish purple-blue, stamped in gold on spine. $300.

AIKEN, Conrad. *Turns and Movies and Other Tales in Verse.* Boston, 1916. Printed wraps over boards. $250.

AIKIN, Anna Laetitia. See *Poems.*

AINSWORTH, William Harrison. See *Sir John Chiverton.*

AINSWORTH, William Harrison. *Cardinal Pole.* London, 1863. 3 vols. $750.

AINSWORTH, W. Harrison. *Jack Sheppard.* London, 1839. Portrait and illustrations by George Cruikshank. 3 vols. $500.

AINSWORTH, W. Harrison. *James the Second.* London, 1848. 3 vols. Integral ad leaf precedes half title, and list of illustrations follows title leaf. $500.

AINSWORTH, W. Harrison. *Merry England or Nobles and Serfs.* London, 1874. 3 vols. Green cloth with "Merrie" on spines. $500.

AINSWORTH, W. Harrison. *The Tower of London.* London, 1840. Illustrated by George Cruikshank. 13 parts in 12, wraps. $1,000. London, 1840. First book edition. Purple cloth. $600.

AKEN, David. *Pioneers of the Black Hills.* (Milwaukee, 1920.) Pictorial wraps. $125.

AKERLY, Samuel. *An Essay on the Geology of the Hudson River . . .* New York, 1820. Map. $300.

ALARIC at Rome: A Prize Poem. Recited in Rugby School. June XII, MDCCCXL. Rugby (England), 1840. (By Matthew Arnold.) Author's first book. 12 pages, pink pictorial and printed wraps. $10,000.

ALBEE, Edward. *The American Dream.* New York (1961). Cloth. $175. Wraps. $40. London (1962). Wraps. $40.

ALBEE, Edward. *Who's Afraid of Virginia Woolf?* New York, 1962. Cloth. $750. Wraps. $125. London (1964). $125. Charlestown, W. Va. (1980). One of 100 signed copies (broadside with drawing by e. e. cummings). $100.

ALBEE, Edward. *The Zoo Story and the Sandbox.* (New York, 1960.) Author's first book. Wraps. $175.

ALBEE, Edward. *The Zoo Story. The Death of Bessie Smith. The Sandbox: Three Plays.* New York (1960). Cloth. Dustwrapper price $2.75. $300. Dustwrapper price clipped and $3.50 added. $250. Wraps. $40. London (1962). $100.

ALBERT, James. *A Narrative of the Most Remarkable Particulars in the Life of James Albert, Akawsaw, Cranwasa; as Dictated by Himself.* Catskill, 1810. $1,250.

ALBERT, Neil. *January Corpse.* New York, 1991. Author's first book. $150.

ALBERT EINSTEIN, Philosopher-Scientist. Evanston, 1949. (25 essays on Einstein by various contributors.) One of 760 copies signed by Einstein. In slipcase. $4,000.

ALCOHOLICS Anonymous: The Story of How More Than One Hundred Men Have Recovered from Alcoholism. New York, 1939. (By Bill Wilson.) Red cloth. In dustwrapper. $7,500.

ALCOTT, Amos Bronson. *Observations on the Principles and Methods of Infant Instruction.* Boston, 1830. Author's first book. Wraps. $1,000.

ALCOTT, Amos Bronson. *Sonnets and Canzonets.* Boston, 1882. Illustrated with photographs. One of 50 signed copies. $1,000. Trade edition, lacking photographs. $150.

ALCOTT, Louisa May. *Flower Fables.* Boston, 1855. Frontispiece and 5 plates. Gift binding. $3,500. Regular binding. $2,000.

ALCOTT, Louisa May. *Hospital Sketches.* Boston, 1863. Ad on back announcing Wendell Phillips' *Speeches* at $2.50 (not $2.25) (VAB). BAL—Boards with ad for "Speeches" on book cover, no price mentioned. Johnson had cloth first because ad for "Speeches" had "as ready for September"; and stated boards had "reviews" of "Speeches" on back, whereas BAL stated cloth had advertisement for fourth edition of "Speeches." Assume BAL is correct. $750.

ALCOTT, Louisa May. *Little Men.* London, 1871. Frontispiece. Blue cloth. $250. Boston, 1871. Green cloth. First American edition, first issue, with ads at front listing *Pink and White Tyranny* as nearly ready. $750.

ALCOTT, Louisa May. *Little Women.* Boston, 1868–69. Frontispiece and 3 plates, 2 vols. First edition, without "Part One" on spine of vol. 1 and with vol. 2 having no notice of *Little Women, Part First,* on page iv. $15,000. ($19,000 at auction in 1996.) London, 1869. First English edition. $1,500. Limited Editions Club, New York, 1967. In slipcase. $150.

ALCOTT, Louisa May. *The Rose Family.* Boston, 1864. 47 pages, printed wraps. $1,000. Johnson stated this was also published in cloth, but BAL disputes this.

ALCUIN: A Dialogue. (By Charles B. Brown.) New York, 1798. Author's first book. $5,000.

ALDIN, Cecil. *An Artist's Model.* London, 1930. One of 310 signed copies. In slipcase. $400.

ALDINGTON, Richard. *A. E. Housman and W. B. Yeats, Two Lectures.* (Hurst, England): Peacocks Press, 1955. One of 350 copies. In glassine dustwrapper. $150.

ALDINGTON, Richard. *All Men Are Enemies.* London, 1933. One of 110 signed copies. $200.

ALDINGTON, Richard. *Death of a Hero.* London, 1929. $250. Paris, 1930. 2 vols. Printed wraps. Unexpurgated text. One of 300 copies. $600.

ALDINGTON, Richard. *Ezra Pound and T. S. Eliot: A Lecture.* London: Peacocks Press, 1954. One of 350 copies. $250. Full morocco. One of 10 trial copies on azure paper, signed. $500.

ALDINGTON, Richard. *Images (1910–1915).* (Cover title.) (London, 1915.) Author's first book. Pictorial wraps. $300. Boston, 1916. Wraps. $175.

ALDINGTON, Richard. *Images of War.* London, 1919. Illustrated. Boards and cloth. One of 120 copies on paper. $350. One of 50 copies with hand-colored illustrations. $750. One of 30 copies on vellum, signed. $1,500.

ALDISS, Brian W. *The Brightfount Diaries.* London (1955). Author's first book. $200.

ALDISS, Brian W. *Greybeard.* New York (1964). $125. London (1964). $100.

ALDISS, Brian W. *Non-Stop.* London (1958). Red boards (second printing in brown cloth). $350.

ALDISS, Brian. *Space, Time and Nathaniel.* London (1957). Author's first science fiction title. Gray cloth. $300.

ALDISS, Brian W. *Starship.* New York (1959). First U.S. edition of *Non-Stop* with textual changes. $125.

ALDRICH, Thomas Bailey. See A., T.B.

ALDRICH, Thomas Bailey. *The Ballad of Babie Bell and Other Poems.* New York, 1859. First issue, with Broadway address for publisher (Johnson). BAL doesn't show two issues. $150.

ALDRICH, Thomas Bailey. *The Story of a Bad Boy.* Boston, 1870. First issue, with line 20 on page 14 reading "scattered" and line 10 on page 197 reading " abroad." $1,250. Second state, "scatter and aboard." $250. Boston, 1895. Illustrated by A. B. Frost. Decorated cloth. $125.

ALDRIDGE, Reginald. *Life on a Ranch.* New York, 1884. Frontispiece and 3 plates. Stiff wraps. $750.

ALDRIDGE, Reginald. *Ranch Notes in Kansas . . .* London, 1884. First English edition of *Life on a Ranch.* 4 plates. Pictorial cloth. $750.

ALEXANDER, E. P. *Military Memoirs of a Confederate.* New York, 1907. Maps, 3 plates. Cloth. $350.

ALEXANDER, Hartley B. (editor). *Sioux Indian Painting.* Nice, France (1938). 50 color plates. 2 vols. One of 400, but many destroyed during war. $6,000.

ALEXANDER, James Edward. *Travels from India to England . . .* Parbury, 1827. 2 engraved maps, 14 lithographic plates, 5 of which are hand-colored. Errata and author's ad on last leaf. $1,750.

ALEXANDER, John H. *Mosby's Men*. New York, 1907. $600.

ALEXANDER, William. *The Costume of China*. London, 1805. With engraved title and 48 hand-colored plates. (One copy at auction in 1985 had 60 plates while all the rest had 48.) $3,500.

ALEXANDER, William. *Picturesque Representations of the Dress and Manners of the Russians*. London (about 1823). 64 color plates. $1,000.

ALEXANDRE, Arsene. *The Decorative Art of Leon Bakst*. London, 1913. Notes on the Ballets by Jean Cocteau. Translated by Harry Melvill. Portrait. 77 plates, 50 in color. Folio, half vellum. $1,750. One of 80 copies with an original watercolor. $9,000.

ALEXANDRE, Arsene. *The Modern Poster*. New York, 1895. Frontispiece by Will Bradley. One of 1,000 copies on enameled book paper. $350.

ALGER, Horatio, Jr. See Starr, Julian. See also *Timothy Crump's Ward*.

ALGER, Horatio, Jr. *Abraham Lincoln, The Backwoods Boy*. New York, 1883. Illustrated. Pictorial cloth. With ads listing this book as no. 2 in "Boyhood and Manhood" series. $850.

ALGER, Horatio, Jr. *Bertha's Christmas Vision: An Autumn Sheaf*. Boston, 1856. Author's first book. Blindstamped cloth. $2,500.

ALGER, Horatio, Jr. *Dan, the Detective*. New York, 1884. $1,250.

ALGER, Horatio, Jr. *The Five Hundred Dollar Check*. New York: United States Book Co. (1891). First book edition, first issue, with "Porter & Coates" on spine. $1,250. Later issue, with "Lovell" on spine. $300.

ALGER, Horatio, Jr. *Grand'ther Baldwin's Thanksgiving*. Boston: Loring Publisher (1875). $750.

ALGER, Horatio, Jr. *Ragged Dick; or Street Life in New York with the Boot-Blacks*. Boston: Loring Publisher (1868). With *Fame and Fortune* listed in ads for publication in December and Dick standing alone on pictorial title page. $4,500.

ALGER, Horatio, Jr. *Robert Coverdale's Struggle*. New York: Street & Smith (1910). Pictorial colored wraps with "New Medal Library No. 555/15 cents" on cover. $1,000.

ALGER, Horatio, Jr. *The Western Boy*. (New York, 1878.) With G. W. Carleton ad at front of book and American News Company in gold at bottom of spine. $850.

ALGREN, Nelson. *The Man with the Golden Arm*. Garden City, 1949. Signed on tipped-in sheet. $450. Trade. $300. London, 1959. $150.

ALGREN, Nelson. *The Neon Wilderness*. Garden City, 1947. Green cloth. Ads for other books on back of dustwrapper. $300. With reviews of this book on back of dustwrapper. $150. London (1965). $75.

ALGREN, Nelson. *Never Come Morning*. New York (1942). Introduction by Richard Wright. $400. London (1958). $100.

ALGREN, Nelson. *Somebody in Boots*. New York (1935). Author's first book. $2,000. London (1937). $750.

ALHAMBRA (The). See Crayon, Geoffrey.

ALISON, Archibald. *Essays on the Nature and Principles of Taste*. Edinburgh, 1790. $1,750.

ALKEN, Henry. *The National Sports of Great Britain*. London, 1820 (–21). 50 colored plates. Folio. First issue, with engraved 1820 title page and with watermarks dated 1816 and 1818. $30,000. London, 1821. Second issue, without 1820 title page. $20,000. London, 1823. $7,500. London, 1825. First octavo edition. $3,500.

ALKEN, Henry. *Scraps from the Sketch-Books of Henry Alken*. London, 1821. 42 colored plates. $3,500. London, 1822. $2,000.

ALLAHAKBARRIE Book of Broadway Cricket for 1899. (London, 1899.) (By Sir James M. Barrie.) Japanese vellum wraps. One of 520 copies. $4,500.

ALLAN, J. T. (compiler). *Central and Western Nebraska, and the Experiences of Its Stock Growers*. (Cover title.) Omaha, 1883. 16 pages, pictorial wraps. (Note: A Union Pacific Land Department pamphlet.) $400.

ALLAN, J. T. (compiler). *Western Nebraska and the Experiences of Its Actual Settlers*. Omaha, 1882. 16 pages, wraps. $400.

ALLBEURY, Ted. *A Choice of Enemies*. New York, 1972. Author's first book. $250. London (1973). $200.

ALLEN, Miss A. J. (compiler). *Ten Years in Oregon*. Ithaca, N.Y., 1848. Portrait. $250. Second issue, same date, portrait omitted, pages added to included Frémont extracts. $200. Ithaca, 1850. $100.

ALLEN, Gracie. *How to Become President*. New York (1940). $200.

ALLEN, Grant. *An African Millionaire*. London, 1897. Pictorial binding. $650.

ALLEN, Grant. *The Great Taboo*. London, 1890. $300. New York, 1891. $250.

ALLEN, Hervey. *Anthony Adverse*. New York, 1933. With publisher's monogram on copyright page and with numerous typographical errors, among them "Xaxier" for "Xavier" in line 6 of page 352, "ship" for "shop" in line 18 of page 1086, and the word "found" repeated in line 22 of page 397. $125. Deluxe issue: 3 vols. Suede boards. One of 105 signed copies. $600. Limited Editions Club, New York, 1937. 3 vols. Orange cloth. In slipcase. $125.

ALLEN, (William) Hervey. *Ballads of the Border*. (El Paso), 1916. Author's first book. Author's name misspelled "Hervy" on copyright page. Printed wraps. $750.

ALLEN, Hervey. *Israfel: The Life and Times of Edgar Allan Poe*. New York, 1926. 2 vols. First state, with wineglass on table in Longfellow portrait facing page 529. $250. Deluxe issue: three-quarter leather. One of 250 copies. In dustwrapper and slipcase. $450.

ALLEN, Hervey. *Wampum and Old Gold*. New Haven, 1921. Stiff wraps. One of 500 copies. $125.

ALLEN, Ira. *The Natural and Political History of the State of Vermont*. London, 1798. Folding map. $1,250.

ALLEN, Ira. *Particulars of the Capture of the American Ship, Olive Branch*. (Philadelphia, 1804.) $600.

ALLEN, J. A. *Notes on the Natural History of Portions of Montana and Dakota.* Boston, 1874. 61 pages, wraps. $350.

ALLEN, John Fisk. *Victoria Regia; or the Great Water Lily of America.* Boston, 1854. 6 chromolithographed plates by William Sharp. Elephant folio. In boards or wraps. $40,000.

ALLEN, Lewis M. *Printing with the Handpress.* Kentfield, 1969. One of 140 copies. $2,500.

ALLEN, Phoebe. *Gilmory.* London, 1876. 3 vols. Author's first book. $250.

ALLEN, Samuel. See Vesey, Paul.

ALLEN, William A. *Adventures with Indians and Game.* Chicago, 1903. 25 plates. Cloth, or half leather. $450.

ALLEN, Woody. *Don't Drink the Water.* New York: French 1967. Author's first book. Wraps. $100. New York: Random House (1967). $500.

ALLEN, Woody. *Play It Again, Sam.* New York (1969). $450.

ALLENDE, Isabel. *The House of the Spirits.* New York, 1985. Author's first book. $150.

ALLIES' Fairy Book (The). London (1916). 12 colored plates, other illustrations by Arthur Rackham. Buckram. One of 525 copies signed by the artist. $1,750. Trade edition. Blue cloth. First issue, with pictorial endpapers. $400.

ALLINGHAM, Margery. *Black'er Chief Dick.* London, 1923. Author's first book. $1,000. Garden City, 1923. $750.

ALLINGHAM, Margery. *Mr. Campion: Criminologist.* New York: Crime Club, 1937. $500.

ALLINGHAM, William. *Poems.* London, 1850. Author's first book. $450.

ALLINGHAM, William. *Sixteen Poems.* Dundrum, Ireland: Dun Emer Press, 1905. Selected by William Butler Yeats. Boards and linen. One of 200. $400.

ALLISON, Dorothy. *Bastard Out of Carolina.* New York, 1992. $200.

ALLISON, Dorothy. *The Women Who Hate Me.* Brooklyn, 1983. Wraps. $750.

ALLISON, Dorothy. *The Women Who Hate Me: Poetry 1980–1990.* Ithaca, 1991. Expanded version. Cloth. $75. Wraps. $50.

ALLISON, William. *The British Thoroughbred Horse.* London, 1901. $400. London, 1907. Second edition. $300.

ALLSTON, Washington. *Outlines and Sketches.* Boston, 1850. 18 plates. $750.

ALNWICK Castle, with Other Poems. New York, 1827. (By FitzGreene Halleck.) Printed tan wraps bound in. $350.

ALPHA and Omega. Blight, the Tragedy of Dublin. Dublin, 1917. (By Oliver St. John Gogarty.) Author's first book written with Joseph O'Connor. $300.

ALTER, J. Cecil. *James Bridger: Trapper, Frontiersman, Scout, and Guide.* Salt Lake City (1925). 18 plates. One of 1,000 signed copies. $350.

ALTOWAN; Or Incidents of Life and Adventure in the Rocky Mountains. New York, 1846. By an Amateur Traveller. Edited by J. Watson Webb. (By Sir William Drummond Stewart.) Howes states this was "probably actually written by Webb," however. 2 vols. Cloth. $1,750.

ALTSHELER, Joseph Alexander. *The Hidden Mine.* New York, 1896. Author's first book. $350.

ALTSHELER, Joseph Alexander. *The Sun of Saratoga.* New York, 1897. Author's first book. $150.

ÁLVAREZ, A. *(Poems).* Oxford, 1952. Author's first book. Fantasy Poets. Wraps. $125.

ALVAREZ, Julia. *Homecoming.* New York, 1984. Author's first book. $350

ALVAREZ, Julia. *How the García Girls Lost Their Accents.* (Chapel Hill) 1991. $100.

ALVORD, Clarence W. *The Mississippi Valley in British Politics . . .* Cleveland, 1917. 2 vols. Illustrated with colored maps. In original cloth. $350.

AMBLER, Eric. *Background to Danger.* New York, 1937. (First American edition of *Uncommon Danger.*) $2,000.

AMBLER, Eric. *Cause for Alarm.* London, 1938. $2,500.

AMBLER, Eric. *A Coffin for Dimitrios.* New York, 1939. $2,500. (U.S. first of *The Mask of Dimitrios.*)

AMBLER, Eric. *The Dark Frontier.* London, 1936. Author's first book. $5,000.

AMBLER, Eric. *Epitaph for a Spy.* London, 1938. $2,500.

AMBLER, Eric. *The Mask of Dimitrios.* London, 1937. $7,500.

AMBLER, Eric. *Uncommon Danger.* London, 1937. $5,000.

AMERICANA Beginnings: A Selection from the Library of Thomas W. Streeter. Morristown, N.J., 1952. 97 pages, wraps. One of 325 copies. $250.

AMERICAN Arguments for British Rights. London, 1806. (By William Loughton Smith.) $350.

AMERICAN Caravan (The). New York, 1927. $250.

AMERICAN Caravan (The Second). New York, 1928. $200.

AMERICAN Chap-Book, The. Jersey City, 1904–1905. Volumes I and II in 12 numbers. (Will Bradley.) $1,000.

AMERICAN Shooter's Manual (The). Philadelphia, 1827. By a Gentleman of Philadelphia County (Jesse Y. Kester). Frontispiece, 2 plates, errata. With "ribbon" misspelled on page 235. $2,500. Second printing. $1,500.

AMES, Joseph. *Catalogue of English Heads; or An Account of About Two Thousand Prints, Describing What Is Peculiar to Each . . .* London, 1848. $300.

AMIS, Kingsley. *Bright November.* London (1947). Author's first book. $2,000.

AMIS, Kingsley. *Lucky Jim.* London, 1953. $3,000. Garden City, 1954. $400.

AMIS, Martin. *Dead Babies.* London (1975). $500. New York, 1976. $150.

AMIS, Martin. *The Rachel Papers.* London, 1973. Author's first book. $750. New York, 1974. $250.

AMIS, Martin. *Success.* London, 1978. $200.

AMMONS, A. R. *Ommateum: With Doxology.* Philadelphia (1955 [actually 1954]). The poet's first book. One of 300 copies, 200 reportedly destroyed. $1,500.

AMSDEN, Charles A. *Navaho Weaving.* Santa Ana, 1934. 122 plates, many in color. $400. Albuquerque, 1948 (actually 1949). $250. Chicago (1964). $60.

AMUNDSEN, Roald. *"The Northwest Passage."* London, 1908. 2 vols. First edition in English. Illustrated, 2 folding maps in pocket. Cloth. $850. New York, 1908. $600.

AMUNDSEN, Roald. *The South Pole . . .* London, 1912. 2 vols. 2 frontispieces, 100 photographic plates, 6 maps (4 folding). $2,250.

ANALYSIS of the Hunting Field (The). London, 1846. (By Robert Smith Surtees.) 7 colored plates (including title page) by Henry Alken, 43 woodcuts. First issue in green cloth (some copies with preface dated 1846, some dated 1847—VAB). $1,000. Second issue, red cloth. $850.

ANAND, Mulk Raj. *The Coolie.* London (1936). $300.

ANAYA, Rudolfo. *Bless Me. Ultima.* (Berkeley), 1972. $600. Wraps. $125.

ANAYA, Rudolfo. *Heart of Aztlán.* (Berkeley, 1976.) $250. Wraps. $100.

ANBUREY, Thomas. *Travels Through the Interior Parts of America . . .* London, 1789. 2 vols. Large folding engraved map, and 7 plates. $1,500.

ANCIENT and Modern Michilimackinac . . . (Cover title.) (St. James, Mich.), MDCLIV (1854). (By James Jesse Strang.) 48 pages. Wraps. First issue. $6,000. Another, dated 1854, obviously on later paper. $600. Later printings. $250.

ANDERSEN, Hans Christian. *The Complete Andersen.* Limited Editions Club, New York, 1949. Translated by Jean Hersholt. Hand-colored illustrations by Fritz Kredel. 6 vols. Buckram and boards. In slipcase. $450.

ANDERSEN, Hans Christian. *Fairy Tales.* London, no date [1924]. 12 tipped-in color plates, numerous black-and-white illustrations by Kay Nielsen. White vellum. One of 500 copies signed by the artist. $5,000. Trade. Green ribbed cloth. $750. London (1932). 12 colored plates and numerous black-and-white illustrations by Arthur Rackham. Vellum. $500. One of 525 copies signed by the artist. $4,000.

ANDERSEN, Hans Christian. *Stories from Hans Andersen.* London (1911). 28 color plates by Edmund Dulac. Vellum, silk ties. One of 750 copies signed by Dulac. $2,500. Pigskin. One of 100 copies on Japan paper. $4,000.

ANDERSON, David. *The Enchanted Galleon*. (San Francisco, 1930.) Signed frontispiece photo by Ansel Adams. One of 60 copies. In slipcase. $1,000.

ANDERSON, Forrest. *Sea Pieces* . . . New York, 1935. Author's first book. (155 copies.) $175.

ANDERSON, Frederick Irving. *Adventures of the Infallible Godahl*. New York (1914). Author's first book. $2,000.

ANDERSON, Jessica. *An Ordinary Lunacy*. Sydney, 1963. Author's first book. $150.

ANDERSON, Jessica. *Tirra Lirra by the River*. Sydney, 1978. $250.

ANDERSON, Kent. *Sympathy for the Devil*. Garden City, 1987. $250.

ANDERSON, Laurie. *The Package*. Indianapolis (1971). $350.

ANDERSON, Maxwell. *Key Largo*. Washington, 1939. First edition stated. $300.

ANDERSON, Maxwell. *You Who Have Dreams*. New York, 1925. Author's first book, preceded by four collaborations in 1924/25. One of 975 copies. $75. One of 25 signed copies. $300.

ANDERSON, Patrick. *A Tent for April*. Montreal, 1945. First regularly published book, preceded by two published items in his teens. Stiff wraps and dustwrapper. $250.

ANDERSON, Poul. *Brain Wave*. London (1955). $400. New York (1969). $150.

ANDERSON, Poul. *The Enemy Stars*. Philadelphia, 1959. $350.

ANDERSON, Poul. *The Fox, The Dog and The Griffin* . . . Garden City (1966). $250.

ANDERSON, Poul. *Vault of the Ages*. Philadelphia (1952). Author's first book. $200.

ANDERSON, Robert. *Tea and Sympathy*. New York (1953). First edition not stated. $250.

ANDERSON, Sherwood. *Beyond Desire*. New York (1932). One of 165 signed copies. In slipcase. $350. Trade edition. $200.

ANDERSON, Sherwood. *Dark Laughter*. New York, 1925. One of 350 signed copies. In slipcase. $400. One of 20 copies lettered and signed by the author. In slipcase. $1,000. Trade edition. $200. London (1926). $125.

ANDERSON, Sherwood. *Horses and Men*. New York, 1923. First issue, with top edges stained orange. $350. London, 1924. $200.

ANDERSON, Sherwood. *Many Marriages*. New York, 1923. $250.

ANDERSON, Sherwood. *Marching Men*. New York, 1917. Crimson cloth. In dustwrapper. $1,000. Without dustwrapper. $200.

ANDERSON, Sherwood. *Mid-American Chants*. New York, 1918. Yellow cloth. In dustwrapper. $750. Without dustwrapper. $100. New York, 1923. $125.

ANDERSON, Sherwood. *The Modern Writer*. San Francisco, 1925. One of 950 copies. $150. One of 50 copies on Japan vellum, signed. In slipcase. $600.

ANDERSON, Sherwood. *Nearer the Grass Roots.* San Francisco, 1929. Half cloth. Grabhorn printing. One of 500 signed copies. $250.

ANDERSON, Sherwood. *A New Testament.* New York, 1927. One of 265 large-paper copies, signed. In slipcase. $300. Trade edition. $150.

ANDERSON, Sherwood. *Poor White.* New York, 1920. First issue with top edges stained blue (Johnson). Sheehy and Lohf don't consider this an issue point. $500. Unstained. $450. London (1921). $250.

ANDERSON, Sherwood. *Windy McPherson's Son.* New York, 1916. Author's first book. $500. London, 1916. $300.

ANDERSON, Sherwood. *Winesburg, Ohio.* New York, 1919. Yellow cloth, paper label on spine. First issue, with line 5 of page 86 reading "lay," and with broken type in the word "the" in line 3 of page 251. Presumed to have top stained yellow, and endpaper map at front. In dustwrapper. $20,000. Without dustwrapper. $600. Second issue, top unstained. In dustwrapper. $17,500. Without dustwrapper. $250. Limited Editions Club, New York, 1978. In slipcase. $125.

ANDERSON, William. *The Pictorial Arts of Japan.* London, 1886. $1,500.

ANDERSSON, Charles. *The Okavango River . . .* London, 1861. $350. New York, 1861. Folding colored map. 15 plates. (Chronology and distances not in the London edition.) $450.

ANDRE, John. *Major Andre's Journal.* Boston, 1903. Edited by Henry Cabot Lodge. Facsimile maps, plans, and other illustrations. 2 vols. Full vellum. One of 488 copies. In slipcase. $750. One of 10 copies on Japan vellum. $1,500.

ANDREAS, A. T. *Atlas Map of Peoria County, Illinois.* Chicago, 1873. 25 maps in color. $600.

ANDREAS, A. T. *History of Chicago.* Chicago, 1884–86. Illustrated. 3 vols. Morocco and cloth. $1,250. Full morocco. $2,000.

ANDREAS, A. T. *History of the State of Kansas.* Chicago, 1883. Morocco or pictorial boards. Folding map. $750.

ANDREAS, A. T. *Illustrated Historical Atlas of the State of Iowa.* Chicago, 1875. Colored maps and views. Three-quarter morocco. $1,500.

ANDREWS, Eliza Frances. *The War-Time Journal of a Georgia Girl, 1864–65.* New York, 1908. 16 plates. $125.

ANDREWS, Jane. *The Seven Little Sisters . . .* Boston, 1861. Author's first book. $250.

ANDREWS, Jane. *Ten Boys Who Lived on the Road from Long Ago to Now.* Boston, 1886. Illustrated by Charles Copeland. Pictorial cloth. $450.

ANDREWS, John. *History of the War with America, France, Spain, and Holland; Commencing in 1775 and Ending In 1783.* London, 1785–86. 4 vols. 24 plates, 6 folding maps, and 1 single-page map (maps partially hand-colored). $2,000.

ANDREWS, Michael. *River Run.* (Hermosa Beach, CA, 1977). Folio, 10 original color photographs, each numbered and signed by Andrews. One of 100 copies signed by Andrews. The text and prints are loose within a custom wood box. $600.

ANDREWS, William Loring. *Among My Books.* New York, 1894. One of 50 copies. 14 engravings and 13 other illustrations. $450.

ANDREWS, William Loring. *Bibliopegy in the United States and Kindred Subjects.* New York, 1902. One of 36 copies in dustwrapper. $1,250. One of 141 copies in dustwrapper. $550.

ANDREWS, William Loring. *A Choice Collection of Books from the Aldine Presses.* New York, 1885. Author's first book. Wraps. One of 50 copies. $600.

ANDREWS, William Loring. *An English XIX Century Sportsman, Bibliopole and Binder of Angling Books.* New York, 1906. One of 32 copies. $1,000. One of 125 copies. $450.

ANDREWS, William Loring. *Gossip About Book Collecting.* New York, 1900. 2 vols. Wraps. Limited to 157 copies for subscribers. 5 plates in first vol., 7 plates in second vol. One of 32 copies. $1,250. One of 125 copies. $450.

ANDREWS, William Loring. *The Old Booksellers of New York and Other Papers.* New York, 1895. 84 pages and four plates. Limited to 142 copies. $450.

ANGEL in the House (The). London, 1854. (By Coventry Patmore.) Cloth, paper label. $600. London, 1863. 2 vols. $400.

ANGELO, Valenti. *The Book of Esther.* New York, 1935. One of 135 signed copies. $350.

ANGELOU, Maya. *I Know Why the Caged Bird Sings.* New York (1969). Top edge stained magenta, text bulks 1/16 inch. $350.

ANNEBERG, Maurice. *Type Foundries of America and Their Catalogs.* Baltimore, 1975. One of 500 copies. $150.

ANONYMOUS. Paris (1930). (By Michael Fraenkel.) Author's first book. (First Carrefour Editions book, with Walter Lowenfels.) Wraps. $250.

ANSON, George. *A Voyage Round the World, in the Years MDCCXL, I, II, III, IV.* London, 1748. First edition has 42 folding copper-engraved plates, maps, plans, and charts. $6,000.

ANSTEY, Christopher. See *The New Bath Guide . . .*

ANSTEY, F. *The Pariah.* London, 1889. (By Thomas Anstey Guthrie.) 3 vols. $750.

ANSTEY, F. *Vice Versa.* London, 1882. (By Thomas Anstey Guthrie.) $350.

ANTHOLOGY of Younger Poets (An). Philadelphia, 1932. Edited by Oliver Wells. Boards. One of 500 copies. In glassine dustwrapper. $300. (Contains five poems by William Faulkner.)

ANTHONY, Peter. *The Women in the Wardrobe.* London, 1951. (By Peter and Anthony Shaffer.) Author's first book. $200.

ANTIN, Mary. *From Plotzk to Boston.* Boston, 1899. Author's first book. Cloth. $350. Wraps. $250.

ANTIN, Mary. *The Promised Land.* Boston, 1912. "Published April 1912" on copyright page. $100. London, 1912. $100.

ANTI-TEXASS Legion (The): Protest of Some Free Men, States, and Presses Against the Texass Rebellion. New York, 1844. 72 pages, wraps. $500.

ANTONINUS, Brother. See Everson, William.

ANTONINUS, Brother. *An Age Insurgent.* San Francisco (1959). (By William Everson.) 500 copies, of which all but 60 to100 copies were destroyed. $600.

ANTONINUS, Brother. *The Poet Is Dead: A Memorial for Robinson Jeffers.* San Francisco: Auerhahn Press, 1964. Boards and leather. (By William Everson.) One of 205 signed copies. In plain white dustwrapper. $250.

ANTONINUS, Brother. *A Privacy of Speech.* Berkeley, 1949. (By William Everson.) One of 100 signed copies. (Issued without dustwrapper.) $3,500.

ANTONINUS, Brother. *Who Is She That Looketh Forth as the Morning.* Santa Barbara, 1972. (By William Everson.) One of 250 signed copies. In acetate dustwrapper. $175.

ANTRIM, Benajah J. *Pantography, Or Universal Drawings, in the Comparison of Their Natural and Arbitrary Laws . . .* Philadelphia, 1843. $200.

APES, William. *The Experience of William Apes . . .* New York, 1829. Author's first book. $1,750.

APOCRYPHA (The). London: Cresset Press, 1929. Authorized version. Full-page woodcuts by Stephen Gooden, Eric Jones, et al. Folio, black vellum. One of 30 copies on handmade paper with an extra set of illustrations signed by the artists. In slipcase. $3,500. Boards. One of 450 copies. In slipcase. $600.

APOLLINAIRE, Guillaume. *The Poet Assassinated.* New York, 1968. Illustrated by Jim Dine. 8 drawings. Loose wraps. One of 250 copies. $1,000.

APPEAL (An) to the Clergy of the Church of Scotland. Edinburgh, 1875. (By Robert Louis Stevenson.) 12 pages, stitched, without wraps. $6,000.

APPEL, Benjamin. *Brain Guy.* New York, 1934. Author's first book. $200.

APPERLEY, C. J. See Nimrod. See also *Memoirs of the Life of the Late John Mytton, Esq.*

APPLEGATE, Jesse. *A Day with the Cow Column in 1843.* Chicago, 1934. Caxton Club. Pictorial cloth. One of 300 copies. $350. Another edition. (Portland), 1952. One of 225 copies. $150.

APPLEGATE, Jesse. *Recollections of My Boyhood.* Roseburg, Ore., 1914. 99 pages, pictorial wraps. $1,250.

ARAGON, Louis. *Henry Matisse, A Novel.* London, 1972. 2 vols. 541 illustrations, including 155 in color. $350. New York (1972). 2 vols. $300.

ARAGON, Louis. *The Red Front.* Chapel Hill (1933). Translated by e. e. cummings. First American edition. Stapled red wraps. $300.

ARCHBOLD, Ann. *A Book for the Married and Single, the Grave and the Gay and Especially Designed for Steamboat Passengers.* East Plainfield, Ohio, 1850. $750.

ARCHER, Jeffrey. *Not a Penny More, Not a Penny Less.* London, 1976. Author's first book. $300. New York, 1976. $150.

ARCHITEC-TONICS . . . New York, 1914. First book illustrated by Rockwell Kent. $350.

ARDIZZONE, Edward. *In a Glass Darkly.* London, 1929. (By J. Sheridan Le Fanu.) First book illustrated by Ardizzone. $350.

ARDIZZONE, Edward. *Little Tim and the Brave Sea Captain.* London, 1936. Author's first book. $450.

ARIAS, Ron. *The Road to Tamazunchale.* Reno, 1975. First issue in stapled wraps. $175. Second issue in orange perfect-bound wraps, no blurbs. $75. Third issue in tan perfect-bound wraps, rear blurbs. $50.

ARISTOPHANES. *Lysistrata.* London, 1896. 8 plates by Aubrey Beardsley. Boards. One of 100 copies. $7,500. London (1926). Translated by Jack Lindsay. Illustrated by Norman Lindsay. Half morocco. One of 725 copies signed by the artist. $1,000. Limited Editions Club, New York, 1934. Translated by Gilbert Seldes. Illustrated by Pablo Picasso. Boards. In slipcase. $7,500. (There also were 150 sets of 6 proofs, each set signed by Picasso, issued in cloth portfolio and sold separately.) $15,000.

ARISTOTLE. *The Organon; or Logical Treatises.* London, 1807. First edition in English. $3,000.

ARISTOTLE. *Politics and Poetics.* Limited Editions Club, Lunenburg, 1964. Illustrated by Leonard Baskin. Buckram. In slipcase. $200.

ARKWRIGHT, William. *The Pointer & His Predecessors.* London, 1906. Illustrated. One of 750 copies. $1,000.

ARLEN, Michael. *The Green Hat.* London (1924). $175. New York, 1925. (Acting version.) Boards. One of 175 signed copies. $150.

ARLEN, Michael. *The London Venture.* London, 1920. (Reportedly, the edition dated "1919" was actually printed later.) Author's first book. $250. New York (1920). $150.

ARMAGEDDON: A Fragment: Avalon. Charleston, S.C., 1923. Wraps. Contains poems by John Crowe Ransom and others. $750.

ARMES, George A. *Ups and Downs of an Army Officer.* Washington, 1900. Illustrated. Pictorial cloth. $250.

ARMITAGE, John. *The History of Brazil.* London, 1836. 2 portraits. 2 vols. London, 1836. $1,000.

ARMITAGE, Merle. *The Art of Edward Weston.* New York, 1932. One of 550 copies signed by Weston. $3,500.

ARMITAGE, Merle. *Brett Weston: Photographs.* New York, 1956. $1,750.

ARMSMEAR: The Home, the Arm and the Armory of Col. Samuel Colt: A Memorial. New York, 1866. Plates. Cloth. $1,500. Full morocco. Presentation binding. $2,500.

ARMSTRONG, A. N. *Oregon: A Brief History and Description of Oregon and Washington.* Chicago, 1857. $750.

ARMSTRONG, Elizabeth. *Robert Estienne, Royal Printer: An Historical Study of the Elder Stephanus.* Cambridge, 1954. $150.

ARMSTRONG, Margaret. *Western Wild Flowers.* New York/London, 1915. Written with J. J. Thornburg. $500.

ARMSTRONG, Martin. *Exodus+.* London, 1912. $175.

ARMSTRONG, Moses K. *History and Resources of Dakota, Montana and Idaho.* Yankton, Dakota Territory, 1866. Map. Printed wraps. $7,500.

ARMSTRONG, Perry A. *The Sauks and the Black War.* Springfield, 1887. $300.

ARNETT, John Andrews. *Bibliopegia; Or, the Art of Bookbinding . . .* London, 1835. 9 plates. $600.

ARNETT, John. *An Inquiry into the Nature and Form of the Books of the Ancients . . .* London, 1837. 14 plates. $650.

ARNO, PETER. *Whoops, Dearie!* (New York, 1927.) (By Curtis Arnoux Peters.) Author's first book. $150.

ARNOLD, Arthur. *Through Persia by Caravan.* London, 1877. 2 vols. $1,000.

ARNOLD, Elliot. *Blood Brother.* New York, 1936. $150.

ARNOLD, Henry V. *The Early History of the Devil's Lake Country.* Larimore, N.D., 1920. 105 pages, printed wraps. $200.

ARNOLD, Henry V. *The History of Old Pembina, 1780–1872.* Larimore, N.D., 1917. Wraps. $200.

ARNOLD, Matthew. See A. (pseudonym-first entry in list). See also *Alaric at Rome.*

ARNOLD, Matthew. *Cromwell: A Prize Poem.* Oxford, 1843. Wraps. $1,750.

ARNOLD, Matthew. *Essays in Criticism.* London, 1865. $200.

ARNOLD, Matthew. *Merope: A Tragedy.* London, 1858. First issue with ads dated November 1857. $200.

ARNOLD, Matthew. *Poems.* London, 1853. $300. London, 1855. (Second series.) $200. Boston, 1856. $100. 3 vols. London, 1895. $500.

ARNOLD, Oren, and HALE, John P. *Hot Irons: Heraldry of the Range.* New York, 1940. $200.

ARNOLD, R. Ross. *Indian Wars of Idaho.* Caldwell, Idaho, 1932. 85 illustrations. $300.

ARNOLD, William Harris. *First Report of a Book-Collector; Comprising a Brief Answer to the Frequent Question "Why First Editions?"* New York, 1897–98. One of 85 copies. $350. Second edition. Limited to 220 copies. $200.

ARNOW, Harriette. See Simpson, Harriette.

ARNOW, Harriette. *The Dollmaker.* New York, 1954. $350.

ARNOW, Harriette. *Hunter's Horn.* New York, 1949. Author's second book, first under real name. (First edition stated.) $125.

AROUND the Horn in '49. See *Journal of the Hartford Union Mining and Trading Company.*

ARP, Jean. *Dreams and Projects.* New York (1952). 15 pages of text and 28 folded sheets with woodcuts by Arp, laid-in wrapper, and blue board folder. One of 320 signed copies. $1,750.

ARRANGEMENT of Places: Will Each Gentleman Kindly Take in to Dinner the Lady Seated on His Right. (New York), 1905. 12 pages, wraps. (Program of Seventieth birthday dinner for Mark Twain at Delmonico's.) $500.

ARTHUR, T. S. See *INSUBORDINATION . . .*

ARTHUR, T. S. *Ten Nights in a Bar-Room, and What I Saw There.* Philadelphia, 1854. First issue, with both Lippincott and Bradley named in imprint and woodcut frontispiece by Van Ingen (VAB). $600.

ARTHUR Mervyn; or Memoirs of the Year 1793. Philadelphia, 1799–1800. By the Author of *Wieland* (Charles Brockden Brown). 2 vols. (For first English edition, see author entry). $2,000.

ASBJÖRNSEN, Peter Christen. See *East of the Sun and West of the Moon.*

ASHBEE, C. R. *Jerusalem, 1920–1922.* London, 1924. 25 plates. $600.

ASHBEE, C. R. *The Private Press: A Study In Idealism. To Which Is Added a Bibliography of the Essex House.* (London, 1909.) One of 127 copies. $850.

ASHBEE, Henry Spencer. *An Iconography of Don Quixote, 1605–1895.* London, 1895. Half cloth or wraps. $350.

ASHBERY, John. *Fragment.* Los Angeles, 1969. Illustrated by Alex Katz. One of 250 copies signed by both. Hardbound. Acetate dustwrapper. $300.

ASHBERY, John. *A Nest of Ninnies.* New York, 1969. $100.

ASHBERY, John. *The New Spirit.* New York (1970). Pictorial wraps. One of 65 signed copies. $350. Also, 100 unsigned copies. $125.

ASHBERY, John. *Some Trees.* Foreword by W. H. Auden. New Haven, 1956. $600.

ASHBERY, John. *Sunrise in Suburbia.* New York, 1968. Wraps. One of 100 signed copies. $350. One of 26 lettered and signed copies. $600.

ASHBERY, John. *Turandot and Other Poems.* New York, 1953. Author's first book. Illustrated. Wraps. One of 300 copies. $1,250.

ASHDOWN, Clifford. *The Adventures of Romney Pringle.* London, 1902. (By R. Austin Freeman and J. J. Pitcairn.) $1,500.

ASHE, Thomas. *Travels in America.* London, 1808. 3 vols. $1,000. Newburyport, 1808. 3 vols. $1,000. Pittsburgh, 1808. $750.

ASHLEY, Clifford W. *The Yankee Whaler.* Boston, 1926. Plates, some in color. Half cloth and boards. One of 156 signed copies, with an original drawing. In slipcase. $1,000. Trade, in dust-wrapper. $450.

ASHLEY, William H. *The West of William H. Ashley.* Denver, 1964. Edited by Dale L. Morgan. Illustrated. Pictorial buckram. One of 750 copies. $350. Deluxe issue: Half calf. One of 250 signed copies. In slipcase. $750.

ASHTON, Warren T. *Hatchie, the Guardian Slave.* Boston, 1853. (By William Taylor Adams.) Author's first book. Black cloth. $1,250.

ASIMOV, Isaac. *The End of Eternity.* Garden City, 1955. $350.

ASIMOV, Isaac. *Foundation.* New York (1951). First binding, in cloth with sheets bulking 1.9 cm. $1,500.

ASIMOV, Isaac. *Foundation and Empire.* New York (1952). First binding in red boards with spine imprint 2.2 cm across (2.8 cm. in second binding). First issue dustwrapper with 26 titles on back. $500.

ASIMOV, Isaac. *I, Robot.* New York (1950). Cloth. $1,500. Wraps. $200.

ASIMOV, Isaac. *Little Brothers.* (Rochester, Mich.): Pretentious Press, 1988. One of 26 signed copies. $350. One of 100 signed copies. $200.

ASIMOV, Isaac. *Pebble in the Sky.* Garden City, 1950. Author's first book. $750.

ASIMOV, Isaac. *Second Foundation.* (New York, 1953.) First binding, blue boards. $450.

ASINOF, Eliot. *Eight Men Out.* New York (1963). $250.

ASKIN, John. *The John Askin Papers 1747–1820.* Detroit, 1928–1931. 2 vols. 13 plates and maps. $300.

"ASK Mama"; or, The Richest Commoner in England. London (1857) and 1858. (By Robert Smith Surtees.) 13 full-page color plates and 6 woodcuts by John Leech. 13 parts, red wraps. $1,750. London, 1858. Pictorial cloth. First book edition. $300.

ASQUITH, Cynthia. *The Ghost Book . . .* London, 1926. Author's first book. $750. New York, 1927. $500.

ASTLE, Thomas Astle. *The Origin and Progress of Writing, as Well Hieroglyphic . . .* London, 1784. 31 plates. $600. London, 1803. Portrait. 32 plates. $450.

ASTON, James. *First Lesson.* London, (1932). (By T. H. White.) $1,250. New York, 1933. $750.

ASTON, James. *They Winter Abroad.* London, 1932. (By T. H. White). $1,250. New York, 1932. $750.

ATALANTIS. New York, 1832. (By William Gilmore Simms.) In original wraps. $1,500.

ATGET, Eugène. *Atget Photographie de Paris.* New York (1930). $750.

ATHERTON, Gertrude. See Lin, Frank.

ATHERTON, Gertrude. *Black Oxen.* New York (1923). One of 250 signed copies. $400.

ATHERTON, Gertrude. *The Conqueror.* New York, 1902. First state, with page numerals on page 546 in upper left corner. $150.

ATHERTON, Gertrude. *Hermia Suydam.* New York, 1889. Second book, first under her own name. Wraps. $250.

ATHERTON, Gertrude. *What Dreams May Come.* London, 1889. First English edition (of author's first book, which was issued in America under the pseudonym Frank Lin). $300.

ATHERTON, William. *Narrative of the Suffering & Defeat of the North-Western Army, Under General Winchester.* Frankfort, Ky., 1842. Leather-backed boards, printed paper label. $600.

ATKINSON, George H. *Address . . . Upon The Possession, Settlement, Climate and Resources of Oregon and the Northwest Coast including Some Remarks Upon Alaska.* New York, 1868. 17 pages. $350.

ATKINSON, Thomas Witlam. *Travels in the Regions of the Upper and Lower Amoor . . .* New York, 1860. Folding map. $500.

ATLAS of Long Island. New York: Beers, Comstock & Cline, 1873. $2,000.

ATLEE, Edwin A. *An Inaugural Essay on the Influence of Music in the Cure of Diseases.* Philadelphia, 1804. $1,250.

ATLEE, Philip. *The Inheritors.* New York, 1940. Author's first book. $125.

ATTACHÉ (The); or, Sam Slick in England. (Second series.) London, 1844. (By Thomas Chandler Haliburton.) 2 vols. Ribbed plum-colored cloth. With 48 pages of ads at end of vol. 2 (VAB). $600.

ATTANASIO, A. A. *Radix.* New York, 1981. Author's first book. Hardback. $400. Wraps. $40.

ATTAWAY, William. *Blood on the Forge.* Garden City, 1941. $300.

ATTAWAY, William. *Let Me Breathe Thunder.* New York, 1939. Author's first book. $400.

ATTERLEY, Joseph. *A Voyage to the Moon.* New York, 1827. (By George Tucker.) $1,500.

ATWATER, Caleb. *A History of the State of Ohio.* Cincinnati (1838). $250.

ATWATER, Caleb. *Mysteries of Washington City.* Washington, 1844. Boards and leather. $300.

ATWATER, Caleb. *Remarks Made on a Tour to Prairie du Chien; Thence to Washington City.* Columbus, Ohio, 1831. $750.

ATWOOD, Daniel Topping. *Atwood's Modern American Homesteads.* New York, 1876. 46 plates. $750.

ATWOOD, Margaret. *The Animals in That Country.* Toronto, 1968. Cloth. In Dustwrapper. $400. Wraps. $100. Boston (1968). $125.

ATWOOD, Margaret. *The Circle Game.* (Bloomfield Hills, 1964.) One of 2 signed copies on handmade paper. $7,500. One of 13 signed copies on Rives paper. $6,500. Contact Press. Toronto (1966). One of 50 copies. Hardbound in dustwrapper. $1,500. Stiff wraps. $500. House of Anasi. Toronto, 1967. One of 100 signed copies. Issued without dustwrapper. $400. Wraps. $40.

ATWOOD, Margaret. *Double Persephone.* Toronto, 1961. Author's first book. Wraps. $3,500.

ATWOOD, Margaret. *The Edible Woman.* Toronto, 1969. (U.K. sheets.) $750. London, 1969. $500. Boston, 1969. $450.

ATWOOD, Margaret. *Power Politics.* Toronto (1971). Cloth. $300. Wraps. $50. New York (1973). (Copyright 1971.) Cloth. $100. Wraps. $35.

ATWOOD, Margaret. *Snake Poems.* Toronto, 1983. 16 pages in accordion binding. One of 100 signed copies. $250.

ATWOOD, Margaret. *Unearthing Suite.* Toronto, 1983. 16 pages in accordion binding without dustwrapper. One of 150 signed copies. $250.

AUBREY-FLETCHER, Henry Lancelot. See Wade, Henry.

AUCHINCLOSS, Louis. See Lee, Andrew.

AUCHINCLOSS, Louis. *The Injustice Collectors.* Boston, 1950. Author's second book, first under own name. $200.

AUCHINCLOSS, Louis. *Sybil.* Boston, 1952. $250.

AUDEN, W. H. See Baudelaire, Charles; Rich, Adrienne Cecile.

AUDEN, W. H. *The Age of Anxiety.* New York (1947). $250. London (1948). $200.

AUDEN, W. H. *Another Time.* New York (1940). $350. London (1940). $250.

AUDEN, W. H. *The Collected Poetry.* New York (1945). $350.

AUDEN, W. H. *Collected Shorter Poems, 1930–1944.* London (1950). $350.

AUDEN, W. H. *The Dance of Death.* London (1933). $600.

AUDEN, W. H. *Epithalamion.* Princeton, 1939. Single sheet, printed both sides, folded to make 4 pages. (About 100 printed.) $2,500.

AUDEN, W. H. *Look, Stranger!* London (1936). $350. (First American edition of *On This Island.*)

AUDEN, W. H. *Louis MacNeice: A Memorial Address.* London, 1963. Printed wraps. $250.

AUDEN, W. H. *Marginalia.* (Cambridge, Mass., 1966.) Engravings by Laurence Scott. Oblong printed wraps. One of 150 copies signed by author and artist, of which 45 copies were hors de commerce. $500.

AUDEN, W. H. *On This Island.* New York (1937). Brown cloth. (First published in London, as *Look, Stranger!*) $300.

AUDEN, W. H. *The Orators: An English Study.* London (1932). $750. London (1934). Revised edition. $300.

AUDEN, W. H. *Our Hunting Fathers.* (Cambridge) 1935. Wraps. One of 22 copies. $1,500. Also, one of 5 copies (from the 22) on Incudine paper and lettered A to E. $3,000.

AUDEN, W. H. *A Platonic Blow.* New York, 1965. Pamphlet. One of 300 (of 310) copies. $250.

AUDEN, W. H. *Poems.* (Hampstead, England), 1928. Wraps. 12 copies recorded. $30,000.

AUDEN, W. H. *Poems.* London (1930). Wraps with flaps. Author's first regularly published book. $750. New York (1934). Different contents. Orange cloth. $300.

AUDEN, W. H. *Three Songs for St. Cecilia's Day.* (New York), 1941. Wraps. One of 250 copies. $500.

AUDEN, W. H. *Two Songs.* New York, 1968. Wraps. One of 26 signed, lettered copies. $750. One of 100 signed copies. $300.

AUDEN, W. H., and ISHERWOOD, Christopher. *The Dog Beneath the Skin, or, Where Is Francis?* London (1935). $350. New York, 1935. $250.

AUDSLEY, George Ashdown. *The Art of Chromolithography Popularly Explained.* New York, 1883. Folio, 44 plates. $2,000.

AUDSLEY, George Ashdown. *The Art of Organ-Building.* New York, 1905. 2 vols. Illustrated. $750.

AUDSLEY, George Ashdown. *The Ornamental Arts of Japan.* New York, 1882–84. 2 vols. 70 plates in gold and colors, 31 in monochrome, loose in 4 cloth portfolios. Folio. $1,500. Artist's proofs edition. One of 50 signed copies. $2,500. 2 vols. morocco. (Not signed.) $2,000.

AUDSLEY, George Ashdown, and AUDSLEY, Maurice Ashdown. *The Practical Decorator and Ornamentist.* Glasgow: Blackie & Son, no date [1892]. Plates A and B, and 100 numbered chromolithographic plates. Folio. In cloth box. $2,600.

AUDSLEY, George Ashdown, and BOWES, J. L. *The Keramic Art of Japan.* Liverpool, 1875. (80) 63 plates, 42 in gold and colors; 4 plates of potters' marks, other illustrations. Half morocco. $2,000. London, 1881. Cloth. $1,000.

AUDSLEY, William James. *Cottage, Lodge, and Villa Architecture.* London (circa 1870). Half leather and cloth. $500.

AUDUBON, John James. *The Birds of America from Original Drawings.* London, 1827–38. 435 double elephant folio hand-colored plates without text. 87 parts in wraps, or 4 leather-bound double elephant folio vols. Rare in the original parts. $7,500,000. New York, 1840–44. 500 colored plates. 100 parts in wraps or 7 vols., full or half leather. First American and first octavo edition. $100,000. New York, 1860. Second edition of large folio. $100,000. New York, 1870. 8 vols. $25,000. New York (c. 1870–1871). 11 vols. (8 vols. with 500 hand-colored plates. 3 vols. with 155 tinted plates). Published by George R. Lockwood. $30,000. New York, 1937. Edited by William Vogt. 500 plates in color. One-volume edition. Buckram. One of 2,500 copies on all-rag paper. In slipcase. $300. Trade edition. Buckram. In dustwrapper. $150. New York, 1966. 2 vols. $200. New York and Amsterdam, 1971–72. Johnson Reprint Corporation and Theatrum Orbis Terrarum. 4 vols. Double elephant folio or 36 paper folios in 6 wooden files. One of 250 copies. $30,000. London, 1972–73. *(The Birds of America: A Selection of Plates.)* 2 vols., Ariel Press, folio, half cloth. One of 250 copies. $4,500. One of 1,000 copies. $3,000.

AUDUBON, John James. *Journal of John James Audubon, Made During His Trip to New Orleans in 1820–21* with *Journal of John James Audubon, Made While Obtaining Subscriptions to His "Birds of America," 1840–1843.* Boston, 1929. Edited by Howard Corning. 2 vols. 250 copies. Usually sold as a set. $600.

AUDUBON, John James. *The Original Water-Color Paintings by John James Audubon for the Birds of America.* New York, 1966. Edited by Marshall B. Davidson. 2 vols. Brown cloth. In slipcase. $450.

AUDUBON, John James. *Ornithological Biography; or, An Account of the Habits of the Birds of the United States of America.* Edinburgh, 1831–49 (actually 1839). 5 vols. The text volumes to accompany the double elephant folios of *The Birds of America.* $3,000.

AUDUBON, John James. *The Quadrupeds of North America.* See Audubon and Bachman, *The Viviparous Quadrupeds,* etc.

AUDUBON, John James. *A Synopsis of the Birds of America.* Edinburgh, 1839. $1,000.

AUDUBON, John James, and BACHMAN, John. *The Viviparous Quadrupeds of North America.* New York, 1845–48. 150 colored plates without text. 30 parts in wraps, or 3 vols. (vol. 1, 1845; vol. 2, 1846; vol. 3, 1848). Folio set. $300,000. Octavo in wraps. $30,000. New York, 1849–54. 155 hand-colored plates. 3 vols. $12,500. Later octavo editions. $10,000.

AUDUBON, John Woodhouse. *Audubon's Western Journal, 1849–50.* Cleveland, 1906. Edited by Maria R. Audubon. Folding map, 6 plates. Reprint of Audubon's extremely rare and virtually unobtainable *Illustrated Notes of an Expedition Through Mexico and California.* $350.

AUDUBON, John Woodhouse. *The Drawings of John Woodhouse Audubon, Illustrating His Adventures Through Mexico and California.* San Francisco: Book Club of California, 1957. 34 full-page illustrations, including 2 in color. Folio, boards, and cloth. Grabhorn printing. One of 400 copies. In plain dustwrapper. $350.

AUDUBON, Maria R. *Audubon and His Journals.* New York, 1897. Edited by Elliot Coues. 2 vols. Plates. Cloth. $350. New York, 1900. 2 vols. Cloth. $250.

AUEL, Jean M. *The Clan of the Cave Bear.* New York (1980). $150.

AUER, Alois. *The Discovery of the Natural Printing Process.* Wien, 1854. 75 pages and 19 plates (one is double-page) in folio. $3,000.

AUGUSTINE, Saint. *Of the Citie of God. With the Learned Comments of Io. Lod. Vives. Englished by J[ohn] H[ealy].* (London) 1610. Folio. With index and errata (often lacking). $5,000. London, 1620. Second edition. Folio. $2,000.

AUSCHER, Ernest Simon. *A History and Description of French Porcelain.* London, 1905. 24 plates in color. Morocco. $400.

AUSTEN, Jane. See *Elizabeth Bennet; Emma; Mansfield Park; Northanger Abbey and Persuasion; Pride and Prejudice; Sense and Sensibility.*

AUSTEN, Jane. *Persuasion. By Miss Austen.* Philadelphia, 1832. 2 vols. First separate edition. Purple quarter cloth. $4,500. Rebound. $1,500.

AUSTEN, Ralph. *A Treatise of Fruit-Trees Shewing the Manner of Grafting* . . . Oxford, 1653. $2,000.

AUSTIN, Jane Goodwin. *Fairy Dreams* . . . Boston (1859). Author's first book. $150.

AUSTIN, Mary. See Adams, Ansel.

AUSTIN, Mary. *The Land of Little Rain*. Boston, 1903. Author's first book. $500. Boston, 1950. Illustrated by Ansel Adams. $250.

AUSTIN, Mary. *What the Mexican Conference Really Means*. New York (1915). Wraps. $300.

AUSTIN, Mary, and MARTIN, Ann. *Suffrage and Government*. New York, 1914. Printed wraps. $300.

AUTHENTIC Narrative of the Seminole War (An), and of the Miraculous Escape of Mrs. Mary Godfrey, and Her Four Female Children. Providence, R.I., 1836. Folding frontispiece in color, 24 pages, plain wraps. $3,500. New York, 1836. $2,000.

AUTHORSHIP of the Imprecatory Psalms. Boston (1852). (By Thomas Bulfinch.) Author's first book. Wraps. $450.

AUTHORS Take Sides on the Spanish War. London: Left Review (1937). Wraps. $450.

AUTOBIOGRAPHY of an Ex-Colored Man, The. Boston, 1912. (By James W. Johnson.) Author's first book. $3,000.

AUTOCRAT of the Breakfast Table (The). Boston, 1858. (By Oliver Wendell Holmes.) With engraved half title, with period after word "Company" on title page, and with left endpaper at back headed "Poetry and the Drama" and right "School Books." $750. Boston, 1859. Illustrated. Large-paper edition. $1,250. Limited Editions Club, New York, 1955. $75.

AVEDON, Richard (photographer). See Baldwin, James; Capote, Truman.

AVEDON, Richard. *An Autobiography*. New York (1993). One of 250 signed copies with a print of Marilyn Monroe laid in. Folio. 284 full-page plates in black and white. Not paginated. White cloth with paste-down portrait of Avedon on rear board. $750.

AVEDON, Richard. *Avedon Photographs 1947–1977*. Lausanne (1978). $300. (New York, 1978.) $350.

AVEDON, Richard (photographer). *Observations*. New York, 1959. Text by James Baldwin. Glassine dustwrapper. In slipcase. Avedon's first book. $600.

AVERY, Milton. *Milton Avery: Paintings 1930–1960*. New York/London (1962). Full black oasis morocco, handbound, gilt, in cloth slipcase. Deluxe edition, one of 90 copies, specially bound and containing a loosely inserted original signed and numbered engraving by Avery. $3,000.

AVIRETT, James B. *The Memoirs of Gen. Turner Ashby and His Compeers*. Baltimore, 1867. Portrait. Cloth. $500.

AWAHSOOSE the Bear. *Forest and Stream Fables*. (By Rowland Evans Robinson.) New York (1886). Author's first book. Wraps. $850.

AXTON, David. *Prison of Ice.* Philadelphia (1976). (By Dean Koontz.) $450.

AYDY, Catherine. *The Colour of Rain.* London, 1964. (By Emma Tennant, her first book.) $300.

AYESHA, The Maid of Mars. London, 1834. By the Author of *"Zohrab"* . . . (By James Morier.) 3 vols. $1,000.

AYRTON, Michael. *Gilles de Rais.* London (1945). (By Cecil Gray.) First book illustrated by Ayrton. Stiff wraps and dustwrapper. One of 200 signed copies. $450.

B

B., E.B. *Sonnets.* Reading, England, 1847 (actually 1890). By E.B.B. (By Elizabeth Barrett Browning.) 47 pages, without wraps. Thomas J. Wise's forgery of "Sonnets from the Portuguese," which actually appeared first in the second edition of *Poems,* 1850. $3,500.

B., F. *The Kasidah of Haji Abdu El-Yezdi.* London (1880). Translated and annotated by his friend and pupil, F. B. (Sir Richard Burton). Yellow wraps. First issue, without Quaritch imprint. $3,000.

B., H. *The Bad Child's Book of Beasts.* Oxford (1896). (By Hilaire Belloc.) Pictorial boards. $400.

B., H.M. *Carmen Becceriense* . . . (Surrey, 1890.) (By Max Beerbohm.) Author's first book. 4 pages, Latin with notes in English. 2 known copies. $7,500.

B., J.K. *The Lorgnette.* By J.K.B. New York (1886). (By John Kendrick Bangs.) Author's first book. $500.

B., M. *Damozel Blanche.* (Eton, 1891.) (By Maurice Baring.) Author's first book. Wraps. $200.

BABBAGE, Charles. *On the Economy of Machinery and Manufactures.* London, 1832. $1,500.

BABBIT, E. D. *The Principles of Light and Color.* New York, 1878. $750.

BABBITT, E. L. *The Allegheny Pilot.* Freeport, Pa., 1855. 16 maps. 64 pages, wraps. $500.

BABCOCK, Rufus. *Forty Years of Pioneer Life: Memoir of John Mason Peck.* Philadelphia, 1864. $300.

BABEL, Isaac. *Red Calvary.* New York, 1929. $750.

BACA, Jimmy Santiago. *Jimmy Santiago Baca.* No place [Santa Barbara] (1978). $125.

BACH, Richard. *Jonathan Livingston Seagull.* (New York, 1970.) $350.

BACHELLER, Irving. *The Master of Silence.* New York, 1892. Author's first book. $125.

BACK, Sir George. *Narrative of the Arctic Land* . . . London, 1836. Folding map and 16 plates. $1,500.

BACKHOUSE, Janet. *The Madresfield Hours.* London: Roxburghe Club, 1975. $350.

BACON, Sir Francis. *Letters . . .* London, 1702. $500.

BACON, Sir Francis. *The Twoo Bookes of Francis Bacon.* London, 1605. $5,000.

BACON, Leonard. *The Ballad of Blonay . . .* Vevy, 1906. Author's first book. Wraps. $300.

BACON, Peggy. *Funeralities.* New York (1925). Original etching signed as the frontispiece. One of 250 copies. $600.

BACON, Peggy. *The True Philospher . . .* Boston, 1919. Author's first book. $75.

BADDELEY, John F. *The Rugged Flanks of Caucasus.* London, 1940. 2 vols. 9 maps (8 extending) and 38 plates. $2,000.

BADEN-POWELL, S. S. *Aids to Scouting for N.C.O.s and Men.* Gale & Polden, no date [1899]. Small pocket size, red cloth wraps. Ads on endpapers. $1,500.

BADGER, Mrs. C. M. *Floral Bells from the Green-House & Garden.* New York, 1867. With 16 hand-colored lithographed plates. $2,000.

BADGER, Mrs. C. M. *Wild Flowers Drawn and Coloured from Nature.* New York and London, 1859. With 22 full-page color lithographs. $2,000.

BAER, Elizabeth. *Seventeenth Century Maryland: A Bibliography.* Baltimore, 1949. One of 300 copies. $300.

BAGNOLD, Enid. *National Velvet.* London, 1935. $1,250. New York, 1935. $450.

BAGSTER, Samuel. *The Management of Bees.* London, 1834. Hand-colored frontispiece. $750.

BAHR, Howard. *The Black Flower.* Baltimore, 1997. First issue without *Southern Living* blurb on dustwrapper. $250.

BAHR, Jerome. *All Good Americans.* New York, 1937. Preface by Ernest Hemingway. Blue cloth. $250. Reissued in yellow cloth, 1939 (with "A" on copyright page, an exception to the Scribner method of marking only first editions with an "A"). $75.

BAILEY, H. C. *The Great Game.* London, 1939. $600.

BAILEY, Washington. *A Trip to California in 1853.* (LeRoy, Ill.), 1915. Portrait. Printed wraps. $750.

BAILY, Francis. *Journal of a Tour in Unsettled Parts of North America in 1796 & 1797.* London, 1856. $750.

BAIN, Alexander. *The Emotions and the Will.* London, 1859. Blind-embossed brown cloth. $300.

BAINBRIDGE, Beryl. *A Weekend with Claude.* (London), 1967. Author's first book. $125.

BAINBRIDGE, George C. *The Fly-Fisher's Guide.* Liverpool, 1816. 8 colored plates. $1,500. One of 12 large-paper copies. $2,500.

BAINES, Thomas. *The Gold Regions of South Eastern Africa.* London, 1877. Folding map in rear pocket. $750.

BAIRD, Joseph A. *California's Pictorial Letter Sheets, 1849–1869.* San Francisco, 1967. Grabhorn printing. One of 475 signed copies. In plain dustwrapper. $350.

BAIRD, Spencer F., BREWER, T. M.; and RIDGWAY, R. *A History of North American Birds.* Boston, 1874. 3 vols. 64 hand-colored plates. $2,000. Boston, 1875. 3 vols. Second edition. 36 hand-colored and unnumbered plates and 64 chromolithographed numbered plates. $2,500.

BAIRD, Spencer F., BREWER, T. M., and RIDGWAY, R. *The Water Birds of North America.* Boston, 1884. 2 vols. Hand-colored illustrations. Cloth. $2,500.

BAKER, Asa. *Mum's the Word for Murder.* New York, 1938. (By Davis Dresser.) Author's first book. $750.

BAKER, Carlos H. *Shadows in the Stone.* Hanover, N.H. 1930. Author's first book. Wraps. One of 125 signed copies. $150.

BAKER, Charles H. Collins. *Lely and the Stuart Portrait Painters.* London, 1912. 2 vols. 240 reproductions. One of 350 copies (50 for U.S.). $750. Vellum. One of 30 copies, with an extra set of plates. $1,250.

BAKER, D. W. C. (compiler). *A Texas Scrap-Book.* New York (1875). $450.

BAKER, David Erskine. *Biographia Dramatica, Or, A Companion to the Playhouse . . .* Various publishers. London, 1812. 3 vols. Third edition. $500.

BAKER, Dorothy. *Young Man with a Horn.* (Boston) 1938. $300. London, 1938. $200.

BAKER, Elliott. *A Fine Madness.* New York (1964). $125. London (1964). $75.

BAKER, George. *The History and Antiquities of the County of Northampton.* London, 1822–41. 2 vols. 39 plates. $1,250.

BAKER, Howard. *Orange Valley.* New York (1931). $750.

BAKER, Hozial H. *Overland Journey to Carson Valley, Utah.* Seneca Falls, N.Y., 1861. Woodcut frontispiece and other illustrations. 38 pages, yellow printed wraps. $6,000. San Francisco: Book Club of California, 1973. In plain dustwrapper. $75.

BALDWIN, James. *Giovanni's Room.* New York, 1956. $500. London (1957). $150.

BALDWIN, James. *Go Tell It on the Mountain.* New York, 1953. Author's first book. $3,000. London, 1954. $400.

BALDWIN, James. *If Beale Street Could Talk.* New York, 1974. Leatherette. One of 250 signed copies in slipcase. $350. Trade. $75.

BALDWIN, James. *Notes of a Native Son.* Boston (1955). First issue dustwrapper without blurbs. $750. In later dustwrapper. $450.

BALDWIN, James. *Nothing Personal.* New York, 1964. Illustrated by Richard Avedon. Boards. Issued without dustwrapper. In slipcase. $450.

BALDWIN, James. *The Story of Siegfried.* New York, 1882. Illustrated by Howard Pyle. Pictorial cloth. $150.

BALDWIN, Joseph G. *The Flush Times of Alabama and Mississippi.* New York, 1853. $300.

BALDWIN, Joseph G. *Remarks of Mr. Baldwin . . .* No place or date [Montgomery, AL, 1843–44]. 16-page pamphlet. Author's first book. $750.

BALFOUR, James. *Reminiscenses of Golf on St. Andrews Links.* Edinburgh, 1887. Original wraps. $6,000.

BALL, John. *In the Heat of the Night.* New York (1965). $750.

BALLANTYNE, Robert Michael. *Hudson's Bay . . .* Edinburgh, 1848. Author's first book. $2,500. Edinburgh/London, 1848. $750.

BALLANTYNE Press and Its Founders, The. Edinburgh, 1909. $200.

BALLARD, Ellis Ames. *Catalogue, Intimate and Descriptive of My Kipling Collection . . .* Philadelphia, 1935. One of 120 copies. $250.

BALLARD, J. G. *The Atrocity Exhibition.* London (1970). $300.

BALLARD, J. G. *The Crystal World.* London (1966). $500.

BALLARD, J. G. *The Day of Creation.* London, 1987. One of 100 signed copies. In slipcase. $250. Trade. $40.

BALLARD, J. G. *The Drought.* London (1965). $600.

BALLARD, J. G. *The Drowned World.* London, 1962. First issue: red boards. $1,000. New York (1962). $250.

BALLARD, J. G. *Empire of the Sun.* London, 1984. One of 100 copies signed by the author. In slipcase. $750. Trade. $100.

BALSTON, Thomas. *William Balston, Paper Maker, 1759–1849.* London, 1954. $150.

BALTES, F. W. *The Cost of Printing, A System in Practical Operation . . .* Portland, 1894. $175.

BALWHIDDER, The Rev. Micah. *Annals of the Parish; or The Chronicle of Dalmailing.* Edinburgh, 1821. (By John Galt.) $200.

BANCROFT, Edward. *Experimental Researches Concerning the Philosophy of Permanent Colours.* London, 1794. Vol. 1. (All published.) $1,500. Philadelphia, 1814. 2 vols. 1st American ed., enlarged and improved. $750.

BANCROFT, George. *Poems.* Cambridge, Mass., 1823. $250.

BANCROFT, George. *Prospectus of a School . . .* (Cambridge, 1823. With J. C. Coggswell.) Author's first book. Wraps. $250.

BANCROFT, H. H. *History of the North Mexican States and Texas, 1521–1889.* San Francisco, 1883–1889. Two thick volumes. $450.

BANCROFT, Hubert Howe. *The Works of Hubert Howe Bancroft.* San Francisco, 1883–1890. 39 vols. Illustrated. Cloth. $2,000. In half calf or sheep. $3,500.

BANDELIER, Adolph F. *The Gilded Man.* New York, 1893. $150.

BANDINI, Joseph. *A Description of California in 1828.* Berkeley, Calif., 1951. Illustrated. Boards and cloth. One of 400 copies. $100.

BANCS, John Kendrick. See B., J.K.

BANGS, John Kendrick. *Bikey the Skicycle and Other Tales of Jimmie Boy.* New York, 1902. Illustrated by Peter Newell. Decorated cloth. $200.

BANGS, John Kendrick. *Mephistopheles: A Profanation.* New York, 1889. Red wraps. $200.

BANGS, John Kendrick. *Mr. Munchausen.* Boston, 1901. First state, with Small, Maynard copyright. (Not seen by BAL.) $200. Second state overstamped with "Noyes, Platt & Co." $100.

BANGS, John Kendrick. *R. Holmes & Co.* New York, 1906. $250.

BANGS, John Kendrick. *Roger Camerden.* New York, 1887. Wraps. $200.

BANKS, Ian. *The Wasp Factory.* London, 1984. Author's first book. $175.

BANNEKER, The Afric-American Astronomer. From the Posthumous Papers of Martha E. Tyson. Philadelphia, 1884. (Edited by her Daughter.) Introduction by Anne T. Kirk (who is presumably the author). $1,000.

BANNERMAN, Helen. *A New Adventure of Little Black Sambo.* London (1937). $1,000.

BANNERMAN, Helen. *The Story of Little Black Sambo.* London, 1899. Colored plates. Original pale-green cloth lettered and stamped in dark green with ruled borders and vertical stripes. Issued as the fourth volume in "Dumpy Books for Children." $12,500. New York [1901]. $2,500. New York, 1936. $750. London (1937). $750.

BANTA, William, and CALDWELL, J. W., Jr. *Twenty-Seven Years on the Frontier, or Fifty Years in Texas.* Austin, 1893. Frontispiece. Wraps. $2,000.

BANTOCK, Miles. *On Many Greens.* New York: Grossett & Dunlap, 1901. $450.

BANVILLE, John. *Long Lankin.* London, 1970. Author's first book. $750.

BARBE-MARBOIS, François. *The History of Louisiana, Particularly the Cession of That Colony to the U.S.A.* Philadelphia, 1830. First edition in English. $1,000.

BARDIN, John Franklin. *The Deadly Percheron.* New York, 1946. $300.

BARFIELD, Owen. *Dancer, Ugliness and Waste.* (London, no date [circa 1922–24].) Wraps. $350.

BARFIELD, Owen. *History in English Words.* London, 1926. (8 pages of advertisements.) $250.

BARHAM, Richard Harris. See Ingoldsby, Thomas.

BARING, Maurice. See B., M.

BARING, Maurice. *Algae: An Anthology of Phrases.* London, 1928. Wraps, paper label. One of 100 signed copies. In dustwrapper and slipcase. $125.

BARING-GOULD, Sabine. *The Book of Were-Wolves.* London: Smith, Elder and Co., 1865. In original cloth. $1,500.

BARKER, A(udrey) L(illian). *Innocents.* London, 1947. $300. New York, 1948. $75.

BARKER, Clive. *The Books of Blood.* London, 1984–85. Vols. I–VI. Author's first book. Wraps. $300. London (1985–86). 6 vols. Cloth. One of 200 signed copies. $750. Trade edition. $250.

BARKER, Eugene, C. *The Life of Stephen F. Austin.* Nashville, 1925. 2 maps, plan, 6 portraits. Boards and vellum. One of 250 signed copies. $400. Trade edition. $175.

BARKER, George. *Alanna Autumnal.* London, 1932. $150.

BARKER, George (Granville). *Catalog of Emotions.* (London), 1932. Author's first book. Wraps. $400.

BARKER, George. *Poems.* London (1935). $125.

BARKER, George. *Thirty Preliminary Poems.* London, 1933. In glassine dustwrapper. $200.

BARKER, Matthew Henry. *The Old Sailor's Jolly Boat.* London, 1844. 24 full-page engravings by George and Robert Cruikshank. $350.

BARKER, Pat. *Union Street.* London (1982). $250. New York (1983). $100.

BARLOW, Joel. *The Columbiad: A Poem.* Philadelphia, 1807. Portrait and 11 plates. (New edition of *The Vision of Columbus,* see below.) $300.

BARLOW, Joel. *Joel Barlow to His Fellow Citizens of the United States.* (Caption title.) (Philadelphia, 1799.) $250. (Philadelphia, 1801.) Second American edition. $150.

BARLOW, Joel. *The Vision of Columbus: A Poem in Nine Books.* Hartford, 1787. $350. (Reprinted as *The Columbiad.*)

BARLOW, William. *The Navigators Supply.* London, 1597. Author's first book. $12,500.

BARNARD, Edward Emerson. *A Photographic Atlas of Selected Regions of the Milky Way.* Washington, D.C., 1927. 2 vols. 51 mounted glossy photographic plates. Original brown cloth, gilt. One of 700 copies. $2,500.

BARNARD, George. *The Theory and Practice of Landscape Painting . . .* London, 1855. 43 woodcuts and figures. Gilt decorated cover. $400.

BARNARD, George N. *Photographic Views of Sherman's Campaign.* New York (1866). 61 gold-toned albumen prints, mounted, with lithographic captions. Oblong folio, morocco. $45,000.

BARNARD, Marjorie, and ELDERSHAW K. *A House is Built.* London, 1929. $600.

BARNARD, Robert. *Death of an Old Goat.* London, 1974. $350. New York (1977). $150.

BARNES, David M. *The Draft Riots in New York, July, 1863.* New York, 1863. 117 pages, wraps, or cloth. $300.

BARNES, Demas. *From the Atlantic to the Pacific, Overland, A Series of Letters . . . Describing a Trip from New York, Via Chicago, Atchison . . .* New York, 1866. $300.

BARNES, Djuna. See *Ladies Almanack.*

BARNES, Djuna. *A Book.* New York (1923). 6 portraits. Black boards, paper label. $1,500.

BARNES, Djuna. *The Book of Repulsive Women.* (New York, 1915.) Author's first book. Illustrated. Gold wraps. $1,000. Yonkers, 1948. Stiff wraps. One of 1,000 copies. $100.

BARNES, Djuna. *Ladies Almanack.* Paris, 1928. One of 1,000 copies. Pictorial wrappers. $400. One of 40 copies on Rives paper. $3,500. One of 10 copies hand-colored and signed by the author. On Vergé de Vidalon. $5,000.

BARNES, Djuna. *A Night Among the Horses.* New York, 1929. $750.

BARNES, Djuna. *Nightwood.* London (1936). $500. New York (1937). Contains an introduction by T. S. Eliot. $300.

BARNES, Djuna. *Ryder.* New York, 1928. $600.

BARNES, Julian. See also Kavanagh, Dan.

BARNES, Julian. *Flaubert's Parrot.* London (1984). $600. New York, 1985. $150.

BARNES, Julian. *Metroland.* London (1980). Author's first book. $350. New York, 1980. $250.

BARNES, Will C. *Apaches and Longhorns.* Los Angeles, 1941. Edited by Frank C. Lockwood. Illustrated. $200.

BARNES, Will C. *Tales from the X-Bar Horse Camp.* Chicago, 1920. $300.

BARNES, William C., McCANN, Joseph W., and DUG, Alexander. *A Collation of Facts Relative to Fast Typesetting . . .* New York, 1887. $500.

BARNEY, James M. *Tales of Apache Warfare.* (Phoenix) 1933. 45 pages, wraps. $250.

BARNEY, Natalie C. See *Tryphe.*

BARNEY, Natalie C. *The One Who Is Legion.* London, 1930. $350.

BARNEY, Natalie C. *Poems & Poèmes.* Paris & New York (1920). Wraps. Copies on blue paper. $350. White paper. $250.

BARNEY, Natalie C. *Quelques Portraits.* Paris, 1900. Author's first book. $500.

BARNUM, Phineas Taylor. *The Life of P. T. Barnum.* New York, 1855. Author's first book. $175.

BARR, James. *Derricks.* New York (1951). $200.

BARR, Louise Farrow. *Presses of Northern California and Their Books, 1900–1933.* Berkeley, 1934. One of 400 copies. $300.

BARR, Nevada. *Bittersweet.* New York (1984). Author's first book. $500.

BARR, Nevada. *Track of the Cat.* New York (1993). Author's first mystery. $300.

BARR, Robert. *The Triumph of Eugene Valmont.* London, 1906. $300.

BARRETT, E. B. *The Battle of Marathon: A Poem.* London, 1820. (By Elizabeth Barrett Browning.) (50 copies.) $75,000.

BARRETT, Elizabeth. *Poems.* London, 1844. (By Elizabeth Barrett Browning.) 2 vols. With ads in vol. 1 dated June 1. $1,250. No ads. $1,000. London, 1850. 2 vols. Brown cloth. Second edition, first issue, with single address in imprint, called "New Edition." (First appearance of "Sonnets from the Portuguese" in a book.) $1,500.

BARRETT, Elizabeth B. *The Seraphim and Other Poems.* London, 1838. (By Elizabeth Barrett Browning.) Original cloth. $400.

BARRETT, Elizabeth, and BROWNING, Robert. *Two Poems.* London, 1854. (By Elizabeth Barrett Browning.) Printed wrapper. $750.

BARRETT, Ellen C. *Baja California, 1535–1956: A Bibliography.* Los Angeles, 1957. Blue cloth. One of 500 copies. $300. Also, one of 50 signed copies. $500.

BARRETT, Timothy. *Nagashizuki: The Japanese Craft of Hand Papermaking.* North Hills, 1979. (Dard Hunter.) One of 300 copies. $450.

BARRIE, Sir James M. See *The Allahakbarrie Book of Broadway Cricket for 1899.*

BARRIE, Sir James M. *The Admirable Crichton.* London (1914). Illustrated by Hugh Thomson. $250. One of 500 copies signed by Thomson. $750.

BARRIE, Sir James M. *Auld Licht Idylls.* London, 1888. First issue, with black endpapers (VAB). (Bibliographies call for green end papers). $400.

BARRIE, Sir James M. *Better Dead.* London, 1888 (actually 1887). Author's first book. Pictorial glazed yellow (or buff) wraps. $1,500.

BARRIE, Sir James M. *An Edinburgh Eleven.* London, 1889. ("Gavin Ogilvy" on front cover and "J. M. Barrie" on title page.) First issue in wraps. $250. Later issue same date; gray cloth. $200.

BARRIE, Sir James M. *The Little Minister.* London, 1891. 3 vols. Brown cloth. With 16 pages of ads in vol. 1. $750.

BARRIE, Sir James M. *My Lady Nicotine.* London, 1890. First issue, with 6 pages of ads at back. $250.

BARRIE, Sir James M. *Peter and Wendy.* London (1911). $600. New York (1911). $500.

BARRIE, Sir James M. *Peter Pan in Kensington Gardens.* London, 1906. Illustrated in color and black-and-white by Arthur Rackham. Vellum. One of 500 copies signed by Rackham. $8,500. Trade edition in cloth. $1,500. New York, 1906. $1,250.

BARRIE, Sir James M. *Quality Street.* (London, 1913.) Vellum with silk ties. One of 1,000 illustrated and signed by Hugh Thomson. $1,000. Trade issue. Cloth. $200.

BARROW, John. *A Chronological History of Voyages into the Arctic Regions.* London, 1818. Illustrated, folding map. $750.

BARROW, John. *Travels in China . . .* London, 1804. Hand-colored frontispiece and 7 engraved plates (2 folding and 4 hand-colored). $2,500.

BARROW, John. *A Voyage to Cochinchina, 1792–1793.* London, 1806. Double-page map, double-page chart, 19 colored aquatint plates. $3,000.

BARROWS, R. M. (compiler). *The Kitbook for Soldiers, Sailors, and Marines.* Chicago (1942— facing title page). Pictorial boards. In pictorial mailing box. (Contains J. D. Salinger's story "The Hang of It," his first book appearance.) $1,500. Without mailing box. $750. Chicago (1943). With box. $450. More common without box. $150.

BARROWS, Willard. *Notes on Iowa Territory.* Cincinnati, 1845. Folding map. 46 pages, cloth, printed front cover label. $2,500.

BARRY, T. A., and PATTEN, B. A. *Men and Memories of San Francisco, in the "Spring of '50."* San Francisco, 1873. 2 plates. Flexible cloth. $250.

BARTELL, Edmund. *Hints for Picturesque Improvements in Ornamented Cottages and Their Scenery . . .* London, 1804. 6 plates. $750.

BARTH, John. *The End of the Road.* Garden City, 1958. $350. London, 1962. $150.

BARTH, John. *The Floating Opera.* New York (1956). Author's first book. $500. Garden City, 1967. Revised. $100. London (1968). $75.

BARTH, John. *Giles Goat-Boy.* Garden City, 1966. One of 250 signed copies. In slipcase. $350. Trade. With "H18" on last page of text." $125. London (1967). $100.

BARTH, John. *Lost in the Funhouse.* Garden City, 1968. One of 250 signed copies. In slipcase. $175. Trade. $50. London, (1969). $100.

BARTH, John. *The Sot-Weed Factor.* Garden City, 1960. $750. London, 1961. $150.

BARTHELME, Donald. *Come Back, Dr. Caligari.* Boston (1964). Author's first book. $250. London, 1966. $150.

BARTHELME, Donald. *The Slightly Irregular Fire Engine . . .* New York, 1971. $175.

BARTHELME, Donald. *Snow White.* New York, 1967. $125. London, 1968. $75.

BARTLETT, Edward. *A Monograph of the Weaver-Birds . . .* (Maidstone, 1888–89.) Parts 1 to 5 in one volume. 31 plates. Ranges from $1,500 with some plates hand-colored to $6,000 with all hand-colored.

BARTLETT, Edward Everett. *The Typographic Treasures in Europe and a Study of Contemporaneous Book Production . . .* New York, 1925. One of 580 copies. $200.

BARTLETT, John. See *A Collection of Familiar Quotations.*

BARTLETT, John Russell. *Personal Narrative of Explorations and Incidents in Texas, New Mexico, California* . . . New York, 1854. 2 vols. Folding map. 44 plates, pictorial cloth. $1,250. London, 1854. 2 vols. $1,000.

BARTON, James L. *Commerce of the Lakes.* Buffalo, 1847. Folding table. 80 pages. Wraps. $500.

BARTON, William P. C. *Compendium Florae Philadelphicae* . . . Philadelphia, 1818. 2 vols. $600.

BARTON, William P. C. *A Flora of North America.* Philadelphia, 1821–23. 3 vols. 106 hand-colored plates. $4,500.

BARTON, William P. C. *The Vegetable Materia Medica of the U.S.; Or Medical Botany* . . . Philadelphia, 1817–1818. 2 vols. 50 hand-colored plates. $4,500.

BARTRAM, John. *Observations on the Inhabitants* . . . London, 1751. $10,000.

BARTRAM, William. *Travels Through North & South Carolina.* Philadelphia, 1791. Author's first book. Folding map, 8 plates, including frontispiece. $10,000. London, 1792. $5,000. Dublin, 1793. $2,000.

BARZUN, Jacques Martin. *Samplings and Chronicles.* (Edited by J.M.B.) New York, 1927. (500 copies.) $150.

BASKIN, Leonard. *Ars Anatomica, A Medical Fantasia, Thirteen Drawings.* New York (1972). Contains two sets of 13 suites enclosed in portfolio. One of 300 signed sets. $450. One of 2,500 signed copies. $400.

BASKIN, Leonard. *Demons, Imps & Friends.* (Northampton, MA), 1976. 18 plates of illustrations. One of 450 copies signed by Baskin. $300.

BASKIN, Leonard. *To Colour Thought.* New Haven, 1967. One of 300 copies. In slipcase. $450.

BASKIN, Leonard. *The Wood Engravings of Leonard Baskin, 1948–1959.* Northampton, 1961. 168 signed engravings. Folio, loose in half-morocco case. One of 24 copies. $10,000.

BASS, Rick. *The Deer Pasture.* College Station, 1985. Author's first book. $200.

BASS, W. W. (editor). *Adventures in the Canyons of the Colorado by Two of Its Earliest Explorers, James White and H. W. Hawkins.* Grand Canyon, 1920. Frontispiece, plate, facsimiles. 38 pages, wraps. $350.

BATCHELOR, John Calvin. *The Furthur Adventures of Haley's Comet.* New York, 1980. Author's first book. Cloth. $300. Wraps. $50.

BATEMAN, Ed W. *The Instinct Never Dies.* No place, 1931. Full limp cowhide. $3,750.

BATES, Ed. F. *History* . . . *of Denton County Texas.* Denton, Tex. (1918). Plates. Cloth. $750.

BATES, H. E. *The Beauty of the Dead, and One Other Story.* Corvinus Press. London, 1941. One of 25 copies. $1,000.

BATES, H. E. *Flowers and Faces.* London: Golden Cockerel Press. 1935. Engravings by John Nash. One of 325 copies. $500.

BATES, H. E. *A German Idyll.* Waltham Saint Lawrence: Golden Cockerel Press, 1932. $400.

BATES, H. E. *The Last Bread:A Play in One Act.* London (1926). Author's first book. Wraps. $150.

BATES, H. E. *Sally Go Round the Moon.* London, 1932. White Owl Press. One of 21 signed copies. In slipcase. $750. Trade. $300.

BATES, H. E. *The Story Without an End.* (London): White Owl Press, 1932. One of 25 signed copies, with a leaf of manuscript. $1,000.

BATES, H. E. *The Two Sisters.* London, 1926. $350.

BATES, Henry Walter. *The Naturalist on the River Amazon.* London: John Murray, 1863. 2 vols. Folding map. 9 engraved plates. $2,500.

BATES, J. H. *Notes of a Tour in Mexico and California.* New York, 1887. $250.

BATESON, F. W. (editor). *The Cambridge Bibliography of English Literature.* Cambridge, 1940. 5 vols. $300.

BATESON, William. *Mendel's Principles of Heredity.* Cambridge, 1902. In original cloth. $2,500.

BAUDELAIRE, Charles. *Intimate Journals.* London, 1930. Translated by Christopher Isherwood. Introduction by T. S. Eliot. One of 400 copies in slipcase. $450. One of 50 copies signed by Eliot. $2,000. New York, 1930. $300. Hollywood, 1947. Revised edition (with W. H. Auden introduction). $150.

BAUER, Max. *Precious Stones.* London, 1904. Translated from the German by L. J. Spencer. 20 colored plates. Half morocco. $750.

NOTE: **The bibliography is a necessity for the Oz books.**

BAUM, L. Frank. *American Fairy Tales.* Chicago, 1901. Illustrated. Pictorial cloth. $1,250.

BAUM, L. Frank. *The Army Alphabet.* Chicago, 1900. Illustrated by Harry Kennedy. Pictorial boards. $1,500.

BAUM, L. Frank. *The Book of Hamburgs.* Hartford, 1886. Author's first book. $4,500.

BAUM, L. Frank. *The Cowardly Lion and the Hungry Tiger.* Chicago (1913). Color plates. Boards. $500.

BAUM, L. Frank. *Dorothy and the Wizard in Oz.* Chicago (1908). Illustrated by John R. Neill. 16 full-color inserts. First issue, with "The Reilly & Britton Co." at bottom of spine versus "Reilly & Britton." $1,250. Second issue. $750.

BAUM, L. Frank. *Dot and Tot of Merryland.* Chicago, 1901. Illustrated by W. W. Denslow. Gilt-pictorial cloth. $1,750.

BAUM, L. Frank. *The Emerald City of Oz.* Chicago, 1910. $1,500.

BAUM, L. Frank. *The Enchanted Island of Yew.* Indianapolis (1903). Illustrated by Fanny Y. Cory. First state with Braunworth's imprint on copyright page, and illustration on page 238 incorrectly positioned over text. $750. Second state. $350.

BAUM, L. Frank. *Father Goose's Year Book*. Chicago (1907). Illustrated. $350.

BAUM, L. Frank. *The Life and Adventures of Santa Claus*. Indianapolis, 1902. First state with headings "Book First," "Book Second, and "Book Third." $1,500. Second state with headings "Youth," "Manhood," and "Old Age." $750.

BAUM, L. Frank. *The Little Wizard Series*. Chicago (1913). 6 vols. Each a first edition. In wraps stapled in center. Printed on highly calendered, semi-glossy paper stock with shadowed areas below lion and tiger on endpapers printed in solid blue. $5,000. Second issue on slightly rough wove paper stock with shadowed area in blue halftone stipple. $2,500.

BAUM, L. Frank. *Little Wizard Stories of Oz*. Chicago (1914). 6 vols in one. First state in yellow cloth with color pictorial label on front cover and one inch thick. $1,000.

BAUM, L. Frank. *The Marvelous Land of Oz*. Chicago, 1904. First issue, without "Published July, 1904" on copyright page. $6,000. With date on copyright page. $3,500. With title on cover shortened to "The Land of Oz." $350. (All have 1904 on title page.)

BAUM, L. Frank. *The Master Key*. Indianapolis (1901). Illustrated in color by Fanny Cory. Olive-green cloth. First issue, with signatures of 8 pages and second line on copyright page 1²¹⁄₃₂ inches wide. $500. Second issue, signatures of 16 pages. $300. Third issue, second line on copyright page 1²⁵⁄₃₂ inches wide. $200.

BAUM, L. Frank. *Mother Goose in Prose*. Chicago (1897). Illustrated by Maxfield Parrish (his first book of illustrations). Way & Williams. Pictorial cloth. First issue with gatherings of 8 and 4 leaves at end concluding on page (268). $6,000. Chicago: Hill (1901). 12 plates. Pictorial cloth. $1,000.

BAUM, L. Frank. *A New Wonderland*. New York, 1900. Illustrated by Frank Verbeck. $4,500. Secondary binding with blank endpapers. $2,500.

BAUM, L. Frank. *Ozma of Oz*. Chicago (1907). First issue, with illustration in color on page 221, and spine imprint "The Reilly & Britton Co." $1,500. Second issue "Reilly & Britton." $750.

BAUM, L. Frank. *The Patchwork Girl of Oz*. Chicago: Reilly & Britton (1913). Light-green pictorial cloth. First state, with the "C" in chapter 3 touching text. $1,250. Second state with correction, in light-tan cloth. $750.

BAUM, L. Frank. *Queen Zixi of Ix*. New York, 1905. First state with terra-cotta and black text illustrations on pages 169–236. $750. Second state, with illustrations in turquoise and black on pages 169–84 and 221–36. $450.

BAUM, L. Frank. *The Road to Oz*. Chicago: Reilly & Britton (1909). First two pages of ads at end with color-tinted text sheets. $1,500. Later printings have an ad for Rinkitink in Oz (1916), on verso of ownership page.

BAUM, L. Frank. *The Sea Fairies*. Chicago (1911). First issue, with three heads on cover label. $750. Second issue has cover label showing girl on a sea horse. $350.

BAUM, L. Frank. *The Songs of Father Goose*. Chicago, 1900. Illustrated by W. W. Denslow. Colored pictorial boards. $1,000.

BAUM, L. Frank. *The Wishing Horse of Oz*. Chicago (1935). Illustrated by John R. Neill. Includes 12 color plates. Color pictorial label. Dustwrapper repeats cover design. $750.

BAUM, L. Frank. *The Woggle-Bug Book*. Chicago, 1905. Illustrated by Ike Morgan. First state: front cover printed in colors, background is field of gray-green, no printing on back cover. $3,500. Second state: front cover background is field of pale-yellow and yellow lettering on back cover. $3,000.

BAUM, L. Frank. *The Wonderful Wizard of Oz*. Chicago and New York, 1900. Illustrated by W. W. Denslow. Green cloth. First issue, with publisher's ads enclosed in box on page 2 and at end of book, and with an 11-line colophon. Publisher's imprint at base of spine stamped in green. $65,000. Second issue, with no box around ads, colophon in 13 lines, and imprint stamped in red. $30,000. (There are other points, and mixed states seem common.) NY, 1982. One of 500 copies signed by illustrator Michael Hague. In slipcase. $200. West Hatfield: Pennyroyal Press, 1985. First 25 numbered copies (out of 350 copies) with extra suite of 62 wood engravings each signed and numbered by the artist Barry Moser. $6,000. Remaining 325 copies signed by Moser. $1,500.

BAUM, L. Frank. *The Yellow Hen*. Chicago (1916). First state, without ads for 6-vol. series on verso of ownership leaf. $1,000. Second state, with ads. $450.

BAX, Clifford (editor). *Florence Farr, Bernard Shaw and W. B. Yeats*. Dublin: Cuala Press, 1941. Boards, linen spine, paper label. One of 500 copies. In tissue dustwrapper. $250.

BAX, Clifford. *Twenty Chinese Poems*. Hampstead, 1910. $125.

BAXLEY, H. Willis. *What I Saw on the West Coast of South and North America, and at the Hawaiian Islands*. New York, 1865. $400.

BAXTER, Charles. *Chameleon*. New York, 1970. Wraps. $400.

BAXTER, Stephen. *Anti-Ice*. (London, 1993.) $500.

BAY, J. Christian. *A Handful of Western Books with a Second Handful of Western Books with a Third Handful of Western Books*. Cedar Rapids, Iowa, 1935–36–37. 3 vols. Illustrated. Boards and cloth. Limited to 350, 400, and 400 copies, respectively. Issued in tissue dustwrappers. Together, the 3 vols. $300. Odd vols. $50–$100 each.

BAY, J. Christian. *Three Handfuls of Western Books*. (Cedar Rapids) 1941. (Combined 1-vol. edition of preceding items.) Boards. One of 35 copies. $300.

BAYLDON, Oliver. *The Paper Maker's Craft*. Leicester, 1965. Limited to "less than 400 copies." $200.

BAYLEY, Harold. *A New Light on the Renaissance, Displayed in Contemporary Emblems*. London (1909). $250.

BAYLIES, Francis. *A Narrative of General Wool's Campaign in Mexico*. Albany, 1851. Frontispiece. 78 pages, printed yellow wraps. $600.

BEACH, Rex. *Pardners*. New York, 1905. Author's first book. $125.

BEACH, Rex. *Spoilers*. New York, 1905. $125.

BEADLE, Clayton. *Chapters on Papermaking*. London, 1908–9. 5 vols. $150.

BEAGLE, Peter S. *A Fine and Private Place*. New York, 1960. Author's first book. $200. London, 1960. $125.

BEAGLE, Peter S. *The Last Unicorn.* New York (1968). $200.

BEAJEAN, Jean. *Jiu-Jitsu Partie Judo.* Paris, 1954. One of 1,250 copies. $250.

BEALE, Charles Willing. *The Secret of the Earth.* New York (1899). Wraps. $750.

BEALE, Joseph Henry. *A Bibliography of Early English Law Books.* Cambridge (1926). $350.

BEALS, Carleton. *The Crime of Cuba.* Philadelphia (1933). 31 photographs by Walker Evans. His first book appearance. $750.

BEAN, Edwin F. (compiler). *Bean's History and Directory of Nevada County, California.* Nevada, Calif., 1867. Half leather and boards. $2,500.

BEARD, Charles A. *An Economic Interpretation of the Constitution of the United States.* New York, 1913. $350.

BEARD, Charles A. *The Office of the Justice . . .* New York, 1904. Author's first book. Wraps. $200.

BEARD, Charles R. *A Catalogue of the Collection of Martinware Formed by Frederick John Nettlefold.* (London), 1936. 31 color plates, 46 in black-and-white. Half brown morocco. $600. Cloth. $400.

BEARD, James. *Hors D'Oeuvres and Canapes.* New York (1940). Author's first book. $150.

BEARDSLEY, Aubrey. *A Book of Fifty Drawings.* London, 1897. $750. One of 50 on vellum. $2,000.

BEARDSLEY, Aubrey. *A Second Book of Fifty Drawings.* London, 1899. One of 1,000 copies. $450. One of 50 copies on vellum. $3,000.

BEARDSLEY, Aubrey. *Six Drawings Illustrating Theophile Gautier's Romance, "Mademoiselle de Maupin."* London, 1898. 6 plates, loose in half-cloth portfolio, silk ties. One of 50 copies. $1,000.

BEARDSLEY, Aubrey. *The Story of Venus and Tannhauser: A Romantic Novel.* London, 1907. One of 250 copies on handmade paper. $500. One of 50 copies on Japan vellum. $1,500.

BEARDSLEY, Aubrey. *The Uncollected Works.* London (1925). Profusion of plates by Beardsley. Gilt-pictorial cloth. $300. One of 110 copies on Japan vellum. $750.

BEARDSLEY, Aubrey. *Under the Hill and Other Essays in Prose and Verse.* London, 1904. 16 illustrations by the author. One of 50 copies on Japan vellum. $1,250. Trade edition. $650.

BEASLEY, Gertrude. *My First Thirty Years . . .* (Paris, 1925.) Author's first book. Wraps. $500.

BEATON, Cecil. *The Book of Beauty.* London (1930). 27 photographic plates, 90 text drawings. Buckram. One of 110 signed copies. $1,250. Trade edition. $750.

BEATON, George. *Jack Robinson.* London (1933). (By Gerald Brenan.) $400. New York, 1934. $300.

BEATTIE, Ann. *Chilly Scenes of Winter.* Garden City, 1976. (Issued simultaneously with *Distortions.*) $150.

BEATTIE, Ann. *Distortions.* Garden City, 1976. Author's first book. $200.

BEATTIE, Ann. *Jacklighting.* Worcester, 1981. One of 26 signed, lettered copies. In dustwrapper. $600. One of 250 signed copies in wraps. $75.

BEATTIE, William. *Switzerland Illustrated.* London, 1836. 2 vols. With 2 engraved titles, folding map, and 106 plates by W. H. Bartlett. $1,500.

BEAUCHAMPE: or, the Kentucky Tragedy. Philadelphia, 1842. (By William Gilmore Simms.) 2 vols. $600.

BEAUMONT, Charles. *The Hunger and Other Stories.* New York (1957). (By Charles Nutt.) $350.

BEAUMONT, Cyril W. *The History of Harlequin.* London, 1926. With a preface by Sacheverell Sitwell. 44 plates (5 colored), text decorations by Claudia Guercio. Decorated parchment boards, vellum spine. London, 1926. One of 325 copies. $600.

BEAUMONT, Cyril W. *Puppets and the Puppet Stage.* London, 1938. 110 pages of illustrations. Illustrated wraps. $200. Cloth without dustwrapper. $100.

BEAUMONT, Francis, and FLETCHER, John. *Comedies and Tragedies Written by* . . . London, 1647. Folio. Engraved frontispiece portrait of Fletcher by William Marshall with "vates duplex" in line 4 of the lower caption. $5,000.

BEAUMONT, Roberts. *Colour in Woven Design.* London, 1890. Cloth. 32 color plates. $200.

BEAUMONT, William. *Experiments and Observations on the Gastric Juice, and the Physiology of Digestion.* Plattsburg, N.Y., 1833. 3 engravings. $3,000. Boston, 1834. Second issue (first edition sheets with Boston title page). $1,500. Edinburgh, 1838. First English edition. $1,000.

BEAUMONT, William. *The Physiology of Digestion.* Burlington, Vt., 1847. Edited by Samuel Beaumont. Cloth. Second edition of *Experiments and Observations on the Gastric Juice.* $600.

BEAUVOIR, Simone de. *The Mandarins.* New York (1976). One of 500 signed copies. In glassine and slipcase. $300.

BECK, Lewis C. *A Gazetteer of the States of Illinois and Missouri.* Albany, 1823. Folding map, 5 plates. $1,500.

BECKER, Robert H. *Disenos of California Ranchos* . . . San Francisco, 1964. Grabhorn printing. One of 400 copies. $500.

BECKETT, Samuel. See Crowder, Henry; Gorey, Edward.

BECKETT, Samuel. *All Strange Away.* No place [New York], (1976). Illustrated by Edward Gorey. One of 200 copies signed by both. In slipcase. $1,250. One of 26 lettered and signed copies. $3,000.

BECKETT, Samuel. *All That Fall: A Play.* New York (1957). $125. One of 100 specially bound copies. $400. One of 25 signed copies. $1,750. Wraps ("Holiday Greeting"). $100. London, 1957. Wraps. $100.

BECKETT, Samuel. *Beginning to End.* New York, 1988. Illustrated by Edward Gorey. One of 300 signed by both. Pictorial boards. $1,250. One of 26 signed. $2,500.

BECKETT, Samuel. *Come and Go: Dramaticule.* London (1967). One of 100 signed copies. In slipcase. $600.

BECKETT, Samuel. *Echo's Bones and Other Precipitates.* Paris: Europa Press, 1935. 30 pages, printed wraps. One of 25 copies on Normandy vellum, signed. $3,500. One of 250 copies on Alfa paper, unsigned. $1,000. One of 50 hors de commerce. $1,250.

BECKETT, Samuel. *Endgame.* New York (1958). Boards. First American edition. One of 100 copies. $400. London (1958). Translated by the author. One of 26 signed copies. $1,250. Trade. Cloth. $300. Wraps. $40.

BECKETT, Samuel. *How It Is.* New York, 1964. $125. London (1964). (Series A and Series B.) Translated from the French by the author. 2 issues, vellum and morocco. Each, 100 signed copies. In tissue dustwrappers. In slipcase. $850 each.

BECKETT, Samuel. *The Lost Ones.* London, 1972. Half vellum (or half leather). One of 100 signed copies. In slipcase. $750. Stamford, 1984. One of 250 copies with etching by Charles Klabunde. In box. $3,000.

BECKETT, Samuel. *Malone Dies.* New York (1956). Translated by the author. 120 pages, cream-colored canvas. One of 500 copies. In transparent dustwrapper. $600. Trade. $300. London, 1958. $300.

BECKETT, Samuel. *Molloy.* Paris (1951). Printed wraps. First edition (in French). One of 500 copies on Alfa paper. $300. One of 50 copies on vellum. $2,000. Paris: Olympia Press (1955). Wraps. First edition in English. $500. New York (1955). $400.

BECKETT, Samuel. *More Pricks Than Kicks.* London, 1934. $7,500. London (1970). One of 100 signed copies. $1,000.

BECKETT, Samuel. *Murphy.* London (1938). First binding. Green cloth. $5,000. New York (1957). One of 100 signed copies. $1,750. Trade. $400.

BECKETT, Samuel. *No's Knife: Collected Shorter Prose, 1945–1966.* London (1967). One of 100 signed copies. (Series A.) One of 100 signed copies. (Series B.) In slipcases. $650 each.

BECKETT, Samuel. *Poems in English.* London (1961). Mottled tan leather-like cloth boards. One of 100 signed copies. $750. Trade. $200. New York (1963). $150.

BECKETT, Samuel. *Proust.* London, 1931. $750. New York (1957). Limited first American edition. One of 250 signed copies. Issued without dustwrapper. $650. London, 1965. One of 100 signed copies. $850.

BECKETT, Samuel. *The Unnamable.* New York: Grove Press (1958). Translated by the author. One of 26 lettered copies, signed. $1,750. One of 100 copies. $400. Trade, hardbound. $250. Wraps. $50.

BECKETT, Samuel. *Waiting for Godot.* New York (1954). Translated by the author. $2,500. London (1956). Publisher's note tipped in. $750.

BECKETT, Samuel. *Watt.* Collection Merlin: Paris: Olympia Press (1953). Printed wraps. One of 25 copies, lettered A to Y, on fine paper and signed by Beckett. $7,500. First trade edition. Wraps. $600. New York (1959). $300. One of 100 copies signed. $750. One of 26 signed copies. $2,000.

BECKETT, Samuel. *Whoroscope*. Paris, 1930. Hours Press. Author's first separately published work. Stapled wraps, with white (separate) band around the book. One of 100 signed copies (of a total edition of 300). $5,000. One of 200 unsigned copies. $2,500.

BECKETT, Samuel, et al. *Our Exagmination Round His Factifaction for Incamination of Work in Progress*. Paris: Shakespeare and Company, 1929. Printed wraps. $600. One of 96 copies (large-paper) on verge d'Arches paper. $1,750. Norfolk, no date. $450. London, no date. $350. (Both later issues used the Paris sheets and were in cloth with dustwrappers.)

BECKFORD, William. See *Biographical Memoirs* . . .

BEDE, Cuthbert. *Photographic Pleasures, Popularly Portrayed with Pen & Pencil*. London, 1855. Blue gilt-pictorial cloth. 24 black-and-white lithographs. $850.

BEEBE, Henry. *The History of Peru*. Peru, Ill., 1858. Leather. $300.

BEEBE, Lucius. *Fallen Stars*. Cambridge, 1921. Wraps. 50 copies. $300. Boston, 1921. $150.

BEEBE, Lucius. *François Villon* . . . Cambridge, 1921. Wraps. One of 50 copies. $200.

BEEBE, William. *The Arcturus Adventure*. New York, 1926. One of 50 signed copies. Issued without dustwrapper. $600. First trade edition. $150.

BEEBE, William. *Galápagos:World's End*. New York, 1924. One of 100 signed copies. Issued in glassine dustwrapper. In folding box. $1,000. First trade edition. $300.

BEEBE, William. *A Monograph of the Pheasants*. London, 1918–22. 4 vols. 90 color plates, 20 maps, 87 photogravures. Folio, cloth. One of 600 copies. $6,000.

BEEBE, William. *Pheasants:Their Lives and Homes*. Garden City, 1926. 2 vols. 64 plates. Vellum. One of 201 copies on large paper, signed. $1,500. Trade edition. 2 vols. $500. Garden City, 1931. 2 vols. $300. Garden City, 1936. 2 vols. in 1. $150.

BEEBE, William. *Two Bird-Lovers in Mexico*. Boston, 1905. Author's first book. First issue, Charles M. Beebe on cover. $2,500 (one known copy). Second issue, C. William Beebe on cover. $250. Third issue, gold sky background lacking. $150. Fourth issue, lacks pictorial design, just lettered. $100.

BEECHER, Edward. *Narrative of the Riots at Alton*. Alton, Ill., 1838. $300.

BEECHER, Harriet Elizabeth. *Primary Geography for Children* . . . Cincinnati, 1833. (Harriet Beecher Stowe's first book), with C. Beecher. $3,000.

BEECHER, Harriet Elizabeth. *Prize-Tale: A New England Sketch*. Lowell, Mass., 1834. First separate book by Harriet Beecher Stowe. In original plain wraps with cloth spine. $1,250.

BEECHER, Henry Ward. *Norwood, or Village Life in New England*. London, 1867. 3 vols. Green cloth. $600. New York, 1868. $125.

BEECHEY, F. W. *An Account of a Visit to California*. (San Francisco, 1941.) Grabhorn printing. Map, color plates. Half vellum. One of 350 copies. $250.

BEECHEY, F. W. *Narrative of a Voyage to the Pacific and Beering's Strait*. London, 1831. 2 vols. 23 plates, 3 maps. Large-paper (4to) "Admiralty" issue. $6,000. 2 vols. Octavo edition. $3,000. Philadelphia, 1832. $1,500.

BEECHEY, F. W. *A Voyage of Discovery Towards the North Pole.* London, 1843. Folding map, 6 plates. $1,000.

BEEDING, Francis. (John Leslie Palmer and Hilary Saunders.) *The Seven Sleepers.* London, 1925. $200.

BEE-HUNTER (The); or, The Oak Openings. London, 1848. By the author of "The Pioneers" (James Fenimore Cooper). 3 vols. Drab boards. First edition (of the novel published in America as *The Oak Openings*). $1,000.

BEER, Thomas. *The Mauve Decade.* New York, 1926. One of 165 signed copies. In slipcase. $150. One of 15 signed copies. $250. Trade. $75.

BEERBOHM, Max. See B., H.M.

BEERBOHM, Max. *A Book of Caricatures.* London (1907). Frontispiece in color, 48 drawings. $250.

BEERBOHM, Max. *Caricatures of Twenty-five Gentlemen.* London (1896). 25 plates. First issue with "Leonard/Smithers" on spine. $1,000. Second issue adds "& Co." $750.

BEERBOHM, Max. *Cartoons: "The Second Childhood of John Bull."* London [1911], although states that they were drawn in 1901. 15 full-page tinted plates. $400. Second issue. Plates in cloth folder. $300.

BEERBOHM, Max. *Fifty Caricatures.* London, 1913. $250.

BEERBOHM, Max. *The Happy Hypocrite: A Fairy Tale for Tired Men.* New York, 1897. Printed green wraps. Period on cover, after Bodley Booklets No. 1, colophon dated December 1896. $300.

BEERBOHM, Max. *Leaves from the Garland.* New York, 1926. One of 72 copies. $450.

BEERBOHM, Max. *Rossetti and His Circle.* London (1922). 23 colored caricatures. One of 380 signed copies. In dustwrapper. $750. Trade edition. $300.

BEERBOHM, Max. *A Survey.* London, 1921. 52 plates, including colored frontispiece. Purple cloth. One of 275 signed copies. In dustwrapper. $750. Trade edition. $200. New York, 1921. $200.

BEERBOHM, Max. *Things New and Old.* London, 1921. Colored frontispiece, 49 other plates. White buckram. One of 380 copies signed and with extra signed plate. $850. Trade edition. $350. Oxford, 1975. One of 750 copies. $300.

BEERBOHM, Max. *The Works of Max Beerbohm.* New York, 1896. (1,000 copies—400 pulped.) $350. London, 1896. $300.

BEERBOHM, Max. *Zuleika Dobson.* London, 1911. Smooth brown cloth, or rough cloth. (No priority, but there were fewer copies bound in rough cloth.) $400. New York, 1912. $200. Limited Editions Club, New York, 1960. In slipcase. $75. Oxford, 1975. Illustrated and signed by Osbert Lancaster. One of 750 copies. In slipcase. $150.

BEERS, F. W., and Co. *Atlas of the Counties of Lamoille and Orleans, Vermont.* New York, 1878. Maps in color. Half leather. $600.

BEETON, Mrs. Isabella. *The Book of Household Management.* London, 1861. 2 vols. Frontispiece and pictorial title in color, numerous other illustrations. First issue, with "18 Bouverie St." on woodcut title page. $3,000.

BEETON'S *Christmas Annual. 28th Season.* London, 1887. Illustrated. Wraps. (Contains first appearance of A. Conan Doyle's *A Study in Scarlet.*) $75,000 or more.

BEGLEY, Louis. *Wartime Lies.* New York, 1991. $200.

BEHAN, Brendan. *The Hostage.* London, 1958. $125. New York (1958). First American edition. One of 26 signed copies. Issued without dustwrapper. $500. 4 signed copies hors de commerce. $750. Trade edition. $100.

BEHAN, Brendan. *The Quare Fellow.* London (1956). Author's first book. $200. New York (1956). Cloth. One of 100 copies. Issued without dustwrapper. $300. Trade in cloth. $150. Wraps. $35.

BEHN, Mrs. Aphra. *LaMontre; or The Lover's Watch.* London, 1686. $750.

BEHN, Mrs. Aphra. *Poems Upon Several Occasions.* London, 1684. Author's first book. $1,000.

BEHRMAN, Samuel Nathaniel. *Bedside Manner.* New York, 1924. Written with J. K. Nicholson. Wraps. $250.

BEHRMAN, Samuel Nathaniel. *The Second Man.* New York, 1927. Author's first book, preceded by two collaborations. Stiff wraps in dustwrapper. $250. London, 1928. $150.

BELCAMP, Jeremy. *The History of New Hampshire.* Philadelphia, 1784; and Boston, 1791–92. 3 vols. $1,500.

BELCHER, Edward. *The Last of The Arctic Voyages . . .* London, 1855. 2 vols. 4 folding maps and 36 plates. $3,000.

BELCHER, Sir Edward. *Narrative of the Voyage of H.M.S. Samarang . . .* London, 1848. 2 vols. Cloth-backed marbled boards. 5 maps (3 folding), 30 plates. $3,000.

BELCHER, Sir Edward. *Narrative of a Voyage Round the World . . . 1836–1842.* London, 1843. 2 vols. 19 plates, 3 maps in pocket. $3,500.

BELDAM, George W. *The World's Champion Golfers.* London (1924). 11 vols. Illustrated boards. $1,500.

BELKNAP, Jeremy. See *The Foresters . . .*

BELL, Acton. *Agnes Grey.* London, 1847. (By Anne Brontë). The third vol. of *Wuthering Heights.* (1,000 copies). See Bell, Ellis (and Acton).

BELL, Acton. *The Tenant of Wildfell Hall.* London, 1848. (By Anne Brontë, her only separate publication.) 3 vols. In original cloth. $50,000. Rebound. $15,000.

BELL, Charles. *The Hand . . .* Philadelphia, 1833. $300.

BELL, Clive. *Art.* London, 1914. Author's first book. $150. New York (1914). English sheets. $100.

BELL, Clive. *Poems.* Richmond (London): Hogarth Press, 1921. Wraps. One of 350 copies. $400.

BELL, Currer (editor). *Jane Eyre: An Autobiography.* London, 1847. (By Charlotte Brontë.) 3 vols. First issue, with 36-page catalogue at back of first vol., dated June and October, with half titles, and with a leaf advertising the *Calcutta Review* (VAB—Not in Wise or Schwartz.) $65,000. London, 1848. Second edition. (Currer Bell as author instead of editor on title page.) $5,000. Third edition. $3,500. New York, 1848. Wraps. $3,500.

BELL, Currer. *The Professor.* London, 1857. (By Charlotte Brontë.) 2 vols., plum-colored cloth. With 2 pages of ads at end of vol. 1 and 16 pages of ads at end of vol. 2 dated June 1857. $3,500. One-vol. issue. London, 1857 (actually 1858). In a remainder binding, with 1858 ads. $2,000. New York, 1857. First American edition. $750.

BELL, Currer. *Shirley: A Tale.* London, 1849. (By Charlotte Brontë.) 3 vols. Deep claret-colored cloth. With 16 pages of ads dated October 1849, at end of vol. 1. $8,500. New York, 1850. Cloth. $500. Wraps. $750.

BELL, Currer. *Villette.* London, 1853. (By Charlotte Brontë.) 3 vols. Olive-brown cloth. With 12 pages of ads dated January 1853, in vol. 1. $6,000. New York, 1853. $1,000.

BELL, Currer, Ellis, and Acton. *Poems.* London, 1846. (By Charlotte, Emily, and Anne Brontë.) Dark-green cloth. First issue, published by Aylott and Jones. $45,000. London, 1846 (actually 1848). Green cloth. Published by Smith, Elder & Co. Second issue, with 4-line errata slip. $4,000. Philadelphia, 1848. Boards. $2,500.

BELL, Ellis (and Acton). *Wuthering Heights.* London, 1847. 3 vols. Claret-colored cloth (third vol. titled *Agnes Grey,* by Acton Bell). (First two vols. by Emily Brontë, third by Anne Brontë.) (1,000 copies printed.) $75,000. New York, 1848. Cloth. $5,000. Wraps. 2 vols. $6,000. London, 1851. New edition, revised. $5,000. New York, 1931. Illustrated by Clare Leighton. Cloth. One of 450 copies signed by the artist. $600. Limited Editions Club. New York, 1993. One of 300 copies signed by Balthus. $4,000.

BELL, Gertrude. *The Arab War.* London: Golden Cockerel Press, 1924. Half linen. One of 500 copies. $600. One of 30 copies. $2,000.

BELL, Horace. *Reminiscences of a Ranger.* Los Angeles, 1881. $600.

BELL, John. *Discourses on the Nature and Cure of Wounds.* Edinburgh, 1795. $1,500. Walpole, N.H., 1807. 2 vols. in 1. 2 plates. $1,000.

BELL, John. *Travels from St. Petersburg . . .* Glasgow, 1763. 2 vols. $3,000.

BELL, Josephine. (Doris Bell and Collier Ball.) *Murder in Hospital.* London, 1937. $300.

BELL, Marvin. *Two Poems.* Iowa City, 1965. Author's first book. Issued without dustwrapper. $350.

BELL, Solomon. *Tales of Travel West of the Mississippi.* Boston, 1830. (By William J. Snelling.) Map plates. $1,250.

BELL, William A. *New Tracks in North America.* London, 1869. 2 vols. 20 color lithographs, 3 botanical plates, 1 diagrammatic plate and 1 folding map. $2,000.

BELLAMY, Edward. See *Six to One: A Nantucket Idyl.*

BELLAMY, Edward. *Looking Backward, 2000–1887.* Boston, 1888. Pea-green, orange-brown, or gray cloth. First issue, with printer's imprint of "J. J. Arakelyan" on copyright page. $450. Another (second) issue. Gray wraps. $250. Limited Editions Club, New York, 1941. In slipcase. $175.

BELLOC, Hilaire. See B., H.

BELLOC, Hilaire. *Cautionary Tales for Children.* London (1908). Pictorial boards. $250.

BELLOC, Hilaire. *The Highway and Its Vehicles.* London, 1926. Illustrated. One of 1,250 copies. $350.

BELLOC, Hilaire. *New Cautionary Tales.* London, 1930. One of 110 signed copies. $450.

BELLOC, Hilaire. *Verses and Sonnets.* London, 1896. Author's first book. $750.

BELLOW, Saul. *The Adventures of Augie March.* New York, 1953. First issue, with top edges orange. In first dustwrapper without reviews. $350. Second issue. $150.

BELLOW, Saul. *Dangling Man.* New York (1944). Author's first book. $3,000. London, 1946. $450.

BELLOW, Saul. *Henderson the Rain King.* New York, 1959. First issue, top edges yellow. $300. London (1959). $150.

BELLOW, Saul. *Herzog.* New York (1964). Stamped blue cloth. $200. (London, 1965.) $100.

BELLOW, Saul. *The Victim.* New York (1947). $750. London (1948). First English edition. In dustwrapper. $250.

BELLOWS, George. *George W. Bellows: His Lithographs.* New York, 1927. In slipcase. $300.

BELLOWS, George. *The Paintings.* New York, 1929. Color frontispiece, 143 plates. One of 2,000 copies in dustwrapper. $450.

BELOE, William. *Anecdotes of Literature and Scarce Books.* London, 1807–12. 6 vols. $1,250.

BELTRAMI, G. C. *A Pilgrimage in Europe and America.* London, 1828. 2 vols. 6 plates including folding map and plan. $1,500.

BEMELMANS, Ludwig. *Hansi.* New York, 1934. Author's first book. $750.

BEMELMANS, Ludwig. *Madeline.* New York, 1939. Date on title page. Dustwrapper priced $2.99 on front flap. $750.

BEMELMANS, Ludwig. *Small Beer.* New York, 1939. One of 75 copies with original colored illustrations. In slipcase. $750.

BENAVIDES, Alonso de. *The Memorial of Fray Alonso de Benavides, 1630.* Chicago, 1916. Facsimile of Madrid edition of 1630. Boards. One of 300 copies. $350.

BENCHLEY, Peter. *Jaws.* Garden City, 1974. Dustwrapper priced $6.50. $450.

BENCHLEY, Robert. *Love Conquers All.* New York, 1922. Blue pictorial cloth. $1,000.

BENCHLEY, Robert. *Of All Things.* New York, 1921. Author's first book. Two states with and without ads at end, priority unknown. $1,250. London, 1922. $750.

BENCHLEY, Robert. *20,000 Leagues Under the Sea, or David Copperfield.* New York (1928). $750.

BENDIRE, Charles. *Life Histories of North American Birds.* Washington, 1892–95. 2 vols. 19 color plates. Folio, cloth. $750.

BENEDICT, Carl Peters. *A Tenderfoot Kid on Gyp Water.* Austin, 1943. Edited by J. Frank Dobie. One of 550 copies. $350.

BENÉT, Laura. *Fairy Bread.* New York, 1921. $200.

BENÉT, Stephen Vincent. *The Devil and Daniel Webster.* Weston, Vt. (1937). Illustrated by Harold Denison. One of 700 signed copies. In glassine dustwrapper and slipcase. $200. New York (1937). Trade. $75.

BENÉT, Stephen Vincent. *The Drug Shop; or Endymion in Edmonstoun.* (New Haven), 1917. Printed wraps. (100 copies.) $250.

BENÉT, Stephen Vincent. *Five Men and Pompey.* Boston, 1915. Author's first book. Wraps over boards. First state in purple wraps. $250. Second state, brown wraps. $125. (Note: Johnson says there were "a few copies" on handmade paper.)

BENÉT, Stephen Vincent. *John Brown's Body.* (Garden City, 1928.) One of 201 signed copies. In slipcase. $450. Trade. $150. Limited Editions Club, New York. 1948. John Steuart Curry illustrations. One of 1,500 copies. In slipcase. $125.

BENÉT, Stephen Vincent, and BENÉT, Rosemary. *A Book of Americans.* New York, 1933. One of 125 signed copies. In slipcase. $150. Trade edition with publisher's monogram on copyright page. $75.

BEN-GURION, David. *Days of David Ben-Gurion . . .* New York, 1967. One of 150 signed copies. In slipcase. $1,200.

BENJAMIN, Asher. *The American Builder's Compendium.* Boston (1827). Sixth edition. $1,250.

BENJAMIN, Asher. *The Country Builder's Assistant . . .* Boston, 1798. 37 plates. $7,500.

BENJAMIN, Asher. *Practice of Architecture.* Boston, 1833. 60 engraved plates. $1,000.

BENJAMIN, Paul. *Squeeze Play.* London, 1982. (By Paul Auster.) First book under this name. Wraps. $750. New York (1984). Wraps. $125.

BENN, George. *A History of the Town of Belfast.* London, 1877. 2 vols in 1. 8 folding maps and plans and an extending genealogical table. $1,250.

BENNETT, Arnold. See Bennett, E. A.

BENNETT, Arnold. *The Bright Island.* London: Golden Cockerel Press, 1924. Limp vellum. One of 200 signed copies. $350.

BENNETT, Arnold. *Elsie and the Child.* London, 1929. One of 100 signed copies. $750. One of 750 copies. $250.

BENNETT, Arnold. *From the Log of the Velsa.* London, 1920. White cloth. One of 110 signed copies. $350.

BENNETT, Arnold. *Imperial Palace.* London (1930). 2 vols. Vellum. One of 100 signed copies. $250. Trade edition. $100.

BENNETT, Arnold. *The Old Wives' Tale.* London, 1908. $500. London, 1927. 2 vols. Parchment and cloth. Facsimile of the manuscript. One of 500 signed copies. $350. Limited Editions Club, New York, 1941. Illustrated by John Austen. 2 vols. In slipcase. $125.

BENNETT, E. A. *A Man from the North.* London, 1898. Arnold Bennett's first book. Red cloth, stamped in white. $350.

BENNETT, Emerson. *The Bandits of the Osage.* Cincinnati, 1847. Wraps. $750.

BENNETT, Emerson. *The Brigand . . .* New York, 1842. Author's first book. Wraps. $450.

BENNETT, Frederick D. *Narrative of a Whaling Voyage Around the Globe.* London, 1840. 2 vols. Frontispieces, folding map. Cloth. $3,000.

BENNETT, George. *Gatherings of a Naturalist in Australasia.* London, 1860. 7 colored plates, one in sepia, numerous woodcuts. $600.

BENNETT, John. *Master Skylark: A Story of Shakespeare's Time.* New York, 1897. Illustrated by Reginald Birch. Pictorial cloth. $200.

BENNETT, Melba Berry. *Robinson Jeffers and the Sea.* San Francisco, 1936. Grabhorn printing. Decorated boards, morocco spine. One of 300 copies. $350.

BENSON, A. C. See Carr, Christopher.

BENSON, A. C. *William Laud, Archbishop of Canterbury.* London, 1887. (Second book, first under own name.) $350.

BENSON, E(dward) F(redric). *Dodo.* London, 1893. 2 vols. Author's first book. $600.

BENSON, Frank W. (illustrator). *Etchings and Drypoints.* Boston, 1917 (2), 1923, and 1929. Limited to 275, 275, 525, and 600 copies respectively. 4 vols. 285 reproductions. Text by Adam E. M. Paff. Each volume has frontispiece signed by Benson. In dustwrappers. $3,500.

BENSON, Henry C. *Life Among the Choctaw Indians.* Cincinnati, 1860. $500.

BENSON, John Howard. *The First Writing Book, An English Translation & Facsimile Text of Arrighi's Operina, The First Manual of the Chancery Hand.* New Haven, 1955. 300 copies signed by Benson. $150.

BENSON, Mildred. *Ruth Fielding and Her Great Scenario.* New York, 1927. (Better known for Nancy Drew.) $350.

BENSON, Sally. *Meet Me in St. Louis.* New York, 1942. $1,250.

BENTLEY, E. C. See Clerihew, E.

BENTLEY, E. C. *Trent's Last Case*. London (1913). (*Woman in Black* in U.S.). $250.

BENTLEY, E. C. *The Woman in Black*. New York, 1913. (New title.) $200.

BENTLEY, Harry C., and LEONARD, Ruth S. *Bibliography of Works on Accounting by American Authors*. Boston, 1933–35. 2 vols. $250.

BENTON, Frank. *Cowboy Life on the Sidetrack*. Denver (1903). Illustrated. Pictorial cloth. $100.

BENTON, J. A. *California as She Was, as She Is, as She Is to Be*. Sacramento, 1850. 16 pages, wraps. $3,500.

BENTON, Thomas Hart. *The Artist in America*. New York (1937). Special Missouri edition. Signed. $300.

BEPPO, A Venetian Story. London, 1818. (By George Gordon Noel, Lord Byron.) $1,250. (Kentfield): Allen Press, 1963. Oblong folio, loose as issued, with 35 plates. $600.

BERDMORE, Thomas. *A Treatise on the Disorders and Deformities of the Teeth and Gums*. London, 1768. $5,000.

BERENDT, John. *Midnight in the Garden of Good and Evil*. New York, 1994. $200. New York, 1995. One of 2,500 signed copies. In pictorial slipcase. $200.

BERENSON, Bernard. *The Drawings of the Florentine Painters*. London, 1903. 180 full-page tinted plates. Folio, half morocco. One of 300 copies. $3,000. Chicago, 1938. 3 vols. Small folio, boards, vellum spine. Amplified edition. $750.

BERENSON, Bernard. *Italian Pictures of the Renaissance*. London, 1957–68. 7 vols. $3,000.

BERESFORD, J(ohn) D(avys). *The Hampdenshire Wonder*. London, 1911. Author's first book. $250. In dustwrapper. $1,000.

BERETON, Ford. *Dolce Cor . . .* London, 1886. (By S. R. Crockett.) Author's first book. $500.

BERGE, Carol. *The Vulnerable Island*. Cleveland, 1964. Wraps. (105 copies.) $200.

BERGER, John. *A Painter of Our Time*. London, 1958. $250. New York, 1959. $125.

BERGER, Thomas. *Crazy in Berlin*. New York (1958). Author's first book. Dustwrapper without Dial Prize Winner notice. $400. With notice. $200. London, 1963. $75.

BERGER, Thomas. *Little Big Man*. New York, 1964. $500. London, 1965. $200.

BERGMAN, Ray. *Trout*. Philadelphia, 1938. Flies in color. Full morocco. One of 149 signed copies. $1,750. Trade. $500.

BERKELEY, Anthony. See *The Layton Court Mystery*.

BERKELEY, Anthony. *Death in the House*. London, 1939. $1,000.

BERKELEY, Anthony. *Murder in the Basement*. London, 1937. $1,250.

BERKELEY, Anthony. *Not to Be Taken.* London, 1938. $1,000.

BERLESE, Abbe. *Monography of the Genus Camellia, or An Essay on Its Culture, Description &*
Classification . . . Boston, 1838. $750.

BERNARD, Auguste. *Geofroy Tory, Painter and Engraver.* (Cambridge, Mass.) 1909. Translated
by George B. Ives. One of 370 copies designed by Bruce Rogers. $600.

BERNE, Victoria. *Touch and Go.* New York, 1939. (By M. F. K. Fisher.) $1,250.

BERNERS, Dame Juliana. *A Treatyse of Fysshynge with an Angle.* London (Chelsea): Ashendene
Press, 1903. Woodcuts. Full green morocco. One of 25 copies on vellum. $4,500. Vellum. One
of 150 copies on paper. In slipcase. $1,750.

BERNIER, R. L. *Art in California* . . . San Francisco, 1916. 332 plates. $750.

BERNSTEIN, Anne. *Three Blue Suits.* New York, 1933. Author's first book. One of 600
signed copies. In slipcase. $150.

BERQUIN-DUVALLON. See *Travels in Louisiana and the Floridas.*

BERRIGAN, Ted. (Edmund J.) *The Sonnets.* (New York), 1964. (300 copies.) Stapled mimeographed sheets with a back wrapper. $1,000. Grove Press, New York (1964). Wraps. (Preceded
by at least 2 privately printed pamphlets.) $60.

BERRY, W. Turner, and JOHNSON, A. F. *Catalogue of Specimens of Printing Types by English and*
Scottish Printers . . . London, 1935. $350.

BERRY, Wendell. *The Long-Legged House.* New York (1969). $250.

BERRY, Wendell. *Nathan Colter.* Boston, 1960. Author's first book. $350. San Francisco, 1985.
Revised. One of 26 signed copies. $350. One of 100 signed copies. $150.

BERRY, Wendell. *November Twenty Six Nineteen Hundred Sixty Three.* New York (1964). Illustrated by Ben Shahn. Limited issue signed by Shahn and Berry. In slipcase. $250. Trade edition.
$150.

BERRYMAN, John. See *Five Young American Poets.*

BERRYMAN, John. *The Dispossessed.* New York (1948). $400.

BERRYMAN, John. *His Thought Made Pockets and the Plane Buckt.* Pawlet, Vt., 1958. Boards,
leather spine. One of 26 lettered copies. $3,000. Wraps. One of 500 copies. 20 copies in
printed envelope. $200.

BERRYMAN, John. *Homage to Mistress Bradstreet.* New York (1956). Illustrated by Ben Shahn.
Boards. $250.

BERRYMAN, John. *Love and Fame.* New York, 1970. One of 250 signed copies. In slipcase.
$300. Trade edition. $750.

BERRYMAN, John. *Poems.* Norfolk, Conn.: New Directions (1942). Author's first book.
Printed blue wraps. Poet of the Month series. In dustwrapper. $150. Boards. One of 500 hard-
bound copies. In dustwrapper. $450.

BERRYMAN, John. *Stephen Crane.* (New York, 1950.) $250.

BERT, Edmund. *An Approved Treatise of Hawks and Hawking.* London, 1619. $7,500. London, 1891. Illustrated. Boards, leather spine. One of 100 copies. $1,250.

BESSIE, Alvah C. *Dwell in the Wilderness.* New York (1935). Author's first book other than translations. $300.

BESTER, Alfred. *The Demolished Man.* Chicago (1953). Author's first book. One of 200 signed copies. $600. Unsigned copies. $350. London (1953). $100.

BESTER. Alfred. *Tiger, Tiger.* London (1956). $1,000. (U.S. edition was published the following year as *The Stars My Destination.*)

BETJEMAN, John. See O'Betjeman, Deirdre.

BETJEMAN, John. *Antiquarian Prejudice.* London: Hogarth Press, 1939. Wraps. $150.

BETJEMAN, John. *Continual Dew.* London (1937). $400.

BETJEMAN, John. *A Few Late Chrysanthemums.* London, 1954. White buckram. One of 50 signed copies. $600. Trade edition. $100.

BETJEMAN, John. *Ghastly Good Taste.* London, 1933. Folding plate. Printed pink boards and cloth. First issue, with pages 119–20 not canceled. $500. London, 1970. Half leather. One of 200 signed copies. In slipcase. $350.

BETJEMAN, John. *John Betjeman's Collected Poems.* London, 1958. Compiled by the Earl of Birkenhead. Scarlet leather. One of 100 signed copies. In slipcase. $500. Trade edition. $100.

BETJEMAN, John. *Mount Zion, or In Touch with the Infinite.* London (1931). Author's first book. Blue-and-gold pattern cover. $1,250. Striped paper cover. $600. Issued without dustwrapper.

BETJEMAN, John. *New Bats in Old Belfries.* London, 1945. Red cloth, paper label. One of a few signed copies on special paper with colored title page. $500. Unsigned. $100.

BETJEMAN, John. *Old Lights for New Chancels.* London (1940). Portrait frontispiece. Wraps. In dustwrapper. $300.

BETJEMAN, John. *An Oxford University Chest.* London (1938). Photographs by Moholy-Nagy. Illustrations by Osbert Lancaster, etc. Marbled boards, cloth spine, gilt top. $350.

BETJEMAN, John. *Selected Poems.* London, 1948. One of 18 signed copies. $1,250. Trade edition. $100.

BETJEMAN, John. *Summoned by Bells.* London, 1960. Illustrated, Full green leather, gilt top. One of 125 signed copies. $600. Trade. $75.

BETTS, Doris. *The Gentle Insurrection . . .* New York, 1954. Author's first book. $175.

BEVERIDGE, Albert J. *The Life of John Marshall.* Boston, 1919. 4 vols. Autograph edition. One of 500 signed copies. $350.

BEVIER, Robert S. *History of the First and Second Missouri Confederate Brigades, 1861–1865.* St. Louis, 1879. $1,250.

BEWICK, Thomas. *The Fables of Aesop* . . . Newcastle, 1818. 323 wood-engraved vignettes including headpieces and tailpieces. "Thumbprint" edition. $1,500.

BEWICK, Thomas. *A General History of Quadrupeds.* Newcastle, 1790. $1,250.

BEWICK, Thomas. *A History of British Birds.* Newcastle, 1797–1804. 2 vols. Woodcuts. $1,250.

BEWICK, Thomas. *Vignettes.* Newcastle Upon Tyne, 1827. Folio. 205 vignettes. $1,500.

BEWICK Gleanings. Newcastle, 1886. (By Thomas Bewick.) Edited by Julia Boyd. 53 plates. Green morocco. Large-paper edition, signed. $500.

BEYER, Edward. *Album of Virginia.* Richmond, 1858. Lithograph title and 44 views on 40 tinted lithograph sheets in folio plate volume and octavo text volume (seldom seen with text volume, which adds little to the price). $15,000.

BEYNON, John. *The Secret People.* London (1935). (By John Beynon Harris, his first book.) $650. Second issue in green binding with black letters with dustwrapper priced 2/6. $350.

BEZZERIDES, A. I. *Long Haul.* New York (1938). $450.

BIANCO, Margery (Williams). *The Little Wooden Doll.* New York, 1925. (First under this name.) $300.

BIANCO, Margery Williams. *Poor Cecco.* New York (or London) (1925). 7 mounted color plates by Arthur Rackham. First issue, with pictorial endpapers (VAB). In dustwrapper. $1,000. Second issue, plain endpapers. $750. Deluxe signed issue. Half vellum and blue boards. One of 105 copies signed by the author. In slipcase. $12,500.

BIBLIOGRAPHICA, Papers on Books, Their History And Art. London, 1895–97. 12 parts bound in 3 vols. $750.

BIBLIOGRAPHICAL and Retrospective Miscellany . . . , The. London, 1830. $250.

BIBLIOPHILE, The: A Magazine and Review for the Collector, Students and General Readers. London, 1809–1909. 3 vols. $250.

BIBLIOPHOBIA; Remarks on the Present Languid and Depressed State of Literature and the Book Trade . . . London, 1832. (Thomas Frognall Dibdin.) $600.

BIBLIOTHECA Americana, Catalogue of the John Carter Brown Library in Brown University . . . Providence, various reprints. 7 vols. constitute a complete set. (An invaluable reference tool.) $1,000.

BICKHAM, George. *The Universal Penman; or, The Art of Writing Made Useful* . . . London, 1733–1741. $4,500. London, 1743. Contains frontispiece and 212 engraved plates. $2,250.

BICKNELL, A. J. *Detail, Cottage and Constructive Architecture.* New York, 1873. $500.

BIDDLE, Owen. *The Young Carpenter's Assistant.* Philadelphia, 1805. 46 plates. $1,500.

BIDWELL, George H. *The Printers' New Hand-Book: A Treatise on the Imposition of Forms . . .* New York (1875). $350.

BIDWELL, John. *A Journey to California . . .* San Francisco, 1937. $200. (Note: Only one copy is known of the 1842 original of this narrative, and it is imperfect.)

BIERCE, Ambrose. See Bowers, Mrs. Dr. J. Milton; Grile, Dod; Herman, William.

BIERCE, Ambrose. *Battle Sketches.* London: Shakespeare Head Press, 1930. Vellum. One of 350 copies. In slipcase. $300.

BIERCE, Ambrose. *Black Beetles in Amber.* San Francisco: Western Authors Publishing Company, 1892. $450. Second issue. Printed gray wraps. Published by Johnson & Emigh. $300.

BIERCE, Ambrose. *The Cynic's Word Book.* New York, 1906. Presumed first issue, without frontispiece (Johnson). $450. Frontispiece inserted. $350. (Reissued as *The Devil's Dictionary.*)

BIERCE, Ambrose. *Fantastic Fables.* New York, 1899. Tan-yellow cloth. With ads at back headed by "By Anna Fuller." $500.

BIERCE, Ambrose. *A Horseman in the Sky.* San Francisco, 1920. John Henry Nash printing. One of 400 copies. $200.

BIERCE, Ambrose. *In the Midst of Life.* London, 1892. Blue cloth. (VAB.) First English edition (of *Tales of Soldiers and Civilians*). $450. (Second issue in colored boards—VAB). New York, 1898. (Reprint of the *Tales* with 3 added stories.) $200.

BIERCE, Ambrose. *My Favorite Murder.* (New York, 1916.) First separate edition. Wraps. $200.

BIERCE, Ambrose. *Nuggets and Dust . . .* London (1873). Pictorial yellow wraps. $1,500.

BIERCE, Ambrose. *The Shadow on the Dial and Other Essays.* San Francisco, 1909. Edited by S. O. Howes. Green buckram. In dustwrapper. $400. Without dustwrapper. $250.

BIERCE, Ambrose. *Shapes of Clay.* San Francisco, 1903. First issue, with transposed lines 5 and 6 on page 71. $450. Second issue, corrected. $300.

BIERCE, Ambrose. *Tales of Soldiers and Civilians.* San Francisco: E.L.G. Steele, 1891. $450. Some copies imprinted "Compliments of" on preliminary leaf and signed by Bierce—the so-called "limited" edition (Johnson). $1,750. Limited Editions Club, New York, 1943. Boards and leather. In slipcase. $400. (For first English edition see Bierce, *In the Midst of Life.*)

BIERCE, Ambrose. *Write It Right: A Little Blacklist of Literary Faults.* New York, 1909. First issue 5¾ by 3 inches in size (VAB). (Johnson, 5½ inches tall.) $500. Second printing 6 by 3⅞ inches. $250. San Francisco, 1971. Grabhorn printing. One of 400. $150.

BIERCE, Ambrose, and DANZIGER, Gustav Adolph. (A pseudonym for Adolphe De Castro.) *The Monk and the Hangman's Daughter.* Chicago, 1892. Illustrated by Theodore Hampe. Printed yellow wraps. $500. Gray cloth. $350. New York, 1907. New introduction by Bierce. $200. Limited Editions Club, New York, 1967. In slipcase. $100.

BIERSTADT, O. A. *The Library of Robert Hoe . . .* New York, 1895. One of 350 copies. $350.

BIGELOW, Jacob. *American Medical Botany.* Boston, 1817–20. 3 vols. or 6 parts. 60 color plates. The first U.S. horticulture book printed in color. $7,500.

BIGELOW, Jacob. *Insensibility During Surgical Operations.* Boston, 1847. $3,500.

BIGGERS, Don H. *From Cattle Range to Cotton Patch.* Abilene, Tex. (1905). Illustrated. Stiff wraps. $4,500. Bandera, Tex., 1944. $250.

BIGGERS, Earl Derr. *Behind That Curtain.* Indianapolis (1928). With Bobbs-Merrill symbol on copyright page. $1,500. London, 1928. $750.

BIGGERS, Earl Derr. *The Black Camel.* Indianapolis, 1929. $750.

BIGGERS, Earl Derr. *The Chinese Parrot.* Indianapolis (1926). $1,750.

BIGGERS, Earl Derr. *The House Without a Key.* Indianapolis (1925). First edition not stated. $1,750. London, 1926. $750.

BIGGERS, Earl Derr. *If You're Only Human.* 1912. Author's first book. $400.

BIGGERS, Earl Derr. *Seven Keys to Baldpate.* Indianapolis (1913). $200.

BIGGS, William. *Narrative of William Biggs, While He Was a Prisoner with the Kickepoo Indians.* (No place), June 1825. (Howes.) Copy in worn wraps at auction in 1999 for $17,000. as (Edwardsville, Ill.), 1826.

BIGSBY, John Jeremiah. *The Shoe and Canoe.* London, 1850. 2 vols. 20 engraved plates, 4 maps, 1 plan. Blue cloth. $1,500.

BINDINGS of To-Morrow: A Record of the Work of the Guild of Women-Binders . . . London, 1902. (By George Eliot Anstruther.) $850.

BINYON, Laurence. *The Art of Botticelli.* London, 1913. Muirhead Bone etching, 23 color plates. Folio, cloth, vellum spine. One of 275 copies. $750.

BINYON, Laurence. *The Engraved Designs of William Blake.* London, 1926. Plates. Half cloth and boards. One of 100 copies with an extra set of plates. $750. Without the extra plates. $400. Trade edition. $250.

BINYON, Laurence. *The Followers of William Blake.* London, 1925. 79 plates, 7 colored. Issued without dustwrapper. $300. One of 100 copies. $750.

BINYON, Laurence. *Lyric Poems.* London, 1894. $250.

BINYON, Laurence. *Persephone.* London, 1890. Author's first book. (Newdigate Prize.) Wraps. $500.

BINYON, Laurence. *Poems.* Oxford: Daniel Press, 1895. Wraps. One of 200 copies. $300.

BINYON, Laurence, and SEXTON, J.J. O'Brien. *Japanese Colour Prints.* London, 1923. 46 plates, some in color. $250. Pigskin. One of 100 signed copies, with an extra set of plates. $1,000.

BINYON, Laurence; WILKINSON, J.V.S.; and GRAY, Basil. *Persian Miniature Painting.* London, 1923. Illustrated, including color plates. Folio, cloth. In dustwrapper. $1,500.

BIOGRAPHICAL Memoirs of Extraordinary Painters. London, 1780. (By William Beckford.) Author's first book. $1,500.

BIOGRAPHICAL Souvenir of the State of Texas. Chicago, 1889. Illustrated. Full leather. $750.

BIOGRAPHY of Joseph Lane. Washington, 1852. By Western. $1,500. Howes lists another copy same date but with pseudonym "A Westerner" and notes authorship as being attributed to Robert Dale Owen.

BION and MOSCHUS. *Poems.* Bristol, 1794. (By Robert Lovell and Robert Southey, their first book.) $2,000.

BIRD, Bessie Calhoun. *Airs from the Wood Winds.* Philadelphia (1935). Author's only book. One of 25 signed, lettered copies, $750. One of 300 copies, $300.

BIRD, Isabella. See *The Englishwoman in America.*

BIRD, Robert Montgomery. See *The Adventures of Robin Day; Calavar; The Infidel; Nick-of-the-Woods; Peter Pilgrim; Sheppard Lee.*

BIRD, William. *A Practical Guide to French Wine.* Paris, no date [1922?]. Author's first book. Wraps. $250.

Bird & Bull Commonplace Book, The. North Hills, 1971. One of 255 copies. Envelope on inside rear cover with brass token inserted. In slipcase. $450.

Bird & Bull Number 13. North Hills, 1972. One of 140 copies. First Bird & Bull publication to use paste paper for the cover. $450.

BIRKBECK, Morris. See *An Impartial Appeal.*

BIRKBECK, Morris. *An Appeal to the People of Illinois, on the Question of a Convention.* Shawnee-town, 1823. 25 pages, wraps. (Howes B 465.) $1,500.

BIRKBECK, Morris. *Extracts from a Supplementary Letter from the Illinois.* New York, 1819. 29 pages, half leather. First edition. $1,500.

BIRKBECK, Morris. *Letters from Illinois.* Philadelphia, 1818. 2 folding maps. Boards and calf. $500.

BIRKBECK, Morris. *Notes on a Journey in America from the Coast of Virginia to the Territory of Illinois.* Philadelphia, 1818. $450. London, 1818. Map. $250. (Map in auction copies not noted in Howes.)

BIRNEY, Earle. See Robertson, E.

BIRNEY, Earle. *David . . .* Toronto, 1942. (500 copies.) $300.

BIRNEY, Earle. *Now Is Time.* Toronto (1945). $175.

BISHOP, Elizabeth. *North & South.* Boston, 1946. Author's first book. $850.

BISHOP, Elizabeth. *Poem.* New York, 1973. One of 26 signed copies. $2,000. One of 100 signed copies. $1,000.

BISHOP, Elizabeth. *Poems*. London, 1956. $750.

BISHOP, J. Leander. *A History of American Manufactures from 1608 to 1860*. Philadelphia, 1864. 2 vols. $750.

BISHOP, John Peale. *Act of Darkness*. New York, 1935. Author's first and only novel. $200.

BISHOP, John Peale. *Green Fruit*. Boston, 1917. Author's first book. Boards and cloth. $200.

BISHOP, John Peale. *Minute Particulars*. New York, 1935. Wraps. One of 165 signed copies. In glassine dustwrapper. $200.

BISHOP, John Peale, and WILSON, Edmund. *The Undertaker's Garland*. New York, 1922. Wilson's first book and Bishop's second. In dustwrapper. $500. Boards. One of 50 copies for "bookseller friends." Issued without dustwrapper. $250.

BISHOP, Richard E. *Bishop's Birds: Etchings of Waterfowl and Upland Game Birds*. Philadelphia, 1936. 73 reproductions. One of 1,050 copies. $350. One of 135 signed copies, with signed Bishop etching tipped in. $750.

BISHOP, Richard E. *Bishop's Wildfowl . . . Etchings and Oil Painting Reproductions*. (St. Paul), 1948. Text by E. Prestrud and R. Williams. Color plates. Full calf. $300.

BISHOP, Zealia. *The Curse of Yig*. Sauk City, Wis., 1953. Arkham House. $175.

BISLAND, Elizabeth (editor). *The Life and Letters of Lafcadio Hearn*. Boston, 1906. 2 vols. One of 200 copies with a page of an original manuscript by Hearn. $2,500. Trade. $350.

BISSET, Robert. *Douglas; or, the Highlander*. Anti-Jacobin Press, 1800. 4 vols. Half titles in vols. 3 and 4 (no others called for). $2,000.

BITTING, Katherine. *Gastronomic Bibliography*. San Francisco, 1939. $600.

BLACK, Campbell. *Assassins and Victims*. (London, 1969.) $150.

BLACK, E. L. *Why Do They Like It . . .* (Dijon, 1927.) (By Sir John Ellerman.) Author's first book. Wraps. $350.

BLACK, Mansell. *Sinister Cargo*. London, 1951. (By Elleston Trevor.) Author's first book. $250.

BLACKBIRD, Andrew J. *History of the Ottawa and Chippewa Indians of Michigan*. Ypsilanti, Mich., 1887. $400.

BLACKBURN, Henry. *Randolph Caldecott: A Personal Memoir of His Early Art Career*. London, 1886. $300.

BLACKBURN, John. *A Scent of New-Mown Hay*. London, 1958. $350. New York, 1958. $50.

BLACKBURN, Paul. *The Dissolving Fabric*. Divers Press. (Mallorca), 1955. Author's first book of poetry. Wraps. $300.

BLACKBURN, Paul. *Proensa*. (Majorca), 1953. Author's first book. (Translation.) $275.

BLACKER, William. *Art of Angling and Complete System of Fly-Making*. London, 1842. $3,000.

BLACKMORE, Richard Doddridge. See Melanter.

BLACKMORE, Richard D. *Lorna Doone: A Romance of Exmoor.* London, 1869. 3 vols. Blue cloth. $3,000.

BLACKMORE, William. *Colorado: Its Resources, Parks, and Prospects as a New Field for Emigration; With an Account of the Trenchara and Costilla Estates . . .* London, 1869. 3 folding maps and mounted frontispiece portrait of author. $1,250.

BLACKMUR, R. P. *Dirty Hands or The True Born Censor.* Cambridge, 1930. Wraps. $175.

BLACKMUR, R. P. *From Jordan's Delight.* New York, 1937. $150.

BLACKMUR, R. P. *The Good European . . .* Cummington, Mass., 1947. Cloth, paper label. Issued without dustwrapper. One of 40 signed copies. $400.

BLACKMUR, R. P. *T. S. Eliot.* (Cambridge, Mass.), 1928. Author's first book. Wraps. Offprint from "Hound & Horn." $250.

BLACKSTONE, William. *Commentaries on the Laws of England.* Oxford, 1765–69. 4 vols., including 8-page "supplement to the first edition." $20,000. Oxford, 1773. 4 vols. $3,500. London, 1803. 4 vols. $1,750.

BLACKWATER Chronicle . . . (The). New York, 1853. (By the Clerke of Oxenforde.) Written and illustrated by Dard Hunter Strother. Sometimes attributed to John Kennedy Pendleton. Frontispiece, engraved title page. $400.

BLACKWELL, Elizabeth. *A Curious Herbal.* (London), 1737–39. 2 vols. Containing 500 hand-colored engraved plates. $30,000. London, 1739. Second edition. 2 vols. $7,500.

BLACKWELL, Elizabeth. *The Laws of Life . . .* New York, 1852. Author's first book. $10,000.

BLACKWOOD, Algernon. *The Empty House and Other Ghost Stories.* London, 1906. Author's first book. $1,000. New York, 1917. $500.

BLACKWOOD, Algernon. *The Fruit Stoners.* New York, 1935. $300.

BLACKWOOD, Algernon. *Jimbo: A Fantasy.* London, 1909. $250.

BLACKWOOD, Algernon. *The Listener and Other Stories.* London, 1907. $600.

BLACKWOOD, Algernon. *Shocks.* New York (1936). $300.

BLADES, William. *The Enemies of Books.* London, 1880. In vellum wraps. $300.

BLADES, William. *The Life And Typography of William Caxton . . .* London, 1861–63. 2 vols. $600.

BLAIR, Robert. *The Grave: A Poem.* London, 1808. Folio. Portrait after T. Phillips. Engraved title and 11 plates by Schiavonetti after designs by Blake. $7,500. Quarto. $2,500. London, 1813. Folio. $6,500. Quarto. $2,000.

BLAKE, Alexander V. *The American Bookseller's Complete Reference Trade List, and Alphabetical Catalogue of Books Published in This Country . . .* Claremont, N.H., 1847. $550.

BLAKE, Nicholas. *The Beast Must Die.* London (1938). $1,500.

BLAKE, Nicholas. *A Question of Proof.* London, 1935. (By C. Day-Lewis.) (First book under this name.) $1,750.

BLAKE, W. O. *The History of Slavery and the Slave Trade.* Columbus, Ohio, 1857. $600.

BLAKE, William. *America: A Prophecy.* Lambeth, 1793. Rebound copy at auction in 1987. $160,000. Facsimile by William Muir. Edmonton, Canada, 1887. Wraps. One of 50 copies. $1,250. London, 1963. One of 526 copies. $750.

BLAKE, William. *Illustrations of the Book of Job.* London, 1825. Title page and 21 other plates engraved by Blake. While title page states "1825," the plates were not issued until 1826 and a label dated "1826" was pasted on. Folio. $40,000. London, 1902. Facsimile. Wraps. $600. New York, 1935. 6 parts, folio, wraps. One of 200 copies. In slipcase. $1,500.

BLAKE, William. *Jerusalem.* London, 1974. One of 500 copies. In slipcase. $750.

BLAKE, William. *The Marriage of Heaven and Hell.* (London, 1868.) Facsimile of 1790 edition. 27 hand-colored plates. $1,000. London, 1960. One of 26 copies. $1,500. One of 500 copies. $750.

BLAKE, William. *The Note-Book of William Blake Called the Rossetti Manuscript.* London: Nonesuch Press, 1935. Edited by Geoffrey Keynes. 120 pages in facsimile. Buckram. One of 650 copies. In dustwrapper. $300.

BLAKE, William. *Pencil Drawings.* London: Nonesuch Press, 1927. Edited by Geoffrey Keynes. 82 facsimile plates. Half buckram. One of 1,550 copies. In dustwrapper. $400. Second Series: London, 1956. One of 1,440 copies. In dustwrapper. $300.

BLAKE, William. *Songs of Innocence and Experience.* London, 1789. One of 3 known copies with final plate "A Divine Image." $1,200,000 at auction in 1989. Three regular copies auctioned for $300,000 to $500,000 in 1989 and 1990. (No record since.) London, 1954. One of 1,600 copies. $350. London: Trianon Press, 1955. Facsimile reproduction from the 1789 original. Full morocco. One of 26 copies. In slipcase. $1,500. One of 500 copies. In slipcase. $750.

BLAKE, William. *Williams Blake's Water-Colour Designs for the Poems of Thomas Gray.* Trianon Press, 1972. 3 vols. One of 518 copies. Folio. Introduction and commentary by Geoffey Keynes. $2,000. One of 100 copies. $2,750.

BLAKE, William. *The Writings of William Blake.* London: Nonesuch Press, 1925. Edited by Geoffrey Keynes. 3 vols. Half vellum and marbled boards. One of 1,500 copies. In slipcase. $750. Thin-paper issue: 3 vols. in 1, morocco or limp vellum. One of 75 copies. $1,250.

BLAKEY, Dorothy. *Minerva Press, 1790–1820.* London, 1939. $200.

BLANCHARD, Rufus (publisher). *Citizen's Guide for the City of Chicago; Companion to Blanchard's Map of Chicago.* Chicago (1868). Printed stiff wraps, with the folding map bound in. $2,000.

BLANCK, Jacob. *Peter Parley to Penrod.* New York, 1938. One of 500 copies. $250. New York, 1956. Second edition. Cambridge, Mass., 1961. $125.

BLAND, David. *A History of Book Illustration.* London (1958). $200. Cleveland (1958). $150.

BLANTON, Wyndham B. *Medicine in Virginia in the Eighteenth Century.* Richmond, 1931–33. 2 vols. $300.

BLASCO IBÁÑEZ, Vicente. *The Four Horsemen of the Apocalypse.* New York, 1918. First American edition. In dustwrapper. $750. Without dustwrapper. $150.

BLATTY, William Peter. *The Exorcist.* New York (1971). $200.

BLEDSOE, A. J. *History of Del Norte County, California.* Eureka, Calif., 1881. Wraps. $3,500. (Howes notes that with one possible exception this is the rarest California local history.)

BLEDSOE, A. J. *Indian Wars of the Northwest.* San Francisco, 1885. Leather. $600. Cloth. $450.

BLEW, William C. A. *A History of Steeple-Chasing.* London, 1901. 28 illustrations, 12 hand-colored plates. $300.

BLIGH, William. *The Log of the Bounty* . . . Golden Cockerel Press, 1937. 2 vols. Small folio, with 4 wood engravings by Lynton Lamb. One of 300 copies. $4,000. (Guildford) 1975. One of 50 copies in morocco. $1,750. One of 500 copies. $1,250.

BLIGH, William. *A Narrative of the Mutiny on Board His Majesty's Ship Bounty* . . . London, 1790. With folding plate and 3 charts. $8,500.

BLIGH, William. *A Voyage to the South Sea* . . . London, 1792. With frontispiece and 6 maps/plans (4 folding), and 1 plate showing breadfruit. $10,000. Limited Editions Club, Adelaide, 1975. One of 2,000 copies. In slipcase. $200.

BLISH, James. *A Case of Conscience.* London (1959). $650. New York (1969). $200.

BLISS, Edward. *A Brief History of the New Gold Regions of Colorado Territory. Map.* New York, 1864. 30 pages, wraps. $5,000.

BLISS, William R. *Paradise in the Pacific; A Book of Travel, Adventure and Facts in the Sandwich Islands.* New York, 1873. Mounted photographic frontispiece. $600.

BLITZSTEIN, Marc. *The Cradle Will Rock.* New York, 1938. $1,250.

BLIXEN, Karen. *Out of Africa.* London (1937). First stated. $1,000. (See Isak Dinesen for U.S. edition.)

BLOCH, Robert. *The Eighth Stage of Fandom* . . . Chicago, 1962. First edition stated. Issued without dustwrapper. One of 125 signed copies. $400. One of 200 hardbound copies. $200. One of 400 copies in wraps. $60.

BLOCH, Robert. *The Opener of the Way.* Sauk City, Wis., 1945. $600.

BLOCH, Robert. *Psycho.* New York, 1959. $1,250. London, 1960. $500. Springfield, 1994. 35th Anniversary edition. One of 500 copies signed by Block and Richard Matheson (introduction). In slipcase. $200.

BLOCH, Robert. *Sea Kissed.* (London, 1945.) Author's first book. Wraps. First issue, 39 pages, "Printed in Great Britain" on page 39. $750. Second issue, 36 pages, "Printed in Eire" on page 36. $450.

BLOCK, Lawrence. *The Burglar Who Liked to Quote Kipling.* New York, 1979. $125.

BLOCK, Lawrence. *Eight Million Ways to Die.* New York, 1982. $500.

BLOCK, Lawrence. *Ronald Rabbit Is a Dirty Old Man.* New York, 1971. $600.

BLOCK, Lawrence. *A Stab in the Dark.* New York, 1981. $400.

BLOCK, Lawrence. *Time to Murder and Create.* London, 1979. $600. Illinois, 1993. One of 300 signed copies. In slipcase. $100.

BLODGET, Lorin. *Climatology of the United States, and of the Temperate Latitudes of the North American Continent . . .* Philadelphia, 1857. Folding map. $400.

BLOME, Richard. *A Description of the Island of Jamaica.* London, 1672. 3 folding maps. $10,000. London, 1678. Portrait. 4 folding maps. $6,000.

BLOME, Richard. *Hawking or Faulconry.* London: Cresset Press, 1929. One of 650 copies. $350.

BLOWE, Daniel. *A Geographical, Commercial, and Agricultural View of the United States of America.* Liverpool (1820). Portrait, 2 maps, 4 plans. $1,000.

BLUE Grotto (The) and Its Literature. London, 1904. (By Norman Douglas.) 18 pages, printed red wraps. $350.

BLUNDELL, John W. F. *The Muscles and Their Story.* London, 1864. $300.

BLUNDEN, Edmund. *Dead Letters.* London: Pelican Press, 1923. Decorated wraps, paper label. One of 50 copies. $250.

BLUNDEN, Edmund. *Japanese Garland.* London: Beaumont Press, 1928. 6 color plates. Boards and vellum. One of 80 signed copies. $450. Also, one of 310 signed. $250.

BLUNDEN, Edmund. *Masks of Time.* London: Beaumont Press, 1925. Illustrated by Randolph Schwabs. Boards and vellum. One of 80 copies on vellum, signed. $450. One of 310 copies on paper. In plain dustwrapper. $250.

BLUNDEN, Edmund. *Pastorals: A Book of Verses.* London (1916). Wraps. $125.

BLUNDEN, E(dmund) C. *Poems 1913 and 1914.* (Horsham, 1914.) Author's first book. Wraps. (100 copies.) $1,500.

BLUNDEN, Edmund. *Retreat: New Sonnets and Poems.* (London, 1928.) One of 112 signed copies. $300. Garden City. $150.

BLUNDEN, Edmund. *Undertones of War.* London, 1928. $600.

BLUNT, Edmund M. *Traveller's Guide to and Through the State of Ohio, with Sailing Directions for Lake Erie.* New York, 1832. 16 pages. $1,500. New York, 1833. Folding map in color. 28 pages. $1,000.

BLUNT, Wilfrid Scawen. See Proteus.

BLUNT, Wilfrid Scawen. *The Celebrated Romance of the Stealing of the Mare.* London, 1892. One of 50 copies. $3,000. Newtown, Wales: Gregynog Press, 1930. Translated from the Arabic by Lady Anne Blunt and done into verse by W.S.B. Boards and leather. One of 275 copies. $1,000. One of 25 copies (of this edition) especially bound in morocco. $4,000.

BLUNT, Wilfrid Scawen. *The Love-Lyrics and Songs of Proteus . . . with the Love-Sonnets.* London: Kelmscott Press, 1892. Woodcut borders and initials. Stiff vellum with ties. One of 300 copies. $1,500.

BLY, Robert. *The Light Around the Body.* New York (1967). $200.

BLY, Robert. *The Lion's Tail and Eyes.* Madison, 1962. (Author's first book with J. Wright and W. Duffy.) $200.

BLY, Robert. *The Silence in the Snowy Fields.* Middletown, 1962. Author's first solely authored book. Cloth. $200. Wraps. $60.

BOCCACCIO, Giovanni. *The Decameron.* London, 1620. 2 vols. $10,000. London: Ashendene Press, 1920. Folio, boards and linen. One of 105 copies on paper. $2,500. One of 6 copies on vellum. $5,000. Limited Editions Club, New York, 1930. Translated by Frances Winwar. 2 vols. In slipcase. $450. Another Limited Editions Club, New York, 1940. Woodcuts by Fritz Kredel. One of 530 copies. In slipcase. $500.

BOCCACCIO, Giovanni. *Life of Dante.* (Boston, 1904.) Translated by Philip Henry Wicksteed. Woodcut title portrait. Boards and vellum. One of 325 copies designed by Bruce Rogers. In slipcase. $350.

BOCKSTOCE, John R. *American Whalers in the Western Arctic.* Fairhave, 1983. One of 30 copies. 12 signed reproductions (extra suite laid in) and 2 original signed pencil sketches by artist, William Gilkerson. In portfolio and clamshell case. $2,000. One of 348 copies. As above without 2 original sketches. $1,500.

BODE, Winston. *A Portrait of Pancho.* Austin, Tex., 1965. Illustrated. Full leather. One of 150 signed copies. In slipcase. $250. Trade edition. $75.

BODENHEIM, Maxwell. See Hecht, Ben.

BODENHEIM, Maxwell. *Minna and Myself.* New York, 1918. Author's first book. First issue, with "Master-Posner" for "Master-Poisoner" on page 67. $125.

BODENHEIM, Maxwell. *The Sardonic Arm.* Chicago, 1923. Issued without dustwrapper. One of 575 copies. $200.

BODKIN, M. McDonald. *Paul Beck: The Rule of Thumb Detective.* London, 1898. $750.

BODKIN, M. McDonald. *White Magic.* London, 1897. Author's first book. $250.

BOGAN, Louise. *Body of This Death: Poems.* New York, 1923. Author's first book. $600.

BOGAN, Louise. *Dark Summer.* New York, 1929. $400.

BOGAN, Louise. *The Sleeping Fury.* New York, 1937. $300.

BOGDANOVICH, Peter. *The Cinema of Orson Welles.* New York (1961). Wraps. $150.

BOGGS, Mae Helene Bacon (compiler). *My Playhouse Was a Concord Coach*. (Oakland, 1942.) Maps, illustrations. $750.

BOLDREWOOD [*sic*] Rolf (Bolderwood). *Robbery Under Arms: A Story of Life and Adventure in the Bush and in the Goldfields of Australia*. London, 1888. (By Thomas A. Browne.) 3 vols. Decorated green cloth. $2,500.

BOLLER, Henry A. *Among the Indians*. Philadelphia, 1868. Folding map, cloth, paper label. $4,500.

BOLTON, Arthur T. *The Architecture of Robert & James Adam*. London, 1922. 2 vols. $750.

BOLTON, George G. *A Specialist in Crime*. London, 1904. Author's only book. $175.

BOLTON, Herbert Eugene. *Anza's California Expeditions*. Berkeley, 1930. 5 vols. Folding map, illustrations. $1,000.

BOLTON, Herbert Eugene. *Athanase de Mezieres and the Louisiana-Texas Frontier*. Cleveland, 1914. 2 vols. Map, 2 facsimiles. $750.

BOLTON, Herbert Eugene. *The Rim of Christendom*. New York, 1936. 12 plates, 3 facsimiles. $200.

BOLTON, Herbert Eugene (translator). *Font's Complete Diary of the Second Anza Expedition*. Berkeley, 1936. Maps, plates, facsimiles. $250.

BOLTON, Theodore. *American Book Illustrators, Bibliographical Check Lists of 123 Artists*. New York, 1938. $150.

BOND, J. Wesley. *Minnesota and Its Resources*. Chicago, 1856. Folding map, 6 plates, cloth. $175.

BOND, Michael. *Bear Called Paddington*. London, 1958. Author's first book. $350. Boston, 1960. $250.

BOND, Nelson. *Exiles of Time*. Philadelphia, 1949. $75. One of 112 signed copies. In slipcase. $200.

BOND, Nelson. *Lancelot Biggs: Spaceman*. New York, 1950. $100. One of 4 signed copies specially bound in gray and black. $1,000.

BOND, Nelson. *Mr. Mergenthwirker's Lobblies and Other Fantastic Tales*. New York (1946). Author's first book. $100.

BOND, Nelson. *Nightmares and Daydreams*. Sauk City (1968). $100.

BOND, Nelson. *The Thirty-first of February*. New York (1949). $125. One of 112 signed copies. In slipcase. $350.

BONFILS, Winifred B. *The Life and Personality of Phoebe Apperson Hearst*. San Francisco, 1928. John Henry Nash printing. Vellum. One of 1,000 copies. In original tan flannel bag. $400.

BONNELL, George W. *Topographical Description of Texas*. Austin, 1840. Cloth. $18,000 at auction in 1999. Boards. $11,000 at auction in 1999.

BONNER, T. D. *The Life and Adventures of James P. Beckwourth, Mountaineer, Scout and Pioneer . . .* New York, 1856. Frontispiece and plates. $750.

BONNEY, Edward. *Banditti of the Prairies; or, The Murderer's Doom!* Chicago, 1850. Pictorial wraps. With imprint "Chicago, W.W. Dannenhauer 1850" on front cover. $12,500. Chicago, 1853. $10,000. Philadelphia (1855). $1,000. Chicago, 1856. "25th or 30th thousand." $400. Chicago, 1858. 13 plates. Wraps. $2,500.

BONTEMPS, Arna. *Black Thunder.* New York, 1936. $1,250.

BONTEMPS, Arna. *God Sends Sunday.* New York, 1931. Author's first book. $1,500.

BONTEMPS, Arna, and CONROY, Jack. *Slappy Hooper, The Wonderful Signer Painter.* Boston, 1946. $650.

Book Collector, The. London, 1947–84. Complete run from vol. 1, no.1, to vol. 33, no.1, and *The Book Handbook,* 9 issues bound in 1 vol. Wraps. $1,250.

Book-Lore, A Magazine Devoted to Old Time Literature. London, 1885–87. 6 vols. $250.

BOOK of Commandments (A), for the Government of the Church of Christ. Zion (Independence, Mo.) 1833. (By Joseph Smith, Jr.) Boards. $30,000 and up.

BOOK of Common Prayer (The). Merrymount Press. New York (Boston), 1928. One of 500 copies. $1,250.

BOOK of Job (The). Limited Editions Club, New York, 1946. Illustrated in color by Arthur Szyk. In slipcase. $400.

BOOK of Jonah (The). Waltham Saint Lawrence: Golden Cockerel Press, 1926. Illustrated by David Jones. Buckram. One of 175 copies. In dustwrapper. $2,000.

BOOK of Princeton Verse 1916 (A). Princeton, 1916. Edited by Alfred Noyes. (Includes poems by Edmund Wilson, John Peale Bishop, and others.) $125.

BOOK of Princeton Verse II (A). Princeton (1919). (First book appearance of three poems by F. Scott Fitzgerald.) In dustwrapper. $1,250. Without dustwrapper. $300.

BOOK of Psalms (The). Limited Editions Club, New York, 1960. Illustrated by Valenti Angelo. One of 1,500 copies. In slipcase. $175.

BOOK of Ruth (The). London: Nonesuch Press, 1923. One of 250 copies. In slipcase. $450. Limited Editions Club, New York, 1947. Introduction by Mary Ellen Chase. Illustrated by Arthur Szyk. One of 1,950 copies. In slipcase. $400.

BOOK of the Law of the Lord (The). Saint James, A.R.I. (Beaver Island, Lake Michigan, 1851.) (By James Jesse Strang.) 3 copies known. $25,000. (Beaver Island, 1856.) Second issue, original sheets, lacking title page (some supplied, and with preface, in modern type, circa 1920). $5,000. For a later edition, see James J. Strang entry.

BOOK of the Poets' Club (The). London, 1909. (Includes first printings of four Ezra Pound poems.) Orange wraps. $750.

BOOK of Vassar Verse (A). (Poughkeepsie, 1916.) (With 3 poems by Edna St. Vincent Millay.) $100.

BOOLE, George. *An Investigation of the Laws of Thought* . . . London, 1854. Imprint reads "London: Walton and Maberly, Upper Gower-Street, and Ivy Lane, Paternoster Row. Cambridge: Macmillan and Co." Errata leaf bound in the back. (The "Note" leaf is found in later editions.) $5,000.

BOOTH, Edward Thomas. *Rough Notes on the Birds.* London, 1881–87. 3 vols. 2 hand-colored maps and 114 plates. $8,500.

BOOTH, Stephen. *The Book Called Holinshed's Chronicles.* San Francisco, 1968. Woodcut reproductions and original leaf from the 1587 edition. Decorated boards and cloth. One of 500 copies. $250.

BOOTH, William. *In Darkest England and the Way Out.* London (1890). Author's first book. Large folding color map. First issue with last line of dedication in smaller type than preceding line. $300.

BORDEN, Gail, Jr. *Letters of . . . to Dr. Ashbel Smith.* Galveston, 1850. 9 pages, wraps. $2,000.

BORDEN, Spencer. *The Arab Horse.* New York, 1906. $200.

BORDER Beagles: A Tale of Mississippi. Philadelphia, 1840. 2 vols. (By William Gilmore Simms.) $200.

BORGES, Jorge Luis. *The Congress.* London, 1974. Translated by Norman Thomas di Giovanni and Borges. Illustrated by Hugo Manning. Cloth. One of 50 signed copies. $750. One of 250 copies. $300.

BORGES, Jorge Luis. *Deathwatch on the Southside.* Cambridge (1968). Wraps. One of 150 signed copies. $500.

BORGES, Jorge Luis. *Ficciones.* London (1962). Author's first book. $600. New York (1962). $350. Limited Editions Club, New York (1984). $500.

BORGES, Jorge Luis. *Labyrinths.* New York: Grove Press (1962). $400.

BORN, Max. *The Constitution of Matter Modern Atomic and Electron Theories.* London, 1923. $175.

BORNEMAN, Henry S. *Pennsylvania German Illuminated Manuscripts.* Norristown, Pa., 1937. 38 colored reproductions. Oblong folio, cloth. $350.

BORROW, George. See *Celebrated Trials.*

BORROW, George. *The Bible in Spain.* London, 1843. 3 vols. Red cloth, paper labels. $500.

BORROW, George. *Faustus: His Life, Death and Descent into Hell.* London, 1825. (Translated by Borrow.) $600.

BORROW, George. *Lavengro; the Scholar—the Gypsy—the Priest.* London, 1851. 3 vols. Blue cloth, paper labels. $400. Limited Editions Club, New York, 1936. 2 vols. In slipcase. $100.

BORROW, George. *The Romany Rye.* London, 1857. 2 vols. $350.

BORROW, George. *Wild Wales: Its People, Language, and Scenery.* London, 1862. 3 vols. Blue cloth, paper labels. $400.

BOSCANA, Father Geronimo. *Chinigchinich*. Santa Ana, 1933. Translated by Alfred Robinson. Color plates, maps. Folio, boards, and cloth. $400.

BOSQUI, Edward. *Memoirs*. (Oakland): Grabhorn Press, 1952. One of 350 copies. $250.

BOSSCHERE, Jean de. *12 Occupations*. London, 1916. Decorated wraps. (Translated anonymously by Ezra Pound.) $1,000. One of 50 copies. Boards. 12 hand-colored illustrations. $2,500.

BOSSERT, Helmuth T. *Peasant Art in Europe*. London, 1927. First English edition. (Originally Berlin, 1926). 100 full-color plates and 32 plates in black-and-white. Folio, cloth. $250. New York, 1927. $200.

BOSWELL, James. *An Account of Corsica* . . . Glasgow, 1768. Map. $2,000.

BOSWELL, James. *Boswell in Search of a Wife*. London, 1957. Edited by F. Brady and Frederick A. Pottle. Blue buckram and calf. Yale deluxe edition. One of 400 copies. In slipcase. $200.

BOSWELL, James. *Boswell on the Grand Tour: Germany and Switzerland*. London, 1953. Edited by Frederick A. Pottle. Illustrated, folding map. Blue buckram and calf. London, 1953. Yale deluxe edition. One of 1,000 copies. In slipcase. $200.

BOSWELL, James. *Boswell on the Grand Tour: Italy, Corsica, and France*. London, 1955. Edited by F. Brady and Frederick A. Pottle. Illustrated, folding maps. Blue buckram and calf. Yale deluxe edition. One of 400 copies. In slipcase. $250.

BOSWELL, James. *Journal of a Tour to the Hebrides with Samuel Johnson, LL.D.* London, 1785. $1,750. New York, 1936. First complete edition. One of 816 copies. In slipcase. $350.

BOSWELL, James. *The Life of Samuel Johnson*. London, 1791. 2 vols., with the "gve" reading on page 135 of vol. 1. $12,500. With "give." $7,500. Boston, 1807. First American edition. $1,500. Limited Editions Club, New York, 1938. 3 vols. In slipcase. $300.

BOSWORTH, Newton. *Hochelaga Depicta: The Early History and Present State of the City and Island of Montreal*. Montreal, 1839. Illustrated, including 2 folding maps. $350.

BOTTA, Charles. *History of the War of Independence of the United States of America*. Philadelphia, 1820. 3 vols. $750.

BOTTOMLEY, Gordon. *Poems of Thirty Years*. London, 1925. One of 75 signed copies. $250.

BOUCHER, Anthony. *The Case of the Baker Street Irregulars*. New York, 1940. $350.

BOUCHER, Anthony. *The Case of the Seven of Calvary*. New York, 1937. Author's first book. $750.

BOUCHETTE, Joseph. *The British Dominions in North America; Or a Topographical and Statistical Description of the Provinces of Lower and Upper Canada, New Brunswick, Nova Scotia* . . . London, 1831. 2 vols. Portrait. 10 maps and plans, 20 plates and 3 tables. $2,000.

BOUCHETTE, Joseph. *A Topographical Description of the Province of Lower Canada, with Remarks Upon Upper Canada*. London, 1815. First English edition with portrait and 17 plates. $1,000. London, 1832. 2 vols. 30 plates and plans. $1,500.

BOUGAINVILLE, Louis Antoine. *A Voyage Around the World, Performed by Order of His Most Christian Majesty, in the Years 1766, 1767, 1768, And 1769.* London, 1772. First edition in English. With 1 double-page plate and 5 folding maps. $5,000.

BOUGARD, R. *The Little Sea Torch.* London, 1801. First English edition, with 20 hand-colored plates and 24 hand-colored charts. $7,500.

BOULLE, Pierre. *The Bridge Over the River Kwai.* London, 1954. (First translation in English.) $300. New York, 1954. $200.

BOULTER, Hugh. *Letters . . .* Oxford, 1769–70. 2 vols. $600. Dublin, 1770. 2 vols. $500.

BOURDILLON, Francis W. *Among the Flowers, and Other Poems.* London, 1878. Author's first book. Decorated white cloth. $200.

BOURJAILY, Vance. *The End of My Life.* New York, 1947. Author's first book. $100.

BOURKE, John G. *An Apache Campaign in the Sierra Madre.* New York, 1886. 12 plates. Printed wraps or pictorial cloth. $1,250.

BOURKE, John G. *Mackenzie's Last Fight with the Cheyennes.* Governor's Island, N.Y., 1890. Portrait. 44 pages, printed wraps. $2,000.

BOURKE, John G. *On the Border with Crook.* New York, 1891. Frontispiece portrait, other plates. $600.

BOURKE, John G. *Scatologic Rites of All Nations.* Washington, 1891. $400.

BOURKE, John G. *The Snake-Dance of the Moquis of Arizona.* New York, 1884. 33 plates, some in color. Pictorial cloth. $500. London, 1884. Half calf. First English edition. $350.

BOURKE-WHITE, Margaret. *Eyes on Russia.* New York, 1931. Author's first book. $500.

BOURNE, Randolph. *The History of a Literary Radical.* New York, 1920. Edited by Van Wyck Brooks. In dustwrapper. $250.

BOURNE, Randolph. *Youth and Life.* Boston, 1913. Author's first book. $200.

BOVA, Ben. *Star Conquerors.* Philadelphia (1959). Author's first book. $400.

BOWDEN, Charles. *Killing the Hidden Waters.* Austin (1977). $300.

BOWDICH, Thomas Edward. *Excursions in Madeira and Porto Santo . . .* London, 1825. 22 plates (4 hand-colored, 3 folding). $3,000.

BOWDICH, Thomas Edward. *Mission from Cape Coast Castle to Ashantee.* John Murray, 1819. 7 hand-colored plates (2 folding), 2 engraved maps (1 folding), folding facsimile and 3 plates of music. $3,000.

BOWDITCH, Nathaniel. *The New American Practical Navigator.* Newburyport, Mass., 1802. Folding frontispiece map, 7 plates. $4,500.

BOWEN, Abel. *The Naval Monument.* Boston, 1816. 25 woodcuts. $250.

BOWEN, Catherine Drinker. *A History of Lehigh University.* (Bethlehem, Pennsylvania), 1924. $200.

BOWEN, Elizabeth. *Ann Lee's and Other Stories.* London, 1926. $750. New York, 1927. $500.

BOWEN, Elizabeth. *The Death of the Heart.* London, 1938. $300.

BOWEN, Elizabeth. *Encounters.* London, 1923. Author's first book. In dustwrapper. $1,250.

BOWEN, Elizabeth. *Seven Winters.* Dublin: Cuala Press, 1942. Boards and linen. One of 450 copies. In tissue dustwrapper. $350.

BOWEN, Peter. *Yellowstone Kelly . . .* Ottawa, 1987. $125.

BOWER, B. M. *Chip of the Flying U.* New York: Street & Smith (1906). (By Bertha Muzzy Sinclair.) $250. (Red-bound G. W. Dillingham edition is later.)

BOWER, B. M. *Happy Family.* New York (1910). (By Bertha Muzzy Sinclair.) $75.

BOWER, B. M. *Lure of the Dim Trails.* New York (1907). (By Bertha Muzzy Sinclair.) In light-brown pictorial cloth. $100. (Red-bound G. W. Dillingham edition is later.)

BOWERING, George. *Sticks and Stones.* Vancouver [1962]. Wraps. $2,000.

BOWERS, Dorothy. *Postscript to Poison.* London (1938). $300.

BOWERS, Mrs. Dr. J. Milton. *The Dance of Life: An Answer to the "Dance of Death."* San Francisco, 1877. Red or green cloth. (By Ambrose Bierce?) $200.

BOWERS, Edgar. *The Form of Loss.* Denver, 1956. $250.

BOWLES, Jane. *In the Summer House.* New York (1954). $250.

BOWLES, Jane. *Plain Pleasures.* London (1966). $125.

BOWLES, Jane. *Two Serious Ladies.* New York, 1943. Author's first book. $2,000. London, 1965. $125.

BOWLES, Paul. *Collected Stories 1939–1976.* Santa Barbara, 1979. Introduction by Gore Vidal. One of 60 copies signed by both Bowles and Vidal. In clear acetate dustwrapper. $750. One of 300 copies signed by Bowles. $300. One of 750 copies unsigned. $75. Wraps. $30.

BOWLES, Paul. *The Delicate Prey and Other Stories.* (New York, 1950.) $600.

BOWLES, Paul. *Let It Come Down.* New York (1952). $250. Santa Barbara, 1980. One of 350 signed copies. $175.

BOWLES, Paul. *A Little Stone.* London (1950). First issue binding is light-green cloth. $350.

BOWLES, Paul. *The Sheltering Sky.* London (1949). $3,500. New York (1949). $1,750.

BOWLES, Paul. *Too Far from Home.* London, 1994. One of 100 signed copies. $250.

BOWLES, Paul. *Two Poems.* (New York, 1934.) Author's first book. Wraps. $7,500.

BOWLES, Paul. *Yallah.* Zurich, 1956. Illustrated with photos. $450. New York, 1957. $350.

BOWMAN, David. *Let the Dog Drive.* New York (1992). Author's first book. $150.

BOWYER, William. *The Origin of Printing in Two Essays . . .* London, 1774. $350.

BOX, Capt. Michael James. *Capt. James Box's Adventures and Explorations in New and Old Mexico.* New York, 1861. $2,000. New York, 1869. Second issue (original sheets with cancel title leaf). $600.

BOX, Edgar. *Death Before Bedtime.* New York, 1953. (By Gore Vidal.) $300.

BOX, Edgar. *Death in the Fifth Position.* New York, 1952. (By Gore Vidal.) $350.

BOX, Edgar. *Death Likes It Hot.* New York, 1954. (By Gore Vidal.) $300.

BOYD, James. *Bitter Creek.* New York, 1939. $150.

BOYD, James. *Drums.* New York–London, 1925. Author's first book. $350. New York (1928). Illustrated by N. C. Wyeth. One of 525 copies signed by author and artist. In slipcase. $1,500. Trade. $250.

BOYD, Martin. *A Difficult Young Man.* London, 1955. $200.

BOYD, Nancy. *Distressing Dialogues.* New York (1924). (By Edna St. Vincent Millay.) First edition stated. $500.

BOYD, Thomas. *Through the Wheat.* New York, 1923. $300.

BOYD, William. *A Good Man in Africa.* London, 1981. Author's first book. $650. New York, 1982. $125.

BOYDELL, John, and BOYDELL, Josiah. *An History of the River Thames.* London, 1794–96. Dedication to George III. Frontispiece, 2 folding maps and 76 hand-colored plates. $10,000.

BOYLE, Jack. *Boston Blackie.* New York (1919). Author's first book. In dustwrapper. $2,500. Without dustwrapper. $450.

BOYLE, Kay. See Brook, Gladys Palmer.

BOYLE, Kay. *The Crazy Hunter.* New York (1940). $250.

BOYLE, Kay. *The First Lover and Other Stories.* New York (1933). $250.

BOYLE, Kay. *Gentlemen, I Address You Privately.* New York, 1933. $400.

BOYLE, Kay. *Monday Night.* New York (1938). $250.

BOYLE, Kay. *Plagued by the Nightingale.* New York, 1931. Her first novel. $400. London, 1931. $250.

BOYLE, Kay. *Short Stories.* Paris: Black Sun Press, 1929. Author's first book. Printed wraps in gold- or silver-tied protective boards. One of 15 signed copies on Japan paper. $1,500. One of

150 on Van Gelder paper. In tissue dustwrapper. In slipcase. $750. One of 20 copies on Arches paper, for France. $1,250.

BOYLE, Kay. *Wedding Day and Other Stories.* New York (1930). Decorated boards, cloth spine. (The author's first book, retitled as shown, also variant spine title, "Short/Stories.") Priority unknown. $450. London, 1932. $250.

BOYLE, Kay. *The White Horses of Vienna.* New York (1936). $250.

BOYLE, T. Coraghessan. *Descent of Man.* Boston (1979). Author's first book. $750. London, 1980. $150.

BOYLES, Kate and Virgil. *Homesteaders.* Chicago, 1909. $150.

BOYLES, Kate and Virgil. *Lansford of the Three Bars.* Chicago, 1907. $75.

"BOZ." See Dickens, Charles. See also *Sketches by "Boz."*

"BOZ." *Master Humphrey's Clock.* London, 1840–41. (By Charles Dickens.) 88 weekly parts, white wraps. $2,500. Second edition, 20 monthly parts in 19, green wraps. $2,500. (First book edition, issued under Dickens' name, which see.)

"BOZ." *Oliver Twist; or, The Parish Boy's Progress.* London, 1838. (By Charles Dickens.) Illustrated by George Cruikshank. 3 vols. In original reddish-brown cloth. First issue, with "Rose Maylie and Oliver" plate in vol. 3 showing them at fireside. $10,000. Rebound in nice old half calf. $2,000. In new "Bayntun-style" morocco. $3,500. Second issue showing them at church. $4,500. (For later editions, see Dickens entries for *The Adventures of Oliver Twist* and *Oliver Twist.*)

BRACKENRIDGE, H. H. See *A Poem on the Rising Glory . . .* and *Strictures on a Voyage to South America, etc.*

BRACKENRIDGE, Hugh Henry. *Gazette Publications.* Carlisle, Pa., 1806. $750.

BRACKENRIDGE, H. M. *Journal of a Voyage up the Missouri.* Baltimore, 1815. First edition (actually second appearance of the journal, which first appeared in author's *Views of Louisiana,* which see). $1,500. Baltimore, 1816 (cover date 1815). Second edition. Boards. $750.

BRACKENRIDGE, H. M. *Views of Louisiana; Together with a Journal of a Voyage up the Missouri River, in 1814.* Pittsburgh, 1814. $2,000. Baltimore, 1817. (Revised.) $750.

BRACKETT, Leigh. *No Good for a Corpse.* New York (1944). $1,500.

BRADBURY, John. *Travels in the Interior of America.* Liverpool, 1817. With errata slip. $2,500. London, 1819. Second edition. Folding map. $2,000.

BRADBURY, Ray. *The Anthem Sprinters.* New York: Dial Press, 1963. Cloth. $300. Wraps actually precedes by a month or so. $75.

BRADBURY, Ray. *Dandelion Wine.* Garden City, 1957. $450. London, 1957. $250.

BRADBURY, Ray. *Dark Carnival.* Sauk City, 1947. Author's first book. $1,250. London (1948). $450.

BRADBURY, Ray. *Fahrenheit 451.* New York (1953). (About 50 author's copies were bound in cloth.) $3,500. Asbestos boards. One of 200 signed copies. Issued without dustwrapper. $6,000 or more if perfect. Very nice copies. $3,500. Trade. In cloth. $1,750. Simultaneous issue by Ballantine in wraps. (Actually true first.) $75. London, 1954. $1,000. Limited Editions Club, New York, 1982. $400.

BRADBURY, Ray. *The Golden Apples of the Sun.* Garden City, 1953. $600. London, 1953. $200.

BRADBURY, Ray. *The Illustrated Man.* Garden City, 1951. $1,000. London, 1952. $300.

BRADBURY, Ray. *The Machineries of Joy.* New York, 1964. $250. London, 1964. $150.

BRADBURY, Ray. *The Martian Chronicles.* Garden City, 1950. First state in green binding. $2,000. Second state in blue binding. $1,500. Limited Editions Club, New York, 1974. 2,000 copies signed by author and illustrator. $350.

BRADBURY, Ray. *A Medicine for Melancholy.* Garden City, 1959. $350.

BRADBURY, Ray. *The October Country.* New York (1955). One of 50 copies bound for author in full red cloth with gold stamping. $2,500. Trade. First state has Ballantine logo on spine inverted. $600. Second state with logo corrected. $400. London, 1956. $250.

BRADBURY, Ray. *The Silver Locusts.* London, 1951. First British edition (of *The Martian Chronicles*). $350.

BRADBURY, Ray. *Switch on the Night.* (New York, 1955.) $500. Later printings have pictorial covers without dustwrapper. (London), 1955. $250.

BRADBY, Anne. *Shakespeare Criticism 1919–1935.* London, 1936. (By Anne Ridler.) Author's first book. $75.

BRADDON, Mary Elizabeth. *Garibaldi . . .* London, 1861. Author's first book. $1,250.

BRADDON, Mary Elizabeth. *Lady Audley's Secret.* London, 1862. (3 vols.) $3,500. New York (1863). $1,250.

BRADFORD, Gamaliel. *Daughters of Eve.* Boston (1930). Illustrated. Cloth. One of 200 signed copies. $200.

BRADFORD, Gamaliel. *Types of American Character.* New York, 1895. Author's first book. $125.

BRADFORD, Roark. *Ol' Man Adam and His Chillun.* New York, 1928. Author's first book. $125.

BRADFORD, William. *The Arctic Regions.* (London, 1873.) 129 albumen prints. Folio, morocco. $12,500. (Also at auction with 141 prints 1991 [Manney].)

BRADLEY, David. *South Street.* New York, 1975. Author's first book. $250.

BRADLEY, Edward. *College Life.* Oxford, 1849–50. Author's first book. (6 parts in 5.) $1,000.

BRADLEY, James. *The Confederate Mail Carrier.* Mexico, Mo., 1894. 15 plates. $450.

BRADLEY, John W. *A Dictionary of Miniaturists.* London, 1887–89. 3 vols. Half leather. $750.

BRADLEY, Joshua. *Accounts of Religious Revivals in Many Parts of the United States from 1815 to 1818.* Albany, 1819. $300.

BRADLEY, Omar Nelson. *A Soldier's Story.* New York (1951). One of 750 signed copies. In slipcase. $500.

BRADLEY, Van Allen. *The Book Collector's Handbook of Values.* New York (1982). The fourth, revised, and enlarged edition. $100.

BRADLEY, Will. *The American Chap-Book.* Jersey City, September 1904–August 1905. Volumes I and II, each in 6 numbers. Original wraps. $1,250. Original wraps bound in one volume. $1,000.

BRADLEY, William Aspenwall. *The Etching of Figures.* Marlborough-on-Hudson, N.Y., 1915. Half vellum. Dard Hunter paper and printing. One of 250. $1,000.

BRADSTREET, Anne. See *The Tenth Muse . . .*

BRADY, Cyrus Townsend. *Arizona.* New York, 1914. $200.

BRADY, William. *Glimpses of Texas.* Houston, 1871. Folding map in color. Stiff wraps, or cloth. $2,500.

BRAINE, John. *Room at the Top.* London, 1957. Author's first book. (Some with wraparound band.) $250. Boston, 1957. $75.

BRAIT, John. *Trails of Yesterday.* Lincoln, Chicago, Dallas, 1921. 26 photographs and illustrations. In slipcase. $400.

BRAITHWAITE, William S. *Lyrics of Life and Love.* Boston, 1904. Author's first book. $400.

BRAITHWAITE, William S. (editor). *Anthology of Magazine Verse for 1913.* Cambridge, Mass. (1913). (First of the Braithwaite anthologies.) Wraps. $250. Boards. $150.

BRAITHWAITE, William S. (editor). *Anthology of Magazine Verse for 1923.* Boston, 1923. Boards and cloth. Issued without dustwrapper. One of 245 copies signed by Braithwaite. $250. Trade edition in dustwrapper. $150.

BRAMAH, Ernest. *English Farming and Why I Turned It Up.* London, 1894. Author's first book. Issued without dustwrapper. $250.

BRAMAH, Ernest. *The Eyes of Max Carrados.* London, 1923. $3,500. New York (1924). $1,000.

BRAMAH, Ernest. *Kai Lung's Golden Hours.* London, 1924. One of 250 signed copies. $1,000. Trade. $350.

BRAMAH, Ernest. *Max Carrados.* London (1914). With ads dated "Autumn 1913." $750.

BRAMAH, Ernest. *The Transmutation of Ling.* London (1911). One of 500. $250.

BRAMAH, Ernest. *The Wallet of Kai Lung.* London (1900). Light-green cloth. First issue, measuring 1½ inches thick. $500. London, 1923. Boards. One of 200 signed copies. $600.

BRAMAN, D. E. E. *Information About Texas.* Philadelphia, 1857. $1,000. Philadelphia, 1858. Second edition. Cloth. $600.

BRAMMER, William. *The Gay Place.* Boston, 1961. Author's first book. First issue, rear dustwrapper flap has name of designer, $350. Second issue, rear dustwrapper flap has name of designer covered by design, $150. Third issue, rear dustwrapper flap has name of designer removed. $100.

BRANCH, Douglas. *The Cowboy and His Interpreters.* New York and London, 1926. Illustrated by Will James, Joe de Young, and Charles M. Russell. 21 illustrations in text plus frontispiece. $200.

BRAND, Christianna. (Mary Christianna Lewis.) *Death in High Heels.* London, 1941. $250. New York, 1954. $100.

BRAND, Max. *Calling Dr. Kildare.* New York, 1940. (By Frederick Faust.) $500.

BRAND, Max. *Destry Rides Again.* New York, 1930. $750.

BRAND, Max. *Night Horseman.* New York, 1920. In dustwrapper. $500.

BRAND, Max. *The Untamed.* New York, 1919. Author's first book. Pseudonym of Frederick S. Faust. In dustwrapper. $1,500. Without dustwrapper. $300.

BRANDEIS, Louis D. *Other People's Money . . .* New York (1914). Author's first book. $300.

BRANDT, Bill. *Camera in London.* London & New York (1948). $600.

BRANDT, Bill. *The English at Home.* London (1936). Author's first book. Issued in glassine dustwrapper. $450. New York, 1936. Issued in tissue dustwrapper. $350.

BRANDT, Bill. *Perspective of Nudes.* New York (1961). $600.

BRANDT, Herbert. *Arizona Bird Life.* Cleveland, 1951. Illustrated, including map and color plates. Green cloth. $250.

BRANGWYN, Frank. *The Etched Work of Frank Brangwyn.* London, 1908. One of 100 copies. $1,250.

BRANGWYN, Frank. *The Historical Paintings in the Great Hall of the Worshipful Company of Skinners.* London, 1909. One of 525 copies. $1,000. One of 25 copies on vellum. $2,000.

BRANGWYN, Frank. *The Way of the Cross.* London (1935). 14 plates. One of 250 copies. $1,000.

BRASHER, Rex. *Birds and Trees of North America.* (Kent, CN, 1929–32). 12 vols. 867 hand-colored plates. Oblong folio, half leather folders. $20,000. New York, 1961–62. 4 vols. with 875 colored plates. $350.

BRASIL, Angela. *A Terrible Tomboy.* London, 1904. $300.

BRASSINGTON, Salt. *A History of the Art of Bookbinding . . .* London, 1894. $500.

BRATHWAITE, Richard. *The English Gentleman . . .* London, 1630. $2,000.

BRATT, John. *Trails of Yesterday.* Lincoln, Neb., 1921. Portrait frontispiece and plates. Pictorial cloth. $350.

BRAUN, Lilian Jackson. *The Cat Who Could Read Backwards.* New York, 1966. Author's first book. $300.

BRAUTIGAN, Richard. *All Watched Over by Machines of Loving Grace.* San Francisco, 1967. One of 1,500 copies. Illustrated yellow wraps. $500.

BRAUTIGAN, Richard. *A Confederate General at Big Sur.* New York (1964). $400.

BRAUTIGAN, Richard. *The Galilee Hitch-Hiker.* San Francisco (1958). Wraps. $2,500. San Francisco, 1966. Illustrated by Kenn Davis. One of 16 signed copies with a small drawing on separate folded 8½-by-11–inch thin brown paper. $1,000. One of 700 copies. $350.

BRAUTIGAN, Richard. *In Watermelon Sugar.* San Francisco (1968). One of 50 signed copies. $1,750.

BRAUTIGAN, Richard. *Lay the Marble Tea.* San Francisco (1959). Printed wraps. $1,500.

BRAUTIGAN, Richard. *Loading Mercury with a Pitchfork.* New York, 1976. $250.

BRAUTIGAN, Richard. *The Octopus Frontier.* San Francisco (1960). Printed wraps. $750.

BRAUTIGAN, Richard. *The Pill Versus the Springhill Mine Disaster.* San Francisco (1968). Tan boards, brown cloth spine. One of 50 signed copies. $1,750.

BRAUTIGAN, Richard. *Please Plant This Book.* San Francisco (1968). Wraps, with eight seed packets enclosed. $750.

BRAUTIGAN, Richard. *The Return of the Rivers.* (San Francisco, 1958.) Author's first book. Wraps. $2,500.

BRAVO (The): A Venetian Story. London, 1831. (By James Fenimore Cooper.) 3 vols. $750. Philadelphia, 1831. 2 vols. First American edition. $500.

BRAYTON, Matthew. *The Indian Captive.* Cleveland, 1860. 68 pages, printed green wraps. $5,000. Boards. $3,000. Fostoria, Ohio, 1896. Second edition. $1,000.

BRENAN, George. See Beaton, George.

BRENNAN, Joseph Payne. *Heart of Earth.* Prairie City (1949). Author's first book. $200.

BRENNAN, Joseph Payne. *Nine Horrors and a Dream.* Sauk City, 1958. $225.

BRENNER, Anita. *Idol Behind Altar.* New York, 1929. $300.

BRENNER, Anita. *The Wind That Swept Mexico.* New York (1943). Illustrated with photographs. $250.

BRETON, André. *What Is Surrealism?* London, 1936. $200.

BRETON, André. *Young Cherry Trees Secured Against Hares.* New York, 1946. $500.

BRETT, Simon. (Anthony Lee.) *Cast, In Order of Disappearance.* London, 1975. $150. New York (1976). $75.

BRETTON, James J. (editor). *Voices from the Press: A Collection of Sketches, Essays* . . . New York, 1850. $350.

BREVOORT, Elias. *New Mexico: Her Natural Resources* . . . Sante Fe, 1874. Wraps. $750.

BREWSTER, Sir David. *A Treatise on the Kaleidoscope.* Edinburgh, 1819. 7 plates. $750.

BREWSTER, Ralph H. *The Good Beards of Athos.* London, Hogarth, 1935. $150.

BREYTENBACH, Breyten. *Sinking Ship Blues.* Oakville, Ontario, 1977. Wraps. $125.

BRICE, Wallace. *A History of Fort Wayne.* Fort Wayne, Ind., 1868. 7 plates. Cloth. $400.

BRIDGENS, Richard. *Furniture, with Candelabra and Interior Decoration.* London, 1838. 60 full-page color plates (including title). Folio. $4,500.

BRIDGES, Robert. *Eros and Psyche: A Poem.* Newtown, Wales: Gregynog Press, 1935. Woodcuts from drawings by Edward Burne-Jones. White pigskin. One of 300 copies. In buckram case. $1,750. One of 15 copies specially bound by George Fisher. $3,000.

BRIDGES, Robert. *Poems.* London, 1873. Author's first book (suppressed by him in 1878). $600.

BRIDGES, Robert. *Poems Written in the Year MCMXIII.* (London): Ashendene Press, 1914. Blue printed boards and cloth. One of 85 copies with initials in red or blue. In slipcase. $2,500. One of 6 copies on vellum. $8,500.

BRIDGES, Robert. *The Testament of Beauty.* Oxford, 1929. One of 50 signed copies. $750. One of 200 copies, unsigned. $150. Trade edition. $125. New York, 1929. One of 250 copies. $300.

BRIDWELL, J. W. (compiler). *The Life and Adventures of Robert McKimie.* Hillsboro, Ohio, 1878. 56 pages, pictorial wraps. $1,500.

BRIEF Description of Western Texas (A). San Antonio, 1873. (By W. G. Kingsbury.) Pictorial wraps. $1,500.

BRIGGS, Charles Frederick. See *The Adventures of Harry Franco* . . .

BRIGGS, Clare. *Golf: The Book of a Thousand Chuckles.* Chicago (1916). $250.

BRIGGS, E. C., and ATTWOOD, R. M. *Address to the Saints In Utah and California, Polygamy Proven an Abomination by Holy Writ, Is Brigham Young President of the Church of Jesus Christ* . . . Plano, Il., 1869. Wraps. Third edition (noted as "Revised by Joseph Smith and Wm. W. Blair"). $750.

BRIGGS, L. Vernon. *History of Shipbuilding on North River, Plymouth County, Massachusetts.* Boston, 1889. $300.

BRIGHAM, Clarence S. *Paul Revere's Engravings.* Worcester, Mass., 1954. 77 plates (some in color). $175.

BRIGMAN, Anne. *Songs of a Pagan.* Caldwell, Idaho, 1949. $300.

BRILLAT-SAVARIN, J. A. *The Physiology of Taste.* Philadelphia, 1854. $1,000. London, 1925. Introduction by Arthur Machen. Portrait, other illustrations. Boards. One of 750. $350. New York, 1926. One of 500 copies. $350. Limited Editions Club, New York, 1949. Translated by M.F.K. Fisher. Half leather. 1,500 copies. Slipcase. $300.

BRILLIANT, Ashley. *I May Not Be Totally Perfect, But . . .* Santa Barbara (1979). Cloth. Issued without dustwrapper. (1,000 copies.) $150. Wraps. $30.

BRINK, André (Philippus). *The Ambassador.* (Cape Town), 1964. First English translation. $150.

BRINK, André. (Phillippus). *File on a Diplomat.* London, 1967. $50.

BRIQUET Album: A Miscellany on Watermarks . . . , The. Hilversum, 1952. One of 400 copies. Vol. 2 (one of the more difficult to find). $300.

BRISBANE, Albert. *Social Destiny of Man . . .* Philadelphia, 1840. Author's first book. $600.

BRISBIN, James S. *The Beef Bonanza.* Philadelphia, 1881. 8 plates. Pictorial cloth. $350.

BRITISH Librarian: Exhibiting A Compendious Review or Abstract of Our Most Scarce . . . London, 1738. 6 vols. bound in 1. $600.

BRITTAIN, Vera M. *Verses of a V.A. D.* London, 1918. $150.

BRITTON, Wiley. *Memoirs of the Rebellion on the Border, 1863.* Chicago, 1882. $300.

BROCH, Hermann. *The Death of Virgil.* New York, 1945. $2,000.

BROCH, Hermann. *The Sleepwalkers.* London, 1932. Translated from the German by Willa and Edwin Muir. $250. Boston, 1932. $200.

BRODER, Patricia Janis. *Bronzes of the American West.* New York (1974). 511 illustrations, including 48 plates in color (not including sculpture). One of 262 copies. $400.

BRODIE, Walter. *Pitcairn's Island and the Islanders in 1850.* London, 1851. 4 plates. Cloth, paper label. $450. London, 1851. Second edition. $250.

BRODKEY, Harold. *First Love & Other Sorrows.* New York (1957). Author's first book. $300. London, 1958. $125.

BROMFIELD, Louis. *The Green Bay Tree.* New York, 1924. Author's first book. $350.

BRONK, William. *Light and Dark.* (Ashland, Mass.), 1956. Author's first book. Wraps. $200.

BRONTË, Anne. See Bell, Acton; Bell, Currer.

BRONTË, Charlotte. See Bell, Currer.

BRONTË, Emily. See Bell, Ellis.

BROOK, Gladys Palmer. *Relations & Complications . . .* London (1929). Ghostwritten by Kay Boyle. $450.

BROOKE, Arthur De Capell. *Travels Through Sweden, Norway, and Finmark, to the North Cape.* London, 1823. Map, 21 plates (2 colored). $1,250. London, 1831. Second edition. $750.

BROOKE, Arthur De Capell. *A Winter in Lapland and Sweden.* London, 1826. With frontispiece, folding map, and 24 plates. $3,000. London, 1827. Second edition. With 21 plates. $1,500.

BROOKE, H. K. *Annals of the Revolution.* Philadelphia, 1843. Boards. First issue with "88½ N. Second St." for publisher's address. $600. Second issue [1848] "198 Market St." $300.

BROOKE, James. *Narrative of Events in Borneo and Celebes.* London, 1848. 2 vols. 18 plates and 5 maps (1 folding, 4 extending). $1,000.

BROOKE, Jocelyn. *Six Poems.* Oxford, 1928. Author's first book. Wraps. $350.

BROOKE, Rupert. *The Bastille.* Rugby: A. J. Lawrence, 1905. Wraps. $4,000. Rugby: George E. Over, 1905 (1920). Wraps. $1,000.

BROOKE, Rupert. *Collected Poems.* New York, 1915. $400. (Of the first edition, 100 copies were especially bound for members of the Woodberry Society. Value: $1,000.) London, 1919. Illustrated by Gwen Raverat. One of 1,000 copies. $450. One of 13 copies on vellum. $2,500.

BROOKE, Rupert. *Lithuania: A Drama in One Act.* (Chicago): Chicago Little Theatre, 1915. Pictorial brown wraps. $750.

BROOKE, Rupert. *1914 and Other Poems.* London, 1915. Portrait frontispiece. Dark-blue cloth, paper label. $400. In dustwrapper (which is usually short). $1,000. New York, 1915. American copyright edition, 87 copies, folded sheets. Bound in morocco. $1,750. In cloth and boards. $1,500. Unbound sheets. $750.

BROOKE, Rupert. *"1914": Five Sonnets.* London, 1915. Printed wraps. In printed envelope. $200.

BROOKE, Rupert. *The Old Vicarage, Grantchester.* London, 1916. Gray wraps. $200.

BROOKE, Rupert. *Poems.* London, 1911. Author's first book of verse and first commercial publication. Dark-blue cloth, paper label. (Issued without dustwrapper.) $750.

BROOKE, Rupert. *The Pyramids.* Rugby, 1904. Author's first book. Wraps. $15,000.

BROOKNER, Anita. *Watteau.* London, 1967. Author's first book. $150.

BROOKS, Bryant B. *Memoirs of Bryant B. Brooks.* Glendale, Calif., 1939. Plates. One of 150 copies. $300.

BROOKS, Cleanth. *The Relations of the Alabama-Georgia Dialect . . .* Baton Rouge, 1935. Author's first book. Issued without dustwrapper. $125.

BROOKS, Gwendolyn. *Annie Allen.* New York (1949). $300.

BROOKS, Gwendolyn. *The Bean Eaters.* New York (1960). $400.

BROOKS, Gwendolyn. *Bronzeville Boys and Girls.* New York (1956). First edition not stated. $250.

BROOKS, Gwendolyn. *Maud Martha.* New York (1953). $300.

BROOKS, Gwendolyn. *Song After Sunset.* 1936. (One known copy.) $6,000.

BROOKS, Gwendolyn. *A Street in Bronzeville.* New York, 1945. Author's first regularly published book. $750.

BROOKS, Noah. *The Fairport Nine.* New York, 1880. $1,250.

BROOKS, Terry. *The Sword of Shannara.* New York (1977). $300.

BROOKS, Walter R. *Freddy and the Flying Saucer Plans.* New York, 1957. $450.

BROOKS, Walter R. *Freddy and the Men from Mars.* New York, 1954. $500.

BROSSARD, Chandler. *Who Walk in Darkness.* (New York, 1952.) Author's first book. Cloth. $150. Wraps. $40. London (1952). $75.

BROTHERHOOD, W. *Forty Years Among the Old Booksellers of Philadelphia, With Bibliographic Remarks.* Philadelphia, 1891. $150.

BROTHER Jonathan. Edinburgh, 1825. (By John Neal.) 3 vols. $600.

BROTHERS (The): A Tale of the Fronde. New York, 1835. 2 vols. (By Henry William Herbert.) Author's first book. First issue, in original brown cloth. $450.

BROUGHTON, James. *Songs for Certain Children.* San Francisco, 1947. Author's first book. $350.

BROUGHTON, William Robert. *A Voyage of Discovery to the North Pacific Ocean.* London, 1804. 9 plates and maps (7 folding). $17,500.

BROUILLET, J.B.A. *Authentic Account of the Murder of Dr. Whitman and Other Missionaries.* Portland, 1869. 108 pages, wraps. Second edition of *Protestantism in Oregon* (see item following). $4,000.

BROUILLET, J.B.A. *Protestantism in Oregon: Account of the Murder of Dr. Whitman, and the Ungrateful Calumnies of H. H. Spalding, Protestant Missionary.* New York, 1853. Wraps. $4,500.

BROWER, Jacob V. *Memoirs of Explorations in the Basin of the Mississippi.* Maps. St. Paul, Minn., 1898–1904. 8 vols. Cloth. One of 300 copies. $1,250.

BROWN, Alice. *Fools of Nature.* Boston, 1887. Author's first book to be published with her name on a title page. $100.

BROWN, Benjamin. *Testimonies for the Truth: A Record of Manifestations of the Power of God . . . High Priest in the Church of Jesus Christ of Latter Day Saints.* Liverpool, 1853. $850.

BROWN, Bob. *Demonics.* Cagnes-sur-Mer, France, 1931. Wraps. $300.

BROWN, Bob. *Readies for Bob Brown's Machine.* Cagnes-sur-Mer, France, 1931. Wraps. One of 300 copies. $750.

BROWN, Bob. *The Remarkable Adventures of Christopher Poe.* Chicago, 1913. Author's first book. $125.

BROWN, Bob. *What Happened to Mary.* New York (1913). $125.

BROWN, Bob. *Words.* Paris: Hours Press, 1931. One of 150 signed copies. $300.

BROWN, Charles Brockden. See *Alcuin . . .* ; *Wieland . . .*

BROWN, Charles Brockden. *Arthur Mervyn: A Tale.* London, 1803. 3 vols. First English edition. $750. (The first edition was issued anonymously in America. See *Arthur Mervyn.*)

BROWN, Christie. *My Left Foot.* London, 1954. Author's first book. $350.

BROWN, Dee. *Bury My Heart at Wounded Knee.* New York (1970). 9½ inches x 6½ inches. Fore edges rough. Dustwrapper has "0171" at bottom of front flap. $250. Second issue. Without "0171" and 9¼ inches x 6¼ inches. Fore edges smooth. $125. (Both state "First Edition" and are in priced dustwrapper.)

BROWN, Fredric. *The Dead Ringer.* New York, 1948. $600. London (1950). $350.

BROWN, Fredric. *The Fabulous Clipjoint.* New York, 1947. Author's first book. $750.

BROWN, Fredric. *Martians, Go Home.* New York, 1955. $400.

BROWN, Fredric. *Murder Can Be Fun.* New York, 1948. $400. London (1951). $350.

BROWN, Fredric. *What Mad Universe.* New York, 1949. $450. London (1951). $350.

BROWN, George MacKay. *Let's See the Orkney Island.* Port William, no date [1948]. Wraps. $150.

BROWN, Henry. *A History of Illinois.* New York, 1844. Map. Cloth. $500.

BROWN, Henry. *A Narrative of the Anti-Masonick . . .* Batavia, 1829. $300.

BROWN, J. Cabell. *Calabazas, or Amusing Recollections of an Arizona "City."* San Francisco, 1892. Printed wraps. $250.

BROWN, J. Willard. *The Signal Corps, U.S.A., in the War of the Rebellion.* Boston, 1896. $200.

BROWN, James S. *California Gold: An Authentic History of the First Find.* Oakland, 1894. Portrait frontispiece. 20 pages, printed wraps. $1,500.

BROWN, James S. *Life of a Pioneer.* Salt Lake City, 1900. Portrait. 2 plates. $400.

BROWN, Jesse, and WILLARD, A. M. *The Black Hills Trails.* Rapid City, S.D., 1924. Numerous illustrations. $250.

BROWN, John Arthur. *Short History of Pine Valley.* New Jersey, 1963. Privately printed. $150.

BROWN, John Henry. *History of Dallas County from 1837 to 1887.* Dallas, 1887. 114 pages, wraps. $750.

BROWN, John Henry. *History of Texas, 1685–1892.* St. Louis (1892–93). 2 vols. 25 plates. Cloth. $400.

BROWN, John Henry. *Indian Wars and Pioneers of Texas.* Austin, Tex. (1896). Plates. $1,250.

BROWN, John Henry. *Political History of Oregon.* Portland, Ore., 1892. Vol. 1 (All published.) Illustrated, folding map. $600.

BROWN, John H(enry). *Reminiscences and Incidents, of "The Early Days" of San Francisco.* San Francisco (1886). Folding frontispiece plan. $1,000. San Francisco (1933). Grabhorn printing. Half cloth. One of 500 copies. $150. One of 25 copies in morocco, with additional reproductions. $500.

BROWN, John Henry, and SPEER, W. S. *The Encyclopedia of the New West.* Marshall, Tex., 1881. In calf. $1,000.

BROWN, Joseph M. *Astyanax: An Epic Romance of Llion, Atlantis, and Amaraca.* New York, 1907. Illustrated. Cloth. $200.

BROWN, Larry. *Facing the Music.* Chapel Hill, 1988. $250.

BROWN, Norman O. *Hermes the Thief.* (Madison, Wisconsin), 1947. $200.

BROWN, Oliver Madox. *Gabriel Denver.* London, 1873. Author's first book. $1,500.

BROWN, Paul. *Aintree.* New York: Derrydale Press, 1930. One of 850 copies. $600. One of 50 large-paper copies with an initialed drawing by Brown. $2,500.

BROWN, Richard. *Domestic Architecture . . .* London (1942). Preface dated 2 May 1842. 63 plates. $750.

BROWN, Richard. *The Principles of Practical Perspective . . .* London, 1815. 51 plates. $1,000.

BROWN, Richard. *The Rudiments of Drawing Cabinet and Upholstery Furniture . . .* London, 1820. $3,500.

BROWN, Rita Mae. *The Hand That Cradles the Rock.* New York, 1971. $200.

BROWN, Robert Carlton. See Brown, Bob.

BROWN, Samuel J. *In Captivity: The Experience, Privations and Dangers of Sam'l J. Brown . . .* Mankato, Minn. (1896). Full leather. $1,000.

BROWN, Samuel R. *The Western Gazetteer, or Emigrant's Directory.* Auburn, N.Y., 1817. First issue, with 3-line errata slip. $1,000. Second issue, with 4-line errata. $600. Third issue, with advertisements. $500.

BROWN, Sterling. *Southern Road.* New York, 1932. Author's first book. $2,000.

BROWN, William C. *The Sheepeater Campaign in Idaho.* Boise, 1926. Folding map. 32 pages, wraps. One of 50 copies. $300.

BROWN, William H. *The Early History of the State of Illinois.* Chicago, 1840. 16 pages, printed wraps. $2,000.

BROWN, William Hill. See *The Power of Sympathy.*

BROWN, William Robinson. *The Horse of the Desert.* New York: Derrydale Press, 1929. Illustrated. Cloth. One of 750 copies. In dustwrapper. $750. One of 75 signed copies. $4,500.

BROWN, William Wells. *Clotel: or, The President's Daughter.* London, 1853. $6,000.

BROWN, William Wells. *Clotelle: A Tale of the Southern States.* (New title.) Boston/New York (1864). $4,000.

BROWN, William Wells. *The Narrative of . . . Fugitive Slave.* Boston, 1847. $2,000.

BROWN, Zenith Jones. See Frome, David.

BROWNE, Francis F. *Volunteer Grain.* Chicago: Way & Williams, 1895. Green cloth. One of 160 copies. (First book by the publisher.) $750.

BROWNE, J. Ross. *Adventures in the Apache Country.* New York, 1869. $350.

BROWNE, J. Ross. *Etchings of a Whaling Cruise.* New York, 1846. 13 plates. $600. New York, 1850. $500.

BROWNE, J. Ross. *Report of the Debates in the Convention of California on the Formation of the State Constitution.* Washington, 1850. $400.

BROWNE, Thomas A. See Boldrewood, Rolf.

BROWNE, Sir Thomas. *Religio Medici.* (London), 1642. 97 leaves. $10,000. Second edition. 81 leaves. $7,500. (London), 1643. First authorized edition. $7,500. Waltham Saint Lawrence: Golden Cockerel Press, 1923. One of 115 copies. $1,500. Limited Editions Club, New York, 1939. John Henry Nash printing. In slipcase. $150.

BROWNING, Elizabeth Barrett. See B., E. B.; Barrett, E. B.; Barrett, Elizabeth B.; Browning, Elizabeth Barrett. See also *An Essay on Mind; Prometheus Bound.*

BROWNING, Elizabeth Barrett. *Aurora Leigh.* London, 1857 (actually 1856). $600.

BROWNING, Elizabeth Barrett. *Casa Guidi Windows: A Poem.* London, 1851. $400.

BROWNING, Elizabeth Barrett. *Poems Before Congress.* London, 1860. Red cloth. With page 25, line 1 having single quote mark '. . . different scarce." (Second impression, lines 1, 2, 3, and 5 reset and reads ". . . different scarce."). In some copies. 32-page publisher's catalogue dated February 1860 (no priority). $300.

BROWNING, Elizabeth Barrett. *Sonnets from the Portuguese.* The following are some separate editions. (Boston): Copeland & Day, 1896. Hand-colored illustrations. One of 750 copies. $1,000. London (1909). One of 500 copies. $500. Montagnola, 1925. Morocco. One of 225 copies. $1,000. San Francisco, 1925–27. 2 vols. Half vellum (including facsimile volume). One of 250 copies. $300. Limited Editions Club, New York, 1948. In slipcase. $350.

BROWNING, Robert. See Barrett, Elizabeth, and Browning, Robert. See also *Pauline: A Fragment of a Confession.*

BROWNING, Robert. *Bells and Pomegranates.* London, 1841–46. 8 parts, printed wraps. First edition, with half title for second part. $1,250. First book edition (parts bound in 1 vol., cloth, with the half title to the second part). $400.

BROWNING, Robert. *Dramatic Romances and Lyrics.* London: Ballantyne Press, 1899. Illustrated. Morocco. One of 10 copies on vellum. $2,000. Buckram. One of 210 copies. In vellum. $750. In morocco. $1,750.

BROWNING, Robert. *Dramatis Personae.* London, 1864. Red cloth. $500. Doves Press. (London, 1910.) Vellum. One of 250 copies on paper. $750. One of 15 copies on vellum. $15,000.

BROWNING, Robert. *Paracelsus.* London, 1835. Author's first acknowledged book. First issue, with 8 pages of ads at front dated Dec. 1, 1842. In original drab boards, paper label. $1,250. Rebound. $750.

BROWNING, Robert. *The Pied Piper of Hamelin.* London (1888). 35 colored illustrations by Kate Greenaway. Pictorial boards. $350. London, 1934. Illustrated by Arthur Rackham. Limp vellum. One of 410 copies. In slipcase. $2,000. Trade. $300.

BROWNING, Robert. *The Ring and the Book.* London, 1868–69. 4 vols. Dark-green cloth. London, 1868–69. First edition, first binding, with spines of first 2 vols. in Arabic numerals and of next 2 in Roman numerals (VAB). All Roman numerals according to Schwartz, who states later have Arabic on first 2 vols. Wise just states second edition was in brown cloth. $750. Limited Editions Club, New York, 1949. 2 vols. Boards and morocco. In slipcase. $100.

BROWNING, Robert. *Sordello.* London, 1840. First issue, in boards, paper label. $1,250. Cloth. $600.

BROWNING, Robert H. K. *History of Golf.* London, 1955. $200. New York (1955). $100.

BROWNLOW, William G (annaway). *Helps to the Study of Presbyterianism . . .* Knoxville, 1834. $400.

BROWNLOW, William. *A Political Register.* Jonesborough, Tenn., 1844. Boards. $450.

BROWNSON, Orestus Augustus. *An Address, On the Fifty-fifth . . .* Ithaca, 1831. Author's first book. In original wraps. $350.

BROWNSTEIN, Michael. *Behind the Wheel.* (New York, 1967.) Author's first book. Wraps. One of 6 signed, lettered copies, $250. One of 10 signed copies, $175. 184 unsigned copies, $60.

BRUCE, James. *Travels to Discover the Source of the Nile.* Edinburgh, 1790. 5 vols. 3 folding maps. Portrait and 58 plates. $6,000. Edinburgh, 1804–5. 8 vols. $2,500.

BRUCE, Lenny. *How to Talk Dirty and Influence People.* Chicago, 1965. $125.

BRUCE, Leo. *Release the Lions.* London, 1933. (By Ruper Croft-Cooke.) Author's first mystery. $750.

BRUEHL, Anton. *Photographs of Mexico.* New York, 1933. Full-page photos by Bruehl. One of 1,000 signed. In slipcase. $750.

BRUFF, J. Goldsborough. *Gold Rush: The Journals, Drawings and Other Papers of J. Goldsborough Bruff.* New York, 1944. Edited by Georgia W. Read and Ruth Gaines. 2 vols. 21 plates. In boards and slipcase. $450.

BRUFFEY, George A. *Eighty-one Years in the West.* Butte, 1925. Portrait. Wraps. $175.

BRUNEFILLE, G. E. *Topo.* London, 1880. (By Gertrude Elizabeth Cambell.) Illustrated by Kate Greenaway. Cloth. $1,000.

BRUNSON, Alfred. *A Western Pioneer.* Cincinnati, 1872 and 1879. 2 vols. Cloth. $200.

BRUNSON, Edward. *Profits in Sheep and Cattle in Central and Western Kansas.* Kansas City, 1883. 16 pages, wraps. $300.

BRUNTON, Mary. See *Self-Control.*

BRUTUS. *The Crisis; or, Essays on the Usurpation of the Federal Government.* Charleston, 1827. (By Robert J. Turnbull.) $500.

BRYAN, Daniel. *The Mountain Muse.* Harrisonburg, 1813. $350.

BRYANT, Edwin. *What I Saw in California.* New York, 1848. $1,000. New York, 1848. Second edition. $500. Santa Ana, Calif., 1936. Half morocco. $350.

BRYANT, Gilbert Ernest. *The Chelsea Porcelain Toys.* London, 1925. 63 plates, 47 in color. One of 650 signed copies. $600.

BRYANT, William Cullen. See *The Embargo.*

BRYANT, William Cullen. *The Embargo: or, Sketches of the Times: A Satire.* (Cover title.) Boston, 1809. Second edition. $750. (For first edition, see title entry *The Embargo.*)

BRYANT, William Cullen. *Hymns.* (New York, 1864.) Brown-orange or blue cloth. First state, with reading "Dwells on Thy works in deep delight" in second line of fourth stanza on page 9. $350.

BRYANT, William Cullen. *Picturesque America.* New York (1872–74). 2 vols. $1,000.

BRYANT, William Cullen. *Poems.* Cambridge, Mass., 1821. $1,000. New York, 1832. Second edition. $400. Limited Editions Club, New York, 1947. Illustrated by Thomas Nason. Leather. In slipcase. $100.

BRYANT, W. N. *Bryant's Texas Almanac and Railway Guide, 1881–1882.* (Cover title.) Dallas, 1881. Wraps. $450.

BRYANT, W. N. *Bryant's Texas Guide!* Austin, 1875. 2 folding maps. Wraps. $750.

BRYCE, James. *The American Commonwealth.* London, 1888. 3 vols. First printing with the chapter in vol. 3 on the Tweed Ring (later suppressed). $600. Second, with Tweed Ring matter omitted. $250.

BRYDGES, Sir Egerton. *Restituta; Or, Titles, Extracts, and Characters of Old Books in English Literature, Revived.* London, 1814–16. 28 numbers in 4 vols. $300.

BRYHER. See Ellerman, Annie Winifred.

BRYHER. *Civilians.* Territet, Switzerland (1927). (Pseudonym of Winifred Ellerman.) Wraps. $400.

BRYHER. *Development.* London, 1920. $650.

BRYHER, Winifred. *The Lament for Adonis.* London, 1918. Translated from the Greek. Wraps. $750. Also copies on handmade paper. $1,000.

BUBER, Martin. *I and Thou.* Edinburgh, 1937. Wraps. $250.

BUCANIERS OF AMERICA . . . London, 1684–1685. (By Alexandre Olivier Esquemeling [a.k.a. John Esquemeling, Basil Ringrose].) Two vols. in one. 16 maps, 3 of which are folding. $12,500.

BUCHAN, John. *Greenmantle.* London, 1916. Issued without front endpaper. $500.

BUCHAN, John. *The Pilgrim Fathers: The Newdigate Prize Poem, 1898.* Oxford, 1898. Wraps. $350.

BUCHAN, John. *The Runagates Club.* London (1928). $500.

BUCHAN, John. *Sir Quixote of the Moors.* London, 1895. Author's first book. Assumed first issue with title running down spine. $750. Second issue with "*Sir Quixote*" on spine. $400. New York, 1895. $300.

BUCHAN, John. *The Thirty-nine Steps.* Edinburgh and London (1915). $1,000.

BUCHANAN, Robert. *The Devil's Case.* London (1896). $125.

BUCHANAN, Robert. *The Fleshly School of Poetry.* London, 1872. Pink or violet pictorial wraps. $500.

BUCHANAN, Robertson. *Practical and Descriptive Essays on the Economy of Fuel, and Management of Heat.* Glasgow, 1810. 2 plates. $1,500.

BUCHANAN, Robertson. *A Practical Treatise on Propelling Vessels by Steam.* Glasgow, 1816. 17 plates, 1 folding. $1,000.

BUCK, Irving A. *Cleburne and His Command.* New York, 1908. Plates. $850.

BUCK, Pearl S. *East Wind: West Wind.* New York (1930). Author's first book. $500.

BUCK, Pearl S. *The Good Earth.* New York (1931). First issue, with "flees" for "fleas" in line 17 of page 100, with "John Day Publishing Company" on copyright page, and with top edges stained brown. $2,500. Later issue, green top edges. $2,000.

BUCK, Pearl S. *Sons.* New York (1932). One of 371 deluxe copies, signed. In dustwrapper and slipcase. $450.

BUCKINGHAM, Nash. *De Shootinest Gent'man and Other Tales.* Edited by Col. Harold P. Sheldon. New York: Derrydale Press (1934). One of 950 copies. $750. New York (1961). One of 260 copies. $350.

BUCKINGHAM, Nash. *Mark Right!* New York: Derrydale Press (1936). One of 1,250 copies. $400.

BUCKINGHAM, Nash. *Ole Miss.* New York: Derrydale Press (1937). Edited by Paul A. Curtis. One of 1,250 copies. $400.

BUCKLER, Ernest. *The Mountain and the Valley.* New York, 1952. $250.

BUCKLEY, Francis. *English Baluster Stemmed Glasses of the 17th and 18th Centuries.* Edinburgh, 1912. 18 plates. Buckram. $500.

BUCKLEY, Francis. *Old London Drinking Glasses.* Edinburgh, 1913. 14 plates. Buckram. $450.

BUCKLEY, Wilfred. *Diamond Engraved Glasses of the 16th Century.* London, 1929. 33 plates. Boards. One of 250 copies. $600.

BUCKLEY, William F., Jr. *God and Man at Yale.* Chicago, 1951. Author's first book. $150.

BUDGE, Sir E. A. Wallis. *Amulets and Superstitions.* London, 1930. 22 plates, 300 other illustrations. $400.

BUDGE, Sir E. A. Wallis. *The Gods of the Egyptians, or Studies in Egyptian Mythology.* London, 1904. 2 vols. 98 color plates. Pictorial cloth. $1,000.

BUDGE, Jesse R. S. *The Life of William Budge by His Son.* Salt Lake City, 1915. $400.

BUECHNER, Frederick. *A Long Day's Dying.* New York, 1950. Author's first book. $100.

BUECHNER, Thomas S. *Norman Rockwell, Artist and Illustrator.* New York (1970). 614 plates. "Special Leatherbound Edition." One of 1,100 copies signed by Rockwell and Buechner. Large color collotype created especially for this edition, hand-numbered and signed by Rockwell. In slipcase. $1,500. Trade. $250.

BUEL, J. W. *The Border Outlaws.* St. Louis, 1881. $850.

BUEL, J. W. *Life and Marvelous Adventures of Wild Bill, the Scout.* Chicago, 1880. Frontispiece and plate. 93 pages, pictorial wraps. Presumed first issue, with cover dated 1880. $2,500.

BUFFET, Bernard. *Lithographs, 1952–1966.* New York (1968). One of 125 copies with 2 additional lithographs signed by Buffet. $3,500. Wraps in dustwrapper and slipcase. $850.

BUFFUM, E. Gould. *Six Months in the Gold Mines.* Philadelphia, 1850. Printed wraps. $1,000. Cloth. $850.

BUKOWSKI, Charles. *All the Assholes in the World and Mine.* (Bensonville, 1966.) Wraps. One of 400 copies. $500. "Author's Edition" created later with an original drawing by Bukowski tipped in. $750.

BUKOWSKI, Charles. *At Terror Street and Agony Way.* Los Angeles: Black Sparrow Press, 1968. One of 75 copies with an original illustration signed by the author, issued in glassine dustwrapper. $1,500. One of 800 copies in wraps. $300. (Also 16 or 18 review copies with front wrap misspelling of "sreet." $1,000.

BUKOWSKI, Charles. *Cold Dogs in the Courtyard*. (Chicago), 1965. Wraps. One of 500 copies. $350. "Author's Edition" created later by author tipping in an illustration or signed poem. $750.

BUKOWSKI, Charles. *Confessions of a Man Insane Enough to Live with Beasts*. Bensenville, 1965. One of 475. Decorated wraps. $600. One of 25 copies with "specially autographed drawings by Buk." $1,500.

BUKOWSKI, Charles. *Cornered*. (No place): Burn Again Press [actually Black Sparrow Press], (no date). One of 30 signed copies. Wraps. $750.

BUKOWSKI, Charles. *Crucifix in a Deathhand*. New Orleans: Loujon Press (1965). Pictorial wraps. One of 3,100 signed copies. $500. (Some copies, with special inscriptions, at higher prices.) One of 26 signed copies. $1,500.

BUKOWSKI, Charles. *The Curtains Are Waving* . . . (Los Angeles): Black Sparrow Press, 1967. Printed brown wraps. One of 122 signed copies. $1,250. Some with an original drawing. $1,500. 3 signed, lettered copies. $2,000.

BUKOWSKI, Charles. *The Days Run Away Like Wild Horses Over the Hills*. Los Angeles, 1969. One of 250 signed copies. In acetate dustwrapper. $750. One of 50 copies with a drawing by the author. $1,750. One of 1,250 copies in tan wraps. $125.

BUKOWSKI, Charles. *Flower, Fist and Bestial Wail*. (Eureka, CA, 1959.) Author's first book. Wraps. (Two previous broadsides, 1950 and 1956.) $1,250. One of 3 or 5 with original drawing or poem tipped in. $2,000.

BUKOWSKI, Charles. *A Genius of the Crowd*. (Cleveland, 1966.) Pamphlet. One of 103 copies. $2,000.

BUKOWSKI, Charles. *Heat Wave*. Santa Rosa, 1995. One of 170 copies signed by Ken Price. Tray case built into back of book holding 15 original serigraphs laid in loose. Inside front cover has envelope holding compact disc of Bukowski reading his poetry. In plexiglass slipcase. $1,250. One of 26 signed, lettered copies. $3,000.

BUKOWSKI, Charles. *Horsemeat*. Santa Barbara, 1982. Folio. One of 125 copies signed by both Bukowski and the photographer, Michael Montfort. $1,500. A prospectus for the book. One sheet folded. 1 of 26 signed copies. $750.

BUKOWSKI, Charles. *Post Office*. Los Angeles, 1971. Boards. In acetate dustwrapper. One of 250 signed copies. $1,000. One of 50 signed copies, with an original drawing by the author. $1,500.

BUKOWSKI, Charles. *Run with the Hunted*. Chicago (1962). Pictorial wraps. $1,000. Harper-Collins. (New York, 1993.) One of 26 signed copies. $750. One of 200 signed copies. $350. Trade edition. $40. Santa Rosa, Black Sparrow Press (1992). One of 26 signed copies. $750. One of 300 signed copies. $300.

BULFINCH, Thomas. See *Authorship*.

BULFINCH, Thomas. *The Age of Chivalry*. Boston, 1859. 6 illustrations. Brown cloth. $400.

BULFINCH, Thomas. *The Age of Fable*. Boston, 1855. First state, with names of both printer and stereotyper on copyright page. $500. Limited Editions Club, New York, 1958. Illustrated by Joe Mugnaini. In slipcase. $125.

BULKELEY, John, and CUMMINS, John. *A Voyage to the South Seas, in the Years 1740 . . .* London, 1743. $3,000. Dublin, 1743. $2,500. Philadelphia, 1757. First American edition. $2,000.

BULLAR, Joseph. *A Winter in the Azores . . .* John Van Voorst, 1841. 2 vols. Cloth. $850.

BULLEN, Frank T. *The Cruise of the "Cachalot."* London, 1898. Author's first book. Folding map and plates. $300. New York, 1899. $150.

BULLEN, Henry Lewis. *Nicolas Jenson, Printer of Venice . . .* San Francisco, 1926. One of 207 copies with an original folio leaf from Plutarch's *Vitae Parallelae Illustrium Virorum* loosely inserted. $1,000.

BULLER, Sir Walter Lawry. *A History of the Birds of New Zealand.* London, 1873. 35 hand-colored plates. $4,500. London, 1887–88. 48 colored plates, 2 plain plates. 13 parts in 8, wraps. $4,000. London, 1888. 2 vols. Second edition. Half morocco. $3,500.

BULLOCK, William. *Six Months' Residence and Travels in Mexico.* London, 1824. Frontispiece, 15 plates (4 hand-colored), a folding table, and 2 folding maps. $1,000.

BULLOCK, Wynn. *The Photograph as Symbol.* Mountain View, 1976. One of 200 copies (but only 100 copies printed). Each initialed by Bullock (on mounted slip) and signed by publisher. In slipcase. $1,000.

BULL-US, Hector. *The Diverting History of John Bull . . .* New York, 1812. (By James K. Paulding, his first book.) $1,000.

BULWER, John. *Chirologia, or the Natural History of the Hand . . .* London, 1644. 2 engraved additional titles, 6 full-page engraved illustrations. $5,000.

BULWER-LYTTON, Edward George. See Caxton, Pisistratus. See also *The Coming Race; Falkland; The Last Days of Pompeii.*

BULWER-LYTTON, Edward George. *Falkland.* London, 1827. $850.

BULWER-LYTTON, Edward George. *Ismael: an Oriental Tale.* London, 1820. Author's first book. Boards. $600.

BULWER-LYTTON, Edward Robert. See *Clytemnestra.*

BUNIN, I. A. *The Gentleman from San Francisco.* Boston, 1918. $100. (Richmond): Hogarth Press, 1922. Translated by Leonard Woolf. Boards. Issued without dustwrapper. With errata slip. $300.

BUNNER, H. C. *A Woman of Honor.* Boston, 1883. Author's first regular book. $200. (Previous pamphlets and collaborations.)

BUNTING, Basil. *Briggflatts.* London (1966). Wraps. One of 100 copies in black cloth and dustwrapper. $1,250. Leather. One of 26 signed, lettered copies. $3,000.

BUNTING, Basil. *First Book of Odes.* London (1965). Green boards. Issued without dustwrapper. One of 125 copies. $200. Another issue, one of 50 copies in black boards and green dustwrapper. $450. One of 26 signed and lettered copies. In black leather and dustwrapper. $1,500.

BUNTING, Basil. *Loquitur.* London (1965). Full morocco. One of 26 signed copies. In dust-wrapper. $1,750. One of 200 copies. In cloth and dustwrapper. $350.

BUNTING, Basil. *Redimiculum Matellarum.* Milan, 1930. Author's first book. Wraps. $4,000.

BUNTING, Basil. *Two Poems.* (No place): Unicorn Press, 1967. Wraps. One of 220 copies. $250. One of 30 signed copies. $750.

BUNTING, Basil, and WILLIAMS, Jonathan. *Descant on Rawthey's Madrigal: Conversations with Basil Bunting.* Lexington, Ky. (1968). One of 25 copies signed by Bunting and Williams. In boards and dustwrapper. $1,250. One of 475 in white wraps, in light-brown printed wrapper. $125.

BUNYAN, John. *The Pilgrim's Progress.* London, 1678. $150,000. London: Chiswick Press, 1899. One of 750 copies. $500. London: Cresset Press, 1928. 2 vols. 10 wood engravings. Folio, cloth. One of 195 copies. $1,000. One of 10 copies on vellum with an extra suite of plates. $20,000. Limited Editions Club, New York, 1941. 29 William Blake illustrations in color. One of 1,500 copies. In slipcase. $200.

BURCH, R. M. *Colour Printing and Colour Printers.* London, 1910. Second edition. $300. New York, 1910. $250.

BURCHELL, William J. *Travels in the Interior of Southern Africa.* London, 1822–24. 2 vols. Large folding map, 20 hand-colored aquatint plates (5 folding). Contemporary calf. $3,500.

BURCKHARDT, John Lewis. *Travels in Nubia.* London, 1819. 2 folding maps. $2,000.

BURDICK, William. *An Oration on the Nature and Effects of the Art of Printing.* Boston, 1802. The earliest book on printing history with a U.S. imprint. $1,500.

BURGESS, Anthony. See Kell, Joseph.

BURGESS, Anthony. *Beds in the East.* London (1959). $250.

BURGESS, Anthony. *A Clockwork Orange.* London (1962). In dustwrapper with price of 16 shillings. $4,000. New York (1963). $750.

BURGESS, Anthony. *The Doctor Is Sick.* London (1960). $250. New York (1960). $100.

BURGESS, Anthony. *The Enemy in the Blanket.* London (1958). $350.

BURGESS, Anthony. *Honey for the Bears.* London (1963). $250. New York (1964). $100.

BURGESS, Anthony. *The Right to an Answer.* London (1960). $200. New York (1961). $100.

BURGESS, Anthony. *Time for a Tiger.* London, 1956. Author's first book. $850.

BURGESS, Anthony. *The Worm and the Ring.* London, 1961. (Suppressed.) $750. A revised edition was issued in 1970.

BURGESS, Gelett. *The Nonsense Almanack for 1900.* New York (1899). Wraps. $250.

BURGESS, Gelett. *The Purple Cow!* (San Francisco, 1895.) Author's first publication. Illustrated. 8 leaves. First state of first printing (printed on both sides of leaf) on rough China paper. $350. Second state (printed on one side of leaf only). $125.

BURGESS, Gelett. *Vivette, or the Memoirs of the Romance Association*. Boston, 1897. Author's first book, aside from *The Purple Cow* leaflet. $200.

BURGESS, Thornton Waldo. *Old Mother West Wind*. Boston (1910). Author's first book for children. Pictorial tan cloth. $600.

BURGOYNE, Lieut. Gen. John. *A State of the Expedition from Canada . . .* London, 1780. Quarto. Large folding map, 5 folding plans. $5,000. Octavo. $2,500.

BURK, John. *The History of Virginia*. Petersburg, 1804–16. 4 vols. $1,250.

BURKE, Edmund. *Reflections on the Revolution in France . . .* London, 1790. First state title page has "M" in imprint date immediately below the "D" of Dodsley, instead of slightly to the right. $1,750.

BURKE, James Lee. *The Convict*. Baton Rouge, 1985. Cloth. $3,500. Wraps. $350.

BURKE, James Lee. *Half of Paradise*. Boston, 1965. Author's first book. $2,250.

BURKE, James Lee. *Neon Rain*. New York, 1987. $300.

BURKE, James Lee. *To the Bright and Shining Sun*. New York (1970). $1,250.

BURKE, Kenneth. *The White Oxen and Other Stories*. New York, 1924. Author's first book. $350.

BURKE, Leda. *Dope-Darling*. London, 1919. (By David Garnett, his second book.) $200.

BURKE, Thomas. *Nights in Town*. London, 1915. $150.

BURKE, Thomas. *Verses*. (Guilford, 1906.) Author's first book. Wraps. One of 25 copies. $1,500.

BURKE, Thomas. *Whispering Windows*. London, 1921. $500. (*More Limehouse Nights* in the U.S.)

BURKE, W. S. (compiler). *Directory of the City of Council Bluffs and Emigrants' Guide to the Gold Regions of the West*. Council Bluffs, Iowa, 1866. Folding map. 32 pages, plus ads, patterned cloth. $4,500.

BURKE, William. See *Memoirs of William Burke . . .*

BURLEND, Rebecca. *A True Picture of Emigration*. London (1848). Wraps. $400.

BURLEY, W. J. *A Taste of Power*. London, 1966. $400.

BURLINGAME, H. J. *Herrmann the Great*. Chicago (1897). 43 figures, original chromolithograph wrappers. $350.

BURNET, Bishop [Gilbert]. *Bishop Burnet's History of His Own Time*. London, 1724–34. 2 vols. $1,000.

BURNETT, Frances Hodgson. *The Drury Lane Boys' Club*. Washington, 1892. Blue wraps. $600.

BURNETT, Frances Hodgson. *Little Lord Fauntleroy.* New York, 1886. Illustrated by Reginald B. Birch. First issue, with De Vinne Press imprint at end. $1,500.

BURNETT, Frances Hodgson. *The Secret Garden.* New York (1911). $1,500. London, 1911. 8 full-color plates by Charles Robinson. $1,000. New York (1987). Illustrated by Michael Hague. $75.

BURNETT, Frances Hodgson. *That Lass O'Lowrie's.* New York, 1877. Author's first book. First state, with illustrator's name on title page. $150. Without name, second state. $75.

BURNETT, Peter H. *Recollections and Opinions of an Old Pioneer.* New York, 1880. $850.

BURNETT, W. R. *The Asphalt Jungle.* New York, 1949. $500.

BURNETT, W. R. *The Goodhues of Sinking Creek.* New York, 1934. $300.

BURNETT, W. R. *High Sierra.* New York, 1940. $500.

BURNETT, W. R. *Little Caesar.* New York, 1929. Author's first book. $1,250.

BURNEY, Fanny (Frances). *Camilla: Or a Picture of Youth.* London, 1796. 5 vols. $2,000. New York, 1797. 5 vols. $1,500.

BURNEY, Fanny (Frances). *Cecilia, or Memoirs of an Heiress.* London, 1782. 5 vols. $1,750. Boston, 1793. 3 vols. $950.

BURNEY, Fanny (Frances). *Evelina.* London, 1778. 3 vols. $8,500.

BURNEY, James. *A Chronological History of the Discoveries in the South Sea or Pacific Ocean.* London, 1803–17. With 41 maps, charts, or plates. 5 vols. $14,500.

BURNEY, James. *History of the Buccaneers of America.* London, 1816. 3 maps (2 folding). First separate edition. Large-paper issue. $2,000. Ordinary. $1,000.

BURNHAM, Daniel H., and BENNETT, Edward H. *Plan of Chicago.* Chicago, 1909. Illustrated. Leather and/or cloth. One of 1,650 copies. $1,000. Full vellum. $1,250.

BURNS, John H. *Memoirs of a Cow Pony.* Boston (1906). Illustrated. Pictorial cloth. $1,000.

BURNS, John Horne. *The Gallery.* New York (1947). Author's first book. $200.

BURNS, Martin. *The Life Work of "Farmer Burns."* Omaha, 1911. $150.

BURNS, Robert. *Poems Ascribed to Robert Burns.* Glasgow, 1801. $500.

BURNS, Robert. *Poems, Chiefly in the Scottish Dialect.* Kilmarnock edition, 1786. Author's first book. $36,000 at auction in 1996. Edinburgh, 1787. Second edition, first issue, with "skinking" on page 263. $2,500. Second issue, with "stinking" on page 263. $1,500. London, 1787. $1,000. Philadelphia, 1788. $1,250.

BURNS, Robert. *Tam O'Shanter.* London: Essex House Press, 1902. Illustrated, colored by hand. Stiff vellum. One of 150 copies on vellum. $750.

BURNS, Tex. *Hopalong Cassidy & the Riders of High Rock.* New York, 1951. (By Louis L'Amour.) $1,000.

BURNS, Tex. *Hopalong Cassidy and the Trail to Seven Pines.* New York, 1951. (By Louis L'Amour.) $750.

BURNS, Tex. *Hopalong Cassidy, Trouble Shooter.* New York, 1952. (By Louis L'Amour.) $600.

BURNSHAW, Stanley. *Poems.* Pittsburgh, 1927. Author's first book. $200.

BURPEE, Lawrence J. *The Search for the Western Sea.* London, 1908. 6 maps, 51 plates. $500. New York, 1908. $400. New York, 1936. 2 vols. Maps and plates. $300.

BURR, Aaron. *The Private Journal of Aaron Burr.* Rochester, 1903. Edited by W. K. Bixby. 2 vols. Portraits. Half cloth. One of 250 copies signed by Bixby. $600.

BURR, Frederic M. *Life and Works of Alexander Anderson, M.D., The First American Wood Engraver.* New York. 1893. One of 700 signed copies. $350. One of 25 signed copies on Japan vellum. $750.

It should be noted that the prices for Burroughs shown below assume some chipping and wear. Fine copies would be significantly higher.

BURROUGHS, Edgar Rice. *At the Earth's Core.* Chicago, 1922. With "M.A. Donohue & Co." at bottom of copyright page. In dustwrapper. $4,500.

BURROUGHS, Edgar Rice. *Back to the Stone Age.* Tarzana, Calif. (1937). $650.

BURROUGHS, Edgar Rice. *Bandit of Hell's Bend.* Chicago, 1925. $4,000.

BURROUGHS. Edgar Rice. *The Beasts of Tarzan.* Chicago, 1916. With "W. F. Hall Printing Company, Chicago" at bottom of copyright page. In dustwrapper. $10,000. Without dustwrapper. $250.

BURROUGHS, Edgar Rice. *The Chessmen of Mars.* Chicago, 1922. $7,500.

BURROUGHS, Edgar Rice. *The Eternal Lover.* Chicago, 1925. With "M.A. Donohue . . ." on copyright page. $4,500.

BURROUGHS, Edgar Rice. *A Fighting Man of Mars.* New York (1931). With Metropolitan Books imprint. $1,500.

BURROUGHS, Edgar Rice. *The Girl from Hollywood.* New York (1923). Pebbled red cloth, lettered in green. In first-issue dustwrapper with "The Macauley Company, New York" within a box at the bottom of the spine. $3,000. (Later in smooth red cloth. The later dustwrapper has the Macauley shield on the spine.)

BURROUGHS, Edgar Rice. *The Gods of Mars.* Chicago, 1918. In dustwrapper. $7,500. Without dustwrapper. $350.

BURROUGHS, Edgar Rice. *Jungle Tales of Tarzan.* Chicago, 1919. In orange cloth with publisher's imprint on spine in three lines. In dustwrapper. $2,500. Without dustwrapper. $350. Second issue, in two lines. $1,750. Without. $150. (Later in green cloth.)

BURROUGHS, Edgar Rice. *The Lad and the Lion.* Tarzana, Calif. (1938). In laminated dust-wrapper. $650.

BURROUGHS, Edgar Rice. *The Land That Time Forgot.* Chicago, 1924. $8,500.

BURROUGHS, Edgar Rice. *Lost on Venus.* Tarzana, Calif. (1935). $750.

BURROUGHS, Edgar Rice. *The Mad King.* Chicago, 1926. (5,000 copies printed.) $3,000.

BURROUGHS, Edgar Rice. *The Master Mind of Mars.* Chicago, 1928. $4,000.

BURROUGHS, Edgar Rice. *The Monster Men.* Chicago, 1929. $3,500.

BURROUGHS, Edgar Rice. *The Mucker.* Methuen. London (1921). In dustwrapper. (Precedes American.) $5,000. Chicago. 1921. $7,500.

BURROUGHS, Edgar Rice. *The Outlaw of Torn.* Chicago, 1927. First edition not stated. Publisher's acorn on copyright page. $3,000.

BURROUGHS, Edgar Rice. *Pellucidar.* Chicago, 1923. $3,500.

BURROUGHS, Edgar Rice. *A Princess of Mars.* Chicago, 1917. With "W. F. Hall . . ." at bottom of copyright page. In dustwrapper. $10,000 or more. Without dustwrapper. $850.

BURROUGHS, Edgar Rice. *The Return of Tarzan.* Chicago, 1915. With "W. F. Hall . . ." at bottom of copyright page. In dustwrapper. $10,000 or more. Without jacket. $850.

BURROUGHS, Edgar Rice. *The Son of Tarzan.* Chicago, 1917. With "W. F. Hall . . ." at bottom of copyright page and lacking dedication leaf (to Hubert Burroughs). In dustwrapper. $7,500. Lacking jacket. $500.

BURROUGHS, Edgar Rice. *Tanar of Pellucidar.* New York, 1929. $2,000.

BURROUGHS, Edgar Rice. *Tarzan and the Ant Men.* Chicago, 1924. With "A. C. McClurg/ & Co." on spine. $3,500.

BURROUGHS, Edgar Rice. *Tarzan and the Golden Lion.* Chicago, 1923. With "M. A. Donohue . . ." at bottom of copyright page. $4,500.

BURROUGHS, Edgar Rice. *Tarzan and the Jewels of Opar.* Chicago, 1918. With "W. F. Hall . . ." at bottom of copyright page. In dustwrapper. $4,000. Without jacket. $500.

BURROUGHS, Edgar Rice. *Tarzan and the Leopard Men.* Tarzana, Calif. (1935). $600.

BURROUGHS, Edgar Rice. *Tarzan at the Earth's Core.* New York: Metropolitan Books, (1930). Green cloth lettered in black. $2,000.

BURROUGHS, Edgar Rice. *Tarzan, Lord of the Jungle.* Chicago, 1928. $4,000.

BURROUGHS, Edgar Rice. *Tarzan of the Apes.* Chicago, 1914. Author's first book. Frontispiece. Red cloth. First edition with printer's name on copyright page in Old English letters. In dustwrapper. $50,000 or more. Without dustwrapper. $5,000. London (1917). Orange-colored cloth. With ads dated Autumn. $1,500.

BURROUGHS, Edgar Rice. *Tarzan Triumphant.* Tarzana (1932). Illustrated by Stanley Burroughs. First edition not stated. $500.

BURROUGHS, Edgar Rice. *Thuvia, Maid of Mars.* Chicago, 1920. With "M. A. Donohue . . ." at bottom of copyright page. In dustwrapper. $5,000.

BURROUGHS, Edgar Rice. *The War Chief.* Chicago, 1927. First edition not stated. Publisher's acorn on copyright page. $2,500.

BURROUGHS, Edgar Rice. *The Warlord of Mars.* Chicago, 1919. First issue, with "W. F. Hall" on copyright page. In dustwrapper. $4,500. Without dustwrapper. $500.

BURROUGHS, John. *Notes on Walt Whitman as Poet and Person.* New York, 1867. Blue wraps with leaves trimmed to 6⁹⁄₁₆ inches high. $1,250. Later, 1867, cloth bound, leaves 7¼ inches high. $750.

BURROUGHS, John. *Wake-Robin.* New York, 1871. $350.

BURROUGHS, William. See Lee, William.

BURROUGHS, William S. *Ali's Smile.* (Brighton), 1971. Oblong, boards and cloth. One of 99 signed copies. (Issued with a Burroughs LP record.) $3,000.

BURROUGHS, William S. *The Last Words of Dutch Schultz.* London, 1970. One of 100 signed copies. In tissue dustwrapper. $450. Trade. Cloth. $150. Wraps. $75. New York (1975). $125.

BURROUGHS, William S. *The Naked Lunch.* Paris: Olympia Press (1959). Wraps. Green border on title page, "Francs 1500" on back cover. In dustwrapper. $3,500. New York [1962]. Copyright page dated 1959, but this edition actually published March 21, 1962 [Maynard and Miles, A2b]. $1,000. London, 1964. $300.

BURROUGHS, William S. *The Soft Machine.* Paris: Olympia Press (1961). "Printed in France June 1961" on page 4. Wraps. In dustwrapper. $750. New York (1966). New edition. Revised and augmented. $125. London (1968). Adds an appendix. Cloth. $150. Wraps. $25.

BURROUGHS, William S. *The Ticket That Exploded.* Paris: Olympia Press (1962). Wraps. In dustwrapper. $750. New York (1967). $125.

BURROUGHS, William S. *Time.* New York, 1965. Illustrated by Brion Gysin. Wraps. One of 100 signed copies. $750. Ordinary copies. $175. One of 10 signed, lettered copies. $2,000.

BURRUS, Ernest. *Kino and the Cartography of Northwestern New Spain.* (Tucson), 1965. One of 750 copies designed and printed by Lawton and Alfred Kennedy. Glassine wrapper. $400.

BURT, (Maxwell) Struthers. *The Man from Where.* Philadelphia, 1904. Pictorial wraps. $250.

BURTON. Alfred. *The Adventures of Johnny Newcome in the Navy.* London, 1818. 16 colored plates by Rowlandson. (By John Mitford.) $750. (See John Mitford entry for second and third editions.)

BURTON, Harley True. *A History of the JA Ranch.* Austin, 1928. Portrait, map. $1,000.

BURTON, Isabel. *The Life of Captain Sir Richard F. Burton . . .* London, 1893. 2 vols. $600.

BURTON, John Hill. *The Book-Hunter.* Edinburgh & London, 1862. One of 25 copies on large paper. Bookplate of Robert Buchanan Stewart. $350.

BURTON, Miles. (Cecil John Charles Street.) *The Hardway Diamonds Mystery.* London, 1930. $400. New York, 1930. $100.

BURTON, Sir Richard. *Abeokuta and the Camaroons Mountains.* London, 1863. 2 vols. Portrait, 4 plates and folding map. $5,000.

BURTON, Sir Richard F. *The Book of the Sword.* London, 1884. $2,000.

BURTON, Sir Richard F. *The City of the Saints and Across the Rocky Mountains to California.* London, 1861. 8 plates. Folding map, folding plan. $3,500. New York, 1862. $1,500.

BURTON, Sir Richard. *Explorations of the Highlands of the Brazil.* London, 1869. 2 vols. Green cloth with gilt-stamped figure on covers, pages untrimmed. $2,500.

BURTON, Sir Richard F. *Falconry in the Valley of the Indus.* London, 1852. Frontispiece, other plates. $4,000.

BURTON, Sir Richard F. *First Footsteps in East Africa; or, an Exploration of Harar.* London, 1856. With 2 maps and 4 colored plates. First issue, in dull-violet cloth, with all edges uncut. $7,500. Second issue. Red cloth with bottom edge trimmed. $3,000.

BURTON, Sir Richard F. *Goa, and the Blue Mountains.* London, 1851. Author's first book. Folding map and 4 plates. First issue, in fawn cloth, 5 by 8⅛ inches. $4,000. Second issue in light blue cloth, 4¾ by 8 inches. $3,000.

BURTON, Sir Richard F. *The Gold-Mines of Midian and the Ruined Midianite Cities.* London, 1878. Folding map. $3,000.

BURTON, Sir Richard F. *The Lake Regions of Central Africa.* London, 1860. Folding map. 12 colored plates. 2 vols. Red cloth. $4,000. (There is also a trial or first issue in purple cloth, few copies known.) New York, 1860. $1,500.

BURTON, Sir Richard F. *The Land of Midian (Revisited).* London, 1879. Folding map. 16 plates (6 colored). 2 vols. First issue, with ads dated "9.78." $3,500.

BURTON, Sir Richard F. *Letters from the Battlefields of Paraguay.* London, 1870. Engraved title, frontispiece, folding map. $2,500.

BURTON, Sir Richard F. *A Mission to Gelele, King of Dahome.* London, 1864. 2 vols. Two plates. Plum-colored cloth. $3,000.

BURTON, Sir Richard F. *Personal Narrative of a Pilgrimage to El-Medinah and Meccah.* London, 1855–56. 3 vols. 15 plates (4 colored), 4 maps and plans (3 folding). Cloth. $9,000. London, 1857. Second edition. 2 vols. Folding map. Maroon pebbled cloth with gilt designs on spine and covers. $2,500. New York, 1856. $1,500.

BURTON, Sir Richard F. *Wanderings in West Africa.* London, 1863. 2 vols. Folding map in vol. 1 and frontispiece in vol 2. $4,000.

BURTON, Sir Richard F. (translator). *The Book of the Thousand Nights and a Night.* (Arabian Nights.) (London, 1885–88.) 16 vols. $3,500. London, 1897. 12 vols. $1,750. Denver, 1900–

1901. 16 vols. One of 1,000 copies. $1,750. Limited Editions Club, New York, 1934. Illustrated by Valenti Angelo. 6 vols., boards, cowhide spines. In slipcase. $200. Another edition. New York, 1954. 4 vols. Illustrated in color by Arthur Szyk. One of 1,500 copies. In slipcase. $350.

BURTON, Robert. *The Anatomy of Melancholy.* London, 1621. $35,000. Oxford, 1624. $4,500. Philadelphia, 1836. First American edition. 2 vols. $1,500. London: Nonesuch Press, 1925–26. Illustrated by E. McKnight Kauffer. 2 vols. Half vellum and boards. One of 750 copies. $600. 2 vols. in 1. One of 40 copies on vellum. $1,750.

BURTON, W. *Josiah Wedgwood and His Pottery.* London, 1922. 32 color plates, 84 in black-and-white. One of 1,500 copies. In dustwrapper. $400.

BURY, Mrs. Edward. *A Selection of Hexandrian Plants . . .* (London), 1831–34. Large folio. 51 hand-colored aquatints by Robert Havell. $125,000.

BUSH, Christopher. *Dead Man's Music.* London, 1991. $1,350.

BUTCHER, S. D. *S. D. Butcher's Pioneer History of Custer Country.* Broken Bow, Neb., 1901. Cloth, or leather. $200.

BUTLER, Arthur G. *Foreign Finches in Captivity.* London, 1894. 60 hand-colored plates. $5,000. London, 1899. Second edition, illustrated with chromolithographs. $450.

BUTLER, Arthur G. *Lepidoptera Exotica.* London, 1874. Author's first book. 64 colored plates. $1,500.

BUTLER, Ellis Parker. See *Pigs Is Pigs.*

BUTLER, Ellis Parker. *Philo Gubb: Correspondence School Detective.* Boston (1918). $300.

BUTLER, Henry. *South African Sketches . . .* London, 1841. Engraved title page and 15 plates (some hand-colored). $2,000.

BUTLER, Mann. *A History of the Commonwealth of Kentucky.* Louisville, 1834. Portrait. $400.

BUTLER, Octavia E. *Pattern-Master.* Garden City, 1976. Author's first book. $300.

BUTLER, Robert Olen. *The Alleys of Eden.* New York (1981). Author's first book. $250.

BUTLER, Samuel. See *Erewhon.*

BUTLER, Samuel. *The Authoress of the Odyssey.* London, 1897. Maps and illustrations. $200.

BUTLER, Samuel. *A First Year in Canterbury Settlement.* London, 1863. Author's first book. Folding map. Red cloth. With 32 pages of ads and light-brown endpapers. $600.

BUTLER, Samuel. *Seven Sonnets and a Psalm of Montreal.* Cambridge, 1904. Unbound, or printed wraps. $200.

BUTLER, Samuel. *The Way of All Flesh.* London, 1903. Red cloth, top edges gilt. $600. Limited Editions Club, New York, 1936. 2 vols. Leather. In slipcase. $125.

BUTORINA, Evgenia. *The Lettering Art, Works by Moscow Book Designers, 1959–1974.* Kniga, 1977. In slipcase. $350.

BUTTERFIELD, C. W. *An Historical Account of the Expedition Against Sandusky.* Cincinnati, 1873. Portrait. $200.

BUTTERFIELD, C. W. *History of the Discovery of the Northwest.* Cincinnati, 1881. $200.

BUTTERFIELD, C. W. *History of Seneca County, Ohio.* Sandusky, Ohio, 1848. $150.

BUTTERWORTH, Benjamin J. *The Growth of Industrial Art.* Washington, 1888. 200 full-page plates. Folio. $1,000. Washington, 1892. $750.

BUTTERWORTH, E. *Butterworth's Young Writer's Instructor. Designed for the Improvement of Youth.* (No place), 1800. $350.

BUTTERWORTH, E. *Elegant Extracts for Butterworth & Son's Universal Penman . . .* (No place), 1809. $250.

BUTTERWORTH, Hezekiah. *Zig-Zag Journeys in Europe.* Boston, 1880. $250.

BUTTS, Mary. *Armed with Madness.* London, 1928. Drawings by Jean Cocteau. One of 100 copies. $400.

BUTTS, Mary. *The Crystal Cabinet.* London (1937). $250.

BUTTS, Mary. *Imaginary Letters.* Paris, 1928. Illustrated by Jean Cocteau. Cloth, paper label. Paris, 1928. One of 250 copies. In glassine dustwrapper and slipcase. $250.

BUTTS, Mary. *Scenes from the Life of Cleopatra.* London (1937). $200.

BUTTS, Mary. *Speed the Plow and Other Stories.* London, 1923. Author's first book. Yellow or red cloth. $500.

BYAM, Mrs. Lydia. *A Collection of Exotics from the Island of Antigua.* (London, 1797.) 12 hand-colored plates. $12,500.

BYAM, Mrs. Lydia. *A Collection of Fruits from the West Indies.* London, 1800. 2 vols. in 1. 9 hand-colored plates. $8,500.

BYATT, A. S. *Possession . . .* London (1990). $200. New York (1990). $100.

BYATT, A. S. *Shadow of a Sun.* London, 1964. Author's first book. $350. New York (1964). $200.

BYERS, William N., and KELLOM, John H. *A Hand Book to the Gold Fields of Nebraska and Kansas.* Chicago, 1859. Map. Blue pictorial printed wraps. $12,500.

BYLES, Mather. *A Poem on the Death of His Late Majesty King George.* (Boston, 1727.) Author's first book. $2,000.

BYNNER, Witter. See Morgan, Emanuel, and Knish, Anne.

BYNNER, Witter. *An Ode to Harvard and Other Poems.* Boston, 1907. Author's first book. Cloth, or leather. $100.

BYNNER, Witter. *The Persistence of Poetry.* San Francisco: Book Club of California, 1929. Full red buckram. One of 325 signed copies. In slipcase. $175.

BYRD, Richard E. *Discovery . . .* New York, 1935. Photographic plates. One of 500 copies signed by Byrd. In slipcase. $750. Trade. $200.

BYRD, Richard E. *Little America.* New York, 1930. 74 maps and plates. Half vellum. One of 1,000 signed copies. In slipcase. $600. Trade with "E" left out of Eleanor E. Bolling's name in dedication. $200. Corrected. $125.

BYRD, Richard E. *Skyward.* New York, 1928. Boards. 58 maps and plates. One of 500 signed copies. In glassine dustwrapper. With extra set of plates. Boxed. $750. Trade. $150.

BYRD, William (of Westover). *The Writings of "Colonel William Byrd of Westover in Virginia, Esqr."* New York, 1901. Edited by John Spencer Bassett. Half vellum. One of 500 copies. $300.

BYRNE, B. M. *Florida and Texas: A Series of Letters Comparing the Soil, Climate, and Productions of These States.* Ocala, Fla., 1866. 40 pages, wraps. Third edition (of *Letters on the Climate, etc.;* see below). $350.

BYRNE, B. M. *Letters on the Climate, Soils, and Productions of Florida.* Jacksonville, 1851. Second edition. 28 pages, wraps. $500. (The first edition was published in Ralston, Pa., according to Howes, who gives no date.)

BYRNE, Donn. *Brother Saul.* New York (1927). One of 500 signed copies. In slipcase. $100.

BYRNE, Donn. *The Foolish Matrons.* New York (1920). First edition, first issue with "I-U" on copyright page. In dustwrapper. $150.

BYRNE, Donn. *Messer Marco Polo.* New York, 1921. Illustrated by C. B. Falls. Rust-colored cloth. With perfect type in the word "of" in the last line of page 10 (Johnson, not in BAL). In dustwrapper. $150.

BYRNE, Donn. *Stories Without Women.* New York, 1915. Author's first book. Frontispiece. Red ribbed cloth. $125.

BYRNE, William S. *Directory of Grass Valley Township for 1865.* San Francisco, 1865. 144 pages, boards. $1,500.

BYRNES, Thomas. *Professional Criminals of America.* NY (1886). $750.

BYRON, George Gordon Noel, Lord. See *The Age of Bronze; Beppo; English Bards and Scotch Reviewers; Ode to Napoleon Buonaparte; The Siege of Corinth.*

BYRON, George Gordon Noel, Lord. *The Bride of Abydos.* London, 1813. 72 pages. First issue, with errata slip and with only 20 lines on page 47. $750. Second issue, without errata slip and with 22 lines on page 47. $500.

BYRON, George Gordon Noel, Lord. *Childe Harold's Pilgrimage: A Romaunt.* (Containing Cantos I and II.) London, 1812. First issue; with "Written beneath a Picture of J-V-D" on page 189 ("of J-V-D" omitted later). $750.

BYRON, George Gordon Noel, Lord. *Childe Harold's Pilgrimage: Canto the Third.* London, 1816. First issue with "L" in "Lettre" under the word "La" in line above on title page; at the end of the first line of the second stanza on page 4, there is no exclamation mark. $400. Second issue, "L" under "U" in "CGLU"; and exclamation mark added. $300.

BYRON, George Gordon Noel, Lord. *Childe Harold's Pilgrimage: Canto the Fourth.* London, 1818. First issue, with page 155 ending with "the impressions of." $1,000.

BYRON, George Gordon Noel, Lord. *Fugitive Pieces.* London, 1806. Author's first book. Three known copies. $75,000? London, 1886. (100 copies.) $1,000.

BYRON, George Gordon Noel, Lord. *Hebrew Melodies.* London, 1815. First issue, with ad for *Roger's Jacqueline.* $1,500. Second issue, without *Jacqueline* ad. $750.

BYRON, George Gordon Noel, Lord. *Hours of Idleness.* Newark, England, 1807. First issue, with line 2 of page 22 reading "Those tissues of fancy . . .". $2,500. Second issue, reading "Those tissues of falsehood . . .". $2,000. London, 1820. $300.

BYRON, George Gordon Noel, Lord. *Manfred, a Dramatic Poem.* London, 1817. 80 pages (originally in plain wraps). First issue, without quotation on title page and with printer's imprint in 2 lines on back of title page. $1,000. Second issue, with printer's imprint in one line. $500. Third issue, with *Hamlet* quotation on title page. $250.

BYRON, George Gordon Noel, Lord. *Mazeppa: A Poem.* London, 1819. (Originally in plain drab wraps.) First issue, with imprint on page 70. $1,000. Second issue, with imprint on back of page 71. $450.

BYRON, George Gordon Noel, Lord. *The Parliamentary Speeches of Lord Byron.* London, 1824. $650.

BYRON, George Gordon Noel, Lord. *The Prisoner of Chillon, and Other Poems.* London, 1816. (Originally in drab plain wraps.) First issue, with ads on back of last page. $600. Second issue, with ads on front of last page. $400.

BYRON George Gordon Noel, Lord. *Sardanapalus, The Two Foscari, Cain.* London, 1821. $400.

BYRON, George Gordon Noel, Lord. *Werner: A Tragedy.* London, 1823. First issue, without the words "The End" on page 188. $750. Second issue, without "The End." $400.

BYRON, Robert. *An Essay on India.* London (1931). $1,000.

BYRON, Robert. *Europe in the Looking Glass . . .* London, 1926. Author's first book. $1,250.

BYRON, Robert. *The Road to Oxiana.* London, 1937. $2,500.

C

C., C. *Poems for Harry Crosby.* Paris: Black Sun Press, 1931. (By Caresse Crosby.) Frontispiece. Boards. One of 22 copies on Van Gelder paper. $1,750. One of 500 copies on Lafuma paper. $750.

C.3.3. *The Ballad of Reading Gaol.* London (1898). (By Oscar Wilde.) Cinnamon-colored cloth, vellum spine. One of 30 copies on Japanese vellum. $10,000. Two-toned cloth. One of 800 copies. $2,000. London, 1898. Second edition. $350. London, 1898. Third edition (bearing Wilde's name). One of 99 signed copies. $8,000. Limited Editions Club, New York, 1937. In slipcase. $125.

CABALLERIA Y COLLELL, Juan. *History of the City of Santa Barbara from Its Discovery to Our Own Days.* Santa Barbara, 1892. Translated by Edmund Burke. Plate, facsimile. 111 pages, wraps. $300.

CABELL, James Branch. *Branchiana.* Richmond, Va. (1907). 147 copies issued. One of 10 copies in red cloth. $1,250. One of 30 copies in buff cloth. $750. Balance in green cloth. $400.

CABELL, James Branch. *Chivalry.* New York, 1909. Illustrated by Howard Pyle and others. Flexible red cloth. $1,250. Trade. Gilt lettering. $125. Black lettering. $75.

CABELL, James Branch. *The Cords of Vanity.* New York, 1909. First state, with "The" omitted on spine and cover. $150. London (1925). $100.

CABELL, James Branch. *The Eagle's Shadow.* New York, 1904. Author's first book. First state, with dedication "M.L.P.B." and frontispiece of seated figure. $150. Second state, dedicated to "Martha Louise Branch." $60.

CABELL, James Branch. *Gallantry.* New York, 1907. Illustrated in color by Howard Pyle. Decorated cloth, gilt top. First binding, silver-gray cloth, stamped with white, silver, and gold lettering. In printed glassine dustwrapper. In slipcase. $300. Without dustwrapper and slipcase. $150.

CABELL, James Branch. *Hamlet Had an Uncle.* New York (1940). $75. One of 125 signed copies. In slipcase. $250.

CABELL, (James) Branch. *Jurgen.* New York, 1919. Reddish-brown cloth. First state, with line rules on page 144 intact and 1¼ inches across. In dustwrapper. $2,000. Without dustwrapper. $350. Second state with line rules broken, 1½ inches. $1,250. Without dustwrapper. $150. London, 1921. Illustrated by Frank C. Pape. First English edition. $500. London: Golden Cockerel Press, 1949. Half morocco. One of 350 copies. $250. One of 100 copies. With an extra engraving. In slipcase. In full leather. $1,000. In quarter purple calf. $250. One of 50 copies. In green and pink boards. $500. Limited Editions Club, Westport (1976). One of 2,000 copies signed by the artist, Virgil Burnett. In glassine and slipcase. $75.

CABELL, James Branch. *The Line of Love.* New York, 1905. Illustrated in color by Howard Pyle. Decorated green cloth, pictorial label. First state, binding stamped with white decoration and gold lettering. $250. Advance copies in red flexible cloth. $1,250.

CABELL, James Branch. *The Majors and Their Marriages.* Richmond (1915). Wraps. (200 copies.) $400. One of 100 signed copies in green cloth. $500.

CABELL, James Branch. *Of Ellen Glasgow.* New York (1938). Wraps. $400.

CABELL, James Branch. *Smith.* New York, 1935. $100. One of 153 signed copies. In slipcase. $300. Trade. $100.

CABEZA DE VACA, Álvar Núñez. *The Narrative of Álvar Núñez Cabeza de Vaca.* Washington, 1851. Translated by Buckingham Smith. 8 maps. One of 110 copies. $2,000. New York 1871. Three-quarters morocco. One of 100 copies. $1,000. (For another issue, under another title, see following entry.)

CABEZA DE VACA, Álvar Núñez. *Relation . . . of What Befel the Armament in the Indias Whither Pamphilo de Narvaez Went for Governor, etc.* San Francisco, 1929. Grabhorn printing. Hand decorations in color by Valenti Angelo. Boards. One of 300 copies. In slipcase. $750.

CABINET of Natural History and American Rural Sports (The). Philadelphia, 1830–32–33. First book edition. 3 vols. Published by J. and T. Doughly; includes 29 monthly parts [dated 1830 to 1834]. 57 plates, 54 colored. $9,500.

CABLE, George W. *The Creoles of Louisiana.* New York, 1884. $300. London, 1885. $200.

CABLE, George W. *Old Creole Days.* New York, 1879. Author's first book. First state, with no ads at back. $250. Second state with ads. $125. New York, 1897. Vellum. One of 204 copies. $200. Limited Editions Club, New York, 1943. In slipcase. $100.

CABLE, George W. *The Southern Struggle for Pure Government.* Boston, 1890. Wraps. $400.

CABLE, George W. *Strange True Stories of Louisiana.* New York, 1889. Illustrated. Pictorial cloth, paper label. $250. London, 1890. $150.

CABRERA INFANTE, Guillermo. *Three Trapped Tigers.* New York (1971). Author's first book. $125.

CAGE, John. *Another Song.* (New York, 1981.) One of 35 copies signed by author and photographer, Susan Barron. Illustrated with 39 original photographs. In windowed tray case. $3,750.

CAHAN, Abraham. *Yekl . . .* New York, 1896. Author's first book. $400.

CAHOON, Herbert. *The Overbrook Press Bibliography, 1934–1959.* Stamford (1963). One of 150 copies. $600.

CAIDIN, Martin. *Cyborg.* New York (1972). $300.

CAIN, James M. *Mildred Pierce.* New York, 1941. $750. London (1943). $350.

CAIN, James M. *Our Government.* New York, 1930. Author's first book other than a collaboration. First issue in printed dustwrapper. $750. Second issue in pictorial dustwrapper. $600.

CAIN, James M. *The Postman Always Rings Twice.* New York, 1934. $3,500. London (1934). $1,000.

CAIN, James M. *Serenade.* New York, 1937. Three variant colors on dustwrapper (no priority). $600. London (1938). $350.

CAIN, James M. *Three of a Kind.* New York, 1943. $400. London (1945). $200.

CAIN, Paul. *Fast One.* Garden City, 1933. Author's first book. $5,000.

CAIN, Paul. *Seven Slayers.* Hollywood (1946). Wraps. "First Book Publication" on copyright page. (By Peter Ruric.) $500. Los Angeles, 1987. One of 250 copies signed by William Nolan (introduction). $75.

CAIRD, James. *Prairie Farming in America . . .* London, 1859. Folding map. $500. New York, 1859. Printed wraps. $250.

CALAVAR: or, The Knight of the Conquest. Philadelphia, 1834. (By Robert Montgomery Bird.) Author's first book. 2 vols. Purple cloth, printed paper labels. $500. Philadelphia, 1847. 2 vols. Revised edition. Printed wraps. $200.

CALDCLEUGH, Alexander. *Travels in South America* . . . London, 1825. 2 vols. 2 folding maps, 9 plates. Frontis of vol. 1 in color. $1,000.

CALDER, Alexander. *Animal Sketching.* Pelham, N.Y. (1926). Author's first book. $500.

CALDER, Alexander. *A Bestiary.* New York (1955). Illustrated by Calder. Small folio, decorated cloth. In slipcase. One of 750 copies signed by Wilbur and Calder. $500. One of 26 signed, lettered copies. $750.

CALDER, Alexander. *Calder's Circus.* New York (1972). Folio. One of 100 copies signed by Calder. $1,000.

CALDER, Alexander. *Fables of Aesop.* (Paris, 1931.) 50 drawings by Alexander Calder. Decorated paper dustwrapper, slipcase, and matching sleeve. One of 495 copies. $1,250. One of 50 copies with original drawing tipped in. $8,500.

CALDER, Alexander. *Fits and Starts.* (Salisbury, 1973.) Translated by Paul Auster. Color lithograph frontispiece by Calder, signed by him in pencil. Board slipcase. One of 100 copies with lithograph by Calder, also signed by Dupin and Auster. $1,750. One of 1,000 copies. Wraps. $175.

CALDWELL, Erskine. *American Earth.* New York, 1931. First edition, with code letter "A" on copyright page. $250.

CALDWELL, Erskine. *The Bastard.* New York (1929). Author's first book. One of 200 signed copies. In glassine dustwrapper. $1,000. One of 900 unsigned copies. $300.

CALDWELL, Erskine. *God's Little Acre.* New York, 1933. $2,500.

CALDWELL, Erskine. *Kneel to the Rising Sun and Other Stories.* New York, 1935. One of 300 signed copies. Issued without dustwrapper. In slipcase. $250. Trade edition. $150.

CALDWELL, Erskine. *Mama's Little Girl.* Mount Vernon, Me., 1932. 2 drawings by Alfred Morang. Printed wraps. One of 75 copies. $750.

CALDWELL, Erskine. *A Message for Genevieve.* Mount Vernon, 1933. Drawing by Alfred Morang. Printed wraps. One of 100 copies. $600.

CALDWELL, Erskine. *North of the Danube.* New York (1939). Photographs by Margaret Bourke-White. Linen. $250.

CALDWELL, Erskine. *Poor Fool.* New York, 1930. Illustrated. Blue buckram. Issued without dustwrapper. One of 1,000 copies. $350.

CALDWELL, Erskine. *Tenant Farmer.* New York (1935). Green wraps. $150.

CALDWELL, Erskine. *Tobacco Road.* New York, 1932. With code letter "A" on copyright page. $1,500. London, 1933. In printed glassine dustwrapper with paper flaps. $750.

CALDWELL, Erskine. *We Are the Living.* New York, 1933. One of 250 signed copies. In glassine dustwrapper. In slipcase. $300. Trade edition. $150.

CALDWELL, Erskine, and BOURKE-WHITE, Margaret. *Say, Is This the U.S.A.* New York (1941). Illustrated. Pictorial boards. $250.

CALDWELL, J. A. *History of Belmont and Jefferson Counties, Ohio.* Wheeling, Ohio, 1880. Half leather. $500.

CALDWELL, J. F. J. *History of a Brigade of South Carolinians.* Philadelphia, 1866. Cloth. $2,000.

CALDWELL, Taylor. *Dynasty of Death.* New York, 1938. Author's first book. $125. London, 1939. $100.

CALEF, Robert. *More Wonders of the Invisible World . . .* London, 1700. $6,500.

CALHOUN, James S. *Official Correspondence of James S. Calhoun While Indian Agent at Santa Fe.* Washington, 1915. Illustrated, 4 maps. Cloth. $250.

CALIFORNIA Gold Regions, with a Full Account of Their Mineral Resources . . . (New York, 1849.) $3,000.

CALIFORNIA Illustrated. New York, 1852. By a Returned Californian. (By J. M. Letts.) First issue, anonymous. 48 plates. $1,250. Later issue, same year, author named. $750. New edition. *Pictorial View of California,* 1853, with fewer plates. $350.

CALIFORNIA Sketches, with Recollections of the Gold Mines. Albany, 1850. Half leather. (By Leonard Kip.) $2,000.

CALISHER, Hortense. *In the Absence of Angels.* Boston, 1951. $125.

CALLAGHAN, Morley. *A Native Argosy.* New York, 1929. $350.

CALLAGHAN, Morley. *No Man's Meat.* Paris, 1931. Boards and cloth, paper label. One of 500 signed copies. In tissue dustwrapper. In slipcase. $200. One of 25 copies for presentation. $500.

CALLAGHAN, Morley. *Strange Fugitive.* New York, 1928. Author's first book. $500.

CALLAHAN, Harry. *Photographs.* Santa Barbara (1964). (1,500 copies.) In slipcase. $1,500.

CALVERT, A. F. *Southern Spain.* London, 1908. 75 color plates and folding map. $400. (Listed on Internet as 1907. Bibliography shows 1908.)

CALVERT, Frederick. *The Isle of Wight Illustrated.* London, 1846. Sepia lithograph frontispiece, colored map. 20 colored aquatint plates. First issue with plate four titles "Ryde" (later issued "Ryde/ Plate 1"). $3,000.

CALVERT, George Henry. *Illustrations of Phrenology.* Baltimore, 1832. (Edited by Calvert.) Author's first book. $200.

CALVIN, Ross. *Sky Determines.* New York, 1934. Author's first book. $200.

CALVINO, Italo. *The Path to the Nest of Spiders.* Boston (1957). First English translation. $500.

CAMBERG, Muriel. *Out of a Book.* Leith, [1933?] (By Muriel Spark, her first book.) $1,500.

CAMERA Work, Number 1. New York, 1903–17. 1–50. $135,000. Suffice it to say that runs or individual issues are worth checking out.

CAMERON, Caddo. *Rangers Is Powerful Hard to Kill.* New York, 1936. $150.

CAMERON, Julia M. *Victorian Photographs of Famous Men and Fair Women.* London, 1926. (Contains an introduction by Virginia Woolf.) One of 450 copies. Issued without dustwrapper. $1,750. New York, 1926. One of 250 copies. Issued without dustwrapper. $750.

CAMP, Charles L., et al. *Essays for Henry R. Wagner.* San Francisco, 1947. One of 260 copies. $150.

CAMP, Charles L. *James Clyman* . . . San Francisco, 1928. $500. Portland, 1960. One of 1,450 copies. $175.

CAMP, Walter. *American Football.* New York, 1891. $800. New York, 1892. $250.

CAMP, Walter, and BROOKS, Lillian. *Drives & Putts: A Book of Golf Stories.* Boston, 1899. $400.

CAMPBELL, Alexander. *A Journey from Edinburgh* . . . London, 1802. 2 vols. $1,000.

CAMPBELL, Alexander, and OWEN, Robert. *Debate on the Evidence of Christianity.* Bethany, Va., 1829. 2 vols. in 1. $1,000.

CAMPBELL, Alexander, and RICE, N. L. *A Debate* . . . *on the Action, Subject, Design and Administration of Christian Baptism.* Lexington, Ky., 1844. $300.

CAMPBELL, Alice. *Juggernaut.* London [1928]. Author's first book. $150. New York, 1929. $100.

CAMPBELL, Archibald. *A Voyage Round the World* . . . Edinburgh, 1816. Folding frontispiece map. $2,000. New York, 1817. Map. $1,500.

CAMPBELL, George. *First Poems.* Kingston, 1945. Green boards. $500.

CAMPBELL, J. L. *The Great Agricultural & Mineral West.* Chicago, 1866. Folding ad leaf and map. Printed Wraps. "Third Annual Edition." $2,000.

CAMPBELL, J. L. *Idaho and Montana Gold Regions.* Chicago, 1865. Second edition. Map. Half morocco. $5,000.

CAMPBELL, J. L. *Idaho: Six Months* . . . New York, 1864. Wraps. $12,500.

CAMPBELL, J. Ramsey. *The Inhabitant of the Lake.* Sauk City, 1964. Author's first book. $150.

CAMPBELL, John. *An Account of the Spanish Settlements in America.* Edinburgh, 1762. $1,250.

CAMPBELL, John. *Travels in South Africa Undertaken at the Request of the Missionary Society.* London, 1815. Folding map and 10 plates. $1,000.

CAMPBELL, John W., Jr. *The Mightiest Machine.* Providence (1947). $350.

CAMPBELL, Patrick. *Travels in the Interior Inhabited Parts of North America.* Edinburgh, 1793. $15,000 in original (cracked) boards at auction in 1999. Toronto, 1937. 3 plates. One of 550 copies. $350.

CAMPBELL, Roy. *Adamastor: Poems.* London (1930). One of 90 signed. $300. Trade edition. In first issue dustwrapper with author's name twice on spine. $150. Second issue jacket, corrected. $100. Cape Town, 1950. Half calf. Illustrated edition. $200.

CAMPBELL, Roy. *Broken Record*. London, 1934. $150. Vellum. One of 50 signed copies. $350. One of 8 signed copies. $500.

CAMPBELL, Roy. *The Flaming Terrapin*. London, 1924. Author's first book. Boards, cloth spine, paper label. $175. New York, 1924. $125.

CAMPBELL, Roy. *Flowering Reeds: Poems*. London, 1933. One of 69 signed copies. Issued without dustwrapper. $300. One of 8 signed copies. $500. Trade edition. In dustwrapper. $100.

CAMPBELL, Roy. *The Georgiad*. London, 1931. Boards and cloth. Issued without dustwrapper. One of 150 signed copies. $250. Vellum. One of 20 copies on goatskin parchment paper, signed. $500.

CAMPBELL, Roy. *Poems*. Paris: Hours Press, 1930. Decorated boards and morocco. One of 200 signed copies. $400.

CAMUS, Albert. *The Fall*. New York, 1957. $150. Allen Press. (Kentfield, Calif., 1966.) Folio, boards. One of 140 copies. $850.

CAMUS, Albert. *The Outsider*. London (1946). (C. Connolly introduction.) Author's first English publication. $600.

CAMUS, Albert. *September 15th, 1937*. Bronxville, 1963. Wraps. One of 50 copies for presentation, privately printed by Valenti Angelo. $300.

CAMUS, Albert. *The Stranger*. (U.S. edition of *The Outsider*.) New York, 1946. (Does not include Connolly introduction.) With dustwrapper priced at $2.00 and no reviews on front flap. $500.

CANFIELD, Chauncey L. (editor). *The Diary of a Forty-Niner*. San Francisco, 1906. Colored map. Pictorial boards. $300.

CANNELL, Dorothy. *The Thin Woman . . .* New York, 1984. Author's first book. $300.

CANNON, George Q. *Life of Joseph Smith . . .* Salt Lake City, 1888. Leather. $150.

CANNON, George Q. *Writings from the "Western Standard." Published in San Francisco*. Liverpool, 1864. Full morocco. $1,500.

CANNON, J. P. *Inside of Rebeldom: The Daily Life of a Private in the Confederate Army*. Washington, D.C., 1900. Cloth. $200.

CANOVA, Andrew. *Life and Adventures in South Florida*. Palatka, Fla., 1885. 4 plates. Printed light-green wraps. $450.

CANTWELL, Robert. *Laugh and Lie Down*. New York, 1931. Author's first book. First issue dustwrapper is pictorial. $500. Second-issue dustwrapper is printed with reviews. $300.

CAPA, Robert. *Death in the Making*. New York (1938). Author's first book. $750.

CAPA, Robert. *Slightly Out of Focus*. New York, 1947. Photo-illustrated. $350.

CAPE, Judith. *The Sun and the Moon*. Toronto, 1944. $350. New York, 1944. $100.

CAPEK, Karel. *Krakatit*. London (1925). $600. New York, 1925. $350.

CAPEK, Karel. *The Makropoulos Affair.* London, 1922. (First English translation.) $350. Boston, 1925. $150.

CAPEK, Karel. *R.U.R.* Garden City, 1923. $1,250. London, 1923. Wraps. $750.

CAPEK, Karel. *War with the Newts.* London (1937). $600. New York (1937). $300.

CAPOTE, Truman. *Breakfast at Tiffany's.* New York (1958). $1,000. London (1958). $250.

CAPOTE, Truman. *A Christmas Memory.* New York (1966). One of 600 signed copies. Bright-red slipcase. $600. Trade edition. Beige boards with teal-blue cloth spine, maroon slipcase (also noted in black cloth in bright-red slipcase). First edition not stated. Copyright 1956. $100. London [1966]. $75.

CAPOTE, Truman. *In Cold Blood.* New York (1965). One of 500 signed copies. In slipcase. $1,500. Trade edition with signed extra leaf inserted. $600. Trade edition. $200. London (1966). $125.

CAPOTE, Truman. *The Grass Harp.* (New York, 1951.) Rough beige cloth. $450. Second binding: smooth, fine-grained beige cloth. $200. London (1952). $200.

CAPOTE, Truman. *The Grass Harp: A Play.* New York (1952). (Reportedly only 500 copies.) $500.

CAPOTE, Truman. *Local Color.* New York (1950). $450. London (1950). One of 200 copies in full leather. $500.

CAPOTE, Truman. *Observations.* New York (1959). Photographs by Richard Avedon. Acetate dustwrapper. In slipcase. $600. London (1959). Acetate dustwrapper. In slipcase. $450.

CAPOTE, Truman. *Other Voices, Other Rooms.* New York (1948). Author's first book. $750. London (1948). $250. Franklin Library, 1979. Signed "Limited Edition." $300.

CAPOTE, Truman. *The Thanksgiving Visitor.* New York (1968). One of 300 signed copies. In slipcase. (Note: published 11/21/68, last date copyright page is 1967.) $750. Trade edition. In green or brown slipcase (priority unknown). $125. London (1969). $75.

CAPOTE, Truman. *A Tree of Night and Other Stories.* New York (1949). $450. London (1950). $150.

CAPPS, Benjamin. *Trail to Ogalla.* New York, 1964. $75.

CAPRON, Elisha S. *History of California.* Boston, 1854. Colored map. $1,250.

CARD, Orson Scott. *Ender's Game.* (New York, 1985.) $1,000.

CARELESS, John. *The Old English 'Squire: A Poem in Ten Cantos.* London, 1821. (By William A. Chatto.) 24 colored plates. $1,250.

CAREW, Thomas. *Poems.* London, 1640. $3,000.

CAREY, David. *Life in Paris.* London, 1822. Illustrated by George Cruikshank. $1,250. Large paper. $1,750.

CAREY, Mathew. *Carey's American Atlas.* Philadelphia, 1795. Folio, chart, and 20 maps. $20,000.

CAREY, Mathew. *Carey's General Atlas, Improved and Enlarged.* Philadelphia, 1814. Folio, 58 engraved maps. Calf-backed boards; worn, repaired. Folding box. $12,500.

CAREY, Peter. *Bliss.* Brisbane. 1981. $250.

CAREY, Peter. *The Fat Man in History.* Brisbane, 1974. Author's first book. $450. London, 1980. $200. New York, 1980. $100.

CARLETON, James Henry. *The Battle of Buena Vista, with the Operations of the "Army of Occupation" for One Month.* New York, 1848. 2 folding maps. Original wraps. $450.

CARLETON, William M. *Fax: A Campaign Poem.* Chicago, 1868. Author's first book. Illustrated. Printed wraps. $750.

CARLTON, Robert. *The New Purchase: or, Seven and a Half Years in the Far West.* New York, 1843. (By Baynard R. Hall.) 2 vols. $300.

CARLYLE, Thomas. See *The Life of Friedrich Schiller.* See also *Sartor Resartus.*

CARLYLE, Thomas. *The French Revolution.* London, 1837. 3 vols. First issue, with 2 pages of ads at end of vol. 2. $1,750. New York: Little, Brown, 1838. 2 vols. $450. London, 1910. 2 vols. Illustrated. Half vellum. One of 150 copies on large paper. $450. Limited Editions Club, New York, 1956. In slipcase. $100.

CARLYLE, Thomas. *Occasional Discourse on the Nigger Question.* London, 1853. Wraps. $1,500.

CARLYLE, Thomas. *Past and Present.* London, 1843. $300.

CARLYLE, Thomas. *Shooting Niagara: and After?* London, 1867. Printed green wraps. $200.

CARMAN, Bliss. See Carmen [sic], Bliss.

CARMAN, Bliss. *The Gate of Peace: A Poem.* New York, 1907. Boards and cloth. One of 112 signed copies. $750. (Note: All except 24 destroyed by fire, says Johnson.)

CARMAN, Bliss. *Poems.* New York, 1904. 2 vols. Half leather. One of 500 signed copies. $300. Boston, 1905. 2 vols. Boards. One of 500 signed copies. $300.

CARMAN, Bliss. *The Princess of the Tower.* New York, 1906. Boards. One of 62 signed copies. $600.

CARMEN, Bliss. *Low Tide on Grand Pre.* Toronto (1889? 1890?). (By Bliss Carman.) Author's first book, with his name misspelled. 13 pages. Wraps. First edition (pirated). $4,500. New York, 1893. Lavender cloth. $350. London, 1893. $250.

CARNE, John. *Syria, the Holy Land . . .* London (1836–38). 3 vols. 3 engraved titles, 2 maps and 121(?) plates. $1,000.

CARNEVALI, Emanuel. *A Hurried Man.* Paris: Contact Editions (1925). Author's first book. Wraps. $300.

CARPENTER, Edward. *Narcissus . . .* London, 1873. Author's first book. $400.

CARPENTER, William B. *The Microscope and Its Revelations.* Philadelphia, 1856. Illustrated by 434 engravings on wood. $250.

CARR, Christopher. *Memoirs of Arthur Hamilton.* London, 1886. (By A. C. Benson, his first book.) $200.

CARR, Mrs. Comyns (Alice). *North Italian Folk Sketches of Town and Country Life.* London, 1878. Hand-colored illustrations by Randolph Caldecott. Boards. One of 400 copies. $200. (New York), 1878. First American edition. (250 copies.) $150.

CARR, Gyln. *Death on Mileston Buttress.* London, 1951. $750.

CARR, Gyln. *Death Under Snowden.* London, 1954. $750.

CARR, John. *Early Times in Middle Tennessee.* Nashville, 1857. $250.

CARR, John. *Pioneer Days in California.* Eureka, Calif., 1891. $450.

CARR, John Dickson. See Dickson, Carter.

CARR, John Dickson. *The Blind Barber.* New York, 1934. $2,000. London, 1934. $600.

CARR, John Dickson. *Castle Skull.* New York, 1931. $3,000.

CARR, John Dickson. *Death Watch.* New York, 1935. $1,500. London, 1935. $500.

CARR, John Dickson. *The Eight of Swords.* New York, 1934. $1,750. London, 1934. $600.

CARR, John Dickson. *It Walks by Night.* New York, 1930. Author's first book. $3,500. London (1930). $2,000.

CARR, John Dickson. *The Lost Gallows.* New York, 1931. $3,000. London, 1931. $1,000.

CARR, John Dickson. *The Murder of Sir Edmund Godfrey.* New York, 1936. $600. London, 1936. $300.

CARR, John Dickson. *The Problem of the Wire Cage.* New York, 1939. $600.

CARR, Sir John (1772–1832). *The Stranger in Ireland.* London, 1806. With hand-colored map and 16 plates. $1,250.

CARR, Spencer. *A Brief Sketch of La Crosse, Wisconsin.* La Crosse, 1854. 28 pages, sewn. $600.

CARRINGTON, Mrs. Henry B. See *Ab-Sa-Ra-Ka.*

CARRINGTON, John Bodman, and HUGHES, George Ravensworth. *The Plate of the Worshipful Company of Goldsmiths.* Oxford, 1926. Illustrated. Red cloth. $350. Morocco. $500.

CARROLL, H. Bailey. *The Texan Santa Fe Trail.* Canyon, Tex., 1951. Illustrated. In slipcase. $200.

CARROLL, Jim. *The Basketball Diaries.* (Bolinas, 1978.) Wraps. $850.

CARROLL, Jim. *Organic Trains.* (New York, 1968.) Author's first book. Mimeographed sheets in stapled wraps. $500.

CARROLL, John, Archbishop. *An Address to the Roman Catholics* . . . Annapolis, 1784. $2,000.

CARROLL, Lewis. See Dodgson, Charles L.

CARROLL, Lewis. *Alice's Adventures in Wonderland.* London, 1865. (By Charles L. Dodgson.) 42 illustrations by John Tenniel. Red cloth. First edition (suppressed by the author). $750,000 ($1,400,000, rebound with 10 original signed Tenniel drawings at auction in 1998). New York, 1866. Red cloth. First American edition made up from the sheets of the English suppressed edition. $45,000. Rebound and stamped with original design. $25,000. London, 1866. Red cloth. Second edition (and first published English edition). $25,000. Boston, 1869. Green cloth. First edition printed in America. $2,000. London (1907). Illustrated by Arthur Rackham. Cloth. $600. One of 1,130 copies signed by Rackham. $1,500. New York (1907). Half cloth. One of 550 copies. $1,750. London, 1914. Tenniel illustrations. Vellum. One of 12 copies on vellum. $5,000. Ordinary issue. One of 1,000. $350. Paris, 1930. One of 350 copies. $2,500. One of 50 copies on vellum. $5,000. One of 20 copies with extra suite. $15,000. Limited Editions Club, New York, 1932. Signed by Alice Hargreaves, the original "Alice." $2,500. Unsigned. $600. New York, 1969. Salvador Dali illustrations (13 plates). Folio (13 plates), loose signatures in folder and leather-backed case. One of 200 copies signed by Dali. $12,500. One of 2,500 signed copies by Dali. $4,000. West Hatfield: Pennyroyal Press, 1982. Large folio, with separate cloth portfolio for the extra suite of plates, in matching cloth and purple leather dropcase. One of 50 copies signed by Barry Moser. $7,500. One of 350 copies. $3,500. Berkeley (1982). 2 vols. One of 750 copies. $500.

CARROLL, Lewis. *Alice's Adventures Under Ground.* London, 1886. (By Charles L. Dodgson.) 37 illustrations by the author. Red cloth, gilt edges. $1,500. (Note: This is a facsimile of the original manuscript from which *Alice's Adventures in Wonderland* was developed.)

CARROLL, Lewis. *Curiosa Mathematica.* Part I. London, 1888. (By Charles L. Dodgson.) Gray or tan cloth. $1,500.

CARROLL, Lewis. *Curiosa Mathematica.* Part II. London, 1893. First edition rare, author recalled. $7,500.

CARROLL, Lewis. *Feeding the Mind.* London, 1907. (By Charles L. Dodgson.) Full flexible maroon morocco. $500. Boards or wraps. $300.

CARROLL, Lewis. *The Game of Logic.* London, 1886. (By Charles L. Dodgson.) With envelope containing 9 counters and board diagram. First (private) edition. $4,000. Only a few copies known. London, 1887. Second edition (only 500 copies). $1,500.

CARROLL, Lewis. *The Hunting of the Snark.* London, 1876. (By Charles L. Dodgson.) Illustrated by Henry Holiday. Pictorial cloth, gilt edges. $1,500. Vellum. $2,000. New York, 1903. Illustrated by Peter Newell. $450.

CARROLL, Lewis. *Logical Nonsense* . . . New York (1934). One of 125. In slipcase. $750. Trade edition. $150.

CARROLL, Lewis. *Phantasmagoria and Other Poems.* London, 1869. (By Charles L. Dodgson.) Without "Author of/Alice's . . ." on title page. $1,250. Second issue with statement added. $500.

CARROLL, Lewis. *Rules for Court Circular.* [No place, January 1860.] 4-page leaflet. $1,000.

CARROLL, Lewis. *Sylvie and Bruno.* London, 1889. (By Charles L. Dodgson.) Illustrated by Harry Furniss. $450.

CARROLL, Lewis. *Sylvie and Bruno Concluded.* London, 1893. (By Charles L. Dodgson.) Red cloth (white for presentation). Illustrated by Harry Furniss. First issue, with error in table of contents showing chapter 8 at page 110 (vs. 113). $250.

CARROLL, Lewis. *A Tangled Tale.* London, 1885. (By Charles L. Dodgson.) Illustrated by A. B. Frost. Pictorial cloth. $600.

CARROLL, Lewis. *Three Sunsets and Other Poems.* London, 1898. (By Charles L. Dodgson.) Frontispiece and other illustrations. $600.

CARROLL, Lewis. *Through the Looking Glass, and What Alice Found There.* London, 1872. (By Charles L. Dodgson.) 50 illustrations by John Tenniel. Red cloth. First issue, with "wade" on page 21. $4,000. Boston, 1872. First American edition. $1,250. New York, 1902. Illustrated by Peter Newell. $400. Limited Editions Club, New York, 1935. Signed by Alice Hargreaves. In slipcase. $2,000. Unsigned. $400. West Hatfield, 1982. One of 350 copies signed by Barry Moser (illustrator). $3,000. One of 50 copies signed by Barry Moser (illustrator). $6,000.

CARRUTH, (Fred) Hayden. *The Adventures of Jones.* New York, 1894. Author's first book. Pictorial tan cloth. $175.

CARRUTHERS, George. *Paper-Making. Part I. First Hundred Years of Paper-Making. Part II. First Century of Paper-Making in Canada.* Toronto, 1947. $200.

CARSON, Christopher. See Grant, Blanche C.

CARSON, James H. *Early Recollections of the Mines, and a Description of the Great Tulare Valley.* Stockton, Calif., 1852. Folding map. 64 pages. printed wraps (with cover title reading "Second Edition. Life in California, etc."). First edition (in book form; earlier appearance in the San Joaquin *Republican*). $30,000 at auction in 1994. Oakland, 1950. One of 750 copies. Issued without dustwrapper. $100.

CARSON, Joseph. *Illustrations of Medical Botany . . .* Philadelphia, 1847. 2 vols. 100 hand-colored plates. $6,500.

CARSON, Rachel. *Silent Spring.* Boston, 1962. First edition stated. $750.

CARSON, Rachel. *Under the Sea Wind.* New York, 1941. Author's first book. $450.

CARSTARPHEN, J. E. *My Trip to California in '49.* (Louisiana, Mo., 1914.) Limited edition. 8 pages, wraps. $500.

CARTER, Angela. *The Magic Toyshop.* London (1967). $600. New York, 1967. $200.

CARTER, Angela. *Shadow Dance.* London, 1966. $500.

CARTER, Angela. *Unicorn.* Leeds, 1966. Author's first book. One of 150 copies. Stapled mimeographed sheets. $450.

CARTER (Asa). See *George and Lurleen Wallace.*

CARTER, E. S. *The Life And Adventures of E. S. Carter Including a Trip Across the Plains and Mountains in 1852 . . .* St. Joseph, 1896. Wraps. $2,000.

CARTER, Forrest. *The Education of Little Tree.* (New York, 1976.) $450.

CARTER, Forrest. *Gone to Texas.* New York (1973). $350. (New title for *The Rebel Outlaw* . . .)

CARTER, Forrest. *The Rebel Outlaw: Josey Wales.* (Gannt, Alabama, 1973.) Author's first book. $1,000.

CARTER, Forrest. *The Vengeance Trail of Josey Wales.* (New York, 1976.) $350.

CARTER, Frederick. *D. H. Lawrence and the Body Mystical.* London (1932). Frontispiece. Vellum. One of 75 on vellum. In glassine dustwrapper. $300. One of 250. Japan vellum and boards. $125.

CARTER, Harry (editor). *Founier on Typefounding; the Text of the Manuel Typographique (1764– 1766) Translated* . . . London, 1930. 16 double-page plates. One of 260 copies. $300.

CARTER, Howard, and MACE, A. C. *The Tomb of Tutankhamen.* London, 1923–33. 3 vols. Large octavo. Brown cloth. $2,500.

CARTER, John. *Binding Variants in English Publishing, 1820–1900.* London, 1932. Limited to 500 copies. $300.

CARTER, John (editor). *New Paths in Book Collecting; Essays by Various Hands.* London (1934). $150.

CARTER, John, and MUIR, Percy H. *Printing and the Mind of Man.* (London), 1967. $350. (New York, 1967.) English sheets. $250.

CARTER, John, and POLLARD, Graham. *An Enquiry into the Nature of Certain 19th Century Pamphlets.* London, 1934. 4 plates. In dustwrapper. $350. London and Berkeley, 1983. 2 vols. One of 80 copies in black morocco. In slipcase with copy of Wise-Forman forgery of Brownings' *Two Poems* enclosed in chemise. $750.

CARTER, Robert G. *Four Brothers in Blue.* Washington, 1913. Frontispiece. $1,250. Washington, 1913. Second edition (so-called "Imperfect Edition" made up of magazine installments bound with first edition text). $1,750.

CARTER, Robert G. *Massacre of Salt Creek Prairie and the Cowboy's Verdict.* Washington, 1919. 48 pages, wraps. $750.

CARTER, Robert G. *The Old Sergeant's Story: Winning the West from the Indians and Badmen in 1870 to 1876.* New York, 1926. Portrait, plates. $750.

CARTER, Robert G. *On the Border with Mackenzie.* Washington (1935). 3 portraits. Cloth. $4,000. New York, 1961. One of 750 copies. $200.

CARTER, Robert G. *On the Trail of Deserters.* Washington, 1920. Printed wraps. One of 250 copies. $750.

CARTER, Robert G. *Pursuit of Kicking Bird: A Campaign in the Texas "Bad Lands."* Washington, 1920. 44 pages, wraps. (100 copies printed.) $750.

CARTER, Susannah. *The Frugal Housewife: or, Complete Woman Cook.* London, no date. $2,500. London, 1795. $2,000. New York (1795). $1,750. Philadelphia, 1796. $1,500. Philadelphia, 1802. Revised. $1,250.

CARTER, Thomas Francis. *The Invention of Printing in China and Its Spread Westward.* New York: Columbia University Press, 1925. $200. New York (1931). Revised with an introduction by Douglas McMurtrie on Carter. $200.

CARTER, W. A. *History of Fannin County, Texas.* Bonham, Tex., 1885. $1,000.

CARTER, William H. *From Yorktown to Santiago with the Sixth U.S. Cavalry.* Baltimore, 1900. Pictorial cloth. $1,000.

CARTIER-BRESSON, Henri. *Beautiful Jaipur.* Jaipur (1948). $750.

CARTIER-BRESSON, Henri. *The Decisive Moment.* New York (1952). Illustrated. Boards. In Matisse dustwrapper. With pamphlet of captions laid in. $1,500.

CARTIER-BRESSON, Henri. *The Europeans.* New York (1955). With pamphlet of captions laid in. $750.

CARTIER-BRESSON, Henri. *The People of Moscow.* New York, 1955. $150.

CARTIER-BRESSON, Henri. *Photographs of Henri Cartier-Bresson.* New York: MoMA, 1947. Author's first book. Cloth in dustwrapper. $300. Wraps. $150.

CARTLAND, Barbara. *Jig-Saw.* London (1925). Author's first book. $750.

CARTWRIGHT, George. *A Journal of Transactions and Events . . .* Newark, 1792. 2 vols. $5,000.

CARUSO, Enrico. *Caricatures.* New York, 1908. Folio. $1,500.

CARUTHERS, William Alexander. *The Kentuckian in New York.* New York, 1834. 2 vols. $750.

CARVER, Jonathan. *Three Years Travels, Through the Interior Parts of North America . . .* Philadelphia, 1784. First American edition. $850.

CARVER, Jonathan. *Travels Through the Interior Parts of North America in the Years 1766, 1767, and 1768.* London, 1778. Two large folding maps and four engraved plates. $4,000. London, 1770. Second edition. With added plate. $2,500. London, 1781. Third Edition. With added plate. $2,000. (Hand-colored maps or plates would be more.)

CARVER, Raymond. *Near Klamath.* Sacramento, 1968. Author's first book. Wraps. $2,500.

CARVER, Raymond. *Put Yourself in My Shoes.* Santa Barbara, 1974. One of 75 hardcover copies signed by Carver. $1,500. Wraps. $150.

CARVER, Raymond. *What We Talk About When We Talk About Love.* New York, 1981. $200.

CARVER, Raymond. *Where I'm Calling From.* New York (1988). One of 250 signed copies. In slipcase. $350. Trade edition. $100. Franklin Library. Pennslvania, 1988. Unspecified number published. Signed. $150.

CARVER, Raymond. *Will You Please Be Quiet, Please?* New York, 1976. $600.

CARVER, Raymond. *Winter Insomnia.* (Santa Cruz, 1970.) Wraps. $300.

CARY, Arthur. *Verse*. Edinburgh, 1908. (Joyce Cary's first book.) $4,000.

CARY, Joyce. *The African Witch*. London, 1926. $300. New York, 1936. $125.

CARY, Joyce. *Aissa Saved*. London, 1932. $750. New York (1962). $75.

CARY, Joyce. *An American Visitor*. London, 1933. $350.

CARY, Joyce. *The Horse's Mouth*. London (1944). $400. New York (1944). $150. London, 1957. One of 1,500 copies. In slipcase. $150.

CASLER, John. *Four Years in the Stonewall Brigade*. Guthrie, Okla., 1893. Folding facsimile. $750.

CASPARA, Vera. *Laura*. London, 1944. $1,000.

CASPER, C. N. *Directory of the Antiquarian Booksellers and Dealers in Second-Hand Books of the United States . . .* Milwaukee, 1885. $150.

CASSON, Stanley. *Murder by Burial*. New York, 1938. $350.

CASTANEDA, Carlos. *The Teachings of Don Juan: Yaqui Way of Knowledge*. Berkeley, 1968. Author's first book. $500. London, 1971. $150.

CASTANEDA, Carlos E. *Our Catholic Heritage in Texas, 1519–1810*. Austin, 1936–50. 6 vols. $1,000.

CASTILLO, Ana. *The Mixquiahuala Letters*. Binghamton (1986). Issued without dustwrapper. $75.

CASTLE Dismal; or, the Bachelor's Christmas. New York, 1844. (By William Gilmore Simms.) $350.

CASTLE of Otranto, A Story (The). London, 1765. (By Horace Walpole.) No mention of this being a Gothic novel on title page. $6,000.

CASTLE Rackrent: An Hibernian Tale. London, 1800. (By Maria Edgeworth.) $1,000.

CASTLEMAN, Alfred L. *Army of the Potomac: Behind the Scenes*. Milwaukee, 1863. $300.

CASTLEMON, H. C. (Harry). *Frank on the Lower Mississippi*. Cincinnati, 1867. (By Charles Austin Fosdick.) $300.

CASTLEMON, H. C. *Frank, the Young Naturalist*. Cincinnati, 1865. (By Charles Austin Fosdick, his first book.) $450.

CASTLEMON, Harry. *Guy Harris, the Runaway*. New York, 1887. (By Charles Austin Fosdick.) Printed wraps. $300.

CASTLEMON, Harry. *The Sportsman's Club Among the Trappers*. Philadelphia, 1874. (By Charles Austin Fosdick.) Plates. $200.

CATALOG of the Avery Architectural Library, A Memorial Library of Architecture, Archaeology, and Decorative Art. New York, 1895. Limited to 1,000 copies. $400.

CATALOGUE of Books & Manuscripts in the Estelle Doheny Collection. Los Angeles, 1940, 1946, 1955. 3 vols. Each vol. limited to 100 copies. $1,500.

CATALOGUE of a Collection of Early German Books in the Library of C. Fairfax Murray. London, 1962. (Completed copies done up in 1981.) 2 vols. $250.

CATALOGUE of First Editions of American Authors. New York, 1885. $200.

CATALOGUE of the Library of Robert Hoe of New York. New York, 1911–12. 8 vols. $500.

CATALOGUE of Valuable Printed Books and Fine Bindings from the Celebrated Collection . . . J. R. Abbey. London, 1965–1989. 11 vols. $750.

CATALOGUE of the Wheeler Gift of Books, Pamphlets and Periodicals in the Library of the American Institute of Electrical Engineers. New York, 1909. 2 vols. $250.

CATES, Cliff D. *Pioneer History of Wise County, Texas.* Decatur, Tex., 1907. Illustrated. Stiff wraps. $250.

CATESBY, Mark. *The Natural History of Carolina, Florida and the Bahama Islands . . .* London (1730–) 1731–43 (–1747). 2 vols. 220 hand-colored engraved plates. $350,000. London, 1754. Second edition. 2 vols. $200,000. London, 1771. Third edition. $125,000. Savannah, 1974. One of 500 copies. $1,250.

CATHER, Willa. See McClure, S. S.; Milmine, Georgine. See also *The Sombrero.*

CATHER, Willa. *Alexander's Bridge.* Boston, 1912. Coarse blue, or purple-mesh, cloth. With "Willa S. Cather" on spine and half title before title page or after title page. (Priority unresolved.) $750. London, 1912. First English edition. $350.

CATHER, Willa. *April Twilights.* Boston, 1903. Brown boards, paper labels. Author's first book. Issued without dustwrapper. $2,500. New York, 1923. First revised edition. Boards and parchment. One of 450 signed copies. In slipcase. $750. Trade edition. $200. London, 1924. $400.

CATHER, Willa. *Death Comes for the Archbishop.* New York, 1927. $1,750. Also, boards and cloth. One of 175 signed copies. In dustwrapper and slipcase. $3,500. One of 50 copies on Japan vellum, signed. In slipcase. $7,500. London, 1927. $750. New York, 1929. Illustrated by Harold von Schmidt. Vellum. One of 170 signed copies. In slipcase. $2,000. Trade. $350.

CATHER, Willa. *A Lost Lady.* New York, 1923. First issue, in green cloth with title at top of spine, and pages 164, 171, 173, and 174 too closely crammed. $600. Second issue with Cather's name at top of spine. In green or tan cloth. $350. Boards and cloth. With pages 164 and 173 reset. $125. One of 20 copies lettered A to T, signed. In glassine dustwrapper. In slipcase. $3,500. One of 200 signed copies. In slipcase. $1,500.

CATHER, Willa. *My Antonia.* Boston, 1918. Illustrated by W. T. Benda. Brown cloth. First issue, with illustrations on glazed or coated paper inserted. In dustwrapper. $3,000. Lacking jacket. $600. (Later dustwrapper has 4 reviews on front cover.) Second state with illustrations on text paper. $2,000. London, 1919. $2,500. Lacking jacket. $400.

CATHER, Willa. *Not Under Forty.* New York, 1936. $100. One of 333 large-paper copies on Japan vellum, signed. In dustwrapper. In slipcase. $850. Trade. $125.

CATHER, Willa. *The Novels and Stories of Willa Cather.* Boston, 1937–41. 13 vols., two-toned cloth. Autograph edition. One of 970 signed copies. In dustwrappers. $4,000. Three-quarter morocco. $5,000. Full morocco. $6,000.

CATHER, Willa. *Obscure Destinies.* New York, 1932. $200. Vellum and boards. One of 260 copies on Japan vellum, signed. In dustwrapper. In slipcase. $850. London (1932). $250.

CATHER, Willa. *One of Ours.* New York, 1922. One of 35 copies on Japan vellum, signed. $4,000. One of 310 copies on handmade paper, signed. In numbered slipcase. $2,000. "One of 250" copies. In mottled gray boards "Made for bookseller friends . . ." 155 copies in U.S. $1,250. 95 copies issued with Toronto: Macmillan, 1922 and without limitation leaf. $750. First trade edition states "Second printing, September 1922." In dark-orange dustwrapper. $1,000 (Also noted in dark-green dustwrapper.)

CATHER, Willa. *O Pioneers!* Boston, 1913. First issue in light-yellow brown vertical ribbed cloth. With period after "Co." on spine touching "o." $750. Second issue in pale cream-yellow vertical ribbed cloth ("Co" same). $600. Third issue in yellow-brown linen cloth, with period separated from "o." $400. "Willa S. Cather" on spine. Later reprints have "Willa Cather." London, 1913. $600.

CATHER, Willa. *The Professor's House.* New York, 1925. $750. Buckram and boards. One of 40 copies on Japan vellum, signed. In slipcase. $4,000. One of 185 signed copies. In slipcase. $2,500. London (1925). $400.

CATHER, Willa. *Shadows on the Rock.* New York, 1931. First edition, advance issue bound in dustwrapper, mislabeled "Second edition" on copyright page. $500. Also advance issue labeled "First Edition." $400. Regular trade edition ("First edition" on copyright page). $250. Marbled boards. Leather label. One of 619 signed copies. In dustwrapper. In slipcase. $750. Full orange vellum. One of 199 copies on Japan vellum, signed. In dustwrapper. In slipcase. $1,250.

CATHER, Willa. *The Song of the Lark.* Boston, 1915. First issue, with boxed ads for 3 books on copyright page and "moment" for "moments" in third line from bottom on page 8. $400. Second issue, ads face half title and page 8 corrected. $200. London (1916). $350.

CATHER, Willa. *The Troll Garden.* New York, 1905. First issue, with "McClure Phillips & Co." at foot of spine. $1,500. Second issue has "Doubleday, Page & Co." $500.

CATHER, Willa, and CANFIELD, Dorothy. *The Fear That Walks by Noonday.* New York, 1931. Boards, paper label. One of 30 copies. $3,500.

CATHERWOOD, Frederick. *Views of Ancient Monuments in Central America, Chiapas, and Yucatán.* London, 1844. Colored title page, engraved map, 25 lithographs. Folio, half morocco. Price depends on whether sets are full-colored. $100,000–$125,000. Or, only tinted. $40,000–$50,000. Book very susceptible to foxing and discoloration, which badly affects many copies and greatly reduces value. Barre, Mass., 1965. One of 500 facsimile copies. $1,250.

CATHOLIC Anthology 1914–1915 (The). London, 1915. Edited by Ezra Pound. Gray boards. (Includes T. S. Eliot's "The Love Song of J. Alfred Prufrock" and 4 other poems.) $1,500.

CATICH, Edward M. *Eric Gill, His Social and Artistic Roots.* Iowa City, 1964. $100.

CATICH, Edward M. *Letters Redrawn from the Trajan Inscription in Rome.* Davenport, Iowa (1961). 2 parts (book and 93 plates) in case. $450.

CATICH, Edward M. *The Origin of the Serif; Brush Writing & Roman Letters.* Davenport, Iowa, 1968. $300. One of 50 copies with extra suite of plates. $850.

CATICH, Edward M. *Reed, Pen, & Brush Alphabets for Writing and Lettering.* Davenport, Iowa (1972). 2 vols. 32 pages in book and 28 heavy leaves loosely inserted in portfolio. $400.

CATICH, Edward M. *The Trajan Inscription, an Essay by Edward M. Catich Together with an Original Rubbing from the Inscription.* Boston, 1973. One of 130 copies signed by Catich. $300.

CATLIN, George. *Last Rambles Among the Indians of the Rocky Mountains and the Andes.* London or New York, 1867. $400

CATLIN, George. *Letters and Notes on the Manners, Customs, and Conditions of the North American Indians.* London, 1841. 2 vols. 2 maps (one folding), and one chart, 309 illustrations. First issue with "Frederick" for "Zacharias" on page 104. $2,000. All early editions. $750–$1,000. New York. 1841. 2 vols. First American edition. Cloth. $1,500.

CATLIN, George. *North American Indian Portfolio.* London or New York, 1844. Either 25 or 31 hand-colored plates mounted on cardboard. Text in cloth-backed wraps. Large folio. With excellent color: $100,000–$125,000. Tinted. $30,000–$40,000. Often subject to poor color, in which case price goes down drastically. Philadelphia, 1913. 2 vols. $1,750. Facsimile edition. New York, 1989. One of 950 copies. $1,500.

CATLIN, George. *O-Kee-Pa, a Religious Ceremony.* London, 1867. 13 colored lithographs, with "folio reservatum" laid in. $25,000 at auction in 1999. Without "reservatum." $10,000. Philadelphia, 1867. $5,000. Often subject to poor color, in which case price goes down drastically.

CATON, John Dean. *The Last of the Illinois, and a Sketch of the Pottawatomies.* Chicago, 1870. 36 pages. Wraps. $250.

CATTLE Raising in South Dakota. (Forest City, 1904.) 32 pages, wraps. $250.

CAUDWELL, Sarah. *Thus Was Adonis Murdered.* London (1981). Author's first book. $750. New York, 1981. $75.

CAWEIN, Madison J. *Blooms of the Berry.* Louisville, 1887. Author's first book. Cloth. $125.

CAXTON, Pisistratus. *What Will He Do with It?* Edinburgh (1859). (By Edward Bulwer-Lytton.) 4 vols., cloth. $400.

CECIL, Henry. *Full Circle.* London, 1948. Author's first book. $250.

CELEBRATED Collection of Americana Formed by the Late Thomas Winthrop Streeter (The). New York, 1966–69. 8 vols. $650.

CELEBRATED Trials and Remarkable Cases. (By George Borrow.) London, 1825. 6 vols. Author's first book. $1,250.

CÉLINE, Louis Ferdinand. *Journey to the End of the Night.* London, 1934. Author's first book. $450. Boston, 1934. $300.

CELIZ, Fray Francisco. *Diary of the Alarcón Expedition into Texas, 1718–1719.* Los Angeles, 1935. Translated by Fritz L. Hoffman. 10 plates. One of 600 copies. $350.

CELLINI, Benvenuto. *The Life of Benvenuto Cellini.* London, 1771. 2 vols. First edition in English. $500. London: Vale Press, 1900. 2 vols. One of 300 copies. $350. One of 10 copies on vellum. $1,250. Garden City, 1946. One of 1,000 copies signed by Salvador Dali. $1,000.

CENDRARS, Blaise. *Panama or the Adventures of My Seven Uncles.* New York, 1931. Translated from the French and illustrated by John Dos Passos. Stiff pictorial wraps. New York, 1931. One of 300 copies signed by Cendrars and Dos Passos. In slipcase. $400. Trade. $200.

CERVANTES, Lorna Dee. *Emplumada.* (Pittsburgh, 1981.) Cloth. $125. Wraps. $25.

CERVANTES, Miguel de. *The History of the Valorous and Wittie Knight-Errant, Don Quixote of the Mancha.* (Note: The 1612 English edition of the first part is now virtually unobtainable. We could find only one at auction for the past 25 years. $11,000 in 1985.) London, 1620. 2 vols. Octavo. Second edition of the first part and first edition of the second part (many issued without engraved title page). $40,000. Nice copies published in the 18th century: $1,000–2,000. London: Ashendene Press, 1927–28 Thomas Shelton translation. 2 vols. Woodcut initials and borders by Louise Powell. Pigskin. One of 225 copies on paper. $3,500. One of 20 copies on vellum. $25,000. London: Nonesuch Press, 1930. P. A. Motteux's translation revised anew (1743). 21 illustrations by E. McKnight Kauffer. 2 vols. Morocco. $1,000.

CHABOT, Frederick Charles. *Pictorial Sketch of Mission San Jose de San Miguel de Aguayo on the San Antonio River.* San Antonio, 1935. Illustrated, including color plates and photographs. Full leatherette. One of 12 copies. $1,250.

CHABOT, Frederick Charles. *With the Makers of San Antonio.* San Antonio, 1937. Illustrated. One of 25 copies (India proof issue) for presentation. $750. Trade. $300.

CHADWICK, Henry. *The Game of Base Ball; How to Learn It, How to Play It, and How to Teach It.* New York (1868). First edition, with rules for 1868. $2,500.

CHAGALL, Marc (illustrator). *Drawings for the Bible.* (French issue: *Dessins pour la Bible.*) New York (and Paris), 1960. Text by Gaston Bachelard. Boards. (Constituting *Verve, No. 37/38.*) $5,000.

CHAGALL, Marc (illustrator). *Illustrations for the Bible.* New York (or Paris), 1956. Edited by Jean Wahl. Translated by Samuel Beckett from the Paris title of the same year (*Eaux-fortes pour la Bible*). 29 lithographs (17 in color), 105 plates. Pictorial boards in color. $4,500. (This is *Verve, No. 33/34,* issued in French and in English.)

CHAGALL, Marc (illustrator). *The Jerusalem Windows.* (French: *Vitraux pour Jerusalem.*) New York (or Monte Carlo), 1962. Text by Jean Leymarie. $1,500.

CHAGALL, Marc (illustrator). *The Lithographs of Chagall.* Monte Carlo and New York or Boston, 1960–84. Text by Fernand Mourlot. 27 original lithographs. 5 vols. Quarto, cloth. $6,000.

CHAINBEARER (The), or, The Littlepage Manuscripts. London, 1845. (By James Fenimore Cooper.) 3 vols. $500. New York, 1845. 2 vols. Wraps. $750. (Note: Name is misspelled "Fennimore" on front cover.)

CHALLONER, Bishop Richard. *The True Principles of a Catholic . . .* Philadelphia, 1789. $500.

CHALMERS, George. *The Life of Thomas Ruddimann, A.M., The Keeper, for Almost Fifty Years, of the Library . . .* London, 1794. $400.

CHAMBERS, Andrew Jackson. *Recollections.* No place (1947). 40 pages, stapled. $175.

CHAMBERS, Charles E. S. *Golfing: A Handbook* . . . Edinburgh, 1887. $1,250.

CHAMBERS, Robert. *A Few Rambling Remarks on Golf* . . . Edinburgh, 1862. Illustrated Wraps. $7,500, although a copy in half morocco brought $11,600 at auction in 1989.

CHAMBERS, Robert W. *In the Quarter.* Chicago, 1893. Author's first book. $600.

CHAMBERS, Robert W. *The King in Yellow.* Chicago, 1895. Green cloth with lizard design (preferred binding, perhaps earliest). $600. Second binding. $450.

CHAMBERS, Robert W. *The Red Republic: A Romance of the Commune.* New York, 1895. Pictorial cloth. $250.

CHAMISSO, Adelbert von. *A Sojourn at San Francisco Bay 1816.* San Francisco, 1936. Grabhorn printing. One of 250 copies. $150.

CHAMPION, Joseph. *The Young Penman's Daily Practice* . . . (London) 1759. $350.

CHANDLER, Francis W. *Municipal Architecture in Boston,* . . . Boston, 1898. 2 vols. $1,250.

CHANDLER, Raymond. *The Big Sleep.* New York, 1939. Author's first book. $12,500. London (1939). $3,000. San Francisco, 1986. 425 copies. $500.

CHANDLER, Raymond. *Farewell, My Lovely.* New York, 1940. $8,500. London (1940). $1,500.

CHANDLER, Raymond. *The High Window.* New York, 1942. $6,000. London (1943). $1,500.

CHANDLER, Raymond. *The Lady in the Lake.* New York, 1943. $7,500. London (1944). $1,500.

CHANDLER, Raymond. *The Little Sister.* London (1949). $2,500. Boston, 1949. $1,500.

CHANDLER, Raymond. *The Long Good-Bye.* London (1953). $1,750. Boston, 1954. $1,500.

CHANDLER, Raymond. *Playback.* London (1958). $500. Boston, 1958. $350.

CHANDLER, Raymond. *The Smell of Fear.* London (1965). $450.

CHANDLESS, William. *A Visit to Salt Lake: Being a Journey Across the Plains and a Residence in the Mormon Settlements of Utah.* London, 1857. Folding map. $750.

CHANNING, Walter. *A Treatise on Etherization in Childbirth.* Boston, 1848. $1,250.

CHANNING, William Ellery (1780–1842). *The Duties of Children.* Boston, 1807. Author's first book. Wraps. $350.

CHANNING, William Ellery (1780–1842). *A Sermon Delivered at the Ordination of the Rev. Jared Sparks* . . . Baltimore, 1819. $250.

CHANNING, William Ellery (1780–1842). *Slavery.* Boston, 1835. $400.

CHANNING, William Ellery (1818–1901). *John Brown, and the Heroes of Harper's Ferry: A Poem.* Boston, 1886. $350.

CHANTICLEER: A Bibliography of the Golden Cockerel Press. Waltham Saint Lawrence, 1936. One of 300 copies. $400.

CHANUTE, Octave. *Progress in Flying Machines.* New York (1894). 85 illustrations. $1,250. Long Beach, 1976. $50.

CHAPELLE, Howard I. *The Baltimore Clipper.* Salem, Mass., 1930. Cloth. 36 plates and 48 plans. $300. Marbled boards. One of 97 copies (VAB). $450.

CHAPMAN, John Jay. See *The Two Philosophers.*

CHAPMAN, R.W. *Cancels.* London, 1930. One of 500 copies. $200.

CHAPPE D'AUTAEROCHE, Jean. *A Voyage to California, to Observe the Transit of Venus . . .* London, 1778. Folding plan of Mexico City. First English translation from the French of 1772. $2,500.

CHAPPELL, Fred. *It Is Time, Lord.* New York, 1963. $200. London, 1965. $150.

CHAPPELL, Fred. *Renaissance Paper . . .* No place [1962]. Author's first book. Wraps. $200.

CHAPPELL, George S. *Colonial Architecture in Vermont.* New York, 1918. Wraps. $250.

CHARLES Auchester. London, 1853. (By Elizabeth Sara Shepard, her first book.) 3 vols $600.

CHARLES, Will. *The Hombre from Sonora.* (New York), 1971. (By Charles Willeford.) $3,000.

CHARLEVOIX, Francis Xavier. *A Voyage to North America, Under the Command of the Present King of France . . .* Dublin, 1766. 2 vols. 8 folding maps. 2 plates. $4,500.

CHARLEVOIX, Pierre F. X. *Journal of a Voyage to North America.* London, 1761. Folding map. 2 vols. $1,750. Chicago, 1923. One of 200 copies. $300.

CHARLOT, Jean. *Picture Book.* New York, 1933. Illustrated with 32 original multicolor lithographic plates. One of 500 copies signed by Charlot and Lynton R. Kistler, the printer. Wraps. In slipcase. $2,500.

CHARTERIS, Leslie. *Enter the Saint.* London [1930]. $1,500. New York, 1931. $1,000.

CHARTERIS, Leslie. *The Last Hero.* London [1930]. $1,750. New York, 1931. $1,250.

CHARTERIS, Leslie. *Meet the Tiger.* London (1928). 4,500. New York, 1929. $3,000.

CHARTERIS, Leslie. *X Esquire.* London, 1927. (By Charles Bowyer Lin, his first book.) $2,500.

CHASE, Charles M. *The Editor's Run in New Mexico and Colorado.* Lyndon, Vt., 1882. Illustrated. Pictorial wraps. $350.

CHASE, James Hadley. *No Orchids for Miss Blandish.* London, 1939. $1,500. (New York, 1942.) $1,000.

CHASE, Owen (and others). *Narratives of the Wreck of the Whale Ship "Essex."* Golden Cockerel Press. London, 1935. 12 wood engravings by Robert Gibbings. One of 275 copies. Issued without dustwrapper. $1,000.

CHATEAUBRIAND, François A. *Travels in America and Italy* . . . London, 1828. 2 vols. $750.

CHATHAM, Russell. *The Angler's Coast.* Clark City Press (1990). One of 150 signed deluxe copies. In slipcase. $250.

CHATTERTON, E. Keble. *Ship-Models.* London, 1923. Edited by Geoffrey Holme. 142 plates, many in color. One of 1,000 copies. $250.

CHATTERTON, E. Keble. *Steamship Models.* London, 1924. 128 plates, some in color. One of 1,000 signed copies. $350.

CHATTO, William A. See Careless, John.

CHATTO, William A. *A Treatise on Wood Engraving* . . . London, 1839. Engravings by John Jackson. $750. London (1861). $350.

CHATWIN, Bruce. *The Attractions of France.* (London), 1993. One of 10 signed, (Roman-) numbered copies. Issued without dustwrapper. $750. One of 26 signed, lettered copies. $350. One of 175 copies. Wraps. $150.

CHATWIN, Bruce. *In Patagonia.* London, 1977. Author's first book. With map endpapers. $1,250. White endpapers. $1,000. New York (1978). $200.

CHATWIN, Bruce, and THEROUX, Paul. *Patagonia Revisited.* (Great Britain, 1985.) One of 250 copies signed by both authors. Without dustwrapper. $400.

CHAUCER, Daniel. *The New Humpty-Dumpty.* London, 1912. (By Ford Madox Ford.) Brick brown cloth, stamped in black and gilt. Copies seen with both 14 pages or 8 pages of ads at rear. $1,000.

CHAUCER, Geoffrey. *The Canterbury Tales.* (Westminister: Caxton, 1478.) Almost $7,000,000 at auction in 1998. London, 1913. Riccardi Press. Colored plates by W. Russell Flint. 3 vols. Limp vellum, silk ties. One of 500 copies. $750. Also, one of 12 copies on vellum, and with extra plates in cloth portfolio. $5,000 or more. New York, 1930. Illustrated by Rockwell Kent. 2 vols. Pigskin. One of 75 signed copies. $4,000. Another issue, cloth. One of 924 signed copies. $600. Waltham Saint Lawrence: Golden Cockerel Press, 1929–31. 4 vols. Eric Gill engravings. Folio, boards, morocco spine. One of 485 copies. $6,000. One of 15 copies on vellum. In slipcase. $35,000 or more. Limited Editions Club, New York, 1946. Illustrated by Arthur Szyk. Half pigskin. In slipcase. $450. London, 1972. Cloth portfolio with 19 etchings by Elizabeth Frink. One of 50 signed copies. $1,500. One of 175 copies. $750.

CHAUCER, Geoffrey. *Troilus and Criseyde.* Waltham Saint Lawrence: Golden Cockerel Press, 1927. 5 full-page illustrations, 5 half-page decorations, and engraved title page by Eric Gill. Folio, boards, and morocco. One of 219 copies. $7,500. Limited Editions Club, London, 1939. $125.

CHAUCER, Geoffrey. *The Workes* (or *Works*) *of Our Ancient and Learned English Poet, Geffrey Chaucer, Newly Printed.* London (1545?). $10,000 or more. London, 1598. Edited by Thomas Speght. $7,500. London, 1602. Second edition. $4,000. London, 1687. Adds for the first time the conclusions to the Cook's and the Squire's Tale, on the verso of the last leaf. $3,000.

CHAUCER, Geoffrey. *The Works of Geoffrey Chaucer.* London, 1721. Three tales that were previously unprinted. Folio. $2,000. (Hammersmith: Kelmscott Press, 1896.) 425 copies issued in blue paper on boards with paper label on spine. $75,000. 13 copies on vellum. $600,000. 46 copies bound in white pigskin at Doves Bindrey. $150,000. London, 1975. 2 vols. One of 515 copies. $1,750.

CHAVEZ, Fray Angelico. *Eleven Lady Lyrics.* Paterson, 1945. $75.

CHEEVER, Henry T. *The Island World of the Pacific.* Glasgow (1851?). Frontispiece. Calf. $350. New York, 1851. $250.

CHEEVER, John. *The Enormous Radio and Other Stories.* New York, 1953. "I" on copyright page. $450. London, 1953. $200.

CHEEVER, John. *The Housebreaker of Shady Hill and Other Stories.* New York, 1958. $200. London, 1958. $100.

CHEEVER, John. *The Leaves, the Lionfish and the Bear.* Los Angeles, 1980. One of 4 copies with printed name of recipient. $750. One of 26 signed, lettered copies. $450. 300 signed copies. $125.

CHEEVER, John. *Some People, Places and Things That Will Not Appear in My Next Novel.* New York (1961). $200. London, 1961. $125.

CHEEVER, John. *The Wapshot Chronicle.* New York (1957). $250. London, 1957. $150. Franklin Library, 1978. Signed "Limited Edition." $125.

CHEEVER, John. *The Way Some People Live.* New York (1943). Author's first book. $2,000.

CHENG Man-ch'ing and SMITH, Robert W. *T'ai-chi: The Supreme Exercise for Health, Sport, and Self-Defense.* Tokyo, 1967. First edition stated. $200.

CHERRY-GARRARD, Apsley. *The Worst Journey in the World: Antarctic, 1910–1913.* London, 1922. 2 vols. Maps and panoramas, color plates. Boards, paper labels. $2,000. New York (1922). $1,500.

CHESNUTT, Charles W. *The Colonel's Dream.* New York, 1905. Name spelled "Chestnutt" on spine and front. $600. Name spelled correctly. $400. London, 1905. $350.

CHESNUTT, Charles W. *The Conjure Woman.* Boston, 1899. Author's first book. 150 large-paper copies. $1,750 (one in dustwrapper catalogued for $3,700). Trade edition. $600. London, 1899. $600. New York, 1927. $125.

CHESNUTT, Charles W. *Frederick Douglass.* Boston, 1899. Limp leather. $1,250. London, 1899. $450.

CHESNUTT, Charles W. *The House Behind the Cedars.* Boston, 1900. $600.

CHESNUTT, Charles W. *The Wife of His Youth and Other Stories.* Boston, 1899. $750.

CHESTER, Alfred. *Here Be Dragons.* Paris, 1955. Author's first book. Wraps. One of 125 deluxe copies, $450. One of 1,000 copies, $150.

CHESTERFIELD, Lord. *Letters Written by the Late Right Honourable . . . Chesterfield, to his Son, Philip Stanhope, Esq.* London, 1774. 2 vols. $2,500.

CHESTERTON, G. K. *Charles Dickens Fifty Years After.* No place, 1920. Wraps. One of 25 copies. $450.

CHESTERTON, G. K. *Club of Queer Complaints.* London, 1905. $500.

CHESTERTON, G. K. *Collected Poems.* London, 1927. Boards and parchment. One of 350 signed copies. $250.

CHESTERTON, G. K. *The Coloured Lands.* London, 1938. Illustrated by the author. Boards. In dustwrapper. $150.

CHESTERTON, G. K. *Graybeards at Play: Rhymes and Sketches.* London, 1900. Author's first book. $750.

CHESTERTON, G. K. *The Incredulity of Father Brown.* London (1926). $1,500. New York, 1926. $600.

CHESTERTON, G. K. *The Innocence of Father Brown.* London, 1911. Illustrated by S. S. Lucas. Red cloth. $750. New York, 1911. $350.

CHESTERTON, G. K. *London.* London, 1914. 10 tipped-in photogravure plates by Alvin Langdon Coburn. $450.

CHESTERTON, G. K. *The Poet and the Lunatics.* London, 1929. $1,250.

CHESTERTON, G. K. *The Scandal of Father Brown.* London (1935). $1,250. New York, 1935. $450.

CHESTERTON, G. K. *The Secret of Father Brown.* London (1927). $1,500. New York, 1927. $750.

CHESTERTON, G. K. *The Wisdom of Father Brown.* London, 1914. $350. New York, 1915. $150.

CHEW, Beverly. *Essays & Verses About Books.* New York, privately printed, 1926. Limited to 275 copies. (Printed by D. B. Updike at Merrymount Press.) $75.

CHICAGO Illustrated. (Cover title.) (Chicago, 1866–67.) 52 tinted lithograph views. Text by James W. Sheahan. Oblong folio, morocco. Jevne and Almini, publishers. First edition, second issue. $15,000. (The original issue was in 13 parts and is now very rare.) New York, 1952. 12 plates. Portfolio. Reprint edition. $500.

CHIDSEY, Donald Barr. *John the Great: The Times and Life of a Remarkable American, John L. Sullivan.* Garden City, 1942. $100.

CHILD, Andrew. *Overland Route to California.* Milwaukee, 1852. Full leather. $7,500.

CHILD, Lydia Maria. See *Emily Parker; Evenings in New England; The First Settlers in New England; The Frugal Housewife; Hobomok.*

CHILD, Lydia Maria. *An Appeal in Favor of That Class of Americans Called Africans.* Boston, 1833. Errata slip and tipped-in frontispiece. $2,750.

CHILDERS, Erskine. *The Riddle of the Sands.* London, 1903. $6,000. New York, 1915. $500.

CHILDRESS, Alice. *Like One of the Family.* Brooklyn (1956). Author's first book. One of 100 copies. In slipcase. $300. Trade. $150.

CHILDS, C. G. (engraver). *Views in Philadelphia and Its Vicinity.* Philadelphia, 1827–(30). Engraved title page, plan, 24 engraved views. $2,000.

CHINESE Poems. London, 1916. (By Arthur Waley, his first book.) Wraps. (About 50 copies.) $4,500.

CHIPPENDALE, Thomas. *The Gentleman and Cabinetmaker's Director.* London, 1754. Engraved dedication and 161 plates. $12,500. London, 1755. $10,000. London, 1762. Engraved dedication and 200 plates. $7,500. New York, 1938. Folio, cloth. A sketch of Chippendale's Life and Works by Walter Rendell Storey. With more than 400 plates. $350.

CHITTENDEN, Hiram M. *The American Fur Trade of the Far West.* New York, 1902. 3 vols. Folding map, plan, 3 facsimiles, 6 plates. Green cloth. $1,500. New York, 1935. 2 vols. Plates. In slipcase. $450.

CHITTENDEN, Hiram M. *History of Early Steamboat Navigation on the Missouri River.* New York, 1903. 16 plates. 2 vols. One of 950 copies. $600.

CHIVERS, Thomas Holley. *The Lost Pleiad and Other Poems.* New York, 1845. Printed tan wraps. $750.

CHIVERS, Thomas Holley. *Memoralia.* Philadelphia, 1853. Boards. $400.

CHIVERS, Thomas Holley. *Nacoochee: or, The Beautiful Star.* New York, 1837. $400.

CHIVERS, Thomas Holley. *The Path of Sorrow.* Franklin (Tenn.), 1832. Author's first book. $1,250.

CHOMSKY, Noam. *Syntactic Structures.* (The Hague) 1957. Wraps. $450.

CHOPIN, Kate. *At Fault.* St. Louis, 1890. Author's first book. Wraps. $4,000.

CHOPIN, Kate. *The Awakening.* Chicago, 1899. Decorated cloth covers. $3,000.

CHOPIN, Kate. *Death Comes as the End.* Boston, 1894. $1,250.

CHRISTIANISM: Or Belief and Unbelief Reconciled. (London, 1832.) (By Leigh Hunt.) 59 pages, in original cloth, paper label. (75 copies printed.) $1,250.

CHRISTIE, Agatha. *Hercule Poirot's Christmas.* London (1939). $5,000.

CHRISTIE, Agatha. *The Hound of Death and Other Stories.* London: Odams (1933). $1,250. London, no date [1937]. Odahms' sheets with Collins title page. $300.

CHRISTIE, Agatha. *The Man in the Brown Suit.* London, 1924. $3,500. New York, 1924. $2,500.

CHRISTIE, Agatha. *Murder for Christmas: A Poirot Story.* New York, 1939. U.S. title for *Hercule Poirot's Christmas.* $2,500.

CHRISTIE, Agatha. *Murder in Mesopotamia.* London (1936). $7,500. New York, 1936. $3,000.

CHRISTIE, Agatha. *Murder in the Calais Coach.* New York, 1934. U.S. title for *Murder on the Orient Express.* $2,000.

CHRISTIE, Agatha. *Murder of Roger Ackroyd.* London, 1926. $8,500. New York, 1926. $3,500.

CHRISTIE, Agatha. *Murder on the Links.* London, 1923. $8,500. New York, 1923. $5,000.

CHRISTIE, Agatha. *Murder on the Orient Express.* London (1934). $17,500. New York, 1934. $7,500. (Reportedly there was a presentation edition under this title. For U.S. trade edition, see *Murder in the Calais Coach* above.)

CHRISTIE, Agatha. *The Mysterious Affair at Styles.* New York, 1920. Author's first book. In dustwrapper. $25,000 or more. Without dustwrapper. $4,000. London, 1921. In dustwrapper. $25,000. Without dustwrapper. $5,000.

CHRISTIE, Agatha. *Sad Cypress.* London [1940]. $2,500. New York, 1940. $1,000.

CHRISTIE, Agatha. *Secret Adversary.* London, 1922. $8,500. New York, 1922. $5,000.

CHRONICLES of the City of Gotham. New York, 1830. (By James Kirke Paulding.) $350.

CHUBB, Ralph. *Manhood.* Curridge, 1924. Author's first book. Wraps. One of 45 copies on handmade paper. $600. Regular edition (200 copies?). $250.

CHURCHILL, Sir Winston S. *Addresses Delivered in the Year 1940 to the People of Great Britain.* London, 1940. Wraps. $350. New York, 1940. Wraps. $350. Los Angeles, 1964. Morocco. $600.

CHURCHILL, Sir Winston S. *Amid These Storms.* New York, 1932. U.S. title of *Thoughts and Adventures.* $1,000.

CHURCHILL, Sir Winston S. *Arms and the Covenant: Speeches.* London, 1938. Dark-blue cloth, top edge stained blue. In red on yellow dustwrapper. $1,250. First issue sheets used in a "cheap" edition. In blue dustwrapper. $750.

CHURCHILL. Sir Winston S. *Beating the Invader.* (London, 1941.) Single leaf, printed on both sides. (There is a later issue, overprinted in red in the top left-hand corner, regarding the evacuation of invaded areas. Both issues dated 5/41.) $750.

CHURCHILL, Sir Winston S. *Great Contemporaries.* London (1937). Dark-blue buckram, top edge stained blue. $1,000. New York, 1937. $500. London: Butterworth (1938). "Revised Edition 1938." $450. London: Macmillan, 1943. (Omits articles on Trotsky and Roosevelt.) $300.

CHURCHILL, Sir Winston S. *Ian Hamilton's March.* London, 1900. Dark-red cloth, black endpapers. Folding map tipped in preceding 4 pages of ads, then 32–page catalogue on thinner paper. $1,250. New York, 1900. $750.

CHURCHILL, Sir Winston S. *India: Speeches.* London (1931). Orange cloth. $1,500. Orange wraps with price of 1/-net (second printing in green wraps. No other difference). $850.

CHURCHILL, Sir Winston S. *Liberalism and the Social Problem.* London, 1909. Plum buckram. $1,250. New York: Hodder and Stoughton, 1909. To protect copyright. $2,500. New York, 1910. $1,000.

CHURCHILL, Sir Winston S. *London to Ladysmith via Pretoria.* London, 1900. Maps and plans. Fawn-colored cloth. $1,250. "New Impression" added to title page. $500. New York, 1900. $750. Toronto (1900). Smooth light-brown cloth. $600.

CHURCHILL, Sir Winston S. *Lord Randolph Churchill.* London, 1906. 2 vols. $850. New York, 1906. 2 vols. $600.

CHURCHILL, Sir Winston S. *Marlborough: His Life and Times.* London (1933–38). 4 vols. Vol. 1 is signed. 155 copies issued of each volume. In slipcases (label on slipcase of vol. 1 has number of set). The set. $15,000. Trade edition. 4 vols. $2,500. New York, 1933–38. 6 vols. $2,000.

CHURCHILL, Sir Winston S. *My African Journey.* London, 1908. Pictorial red cloth. $1,500. New York: Hodder & Stoughton, 1908. To protect copyright. $2,000. New York: Doran (1909). $2,000.

CHURCHILL, Sir Winston S. *My Early Life.* London, 1930. With boxed list of 11 of Churchill's works on verso of half title. $1,500. Second issue adds 12th title, *The World Crisis.* $1,000.

CHURCHILL, Sir Winston S. *The People's Rights.* London (1910). Cherry-red cloth. Index at rear. $2,000. Wraps. Published simultaneously. $1,250. Second issue with index deleted and a second appendix added. $1,000. New York (1971). $100.

CHURCHILL, Sir Winston S. *The River War.* London, 1899. 2 vols. $7,500. New York, 1899. $6,000. London, 1902. "New and Revised Edition." 1 vol. 40–page catalogue at rear. $1,500.

CHURCHILL, Sir Winston S. *A Roving Commission.* New York, 1930. U.S. title for *My Early Life.* $750.

CHURCHILL, Sir Winston S. *Savrola.* New York, 1900. Dark-blue cloth. (Also noted in dark-green cloth.) $2,000. London, 1900. First state without copyright notice. $2,250. Second state with copyright notice. $1,000. Colonial Edition. $1,000. London (1908). First illustrated edition. Wraps. $500. New York (1956). New foreword. $150.

CHURCHILL, Sir Winston S. *Step by Step, 1936–1939.* London, 1939. Green cloth. $1,000. New York, 1939. $500.

CHURCHILL, Sir Winston S. *The Story of the Malakand Field Force.* London, 1898. $6,000. Second state, errata slip tipped in immediately preceding first folding map. $5,000. Colonial Library edition. Front cover and spine have "1897" but actually distributed afterward. $2,500.

CHURCHILL, Sir Winston S. *Thoughts and Adventures.* London (1932). Sandy-brown cloth. $1,500.

CHURCHILL, Sir Winston S. *While England Slept.* New York, 1938. Blue cloth with top edge stained red. U.S. title for *Arms and the Covenant.* $250. (Believe there was a large Book-of-the Month Club edition without price on dustwrapper.)

CHURCHILL, Sir Winston S. *The World Crisis.* London, 1923–31. 6 vols. In dustwrapper. $6,000. Without dustwrappers. $1,500. New York, 1923–31. 6 vols. In dustwrapper. $3,000. Without dustwrappers. $600.

CHURTON, Henry. *Toinette.* New York, 1874. (By Albion W. Tourgee, his first novel.) $250.

CHUTE, Carolyn. *The Beans of Egypt, Maine.* New York, 1985. Author's first book. $300.

CINCINNATUS. *Travels on the Western Slope of the Mexican Cordillera.* San Francisco, 1857. (By Marvin T. Wheat.) Engraved title page. Cloth. $500.

CINDERELLA. Retold by C. S. Evans. London, 1919. Frontispiece in color and numerous silhouette illustrations by Arthur Rackham. One of 525 copies. Half cloth. In dustwrapper. $2,000. Half vellum; one of 325 copies on Japan vellum, signed by Rackham, with an extra plate. $3,000.

CISNEROS, Sandra. *The House on Mango Street.* Houston, 1984. Wraps. $250. New York, 1994. Cloth. $50.

CLAMPITT, Amy. *Multitudes, Multitudes.* New York (1973). Author's first book. Wraps. $400.

CLANCY, Tom. *Armored Cav.* New York (1994). One of 150 signed copies. Issued without dustwrapper. In slipcase. $300.

CLANCY, Tom. *The Hunt for Red October.* Annapolis (1984). Author's first book. No statement of edition, no series of numbers on copyright page, weighing two pounds, and no price on dustwrapper. (Book club edition matches this description but weighs one pound and printed at Berryville, Va.) $1,000. London, 1985. $400.

CLANCY, Tom. *Submarine.* New York (1993). One of 300 signed copies. Issued without dustwrapper. In slipcase. $250.

CLAPCOTT, C. B. *Rules of the Ten Oldest Golf Clubs.* Edinburgh, 1935. One of 500 copies. Wraps. $750.

CLAPPE, Louise A.K.S. *California in 1851 (in 1852): The Dame Shirley Letters.* San Francisco, 1933. 2 vols. Grabhorn printing. One of 500 copies. $350.

CLAPPERTON, R. H. *Paper, An Historical Account of Its Making by Hand from the Earliest Times Down to the Present Day.* Oxford, 1934. One of 250 copies. $1,750.

CLAPPERTON, R. H. *The Paper-Making Machine, Its Invention, Evolution and Development.* Oxford (1967). 18 foldout plates. $350.

CLARE, John. *Poems Descriptive of Rural Life . . .* London, 1820. Author's first book. $1,750.

CLARE, John. *The Village Minstrel and Other Poems.* London, 1821. 2 vols. $500.

CLARK, Charles E. *Prince and Boatswain: Sea Tales from the Recollection of Rear-Admiral Charles E. Clark.* Greenfield, Mass. (1915). (Edited by John P. Marquand and James M. Morgan.) Marquand's first book. Blue cloth. $250.

CLARK, Charles M. *A Trip to Pike's Peak and Notes by the Way.* Chicago, 1861. Frontispiece, 18 woodcuts. $2,500.

CLARK, Daniel. *Proofs of the Corruption of Gen. James Wilkinson, and of His Connexion with Aaron Burr.* Philadelphia, 1809. $1,000.

CLARK, Daniel. *Railway Machinery . . .* London, 1860–62. 2 vols. $750.

CLARK, Daniel M. *The Southern Calculator, or Compendious Arithmetic.* Lagrange, Ga., 1844. Boards. $250.

CLARK, John Willis. *The Care of Books: An Essay on the Development of Libraries and Their Fittings* . . . Cambridge, 1901. $350. Cambridge,1909. Second edition. $200.

CLARK, Larry. *Tulsa (Photographs).* (New York, 1971.) Author's first book. Stiff wraps. $1,500. (New York, 1979.) Hardback in dustwrapper. $1,000.

CLARK, Mary Higgins. *Aspire to the Heavens.* New York (1968). Author's first book. $500.

CLARK, Mary Higgins. *Where Are the Children?* New York, 1975. $250. London (1975). $250.

CLARK, Robert. *Golf: A Royal & Ancient Game.* Edinburgh, 1875. One of 50 large-paper copies. $7,500. Trade edition. $3,000. Edinburgh, 1893. Second edition. Large paper. $750.

CLARK, Roland. *Gunner's Dawn.* New York: Derrydale Press, 1937. Signed frontispiece. Leatherette. One of 950 copies. In slipcase. $750. One of 50 signed copies with 8 signed engravings. $4,500.

CLARK, Roland. *Pot Luck.* West Hartford, Vt. (1945). Illustrated, including signed frontispiece etching. Half leather. One of 150 copies. $450. Another issue, one of 460 signed. In slipcase. $250. Trade edition. $100.

CLARK, Roland. *Roland Clark's Etchings.* New York: Derrydale Press (1938). Illustrated, with a signed frontispiece etching. Folio, cloth. One of 800 copies. In slipcase. $1,250. Half morocco. One of 50 (presentation) copies with 2 signed etchings. $5,000.

CLARK, Stanley. *The Life and Adventures of the American Cowboy.* (Providence) 1897. Illustrated. Pictorial wraps. $1,750. Another edition, title changed to *True Life in the Far West by the American Cowboy.* Wraps with author's photo. (Providence, about 1898?) $750.

CLARK, Thomas D. *Travels in the Old South, A Bibliography.* Norman (1956–59). 3 vols. $350. Norman (1969). 3 vols. In slipcase. $350.

CLARK, Tom. *Airplanes.* (Essex, England), 1966. Wraps. One of 4 signed, numbered copies. $500. Trade edition. $75.

CLARK, Tom. *The Sand Burg.* London (1966). Wraps. One of 60 signed copies. $300. Trade edition. (440 copies.) $75.

CLARK, Tom. *To Give a Painless Light.* No place, 1963. Author's first book. Typescript carbon (3 copies). $1,000.

CLARK, Walter (editor). *Histories of the Several Regiments and Battalions from North Carolina in the Great War, 1861–1865.* Raleigh, 1901. 5 vols. Plates. $750.

CLARK, Walter Van Tilburg. *Christmas Comes to Hjalsen.* Reno, 1930. Author's first book. Pictorial wraps. In original mailing envelope. $600.

CLARK, Walter Van Tilburg. *The Ox-Bow Incident.* New York (1940). $1,250.

CLARK, Walter Van Tilburg. *Ten Women in Gale's House.* Boston (1932). First edition not stated. $600.

CLARKE, A. B. *Travels in Mexico and California.* Boston, 1852. Printed tan wraps. $2,750. Cloth. $2,500.

CLARKE, Arthur C. *Against the Fall of Night.* Gnome Press, 1953. $300.

CLARKE, Arthur C. *Earthlight.* New York (1955). Cloth. $750. Wraps. $75. London, 1955. $450.

CLARKE, Arthur C. *Expedition to Earth.* New York (1953). Cloth. $650. Wraps. $50.

CLARKE, Arthur C. *A Fall of Moondust.* New York (1961). $300. London, 1961. $150.

CLARKE, Arthur C. *Interplanetary Flight.* London, 1950. Author's first book. $600. New York (1951). $300.

CLARKE, Arthur C. *Rendezvous with Rama.* London, 1973. Green boards. $500. New York (1973). $150.

CLARKE, Arthur C. *2001: A Space Odyssey.* New York, 1968. $1,250. London, 1968. $450.

CLARKE, Austin. *The Vengeance of Fiona.* Dublin, 1917. Author's first book. $450.

CLARKE, H. C. *The Confederate States Almanac, and Repository of Useful Knowledge, for 1862.* Vicksburg, 1861. Wraps. $450.

CLARKE, Mrs. J. Sterling. *The Ladies' Equestrian Guide.* London (1857). 8 plates (including the frontispiece). Green cloth, ornately gilt with a figure of a woman on horseback (the author's name only appears on the cover). $750.

CLARKE, Lewis. *Narrative of the Sufferings of Lewis Clarke During a Captivity of More Than Twenty-five Years.* Boston, 1845. Portrait. Wraps. $2,000.

CLARKE, Lewis, and CLARKE, Milton. *Narrative of the Sufferings of Lewis Clarke During a Captivity of More Than Twenty-five Years.* Boston, 1846. Adds brother's narrative. Cloth boards. $1,250.

CLARKSON, Thomas. *An Essay on the Slavery* . . . London, 1786. $1,500. Philadelphia, 1786. $1,250.

CLARKSON, Thomas. *The History of the Rise, Progress, and Accomplishment of the Abolition of the African Slave-Trade* . . . London, 1808. 2 vols. 3 plates, two folding. $1,500.

CLASS Poem. (Cambridge, Mass.) 1838. (By James Russell Lowell.) Author's first published work. Printed wraps. $1,500.

CLAVELL, James. *King Rat.* Boston (1962). Author's first book. $750. London (1963). $200.

CLAVELL, James. *Tai-Pan: A Novel of Hong Kong.* New York, 1966. $150. London, 1966. $100. (May precede.)

CLAY, John. *My Life on the Range.* Chicago (1924). $600.

CLAYTON, W(illiam). *The Latter-Day Saints' Emigrants' Guide.* St. Louis, 1848. 24 pages, plain wraps. $6,000.

CLELAND, John. See *Memoirs of a Coxcomb.*

CLEMENS, Samuel Langhorne, See Twain, Mark. See also *Date 1601; What Is Man?*

CLEMENT, Hal. *Needle.* Garden City, 1950. Author's first book. $250.

CLERIHEW, E. *Biography for Beginners.* London (1905). (By E. C. Bentley, his first book.) Illustrated by G. K. Chesterton. Wraps. $400.

CLERK, N. W. *A Grief Observed.* London, 1961. (By C. S. Lewis.) $450.

CLEVELAND, H. W. S. *Landscape Architecture . . .* Chicago, 1873. $600.

CLEVELAND, Henry W. *Village and Farm Cottages . . . American Village Homes.* New York, 1856. Frontispiece, plates. $500.

CLEVELAND, Richard J. *A Narrative of Voyages and Commercial Enterprises.* Cambridge, Mass., 1842. 2 vols. $1,250.

CLOCKMAKER (The); or the Sayings . . . Halifax, 1836. (By Thomas Chandler Haliburton.) $750. Philadelphia, 1839–40. 3 vols. $250. Boston, 1838. $200.

CLOUGH, A. H. *A Consideration of Objections Against . . .* Oxford, 1847. Author's first book. Wraps. $600. (Two previous pamphlets at Rugby.)

CLUM, Woodworth. *Apache Agent: The Story of John P. Clum.* Boston, 1936. Illustrated, including frontispiece in color of Geronimo. $200.

CLUTTERBUCK, Captain. *The Monastery.* Edinburgh, 1820. (By Sir Walter Scott.) 3 vols. $450.

CLYMER, W. B., and GREEN, Charles R. *Robert Frost: A Bibliography.* Amherst, 1937. Limited to 650 copies. $350. One of 150 copies signed by Frost. $1,000.

CLYTEMNESTRA . . . (By Edward Robert Bulwer-Lytton.) London, 1855. Author's first book. $750.

COATES, Robert M. *The Eater of Darkness.* (Paris), Contact Editions (1926). Author's first book. Wraps, paper labels. $750. New York, 1929. $450.

COATES, Robert M. *The Outlaw Years.* New York: Macaulay (1930). $300.

COATES, Robert M. *Yesterday's Burdens.* New York (1933). $300.

COBB, Humphrey. *Paths of Glory.* New York, 1935. First dustwrapper blank on verso $200. Second with comments on verso. $150. London (1935). $150. His only book.

COBB, Irvin S. *Back Home.* New York (1912). Author's first book. First printing with "Plimpton Press" slug on copyright page, and first binding, with publisher's name in 3 lines on spine. $75.

COBBETT, Thomas B. *Colorado Mining Directory.* Denver, 1879. $750.

COBBETT, William. *Rural Rides . . .* London, 1830. Woodcut map. $1,000.

COBDEN-SANDERSON, T. J. *Amantium Irae: Letters to Two Friends, 1864–1867.* Hammer-smith (London), 1914. Doves Press. Frontispiece portrait. Limp vellum. One of 150 copies. $850. In a Doves binding of morocco. $2,500.

COBDEN-SANDERSON, T. J. *Credo.* London, 1908. Doves Press. One of 250 copies. $500.

COBDEN-SANDERSON, T. J. *The Ideal Book or Book Beautiful.* London: Doves Press, 1900. Vellum. One of 300 copies. $750. One of 10 copies on vellum. $5,000.

COBURN, Alvin Langdon. See Wells, H. G.

COBURN, Alvin Langdon. *London.* New York/London (1909). Introduction by Hilaire Bel-loc. 20 tipped-in Coburn photogravures. Folio, boards. $6,000. London, 1914. $600.

COBURN, Alvin Langdon. *Men of Mark.* London, 1913. With 33 tipped-in photogravures. $1,750.

COBURN, Alvin Langdon. *More Men of Mark.* London (1922). With 33 mounted collotype portraits. $750. New York, 1922. $600.

COBURN, Alvin Langdon. *New York.* London and New York (1910). 20 tipped-in pho-togravures. Folio. Foreword by H. G. Wells. $9,500.

COBURN, Alvin Langdon. *A Portfolio of Sixteen Photographs.* Rochester (1962). One of 200 copies. Portfolio with text in wraps laid in. $500. Rochester (1963). One of 2,000 copies. $250.

COBURN, Wallace D. *Rhymes from the Round-up Camp.* (Great Falls, Mont.), 1899. 8 Charles M. Russell drawings. Limp pictorial morocco. First issue, with "the" instead of "a" in title. $3,000. Second issue, with "a." $2,000. Second edition. $500.

COCHRANE, Charles Stuart. *Journal of a Residence and Travels in Colombia.* London, 1825. 2 vols. $1,500.

COCKBURN, Catherine Trotter. See *Agnes de Castro.*

COCKERELL, S. C. (editor). *Laudes Beatae Mariae Virginis.* London: Kelmscott Press, 1896. Printed in red, black, and blue. Boards and linen. One of 250 copies. $1,500. One of 10 copies on vellum. $5,000.

COCKERELL, S. C. (editor). *Some German Woodcuts of the 15th Century.* London: Kelmscott Press, 1897. 35 reproductions. Boards and linen. One of 225 copies. $1,500. One of 8 copies on vellum. $6,000.

COCKTON, Henry. *The Life and Adventures of Valentine Vox . . .* London (1840). Author's first book. $200.

COCTEAU, Jean. *Orphée.* London, 1933. First edition in English. Translated by Carl Wildman. Frontispiece by Pablo Picasso. Boards. One of 100 copies signed by Cocteau and Picasso. $2,500. London, 1953. One of 100 copies. $1,000.

CODY, Liza. *Dupe.* London (1980). $750.

COESTLER, A. See Costler, Dr. A.

COETZEE, J. M. *Dusklands.* Johannesburg, 1974. Author's first book. $400. New York (1985). Wraps. $100.

COFF, Geoffrey. *Murder in the Senate.* New York, 1935. (By Van Wyck Mason.) $600.

COFFEY, Brian. *Blood Risk.* Indianapolis, 1973. (By Dean Koontz.) $350.

COFFEY, Brian. *The Face of Fear.* Indianapolis (1977). (By Dean Koontz.) Dustwrapper. $300.

COFFIN, Joshua. *A Sketch of the History of Newbury, Newburyport, and West Newbury.* Boston, 1845. Map, tables. $175.

COFFIN, Peter. *The Search for My Great Uncle's Head.* New York, 1937. (By Jonathan Latimer.) $750.

COFFINBERRY, Andrew. *Forest Rangers.* Columbus, 1842. Wraps. $500.

COGHLAN, Margaret. *Memoirs of Mrs. Coghlan . . .* London, 1794. 2 vols. $750.

COGSWELL, Joseph Green. *Life of Joseph Green Cogswell as Sketched in His Letters.* New York, 1874. Tipped-in photograph frontispiece. One of 322 copies. $300.

COHEN, Leonard. *Let Us Compare Mythologies.* Montreal (1956). Author's first book. $1,500.

COHN, Albert M. *A Bibliographical Catalogue of the Printed Works Illustrated by George Cruikshank.* London, 1914. $300.

COHN, Albert M. *George Cruikshank:A Catalogue Raisonné.* London, 1924. One of 500 copies. $500.

COHN, David L. *New Orleans and Its Living Past.* Boston, 1941. One of 1,000 signed copies. Signed by Cohn and the artist, Clarence John Laughlin (his first book). $750.

COKE, Henry J. *A Ride Over the Rocky Mountains to Oregon and California.* London, 1852. $450.

COLBERT, E. *Chicago: Historical and Statistical Sketch of the Garden City.* Chicago, 1868. 120 pages, wraps. $300.

COLE, G.D.H. *The Brooklyn Murders.* London, 1923. Author's first book. $1,250.

COLE, George Watson. *Catalogue of Books Relating to the Discovery and Early History of North and South America . . .* New York, 1907. 5 Vols. One of 150 copies. $1,500. New York, 1951. 5 vols. Reprint. $250.

COLERIDGE, Hartley. *Poems.* (Vol. 1, all published.) Leeds, 1833. Author's first book. $600.

COLERIDGE, Samuel T. See *Lyrical Ballads.*

COLERIDGE, Samuel T. *Biographia Literaria.* London, 1817. 2 vols. $1,000.

COLERIDGE, Samuel T. *Christabel: Kubla Khan, A Vision: The Pains of Sleep.* London, 1816. Wraps. First issue, with 4 pages of February ads at back, and with a half title. $3,500. With

March ads. $2,500. London: Eragny Press, 1904. Colored frontispiece. Boards. One of 226 copies on paper. $1,500. One of 10 copies on vellum. $6,000. Boston, 1816. $1,500.

COLERIDGE, Samuel T. *The Fall of Robespierre*. London, 1794. Author's first book. Written with Robert Southey. $12,500.

COLERIDGE, Samuel T. *Notes, Theological, Political, and Miscellaneous*. London, 1853. $250.

COLERIDGE, Samuel T. *Osorio: A Tragedy*. London, 1873. $250.

COLERIDGE, Samuel T. *Poems Chosen Out of the Works of Samuel Taylor Coleridge*. London: Kelmscott Press, 1896. Woodcut borders and initial letters. Vellum. One of 300 copies. $2,500. One of 8 copies on vellum. $8,000.

COLERIDGE, Samuel Taylor. *Remorse: A Tragedy in Five Acts*. London, 1813. $750.

COLERIDGE, Samuel T. *The Rime of the Ancient Mariner*. New York, 1877. Illustrated by Gustave Doré. $1,000. London: Vale Press, 1899. Illustrated by Charles Ricketts. Boards. One of 210 copies. $2,000. London: Essex House, 1903. Frontispiece. One of 150 copies on Japan vellum. $1,500. London (1910). Illustrated by Willy Pogany. Calf. One of 525 copies signed by Pogany. $1,000. One of 25 copies in Japan vellum. $5,000. Clothbound. $500. Bristol, England, 1929. 10 engravings by David Jones. Canvas. One of 60 copies with extra set of engravings, signed by the artist. $5,000. Boards and cloth. One of 400 copies signed by Jones. $1,250. London: Corvinus Press, 1944. Half buckram. One of 21 copies. $2,000.

COLERIDGE, Samuel T. *Sibylline Leaves: A Collection of Poems*. London, 1817. With errata leaf. $2,500.

COLERIDGE, Samuel T. *Specimens of the Table Talk of the Late Samuel Taylor Coleridge*. London, 1835. Frontispiece. 2 vols. $450. New York, 1835. $350.

COLERIDGE, Samuel T. *Zapolya*. London, 1817. $1,500.

COLES, Manning. *Drink to Yesterday*. London (1940). (By Cyril Henry Coles and Adelaide Manning, their first book.) $750. New York, 1941. $250.

COLETTE. *The Vagrant*. London, 1912. Author's first book. $750.

COLLECTED *Catalogues of Dr. A.S.W. Rosenbach, 1904–1951 (The)*. New York (1967). 10 vols. $600.

COLLECTION *of Book Plate Designs by Louis Rhead*. Boston, 1907. Limited to 150 copies. $450.

COLLECTION *of Familiar Quotations (A)*. Cambridge, Mass., 1855. (By John Bartlett.) $600.

COLLECTION *of Receipts . . . (A)*. Philadelphia, 1958. First book of Henry Morris (Bird & Bull Press). $1,250.

COLLES, Christopher. *A Survey of the Roads of the United States of America*. (New York), 1789. Engraved title and 83 map sheets in portfolio. $45,000.

COLLIER, Jane. See *Essay on the Art of Ingeniously Tormenting*.

COLLIER, John. *Green Thoughts.* London, 1932. One of 50 signed presentation copies. In glassine dustwrapper. $500. One of 550 signed copies. With errata slip. $150.

COLLIER, John. *His Monkey Wife.* London, 1930. Author's first book. $750. New York, 1931. $500.

COLLIER, John. *Pictures in the Fire.* London, 1958. $125.

COLLIER, John. *Tom's A-Cold.* London, 1933. $300.

COLLIER, John. *Witch's Money.* New York, 1948. One of 350 signed copies. In glassine dustwrapper. $300.

COLLINS, Charles. *Collins' History and Directory of the Black Hills.* Central City, Dakota Territory, 1878. 91 pages, printed yellow wraps. $3,000.

COLLINS, Charles (compiler). *Collins' Omaha Directory.* (Omaha, 1866.) Printed boards. $1,250.

COLLINS, David. *An Account of the English Colony in New South Wales.* London, 1798–1802. 2 vols. 34 maps, plans and plates. $15,000. London, 1804. $4,500.

COLLINS, Dennis. *The Indians' Last Fight; or, the Dull Knife Raid.* (Girard, Kan., about 1915.) 8 plates. Cloth. $500.

COLLINS, John S. *Across the Plains in '64.* Omaha, 1904. Pictorial cloth. $450.

COLLINS, Mrs. Nat. *The Cattle Queen of Montana.* St. James, Minn., 1894. Compiled by Charles Wallace. Illustrated. Stiff wraps. $17,500. Spokane (about 1898–1902). Plates. Pictorial wraps with cloth spine. $3,500.

COLLINS, Wilkie. *After Dark.* London, 1856. 2 vols. $1,500.

COLLINS, Wilkie. *Antonina.* London, 1850. 3 vols. Author's first novel. Cloth. $3,000. New York, 1850. $750.

COLLINS, Wilkie. *The Dead Secret.* London, 1857. 2 vols. $1,750.

COLLINS, Wilkie. *The Evil Genius.* London, 1886. 3 vols. First English edition. $1,500.

COLLINS, Wilkie. *The Law and the Lady.* London, 1875. 3 vols. $2,000. New York, 1875. First American edition. Illustrated. Wraps. $600.

COLLINS, Wilkie. *Memoirs of the Life of William Collins, R.A.* London, 1848. Author's first book. 2 vols. $1,500.

COLLINS, Wilkie. *Mr. Wray's Cash-Box.* London, 1852. Frontispiece. $1,250.

COLLINS, Wilkie. *The Moonstone: A Romance.* London, 1868. 3 vols. Purple cloth. First issue, with half titles, with misprint "treachesrouly" on page 129 of vol. 2, and with ads in vols. 2 and 3. $15,000. New York, 1868. $1,000. Limited Editions Club, New York, 1959. $100.

COLLINS, Wilkie. *No Name.* London, 1862. 3 vols. Red cloth. $2,500. Boston, 1863. 2 vols. $750.

COLLECTED BOOKS 143

COLLINS, Wilkie. *The Queen of Hearts.* London, 1859. 3 vols. $7,500. New York, 1859. $450.

COLLINS, Wilkie. *The Woman in White.* New York, 1860. Illustrated by John McLenan. Brown cloth. First issue, with the woman on spine in white. $2,000. London, 1860. 3 vols. Cloth. First English edition (published a month after the first American edition), first issue, with ads at end of vol. 3 dated May 1, 1860, with "*The Woman in White* to be published shortly" (catalogued by Heritage Bookshop). Previously it was thought that the book with ads dated August 1, 1860, was the first. $15,000. London, 1861. $400. Limited Editions Club, Woodstock, 1964. $75.

COLLODI, Carlo. *The Story of a Puppet or The Adventures of Pinocchio.* London, 1892. First edition in English. $7,500. New York, 1892. Off-white cloth stamped in blue with matching endpapers and edges. $6,000.

COLMAN, George, the Younger. See Mathers, John.

COLNETT, James. *A Voyage to the South Atlantic . . .* London, 1798. 9 maps and plates. $10,000.

COLOPHON (The): A Book Collector's Quarterly. New York, 1930–50. 48 vols. Boards, including clothbound indexes and *The Annual of Bookmaking.* Complete set. $1,250.

COLT, Harry S., and ALLISON, C. H. *Some Essays on Golf Course Architecture.* London, 1920. $3,500. Without dustwrapper. $1,750.

COLT, Miriam Davis. *Went to Kansas.* Watertown, N.Y., 1862. $650.

COLTON, Calvin. *Tour of the American Lakes.* London, 1833. 2 vols. Boards. $1,250.

COLTON, J. H. (publisher). See *The State of Indiana Delineated.*

COLTON, J. H. (publisher). *Particulars of Routes, Distances, Fares . . .* New York, 1849. 12 pages. (11 of text.) (Caption title.) With Colton's Map of the United States . . . and a Plan of the Gold Region. Map folded into brown cloth covers, with printed paper label; text attached to inside of front cover. First issue, with "longitude West from Greenwich" at top of map. $4,500.

COLTON, James. *Lost on Twilight Road.* Fresno (1964). (By Joseph Hansen.) Author's first book. Wraps. $250.

COLTON, Walter. *Three Years in California.* New York, 1850. Map, 6 portraits, 6 plates, folding facsimile. $500.

COLUMBUS, Christopher. *The Voyages of Christopher Columbus; Being the Journals . . .* London: Argonaut Press, 1930. Translated by Cecil Jane. 5 maps. One of 1,050 copies. $300.

COLWIN, Laurie. *Passion and Affect.* New York (1974). $150.

COMBE, William. See Syntax, Doctor. See also *The Dance of Life; The English Dance of Death; A History of Madeira; Journal of Sentimental Travels, etc.; The History of Johnny Quae Genus.*

COMBS, Leslie. *Narrative of the Life of Gen. Leslie Combs.* (Cover title.) (New York, 1852.) 23 pages, plus errata leaf, wraps. $750. (Washington), 1852. 20 pages, printed wraps. $600.

COMFORT, Will L. *Apache.* New York, 1930. $400.

COMING Race (The). Edinburgh (1871). (By Edward Bulwer-Lytton.) Scarlet-orange cloth, blocked in black and gold. $300.

COMMERCIAL Tourist (The); or, Gentleman Traveller; A Satirical Poem. London, 1822. (By Charles William Hempel.) Frontis and 4 hand-colored plates by Cruikshank. $500.

COMMON Sense. Philadelphia: Robert Bell, 1776. (By Thomas Paine.) 79 pages plus last page with publisher's catalogue. Page 63, line 12, last words "pedling politi-". Page [80], line 3: "There volumes." Pamphlet. $250,000. Second issue. Last words page 63 line 13 "pidling po-". Page [80], line 3: "Three volumes." $175,000. "Second Edition" so stated on title page. 125,000. "Third Edition" so stated on title page. $100,000. For further editions by Bell and Bradford, see Gimbel. Any of the 1776 editions/printings/issues have value.

COMPLETE Art of Boxing According to the Modern Method . . . (The). London, 1788. By an Amateur of Eminence. $2,500.

COMPOSITOR'S Handbook: Designed as a Guide in the Composing Room . . . London, 1854. $350.

COMPTON-BURNETT, Ivy. *Dolores.* Edinburgh, 1911. Author's first book, written with her brother (suppressed by her). $600.

COMPTON-BURNETT, Ivy. *Pastors and Masters.* London, 1925. $300.

CONARD, Howard Louis. *"Uncle Dick" Wootton, the Pioneer Frontiersman of the Rocky Mountain Region.* Chicago, 1890. Portrait, 31 plates. Decorated cloth, or leather and cloth. $600.

CONCISE History of the Origin and Progress of Printing with Practical Instructions to the Trade in General. London, 1770. $450.

CONCLIN, George. *Conclin's New River Guide, or a Gazeteer of All the Towns on the Western Waters.* Cincinnati, 1848. 44 full-page route maps. 128 pages, wraps. $1,500. Cincinnati, 1850. Second edition. $1,000.

CONDER, Josiah. *Landscape Gardening in Japan.* Tokyo, 1893. 2 vols., including supplement. $750.

CONDON, Richard. *The Manchurian Candidate.* New York (1959). $300.

CONEY, John. *Engravings of Ancient Cathedrals . . .* London, 1832. Folio. $1,250.

CONFEDERATE Receipt Book. Richmond, 1863. Wraps. $850.

CONFESSIONS of an English Opium-Eater. London, 1822. (By Thomas De Quincey.) First issue, with ad leaf at end. $3,000. Second issue, lacking ad leaf. $2,000. Philadelphia, 1823. First American edition. $500. Limited Editions Club, New York, 1930. Boards. In slipcase. $200.

CONFESSIONS of Harry Lorrequer (The). Dublin, 1839. (By Charles Lever.) Author's first book. Illustrated by Phiz. 11 parts, pictorial pink wraps. $500. First edition in book form. $400. Cloth. $300.

CONFESSIONS of J. Lackington, Late Bookseller, at the Temple of the Muses, in a Series of Letters to a Friend . . . London, 1804. $250.

CONGREVE, William. *The Way of the World.* London, 1700. $2,500.

CONJECTURAL *Observations on the Origin and Progress of Alphabetic Writing.* London, 1772. 3 foldout plates. $500.

CONKLIN, E. *Picturesque Arizona.* New York, 1878. Illustrated. Green cloth. $300.

CONNELL, Evan S., Jr. *The Anatomy Lesson.* New York, 1957. Author's first book. $300. London (1958). $125.

CONNELL, Evan S., Jr. *Mrs. Bridge.* New York, 1959. $250.

CONNELL, Evan S., Jr. *Son of Morning Star.* San Francisco, 1984. No statement of edition. First dustwrapper parchment-like paper. (Later glossy.) $200.

CONNELLEY, William E. *Doniphan's Expedition and the Conquest of New Mexico and California.* Kansas City, 1907. $300.

CONNELLEY, William E. *Quantrill and the Border Wars.* Cedar Rapids, Iowa, 1910. $250.

CONNELLEY, William E. *The War with Mexico, 1846–47; Doniphan's Expedition.* Topeka, 1907. 2 maps, illustrations. $300.

CONNELLEY, William E. *Wild Bill and His Era.* New York, 1933. 12 plates. One of 200 copies. $300.

CONNELLY, Marc. *Dulcy.* New York, 1921. Author's first book, written with G. S. Kaufman. $750.

CONNELLY, Marc. *The Green Pastures.* New York, 1930. Illustrated in color by Robert Edmond Jones. Green boards. One of 550 signed copies. In slipcase. $350. Some signed copies issued in morocco. $500. Trade edition. $250.

CONNELLY, Michael. *The Black Echo.* Boston (1992). Author's first book. $150.

CONNELLY, Michael. *Blood Work.* Tucson (1997). One of 26 signed, lettered copies. In quarter morocco, dustwrapper and slipcase. $600. One of 300 signed copies. In dustwrapper and slipcase. $300. Boston (1998). $25.

CONNETT, Eugene V. *Magic Hours.* New York: Derrydale Press, 1927. 2 mounted plates by the author. 20 pages, gray boards, paper label. One of 100 copies. (First Derrydale Press book.) $10,000.

CONNETT, Eugene V. (editor). *American Big Game Fishing.* New York: Derrydale Press (1935). Illustrated, including color plates. In dustwrapper. In slipcase. $750.

CONNETT, Eugene V. (editor). *Upland Game Bird Shooting in America.* New York: Derrydale Press, 1930. Illustrated, including color plates. Pictorial cloth. One of 850 copies. $850. Brown morocco. One of 75 copies with 6 original signed etchings. $3,500.

CONNICK, Charles J. *Adventures in Light and Color.* New York (1937). Color plates and collotype plates. Buckram. Deluxe issue, one of 300 copies with 42 plates in color, 48 in collotype. $750. Trade edition with 36 colored plates. $350. London, 1937. 36 color plates, 48 in collotype. $200.

CONNOLLY, A. P. *A Thrilling Narrative of the Minnesota Massacre and the Sioux War of 1862–1863.* Chicago (1896). Illustrated. $250.

CONNOLLY, Cyril. See Palinurus.

CONNOLLY, Cyril. *Enemies of Promise.* London, 1938. $600. Boston, 1938. $200.

CONNOLLY. Cyril. *The Rock Pool.* Obelisk Press. Paris (1936). Wraps. Author's first book. $750. New York, 1936. $250. London, 1947. New postscript. $125.

CONOLLY, John. *The Treatment of the Insane Without Mechanical Restraints.* London, 1856. $2,000.

CONOVER, George W. *Sixty Years in Southwest Oklahoma.* Andarko, 1927. Illustrated. Issued without dustwrapper. $250.

CONQUEST (The) . . . By A Negro Pioneer (Oscar Micheaux). Lincoln, Nebr., 1913. Author's first book. $2,500.

CONRAD, Joseph. See *The Nigger of the "Narcissus," Preface.*

CONRAD, Joseph. *"Admiralty Paper."* (New York, 1925.) Facsimile plate. Blue wraps. One of 93. $1,500.

CONRAD, Joseph. *Almayer's Folly: A Story of an Eastern River.* London, 1895. Author's first book. Dark-green cloth. First issue, with first "e" missing in "generosity" in the second line from last on page 110. $2,000. New York, 1895. Spine reads "Macmillan & Co." $1,000. Second binding. "The Macmillan Company." $750. London, 1895. Colonial issue. $1,250.

CONRAD, Joseph. *The Arrow of Gold: A Story Between Two Notes.* Garden City, 1919. Dark-blue cloth. First issue, with the reading "credentials and apparently" in line 16 of page 5. In dustwrapper. $600. Second issue ("credentials and who") in dustwrapper. $500. London (1919). In dustwrapper. $600. Without dustwrapper. $125.

CONRAD, Joseph. *Chance: A Tale in Two Parts.* London (1913). Sage-green cloth. First issue, with "First published in 1913" on verso of integral title page and "Methven" on spine and 32-page catalogue dated July 1913. $2,750. Second issue with "Methuen" on spine and no catalogue. $2,250. Third issue with "Methuen" on spine and "First published in 1914" on tipped-in page. $750. Garden City, 1913. Dark-blue cloth. First American edition. One of 150 copies issued for copyright purposes. $1,000. New York, 1914. $200.

CONRAD, Joseph. *The Children of the Sea.* New York, 1897. First edition of the book published in England in 1898 as *The Nigger of the "Narcissus."* Mottled blue-gray cloth. $750. New York, 1898. Second issue. $500.

CONRAD, Joseph. *A Handbook of Cookery for a Small House.* By Jessie Conrad. With a preface by Joseph Conrad. London, 1923. Cloth. $250.

CONRAD, Joseph. *Joseph Conrad's Letters to His Wife.* London, 1927. Limp imitation leather. Issued without dustwrapper. One of 220 copies signed by Jessie Conrad. $450.

CONRAD, Joseph. *Laughing Anne: A Play.* London, 1923. Full vellum, gilt top. One of 200 signed copies. In folding box. $750.

CONRAD, Joseph. *Laughing Anne & One Day More.* London, 1924. $200. Garden City, 1925. $150.

CONRAD, Joseph. *Lord Jim.* Edinburgh and London, 1900. Gray-green cloth. $2,500. New York, 1900. Copyright 1900. $1,000. Copyright 1899 and 1900. $500. Limited Editions Club, New Haven, 1959. In slipcase. $175.

CONRAD, Joseph. *The Mirror of the Sea: Memories and Impressions.* London (1906). Light-green cloth. First edition, with 40 pages of ads dated August 1906. $500. Ads dated July. $400. New York, 1906. Blue cloth. $250.

CONRAD, Joseph. *The Nigger of the "Narcissus."* London, 1898. First published English edition of *The Children of the Sea.* With "H" in "Heinemann" on spine 5.5 mm (the following letters 4 mm), 16-page catalogue. $500. Second-issue letters all 3 mm high. 16-page catalogue. $400. Third issue same as second but 32–page catalogue. "New York, 1914" on title page. Contains suppressed preface and adds new prefatory note. $350. Limited Editions Club, New York, 1965. In slipcase. $125. (See also title entry, anonymous.)

CONRAD, Joseph. *Nostromo: A Tale of the Seaboard.* London, 1904. Bright-blue cloth. $1,500. New York, 1904. $350. Limited Editions Club, New York, 1961. In slipcase. $100.

CONRAD, Joseph. *Notes by Joseph Conrad in a Set of His First Editions in the Possession of Richard Curle.* London, 1925. Buckram, paper label. One of 100 copies signed by Curle. $450.

CONRAD, Joseph. *Notes on Life and Letters.* Dent, London, 1921. Green cloth. Advance printing with "Privately printed" on copyright page. $2,250. London, 1921. First issue of trade edition with "S" and "a" missing from the word "Sea" in "Tales of the Sea" in eighth line of table of contents. $300. Third issue, with corrected page on canceled leaf. $175.

CONRAD, Joseph. *Notes on My Books.* London, 1921. Boards, parchment spine, paper labels. First English edition. One of 250 signed copies. In dustwrapper. $600. Garden City, 1921. One of 250 signed copies. In dustwrapper. $600.

CONRAD, Joseph. *One Day More: A Play in One Act.* London, 1917. Blue wraps. One of 25 copies signed by Clement Shorter, who had it printed privately. $2,500. London: Beaumont Press (1919). Boards. First published edition. One of 24 on vellum. $3,500. One of 250 copies. $350. Garden City, 1920. One of 377 signed copies. $400.

CONRAD, Joseph. *An Outcast of the Islands.* London, 1896. $1,000. New York, 1896. First American edition. Wraps. $750. Green cloth. $600. Deluxe edition in three-quarter roan and marbled boards. $1,000. Limited Editions Club, Avon, 1975. In slipcase. $100.

CONRAD, Joseph. *The Point of Honor: A Military Tale.* New York, 1908. Decorated cloth. With "McClure" at base of spine. $250. With "Doubleday/Page & Co." at base of spine. $150.

CONRAD, Joseph. *The Rescue: A Romance of the Shallows.* Garden City, 1920. Dark-blue cloth. In dustwrapper. Priced "Net $1.90." $750. In dustwrapper. With "Net $2.00" overprinted. $250. London, 1920. Flexible red wraps (text differing from other editions). First English edition. One of 40 privately printed advance copies. $2,000. London, 1920. Green cloth. First published English edition. In dustwrapper. $450.

CONRAD, Joseph. *The Rover.* Garden City, 1923. Boards. First American edition. One of 377 signed copies. Slipcase. $750. Trade edition. $250. London (1923). Green cloth. $300.

CONRAD, Joseph. *The Secret Agent: A Drama in Three Acts.* London, 1923. Portrait frontispiece. Boards and parchment. One of 1,000 signed copies. In dustwrapper. $750.

CONRAD, Joseph. *The Secret Agent: A Simple Tale.* London (1907). Red cloth. First edition, with 40 pages of ads at end dated September. $2,500. New York, 1907. $500.

CONRAD, Joseph. *A Set of Six.* London (1908). First issue, with ads dated February 1908, and with the list of Conrad's works, including "The Secret Agent" (with Ford M. Hueffer). $1,250. Second issue, with ads dated February 1908, with Hueffer's name between "The Secret Agent" and "The Inheritors." $600. Third issue with ads dated June 1908. $500. With ads dated August 1908. $300. New York, 1915. $200.

CONRAD, Joseph. *Suspense.* Garden City, 1925. One of 377. In plain blue dustwrapper. In slipcase. $600. Trade edition. $350. London, 1925. Dark-red cloth. $350.

CONRAD, Joseph. *Tales of Unrest.* New York, 1898. $500. London, 1898. Dark-green cloth. First English edition, first issue top edge gilt, other edges untrimmed. $500. Plain top edge, other edges rough-trimmed. $350.

CONRAD, Joseph. *'Twixt Land and Sea Tales.* London, 1912. Olive-green cloth. First issue, with "Secret" instead of "Seven" on front cover. $2,500. Second issue, with "Seven" stamped over erased word "Secret." $350. Third issue with cover corrected. $150. New York (1912). First edition not stated (nor is Doran colophon present on copyright page). $300.

CONRAD, Joseph. *Typhoon.* New York, 1902. First issue in dark-green cloth with 4 pages of ads. $600. Second issue in maroon cloth (ghost?). $500. London, 1903. Dark-gray cloth. First English edition, first issue, with windmill device and without "Reserved for the Colonies only" on verso of half title, front and bottom edges untrimmed. $750. Second issue all edges trimmed. $500.

CONRAD, Joseph. *Within the Tides: Tales.* London, 1915. Sage-green cloth. $200. New York, 1916. $100.

CONRAD Joseph. *Youth: A Narrative and Two Other Stories.* Edinburgh, 1902. Light-green cloth. With ads dated "10/02" at end. $1,250. With "11/02." $750. Without ads. $600. New York, 1903. $300. Kentfield, 1959. One of 140 copies. $1,000.

CONRAD, Joseph, and HUEFFER, Ford M. *The Inheritors: An Extravagant Story.* New York, 1901. Advance copies in beige pictorial cloth with sky in gold and with the dedication leaf reading "To Boys and Christina." Only a few copies known. $4,500. First published edition, with a corrected dedication, on a stub: "To Borys and Christina" and sky in gold. $600. Second issue with sky in cover cloth color. $400. London, 1901. Yellow cloth. First issue, without dedication leaf (most copies including later issues). With 32 pages of ads and publisher's device on spine with initials. Top edge untrimmed. $750. Without catalogue. Top edge trimmed. $600. Without initials in publisher's device. $500. Also, remaindered in smooth yellow nonpictorial cloth. $250.

CONRAD, Joseph, and HUEFFER, Ford M. *Romance: A Novel.* London, 1903. Bright-blue cloth. $400. Red cloth. $300. Red wraps. $300. New York, 1904. $400.

CONROY, Jack. *The Disinherited.* (New York, 1933.) Author's first book. Pictorial dustwrapper. $300. Printed dustwrapper. $200. London (1934). $250.

CONROY, Pat. *The Boo.* Verona (1970). Author's first book. First edition stated. $3,500. New York, 1981. Wraps. New introduction. $150. Atlanta, 1988. One of 250 copies signed without dustwrapper. In slipcase. $500. One of 20 signed copies with original page or manuscript. $1,500. Trade. In dustwrapper. $75.

CONROY, Pat. *The Water Is Wide.* Boston, 1972. $1,250.

CONSIDERANT, Victor. *European Colonization in Texas.* New York, 1855. First edition in English. 38 pages, wraps. $850.

CONSIDERATIONS on Some Recent Social Theories. Boston, 1853. (By Charles Eliot Norton.) Author's first book. $300.

CONSTABLE, Henry. *Poems and Sonnets.* London, 1897. Woodcut border, ornamental woodcut initials. White pigskin. One of 210 copies. $600.

CONSTANTINE, K. C. (pseudonym). *The Blank Page.* (New York), 1974. $200.

CONSTANTINE, K. C. (pseudonym). *The Rocksburg Railroad Murders.* New York, 1972. Author's first book. First issue, no reviews on back of dustwrapper. $750. Second issue, reviews on back of dustwrapper. $250.

CONSTITUTION and Laws of the Cherokee Nation. St. Louis, 1875. Leather. $400.

CONSTITUTION and Laws of the Muskogee Nation. St. Louis, 1880. Sheep. $350.

CONSTITUTION and Playing Rules of the International Baseball Association . . . and Championship Record for 1877. Jamaica Plain, Mass., 1878. 77 pages, wraps. $1,000.

CONSTITUTION of the Republic of Mexico and the State of Coahuila and Texas (The). New York, 1832. Half calf. $1,250.

CONSTITUTION of the State of Sequoyah. (Muscogee, Indian Territory, 1905.) Folding map in color. 67 pages, self-wraps. First edition, with last page numbered. $2,500. Second edition, same date, no page number on last page. $1,000.

CONSTITUTION of the State of West Texas. (Cover title.) Austin (1868). 35 pages, wraps. $600.

CONSTITUTION of the U.S.A . . . Also, an Act to Establish a Territorial Government for Utah. Salt Lake City, 1852. 48 pages, sewn. $1,000.

CONTACT Collection of Contemporary Writers. (Paris): Contact Editions (1925). Edited by Robert McAlmon. Wraps. One of 300 copies. $1,500. (Contains work by Ernest Hemingway, James Joyce, Ezra Pound, Gertrude Stein, William Carlos Williams, and others.)

COOK, Clarence. *The House Beautiful.* New York, 1878. $500.

COOK, D. J. *Hands Up, or 20 Years of Detective Life in the Mountains and on the Plains.* Denver, 1882. 32 plates. Wraps. $750. Cloth, same date, later issue. $450. Denver, 1897. Second edition, enlarged, with *20 Years* changed to *35 Years* in title. $350.

COOK, Frederick A. *My Attainment of the Pole.* New York, 1911. $600.

COOK, Frederick A. *Through the First Antarctic Night 1898–1899.* London, 1900. Map, 4 colored and 72 monochrome illustrations. $1,000. New York, 1900. $750.

COOK, Captain James. See Ellis, William; Magra, James; Parkinson, Sydney.

COOK, James. *A Voyage Towards the South Pole, and Round the World* . . . London, 1777. 2 vols. $5,500.

COOK, Captain James. *Complete Set, Official Accounts of the Three Voyages Round the World.* London, 1773–85. 8 vols. The Atlas format for the plates of the first and second voyages are extremely rare. See bibliographies for further detail. $30,000.

COOK, James. *History of North Dakota.* Chicago and New York, 1931. 3 vols. $500.

COOK, James H. *Fifty Years on the Old Frontier.* New Haven, 1923. Plates. $350.

COOK, John R. *Border and the Buffalo.* Topeka, 1907. Plates. $250.

COOK, Robin. *The Crust and Its Uppers.* London, 1962. $250.

COOKE, Edward. *A Voyage to the South Seas* . . . London, 1712. Folding frontispiece map. 15 plates. 4 maps and plans (2 folding). $3,000.

COOKE, John Esten. See Effingham, C. See also *Leather Stocking and Silk; The Life of Stonewall Jackson.*

COOKE, John Esten. *The Last of the Foresters* . . . New York, 1856. $500.

COOKE, John Esten. *A Life of General Robert E. Lee.* New York, 1871. $300.

COOKE, John Esten. *Stonewall Jackson: A Military Biography* . . . New York, 1876. With appendix, 13 tissue-guarded portraits, 6 maps, and an engraved illustration. $1,000.

COOKE, John Esten. *Surry of Eagle's Nest.* New York, 1866. Illustrated by Winslow Homer. With Bunce and Huntington imprint. $750.

COOKE, Philip St. George. *The Conquest of New Mexico and California.* New York, 1878. Folding map. $450.

COOKE, Philip St. George. *Scenes and Adventures in the Army.* Philadelphia, 1857. $750.

COOKSON, Mrs. James. *Flowers Drawn and Painted in India.* London (1835). 31 hand-colored lithographs. $10,000.

COOLBRITH, Ina Donna. *A Perfect Day* . . . San Francisco, 1881. Author's first book. Folio issue. $600. Regular issue. $300.

COOLIDGE, Calvin. *Address Delivered By* . . . Boston, 1916. $450.

COOLIDGE, Calvin. *The Autobiography of Calvin Coolidge.* New York, 1929. One of 1,000 signed. $500. Trade edition. $75.

COOLIDGE, Dane. *The Fighting Fool.* New York, 1918. $75.

COOLIDGE, Dane. *Hidden Water.* Chicago, 1910. Author's first book. $100.

COOLIDGE, Dane. *The Texican.* Chicago, 1911. $75.

COON, James Churchill. *Log of the Cruise of 1889 D.T.S.C., New Smyrna to Lake Worth, East Coast of Florida.* Lake Helen, Fla., 1889. Wraps. $300.

COOPER, (A.) Distiller. *The Complete Distiller . . .* London, 1757. $1,000.

COOPER, J. W. *Game Fowls, Their Origin and History.* West Chester, Pa. (1869). Colored lithographs. Pictorial green cloth, gilt. $300.

COOPER, James Fenimore. See *The Bee-Hunter; The Bravo; The Chainbearer; The Deerslayer; The Headsman; The Last of the Mohicans; The Monikins; The Pathfinder; The Pilot; The Pioneers; The Prairie; Precaution; Ravensnest; The Redskins; Satanstoe; The Spy; The Two Admirals; The Water Witch; The Wept of Wish Ton-Wish; The Wing-and-Wing; Wyandotte.*

COOPER, James Fenimore. *The American Democrat.* Cooperstown, 1839. $500.

COOPER, James Fenimore. *The Battle of Lake Erie.* Cooperstown, N.Y., 1843. Printed wraps. $1,000.

COOPER, James Fenimore. *The History of the Navy of the United States of America.* Philadelphia, 1839. 2 vols. Maps. In original cloth. $600. London, 1839. 2 vols. First English edition. In original cloth. $500.

COOPER, James Fenimore. *The Jack O'Lantern.* London, 1842. 3 vols. Drab-brown boards, purple cloth, paper spine labels. First edition (of the novel issued anonymously in America as *The Wing-and-Wing,* which see as title entry). $600.

COOPER, James Fenimore. *Lives of Distinguished American Naval Officers.* Philadelphia, 1846. 2 vols. Cloth. $500. Wraps. $750.

COOPER, James Fenimore. *Notions of the Americans.* London, 1828. 2 vols. $500. Philadelphia, 1828. 2 vols. $350.

COOPER, Susan Rogers. *The Man in the Green Chevy.* New York, 1988. Author's first book. $600.

COOPER, Thomas. *Tracts on Medical Jurisprudence.* Philadelphia, 1819. $750.

COOVER, Robert. *The Origin of the Brunists.* New York (1966). Author's first book. $250. London, 1967. $125.

COOVER, Robert. *The Universal Baseball Association, J. Henry Waugh, Proprietor.* New York (1968). $250. London (1970). $150.

COPE, Wendy. *Across the City.* London, 1980. Wraps. 30 signed and numbered copies. $350. 150 copies. Wraps. $150.

COPPARD, A. E. *Adam and Eve and Pinch Me.* Waltham Saint Lawrence: Golden Cockerel Press, 1921. White buckram. One of 160 copies (from an edition of 500). $500. Orange boards. One of 340 copies. $250. New York, 1922. Boards and cloth. $125.

COPPARD, A. E. *Pink Furniture.* London, 1930. Illustrated. Vellum. One of 260 signed copies. In dustwrapper. $250. Trade edition. $125.

COPPARD, A. E. *Silver Circus.* (London, 1928.) Full vellum. Issued without dustwrapper. One of 125 signed copies. $250. Trade edition. $150.

CORBETT, James J. *The Roar of the Crowd: The True Tale of the Rise and Fall of a Champion.* New York, 1925. $250.

CORELLI, Marie. *Barabbas.* London (1893). 3 vols. $750.

CORK, Richard. *Vorticism and Abstract Art* . . . London, 1976. 2 vols. In dustwrapper. In slipcase. $500. Berkeley (1976). 2 vols. In dustwrapper. $450.

CORLE, Edwin. *Death Valley* . . . Los Angeles (1962). Ansel Adams Illustrations. $200.

CORLE, Edwin. *Fig Tree John.* New York, 1935. $200.

CORLE, Edwin. *Mojave.* New York, 1934. Author's first book. $350.

CORLE, Edwin. *People of the Earth.* New York, 1937. $150.

CORMAN, Cid. *Clocked Stone.* Ashland, Mass., 1959. One of 210 copies signed by Corman and the artist. In slipcase. $650.

CORNER, William. *San Antonio de Bexas.* San Antonio, 1890. Map, 16 plates. $150.

CORNFORD, Frances. See D., F.C.

CORNFORD, Frances. *Autumn Midnight.* London, 1923. Woodcuts by Eric Gill. Wraps. $200.

CORNFORD, Frances. *Poems.* Hampstead (1910). $200.

CORNISH, Geoffrey S., and WHITTEN, Ronald W. *The Golf Course.* New York, 1981. $75. London, 1984. One of 200 copies signed by Cornish. In leather slipcase. $250.

CORNWALL, Bruce. *Life Sketch of Pierre Barlow Cornwall.* San Francisco, 1906. 6 portraits. $250.

CORNWELL, Bernard. *Sharpe's Eagle.* London, 1981. Author's first book. $400. New York, 1981. $150.

CORNWELL, Bernard. *Sharpe's Gold.* London, 1981. $350. New York (1982). $100.

CORNWELL, Bernard. *Sharpe's Sword.* London, 1981. $500. New York, 1983. $300.

CORNWELL, Patricia. *Postmortem.* New York, 1990. First mystery. $1,250. (London, 1990.) $400.

CORNWELL, Patricia. *A Time for Remembering* . . . San Francisco (1983). Author's first book. $400.

CORRILL, John. *A Brief History of the Church of Christ of Latter Day Saints.* St. Louis, 1839. Sewn, as originally issued. $7,500.

CORSO, Gregory. *Ankh.* New York, 1971. Oblong, magenta wraps. One of 100 signed copies. $100. One of 26 signed copies. $250.

CORSO, Gregory. *Gasoline.* City Lights Books. San Francisco (1958). Wraps. $125.

CORSO, Gregory. *The Vestal Lady on Brattle and Other Poems.* Cambridge, Mass., 1955. Printed wraps. Author's first book. $400.

CORVO, Baron (Frederick William Rolfe). See Rolfe, Fr. See also *Tarcissus.*

CORVO, Baron. *Chronicles of the House of Borgia.* London, 1901. (By Frederick William Rolfe.) 10 plates. Pictorial red buckram. First issue has Appendix III on Homosexuality (3 or 4 copies). $2,000. Second issue has Appendix III entitled "Papal Tribute." $500. New York, 1901. First American edition. Dark-red or black cloth. $400. London, 1957. One of 250 copies. $300.

CORVO, Baron. *The Desire and Pursuit of the Whole.* London (1934). (By Frederick William Rolfe.) First binding in veridian (dark-green) cloth. $350. Remainder binding in light-green. Issued without dustwrapper. $150. London (1953). Cloth. $75.

CORVO, Baron. *Hadrian the Seventh.* London, 1904. One of 700 copies. $1,000.

CORVO, Baron. *In His Own Image.* London, 1901. (By Frederick William Rolfe.) With 1 ad leaf at end. $350.

CORVO, Baron. *Letters to Grant Richards.* (Hurst, England): Peacocks Press (1952). (By Frederick William Rolfe.) Boards. Issued without dustwrapper. One of 200 copies. $400.

CORVO, Baron. *Stories Toto Told Me.* London, 1898. (By Frederick William Rolfe.) Printed green wraps. No. 6 of the Bodley Booklets. $600.

COSTAIN, Thomas B. *The Silver Chalice.* Garden City (1952). One of 750 signed copies. In slipcase. $300.

COSTAKIS, George Collection. *Russian Avant-Garde Art.* New York, 1981. $200.

COSTANSO, Miguel. *The Spanish Occupation of California.* (San Francisco), 1934. Portraits, folding maps. Boards. One of 550 copies. In slipcase. $250.

COSTLER, Dr. A. *Encyclopedia of Sexual Knowledge.* London (1934). (By Arthur Koestler, his first book.) $600.

COSTLER, Dr. A. *The Practice of Sex.* London (1936). (By Arthur Koestler.) ("Coester" on title page.) $450.

COTTA, John. *The Triall of Witch-Craft, Shewing the Trve and Right Methode of the Discovery.* (London, 1616.) $4,000.

COTTEN, Bruce. *Housed on the Third Floor, Being a Collection of North Carolinians.* Baltimore, 1941. 100 facsimiles of title pages. One of 250 copies. $450.

COTTON, Rev. Henry. *A Typographical Gazetteer.* Oxford, 1831. Second edition, corrected and much enlarged. $250.

COTTON, John. *God's Promise . . .* London, 1630. Author's first book. $1,250.

COUES, Elliott. *Forty Years a Fur Trader . . .* New York, 1898. 2 vols. $650.

COUES, Elliott (editor). *New Light on the Early History of the Greater Northwest.* New York, 1897. 3 vols. Frontispiece, facsimile, 3 maps in pocket of vol. 3. Cloth. One of 1,000 copies. $1,500. Half vellum. One of 100 copies on large paper. $2,500.

COUES, Elliott (editor). *On the Trail of a Spanish Pioneer: The Diary and Itinerary of Francisco Garces* . . . New York, 1900. 2 vols. One of 950 copies. $400.

COULTANT, C. G. *The History of Wyoming from the Earliest Known Discoveries* . . . *Volume I* (all published). Laramie, 1899. $400.

COURTAULD, George. *Address to Those Who May Be Disposed to Remove to the United States of America.* Sudbury, 1820. 40 pages. $1,500.

COUSINS, Sheila. *To Beg I Am Ashamed.* New York (1938). (By Graham Greene and Ronald Matthews.) $450.

COUTS, Cave J. *From San Diego to the Colorado in 1849.* Los Angeles, 1932. 3 maps on 2 sheets. $200.

COUTS, Joseph. *A Practical Guide for the Tailor's Cutting Room.* Glasgow (1848). 27 plates, 13 colored, and 18 diagrammatic plates. Half morocco. $1,500.

COVARRUBIAS, Miguel. *Negro Drawings.* New York, 1927. $1,500.

COWAN, Robert E. *A Bibliography of the History of California and the Pacific West, 1510–1906.* San Francisco, 1914. One of 250 copies. In slipcase. $400. San Francisco, 1933. 3 vols. Boards and cloth. $600.

COWARD, Noel. *"I'll Leave It to You."* London, 1920. Author's first book. Wraps. $600.

COWARD, Noel. *Present Indicative.* Garden City, 1937. One of 250 signed copies. In slipcase. $500.

COWLEY, Malcolm. *Blue Juniata: Poems.* New York (1929). Cloth. $400.

COWLEY, Malcolm. *Exile's Return.* New York (1934). $600. Limited Editions Club, New York, 1981. One of 2,000 copies signed by author and photographer. $300.

COWLEY, Malcolm. *Racine.* Paris, 1923. Author's first book. Wraps. $2,500.

COWLEY, Malcolm, and MANNIX, Daniel P. *Black Cargo* . . . New York (1962). $1,000.

COWTAN, Robert. *Memories of the British Museum.* London, 1872. $200.

COX, A. B. See *The Layton Court Mystery.*

COX, David. *A Treatise on Landscape Painting and Effect in Water Colours* . . . London, 1813–14. 12 parts in one volume. 16 hand-colored aquatints. First issue has plates incorrectly numbered and etching of Convict Hulks on the Thames. $4,000. Second issue has plates correctly numbered and Haymaking and Reaping etching replacing Convict Hulks . . . $3,500.

COX, Edward Godfrey. *A Reference Guide to the Literature of Travel* . . . Seattle, 1948–50. 3 vols. Reprint of the first (1935) edition. $350.

COX, Isaac. *The Annals of Trinity County.* San Francisco, 1940. John Henry Nash printing. One of 350 copies. In slipcase. $250.

COX, James. *Historical and Biographical Record of the Cattle Industry and the Cattlemen of Texas and Adjacent Territory.* St. Louis, 1895. Colored frontispiece, other illustrations. Decorated leather.

$8,500. Without frontis. $6,500. New York, 1959. 2 vols. Half leather. In slipcase. One of 500 copies. $350.

COX, Palmer. *The Brownies Around the World.* New York (1894). $350.

COX, Palmer. *The Brownies at Home.* New York (1893). Pictorial boards. $450.

COX, Palmer. *The Brownies: Their Book.* New York (1887). Green glazed pictorial boards. First issue, with DeVinne Press seal immediately below copyright notice. $750. Second issue, with seal about 2½ inches from bottom of page. $500.

COX, Palmer. *Queer People with Wings and Stings and Their Kweer Kapers.* Philadelphia (1888). Pictorial boards. $300.

COX, Palmer. *Squibs of California.* Hartford, 1874. Author's first book. $400.

COX, Ross. *Adventures on the Columbia River.* London, 1831. 2 vols. $1,000. New York, 1832. $1,750.

COX, Sandford C. *Recollections of the Early Settlement of the Wabash Valley.* Lafayette, Ind., 1860. $200.

COX, William D. *Boxing in Art and Literature.* New York, 1935. $250.

COXE, Daniel. *A Description of the English Province of Carolana . . .* London, 1722. Folding map. $6,000.

COXE, George Harmon. *Murder with Pictures.* New York, 1935. Author's first hardcover book. $750.

COXE, John Redman. *The American Dispensatory . . .* Philadelphia, 1806. $600.

COXE, Louis O. *Uniform of Flesh.* Princeton, 1947. Author's first book (written with R. H. Chapman). Mimeographed sheets in stiff wraps. $250.

COXE, William. *Travels in Switzerland, And in the Country of the Grisons.* London, 1789. 3 vols. $1,000.

COXE, William. *Travels into Poland, Russia, Sweden and Denmark . . .* London, 1784. 2 vols. 13 engraved plates, 7 maps (6 folding), and 4 folding city plans. $2,000.

COXE, William. *A View of the Cultivation of Fruit Trees . . .* Philadelphia, 1817. $600.

COY, Owen C. *Pictorial History of California.* Berkeley (1915). 261 photographs. $400.

COYLE, Kathleen. *Picadilly.* London, 1923. Author's first book. $350. New York (1923). $350.

COYNER, David H. *The Lost Trappers.* Cincinnati, 1847. $750. Cincinnati, 1850. Second edition. $350.

COZZENS, Frederick S. See Haywarde, Richard.

COZZENS, Frederick S. *Acadia.* New York, 1859. 2 plates. $200.

COZZENS, James Gould. *Cock Pit.* New York, 1928. $450.

COZZENS, James Gould. *Confusion.* Boston, 1924. Author's first book. Gray-green cloth. Top edge red. $850.

COZZENS, James Gould. *Michael Scarlett.* New York, 1925. $250.

CRABBE, George. *Tales of the Hall.* London, 1819. 2 vols. $300.

CRACKANTHORPE, Hubert. *Wreckage.* London, 1893. Author's first book. With 16 pages of ads dated October 1892. $150.

CRAIG, Edward Gordon. *Ellen Terry and Her Secret Self.* London, 1931. White cloth. One of 256 signed copies. With 8 plates and "A Plea for G.B.S." Loosely inserted in wallet at end. In slipcase. $600. Trade edition. $150.

CRAIG, Edward Gordon. *Nothing or the Bookplate.* London, 1924. One of 280 copies. $500. London (1931). $150.

CRAIG, John R. *Ranching with Lords and Commons.* Toronto (1903). 17 plates. Pictorial cloth. $750.

CRAIG, Maurice. *Irish Bookbindings, 1600–1800.* London, 1954. 58 plates, full-color frontispiece. $400.

CRAIK, Dinah M. See *The Adventures of a Brownie; The Fairy Book; John Halifax, Gentleman; The Ogilvies.*

CRAIS, Robert. *Lullaby Town.* New York (1992). $600.

CRAKES, Sylvester. *Five Years a Captive Among the Black-Feet Indians.* Columbus, Ohio, 1858. 6 plates. $2,500.

CRAM, Ralph Adams. *Ruined Abbeys of Great Britain.* Boston, 1927. Full calf. One of 350 signed copies. $300.

CRANCH, Christopher Pearse. *Giant Hunting: or, Little Jacket's Adventures.* Boston, 1860. Illustrated. Pictorial cloth. $400.

CRANCH, Christopher Pearse. *The Last of the Huggermuggers.* Boston, 1856. $600.

CRANCH, Christopher Pearse. *A Poem Delivered in the First Congregation Church . . .* Boston, 1840. Author's first book. Wraps. $350.

CRANE, Hart. See *A Pagan Anthology.*

CRANE, Hart. *The Bridge.* Paris: Black Sun Press, 1930. 3 photographs by Walker Evans. Stiff printed wraps. One of 200 copies (weighing 19¼ ounces). In glassine dustwrapper. In silver slipcase. $4,000. Also, 25 advance copies not for sale, on thin paper and weighing 15¼ ounces. $3,500. One of 50 on Japan vellum; signed. In glassine dustwrapper and slipcase. $12,500. Also, 8 lettered copies on vellum, signed by the poet. $20,000. New York (1930). First American edition. $750. Limited Editions Club, New York, 1981. Folio. One of 2,000 copies signed by Richard Benson (photographer). $150.

CRANE, Hart. *The Collected Poems of Hart Crane.* New York: Liveright Inc. Publishers (1933). Edited by Waldo Frank. Portrait frontispiece. Red cloth. $400. Second printing with imprint of "Liveright Publishing Corporation." $150. Brown cloth. One of 50 copies "for presentation to the friends . . ." $750. London (1938). $350.

CRANE, Hart. *Two Letters.* Brooklyn Heights, 1934. Leaflet, 4 pages. One of 50 copies. $1,000.

CRANE, Hart. *Voyages: Six Poems* . . . New York, 1957. Illustrated by Leonard Baskin. Oblong, wraps in board folder. One of 975 copies. $350. One of 25 review copies. $500.

CRANE, Hart. *White Buildings.* (New York), 1926. Author's first book. Foreword by Allen Tate. First issue, with Tate's first name misspelled "Allan." $3,500. Second issue, with tipped-in title page, Tate's name spelled correctly. $1,750. Paris, 1930. Wraps and dustwrapper. (200 copies.) $1,000.

CRANE, Stephen. See Smith, Johnston. See also *The Lanthorn Book; Pike County Puzzle.*

CRANE, Stephen. *Active Service.* New York (1899). $250. London, 1899. $150.

CRANE, Stephen. *The Black Riders and Other Lines.* Boston, 1895. Gray paper boards with first line of title on front cover indented one space to right has been presumed to be the first, but Pastore believes cream laid paper over yellow boards is the first. $1,500. There are variants in pale-yellow paper over boards, pale-yellow cloth (no known copies), gray laid paper (assume the "other first"), light-gray paper over boards (one known copy), and publisher leather (Williams & Starrett call for black morocco). We would assume all the variants would be about the same value as the first except the leather, which would be somewhat more. Plain boards, paper label. One of 50 copies in white paper over boards and printed in green ink on Japan vellum. $5,000. One of 3 copies bound in white vellum. $7,500. One of 3 copies bound in full green levant. $7,500. (For further detail see Stephen R. Pastore's bibliographical study of this title in *Stephen Crane Studies* vol. 6, no. 2 [Fall 1997].) London, 1896. 500 copies in black morocco. $1,250.

CRANE, Stephen. *George's Mother.* New York, 1896. $300. London, 1896. $150.

CRANE, Stephen. *Great Battles of the World.* Philadelphia, 1901. Illustrated by John Sloan. $300. London, 1901. Pictorial cloth. $400. Plain cloth. $200.

CRANE, Stephen. *Last Words.* London, 1902. Maroon cloth stamped in gold and blind. $750. Red, brown, blue, or green cloth stamped in black, presumed remainder bindings. $500.

CRANE, Stephen. *The Little Regiment and Other Episodes of the American Civil War.* New York, 1896. First printing, with ads at back, headed "Gilbert Parker's Best Books." $350. Second state advertises "The Beginners of the Nation." $200. London, 1897. $200.

CRANE, Stephen. *Maggie:A Girl of the Streets.* New York, 1896. Cream-yellow buckram. Second (revised) edition, first state, with title page printed in 8-lines capital and lower-case letters. $750. Second state, 11 lines, capital letters only. $350. London, 1896. First English (revised) edition (as *Maggie:A Child of the Street*). $750. (For first edition, see Johnston Smith, *Maggie:A Girl of the Streets.*)

CRANE, Stephen. *The Monster and Other Stories.* New York, 1899. $350. London, 1901. Revised edition, with 4 stories added. $200.

CRANE, Stephen. *The Open Boat and Other Tales of Adventure.* New York, 1898. Dark-green pictorial cloth. $450. London, 1898. First English edition, with 9 added stories. Light-green cloth. $300. Tan linen. $200.

CRANE, Stephen. *The Red Badge of Courage.* New York, 1895. "Gilbert Parker's Best Books . . ." in ads at back with perfect type in the last line on page 225. $4,500. Second printing includes this title in ads. $2,000. New York, 1896. $450. London, 1896. $750. New York, 1931. One of 980 copies. $250. Limited Editions Club, New York, 1944. Illustrated. Embossed morocco. In slipcase. $300.

CRANE, Stephen. *The Third Violet.* New York, 1897. $250. London, 1897. $150.

CRANE, Stephen. *War Is Kind.* New York, 1899. Illustrated by Will Bradley. Pictorial gray boards. $1,250.

CRANE, Stephen. *Whilomville Stories.* New York, 1900. (Copyright William Howe Crane.) $300. (Note: One known copy, copyright "Stephen Crane," would be much more.) London, 1900. $200.

CRANE, Stephen. *Wounds in the Rain.* London, 1900. With catalogue dated "August 1900." $450. Printed from American plates, but preceded that edition by three days. Second binding has "October, 1908." $400. New York (1900). $300.

CRANE, Stephen, and BARR, Robert. *The O'Ruddy.* New York (1903). $150.

CRANE, Walter. *The Bases of Design.* London, 1898. Blue-gray cloth. $400.

CRANE, Walter. *Flora's Feast.* London, 1889. Illustrated by the author. $400.

CRANE, Walter. *Of the Decorative Illustration of Books Old and New.* London, 1896. Illustrated. Cloth. One of 130 copies. $500.

CRANE, Walter. *Slate and Pencil-Vania.* London, 1885. Illustrated. Pictorial half cloth. $250.

CRANE, Walter. *Triplets.* London, 1899. Designs in color by Crane. Half vellum. One of 750 copies. $600. One of 20 copies on Japan vellum. $1,500.

CRANFORD. London, 1853. By the author of "Mary Barton," "Ruth," etc. (By Elizabeth C. Gaskell.) Green cloth. $3,500. New York, 1853. $600.

CRAPSEY, Adelaide. *Verse.* Rochester, 1915. Author's first book. $125.

CRARY, Mary. *The Daughters of the Stars.* London, 1939. Illustrated by Edmund Dulac. Half vellum. One of 500 copies signed by the author and the artist. In dustwrapper. $750.

CRAWFORD, F. Marion. *Katharine Lauderdale.* London, 1894. 3 vols. $300.

CRAWFORD, F. Marion. *Our Silver . . .* New York, 1881. Author's first book. Wraps. $400.

CRAWFORD, F. Marion. *Uncanny Tales.* London, 1911. $350.

CRAWFORD, F. Marion. *Wandering Ghosts.* New York (1911). $300. (U.S. title for *Uncanny Tales.*)

CRAWFORD, Lewis F. *Rekindling Camp Fires.* Bismarck, N.D. (1926). One of 100 signed copies. In slipcase. $750. Trade edition. Cloth. In dustwrapper. $200.

CRAWFORD, Lucy. *The History of the White Mountains.* Portland, Maine, 1846. $500.

CRAWSHAY, Richard. *The Birds of Tierra del Fuego.* London, 1907. 21 color plates by J. G. Keulemans, 23 photographic views, map. Half morocco. One of 300 copies. $2,000.

CRAYON, Geoffrey. *The Alhambra.* London, 1832. (By Washington Irving.) 2 vols. $400. Philadelphia, 1832. Anonymously published ("By the Author of 'The Sketch-Book'"). 2 vols. $350. Priority uncertain (BAL has U.K. first; Johnson, et al. have U.S. first.)

CRAYON, Geoffrey. *Bracebridge Hall, or The Humourists.* New York, 1822. (By Washington Irving.) 2 vols. $400. London, 1822. Text ending on page 403, vol. 2. $300. New York, 1896. Surrey Edition. 2 vols. Arthur Rackham illustrations. Pictorial cloth. $400. New York, 1896. 2 vols. $300.

CRAYON, Geoffrey. *The Sketch Book of Geoffrey Crayon, Gent.* New York, 1819–20. 7 parts, wraps. (By Washington Irving.) Parts 1 through 5 dated 1819, parts 6 and 7 dated 1820. $13,000 at auction in 1995. Rebound in book form. $1,000. (Note: Second editions so identified on wraps. See BAL.)

CREASEY, John. *Seven Times Seven.* London, 1932. Author's first book. $750.

CREELEY, Robert. *All That Is Lovely in Men.* Asheville, 1955. Drawings by Dan Rice. Pictorial wraps. Jargon No. 10. One of 200 copies signed by Creeley and Rice. In dustwrapper. $300.

CREELEY, Robert. *The Charm.* (Mt. Horeb, Wis.): Perishable Press, 1967. Leather-backed cloth. One of 250 signed copies. Issued without dustwrapper. $300. San Francisco, 1969. Wraps. One of 100 signed copies. $200.

CREELEY, Robert. *Divisions and Other Early Poems.* (Mt. Horeb), 1968. Wraps. One of 110 copies. $250.

CREELEY, Robert. *For Love: Poems 1950–1960.* New York (1962). Cloth. $250. Wraps. $50.

CREELEY, Robert. *The Gold Diggers.* (Mallorca): Divers Press, 1954. Wraps. $200. New York (1965). Cloth. $125. Wraps. $40.

CREELEY, Robert. *The Immoral Proposition.* (Baden, Germany, 1953.) Wraps. (200 copies.) $1,000.

CREELEY, Robert. *Le Fou.* Columbus, Ohio, 1952. Frontispiece. Decorated wraps. Author's first book. $750.

CREELEY, Robert. *Poems, 1950–1965.* London (1966). Vellum and boards. One of 100 signed copies. In slipcase. $500.

CREELEY, Robert. *The Whip.* (Worcester, England), 1957. Cloth. One of 100 copies. $600. Wraps. One of 500 copies. $150.

CREMONY, John C. *Life Among the Apaches.* San Francisco, 1868. $400.

CREUZBAUR, Robert (compiler). *Route from the Gulf of Mexico and the Lower Mississippi Valley to California and the Pacific Ocean.* New York, 1849. 5 maps in pocket. $7,500.

CREVECOEUR, Michael Guillame Jean de. See *Letters from . . .*

CREVEL, Rene. *Mr. Knife, Miss Fork.* Paris: Black Sun Press, 1931. With 19 photograms. Translated by Kay Boyle. Illustrated by Max Ernst. One of 200 copies. $6,000. One of 50 specially bound copies, signed by Crevel and Ernst. $15,000.

CREW, Benjamin J. *A Practical Treatise on Petroleum* . . . Philadelphia, 1887. Two folding plates. $500.

CREWS, Harry. *The Gospel Singer.* New York, 1968. Author's first book. $1,500.

CREWS, Harry. *Karate Is a Thing of the Spirit.* New York, 1971. $350.

CREWS, Harry. *Naked in Garden Hills.* New York, 1969. Without two dots at bottom of copyright page and in dustwrapper without reviews for this title on back. $350. In dustwrapper with reviews of this book. $150. London, 1973. Wraps. $100.

CREWS, Harry. *This Thing Don't Lead to Heaven.* New York, 1970. $350.

CREYTON, Paul. *Paul Creyton's Great Romance!! Kate the Accomplice; or, the Preacher and the Burglar.* Boston (1849). (By John Townsend Trowbridge.) Author's first book. With 1849 cover date. Pictorial pink wraps. $2,000.

CRICHTON, Michael. See Hudson, Jeffrey; Lange, John.

CRICHTON, Michael. *The Andromeda Strain.* New York, 1969. $300.

CRISP, Quentin. *Colour in Display.* London, 1938. Author's first book. $350.

CRISPIN, Edmund. *The Case of the Gilded Fly.* London, 1944. (By Robert Bruce Montgomery.) Author's first book. $750.

CRISPIN, Edmund. *Holy Disorders.* (By Robert Bruce Montgomery.) London (1945). $400.

CRISPIN, Edmund. *The Long Divorce.* (By Robert Bruce Montgomery.) London, 1951. $200.

CRISPIN, Edmund. *The Moving Toyshop.* London (1946). (By Robert Bruce Montgomery.) $650. Philadelphia, 1946. $350.

CRISPIN, Edmund. *Obsequies at Oxford.* Philadelphia, 1945. (By Robert Bruce Montgomery.) First U.S. of author's first book with new title. $350.

CROAKER, Croaker & Co., and CROAKER, Jun. *Poems.* New York, 1819. (By Joseph Rodman Drake and Fitz-Greene Halleck.) First book by each author. 36 pages. $500.

CROCKET, George L. *Two Centuries in East Texas.* Dallas (circa 1932). $250.

CROCKETT, David. See *Davy Crockett's Almanac.*

CROCKETT, David. *An Account of Col. Crockett's Tour to the North and Down East.* Philadelphia, 1835. $1,000.

CROCKETT, David. *David Crockett's 1838 Almanac.* Nashville (1837). Wraps. $1,500.

CROCKETT, David. *A Narrative of the Life of Col. David Crockett.* Philadelphia, 1834. Written by Himself. With 22 pages of ads at end. $1,250.

CROCKETT, S. R. See Bereton, Ford.

CROFT-COOKE. See Bruce, Leo.

CROFT-COOKE, Rupert. *Songs of a Sussex Tramp.* Steyning, 1922. Author's first book. One of 600 copies. $175.

CROFTS, Freeman Wills. *The Cask.* London (1920). Author's first book. 2 pages of ads at back, "Spring List 1920." In dustwrapper. $5,000. Without dustwrapper. $1,000.

CROFTS, Freeman Wills. *Found Floating.* London, 1937. $1,250. New York, 1937. $400.

CROFTS, Freeman Wills. *Golden Ashes.* London, 1940. $1,500.

CROFTS, Freeman Wills. *The Groote Park Murder.* London (1923). $2,500. New York, 1925. $1,000.

CROFTS, Freeman Wills. *Man Overboard.* London, 1936. $1,500.

CROFTS, Freeman Wills. *The Pit-Prop Syndicate.* London (1922). $3,000.

CROLL, Robert Henderson. *Tom Roberts—Father of Australian Landscape Painting.* Melbourne, 1935. 6 tipped-in color plates. $750.

CROMBIE, Charles. *Rules of Golf Illustrated.* (London, 1905.) 24 colored plates. $3,500.

CROMPTON, Richmal. *Just—William.* London, 1922. Author's first book. $450.

CROMWELL: An Historical Novel. New York, 1838. (By Henry William Herbert.) 2 vols. First issue, with 12 pages of ads. $200.

CRONIN, A. J. *Dust Inhalation by Hematite Miners.* (London), 1926. Author's first book. Wraps. Offprint. $350.

CRONIN, A. J. *Hatter's Castle.* London, 1931. $450. New York, 1931. $350.

CROSBY, Caresse. See C., C.

CROSBY, Caresse. *Crosses of Gold: A Book of Verse.* Paris, 1925. Author's first book. Hand-colored illustrations. Green parchment. One of 100 copies. $1,500. Exeter (England), 1925. Wraps. $350.

CROSBY, Caresse. *Graven Images.* Boston, 1926. $600.

CROSBY, Caresse. *Painted Shores.* Paris, 1927. Illustrated with 3 watercolors. Wraps. One of 222 copies on Arches paper. In tissue dustwrapper. $650.

CROSBY, Everett. *Susan's Teeth and Much About Scrimshaw.* (Nantucket, 1955.) Cloth and boards in glassine dustwrapper. $1,500.

CROSBY, Harry. *Chariot of the Sun.* Paris: Black Sun Press, 1931. Introduction by D. H. Lawrence. Wraps. One of 500 copies. $750.

CROSBY, Harry. *The Collected Poems.* Paris, 1931. 4 vols. One of 500 copies. $2,000.

CROSBY, Harry. *Mad Queen:Tirades.* Paris: Black Sun Press, 1929. Drawing by Caresse Crosby. Stiff wraps. One of 20 signed copies. $3,000. One of 100 copies. $1,500. Trade. $600.

CROSBY, Harry. *Shadows of the Sun.* Paris: Black Sun Press, 1928–30. 3 vols. Printed wraps. One of 44 copies. In glassine dustwrapper. $1,500. Santa Barbara, 1977. Trade edition. One of 1,300 copies. $150.

CROSBY, Harry. *Sleeping Together:A Book of Dreams.* Paris: Black Sun Press, 1931. Wraps. One of 500 copies. $750.

CROSBY, Harry. *Sonnets for Caresse.* Paris, 1927. $1,500.

CROSBY, Harry. *Torchbearer.* Paris: Black Sun Press, 1931. Notes by Ezra Pound. Wraps. One of 500 copies. $750.

CROSBY, Harry. *Transit of Venus.* Paris: Black Sun Press, 1929. Second edition, with 10 new poems. One of 200 copies. Printed wraps with glassine. In gold and silver slipcase. $350.

CROSBY, Henry Grew. *Anthology.* (Paris, 1924.) Author's first book. Wraps. $2,500.

CROSBY, Sylvester S. *The Early Coins of America.* Boston, 1875. With 2 folding facsimiles and 10 plates. $750. New York, 1983. $75.

CROTCHET Castle. London, 1831. By the author of *Headlong Hall.* (Thomas Love Peacock.) $1,000.

CROTHERS, Samuel McCord. *Miss Muffet's Christmas Party.* St. Paul [1891]. Author's first book. Pictorial vellum wraps. $250. Boston, 1902. $75.

CROTTY, D. G. *Four Years Campaigning in the Army of the Potomac.* Grand Rapids, 1894. $300.

CROWDER, Henry; BECKETT, Samuel; ALDINGTON, Richard; and others. *Henry-Music.* Paris: Hours Press, 1930. Pictorial boards. One of 100 copies signed by Crowder. (Includes poems by the authors set to music by Crowder, a black musician.) $7,500.

CROWE, Eyre. *With Thackeray in America.* New York, 1893. $300.

CROWLEY, Aleister. See *Therion,The Master.* See also *Aceldama.*

CROWLEY, Aleister. *Ahab and Other Poems.* London, 1903. Wraps. $300. Vellum. Printed on vellum. $1,500.

CROWLEY, Aleister. *The Diary of a Drug Fiend.* London, 1922. $3,500. New York (1923). $1,250.

CROWLEY, Aleister. *Magick in Theory and Practice.* London, 1929. $1,250.

CROWLEY, Aleister. *Moonchild:A Prologue.* London, 1929. $1,500.

CROWLEY, Aleister. *Olla: An Anthology of Sixty Years of Song.* London (1946). One of 500 copies. $400. One of 20 copies on handmade paper. $1,500.

CROWLEY, Aleister. *Songs of the Spirit.* London, 1898. One of 50 copies. $1,500. One of 300 copies. $600.

CROWLEY, Aleister. *The Soul of Osiris.* London, 1901. Boards, cloth spine, paper label. $1,250.

CROWLEY, John. *The Deep.* Garden City, 1975. Author's first book. $300.

CROWLEY, John. *Little, Big.* New York (1981). Wraps. $250. London, 1982. First hardback. $750.

CROWLEY, Mart. *The Boys in the Band.* New York (1968). $200.

CRUIKSHANK, George. See *The Humourist.*

CRUIKSHANK, George. *George's Table Book.* London, 1845. $600.

CRUIKSHANK, George. *Illustrations of Time.* London, 1827. 6 leaves of illustrations. Oblong, wraps. $500.

CRUISE, Richard A. *Journal of a Ten Months' Residence in New Zealand.* London, 1823. $750.

CRUMLEY, James. *The Muddy Fork: A Work In Progress.* Northridge, 1984. One of 50 signed copies. $350. One of 200 signed copies. $150. Livingston (1991). Adding "And Other Things." One of 125 copies in slipcase. $200.

CRUMLEY, James. *One to Count Cadence.* New York, 1969. Author's first book. $450.

CRUMLEY, James. *The Pigeon Shoot.* Santa Barbara, 1987. One of 26 signed, lettered copies. In slipcase. $500. One of 350 signed copies. $200.

CRUMLEY, James. *The Wrong Case.* New York, 1975. $1,000. London (1976). $200.

CRUNDEN, John. *Convenient and Ornamental Architecture . . .* London, 1767. 57 plates (11 folding) numbered 1–70 (some plates have two numbers). $1,750. London, 1770. $1,500. London, 1791. $600.

CRYSTAL Age (A). London, 1887. (By W. H. Hudson.) First edition, with 32 pages of ads at end. Black or red cloth. $1,500.

CUFFE, Paul. *Narrative of the Life and Adventures of Paul Cuffe, a Pequot Indian.* New York, 1839. In original wraps. $1,250.

CUILD, John, Major. *New-Englands' Jonas Cast Up at London . . .* London, 1647. $10,000.

CUISINE Creole (La). New York (1885). (Compiled by Lafcadio Hearn.) Pictorial cloth. $4,000. New Orleans, 1885 [but 1922]. Second edition. $400.

CULIN, Stewart. *Games of the North American Indians.* Washington, 1907. Original half leather. Plates, photographic illustrations. $450.

CULLEN, Countee. *The Ballad of the Brown Girl.* New York, 1927. One of 500 copies. Issued without dustwrapper in slipcase. $500. Trade edition without dustwrapper in slipcase. $300.

CULLEN, Countee. *The Black Christ and Other Poems.* New York, 1929. One of 128 signed copies. In slipcase. $1,250. Trade edition. $350.

CULLEN, Countee. *Color.* New York, 1925. Author's first book. First edition stated. $1,500.

CULLEN, Countee. *Copper Sun*. New York, 1927. One of 100 signed copies. In slipcase. $1,250. One of 500 copies. In slipcase. $600. Trade edition. $450.

CULLEN, Countee. *One Way to Heaven*. New York, 1932. $1,500.

CULLEN, Countee, and Christopher Cat. *The Lost Zoo (A Rhyme for the Young, But Not Too Young)*. New York (1940). $450.

CUMING, F(ortescue). *Sketches of a Tour to the Western Country*. Pittsburgh, 1810. $3,000.

CUMINGS, Samuel. *The Western Pilot*. Philadelphia, 1822. 2 vols. $3,500. (Note: Issued under various titles and authors from 1825 to 1860. Earlier more valuable, ranging from $1,000 down to $250.)

CUMMING, Alexander. *The Elements of Clock and Watch Work*. London, 1766. $2,500.

CUMMING, Roualeyng. *Five Years of a Hunter's Life . . .* New York, 1850. 2 vols. $650.

CUMMINGS, E. E. See *Eight Harvard Poets*. See also Aragon, Louis.

CUMMINGS, E. E. *&*. New York, 1925. Green gold-flecked boards. One of 111 copies on Vidalon paper, signed. Slipcase. $1,500. One of 222 copies on rag paper, signed. In slipcase. $1,000.

CUMMINGS, E. E. *Anthropos: The Future of Art*. (New York, 1944.) Half cloth. One of 222 copies. In cloth dustwrapper. Slipcase. $400.

CUMMINGS, E. E. *Christmas Tree*. New York, 1928. Green decorated boards. In glassine dustwrapper. $600.

CUMMINGS, E. E. *CIOPW*. New York, 1931. Cloth. Issued without dustwrapper. One of 391 signed copies. $1,500.

CUMMINGS, E. E. *Complete Poems*. Bristol (1968). 2 vols. One of 150 copies. In glossy dustwrapper and slipcase. $300.

CUMMINGS, E. E. *Eimi*. (New York, 1933.) Yellow cloth. One of 1,381 signed copies. In dustwrapper. $600. New York (1958). Boards and cloth. One of 26 lettered and signed copies. In glassine dustwrapper. $750.

CUMMINGS, E. E. *The Enormous Room*. New York (1922). With word ("shit") in last line on page 219. $3,000. Word inked out. $750. London, 1928. Includes Robert Graves introduction. $750.

CUMMINGS, E. E. *50 Poems*. New York (1940). One of 150 signed copies. In glassine dustwrapper. Slipcase. $1,250. Trade edition. $350.

CUMMINGS, E. E. *XLI Poems*. New York, 1925. $750.

CUMMINGS, E. E. *Him*. New York, 1927. Decorated boards, vellum spine and corners. One of 160 signed copies. In slipcase. $750. Trade edition. $350.

CUMMINGS, E. E. *is 5*. New York, 1926. Gold-flecked orange boards, cloth spine. $450. Black boards. One of 77 signed copies. In slipcase. $2,500.

CUMMINGS, E. E. *95 Poems.* New York (1958). One of 300 signed copies. In glassine dustwrapper. In slipcase. $500. Trade edition. $100.

CUMMINGS, E. E. *No Thanks.* (New York, 1935.) One of 90 copies on handmade paper, signed. In glassine dustwrapper. $1,250. Morocco. One of 9 copies on Japan vellum, signed. With a manuscript page. $3,000. First trade edition. One of 900 copies on Riccardi Japan paper. In dustwrapper. $250.

CUMMINGS, E. E. *Poems 1905–1962.* London, 1963. Edited by George J. Firmage. Half calf. One of 225 copies. With errata slip. In acetate dustwrapper. $450.

CUMMINGS, E. E. *Santa Claus.* New York (1946). Frontispiece. One of 250 signed copies. In glassine dustwrapper. $500. Trade edition. $200. Paris, 1974. One of 175 copies illustrated with 9 full-page original etchings signed and numbered by Alexander Calder. Very large folio, loose sheets, wraps, in illustrated cloth box. $5,000.

CUMMINGS, E. E. *Six Nonlectures.* Cambridge, 1953. One of 350 signed copies. $500. Trade edition. $125.

CUMMINGS, E. E. *Tulips and Chimneys.* New York, 1923. $1,000. Mount Vernon, N.Y., 1937. Boards, vellum spine. One of 481 copies. In dustwrapper. $500. (Of this edition, there were supposed to have been 629 signed by the author, but 148 sets of sheets were lost between printer and binder.)

CUMMINGS, E. E. *W [Viva: Seventy New Poems].* New York, 1931. Folio, buckram, and boards. One of 95 signed copies. In glassine dustwrapper. $1,250. Trade edition. $350.

CUMMINGS, Marcus. *Architecture: Designs for Street Fronts . . .* Troy, 1865. $750.

CUMMINGS, Maria. See *The Lamplighter.*

CUMMINGS, Ray. *The Girl in the Golden Atom.* London (1922). Author's first book. $750. New York, 1923. In light yellow-brown cloth with "I–X" on copyright page. $500.

CUMMINGTON Poets. (Northampton, Mass., 1939.) Wraps. One of 300 copies. $300.

CUMMINS, Ebenezer H. *A Summary Geography of Alabama.* Philadelphia, 1819. $3,000.

CUMMINS, Ella Sterling. *The Story of the Files: A Review of California Writers and Literature.* (San Francisco), 1893. Illustrated. Decorated boards or cloth. $250.

CUMMINS, Jim. *Jim Cummins' Book.* Denver, 1903. 13 plates. $1,000.

CUMMINS, Mrs. Sarah J. W. *Autobiography and Reminiscences.* (La Grande, Ore., 1914.) Portrait. Wraps. $100.

CUNARD, Nancy. *Black Man and White Ladyship: An Anniversary.* (Toulon), 1931. 10 pages, red wraps. $600. London, 1931. $300.

CUNARD, Nancy. *Outlaws.* London, 1921. Author's first book. Assumed issued without dustwrapper. $350.

CUNARD, Nancy. *Parallax.* London: Hogarth Press, 1925. Pictorial boards. Issued without dustwrapper. $500.

CUNARD, Nancy (editor). *Negro: Anthology.* London, 1934. Illustrated, including colored folding map. Brown buckram. Issued without dustwrapper. $8,500.

CUNDALL, H. M. *Birket Foster, R.W.S.* London, 1906. One of 500 copies signed by the publisher and containing an original etching. $300.

CUNDALL, Joseph. See also Percy, Stephen.

CUNDALL, Joseph. *A Booke of Christmas Carols.* London, 1846. $1,250.

CUNDALL, Joseph. *On Bookbindings, Ancient and Modern.* London, 1881. $200.

CUNNINGHAM, A. B. *Murder at Deer Lick.* New York, 1939. $350.

CUNNINGHAM, A. B. *Singing Mountains.* New York, 1919. Author's first book. In dustwrapper. $600.

CUNNINGHAM, Eugene. *Diamond River Man.* Boston, 1934. $250.

CUNNINGHAM, Eugene. *Famous in the West.* El Paso, 1926. Illustrated. Printed wraps. $300.

CUNNINGHAM, Eugene. *The Ranger Way.* Boston, 1937. $200.

CUNNINGHAM, Eugene. *Spiderweb Trail.* Boston, 1934. $200.

CUNNINGHAM, Eugene. *Texas Sheriff.* Boston, 1925. $300.

CUNNINGHAM, Eugene. *Triggernometry: A Gallery of Gunfighters.* New York, 1934. 21 plates. Pictorial cloth. $400.

CUNNINGHAM, J. V. *The Helmsman.* San Francisco, 1942. Author's first book. (300 copies in total.) Cloth. $750. Wraps. Beige floral design. $350. Plain green. $300.

CUNNINGHAME GRAHAM, R. B. See Graham.

CURIE, Marie. *Pierre Curie.* New York, 1923. One of 100 signed copies. In slipcase. $2,000. Trade edition. $250.

CURLEY, Edwin A. *Nebraska: Its Advantages, Resources and Drawbacks.* London, 1875. Illustrated. $400. New York, 1876. $300.

CURRIE, Barton. *Fishers of Books.* Boston, 1931. 2 vols. One of 365 signed copies. $175.

CURTIES. *The Friar's Tale.* London, 1805. (By T. J. Horsley.) 2 vols. $5,000.

CURTIES. *The Monk of Udolpho: A Romance.* London, 1807. (By T. J. Horsley.) 4 vols. $7,500.

CURTIS, Edward S. *The North American Indian.* Cambridge, Mass., 1907–30. Preface by Theodore Roosevelt. More than 1,500 plates. 20 quarto vols., half morocco, and 20 half-morocco portfolios of plates. One of 500 sets (about half this number actually issued). Signed by Curtis and Roosevelt (some by Curtis only). Mixed set with most of the photogravures in rarest state brought $420,000 at auction in 1995.

CURTIS, George William. See *Nile Notes of a Howadji.*

CURTIS, W., and others. *The Botanical Magazine.* London, 1787–1982. A complete run. Vols. 1–184, plus 5 vols. of Index, etc. Nearly 10,000 hand-colored plates and over 500 printed in color. $75,000. Individual vols. $100 to $1,000.

CURTISS, Daniel S. *Western Portraiture, and Emigrants' Guide.* New York, 1852. Illustrated. Folding map. $450.

CURTISS, Frederick, and HEARD, John. *The Country Club 1882–1932.* Brookline, 1932. $300.

CURWEN, Henry. *A History of Booksellers, the Old and the New.* London (1873). $175.

CURWOOD, James Oliver. *The Courage of Captain Plum.* Indianapolis, 1910. $125.

CURWOOD, James Oliver. *Danger Trail.* Indiana, 1910. $100.

CURWOOD, James Oliver. *Gold Hunters.* Indiana, 1909. $100.

CURWOOD, James. *Wolf Hunters.* Indianapolis, 1908. $150.

CUSHING, Frank Hamilton. *My Adventures in Zuñi.* Santa Fe (1941). One of 400 copies. $450.

CUSHING, Harvey. *The Pituitary Body and Its Disorders.* Philadelpha (1912). Author's first book. $750.

CUSHING, Luther S. *Manual of Parliamentary Practice.* Boston, 1845. Leather. $750.

CUSHMAN, H. B. *A History of the Choctaw, Chickasaw and Natchez Indians.* Greenville, Tex., 1899. $300.

CUSSLER, Clive. *Iceberg.* New York (1975). $2,000.

CUSSLER, Clive. *Raise the Titanic!* New York, 1976. $200.

CUSTER, Elizabeth B. *"Boots and Saddles," or Life in Dakota with General Custer.* New York, 1885. $250. Later printing, same date but adds portrait and map (Howes). $1,000.

CUSTER, Elizabeth B. *Tenting on the Plains.* New York, 1887. Frontispiece. Gray cloth. $300. In three-quarter morocco. $500.

CUSTER, George A. *My Life on the Plains.* New York, 1874. 8 illustrations. $2,500.

CUTBUSH, James. *The American Artist's Manual.* Philadelphia, 1814. 2 vols. 39 plates. $600.

CUTTS, James M. *The Conquest of California and New Mexico.* Philadelphia, 1847. 4 battle plans. $1,000.

CYNWAL, Wiliam [*sic*]. *In Defence of Woman.* London: Golden Cockerel Press (1956). 10 colored engravings. Full blue morocco. One of 100 copies with an extra engraving. $650. Another issue. One of 500 copies. $250.

D

D., F.C. *The Holtbury Idyll.* No place, circa 1908. (By Frances Crofts Darwin Cornford, her first book.) $2,000.

D., H. *Choruses from Iphigeneia in Aulis.* London, 1916. Translated from the Greek of Euripides. (By Hilda Doolittle.) Stiff wraps. $300. Cleveland, 1916. One of 40 wraps. Wraps. $2,000.

D., H. *Collected Poems.* New York, 1925. (By Hilda Doolittle.) $450.

D., H. *Hedylus.* Stratford-on-Avon (Oxford), 1928. (By Hilda Doolittle.) Decorated boards and cloth. One of 775 copies. $300.

D., H. *Hymen.* New York, 1921. (By Hilda Doolittle.) Pale-green wraps. $400. London, 1921. Boards. $300.

D., H. *Kora and Ka.* (Dijon, 1934.) (By Hilda Doolittle.) Printed wraps. One of 100 copies. $500.

D., H. *Palimpsest.* Contact Editions. (Paris), 1926. (By Hilda Doolittle.) Wraps. $400. Boston, 1926. Decorated boards and cloth. One of 700 copies. $350.

D., H. *Sea Garden: Imagist Poems.* London, 1916. (By Hilda Doolittle.) Except for a translation, her first book. Laid green paper over boards. $850. Red paper wraps (with flaps) over cardboard. $500. Boston, 1916. English sheets. $350.

D., H. *Selected Poems.* New York (1957). (By Hilda Doolittle.) One of 50 signed copies. $500. (Issued without dustwrapper.)

D., H. *The Usual Star.* London, 1928 (1934). (By Hilda Doolittle.) One of 100 copies. Wraps. $500.

DABNEY, Owen P. *True Story of the Lost Shackle.* (Salem, 1897.) Blue printed wraps. $500.

DACUS, J. A. *Life and Adventures of Frank and Jesse James.* St. Louis, 1880. $750.

DADDOW, Samuel Harries, and BANNAN, Benjamin. *Coal, Iron, and Oil . . .* Pottsville, 1866. Large colored folding map. $750.

DAGUERRE, Louis. *A Full Description of the Daguerreotype Process.* New York, 1840. Wraps. $3,000.

DAGUERRE, Louis. *Practical Description of That Process Called the Daguerreotype.* London, 1839. Wraps. $4,000.

DAHL, Roald. *Charlie and the Great Glass Elevator.* New York, 1972. $450. London, 1972. $350.

DAHL, Roald. *The Gremlins.* New York (1943). Author's first book. $2,500. London (1944). $1,750.

DAHL, Roald. *Over to You . . .* New York (1946). $350. London, 1946. $350.

DAHL, Roald. *Some Time Never.* New York, 1948. $350.

DAHL, Roald. *Someone Like You.* New York, 1953. $150. London, 1954. $350.

DAHLBERG, Edward. *Bottom Dogs.* London (1929). Introduction by D. H. Lawrence. Author's first book. One of 520 copies. $350. New York (1930). $175.

DAHLBERG, Edward. *The Confessions of Edward Dahlberg.* New York (1971). One of 200 signed copies. In slipcase. $250.

DAHLBERG, Edward. *Do These Bones Live?* New York (1941). $150.

DAHLBERG, Edward. *The Flea of Sodom.* London (1950). $150.

DAHLBERG, Edward. *From Flushing to Calvary.* New York (1932). $200.

DAHLBERG, Edward. *Kentucky Blue Grass Henry Smith.* Cleveland, 1932. Drawings by Augustus Peck. One of 10 signed copies. In dustwrapper. $1,000. One of 85 copies (not signed). In dustwrapper. $500.

DAHLBERG, Edward. *The Sorrows of Priapus.* (New York): Thistle Press (1957). Illustrated by Ben Shahn. Printed white boards. One of 150 copies signed by author and artist. Extra signed lithograph laid in. In glassine dustwrapper. In slipcase. $750.

DALE, Edward Everett. *The Range Cattle Industry.* Norman, Okla., 1930. Plates. $350.

DALE, Harrison Clifford (editor). *The Ashley-Smith Explorations.* Cleveland, 1918. 2 maps, 3 plates. One of 750 copies. $400. Glendale, Calif., 1941. Revised edition. One of 750 copies. $400.

DALI, Salvador. *Fifty Secrets of Magic Craftmanship.* Dial, 1948. $400.

DALI, Salvador. *Hidden Faces.* New York, 1944. $100. London, 1973. Half vellum. One of 100 copies signed by Dalí. With limited pamphlet *Postface to Hidden Faces.* In slipcase. $1,250. Trade. $150.

DALI, Salvador. *The Secret Life of Salvador Dali.* New York, 1942. Illustrated. Cloth, pictorial labels. One of 119 copies with an original Dalí drawing. In dustwrapper. In slipcase. $4,500. Trade edition. $300.

DALRYMPLE, Alexander. *An Historical Collection of Several Voyages . . .* London, 1770–71. 2 vols. 6 folding maps (one as frontispiece) and 12 plates. $10,000.

DALTON Brothers and Their Astounding Career of Crime (The). Chicago, 1892. By an Eye Witness. Pictorial wraps. $750.

DALTON, Emmett. *When the Daltons Rode.* Garden City, 1931. Portrait and plates. Pictorial cloth. $600.

DALTON, John. *A New System of Chemical Philosophy.* Manchester, 1808–27. Part 1 and 2 of vol. I, and part 1 of vol. II (all published). $22,000 at auction in 1998.

DALY, Carroll John. *The Hidden Hand.* New York, 1929. $1,500.

DALY, Elizabeth. *Deadly Nightshade.* New York (1940). $500.

DALY, Victor. *Not Only War.* Boston (1932). $600.

DAMON, S. Foster. *William Blake: His Philosophy and Symbols.* Boston, 1924. First American edition. Boards. $250. London, 1924. (Same sheets.) $200.

DAMON, Samuel C. *A Journey to Lower Oregon and Upper California, 1848–49.* Honolulu, 1849. Sheets from the periodical *The Friend,* with title page added. $1,250. San Francisco, 1927. Grabhorn printing. One of 250 copies. $350.

DAMPIER, William. *A Collection of Voyages.* London, 1729. 4 vols. 64 maps, plans, or plates. $7,500.

DAMPIER, William. *A New Voyage Round the World.* London, 1927. 4 maps, portrait. Half vellum. One of 975 copies on vellum. $350.

DANA, Edmund. *Geographical Sketches on the Western Country: Designed for Emigrants and Settlers.* Cincinnati, 1819. Boards. $1,500.

DANA, J. G., and THOMAS, R. S. *A Report of the Trial of Jereboam O. Beauchamp.* Frankfort, Ky. (1826). 153 pages. $1,000.

DANA, James Dwight. *A System of Minerology.* New Haven, 1837. $3,500. New York, 1844. Second edition. $750. New York, 1850. Third edition. $500. New York, 1854. Fourth edition. $350.

DANA, Richard H., Sr. *Poems.* Boston, 1827. Author's first book, preceded by several pamphlets. $300.

DANA, Richard Henry, Jr. Also see *Two Years Before the Mast.*

DANA, Richard Henry, Jr. *To Cuba and Back: A Vacation Voyage.* Boston, 1859. $350.

DANA, Richard Henry, Jr. *Two Years Before the Mast.* Boston, 1869. First under his name. With new preface and added chapter. $450.

DANCE of Life (The). London, 1817. (By William Combe.) Frontispiece. Engraved title, 26 hand-colored plates by Thomas Rowlandson. $1,750.

DANIEL, John W. *Character of Stonewall Jackson.* Lynchburg, Va., 1868. $200.

DANIELL, Thomas and William. *A Picturesque Voyage to India; by the Way of China.* London, 1810. Oblong folio with 50 colored plates. $8,500.

DANIELS, Jonathan. *Devil Trends.* Chapel Hill, 1922. Author's first book. $150.

DANIELS, William M. *A Correct Account of the Murder of Generals Joseph and Hyrum Smith, at Carthage, on the 27th Day of June, 1844.* Nauvoo, Ill., 1845. 24 pages, wraps. First edition, first issue, without plates. $6,000. Second issue, with 2 woodcut engravings added. $6,000.

DANISH Eighteenth Century Bindings, 1730–1780. Copenhagen, 1930. 102 plates. $350.

DANNAY, Frederic. See Queen, Ellery.

DARBY, William. *The Emigrant's Guide to the Western and Southwestern States and Territories.* New York, 1818. 3 maps, 2 tables. $2,500.

DARBY, William. *A Geographical Description of the State of Louisiana.* Philadelphia, 1816. Map. $1,000. New York, 1817. Second edition, with 3 maps and including a large folding map. $2,500.

DARBY, William. *A Tour from the City of New York, to Detroit, in the Michigan Territory.* New York, 1819. 3 folding maps (1 in some copies). $600.

DARLINGTON, Mary Carson (editor). *Fort Pitt and Letters from the Frontier.* Pittsburgh, 1892. 3 maps, 3 plates. 1 of 100 large-paper copies. $500. Ordinary issue, one of 200 copies. $400.

DARLOW, T. H., and MOULE, H. F. *Historical Catalogue of the Printed Editions of Holy Scripture in the Library . . .* New York, 1963. Reprint of the 1903 first edition. $750.

DARROW, Clarence. *Crime: Its Cause and Treatment.* New York, 1922. $750.

DARROW, Clarence. *Farmington.* Chicago, 1904. $300.

DARROW, Clarence. *A Persian Pearl.* Chicago, 1899. (Edited by.) $300.

DARROW, Clarence. *Realism in Literature and Art.* Chicago (1899). Author's first book. Wraps. First stated. $300.

DARROW, Clarence. *Resist Not Evil.* Chicago, 1903. $250.

DARROW, Clarence. *The Story of My Life.* New York and London, 1932. Ivory cloth. 294 signed copies. $2,500.

DARWIN, Bernard. *The Golf Courses of the British Isles.* London, 1910. $1,250. New York, 1911. $500.

DARWIN, Bernard. *Green Memories.* London (1928). $500.

DARWIN, Bernard. *Tee Shots and Others.* London, 1911. $400.

DARWIN, Bernard, and others. *History of Golf in Britain.* London (1952). $300.

DARWIN, Charles. *The Descent of Man.* London, 1871. 2 vols. Illustrated. Green cloth. First issue, with "transmitted" on line 1 of page 297 of vol. 1, errata on back of title page in vol. 2, and with ads in each volume dated January. $2,500. Second issue has list of nine works by Darwin and no errata. $1,250. New York, 1871. 2 vols. $1,000.

DARWIN, Charles. *The Different Forms of Flowers on Plants of the Same Species.* London, 1877. Green cloth. $1,250.

DARWIN, Charles. *The Expression of the Emotions in Man and Animals.* London, 1872. Plates. $1,500. New York, 1873. $500.

DARWIN, Charles. *Extracts from Letters Addressed to Prof Henslow . . .* Cambridge (1835). Author's first book. $28,000 at auction in 1998.

DARWIN, Charles. *Insectivorous Plants.* London, 1875. $1,000. New York, 1875. $650.

DARWIN, Charles. *Journal of Researches* . . . London, 1839. 2 folding engraved maps. $12,500. New York, 1846. 2 vols. (Vol. III of *Narrative* . . . with new title page.) $2,000.

DARWIN, Charles. *On the Origin of Species by Means of Natural Selection.* London, 1859. Green cloth. Two quotations on page (ii) and with ads at end dated June. Folding diagram at page 117. $50,000. London, 1860. Folding diagram. Second edition with 3 quotations on page (ii) and no ads. $4,500. Second issue of this edition with "Fifth Thousand" on title page. $4,000. New York, 1860. Folding diagram. First American edition with 2 quotations facing title page. $6,000. New York, 1860. Second issue with 3 quotations on verso of half title. Folding diagram at page 108. $2,000. Limited Editions Club, New York, 1963. Leather. In slipcase. $300.

DARWIN, Charles. *The Variation of Animals and Plants* . . . London, 1868. 2 vols. First issue in green cloth with publisher's imprint in one line. 4 lines errata in vol. I, 7 lines in vol. II. $1,250. Second issue in green cloth but publisher's imprint in two lines. One-line erratum in vol. I, none in vol. II. $750. New York (1868). 2 vols. 43 illustrations. $600.

DARWIN, Charles. *The Voyage of H.M.S. Beagle.* Limited Editions Club, New York, 1956. Illustrated by Robert Gibbings. Folio, decorated sailcloth. One of 1,500 copies. In slipcase. $350.

DARWIN, Charles and others. *Narrative of the Surveying Voyages* . . . London, 1839. 4 vols. Original cloth. (Includes Darwin's *"Journal of Researches* . . .*"* as vol. III.) $30,000.

DARWIN, Erasmus. *The Temple of Nature* . . . London, 1803. $1,000.

DATE 1601. *Conversation, as It Was by the Social Fireside, in the Times of the Tudors.* (West Point, N.Y., 1882.) First authorized edition. 7 single leaves, with title on front of first leaf, unbound. (By Samuel Langhorne Clemens.) $10,000 at auction in 1991. There have been numerous printings of this item. The first 2 in 1880 by Alexander Gunn in Cleveland, Ohio, were 8 9/16 by 7 inches on wove paper in self-wraps (first printing). $20,000. Second printing, 8 7/16 by 7 1/16 inches on laid paper in self-wraps. $15,000.

DAUBENY, Charles. *Journal of a Tour Through the United States and Canada* . . . *1837–1838.* Oxford, 1843. Folding map. $1,750.

DAVENPORT, Cyril. *Cameo Book-Stamps Figured and Described.* London, 1911. $350.

DAVENPORT, Cyril. *English Embroidered Bookbindings.* London, 1899. $350. Another issue. One of 50 copies. $750.

DAVENPORT, Cyril. *English Heraldic Book-Stamps, Figured and Described.* London, 1909. $450.

DAVENPORT, Cyril. *Roger Payne: English Bookbinder of the Eighteenth Century.* Chicago: Caxton Club, 1929. One of 250 copies. $750.

DAVENPORT, Cyril. *Royal English Bookbindings.* London, 1896. Frontispiece, 7 other color plates, 27 other illustrations. $250.

DAVENPORT, Cyril. *Thomas Berthelet, Royal Printer and Bookbinder to Henry VIII* . . . Chicago, 1901. One of 252 copies. $600.

DAVENPORT, Guy. *Carmina Archilochi.* Berkeley/Los Angeles, 1964. Author's first book. Cloth. $250. Wraps. $75.

DAVENPORT, Homer. *My Quest of the Arab Horse.* New York, 1909. Cloth. $350.

DAVID, Elizabeth. *French Country Cooking*. Macdonald, 1951. $600.

DAVID, Robert Beebe. *Finn Burnett: Frontiersman*. Glendale, Calif., 1937. $250.

DAVIDSON, Bruce. *East 100th Street*. Cambridge, 1970. In printed acetate dustwrapper. $150.

DAVIDSON, Diane Mott. *Catering to Nobody*. New York, 1990. $250.

DAVIDSON, Donald. *Lee in the Mountains and Other Poems*. Boston, 1938. $250.

DAVIDSON, Donald. *An Outland Piper*. Boston, 1924. Author's first book. Boards. $300.

DAVIDSON, Donald. *The Tall Men*. Boston, 1927. $350.

DAVIDSON, Donald. *The Tennessee*. New York, 1946–48. 2 vols. $200.

DAVIDSON, Gordon Charles. *The North West Company*. Berkeley, 1918. 5 folding maps. $600.

DAVIDSON, James Wood. *The Living Writers of the South*. New York, 1869. (Contains first book appearance of Joel Chandler Harris.) $450.

DAVIDSON, John. *Diabolus Amans*. Glasgow, 1885. Author's first book. $750.

DAVIDSON, John. *Plays*. London, 1894. Aubrey Beardsley frontispiece. Pictorial cloth. One of 500 copies. $450.

DAVIE, Donald. *(Poems) Fantasy Poets*. (Oxford, 1954.) Cloth. $450. Wraps. $250.

DAVIES, Gen. Henry. *Ten Days on the Plains*. New York, no date [1872]. 18 photographs and folding map. $3,500.

DAVIES, Hugh W. *Catalogue of a Collection of Early French Books in the Library of C. Fairfax Murray*. London, 1910. One of 100 copies. $2,000. London, 1913. $1,500. London, 1961. $300.

DAVIES, Rhys. *The Song of Songs and Other Stories*. London (1927). Author's first book. Wraps. One of 100 signed copies. $250. One of 900 unsigned copies. $60.

DAVIES, Robertson. *At My Heart's Core*. Toronto, 1950. Cloth. $350. Wraps in dustwrapper. $150.

DAVIES, Robertson. *Eros at Breakfast* . . . Toronto, 1949. $250.

DAVIES, Robertson. *Shakespeare for Young Players* . . . Toronto, 1942. Issued without dustwrapper. $1,000.

DAVIES, Robertson. *Shakespeare's Boy Actors*. London (1939). Author's first book. $2,500. New York. $1,500.

DAVIES, Robertson. *Tempest Tost*. Toronto, 1951. $250. London, 1952. $150. New York (1952). $150.

DAVIES, Valentine. *Miracle on 34th Street*. New York (1947). $150.

DAVIES, W. H. *The Autobiography of a Super-Tramp*. London, 1908. Preface by Bernard Shaw. $200.

DAVIES, W. H. *The Soul's Destroyer, and Other Poems.* (London, 1905.) Buff printed wraps. Author's first book. $750.

DAVIOT, Gordon. *The Man in the Queue.* London, 1929. Author's first mystery. $1,200. New York, 1929. $1,000.

DAVIS, C. H. (editor). *Narrative of the North Polar Expedition.* Washington, 1876. $600.

DAVIS, Charles Thomas. *The Manufacture of Leather, Being a Description . . .* Philadelphia, 1885. Includes 12 tipped-in samples of dyed leathers. $600.

DAVIS, Charles Thomas. *The Manufacture of Paper; Being A Description . . .* Philadelphia, 1886. $250.

DAVIS, Don. *Return of the Rio Kid.* New York, 1940. (By Davis Dresser.) $250.

DAVIS, Duke. *Flashlights from Mountain and Plain.* Bound Brook, N.J., 1911. Illustrated by Charles M. Russell. $150.

DAVIS, Edmund. W. *Salmon-Fishing on the Grand Cascapedia.* (New York), 1904. Half vellum. One cf 100 copies. $2,000.

DAVIS, H. L. *Honey in the Horn.* New York, 1935. $600.

DAVIS, Hubert. *The Symbolic Drawings . . . for "An American Tragedy."* (New York, 1930.) Foreword by Theodore Dreiser. 20 drawings. Folio, gold and silver boards, cloth spine. One of 525 copies signed by Dreiser and Davis. $350.

DAVIS, Jefferson. *The Rise and Fall of the Confederate Government.* New York, 1881. 2 vols. $650. London, 1881. 2 vols. 14 maps. $600.

DAVIS, John. *Travels of Four Years and a Half in the United States of America . . .* London, 1803. Large folding map. $1,200. Boston, 1910. One of 487 copies. $200.

DAVIS, Lindsey. *Shadows in Bronze.* London, 1990. $500.

DAVIS, Lindsey. *Silver Pigs.* London, 1989. Author's first book. $1,250. New York, 1989. $125.

DAVIS, Paris M. *An Authentick History of the Late War Between the United States and Great Britain.* Ithaca, 1829. $200.

DAVIS, Rebecca Harding. *Margaret Howth: A Story of To-Day.* Boston, 1862. Author's first book. $125.

DAVIS, Richard Harding. *The Adventures of My Freshman.* (Bethlehem, Pa., 1883.) Author's first book. Wraps. (About 10 copies known to exist.) $3,000.

DAVIS, Richard Harding. *Cuba in War Time.* New York, 1897. Illustrated by Frederic Remington. Boards. $250.

DAVIS, Richard Harding. *Dr. Jameson's Raiders vs. the Johannesburg Reformers.* New York, 1897. Wraps. $400.

DAVIS, Richard Harding. *Gallegher and Other Stories.* New York, 1891. First issue in yellow wraps. $450. Later, cloth. $200. London, 1891. $150.

DAVIS, William Heath. *Sixty Years in California*. San Francisco, 1889. $500. San Francisco, 1929. 44 maps and plates. Half morocco. Second edition. One of 2,000 (with title changed to *Seventy-five Years in California*). $300.

DAVIS, William J. (editor). *The Partisan Rangers of the Confederate States Army*. Louisville, 1904. 65 plates. (By Adam R. Johnson.) $500.

DAVIS, William W. H. *El Gringo; or New Mexico and Her People*. New York, 1857. Frontispiece. $450.

DAVIS, William W. H. *The Fries Rebellion*. Doylestown, Pa., 1899. 10 plates. $350.

DAVIS, William W. H. *The Spanish Conquest of New Mexico: 1527–1703*. Doylestown, 1869. Folding map, plate. $750.

DAVISON, Lawrence H. *Movements in European History*. London, 1921. (By D. H. Lawrence.) First binding in brown cloth. Issued without dustwrapper. $750. Second binding, light-blue cloth. $350.

DAVY, Sir Humphry. *On the Safety Lamp for Coal Miners*. London, 1818. Folding plate. $2,000.

DAVY, Sir Humphry. *Researches, Chemical and Philosophical . . .* London, 1800. Author's first book. $7,500.

DAVY Crockett's Almanac, of Wild Sports in the West. Nashville (1834 to 1841). Pictorial wraps. Depending on condition, the Nashville almanacs for these years are worth individually from $750 to $1,250 each, possibly more. Other Crockett Almanacs with Boston and Philadelphia imprints through the 1830s and into the 1850s retail at $100 to $500.

DAWSON, Fielding. *A Simple Wish for a Sincere . . .* Black Mountain (1949). Author's first book. Wraps. $350.

DAWSON, Fielding. *6 Stories of the Love of Life*. Black Mountain (1949). Wraps. $300.

DAWSON, Capt. Francis W. *Reminiscences of Confederate Service, 1861–65*. Charleston, 1882. One of 100 copies. $4,500.

DAWSON, Lionel. *Sport in War*. London, 1936. Illustrated by Lionel Edwards. Half leather. One of 75 signed copies. $1,000.

DAWSON, Moses. *A Historical Narrative of the Civil and Military Services of Maj. Gen. William Henry Harrison*. Cincinnati, 1824. First issue, with 15-line errata slip. $1,250. Later issue, with 24-line errata slip. $1,000.

DAWSON, Nicholas. *California in '41. Texas in '51. Memoirs*. (Austin, Tex., [about 1910].) Frontispiece. $750.

DAWSON, Peter. *Crimson Horseshoe*. (By Jonathan H. Glidden.) New York, 1914. $150.

DAWSON, Simon J. *Report on the Exploration of the Country Between Lake Superior and the Red River Settlement and the Assiniboine and Saskatchewan*. Toronto, 1859. Illustrated. Folding maps. $850.

DAWSON, Thomas F., and SKIFF, F.J.V. *The Ute War: A History of the White River Massacre, etc.* Denver, 1879. 184 pages. Wraps. $2,500.

DAWSON, William Leon. *The Birds of California*. San Diego, 1923. 4 vols. Illustrated. Folio. Cloth. $750. Half leather. One of 350 copies. $1,250. One of 100 signed copies. $1,500.

DAWSON, William Leon. *The Birds of Ohio*. Columbus, Ohio, 1903. 2 vols. Illustrated. $250.

DAWSON, William Leon, and BOWLES, John H. *The Birds of Washington*. Seattle, 1909. 2 vols. Boards. One of 200 signed copies. $750. "Edition De Luxe." One of 85 copies. $1,500. One of 22 copies. $2,000.

DAY, Sherman. *Report of the Committee on Internal Improvements, on the Use of the Camels on the Plains, May 30, 1885*. (Sacramento), 1885. 11 pages. $500.

DAY-LEWIS, Cecil. See Blake, Nicholas.

DAY-LEWIS, Cecil. *Beechen Vigil & Other Poems*. London (1925). Author's first book. Green wraps (although at least one copy in cloth). $600.

DAY-LEWIS, Cecil. *Country Comets*. London, 1928. Boards. In slipcase. $200.

DAY-LEWIS, Cecil. *Dick Willoughby*. London (1933). $1,000. New York, 1938. $200.

DAY-LEWIS, Cecil. *The Magnetic Mountain*. London: Hogarth Press, 1933. Boards. One of 100 signed copies. Issued without dustwrapper. $450. Trade edition issued without dustwrapper. $175.

DAY-LEWIS, Cecil. *Noah and the Waters*. London: Hogarth Press, 1936. One of 100 signed copies. In dustwrapper. $400. Trade edition, in dustwrapper. $125.

DAY-LEWIS, Cecil (translator). *The Graveyard by the Sea*. London (1945—actually 1947). (With title page for Paul Valéry's *Le Cimetiere Marin* as right-hand page beside the title page for Day-Lewis's translation.) Marbled wraps. One of 500 copies. In fawn envelope. $450.

DEAN, Bashford. *A Bibliography of Fishes*. New York, 1916–23. 3 vols. In leather. $600.

DEAN, Henry. *Dean's Recently Improved Analytical Guide to the Art of Penmanship* . . . New York (1808). Second edition. $350.

DEAN, Henry. *Hocus Pocus* . . . Glasgow, no date [1758]. Fourth edition. $7,500. Glasgow, 1772. $5,000. Glasgow, 1806. $4,500. New York, 1846. $3,500. Omaha, 1983. One of 200 copies. $350.

DEARBORN, Henry. *The Revolutionary War Journals of Henry Dearborn, 1775–1783*. Chicago: Caxton Club, 1939. One of 350 copies. 6 plates. In slipcase. $250.

DEARDEN, Robert R., Jr., and WATSON, Douglas S. *An Original Leaf from the Bible of the Revolution and an Essay Concerning It*. San Francisco, 1930. Grabhorn printing. One of 515 copies with leaf from 1782 Bible. $350. One of 50 copies with 2 leaves. $1,000. One of 15 copies with 2 leaves plus a leaf from the Benjamin Franklin printing of the "Confession of Faith." $1,500.

DEBAR, J. H. *The West Virginia Handbook and Immigrant's Guide*. Parkersburg, W.Va., 1870. Folding map. $350.

DE BARTHE, Joe. *The Life and Adventures of Frank Grouard, Chief of Scouts*. St. Joseph., Mo. (1894). Frontispiece, 67 plates. Pictorial cloth. $600.

DE BERNIERES, Louis. *The War of Don Emmanuel's Nether Parts.* London, 1990. 2,500 copies. $350. New York (1991). $75.

DEBURY, Richard. *Philobiblon: A Treatis on the Love of Books.* London, 1832. First translation into English. $650. Albany, 1861. One of 230 copies. $450.

DEBURY, Richard. *Philobiblon of Richard DeBury, Bishop of Durham.* (San Francisco, 1925.) One of 250 copies. $300.

DEBURY, Richard. *The Philobiblon of Richard DeBury, Edited from . . .* New York, 1889. 3 vols. One of 300 copies. $500.

DEBURY, Richard. *Philobiblon, Richard DeBury, The Text and Translation of E. C. Thomas . . .* Oxford (1960). One of 500 copies. $200.

DE CAMP, L. Sprague. *Demons and Dinosaurs.* Sauk City, Wis., 1970. (500 copies.) $450.

DE CAMP, L. Sprague. *A Gun for Dinosaur . . .* Garden City, 1963. $250.

DE CAMP, L. Sprague, and PRATT, Fletcher. *Land of Unreason.* New York (1942). $350.

DE CHAIR, Somerset. *The Golden Carpet.* London: Golden Cockerel Press, 1943. Frontispiece. Half morocco. One of 470 copies. $250. One of 30 copies specially bound and inscribed. $400.

DECKER, Peter. *A Descriptive Check List Together with Short Title Index . . . 7500 Items of Western Americana . . .* New York, 1960. One of 550 copies. $350.

DECLARATION of Independence (The). Philadelphia (1776). $2,200,000 at auction in 1991.

DECLARATION of the Immediate Cause Which Induce and Justify the Secession of South Carolina from the Federal Union, and the Ordinance of Secession. Charleston, 1860. Wraps. First issue, with misprinted "Cause" for "Causes." $5,000.

DECORATIONS of the Garden-Pavilion . . . London, 1846. (By Louis Gruner.) 6 hand-colored plates. $2,500.

DE CORDOVA, J. *Texas: Her Resources and Her Public Men.* Philadelphia, 1858. Tables. First issue, without index. $750.

DE CORDOVA, J. *The Texas Immigrant and Traveller's Guide Book.* Austin, 1856. $2,500.

DEERSLAYER (The): or, The First War-Path. Philadelphia, 1841. By the Author of *"The Last of the Mohicans,"* James Fenimore Cooper. 2 vols., purple cloth, paper labels on spine. $2,000. London, 1841. 3 vols. $1,500. New York, 1925. Illustrated by N. C. Wyeth. $500.

DEFOE, Daniel. See *The Life and Strange Surprising Adventures of Robinson Crusoe.*

DEFOE, Daniel. *Robinson Crusoe.* Limited Editions Club, New York, 1930. In slipcase. $250.

DEFOE, Daniel. *A Treatise Concerning the Use and Abuse of the Marriage Bed . . .* London, 1727. First edition, second issue with *Conjugal Lewdness: Or, Matrimonial Whoredom* dropped from the title. $2,500.

DE FOREST, John W. *History of the Indians of Connecticut* . . . Hartford, 1851. Author's first book. First issue, page vii misnumbered iiv. $350.

DE FOREST, John W. *Miss Ravenel's Conversion from Secession to Loyalty.* New York, 1867. Cloth. $300.

DE GIVRY, G. *Witchcraft, Magic and Alchemy.* London (1931). Translated by J. C. Locke. 366 illustrations, 10 color plates. In dustwrapper. $500.

DE GOURMONT, Remy. *The Natural Philosophy of Love.* New York (1922). Translated by Ezra Pound. Boards with label with a 14-unit ornament (later 6) in dustwrapper. $750. London, 1926. $450.

DE GOUY, L. P. *The Derrydale Cook Book of Fish and Game.* New York (1937). 2 vols. Buckram. One of 1,250 copies in slipcase. $400.

DE GRAZIA, Ted. *Padre Kino.* Los Angeles, 1962. One of 250 signed copies with an original ink drawing. $450.

DE HASS, Wills. *History of the Early Settlement and Indian Wars of Western Virginia.* Wheeling, W.Va., 1851. 4 plates, folding facsimile. Decorated cloth. $600.

DEIGHTON, Len. *Horse Under Water.* London (1963). Endpapers illustrated with crossword clues. Noted with crossword competition leaf laid in. $200.

DEIGHTON, Len. *The Ipcress File.* London (1962). Author's first book. First issue, no reviews on front dustwrapper flap. $1,000. New York, 1963. $300.

DEIGHTON, Len. *Only When I Larf.* No place or date [1967]. One of 150 signed copies. Issued in ring-bound stiff, glossy, pictorial wraps, printed on rectos only. This edition was privately printed by Deighton to establish the copyright while negotiating the motion picture deal with Paramount Pictures. $1,500. London (1968). $250. Wraps. $75. New York, 1987. One of 250 signed copies. In slipcase. $150.

DELAFIELD, John, Jr. *An Inquiry into the Origin of the Antiquities of America.* New York, 1839. 11 plates, including 18-foot-long folding tissue-paper plate. $1,250.

DE LA MARE, Walter. See Ramal, Walter.

DE LA MARE, Walter. *Broomsticks and Other Tales.* London, 1925. Wood engravings. Half cloth, leather label on spine. One of 278 signed copies. $250.

DE LA MARE, Walter. *Desert Islands and Robinson Crusoe.* London, 1930. Engravings by Rex Whistler. One of 650 signed copies. $250. Trade edition. $150.

DE LA MARE, Walter. *Down-Adown-Derry.* London, 1922. Illustrated by Dorothy P. Lathrop. Blue cloth. In dustwrapper. $450.

DE LA MARE, Walter. *Henry Brocken.* London, 1904. First issue, without gilt on top edges. $200.

DE LA MARE, Walter. *The Lord Fish.* London (1933). Illustrated by Rex Whistler. Parchment. One of 60 signed copies. In dustwrapper. In slipcase. $1,000. Trade edition. $250.

DE LA MARE, Walter. *Songs of Childhood.* London, 1923. (Published earlier under his pen name, Walter Ramal.) Colored plates. Vellum and boards. One of 310 signed copies. In dust-wrapper. $300.

DE LA MARE, Walter. *The Three Mulla-Mulgars.* London, 1910. First issue, with errata slip. $175. London (1925). Illustrated by J. B. Shepherd. Boards. One of 250 signed copies. $250.

DELAND, Margaret. *The Old Garden and Other Verses.* Boston, 1886. Author's first book. White cloth and flowered cloth. $150. London, 1893. Illustrated by Walter Crane. $250. Boston, 1894. $200.

DELANEY, Shelagh. *A Taste of Honey.* New York (1959). Author's first book. One of 50 copies. Cloth. Issued without dustwrapper. $200. Wraps. $75.

DELANO, Alonzo. See *Pen-Knife Sketches.*

DELANO, Alonzo. *Life on the Plains and Among the Diggings.* Auburn, N.Y., 1854. Frontispiece and 3 plates. First issue, with page 219 misnumbered 119 and with no mention of number of thousands printed. $750. Later issue. $350.

DELANO, Alonzo. *A Narrative of Voyages and Travels, in the Northern and Southern Hemispheres.* Boston, 1817. 2 portraits, folding map, errata leaf. $2,500.

DELANO, Judah. *Washington (D.C.) Directory.* Washington, 1822. $1,500.

DELANO, Reuben. *Wanderings and Adventures of Reuben Delano.* Worcester, Mass., 1846. 3 plates. 102 pages, pictorial wraps. $2,800 at auction in 1996.

DELAVAN, James. See *Notes on California and the Placers.*

DELAY, Peter J. *History of Yuba and Sutter Counties, California.* Los Angeles, 1924. Illustrated. Three-quarter leather. $300.

DeLILLO, Don. *Americana.* Boston, 1971. Author's first book. $1,000.

DeLILLO, Don. *End Zone.* Boston, 1972. $450.

DELL, Floyd. *Runaway.* New York (1925). One of 250 signed copies. In slipcase. $175.

DELL, Floyd. *Women as World Builders.* Chicago, 1913. Author's first book. $200.

DE LONG, Emma. *The Voyage of the Jeanette* . . . Boston, 1884. 2 vols. Copper-colored cloth. $750.

DELORIA, Vine, Jr. *Custer Died for Your Sins.* New York, 1969. Author's first book. $200.

DEMIJOHN, Thom. *Black-Alice.* Garden City, 1968. (By Thomas K. Disch and John T. Sladek.) $300.

DEMOCRACY: An American Novel. New York, 1880. (By Henry Adams.) No. 112 in "Leisure Hour Series." Presumed first issue in white cloth, and printed red endpapers, with March 31, 1880, in last line on front pastedown, and signature mark "F" on page 65. $1,000.

DE MORGAN, August. *An Essay on Probabilities* . . . London, 1838. $750.

DE MORGAN, August. *Formal Logic* . . . London, 1848. Blindstamped cover decoration. $1,000.

DEMOS:A Story of English Socialism. London, 1886. (By George Gissing.) 3 vols. Brown cloth. $3,000.

DEMPSEY, Jack. *Round-by-Round: An Autobiography.* New York, 1940. $200.

DENBY, Major Dixon; CLAPPERTON, Captain Hugh, and OUDNEY, Doctor. *Narrative of Travels and Discoveries in Northern and Central Africa* . . . London, 1826. 34 engraved plates (one hand-colored), 3 sketch maps, 6 engraved vignettes, and a large engraved route map. $3,000.

DENBY, Edwin. *In Public, in Private: Poems.* Prairie City, Ill. (1948). Illustrated. Blue cloth. $600. Gray cloth. $500.

DENBY, Edwin. *Second Hurricane.* Boston (1938). Author's first book. Lyrics from a play. Wraps. $500.

DENNIE, Joseph. *The Lay Preacher* . . . Walpole, New Hampshire, 1796. Author's first book. $600. Philadelphia, 1817. (Different content.) $450.

DENNIS, Patrick. *Auntie Mame.* New York (1955). Author's first book. $300.

DENNY, Arthur A. *Pioneer Days on Puget Sound.* Seattle, 1888. $500.

DENTON, Sherman F. *As Nature Shows Them: Moths and Butterflies of the United States East of the Rocky Mountains.* Boston (1898–1900). 2 vols. 56 colored plates. Half leather. One of 500 copies. $5,000. Boston (1900). 3 vols. $2,500.

DEPONS, François. *Travels in Parts of South America, During the Years 1801–1804.* London, 1806. Folding map and plan. $450. London, 1807. 2 vols. $400.

DEPONS, François. *A Voyage to the Eastern Part of Terra Firma* . . . New York, 1806. Translated by an American Gentleman. 3 vols. Map. (Translated by Washington Irving, Peter Irving, and George Caines.) First edition in English. Washington Irving's first book. $1,500.

DEPREDATIONS and Massacre by the Snake River Indians. (Washington), 1861. 16 pages, sewn. $250.

DE QUILLE, Dan. *History of the Big Bonanza.* Hartford, 1876. Illustrated. Decorated cloth. (By William Wright.) First issue, without plate no. 44. $250.

DE QUILLE, Dan. *A History of the Comstock Silver Lode and Mines.* Virginia (City, Nev., 1889). (By William Wright.) Printed wraps. $350.

DE QUINCEY, Thomas. See *Confessions of an English Opium Eater; Klosterheim, or, The Masque.*

DE QUINCEY, Thomas. *The Logic of Political Economy.* Edinburgh, 1844. $2,000.

DE RICCI, Seymour. *A Census of Caxtons.* Oxford, 1909. Wraps. $450.

DE RICCI, Seymour. *French Signed Bindings in the Mortimer L. Schiff Collection.* New York, 1935. 3 vols. and *British and Miscellaneous Signed Bindings in the Mortimer L. Schiff Collection.* New York, 1935. 1 vol. The 4 vols. $2,500.

DERLETH, August. *In Re: Sherlock Holmes.* Sauk City, 1945. $300.

DERLETH, August. *The Memoirs of Solar Pons.* Sauk City, 1951. Foreword by Ellery Queen. $250.

DERLETH, August. *Murder Stalks the Wakely Family.* New York, 1934. $1,250.

DERLETH, August. *Not Long for This World.* Sauk City, 1948. $175.

DERLETH, August. *The Reminiscences of Solar Pons.* Sauk City, 1961. $200.

DERLETH, August. *The Return of Solar Pons.* Sauk City, 1958. $200.

DERLETH, August. *Someone in the Dark.* (Sauk City, Wis.), 1941. Arkham House. First issue, 17.6 cm tall. $1,250. Later: Falsely issued "first edition," a facsimile, bound with a headband (not on the first binding) and 18.35 cm tall. $300.

DERLETH, August. *Something Near.* Sauk City, 1945. $200.

DERLETH, August. *Three Problems for Solar Pons.* Sauk City, Wis., 1952. $450.

DERLETH, August. *To Remember.* Vermont, 1931. Author's first book. 29-page pamphlet. Wraps. $1,000.

DERLETH, August, and LOVECRAFT, H. P. *The Lurker at the Threshold.* Sauk City, 1945. $250.

DE ROOS, Fred F. *Personal Narrative of Travels in the United States and Canada in 1826.* London, 1827. 14 plates and plans. $750. Second edition, same date. 14 lithographs, 2 maps. $600.

DERRY, Derry Down. *A Book of Nonsense.* London (1846). Author's first book for children. Illustrated. Oblong, printed wraps. (By Edward Lear.) One of 175 copies. (For second edition, see Lear listing.) $7,500.

DESCENDANT (The). New York, 1897. (By Ellen Glasgow.) Author's first book. First printing, with single imprint on title page, and first binding, with author's name omitted from spine. $300.

DESCRIPTION of Central Iowa (A), with Especial Reference to Polk County and DesMoines, the State Capital. Des Moines, 1858. 32 pages, stitched. $600.

DESCRIPTIVE Account of the City of Peoria (A). Peoria, 1859. 32 pages, wraps. $350.

DESCRIPTIVE Bibliography of the Books Printed at the Ashendene Press, 1895–1935. Chelsea, 1935. 15 collotype plates, 10 of bindings; 2 photogravures, and numerous specimen pages, initial letters, woodcuts, etc. Cowhide. One of 390 copies. In slipcase. $3,500.

DESCRIPTIVE, Historical, Commercial, Agricultural, and Other Important Information Relative to the City of San Diego, California. (San Diego), 1874. 22 photographs. 51 pages, wraps. $2,000.

DE SHIELDS, J. T. *Border Wars of Texas.* Tioga, Tex., 1912. $400.

DE SHIELDS, J. T. *Cynthia Ann Parker.* St. Louis, 1886. Frontispiece, 3 portraits. $750.

DES IMAGISTES:An Anthology. New York, 1914. (Edited by Ezra Pound including poems by Pound and James Joyce.) $1,000. London, 1914. First English issue (American sheets). $500.

DE SMET, Pierre-Jean. *Letters and Sketches* . . . Philadelphia, 1843. With folded allegorical leaf and 12 plates. First with 252 (later 244) pages. $3,000.

DE SMET, Pierre-Jean. *Life, Letters and Travels of Father Jean-Pierre de Smet.* New York, 1905. 4 vols. Edited by Hiram M. Chittenden. Map, 3 plates, 3 facsimiles. $1,250.

DE SMET, Pierre-Jean. *Oregon Missions and Travels over the Rocky Mountains* . . . New York, 1847. Folding map, 12 plates. $1,000.

DESPERATE Remedies: A Novel. London, 1871. 3 vols. (By Thomas Hardy.) Author's first book. Red cloth. (500 printed.) $17,500. New York, 1874. Yellow cloth. With "Author's Edition" on copyright page. $750.

DESTINY; or The Chief's Daughter. Edinburgh, 1831. (By Susan Edmonstone Ferrier.) 3 vols. $350.

DEUTSCH, Babette. *Banners.* New York (1919). Author's first book. Boards, paper label. In dustwrapper. $300. Without dustwrapper. $75.

DEUTSCH, Babette. *A Brittle Heaven.* New York (1926). $200.

DEUTSCH, Babette. *Fire for the Light.* New York (1930). $125.

De VINNE, Theodore L. *The Invention of Printing.* New York, 1876. Half morocco. $450. New York, 1878. Second edition. $450.

DE VINNE, Theodore L. *The Printers' Price List, A Manual* . . . New York, 1871. Second edition. $350.

DE VINNE, Theodore L. *Title Pages as Seen by a Printer.* New York, 1901. One of 325 copies. $350.

DEVOTO, Bernard. *Across the Wide Missouri.* Boston, 1947. 81 plates, some in color. One of 265 copies. In slipcase. $200. Trade edition in cloth. $100.

DEVOTO, Bernard. *The Crooked Mile.* New York, 1924. Author's first book. $125.

DEVRIES, Hugo. *The Mutation Theory.* Chicago, 1909–10. 2 vols. 12 color plates, text illustrations. $500.

DEVRIES, Peter. *Angels Can't Do Better.* New York (1944). $300.

DEVRIES, Peter. *But Who Wakes the Bugler?* Boston, 1940. Author's first book. Illustrated by Charles Addams. Cloth. $400.

DEVRIES, Peter. *The Handsome Heart.* New York (1943). $350.

DEVRIES, Peter. *No, But I Saw the Movie.* Boston, 1952. $250.

DEWEES, William P. *A Treatise on the Physical and Medical Treatment of Children.* Philadelphia, 1825. $1,250.

DEWEY, John. *Psychology.* New York, 1887. Author's first book. $300.

DEWEY, Neville. *A Classification and Subject Index for Cataloguing . . .* Amherst, Mass., 1876. $600.

DE WITT, David Miller. *The Judicial Murder of Mary E. Surratt.* Baltimore, 1895. $250.

DE WOLFF, J. H. *Pawnee Bill (Maj. Gordon W. Lillie): His Experience and Adventures on the Western Plains.* No place, 1902. Illustrated. Pictorial boards. $200.

DEXTER, A. Hersey. *Early Days in California.* (Denver), 1886. Pictorial cloth. $1,000.

DEXTER, Colin. *Last Bus to Woodstock.* London (1975). Author's first book. $1,750. (New York, 1975.) $1,000.

DEXTER, Colin. *Last Seen Wearing.* (London, 1976.) $1,750. New York (1976). $1,000.

DEXTER, Colin. *The Silent World of Nicholas Quinn.* London (1977). $1,500. New York (1977). $750.

DIARY of Isaiah Thomas, 1805–1828 (The). Worcester, 1909. 2 vols. $300.

DIAZ DEL CASTILLO, Bernal. *The Discovery and Conquest of Mexico, 1517–1521.* Limited Editions Club, New York, 1942. Translated by A. P. Maudslay. Illustrated by Miguel Covarrubias. Leather. In slipcase. $350.

DIAZ DEL CASTILLO, Bernal. *The True History of the Conquest of Mexico.* London, 1800. First edition in English. Translated by Maurice Keatinge. Map, errata leaf. $1,000. Salem, 1803. 2 vols. $1,000.

DIBDIN, Thomas Frognall. *A Bibliographical, Antiquarian and Picturesque Tour in France and Germany.* London, 1821. 3 vols. $750. London, 1829. 3 vols. Second edition. $250.

DIBDIN, Thomas Frognall. *A Bibliographical, Antiquarian and Picturesque Tour in the Northern Counties of England and in Scotland.* London, 1838. 2 vols. $600.

DIBDIN, Thomas Frognall. *The Bibliographical Decameron.* London, 1817. 3 vols. $1,250.

DIBDIN, Thomas Frognall. *Bibliography: A Poem.* (London, 1812). One of 50 copies. $2,500.

DIBDIN, Thomas Frognall. *Bibliomania; Or, Book Madness . . .* London, 1809. $600. London, 1811. Second edition. $500. London, 1842. (Includes a reprint of the 1809 edition.) $500. London, 1876. Revision of the 1842 edition. $250. Boston, 1903. 4 vols. Reprint of the 1842 edition. One of 489 copies. $400.

DIBDIN, Thomas Frognall. *Bibliotheca Spenceriana.* 7 vols. London, 1814–23. $2,500. One of 50 large-paper sets. $5,000.

DIBDIN, Thomas Frognall. *An Introduction to the Knowledge of Rare and Valuable Editions of the Greek and Roman Classics . . .* Oxford, 1802. $500.

DIBDIN, Thomas Frognall. *Poems.* London, 1797. Author's first book. (500 copies.) $1,000.

DIBDIN, Thomas Frognall. *Reminiscences of a Literary Life.* London, 1836. 2 vols. $400.

DICK, Philip K. *Confessions of a Crap Artist* . . . New York, 1975. Issued without dustwrapper. One of 90 signed copies. $1,250. One of 410 copies. $400. Wraps. One of 500 copies. $200.

DICK, Philip K. *Do Androids Dream of Electric Sheep?* Garden City, 1968. $6,000. London (1969). $1,500.

DICK, Philip K. *A Handful of Darkness.* London (1955). First issue, blue boards, lettered in silver, $1,250. Second issue, orange boards, lettered in black. $1,000. (Later dustwrapper has *"World of Chance"* on rear panel.) Also variant in blue boards with black lettering. $500. Boston, 1978. Issued without dustwrapper. $300.

DICK, Philip K. *The Man in the High Castle.* New York (1962). $1,250.

DICK, Philip K. *A Maze of Death.* Garden City, 1970. $1,000.

DICK, Philip K. *The Three Stigmata of Palmer Eldritch.* Garden City, 1965. $2,000.

DICK, Philip K. *Time Out of Joint.* Philadelphia (1959). $1,000.

DICK, Philip K. *World of Chance.* London 1956. Blue boards titled in silver. First hardback edition of author's first book. $2,500. Published in paperback in U.S. as *Solar Lottery.*

DICK, R. A. *The Ghost and Mrs. Muir.* Chicago/New York (1945). (By Josephine A. Lincoln.) $750. London, 1946. $600.

DICKENS, Charles. See "Boz"; "Sparks, Timothy." See also *Sketches by "Boz."*

DICKENS, Charles. Note: The "Parts" price estimates below assume that the "points" are correct, but not necessarily all of the ad placements called for by Hatton & Cleaver may be exact. Although we have tried hard on these, one should have the bibliographies. Prices on rebound copies assume nice old calf bindings. New "Bayntun-style" morocco copies would be perhaps 50 percent more.

DICKENS, Charles. *The Adventures of Oliver Twist.* London, 1846. 24 illustrations by George Cruikshank. 10 monthly parts, green wraps. "New edition." Revised and Corrected. (For earlier editions see *Oliver Twist* under "Boz" and Dickens.) $20,000. London, 1846. Slate-colored cloth. $2,500. Rebound. $500.

DICKENS, Charles. *American Notes for General Circulation.* London, 1842. 2 vols. Horizontally ribbed or vertically ribbed (variant), brown cloth. First state, with initial pages misnumbered with page 10 (x) as "xvi." $1,750. Second state corrected. $750.

DICKENS, Charles. *The Battle of Life: A Love Story.* London, 1846. Engraved title page and frontispiece by Maclise. First issue imprint on engraved title page in 3 lines, with "A Love Story" printed in heavy type. A rebound copy was catalogued a few years ago for $45,000. No copy at auction in 50 years. We do not know what the price should be, but the first and second issues are both rare and the third is certainly scarce. Second issue with "A Love Story" in light type. $7,500. Third issue, with imprint in 3 lines and " A Love Story" engraved on a scroll. $1,250. Other variants have imprint on one line and Cupid carrying the scroll. $600.

DICKENS, Charles. *Bleak House.* London, 1852–53. Illustrated by H. K. Browne. 20 parts in 19, blue pictorial wraps. $3,500. London, 1853. First book edition. Olive-green cloth with vignette. Title page dated "1853." $4,500. Rebound. $600. New York, 1853. 2 vols. $2,000.

DICKENS, Charles. *A Child's History of England*. London, 1852–53–54. Frontispiece. 3 vols. Reddish cloth. First state of vol. I with ad page (211) listing 4 books plus the 5 Christmas books, and ad page (324) in vol. III has "Collected and Revised" for this title. $3,000. Second state, vol. I ad begins with this title plus 7 works and the Christmas books. Vol. III states "Corrected and Revised." $1,250.

DICKENS, Charles. *The Chimes*. London, 1845. 13 illustrations. Engraved title page. Red cloth. First issue, with imprint as part of engraved title. $1,000. Second issue, publisher's name printed below engraving. $450. Limited Editions Club, New York, 1931. Illustrated by Arthur Rackham. Signed by Rackham. In slipcase. $750.

DICKENS, Charles. *A Christmas Carol*. London, 1843. 4 colored plates and 4 woodcuts by John Leech. Brown cloth. There doesn't seem to be a final agreement on the first issue and would suggest some detailed research in any copy in original cloth with 1843 or 1844 on title page. The prices can vary from $5,000 to $35,000, depending on issues and condition, and many believe the green endpapers are first. In spite of this comment, most seem to believe the first is dated 1843. "Stave I" (not "Stave One") on first text page, with red-and-blue lettered title page and yellow endpapers. $15,000. Second issue, same but green endpapers. $12,500. Third issue with 1844 title page, yellow endpapers. $10,000. Fourth issue, with "Stave one." $4,500. Philadelphia, 1844. First American edition. Blue cloth. $3,500. London (1915). Illustrated in color by Arthur Rackham. Pictorial vellum. Large-paper edition. One of 525 copies. $2,500. One of 100 signed copies. Pictorial vellum. $3,500. Limited Editions Club, Boston, 1934. In slipcase. $125.

DICKENS, Charles. *The Complete Works of Charles Dickens*. Nonesuch Press. Bloomsbury, London, 1937–38. 23 vols. Edited by Arthur Waugh, Hugh Walpole, Walter Dexter, and Thomas Halton. Illustrated. Buckram (each volume a different color), leather labels, gilt, with an original engraved steel plate. One of 877 sets. $12,500.

DICKENS, Charles. *The Cricket on the Hearth*. London, 1846. Crimson cloth. First state, with ad page (175) without heading "New Edition of Oliver Twist." $750. Second state. $450. Limited Editions Club, New York, 1933. In slipcase. $250.

DICKENS, Charles. *Dombey and Son*. London, 1846–47–48. Illustrated by H. K. Browne. 20 parts in 19, green pictorial wraps. With 12-line errata slip in part V. $2,000. New York, 1846–48. First American edition. 20 parts in 19, wraps. $3,000. London, 1848. First book edition. Dark-green cloth. $3,500. Rebound. $450. Limited Editions Club, New York, 1957. 2 vols. In slipcase. $125.

DICKENS, Charles. *Great Expectations*. London, 1861. 3 vols. Violet (or yellow-green variant) cloth. First issue, with 32 pages of ads dated May, 1861 (in three places). (Later issues/editions had the edition on the title page and later ad dates.) $35,000. Rebound with original title pages. $10,000. (Note: This is a complicated book and individual copies should be checked carefully.) Limited Editions Club, New York, 1937. In slipcase. $200.

DICKENS, Charles. *Hard Times, for These Times*. Bradbury & Evans. London, 1854. Olive-green cloth with "Price 5/" on spine. $1,500. Without price on spine. $750. Harper & Brothers. New York, 1854. $1,000. Limited Editions Club, New York, 1966. In slipcase. $100.

DICKENS, Charles. *The Life and Adventures of Martin Chuzzlewit*. London, 1844. Illustrated by "Phiz," 20 parts in 19, green wraps. (There is no priority assigned to copies with English pound sign after "100" in reward notice on engraved title page.) $2,000. London, 1844. First book edition. Blue cloth (later, brown). $3,500. Rebound. $400.

DICKENS, Charles. *The Life and Adventures of Nicholas Nickleby.* London, 1838–39. Frontispiece portrait by Maclise, illustrations by "Phiz." 20 parts in 19, green pictorial wraps. First issue, with "vister" for "sister" in line 17, page 123, part IV, and "Chapman and Hall" on frontispiece and first 4 plates. $3,000. London, 1839. 1 vol. First book edition. In original dark olive-green cloth. $3,500. Rebound. $750.

DICKENS, Charles. *Little Dorrit.* London, 1855–57. Illustrated by H. K. Browne. 20 parts in 19, blue wraps. First issue, with errata slip in part XVI ("Rigaud" should have been "Blandois"), and uncorrected errors in part XV. $3,000. London, 1857. Olive-green cloth. First book edition. Errors as above and page 371 signature is "B2" vs. "2B2." $3,500. With "Blandois" and "2B2." $1,000.

DICKENS, Charles. *Master Humphrey's Clock.* London, 1840–41. 20 parts. In printed green self-wrappers. $2,500. 3 vols. First book edition. Illustrated by George Cattermole and H. K. Browne, Brown cloth. With clock on front pointing to volume numbers. $2,000. No hands on clock on variant binding. $500. (See entry under "Boz" for editions in parts.) Rebound. $400.

DICKENS, Charles. *The Mystery of Edwin Drood.* London, 1870. 12 illustrations by S. L. Fildes. 6 parts, green pictorial wraps. $1,250. London, 1870. First book edition. Green cloth with sawtooth border around front cover. $1,000. Without border. $600. Boston, 1870. $600.

DICKENS, Charles. *Oliver Twist.* London, 1838. 3 vols. In original brown cloth. Second edition (or third issue of the 1838 original, see "Boz" entry). With "Dickens" on title page instead of "Boz." $3,000. Same with 1839 on title page. $1,000. (For first octavo edition, see Dickens, *The Adventures of Oliver Twist.*)

DICKENS, Charles. *Our Mutual Friend.* London, 1864–65. Illustrations by Marcus Stone. 20 parts in 19, green pictorial wraps. $2,500. London, 1865. 2 vols. First book edition. Reddish-brown cloth. $2,500. Rebound. $450.

DICKENS, Charles. *The Personal History of David Copperfield.* London, 1849–50. Illustrated by H. K. Browne. 20 parts in 19, green pictorial wraps. $8,500. London, 1850. Dark-green cloth. First book edition, first state, with engraved title page dated 1850. $7,500. Later state. $3,000. Rebound. $1,000.

DICKENS, Charles. *Pictures from Italy.* London, 1846. Illustrations on wood by Samuel Palmer. Blue cloth. $850.

DICKENS, Charles. *The Posthumous Papers of the Pickwick Club.* London, 1836. Illustrated by R. Seymour and Phiz. 20 parts in 19, green wraps. Complicated book; one should check further. $5,000. London, 1837. In original slate or purplish-black cloth. First book edition, first issue, with "S. Veller" on page 342, line 5; "this friends" for "his friends" on page 400, line 21; and "f" in "of" imperfect in the headline on page 432. $5,000 or more. Rebound. $600. Philadelphia, 1836–37. 5 vols. First American edition. In original boards. $2,500. Limited Editions Club, New York, 1933. 2 vols. Cloth. In slipcase. $150.

DICKENS, Charles. *A Tale of Two Cities.* London, 1859. Illustrated by H. K. Browne, 8 parts in 7, blue wraps. First state, with page 134, line 12, "affetcionately" and page 213 misnumbered "113." $12,500. London, 1859. Red cloth. First book edition, first state. $15,000. In green cloth. $7,500. Rebound. $1,500.

DICKENS, Charles. *The Uncommercial Traveller.* London, 1861. Reddish-purple cloth. With ads dated December 1860. $1,750.

DICKENS, Charles. *The Village Coquettes: A Comic Opera*. London, 1836. Gray boards. Original boards. $4,500. Rebound. $1,500. Facsimile in sheets (1878). $750.

DICKENSON, Luelia. *Reminiscences of a Trip Across the Plains in 1846*. San Francisco, 1904. First edition. Pictorial cloth. $1,500.

DICKERSON, Philip J. *History of the Osage Nation*. (Cover title.) (Pawhuska, Oklahoma Indian Territory, 1906.) Illustrations and map. 144 pages, wraps. $400.

DICKEY, James. *Buckdancer's Choice*. Middletown, Conn. (1965). $350. Wraps. $150.

DICKEY, James. *Deliverance*. Boston, 1970. $250.

DICKEY, James. *Drowning with Others*. Middleton, Conn., 1962. Author's first book. Cloth. $300. Wraps. $125.

DICKEY, James. *Two Poems of the Air*. Portland, Or. (1964). Calligraphic text. Decorated boards. Oblong, decorated boards. One of 300 copies signed by the poet and the calligrapher, Monica Moseley Pincus. In slipcase. $300.

DICKINSON, Emily. See *A Masque of Poets*.

DICKINSON, Emily. *Further Poems of Emily Dickinson*. Boston, 1929. One of 465 copies. In slipcase. $750. Trade. $150.

DICKINSON, Emily. *Letters of Emily Dickinson*. Boston, 1894. 2 vols. Edited by Mabel Loomis Todd. Medium yellowish-green buckram. With Roberts Brothers imprint on spine. First printing and first issue of second printing the same. $600. (Later in brown cloth and still later by Little Brown.) Cleveland (1951). $100.

DICKINSON, Emily. *Poems*. Boston, 1890. Edited by Mabel Loomis Todd and T. W. Higginson. Author's first book. White and gray cloth. $7,500. London, 1891. First English edition. (480 copies.) $3,000. Limited Editions Club, New York, 1952. Morocco. In slipcase. $300.

DICKINSON, Emily. *Poems: Second Series*. Boston, 1891. Edited by T. W. Higginson and Mabel Loomis Todd. $1,500. Some special copies issued in decorated boards, calf spine. $2,000.

DICKINSON, Emily. *Poems: Third Series*. Roberts Brothers. Boston, 1896. Edited by Mabel Loomis Todd. First binding. Gilt stamped with Indian pipes vignette. $750. ("Second edition" so stated.)

DICKINSON, Emily. *The Single Hound: Poems of a Lifetime*. Boston, 1914. $1,000.

DICKINSON, Emily. *Unpublished Poems*. Boston, 1935. Edited by Martha Dickinson Biachi and Alfred Leete Hampson. One of 525 deluxe copies. In slipcase. $500. Boston, 1936. $150.

DICKINSON, Peter. *Skin Deep*. London (1968). Author's first mystery. $200.

DICKSON, Carter. *The Peacock Feather Murders*. New York, 1937. (By John Dickson Carr.) $1,000.

DICKSON, H.R.P. *Kuwait and Her Neighbours*. London, 1968. With 5 maps and 2 genealogical tables and 4 maps in pocket at rear. $1,000.

DIDIMUS, H. *New Orleans as I Found It.* New York, 1845. (By Edward H. Durrell.) Double columns, 125 pages, wraps. $750.

DIDION, Joan. *Run River.* New York (1963). Author's first book. $200. London (1964). $150.

DIDION, Joan. *Slouching Towards Bethlehem.* New York (1968). $150. (London, 1969.) $100.

DI DONATO, Pietro. *Christ in Concrete.* Chicago: Esquire Publishers (1937). Author's first book. In glassine dustwrapper. $150. Indianapolis (1939). $35. Expanded. Signed tipped-in leaf. $75. Trade. $35.

DIEHL, Edith. *Bookbinding: Its Background and Technique.* New York, 1946. 2 vols. $300.

DIETZ, August. *The Postal Service of the Confederate States of America.* Richmond, 1929. 2 color plates. Half leather. $350.

DIGBY, Kenelm. *Of Bodies, and of Mans Soul . . .* London, 1669. $1,500.

DILLARD, Annie. *Tickets for a Prayer Wheel.* Columbia (Mo., 1974). Author's first book. $750.

DiMAGGIO, Joe. *The DiMaggio Album.* New York (1989). 2 vols. Full leather in slipcase with cloth pinstripe number 5 affixed. One of 700 signed copies. $1,250.

DIMSDALE, Thomas J. *The Vigilantes of Montana.* Virginia City, Mont., 1866. 228 pages, printed wraps. $10,000. Rebound in half calf, $3,500. Virginia City, 1882. 241 pages, printed wraps. Second edition. $850. Cloth. $500.

DINE, Jim. *The Apocalypse: The Revelation of Saint John the Divine.* San Francisco, 1982. Folio, pigskin spine, matching slipcase edged in pigskin. One of 150 copies signed by Dine and Andrew Hoyem. $6,000.

DINESEN, Isak. See Blixen, Karen.

DINESEN, Isak. *Out of Africa.* New York (1938). $500.

DINESEN, Isak. *Seven Gothic Tales.* New York, 1934. One of 1,010 copies in slipcase. In leather. $500. In black cloth. $300. Trade edition. $350. London, 1934.

DINSDALE, Alfred. *Television: Seeing by Wireless.* London, 1926. 12 plates. Stiff wraps in dustwrapper. $5,000.

DIOMEDI, Alexander. *Sketches of Modern Indian Life.* (Woodstock, Md, [1894?]) 79 pages, wraps. $750.

DiPRIMA, Diane. *New Mexico Poems.* (New York, 1968.) Wraps. One of 50 signed copies. $250.

DiPRIMA, Diane. *This Kind of Bird Flies Backward.* (New York, 1958). Author's first book. Wraps. $150.

DIRECTORY of Newark for 1835–6. Newark, N.J., 1835. Half leather. $750 and up.

DIRECTORY of the City of Mineral Point for the Year 1859. Mineral Point, Wis., 1859. Map. 64 pages, sewn. $350.

DIRINGER, David. *The Alphabet, a Key to the History of Mankind.* London (1968). 2 vols. Third edition, completely revised. $350.

DISCH, Thomas M. See Demijohn, Thom.

DISCH, Thomas M. *Camp Concentration.* London, 1968. $350. Garden City, 1969. $175.

DISCH, Thomas M. *The Genocides.* New York (1965). Author's first book. Wraps. $50. London, 1967. $750.

DISCH, Thomas M. *Under Compulsion.* London, 1968. $300.

DISCOURSE on the Aborigines of the Valley of the Ohio (A). Cincinnati, 1838. (By William Henry Harrison.) Folding map, 51 pages, wraps. $750. Some copies with corrections in Harrison's hand. $1,500.

DISNEY, Walt. See Disney, Walter; Taylor, Deems.

DISNEY, Walt (or Disney Studios). *The Adventures of Mickey Mouse: Book I.* Philadelphia (1931). Illustrated. Pictorial boards. $3,500. London, 1931. $2,500.

DISNEY, Walt. *Little Red Riding Hood and the Big Bad Wolf.* Philadelphia (1934). Illustrated. Boards. $750.

DISNEY, Walt. *Mickey Mouse.* Racine, Wis. (1933). Illustrated. Pictorial wraps. $1,000.

DISNEY, Walt. *Pinocchio.* New York [1939]. One of 100 copies. Spiral-bound. $1,500. New York (1939). In dustwrapper. $300.

DISNEY, Walt. *The Pop-Up Mickey Mouse.* New York (1933). Illustrated with 3 double-page pop-up cutouts. Pictorial boards. Issued without dustwrapper. $750.

DISNEY, Walter. *Mickey Mouse Book.* New York: Bibo and Lang, 1930. Author's first book. Wraps with green background (or white background). Without illustrated strip on back cover. (Priority uncertain, although white is less common.) $5,000.

DISRAELI, Benjamin. See *Henrietta Temple; The Letters of Runnymede; The Tragedy of Count Alarcos; Vivian Grey; The Young Duke.*

DISRAELI, Benjamin. *Coningsby; or, The New Generation.* London (1844). 3 vols. Boards. $1,000.

DISRAELI, Benjamin. *Sybil, or The Two Nations.* London (1845). 3 vols. $1,000.

DISSERTATION on the History . . . of the Bible . . . (A). New Haven, 1772. (By Timothy Dwight.) Author's first book. Wraps. $350.

DISTURNELL, John. *The Influence of Climate in North and South America.* New York, 1867. $150.

DISTURNELL, John (publisher). *Disturnell's Guide Through the Middle, Northern, and Eastern States.* New York, June, 1847. Map of New York City, folding map. Cloth. $450.

DISTURNELL, John (publisher). *The Emigrant's Guide to New Mexico, California, and Oregon.* New York, 1849. Cloth. Folding map, 46 pages. First issue, with map published by Colton. $3,500. Second issue, wraps with map by Disturnell. $3,000.

DISTURNELL, John (publisher). *The Great Lakes or Inland Seas of America.* New York, 1868. Cloth. $750.

DISTURNELL, John (publisher). *The Upper Lakes of North America: A Guide.* New York, 1857. Cloth. $500.

DIX, John Ross. See Jones, J. Wesley.

DIXON, Captain George. *A Voyage Round the World* . . . London, 1789. Ghostwritten by William Beresford, but usually cited as by Capt. Dixon (Howes). First issue: 22 plates and charts. Quarto. $4,000. Second issue: on large and thick paper with some plates colored and much of the errata corrected. $6,500.

DIXON, Richard W. *Odes and Eclogues.* Oxford: Daniel Press, 1884. Wraps. One of 100 copies. $500.

DIXON, Sam Houston. *The Heroes of San Jacinto.* Houston, 1932. $150.

DIXON, Sam Houston. *The Poets and Poetry of Texas.* Austin, 1885. Illustrated. $300.

DIXON, Thomas, Jr. *The Clansman.* New York, 1905. $200.

DOBBS, Michael. *House of Cards.* London, 1989. Author's first book. $250.

DOBIE, J. Frank. *Apache Gold and Yaqui Silver.* Boston, 1939. Illustrated by Tom Lea. First (Sierra Madre) edition. One of 265 copies signed by author and artist. In slipcase. $1,500. Trade. $250.

DOBIE, J. Frank. *Bigfoot Wallace and the Hickory Nuts.* Austin, 1936. 7 pages, wraps. One of 300 signed copies. $500.

DOBIE, J. Frank. *Carl Sandburg and Saint Peter at the Gate.* Austin, 1966. Illustrated. Boards. One of 750 copies. Slipcase. $200.

DOBIE, J. Frank. *Coronado's Children.* Dallas (1930). Maps, illustrated. First issue, without the word "clean" in dedication. $300.

DOBIE, J. Frank. *Cow People.* Boston (1964). Fabrikoid. In dustwrapper $150. One of 15 signed copies. In slipcase. $1,500.

DOBIE, J. Frank. *John C. Duval, First Texas Man of Letters.* Dallas, 1939. Illustrated. One of 1,000 copies. In dustwrapper. $200.

DOBIE, J. Frank. *The Longhorns.* Boston, 1941. 16 plates by Tom Lea. Rawhide. One of 265 signed copies. In slipcase. $3,500. Trade edition, pictorial cloth. $125.

DOBIE, J. Frank. *The Mustangs.* Boston (1952). Illustrated. Leather. One of 100 copies with original drawing. In slipcase. $4,500. Trade edition. $150.

DOBIE, J. Frank. *Tales of the Mustang.* Dallas, 1936. Boards. One of 300 copies for the Book Club of Texas. In slipcase. $1,500.

DOBIE, J. Frank. *Tongues of the Monte.* New York, 1935. $250.

DOBIE, J. Frank. *A Vaquero of the Brush Country.* Dallas, 1929. Author's first commercially published book. First issue, with "Rio Grande River" on map. $500. With "Rio Grande." $300.

DOBIE, J. Frank, and others (editors). *Mustangs and Cow Horses.* Austin, 1940. $200.

DOBSON, Austin. *Horace Walpole: A Memoir.* New York, 1890. Illustrated by Percy and Leon Moran. Boards. One of 50 copies on Japan paper. $250. One of 484 copies. $100.

DOBSON, Austin. *Vignettes in Rhyme.* London, 1873. Author's first book. $250.

DOCTOROW, E. L. *Bad Man from Bodie.* London, 1961. Author's first book with new title. $450.

DOCTOROW, E. L. *Big as Life.* New York (1966). $500.

DOCTOROW, E. L. *Ragtime.* New York (1975). One of 150 signed copies. Issued without dustwrapper. In slipcase. $300. Unspecified number in brown cloth with signed tipped-in sheet. $125. Trade edition. $75. London, 1976. $75.

DOCTOROW, E. L. *Welcome to Hard Times.* New York, 1960. Author's first book. $750.

DODDRIDGE, Joseph. *Notes, on the Settlement and Indian Wars, of the Western Parts of Virginia and Pennsylvania . . .* Wellsburgh, Va., 1824. $1,250.

DODGE, Alfred. *Pianos and Their Makers.* Covina, Calif., 1911. $250.

DODGE, Grenville M. *Biographical Sketch of James Bridger, Mountaineer, Trapper and Guide.* Kansas City (1905). 2 plates. 10 leaves, wraps. First edition, without preface. $250. New York, 1905. 3 plates, one folding. 27 pages, wraps. $150.

DODGE, Grenville M. *How We Built the Union Pacific Railway.* Council Bluffs, Iowa (1908?). 30 plates. Printed wraps. First edition, first issue, without printer's name on page before title page. $250. Second issue. $150.

DODGE, Grenville M. *Union Pacific Railroad: Report of G. M. Dodge, Chief Engineer, to the Board of Directors on a Branch Line from the Union Pacific Railroad to Idaho, Montana, Oregon, and Puget's Sound.* Washington, 1868. Large folding map. 13 pages, wraps. $600. Second edition, same date. $500.

DODGE, M. E. *Hans Brinker; or, The Silver Skates.* New York, 1866. (By Mary Mapes Dodge.) Frontispiece with either one or two leaves of ads (no priority). 3 plates by Thomas Nast. $2,500.

DODGE, M. E. *The Irvington Stories.* New York, 1865. (By Mary Mapes Dodge.) Author's first book. Frontispiece, 4 plates. $300.

DODGE, Mary Abigail. See Hamilton, Gail.

DODGE, Mary Mapes. See Dodge, M. E.

DODGE, Orvil. *Pioneer History of Coos and Curry Counties, Oregon.* Salem, Ore., 1898. Illustrated. $350.

DODGE, Richard Irving. See *A Living Issue.*

DODGE, Richard Irving. *The Black Hills.* New York, 1876. 14 tinted plates, folding map. $300.

DODGE, Richard Irving. *Our Wild Indians.* Hartford, 1882. Illustrated. Cloth. $250. Hartford, 1883. Second edition. $200.

DODGE, Richard Irving. *The Plains of the Great West and Their Inhabitants.* New York, 1877. Illustrated. Folding map. $300.

DODGE, Theodore A. *Riders of Many Lands.* New York, 1894. 19 illustrations by Frederic Remington. $150.

DODGSON, Campbell (editor). *An Iconography of the Engravings of Stephen Gooden.* London, 1944. Illustrated. Buckram. One of 500 copies. $350. Buckram vellum spine, with original proof frontispiece (etching) signed by Gooden. One of 160 copies in half vellum. Gilt. In slipcase. $600.

DODGSON, Charles L. See Carroll, Lewis.

DODGSON, Charles L. *Curiosa Mathematica.* London, 1888. $3,500.

DODGSON, Charles L. *The Dynamics of a Particle.* Oxford, 1865. Wraps. $5,000.

DODGSON, Charles L. *The Game of Logic.* London, 1886. Red Cloth. With lettered envelope. $3,500. London, 1887. With envelope. $750.

DODGSON, Charles L. *Lawn Tennis Tournaments.* London, 1883. 10 pages, sewn, without wraps. $2,500.

DODSON, Owen. *Powerful Long Ladder.* New York, 1946. Author's first book. $300.

DODSON, W. C. (editor). *Campaigns of Wheeler and His Cavalry, 1862–1865.* Atlanta, 1899. $200.

DOERR, Harriet. *Stones for Ibarra.* New York, 1984. $150. London (1985). $50.

DOHERTY, P. C. *Dove Among the Hawkes.* London, 1990. $450.

DOHERTY, P. C. *Satan in St. Mary's.* London, 1986. $750.

DOIG, Ivan. *A History of the Pacific Northwest Forest . . .* (Portland, 1977). Stapled wraps. $250.

DOIG, Ivan. *The House of Sky.* New York, 1978. $200.

DOLCE, Lodovico. *Aretin: A Dialogue on Painting, from the Italian . . .* London, 1770. First English-language edition. $850.

DOMENECH, Emmanuel. *Seven Years' Residence in the Great Deserts of North America.* London, 1860. Author's first book. Folding map, 5 tinted plates. 2 vols. $1,250.

DOMESTIC Manners of the Americans. London, 1832. 2 vols. (By Frances Trollope.) 24 plates. $850. New York, 1832. First American edition. $500.

DONALDSON, D. J. *Cajun Nights.* New York, 1988. Author's first mystery. $250.

DONAN, P. *Gold Fields of Baker County, Eastern Oregon.* Portland (1898). Folding map, 36 pages, wraps. $400.

DONDERS, Franciscus Cornelius. *On the Anomalies of Accomodation* . . . London, 1864. $400.

DONLEAVY, J. P. *The Ginger Man.* Paris: Olympia Press (1955). Author's first book. Green wraps. With "1500 francs" on rear cover. $850. London, 1956. $250. Paris, 1958. Original dustwrapper flaps. $600. New dustwrapper flaps glued on. $200. New York (1958). $150. Franklin Library, 1978. Signed. $175.

DONNE, John. *The Holy Sonnets of John Donne.* London (1938). One of 550 copies signed by Eric Gill. $750.

DONNE, John. *Juvenilia* . . . London, 1633. $4,500.

DONNE, John. *Poems . . . with Elegies on the Author's Death.* London, 1633. $8,500.

DONNE, John. *Pseudo-Martyr* . . . London, 1610. Author's first book. $12,500.

DONNELLY, I(gnatius). *The Mourner's Vision.* Philadelphia, 1850. Gray boards. $300.

DONOHO, M. H. *Circle-Dot, a True Story of Cowboy Life 40 Years Ago.* Topeka, 1907. Frontispiece. $200.

DONOVAN, Dick. *The Chronicles of Michael Danevitch of the Russian Secret Service.* London, 1897. $150.

DONOVAN, Dick. *The Man Hunter.* London, 1888. (By Joyce E. Muddock her first book.) $450.

DONOVAN, Edward. *An Epitome of the Natural History of Insects . . . of China.* London, 1798. 58 hand-colored plates. $12,500.

DOOLITTLE, Hilda. See D., H.; Helforth, John.

DORING, Ernest N. *The Guadagnini Family of Violin Makers.* Chicago, 1949. Original half leather. One of 1,500 copies. Illustrated. $1,750.

DORING, Ernest N. *How Many Strads?* . . . Chicago, 1945. One of 1,400 copies. In slipcase. $1,250.

DORN, Edward. *The Shoshoneans.* New York, 1966. Photographs. Oblong, cloth. In dustwrapper. $400.

DORN, Edward. *What I See in the Maximus Poems.* (Ventura, Calif.), 1960. Author's first book. Wraps. $200.

DOS PASSOS, John. See Cendrars, Blaise.

DOS PASSOS, John. *Airways, Inc.* New York (1928). $350.

DOS PASSOS, John. *Facing the Chair: Story of the Americanization of Two Foreign-born Workmen.* Boston, 1927. Stiff olive-drab wraps. $200.

DOS PASSOS, John. *The 42nd Parallel.* New York, 1930. Decorated orange boards. Code "A-E" on copyright page. $750. London (1930). $300.

DOS PASSOS, John. *Henry and William Ford and Hearst* . . . San Francisco, 1940. One of 35 copies. Wraps. $600.

DOS PASSOS, John. *Manhattan Transfer.* New York, 1925. $750.

DOS PASSOS, John. *1919.* New York (1932). $600. London (1932). $300.

DOS PASSOS, John. *One Man's Initiation—1917.* London (1920). Pale-blue mesh cloth. First state has a broken "d" and the word "flat" obliterated on page 35, line 32. $1,000. Second state: perfect "d" and "flat." $600. New York, 1922. Title page is a cancel on a stub; verso of title page is blank. First state with broken "d" and obliterated "flat" at page 35, line 32. $750. Second state with perfect "d" and "flat" on page 35, line 32. $500.

DOS PASSOS, John. *Orient Express.* New York (1927). Code "M-A" on copyright page. Lavender boards and lavender paper label on shiny blue cloth spine, top edge trimmed and stained wine-colored. $350. Second-state binding: blue cloth with paper label on spine. $200. London (1928). states "First issued in Traveler's Library." $200.

DOS PASSOS, John. *A Pushcart at the Curb.* New York (1922). Colored pictorial boards, cream-colored paper label on black cloth spine. $450.

DOS PASSOS, John. *Rosinante to the Road Again.* New York (1922). Yellow boards. $500.

DOS PASSOS, John. *Three Soldiers.* New York (1921). Publisher's colophon not found in any state of first printing. 3 blank integral leaves at front, none at back, endpapers front and back. "Signing" for "singing" on page 213 line 31. First-state dustwrapper has publisher's blurb on front, spine, and back. $1,250. Second state: 2 blank integral leaves in front, none in back, endpapers front and back, pages 9–10 tipped onto pages 11–12, "signing" for "singing" page 213:31. Dustwrapper has a quotation from the *Brooklyn Daily Eagle* as last item on front panel. $750. Third state: like first, has 3 blank integral leaves in front and none in back, endpapers front and back, "signing" has been corrected to "singing." Dustwrapper same as second state except the quote from the *Brooklyn Daily Eagle* has been replaced by one from *Stars and Stripes.* $450. Fourth state: 2 integral blank leaves at front and 3 at back, no endpapers (the first and last leaves being pastedowns); "Singing" at page 213:31. Dustwrapper as in third state but with price on spine blacked over. $350. Fifth state: 3 blank integral leaves in front and four in back, endpapers in front and back. $300. (Note: priority of third, fourth, and fifth states presumed.) London (1922). Page 383 "Printed by Anchor Press Ltd. . . ." $600.

DOS PASSOS, John. *U.S.A. (The 42nd Parallel, 1919, The Big Money).* New York (1938). 1 vol. trilogy. First appearance of short sketch by Dos Passos. Last copyright date 1937, but not published until January 1938. $250. London (1938). $200. Boston, 1946. 3 vols. Illustrated by Reginald Marsh. One of 365 copies, signed by Dos Passos and Marsh. In slipcase. $750. Trade edition. 3 vols. In slipcase. $350.

DOSTOEVSKY, Feodor. *Crime and Punishment.* New York: Crowell [1886]. First edition in English. $3,000.

DOSTOEVSKY, F. *The Grand Inquisitor.* (London) 1930. Translated by S. S. Koteliansky. Introduction by D. H. Lawrence. One of 300 copies. In slipcase. $350.

DOSTOEVSKY, F. *Poor Folk.* London, 1894. First English publication. (Beardsley cover.) $500. Boston, 1984. Translated by Lena Millman. $500.

DOTY, M. R. *An Alphabet.* Ithaca (1979). (By Mark and Ruth Doty.) Authors' first book. One of 600 copies. Wraps. $600.

DOTY, M. R. *An Introduction to the Geography of Iowa*. Fort Kent, 1979. (By Mark and Ruth Doty.) Stapled wraps. $400.

DOTY, Mark. *Turtle, Swan*. Boston (1987). $600. Wraps. $150.

DOUGHTY, Charles M. *Travels in Arabia Deserta*. Cambridge, 1888. Illustrated, folding map in pocket. 2 vols. $7,500. London/Boston, 1921. 2 vols. Introduction by T. E. Lawrence. $1,500. New York/London, 1923. Introduction by T. E. Lawrence. 2 vols. $750. Limited Editions Club, New York, 1953. $300. London, 1936. New and definitive issue. $450.

DOUGLAS, Lord Alfred. *The City of the Soul*. London, 1899. Vellum boards. $200.

DOUGLAS, Lord Alfred. *My Friendship with Oscar Wilde*. New York, 1932. $350.

DOUGLAS, Lord Alfred. *Poems*. Paris, 1896. Author's first book. Text in English and French. Portrait frontispiece. Wraps. One of 20 copies on Hollande paper. (Usually inscribed.) $1,250. Ordinary issue. $500.

DOUGLAS, C. L. *Cattle Kings of Texas*. Dallas (1939). Illustrated. $125. Second edition, same date. Rawhide. Limited. $400.

DOUGLAS, C. L. *Famous Texas Feuds*. Dallas (1936). Illustrated. Decorated cloth and leather. In dustwrapper. $125.

DOUGLAS, C. L. *The Gentlemen in White Hats*. Dallas (1934). $200.

DOUGLAS, David. *Journal Kept by David Douglas During His Travels in North America, 1823–27*. London, 1914. Portrait. $1,250. New York, 1959. One of 750 copies. $250.

DOUGLAS, Ellen. *A Family Affair*. Boston, 1962. Author's first book. $200. London (1963). $150.

DOUGLAS, James. *The Gold Fields of Canada*. Quebec, 1863. 18 pages, wraps. $600.

DOUGLAS, Margaret. *Stoneman*. New York (1941). Signed numbered copies. $1,750.

DOUGLAS, Norman. See Douglass, G. Norman; Normyx. See also *The Blue Grotto . . . ; Some Antiquarian Notes; Three Monographs*.

DOUGLAS, Norman. *The Angel of Manfredonia*. San Francisco, 1929. One of 225 signed copies. Issued without dustwrapper. $300.

DOUGLAS, Norman. *Birds and Beasts of the Greek Anthology*. (Florence, Italy), 1927. Frontispiece. Blue boards, paper label. One of 500 signed copies. In dustwrapper. $350. London, 1928. $250.

DOUGLAS, Norman. *Experiments*. (Florence), 1925. Boards, paper label. One of 300 signed copies. In dustwrapper. $300. London, 1925. One of 300 signed copies. $300.

DOUGLAS, Norman. *How About Europe?* (Florence), 1929. Decorated boards. One of 550 signed copies. $200. London, 1930. Orange cloth. In dustwrapper. $200.

DOUGLAS, Norman. *In the Beginning*. (Florence), 1927. Printed boards, leather label. One of 700 signed copies. $300. New York (1928). Boards. First American edition. $150. London, 1928. $200.

DOUGLAS, Norman. *London Street Games.* London: St. Catherine Press (1916). Buckram. One of 500 copies. $300. London (1931). Second edition. Boards and cloth. One of 110 signed copies. $350. Trade issue. $75.

DOUGLAS, Norman. *Looking Back: An Autobiographical Excursion.* London, 1933. 2 vols. Boards and buckram. One of 535 signed copies. $350. New York, 1933. $125.

DOUGLAS, Norman. *One Day.* Chapelle-Reanville, France: Hours Press, 1929. Portraits. Full scarlet leather. One of 200 copies on Rives paper, signed. $500. Boards. One of 300 copies. $175.

DOUGLAS, Norman. *Paneros.* Florence (1930). Gold cloth and boards, leather label. One of 250 signed copies. In dustwrapper. In slipcase. $500. London, 1931. First English edition. Boards and cloth. One of 650 copies. $175. New York, 1932. First American edition. Illustrated. Vellum. One of 750 copies. In slipcase. $100.

DOUGLAS, Norman. *Some Limericks.* (Florence), 1928. Gold-colored linen. One of 110 signed copies. $600. (New York), 1928. Cloth. First American edition. $175. (Florence), 1929. Wraps. $150. Buckram. $150.

DOUGLAS, Norman. *South Wind.* London (1917). $150. London (1922). One of 150 copies on blue paper, signed. $600. New York, 1928. Illustrated by Valenti Angelo. One of 250 copies signed by Douglas. In slipcase. $400. 2 vols. in 1. Half morocco. One of 40 signed copies. $750. Limited Editions Club, New York, 1932. In slipcase. $100.

DOUGLASS, Frederick. *The Narrative of the Life of Frederick Douglass . . .* Boston, 1845. $3,500. Published in the U.K. as *The Narrative of Frederick Douglass . . .* Wortley, Near Leeds, 1846. $3,000.

DOUGLASS, G. Norman. *On the Herpetology of the Grand Duchy of Baden.* London, 1894. (By Norman Douglas.) 64 pages, pale gray-blue wraps. $1,500.

DOUGLASS, G. Norman. *Report on the Pumice Stone Industry of the Lipari Islands.* 8 pages. London, 1895. (By Norman Douglas.) One of 125 copies. $1,250.

DOVE, Rita. *Museum.* Pittsburgh, 1983. $350. Wraps. $60.

DOVE, Rita. *Ten Poems.* Lisbon, Iowa, 1977. One of 200 copies. Pamphlet in printed envelope. $1,250.

DOVE, Rita. *Thomas and Beulah, Poems.* Pittsburgh, 1986. Cloth. First issue dustwrapper does not have the Pulitzer Prize notice. $750. Second issue. $500. Wraps. $100.

DOW, Francis. *The Arts and Crafts in New England.* Topsfield, 1927. $200.

DOW, George Francis. *The Sailing Ships of New England: Series I–III.* Salem, 1922–24–28. 3 vols. In dustwrapper. Written with John Robinson. $600.

DOW, George Francis. *Slave Ships and Slaving.* Salem, 1923. Illustrated. Buckram. Issued without dustwrapper. $350. Half cloth. Large paper. One of 97 copies. $500.

DOW, George Francis. *Whale Ships and Whaling.* Salem, 1925. Illustrated. Buckram. Issued without dustwrapper. One of 950 copies. $300. Half cloth. Large paper. One of 97 copies. Issued without dustwrapper. $500.

DOW, Lorenzo. *The Life and Travels of Lorenzo Dow.* Hartford, 1804. $600.

DOWDEN, Edward. *Mr. Tennyson and Mr. Browning.* (London), 1863. Author's first book. $350.

DOWDEN, Edward. *Poems.* London, 1860. $200.

DOWDEN, Edward. *A Woman's Reliquary.* Dundrum, Ireland: Cuala Press, 1913. One of 300 copies. $350.

DOWNEY, Fairfax. *Indian-Fighting Army.* New York, 1941. $200.

DOWNIE, William. *Hunting for Gold: Personal Experiences in the Early Days on the Pacific Coast.* San Francisco, 1893. Frontispiece. Half morocco or cloth. $450.

DOWNING, Andrew Jackson. *The Architecture of Country Houses.* New York, 1850. Illustrated. Pictorial cloth. $500.

DOWNING, Andrew Jackson. *Cottage Residences* . . . New York, 1842. $600.

DOWSON, Ernest. *Decorations: In Verse and Prose.* London, 1899. $750.

DOWSON, Ernest. *The Pierrot of the Minute.* London, 1897. Illustrated by Aubrey Beardsley. One of 300 copies on handmade paper. $1,500. One of 30 copies on Japanese vellum. $6,000. New York, 1923. Grolier Club. One of 300 copies designed by Bruce Rogers. In slipcase. $500.

DOWSON, Ernest. *The Poems of Ernest Dowson.* London, 1905. Illustrated by Aubrey Beardsley. $350.

DOWSON, Ernest. *Verses.* London, 1896. Cover decorations by Aubrey Beardsley. Vellum. One of 30 copies on Japan paper. $7,500. One of 300 copies on handmade paper. $750.

DOYLE, A. Conan. See *Beeton's Christmas Annual; Dreamland and Ghostland.*

DOYLE, A. Conan. Note: Many of the early Doyle titles have colonial issues in cloth and wraps and other variants. See the bibliography or our Author Price Guide on Doyle.

DOYLE, A. Conan. *The Adventures of Sherlock Holmes.* London, 1892. Illustrated by Sidney Paget. Light-blue cloth. With no name on street sign on front cover. Gray flower-and-leaf endpapers. $4,000. New York, 1892. First issue, with "if had" on page 65, line 4. $1,250. Second issue with "if he had." $600.

DOYLE, A. Conan. *The Case-Book of Sherlock Holmes.* London (1927). Pink cloth, lettered in gilt. $3,000. Colonial issue in light-gray cloth, lettered in black. $2,500. New York (1927). With Doran colophon on copyright page. $1,500.

DOYLE, A. Conan. *The Complete Sherlock Holmes.* New York, 1953. 2 vols. Original cloth, leather backs lettered in gilt, publisher's cardboard slipcase. One of 147 numbered sets signed by Doyle. $4,000.

DOYLE, A. Conan. *The Crowborough Edition of the Works of Sir Arthur Conan Doyle.* Garden City, 1930. 24 volumes. One of 760 signed copies. $6,000.

DOYLE, A. Conan. *The Doings of Raffles Haw.* London, 1892. Dark-blue cloth. First edition not stated. $600. New York: Lovell (1892). Address of "East 10th" (later "Sixth Avenue"). Wraps. $600. Cloth. $500.

DOYLE, A. Conan. *The Firm of Girdlestone.* London, 1890. 32-page catalogue dated January 1890. $500. With later ads. $400. New York, 1890. Wraps. $400. Cloth. $750.

DOYLE, A. Conan. *The Great Shadow.* Bristol, England, 1892. Pictorial wraps. $750. Later printing in cloth with dark-brown endpapers. $300.

DOYLE, A. Conan. *His Last Bow.* London: John Murray, 1917. $750. G. Bell. London, 1917. Colonial issue. $450. New York (1917). Orange cloth. First edition not stated. $150. In dustwrapper. $4,500. Later in dark-red cloth in dustwrapper. $2,500. Without dustwrapper. $100.

DOYLE, A. Conan. *The History of Spiritualism.* London (1926). 2 vols. $1,000. New York (1926). 2 vols. $750.

DOYLE, A. Conan. *The Hound of the Baskervilles.* London: George Newnes, Ltd., 1902. Illustrated by Sidney Paget. Decorated red cloth. $6,000. London: Longman's Green, 1902. Colonial issue. $1,250. New York (1902). First issue, without the "Published 1902" line on copyright page. $1,250. Second issue. $500. Third issue with tipped-in title page, with "illustrated." $400. Fourth state same as third, but title page integral. $300.

DOYLE, A. Conan. *The Land of Mist.* London (1926). Green cloth. $3,500. New York (1926). $1,250.

DOYLE, A. Conan. *The Last Galley.* London: Smith, Elder & Co., 1911. Pictorial red cloth. Color frontispiece and one inserted black-and-white plate by N. C. Wyeth. [14] pages of undated publisher's ads bound in at rear. $500. London: G. Bell & Sons, 1911. Cloth or wraps. $350. New York, 1911. $300.

Doyle, A. Conan. *The Lost World.* London (1912). Light-blue cloth. $1,250. One of 190 large-paper copies. In light-blue boards. $3,000. One of 810 large-paper copies in light-brown cloth. $1,500. New York (1912). $600.

DOYLE, A. Conan. *The Maracot Deep and Other Stories.* London, 1929. Ads at rear. $1,750. Garden City, 1929. $750.

DOYLE, A. Conan. *The Memoirs of Sherlock Holmes.* London, 1894. Illustrated by Sidney Paget. Blue cloth, gold letters. $2,500. New York, 1894. First American edition. Including 1 story not in English edition or later American editions. Blue cloth. 281 pages. $1,500.

DOYLE, A. Conan. *My Friend the Murderer.* New York (1893). Wraps. $1,000. Blue cloth. $750.

DOYLE, A. Conan. *Our African Winter.* London, 1929. Dark-blue cloth stamped in blind and gilt. $1,250. Cover ruled and titled in white. $1,000.

DOYLE, A. Conan. *The Poison Belt.* London, 1913. Red cloth. $600.

DOYLE, A. Conan. *The Refugees: A Tale of Two Continents.* London, 1893. 3 vols. Green cloth. $6,000. New York, 1893. $300.

DOYLE, A. Conan. *The Return of Sherlock Holmes.* New York: McClure, Phillips & Co., 1905. (Preceding English edition by a month.) Black cloth. $1,000. Dark-blue cloth. "Special Edition." $400. George Newnes, Ltd., London, 1905. $3,500.

DOYLE, A. Conan. *The Sign of Four.* London: Spencer Blackett, 1890. Frontispiece. Dark-red cloth. First issue, with "Spencer Blackett's Standard Library" on spine. Probable early issue with "8" missing on page "138." $10,000. Remainder sheets issued by Griffin Farran & Co. (on spine), with same title page as first. $4,000. Remainder sheets issued by George Newnes. London, 1892. With "Griffin . . ." cover. $2,500. Collier. New York, 1891. Wraps. $6,000. Philadelphia: Lippincott, 1893. Cloth. $1,500. Wraps. $2,000.

DOYLE, A. Conan. *The Speckled Band.* London: Samuel French, Ltd., "Copyright 1912" on title page of all printings. Stage diagrams. Printed light-green wraps. $7,500. Second printing with dark-green wraps. (Both have publisher's address as "West 38th Street.") $3,000. Later in brown wraps with "West 45th Street." $350.

DOYLE, A. Conan. *A Study in Scarlet.* London, 1888. Illustrated. White wraps. First edition in book form, first issue, with "younger" correctly spelled in the preface. $100,000. With "youuger." $40,000. Philadelphia, 1890. Wraps. $10,000. Cloth. $7,500. London, 1891. Second edition. $500.

DOYLE, A. Conan. *The Valley of Fear.* New York (1914). Red cloth. $500. London: Smith, Elder & Co., 1915. First English edition. $1,000. London: G. Bell, 1915. Cloth. $500. Wraps. $600.

DOYLE, A. Conan. *The White Company.* London, 1891. 3 vols. Dark-red cloth. $7,500. New York: John Lovell Co. (1891). Tan wraps. $1,000. Lovell, Coryell & Co. (1892). White pictorial wraps. $750.

DOYLE, A. Conan, and BARRIE, James M. *Jane Annie: Or the Good Conduct Prize.* London, 1893. Wraps. 53 pages of text, 3 pages of ads. $1,500. 50 pages of text, 2 pages of ads. $1,000. 48 pages of text, 2 pages of ads. $750. 52 pages of text, no ads. $500.

DOYLE, Roddy. *The Commitments.* Dublin, 1987. Author's first book. Wraps. $600.

DOYLE, Roddy. *The Snapper.* London, 1990. $450.

DRABBLE, Margaret. *A Summer Bird-Cage.* London, 1963. Author's first book. $250. New York, 1964. $150.

DRABBLE, Margaret. *Virginia Woolf: A Personal Debt.* New York, 1973. Wraps. One of 110 signed copies. $400.

DRAEGER, Donn F. and SMITH, Robert W. *Asian Fighting Arts.* Tokyo, 1969. First edition stated. $100.

DRAGO, Harry Sinclair. *Following the Free Grass.* New York, 1924. $250.

DRAGO, Harry Sinclair. *Outlaws on Horseback.* New York, 1964. Illustrated, map. One of 150 signed copies. In slipcase. $250.

DRAGO, Harry Sinclair. *Suzanna.* New York, 1922. Author's first book. $450.

DRAGO, Harry Sinclair. *Wild, Woolly & Wicked.* New York, 1960. Illustrated by Nick Eggenhofer. One of 250 signed copies. $200. Trade edition. $60.

DRAGOON Campaigns to the Rocky Mountains. New York, 1836. By a Dragoon. (By James Hildreth.) Blue cloth. $1,250.

DRAKE, Benjamin. *The Life and Adventures of Black Hawk.* Cincinnati, 1838. Portrait and plates. $350.

DRAKE, Benjamin. *Life of Tecumseh, and His Brother the Prophet.* Cincinnati, 1841. $350.

DRAKE, Benjamin, and MANSFIELD, E. D. *Cincinnati in 1826.* Cincinnati, 1827. 2 plates. $450.

DRAKE, Daniel. *An Account of Epidemic Cholera, as It Appeared in Cincinnati.* Cincinnati, 1832. 46 pages, in original wraps. $1,500.

DRAKE, Daniel. *Natural and Statistical View, or Picture of Cincinnati and the Miami Country.* Cincinnati, 1815. 2 folding maps. $2,000.

DRAKE, Daniel. *Pioneer Life in Kentucky: A Series of Reminiscential Letters from Daniel Drake, M.D., of Cincinnati to His Children.* Cincinnati, 1870. Portrait. Cloth. $500.

DRAKE, Daniel. *A Practical Treatise on the History, Prevention, and Treatment of Epidemic Cholera.* Cincinnati, 1832. $1,500.

DRAKE, Daniel. *A Systematic Treatise: Historical, Etiological, and Practical, on the Principal Diseases of the Interior Valley of North America.* (First series.) Cincinnati, 1850. Maps and plates. Full leather. $1,500. Philadelphia, 1854. (Second series.) $1,000.

DRAKE, Joseph Rodman. See Croaker.

DRAKE, Joseph Rodman. *The Culprit Fay and Other Poems.* New York, 1835. Frontispiece, vignette title page. Blue or purple cloth. $175. Also bound in leather. $300. New York, 1923. Grolier Club. One of 300 copies. $150.

DRAKE, Leah Bodine. *A Hornbook for Witches.* Sauk City, Wis., 1950. $1,750.

DRAKE, Morgan. *Lake Superior Railroad: Letter to the Hon. Lewis Cass.* Pontiac, 1853. 24 pages, wraps. $400.

DRANNAN, Capt. William F. *Thirty-one Years on the Plains and in the Mountains.* Chicago, 1899. Illustrated. $350.

DRAPER, John William. *Human Physiology.* New York, 1856. $500.

DRAYSON, Capt. Alfred W. *Sporting Scenes Amongst the Kaffirs of South Africa.* London, 1858. 8 colored plates by Harrison Weir. $1,250.

DRAYTON, John. *Memoirs of the American Revolution.* Charleston, 1821. 2 vols. Portrait, 2 folding maps. $2,500.

DRAYTON, John. *A View of South-Carolina.* Charleston, 1802. 2 folding maps, 2 folding tables, 3 plates. $9,500 at auction in 1999.

DRAYTON, Michael. *The Battle of Agincourt . . .* London, 1627. $1,500.

DREAM Drops, or Stories from Fairy Land. Boston (1887). By a Dreamer. (By Amy Lowell, her first book.) Wraps (151 copies). $2,250. Cloth (99 copies). $3,000.

DREAMLAND and Ghostland: An Original Collection of Tales and Warnings. London (1887). 3 vols. Pictorial red cloth. First edition, first binding (red cloth). (Contains 6 stories by A. Conan Doyle.) $10,000 at auction in 1998.

DREAM of Gerontius (The). London, 1866. (By John Henry, Cardinal Newman.) Wraps or brown cloth. First edition, printed dedication "J. H. N." $3,500 at auction in 1990.

DREISER, Theodore. See Davis, Hubert.

DREISER, Theodore. *An American Tragedy.* New York, 1925. 2 vols. Black cloth, white end-papers. First issue, with Boni & Liveright imprint. In slipcase. $2,000. Another (later) issue, 2 vols. Blue boards and cloth. First limited edition. One of 795 signed copies. In slipcase. $1,000. London, 1926. $450. Limited Editions Club, New York, 1954. In slipcase. $200.

DREISER, Theodore. *The Carnegie Works at Pittsburgh.* New York, 1927. One of 150 copies. $250. One of 27 copies with page of original manuscript. $1,000.

DREISER, Theodore. *Chains: Lesser Novels and Stories.* New York, 1927. Decorated boards and cloth. One of 440 signed copies. In slipcase. $450. Trade edition. $300.

DREISER, Theodore. *Dawn: A History of Myself.* New York (1931). One of 275 signed copies. In slipcase. $400. Trade edition. $200. London, 1931. $250.

DREISER, Theodore. *Dreiser Looks at Russia.* New York, 1928. $350.

DREISER, Theodore. *Epitaph: A Poem.* New York, 1929. One of 200 copies in leather signed by Dreiser and the illustrator, Robert Fawcett. In slipcase. $350. One of 200 signed copies, in silk. In slipcase. $250. One of 700 signed copies, in cloth. In slipcase. $175.

DREISER, Theodore. *The Financier.* New York, 1912. With "Published October, 1912" and "K–M" on copyright page. $500.

DREISER, Theodore. *Free, and Other Stories.* New York, 1918. In dustwrapper. $1,000. Without dustwrapper. $200.

DREISER, Theodore. *A Gallery of Women.* New York, 1929. 2 vols. Boards and vellum. One of 560 signed copies. In slipcase. $600. Trade edition. 2 vols. In slipcase. $600. (Precedes limited edition.)

DREISER, Theodore. *The "Genius."* New York, 1915. First issue, 1¾ inches thick, and with page 497 so numbered. $200. Second issue, 1½ inches thick, no number on page 497. $100. London, 1915. Same issue points. First issue. $250. Second issue. $125.

DREISER, Theodore. *The Hand of the Potter.* New York, 1918. First issue. Last word on page 191 "that." In dustwrapper. $750. Second issue. Last word on page 191 "it." In dustwrapper. $500.

DREISER, Theodore. *Hey, Rub-A-Dub-Dub!* New York, 1920. In dustwrapper. $1,000.

DREISER, Theodore. *Jennie Gerhardt.* New York, 1911. Frontispiece. Mottled light-blue cloth. First issue, with "is" for "it" in line 30 of page 22 and "Theodore Dreiser" on spine. $1,000. Second issue, text corrected and "Dreiser" on spine. $500.

DREISER, Theodore. *My City.* New York (1929). Colored etchings by Max Pollak. Folio, boards, and cloth. Issued without dustwrapper. In slipcase. One of 275 signed copies. $600.

DREISER, Theodore. *Sister Carrie.* New York, 1900. Author's first book. Dark-red cloth. $6,000. London, 1901. $1,250. New York, 1907. First illustrated edition. Colored frontispiece. $350. Limited Editions Club, New York, 1939. In slipcase. $350.

DREYFUS, John. *The Survival of Baskerville's Punches.* Cambridge, 1949. Limited to 250 copies. $200.

DREYFUS, John. *The Work of Jan Van Krimpen* . . . London, 1952. $200.

DREYFUS, John (editor). *Typographical Partnership* . . . New York, 1971. One of 350 copies. $200.

DRIFTWOOD Flames. Nashville (1923). (Includes 5 poems by Robert Penn Warren, his first book appearance.) $500.

DRINKWATER, John. *A History of the Late Siege of Gibraltar.* London, 1785. 10 folding plates and plans. $1,250. London, 1786. $1,000. Dublin, 1786. $1,000. London, 1790. $850.

DRINKWATER, John. *Loyalties.* (London): Beaumont Press, 1918. Illustrated. Vellum and boards. One of 30 copies on Japan vellum, signed. $1,500. Boards and cloth. One of 120 copies. $500. One of 50 copies with hand-colored illustrations. $1,000.

DRINKWATER, John. *Poems.* Birmingham, England, 1903. Author's first book. $350.

DRINKWATER, John. *Tides: A Book of Poems.* (London): Beaumont Press, 1917. One of 250 copies. $300. Full vellum. One of 20 copies on vellum, signed. $2,000.

DRINKWATER, John, and RUTHERSTON, Albert. *Claud Lovat Fraser: A Story of His Life.* London, 1923. Portrait frontispiece by Rutherston, 39 Fraser illustrations, 20 in color. One of 450 signed copies. $400.

DRIPS, Joseph H. *Three Years Among the Indians in Dakota.* Kimball, S.D., 1894. 139 pages, wraps. $3,500.

DROPE, Francis. *A Short and Sure Guide in the Practice of Raising and Ordering of Fruit-Trees.* Oxford, 1672. $1,750.

DRUMHELLER, "Uncle Dan." *"Uncle Dan" Drumheller Tells Thrills of Western Trails in 1854.* Spokane, 1925. Portraits. First issue with only one foreword. $200. Second issue. $150.

DRURY, Dru. *Illustrations of Exotic Entomology.* London, 1837. 3 vols. Edited by J. O. Westwood. 1 plain plate and 150 hand-colored plates. $6,000.

DRURY, The Rev. P. Sheldon (editor). *The Startling and Thrilling Narrative of the Dark and Terrible Deeds of Henry Madison, and His Associate and Accomplice Miss Ellen Stevens, Who Was Executed by the Vigilance Committee of San Francisco, on the 20th September Last.* Cincinnati (1857). Illustrated. 36 pages, pictorial wraps. $750. Philadelphia, 1865. $500.

DRYDEN, John. *Alexander's Feast.* London, 1697. $1,000. London: Essex House, 1904. Vellum. One of 140 copies on vellum. $600.

DRYDEN, John. *All for Love*. San Francisco, 1929. 2 vols. Folio, half vellum. John Henry Nash printing. One of 250 copies. $250.

DRYDEN, John. *Dramatic Works*. London: Nonesuch Press, 1931–32. 6 vols. Edited by Montague Summers. Buckram and marbled boards. $500. One of 50 sets on Van Gelder paper. $750.

DRYDEN, John. *Of Dramatick Poesie*. London, 1668. $3,500. Another edition: London, 1928. Preceded by a *Dialogue on Poetic Drama by T. S. Eliot*. Marbled boards, cloth spine. One of 580 copies. In dustwrapper. In slipcase. $500. Boards and vellum. One of 55 copies signed by Eliot. In dustwrapper. In slipcase. $2,000.

DU BOIS, John. *Campaigns in the West, 1856–61: The Journal and Letters of Col. John Du Bois with Pencil Sketches by Joseph Heger*. Tucson, 1949. Plates, folding map. Boards and leather. Grabhorn Printing. One of 300 copies signed by George P. Hammond as editor. $500.

DU BOIS, John Witherspoon. *Life and Times of William Lowndes Yancey*. Birmingham, Ala., 1892. 9 plates. $300.

DU BOIS, W. E. Burghardt. *The Gift of Black Folk in the Making of America*. Boston, 1924. $2,500.

DU BOIS, W. E. Burghardt. *The Souls of Black Folk*. Chicago, 1903. $2,000. London, 1905. $1,500. New York, 1953. Signed limited edition. $750.

DU BOIS, W. E. Burghardt. *Suppression of the American Slave Trade*. New York, 1896. Author's first book. $2,500.

DUBUS, André. *The Lieutenant*. New York, 1967. Author's first book. $500.

DUBUS, André. *Separate Flights*. Boston (1975). First issue dustwrapper priced $8.95 on flap. $200.

DU CHAILLU, Paul. *The Land of the Midnight Sun*. New York, 1882. 2 vols. Folding map. $300.

DU CHAILLU, Paul. *Stories of the Gorilla Country*. New York, 1868. Woodcuts. Pictorial cloth. $500.

DUDLEY-SMITH, T. See Smith, T. Dudley.

DUFF, E. Gordon. *Early English Printing*. London, 1896. Illustrated. Folio, half morocco. One of 300 copies. $450.

DUFF, E. Gordon. *William Caxton*. Chicago: Caxton Club, 1905. Boards and cloth. One of 145 copies with an original leaf from Chaucer's *Canterbury Tales* of 1478. $10,000. One of 107 copies without the leaf. $500.

DUFLOT DE MOFRAS, Eugene. *Exploration du Territoire de l'Oregon*. Paris, 1844. Illustrated. 2 vols., leather; plus atlas, folio, cloth. $6,000 to $16,000 at auction in recent years.

DUFLOT DE MOFRAS, Eugene. *Travels on the Pacific Coast*. Santa Ana, 1937. 2 vols. Translated by Marguerite E. Wilbur. 2 folding maps, 8 plates. Half leather. $1,250.

DULAC, Edmund. See *Sleeping Beauty*. See also Andersen, Hans Christian.

DULAC, Edmund. *Edmund Dulac's Fairy Book*. New York or London (1916). 15 color plates. Ivory cloth. One of 350 signed copies. $1,250.

DULAC, Edmund. *Sinbad the Sailor and Other Stories from the Arabian Nights*. London (1911). Illustrated by Dulac. Vellum. One of 500 signed copies. $1,500.

DUMAS, Alexandre. *The Count of Monte-Cristo*. London, 1846. 2 vols. First English edition. $4,500. London, 1934. Photoplay edition. $300. Limited Editions Club, New York, 1941. 4 vols. $300.

DU MAURIER, Daphne. *I'll Never Be Young Again*. London, 1932. $350.

DU MAURIER, Daphne. *The Loving Spirit*. London, 1931. Author's first book. $400.

DU MAURIER, Daphne. *Rebecca*. London, 1938. $3,000. Garden City, 1938. $600.

DU MAURIER, George. *Sir Gawaine Hys Penance: A Legend of Camelot*. (London), 1866. Author's first book. Wraps. $1,000.

DU MAURIER, George. *Trilby*. London, 1894. 3 vols. $750. London, 1895. Illustrated. Half vellum. One of 250 signed copies. $1,000. New York, 1894. $150. New York, 1895. Vellum. One of 250 signed copies. $750.

DUNBAR, Alice. *The Goodness of Saint Rocque*. New York, 1899. $1,500.

DUNBAR, James. *The Practical Papermaker: A Complete Guide to the Manufacture of Paper*. Leith, Scotland 1881. Second edition. $200.

DUNBAR, Paul Laurence. *Howdy, Honey, Howdy*. New York, 1905. $450.

DUNBAR, Paul Laurence. *Joggin 'Erlong*. New York, 1906. Illustrated. $450.

DUNBAR, Paul Laurence. *Li'l Gal*. New York, 1904. Photographs by Leigh Richmond Miner. Pictorial green cloth. $400.

DUNBAR, Paul Laurence. *Lyrics of Lowly Life*. New York, 1896. $750. London, 1897. $400.

DUNBAR, Paul Laurence. *Majors and Minors: Poems*. (Toledo, 1895.) Frontispiece portrait. $3,000.

DUNBAR, Paul Laurence. *Oak and Ivy*. Dayton, Ohio, 1893. Author's first book. Blue cloth. $7,500. (Reportedly 500 copies printed. 250 were destroyed by fire.)

DUNBAR, Paul Laurence. *Poems of Cabin and Field*. New York, 1899. Illustrated. Pictorial cloth. $300.

DUNBAR, Paul Laurence. *The Sport of the Gods*. New York, 1902. $1,000.

DUNBAR, Paul Laurence. *The Strength of Gideon and Other Stories*. New York, 1900. Illustrated by E. W. Kemble. $750.

DUNBAR, Paul Lawrence. *The Uncalled*. New York, 1898. With "Lawrence" on cover. $1,000. With "Laurence." $750.

DUNCAN, David James. *The River Why.* San Fransisco (1983). $300.

DUNCAN, Isadora. *Art of the Dance.* New York, 1928. $1,000.

DUNCAN, Isadora. *My Life.* New York, 1927. One of 650 copies. In slipcase. $600.

DUNCAN, John M. *Travels Through Part of the United States and Canada in 1818 and 1819.* Glasgow, 1823. 2 vols. 14 maps and plates. $500. New York, 1823. 2 vols. $400.

DUNCAN, L. Wallace. *History of Montgomery County, Kansas.* Iola, Kan., 1903. Half leather. $250.

DUNCAN, L. Wallace. *History of Wilson and Neosho Counties, Kansas.* Fort Scott, Kan., 1902. $250.

DUNCAN, Robert. *A Book of Resemblances.* New Haven, 1966. Illustrated by Jess (Collins). Cloth. One of 203 signed copies. In tissue dustwrapper. $350.

DUNCAN, Robert. *Caesar's Gate: Poems, 1949–1950.* (Mallorca): Divers Press, 1955. Illustrated by "Jess" (Collins). Wraps. One of 200 copies. $450. One of 13 copies signed with original collage by "Jess." $7,500.

DUNCAN, Robert. *Derivations.* London: Fulcrum Press (1968). One of 162 signed copies. $300. Trade edition. $100.

DUNCAN, Robert. *The First Decade.* (London): Fulcrum Press (1968). Cloth. One of 150 signed copies. In dustwrapper. $300. Trade edition. $50.

DUNCAN, Robert. *Heavenly City, Earthly City.* (Berkeley), 1947. Author's first book. Illustrated by Mary Fabilli. White boards. $1,000. One of 100 signed copies. Green cloth. $2,000.

DUNCAN, Robert. *Letters.* (Highlands, N.C., 1958.) Decorated wraps. One of 450 copies. $250. Boards and calf. One of 60 signed copies, with an original drawing by Duncan on endpapers. $1,000.

DUNCAN, Robert. *Medieval Scenes.* San Francisco (1950). Wraps. One of 250 signed copies. $350.

DUNCAN, Robert. *A Selection of 65 Drawings.* Los Angeles, 1970. One of 300 signed copies in cloth portfolio. $200. One of 26 lettered copies, signed, with an original drawing. $600.

DUNDASS, Samuel. *Journal of Samuel Rutherford Dundass.* Steubenville, Ohio, 1857. 60 pages, wraps. $12,000 at auction in 1996.

DUNHILL, Alfred. *The Pipe Book.* London, 1924. $200.

DUNIWAY, Mrs. Abigail J. *Captain Gray's Company; or, Crossing the Plains and Living in Oregon.* Portland, 1859. $2,500.

DUNLAP, William. *Diary: Memoirs of a Dramatist.* New York, 1931. 3 vols. Buckram. One of 100 copies. Issued without dustwrapper. $350.

DUNLAP, William. *A History of the American Theatre.* New York, 1832. $500. London, 1833. 2 vols. First English edition. $350.

DUNLAP, William. *A History of the New Netherlands.* New York, 1839–1840. 2 vols. 2 folding maps. With errata leaf. $400.

DUNLAP, William. *History of the Rise and Progress of the Arts of Design in the United States.* New York, 1834. 2 vols. $500. Boston, 1918. 3 vols. Plates. $300.

DUNLAP, William. *The Life of Charles Brockden Brown.* Philadelphia, 1815. 2 vols. Frontispiece. (Note: Contains first printing of "Memoirs of Carwin" and other Brown items). $500.

DUNLAP, William. *Memoirs of the Life of George Frederick Cooke.* New York, 1813. 2 vols. Frontispieces. $600.

DUNLAP, William. *A Narrative of the Events Which Followed Bonaparte's Campaign . . .* Hartford, 1814. Frontispiece. 5 plates. $450.

DUNN, Jacob Piatt. *Massacres of the Mountains.* New York, 1886. Folding map and illustrations. Pictorial cloth. $600.

DUNN, John. *History of the Oregon Territory and British North-American Fur Trade.* London, 1844. Folding map. $1,250.

DUNN, John. *The Oregon Territory and the British North American Fur Trade.* Philadelphia, 1845. First American edition (of *History of the Oregon Territory, etc.*). Wraps. $750.

DUNN, Katherine. *Attic.* New York, 1970. Author's first book. $350. (London, 1970.) $125.

DUNNE, Finley Peter. See *Mr. Dooley in Peace and in War.*

DUNNE, Finley Peter. *Mr. Dooley at His Best.* New York, 1938. One of 520 copies, with a page of the original manuscript. $400.

DUNNE, John Gregory. *Delano: The Story of the California Grape Strike.* New York, 1967. Author's first book. $100.

DUNNING, John. *Booked to Die.* New York, 1992. $850.

DUNNING, John. *The Holland Suggestions.* Indianapolis, 1975. Author's first book. $1,000.

DUNNING, Ralph Cheever. *Rococo.* Paris: Black Manikin Press, 1926. Author's first book. (First book of this press.) One of 500 to be signed by artist and author; however, Dunning reportedly only signed 25 or so. Signed by artist. $175. Signed by both. $350.

DUNSANY, Lord. *The Book of Wonder.* London, 1912. Illustrated by Sidney H. Sime. $350.

DUNSANY, Lord. *The Chronicles of Rodriguez.* London/New York, 1922. Frontispiece. Light-brown cloth, vellum spine, leather label. One of 500 signed copies. $750.

DUNSANY, Lord. *The Gods of Pegana.* London, 1905. Author's first book. Drummer blind-stamped on front cover. $750. Without drummer. $350.

DUNSANY, Lord. *The King of Elfland's Daughter.* London (1924). Frontispiece. Orange cloth, vellum spine, leather label. One of 250 signed copies. In dustwrapper. $750.

DUNSANY, Lord. *The Old Folks of the Centuries: A Play.* London, 1930. One of 100 signed copies. $750. One of 800 copies. $100.

DUNSANY, Lord. *Selections from the Writings of Lord Dunsany.* Churchtown, Dundrum, Ireland: Cuala Press, 1912. Edited and with introduction by William Butler Yeats. Boards and linen. One of 250 copies. $500.

DUNSANY, Lord. *The Sword of Welleran and Other Stories.* London, 1908. Illustrated by Sidney Sime. First binding. Blue cloth. "George Allen & Sons" base of spine. $300. Second binding. Green cloth. "George Allen" base of spine. $200.

DUNSANY, Lord. *Time and the Gods.* London, 1906. Illustrated by Sidney Sime. In brown boards with green cloth spine. $350. Second binding in green boards. $250. London (1922). Illustrated. Orange cloth, vellum spine, leather label. One of 250 signed copies. $600.

DUNTHORNE, Gordon. *Flower and Fruit Prints of the 18th and Early 19th Centuries.* Washington, 1938. Illustrated. Folio, cloth. One of 750 copies, with folding plate listing subscribers. In slipcase. $750. Washington or London. Regular issue. $600. New York, 1970. $500.

DUNTON, John. *The Life and Errors of John Dunton, Citizen of London . . .* London, 1705. $1,000. London, 1818. 2 vols. In 1. Contains much of the 1705 edition with the addition of a memoir and a few omissions. $500.

DU PONT, S. F. *Extracts from Private Journal-Letters of Capt. S. F. Du Pont During the War with Mexico.* Wilmington, 1885. Boards. $2,500.

DU PONT, Samuel F. *Official Dispatches and Letters of Rear Admiral DuPont, 1846–48; and 1861–63.* Wilmington, 1883. Half leather. $2,500.

DU PRE, Ann. *Some Take a Lover.* New York (1933). (Pseudonym of Grace Lumpkin.) $400.

DU PRE, Ann. *Timid Woman.* New York (1933). (Pseudonym of Grace Lumpkin.) $400.

DURANTE, Castore. *A Treasure of Health . . . Wherein Is Shewn How to Preserve Health . . .* London, 1686. $3,000.

DURRELL, Lawrence. See Norden, Charles; Peeslake, Gaffer.

DURRELL, Lawrence. *The Alexandria Quartet.* London (1962). Buckram. First collected edition of *Justine, Balthazar, Mountolive,* and *Clea.* Includes some revisions to the original versions. One of 500 signed copies. In slipcase. $750. New York (1962). First American edition. Marbled boards. One of 199 signed copies. In slipcase. $850.

DURRELL, Lawrence. *Beccafico Le Becfigue.* Montpelier, 1963. Translated and edited by F.-J. Temple. Wraps. One of 150 signed copies. $350.

DURRELL, Lawrence. *Bitter Lemons.* London, 1957. Illustrated. $200. New York, 1957. $100.

DURRELL, Lawrence. *The Black Book.* Paris: Obelisk Press (1938). Wraps. $1,000. Paris (1959). Wraps and dustwrapper. $100. New York, 1960. $100.

DURRELL, Lawrence. *Clea.* London (1960). $200.

DURRELL, Lawrence. *Collected Poems 1931–1974.* (London, 1980.) One of 100 signed copies bound in full oasis goatskin. This issue contains original signed etching by Henry Moore bound in as frontispiece. Slipcase. $2,500.

DURRELL, Lawrence. *Deus Loci.* Ischia, Italy, 1950. Printed blue-gray wraps. One of 200 signed copies. $600.

DURRELL, Lawrence. *In Arcadia.* London: Turret Books, 1968. Music by Wallace Southam. Wraps. One of 100 signed copies. $300.

DURRELL, Lawrence. *Justine.* London, 1957. $750. New York, 1957. $250.

DURRELL, Lawrence. *Mountolive.* London (1958). $350.

DURRELL, Lawrence. *Nothing Is Lost, Sweet Self.* Turret Books. (London, 1967.) Music by Wallace Southam. Pictorial wraps. One of 100 signed copies. $250.

DURRELL, Lawrence. *Pied Piper of Lovers.* London, 1935. Author's first novel. $4,000.

DURRELL, Lawrence. *A Private Country: Poems.* London (1943). Gray cloth. $2,500.

DURRELL, Lawrence. *Private Drafts.* (Nicosia, Cyprus): Proodos Press, 1955. Illustrated. Very small, pictorial wraps. One of 100 signed copies. $750.

DURRELL, Lawrence. *Quaint Fragment.* (London): Cecil Press, 1931. Author's first book. Portrait. Blue wraps or red boards. $40,000.

DURRELL, Lawrence. *Six Poems, from the Greek of Sekillianos and Seferis.* Rhodes, 1946. Pictorial wraps. $1,250.

DURRELL, Lawrence. *Ten Poems.* London: Caduceus Press, 1932. One of 12 signed copies in buckram. $30,000. Wraps. $6,000.

DURRELL, Lawrence. *Transition: Poems.* London, 1934. $5,000.

DURRELL, Lawrence. *Zero and Asylum in the Snow.* Rhodes, 1946. Wraps. $1,250. Berkeley, 1947. White coated paper-covered boards. In dustwrapper. $300.

DUSTIN, Fred. *The Custer Tragedy.* Ann Arbor, 1939. 3 folding maps in pocket. Blue cloth. One of 200 copies. $1,250.

DUVAL, John C. *The Adventures of Big-Foot Wallace.* Philadelphia, 1871. 8 plates. Green cloth. $2,000. (Note: there is a later reprint with the date 1870 on title page.) Austin (1947). $500.

DUVAL, John C. *Early Times in Texas.* Austin, 1892. Cloth. $350. Wraps. $450.

DUVAL, K. D., and SMITH, Sydney Goodsir (editors). *Hugh MacDiarmid: A Festschrift.* Edinburgh (1962). Cloth. One of 50 copies with holograph poem signed by MacDiarmid tipped in. In dustwrapper. $500.

DWIGGINS, W. A. *Towards a Reform of the Paper Currency.* Limited Editions Club, New York, 1932. One of 452 signed copies. In dustwrapper. In slipcase. $600.

DWIGHT, Theodore. *An Oration, Spoken Before the Society of the Cincinnati*. New Haven, 1792. Author's first book. $250.

DWIGHT, Timothy. *Travels in New-England and New York*. New Haven, 1821–22. 4 vols. 3 maps. With errata slip in last vol. $850.

DWINELLE, John W. *The Colonial History of the City of San Francisco*. San Francisco, 1863. Map. Printed wraps. $1,000. San Francisco, 1866. 3 maps (one folding), 3 plates, errata and addenda slips. $1,250.

DWYER, Charles P. *The Economy of Church, Parsonage and School Architecture* . . . Buffalo, 1856. $750.

DWYER, K. R. *Chase*. New York, 1972. (By Dean Koontz.) $350.

DWYER, K. R. *Dragonfly*. New York, 1975. (By Dean Koontz.) $250. London, 1977. $200.

DYE, Eva Emery. *The Conquest*. Chicago, 1902. $125.

DYER, Mrs. D. B. *"Fort Reno," or Picturesque "Cheyenne and Arrapahoe Army Life," Before the Opening of Oklahoma*. New York, 1896. 10 plates. $500.

DYKES, W. R. *The Genus Iris*. Cambridge, 1913. 48 colored plates. Folio, cloth. $1,000. Half morocco. $1,250.

E

E., A. *The Dublin Strike*. (Caption title.) (London, 1913.) (By George W. Russell.) 8 pages, self-wraps. $300.

E., A. *Gods of War, with Other Poems*. Dublin, 1915. (By George W. Russell.) Brown wraps. $250.

E., A. *Homeward Songs by the Way*. Dublin, 1894. (By George W. Russell.) Author's first book. Wraps. $400.

E., A. *Midsummer Eve*. New York, 1928. (By George W. Russell.) Boards. One of 450 signed copies. $200. One of 8 signed copies. On green paper. $1,000.

E., A. *Salutation: A Poem on the Irish Rebellion of 1916*. London 1917. (By George W. Russell.) Wraps. One of 25 signed copies. $600.

EAKINS, Thomas. *21 Photographs*. Atlanta, 1979. One of 200 copies. 21 original photographs tipped in. In slipcase. $1,250.

EARHART, Amelia. *The Fun of It: Random Records of My Own Flying and of Women in Aviation*. New York, 1932. With broadcast record in pocket at back. $1,000.

EARHART, John F. *The Color Printer: A Treatise on the Use of Colors in Typographic Printing*. Cincinnati, 1892. 92 full-color plates. $900.

EARHART, John F. *The Harmonizer*. Cincinnati, 1897. $250.

EARL, George Windsor. *The Eastern Seas.* London, 1837. $1,250.

EARLE, Ferdinand (editor). *The Lyric Year.* New York, 1912. First state, with "careful gentlemen" for "polite gentleman" in line 13 of page 25. (Contains first appearance of Edna St. Vincent Millay's "Renascence.") $200.

EARLE, Thomas (compiler). *The Life, Travels and Opinions of Benjamin Lundy.* Philadelphia, 1847. Colored folding map. $1,000.

EARLY, Gen. Jubal A. *Autobiographical Sketch and Narrative of the War Between the States.* Philadelphia, 1912. $500.

EARLY, Gen. Jubal A. *A Memoir of the Last Year of the War for Independence in the Confederate States of America.* Toronto, 1866. $600. Lynchburg, 1867. Wraps. $400.

EAST of the Sun and West of the Moon. London (1914). (By Peter Christen Asbjörnsen and Jörgen Ingebreksten Moe.) 25 mounted color plates by Kay Nielsen. $4,500. New York, no date [1927?]. In dustwrapper. $1,750.

EASTLAKE, William. *Go in Beauty.* New York (1956). Author's first book. $500. London, 1957. $150.

EASTMAN, Mary H. *The American Aboriginal Portfolio.* Philadelphia (1853). Engraved title page; 26 plates. $1,500.

EASTMAN, Mary. *Dahcotah; or, Life and Legends of the Sioux Around Fort Snelling.* New York, 1849. 4 steel-engraved plates by Eastman's husband, Captain Seth Eastman. $750.

EATON, Daniel Cady. *The Ferns of North America.* Salem, Mass., 1879, and Boston, 1880. 2 vols. $1,250.

EBERHART, Mignon G. *The Patient in Room 18.* Garden City, 1929. Author's first book. $750.

EBERHART, Richard. *A Bravery of Earth.* London (1930). Author's first book. $400. New York (1930). $200.

EBERHART, Richard. *Brotherhood of Men.* Banyan Press. (Pawlet, Vt., 1949.) Wraps. One of 200 signed copies. $300. One of 26 signed copies. $500.

EBERHART, Richard. *Collected Verse Plays.* Chapel Hill (1962). Boards and cloth. One of 100 signed copies. In glassine dustwrapper. $300.

EBERHART, Richard. *An Herb Basket.* Cummington, 1950. One of 155 signed copies. $750.

EBERHART, Richard. *Reading the Spirit.* London, 1936. $250. New York, 1937. $175.

EBERHART, Richard. *Thirty-one Sonnets.* New York (1967). One of 99 signed copies. In slipcase. $300. Trade edition. $60.

EBERHART, Walter. *The Jig-Saw Puzzle Murder.* New York: Grosset & Dunlap, 1933. One volume and boxed 200-piece jigsaw puzzle in slipcase. $300.

ECHOES. By Two Writers. (Lahore, India, 1884.) Printed light-brown wraps. (By Rudyard Kipling, with eight poems credited to his sister Beatrice.) First edition, printed at the Civil and Military Gazette Press. $1,750.

ECKEL, John C. *The First Editions of the Writings of Charles Dickens.* London/New York, 1932. Revised and enlarged edition. One of 750 copies. $350.

ECO, Umberto. *The Name of the Rose.* New York (1983). $150.

ECO, Umberto. *The Picture History of Inventions.* New York, 1962. Author's first book. $200.

ECO, Umberto. *A Theory of Semiotics.* Bloomington (1976). 7 vols. $250.

EDDINGTON, Arthur Stanley. *Stellar Movements and the Structure of the Universe.* London, 1914. Author's first book. $250.

EDDISON, E. R. *A Fish Dinner in Memison.* New York, 1941. One of 998 copies. $200.

EDDISON, E. R. *Poems, Letters and Memories of Philip Sidney Nairn.* London, 1916. Author's first book. (109–page introduction by Eddison.) Issued without dustwrapper. $250.

EDDISON, E. R. *The Worm Ouroboros.* London (1922). First issue, no blindstamped windmill on rear cover. $600. Second issue, with windmill. $400. New York, 1926. $200.

EDDY, Mary Baker. See Glover, Mary Baker.

EDDY, Mary Baker. *Pulpit and Press.* Concord, 1895. $750.

EDE, Charles (editor). *The Art of the Book.* London (1951). In slipcase. $150.

EDE, Harold Stanley. *A Life of Gaudier-Brzeska.* London, 1930. Numerous plates (some colored), other illustrations. One of 350 copies. In dustwrapper. In slipcase. $750.

EDE, Harold Stanley. *Shaw-Ede. T. E. Lawrence's Letters to H. S. Ede.* (London, 1942.) One of 470 copies in half morocco. In slipcase. $750. One of 30 copies in full morocco. In slipcase. $2,750.

EDELMAN, George W. *Guide to the Value of California Gold.* Philadelphia, 1850. Unbound. $2,500.

EDEN, Sir Frederic Morton. *The State of the Poor . . .* London, 1797. 3 vols. $12,500.

EDGAR, Patrick Nisbett. *The American Race-Turf Register.* New York, 1833. Vol. 1. (All published.) $3,000.

EDGERTON, Clyde. *Raney.* Chapel Hill, 1985. $450.

EDGEWORTH, Maria. See *Castle Rackrent; The Modern Griselda.*

EDGEWORTH, Maria. *Harrington, a Tale; and Ormond, a Tale.* London, 1817. 3 vols. Page 118 lacks page number. $500.

EDGEWORTH, Maria. *Leonora.* London, 1806. 2 vols. $600.

EDGEWORTH, Richard Lovell. *Memoirs of Richard Lovell Edgeworth, Esq.* London, 1820. 2 vols. $500.

EDMONDS, Walter D. *Drums Along the Mohawk*. Boston, 1936. $350.

EDMONDS, Walter D. *Rome Haul*. Boston, 1929. Author's first book. With "Published February, 1929" on copyright page. (Presentation) edition. One of 1,001 copies. $450. Trade edition. $350.

EDWARD, David B. *The History of Texas*. Cincinnati, 1836. Folding map in color. $6,000.

EDWARDS, Billy. *Gladiators of the Prize Ring or Pugilists of America*. Chicago (1895). Illustrated. Folio, red cloth. $450.

EDWARDS, Bryan. *The History, Civil and Commercial, of the British Colonies in the West Indies . . .* London, 1793. 2 vols. 2 folding maps, 5 folding tables. $1,750.

EDWARDS, E. I. *Desert Voices: A Descriptive Bibliography*. Los Angeles, 1958. Illustrated. Tan buckram. One of 500 copies. In dustwrapper. $175.

EDWARDS, E. I. *The Valley Whose Name Is Death*. Pasadena, 1940. Map. One of 1,000 copies. Issued without dustwrapper. $175.

EDWARDS, Edward. *Free Town Libraries, Their Formation, Management, and History . . .* London, 1869. $150.

EDWARDS, Frank S. *A Campaign in New Mexico with Col. Doniphan*. Philadelphia, 1847. Folding map. $1,000. Philadelphia, 1848. (Cover date.) Wraps. $850.

EDWARDS, John. *A Select Collection of One Hundred Plates, Consisting of the Most Beautiful and Exotic British Flowers Which Grow in Our English Gardens*. London, 1775. 100 hand-colored plates. $50,000.

EDWARDS, John N. *Shelby and His Men, or The War in the West*. Cincinnati, 1867. Portrait. Folding map. $400.

EDWARDS, John N. *Shelby's Expedition to Mexico*. Kansas City, 1872. $400.

EDWARDS, Philip Leget. *California in 1837*. Sacramento, 1890. Wraps. $500.

EDWARDS, Philip Leget. *The Diary of Philip Leget Edwards: The Great Cattle Drive from California to Oregon in 1837*. San Francisco: Grabhorn Press, 1932. Boards. One of 500 copies. (This reprints *California in 1837*.) $200.

EDWARDS, Samuel E. *The Ohio Hunter*. Battle Creek, 1866. $2,000.

EDWARDS, Sydenham Teak, and others. *The Botanical Register*. 1815–1847. 33 vols. 2,719 hand-colored and engraved plates. $50,000.

EDWARDS, Sydenham Teak. *The New Botanic Gardens*. London, 1812. 2 vols. 61 hand-colored plates. $8,500.

EDWARDS, W. F. (publisher). *W. F. Edwards' Tourists' Guide and Directory of the Truckee Basin*. Truckee, Calif., 1883. Illustrated. Cloth. $1,750.

EDWARDS Chicago Directory (The). Chicago, 1871. "Fire edition." 40 pages, boards. $600.

EFFINGHAM, C. *The Virginia Comedians.* New York, 1854. (By John Esten Cooke.) 2 vols. Wraps, or cloth. Wraps. (Cover date 1855—VAB). Not seen (BAL). $750. Cloth. $500.

EGAN, Pierce. *Anecdotes of the Turf . . .* London, 1827. With 13 hand-colored plates. $850.

EGAN, Pierce. *Boxiana: or, Sketches of Ancient and Modern Pugilism.* London, 1812–29. 5 vols. $3,000.

EGAN, Pierce. *Real Life in London.* London, 1821–22. $2,000.

EGGLESTON, Edward. *The Book of Queer Stories, and Stories Told on a Cellar Door.* Chicago, 1871. $350.

EGGLESTON, Edward. *The Hoosier School-Boy.* New York, 1883. Illustrated by George D. Bush. Pictorial cloth. First edition, first issue, with "Cousin Sukey" frontispiece and first chapter ending on page 16. $600.

EGGLESTON, Edward. *Mr. Blake's Walking-Stick.* Chicago, 1870. Frontispiece and one plate. Light-gray wraps. $350.

EGGLESTON, Edward. *To the Friends of the Sanitary Commission in Minnesota.* [1865?] Author's first book. 4–page appeal for funds. $750.

EGLE, William H. *History of the Counties of Dauphine and Lebanon (Pennsylvania).* Philadelphia, 1883. $300.

EGLINTON, John. *Irish Literary Portraits.* London, 1935. (By William C. Magee.) $175.

EGLINTON, John. *Some Essays and Passages.* Dundrum, Ireland: Cuala Press, 1905. Selected by William Butler Yeats. Boards, linen spine. (By William C. Magee.) One of 200 copies. $350.

EHLE, John. *Move Over, Mountain.* New York, 1957. Author's first book. $250.

EICHENBERG, Fritz. *Dance of Death.* West Hatfield, 1983. Loose sheets. Complete text and 17 signed and numbered wood engravings. In portfolio (with ties). One of 50 signed copies. $4,000.

EIGHT Harvard Poets. New York, 1917. Boards. (Contains poems by e. e. cummings, John Dos Passos, and others.) $200.

EIGNER, Larry. *From the Sustaining Air.* (Mallorca), 1953. One of 250 copies. Wraps. $400.

EIGNER, Larry. *Poems.* Canton, Mass., 1941. Author's first book. Wraps. One of 25 copies. $2,000.

EINSTEIN, Albert. See *Albert-Einstein, Philosopher-Scientist.*

EISELEY, Loren. *The Immense Journey.* New York (1957). Author's first book. $250.

EISENHOWER, Dwight D. *Crusade in Europe.* Garden City, 1948. One of 1,426 signed copies. In slipcase. $1,750.

EISENHOWER, Dwight D. *The White House Years: Mandate for Change, 1953–1956.* Garden City, 1963. Cloth. One of 1,434 signed copies. In slipcase. $1,000.

EISENHOWER, Dwight D. *The White House Years: Waging Peace, 1956–1961.* Garden City, 1965. One of 1,434 signed copies. In slipcase. $1,000.

ELEGY Written in a Country Church-Yard. San Francisco, 1925. (By Thomas Gray.) 2 vols. One of 200 copies. $500. Limited Editions Club, London, 1938. Illustrated by Agnes Miller Parker. One of 1,500 copies signed by Parker. Issued in slipcase. $450. [See next entry.]

ELEGY Wrote in a Country Church Yard (An). London, 1751. (By Thomas Gray.) $30,000.

EL GABILÁN. Salinas, Calif., 1919. Salinas High School Year Book, with 3 contributions by John Steinbeck, his first appearance in print. Pictorial cloth. $3,000.

ELIOT, George. See Strauss, David Friedrich, and Evans, Marian.

ELIOT, George. *Adam Bede.* Edinburgh, 1859. (By Mary Ann Evans.) 3 vols., orange-brown cloth. $4,000.

ELIOT, George. *Daniel Deronda.* Edinburgh, 1876. (By Mary Ann Evans.) 8 parts, wraps. With erratum slip in part 3. $5,000. First book edition. 4 vols. Maroon cloth. Without inserted "contents" leaves. $2,500.

ELIOT, George. *Felix Holt, the Radical.* Edinburgh, 1866. (By Mary Ann Evans.) 3 vols. Red-brown cloth. $1,250.

ELIOT, George. *Middlemarch: A Study of Provincial Life.* Edinburgh, 1871. (By Mary Ann Evans.) 8 parts, pictorial wraps. $6,000. Edinburgh, 1871–72. 4 vols. First book edition. Blue cloth. $5,000.

ELIOT, George. *The Mill on the Floss.* Edinburgh, 1860. (By Mary Ann Evans.) 3 vols. Orange-brown cloth. $2,500.

ELIOT, George. *Romola.* London, 1863. (By Mary Ann Evans.) 3 vols. Green cloth. First issue, with 2 pages of ads at end of vol. 2. $2,500.

ELIOT, George. *Scenes of Clerical Life.* Edinburgh, 1858. (By Mary Ann Evans.) 2 vols. Author's first book. (Preceded by 2 translations.) Maroon cloth. $17,500. New York, 1859. Wraps. $1,500.

ELIOT, George. *Silas Marner: The Weaver of Raveloe.* Edinburgh, 1861. (By Mary Ann Evans.) Orange-brown cloth. $2,250.

ELIOT, T. S. See Ridler, Anne; Perse, St. John; Dryden, John. See also *The Catholic Anthology; Ezra Pound: His Metric and Poetry; Harvard Class Day 1910.*

ELIOT, T. S. *After Strange Gods: A Primer of Modern Heresy.* London (1934). $1,000. New York, 1933. (Actually 1934.) $350.

ELIOT, T. S. *Animula.* (London, 1929.) Wraps. $100. (Note: unsold copies reissued in 1938 in green paper envelopes printed in brown "The Original First . . .") London, 1929. Yellow boards. One of 400 signed copies. $750.

ELIOT, T. S. *Ara Vus Prec.* (London, 1920.) One of 30 signed copies (numbered 5–34). Spine label reads *Ara Vos Prec* (which is the correct spelling) title page reads *Ara Vus Prec.* $10,000. 220 numbered (but not signed) copies. Error remains on title page. $4,500. 10 copies not numbered. (There appear to have been more.) $2,500. (Note: There were also 4 presentation copies printed on Japan vellum.)

ELIOT, T. S. *Ash-Wednesday.* New York/London, 1930. One of 600 signed copies. In cellophane dustwrapper with white paper flaps and in plain brown cardboard box (200 copies in English edition/400 copies American). $1,000. London, 1930. $500. New York, 1930. Black cloth. $400. (Variant in blue cloth catalogued for $2,500.)

ELIOT, T. S. *The Cocktail Party.* London (1950). 19,950 copies printed. Gallup notes "about half" of the copies have misprint "here" for "her" page 29, line 1. $150. Misprint corrected. $100. New York (1950). Approximately 10 copies with pages 35–36 printed on uncanceled leaf. $750. Pages 35–36 printed on cancel leaf. $150. (The first edition is not stated but later printings have code letters/numbers below copyright notice.)

ELIOT, T. S. *Dante.* London (1929). In gray dustwrapper. Earliest state of dustwrapper has no review excerpts on front flap and back. $450. 125 signed copies. $1,500.

ELIOT, T. S. *East Coker: A Poem.* London, 1940. *New England Weekly* (supplement). Unbound. $1,500. Wire-stitched, Reprint from the Easter number of *The New English Weekly.* 500 copies printed. $750. London: Faber (1940). Yellow wraps. $500.

ELIOT, T. S. *Elizabethan Essays.* London (1934). First issue, with misprint on half title, "No. 21" for "No. 24." $450. Second issue corrects error. Spine stamped in gold. $350. Third-issue copies measure 18 cm in height, half title correctly reprinted. Spine stamped in silver. $200.

ELIOT, T. S. *For Lancelot Andrewes.* London (1928). $450. Garden City, 1929. $300.

ELIOT, T. S. *Four Quartets.* New York (1943). States "First American edition" on copyright page. $4,000. Second impression does not state "First." Dustwrapper has flap price of $2.00, and the dustwrapper has three states: heavy block letters with 9 titles listed on back through *Possum . . .* Publisher's address as "NY." $750. Lighter type with *Essays Ancient & Modern* as 1 of the 6 titles and publisher's address as "NY." $450. Heavy block letters with *Family Reunion* as 1 of the 6 titles and address as "NY 17." [Note: the dustwrapper noting that Eliot is a Nobel Winner (1948) is not a second issue dustwrapper, it is a later printing.] $300. London (1944). $750. London (1960). One of 290 signed copies in marbled-paper cardboard box. $4,500. (Cambridge, 1966.) One of 200 copies. In slipcase. $200. One of 26 lettered copies. In slipcase. $450.

ELIOT, T. S. *Homage to John Dryden.* London, 1924. Wraps. $350. (New York, 1964.) Wraps. Offprint with no indication of publisher, place, or date. $100.

ELIOT, T. S. *John Dryden: The Poet, the Dramatist, the Critic.* New York, 1932. One of 110 copies, of which 100 are signed. $1,500. New York, 1932. $300.

ELIOT, T. S. *Journey of the Magi.* (London, 1927.) Wraps. (Note: Unsold copies were reissued in 1938 in mauve paper envelopes printed in black "The Original First . . .") $125. (London, 1927.) One of 350 copies (not signed). $300. New York, 1927. One of 27 copies (12 were for sale). $2,000. Iowa City, 1953. One of 260 copies. Wraps. Mailed in blue paper envelope. $300.

ELIOT, T. S. *Marina.* (London, 1930.) Wraps. $125. One of 400 signed copies. $750.

ELIOT, T. S. *Murder in the Cathedral.* No place, 1935. Gray wraps. $750. White wraps. $1,000. London (1935). $600. New York (1935). $300.

ELIOT, T. S. *Old Possum's Book of Practical Cats.* London (1939). $1,750. New York (1939). $1,000. London (1940). First illustrated edition. $500.

ELIOT, T. S. *Poems.* Richmond: Hogarth Press, England, 1919. Wraps of various colors and textures and white printed label. First issue; page 13, line 6, "aestival" for "estivale," and page 13, line 12, "capitaux" for "chapitaux." $12,500. In marbled wraps, most with black printed label. Misprints corrected. $9,500. New York, 1920. In dustwrapper. $3,500.

ELIOT, T. S. *Poems, 1909–1925.* London, 1925. $1,250. One of 85 signed copies. $6,000. New York/Chicago (1932). Laid paper watermarked with a crown and "Antique DeLuxe BCMSH." In cream dustwrapper printed in blue without price at bottom on back flap. $750.

ELIOT, T. S. *A Practical Possum.* Cambridge, Mass., 1947. Wraps. One of 60 copies (states 80 copies, but actually only 60 were printed). $2,000.

ELIOT, T. S. *Prufrock and Other Observations.* London, 1917. Author's first book. Wraps. $20,000.

ELIOT, T. S. *Religious Drama: Medieval and Modern.* New York, 1954. One of 26 signed lettered copies. Limitation page inserted. $2,500. One of 300 signed copies. Limitation page inserted. $750.

ELIOT, T. S. *The Rock.* London (1934). Wraps. Note on Iconoclasm scene laid in some copies. Priced at 1 shilling. Wraps have flaps folded over endpaper. $350. Boards in dustwrapper. $300. New York, 1934. $200.

ELIOT, T. S. *The Sacred Wood.* London (1920). First state with "Methuen" at foot of spine in letters approximately 3 mm and in dustwrapper without subtitle on front. $1,500. Second state with letters 3.5 mm, dustwrapper includes subtitle and adds "Books by A. Clutton-Brock" on back. $750. Third state adds 8 pages of publisher's ads inserted after page 156. $600. New York, 1921. (No dustwrapper mentioned in Gallep but copy in dustwrapper auctioned in 1982.) In dustwrapper. $1,250.

ELIOT, T. S. *Selected Essays, 1917–1932.* London (1932). One of 115 signed copies. $2,500. Trade edition. $500. New York (1932). $450.

ELIOT, T. S. *Thoughts After Lambeth.* London (1931). $350. Wraps. $100.

ELIOT, T. S. *Triumphal March.* (London, 1931.) Wraps. $100. London, 1931. One of 300 signed copies. Issued without dustwrapper. $750.

ELIOT, T. S. *Two Poems.* (Cambridge), 1935. Wraps. 22 copies, 5 on Arches (numbered 1–5); 5 on Normandie (numbered I–V); 5 on Bremen (lettered a–e); 5 on Brussels (lettered A–E); 2 on Brussels (lettered x and xx). $3,500.

ELIOT, T. S. *The Use of Poetry and the Use of Criticism.* London (1933). Top page edge stained blue. $350. Cambridge, 1933. $400.

ELIOT, T. S. *The Waste Land.* New York, 1922. One of 1,000 copies in total. Approximately 500 copies in first state with flexible cloth boards and "mountain" correctly spelled on page 41, number on colophon 5 mm high. $25,000. Approximately 500 copies in second state with stiff cloth boards and "mount in" for "mountain" on page 41. Number on colophon 2 mm high. $20,000. New York (1923). One of 1,000 copies. Misprint "mount in" remains. "Second Edition." $5,000. Richmond, 1923. 3 states of label exist and apparently issued simultaneously.

$6,000. London (1962). One of 300 signed copies. $4,000. London (1971). In slipcase without dustwrapper. $400. Trade edition. $150. New York (1971). One of 250 copies. $300. Trade. $75.

ELIOT, T. S. *What Is a Classic?* London (1945). Wraps. Contains statements on the aims of the Virgil Society by Eliot and others. $350. Cloth. Statements not included. $200.

ELIOT, T. S. *Words for Music.* Bryn Mawr (1935). Wraps. 20 copies. 2 copies lettered "A" and "B." $6,000. 6 copies lettered "a–f." $4,000. 6 copies numbered "1–6." $4,000. 6 copies numbered "I–VI." $4,000. Note: There are indications that the total edition exceeds the above 20 copies.

ELIZABETH Bennet; or, Pride and Prejudice: A Novel. Philadelphia, 1832. (By Jane Austen.) 2 vols. In original boards and linen, paper label. First American edition of *Pride and Prejudice.* $4,500.

ELKIN, Stanley. *Boswell.* New York (1964). Author's first book. $200.

ELKINS, Aaron J. *The Dark Place.* New York, 1983. With $12.95 on front flap of dustwrapper. $750.

ELKINS, Aaron J. *Fellowship of Fear.* New York, 1982. Author's first book. $1,000.

ELKINS, Aaron J. *Murder in the Queen's Armes.* New York, 1985. $400.

ELKUS, Richard J. *Alamos.* San Francisco: Grabhorn Press, 1965. Foreword by Barnaby Conrad. Half suede and cloth. One of 487 copies. $350.

ELLERMAN, Annie Winifred. See Bryher. See also Bryher, Winifred.

ELLERMAN, Annie Winifred. *Region of Lutany . . .* London, 1914. Author's first book. Wraps. $750.

ELLERMAN, Sir John. See Black, E. L.

ELLICOTT, Andrew. *The Journal of Andrew Ellicott.* Philadelphia, 1803. 14 maps and plates. With errata leaf. $6,000. Philadelphia, 1814. Second edition. $4,500.

ELLIN, Stanley. *Dreadful Summit.* New York, 1948. Author's first book. $175. London (1958). $100.

ELLIOT, Daniel Giraud. *A Monograph of the Bucerotidae . . .* London, 1877–82. 3 plain and 57 hand-colored plates. $25,000.

ELLIOT, Daniel Giraud. *A Monograph of the Felidae, or Family of Cats.* London, 1883. 43 hand-colored lithographs. $60,000.

ELLIOT, Daniel Giraud. *A Monograph of the Tetraoninae; or, Family of Grouse.* New York, 1865. 27 hand-colored lithographed plates. $20,000.

ELLIOT, Daniel Giraud. *The New and Heretofore Unfigured Species of the Birds of North America.* New York (1866–69). 72 hand-colored plates. 2 vols., half morocco. $25,000.

ELLIOT, W. J. *The Spurs.* (Spur, Tex., 1939.) Plates and map. Cloth. Issued without dustwrapper. $450.

ELLIOTT, David Stewart. *Last Raid of the Daltons.* Coffeyville, Kan., 1892. Illustrated. 72 pages, wraps. $750.

ELLIOTT, E. N. *Cotton Is King.* Augusta, 1860. Engraved portrait frontis and 4 engraved portraits. $850.

ELLIOTT, Summer Locke. *Careful He Might Hear You.* London, 1963. $250.

ELLIOTT, William. *Address to the People of St. Helena Parish.* Charleston, 1832. Author's first book. Wraps. $450.

ELLIOTT, William. *Carolina Sports, By Land and Water.* Charleston, 1846. In original cloth. $1,250.

ELLIS, Edward S. See *On the Plains.*

ELLIS, Edward S. *The Life and Adventures of Col. David Crockett.* New York, 1861. Half leather. $500.

ELLIS, Edward S. *The Life and Times of Christopher Carson.* New York (1861). Wraps. $350.

ELLIS, Frederick S. *The History of Reynard the Foxe.* London: Kelmscott Press, 1892. Vellum. One of 300 copies. $1,250.

ELLIS, Frederick S. (editor). *Psalmi Penitentiales.* London: Kelmscott Press, 1894. Woodcut designs and initials. Boards and linen. One of 300 copies. $750. One of 12 copies on vellum. $4,000.

ELLIS, Frederick S. (editor). *The Romance of Syr Ysambrace.* London: Kelmscott Press, 1897. Printed in black and red. Woodcut borders and designs by E. Burne-Jones. Boards and linen. One of 350 copies. $750. One of 8 copies on vellum. $6,000.

ELLIS, Havelock. *The New Spirit.* London, 1890. Author's first book. $300.

ELLIS, Henry. *A Voyage to Hudson's-Bay . . .* London, 1748. Octavo. Folding map and 9 engravings. $3,000.

ELLIS, John B. *Free Love and Its Votaries; or, American Socialism Unmasked.* New York (1870). Illustrated. $300.

ELLIS, Martha and Ted. *Alphabet of New York Bookshops.* Buffalo, 1940. One of 40 copies initialed by the authors. $150.

ELLIS, William. *The American Mission in the Sandwich Islands.* Honolulu, 1866. Boards. $500.

ELLIS, William. *An Authentic Narrative of a Voyage Performed by Captain Cook . . .* London, 1782. 2 vols. 21 plates. Folding chart. $7,500.

ELLIS, William. *Polynesian Researches, During a Residence of Nearly Six Years in the South Sea Islands.* London, 1829. 2 vols. 10 plates and maps, 16 woodcuts. $1,000.

ELLISON, Harlan. *The Deadly Streets.* New York (1958). Wraps. $200.

ELLISON, Harlan. *Love Ain't Nothing but Sex Misspelled.* New York (1968). $250.

ELLISON, Harlan. *Rumble.* New York (1958). Pictorial wraps. $250.

ELLISON, Ralph. *Invisible Man.* New York (1952). Author's first book. $3,000.

ELLISON, Ralph. *Shadow and Act.* New York (1964). $250. London, 1967. $150.

ELLSWORTH, Henry W. *Valley of the Upper Wabash, Indiana . . .* New York, 1938. Folding map, folding plan, and 2 folding plates. $850.

ELLSWORTH, Robert. *Chinese Furniture.* New York, 1971. Author's first book. $850.

ELWES, Henry John. *A Monograph of the Genus Lilium . . . 1877–80* [with] *Supplements . . .* 1880, 1933–62. 78 hand-colored lithographed plates and 10 chromolithographed plates, 1 photograph, and 1 colored map. $25,000. (Originally appeared in 7 parts in 1877–80. The supplements were issued in 9 parts.)

ELY, William. *The Big Sandy Valley: A History of the People and Country from the Earliest Settlement to the Present Time.* Catlettsburg, Ky., 1887. $300.

EMBARGO (The), or Sketches of the Times; A Satire. By a Youth of Thirteen. (Cover title.) Boston, 1808. (By William Cullen Bryant.) 12 pages, self-wraps (stitched). $10,000. (For second edition, see author and title.)

EMBURY, Emma C. *American Wild Flowers in Their Native Haunts.* New York and Philadelphia, 1845. 22 lithographed plates with superimposed hand-colored botanical drawings. $1,750.

EMERSON, Charles L. *Rise and Progress of Minnesota Territory.* St. Paul, 1855. 64 pages, pictorial printed wraps. $2,000.

EMERSON, Lucy. *The New-England Cookery.* Montpelier, Vt., 1808. $3,000.

EMERSON, Peter Henry. *Marsh Leaves.* (London, 1895.) 16 photogravures. One of 300 copies. $7,500. One of 100 copies. $12,500.

EMERSON, Ralph Waldo. See *Nature.*

EMERSON, Ralph Waldo. *An Address Delivered Before the Senior Class in Divinity College. Cambridge . . . 15 July, 1838.* Boston, 1838. 31 pages, in original blue wraps. $1,000.

EMERSON, Ralph Waldo. *An Address Delivered in the Court-House in Concord, Massachusetts, on 1st August, 1844, on the Anniversary of the Emancipation of the Negroes in the British West Indies.* Boston, 1844. 34 pages. Tan wraps. $1,000.

EMERSON, Ralph Waldo. *The American Scholar.* ("An Oration Delivered Before the Phi Beta Kappa Society.") Boston, 1837. 26 pages. Original wraps. $1,000. Unlettered cloth. $500.

EMERSON, Ralph Waldo. *The Complete Works of . . .* Cambridge, 1903–14. 22 vols. One of 600 large-paper sets issued with a page of Emerson's manuscript bound into the first volume. $5,000.

EMERSON, Ralph Waldo. *The Conduct of Life.* Boston, 1860. First issue, with ads for this title as "Nearly Ready." $750.

EMERSON, Ralph Waldo. *English Traits.* Boston, 1856. $600.

EMERSON, Ralph Waldo. *Essays.* Boston, 1841. (6 bindings, no priority, but without "First Series" on spine.) $2,000. London: Doves Press, 1906. Vellum. One of 300 copies on paper. $850. One of 25 copies printed on vellum. $4,500. Limited Editions Club, New York, 1934. Includes first and second series. In slipcase. $150.

EMERSON, Ralph Waldo. *Essays: Second Series.* Boston, 1844. First binding, with "2D Series" on spine. $750. Second binding with "Second Series" on spine, in brown or purple cloth. $350.

EMERSON, Ralph Waldo. *Letter from the Rev. R. W. Emerson to . . .* Boston (1832). Author's first book. Wraps. $20,000.

EMERSON, Ralph Waldo. *May-Day and Other Pieces.* Boston, 1867. Various cloth colors. $250. White cloth, which may have been a special binding. $350.

EMERSON, Ralph Waldo. *The Method of Nature.* Boston, 1841. 30 pages, printed tan wraps. $750.

EMERSON, Ralph Waldo. *An Oration Delivered Before the Literary Societies of Dartmouth College, July 24, 1838.* Boston, 1838. Wraps. $750.

EMERSON, Ralph Waldo. *Poems.* London, 1847. First issue, with "Chapman Brothers" on foot of spine and ads dated Nov. 16, 1846. $1,000. Boston, 1847. Glazed boards or black cloth. First issue, with 8 pages preceding title page, including 4 pages of ads dated Jan. 1, 1847. $1,250. Limited Editions Club, New York, 1945. Full leather. In slipcase. $150.

EMERSON, Ralph Waldo. *Representative Men.* Boston, 1850. Black or brown cloth. First printing sheets bulk $^{11}/_{16}$ inch and no ads at end versus ⅞ inch in second printing and 2 pages of ads at end (BAL). $850. London, 1850. Brown or green cloth. First English edition (possibly issued simultaneously). $750.

EMILY Parker, or Impulse, Not Principle. Boston, 1827. (By Lydia Maria Child.) Frontispiece. $400.

EMMA. By the author of "Pride and Prejudice," . . . London, 1816. (By Jane Austen.) 3 vols. $15,000. Limited Editions Club, New York, 1964. Illustrated in color by Fritz Kredel. Buckram. In slipcase. $150.

EMMETT, Chris. *Shanghai Pierce, a Fair Likeness.* Norman (1953). Illustrated, map. $150.

EMMONS, Richard. *The Fredoniad.* Boston, 1827. 4 vols. Author's first book. $300.

EMMONS, Samuel Franklin. *Geology and Mining Industry of Leadville, Colorado.* Washington, 1883–86. 2 vols. Half leather, including atlas with colored maps. $1,000.

EMORY, William H. *Notes of a Military Reconnoissance.* Washington, 1848. 64 plates, 6 maps and plans. Cloth. House or Senate version. $1,500.

EMPSON, William. *Letter IV.* London, 1929. Author's first book. $250.

EMPSON, William. *Poems.* London, 1935. $350. New York, 1949. $125.

ENGELHARDT, Zephyrin. *The Franciscans in Arizona.* Harbor Springs, Mich., 1899. Map, plates. 236 pages, wraps. $250.

ENGELHARDT, Zephyrin. *The Franciscans in California.* Harbor Springs, 1897. Illustrated. Wraps. $250.

ENGELHARDT, Zephyrin. *The Missions and Missionaries of California.* San Francisco, 1908, 1912, 1913, 1915, and 1916. 5 vols. $400.

ENGELS, Friedrich. *Socialism, Utopian, and Scientific.* London, 1892. First edition in English. $500.

ENGLE, Paul. *Worn Earth.* New Haven, 1932. Author's first book. Boards. $150.

ENGLISH Bards and Scotch Reviewers. London (1809). (By George Gordon Noel, Lord Byron.) First issue, without preface. 54 pages. $750. Later issue, with preface. $400.

ENGLISH Dance of Death (The). London, 1815–16. (By William Combe.) 2 vols. Frontispiece, engraved title, and 72 color plates by Thomas Rowlandson. $3,500.

ENGLISH Fairy Tales. Retold by Flora Annie Steel. London, 1918. Illustrated and signed by Arthur Rackham. One of 500 copies. 16 mounted plates. $3,500. New York, 1918. One of 250 signed copies. $2,500.

ENGLISHWOMAN in America (The). London, 1856. (By Isabella Bird.) Author's first book. $500.

ENQUIRY into the Present State of Polite Learning in Europe (An). London, 1759. Oliver Goldsmith's first original work. $1,500.

ENSLIN, Theodore. *The Work Proposed.* (Ashland, Mass.), 1958. Author's first book. One of 250 copies. Stiff wraps. $175.

EPIPSYCHIDION: Verses . . . London, 1821. (By Percy Bysshe Shelley.) $8,500. Montagnola, Italy, 1923. Vellum. One of 222 copies. $1,250.

EPISTLES and Gospels for All Sundays and Holidays Throughout the Year. New Edition . . . Detroit, 1812. By Two Gentlemen . . . "Reprinted from the 6th Edition of Dublin 1794 . . ." $1,850.

EPITOME of Electricity and Galvanism (An). Philadelphia, 1809. By Two Gentlemen of Philadelphia. (By Jacob Green and Ebenezer Hazard.) $1,250.

EPSTEIN, Jacob. *Epstein: An Autobiography.* London, 1955. Illustrated. Leatherette. One of 195 signed copies. Issued without dustwrapper. $450.

EPSTEIN, Jacob. *Let There Be Sculpture: An Autobiography.* (London, 1940.) Vellum. One of 100 signed copies. In slipcase. $600.

EPSTEIN, Jacob. *Seventy-five Drawings.* London, 1929. Oblong, vellum. One of 220 signed copies. Issued without dustwrapper. $750.

ERDRICH, Louise. *Jacklight.* New York (1984). Author's first book. Wraps. $300.

ERDRICH, Louise. *Love Medicine.* New York (1984). $250.

EREWHON, or Over the Range. London, 1872. (By Samuel Butler.) Brown cloth. $400. Newtown, Wales: Gregynog Press, 1932. Illustrated. Sheep. One of 275 copies on Japan vellum.

$1,000. One of 25 copies specially bound in morocco by George Fisher. $4,500. Limited Editions Club, New York, 1934. Introduction by Aldous Huxley. Illustrated by Rockwell Kent. In slipcase. $200.

ERMAN, Adolph. *Life in Ancient Egypt.* London, 1894. 11 plates and 400 text illustrations. $150.

ERMAN, Adolph. *Travels in Siberia; Including Excursions Northwards, Down the Obi, to the Polar Circle, and Southwards, to the Chinese Frontier.* London, 1848. 2 vols. Folding map. $750. Philadelphia, 1850. $500.

ESHLEMAN, Clayton. *Mexico & North.* (New York/San Francisco, 1961.) (New York/San Francisco imprint but actually printed in Tokyo.) Author's first book. Wraps. One of 26 lettered copies. $250. Regular edition. $125.

ESPEJO, Antonio de. *Expedition into New Mexico . . .* Los Angeles, 1929. One of 500 copies. In dustwrapper. $200.

ESPEJO, Antonio de. *New Mexico: Otherwise the Voiage of Anthony Espeio, Who in the Yeare 1583, with His Company, Discovered a Lande of 15 Provinces, etc.* (Lancaster, 1928.) Boards. One of 200 copies. $300.

ESQUIVEL, Laura. *Like Water for Chocolate.* New York (1992). $125.

Essay Concerning Humane Understanding, An. London: Elizabeth Holt for Thomas Basset, 1690. (By John Locke.) The 'Holt' imprint with "ss" correctly printed in "Essay." $45,000. Copies with the inverted "ss" are regarded as the second issue. $35,000.

ESSAY on Mind (An), with Other Poems. London, 1826. (By Elizabeth Barrett Browning.) First issue, with the reading "found" in line 15, page 75. $1,500.

ESSAY on the Art of Ingeniously Tormenting. London, 1753. (By Jane Collier.) $600.

ESSAY on the Principle of Population . . . (An). London, 1798. (By Thomas Robert Malthus.) Blue-tinted paper, errata on verso of A8, Q8 canceled. $80,000. For second editions, see listing under author's name.

ESSAYS from Poor Robert the Scribe. Doylestown, Pa., 1815. (By Charles Miner.) $300.

ESSAYS honoring Lawrence C. Wroth. Portland, 1951. One of 360 copies (stated in prospectus). $150.

ESSE, James. *Hunger: A Dublin Story.* Dublin, 1918. (By James Stephens.) Printed wraps. $125.

ESTIENNE, Henri. *The Frankfort Book Fair.* Chicago: Caxton Club, 1911. One of 303 copies. $500.

EUPHRANOR: A Dialogue on Youth. London, 1851. (By Edward FitzGerald.) Green cloth. $750.

EVANS, C. S. *Cinderella.* [For 1808 first edition, see Perrault, Charles.] London (1919). 325 copies on Japanese vellum, signed by illustrator, Arthur Rackham. With extra plate. $2,500. One of 525 copies. $1,250.

EVANS, C. S. *The Sleeping Beauty.* London, (1920). Illustrated by Arthur Rackham. Edition Deluxe. One of 625 copies with an extra plate, printed on handmade paper and signed by Rackham. $1,500. Philadelphia (1920). First U.S. trade edition. $400.

EVANS, Charles, Jr. *Chick Evans' Golf Book.* Chicago (1921). One of 999 signed copies. Decorative leather. $1,500. Trade edition. (1921). In dustwrapper. $300.

EVANS, Elwood. *History of the Pacific Northwest: Oregon & Washington.* Portland, Oregon, 1889. 2 vols. $850.

EVANS, Elwood. *Puget Sound: Its Past, Present and Future.* Olympia, Wash., 1869. 16 pages, wraps. $350.

EVANS, Elwood. *Washington Territory.* Olympia, 1877. 51 pages, wraps. $750.

EVANS, Estwick. *A Pedestrious Tour, of 4,000 Miles, Through the Western States and Territories.* Concord, N.H., 1819. Portrait. $1,500.

EVANS, Evan. *Montana Rides Again.* New York, 1934. (By Frederick Faust.) $400.

EVANS, Joan. *English Jewellery . . .* London (1921). $450.

EVANS, Joan. *A History of Jewellery, 1100–1870.* New York, 1953. 186 photographic plates. Green cloth, gilt. $350.

EVANS, Marian. *The Essence of Christianity.* London, 1854. Author's first book. First issue, black cloth with "Marian Evans" on spine. $3,000. Second issue, purple cloth with "George Eliot" on spine. $2,000. (Evans's translation of Ludwig Feuerbach's book. The only use of her real name.)

EVANS, Walker. See Beals, Carleton.

EVANS, Walker. *American Photographs.* New York, 1938. $750.

EVANS, Walker. *Many Are Called.* Boston, 1966. $600.

EVANS, Walker. *Message from the Interior.* New York (1966). $750.

EVARTS, Hal. *Cross Pull.* New York, 1920. Author's first book. $400.

EVARTS, Hal. *Painted Stallion.* New York, 1926. $250.

EVELYN, John. *Memoirs, Illustrative of the Life and Writings of John Evelyn, Esq., F.R.S.* London (Bath), 1818. Edited by William Bray. Folding pedigree, 8 plates. 2 vols. $1,000.

EVELYN, John. *Navigation and Commerce . . .* London, 1674. $2,500.

EVELYN, John. *Sculptura; Or, the History and Art of Chalcography, and Engraving in Copper . . .* London, 1662. $4,500. London, 1755. $750.

EVELYN, John. *Sylva . . .* London, 1664. 3 parts. $3,500. York, 1776. $750.

EVENINGS in New England. Boston, 1824. By an American Lady. (Lydia Maria Child.) $600.

EVENTS in Indian History, Beginning with an Account of the Origin of the American Indians . . . Lancaster, Pa., 1841. (By James Wimer.) 8 plates. $450.

EVERARD, Edward. *A Bristol Printing House.* London (1903). Cloth folder with loosely inserted cord-tied book. $200.

EVERARD, Harry S. C. *History of the Royal and Ancient Golf Club, St. Andrews from 1754–1900.* 1907. $2,500.

EVERETT, Edward. *Address of Hon. Edward Everett, at the Consecration of the National Cemetery at Gettysburg . . . with the Dedicatory Speech of President Lincoln . . .* Boston, 1864. First authorized edition. Map and folding plan of battlefield. $1,000. [See also entry after next.]

EVERETT, Edward. *A Defence of Christianity.* Boston, 1814. Author's first book. Boards, paper label. $250.

EVERETT, Edward. *An Oration Delivered on the Battlefield of Gettysburg . . .* New York, 1863. 48 pages, yellow printed wraps. Includes one of the early book appearances of Abraham Lincoln's Gettysburg Address. (See also Lincoln, Abraham.) $7,500.

EVERETT, Horace. *Regulating the Indian Department.* (Washington), 1834. Folding map. $450.

EVERGOOD, Philip. *Evergood: 20 Years.* New York (1946). One of 150 copies. With original color etching bound in and signed, numbered and dated by the artist. In dustwrapper. $600. Trade. $125.

EVERITT, Simon. *Tales of Wild Turkey Hunting.* Chicago, 1928. Illustrated. Original gilt-stamped cloth. $350.

EVERSON, William. See Antoninus, Brother.

EVERSON, Bill (William). *These Are the Ravens.* (Cover title.) San Leandro, Calif., 1935. Author's first book. 11 pages, stapled self-wraps. $450.

EVERSON, William. *Blame It on the Jet Stream.* Santa Cruz, 1978. Illustrated. Oblong, boards. One of 150 signed copies, issued without dustwrapper. $250.

EVERSON, William. *The Blowing of the Seed.* New Haven, 1966. Green or brown flowered boards, leather spine. One of 203 signed copies. $250. Also, 15 numbered copies. $500.

EVERSON, William. *In the Fictive Wish.* (Berkeley, 1967.) Oyez Press. One of 200 signed copies. In plain white dustwrapper. $200.

EVERSON, William. *The Masculine Dead Poems, 1938–1940.* Prairie City, Ill. (1942). With tipped-in errata sheet. $900. Without errata. $750.

EVERSON, William. *A Privacy of Speech.* Berkeley, 1949. Illustrated. Boards. One of 100 copies. $3,500.

EVERSON, William. *The Residual Years.* (Waldport, 1944.) Illustrated by the author. Wraps. One of 330 signed copies. $350. New Directions. (New York, 1948.) Boards. One of 1,000 copies. (A collection of 4 prior works.) $150.

EVERSON, William. *San Joaquin.* Los Angeles, 1939. One of 100 copies. Issued without dustwrapper. $1,250.

EVERSON, William. *Triptych for the Living.* (Oakland, 1951.) Illustrated. Limp vellum. One of 200 copies (actually fewer than 100). $2,000.

EVERSON, William. *War Elegies.* Waldport, 1944. Wraps. Expanded edition of *X War Elegies.* One of 975 copies. $250. One of 30 copies in full calf, signed. (Bound and signed in 1970s.) $750.

EVERSON, William. *X War Elegies.* Waldport, 1943. Wraps. First state, wraps lettered in black and yellow. $350.

EVERTS, Truman C. *Thirty-seven Days of Peril.* San Francisco, 1923. Grabhorn Press. One of 375 copies. $250.

EVERTS and KIRK. *The Official State Atlas of Nebraska.* Philadelphia, 1885. Plates, 207 colored maps. Half calf. $850.

EVERY Man His Own Printer; or, Lithography Made Easy. London, 1854. $600.

EVERYTHING for the Printer. New York, 1902. Includes 49 pages of single color samples. Wraps. $150.

EVIDENCE Concerning Projected Railways Across the Sierra Nevada Mountains. Carson City, Nev., 1865. Calf. $1,500.

EVIL of Intoxicating Liquor (The) and the Remedy. Park Hill, Okla., 1844. 24 pages, sewn. $1,000.

EWART, Gavin. *Poems and Songs.* London (1939). Author's first book. $250.

EWELL, Thomas T. *A History of Hood County, Texas.* Granbury, Tex., 1895. Cloth. $1,250.

EXAMPLES of Modern Book Binding, Designed and Executed by Robt. Riviere & Son. London, 1919. 69 full-page plates and 8 in full color. One of 200 copies. $450.

EXLEY, Frederick. *A Fan's Notes.* New York (1968). Author's first book. $350. London (1970). $150.

EXPEDITION of Humphrey Clinker (The). London, 1671 [for 1771]. (By Tobias George Smollett.) 3 vols. $1,250. (See bibliography.) Boston, 1813. 2 vols. $1,000.

EXQUEMELIN, Alexandre Olivier. *Bucaniers of America . . .* London, 1684–85. 4 parts in 1 vol. First edition in English. 9 plates, 16 maps. $10,000.

EYE WITNESS (An). *Satan in Search of a Wife.* London, 1831. (By Charles Lamb.) 4 full-page woodcuts and 2 vignettes by George Cruikshank. $750.

EZRA Pound: His Metric and Poetry. New York, 1917. (By T. S. Eliot.) Portrait frontispiece by Gaudier-Brzeska. Rose-colored paper boards, lettered in gold on front cover. In plain buff dustwrapper. $1,000. Lacking dustwrapper. $750.

F

F., M.T. *My Chinese Marriage.* New York, 1921. (By Mai Taim Franking, ghosted by Katherine Anne Porter.) Porter's first book. Green boards and cloth. $1,000. Without dustwrapper. $200.

FACSIMILES *of Royal, Historical, Literary, and Other Autographs in the Department of MSS., British Museum.* London, 1899. Edited by George F. Warner, 150 plates. 5 parts, folio, sewn. $500.

FACTS *Concerning the City of San Diego, the Great Southwestern Seaport of the United States, with a Map Showing the City and Its Surroundings.* San Diego (1888). 14 pages, wraps. $600.

FACTS *Respecting Indian Administration in the Northwest (The).* (Victoria, 1886.) 74 pages, wraps. $400.

FAHEY, Herbert. *Early Printing in California.* San Francisco: Grabhorn Press, 1956. Illustrated. One of 400 copies. $350.

FAIR DEATH *(A).* London (1881). (By Sir Henry Newbolt, his first book.) Wraps. $200.

FAIRBAIRN, W. E. *Defendu, Scientific Self-Defense.* Shanghai, 1925. $150.

FAIRBAIRN, W. E. *Scientific Self Defense.* Shanghai, 1931. $150.

FAIRBANKS, George R. *Early History of Florida.* St. Augustine, 1857. 82 pages, sewn. $350.

FAIRBANKS, George R. *The Spaniards in Florida.* Jacksonville, 1868. 120 pages, wraps. $350.

FAIRCHILD, T. B. *A History of the Town of Cuyahoga Falls, Summit County.* Cleveland, 1876. 39 pages. $125.

FAIRFIELD, Asa Merrill. *Fairfield's Pioneer History of Lassen County, California.* San Francisco (1916). 4 plates. Folding map. Pictorial cloth. $250.

FAIRLIE, Gerard. *Mr. Malcolm Presents.* London (1932). $1,250.

FAIRMAN, Henry Clay. *The Third World . . .* Atlanta, 1895. Author's first book. $450. New York, 1896. $200.

FAIRY *Book (The).* New York, 1837. (By Dinah M. Craik.) Frontispiece and 81 woodcuts by Joseph A. Adams. $600.

FAIRY *Garland (A).* London (1928). 12 colored illustrations by Edmund Dulac. Half vellum. One of 1,000 copies signed by the artist. $950.

FALCONER, Thomas. *Letters and Notes on the Texan Santa Fe Expedition, 1841–42.* New York, 1930. Edited by F. W. Hodge. Portrait. Half cloth. Issued without dustwrapper. $200.

FALCONER, Thomas. *On the Discovery of the Mississippi, and On the South-Western, Oregon, and North-Western Boundary of the United States.* London, 1844. Folding map, errata leaf. Cloth. First issue, with the map (later absent). $2,500.

FALCONER, William. *A Universal Dictionary of the Marine.* London, 1769. With 12 folding plates. $1,250.

FALKLAND. London, 1827. (By Edward Bulwer-Lytton.) Author's first novel. $750.

FALKNER: A Novel. London, 1837. (By Mary Wollstonecraft Shelley.) 3 vols. $4,500.

FALKNER, J. Meade. *The Lost Stradivarius.* London, 1895. Author's first book. First issue with ads dated 10/95. $600.

FALKNER, W(illiam) C(lark). *The White Rose of Memphis.* New York, 1881. $350.

FALL, Bernard. *Hell in a Very Small Place.* Philadelphia, 1967. $300.

FALL, Bernard. *Street Without Joy.* Harrisburg (1961). $500.

FALLON, Peter. *Among the Walls.* (Dublin, 1971.) Wraps. $150.

FAMILY Robinson Crusoe (The). London, 1814. Translated from the German of M. Wiss (Johann David Wyss). 2 vols. First edition in English. $4,500. London 1814–16. Second edition. $2,000. See also *The Swiss Family Robinson.*

FANNY. New York, 1819. (By Fitz-Greene Halleck.) Author's first separate book. 49 pages, original printed gray wraps. (Note: There also exists a pirated 1819 edition, 67 pages.) $750. Rebound. $300.

FANSHAWE: A Tale. Boston, 1828. (By Nathaniel Hawthorne.) Author's first book. Brown or buff boards, purple cloth spine, paper labels. $60,000. Rebound. $30,000.

FANTE, John. *Ask the Dust.* New York, 1939. Cloth. $3,500. Santa Barbara, 1980. One of 75 copies signed by Fante and Charles Bukowski. In acetate dustwrapper. $750. One of 750 copies. $200. Wraps. $35.

FANTE, John. *Wait Until Spring, Bandini.* New York (1938). Author's first book. $2,500. Santa Barbara, 1983. One of 26 signed, lettered copies. $500. One of 250 signed copies. $250. (Both in acetate dustwrappers.)

FARINA, Richard. *Been Down So Long It Looks Like Up to Me.* New York (1966). Author's first book. $250.

FARJEON, Eleanor. *Pan-World . . .* London, 1908. $150.

FARMER, Philip José. *The Fabulous Riverboat.* New York (1971). $350.

FARMER, Philip José. *Flesh.* (New York, 1960.) Wraps. $75. Garden City, 1968. Revised, first hardcover. First edition stated. $350.

FARMER, Philip José. *The Green Odyssey.* New York, 1957. Author's first book. Cloth. $1,500. Wraps. $75.

FARNHAM, Eliza W. *California, In-Doors and Out.* New York, 1856. $400.

FARNHAM, S. B. *The New York and Idaho Gold Mining Co.* New York, 1864. Folding map. 23 pages, wraps. $750.

FARNHAM, Thomas J. *History of Oregon Territory.* New York, 1844. Frontispiece map. Wraps. $1,500.

FARNHAM, Thomas J. *Travels in the Californias.* New York, 1844. Map and plates. First edition, second (or clothbound) issue. $1,750.

FARNHAM, Thomas J. *Travels in the Great Western Prairies.* Poughkeepsie, 1841. Cloth, leather label. $2,000. Poughkeepsie, 1843. Tan boards, lavender cloth. $1,500. London, 1843. 2 vols. $750.

FARNIE, H. B. *The Golfers Manual.* Scotland, 1857. (Pseudonym is A Keen Hand.) $7,500. London, 1947. One of 750 copies. Reprint of the original 1857 edition. In dustwrapper and slipcase. $600.

FARQUHARSON, Martha. *Elsie Dinsmore.* New York, 1867. (By Martha Finley.) $6,500 at auction in 1992.

FARRELL, J. G. *A Man from Elsewhere.* London, 1963. Author's first book. $250.

FARRELL, James T. *Calico Shoes and Other Stories.* New York (1934). $400.

FARRELL, James T. *Gas-House McGinty.* New York, 1933. $500.

FARRELL, James T. *Guillotine Party.* New York (1935). $350.

FARRELL, James T. *Judgment Day.* New York, 1935. With "thay" for "they" in third line of page 218 (VAB). $750.

FARRELL, James T. *A Misunderstanding.* New York, 1949. One of 300 signed copies. In tissue jacket. $150. Trade. $60.

FARRELL, James T. *$1,000 a Week and Other Stories.* New York (1942). $250.

FARRELL, James T. *Tommy Gallagher's Crusade.* New York (1939). $150.

FARRELL, James T. *Young Lonigan: A Boyhood in Chicago Streets.* New York, 1932. Author's first book. Brown cloth. $1,250. Reissued in 1935 in blue cloth with new foreword by F. Thrasher inserted, title page still dated 1932. $350.

FARRELL, James T. *The Young Manhood of Studs Lonigan.* New York (1934). Brown cloth. First edition, with errata slip listing 8 typographical errors, among them "Connolly" for "Connell" in line 18 of page 88. $1,000.

FARRINGTON, S. Kip, Jr. *Atlantic Game Fishing.* New York, 1937. Introduction by Ernest Hemingway. In dustwrapper. $350.

FARROW, Edward S. *Mountain Scouting: A Hand-Book for Officers . . .* New York, 1881. $400.

FAST, Howard. *Peekskill: USA. A Personal Experience.* Civil Rights Congress, 1951. One of 500 copies specially bound and signed by Paul Robeson, William L. Patterson, and Howard Fast. $750.

FAST, Howard. *Two Valleys.* New York, 1933. Author's first book. $750.

FAULKNER, J. P. *Eighteen Months on a Greenland Whaler.* New York, 1878. Portrait. Cloth. $350.

FAULKNER, William. See Petersen, Carl.

FAULKNER, William. *Absalom, Absalom!* New York, 1936. One of 300 signed copies. Issued without dustwrapper in slipcase. $7,500. Trade. $4,000. London (1937). Cream-colored cloth stamped in red and black, top edge red. In glassine dustwrapper with glued-on printed flaps. $2,000. Franklin Library, Franklin Center, 1978. $125.

FAULKNER, William. *As I Lay Dying.* New York (1930). Initial capital "I" at page 11, line 1 not aligned (dropped so that the top of the letter is almost at the bottom of the first line of text). Preferred state of binding has lettering complete and undamaged. $7,500. Initial capital "I" at page 11, line 1 correctly aligned. $3,500. London, 1935. Blue cloth stamped in white, top edge blue. $1,500.

FAULKNER, William. *Collected Stories of William Faulkner.* New York (1950). Title page printed in blue and black, top edge stained blue. $1,000.

FAULKNER, William. *Doctor Martino and Other Stories.* New York, 1934. One of 360 signed copies. $3,000. Trade. $1,250. London, 1934. $1,500.

FAULKNER, William. *A Fable.* (New York, 1954.) One of 1,000 signed copies. In slipcase. $2,000. Trade. Maroon cloth, top edge gray. $250. London, 1955. $300.

FAULKNER, William. *Go Down, Moses and Other Stories.* New York (1942). One of 100 signed copies. $25,000. Trade. Black cloth, top edge stained red. $2,500. Various colors of cloth with top unstained. $1,500. London, 1942. $1,000.

FAULKNER, William. *A Green Bough.* New York, 1933. One of 360 signed copies. Issued without dustwrapper. $2,500. Trade. $1,000.

FAULKNER, William. *The Hamlet.* New York, 1940. One of 250 signed copies. In slipcase. $7,500. Trade. Back of dustwrapper has ads for other books. $3,000. Back of dustwrapper has reviews of this book. $1,500. London, 1940. $1,500.

FAULKNER, William. *Idyll in the Desert.* New York, 1931. One of 400 signed. $2,500. (No trade edition.)

FAULKNER, William. *Intruder in the Dust.* New York (1948). $600. London, 1949. $350.

FAULKNER, William. *Jealousy and Episode.* Minneapolis, 1955. One of 500 copies. $500. (No trade edition.)

FAULKNER, William. *Knight's Gambit.* New York (1949). First edition not stated. $450. London, 1951. $200.

FAULKNER, William. *Light in August.* (New York, 1932.) Tan cloth stamped in blue and orange. Issued with a glassine wrapper over dustwrapper. $5,000. Stamped in blue only. $2,500. London, 1933. $1,250.

FAULKNER, William. *The Mansion.* New York (1959). One of 500 signed copies. In acetate dustwrapper without slipcase. $2,500. Trade. $250.

FAULKNER, William. *The Marble Faun.* Boston (1924). $25,000.

FAULKNER, William. *The Marionettes.* (Charlottesville, 1975.) One of 26 copies. Unbound gatherings on Arches paper in box. $1,000. One of 100 copies. Unbound in slipcase. $400. Trade. $50.

FAULKNER, William. *The Marionettes: A Play in One Act.* Oxford, 1975. One of 10 copies. Facsimile edition in boards with monograph by Ben Wasson, *A Memory of Marionettes,* a pamphlet. Laid into box. $1,000. One of 500 copies. $350.

FAULKNER, William. *Mirrors of Chartres Street.* (Minneapolis, 1953.) One of 1,000 copies. $450.

FAULKNER, William. *Miss Zilphia Gant.* (Dallas): Book Club of Texas, 1932. One of 300 copies. $2,500.

FAULKNER, William. *Mosquitoes.* New York: Boni & Liveright, 1927. In red on green dustwrapper with mosquito. $7,500. In dustwrapper with card players on yacht and Boni & Liveright (original publisher) on spine. $10,000. With "Horace Liveright, Inc." on dustwrapper spine. $2,500. (Note: "second printing" done in 1931.)

FAULKNER, William. *New Orleans Sketches.* Tokyo, 1955. Dark-blue and medium-blue cloth bindings. $600. Wraps. $250.

FAULKNER, William. *Notes on a Horsethief.* Greenville, Miss., 1950. One of 975 signed copies. Issued in tissue dustwrapper without slipcase. $1,500.

FAULKNER, William. *Pylon.* New York, 1935. One of 310 signed copies. Issued without dustwrapper in slipcase. $3,500. Trade. (Later printing dustwrapper is blank on back.) $1,250. London, 1935. Rose-brown binding, top edge stained rose; bottom edge untrimmed, two leaves of ads at end. $1,750. Bright red binding, top edge unstained, bottom edge trimmed, no ads. $1,500.

FAULKNER, William. *The Reivers: A Reminiscence.* New York (1962). One of 500 signed. In acetate dustwrapper without slipcase. $2,500. Trade. Red cloth, top edges stained red and without Book of Month Club blind stamp on back cover. $250. London, 1962. $100.

FAULKNER, William. *Requiem for a Nun.* New York (1951). One of 750 signed copies. Issued without dustwrapper or slipcase. $1,750. Trade, with top edge stained gray (presumed first issue). First edition not stated. $250. London, 1953. $200.

FAULKNER, William. *A Rose for Emily and Other Stories.* New York (1945). Wraps. Reportedly the issue with aerial view of home on verso of title page is first. $500. Without view. $300. Tokyo, 1956. Wraps. $200.

FAULKNER, William. *Salmagundi.* Milwaukee, 1932. One of 525 copies. In box. First 26 copies have bottom edge untrimmed and top edge even with top of cover. $3,500. One of the 499. $1,500.

FAULKNER, William. *Sanctuary.* New York (1931). $10,000. London, 1931. Wine-red cloth stamped in gold; four pages of ads. $1,750. Bright-red cloth stamped in black. No ads. $1,500.

FAULKNER, William. *Sartoris.* New York (1929). $7,500. London, 1932. Blue cloth, top edge stained blue. $1,250. Tan cloth, top edge unstained. $1,000.

FAULKNER, William (editor). *Sherwood Anderson & Other Famous Creoles.* New Orleans, 1926. One of 50 copies signed by William Spratling (the caricaturist). Bound in decorative boards with frontispiece and illustrations hand-tinted by Spratling. $7,500. One of 200 copies (limitation notice indicates 250 numbered copies). Green boards. $2,500. Label is pasted over original limitation statement stating "Second Issue 150 copies January 1927." $2,000.

FAULKNER, William. *Soldiers' Pay.* New York, 1926. $45,000. Without dustwrapper. $2,500. London, 1930. $2,500.

FAULKNER, William. *The Sound and the Fury.* New York (1929). Dustwrapper not priced but "Humanity Uprooted" priced "$3.00" on rear panel. $45,000. With "Humanity Uprooted" priced $3.50. $30,000. (Note: Dustwrapper spine usually faded.) London, 1931. Bound in black cloth, top edge stained red. $3,500. Mustard cloth stamped in red. Top edge unstained without publisher's imprint on spine. $1,750.

FAULKNER, William. *These 13.* New York (1931). One of 299 signed copies. In tissue dustwrapper. $4,500. Trade. $1,500. London, 1933. Blue cloth stamped in gold, top edge green. $2,000.

FAULKNER, William. *This Earth.* New York, 1932. Stiff tan wraps in plain white envelope. $400.

FAULKNER, William. *The Town.* New York (1957). One of 450 signed copies in acetate dustwrapper without slipcase. $2,500. Trade. Red cloth, top edge stained gray. Dustwrapper has "5/57" on front flap. Threaded gray endpapers. $350. Various cloths, plain endpapers, various top edge colors. Without dustwrapper point. $100. London, 1958. $150.

FAULKNER, William. *The Unvanquished.* New York (1938). One of 250 signed copies. Issued without dustwrapper or slipcase. $5,000. Trade. $1,500. London, 1938. Dustwrapper is clear with paper flaps. $1,500. Without dustwrapper. $250.

FAULKNER, William. *The Wild Palms.* New York (1939). One of 250 signed copies. Issued in glassine wrapper without slipcase. $5,000. Trade. Tan cloth, stamped in gold and green on spine. $1,500. Tan cloth, stamped in brown and green on spine. $1,000. London, 1939. $1,250.

FAULKS, Sebastian. *A Trick of the Light.* London, 1984. $750.

FAUSET, Arthur Huff. *For Freedom: A Biographical Story of the American Negro.* Philadelphia, 1927. $750. Philadelphia, 1934. Revised. $350.

FAUSET, Jessie. *Comedy:American Style.* New York, 1933. $2,500. Canadian edition. "Canadian Edition For Sale in Canada Only" on title page. $3,000.

FAUSET, Jessie Redmon. *There Is Confusion.* New York, 1924. $2,500.

FAUST, Frederick. See Brand, Max; Evans, Evan; Frederick, John.

FAUST, Frederick. *Dionysus in Hades.* Oxford, 1931. Boards. (The real Max Brand.) One of 500 copies. $250.

FAUST, Frederick. *One of Cleopatra's Nights.* Berkeley, 1914. 15–page pamphlet. $750.

FAUX, William. *Memorable Days in America.* London, 1823. $600.

FAVOURITE of Nature (The). London, 1821. (By Mary Ann Kelty.) 3 vols. Author's first book. $600.

FAWCETT, William. *Rules and Regulations for the Sword Exercise of the Cavalry.* London, 1796. 29 plates. $750.

FAY, Bernard. *Notes on the American Press at the End of the Eighteenth Century.* New York, 1927. One of 325 copies. In slipcase. $250.

FAY, Theodore S(edgwick). *Hoboken: A Romance of New York.* New York, 1843. In original wraps. $1,250.

FEARING, Kenneth. *Angel Arms.* New York, 1929. Author's first book. $250.

FEARING, Kenneth. *The Big Clock.* New York (1946). $200.

FEARING, Kenneth. *Dead Reckoning.* New York (1938). $200.

FEARN, John Russell. See Statton, Vargo.

FEAST of the Poets (The). London, 1814. By the Editor of the Examiner. (By Leigh Hunt.) $1,250.

FEATHERSTONHAUGH, George W. *A Canoe Voyage Up the Minnay Sotor.* London 1847. 2 vols. 2 folding maps. 2 plates. $1,000.

FEDERALIST: A Collection of Essays . . . (The). See Hamilton, Jay . . .

FEIBLEMAN, James K. *Death of the God in Mexico.* New York (1931). Author's first book. $250.

FEIKEMA, Feike. *The Golden Bowl.* St. Paul, 1944. (By Frederick Manfred, his first book.) $100.

FEIST, Raymond. *Magician.* Garden City, 1982. $400.

FELDENKRAIS, M. *Judo.* London, 1944. $125.

FELDENKRAIS, M. *Practical Unarmed Combat.* London, 1942. $150.

FELLOWS-JOHNSTON, Annie. *The Little Colonel.* Boston, 1896. $150.

FENOLLOSA, Ernest F. *Certain Noble Plays of Japan.* Churchtown, Dundrum, Ireland: Cuala Press, 1916. From manuscripts of Fenollosa, chosen and finished by Ezra Pound. Introduction by W. B. Yeats. Boards, linen spine. One of 350 copies. $600.

FENOLLOSA, Ernest F. *The Chinese Written Character as a Medium for Poetry.* London (1936). Foreword by Ezra Pound. Black cloth, parchment spine. $400. New York (1936). Green boards. $300.

FENOLLOSA, Ernest Francisco. *East and West.* New York, 1893. Author's first book. $500.

FENTON, James. *Our Western Furniture.* Oxford (1968). Author's first book. One of 12 signed copies. $1,250. Wraps. One of 200 copies. $500.

FERBER, Edna. *Dawn O'Hara: The Girl Who Laughed.* New York (1911). Colored frontispiece. Author's first book. $300.

FERBER, Edna. *A Peculiar Treasure.* New York, 1939. One of 351 signed copies. In slipcase. $400.

FERBER, Edna. *Show Boat.* Garden City, 1926. Green boards, white vellum spine. One of 201 signed copies. In slipcase. $1,250. One of 1,000 copies for presentation (not numbered or signed). $350. Trade edition. "First Edition" not stated. $250.

FERGUSON, Charles D. *The Experiences of a Forty-Niner During Thirty-Four Years' Residence in California and Australia.* Cleveland, 1888. $300.

FERGUSON, Helen. *A Charmed Circle.* London (1929). (By Helen Woods, who also used the name Anna Kavan.) Author's first book. $450.

FERGUSON, John. *Bibliotheca Chemica; A Bibliography of Books on Alchemy, Chemistry and Pharmaceutics.* London (1954). 2 vols. (Reprint of Glasgow 1906 edition.) Adds a new introduction. $400.

FERGUSSON, Harvey. *Blood of the Conquerors.* New York, 1921. $250.

FERGUSSON, Harvey. *Wolf Song.* New York, 1927. $200. One of 100 signed copies. $450.

FERLINGHETTI, Lawrence. *Pictures of the Gone World.* San Francisco (1955). Author's first book and first City Lights book. Stiff black printed wraps, (priced at $.65) with wraparound label. One of 500 copies. $450. Boards. One of 25 signed copies. $1,500.

FERLINGHETTI, Lawrence. *The Secret Meaning of Things.* (New York, 1968.) One of 150 signed copies. In slipcase. $200. Trade edition. $75.

FERMOR, Patrick Leigh. *The Traveller's Tree.* London, 1950. Author's first book. $250.

FERRIAR, John. *The Bibliomania, An Epistle, To Richard Heber, Esq . . .* London, 1809. $600.

FERRIER, Davis. *The Functions of the Brain.* London, 1876. $2,500. New York, 1876. $1,750.

FERRIER, J. P. *History of the Afghans.* London, 1858. 2 maps (1 folding). Publisher's list dated January 1858. $1,000.

FERRIER, Susan Edmonstone. See *Destiny, or, The Chiefs Daughter; Marriage.*

FERRINI, Vincent. *No Smoke.* Portland, Me., 1941. Author's first book. $100.

FERRIS, Benjamin G. *Utah and the Mormons, The History, Government . . .* New York, 1854. $300.

FEUCHTWANGER, Dr. Lewis. *A Popular Treatise on Gems.* New York, 1859. With frontispiece and 17 plates. $850.

FEUCHTWANGER, Dr. Lewis. *A Treatise on Gems.* New York, 1838. First issue with author's name misspelled on verso of title page (two r's). In original cloth. $1,250.

FICKE, Arthur Davison. See Morgan, Emanuel, and Knish, Anne.

FICKE, Arthur Davison. *From the Isles.* (Surrey) 1907. Wraps. $300.

FICKE, Arthur Davison (and Thomas Newell Metcalf). *Their Book.* (Chicago, 1901.) Author's first book. One of 50 copies. $1,000.

FIELD, Eugene. *A Little Book of Western Verse.* Chicago, 1889. Blue-gray boards and cloth. One of 250 large-paper copies. $250. New York, 1890. Cloth. Trade edition. $75.

FIELD, Eugene. *The Love Affairs of a Bibliomaniac.* New York, 1896. Half vellum. One of 150 copies on Holland paper. $200. Frontispiece. Blue cloth. First issue, with 8 titles listed. $100.

FIELD, Eugene. *Love-Songs of Childhood.* New York, 1894. One of 106 on Van Gelder paper. $250. One of 15 copies on Japan vellum. $600. Trade edition. Blue cloth. $50.

FIELD, Eugene. *Poems of Childhood.* New York, 1904. Frontispiece and 8 color plates by Maxfield Parrish. $300.

FIELD, Eugene. *Tribune Primer.* (Denver, 1881.) Gray-blue wraps. Author's first book. $5,000. Brooklyn, 1882. $400.

FIELD, Joseph E. *Three Years in Texas.* Greenfield, Mass., 1836. $16,000 at auction in 1999.

FIELD, Peter. *Dry Gulch Adams.* New York, 1934. (By Laura and Thayer Hobson.) $450.

FIELD, Peter. *Outlaws Three.* New York, 1934. (By Laura and Thayer Hobson, their first book.) $500.

FIELD, Rachel. *Hitty: Her First Hundred Years.* New York, 1929. Illustrated by Dorothy P. Lathrop. Decorated cloth, paper label. $250.

FIELD, Rachel. *Rise Up, Jennie Smith.* New York (1918). Author's first book. Wraps. $350.

FIELD, Robert. *The Art of Walt Disney.* New York, 1942. $850.

FIELD, Stephen J. *Personal Reminiscences of Early Days in California.* (San Francisco, 1880.) $750. Second edition (Washington, 1893). Half morocco. $450.

FIELD, Thomas W. *An Essay Towards an Indian Bibliography Being a Catalogue of Books Relating to the History . . .* New York, 1873. $600. Columbus, 1951. $150.

FIELDING, Henry. See *History of the Adventures of Joseph Andrews . . . , The.*

FIELDING, Henry. *Amelia.* London, 1752. 4 vols. (There are two identical printings—December 1751 and January 1752.) $2,000.

FIELDING, Henry. *A Clear State of the Case of Elizabeth Canning.* London, 1753. $1,500.

FIELDING, Henry. *The History of Tom Jones . . .* London, 1749. 6 vols. First edition has errata leaf in vol. I and final blank in vol. III, and some leaves are cancels. $7,500. The second edition does not have errata leaf, which is replaced by page xliii. The list of contents are all in vol. I. $3,500.

FIELDING, Henry. *The Journal of a Voyage to Lisbon.* London, 1755. First published edition ending on page 245 (was actually printed second). $1,250. Second published edition (first printed) ending on page 228 (actually 276, as pages 241–76 are misnumbered 193–228). $2,750.

444444

FIELDING, Sarah. See *The Adventures of David Simple*.

FIELDING, T. H. *A Picturesque Description of the River Wye*. London, 1822. 28 colored plates. $10,000. London, 1841. 12 colored plates. In original cloth. $3,000.

FIELDING, T. H., and WALTON, J. *A Picturesque Tour of the English Lakes*. London, 1821. Color title vignette and 48 colored aquatint plates. $4,500. One of 100 copies. Large-paper issue. $5,500.

FIELDS, W. C. *Fields for President*. New York, 1940. Author's first book. $750.

FIFTY Years' Recollections of an Old Bookseller. London, 1837. (Bookseller William West.) Second edition with 11 full-page plates. $350.

FIGUEROA, José. *The Manifesto*. San Francisco, 1855. (Translated from the original as published in Monterey in 1835.) Original sheep. $2,500.

FILISOLA, Gen. Vicente. *Evacuation of Texas*. Columbia, Tex., 1837. (Sometimes called "the first real book published in Texas.") 68 pages, half leather. First edition in English. $5,000, possibly more.

FILLEY, William. *Life and Adventures of William Filley*. Chicago, 1867. 7 plates and half-page cut, 96 pages, wraps. Printed by Fergus. $2,500. Second edition, same place and date; 112 pages, wraps. Printed by Filley & Ballard. $1,000.

FINCHAM, Henry W. *Artists and Engravers of British and American Bookplates* . . . London, 1897. One of 15 copies in wraps. With extra suite of plates. $600. One of 50 copies in half vellum. $400. One of 1,050 copies. $250. New York, 1897. One of 40 copies signed by E. P. Bartlett. $200.

FINDLEY, Timothy. *The Last of the Crazy People*. Toronto, 1967. Author's first book. $300. London (1967). $150. New York (1967). $75.

FINLAY, Ian H. *The Sea-Bed* . . . Edinburgh (1958). Author's first book. Wraps. In dustwrapper. $600.

FINLEY, Ernest L. (editor). *History of Sonoma County*. (California.) Santa Rosa, 1937. Morocco. $200.

FINLEY, James B. *History of the Wyandott Mission at Upper Sandusky, Ohio*. Cincinnati, 1840. $500.

FINLEY, Martha. See Farquharson, Martha.

FINNEY, Charles G. *The Circus of Doctor Lao*. New York, 1935. Author's first book. Illustrated. $500. Limited Editions Club, Lunenberg, 1982. In slipcase. $250. Newark, Vt.: Janus Press, 1984. One of 150 copies. $2,500.

FINNEY, Jack. *The Body Snatchers*. New York (1955). Wraps $75. London, 1955. $500.

FINNEY, Jack. *5 Against the House*. Garden City, 1954. (By Walter Braden Finney.) $500. London, 1954. $500.

FINNEY, Jack. *Time and Again*. New York (1970). (By Walter Braden Finney.) $600.

FINNY, Sterling. *Less Than Nothing* . . . (New York, 1927). (By E. B. White, his first book.) Issued without dustwrapper. $2,000.

FIRBANK, Ronald. *The Flower Beneath the Foot.* London, 1923. $500. New York, 1924. $400.

FIRBANK, Arthur Ronald. *Odette D'Antrevernes.* London, 1905. Author's first book. Pink or blue-gray wraps. $750. Also, large-paper signed copies on vellum. $4,000.

FIRBANK, Ronald. *Odette:A Fairy Tale for Weary People.* London, 1916. Illustrated. Wraps. First separate edition. $350.

FIRBANK, Ronald. *Prancing Nigger.* Introduction by Carl Van Vechten. New York (1924). $400.

FIRBANK, Ronald. *The Princess Zoubaroff.* London, 1920. In dustwrapper. $500.

FIRBANK, Ronald. *Santal.* London, 1921. Wraps. $350.

FIRBANK, Ronald. *Sorrow in Sunlight.* London, 1925. First English edition (of *Prancing Nigger*). One of 1,000 copies. $250.

FIRBANK, Ronald. *A Study in Temperament.* London, 1905. Wraps. $500. Also, one of 10 signed copies on vellum. $2,500.

FIRE Over London . . . London, 1941. (By William Sansom.) Author's first book. Wraps. $125.

FIRST Lessons in Grammar . . . Boston, 1830. (By Elizabeth Peabody.) Author's first book. $300.

FIRST Settlers of New England (The), or, Conquest of the Pequods, Narragansets and Pokanokets. Boston (1829). By a Lady of Massachusetts. (Lydia Maria Child.) First issue, with undated integral title page. $450. Second issue with tipped-in dated title page. $350.

FISH, Daniel. *Lincoln Bibliography.* New York (1906). Red cloth. One of 75 signed copies. In slipcase. $450.

FISH, H. C. *The Voice of Our Brother's Blood: Its Source and Its Summons.* Newark, 1856. 16 pages, sewn. $250.

FISHER, Alfred Young. *The Ghost in the Underblows.* Los Angeles, 1940. 300 copies. $300.

FISHER, Bud (Harry C.). *The Mutt and Jeff Cartoons.* Boston, 1910. First Mutt and Jeff book. Oblong folio, pictorial boards and cloth. $150.

FISHER, Clay. *Yellow Hair.* Boston: Ballantine, 1953. $300.

FISHER, Joshua Brydges. *The Hermitage.* London, 1796. 2 vols. $2,500.

FISHER, M.F.K. See Berne, Victoria.

FISHER, M.F.K. *How to Cook a Wolf.* New York (1942). States "First Edition." In first-issue dustwrapper with author smoking. $450. Second issue, author is not smoking. $300.

FISHER, M.F.K. *Serve It Forth.* New York, 1937. Author's first book. $600.

FISHER, Richard S. *Indiana: In Relation to Its Geography, Statistics* . . . New York, 1852. Including Colton's large folding map in color. $1,500.

FISHER, Rudolph. *The Walls of Jerico.* New York, 1928. $2,500.

FISHER, Vardis. See *Idaho: A Guide in Word and Picture.*

FISHER, Vardis. *Children of God, an American Epic.* Caldwell, 1939. Leather. One of 100 signed copies. $350. New York, 1939. $125.

FISHER, Vardis. *City of Illusion.* New York (1941). $100. Caldwell, 1941. One of 1,000 copies. $100. Morocco. One of 100 signed copies. $250.

FISHER, Vardis. *Forgive Us Our Virtues.* Caldwell, 1938. One of 75 signed copies. In morocco. $350. Trade edition. $100.

FISHER, Vardis. *In Tragic Life.* Caldwell, 1932. $150. Leather. One of 25 signed copies. $450. Garden City, 1932. $100.

FISHER, Vardis. *No Villain Need Be.* Caldwell, 1936. $150. One of 75 signed copies. In full leather. $450. Garden City, 1936. $150.

FISHER, Vardis. *Sonnets to an Imaginary Madonna.* New York, 1927. Author's first book. $350.

FISHER, Vardis. *We Are Betrayed.* Caldwell (1935). First edition (so stated). $150. Morocco. One of 75 signed copies. $250. Garden City, 1935. $125.

FISKE, John. *Tobacco and Alcohol.* New York, 1869. Author's first book. $750.

FITCH, Clyde. *The Knighting of the Twins and Ten Other Tales.* Boston (1891). Author's first book. Decorated cloth. $125.

FITCH, Ensign Clarke. *Saved by the Enemy.* New York, 1898. (By Upton Sinclair, his first book.) $750.

FITE, Emerson D., and FREEMAN, Archibald (editors). *A Book of Old Maps Delineating American History.* Cambridge, Mass., 1926. 74 maps in facsimile, colored frontispiece. Folio, cloth. $400.

FITTON, Sarah Mary. *Conversations on Botany.* London, 1817. 20 color plates. Brown calf and marbled boards. $1,250. London, 1818. Second edition. $1,000. London, 1820. Third edition. $750.

FITTS, Dudley. *Two Poems.* No place (1932). Author's first book. Wraps. One of 100 signed copies. $125.

FITZGERALD, Edward. See Aeschylus. See also *Euphranor; Polonius; Rubaiyat of Omar Khayyam; Salaman and Absal.*

FITZGERALD, Edward. *Letters and Literary Remains of Edward FitzGerald.* London, 1889. 3 vols. Edited by William Aldis Wright. Frontispiece plates. $350. London, 1902–3. 7 vols. One of 775 copies. $350. One of 20 copies with extra plates. $1,500.

FITZGERALD, F. Scott. See *A Book of Princeton Verse II.* See also *Samples.*

FITZGERALD, F. Scott. *All the Sad Young Men*. New York, 1926. Dark-green cloth. Publisher's seal on copyright page (three printings). Earliest dustwrapper has woman's lips on front unbattered. They become progressively more battered in later printings, as does the type on page 38, lines 6–9 (left), page 248, lines 21–24 (right), and the page number 90. $6,000.

FITZGERALD, F. Scott. *The Beautiful and Damned*. New York, 1922. "Published March, 1922" on copyright page. Scribner seal not on copyright page. First printing of dustwrapper has book title on front in white outlined in black. $10,000. In second printing, dustwrapper with front title letters in black. $3,500. London (1922). Blue cloth. $3,500.

FITZGERALD, F. Scott. *The Crack-Up*. No place (1945.) Title page printed in red-brown and black. (Later printings have title page printed in black only and no colophon on page 348.) $250. No place or date. First English issue has paper label pasted on page 2. "This is a New Directions Book distributed through the British Empire . . ." $250.

FITZGERALD, F. Scott, and others. *The Evil Eye: A Musical Comedy in Two Acts*. (Cincinnati/New York/London on cover), 1915. $3,000.

FITZGERALD, F. Scott. *FIE! FIE! FI-FI!* (Cincinnati/New York/London on cover), 1914. $3,500.

FITZGERALD, F. Scott. *Flappers and Philosophers*. New York, 1920. "Published September, 1920" and publisher's seal on copyright page. In dustwrapper. $12,500. London (1922). $3,500.

FITZGERALD, F. Scott. *The Great Gatsby*. New York, 1925. First state includes the following differences: On page 60, line 16: "chatter" vs. "echolalia," page 119, line 22: "northern" vs. "southern"; page 205, lines 9–10: "sick in tired" vs. "sickantired"; page 211, lines 7–8 "Union Street Station" vs. "Union Station." Scribner seal on copyright page. First state of dustwrapper: On back blurb, line 14 has lowercase "j" in "jay Gatsby" which is hand-corrected in ink in most copies or overstamped with a capital "J." $75,000. Second state of dustwrapper has back blurb line 14 corrected to uppercase "J" in "Jay Gatsby." $35,000. Without dustwrapper. $3,000. London (1926). "Published 1926" on copyright page. $7,500. Limited Editions Club, New York (1980). 2,000 copies signed by Fred Meyer, the illustrator. In slipcase. $175.

FITZGERALD, F. Scott. *The Mystery of the Raymond Mortgage*. New York, 1960. 750 copies. Wraps. $400.

FITZGERALD, F. Scott. *Safety First*. Cincinnati/New York/London (1916). $2,500.

FITZGERALD, F. Scott. *Tales of the Jazz Age*. New York, 1922. "Published September, 1922" and Scribner seal on copyright page and "an" page 232, line 6 (first two printings, "and" in third printing). $10,000. London/Glasgow . . . (1923). $2,500.

FITZGERALD, F. Scott. *Taps at Reveille*. New York, 1935. Front dustwrapper flap unpriced or rubber-stamped on front flap of some copies in two sizes: ³⁄₁₆ inch and ⅛ inch high. First state with pages 349–52 not canceled and page 351, line 29–30, reading "Oh, catch it—oh, catch it . . ." $5,000. Second state: dustwrapper price printed; pages 349–52 canceled and page 351, line 29–30, reading "Oh, things like that happen . . ." $3,000.

FITZGERALD, F. Scott. *Tender Is the Night*. New York, 1934. Dustwrapper (front flap) has blurbs by Eliot, Mencken, and Rosenfeld. $10,000. London, 1934. $3,500. New York, 1951. First state has following errors: page xi, line 18 "xett"; page xiv, line 19 "tsandards"; page xviii, line 23 "b each"; page xviii, line 24: "accompanied." (A publisher errata sheet was enclosed in review copies.) $400. Errors in text corrected on 3 cancel leaves. $200. Limited Editions Club, New York, 1983. 2,000 copies signed by Fred Meyer, the illustrator. In slipcase. $200.

FITZGERALD, F. Scott. *This Side of Paradise.* New York, 1920. Author's first book (three previous music scores). "Published April, 1920" on copyright page. Dustwrapper price either "$1.75" or "$1.75 net," priority undetermined. $35,000. Without dustwrapper. $2,500. Third printing has signed "Author's Apology" tipped in. $4,500. London (1921). $3,500.

FITZGERALD, F. Scott. *The Vegetable.* New York, 1923. "Published April, 1923" on copyright page. $1,750.

FITZGERALD, Robert. *Poems.* New York, 1935. Author's first book. $125.

FITZGERALD, Zelda. *Save Me the Waltz.* New York, 1932. Author's first book. Green cloth. $2,500. London (1953). $350.

FITZSIMMONS, Robert. *Physical Culture and Self Defense.* Philadelphia, 1903. $300.

FIVE on Paper: A Collection of Five Essays on Papermaking . . . Bird & Bull Press, 1963. One of 169 copies. (The paper in this edition has some acidity problem.) $750.

FIVE Young American Poets. Norfolk, Conn.: New Directions, 1940. (By John Berryman, et al.) Considered Berryman's first book, as the five "books" were combined by the publisher. $400.

FLACCUS, Kimball. *In Praise of Mara.* Hanover, 1932. Author's first book. Wraps. One of 25 signed copies. (100 copies in total.) $250. 75 unsigned copies. $125.

FLADER, Louis (editor). *Achievement in Photo-Engraving and Letterpress Printing.* Chicago (1927). $400.

FLAGG, Fannie. *Fried Green Tomatoes at the Whistle Stop Cafe.* New York, 1987. $125.

FLANIGAN, J. H. *Mormonism Triumphant! Truth Vindicated, Lies Refuted, the Devil Mad, and Priestcraft in Danger!!! . . .* Liverpool, 1849. Printed self-wraps. $300.

FLANNER, Janet. *An American in Paris . . .* New York (1940). First edition not stated. $500.

FLANNER, Janet. *The Cubical City.* New York, 1926. Author's first book. $1,250.

FLAUBERT, Gustave. *Bouvard and Pecuchet.* London, 1896. First English translation. $300.

FLAUBERT, Gustave. *Salambo.* London: Vizetelly, 1886. First edition in English. $750. London: Golden Cockerel Press, 1931. One of 500 copies. $300.

FLAUBERT, Gustave. *A Sentimental Education.* London, 1898. 2 vols. First English edition. Illustrated. Blue cloth. $450.

FLECKER, James. *The Best Man . . .* Oxford, 1906. Author's first book. Wraps. $350.

FLECKER, James. *The Bridge of Fire: Poems.* London, 1907. Wraps. First issue, no quote from the *Sunday Times.* $150.

FLECKER, James. *God Save the King.* (London, 1915.) Wraps. One of 20 copies. $300.

FLEISCHER, Nat. *Jack Dempsey: The Idol of Fistiana.* New York, 1924. One of 250 copies signed by author and subject. $750.

FLEMING, Alexander. *Penicillin.* London, 1946. $250. Philadelphia, $200.

FLEMING, George. *Travels on Horseback in Mantchu Tartary.* London, 1863. Extending map. $1,250.

FLEMING, Ian. *Casino Royale.* London (1953). Author's first book. Bottom front flap of dust-wrapper blank except for price. $35,000 at auction in 2001. New York, 1954. $2,500.

FLEMING, Ian. *Diamonds Are Forever.* London (1956). $3,500. New York, 1956. $500.

FLEMING, Ian. *Dr. No.* London (1958). Front cover stamped with woman's figure or blank, no clear priority. $3,500. New York, 1958. Title in U.S. is *Doctor No.* $450.

FLEMING, Ian. *From Russia with Love.* London (1957). $2,500. New York, 1957. $400.

FLEMING, Ian. *Live and Let Die.* London (1954). $17,500. New York, 1955. $750. (Note: Second-printing dustwrapper adds two lines to front flap: "Jacket devised by the author . . .")

FLEMING, Ian. *Moonraker.* London (1955). $10,000 with unfaded spine. New York, 1955. $1,500.

FLEMING, Ian. *On Her Majesty's Secret Service.* London (1963). One of 220 signed copies. In plain acetate dustwrapper without slipcase. $8,500. Trade edition. $600. (New York, 1963.) $200.

FLEMING, Oliver. *Ambrotox and Limping Dick.* London, 1920. (By Philip and Ronald Mac-Donald.) Authors' first book. $1,000.

FLEMING, Sandford. *Memorial of the People of Red River to the British and Canadian Governments.* Quebec, 1863. 7 pages, printed front paper cover. $750.

FLEMING, Walter L. *Documentary History of Reconstruction.* Cleveland, 1906–7. 2 vols. 9 facsimiles. Half calf. $350.

FLETCHER, John Gould. *Fire and Wine.* London (May, 1913). Author's first or second book (there were 5 books published in 1913). $150.

FLETCHER, John Gould. *Japanese Prints.* Boston: Four Seas Press, 1918. $100. Full leather. One of 25 copies on vellum in full leather. With a signed manuscript poem by Fletcher. $750.

FLETCHER, William Younger. *English Bookbindings in the British Museum.* London, 1895. One of 500 copies. 63 plates. $600.

FLETCHER, William Younger. *English Book Collectors.* London, 1902. One of 50 copies bound in vellum. $450. Trade edition. $150.

FLETCHER, William Younger. *Foreign Bookbindings in the British Museum.* London, 1896. One of 500 copies. 63 plates. $500.

FLINDERS, Matthew. *A Voyage to Terra Australis* . . . London, 1814. 2 vols., plus atlas. $25,000.

FLINDERS, Matthew. *Narrative of His Voyage in the Schooner Francis.* Waltham Saint Lawrence: Golden Cockerel Press, 1946. Engravings by John Buckland Wright. One of 750 copies. $850. One of 100 copies. $1,250.

FLINT, Timothy. *A Condensed Geography and History of the Western States, or the Mississippi Valley.* Cincinnati, 1828. 2 vols. $1,000.

FLINT, Timothy. *Francis Berrian, or the Mexican Patriot.* Boston, 1926. 2 vols. $2,000.

FLINT, Timothy. *Indian Wars of the West.* Cincinnati, 1833. $750.

FLINT, Timothy. *Recollections of the Last Ten Years.* Boston, 1826. $500.

FLINT, Timothy. *A Sermon, Preached . . .* Newburyport, 1808. Author's first book. $400.

FLINT, W. Russell. *Breakfast in Périgord.* London, 1968. Illustrated. Half morocco. One of 525 signed copies. In slipcase. $450.

FLINT, W. Russell. *Drawings.* London, 1950. 134 plates. Half morocco. One of 125 signed copies by Flint, with an original drawing in folder at end. In slipcase. $1,750. One of 500 copies. $1,250. Trade in cloth. In dustwrapper. $500.

FLINT, W. Russell. *Shadows in Arcady.* London, 1965. With some text illustrations and calligraphic notes. Printed in 3 colors. One of 500 signed copies. Two-toned gilt cloth. In slipcase. $300.

FLOWER, Richard. *Letters from Illinois, 1820–1821.* London, 1822. 76 pages, original wraps. $2,500. Rebound. $1,750.

FOÀ, Edouard. *After Big Game in Central Africa.* London, 1899. $1,250.

FOLEY, Edwin. *The Book of Decorative Furniture.* London, 1910–11. 2 vols. 100 mounted color plates. $400.

FOOL'S Errand (A). By One of the Fools. New York, 1879. (By Albion W. Tourgee.) $125.

FOOTE, Henry Stuart. *Texas and the Texans.* Philadelphia, 1841. 2 vols. $1,500.

FOOTE, Shelby. *The Civil War.* New York (1958, 1963, 1974). 3 vols. $1,000.

FOOTE, Shelby. *The Merchant of Bristol.* (Greenville, 1947.) Author's first book. Wraps. One of 260 signed copies. $1,000.

FOOTE, Shelby. *Tournament.* New York, 1949. $400.

FORBES, Alexander. *California: A History.* London, 1839. Folding map and lithographed plates. $2,000. San Francisco, 1919. Map, 10 plates. One of 250 copies signed by the publisher. $450. San Francisco, 1937. John Henry Nash printing. Marbled boards. One of 650 copies. In dustwrapper. $450.

FORBES, Edwin. *Life Studies of the Great Army.* New York (1876). 40 plates. $1,750.

FORBES, Edwin. *Thirty Years After: An Artist's Story of the Great War.* New York (1890). 4 vols. 80 full-page plates, 20 portraits. Folio. $1,000. Another issue, 2 vols. $450.

FORBES, Sir James. *Oriental Memoirs.* London, 1813. 4 vols. Frontispiece and 93 plates (28 hand-colored). $5,500. Same sheets. Reissued in London (1839) with 27 additional plates. $6,500.

FORBES, James D. *Occasional Papers on the Theory of Glaciers* . . . Edinburgh, 1859. $1,000.

FORBES, James Grant. *Sketches, Historical and Topographical, of the Floridas.* New York, 1821. With the map. $1,500. Without map. $500.

FORBUSH, Edward Howe. *Birds of Massachusetts and Other New England States.* (Boston), 1925, 1927, 1929. 3 vols. Color illustrations by L. A. Fuertes. $500.

FORCHE, Carolyn. *Gathering the Tribes.* New Haven, 1976. Cloth. $350. Wraps. $75.

FORD, Charles Henri. *A B C's.* Prairie City, Ill. (1940). Cover by Joseph Cornell. $600.

FORD, Charles Henri. *The Garden of Disorder and Other Poems.* London (1938). Boards and cloth. One of 30 signed copies. (Issued without dustwrapper.) $500. One of 460 unsigned copies. $250. Also, Norfolk (1938). English edition in New Directions dustwrapper. $200.

FORD, Charles Henri. *A Pamphlet of Sonnets.* Majorca, 1936. Drawing by Pavel Tchelitchew. Printed wraps. One of 50 copies signed by Ford and Tchelitchew. $750. Unsigned. $250.

FORD, Charles Henri, and TYLER, Parker. *The Young and Evil.* Paris (1933). The first book for both authors. One of 50 copies. Wraps. $1,000. Regular edition. In dustwrapper. $500.

FORD, Ford Madox. See Conrad, Joseph, and Hueffer, Ford Madox; "Chaucer, Daniel." (Note: Ford changed his name from Hueffer to Ford in 1919.) See also *The Imagist Anthology.*

FORD, Ford Madox. *The Good Soldier.* London, 1915. $3,000. New York, 1915. $1,500. New York, 1927. One of 300 signed copies. In slipcase. $1,500.

FORD, Ford Madox. *The Great Trade Route.* New York, 1937. First issue, without illustrator's name on title page or dustwrapper. $250.

FORD, Ford Madox. *It Was the Nightingale.* New York, 1933. $200. London (1934). $250.

FORD, Ford Madox. *Joseph Conrad: A Personal Remembrance.* London, 1924. Frontispiece, 2 other plates. $300.

FORD, Ford Madox. *Last Post.* London (1928). $450.

FORD, Ford Madox. *Mister Bosphorus and the Muses.* London (1923). Illustrated by Paul Nash. Half cloth. One of 70 copies signed by the artist. In dustwrapper. $1,250. Trade edition in dustwrapper. $450.

FORD, Ford Madox. *New Poems.* New York, 1927. One of 325 signed copies. In glassine dustwrapper. $400.

FORD, Ford Madox. *No More Parades.* London (1925). $450.

FORD, Ford Madox. *The Queen Who Flew.* London, 1894. One of 25 copies in vellum. $3,000.

FORD, Ford Madox. *When the Wicked Man.* New York (1931). $400.

FORD, Ford Madox. *Women & Men.* Paris: Three Mountains Press, 1923. One of 300 copies. Wraps. $750.

FORD, Henry Chapman. *Etchings of the Franciscan Missions of California.* New York, 1883. 24 matted plates, unbound, 28 pages of text, stitched, in half-morocco portfolio. Imperial edition. One of 50 copies signed by the artist. $4,500.

FORD, Leslie. (Mrs. Zenith Jones Brown.) See Frome, David.

FORD, Leslie. *The Sound of Footsteps.* New York, 1931. (By Zenith Brown.) $500.

FORD, Paul Leicester. See Gaine, Hugh.

FORD, Paul Leicester. *Franklin Bibliography.* Brooklyn, 1889. Half leather. One of 500 copies. $400.

FORD, Paul Leicester. *The Great K & A Train Robbery.* New York, 1897. First state with "Train" missing from the title on title page. $200.

FORD, Paul Leicester (editor). *Webster Genealogy . . . By Noah Webster.* Brooklyn, 1876. Ford's first book, printed by him on his own press at age 11. 16 pages, oversize wraps. (250 copies.) $250.

FORD, Richard. *A Piece of My Heart.* New York, 1976. Author's first book. $500.

FORD, Richard. *The Ultimate Good Luck.* Boston, 1981. $400.

FORD, Thomas. *A History of Illinois . . .* Chicago, 1854. First issue, with "1814" (instead of "1818") in the extended title (VAB). $300.

FORD, Thomas. *Message of the Governor on the Disturbances in Hancock County.* Springfield, Ill., 1844. 21 pages, unbound. $2,500.

FORD, Webster. *Songs & Sonnets.* Chicago, 1910. (By Edgar Lee Masters.) $250.

FORDHAM, Mary Weston. *Magnolia Leaves.* Tuskegee (1897). Author's first book. Introduction by Booker T. Washington. $750.

FOREMAN, Grant. *Advancing the Frontier.* Norman, Okla., 1933. Maps. $150.

FOREMAN, Grant. *Indian Removal.* Norman, 1932. $150.

FOREMAN, Grant. *Pioneer Days in the Early Southwest.* Cleveland, 1926. Illustrated. $300.

FORESTER, C. S. *The African Queen.* London (1935). $3,500. Boston, 1935. Text differs. $2,500.

FORESTER, C. S. *Beat to Quarters.* Boston, 1937. $1,000. (First American edition of first Hornblower novel. Published in England as *The Happy Return.*)

FORESTER, C. S. *Brown on Resolution.* London (1929). $1,250.

FORESTER, C. S. *Flying Colours.* London (1938). $1,000. Boston, 1939. $750.

FORESTER, C. S. *Josephine, Napoleon's Empress.* London (1925). "Published 1925" on copyright page. $1,250. London (1925). Ads dated June 1928. $1,000. New York, 1925. $750.

FORESTER, C. S. *Love Lies Dreaming*. London (1927). $1,000. Indianapolis (1927). First issue has "C. E. Forester" vs. "C. S. Forester" on cover. $750.

FORESTER, C. S. *Marionettes at Home.* London (1936). Sienna cloth. $850. Orange cloth. "3/6 net" on spine of dustwrapper (later). $600.

FORESTER, C. S. *Napoleon and His Court.* London (1924). "Published 1924" on copyright page. First issue is in blue cloth. $1,750. New York, 1924. $1,250.

FORESTER, C. S. *The Paid Piper.* London (1924). Ads dated September 1923. $3,500. Ads dated May 1925. $3,000. Toronto (1924). $2,500.

FORESTER, C. S. *A Pawn Among Kings.* London (1924). Author's first book. $3,000. Toronto (1924). $2,000.

FORESTER, C. S. *Plain Murder.* London (1930). $2,500.

FORESTER, C. S. *The Shadow of the Hawk.* London (1928). $2,000.

FORESTER, C. S. *Single-Handed.* New York, 1929. First American edition of *Brown on Resolution.* $750.

FORESTER, Frank. See Herbert, Henry William.

FORESTER, Frank. *American Game in Its Seasons.* New York, 1853. (By Henry William Herbert.) Illustrated by the author. $300.

FORESTER, Frank. *The Complete Manual for Young Sportsmen.* New York, 1856. (By Henry William Herbert.) Illustrated by the author. $300.

FORESTER, Frank. *Field Sports in the United States, and the British Provinces of America.* London 1848. (By Henry William Herbert.) 2 vols. Green cloth. First issue, with "Provinces of America" on title page (changed later to "Provinces of North America") (VAB). $350. New York, 1849. 2 vols. Green cloth. First American edition, first issue, with "Rutted Grouse" frontispiece and "Burgess, Stringer" on spine (later Stringor). (Issued as *Frank Forester's Field Sports of the United States . . .*) $350.

FORESTER, Frank. *Frank Forester's Fish and Fishing of the United States and British Provinces of North America.* London, 1849. (By Henry William Herbert.) Illustrated by the author. Blue cloth. $250. New York, 1850. $250.

FORESTER, Frank. *Frank Forester's Fugitive Sporting Sketches.* Westfield, Wis., 1879. (By Henry William Herbert.) Edited by Will Wildwood (Fred E. Pond). Wraps. $350. Cloth. $250.

FORESTER, Frank. *Frank Forester's Horse and Horsemanship of the United States and British Provinces of North America.* New York, 1857. (By Henry William Herbert.) 2 vols. Plates, pedigree tables. Purple cloth. $600.

FORESTER, Frank. *Hints to Horse-Keepers.* New York, 1859. Frontispiece, 23 plates. (By Henry William Herbert.) $200.

FORESTER, Frank. *Trouting Along the Catasauqua.* New York: Derrydale Press, 1927. (By Henry William Herbert.) One of 423 copies. In dustwrapper. $600.

FORESTERS. An American Tale (The). (By Jeremy Belknap.) Boston, 1792. 3 variants, no priority. $1,000.

FORGET-Me-Not. *Megda.* Boston, 1891. (By Emma Dunham Kelly.) Author's first book. $1,500. Boston, 1892. $500. Boston (1892). $300.

FORNEY, Col. John W. *What I Saw in Texas.* (Cover title.) Philadelphia (1872). Map and plates. 92 pages, pictorial wraps. $500.

FORREST, Lieut. Col. Charles R. *A Picturesque Tour Along the Rivers Ganges and Jumna, in India.* London, 1824. With folding map, and 24 hand-colored plates. $7,500.

FORREST, Earle R. *Missions and Pueblos of the Old Southwest.* Cleveland, 1929. $250.

FORREST, John. *Explorations in Australia.* London, 1875. With 4 folding maps, and 8 portraits and plates. $1,500.

FORSTER, E. M. *Abinger Harvest.* London (1936). First issue, including "A Flood in the Office" (pages 278–81). $650. Second issue, without "A Flood in the Office," and with pages 277–82 canceled. $350.

FORSTER, E. M. *Alexandria: A History and a Guide.* Alexandria, Egypt, 1922. Folding map in pocket at rear. Boards. Issued without dustwrapper. $750. Alexandria, 1938. Second edition. Boards. One of 250 signed copies. Issued without dustwrapper. $1,000.

FORSTER, E. M. *Anonymity: An Enquiry.* London: Hogarth Press, 1925. Illustrated boards. $300.

FORSTER, E. M. *Desmond McCarthy.* No place: Millhouse Press, 1952. One of 72 copies. Gray wraps. $500.

FORSTER, E. M. *The Eternal Moment and Other Stories.* London, 1928. First binding in maroon cloth with gold stamping. In dustwrapper priced "5s." $650. Second binding, stamped in black. $450.

FORSTER, E. M. *The Government of Egypt.* London (1920). Wraps, paper label. (Official recommendations of a Labour committee, 1919.) $500.

FORSTER, E. M. *Howards End.* London, 1910. First issue with 4 pages of ads (integral). $2,000. Second issue with 8 pages of ads inserted. $1,500.

FORSTER, E. M. *The Longest Journey.* London, 1907. $750.

FORSTER, E. M. *A Passage to India.* London, 1924. Red cloth. In dustwrapper. $6,000. Without dustwrapper. $1,000. Boards and cloth. One of 200 signed copies, issued without dustwrapper. In slipcase. $5,000. New York (1924). $1,500.

FORSTER, E. M. *Pharos and Pharillon.* Richmond: Hogarth Press, 1923. Blue boards with cloth spine. Issued without dustwrapper. $600. New York, 1923. First American edition. Orange cloth. $350.

FORSTER, E. M. *A Room with a View.* London, 1908. $1,500. New York, 1911. $750.

FORSTER, E. M. *The Story of the Siren*. Richmond: Hogarth Press, 1920. Wraps. (500 copies printed.) First state with front label reading *"The Story/of the Siren."* (The other two states have title as single line or *"The Story of the/Siren."*) $1,000. Later states. $600.

FORSTER, E. M. *Where Angels Fear to Tread*. Edinburgh, 1905. Author's first book. First issue, with this title not mentioned in ads at back. $2,500. With title in ads. $1,500. New York, 1920. First American edition. Black or orange cloth. In dustwrapper. $750.

FORSTER, George. *A Voyage Round the World* . . . London, 1777. 2 vols. Folding map. $5,500.

FORSTER, Johann Reinhold. *History of the Voyages and Discoveries Made in the North*. London, 1786. 3 folding maps. $4,500.

FORSTER, Johann Reinhold. *Observations Made During a Voyage Round the World* . . . London, 1778. 2 folding tables. Folding map. $4,500.

FORSYTH, Frederick. *The Biafra Story*. (Middlesex, 1969.) Author's first book. Wraps. $200.

FORSYTH, Frederick. *The Day of the Jackal*. London (1971). $300. New York, 1971. $125.

FORSYTH, James W., and GRANT, F. D. *Report of an Expedition up the Yellowstone River, Made in 1875*. Washington, 1875. Folding map. 17 pages, wraps. $1,250.

FORSYTH, William. *A Treatise on the Culture and Management of Fruit-Trees*. London, 1802. $750. Philadelphia, 1802. $300.

FORT, Charles. *The Book of the Damned*. New York, 1919. In dustwrapper. $450. Without dustwrapper. $75.

FORT, Charles. *The Outcast Manufacturers*. New York, 1909. Author's first book. Blue ribbed cloth lettered in gold. $200. Blue mesh cloth lettered in red. $100.

FORTRESS of Sorrento (The). (By Mordecai M. Noah.) New York, 1808. Author's first book. Wraps. $1,000. Rebound. $350.

FORTUNES of Colonel Torlogh O'Brien (The). Dublin, 1847. (By Joseph Sheridan Le Fanu.) 10 monthly parts, wraps. $2,500. First book edition, illustrated. $1,500.

FORTUNES of Perkin Warbeck (The). London, 1830. (By Mary Wollstonecraft Shelley.) 3 vols. In original boards, cloth spine, printed labels. $4,500. Rebound. $1,750.

FOSTER, B. F. *Foster's System of Penmanship; or, The Art of Rapid Writing* . . . Boston, 1835. 15 plates. $300.

FOSTER, Charles. *The Gold Placers of California*. Akron, Ohio, 1849. Map. Printed wraps. $8,500.

FOSTER, George G. *New-York by Gas-Light*. New York, 1850. Wraps. $600.

FOSTER, George G. (editor). *The Gold Mines of California*. New York, 1848. Frontispiece map. Wraps. $5,000.

FOSTER, George G. (editor). *The Gold Regions of California*. New York, 1848. Frontispiece map. (Reprint of above.) Wraps. $3,000. London (1849). $1,500.

FOSTER, Isaac. *The Foster Family, California Pioneers.* (Santa Barbara, 1925.) $250.

FOSTER, James S. *Advantages of Dakota Territory.* Yankton, 1873. 51 pages, wraps. $2,000.

FOSTER, James S. *Outlines of History of the Territory of Dakota and Emigrant's Guide to the Free Lands of the Northwest.* Yankton, 1870. Folding map. 127 pages, wraps. $3,000.

FOSTER, Myles Birket. *A Day in a Child's Life.* (London, 1881.) Illustrated by Kate Greenaway. Glazed boards and cloth. $250.

FOUNTAIN, Albert J. *Bureau of Immigration of the Territory of New Mexico: Report of Dona Ana County.* Santa Fe, 1882. 34 pages, wraps. $1,000.

FOUQUE, F.H.K. de La Motte. *Undine.* London, 1909. Illustrated in color by Arthur Rackham. Vellum with ties. One of 1,000 copies signed by Rackham. $1,500. Trade. $500. Limited Editions Club, New York, 1930. In slipcase. $150.

FOUR Elegies . . . London, 1760. (By John Scott.) Author's first book. $300.

FOUR Gospels of the Lord Jesus Christ (The). Waltham Saint Lawrence: Golden Cockerel Press, 1931. Decorations by Eric Gill. Half pigskin. One of 488 copies. In slipcase. $7,500. One of 12 copies on vellum. $40,000.

FOURGEAUD, Victor H. *The First Californiac.* San Francisco: Allen Press, 1942. Illustrated. Blue boards and calf. One of 225 copies. $400.

FOURIER, Jean Baptiste Joseph. *The Analytical Theory of Heat.* Cambridge, 1878. $600.

FOWLER, Jacob. *The Journal of Jacob Fowler.* New York, 1898. One of 950 copies. $250.

FOWLER, Laurence Hall, and BAER, Elizabeth. *The Fowler Architectural Collection of the Johns Hopkins University.* Baltimore, 1961. One of 250 copies. First issue (10 or 12 copies) with "Lawrence" on title page. $1,000. Corrected. $500.

FOWLES, John. *The Aristos.* Boston (1964). $200. London, 1964. $600.

FOWLES, John. *The Collector.* London, 1963. Author's first book. In dustwrapper, without publisher's blurbs on front flap. Brown boards (black boards reportedly a trial binding and therefore rare). $1,000. With 4 blurbs. $450. Boston (1963). $200.

FOWLES, John. *The Ebony Tower.* Boston (1974). Signed tipped-in leaf. $300. Without leaf. $75. London (1974). $200.

FOWLES, John. *The French Lieutenant's Woman.* London (1969). $350. Boston (1969). $150.

FOWLES, John. *The Magus.* Boston, 1966. $250. London (1966). $450.

FOX, John. *The New and Complete Book of Martyrs.* New York, 1794. 2 vols. $2,000.

FOX, John, Jr. *A Cumberland Vendetta and Other Stories.* New York, 1896. Author's first book with final entry in contents as "Hell Fer Sartain." $200. With "On Hell-Fer-Sartain Creek." $125.

FOX, John, Jr. *The Little Shepherd of Kingdom Come.* New York, 1903. Illustrated by F. C. Yohn. Smooth red cloth, paper label. One of 100 copies. Signed by Fox and Yohn (VAB). $750. Trade edition. Red cloth with only Scribner device on copyright page and no ads for other Fox books on verso or half title. $300. New York, 1931. Illustrated by N. C. Wyeth. Half vellum. One of 512 copies signed by Wyeth. $2,000.

FOX, Lady Mary. *Account of an Expedition to the Interior of New Holland.* London, 1837. $450.

FRAENKEL, Michael. See *Anonymous* and *Werther's* . . .

FRAENKEL, Michael. *Bastard Death.* Paris (1936). One of 400 copies. Wraps. $200.

FRAME, Janet. *The Lagoon.* Christchurch (1951). Author's first book. $1,250.

FRAME, Janet. *Owls Do Cry.* New York, 1960. $100. London, 1961. $100.

FRANCHERE, Gabriel. *Narrative of a Voyage to the Northwest Coast of America . . .* New York, 1854. First edition in English. 3 plates. $750.

FRANCIS, Dick. *Dead Cert.* London, 1962. Author's first mystery. $7,500. New York, 1962. $2,500. New York (1989). One of 26 signed, lettered copies. Issued without dustwrapper. In slipcase. $350. One of 100 signed copies. Issued without dustwrapper. $150.

FRANCIS, Dick. *For Kicks.* London (1965). $1,250. New York (1965). $750.

FRANCIS, Dick. *Nerve.* London (1964). In dustwrapper with one paragraph (13 lines) on front flap. $1,500. New York (1964). $750.

FRANCIS, Dick. *Sport of Queens.* London, 1957. Author's first book. (Note: The second state dustwrapper has reviews of the book on the front flap.) $1,000. Second state. $500. New York, 1969. $250.

FRANCIS, Grant R. *Old English Drinking Glasses.* London, 1926. 72 plates. Buckram. $450.

FRANCIS, Robert. *Stand with Me Here.* New York, 1936. Author's first book. $175.

FRANK, Anne. *The Diary of a Young Girl.* London, 1952. $750. Garden City, 1952. First edition stated. $600.

FRANK, Robert. *The Americans.* Paris (1958). $3,000. New York (1959). Introduction by Jack Kerouac. 83 plates. Oblong. $2,500. New York, 1968. Wraps. Revised and enlarged. $300. New York, 1969. Cloth. $350. (Note: Preceded in 1958 by the French edition, which brought $3,000 at auction in 1998.)

FRANK, Robert. *The Lines of My Hand.* (New York), 1972. 100 unnumbered pages of black-and-white photos and texts by the photographer. In stiff wraps. $600. (Tokyo, 1972). Japanese translation laid in. Folio, black cloth. In black slipcase. $4,000.

FRANK, Waldo. *The Dark Mother.* New York (1920). In dustwrapper. $350.

FRANK, Waldo. *The Unwelcome Man.* Boston, 1917. Author's first book. $150.

FRANK Fairleigh; or Scenes from the Life of a Private Pupil. London, 1850. (By Frank E. Smedley.) Illustrated by George Cruikshank. 15 parts, blue-green wraps. First issue, with dated title page (VAB). $1,500. Second issue in cloth. $750.

FRANKENSTEIN; or The Modern Prometheus. London, 1818. (By Mary Wollstonecraft Shelley.) 3 vols. In original boards, paper labels. $125,000 or more. Rebound copies. $60,000. London, 1831. Third edition. With a new preface by the author. $7,500. Sheets also bound in 2 vols. With 2 other titles in the Bentley's *Standard Novels*, vols. IX and X. $4,500. Philadelphia, 1833. First American edition. 2 vols. In original boards. $35,000. Rebound. $10,000. New York, 1931. Grosset & Dunlap, photoplay edition. $2,000. Limited Editions Club, New York, 1934. In slipcase. $350. West Hatfield, 1983. One of 350 copies signed by Barry Moser with an extra suite of illustrations. One half leather with cloth boards. In slipcase. $2,000. One of 50 copies. $4,500.

FRANKLIN, Benjamin. *Autobiography.* Philadelphia and London, 1868. $350. One of 100 large-paper copies. $750. Boston, 1906. One of 1,000 copies. $300. Limited Editions Club, San Francisco, 1931. $300.

FRANKLIN, Benjamin. *Experiments and Observations on Electricity . . .* London, 1751–54. 3 parts in 1 vol. $60,000. London, 1769. First complete collected edition. 7 plates (2 folding). $10,000.

FRANKLIN, Benjamin. *Philosophical and Miscellaneous Papers.* London, 1787. 3 folding plates and one folding map. $3,500.

FRANKLIN, Benjamin. *The Private Life of the Late Benjamin Franklin . . . Originally Written by Himself . . .* London, 1793. First edition in English. $2,500.

FRANKLIN, Benjamin. *The Report of Dr. Benjamin Franklin, and Other Commissioners . . .* London, 1785. $1,500.

FRANKLIN, Benjamin. *The Works of the Late Benjamin Franklin.* London, 1793. 2 vols. $2,000. New York (1794). First issue with binder's instructions above the middle of the final page. $1,500. Second issue has binder's instructions moved up to make room for an advertisement. $1,000. Also noted without binding instructions and ads.

FRANKLIN, Colin. *Emery Walker, Some Light on His Theories of Printing . . .* Cambridge, 1973. One of 500 copies. $350.

FRANKLIN, Colin. *Themes in Aquatint.* San Francisco, 1978. One of 500 copies. 16 full-color plates. $300.

FRANKLIN, Miles. *Some Everyday Folk and Dawn.* London, 1909. $1,250.

FRANKS, David. *The New-York Directory . . .* New York, 1786. 82 pages. $6,000. New York, 1909. Folding map. Printed wraps. $250.

FRASCONI, Antonio. *Woodcuts by Antonio Frasconi.* New York, 1957. One of 500 signed copies. In slipcase. $300.

FRASER, George MacDonald. *Flashman.* London (1969). Author's first book. $300. New York, 1969. $150.

FRASER, Louis. *Zoologia Typica, or Figures of New and Rare Mammals and Birds.* London, 1849. Folio. One of 250 copies. Hand-colored title and 70 plates. $17,600 at auction in 1999.

FRAZER, Sir James George. *The Golden Bough: A Study in Comparative Literature.* London, 1890. 2 vols. $1,250. Limited Editions Club, New York, 1970. 2 vols. $200.

FRAZER, Sir James George. *Totemism.* Edinburgh, 1887. Author's first book. $400.

FRAZIER, Charles. *Cold Mountain.* New York (1997). First state: "looking like a man-woman" on page 25, line 16. $250. New York, 1997. 500 signed and numbered. Not issued for sale. Issued in slipcase. $750.

FREDERIC, Harold. *The Damnation of Theron Ware.* Chicago, 1896. Wraps. $1,000. Cloth. $300.

FREDERIC, Harold. *Illumination.* London, 1896. First English edition of *The Damnation of Theron Ware* with some textual differences. $350.

FREDERIC, Harold. *In the Valley.* New York, 1890. 16 plates by Howard Pyle. Cloth. $350.

FREDERIC, Harold. *Seth's Brother's Wife.* New York, 1887. First issue, with 1886 copyright and no ads. Author's first book. $400.

FREDERICK, J. V. *Ben Holladay, the Stagecoach King.* Glendale, Calif., 1940. Folding map. Issued without dustwrapper. $275.

FREDERICK, John. *Riders of the Silences.* New York, 1920. (By Frederick Faust.) In dustwrapper. $750.

FREE-and-Easy Songbook (The). Philadelphia, 1834. Plates. Davy Crockett portrait on title page. $600.

FREEDLEY, Edwin T. (editor). *Leading Pursuits and Leading Men.* Philadelphia (1854). $200.

FREELING, Nicolas. *Love in Amsterdam.* London, 1962. $250.

FREEMAN, Douglas Southall. *Lee's Lieutenants . . .* New York, 1942–44. 3 vols. $350.

FREEMAN, Douglas Southall. *R. E. Lee: A Biography.* New York, 1934–35. 4 vols. $400.

FREEMAN, James W. See *Prose and Poetry of the Live Stock Industry.*

FREEMAN, Mary E. Wilkins. See Wilkins, Mary E.

FREEMAN, R. Austin. See Ashdown, Clifford.

FREEMAN, R. Austin. *As a Thief in the Night.* New York, 1928. $1,250.

FREEMAN, R. Austin. *The Cat's Eye.* London (1923). $2,500. New York, 1927. $1,500.

FREEMAN, R. Austin. *Dr. Thorndyke Intervenes.* London (1927). $1,250. New York, 1933. $750.

FREEMAN, R. Austin. *Felo de Se?* London (1937). $750.

FREEMAN, R. Austin. *John Thorndyke's Cases.* London, 1909. $1,000.

FREEMAN, R. Austin. *A Journey to Bontuku.* (London, 1893.) Author's first book. Wraps. (Offprint.) $1,500.

FREEMAN, R. Austin. *Mr. Polton Explains.* London, 1940. $750. New York, 1940. Red cloth. First American edition. $450.

FREEMAN, R. Austin. *The Red Thumb Mark.* (London, 1907.) Cloth. $1,250. Wraps. $1,000.

FREEMAN, R. Austin. *Travels and Life in Ashanti and Japan.* London, 1898. $1,250.

FREMAUX, Leon J. *New Orleans Characters.* (New Orleans), 1876. Litho title with border, hand-colored oval portrait, and 16 color plates. Folio, cloth, and morocco. $10,000.

FREMONT, Jessie Benton. *A Year of American Travel.* New York, 1878. Buff wraps printed in red and black. $3,500. San Francisco, 1960. One of 450 copies. $200.

FRÉMONT, John Charles. *Geographical Memoir Upon Upper California.* Senate Misc. Doc. No. 148. Washington, 1848. 67 pages, original wraps. With folding map. $1,250. Without map. $400.

FRÉMONT, John Charles. *Narrative of the Exploring Expedition to the Rocky Mountains, in the Year 1842, etc.* London, 1846. $1,250. New York, 1846. Wraps. $1,000.

FRÉMONT, John Charles. *Oregon and California: The Exploring Expedition to the Rocky Mountains, Oregon and California.* Buffalo, 1849. 2 portraits; 2 plates. Cloth. $400. (One of several reprints of *Report of the Exploring Expedition.*)

FRÉMONT, John Charles. *Report of the Exploring Expedition to the Rocky Mountains in the Year 1842.* Washington, 1845. 22 plates, 5 maps (including 1 folding in rear pocket). House or Senate editions. $1,750.

FRÉMONT, John Charles. *Report on an Exploration of the Country Lying Between the Missouri River and the Rocky Mountains . . .* Senate Doc. 243. Washington, 1843. 6 plates, folding map. Wraps. $1,250.

FRENCH, James Weir. *Machine Tools.* London, 1911. 2 vols. 10 multilayered (between 10 and 20 overlays each), die-cut plates. $750.

FRENCH, Capt. W. J. *Wild Jim, the Texas Cowboy and Saddle King.* Antioch, Ill., 1890. Portrait. 76 pages, wraps. $1,250.

FRENCH, William. *Some Recollections of a Western Ranchman.* London (1927). Gray cloth. $600. New York (1928). $500.

FRENEAU, Philip. See *Poem, On the Rising Glory . . .*

FRENEAU, Philip. *The American Village.* New York, 1772. $2,500.

FRENEAU, Philip. *Letters on Various Interesting and Important Subjects . . .* Philadelphia, 1799. With page 74 misnumbered 47. $1,000.

FRESHFIELD, Douglas W. *The Exploration of the Caucasus.* London, 1896. 2 vols. $2,250. One of 100 copies. $3,500.

FRESHFIELD, Douglas W. *Travels in the Central Caucasus and Bashan.* London, 1869. 3 extending maps and 5 plates, including 2 panoramas on one plate. $1,000.

FREUD, Sigmund. *A General Introduction to Psychoanalysis.* New York (1920). First American edition. Blue cloth. In dustwrapper. $1,500.

FREUD, Sigmund. *The Interpretation of Dreams.* New York, 1913. Author's first book. First issue with integral title page. $1,500. London, 1913. $1,250.

FREUD, Sigmund. *The Problem of Lay-Analyses.* New York, 1927. $200.

FREUD, Sigmund. *Psychopathology of Everyday Life.* London, 1914. $350. New York, 1914. $300.

FREUD, Sigmund. *Totem and Taboo.* New York, 1918. Authorized English translation. $400. London, 1919. $300.

FREZIER, Amedée François. *A Voyage to the South Sea . . .* London, 1717. With engraved map frontispiece, 14 copper plates, and 22 maps and plans. $2,500.

FRIDGE, Ike. *History of the Chisum War . . . Cowboy Life on the Frontier.* Electra, Tex. (1927). Stiff wraps. $1,500.

FRIEDLANDER, Lee. *Self Portrait.* New City (1970). With original silver print photograph bound in, signed and numbered by Friedlander, in pencil on mount recto. One of 100 copies (and 20 artist's proofs). $4,500.

FRIEDMAN, Bruce Jay. *Far from the City of Class.* New York, 1963. $125.

FRIEDMAN, Bruce Jay. *Stern.* New York, 1962. Author's first book. $125.

FRIEDMAN, I. K. *The Lucky Number.* Chicago, 1896. Author's first book. $200.

FRIES, Waldemar H. *The Double Elephant Folio: The Story of Audubon's Birds of America.* Chicago, 1973. $300.

FRINK, F. W. *A Record of Rice County, Minnesota, in 1868.* Faribault, Minn., 1868. 24 pages, wraps. $300. Faribault, 1871. Second edition. $150.

FRINK, Margaret A. *Journal of the Adventures of a Party of California Gold-Seekers.* (Oakland, 1897.) 2 frontispieces. $3,000.

FROME, David. *The Murder of an Old Man.* London, 1929. (By Zenith Jones Brown.) Author's first book. $450.

FROST, A(rthur) B(urdette). See Adeler, Max.

FROST, A. B. *A Book of Drawings.* New York, 1904. Illustrated. Folio, boards. $300.

FROST, A. B. *The Golfer's Alphabet.* New York and London, 1898. 28 full-page cartoons. Pictorial boards. $350.

FROST, A. B. *Shooting Pictures.* New York, 1895. 6 parts. Oblong folio, loose in wraps in half-leather portfolio. With 12 mounted chromolithograph plates. $11,000 at auction in 1993.

FROST, A. B. *Sports and Games in the Open.* New York, 1899. 53 color plates. Folio, pictorial cloth porfolio. $1,500.

FROST, John. *History of the State of California.* Auburn, Calif., 1850. 16 plates. $450.

FROST, John. *The Mexican War and Its Warriors.* New Haven, 1849. Colored frontispiece, other plates, map. $450.

FROST, Robert. *A Boy's Will.* London, 1913. Author's first regularly published book. Binding A: bronzed brown pebbled cloth, gilt-stamped. $10,000. Binding B: cream-colored vellum-paper boards stamped in red (including border rule). $3,500. Binding C: cream-colored linen-paper wraps, stamped in black without a border rule. 8–petaled flowers. $2,500. Binding D: cream-colored linen-paper wraps, stamped in black. 4–petaled flowers $1,750. One of 135 signed copies in wraps. $3,000. (Note: 1,000 copies in total for London bindings.) New York, 1915. "Aind" for "And" on last line of page 14. In dustwrapper. $2,500. Without dustwrapper. $600. With "and" on last line of page 14. $250.

FROST, Robert. *Collected Poems.* Random House. New York, 1930. One of 1,000 signed copies. Issued without dustwrapper. $750. New York (1930). States "First trade edition." $350. London, 1930. $300. New York, 1939. $300. London, 1939. $300.

FROST, Robert. *Complete Poems.* New York, 1949. One of 500 signed copies. Issued without dustwrapper. In slipcase. $1,000. Limited Editions Club, New York, 1950. One of 1,500 signed copies. 2 vols. In slipcase. $1,250. London (1951). $200.

FROST, Robert. *A Considerable Speck.* No place (1939). Fewer than 100 copies printed. Single sheet folded to 4 pages. $750.

FROST, Robert. *The Cow's in the Corn.* Gaylordsville, 1929. One of 91 signed copies. Issued with dustwrapper. $2,000.

FROST, Robert. *A Further Range.* New York (1936). One of 803 signed copies. Issued without dustwrapper. In slipcase. $500. Trade edition. $200. London (1937). $150.

FROST, Robert. *The Gold Hesperidee.* (Cortland, 1935.) 8 pages, tan wraps. Colophon page has "Cortland NY/A." Page 7, second line from bottom "Twas Sunday and Square Hale was dressed for meeting." Unnumbered on limitation page. Leaves measure 162 by 114 mm. $1,250. One of 200 copies. Colophon page has "Cortland NY/B." Yellow wraps. Line noted above has been reset so that "for meeting" is on separate line. Leaves measure 183 by 127 mm. $750. Reported 67 copies issued in pale-yellow wraps with the word "English" stamped under "copy number" on page 2. $750.

FROST, Robert. *Hard Not to Be King.* New York, 1951. One of 300 signed copies. $1,000.

FROST, Robert. *In the Clearing.* New York (1962). One of 1,500 signed copies. In slipcase. $400. Trade. $100. London (1962). With introduction by Robert Graves not in U.S. edition. $125.

FROST, Robert. *The Lone Striker.* (New York, 1933.) Wraps. Issued in envelope. (Some used as a Christmas card by Frost.) $100.

FROST, Robert. *A Masque of Reason.* New York (1945). One of 800 signed copies. Issued without dustwrapper. In slipcase. $500. Trade. $125.

FROST, Robert. *Mountain Interval.* New York (1916). First state, page 88, lines 6 and 7 repeated lines; page 93, line 6 from bottom: "Come" for "Gone." In dustwrapper. $2,000. Without dustwrapper. $600. Second state; errors corrected. In dustwrapper. $1,250. Without dustwrapper. $200.

FROST, Robert. *New Hampshire.* New York, 1923. One of 350 signed copies. In white slipcase. $1,500. Trade. $750. London, 1924. $750. Hanover, 1955. One of 750 signed copies. In semitransparent rough white Japanese paper dustwrapper. $750.

FROST, Robert. *North of Boston.* London (1914). First issue, binding A: coarse green cloth. $4,000. New York, 1914. Binding B: drab gray-brown boards backed with brown cloth. U.K. sheets with Holt title page. $2,750. London (1914). First issue, binding C: fine green cloth. $2,500. Binding D: blue cloth. $1,750. Binding E: coarse green cloth, measuring 200 by 145 mm, all edges trimmed, rubber stamp on page iv. $1,250. Binding F: coarse green cloth, measuring 195 by 150 mm, top edge trimmed others rough cut, rubber stamp on page iv. $1,000. New York (1919). First illustrated in dustwrapper. $1,000. Without dustwrapper. $350.

FROST, Robert. *Selected Poems.* New York, 1923. "March, 1923" on copyright page. $1,250. London (1923). $750. New York (1928). $500.

FROST, Robert. *Steeple Bush.* New York, 1947. One of 751 signed copies. Issued without dustwrapper. In slipcase. $500. Trade. $150.

FROST, Robert. *Three Poems.* Hanover, N.H. (1935). Wraps. One of 125 copies. $1,000.

FROST, Robert. *To a Young Wretch.* (New York, 1937.) Wraps. (Christmas poem. Seven imprints with quantities varying from 25 to 275 copies.) $150 to $350.

FROST, Robert (Lee). *Twilight.* (Lawrence, Massachusetts, 1894). 2 known copies. $75,000. Charlottesville, 1966. Facsimile wraps. 20 copies on handmade paper. $500. 150 copies. $250.

FROST, Robert. *A Way Out.* New York: Harbor Press, 1929. One of 485 signed copies. Issued without dustwrapper. $450.

FROST, Robert. *West-Running Brook.* New York (1928). Lacks "First Edition" statement. $600. States "First Edition." $300. One of 1,000 copies signed by Frost and frontispiece and three plates pencil-signed by artist J. J. Lankes. In slipcase. $750.

FRUGAL *Housewife (The).* By the Author of *Hobomok.* Boston, 1829. (By Lydia Maria Child.) $450.

FRY, Christopher. *The Boy with a Cart.* London, 1939. Author's first book. Wraps. $250.

FRY, Edmund. *Pantographia; Containing Accurate Copies of All the Known Alphabets* . . . London, 1799. $1,000.

FRY, Frederick. *Fry's Traveler's Guide, and Descriptive Journal of the Great North Western Territories.* Cincinnati, 1865. $1,500.

FRY, James B. *Army Sacrifices of* . . . New York, 1879. $450.

FRY, Roger E. *Giovanni Bellini.* London, 1899. Author's first book. Illustrated. Boards and cloth. $150.

FRYER, John. *A New Account of East-India and Persia* . . . London, 1698. Portrait, 3 maps and 5 plates (3 double-page). $4,500.

FRYKE, Christopher, and SCHEWITZER, Christopher. *A Relation of Two Several Voyages Made into the East Indies.* London, 1700. $1,750.

FUCHS, Daniel. *Summer in Williamsburg.* New York (1934). Author's first book. $1,500. London (1935). $500.

FUENTES, Carlos. *Where the Air is Clear.* New York (1960). $200.

FUGARD, Athol. *The Blood Knot.* Johannesburg, 1963. Author's first book. Issued without dustwrapper. $300. New York, 1964. $125.

FUGITIVES: An Anthology of Verse. New York (1928). Decorated paper boards, cloth back. Issued in dustwrapper. $1,000. Without dustwrapper. $200.

FULKERSON, H. S. *Random Recollections of Early Days in Mississippi.* Vicksburg, 1885. Wraps. $1,000. Cloth. $750.

FULLER, C. L. *Pocket Map and Descriptive Outline History of the Black Hills of Dakota and Wyoming.* Rapid City, 1887. Folding map. 56 pages, stiff wraps. $1,500.

FULLER, Emeline. *Left by the Indians, or Rapine, Massacre and Cannibalism on the Overland Trail in 1860.* (Cover title.) (Mt. Vernon, Iowa, 1892.) Portrait. 41 pages, printed wraps. First edition. $1,000. New York, 1936. Facsimile reprint. One of 200 copies. $100.

FULLER, Henry Blake. See Page, Stanton.

FULLER, Henry Blake. *The Cliff-Dwellers.* New York, 1893. First issue, with author's name on front cover as "Henry Fuller." $200.

FULLER, R. Buckminster. *Nine Chains to the Moon.* Philadelphia (1938). Author's first book. $350.

FULLER, Roy. *Poems.* London (1940). Author's first book other than a privately printed book. $150.

FULLER, S(arah). M(argaret). *Conversations with Goethe.* Boston, 1839. Author's first book. (Translated by Fuller.) In original cloth. $1,500. Rebound. $500.

FULLER, Sarah Margaret. *Guenderode.* Boston, 1842. (Translated by Fuller.) $750.

FULLER, Sarah Margaret. *Summer on the Lakes . . .* Boston/New York, 1844. Cloth. $750. New York, 1845. Wraps. $750.

FULLER, [Sarah] Margaret. *Woman in the Nineteenth Century.* New York, 1845. Light bluegreen wraps printed in black. Blank on back cover. $3,000. Ad by Greely and McElrath on back cover. $2,500.

FULLMER, John S. *Assassination of Joseph and Hyrum Smith, the Prophet and the Patriarch of the Church of Jesus Christ of Latter-Day Saints.* Liverpool, 1855. 40 pages, half leather. $750.

FULL Vindication of the Measures of the Congress . . . , (A). New York, 1774. (By Alexander Hamilton.) Wraps. $10,000.

FULTON, A. R. *The Red Men of Iowa.* Des Moines, 1882. 26 plates. $400.

FULTON, Robert. *Torpedo War, and Submarine Explosions.* New York, 1810. 5 plates. $15,000 in original wraps at auction in 1991. Rebound. $7,500.

FURBER, George C. *The Twelve Months Volunteer.* Cincinnati, 1848. $450.

FURBER, Robert, and BRADLEY, Richard. *The Flower Garden* . . . London, 1732. Frontispiece, title page and 12 plates, all hand-colored. $6,000. London, 1734. $5,000.

FURLONG, Capt. Lawrence. *The American Coast Pilot.* Newburyport, 1796. Wraps. $9,000 at auction in original wraps in 1991. Later editions. $750 to $1,000.

FURST, Herbert (editor). *The Modern Woodcut.* London, 1924. $350. One of 75 copies with 3 original woodcuts. $650.

FURST, Herbert (editor). *The Woodcut: An Annual.* London, 1927–30. 4 vols. One of 750 copies except for vol. 4, which was one of 700 copies. Contains examples of woodcuts by leading wood engravers. $1,000.

G

GADDIS, William. *The Recognitions.* New York (1955). Author's first book. Cloth. $1,000. London (1962). $350.

GÁG, Wanda. *Millions of Cats.* New York, 1928. $1,000. Another issue. One of 250 signed copies with a signed engraving. $2,500.

GAGE, Thomas. *The English-American: His Travail by Sea and Land.* London, 1648. $3,000.

GAINE, Hugh. *The Journals of Hugh Gaine, Printer.* New York, 1902. Edited by Paul Leicester Ford. 2 vols. Plates. Boards. One of 350 copies. $300. Cloth. One of 30 copies printed on Japan paper. $750.

GAINES, Ernest J. *Catherine Carmier.* New York, 1964. Author's first book. $1,000. London, 1966. $250.

GAINES, Ernest J. *Of Love and Dust.* New York, 1967. $250. London, 1968. $100.

GALE, George. *Upper Mississippi* . . . Chicago, 1867. Frontispiece, maps, plates. $300.

GALL, James. *A Historical Sketch of the Origin and Progress of Literature for the Blind* . . . Edinburgh, 1834. $350.

GALLAGHER, Tess. *Stepping Outside.* Lisbon, Iowa (1974). Author's first book. Wraps. $600. Cloth. $1,000.

GALLAHER, James. *The Western Sketch-Book.* Boston, 1850. Plates. $300.

GALLATIN, A. E., and OLIVER, L. M. *A Bibliography of the Works of Max Beerbohm.* Cambridge, 1952. $150.

GALLATIN, Albert. *Considerations on the Currency and Banking System of the United States.* Philadelphia, 1831. $300.

GALLATIN, Albert. *Letters of Albert Gallatin on the Oregon Question.* Washington, 1846. Stitched pamphlet. $200.

GALLATIN, Albert Eugene. *Art and the Great War.* New York, 1919. Illustrated. Folio, full morocco. One of 100 signed copies. Boxed. $750. Trade edition. $200.

GALLICO, Paul. *Farewell to Sport.* New York, 1938. Author's first book. $300.

GALLICO, Paul. *The Snow Goose.* London, 1946. Illustrated by Peter Scott, including 4 color plates. Morocco. One of 750 signed copies. $400. Trade edition. $100.

GALSWORTHY, John. See Sinjohn, John.

GALSWORTHY, John. *The Forsyte Saga.* London, 1922. First issue, with genealogical table pulling out to the right. Green cloth. In dustwrapper. $500. Red leather in dustwrapper. $600. Green leather. One of 275 signed copies. $850.

GALSWORTHY, John. *The Island Pharisees.* London, 1904. First (unpublished) issue, with "Wold" for "Dolf" as author of *Uriah the Hittite* in list of novels. $1,000. First published edition. $150.

GALSWORTHY, John. *The Man of Property.* London, 1906. First issue, with broken bar of music on page 200. $400. Limited Editions Club. New York, 1964. Signed by Charles Mozley, illustrator. In slipcase. $225.

GALT, John. See Balwhidder, The Rev. Micah. See also *The Provost; Ringan Gilhaize; The Steam-Boat.*

GALT, John. *The Bachelor's Wife.* Edinburgh, 1824. $200.

GALT, John. *Lawrie Todd.* London, 1830. 3 vols. $450. New York, 1830. 2 vols. in 1. First American edition. $250.

GALT, John. *The Spaewife: A Tale of the Scottish Chronicles.* Edinburgh, 1823. 3 vols. $350.

GALTON, Francis. *Finger Prints.* London, 1892. 16 plates. $1,000.

GALTON, Francis. *Hereditary Genius.* London, 1869. Folding table. $750. New York, 1870. $400.

GAMEKEEPER at Home (The). London, 1878. (By Richard Jefferies.) $250.

GANCONAGH. *John Sherman and Dhoya.* London (1891). (By William Butler Yeats.) Buff cloth, lettered in blue. $2,500. Yellow wraps, lettered in black. $1,500. (Note: The cloth issue is scarcer than the one in wraps.)

GANN, Ernest. *Sky Roads.* New York, 1940. Author's first book. $750.

GANN, Ernest. *The High and the Mighty.* New York, 1953. $500.

GANNET(T), William, C. *The House Beautiful.* Rivert Forest, Ill.: (Auvergne Press), 1897. With designs by Frank Lloyd Wright. Folio, half leather. One of 90 copies signed by Wright and William Winslow, the publisher. $13,000 at auction in 1990. Park Forest (1963). Facsimile. $850.

GARCES, Francisco. *On the Trail of the Spanish Pioneer.* New York, 1900. 2 vols. Translated by Elliott Coues. Illustrated. One of 950 copies. $500.

GARCÍA LORCA, Federico. *Bitter Oleander.* London, 1935. Author's first English publication. $750.

GARCÍA MÁRQUEZ, Gabriel. *No One Writes to the Colonel and Other Stories.* New York (1968). Dustwrapper photo by "Jerry Bauer." $750. Photo by Rodrigo Moya. $450. London, 1971. $400.

GARCÍA MÁRQUEZ, Gabriel. *One Hundred Years of Solitude.* New York (1970). Without series of numbers on last leaf of book. (All printings have "First edition" on copyright page.) First issue dustwrapper has an exclamation mark at end of first paragraph on front flap. $4,500. Changed to a period. $1,000. (Although it appears that both dustwrappers were used for the first few printings, we have seen a proof of the dustwapper that had the exclamation mark.) Limited Editions Club. (New York, 1982). Leather spine. In slipcase. $400. London (1970). $600.

GARCÍA VILLA, José. *Footnote to Youth.* New York, 1933. Author's first book. $200.

GARD, Wayne. *Sam Bass.* Boston, 1936. Illustrated. $200.

GARDEN, Alexander. *Anecdotes of the Revolutionary War in America.* Charleston, 1822. First Series. $750. Charleston, 1828. Second Series. $600.

GARDINER, E. Norman. *Athletics of the Ancient World.* Oxford, 1930. $200.

GARDINER, John, and HEPBURN, David. *The American Gardener.* Washington, 1804. $3,000. Washington, 1818. New enlarged edition. $600.

GARDNER, Alexander. See *Photographic Sketch Book of the War.*

GARDNER, Erle Stanley. *The Case of the Lame Canary.* New York, 1937. $1,250.

GARDNER, Erle Stanley. *The Case of the Lucky Legs.* New York, 1934. $3,500.

GARDNER, Erle Stanley. *The Case of the Stuttering Bishop.* New York, 1936. $1,500.

GARDNER, Erle Stanley. *The Case of the Sulky Girl.* New York, 1933. $5,000.

GARDNER, Erle Stanley. *The Case of the Velvet Claws.* New York, 1932. Author's first book. $6,000.

GARDNER, John. *The Complete Works of the Gawain Poet.* Chicago (1965). Translated by Gardner. $300.

GARDNER, John. *The Forms of Fiction.* New York, 1962. (Author's first book [with Lennis Dunlap], preceded by Ph.D. dissertation.) No dustwrapper. $300.

GARDNER, John. *Grendel.* New York, 1971. Illustrated. $400. (London, 1972.) $200.

GARDNER, John. *The Resurrection.* (New York, 1966.) Author's first novel. $600.

GARDNER, John. *The Wreckage of Agathon.* New York (1970). $250.

GARFIELD, Brian. *Death Wish.* New York, 1972. $200. London, 1973. $100.

GARLAND, Hamlin. *The Book of the American Indian*. New York, 1923. First edition stated. Colored frontispiece and 34 plates by Frederic Remington. Folio, boards, and cloth. In dustwrapper. In slipcase. $600.

GARLAND, Hamlin. *Main-Travelled Roads*. Boston, 1891. Gray printed wraps. First issue with "First Thousand" at bottom of front cover. $500. Blue or gray cloth with sheets bulking ⁹⁄₁₆ inches versus ⅞ inch (later). $350. Chicago, 1893. 100 large-paper copies. $350.

GARLAND, Hamlin. *Under the Wheel: A Modern Play in Six Scenes*. Boston, 1890. Author's first book. Wraps. $600.

GARNEAU, Joseph, Jr. *Nebraska: Her Resources, Advantages and Development*. (Cover title.) Omaha, 1893. 24 pages, printed wraps. $125.

GARNER, Alan. *The Weirdstone of Brisingamen*. London, 1960. Author's first book. $500.

GARNER, James W. *Reconstruction in Mississippi*. New York, 1901. $200.

GARNETT, David. See Burke, Leda.

GARNETT, David. *The Grasshoppers Come*. London, 1931. Illustrated. Yellow buckram. One of 200 signed copies. $250. Trade edition. $75. New York, 1931. $100.

GARNETT, David. *The Kitchen Garden . . .* London (1909). (Translated and adapted by Garnett from French work of Prof. Gressent.) Wraps. $300.

GARNETT, Richard. See *Primula*.

GARNETT, Richard. *The Twilight of the Gods and Other Tales*. London, 1888. $300. New York (1924). T. E. Lawrence introduction. $350.

GARRARD, Lewis H. *Wah-To-Yah, and the Taos Trail*. Cincinnati, 1850. First issue, with page 269 misnumbered 26. $3,000. San Francisco: Grabhorn Press, 1936. Boards. One of 550 copies. $250.

GARRETT, Edmund H. (editor). *Victorian Songs*. Boston, 1895. Illustrated by Garrett. Vellum, gilt. One of 225 copies. $250.

GARRETT, George. *King of the Mountain*. New York (1957). Author's first book. $100.

GARRETT, Julia Kathryn. *Green Flag over Texas*. New York, 1939. Maps. $250.

GARRETT, Pat F. *The Authentic Life of Billy, The Kid*. Santa Fe, 1882. Frontispiece and 5 plates. 137 pages, pictorial blue wraps. First edition, with ad inside back wrapper, misnumbered pages at the back, and one errata slip. $13,000 at auction in 1996. New York, 1927. Revised. $250.

GARRUD, W. H. *The Complete Jujitsuan*. New York, 1914. $175.

GARTH, Will. *Dr. Cyclops*. New York, 1940. (House pseudonym attributed to Henry Kuttner.) $600.

GARTH, Will. *Lawless Guns*. New York, 1937. (House pseudonym attributed to Henry Kuttner.) Author's first book. $350.

GARTON, Ray. *Live Girls.* (London, 1987.) $250.

GARVIE, James. *Abraham Lincoln koni kin, qa Aesop tawoyake kin.* (Life of Abraham Lincoln and Aesop's Fables.) Santee [Indian] Agency, Neb., 1893. 17 pages, printed wraps. $450.

GASCOYNE, David. *Opening Day.* London (1932). First binding in buff cloth stamped in gilt. $1,250. Second binding in red cloth stamped in black. $750.

GASCOYNE, David. *Poems, 1937–1942.* (London, 1943.) Illustrations by Graham Sutherland. $350.

GASCOYNE, David. *Roman Balcony . . .* London, 1932. Author's first book. $1,500.

GASH, Jonathan. *Gold from Gemini.* London, 1978. $450.

GASH, Jonathan. *The Grail Tree.* London, 1978. $350.

GASH, Jonathan. *The Judas Pair.* London, 1977. Author's first mystery. $650. New York, 1977. $200.

GASH, Jonathan. *Pontiff.* (London, 1971.) $1,000.

GASKELL, Elizabeth C. See *Cranford; Mary Barton; North and South.*

GASKELL, Elizabeth C. *The Life of Charlotte Brontë.* London, 1857. 2 vols. $850. New York, 1857. 2 vols. With publisher's ads. $450.

GASKELL, Elizabeth C. *Sylvia's Lovers.* London, 1893. 3 vols. $1,000.

GASKELL, Philip. *John Baskerville: A Bibliography.* Cambridge, 1959. $200. Chicheley, 1973. 17 plates and a facsimile of a type specimen in a pocket at the back. Reprinted with additions. $150.

GASS, Patrick. *Gass's Journal of the Lewis and Clark Expedition.* Chicago, 1904. Edited by James K. Hosmer. Illustrated. $400. One of 75 copies on large paper. $600.

GASS, Patrick. *A Journal of the Voyages and Travels of a Corps of Discovery, Under the Command of Capt. Lewis and Capt. Clark . . .* Pittsburgh, 1807. $7,500. London, 1808. First English edition. $5,000. Philadelphia, 1810. Second edition (without plates). $2,500. Philadelphia, 1810. 6 plates added. $2,500.

GASS, William H. *The First Winter of My Married Life.* Northridge, 1979. One of 26 signed, lettered copies. $250. One of 275 signed copies. Issued without dustwrapper or slipcase. $150.

GASS, William H. *Omensetter's Luck.* (New York, 1966.) Author's first book. $300. London, 1967. $150.

GASS, William H. *Willie Masters' Lonesome Wife.* (Evanston, 1968.) One of 100 signed copies. Issued without dustwrapper. $300. One of 300 copies (not signed or numbered). Issued without dustwrapper. $125. Also in wraps. $50. New York, 1971. $125.

GASSET, José Ortega. See Ortega y Gasset, José.

GAUGUIN, Paul. *Intimate Journals.* New York, 1921. Translated by Van Wyck Brooks. 27 illustrations by Gauguin. First edition in English issued without dustwrapper. One of 990 copies. $250. London, 1923. One of 530 copies. $250.

GAUTIER, Théophile. *One of Cleopatra's Nights.* New York, 1882. Translated by Lafcadio Hearn. First issue with publisher's name in capital letters on spine. $750. Chicago, 1929. One of 150 copies. $450.

GAY, Frederick A. *For Gratuitous Distribution: Sketches of California.* (Cover title.) (New York, 1848.) 16 pages, printed wraps. $1,500.

GAY, John. *Trivia* . . . London (1716). One of 250 large-paper copies. $4,000.

GEE, Ernest R. *Early American Sporting Books, 1734 to 1846.* New York: Derrydale Press, 1928. One of 500 copies. $300.

GELLHORN, Martha. *What Mad Pursuit.* New York, 1934. Author's first book. $300.

GEM of the Rockies! (The): Manitou Springs. Manitou Springs, Colo. [about 1885]. Plates and tables, 23 pages, printed wraps. $250.

GENERAL and Statistical Description of Pierce County (Wisconsin). (Prescott, Wis., 1854.) 9 pages, sewn. $300.

GENERAL Instructions to Deputy Surveyors. Little Rock, 1837. Folding diagram. 25 pages, sewn. $500.

GENET, Edmond Charles. *Memorial on the Upward Forces of Fluids.* Albany, 1825. Folding table, 6 plates. $2,500.

GENET, Jean. *Our Lady of the Flowers.* Paris (1949). Author's first English publication. One of 475 copies. First binding in imitation red morocco, issued without dustwrapper. $300. Second binding in tan boards. $150. One of 25 copies. $750.

GENIUS of Oblivion (The), and Other Poems. Concord, N.H., 1823. By a Lady of New-Hampshire. (By Sarah Josepha Hale.) Author's first book. $400.

GENT, Thomas. *The Life of Mr. Thomas Gent, Printer, of York* . . . London, 1832. $400.

GENTHE, Arnold. *As I Remember.* New, York, 1936. 112 photographic illustrations. Half leather. One of 250 signed copies. $450. Trade edition. $200.

GENTHE, Arnold. *The Book of the Dance.* New York (1916). White paper boards. One of 100 signed copies. $1,250. Trade. $250.

GENTHE, Arnold. *Impressions of Old New Orleans: A Book of Pictures.* New York (1926). Foreword by Grace King with 101 plates. Green boards and cloth. $350. One of 200 copies. $750.

GENTHE, Arnold. *Pictures of Old Chinatown.* New York, 1908. Author's first book. Text by Will Irwin. $300. New York, 1913. $200.

GEORGE, Henry. *Our Land and Land Policy, National and State.* San Francisco, 1871. Author's first book. Folding map in black and red. 48 pages, printed wraps. $1,250.

GEORGE, Henry. *Progress and Poverty.* San Francisco, 1879. Green or blue cloth. "Author's Edition." First issue, with the slip asking that no reviews be printed. One of 200 copies. $1,500. Second issue, without the slip referring to reviews. $750.

GEORGE, Mason. *The Young Backwoodsman.* Boston, 1829. (By Timothy Flint.) $200.

GEORGE and Lurleen Wallace. (Centre, Alabama, 1967.) (By Asa Forest Carter.) Author's first book. $600.

GEORGIA Scenes, Characters, Incidents, etc., in the First Half Century of the Republic. Augusta, Ga., 1835. By a Native Georgian. (By Augustus Baldwin Longstreet.) Author's first book. In original brown boards with cloth back and paper labels. $4,000. New York, 1840. Illustrated. Second edition. $600.

GERARD, John. *The Herball or Generall Historie of Plantes.* London, 1597. $10,000 or more. London, 1633. Second and "best edition." $6,000. London, 1636. $3,500. London, 1927. One of 150 copies. $350.

GERHARD, Fred. *Illinois as It Is.* Chicago, 1857. Map. Frontispiece, 3 folding maps. $350.

GERHARDI, William. *Futility.* London (1922). Author's first book. $250. New York, 1923. Preface by Edith Wharton. $300.

GERNING, J. *A Picturesque Tour Along the Rhine . . .* London, 1820. With 24 hand-colored plates, folding map. $6,000.

GERNSBACK, Hugo. *Ralph 124C41: A Romance of the Year 2660.* Boston, 1925. Illustrated. Blue cloth. $2,000.

GERRING, Charles. *Notes on Printers and Booksellers with a Chapter on Chap Books.* London, 1900. $250.

GERSHWIN, George. *George Gershwin's Song-Book.* New York, 1932. Illustrated by Alajolov. Portrait, song reproductions. Full blue morocco. One of 300 copies signed by Gershwin and Alajolov. In Slipcase. $4,500. Trade edition. $400.

GERSHWIN, George. *Porgy and Bess.* New York, 1935. Frontispiece in color. Morocco. One of 250 copies signed by the Gershwins, DuBose Heyward, and others. In slipcase. $7,500.

GERSTAECKER, Friedrich. *Gerstaecker's Travels . . .* London, 1854. $350.

GERSTAECKER, Friedrich. *Scenes of Life in California.* San Francisco: Grabhorn Press, 1942. One of 500 copies. $200.

GESNER, Abraham. *Remarks on the Geology and Minerology of Nova Scotia.* Halifax, 1836. $500.

GHIRARDELLI, Ynez. *The Artist H. Daumier.* San Francisco: Grabhorn Press, 1940. One of 250 copies. $200.

GHOST in the Bank of England (The). London, 1888. (By Eden Philpotts.) Author's first book. $1,750.

GIANNI June 23rd–April 30th 1933. (London) 1933. (By Iris Origo.) Author's first book. $250.

GIBBINGS, Robert. *Iorana! A Tahitian Journal.* Boston, 1932. Author's first book. 385 signed copies. $350. Trade edition in slipcase. $150. London, 1932. $150.

GIBBINGS, Robert. *The Wood Engravings of Robert Gibbings.* London (1959). In acetate dustwrapper. $400.

GIBBON, Edward. *The History of the Decline and Fall of the Roman Empire.* London, 1776–88. 6 vols. Two states (500 copies each). First state had errata uncorrected. $12,500. Second or mixed. $7,500.

GIBBONS, Floyd. *The Red Napoleon.* New York (1929). $250.

GIBBS, Barbara. *The Well.* Albuquerque (1941). Author's first book. Wraps. $250.

GIBBS, George. *A Dictionary of the Chinook Jargon.* New York, 1863. Wraps. One of 100 copies. $400.

GIBRAN, Kahlil. *The Madman: His Parables and Poems.* New York, 1918. Author's first book. $200.

GIBRAN, Kahlil. *Sand and Foam.* New York, 1926. Illustrated by the author. Boards. One of 95 signed copies. Issued without dustwrapper. $750.

GIBRAN, Kahlil. *Twenty Drawings.* New York, 1919. One of 100 copies. $750.

GIBSON, Charles Dana. *Americans.* New York, 1900. Illustrated. Oblong folio, cloth. One of 200 signed copies. $450. Trade edition. $200.

GIBSON, Charles Dana. *Drawings.* New York, 1894. Author's first book. Oblong folio, boards and cloth. $350.

GIBSON, Charles Dana. *Eighty Drawings, Including the Weaker Sex.* New York, 1903. Oblong folio, cloth. One of 250 signed copies. $500.

GIBSON, Charles Dana. *London, as Seen by Gibson.* New York, 1897. Illustrated. Oblong folio, cloth. One of 250 copies. $400.

GIBSON, Wilfrid Wilson. *Urlyn the Harper.* London 1902. Author's first book. Wraps. $200.

GIBSON, William. *Neuromancer.* New York (1984). Author's first book. Wraps (Ace paperback). $150. London, 1984. $1,500. West Bloomfield, 1986. One of 375 signed copies. $750.

GIDE, André. *If It Die: An Autobiography.* New York (1935). One of 100 signed copies. $500. One of 1,400 copies. $100.

GIDE, André. *Prometheus Illbound.* London, 1919. One of 100 copies signed by Gide. Gilt vellum. $300.

GIFFEN, Fannie Reed. *Oo-Mah-Ha Ta-Wa-Tha.* Lincoln (1898). $200.

GILB, Dagoberto. *Winners on the Pass Line.* (El Paso, 1985.) Wraps (no hardback edition). $150.

GILBERT, Frank T. *History of San Joaquin County, California.* Oakland, 1879. Illustrated. Oblong folio, leather. 6 maps and 171 plates. $750.

GILBERT, Jack. *Views of Jeopardy.* New Haven, 1962. Author's first book. $1,000. Wraps. $350.

GILBERT, Michael. *Close Quarters.* London, 1947. Author's first book. $600. New York, 1963. $150.

GILBERT, Paul T., and BRYSON, Charles L. *Chicago and Its Makers.* Chicago, 1929. $250. Full morocco. One of 2,000 copies. $750.

GILBERT, W. S. *The "Bab" Ballads: Much Sound and Little Sense.* London, 1869. First issue, with Hotten imprint on title page. $500.

GILBERT, W. S. *The Mikado.* London, 1928. $450.

GILBERT, W. S. *A New and Original Extravaganza Entitled Dulcamara; or, The Little Duck and the Great Quack.* London, 1866. Author's first published work. Illustration. Orange wraps. $1,250.

GILBERT, William. *On the Magnet, Magnetick Bodies . . .* London, 1900. Woodcuts. Folio, limp vellum, silk ties. One of 250 copies. $1,000.

GILBEY, John F. *Secret Fighting Arts of the World.* Tokyo, 1963. (By Robert W. Smith.) First edition stated. $200.

GILCHRIST, Alexander. *Life of William Blake.* London, 1863. 2 vols. $450. London, 1880. 2 vols. $300.

GILCHRIST, Ellen. *In the Land of Dreamy Dreams.* Fayetteville, 1981. Cloth. $1,250. Wraps. (1,000 copies.) $250. London, 1982. $150.

GILCHRIST, Ellen. *The Land Surveyor's Daughter.* (Fayetteville), 1979. Author's first book. Wraps. $750.

GILHAM, William B. *Manual of Instruction for the Volunteers and Militia of the Confederate States.* Richmond, 1862. Folding charts. $500.

GILHESPY, F. Brayshaw. *Crown Derby Porcelain.* Leigh-on-Sea (1951). One of 600 copies. In dustwrapper. $450.

GILL, Brendan. *Death in April and Other Poems.* Windham, 1935. Author's first book. $300.

GILL, Eric. *Art-Nonsense and Other Essays.* London, 1929. One of 100 signed copies in half calf. $1,250. Trade edition. $300.

GILL, Eric. *Clothes.* London, 1931. One of 160 signed copies. $850.

GILL, Eric. *Clothing Without Cloth: An Essay on the Nude.* London: Golden Cockerel Press, 1931. 4 wood engravings by the author. One of 500 copies. $500.

GILL, Eric. *Drawings from Life.* London (1940). 36 plates. $250.

GILL, Eric. *The Engravings of Eric Gill.* Wellingborough, 1983. 2 vols. One of 85 copies. With additional portfolio of 8 wood engravings. $2,500. One of 1,350 copies. $500.

GILL, Eric. *An Essay on Typography.* (London, 1931.) Illustrated. Cloth. One of 500 signed copies. In dustwrapper. $750.

GILL, Eric. *From the Jerusalem Diary.* (London), 1953. Illustrated. Half cloth. One of 300 copies. $350.

GILL, Eric. *Sculpture.* Ditchling, 1918. Wraps. $1,250.

GILL, Eric. *Serving at Mass.* Sussex, 1916. Author's first book. Wraps. $2,000.

GILL, Eric (illustrator). See *The Four Gospels of the Lord Jesus Christ.*

GILLELAND, J. C. *The Ohio and Mississippi Pilot.* Pittsburgh, 1820. 16 maps. $3,500.

GILLELEN, F.M.L. *The Oil Regions of Pennsylvania.* Pittsburgh [1865?]. 17 maps (one folding), frontispiece, 3 other plates. 67 pages, wraps. $1,500.

GILLETT, James B. *Six Years with the Texas Rangers.* Austin (1921). 8 plates. $400.

GILLIAM, Albert M. *Travels over the Table Lands and Cordilleras of Mexico . . .* Philadelphia, 1846. 3 folding maps and 10 plates. $750.

GILMAN, Charlotte Perkins Stetson. See Stetson, Charlotte Perkins.

GILPIN, Laura. *The Pueblos: A Camera Chronicle.* New York, 1941. Author's first book. $500.

GILPIN, William. *The Central Gold Region: The Grain, Pastoral, and Gold Regions of North America . . .* Philadelphia, 1860. 6 maps. $1,250.

GINSBERG, Allen. *Ankor Wat.* London (1969). Fulcrum Press. 10 photographs by Alexandra Lawrence. One of 100 signed copies. $300.

GINSBERG, Allen. *Careless Love.* Madison, Wis. (1978). Wraps. One of 280 signed copies. $200.

GINSBERG, Allen. *Howl and Other Poems.* San Francisco (1956). Introduction by William Carlos Williams. Printed wraps. Cover price 75 cents. $3,500. (Note: *Howl* appeared originally as *Howl for Carl Solomon.*) San Francisco, 1971. Pictorial cloth. Issued without dustwrapper. One of 275 signed copies. $1,000.

GINSBERG, Allen. *Howl for Carl Solomon.* San Francisco, 1955. Author's first book. Wraps. One of 50 mimeographed copies. $25,000.

GINSBERG, Allen. *The Moments Return.* San Francisco, 1970. Illustrated. Half cloth. One of 200 copies. Issued without dustwrapper. $200. Half leather. One of 14 in a special binding. $750.

GINSBERG, Allen. *Planet News: 1961–1967.* San Francisco, 1968. One of 500 signed copies. In slipcase. $250.

GINSBERG, Allen. *Siesta in Xbalba and Return to the States.* Near Icy Cape, Alaska, July, 1956. Self-wraps, stapled. One of about 56 mimeographed copies. $4,500.

GINSBERG, Allen. *T. V. Baby Poems.* (London, 1967.) Cape Goliard Press. One of 100 signed copies. In dustwrapper. $500. Trade in wraps. $100. New York, 1968. Wraps. $50.

GINX'S Baby: His Birth and Other Misfortunes. London, 1870. (By John Edward Jenkins.) Author's first book. Cloth. $600.

GIPSON, Fred. *Hound-Dog Man.* New York, 1949. Author's first novel. $150.

GISSING, George. See *Demos: A Story of English Socialism.*

GISSING, George. *Born in Exile.* London, 1892. 3 vols. Slate-gray cloth. $1,000.

GISSING, George. *By the Ionian Sea: Notes of a Ramble in Southern Italy.* London, 1901. Illustrated in color and black-and-white. White cloth. $300.

GISSING, George. *Charles Dickens: A Critical Study.* London, 1898. $250.

GISSING, George. *The Emancipated.* London, 1890. 3 vols. Boards and cloth. $2,000.

GISSING, George. *Human Odds and Ends . . .* London, 1898. $500.

GISSING, George. *New Grub Street.* London, 1891. 3 vols. Dark-green cloth. $3,000.

GISSING, George. *The Private Papers of Henry Ryecroft.* Westminster, England, 1903. With three ad leaves. $600. New York, 1903. $200.

GISSING, George. *The Scholar of Bygate: A Tale.* London, 1897. 3 vols. $1,500.

GISSING, George. *Workers in the Dawn.* London, 1880. 3 vols. Author's first book. Light-brown cloth. First edition, with black endpapers. $10,000. Garden City (1935). 2 vols. Blue cloth. In dustwrapper. $350.

GLADSTONE, William. *The State in Its Relations with the Church.* London, 1838. Author's first book. $400.

GLASGOW, Ellen. See *The Descendant.*

GLASGOW, Ellen. *The Freeman and Other Poems.* New York, 1902. $250.

GLASGOW, Ellen. *Phases of an Inferior Planet.* New York, 1898. With erratum slip and verso of last page listing "Jerome" first and the last paragraph beginning "Studies from." $150.

GLASPELL, Susan. *A Jury of Her Peers.* London, 1927. One of 250 signed copies. Buff wraps. $350.

GLEANINGS from the Inside History of the Bonanzas. (San Francisco, 1878.) 40 pages, printed wraps. $300.

GLEESON, William. *History of the Catholic Church in California.* San Francisco, 1871–72. 2 vols. 4 maps and plans, 9 plates. Cloth. $750. San Francisco, 1872. 2 vols. in 1. $450.

GLENARVON. London, 1816. (By Lady Caroline Lamb.) 3 vols. Author's first book. $2,500. Second edition with Preface by Lamb defending her novel. $1,250. Third edition. $600.

GLENN, Allen. *History of Cass County (Missouri).* Topeka, 1917. $250.

GLISAN, R. *Journal of Army Life.* San Francisco, 1874. Folding table, 21 plates. $750.

GLOVER, Mary Baker. *Science and Health, with Key to the Scriptures.* Boston, 1875. (By Mary Baker Eddy.) Black or purple cloth. First issue, with errata slip and without index. $4,000. Lynn, Mass., 1878. Second edition. $1,000. Lynn, 1881. 2 vols., cloth. Third edition. $750.

GLÜCK, Louise. *Firstborn: Poems.* (New York, 1968.) Author's first book. Cloth. $600. Wraps. $50. London, 1969. One of 50 signed copies. $350. Trade edition. Cloth. $125. Wraps. $40.

GODDARD, Paul. *Past Caring.* London (1986). Author's first book. $1,000.

GODDARD, R. H. *A Method of Reaching Extreme Altitudes.* Washington, 1919. 10 plates. Wraps. $4,500.

GODDEN, Rumer. *Chinese Puzzle.* London (1936). $750.

GODWIN, Gail. *The Perfectionists.* New York (1970). Author's first book. $200.

GODWIN, William. *Essay on Sepulchres.* London, 1809. Engraved frontispiece. $600.

GODWIN, William. *Fleetwood: or, The New Man of Feeling.* London, 1805. 3 vols. $850.

GODWIN, William. *Life of Geoffrey Chaucer.* London, 1803. 2 vols. $1,000.

GODWIN, William. *Mandeville: A Tale of the 17th Century in England.* London, 1817. 3 vols. $1,500.

GODWIN, William. *Of Population . . . An Answer to Mr. Malthus' Essay.* London, 1820. $3,000.

GODWIN, William. *Things as They Are; or The Adventures of Caleb Williams.* London, 1794. 3 vols. $3,500.

GOETHE, Johann Wolfgang von. *Faust.* London, 1906–10. 2 vols. One of 300 and 250 copies. $1,500. One of 3 copies on vellum. $15,000. London (1925). With 8 color illustrations and numerous wood engravings. One of 2,000 copies signed by Harry Clarke. $1,000. New York (1925). One of 1,000 copies signed by Clarke. $1,000.

GOFF, Frederick R. *Incunabula in American Libraries . . .* New York, 1964, with first supplement. New York, 1972. 2 vols. First edition of third census. $450.

GOGARTY, Oliver St. John. See *Alpha and Omega.*

GOGARTY, Oliver St. John. *Elbow Room.* Dublin: Cuala Press, 1939. Boards, linen spine. One of 450 copies. In glassine dustwrapper. $200.

GOGARTY, Oliver St. John. *An Offering of Swans.* Dublin: Cuala Press, 1923. Introduction by William Butler Yeats. Boards and cloth, paper label. One of 300 copies. In dustwrapper. $400.

GOGARTY, Oliver St. John. *Wild Apples.* Dublin: Cuala Press, 1930. Preface by William Butler Yeats. Boards and linen. One of 250 copies. In dustwrapper. $300.

GOGOL, Nikolai. See *Home Life in Russia.*

GOGOL, Nikolai. *Dead Souls.* New York, 1886. $500. London (1887). 2 vols. $600.

GOGOL, Nikolai. *Taras Bulba.* Troy, New York, 1889. Translated by Jeremiah Curtin. $200.

GOLD, Michael. *Jews Without Money.* New York (1930). $350.

GOLD, Silver, Lead, and Copper Mines of Arizona. (Philadelphia, 1867.) 40 pages, printed wraps. $750.

GOLDER, Frank Alfred et al. *The March of the Mormon Battalion from Council Bluffs to California* . . . New York (1928). $200.

GOLD-HUNTER'S Adventure . . . *(The)*. (By William Henry Thomes.) Boston, 1864. Author's first book. $600.

GOLDING, W. G. (William). *Poems.* London, 1934. Author's first book. Wraps. $6,000.

GOLDING, William. *Free Fall.* London (1959). $250.

GOLDING, William. *The Inheritors.* London (1955). $600.

GOLDING, William. *The Ladder and the Tree.* London, 1961. Wraps. $3,500.

GOLDING, William. *Lord of the Flies.* London (1954). Author's first book. Red cloth. $6,500. New York (1954). $1,500.

GOLDING, William. *Pincher Martin.* London (1956). $400.

GOLDMAN, Emma. *Anarchism* . . . New York, 1910. Author's first book. $300.

GOLDMAN, William. *The Princess Bride.* New York (1973). $600.

GOLDMAN, William. *Temple of Gold.* New York, 1957. $250.

GOLDSCHMIDT, E. P. *Gothic & Renaissance Bookbindings Exemplified* . . . London/New York, 1928. One of 750 copies. $750.

GOLDSCHMIDT, E. P. *The Printed Book of the Renaissance.* Cambridge, 1950. 7 plates. One of 750 copies. $200.

GOLDSMID, Edmund. *A Bibliographical Sketch of the Aldine Press at Venice* . . . Edinburgh, 1887. Translated. 3 parts in 1 volume. One of 75 large-paper copies. Revised and corrected by Goldsmid from Renouard's *Annales de L'Imprimerie des Aldes.* $250.

GOLDSMITH, Oliver. *Overland in Forty-nine.* Detroit, 1896. 148 pages, pictorial boards. $1,000.

GOLDSMITH, Oliver. See Willington, John.

GOLDSMITH, Oliver. *The Deserted Village: A Poem.* London, 1770. $2,000. London, 1898. One of 10 copies on vellum. $3,500.

GOLDSMITH, Oliver. *An Enquiry into the Present State of Polite Learning in Europe.* London, 1759. Small octavo. Engraved title vignette. $1,500.

GOLDSMITH, Oliver. *She Stoops to Conquer.* London, 1773. $2,000.

GOLDSMITH, Oliver. *The Traveller.* London, 1765. First work with his name as author. $1,750.

GOLDSMITH, Oliver. *The Vicar of Wakefield.* Salisbury, 1766. 2 vols. First issue has misprint "Waekefield" in running headline in vol. II, page 95. $6,000. London (1929). 12 color illustrations and some in black and white by Arthur Rackham. Parchment. One of 775 copies signed by the artist. In slipcase. $1,250. Trade. $600.

GOLDSTONE, Adrian H., and PAYNE, John. *John Steinbeck, A Bibliographical* . . . Austin (1974). One of 1,200 copies. $400.

GOLFIANA, or A Day at Gullane. No place, 1869. Wraps. $10,000.

GOLL, Claire. *The Diary of a Horse.* (Brooklyn, 1946.) 4 illustrations by Chagall. One of 320 copies. $400.

GOLL, Ivan. *Jean sans Terre (Landless John).* Grabhorn Press. San Francisco, 1944. Preface by Allen Tate. Translated by William Carlos Williams and others. Illustrated. Folio, boards. One of 175 copies. $500.

GOOCH, Mrs. *An Appeal to the Public* . . . London, 1788. (By Elizabeth Sara Villa-Real.) Author's first book. $600.

GOOD, P. P. *A Materia Medica Animalia.* Cambridge, Mass., 1853. 24 color plates. $750.

GOODE, G. Brown. *American Fishes.* Boston (1887). Illustrated, with a color frontispiece. Green cloth. $450.

GOODHUE, Bertram Grosvenor. *Book Decorations.* New York, 1931. One of 400 copies. $250.

GOODIS, David. *Dark Passage.* New York, 1946. $1,000. London (1947). $350.

GOODIS, David. *Retreat from Oblivion.* New York, 1939. Author's first book. $2,000.

GOODMAN, Mitchell. *Light from Under a Bushel.* Madison: Perishable Press, 1968. Wraps. One of 100 copies. $200.

GOODMAN, Paul. *The Break-Up of Our Camp and Other Stories.* (Norfolk, 1949.) $100.

GOODMAN, Paul. *The Copernican Revolution.* Saugatuck (1947). Wraps. $125.

GOODMAN, Paul. *The State of Nature.* New York (1946). $200.

GOODMAN, Paul. *Stop-light: 5 Dance Poems.* Harrington Park, N.J., 1941. In first dustwrapper (red and black without "Vinco" on the spine). $350. In later jacket. $150.

GOODMAN, Paul. *Ten Lyric Poems.* (New York, 1934.) Author's first book. 8 leaves, self-wraps. $400.

GOODNER, Ross. *The 75 Year History of Shinnecock Hills Golf Club.* Southhampton (1966). One of 500 copies. $100.

GOODNIGHT, Charles, III. *The Loving Brand Book.* Austin, 1965. Illustrated. Leather. One of 119 copies. In slipcase. $600.

GOODRICH, Lloyd. *Edward Hopper.* New York (1971). Folio. Cloth, dustwrapper. 246 illustrations. $450. New York (1978). $200.

GOODRICH, Samuel G. See Parley, Peter.

GOODSPEED, Charles E. *Angling in America.* Boston, 1939. One of 795 signed copies. $750.

GOODSPEED, Charles E. *Yankee Bookseller, Being the Reminiscences of Charles E. Goodspeed.* Boston, 1937. One of 310 signed copies. In slipcase. $200.

GOODWIN, H. C. *Pioneer History; or Cortland County and the Border Wars of New York.* New York, 1859. 3 portraits. $250.

GOODWIN, Mrs. L. S. *The Gambler's Fate: A Story of California.* Boston, 1864. Woodcuts. 50 pages, pictorial wraps. $300.

GOODYEAR, W. A. *The Coal Mines of the Western Coast of the United States.* San Francisco, 1877. $150.

GORDIMER, Nadine. *Face to Face.* Johannesburg (1949). Author's first book. $1,250.

GORDIMER, Nadine. *The Lying Days.* London, 1953. $350. New York, 1953. $200.

GORDIMER, Nadine. *Six Feet of Country.* London, 1956. $300. New York, 1956. $200.

GORDIMER, Nadine. *The Soft Voice of the Serpent.* New York, 1952. $300. London (1953). $300.

GORDON, Caroline. *Aleck Maury, Sportsman.* New York, 1934. First binding in green cloth. $350. Second binding in blue cloth. $250.

GORDON, Caroline. *The Forest of the South.* New York, 1945. $200.

GORDON, Caroline. *The Garden of Adonis.* New York, 1937. $300.

GORDON, Caroline. *Green Centuries.* New York, 1941. $300.

GORDON, Caroline. *None Shall Look Back.* New York, 1937. $300.

GORDON, Caroline. *Penhally.* New York, 1931. Author's first book. $1,500.

GORDON, J.E.H. *A Practical Treatise on Electric Lighting.* London, 1884. 23 plates, other illustrations. $400.

GORDON, Taylor. *Born to Be.* New York, 1929. First issue without dedication to Van Vechten. $450. Second issue with dedication. $300.

GORDON, William. *The History of the Rise, Progress, and Establishment of the Independence of the United States of America.* London, 1788. 4 vols. 9 engraved folding maps. $2,500.

GORES, Joe. *Marine Salvage.* Garden City, 1971. $125.

GORES, Joe. *A Time of Predators.* New York (1969). Author's first book. $300.

GOREY, Edward. See Beckett, Samuel; Weary, Ogdred.

GOREY, Edward. *Amphigorey.* New York, 1972. One of 50 signed copies. In slipcase. With original watercolor. $2,500. Trade edition, in dustwrapper. $150. New York, 1983. One of 26 signed, lettered copies. In dustwrapper and slipcase. $650. One of 250 signed, numbered copies. In dustwrapper and slipcase. $350.

GOREY, Edward. *The Doubtful Guest.* Garden City, 1957. $450.

GOREY, Edward. *The Iron Tonic.* New York: Albondocani Press, 1969. Decorated wraps. One of 200 signed copies. $750. One of 26 signed copies. $1,000.

GOREY, Edward. *The Listing Attic.* New York (1954). $350.

GOREY, Edward. *The Object Lesson.* Garden City, 1958. $450.

GOREY, Edward. *The Sopping Thursday.* New York, 1970. Cloth. One of 26 copies lettered, signed. In slipcase, with original unpublished drawing. $2,500. Wraps. One of 300 signed copies. $300. Santa Barbara, 1971. "Second Printing April 1971." Wraps. $50.

GOREY, Edward. *The Unstrung Harp.* New York (1953). Illustrated by the author. Decorated boards. Author's first book. $350.

GOREY, Edward. *The Willowdale Handcar.* Indianapolis (1962). Illustrated. Pictorial wraps. No statement of edition. $125.

GOREY, Edward. *The Wuggly Ump.* Philadelphia (1963). Illustrated. Oblong pictorial boards. No statement of edition. In dustwrapper. $150.

GORHAM Golf Book. New York, 1903. $1,250.

GORMAN, Herbert. *James Joyce.* New York, 1924. (Note: Contains new material by Joyce.) $500.

GOSNELL, Harpur Allen (editor). *Before the Mast in the Clippers.* New York: Derrydale Press, 1937. Composed of the Diaries of Charles A. Abbey. Illustrated. Boards. One of 950 copies. $250.

GOSSE, Edmund. *Madrigals, Songs and Sonnets.* London, 1870. Written with John A. Blaikie.) Author's first book. $600.

GOSSE, Philip H. *The Birds of Jamaica.* London, 1847–49. 2 vols. With 52 hand-colored plates. $12,500 or more (see auction records).

GOSSE, Philip H. *Letters from Alabama.* London, 1855. $750.

GOTHEIN, Marie Luise. *A History of Garden Art.* London/Toronto, 1928. 2 vols. Illustrated. $750.

GOTO, Seikichiro. *Japanese Paper and Papermaking.* (No place): Bijutsushuppan-sha (1958). 2 vols. Cord-tied decorated stiff paper wraps contained in cloth folder. Includes 170 tipped-in woodcuts and 59 specimens of Japanese paper. $3,500.

GOTTSCHALK, Laura Riding. *The Close Chaplet.* London, 1926. Author's first book. $750. New York (1926). Tissue dustwrapper. $500.

GOUDY, Frederic W. *Typologia: Studies in Type Design and Type-Making.* Berkeley, 1940. Half morocco. One of 300 signed copies. In slipcase. $250. Trade edition. $100.

GOUGE, William M. *The Fiscal History of Texas.* Philadelphia, 1852. $1,000.

GOULD, E. W. *Fifty Years on the Mississippi.* St. Louis, 1889. Frontispiece. Pictorial cloth. $750.

GOULD, John. *The Birds of Asia*. London, 1850–83. 7 vols. Edited by R. B. Sharpe. 530 hand-colored lithographed plates. Folio, half (or full) morocco. $150,000.

GOULD, John. *The Birds of Australia*. London, 1837–38. 2 vols. With 20 hand-colored plates. $100,000. London, 1840–69. 8 vols. 681 hand-colored lithographed plates. Folio morocco (including 41 parts and supplement volume). $350,000.

GOULD, John. *The Birds of Great Britain*. London, 1862–73. 5 vols. 367 hand-colored lithographed plates. Half morocco. $75,000.

GOULD, John. *Birds of New Guinea and the Adjacent Papuan Islands*. London, 1875–88. 5 vols. 320 hand-colored plates. Folio half morocco. $100,000.

GOULD, John. *A Century of Birds from the Himalaya Mountains*. London (1831), 1832. 80 plates. Author's first book. First issue with backgrounds uncolored. $20,000. Second issue with backgrounds colored. $25,000.

GOULD, Joseph. *The Letter-Press Printer* . . . London, 1876. $200.

GOULD, Stephen. *The Alamo City Guide*. (San Antonio), 1882. Illustrated. Pictorial wraps. $750.

GOVE, Capt. Jesse A. *The Utah Expedition, 1857–58*. Concord, N.H., 1928. 5 plates. $150. One of 50 copies on large paper. $350.

GOYEN, William. *The House of Breath*. New York (1950). Author's first book. $150. London, 1951. $75.

GOYEN, William. *In a Farther Country*. New York (1955). $100. London (1962). $75.

GOYEN, William. *New Work* and *Work in Progress*. (Winston-Salem, 1983.) One of 40 signed copies. Issued without dustwrapper. $125. One of 160 signed copies (not numbered). $60.

GRABHORN, Edwin. *Figure Prints of Old Japan*. San Francisco: Book Club of California, 1959. 52 reproductions. Boards. Grabhorn printing. One of 400 copies. In dustwrapper. $750.

GRABHORN, Edwin. *Landscape Prints of Old Japan*. San Francisco: Book Club of California, 1960. 52 full-color plates. Boards. Grabhorn printing. One of 450 copies. $1,000.

GRABHORN, Robert. *A Short Account of the Life and Work of Wynkyn de Worde*. San Francisco: Grabhorn Press, 1949. One of 375 copies. $600.

GRAFTON, Sue. *"A" Is for Alibi*. New York (1982). $1,500. (London, 1982). $450.

GRAFTON, Sue. *"B" Is for Burglar*. New York (1985). $1,250. London (1986). $350.

GRAFTON, Sue. *"C" Is for Corpse*. New York (1986). $750. London (1987). $250.

GRAFTON, Sue. *"D" Is for Deadbeat*. New York (1987). $400. London (1987). $150.

GRAFTON, Sue. *"E" Is for Evidence*. New York (1988). $250. London (1988). $100.

GRAFTON, Sue. *Keziah Dane*. New York (1967). Author's first book. $1,000. London (1968). $500.

GRAHAM, Benjamin, and DODD, David. *Security Analysis.* New York, 1934. $5,000.

GRAHAM, James. *A Game for Heroes.* (London, 1973.) (By Jack Higgins.) $500.

GRAHAM, Maria. *Journal of a Residence in Chile During the Year 1822 and a Voyage from Chile to Brazil in 1823.* London, 1824. With hand-colored frontispiece and 15 colored plates. $3,000.

GRAHAM, R. B. Cunninghame. *The District of Menteith.* Stirling (Scotland), 1930. Illustrated, including an original etching by Sir D. Y. Cameron. Folio, half calf. One of 250 signed copies. In dustwrapper. In slipcase. $600.

GRAHAM, R. B. Cunninghame. *Notes on the District of Menteith.* London, 1895. Printed gray wraps. $300.

GRAHAM, Tom. *Hike and the Aeroplane.* New York (1912). (By Sinclair Lewis.) Author's first book. Colored illustrations by Arthur Hutchins. Decorated cloth. First issue, with "August, 1912" on copyright page. $6,000.

GRAHAM, W. A. *Major Reno Vindicated.* Hollywood, 1935. 30 pages, wraps. $200. One of 100 signed copies. Full leather. $500.

GRAHAM, W. A. (editor). *The Official Record of a Court of Inquiry Convened . . . by Request of Major Marcus A. Reno to Investigate His Conduct at the Battle of the Little Big Horn, etc.* Pacific Palisades, Calif., 1951. 2 vols. Multigraphed. Folio, cloth. One of 125 copies. $1,500.

GRAHAM, W. S. *Cage Without Grievance.* Glasgow (1942). Author's first book. $500.

GRAHAM, Winston. *Ross Poldark.* London, 1945. $250.

GRAHAME, Kenneth. *Dream Days.* New York, 1899 (actually 1898). First issue, with 15 pages of ads at end dated 1898. $300. London and New York (1902). Illustrated by Maxfield Parrish. $300. London (1930). Illustrated by Ernest H. Shepard. Boards and vellum. One of 275 signed copies. In slipcase. $750.

GRAHAME, Kenneth. *The Golden Age.* London, 1895. $300. London, 1900 (actually 1899). With 16 pages of ads dated 1895. Illustrated by Maxfield Parrish. $200. London (1928). Illustrated by Ernest H. Shepard. Boards and vellum. One of 275 signed copies. $750. Trade edition. $200.

GRAHAME, Kenneth. *Pagan Papers.* London, 1894. Author's first book. Title page designed by Aubrey Beardsley. One of 450 copies. $300.

GRAHAME, Kenneth. *The Wind in the Willows.* London (1908). Frontispiece by Graham Robertson. Pictorial cloth. $5,000. New York, 1909. $1,000. London (1931). Illustrated by Ernest H. Shepard. Map. Gray boards and cloth. One of 200 signed copies. In dustwrapper. In slipcase. $10,000. Trade. $2,000. Limited Editions Club, New York, 1940. Edited by A. A. Milne. Illustrated by Arthur Rackham. Boards and cloth. In slipcase. $1,500. London, 1951. Illustrated by Rackham. Full white calf. One of 500 copies. In slipcase. $3,000.

GRAINGER, M. *Grainger's New Copy-Book or, The Running Hand Made Easy.* London, No date [circa 1730]. Engraved title page, 31 engraved plates numbered 2–32. $750.

GRAND, Sarah. *The Heavenly Twins.* London, 1893. (Pseudonym of Frances Elizabeth McFall.) 3 vols. Green cloth. $500.

GRANDMA Moses: My Life's History. New York (1952). (By Anna Mary Robertson Moses.) One of 275 signed copies. $750.

GRANT, Anne. *Poems of Various Subjects.* Edinburgh, 1803. $350.

GRANT, Blanche C. (editor). *Kit Carson's Olsen Story.* Taos, 1926. Plates. 138 pages, wraps. $350.

GRANT, Marie M. *Artiste.* London, 1871. 3 vols. Author's first book. $350.

GRANT, Maxwell. *The Living Shadow.* New York (1933). (By Walter B. Gibson.) Pictorial boards. First hardbound of *Shadow.* Issued without dustwrapper. $300.

GRANT, U. S. *Personal Memoirs.* New York, 1885–86. 2 vols. Full leather. $500. Trade in cloth. $250. Half leather. $300.

GRANVILLE-SMITH, W. *Drawings.* New York (1898). Large oblong folio, 22 full color reproductions. $500.

GRAPES and Grape Vines of Califronia. San Francisco, 1877. Folio, half morocco. Most copies lost. $10,000 or more. San Francisco, 1980. In original maroon cloth chemise within cloth portfolio. One of fewer than 100 copies. $1,250.

GRASS, Günter. *The Tin Drum.* London, 1961. $150. New York (1962). $100.

GRAU, Shirley Ann. *The Black Prince and Other Stories.* New York, 1955. Author's first book. Dustwrapper without reviews. $175. With reviews. $100.

GRAVES, John. *Goodbye to a River.* New York, 1960. $150. (Austin), 1989. One of 500 signed copies. Issued without dustwrapper. $150.

GRAVES, John. *Home Place.* Ft. Worth, 1958. Author's first book. Wraps. One of 200 copies. $500.

GRAVES, John. *A Memorial . . .* (London, 1706–7). $4,000.

GRAVES, Richard S. *Oklahoma Outlaws.* (Oklahoma City, 1915.) Illustrated. 131 pages, pictorial red wraps. $200.

GRAVES, Robert. See Rich, Barbara; Richards, Frank; Schwarz, George.

GRAVES, Robert. *Adam's Rib.* (London): Trianon Press (1955). One of 26 signed copies. In slipcase. $500. One of 250 copies. In slipcase. $250. Trade. $150. New York (1958). One of 100 signed copies. $250. Trade. $75.

GRAVES, Robert. *Beyond Giving: Poems.* (London), 1969. One of 536 signed copies. In dustwrapper. $175.

GRAVES, Robert. *But It Still Goes On.* London (1930). Refers to "the child she bare" first paragraph on page 157. Dustwrapper is green printed in blue and black. $500. "child she bare" deleted on page 157, which is on a stub. $250. Page 157 is not on a stub. $150. New York (1931). Dark-green cloth with top edge stained black. Also noted in light-blue cloth, top edge red. $250.

GRAVES, Robert. *Claudius the God*. London, 1934. $1,000. New York, 1935. Presumed first state of dustwrapper priced at $3.00 below text (not in corner) with the first word on the back jacket flap "suddenly." Blue cloth blind-stamped on front. $600. Second state of dustwrapper, the same except the first word on the back flap is "At." Dark-blue cloth stamped in gold. $200.

GRAVES, Robert. *Colophon to Love Respelt*. (London), 1967. One of 386 signed copies. $200.

GRAVES, Robert. *Country Sentiment*. London (1920). In dustwrapper. $350. New York, 1920. Higginson called for blue boards, but we have noted two variants in dark-blue pebbled cloth and in a maroon cloth. $350.

GRAVES, Robert. *The English Ballad*. London, 1927. Presumed first issue bound in bright-red cloth, top edge only trimmed; height is 19.5 cm; dustwrapper height is 19.8 cm. $400. Presumed later issue bound in dull-red cloth having a faded appearance; all edges trimmed; height is 19.0 cm; dustwrapper height is 19.0 cm. $300. Note: Higginson describes a book "bound in red cloth," "top edges only trimmed"; height "18.8" cm, which doesn't sound like either of the above.

GRAVES, Robert. *Fairies and Fusiliers*. London (1917). Orange-red cloth stamped in gilt, publisher's imprint on spine ⅝ inch across. $850. Secondary binding in red cloth stamped in green, publisher's imprint ¾ inch across. $750. New York, 1918. $750.

GRAVES, Robert. *The Feather Bed*. Richmond (England), 1923. One of 250 signed copies. $750.

GRAVES, Robert. *Goliath and David*. (London, 1916.) Wraps. (200 copies printed.) $3,000.

GRAVES, Robert. *Good-bye to All That*. London (1929). Contains Sassoon poem on pages 341, 342, and 343. $2,000. Asterisks in shape of v mark deletions on pages 290, 341, 342, and 343. $1,000. London (1930). Type reset to eliminate deletions. $750. New York (1930). Dustwrapper has printed price of $3.00 on front flap; this book in ads on back panel and ad for *The Paris Gun* has price of $3.50. Publisher's logo stamped in middle of front cover and double-ruled lines run diagonally on both front and back cover. $500. (Note: There was a presumed advance copy in dustwrapper without price and *The Paris Gun* listed "To be published . . . Probable price, $3.50.")

GRAVES, Robert. *I, Claudius*. London, 1934. $2,500. New York, 1934. $750.

GRAVES, Robert. *Impenetrability or the Proper Habit of English*. London, 1926. $200.

GRAVES, Robert. *John Kemp's Wager: A Ballad Opera*. Oxford, 1925. Wraps. $300. One of 100 signed copies. $1,250.

GRAVES, Robert. *Lars Porsena, or The Future of Swearing and Improper Language*. London (1927). $350. New York (1927). Higginson calls for blue cloth, but seen in variant bindings. $300. London, 1972. One of 100 signed copies. In glassine dustwrapper. In slipcase. $300.

GRAVES, Robert. *Lawrence and the Arabian Adventure*. Garden City, 1928. First Edition stated. $300.

GRAVES, Robert. *Lawrence and the Arabs*. London (1927). Light orange-yellow cloth. $500. Mustard-colored (dark orange-brown-colored) cloth. $450.

GRAVES, Robert. *Mock Beggar Hall*. London: Hogarth Press, 1924. $750.

GRAVES, Robert. *My Head! My Head!* London, 1925. $500. New York, 1925. $500.

GRAVES, Robert. *Over the Brazier.* London, 1916. Author's first book. Wraps. $1,750. London, 1917. Wraps. $350. London (1920). New For·word, some alterations. $400.

GRAVES, Robert. *The Pier-Glass.* London (1921). $750. New York, 1921. Bound in green cloth. $500. Orange paper-covered boards. $400.

GRAVES, Robert. *Poems (1914–1926).* London, 1927. $400. New York, 1929. $400.

GRAVES, Robert. *Poems (1914–1927).* London, 1927. One of 115 signed copies. Issued with dustwrapper in plain white slipcase. $1,500.

GRAVES, Robert. *Poems 1953.* London (1953). One of 250 signed copies. Issued in transparent parchment wrapper. $350. Trade. $100.

GRAVES, Robert. *The Real David Copperfield.* London (1933). Higginson states spine stamped in gold, Elsworth Mason states gold was trial state. $400. Spine stamped in black. $300.

GRAVES, Robert. *The Shout.* London, 1929. One of 530 signed copies. $500.

GRAVES, Robert. *Treasure Box.* (London, 1919.) Plain blue wraps. $2,750.

GRAVES, Robert. *Welchman's Hose.* London, 1925. In transparent parchment dustwrapper. $500.

GRAVES, Robert. *Whipperginny.* London (1923). $400. New York, 1923. $600.

GRAVES, W. W. *Annals of Osage Mission.* St. Paul, Kan., 1935. Illustrated. $250.

GRAY, A. B. *Charter of the Texas Western Railroad Company . . .* Cincinnati, 1855. $2,000.

GRAY, Alasdair. *Lanark.* Edinburgh, 1981. Author's first book. $600. New York (1981). Wraps. $45. Edinburgh, 1985. One of 1,000 signed copies. $200. New York, 1985. First U.S. hardback. $75.

GRAY, Asa. *Elements of Botany.* New York, 1836. $1,500.

GRAY, Asa. *A Manual of the Botany of the Northern United States.* Boston, 1848. $400.

GRAY, David. *The Sporting Works of David Gray.* New York: Derrydale Press, 1929. Illustrated. 3 vols. One of 750 copies. In slipcase. $250.

GRAY, Henry. *Anatomy, Descriptive and Surgical.* London, 1858. $7,500. Philadelphia, 1859. Illustrated. Calf. $1,500. Philadelphia, 1862. Second edition. $500.

GRAY, John. *Silver Points.* London, 1893. Author's first book. One of 250 copies. $2,250.

GRAY, Thomas. See *An Elegy Written in a Country Church Yard.* See also *An Elegy Wrote in a Country Church Yard.*

GRAY, Thomas. *Poems.* London, 1768. Includes the first appearance of "The Fatal Sisters," "The Descent of Odin," and "The Triumphs of Odin." $500.

GRAYDON, Alexander. *Memoirs of a Life, Chiefly Passed in Pennsylvania, Within the Last 60 Years.* Harrisburg, 1811. $400. Edinburgh, 1822. $200.

GRAZZINI, A. F. *The Story of Doctor Manente*. Florence, 1929. Translated and with introduction by D. H. Lawrence. One of 2 copies on blue paper signed by Lawrence. Vellum boards. $1,500. One of 200 signed copies. Vellum boards $850.

GREAT Eastern Gold Mining Co. (The). New York, 1880. Map. 7 pages, wraps. $300.

GREAT Steam-Duck (The) . . . *An Invention of Aerial Navigation*. Louisville, 1841. By a Member of the LLBB. 32 pages. $3,000.

GREAT Trans-Continental Railroad Guide. Chicago, 1869. Wraps. $1,000.

GREAVES, Richard. *Brewster's Millions*. Chicago, 1903. (By George Barr McCutcheon.) $150.

GRECE, Charles F. *Facts and Observations Respecting Canada, and the United States of America*. London, 1819. $750.

GREELEY, Horace. *An Overland Journey from New York to San Francisco*. New York, 1860. $300.

GREELY, Adolphus W. *Three Years of Arctic Service* . . . New York, 1886. 2 vols. 9 maps. 42 plates. $850.

GREEN, Anna Katharine. *The Circular Study*. New York, 1900. $200. London, 1902. $100.

GREEN, Anna Katharine. *Hand and Ring*. New York, 1883. Wraps. $750. Cloth. $450.

GREEN, Anna Katharine. *The Leavenworth Case: A Lawyer's Story*. New York, 1878. Author's first book. "F" missing from "fresh" last line on page 215. $4,500.

GREEN, Ben K. *Back to Back*. Austin, 1970. Boards. One of 850 signed copies. In slipcase. $250.

GREEN, Ben K. *The Color of Horses*. Flagstaff, Ariz. (1974). Illustrated in color. Half cloth and fabrikoid. One of 150 signed copies. In slipcase. $500. Trade edition. $300.

GREEN, Ben K. *Horse Conformation* . . . (Ft. Worth, 1963.) Author's first book. $300.

GREEN, Ben K. *The Last Trail Drive Through Downtown Dallas*. Flagstaff (1971). Illustrated. Half leather. One of 100 copies signed and with a Joe Beeler drawing in ink and watercolor. In slipcase. $750. Trade. $75.

GREEN, Ben K. *The Shield Mares*. Austin, 1967. One of 750 signed copies. In slipcase. $400.

GREEN, Ben K. *A Thousand Miles of Mustangin'*. Flagstaff (1972). One of 150 signed copies. Boxed. $400. Trade. $200.

GREEN, Ben K. *Wild Cow Tales*. New York, 1969. In dustwrapper. $150. One of 300 signed copies. $250.

GREEN, Henry. *Back*. London, 1946. $300. New York, 1950. $75.

GREEN, Henry. *Blindness*. London, 1926. Author's first book. $3,500. New York (1926). $1,500.

GREEN, Henry. *Concluding*. London, 1948. $350. New York, 1950. $75.

GREEN, Henry. *Living.* London, 1929. $3,000. New York, 1929. $1,000.

GREEN, Henry. *Nothing.* London, 1950. $250. New York, 1950. $125.

GREEN, Henry. *Party Going.* London, 1939. $1,500.

GREEN, Jonathan S. *Journal of a Tour on the Northwest Coast of America in the Year 1829.* New York, 1915. Edited by Edward Eberstadt. Boards, paper label. One of 150 copies. $300. One of 10 copies on Japan vellum. $600.

GREEN Mountain Boys (The). Montpelier, Vt., 1839. (By Daniel Pierce Thompson.) 2 vols. Presumed first issue, with publisher's name misspelled "Waltton" in copyright notice in vol. 2. $1,000.

GREEN, Mowbray A. *The Eighteenth Century Architecture of Bath.* Bath, England, 1904. Plates and plans. Buckram. One of 500 copies. $450.

GREEN, Thomas. *The Universal Herbal, or Botanical, Medical and Agricultural Dictionary.* Liverpool (1816–20). 2 vols. 2 colored frontispieces and 106(?) plates. $3,500. Not colored or partially colored. $2,500. London, 1824. 2 vols. Colored. $2,500. Not colored or partially colored. $1,500.

GREEN, Thomas J. *Journal of the Texian Expedition Against Mier.* New York, 1845. 11 plates, 2 plans. $750.

GREEN, Thomas M. *The Spanish Conspiracy.* Cincinnati, 1891. $350.

GREENAN, Edith. *Of Una Jeffers.* Los Angeles, 1939. 5 photographic illustrations. One of 250 copies. In dustwrapper. $350.

GREENAWAY, Kate. See Harte, Bret; Mavor, William; Spielmann, M. H., and Layard, G. S.; Taylor, Jane and Ann.

GREENAWAY, Kate. *A Apple Pie.* Routledge, London (1886). Colored illustrations. Oblong, half cloth. $600.

GREENAWAY, Kate. *Almanacks.* London (1883–95 and 1897). Illustrated in color by the author. Pictorial boards, wraps, or cloth. (With no *Almanack* issued in 1896.) $7,500. Individual years $500 to $750 each.

GREENAWAY, Kate. *Kate Greenaway's Book of Games.* London (1889). 24 plates. Pictorial boards. $450.

GREENAWAY, Kate. *Marigold Garden.* (London, 1885.) Illustrated in color by the author. Pictorial boards and cloth. $250.

GREENAWAY, Kate. *Under the Window: Pictures and Rhymes for Children.* London (1878). Colored illustrations. Pictorial boards. First issue, with printer's imprint on back of title page and "End of Contents" at foot of page 14. $350.

GREENAWAY, Kate (illustrator). *Language of Flowers.* London (1884). Colored illustrations. Boards. $350.

GREENAWAY, Kate (illustrator). *Mother Goose or The Old Nursery Rhymes.* London (1881). Illustrated in color by Kate Greenaway. Wraps. $750. Later various colors of cloth. $300.

GREENAWAY, Kate, and CRANE, Walter. *The Quiver of Love.* (London): Marcus Ward & Co. (1876.) Colored illustrations. First binding in blue cloth. $1,000. Second binding in green or dark red cloth. $850.

GREENE, Graham. See Cousins, Sheila.

GREENE, Graham. *Babbling April: Collected Poems.* Oxford, 1925. Author's first book. $7,500.

GREENE, Graham. *The Bear Fell Free.* London, 1935. One of 250 signed copies (out of 285 in total). (Dark-green cloth, although the British Library copy of the unnumbered edition is black.) $2,000.

GREENE, Graham. *Brighton Rock.* New York, 1938. "Published in June 1938." Also noted with wraparound band. $2,500. London (1938). "Published July 1938." $9,500.

GREENE, Graham. *Confidential Agent.* London/Toronto (1939). $7,500. New York, 1939. $1,000.

GREENE, Graham. *A Gun for Sale.* London (1936). $10,000. Published one month after American edition, *This Gun for Hire.*

GREENE, Graham. *The Heart of the Matter.* London/Toronto (1948). $750. New York, 1948. "For the friends of Viking Press." Issued without dustwrapper. $200. Trade. Boards covered in maroon embossed paper with spine in ivory cloth. $200.

GREENE, Graham. *It's a Battlefield.* London (1934). In "7/6" dustwrapper. $4,000. With "3/6." $1,750. Garden City, 1934. $1,000.

GREENE, Graham. *The Lawless Roads.* London/New York/Toronto (1939). Red cloth with letters in gold. All but 1 photograph by Greene per acknowledgment on page 8. (Photos vary in later printings.) $3,500. Second binding in red cloth with blue letters. $2,000.

GREENE, Graham. *The Man Within.* London (1929). $4,000. Garden City, 1929. Wobbe calls for a white dustwrapper printed in blue with "Advertisements for other books published by Heinemann." We believe this may have been the description of the U.K. edition (Wobbe A2) as there is no dustwrapper description under A2. The only dustwrapper we have seen on the U.S. edition is primarily green with spine blocks in light green. $2,500. New York: Bantam, 1948. First paperback edition. In dustwrapper. $150.

GREENE, Graham. *May We Borrow Your Husband?* London (1967). One of 500 signed copies. Issued in a clear acetate dustwrapper and slipcase. $350. Trade. $75. New York (1967). $60.

GREENE, Graham. *The Name of Action.* London (1930). Wobbe calls for price of 7s6d and dustwrapper with reviews of *The Man Within* on back cover. $6,000. With "3s6d" on spine and reviews on dustwrapper flap. $1,750. Garden City, 1931. $2,500.

GREENE, Graham. *Orient Express.* Garden City, 1933. $3,000.

GREENE, Graham. *Our Man in Havana.* London (1958). $200. New York (1958). $150.

GREENE, Graham. *The Power and the Glory.* London (1940). $10,000.

GREENE, Graham. *The Quiet American.* London (1955). $400. New York, 1956. $150.

GREENE, Graham. *Stamboul Train.* (*Orient Express* in U.S.) London (1932). Pages 77, 78, 82, 98, and 131 include reference to Q. C. Savory. $5,000. Pages changed to Quin Savory. $3,000.

GREENE, Graham. *This Gun for Hire.* Garden City, 1936. $2,500.

GREENE, Max. *The Kanzas Region.* New York, 1856. 2 maps. Wraps. $1,000. Cloth. $750.

GREENE, W. T. *Parrots in Captivity.* London, 1884–87. 3 vols. $5,000.

GREENEWALT, Crawford H. *Hummingbirds.* Garden City (1960). With 69 mounted color plates. Morocco. One of 500 signed copies. In slipcase. $750. Trade in cloth. In dustwrapper. $500.

GREENHOW, Robert. *The Geography of Oregon and California.* Boston, 1845. Folding map. Wraps. Later edition of his *Memoir.* $1,000.

GREENHOW, Robert. *The History of Oregon and California.* Boston, 1844. Map. Calf. Enlarged edition of his *Memoir.* $1,000. Boston, 1845. Wraps. "Second edition." $750.

GREENHOW, Robert. *Memoir, Historical and Political on the Northwest Coast . . .* Washington, 1840. Folding map. Sewn wraps. (Senate Document 174.) $1,500. Cloth. $750.

GREENWOOD, Lieutenant J. *Narrative of the Late Victorious Campaign in Afghansitan, Under General Pollock.* London, 1844. Extending map. $1,500.

GREER, James K. *Bois d'Arc to Barb'd Wire.* Dallas, 1936. Plates, maps. Pictorial cloth. $250.

GREER, James K. *Colonel Jack Hays: Texas Frontier Leader and California Builder.* New York, 1952. Illustrated. $175.

GREGG, Alexander. *History of the Old Cherraws.* New York, 1867. 4 maps. $500.

GREGG, Asa. *Personal Recollections of the Early Settlement of Wapsinonoc Township and the Murder of Atwood by the Indians.* West Liberty, Iowa (about 1875–80). Tables. Dark-purple wraps. $1,250.

GREGG, Josiah. *Commerce of the Prairies.* New York, 1844. 2 vols. 2 folding maps, 6 plates. Brown pictorial cloth. First issue, with only New York in imprint. $3,000. Second issue, with imprint "New York and London." $2,000. New York, 1845. 2 vols. Cloth. Second edition. $750.

GREGOIRE, H. *An Enquiry Concerning the Intellectual and Moral Faculties, and Literature of Negroes.* Brooklyn, 1810. $2,000.

GREGORY, Horace. *Chelsea Rooming House.* New York (1930). Author's first book. $125.

GREGORY, Isabella Augusta Persse, Lady. *Coole.* Dublin: Cuala Press, 1931. Boards and linen. One of 250 copies. In tissue dustwrapper. $250.

GREGORY, Isabella Augusta Persse, Lady. *The Kiltartan Poetry Book.* Dundrum, Ireland: Cuala Press, 1918. Boards and linen. One of 400 copies. $250.

GREGORY, J. W. *The Dead Heart of Australia . . .* London, 1906. $750.

GREGORY, Joseph W. *Gregory's Guide for California Travellers via the Isthmus of Panama.* New York, 1850. 46 pages, wraps. $2,500.

GREGORY, Thomas Jefferson, and others. *History of Solano and Napa Counties, California.* Los Angeles, 1912. Illustrated. Maps. Three-quarters leather. $300.

GRESHAM, William Lindsay. *Nightmare Alley.* New York (1946). $250.

GRESSENT, Professor. See Garnett, David.

GRESWELL, William Parr. *Annals of Parisian Typography* . . . London, 1818. $350.

GREVILLE, Fulke, Lord Brooke. *Caelica.* Newtown, Wales: Gregynog Press, 1936. Edited by Una Ellis-Fermor. Boards and leather. One of 225 copies. $600. One of 15 copies. Blue morocco, specially decorated by the Gregynog bindery. $5,000.

GREY, George. *Journals of Two Expeditions of Discovery in North-West & Western Australia* . . . London, 1841. 2 vols. 2 frontispieces, 15 plain and 5 colored plates, and 2 folding maps in pocket. $2,000.

GREY OWL. *The Men of the Last Frontier.* New York, 1932. $200.

GREY, Romer. *The Cruise of the "Fisherman."* New York, 1929. $600.

GREY, Zane. *American Anglers in Australia.* New York, 1937. Code letters "B-M" on copyright page. $1,000. London (1937). $850.

GREY, Zane. *Betty Zane.* New York (1903). Author's first book. No mention of edition on the title page. Issued without dustwrapper. $3,500. States "Second Edition" in small letters near the center of the title page. Issued without dustwrapper. $1,000. London, 1903. $1,500.

GREY, Zane. *The Day of the Beast.* New York (1922). Code letters "G-W" on copyright page and states "First Edition." $1,500.

GREY, Zane. *The Desert of Wheat.* New York, 1919. "Published January 1919" and code letters "A-T" on copyright page. In dustwrapper. $1,000.

GREY, Zane. *The Heritage of the Desert.* New York, 1910. No code letters on copyright page. In dustwrapper. $2,000. Without dustwrapper. $350.

GREY, Zane. *The Last of the Plainsmen.* New York, 1908. $500.

GREY, Zane. *The Rainbow Trail.* New York, 1915. "Published August 1915" and code letters "F-P" on copyright page. $300.

GREY, Zane. *Riders of the Purple Sage.* New York, 1912. $1,250. New York (1921). Code letters "K-V" on copyright page. In dustwrapper. $1,500.

GREY, Zane. *The Short Stop.* New York: McClure, 1909. "Published June 1909." $1,000.

GREY, Zane. *Tales of Fishes.* New York (1919). Code letters "F-T" on copyright page. $500.

GREY, Zane. *Tappan's Burro.* New York (1923). States first and contains code letters "I-X" on copyright page. $500.

GREY, Zane. *The Young Forester.* New York, 1910. "Published October 1910." No code letters. $500.

GREYSLAER:A Romance of the Mohawk. London, 1840. (By Charles Fenno Hoffman.) 3 vols. In original boards with paper labels. $750. New York, 1840. 2 vols. In original cloth, and paper labels on spines. $500.

GREYVENSTEIN, Chris. *The Fighters:A Pictorial History of South African Boxing from 1881.* Cape Town, 1981. Stated first. $100.

GRIEVE, C. M. See MacDiarmid, Hugh.

GRIEVE, C. M. *Annals of Five Senses.* Montrose (Scotland), 1923. (By Hugh McDiarmid.) Author's first book. $600.

GRIEVE, Maud. *A Modern Herbal.* London (1931). 2 vols. 96 plates. $300. New York, 1931. 2 vols. $250.

GRIFFIN, John H. *The Devil Rides Outside.* Fort Worth, 1952. Author's first book. $125. London, 1953. $100.

GRIFFITH, D. W. *The Rise and Fall of Free Speech in America.* Los Angeles, 1916. Author's first book. $400.

GRIFFITH, George. *A Honeymoon in Space.* London, 1901. Pictorial cloth. $200.

GRIFFITH, Thomas W. *Sketches of the Early History of Maryland.* Baltimore, 1821. Frontispiece. $400.

GRIFFITHS, A. F. *Bibliotheca Angelo-Poetica; Or, A Descriptive Catalogue . . .* London, 1815. $350. One of 50 copies. $1,250.

GRIFFITHS, D., Jr. *Two Years' Residence in the New Settlements of Ohio.* London, 1835. Frontispiece. In original cloth. $2,500.

GRILE, Dod. *Cobwebs: Being the Fables of Zambri, the Parsee.* (London, about 1884.) (By Ambrose Bierce.) Heavy pictorial printed wraps, or boards. "Fun" Office. Reprint edition of *Cobwebs from an Empty Skull.* $350.

GRILE, Dod. *Cobwebs from an Empty Skull.* London and New York, 1874. (By Ambrose Bierce.) Illustrated. Blue, brown, or green cloth. $750.

GRILE, Dod. *The Fiend's Delight.* London [1872]. (By Ambrose Bierce.) Author's first book. $1,000. New York (1873). Brown or purple-brown cloth. First American edition, without publisher's ads. $750.

GRILE, Dod. *Nuggets and Dust Panned Out in California.* London (1873). (By Ambrose Bierce.) Yellow pictorial wraps. $1,000.

GRIMES, Martha. *The Anodyne Necklace.* Boston (1983). $200.

GRIMES, Martha. *The Man with a Load of Mischief.* Boston (1981). Author's first book. $450.

GRIMES, Martha. *The Old Fox Deceiv'd.* Boston (1982). $250.

GRIMKE, A. E. *Appeal to the Christian Women of the South.* (New York, 1836.) Author's first book. In original wraps. $600.

GRIMM, Jacob L. K. and W. K. *The Fairy Tales of the Brothers Grimm.* London, 1909. Translated by Mrs. Edgar Lucas. Illustrated with color plates by Arthur Rackham. Vellum. One of 750 copies signed by Rackham. $3,500. Trade edition. $1,500. New York, 1909. One of limited number signed by Arthur Rackham. In box. $3,000. Trade. $1,250. Limited Editions Club, New York, 1962–63. 4 vols. In slipcase. $250.

GRIMM, Jacob L. K. and W. K. *Hansel and Gretel and Other Tales.* London, 1920. First separate edition. Illustrated by Arthur Rackham. Without dustwrapper. $750. London (1925). One of 600 copies signed by the illustrator Kay Nielsen. $6,000. New York, 1925. One of 600 copies signed by Nielson. $3,000.

GRIMM, Jacob L. K. and W. K. *Little Brother and Little Sister.* London (1917). Color plates by Arthur Rackham. One of 525 copies signed by Rackham, with an extra plate. $3,500. Lacking extra plate. $1,500. Trade edition. $750. New York, 1917. 12 mounted color plates by Rackham. In slipcase. $750.

GRIMM, M. M. *German Popular Stories.* London, 1823 and 1826. Author's first book. 2 vols. First edition in English. First issue without umlaut over "a" in "märchen" on title page. $12,500.

GRINDLAY, Robert Melville. *Scenery, Costumes, and Architecture . . .* London, 1826–30. 2 vols. 38 hand-colored plates. $10,000.

GRINNELL, George Bird. *The Cheyenne Indians: Their History and Way of Life.* New Haven, 1923. Illustrated. 2 vols. With a folding map and 48 plates. Without dustwrapper. $500.

GRINNELL, George Bird. *The Indians of Today.* Chicago. 1900. Small folio, decorated cloth. Many full-page illustrations. Custom-made sturdy paper-covered board slipcase. $750.

GRINNELL, George Bird. *Pawnee Hero . . .* New York, 1889. Author's first book. $400.

GRINNELL, Joseph, and STORER, Tracy I. *Animal Life in the Yosemite.* Berkeley, 1924. Illustrations (some in color). Without dustwrapper. $300.

GRINNELL, Joseph, et al. *The Game Birds of California.* Berkeley, 1918. 16 color plates, other illustrations. $250.

GRISHAM, John. *The Firm.* New York (1993). $250.

GRISHAM, John. *A Time to Kill.* New York (1989). Dustwrapper priced, bar code on back, no mention of *The Firm* on dustwrapper flap. Author's first book. $2,000. (Book Club edition has Tarrytown, NY on title page.) New York, 1993. One of 350 signed copies. Bound in leather. In slipcase. $850.

GRISWOLD, David D. *Statistics of Chicago, Ill., Together with a Business Advertiser, and Mercantile Directory for July, 1843.* (Chicago), 1843. 24 pages, printed wraps. $1,250.

GRISWOLD, Rufus W. *The Republican Court.* New York, 1856. Morocco. $450.

GRISWOLD, Wayne. *Kansas: Her Resources and Developments.* Cincinnati, 1871. Illustrated. Printed wraps. $350.

GRONOW, Rees Howell. *The Reminiscences and Recollections of Captain Gronow.* London, 1889. 2 vols. One of 870 copies with plates in two states. $750.

GROOM, Winston. *Forrest Gump.* Garden City, 1986. $300.

GROPIUS, Walter. *The New Architecture and the Bauhaus.* (London, 1935.) First English translation of the author's work. $300.

GROPPER, William. *Twelve Etchings.* New York, 1965. One of 100 in large folding box with 12 original signed etchings. $2,500.

GROSS, Samuel. *The Anatomy, Physiology and Diseases of the Bones and Joints.* Philadelphia, 1830. $1,250.

GROSSMITH, George. *The Diary of a Nobody.* Bristol, England (1892). Illustrated by Weedon Grossmith. Light-brown cloth. $600.

GROSZ, George. *Ecce Homo.* New York, 1965. $450.

GROSZ, George. *George Grosz: Twelve Reproductions from His Original Lithographs.* Chicago, 1921. Author's first American publication. Wraps. $600.

GROSZ, George. *Interregnum.* New York, 1936. One of 280 copies with signed 4-color frontispiece. Folio, loose in clamshell box. $4,000.

GROSZ, George. *A Little Yes and a Big No.* New York, 1946. $350.

GROTIUS, Hugo. *Of the Law of Warre and Peace.* London, 1654. $4,000.

GROUPED Thoughts and Scattered Fancies. Richmond, Va., 1845. (By William Gilmore Simms.) Wraps. $450.

GROVER, La Fayette (editor). *The Oregon Archives.* Salem, 1853 (actually 1854). Printed yellow wraps. $1,500.

GROWOLL, A. *Three Centuries of English Booktrade Bibliography* . . . New York, 1903. One of 550 copies. $250.

GRUBB, Davis. *The Night of the Hunter.* (New York, 1953.) Author's first book. 1,000 signed. $350. Regular trade. $250. London (1954). $100.

GRUBB, Davis. *Twelve Tales of Suspense and the Supernatural.* New York (1964). $150.

GRUBER, Frank. *Peace Marshall.* New York, 1939. Author's first book. $400.

GRUELLE, Johnny. *Mr. Twee Deedle.* New York, 1913. Author's first book. $300.

GRUELLE, Johnny. *Raggedy Andy Stories.* Joliet (1920). $400.

GRUELLE, Johnny. *Raggedy Ann's Magical Wishes.* Joliet, 1927. Issued in pictorial box. $350.

GRUELLE, Johnny. *Raggedy Ann Stories.* Joliet (1918). $350.

GRUMBACH, Doris. *The Short Throat, the Tender Mouth.* Garden City, 1964. $200.

GRUMBACH, Doris. *The Spoil of the Flowers.* Garden City, 1962. Author's first book. $250.

GRUNER, Louis. See *The Decorations of the Garden-Pavilion* . . .

GUERIN, Maurice de. *The Centaur.* London: Vale Press, 1899. One of 150 copies. $600. (Montague, Mass.), 1915. Translated by George B. Ives. Boards. One of 135 copies. Bruce Rogers typography. $1,250.

GUIDE for Emigrants to Minnesota (A). By a Tourist. St. Paul, 1857. Map. 16 pages, printed wraps. $750.

GUIDE, Gazetteer and Directory of Nebraska Railroads. Omaha, 1872. Folding map, 6 plates. 210 pages, wraps. (By J. M. Wolfe.) $600.

GUILD, Jo. C. *Old Times in Tennessee.* Nashville, 1878. Green cloth. $300.

GUINEY, Louise Imogen. *"Monsieur Henri": A Footnote to French History.* New York, 1892. One of 50 signed copies. $300.

GUINEY, Louise Imogen. *Songs at the Start.* Boston, 1884. Author's first book. Half morocco. $200. Cloth. $125.

GUNN, Otis B. *New Map and Hand-Book of Kansas and the Gold-Mines.* Pittsburgh, 1859. Large map in color, folding into black cloth covers, and accompanied by text pamphlet *(Gunn's Map and Hand-Book, etc.),* bound in salmon-colored printed wraps. $5,000. Lacking the text pamphlet. $4,500.

GUNN, Thom. *Fighting Terms.* (Oxford, 1954.) First issue, final "t" in "thought" omitted on first line on page 38. Yellow cloth issued without dustwrapper. $850. Second issue, corrected. $350. New York, 1958. Stiff wraps. $150. Berkeley, 1983. One of 25 signed copies. New introduction by Gunn. $1,250.

GUNN, Thom. *A Geography.* Iowa City, 1966. Wraps. One of 220 signed copies. $350.

GUNN, Thom. *Mandrakes.* London (1973). Illustrated by Leonard Baskin. Half vellum. One of 150 signed copies. In slipcase. $450.

GUNN, Thom. *(Poems.)* Fantasy Press. Oxford, 1953. Author's first book. Wraps. $400.

GUNNISON, John W. *The Mormons; or, Latter-Day Saints, in the Valley of the Great Salt Lake.* Philadelphia, 1852. Frontispiece. Dark-blue cloth. $500.

GUNSAULUS, Helen C. *The Clarence Buckingham Collection of Japanese Prints: The Primitives.* Chicago (1955). Plates. Folio, cloth. One of 500 copies. $750. Chicago (1965). One of 1,000 copies. $600.

GURGANUS, Allan. *Breathing Lessons.* Rocky Mount, 1981. Author's first book. Wraps. $200.

GUTENBERG Bible. Mainz (1450–55). Single leaf. $22,000 to 46,000 at auction in 1999. New York, 1961. 2 vols. One of 1,000 copies. $2,500. New York, 1968. 3-vol. facsimile. In slipcase. $400. Munich, 1977. 2 vols. One of 750 copies. $12,500.

GUTERSON, David. *The Country Ahead of Us . . .* New York (1989). Author's first book. $350.

GUTERSON, David. *Snow Falling on Cedars.* New York, 1994. $200.

GUTHRIE, A. B., Jr. *The Big Sky.* New York, 1947. One of 500 signed copies. In additional numbered dustwrapper. "This is your autographed copy . . ." $500. Trade edition. $250.

GUTHRIE, A. B., Jr. *Murders at Moon Dance.* New York, 1943. Author's first book. $1,250.

GUTHRIE, A. B., Jr. *The Way West.* New York, 1949. $250.

GUTHRIE, Woody. *Bound for Glory.* New York, 1945. Author's first book. $400.

GUY *Rivers: A Tale of Georgia.* New York, 1834. (By William Gilmore Simms.) 2 vols. $250.

GUY, Rosa. *Bird at My Window.* Philadelphia, 1966. $300. (London, 1966.) $100.

H

H., H. *Verses.* Boston, 1870. (By Helen Hunt Jackson.) Author's first book. $400.

H., H. (translator). *Bathmendi: A Persian Tale.* Boston, 1867. Translated from the French of Florian. (Translated by Helen Hunt Jackson), her first publication. Printed wraps. $300.

HABBERTON, John. *Helen's Babies.* Boston (1876). Wraps. First issue: measures 1³⁄₁₆ inches. $400.

HABERLY, Loyd. *Anne Boleyn, and Other Poems.* Newtown, Wales: Gregynog Press, 1934. Printed in red and black on handmade paper. Niger morocco. One of 300 copies. $750. One of 15 copies (from the edition) elaborately bound. $2,000.

HABERLY, Loyd. *Artemis: A Forest Tale.* (St. Louis): Mound City Press (1942). Illustrated in color by Haberly. Full green morocco. One of 240 copies. $350.

HABERLY, Loyd. *The Crowning Year and Other Poems.* Stoney Down (England), 1937. Half morocco. One of 150 copies. $450.

HABERLY, Loyd. *Medieval English Pavingtiles.* Oxford, 1937. Half morocco. One of 425 copies. $750.

HABERLY, Loyd. *Poems.* Long Crendon: Seven Acres Press, 1930. Dark-blue morocco. One of 120 copies. $500.

HACKENSCHMIDT, George. *Complete Science of Wrestling.* London, no date. $100.

HACKER, Marilyn. *The Terrible Children.* No place (1967). Stapled wraps. $400.

HACKETT, James. *Narrative of the Expedition Which Sailed from England in 1817, to Join the South American Patriots.* London, 1818. $1,500.

HAEBLER, Konrad. *The Early Printers of Spain and Portugal.* London, 1897 (1896). 33 plates reproducing title pages. $450.

HAFEN, LeRoy R. *The Overland Mail, 1849–1869*. Cleveland, 1926. Map, 7 plates. Issued without dustwrapper. $350.

HAFEN, LeRoy R. *Overland Routes to the Gold Fields*. Glendale, 1942. 7 plates, folding map. Cloth. Issued without dustwrapper. $350.

HAFEN, LeRoy R. (editor). *The Mountain Men and the Fur Trade of the Far West*. Glendale, Calif., 1965–72. 10 vols. In plain dustwrappers. $2,500.

HAFEN, LeRoy R. and Ann W. (editors). *The Far West and the Rockies, 1820–75*. Glendale, 1954–61. 10 vols. $2,750.

HAFEN, LeRoy R., and GHENT, W. J. *Broken Hand: The Life Story of Thomas Fitzpatrick, Chief of the Mountain Men*. Denver, 1931. Map, 8 plates. Cloth-backed boards. One of 100 large paper copies, signed. $850. Cloth. One of 500 copies. In dustwrapper. $500. Denver [1973]. One of 200 signed copies. Revised edition. In slipcase. $400.

HAFEN, LeRoy R., and YOUNG, Francis Marion. *Fort Laramie and the Pageant of the West, 1834–1890*. Glendale, 1938. $350.

HAFEN, Mary Ann. *Recollections of a Handcart Pioneer of 1860*. Denver, 1938. Plates. Cloth. Issued without dustwrapper. $450.

HAGEDORN, Herman, Jr. *The Silver Blade*. Berlin, 1907. Author's first book. Wraps. $250.

HAGEN, Walter. *Walter Hagen Story*. New York, 1956. $100.

HAGGADAH (The). London [1939]. Executed by Arthur Szyk. Edited by Cecil Roth. Vellum sheets, folded, unbound. Pictorial endpapers printed on silk. One of 125 copies signed by Szyk and Roth. $12,500. Bound by Sangorski & Sutcliffe. $17,500. Jerusalem, 1956. Quarto. $300.

HAGGARD, H. Rider. *Allan Quatermain*. London, 1887. With 20 full-page illustrations. Blue cloth. With no footnote on the frontispiece. $750. Brown pebbled cloth. One of 112 copies on large paper. $2,000. New York, 1887. Wraps. $750.

HAGGARD, H. Rider. *Allan's Wife and Other Tales*. London, 1889. One of 100 copies on large paper. In red cloth. $3,000. Trade edition in brown pebbled cloth. $450.

HAGGARD, H. Rider. *Black Heart and White Heart and Other Stories*. London, 1900. $450.

HAGGARD, H. Rider. *Cetywayo and His White Neighbours*. London, 1882. Author's first book. (750 copies.) $2,000.

HAGGARD, H. Rider. *Cleopatra*. London, 1889. Morocco spine and brown cloth. One of 57 copies on large paper. $3,000. Trade edition in blue cloth. With 16-page catalogue dated January 1889. $850.

HAGGARD, H. Rider. *Colonel Quaritch, V.C.: A Tale of Country Life*. London, 1888. 3 vols. Red cloth. $1,000. London, 1889. 1 vol. $250.

HAGGARD, H. Rider. *Dawn*. London, 1884. 3 vols. Author's first novel. Olive-green cloth. $12,500. London, 1887. 1 vol. $600. New York, 1887. $300. New York, 1887. 2 vols. Wraps. $2,750.

HAGGARD, H. Rider. *Heart of the World.* New York, 1895. Green cloth. $250. London, 1896. $200.

HAGGARD, H. Rider. *Jess.* London, 1887. Red cloth. $500.

HAGGARD, H. Rider. *King Solomon's Mines.* London, 1885. Folding colored frontispiece, map. Bright-red cloth. First issue: page 10, line 14: "Bamamgwato" for "Bamangwato"; page 122, line 27: "to let twins to live" for "to let twins live"; and page 307, line 29: "wrod" for "word." Ads dated "5G.8.85." $10,000. Second issue, uncorrected with ads dated "5G.10.85." $4,500. Third issue, with no ads. 500 copies of English sheets, bound in the U.S. Considered to be first American edition. $3,500.

HAGGARD, H. Rider. *Mr. Meeson's Will.* London, 1888. Red cloth. With "Johnson" for "Johnston" in line 1 of page 284 and 32-page catalogue dated "Ocotber 1888." $600. New York, 1888. Wraps. (May have preceded English.) $500.

HAGGARD, H. Rider. *Montezuma's Daughter.* London, 1893. Blue cloth. $250.

HAGGARD, H. Rider. *Queen Sheba's Ring* . . . London, 1910. $400. Garden City, 1910. $200.

HAGGARD, H. Rider. *Red Eve.* London (1911). Red cloth with pictorial paper inlay. Frontispiece and 3 additional color plates. $450.

HAGGARD, H. Rider. *She: A History of Adventure.* New York, 1886. Printed wraps. $1,500. London, 1887. Illustrated. Blue cloth. First English edition, first issue, with "Godness me" in line 38, page 269. $1,250. New York (1926). Photoplay edition. $350.

HAGGARD, H. Rider. *Treasure of the Lake.* London, 1926. $750. New York, 1926. $500.

HAGGARD, H. Rider. *The Witch's Head.* London, 1885. 3 vols. Gray cloth. $15,000. London (1887). $300.

HAIG-BROWN, Roderick. *Silver.* London, 1931. Author's first book. $500.

HAINES, Elijah M. *The American Indian.* Chicago, 1888. Half morocco. $150.

HAINES, Elijah M. *Historical and Statistical Sketches of Lake County, State of Illinois.* Waukegan, Ill., 1852. Folding frontispiece. 112 pages, printed wraps. $1,500.

HAKEWILL, James. *A Picturesque Tour of Italy.* London, 1820. With engraved title and 63 plates. Folio. $1,500.

HAKEWILL, James. *A Picturesque Tour of the Island of Jamaica.* London, 1825. 21 colored aquatint plates. $17,500.

HAKLUYT, Richard. *The Principal Navigations, Voyages* . . . London, 1589. Folding world map, and 6-leaf Drake insert. $45,000. London, 1598–1600. 3 vols. in 2. Folio. Cancel title page in vol. I. Folding map. $27,500. London, 1599–1600. 3 vols. in 2. Folio. Folding map in vol. 3. Second state without mention of the voyage of Cadiz and with date changed to 1599 in volume 1. $20,000.

HALBERSTAM, David. *The Best and the Brightest.* New York (1972). $150.

HALDANE, Charlotte. *Man's World.* London, 1926. Author's first book. $300. New York (1927). $125.

HALDEMAN, Joe. *The Forever War.* New York (1974). $600. London, 1975. $275.

HALE, Edward Everett. See *The Man Without a Country; Margaret Percival in America.*

HALE, Edward Everett. *Kanzas and Nebraska.* Boston, 1854. Folding map. $500.

HALE, Edward Everett. *A Tract for the Day: How to Conquer Texas Before Texas Conquers Us.* Boston, 1845. 16 pages, self-wraps. $150.

HALE, John. *California as It Is.* San Francisco: Grabhorn Press, 1954. One of 150 copies. $250.

HALE, Kathleen. *Orlando, The Marmalade Cat . . .* London, 1938. Author's first book. $400.

HALE, Lucretia P. *The Peterkin Papers.* Boston, 1880. Illustrated by F. G. Attwood. $300.

HALE, Sarah Josepha. See *The Genius of Oblivion.*

HALE, Sarah Josepha. *Northwood: A Tale of New England.* Boston, 1827. 2 vols. $450.

HALE, Sarah Josepha (editor). *The Good Little Boy's Book.* New York (about 1848). Printed flexible boards. $350.

HALE, Will. *Twenty-four Years a Cowboy and Ranchman in Southern Texas and Old Mexico.* Oklahoma Territory: Hedrick (Headrick) (1905). (By William Hale Stone.) 268 pages, stiff purplish-blue wraps. $5,000.

HALEY, Alex. *Roots.* Garden City, 1976. In full leather. Author's first book. One of 500 signed copies. In slipcase. $600. Trade edition. $125.

HALEY, J. Evetts. *Charles Goodnight, Cowman and Plainsman.* Boston, 1936. $850.

HALEY, J. Evetts. *Charles Schriener, General Merchandise: The Story of a Country Store.* Austin, 1944. $200.

HALEY, J. Evetts. *Fort Concho on the Texas Frontier.* San Angelo, 1952. One of 185 signed copies. In dustwrapper. In slipcase. $750. Trade edition. $400.

HALEY, J. Evetts. *The Heraldry of the Range.* Canyon, Tex., 1949. Illustrated by Harold Bugbee. $600.

HALEY, J. Evetts. *Life on the Texas Range.* Austin, 1952. Photographs by Erwin E. Smith. Pictorial cloth. In slipcase. $250.

HALEY, J. Evetts. *The XIT Ranch of Texas.* Chicago, 1929. Author's first book. 2 maps, 30 plates. $600.

HALFORD, Frederic M. *Dry Fly Entomology.* London, 1897. 2 vols. With 18 plain and 28 hand-colored plates, and 100 artificial flies in sunken mounts. Morocco. One of 100 copies, signed. $4,000.

HALFORD, Frederic M. *The Dry-Fly Man's Handbook.* London, 1913. Illustrated. Leather and cloth. One of 100 signed copies. $1,500. Trade edition. 43 black-and-white plates. $450. New York, 1913. $250.

HALFORD, Frederic M. *Modern Development of the Dry Fly.* London (1910). 2 vols. With 43 plates, and 33 mounted flies, 9 in sunken mounts. Leather and cloth. One of 75 signed copies. In slipcase. $4,000.

HALFPENNY, William. *A New and Compleat System of Architecture Delineated . . .* London, 1749. 47 engraved plates. $3,000.

HALIBURTON, Thomas Chandler. See *The Clockmaker.*

HALKETT, John. *Statement Respecting the Earl of Selkirk's Settlement of Kildonan . . .* London (1816). Folding map. First issue without a printer or date on title. $2,000. London, 1817. $1,000.

HALKETT, Samuel, and LAING, John. *Dictionary of Anonymous and Pseudonymous English Literature.* Edinburgh, 1926–1962. 9 vols. New and revised edition by Dr. James Kennedy et al. Complete with index and second supplement volume and other supplements to 1960. $750.

HALL, Arthur Vine. *Table Mountain . . .* Capetown (1896). Author's first book. $200.

HALL, Basil. *The Great Polyglot Bibles.* San Francisco: Book Club of California, 1966. Folio, loose in wraps. One of 400 copies. In slipcase. $600.

HALL, Capt. Basil. *Account of a Voyage of Discovery to the West Coast of Corea . . .* London, 1818. 10 tissue-guarded hand-colored aquatints, and 5 maps. $4,000.

HALL, Capt. Basil. *Forty Etchings, from Sketches Made with the Camera Lucida, in North America, in 1827 and 1828.* Edinburgh, 1829. Folding map, 40 etchings on 20 plates. $1,000.

HALL, Capt. Basil. *Travels in North America.* Edinburgh, 1829. 3 vols. Colored folding map, folding table. $750. Philadelphia, 1829. Illustrated. 2 vols. $300.

HALL, Carroll D. (editor). *Donner Miscellany.* San Francisco: Book Club of California, 1947. (Printed by the Allen Press.) One of 350 copies. $300.

HALL, Charles Francis. *Narrative of the North Polar Expedition . . .* Washington, 1876. 2 steel engravings, 38 wood engravings, 19 tailpieces, 2 photolithographs, 6 maps. Original orange cloth, stamped in gilt. Spine sunned, trace of wear; frontispiece foxed. $600.

HALL, Donald. *Exile.* Swinford (1952). Wraps. $300.

HALL, Donald. *Exiles and Marriages.* New York, 1955. $150.

HALL, Donald. *(Poems.)* Oxford (1952). Fantasy Poets No. 4. Wraps. $350.

HALL, Edward H. *The Great West . . .* New York, 1864. Map. 89 pages. Folding map. Printed wraps. $850. London, 1865. $750.

HALL, Francis. *Travels in Canada and the United States in 1816 and 1817.* London, 1818. Folding map. $350. Boston, 1818. First American edition. $350.

HALL, Frederic. *The History of San José and Surroundings.* San Francisco, 1871. With folding map and 4 plates. $750.

HALL, George Eli. *A Balloon Ascension at Midnight.* San Francisco, 1902. Illustrated by Gordon Ross. One of 30 copies on Japan vellum, signed. $1,250. One of 1,175 copies. $300.

HALL, Halworthy. *Dormie One.* New York, 1917. $250. Limited edition. 1944. $250.

HALL, Henry (editor.) *The Tribune Book of Open-Air Sports.* New York, 1887. (This is the first book printed without using movable type.) $300.

HALL, James. *Letters from the West.* London, 1828. $750.

HALL, James. *Notes on the Western States.* Philadelphia, 1838. (Later edition of *Statistics of the West.*) $300.

HALL, James. *Sketches of History, Life, and Manners in the West.* Cincinnati, 1834. Vol. 1. (All published.) $500. Philadelphia, 1835. 2 vols. Frontispiece. First complete edition. $600.

HALL, James. *Statistics of the West.* Cincinnati, 1836. Purple cloth. $400.

HALL, James Norman. See Nordhoff, Charles B. (For *Mutiny on the Bounty.*)

HALL, James Norman. *Kitchener's Mob.* Boston, 1916. Author's first book. In dustwrapper. $400. Without dustwrapper. $100. London, 1916. $125.

HALL, James Norman, and NORDHOFF, Charles B. (editors). *The Lafayette Flying Corps.* Boston, 1920. 2 vols. Illustrated, including colored plates. Blue cloth. In dustwrappers. $2,500. New York, 1964. 2 vols. One of 500 copies. $600.

HALL, Manly P. *An Encyclopedic Outline of Masonic, Cabbalistic and Rosicrucian Symbolical Philosophy.* San Francisco, 1928. Colored plates, text illustrations. Folio boards and vellum. John Henry Nash printing. One of 550 signed copies. In slipcase. $1,250.

HALL, Marguerite Radclyffe. *The Forgotten Island.* London, 1915. $250.

HALL, (Marguerite) Radclyffe. *The Master of the House.* London (1932). Buckram, vellum spine. One of 172 signed copies. $500. Trade edition. $250. New York (1932). $200.

HALL, Marguerite Radclyffe. *Poems of the Past and Present.* London, 1910. $250.

HALL, Marguerite Radclyffe. *A Sheaf of Verses.* London, 1908. $300.

HALL, Marguerite Radclyffe. *'Twixt Earth and Stars.* London, 1906. Author's first book. $600.

HALL, (Marguerite) Radclyffe. *The Well of Loneliness.* London (1928). First state, with "whip" for "whips" on page 50, line 13. In dustwrapper. $1,000. New York, 1928. Boards and cloth. One of 500 copies. In slipcase. Issued simultaneously with U.K. $500. New York, 1929. 2 vols. Half cloth. One of 225 signed copies. In slipcase. $750.

HALL, Marshall. *New Memoir on the Nervous System.* London, 1843. 5 plates. $500.

HALL, Marshall. *Principles of the Theory and Practice of Medicine.* Boston, 1839. $400. (Contains new material by Oliver Wendell Holmes.)

HALL, Samuel R. *Lectures on School-Keeping.* Boston, 1829. $200.

HALL, Samuel R. *Lectures to Female Teachers on School-Keeping.* Boston, 1832. $150.

HALLECK, Fitz-Greene. See Croaker. See also *Alnwick Castle; Fanny.*

HALLENBECK, Cleve. *The Journey of Fray Marcos de Niza.* Dallas, 1949. $300.

HALPER, Albert. *Chicago Side-Show.* New York, 1932. One of 110 copies. Wraps. $300.

HALSEY, R.T.H. *Pictures of Early New York on Dark Blue Staffordshire Pottery . . .* New York, 1899. 155 illustrations, mostly in color. One of 268 copies on handmade paper. $750. One of 30 copies on vellum. $2,500.

HALSMAN, Philippe. *Jump Book.* New York, 1959. $150.

HALSTEAD, Murat. *The Caucuses of 1860.* Columbus, Ohio, 1860. $200.

HAMADY, Walter. *The Disillusioned Solipsist.* Mt. Horeb, 1954. Author's first book. One of 60 copies. Also first Pershable Press book. $2,500.

HAMADY, Walter. *Hand Papermaking.* Perry, 1982. One of 200 copies signed beneath the plate on page 19. 9 leaves of paper samples. $750.

HAMBLETON, Chalkley J. *A Gold Hunter's Experience.* Chicago, 1898. Green cloth. $500.

HAMERTON, Philip G. *Etching and Etchers.* London, 1868. Illustrated. Half morocco. $2,000. London, 1880. Third edition. (With a Whistler etching.) $2,000.

HAMILTON, Alexander. See *A Full Vindication . . .*

HAMILTON, Alexander. *Report of the Secretary of the Treasury . . .* New York, 1790. $20,000.

HAMILTON, Alexander; JAY, John; and MADISON, James. *The Federalist . . .* New York, 1788. 2 vols. $75,000. Washington, 1818. First edition to contain Madison's corrections. $1,250. Limited Editions Club, New York, 1945. $300.

HAMILTON, Clive. *Spirits in Bondage.* London, 1919. (By C. S. Lewis.) Author's first book. $750.

HAMILTON, Edmond. *The Horror on the Asteroid.* London, 1936. Author's first book. $600.

HAMILTON, Edmond. *The Metal Giants.* Washborn: Swanson Book Co. (1932). Author's first book. 40 mimeographed pages issued as science fiction reprints no.1, but no other printing known. $400.

HAMILTON, Gail. *Country Living and Country Thinking.* Boston, 1862. (By Mary Abigail Dodge.) Author's first book. $400.

HAMILTON, George. *A Voyage Around the World in His Majesty's Frigate Pandora.* Berwick, 1793. $8,500.

HAMILTON, H. W. *Rural Sketches of Minnesota.* Milan, Ohio, 1850. 40 pages, printed wraps. $750.

HAMILTON, Jane. *The Book of Ruth.* New York, 1988. Author's first book. $400.

HAMILTON, John P. *Travels Through the Interior Provinces of Colombia.* London, 1827. 2 vols. Map, 7 plates. $1,000.

HAMILTON, Sinclair. *Early American Book Illustrators and Wood Engravers 1679–1870.* Princeton, 1958–68. 2 vols. $600. Princeton, 1968. 2 vols. $300.

HAMILTON, W. T. *My Sixty Years on the Plains.* New York, 1905. Edited by E. T. Sieber. 8 plates (6 by Charles M. Russell). $300.

HAMILTON, Walter. *Dated Book-Plates (Ex Libris) with a Treatise on Their Origin and Development.* London, 1895. $250.

HAMILTON, The Rev. William, and IRVIN, the Rev. S. M. *An Ioway Grammar.* (Wolf Creek, Neb.): Iowa and Sac Mission Press, 1848. Wraps. $2,500.

HAMMER, Victor. *Concern for the Art of Civilized Man.* Lexington, 1963. One of 109 copies. $500.

HAMMER, William J. *Radium, and Other Radio-Active Substances.* New York, 1903. $600.

HAMMETT, Dashiell. *The Dain Curse.* New York, 1929. With "dopped in" for "dropped in" in line 19 of page 260. (May be in all copies of the first edition.) $15,000. London, 1930. "First published 1930 . . ." Richard Layman calls for a skull and crossbones on front upper right-hand corner but also noted without this. $2,500.

HAMMETT, Dashiell. *The Glass Key.* London/New York, 1931. (Published January 20.) $7,500. New York/London, 1931. (Published April 24.) $3,500.

HAMMETT, Dashiell. *The Maltese Falcon.* New York/London, 1930. $25,000 (although sold for $30,000 at auction in 1992). London/New York, 1930. $4,500.

HAMMETT, Dashiell. *Red Harvest.* New York, 1929. Author's first book. $25,000.

HAMMETT, Dashiell. *Secret Agent X-9.* (Book One.) Philadelphia (1934). No dustwrapper. $2,000.

HAMMETT, Dashiell. *Secret Agent X-9.* (Book Two.) Philadelphia (1934). No dustwrapper. $1,500.

HAMMETT, Dashiell. *The Thin Man.* New York, 1934. No priority on dustwrapper color. $5,000. London, 1934. $1,500.

HAMMETT, Dashiell, and COLODNY, Robert. *The Battle of the Aleutians.* (San Francisco, 1944.) Blue wraps. $300.

HAMMOND, John Martin. *Colonial Mansions of Maryland and Delaware.* Philadelphia, 1914. 65 plates. $300.

HAMSUN, Knut. *Hunger.* London, 1899. Wraps. $350.

HANCOCK, H. Irving, and HIGASHI, K. *The Complete Kano Jiu Jitsu.* New York, 1926. $150.

HANCOCK, R. R. *Hancock's Diary: or, a History of the 2d Tennessee Confederate Cavalry.* Nashville, 1887. 2 plates. $600.

HAND Book of Monterey and Vicinity (The). Monterey, 1875. 152 pages, printed wraps. $300.

HAND-BOOK of Ness County, the Banner County of Western Kansas. Chicago, 1887. 36 pages, wraps. $250.

HANDLEY Cross: or, Mr. Jorrock's Hunt. London, 1853–54. (By Robert Smith Surtees.) 17 color plates and numerous woodcuts by John Leech. 17 parts in pictorial wraps. First illustrated edition. With all the ads and slips and with the words "with the aid of the illustrious Leech" in the preface. $2,500. London, 1854. Cloth. First illustrated hardbound edition. $400.

HANDLEY Cross; or, The Spa Hunt. London, 1843. 3 vols. Boards and cloth. (By Robert Smith Surtees.) $400.

HANDMADE Papers of the World. Tokyo, 1979. Large folio box containing 6 books and cases. Limited to 1,100 copies. $2,000.

HANDY, W. C. *Blues: An Anthology.* New York, 1926. Author's first book. Edited by Handy. $750.

HANFF, Helene. *84, Charing Cross Road.* New York, 1970. $150. London (1971). $200.

HANLEY, James. See Shone, Patric.

HANLEY, James. *Boy.* London, 1931. $300. One of 145 copies. $400. One of 15 signed copies. $750. New York, 1932. $250.

HANLEY, James. *Captain Bottell.* London, 1933. One of 99 signed copies. In dustwrapper. $400.

HANLEY, James. *Drift.* London, 1930. Author's first book. One of 10 signed copies. $1,000. Trade edition. One of 490 copies. $300.

HANLEY, James. *Men in Darkness.* London (1931). Preface by John Cowper Powys. One of 105 signed copies. $250.

HANNA, Charles A. *The Wilderness Trail . . .* New York, 1911. Maps and illustrations. 2 vols. One of 1,000 copies. $500.

HANNAH, Barry. *Geronimo Rex.* New York (1972). Author's first book. $250.

HANNOVER, Emil. *Pottery and Porcelain: A Handbook for Collectors.* London, 1925. 3 vols. Cloth. Issued without dustwrappers. $500.

HANSARD, Thomas C. *Treatises on Printing and Type-Founding.* Edinburgh, 1841. 3 foldout plates. $350.

HANSARD, Thomas C. *Typographia: An Historical Sketch of the Art of Printing . . .* London, 1825. $500.

HANSBERRY, Lorraine. *A Raisin in the Sun.* New York (1959). Author's first book. Wraps. $125. Cloth. First edition not stated. Photographs from the Broadway production. $350. London (1960). $100.

HARASZTHY, Agoston. *Grape Culture, Wines, and Wine-Making.* New York, 1862. Burgundy cloth with grape cluster on front cover. $2,500.

HARDIE, Martin. *English Coloured Books.* London (1906). $200.

HARDIN, John Wesley. *The Life of John Wesley Hardin.* Seguin, Tex., 1896. Portrait, other illustrations. 144 pages, printed wraps. First issue, with portrait of Hardin's brother mislabeled "John." $400. Second issue, with the Hardin portrait tipped in. $250.

HARDIN, Mrs. Philomelia Ann Maria Antoinette. *Everybody's Cook and Receipt Book.* (Cleveland, 1842.) $1,250.

HARDING, George L. *Don Augustin V. Zamorano: Statesman, Soldier, Craftsman, and California's First Printer.* Los Angeles, 1934. $300.

HARDWICK, Elizabeth. *The Ghostly Loves.* New York, 1945. Author's first book. $300.

HARDY, Frank. *Power Without Glory.* No place, 1950. $650.

HARDY, John. *A Collection of Sacred Hymns, Adapted to the Faith and Views of the Church of Jesus Christ of Latter Day Saints.* Boston, 1843. 160 pages, full calf. $4,500.

HARDY, Joseph. *A Picturesque and Descriptive Tour in the Mountains of the High Pyrenees.* London, 1825. Map, 24 hand-colored plates. $2,500.

HARDY, Thomas. See *Desperate Remedies; Under the Greenwood Tree.*

HARDY, Thomas. *A Changed Man.* London, 1913. Frontispiece and map. Green cloth. $200. New York, 1913. Blue cloth. $150.

HARDY, Thomas. *The Dynasts: A Drama of the Napoleonic Wars.* London, 1903–6–8. 3 vols. Green cloth. First issue, with 1903 on title page of vol. 1. $3,500. London, 1927. 3 vols. Portrait etching, signed by Francis Dodd. Half vellum. One of 525 copies signed by Hardy. In clear dustwrappers. In box. $1,750. Lacking dustwrappers. In box. $1,250.

HARDY, Thomas. *Far from the Madding Crowd.* New York, 1874 (published 11 days earlier than the U.K. edition). Cream cloth. $1,500. London, 1874. 2 vols. $2,500. Limited Editions Club, New York, 1958. Half leather. In slipcase. $200.

HARDY, Thomas. *The Hand of Ethelberta.* London, 1876. 11 illustrations by George Du Maurier. 2 vols. Red-brown cloth. $1,750. Green sand-grain cloth. $1,500. New York, 1876. Published simultaneously. $400.

HARDY, Thomas. *Human Shows: Far Phantasies; Songs and Trifles.* London, 1925. $350. New York (1925). $250.

HARDY, Thomas. *Jude the Obscure.* (London, 1896.) Green cloth. $600. New York, 1896. $350. Limited Editions Club, New York, 1969. In slipcase. $150.

HARDY, Thomas. *A Laodicean; or, The Castle of the De Stancys.* London, 1881. 3 vols. Slate-colored cloth. First issue, without the word "or" on half title of vol. 1. $2,000. Second issue, with the word "or" on half title of vol. 1. $1,000. New York: Henry Holt, 1881. First authorized U.S. edition. Wraps. (Preceded by unauthorized Harper edition in wraps.) $500.

HARDY, Thomas. *Late Lyrics and Earlier.* London, 1922. In dustwrapper. $350.

HARDY, Thomas. *Life's Little Ironies.* (London, 1894.) $350. New York, 1894. $150.

HARDY, Thomas. *The Mayor of Casterbridge.* London, 1886. 2 vols. Blue cloth. $6,000. New York, 1886. Wraps. First American edition. $1,000. Limited Editions Club, New York, 1964. Half morocco. In slipcase. $200.

HARDY, Thomas. *Moments of Vision and Miscellaneous Verses.* London, 1917. $250.

HARDY, Thomas. *A Pair of Blue Eyes.* London, 1873. 3 vols. First issue, in green cloth, with "c" dropped or missing from the word " clouds" in last line on page 5 of vol. 2. $8,500. Second issue, in blue cloth. $4,500.

HARDY, Thomas. *Poems of the Past and the Present.* (London, 1902.) White (cream) or dark-green cloth. $2,000.

HARDY, Thomas. *The Return of the Native.* London, 1878. 3 vols. Frontispiece map. Brown cloth. First binding, with double-rule border on back cover. First issue lacking single quote mark after "A Pair of Blue Eyes" on title page (Cutler & Stiles). $10,000. Second binding with 3-rule border. $8,500. New York, 1878. Cream-colored cloth. $500. London, 1929. Illustrated by Clare Leighton. Batik boards, vellum spine. One of 500 copies signed by the artist. In slipcase. $350. American issue. Buckram. One of 1,000 signed copies. $250.

HARDY, Thomas. *Tess of the D'Urbervilles.* (London, 1891.) 3 vols. Brownish-yellow cloth with gilt design on cover. With "Chapter XXV" for "Chapter XXXV" on page 199 of vol. 2. $10,000. (London, 1892.) Second issue or printing, with correction and dated 1892 on verso of title page. $1,750. New York, 1892. $500. London, 1926. 41 wood engravings by Vivien Gribble, folding map. Marbled boards, vellum spine. One of 325 signed copies. In dustwrapper. $1,500. Limited Editions Club, New York, 1956. One of 1,500 copies. $250.

HARDY, Thomas. *The Trumpet-Major.* London, 1880. 3 vols. Decorated red cloth. $10,000. New York, 1880. $400.

HARDY, Thomas. *Two on a Tower: A Romance.* London, 1882. 3 vols. Green cloth. $2,500. New York, 1882. Decorated yellow cloth. $500.

HARDY, Thomas. *Wessex Tales, Strange, Lively and Commonplace.* London, 1888. 2 vols. Green cloth. $2,500. New York/London, 1888. $500.

HARDY, Thomas. *The Woodlanders.* London, 1887. 3 vols. First binding in smooth dark-green buckram cloth with 2-rule border on back. First issue, with ad leaf at end of vol. 1. $2,750. Second binding, pebbled dark-green cloth with single-rule border on back and lacking ad leaf. $1,750.

HARE, Cyril. (Alfred Alexander Gordon Clark.) *Tenant for Death.* London, 1937. $750.

HARFORD, Henry. *Fan: The Story of a Young Girl's Life.* London, 1892. (By W. H. Hudson.) 3 vols. Sage-green cloth. $7,500.

HARGRAVE, Catherine Perry. *A History of Playing Cards* . . . Boston (1930). $600.

HARLAN, Jacob Wright. *California, '46 to '88.* San Francisco, 1888. Portrait frontispiece. $350.

HARLAN, Richard M. D. *Fauna Americana* . . . Philadelphia, 1825. $350.

HARLAN, Robert D. (editor). *Bibliography of the Grabhorn Press* . . . San Francisco, 1977. The third and final volume of the Grabhorn bibliography. One of 225 copies. $750.

COLLECTED BOOKS 297

HARLAND, John Whitfield. *The Printing Arts: An Epitome of the Theory* . . . London, 1892. 12 plates. $250.

HARLAND, Marion. *Alone.* Richmond, 1854. (By Marion Hawes Terhune.) Author's first book. $450.

HARLOW, Alvin F. *Old Towpaths.* New York, 1926. Illustrated. $150.

HARLOW, Neal. *The Maps of San Francisco Bay.* San Francisco: Grabhorn Press, 1950. Folio, half leather. One of 375 copies. In dustwrapper. $750.

HARMAN, S. W. *Hell on the Border.* Fort Smith, Ark. (1898). Portrait, map. Stiff printed green wraps. $1,750.

HARMON, Daniel Williams. *A Journal of Voyages and Travels in the Interiour of North America.* Andover, Mass., 1820. Portrait, folding map. First issue, with map placed opposite title page and with no errata slip. $1,500.

HAROLD the Dauntless. Edinburgh, 1817. (By Sir Walter Scott.) $250.

HARPEL, Oscar H. *Harpel's Typography or Book of Specimens* . . . Cincinnati, 1870. $2,250.

HARPER, Frances E. W. *Iola Leroy, or Shadows Uplifted.* Philadelphia, 1892. (Later printings had Boston imprinted.) $1,500.

HARPER, Frances E. W. *Miscellaneous Poems.* Philadelphia, 1854. Author's first book. $3,000.

HARRINGTON, James. *The Common-Wealth of Oceana.* London, 1656. $1,500.

HARRIS, Frank. *Elder Conklin and Other Stories.* New York, 1894. Author's first book. $150. London, 1895. $125.

HARRIS, Frank. *The Man Shakespeare and His Tragic Life Story.* London, 1909. Boards and vellum. One of 150 on large paper, signed. $250. Trade edition. Green cloth. $100.

HARRIS, Frank. *My Life and Loves.* Paris, 1922–27. 4 vols. Half cloth or wraps with limitations of 425 to 1,000 copies. $600.

HARRIS, Frank. *Oscar Wilde: His Life and Confessions.* New York, 1916. 2 vols. Japan-paper issue. In half morocco and slipcase. $300.

HARRIS, Henry. *California's Medical Story.* San Francisco: Grabhorn Press, 1932. Half morocco. One of 200 copies. $200.

HARRIS, Joel Chandler. See Davidson, James Wood.

HARRIS, Joel Chandler. *Daddy Jake the Runaway.* New York (1889). Pictorial cream-colored glazed boards. $1,000. London, 1890 (actually 1889). $500.

HARRIS, Joel Chandler. *Free Joe and Other Georgian Sketches.* New York, 1887. Pictorial red cloth. $300.

HARRIS, Joel Chandler. *Nights with Uncle Remus.* Boston, 1883. Pictorial gray cloth. $850.

HARRIS, Joel Chandler. *On the Plantation.* New York, 1892. Pictorial cloth. $350.

HARRIS, Joel Chandler. *Tales of the Home Folks in Peace and War.* Boston, 1898. $400.

HARRIS, Joel Chandler. *The Tar-Baby and Other Rhymes of Uncle Remus.* New York, 1904. $500.

HARRIS, Joel Chandler. *Uncle Remus and Brer Rabbit.* New York (1906). Oblong, pictorial boards. $750.

HARRIS, Joel Chandler. *Uncle Remus and His Legends of the Old Plantation.* London, 1881. Olive-green cloth. First English edition of *Uncle Remus: His Songs and His Sayings.* $1,000.

HARRIS, Joel Chandler. *Uncle Remus: His Songs and His Sayings.* New York, 1881. Author's first book. Illustrated by Frederick S. Church and James S. Moser. Various pictorial cloth colors. First issue/printing, with "presumptive" for "presumptuous" in last line, page 9, and with no mention of this book in ads at back. $2,500. Second issue/printing, with "presumptuous" in last line, page 9. $600. (For first English edition, see preceding entry.) New York, 1895. Illustrated by A. B. Frost. Vellum. One of 250 signed copies. $5,000. Trade edition. Red buckram. $450. Limited Editions Club, New York, 1957. Illustrated. Pictorial cloth. In slipcase. $150.

HARRIS, Joel Chandler. *Uncle Remus Returns.* Boston, 1918. In dustwrapper. $1,250. Without dustwrapper. $250.

HARRIS, Joseph. *A Treatise of Navigation.* London, 1730. 12 folding plates. $7,000.

HARRIS, Mark. *The Southpaw.* Indianapolis/New York (1953). First edition stated. $300.

HARRIS, Mark. *Trumpet to the World.* New York (1946). Author's first book. $150.

HARRIS, Mel. *Naked Hollywood.* New York (1953). Photographs by Weegee. $300.

HARRIS, Robert. *Fatherland.* London (1992). $350.

HARRIS, Robert. *Sixty Years of Golf.* London, 1953. $200.

HARRIS, Sarah Hollister. *An Unwritten Chapter of Salt Lake, 1851–1901.* New York, 1901. $750.

HARRIS, Thaddeus Mason. *The Journal of a Tour into the Territory Northwest of the Allegheny Mountains.* Boston, 1805. 4 maps (3 folding) and a folding plate. $1,500.

HARRIS, Thomas. *Black Sunday.* New York (1975). Author's first book. $350. London, 1975. $200.

HARRIS, Thomas M. *Assassination of Lincoln.* Boston (1892). Illustrated. Pictorial cloth. $300.

HARRIS, Captain W. Cornwallis. *Portraits of the Game and Wild Animals of Africa.* London, 1840. 30 hand-colored plates. Elephant folio. $15,000.

HARRIS, William Charles. *The Fishes of North America That Are Captured on Hook and Line.* New York, 1898. Vol. 1. (All published.) Illustrated. Folio, half leather. $3,000.

HARRIS, William R. *The Catholic Church in Utah.* Salt Lake City (1909). Map, 25 plates. Cloth. Also issued in 2 vols. $200.

HARRISON, Bill. *The Galactic Hero.* Garden City, 1965. $200.

HARRISON, E. J. *The Fighting Spirit of Japan.* New York, 1912. $200. London, 1913. Gilt mounted samurai on front. $200.

HARRISON, E. J. *The Thrilling, Startling and Wonderful Narrative of Lieutenant Harrison.* Cincinnati, 1848. Illustration in text. 30 pages, printed buff wraps. $2,500 or more.

HARRISON, Fairfax. *The Belair Stud 1747–1761.* Richmond, 1929. $300.

HARRISON, Jim. *Locations.* New York (1968). Cloth. $300. Wraps. $75.

HARRISON, Jim. *Outlyer and Ghazals.* New York (1971). $500. Wraps. $125.

HARRISON, Jim. *Plain Song.* New York (1965). Author's first book. Cloth. $500. Wraps. $150.

HARRISON, Jim. *Walking.* Cambridge, 1967. One of 26 signed copies. $2,000. One of 100 signed copies. $1,000.

HARROWER, Elizabeth. *Down in the City.* London, 1957. Author's first book. $500.

HART, George. *The Violin: Its Famous Makers and Their Imitators.* London, 1875. $300. Boston, 1884. $250.

HART, Joseph C. See *Miriam Coffin* . . .

HART, Joseph C. *The Romance of Yachting.* New York, 1848. $600.

HARTE, Bret. See *Outcroppings.*

HARTE, Bret. *Condensed Novels and Other Papers.* New York, 1867. Author's first book. Illustrated by Frank Bellew. Violet cloth. $350.

HARTE, Bret. *"Excelsior."* (Cover title.) Five Points, N.Y. (1877). 16 pages, oblong, blue wraps. First edition, first issue, with Donaldson imprint. $600. Later issue, without Donaldson imprint. $300. Also issued in cloth. $300.

HARTE, Bret. *Gabriel Conroy.* Hartford, 1876. First binding in mauve cloth. $250. London: Warne & Co. (1876). 3 vols. $600.

HARTE, Bret. *The Heathen Chinee.* (Chicago) 1870. First separate edition. 9 lithographed cards in envelope. $850.

HARTE, Bret. *The Lost Galleon and Other Tales.* San Francisco, 1867. $600.

HARTE, Bret. *The Luck of Roaring Camp and Other Sketches.* Boston, 1870. Without the story "Brown of Calaveras." $1,000. Boston, 1870. Second edition, with "Brown of Calaveras." $300. San Francisco, 1916. John Henry Nash printing. Half cloth. One of 260 copies. $250. San Francisco, 1948. Grabhorn Press. Folio, half cloth. One of 300. $175.

HARTE, Bret. *Mliss: An Idyl of Red Mountain.* New York (1873). Printed wraps. (Pirated edition of the story, which originally appeared in *The Luck of Roaring Camp.* Contains 50 additional chapters by R. G. Densmore.) First issue, with Harte's name on the title page and front cover. $1,250. Second issue, with Harte's name removed and with page 34 a cancel leaf. $600. San Francisco: Grabhorn Press, 1948. Half cloth. One of 300 copies. $200.

HARTE, Bret. *Poems.* Boston, 1871. With Fields, Osgood monogram on title page and "S.T.K." for "T.S.K." on page 136. $200.

HARTE, Bret. *The Queen of the Pirate Isle.* London (1886). 28 color illustrations by Kate Greenaway. Decorated cloth. First issue, bound in unbleached linen, with green endpapers, gilt edges. $500. Boston, 1887. $400.

HARTE, Bret. *San Francisco in 1866.* San Francisco: Grabhorn Press, 1951. One of 400 copies. Issued without dustwrapper. $150.

HARTE, Bret. *Tales of the Gold Rush.* Limited Editions Club, New York, 1944. In slipcase. $100.

HARTE, Bret. *The Wild West.* Paris: Harrison of Paris (1930). Hand-colored illustrations. Burlap. One of 36 copies on vellum. In slipcase. $500. One of 840 copies. In slipcase. $150.

HARTE, Bret, and TWAIN, Mark. *Sketches of the Sixties.* San Francisco, 1926. One of 250 copies. $350. Trade. $125.

HARTLEY, L. P. *Night Fears . . .* London, 1924. Author's first book. $1,500. New York, 1924. $750.

HARTLEY, L. P. *Simonetta Perkins.* London (1925). $300.

HARTLEY, L. P. *The Traveling Grave and Other Stories.* Sauk City, Wisc., 1948. $125.

HARTLEY, Marsden. *Adventures in the Arts.* New York (1921). Author's first book. $750.

HARTLEY, Marsden. *Twenty-five Poems.* (Paris, 1923.) Wraps. $1,000.

HARTMANN, Karl Robert Eduard von. *Philosophy of the Unconscious . . .* New York, 1884. 3 vols. 1st edition in English, American issue printed on British sheets. $300.

HARTSHORNE, Albert. *Old English Glasses.* London, 1897. Color frontispiece, plates, numerous drawings. Folio, vellum, and cloth. $350.

HARTWELL, Mary. *A Women in Armour.* New York, 1875. Author's first book. $300.

HARTZENBUSCH, Juan Eugenio. *The Lovers of Teruel.* Newtown, Wales: Gregynog Press, 1938. Translated by Henry Thomas. Morocco. One of 175 copies. $600. One of 20 copies specially bound in morocco by George Fisher. $2,250.

HARVARD Class Day 1910. (Cover title.) (Cambridge, Mass.) 1910. Illustrated. 17 leaves, stiff cream wraps, red cord ties. (Includes a class ode by T. S. Eliot, his first contribution to a book.) $5,000.

HARVARD Lyrics. Boston, 1899. (Includes "Vita Mea," the first published work of Wallace Stevens.) $1,500.

HARVEY, Henry. *History of the Shawnee Indians.* Cincinnati, 1855. First issue, without portrait and preface dated "Sept. 21." $350. With portrait and preface dated "Ninth month." $300.

HARVEY, William. *The Anatomical Exercises . . .* London, 1653. First edition in English. $13,000, $19,800 and $5,500 at auction in 1996, 1997, and 1998, respectively. London: Nonesuch Press (1928). Edited by Geoffrey Keynes. Drawing by Stephen Gooden. Full morocco. One of 1,450 copies. $400.

HASHEESH Eater (The). New York, 1857. (By Fitz-Hugh Ludlow.) Author's first book. $600.

HASKINS, C. W. *The Argonauts of California.* New York, 1890. $600.

HASS, Robert. *Field Guide.* New Haven, 1973. Author's first book. Cloth. $750. Wraps. $50.

HASSELL, James. *The Tour of the Grand Junction . . . Description of Middlesex, Hertfordshire.* London, 1819. $2,000.

HASTAIN, E. *Township Plats of the Creek Nation.* Muskogee, Okla., 1910. Full limp morocco. $500.

HASTINGS, Frank S. *A Ranchman's Recollections.* Chicago, 1921. In dustwrapper. $500. Without dustwrapper. $250.

HASTINGS, Lansford W. *The Emigrants' Guide, to Oregon and California.* Cincinnati, 1845. 152 pages, in original wraps, or printed boards. $52,000 at auction in 1993. A defective copy for $13,000 at auction in 1994.

HASTINGS, Lansford W. *A New Description of Oregon and California.* Cincinnati, 1849. Frontispiece. Wraps. $5,000.

HASTINGS, Sally. *Poems, on Different Subjects. To Which Is Added a Descriptive Account of a Family Tour to the West, in the Year 1800.* Lancaster, Pa., 1808. $1,000.

HASWELL, Anthony (editor). *Memoirs and Adventures of Capt. Matthew Phelps.* Bennington, Vt., 1802. $1,250.

HATCH, Benton L. *A Check List of the Publications of Thomas Bird Mosher of Portland, Maine.* Northampton, Mass.: Gehenna Press, 1966. One of 500 copies. In slipcase. $350.

HATFIELD, Edwin F. *History of Elizabeth, New Jersey.* New York, 1868. 8 plates. Morocco. $450.

HATTERAS, Owen. *Pistols for Two.* New York, 1917. Pink wraps. (By H. L. Mencken and George Jean Nathan.) $300.

HATTON, Thomas, and CLEAVER, Arthur H. *A Bibliography of the Periodical Works of Charles Dickens . . .* London, 1933. 250 large-paper copies. $500.

HAUKAL, Ibn. *The Oriental Geography of Ebn Haukal.* London, 1800. Folding map and frontispiece. $1,000.

HAULTAIN, Theodore Arnold. *Mystery of Golf.* Boston, 1908. One of 440 copies. $1,750. London, 1910. $400.

HAVEN, Charles T., and BELDEN, Frank A. *History of the Colt Revolver.* New York, 1940. In slipcase. $300. Morocco. Signed. In slipcase. $750.

HAWBUCK Grange; or, The Sporting Adventures of Thomas Scott, Esq. London, 1847. (By Robert Smith Surtees.) 8 illustrations by "Phiz." Blindstamped pictorial red cloth. With April ads. $450.

HAWES, William Post. *Sporting Scenes and Sundry Sketches.* New York, 1842. 2 vols. Edited by Frank Forester. Illustrated. Cloth. $350.

HAWKER, Peter. *Instructions to Young Sportsmen.* London, 1814. $1,000. London, 1816. Second edition. $1,000. London, 1824. Third edition. $1,000. Philadelphia, 1846. First American edition. $250.

HAWKER, The Reverend Robert S. *The Cornish Ballads and Other Poems.* London, 1869. Green cloth. $200.

HAWKER, The Reverend Robert S. *The Quest of the Sangraal: Chant the First.* Exeter, England, 1864. Cloth. Printed on vellum. $1,250.

HAWKES, J. C. B., Jr. *Fiasco Hall.* Cambridge, Mass., 1943. (By John Hawkes.) Author's first book. Wraps. $1,500.

HAWKES, John. *The Beetle Leg.* (New York, 1951.) First edition not stated. First issue in orange cloth. $250. Second issue in red cloth. $200.

HAWKES, John. *The Cannibal.* (Norfolk, Conn.): New Directions (1949). First edition not stated, first binding in gray cloth. $250. Second printing in rust cloth. $100. (London), 1962. $100.

HAWKES, John. *Lunar Landscapes.* (New York): New Directions (1969). First edition not stated. One of 150 signed copies. Issued without dustwrapper in slipcase. $250. Trade edition. $75.

HAWKES, John. *Second Skin.* (New York): New Directions (1964). First edition not stated. One of 100 signed copies. In slipcase. $250. Trade edition. $75. London, 1966. $75.

HAWKINS, Alfred. *Hawkins's Picture of Quebec; with Historical Recollections.* Quebec, 1834. 14 plates. $400.

HAWKINS, Rush C. *Titles of the First Books from the Earliest Presses . . .* New York, 1884. One of 300 copies. Two frontispieces and 25 plates. $350.

HAWKS of Hawk-Hollow (The). Philadelphia, 1835. (By Robert Montgomery Bird.) 2 vols. In original purple cloth, paper labels. $600.

HAWKSMOOR, Nicholas. *A Short Account of London Bridge . . .* London, 1736. 5 folding plates. $2,250.

HAWLEY, Walter A. *Oriental Rugs: Antique and Modern.* New York, 1913. 102 plates. $400. New York, 1922. $300.

HAWLEY, Zerah. *A Journal of a Tour Through Connecticut, Massachusetts, New York, etc.* New Haven, 1822. $1,500.

HAWTHORNE, Julian. *Bressant.* New York, 1873. Author's first book. $150.

HAWTHORNE, Nathaniel. See *Fanshawe; Peter Parley's Universal History; The Sister Years.*

HAWTHORNE, Nathaniel. *The Blithedale Romance.* London, 1852. 2 vols. $600. Boston, 1852. Tan cloth. First American edition, binding A (BAL 7611) with no ads at rear. $350. With 4 pages of ads dated April, 1852 at end. $300.

HAWTHORNE, Nathaniel. *The Celestial Rail-Road.* Boston: Wilder & Co. or James F. Fish, 1843. 32 pages, buff wraps. First edition and first separate printing. $5,000. (No priority established for two publishers.)

HAWTHORNE, Nathaniel. *Doctor Grimshawe's Secret.* Boston, 1883. Edited by Julian Hawthorne. Pictorial cloth. $250. Large-paper issue. One of 250 copies, some signed by the editor. $600.

HAWTHORNE, Nathaniel. *Famous Old People, Being the Second Epoch of Grandfather's Chair.* Boston, 1841. In original cloth, paper label. $850.

HAWTHORNE, Nathaniel. *The Gentle Boy: A Thrice-Told Tale.* Boston, 1839. Engraved frontispiece. In original wraps. $3,000.

HAWTHORNE, Nathaniel. *Grandfather's Chair: A History.* Boston, 1841. In original cloth, paper label. $1,000.

HAWTHORNE, Nathaniel. *The House of the Seven Gables.* Boston, 1851. Brown cloth. With the last letters ("t" and "h") of the last words in lines 1 and 2 on page 149 battered and not complete. $4,500. Second printing has page 149 corrected; "apparent" on page 50, line 25, with final "t"; and "or" complete on page 278, line 25. $1,250. The type worsens during the second printing to the point where the "t" in "apparent" (page 50, line 25) and the "r" in "or" disappear. They are not present in the third, fourth, and fifth printings. $600. All have 1851 on title page. Limited Editions Club, New York, 1935. In slipcase. $125.

HAWTHORNE, Nathaniel. *Liberty Tree, with the Last Word of Grandfather's Chair.* Boston, 1841. Cloth, paper label. With second line of page 24 ending "Meet in a Con-." $4,000 at auction in 1988. (Second printing had "Meet in Con-.")

HAWTHORNE, Nathaniel. *Life of Franklin Pierce.* Boston, 1852. Frontispiece. Printed wraps. $750. Cloth. $450.

HAWTHORNE, Nathaniel. *The Marble Faun; or The Romance of Monte Beni.* Boston, 1860. 2 vols. Brown cloth. With "Preface" preceding "Contents" and "for" versus "on" on page 225, line 22, in vol. 1. $750. Second printing with "Contents" preceding "Preface" and "on" versus "for." $450. Later printings had "Preface" first and "on" versus "for." (There were 7 printings with "1860" on the title page.)

HAWTHORNE, Nathaniel. *Mosses from an Old Manse.* New York, 1846. With "T.B. Smith . . . and R. Craighead's . . ." on copyright pages. 2 vols. Wraps. $4,000. 1-vol. issue; in cloth. $750.

HAWTHORNE, Nathaniel. *Our Old Home.* Boston, 1863. State 1: Various color cloths. Brown-coated endpapers. Page (399) has ad. $300. London, 1863. 2 vols. $750.

HAWTHORNE, Nathaniel. *Passages from the American Note-Books.* Boston, 1868. 2 vols. Green cloth. With spine reading "Ticknor & Co." (Later, "Fields, Osgood & Co.") $500. London, 1870. 2 vols. First English edition. $250.

HAWTHORNE, Nathaniel. *The Scarlet Letter.* Boston, 1850. Brown cloth. With "reduplicate" in line 20 of page 21; instead of "repudiate" and no preface. $10,000. Boston, 1850. Second edition with new preface by Hawthorne. $1,500. Third edition with "Hobart and Robbins" on copyright page instead of "Metcalf and Co." $750. New York: Grabhorn Press, 1908. One of 300 copies. In slipcase. $300. London, 1920. Illustrated by Hugh Thomson. $350. New York: Grabhorn Press, 1928. Colored woodblocks by Valenti Angelo. Half morocco. One of 980 copies. In dustwrapper. $350. Limited Editions Club, New York, 1941. Illustrated by Henry Varnum Poor. Leather. In slipcase. $250.

HAWTHORNE, Nathaniel. *The Snow-Image and Other Twice-Told Tales.* Boston, 1852. Brown cloth. $500. London, 1851. First English edition. (Issued simultaneously with American first edition, BAL suggests.) Titled *The Snow-Image, and Other Tales.*) $350.

HAWTHORNE, Nathaniel. *Tanglewood Tales, for Girls and Boys.* Boston, 1853. Decorated cloth. Without "George C. Rand" imprint on copyright page. $1,500. London, 1853. Green cloth. First edition (preceding the American edition by a few days). $1,250. London (1918). Illustrated by Edmund Dulac. Half vellum. One of 500 copies signed by Dulac. $1,500. Trade edition in cloth. $450.

HAWTHORNE, Nathaniel. *Transformation.* London, 1860. 3 vols. First English edition of *The Marble Faun.* Published one week earlier. $1,500.

HAWTHORNE, Nathaniel. *Twice-Told Tales.* Boston, 1837. Various cloth colors. $5,000. Limited Editions Club, New York, 1966. Colored illustrations by Valenti Angelo. Blue cloth. In slipcase. $175.

HAWTHORNE, Nathaniel. *A Wonder-Book for Girls and Boys.* Boston, 1852. First printing with "lifed" in line 3 of page 21, instead of "lifted." $2,500. (An "excellent" copy for $4,500 at auction in 1990.) Second printing (there were only two in 1852). Page 21 corrected. $750. London, 1852. 8 engravings. Decorated blue cloth. First English edition. $750. London, 1893. Illustrated by Walter Crane. Decorated cloth. $450. Cambridge, Mass., 1893. Crane illustrations. Vellum. One of 250 copies. $2,000. Ordinary issue, cloth. $350. London (1922). Illustrated by Arthur Rackham. White buckram. One of 600 copies signed by the artist. In slipcase. $1,750.

HAY, John. *Jim Bludso of the Prairie Bell, and Little Breeches.* Boston, 1871. Author's first book. Illustrated by S. Eytinge, Jr. 23 pages, printed orange wraps. $150.

HAY, John. *Letters of John Hay and Extracts from His Diary.* Washington, 1908. 3 vols. Cloth, paper labels. $350.

HAYAKAWA, S. I. *Language in Thought and Action.* Madison, 1939. Author's first book. Blue flexible wraps. $350.

HAYCOX, Ernest. *Brand Fires on the Ridge.* New York, 1929. $450.

HAYCOX, Ernest. *Bugles in the Afternoon.* Boston, 1944. $350.

HAYCOX, Ernest. *By Rope and Lead.* Boston, 1951. $200.

HAYCOX, Ernest. *Chaffee of Roaring Horse.* New York, 1930. $850.

HAYCOX, Ernest. *Free Grass.* New York, 1929. Author's first book. $600.

HAYCOX, Ernest. *Night Raid.* New York, 1929. $500.

HAYDEN, Ferdinand V. *Geological and Geographical Atlas of Colorado.* (Washington), 1877. 20 double-page maps, mostly colored. Three-quarter morocco. $1,750.

HAYDEN, Ferdinand V. *Sun Pictures of Rocky Mountain Scenery.* New York, 1870. 30 mounted photographs. Half morocco. $8,500.

HAYDEN, Ferdinand V. *The Yellowstone National Park.* Boston, 1876. 2 maps. Illustrated in color by Thomas Moran. Folio, half morocco portfolio. $125,000 at auction in 1998.

HAYMOND, Creed. *The Central Pacific Railroad.* San Francisco, 1888. $350.

HAYMOND, Henry. *History of Harrison County, West Virginia.* Morgantown, W. Va. (1910). $200.

HAYNE, Rev. Joseph E. *The Black Man; or, the Natural History of the Hametic Race.* Raleigh, 1894. $600.

HAYNE, Paul H. *Poems.* 1855. Author's first book. $600.

HAYNE, Paul H. *Sonnets . . .* Charleston, 1857. $500.

HAYWARD, John (compiler). *English Poetry: An Illustrated Catalogue of First and Early Editions . . .* Cambridge, 1950. Limited to 550 copies. In dustwrapper. $300.

HAYWARDE, Richard. *Prismatics.* New York, 1853. (By Frederick Swartwout Cozzens, his first book.) $150.

HAYWOOD, John. *The Civil and Political History of the State of Tennessee.* Knoxville, 1823. First edition, with tipped-in copyright slip and inserted printed slip. $2,500.

HAYWOOD, John. *The Natural and Aboriginal History of Tennessee.* Nashville, 1823. Leather. First edition, with errata leaf. $12,000 at auction in 1998.

HAZARD, Ebenezer. *Historical Collections . . .* Philadelphia, 1792–94. 2 vols. $600.

HAZEN, Gen. W. B. *A Narrative of Military Service.* Boston, 1885. Map, illustrations. $350.

HAZEN, Gen. W. B. *Our Barren Lands.* Cincinnati, 1875. 53 pages, printed blue wraps. $1,250.

HAZEN, Gen. W. B. *Some Corrections of "Life on the Plains."* (Cover title.) St. Paul, 1875. 18 pages, wraps. $1,000.

HAZLITT, William. *Characters of Shakespear's Plays.* London, 1817. $350.

HAZLITT. William. *Lectures on the English Poets.* London, 1818. First edition, with 4 pages of ads at end dated May 1, 1818, although some copies also have ads dated April 1818 at the beginning. $500.

HAZLITT, William. *Political Essays, with Sketches of Public Characters.* London, 1819. $500.

HEAD, Sir Francis B. *A Narrative.* London, 1839. Errata slip. Ads dated February 1839. $200.

HEADLONG Hall. London, 1816. (By Thomas Love Peacock.) $1,750.

HEADSMAN (The). London, 1833. (By James Fenimore Cooper.) 3 vols. In original tan boards, or rose-colored cloth. $400. Philadelphia, 1833. 2 vols. First American edition. In original blue boards. $650.

HEAL, Ambrose. *The Signboards of Old London Shops.* London, 1947. One of 250 large-paper copies. $250.

HEALY, Jeremiah. *Blunt Darts.* New York, 1984. Author's first book. $450.

HEANEY, Seamus. *Bog Poems.* One of 150 signed copies. $1,500.

HEANEY, Seamus. *Death of a Naturalist.* London (1966). $750. New York, 1966. (English sheets.) $500.

HEANEY, Seamus. *Door into the Dark.* London (1969). $600. New York, 1969. $450.

HEANEY, Seamus. *Eleven Poems.* Belfast (1965). Author's first book. First issue, laid paper, wraps, red-violet sun. $1,750. Second issue, wove paper, dark-maroon sun, $1,000. Third issue, gray paper in stiff green wraps. $600.

HEANEY, Seamus. *Field Work.* London, 1979. $400.

HEANEY, Seamus. *Hedgeschool.* Vermont, 1979. Color woodcuts by Claire Van Vliet. One of 285 copies signed by both author and artist. Wraps. $1,250.

HEANEY, Seamus. *New Selected Poems, 1966–1987.* London, (1980). One of 100 signed copies. In slipcase. $600.

HEANEY, Seamus. *Wintering Out.* London (1972). Wraps. $750. New York, 1973. $500.

HEAP, Gwin Harris. *Central Route to the Pacific.* Philadelphia, 1854. Folding map (not in all copies), 13 tinted plates. First edition, first issue, with plate IV lacking a plate or page number. $3,000. Another issue, without map. $1,000.

HEARN, Lafcadio. See Bisland, Elizabeth; Gautier, Theophile. See also *Historical Sketch-Book and Guide to New Orleans; La Cuisine Creole.*

HEARN, Lafcadio. *Chita: A Memory of Last Island.* New York, 1889. Salmon-colored cloth. $500.

HEARN, Lafcadio. *Editorials from the Kobe Chronicle.* (Cover title.) (New York, 1913.) Printed white wraps. One of 100 copies, with an addenda slip tipped in. $1,500.

HEARN, Lafcadio. *Gleanings in Buddha-Fields.* Boston, 1897. $350. New York, 1925. In dustwrapper and slipcase. $500.

HEARN, Lafcadio. *Glimpses of Unfamiliar Japan.* Boston, 1894. 2 vols. Black or olive cloth. $450.

HEARN, Lafcadio. *"Gombo Zhebes": Little Dictionary of Creole Proverbs.* New York, 1885. $1,000.

HEARN, Lafcadio. *In Ghostly Japan.* Boston, 1899. Illustrated. Pictorial blue cloth. $350.

HEARN, Lafcadio. *Japan: An Attempt at Interpretation.* New York, 1904. Colored frontispiece. Tan cloth. $300.

HEARN, Lafcadio. *Japanese Fairy Tales.* Tokyo (1898–1903). 5 vols. Wraps. *(The Boy Who Drew Cats, The Goblin Spider, The Old Woman Who Lost Her Dumpling, The Fountain of Youth, Chin Chin Kobakama.)* $3,500 for complete sets. It would be best to look these up in BAL to ascertain first or early printings. Philadelphia: Macrae-Smith Co. (1931). 5 vols. $1,500.

HEARN, Lafcadio. *Japanese Goblin Poetry.* Tokyo, Japan, 1934. One of 500 copies. Folio. 23 tipped-in facsimile reproductions. $1,000.

HEARN, Lafcadio. *A Japanese Miscellany.* Boston, 1901. Pictorial green cloth. Without "October 1901" on copyright page is the first (Perkins). $400. Although BAL states that the sequence is not determined. With "October 1901." $300.

HEARN, Lafcadio. *Kokoro.* Boston, 1896. $350.

HEARN, Lafcadio. *Kotto.* New York, 1902. Illustrated. Pictorial olive cloth. First state, with background of title page upside down, artist's monogram in upper right corner. $500. Second state. $200.

HEARN, Lafcadio. *Kwaidan.* Boston, 1904. Blue-green pictorial cloth. $500. Second printing in tan. $150. Limited Editions Club, New York, 1932. Color plates. Printed silk binding. In silk wraparound case. $350.

HEARN, Lafcadio. *Letters to a Pagan.* Detroit, 1933. One of 550 copies. $500.

HEARN, Lafcadio. *The Life and Letters of Lafcadio Hearn.* Boston, 1906. By Elizabeth Bisland. 200 copies with an original page of Hearn's manuscript tipped in. 2 vols. $3,500. Boston, 1906. 2 vols. Trade edition. $150.

HEARN, Lafcadio. *The Romance of the Milky Way.* Boston, 1905. With "Published October 1905" on copyright page. Gray cloth. $350. London, 1905. $350.

HEARN, Lafcadio. *Shadowings.* Boston, 1900. Pictorial blue cloth. $450.

HEARN, Lafcadio. *Some Chinese Ghosts.* Boston, 1887. Red cloth. $500. Various other colored cloths. $400.

HEARN, Lafcadio. *Stray Leaves from Strange Literature.* Boston, 1884. Author's first book. First issue: "JR O & Co" on spine. $850.

HEARN, Lafcadio. *Two Years in the French West Indies.* New York, 1890. $500.

HEARNE, Samuel. *A Journey from Prince of Wales's Fort in Hudson's Bay, to the Northern Ocean.* London, 1795. Five folding maps (one colored in outline), four engraved plates (three folding). $6,500.

HEARNE, Thomas. *Antiquities of Great Britain . . .* London, 1807. 2 vols. 51 plates. $1,500.

HEARON, Shelby. *At Home After 1840 . . .* Austin, 1966. Author's first book. One of 100 signed copies. $300. (Text by Hearon, drawings by Peggy Goldstein.) Regular edition, 1,000 copies. $75.

HEART, Capt. Jonathan. *Journal.* Albany, N.Y., 1885. Edited by C. W. Butterfield. 94 pages, tan printed wraps. One of 150 copies. $500.

HEARTMAN, Charles F. *The New-England Primer* . . . (New York), 1922. One of 265 copies. $300. New York, 1934. Cloth. One of 300 copies. $150.

HEARTMAN, Charles F., and CANNY, James R. *A Bibliography of the First Printings of Edgar Allan Poe.* Hattiesburg, Miss., 1940. $250.

HEBARD, Grace R. *Sacajawea.* Glendale, 1933. One of 750 copies. $650.

HEBARD, Grace R. *Washakie.* Cleveland, 1930. 7 maps, 16 plates. $300.

HEBARD, Grace R., and BRININSTOOL, E. A. *The Bozeman Trail.* Cleveland, 1922. Plates, 2 folding maps. 2 vols. Without dustwrapper. $850. Glendale, Calif., 1960. 2 vols. in 1. Issued without dustwrapper. $350.

HEBISON, W. C. *Early Days in Texas and Rains County.* Emory, Tex., 1917. 50 pages, wraps. $300.

HECHT, Anthony. *A Summoning of Stones.* New York (1954). Author's first book. $400.

HECHT, Ben. *The Bewitched Tailor.* New York, 1941. Drawing by George Grosz. 8 pages, printed wraps. One of 850 copies signed by author and artist. $600.

HECHT, Ben. *Erik Dorn.* New York, 1921. First issue, yellow lettering on cover. $500.

HECHT, Ben. *Fantazius Mallare.* Chicago, 1922. Illustrated by Wallace Smith. One of 2,000 copies. $200.

HECHT, Ben. *The Hero of Santa Maria.* New York (1920). Author's first book (with Kenneth Goodman). Wraps. $250.

HECHT, Ben. *A Jew in Love.* New York (1931). Cloth. One of 150 signed. In slipcase. $500. Trade edition; first issue, with exactly 34 lines on page 306, as in the signed edition (VAB). $300. Later issue, 32 lines. $250.

HECHT, Ben. *The Kingdom of Evil.* Chicago, 1924. One of 2,000 copies. $150.

HECHT, Ben. *A Thousand and One Afternoons in Chicago.* Chicago (1922). Illustrated. $500.

HECHT, Ben, and FOWLER, Gene. *The Great Magoo.* New York (1933). First binding in black cloth. $200. Second binding in green cloth. $175.

HECHT, Ben, and MACARTHUR, Charles. *The Front Page.* New York, 1928. $1,000.

HECKENDORN & WILSON. *Miners and Business Men's Directory.* (For Tuolumne, Calif.) Columbia, Calif., 1856. 104 pages, printed wraps. $3,500.

HECKETHORN, Charles William. *The Printers of Basle in the XV and XVI Centuries* . . . London, 1897. $400.

HECKEWELDER, John. *An Account of the History, Manners, and Customs of the Indian Nations.* Philadelphia, 1818. Calf. $250. Philadelphia, 1819. Second edition. $150.

HECKEWELDER, John. *A Narrative of the Mission of the United Brethren Among the Delaware and Mohegan Indians.* Philadelphia, 1820. Portrait and errata slip. $750. Cleveland, 1907. 3 maps, 5 plates. Three-quarter leather. One of 160 copies on large paper. $600.

HEGAN, Alice Caldwell. *Mrs. Wiggs of the Cabbage Patch.* New York, 1901. First issue, with gold sky on cover. Author's first book. $200.

HEGGAN, Thomas. *Mister Roberts.* Boston, 1946. $450. London, 1948. $200.

HEINLEIN, Robert A. *Assignment in Eternity.* Reading, Pa. (1953). One of 500 copies signed on tipped-in page. $750. Trade. First binding: brick-red cloth, gilt lettering. "Heinlein" 3 mm high on spine. $500. Second binding: green boards, spine lettered in black. $300. Third binding: red cloth. "Heinlein" 2 mm high on spine (and other variants). $200. London (1955). $250.

HEINLEIN, Robert A. *Beyond This Horizon.* Reading, Pa., 1948. One of 500 signed copies. Brick-red cloth. $1,750. Trade. Brick-red cloth or medium-blue cloth. Priority unknown. Variant blue dustwrapper is a later dustwrapper. $600.

HEINLEIN, Robert A. *The Discovery of the Future.* (Cover title.) (Los Angeles, 1941.) Wraps. "Limited First Edition (200)" on front wrapper. Printed in green ink. $2,000. Adds "Reprint (100)" under original limitation. Peach-colored front cover. 18 pages, including covers. $750.

HEINLEIN, Robert A. *Double Star.* Garden City, 1956. Published at $2.95. $1,750. London (1958). $300.

HEINLEIN, Robert A. *The Green Hills of Earth.* Chicago (1951). Signed on tipped-in page. $1,250. Trade. $750. London, 1954. $300.

HEINLEIN, Robert A. *The Man Who Sold the Moon.* Chicago (1950). Signed on tipped-in page. $1,000. Trade. $500. London (1953). $250.

HEINLEIN, Robert A. *Revolt in 2100.* Chicago (1953). Signed on tipped-in page. $1,000. Trade. $500. London (1964). $150.

HEINLEIN, Robert A. *Rocket Ship Galileo.* New York (1947). Publisher's seal on copyright page. Published at $2.00. $1,500.

HEINLEIN, Robert A. *Starman Jones.* New York (1953). Publisher's seal on copyright page. Published at $2.50. $450. London (1954). $250.

HEINLEIN, Robert A. *Starship Troopers.* New York (1959). $1,500. (London, 1961.) $300.

HEINLEIN, Robert A. *Stranger in a Strange Land.* New York (1961). "C22" on page 408. Dustwrapper priced $4.50. $3,000. London, 1965. $400.

HEINS, Henry Hardy. *A Golden Anniversary Bibliography of Edgar Rice Burroughs.* West Kingston, R.I., 1964. Complete edition, revised. $500.

HELD, John Jr. *I'm the Happiest Girl in the World.* New York (1935). $250.

HELEN'S Babies . . . By Their Latest Victim. Boston, 1876.(By John Habberton.) Author's first book. Wraps. First issue measures 1³⁄₁₆ inches thick. $350.

HELFORTH, John. *Nights.* (Dijon, France, 1955.) Printed wraps. (By Hilda Doolittle.) One of 100 copies. $1,000.

HELLER, Elinor, and MAGEE, David. *Bibliography of the Grabhorn Press, 1915–1940.* San Francisco, 1940. Illustrated. Full leather. One of 210 specially bound copies. $850. See also Dorothy and David Magee entry for a related work.

HELLER, Joseph. *Catch-22.* New York, 1961. Author's first book. Dustwrapper priced "$5.95." $2,500. London (1962). First-issue dustwrapper with blurb about book on back. $450. With comments of other authors. $250.

HELLMAN, Lillian. *The Children's Hour.* New York, 1934. Author's first book. $750.

HELMS, Mary S. *Scraps of Early Texas History.* Austin, 1884. $600.

HELPER, Hinton R. *The Land of Gold.* Baltimore, 1855. $450.

HELPRIN, Mark. *A Dove of the East . . .* New York, 1975. Author's first book. $250. London, 1976. $100.

HEMANS, Felicia. *Poems.* Liverpool, 1808. Author's first book. $250.

HEMENWAY, Charles. *Memoirs of My Day In and Out of Mormondom.* Salt Lake City, 1887. $200.

HEMINGWAY, Ernest. See Bahr, Jerome; Faulkner, William, *Salmagundi;* North, Joseph; Paul, Elliot. See also *Kiki's Memoirs; Somebody Had to Do Something; Senior Tabula.*

HEMINGWAY, Ernest. *Across the River and into the Trees.* London (1950). Precedes American edition by 3 days. $400. New York, 1950. First issue of dustwrapper with yellow lettering on spine. $600. Second issue of dustwrapper with orange lettering on spine. $400.

HEMINGWAY, Ernest. *Death in the Afternoon.* New York, 1932. $4,000. London (1932). $1,000.

HEMINGWAY, Ernest. *A Farewell to Arms.* New York, 1929. One of 510 signed copies. In slipcase. $15,000. Trade. Contains publisher's seal on copyright page. No disclaimer on page [x] ("None of these characters . . ."). $4,500. Second printing with disclaimer. $1,000. London (1929). Page 66, line 28 "seriosu." $1,250.

HEMINGWAY, Ernest. *The Fifth Column and the First Forty-nine Stories.* New York, 1938. $2,500. London (1939). $1,000.

HEMINGWAY, Ernest. *For Whom the Bell Tolls.* New York, 1940. Photographer's name missing from back panel of dustwrapper. $1,500. Photographer's name on back panel. $500. London (1941). $750. Limited Editions Club, Princeton, 1942. One of 15 copies for presentation by the author. (Not signed.) $2,000. One of 1,500 copies signed by Lynd Ward, the illustrator. In slipcase. $400.

HEMINGWAY, Ernest. *God Rest You Merry Gentlemen.* New York, 1933. One of 300 copies. $1,250.

HEMINGWAY, Ernest. *Green Hills of Africa.* New York, 1935. (Price assumes book without usual fading/discoloration of spine.) $2,500. London (1936). $1,000.

HEMINGWAY, Ernest. *In Our Time.* Paris: Three Mountains Press, 1924. One of 170 copies. $25,000. New York, 1925. $10,000. London, 1926. $3,500. New York, 1930. $1,000.

HEMINGWAY, Ernest. *Introduction to Kiki of Montparnasse.* (Cover title.) New York, 1929. Wraps. 8 pages with front cover as title. One of 25 copies. $4,500. Paris, 1930. Stiff wraps with wraparound band. Issued with glassine dustwrapper and unprinted, carboard mailing slipcase. $500.

HEMINGWAY, Ernest. *Men Without Women.* New York, 1927. First issue weighs about 15½ ounces. In dustwrapper without blurbs on orange bands on front. $10,000. Second issue weighing about 15 ounces. $5,000. Second printing weighing 13 to 14 ounces. Dustwrapper has reviews on front panel and publisher comments on front flap. $1,500. London (1928). Slight textual changes. $1,500.

HEMINGWAY, Ernest. *The Old Man and the Sea.* New York, 1952. 30 sets of sheets bound for presentation in black buckram. $16,500. Trade. Deep-blue ink in Hemingway photograph changed to olive in later states of the dustwrapper. $2,000. London (1952). First dustwrapper not printed on both sides. $750. Limited Editions Club (New York, 1990). One of 600 copies signed by Alfred Eisenstaedt. In slipcase. $2,000.

HEMINGWAY, Ernest. *The Spanish Earth.* Cleveland, 1938. Pictorial endpapers showing F.A.I. banner. $2,500. Plain endpapers. $750.

HEMINGWAY, Ernest. *The Sun Also Rises.* New York, 1926. Publisher's seal on copyright page. Page 181, line 26 "stoppped" vs. "stopped." Dustwrapper error, "In Our Times" vs. "Time." $35,000. Errors corrected. $7,500.

HEMINGWAY, Ernest. *Three Stories & Ten Poems.* (Paris, 1923.) Author's first book. Wraps. $35,000. [Broomfield Hills, 1977.] One of 3,000 facsimile copies. $250.

HEMINGWAY, Ernest. *The Torrents of Spring.* New York, 1926. $12,500. Paris, 1932. Large-paper edition (7½ by 5⅝ inches and priced at 125 francs). Wraps. $750. Small paper edition (6¹⁄₁₆ by 4¾ inches and priced 10 francs). $300. London (1933). $1,250.

HENDERSON, Elliot Blaine. *Plantation Echoes.* Columbus, 1904. Author's first book. $300.

HENDERSON, George Wylie. *Ollie Miss.* New York, 1935. Author's first book. $350. London (1935). $250.

HENDERSON, Ian, and STIRPIK, David I. *Golf in the Making.* England, 1979. One of 300 signed copies. $350. Trade. $100.

HENDERSON, Lauren. *Dead White Female.* (London, 1955.) $600.

HENDERSON, Robert W. *Early American Sport: A Chronological Check-List.* Grolier Club. New York, 1937. One of 400 copies. $250.

HENDERSON, Zenna. *The People: No Different Flesh.* London, 1966. $450. Garden City, 1967. $350.

HENDERSON, Zenna. *Pilgrimage.* Garden City, 1961. Author's first book. $500.

HENDRYX, James B. *Connie Morgan in Alaska.* New York, 1916. $200.

HENDRYX, James B. *Gun Brand.* New York, 1917. $200.

HENDRYX, James B. *Promise.* New York, 1915. $250.

HENDRYX, James B. *Texan*. New York, 1918. $175.

HENDY, James, M.D. *A Treatise on the Glandular Disease of Barbados* . . . London, 1784. 2 folding plates. $2,500.

HENLEY, William Ernest. *A Book of Verses*. London, 1888. Author's first book. Stiff printed wraps. One of 20 large-paper signed copies. $850. One of 75 large-paper copies. $600. Regular edition in stiff wraps. $250.

HENLEY, William Ernest. *London Types*. London, 1898. 12 colored illustrations by William Nicholson. Half vellum. $1,250. Half cloth or pictorial boards. $850.

HENNEPIN, Father Louis. *A Description of Louisiana*. New York, 1880. Translated by John G. Shea. One of 250 copies. $350.

HENRIETTA Temple: A Love Story. London, 1837. (By Benjamin Disraeli.) 3 vols. $1,250. Philadelphia, 1837. $250.

HENRY, Alexander. *Travels and Adventures in Canada and the Indian Territories*. New York, 1809. First issue, without the portrait by Maverick. $1,000. Second issue, with portrait. $1,500. Boston, 1901. Cloth. One of 700 copies. $300.

HENRY, Edward Richard. *Classification and Use of Fingerprints*. London, 1900. 11 plates, 3 folding. $450.

HENRY, John Joseph. *An Accurate and Interesting Account of the Hardships and Sufferings of That Band of Heroes, Who Traversed the Wilderness in the Campaign Against Quebec in 1775*. Lancaster, Pa., 1812. $600.

HENRY, John Joseph. *Campaign Against Quebec*. Watertown, N.Y., 1844. Sheep. Revised edition of *An Accurate and Interesting Account* . . . $500.

HENRY, O. *Cabbages and Kings*. New York, 1904. Pictorial cloth. (By William Sidney Porter.) Author's first book. First issue, with "McClure, Phillips & Co." on spine. $400.

HENRY, O. *The Four Million*. New York, 1906. (By William Sidney Porter.) $300.

HENRY, O. *The Gentle Grafter*. New York, 1908. (By William Sidney Porter.) $200.

HENRY, O. *Heart of the West*. New York, 1907. (By William Sidney Porter.) $175.

HENRY, O. *The Hiding of Black Bill*. New York (about 1913?). (By William Sidney Porter.) Pictorial wraps. $500.

HENRY, O. *Roads of Destiny*. New York, 1909. (By William Sidney Porter.) First state, with "h" missing in line 6 on page 9. $150.

HENRY, O. *The Voice of the City*. New York, 1908. (By William Sidney Porter.) First binding, with McClure imprint on spine. $200. Limited Editions Club, New York, 1935. Signed by illustrator George Grosz. Buckram. In slipcase. $750.

HENRY, O. *Waifs and Strays: 12 Stories*. Garden City, 1917. (By William Sidney Porter.) One of 200. $300.

HENRY, Samuel. *A New and Complete American Medical Family Herbal.* New York, 1814. $1,250.

HENRY, Samuel J. *Foxhunting Is Different.* New York: Derrydale Press (1938). Pictorial cloth. One of 950 copies. $250.

HENRY, Will. *Fourth Horseman.* New York, 1954. $200.

HENRY, Will. *I Tom Horn.* Philadelphia, 1975. $400.

HENRY, Will. *No Survivors.* New York, 1950. (By Henry Allen.) Author's first book. $500.

HENSON, Matthew A. *A Negro Explorer at the North Pole.* New York (1912). $1,500.

HENTY, G. A. *All But Lost.* London, 1869. 3 vols. $3,500.

HENTY, G. A. *By Conduct and Courage.* New York, 1904. $200. London, 1905. $200.

HENTY, G. A. *A Jacobite Exile.* New York, 1893. $250. London, 1894. $250.

HENTY, G. A. *A March on London.* London, 1898 (1897). 8 plates. $400. New York (1897). $150.

HENTY, G. A. *The March to Magdala.* London, 1868. $1,500.

HENTY, G. A. *The Queen's Cup.* London, 1897. 3 vols. With ads dated Nov. 1896. $2,000.

HENTY, G. A. *Rujub, the Juggler . . .* London, 1893. 3 vols. $3,000.

HENTY, G. A. *A Search for a Secret.* London, 1867. 3 vols. Author's first book. $6,000.

HENTY, G. A. *The Tiger of Mysore.* London, 1896 (actually 1895). Map, 12 plates. $500. New York, 1895. $125.

HENTY, G. A., et al. *Brains and Bravery.* London, 1903. 8 plates by Arthur Rackham. $750.

HEPPLEWHITE, Alice. *The Cabinet-Maker and Upholsterer's Guide . . .* London, 1788. With 127 (one folding) plates. $12,500. London, 1789. Second edition. $10,000. London, 1794. Third edition. 127 plates, about a quarter of which were changed. $4,000.

HERBERT, Sir A. P. *Poor Poems and Rotten Rhymes.* Winchester, England. 1910. Author's first book. Wraps. $300.

HERBERT, Edward, Lord. *The Autobiography of Edward, Lord Herbert of Cherbury.* Newtown, Wales: Gregynog Press, 1928. Wood engravings by H. W. Bray. Folio, buckram. One of 300 copies. $750. One of 25 copies specially bound in morocco. $2,500.

HERBERT, Frank. *The Dragon in the Sea.* Garden City, 1956. $450. London, 1960. $125.

HERBERT, Frank. *Dune.* Philadelphia (1965). $7,500. First edition stated, but also states that the book is published in Canada by Ambassador (later Thomas Nelson) and does not have an ISBN number (added later). London, 1966. $500.

HERBERT, Frank. *Survival and the Atom.* (Santa Rosa, 1950). Author's first book. Wraps. An offprint. $500.

HERBERT, George. *Poems.* Newtown, Wales: Gregynog Press, 1923. Illustrated. Marbled boards and cloth. One of 300 copies. $350. One of 43 copies specially bound in morocco. $2,500.

HERBERT, Henry William. See Forester, Frank; Hawes, William Post. See also *The Brothers; Cromwell.*

HERBERT, Henry William. *The Quorndon Hounds.* Philadelphia, 1852. Frontispiece, 3 plates. $500.

HERBERT, Henry William. *The Warwick Woodlands.* Philadelphia, 1845. Wraps. $1,500. Rebound. $600. New York, 1934. One of 250 copies. Hand-colored frontis and title page, plus 6 plates. $300.

HERBERT, J. A. *Illuminated Manuscripts.* London, 1911. Color frontispiece, 50 other plates. $125.

HERBERT, James. *The Fog.* (London, 1975.) $350.

HERBERT, James. *The Rats.* (London, 1974.) Author's first book. $500.

HERBERT, Xavier. *Capricornia.* Sydney, 1938. Author's first book. One of 150 copies. $1,250. Trade. $750. New York, 1974. $100.

HERBST, Josephine. *Nothing Is Sacred.* New York, 1928. Author's first book. $250.

HERDMAN, William. *Picturesque Views in Liverpool.* Liverpool, 1864. 28 plates. $1,250.

HERFORD, Oliver. *Artful Anticks.* New York, 1888. Author's first book. $200.

HERGESHEIMER, Joseph. *Berlin.* New York, 1932. One of 125 signed copies. In slipcase. $200.

HERGESHEIMER, Joseph. *The Lay Anthony.* New York, 1914. Author's first book. $100.

HERGESHEIMER, Joseph. *The Limestone Tree.* New York, 1931. One of 225 signed copies. In dustwrapper. In slipcase. $150. One of 75 signed copies on Japan vellum. $250.

HERIOT, George. *Travels Through the Canadas . . .* London, 1807. 27 plates, folding colored map. $4,000.

HERMAN, William. *The Dance of Death: Author's Copy.* (San Francisco, 1877.) Brown or green cloth. (By Ambrose Bierce and Thomas A. Harcourt.) $1,000. San Francisco, 1877. Red or blue cloth. Second edition, with dated title page. $300.

HERNDON, William H., and WEIK, Jesse W. *Herndon's Lincoln: The True Story of a Great Life.* Chicago (1889). 3 vols. 63 plates, blue cloth. $1,250. Chicago, 1890. 3 vols. Second edition. $300.

HERR, Michael. *Dispatches.* New York, 1977. Author's first book. $250. London (1978). Wraps. $75.

HERRICK, Robert. *One Hundred and Eleven Poems.* London: Golden Cockerel Press, 1955. Illustrated by W. Russell Flint. Sheep. One of 105 copies issued with 8 extra plates signed by Flint. In slipcase. $1,500. Cloth, parchment spine. One of 445 copies. In slipcase. $750.

HERRICK, Robert. *Poems.* (London) Kelmscott Press (1895). Woodcut title page. Vellum. One of 250 copies. $1,750. One of 8 copies on vellum. $7,500.

HERRICK, Robert. *Selections from the Poetry of Robert Herrick.* New York, 1882. $250.

HERRING, Richard. *Paper & Paper Making, Ancient and Modern.* London, 1856. 30 specimens of paper. 24 pages of publisher's ads. $750.

HERRING, Richard. *A Practical Guide to the Varieties and Relative Values of Paper . . .* London, 1860. 230 specimens of paper bound in at end. $2,000.

HERSEY, John. *Hiroshima.* New York, 1946. Offprint from *New Yorker.* Wraps. $200. New York, 1948. $150. Limited Editions Club, New York, 1983. One of 1,500 copies. $750.

HERSEY, John. *Men on Bataan.* New York, 1942. Author's first book. $300.

HESSE, Herman. *Demian.* New York, 1923. $1,000.

HESSE, Herman. *In Sight of Chaos.* Zurich, 1923. Issued without dustwrapper. $750.

HESSE, Herman. *Steppenwolf.* London (1929). First English edition. $1,750. New York (1929). $1,000. Limited Editions Club, Westport, Ct., 1977. $150.

HEWATT, Alexander. *Historical Account of the Rise and Progress of the Colonies of South Carolina and Georgia . . .* London, 1779. 2 vols. $3,500.

HEWITSON, William. *Illustrations of New Species of Exotic Butterflies.* London (1856)–76. 5 vols. 300 plates. Half morocco. $6,500.

HEWITT, Edward R. *Secrets of the Salmon.* New York, 1922. One of 780 copies. In dustwrapper. $600.

HEWITT, Graily. *Lettering for Students and Craftsmen.* London, 1930. Illustrated. White buckram. One of 380 signed copies. Issued without dustwrapper. $500.

HEWITT, Graily. *The Pen & Type-Design.* London, 1928. One of 250 copies. $350.

HEWITT, Randall H. *Across the Plains and Over the Divide.* New York (1906). Folding map, portrait, 58 plates (copy noted in 1997 auction with 59 plates). Pictorial cloth. $750.

HEWITT, Randall H. *Notes by the Way: Memoranda of a Journey Across the Plains, from Dundee, Ill., to Olympia, W. T. May 7 to November 3, 1862.* Olympia, Wash., 1863. 58 pages, printed wraps. $5,000. New York, 1906. $400.

HEWITT, Robert. *Coffee: Its History, Cultivation and Uses.* New York, 1872. Color frontispiece, several illustrations, and a large hand-colored 5-section folding map. $250.

HEWLETT, Maurice. *The Song of the Plow.* London (1916). One of 100 signed copies. In dustwrapper. In slipcase. $125.

HEYER, Georgette. *The Black Moth.* Boston, 1921. Author's first book. $750.

HEYER, Georgette. *Death in the Stocks.* London, 1935. $1,000.

HEYER, Georgette. *Footsteps in the Dark.* London (1932). First mystery. $1,250.

HEYERDAHL, Thor. *The Kon-Tiki Expedition.* London, 1950. One of 350 signed copies. $750.

HEYWARD, Du Bose. See Gershwin, George.

HEYWARD, Du Bose. *Brass Ankle.* New York (1931). One of 100 signed copies. In slipcase. $250. Trade edition. $75.

HEYWARD, Du Bose. *The Half Pint Flask.* New York, 1929. One of 175 signed copies. In dustwrapper. $175.

HEYWARD, Du Bose. *Porgy.* New York (1925). First printing in dark-brown cloth with Doran logo on copyright page. $1,000.

HEYWARD, Du Bose. *Skylines and Horizons.* New York, 1924. Author's first book. $200.

HEYWARD, Du Bose and Dorothy. *Porgy: A Play in Four Acts.* Garden City, 1927. $1,000.

HIAASEN, Carl. See Shulman, Neil.

HIAASEN, Carl. *Tourist Season.* New York, 1986. First solely authored title. $300.

HIAASEN, Carl, and MONTALBANO, William. *Powder Burn.* New York, 1981. $600.

HIBBERT, Thomas, and BUIST, Robert. *The American Flower Garden Directory.* Philadelphia, 1832. Color frontispiece. $400.

HICKMAN, William. *Brigham's Destroying Angel* . . . New York, 1872. Pictorial cloth. $450.

HIGBEE, Elias, and THOMPSON, R. B. *The Petition of the Latter-Day Saints.* Washington, 1840. 13 pages, sewn. $600.

HIGGINS, F. R. *Arable Holdings: Poems.* Dublin: Cuala Press, 1933. Boards and linen. One of 300 copies. In tissue dustwrapper. $250.

HIGGINS, Godfrey. *Anacalypsis, an Attempt to Draw Aside the Veil of the Saitic Isis.* London, 1836. 2 vols. 6 engraved plates. With errata slip. $750.

HIGHSMITH, Patricia. *The Blunderer.* New York, 1954. $600. London, 1956. $350.

HIGHSMITH, Patricia. *Strangers on a Train.* New York, 1950. Author's first book. $3,500. London, 1950. $1,500.

HIGHSMITH, Patricia. *The Talented Mr. Ripley.* New York, 1955. $1,500. London, 1957. $1,000.

HIJUELOS, Oscar. *Our House in the Last World.* New York (1983). $250.

HILDEBRAND, Samuel S. *Autobiography of Samuel S. Hildebrand, the Renowned Missouri "Bushwacker"* . . . Jefferson City, Missouri, 1870. $350.

HILDRETH, Richard. See *The Slave.*

HILDRETH, Richard. *The History of Banks.* Boston, 1837. $300.

HILDRETH, Samuel P. *Biographical and Historical Memoirs of the Early Pioneer Settlers of Ohio.* Cincinnati, 1852. 6 plates. $300.

HILDRETH, Samuel P. *Genealogical and Biographical Sketches of the Hildreth Family.* Marietta, Ohio, 1840. $300.

HILDRETH, Samuel P. *Memoirs of the Early Pioneer Settlers of Ohio.* Cincinnati, 1854. Leather. Later reprint of *Biographical and Historical Memoirs.* $200.

HILDRETH, Samuel P. *Pioneer History.* Cincinnati, 1848. Folding map, 8 plates. Half leather. $1,000.

HILL, Geoffrey. *Collected Poems.* (London, 1959.) One of 100 signed copies. In slipcase. $350.

HILL, Geoffrey. *For the Unfallen.* London, 1959. $400.

HILL, Geoffrey. *Mercian Hymns.* London (1971). $750. Wraps. $150.

HILL, Geoffrey. *(Poems).* Swinford, 1952. Author's first book. The Fantasy Poets—Number Eleven. Wraps. $600.

HILL, John, M.D. *The British Herbal . . .* Gray's-Inn, 1756. Frontispiece and 75 copper plates. $2,000.

HILL, Reginald. *A Clubable Woman.* London (1970). Author's first book. $1,500.

HILL, Reginald. *Fell of Dark.* London (1971). $750.

HILL, Rowland. *Post Office Reform . . .* London, 1837. $4,000.

HILL, William Henry, and others. *Antonio Stradivari: His Life and Work.* London, 1902. Morocco. One of 100 copies. $2,000. London, 1909. Half vellum. $1,000.

HILL, William Henry, et al. *The Violin-Makers of the Guarnieri Family.* London, 1931. Plates. Half vellum. Issued without dustwrapper. $1,250.

HILL, Wilson, and CHAMBERS, Robert. *The Land of Burns: A Series of Landscapes . . .* Glasgow, 1840. 2 vols. 81 engraved plates and titles. $350.

HILLARD, Reverend Elias Brewster. *Last Men of the Revolution (The).* Hartford, 1864. Original pebbled cloth over boards, leather spine and tips. $1,500.

HILLERMAN, Tony. *The Blessing Way.* New York, 1970. Author's first book. States "First Edition" on all early printings. First has "70 71 . . . 3 2 1" on last blank page. $2,000. (London, 1970.) $500. New York, 1989. One of 26 signed, lettered copies. In slipcase. $350. One of 100 signed copies. In slipcase. $150.

HILLERMAN, Tony. *The Boy Who Made Dragonfly.* New York (1972). $750.

HILLERMAN, Tony. *The Dance Hall of the Dead.* New York, 1973. $1,500. New York, 1991. One of 26 signed, lettered copies. In slipcase. $350. One of 100 signed copies. In slipcase. $150.

HILLERMAN, Tony. *The Fly on the Wall.* New York, 1971. $1,500.

HILLERMAN, Tony. *The Great Taos Bank Robbery.* Albuquerque (1973). $500.

HILLS, Sir John. *Points of a Racehorse.* London, 1903. Illustrated. Folio. $500.

HILLS, John Waller. *A History of Fly-Fishing for Trout.* London, 1921. One of 50 copies. Issued without dustwrapper. $450.

HILLS, John Waller. *A Summer on the Test.* London (1924). 12 plates by N. Wilkinson. One of 300 signed copies. Issued without dustwrapper. $1,000. One of 25 copies, with plates signed by the artist. $2,500.

HILLYER, Robert. *Sonnets and Other Lyrics.* Cambridge, Mass., 1917. Author's first book. $100.

HILTON, Conrad. *Inspirations of an Innkeeper.* (Los Angeles, 1963.) One of 312 signed copies. $300.

HILTON, Harold H. *My Golfing Reminiscenses.* London, 1907. $400.

HILTON, Harold H., and SMITH, Garden C. *Royal and Ancient Game of Golf.* London, 1912. One of 100 copies. $8,000 at auction in 1998. One of 900 copies. $2,000.

HILTON, James. See Trevor, Glen.

HILTON, James. *Catherine Herself.* London (1920). Author's first book. In dustwrapper. $1,250. London, 1935. Second edition. With new preface. $300.

HILTON, James. *Good-bye, Mr. Chips.* Boston, 1934. $500. London, 1934. $600.

HILTON, James. *Lost Horizon.* London, 1933. $4,000. New York, 1933. $3,000.

HIMES, Chester B. *Cotton Comes to Harlem.* New York (1965). $300. London (1966). $175.

HIMES, Chester B. *If He Hollers Let Him Go.* New York, 1947. Author's first book. $750. London, 1947. $200.

HIMES, Chester. *Pinktoes.* Olympia Press. Paris (1961). Wraps. "Printed in July 1961" on back page. $300. New York (1965) $150. London, 1965. $75.

HIMSELF. See *Sheppard Lee.*

HIND and the Panther . . . (The). London, 1687. (By Matthew Piror and Charles Montagu.) Author's first book. $600.

HIND, Arthur M. *Engraving in England . . .* Cambridge, 1952–64. 1,403 photographic illustrations. 3 vols. $1,000.

HIND, Arthur M. *Giovanni Battista Piranesi . . .* London, 1922. Frontispiece and 146 illustrations on 74 plates. One of 500 copies. In dustwrapper. $750.

HIND, Arthur M. *An Introduction to a History of Woodcut . . .* London, 1935. 2 vols. $450.

HIND, Henry Youle. *Narrative of the Canadian Red River Exploring Expedition of 1857 . . .* London, 1860. 2 vols. Plates, 8 maps (2 folding), 1 folding plan. Brown cloth. $1,500.

HIND, Henry Youle. *North-West Territory.* Toronto, 1859. 8 folding maps and plans, and 3 plates. $750.

HIND, Henry Youle. *A Sketch of an Overland Route to British Columbia.* Toronto, 1862. Folding map. Dark-green flexible cloth, paper label on front cover. First edition, with errata slip. $1,500.

HINDLEY, Charles. *The History of the Catnach Press . . .* London, 1886. One of 250 large-paper copies signed by the author. $250.

HINE, Daryl. *Five Poems.* Toronto (1954). Author's first book. Wraps. $350.

HINE, Lewis. *Men at Work.* New York, 1932. 50 black-and-white plates. $3,250.

HINKLE, James F. *Early Days of a Cowboy on the Pecos.* Roswell, N.M., 1937. Illustrated. 35 pages, pictorial wraps. One of 35 copies. $2,500.

HINTON, Richard J. *The Hand-Book of Arizona.* San Francisco, 1878. 4 maps, 16 plates. $600.

HINTON, S. E. *The Outsiders.* New York (1967). Author's first book. $250. Also issued without dustwrapper. $125.

HINTS Towards Forming the Character of a Young Princess. London, 1805. (By Hannah More.) 2 vols. $350.

HIPKINS, A. J., and GIBB, William. *Musical Instruments: Historic, Rare, and Unique.* London, 1888. 50 color plates. Half leather. One of 1,040 copies. $1,000.

HIRSCHFELD, Al. *Harlem as Seen by Hirschfeld.* New York, 1941. 1,000 copies. 24 mounted lithographs. Text by William Saroyan. Folio. $3,500.

HIRSCHFELD, Al. *Show Business Is No Business.* New York (1951). $250.

HIRSCHMAN, Jack. *Fragments.* (New York, 1952.) Author's first book. (Privately published.) Wraps. $300.

HIRSHBERG, Dr. L. K. *What You Ought to Know About Your Baby.* New York, 1910. (Written by or in collaboration with H. L. Mencken.) $2,500.

HISTORICAL and Descriptive Review of the Industries of Tacoma, 1887. Los Angeles, 1887. 108 pages, unbound. $250.

HISTORICAL and Descriptive Review of the Industries of Walla Walla. No place, 1891. 112 pages, wraps. $250.

HISTORICAL and Scientific Sketches of Michigan. Detroit, 1834. $750.

HISTORICAL Record of the Light Horse Volunteers (An). London, 1843. 7-color uniform plate. Cloth. $350.

HISTORICAL Sketch Book and Guide to New Orleans and Environs. New York, 1885. Plates, folding map. (By Lafcadio Hearn, George W. Cable et al.) First issue, with spelling "Bizoin" (instead of "Bisoin") at head of title page. In reddish-brown stiff wraps, with map laid in. $1,750. Later issues in wraps or cloth with map. $1,000. Without map. $500.

HISTORICAL War Map (The). Indianapolis: Asher & Co., 1862. Folding maps, plus maps in text. 56 pages, printed boards. $600.

HISTORY of Alameda County, California. Oakland, 1883. Portraits. (By J. P. Munro-Fraser.) $450.

HISTORY of Amador County, California. Oakland, 1881. Full leather. $850.

HISTORY of Arizona Territory Showing Its Resources and Advantages . . . San Francisco, 1884. 60 lithographed plates (2 double-page). Folding map. $3,000.

HISTORY of a Six Weeks' Tour Through a Part of France, Switzerland, Germany, and Holland. London, 1817. (By Mary Shelley.) $3,000.

HISTORY of Crawford and Richland Counties, Wisconsin. Springfield, Ill., 1884. Cloth. (By C. W. Butterfield and George A. Ogle.) $250.

HISTORY of Franklin, Jefferson, Washington, Crawford and Gasconade Counties, Missouri. Chicago, 1888. Illustrated. Half leather. $250.

HISTORY of Henry Esmond (The). London, 1852. 3 vols. Brown cloth, paper labels. (By William Makepeace Thackeray.) First edition, with 16 pages of ads dated September (VAB). Dated October (Van Duzer). $750. Limited Editions Club, Cambridge, 1956. $100. New York, 1852. Tan printed wraps. $450.

HISTORY of Idaho Territory. San Francisco, 1884. 2 maps, 69 plates, 2 facsimiles. Half morocco. $750.

HISTORY of Ink. New York [1860]. (By Thaddeus Davids.) 16 plates (with full-color title page and 1 plate in color). 7 pages of notices from the press. $350.

HISTORY of Johnny Quae Genus (The). London, 1822. (By William Combe.) 24 colored plates by Thomas Rowlandson. 8 parts, in original wraps. $1,250. London, 1822. First book edition. Boards. $500.

HISTORY of Los Angeles County, California. Oakland, 1880. Colored folding map, 113 lithographs. Morocco and cloth. $2,500.

HISTORY of Madeira (A). London, 1821. (By William Combe.) 27 colored plates. $3,500.

HISTORY of Marin County, California. San Francisco, 1880. (By J. P. Munro-Fraser.) Frontispiece, 35 portraits. Full sheep. $750.

HISTORY of Mendocino County, California. San Francisco, 1880. Portraits. Sheep. $600.

HISTORY of Montana, 1739–1885. Chicago, 1885. Folding map, plates. Half morocco. (Edited by Michael A. Leeson.) $1,250.

HISTORY of Napa and Lake Counties, California. San Francisco, 1881. Illustrated. Full sheep. $1,500.

HISTORY of Nevada. Oakland, 1881. (Edited by Myron Angel.) 116 plates. Half morocco. $1,250.

HISTORY of Pike County, Missouri. Des Moines, 1883. Half leather. $200.

HISTORY of Sangamon County, Illinois. Chicago, 1881. Illustrated. Half leather. $250.

HISTORY of San Luis Obispo County, California. Oakland, 1883. (By Myron Angel.) Portraits and scenes. Half leather. $1,250.

HISTORY of Santa Barbara County, California. Oakland, 1883. Half leather. 88 plates, 15 portraits and 2 litho titles. $1,750.

HISTORY of Sir Thomas Thumb . . . (The). Edinburgh, 1855. (By Charlotte M. Yonge.) $250.

HISTORY of Sonoma County, California. San Francisco, 1880. Illustrated. Three-quarter leather. $400.

HISTORY of Texas (A), or The Emigrant's Guide to the New Republic, by a Resident Emigrant. New York, 1844. Frontispiece colored. $2,000.

HISTORY of the Adventures of Joseph Andrews . . . , The. London, 1742. (By Henry Fielding.) 2 vols. $6,000.

HISTORY of the Arkansas Valley, Colorado. Chicago, 1881. Illustrated. Half leather. $500.

HISTORY of the City of Denver, Arapahoe County, and Colorado. Chicago, 1880. Illustrated. Half morocco. $600.

HISTORY of the Counties of Woodbury and Plymouth, Iowa. Chicago, 1890–91. Half leather. $350.

HISTORY of the Detection and Trial of John A. Murel, the Great Western Land Pirate. (Lexington, Ky., 1835.) Wraps. (By Augustus Q. J. Walton.) Athens, Tenn., 1835. $1,000.

HISTORY of the Great Lakes. Chicago, 1899. 2 vols. Plates, 5 double-page maps. Cloth. (Edited by John B. Mansfield.) $750.

HISTORY of the Indian Wars with the First White Settlers of the United States (A). Montpelier, Vt., 1812. (By Daniel C. Sanders.) Leather. $1,750. Rochester, 1828. Second edition. Boards. (Chapter 27 omitted.) $350.

HISTORY of the Late Expedition to Cuba . . . New Orleans, 1850. Second issue with appendix not contained in the first issue. $1,500.

HISTORY of the Late War in the Western Country. Lexington, Ky., 1816. (By Robert B. McAfee.) Boards or leather. First edition, with the "extra" printed leaf (of Gen. Winchester's criticism) at end. $1,750. Bowling Green, Ohio (1919). Cloth. One of 300 copies. $350.

HISTORY of the Regulators of Northern Indiana. Indianapolis, 1859. 67 pages, printed yellow wraps. $1,500.

HISTORY of Waukesha County, Wisconsin. Chicago, 1880. Illustrated. Half leather. $300.

HISTORY of Wayne County, New York. Philadelphia, 1877. Illustrated. Half leather. $200.

HITTELL, John S. *The Commerce and Industries of the Pacific Coast of North America.* San Francisco, 1882. Folding colored map, plates. $350.

HITTELL, John S. *A History of the City of San Francisco.* San Francisco, 1878. Cloth. $300.

HITTELL, John S. *The Resources of Vallejo.* (Vallejo, Calif., 1869.) Folding map. Printed wraps. $1,500.

HITTELL, John S. *Yosemite: Its Wonders and Its Beauties.* San Francisco, 1868. 20 mounted photographic views by "Helios." Green cloth. $2,000.

HITTELL, Theodore H. (editor). *Adventures of James Capen Adams, Mountaineer and Grizzly Bear Hunter, of California.* San Francisco, 1860. 12 wood engravings. $500. Boston, 1860. 12 plates. $300.

HOAG, Jonathan E. *The Poetical Works of Jonathan E. Hoag.* New York, 1923. Preface by H. P. Lovecraft and contains 6 of his poems. $500.

HOAGLAND, Edward. *Cat Man.* Boston, 1956. Author's first book. $250.

HOBAN, Russell. *Riddley Walker.* London (1980). $150.

HOBAN, Russell. *What Does It Do . . .* New York, 1959. Author's first book. $350.

HOBBES, Thomas. *Leviathan, or The Matter, Forme, & Power of a Commonwealth . . .* London, 1651. Folio. First issue has typographical "head" ornament on printed title page. $20,000. Second issue with additional engraved title, and folding table. $4,500.

HOBBS, James. *Wild Life in the Far West.* Hartford, 1872. 20 plates, colored frontispiece. $500. Hartford, 1873. Second edition. $250.

HOBOMOK, a Tale of Early Times. Boston, 1824. (By Lydia Maria Child.) Author's first book. $1,500.

HOBSON, Geoffrey D. *Bindings in Cambridge Libraries . . .* Cambridge, 1929. One of 230 copies. 72 full-page plates. $1,500.

HOBSON, Geoffrey D. *English Binding 1490–1940.* London, 1940. One of 180 copies. Folio. Cloth. $3,000. One of 25 copies. $4,500.

HOBSON, Geoffrey D. *Thirty Bindings.* First Edition Club, London, 1926. 30 plates. One of 600 copies. $400.

HOBSON, Laura Z. See Field, Peter.

HOBSON, Laura Z. *A Dog of His Own.* New York, 1941. $300.

HOBSON, R. L. *A Catalogue of Chinese Pottery and Porcelain in the Collection of Sir Percival David.* London, 1934. 180 plates, mostly in color. Folio, linen. In portfolio box. One of 650 copies. $2,250. Silk boards. One of 30 copies on vellum, signed by Hobson. In slipcase. $3,500.

HOBSON, R. L. *Chinese Art.* London, 1927. 100 color plates. $350. New York, 1927. $250.

HOCKNEY, David. *The Erotic Arts.* London, 1975. Full green crushed morocco. In cloth slip-case. One of 126 copies containing a signed 14-color screen print by Allen Jones and a signed copper plate engraving of a highly homoerotic nature by Hockney. $2,500.

HODDER, Reginald. *The Vampire.* London, 1913. $600.

HODGE, Frederick W. *Handbook of American Indians North of Mexico.* Map. Washington, 1907–10. 2 vols. $450. Washington, 1911. 2 vols. $350.

HODGE, Hiram C. *Arizona as It Is.* New York, 1877. Frontispiece, 2 plates and double-page map. $250.

HODGINS, Eric. *Mr. Blandings Builds His Dream House.* New York (1946). $250.

HODGSON, Adam. *Letters from North America.* London, 1824. 2 vols. Map, plate. (First English edition of *Remarks During A Journey . . .*) With 2 errata slips. $750.

HODGSON, Adam. *Remarks During a Journey Through North America in the Years 1819–21 . . .* New York, 1823. First (pirated) edition. $750.

HODGSON, J. E. *The History of Aeronautics in Great Britain.* Oxford, 1924. Colored frontispiece, 150 plates, some colored. Buckram. Dustwrapper. One of 1,000 copies. $750.

HODGSON, Joseph. *The Alabama Manual and Statistical Register for 1869.* Montgomery, 1869. Printed boards. $450.

HODGSON, Joseph. *The Cradle of the Confederacy.* Mobile, 1876. Cloth. $350.

HODGSON, Ralph. *The Last Blackbird and Other Lines.* London, 1907. Author's first book. First issue, edges uncut. $150. New York, 1907. $50.

HODGSON, William Hope. *The Boats of the 'Glen Carrig.'* London, 1907. Author's first book. $1,000.

HODGSON, William Hope. *The Calling of the Sea.* London (1920). In dustwrapper. $600.

HODGSON, William Hope. *Captain Gault.* New York, 1918. $350.

HODGSON, William Hope. *Carnacki the Ghost-Finder.* London, 1913. $750. Sauk City, 1947. $300.

HODGSON, William Hope. *The House on the Borderland and Other Novels.* London, 1908. $3,000. Sauk City, Wis., 1946. $600.

HODGSON, William Hope. *The Night Land.* London, 1912. $750.

HODNETT, Edward. *English Woodcuts, 1480–1535.* London, 1935. $150.

HOE, Robert. *A Lecture on Bookbinding as a Fine Art.* New York, 1886. 63 full-page plates. Limited to 200 copies. $450.

HOFFMAN, Alice. *Property of.* New York (1977). $150. London, 1978. $100.

HOFFMAN, Charles Fenno. See *Greyslaer; A Winter in the West.*

HOFFMAN, Charles Fenno. *The Pioneers of New York.* New York, 1848. 55 pages, printed tan wraps. With seal on front cover 1⅜ inches wide. (In later reprint seal was 1⅛ inches.) $300.

HOFFMAN, Charles Fenno. *Wild Scenes in the Forest and Prairie.* London, 1839. 2 vols., in original boards, paper label on spine. $300. New York, 1843. 2 vols. Boards. First American edition. $250.

HOFFMANN, Carl. *A Practical Treatise on the Manufacture of Paper in All Its Branches.* Philadelphia, 1873. 129 wood engravings and 5 large folding plates. $600.

HOFFMANN, Professor. *Modern Magic.* London (1876). $750.

HOGARTH, William. *The Analysis of Beauty.* London, 1753. 2 large folding plates. $2,000.

HOGG, James. *Scottish Pastorals . . .* Edinburgh, 1801. Author's first book. $1,000.

HOGG, Robert, and BULL, H. G. (editors). *The Herefordshire Pomona, Containing Original Figures and Descriptions of the Most Esteemed Kinds of Apples and Pears.* London, 1876–85. 77 colored plates, 4 plain plates. 2 vols., wraps or leather. $10,000.

HOLBROOK, John Edwards. *Ichthyologia of South Carolina.* Vol. I (all published). Charleston, 1855–(57). 28 colored plates. Three-quarter morocco. $12,500. Charleston, 1860. Second edition. $8,500.

HOLCOMBE, W(illiam) H(enry). *A Mystery of New Orleans.* Philadelphia, 1890. $300.

HOLDEN, W. C. *Rollie Burns; or, An Account of the Ranching Industry on the South Plains.* Dallas (1932). Maps, illustrations. Tan cloth. $350. Green cloth, without frontispiece. $250.

HOLDEN, W. C. *The Spur Ranch.* Boston (1934). $450.

HOLDER, Charles F. *All About Pasadena and Its Vicinity.* Boston, 1889. Wraps. $500.

HOLIDAY, Henry. *Stained Glass as an Art.* London, 1896. Folding colored frontispiece, 20 colotype plates. $400.

HOLLADAY, Benjamin. *Table of Distances of the Overland Daily Stage Line from Atchinson . . .* New York, 1863. Leaflet. $5,000.

HOLLEY, Mary Austin. *Texas: Observations, Historical, Geographical and Descriptive.* Baltimore, 1833. Folding map. $10,000. Lexington, Ky., 1836. Map in color. Gray cloth. Second edition (but essentially different). $7,500. Austin, 1981. One of 350 copies. In dustwrapper. $300.

HOLLIDAY, George H. *On the Plains in '65.* Wheeling, W.Va., 1883. 97 pages, printed wraps. $2,500.

HOLLINGHURST, Alan. *Confidential Chats With Boys.* Oxford, 1982. Wraps. $250.

HOLLINGSWORTH, John McHenry. *Journal.* San Francisco, 1923. Frontispiece in color. Half buckram. One of 300 copies. $250. One of 50 large-paper copies. Half vellum. $450.

HOLLISTER, Ovando J. *History of the First Regiment of Colorado Volunteers.* Denver, 1863. 178 pages, printed wraps. $8,500 at auction in 1999. (See *The March of the First.*)

HOLLISTER, Ovando J. *The Mines of Colorado*. Springfield, Mass., 1867. Enlarged edition of "The Silver Mines . . ." $500.

HOLLISTER, Ovando J. *The Silver Mines of Colorado*. Central City, 1867. 87 pages, printed wraps. $1,500.

HOLLISTER, Uriah S. *The Navajo and His Blanket*. Denver, 1903. 10 color plates, other illustrations. $600.

HOLLO, Anselm. *Sateiden Valilla*. Helsinki, 1956. Author's first book. $200.

HOLLO, Anselm. *Text and Fin Poems*. Birmingham (England), 1961. Wraps. (300 copies.) $150.

HOLLY, H. Hudson. *Modern Dwellings in Town & Country* . . . New York, 1878. 114 wood engravings. $500.

HOLMAN, Louis A. *The Graphic Processes* . . . Boston, 1926. 37 loose specimens in a cloth-covered case. $1,500.

HOLMAN, William R. *Library Publications*. San Francisco (1965). One of 350 copies. 16 tipped-in examples in text and 16 additional examples in rear pocket of book. $400.

HOLMES, John Clellon. *Go*. New York, 1952. Author's first book. $1,000.

HOLMES, Oliver Wendell. See Hall, Marshall. See also *The Autocrat of the Breakfast-Table; The Poet at the Breakfast-Table*.

HOLMES, Oliver Wendell. *The Benefactors of the Medical School of Harvard University*. Boston, 1850. Tan wraps. $600.

HOLMES, Oliver Wendell. *Border Lines of Knowledge in Some Provinces of Medical Science*. Boston, 1862. First edition, with Ticknor & Co. imprint on spine. $300.

HOLMES, Oliver Wendell. *The Claims of Dentistry*. Boston, 1872. Tan wraps. $450.

HOLMES, Oliver Wendell. *The Contagiousness of Puerperal Fever*. (Caption title.) (Boston, 1844). An offprint. 28 pages, printed buff wraps. $80,000 at auction in 1998.

HOLMES, Oliver Wendell. *Currents and Counter-Currents in Medical Science: An Address* . . . *Before the Massachusetts Medical Society*. Boston, 1860. Printed salmon-colored wraps. 55 or 48 pages, priority unknown but the 55-page may have been earlier. It is scarcer than the 48-page version. $750. Boston, 1861. (*With Other Addresses* . . .) Cloth. $400.

HOLMES, Oliver Wendell. *Elsie Venner: A Romance of Destiny*. Boston, 1861. 2 vols. Brown cloth. "Probable" first printing, with ads dated January 1861. $300.

HOLMES, Oliver Wendell. *Homoeopathy, and Its Kindred Delusions*. Boston, 1842. Tan boards, paper label. $350.

HOLMES, Oliver Wendell. *Humorous Poems*. Boston, 1865. Portrait frontispiece. Printed wraps. $250. Cloth. $200.

HOLMES, Oliver Wendell. *Poems.* Boston, 1836. Author's first book. In original decorated cloth, paper label. With Boston imprint only. $600. Later 1836 issue. Boston and New York imprint. $300. London, 1846. $250.

HOLMES, Oliver Wendell. *The Position and Prospects of the Medical Student.* Boston, 1844. Printed tan wraps. $750.

HOLMES, Oliver Wendell. *The Professor at the Breakfast-Table.* Boston, 1860. Cloth. $250. Beveled cloth, edges gilt. Large paper. $450.

HOLMES, Oliver Wendell. *Puerperal Fever, as a Private Pestilence.* Boston, 1855. Original printed wraps. $4,500.

HOLMES, (Justice) Oliver Wendell (1841–1935). *The Common Law.* Boston, 1881. Author's first book. First issue: green cloth. Reading "John Wilson . . ." $2,500. Second issue: russet cloth. Reading "University Press." $1,750. Third issue: russet cloth. Reading "S. J. Park Hill & Co." $1,250.

HOLMES, Roberta E. *The Southern Mines of California.* San Francisco: Grabhorn Press, 1930. Plates and maps. Boards. One of 250 copies. $600.

HOLY *Bible, The.* London, 1611. Authorized (i.e., the "King James Version"). First edition, first issue is printed in large black-letter font, in double columns within a ruled frame. $35,000.

HOMAGE *to a Bookman, Essays on Manuscripts* . . . Berlin (1967). $300.

HOME *Life in Russia.* London, 1854. (By Nikolai Gogol.) 2 vols. Author's first book. $2,000.

HOMER. *The Odyssey of Homer.* Boston, 1929. Translated by George H. Palmer. Illustrated by N. C. Wyeth. $450. (London), 1932. Translated by T. E. Shaw (T. E. Lawrence). With 25 large rondelles in gold and black. Small folio, black morocco. One of 530 copies designed by Bruce Rogers. In slipcase. $3,500. Note: A few copies were signed by Lawrence, "T. E. Shaw," and Rogers. $8,500. New York, 1932. Morocco (11 copies). Calf (about 23 copies). First American edition (for copyright purposes). Either issue. $7,500. Trade. $350. London (1935). $250. One of 550 signed copies. With an extra set of color plates. $2,000. Limited Editions Club, New York, 1981. $250.

HOMES *in Texas on the Line of the International and Great Northern Railroad.* Chicago, 1879. 79 pages, wraps. (By N. W. Hunter.) $500.

HONCE, Charles. *Books and Ghosts* . . . Mount Vernon, New York, 1948. One of 111 copies. $250.

HONCE, Charles. *For Loving a Book* . . . Mount Vernon, New York, 1945. One of 111 copies. $350.

HONCE, Charles. *Notes from a Bookman's Cuff* . . . New York, 1949. One of 111 copies. $350.

HONCE, Charles. *The Public Papers of a Bibliomaniac* . . . Mount Vernon, New York, 1942. One of 100 copies. $325.

HONCE, Charles. *A Vincent Starrett Library* . . . Mount Vernon, New York, 1941. One of 100 copies. $350.

HOOD, Thomas. *Humorous Poems.* London, 1893. One of 250 copies on large paper. $250.

HOOKER, Joseph Dalton. *Exotic Flora.* Edinburgh, 1823–27. 3 vols. 233 hand-colored plates, some folding. $11,830 at auction in 1998.

HOOKER, Joseph Dalton. *Illustrations of Himalayan Plants.* (London, 1855.) Lithographed title within hand-colored border and 24 hand-colored plates. $54,000 at auction in 1998.

HOOKER, Joseph Dalton. *On the Flora of Australia . . .* London, 1859. $10,000.

HOOKER, Joseph Dalton. *The Rhododendrons Of Sikkim-Himalaya.* 1849–51. 3 parts. Vignette title, 30 hand-colored lithographed plates. $17,500.

HOOKER, Richard. *M.A.S.H.* New York, 1968. (By H. Richard Hornberger.) Author's first book. $600.

HOOVER, Herbert C. *Fishing for Fun.* New York (1963). One of 200 signed copies. In slipcase. $600. Trade. $100.

HOOVER, Herbert C. *The Principles of Mining.* New York, 1909. Author's first book (with Lou Henry Hoover). $300.

HOOVER, Herbert C. *A Remedy for Disappearing Game Fish.* New York, 1930. Woodcuts. Marbled boards and cloth. One of 990 copies. In slipcase. $350.

HOOVER, Herbert C., and HOOVER, Lou Henry (translators). *De Re Metallica.* London, 1912. First English edition. From the Latin of Georgius Agricola. Illustrated. Parchment boards. $850.

HOPE, Anthony. *The Dolly Dialogues.* London, 1894. (By A. H. Hawkins.) 4 plates by Arthur Rackham. Tan wraps. First issue, with "Dolly" as running headband on left-hand pages (VAB). $1,000. Blue cloth. $400.

HOPE, Anthony. *The Man of Mark.* London, 1890. (By A. H. Hawkins.) Author's first book. $400.

HOPE, Anthony. *The Prisoner of Zenda.* Bristol [1894]. (By A. H. Hawkins.) Dark-red cloth. First issue, with list of 17 (not 18) titles on page 311 (VAB). $450. Second issue. $200. Limited Editions Club, Baltimore, 1966. $75.

HOPKINS, Gerard Manley. *Poems.* London (1918). Edited by Robert Bridges. Author's first book. 2 portraits, 2 double-page facsimiles. Blue-gray boards and linen. In dustwrapper. $5,000. Without dustwrapper. $3,000. London, 1930. Second edition. Adds appendix of 16 poems. $750.

HOPKINS, Gerard Manley. *Selected Poems.* London: Nonesuch Press, 1954. One of 1,100 copies. $350.

HOPKINS, Gerard T. *A Mission to the Indians, from the Indian Committee of Baltimore Yearly Meeting, to Fort Wayne in 1804.* Philadelphia, 1862. Edited by Martha E. Tyson. 198 pages, wraps. $2,000.

HOPKINS, Harry C. *History of San Diego: Its Pueblo Lands and Water.* San Diego (1929). Issued without dustwrapper. $200.

HOPKINS, Pauline E. *Contending Forces: A Romance Illustrative of Negro Life North and South.* Boston, 1900. Green cloth decorated in red and yellow. $3,500.

HOPKINSON, Cecil. *Collecting Golf Books 1743–1938.* London (1938). $4,500. Worcestershire, 1980. One of 250 copies. $750.

HOPPE, E. O. (photographer). See King, Richard.

HOPPE, E. O. *Studies from the Russian Ballet.* London (1911). Folio. $750.

HORBLIT, Harrison D. *One Hundred Books Famous in Science.* New York, 1964. Limited to 1,000 copies. $1,000.

HORGAN, Paul. *The Fault of Angels.* New York (1933). $175.

HORGAN, Paul. *Great River: The Rio Grande in American History.* New York, 1954. 2 vols. Illustrated, including color plates. Tan cloth. One of 1,000 signed copies. In slipcase. $350. Trade edition. 2 vols. Black cloth. In slipcase. $100.

HORGAN, Paul. *The Habit of Empire.* New Mexico, 1938. $150.

HORGAN, Paul. *Lamb of God.* Roswell, 1927. Wraps. (60 copies.) $1,500.

HORGAN, Paul. *Men of Arms.* Philadelphia (1931.) (500 copies.) $1,000.

HORGAN, Paul. *The Return of the Weed.* New York and London, 1936. One of 350 copies signed by Horgan and Peter Hurd. 6 full-page and tipped-in frontispiece black-and-white lithographs by Hurd. $450.

HORGAN, Paul. *Villanelle of Evening.* No place, 1926. Author's first book. Wraps. (200 copies.) $1,250.

HORN, Hosea B. *Horn's Overland Guide . . .* New York, 1852. Folding map. First issue, 78 pages. $3,000. Second issue, same date, 83 pages. $2,500.

HORN, Tom. *Life of Tom Horn . . .* Denver, 1904. Photographs and frontispiece portrait, pictorial wrappers. $250.

HORNBY, C. H. St. J. *A Descriptive Bibliography of the Books Printed at the Ashendene Press, MDCCCXV-MCMXXXV.* Chelsea, 1935. One of 390 signed copies. Last book of the press. In slipcase. $2,000. San Francisco, 1976. One of 375 copies. $150.

HORNE, Bernard S. *The Compleat Angler, 1653–1967.* Pittsburgh, 1970. One of 300 copies bound in cloth (out of 500 total). In dustwrapper. $200.

HORNE, Henry. *Essays Concerning Iron and Steel . . .* London, 1773. $2,500.

HORNE, Herbert P. *The Binding of Books.* London, 1894. Large octavo, cloth and parchment spine. One of 150 copies, printed on Dutch handmade paper. $350.

HORNE, Thomas Hartwell. *An Introduction to the Study of Bibliography . . .* London, 1814. 2 vols. 11 plates. $300.

HORNUNG, E. W. *Mr. Justice Raffles.* London, 1909. $300.

HORSBRUGH, Boyd R. *The Game-birds & Waterfowl of South Africa*. London, 1912. 67 color plates. $1,000.

HORSE-Shoe Robinson. Philadelphia, 1835. (By John Pendleton Kennedy.) 2 vols. In original purple cloth, paper labels on spines. $750.

HOSACK, David. *Essays on Various Subjects of Medical Science*. New York, 1824–30. 3 vols. $750.

HOSMER, Hezekiah L. *Early History of the Maumee Valley*. Toledo, Ohio, 1858. 70 pages, printed wraps. $600.

HOSMER, Hezekiah L. *Montana: An Address . . . Before the Travellers' Club, New York City, January, 1866*. (Cover title.) New York, 1866. 23 pages, printed wraps. $1,000.

HOSMER, John Allen. *A Trip to the States, by the Way of the Yellowstone and Missouri*. Virginia City, Mont., 1867. Cloth, or tan printed boards. $26,000 at auction in 1999.

HOUDINI, Harry. *A Magician Among the Spirits*. New York, 1924. (By Ehrich Weiss.) $1,000.

HOUDINI, Harry. *The Right Way to Do Wrong: An Exposé of Successful Criminals*. Boston, 1906. (By Ehrich Weiss.) Author's first book. Wraps. $1,500.

HOUDINI, Harry. *The Unmasking of Robert-Houdin*. New York, 1908. (By Ehrich Weiss.) $750.

HOUGH, Emerson. *54-40 or Fight*. Indianapolis, 1909. $125.

HOUGH, Emerson. *The Singing Mouse Stories*. New York, 1895. Author's first book. Cover by Will Bradley. $150.

HOUGH, Emerson. *The Story of the Cowboy*. New York, 1897. Decorated cloth. $250.

HOUGH, Emerson. *The Story of the Outlaw*. New York, 1907. With printer's rule in heading at top of page v. $200.

HOUGH, Franklin B. *History of Jefferson County, New York*. Albany, 1854. Half leather. $300.

HOUGH, Franklin B. *History of St. Lawrence and Franklin Counties, New York*. Albany, 1853. With 3 folding maps. Half leather. $300.

HOUGH, Franklin B. *Washingtonia*. Roxbury, Mass., 1865. Plates, folding map. 2 vols., half morocco. One of 91 copies. $500. Wraps. One of 200 copies on large paper. $350.

HOUGHTON, Jacob. *The Mineral Region of Lake Superior*. Buffalo, 1846. 2 maps on one folding sheet. $350.

HOUGHTON, T. S. *The Printers' Practical Every-Day-Book*. London, 1841. $400.

HOUGHTON, W. *British Fresh-Water Fishes*. London (1879). 2 vols. Illustrated. With 41 color plates. $2,500.

HOUSE, Homer D. *Wild Flowers of New York*. Albany, 1918–20. 2 vols. Illustrated in color. $200.

HOUSEHOLD, Geoffrey. *Rogue Male*. London, 1939. $1,500. Boston, 1939. $600.

HOUSEHOLD, Geoffrey. *The Terror of Villedonga*. London (1936). Author's first book. $500.

HOUSEHOLD, Geoffrey. *The Third Hour*. London, 1937. $250. Boston, 1938. $200.

HOUSMAN, A. E. *Fragment of a Greek Tragedy*. Cambridge, 1921. Printed wraps. $500.

HOUSMAN, A. E. *Last Poems*. London, 1922. First issue, with comma and semicolon missing after "love" and "rain," respectively, in the first two lines on page 52. In dustwrapper. $200.

HOUSMAN, A. E. *More Poems*. London (1936). Portrait. Morocco and cloth. One of 379. In dustwrapper. $350. Trade. $125. New York, 1936. First American edition. $100.

HOUSMAN, A. E. *A Shropshire Lad*. London, 1896. Gray-blue boards, vellum spine, paper label. Author's first book. First state, with the word "Shropshire" on the label exactly 33 mm wide. $2,500. Second state, measuring 37 mm. $2,000. New York, 1897. Boards, vellum spine. $2,000. (Note: The entire first edition was 500 copies, 350 for England and 150 for America, with a substitute New York title page.)

HOUSMAN, Clemence. *The Were-Wolf*. New York, 1895. $500. London, 1896. Silk-like brown cloth. $350. Second state of binding in brown cloth. $150.

HOUSMAN, Laurence. *False Premises*. Oxford, 1922. One of 150 signed copies. Issued without dustwrapper. $150.

HOUSMAN, Laurence. *A Farm in Fairyland*. London, 1894. Author's first book. $500. One of 50 large-paper copies. $1,000.

HOUSMAN, Laurence. *Followers of St. Francis*. London, 1923. $200.

HOUSMAN, Laurence. *Stories from the Arabian Nights*. London (1907). Mounted color plates by Edmund Dulac. $750. Vellum with silk ties. One of 350 signed copies. $1,750.

HOUSTON, Pam. *Cowboys Are My Weakness*. New York (1992). Author's first book. $250.

HOUSTOUN, Mrs. Matilda C. *Texas and the Gulf of Mexico* . . . London, 1844. 2 vols. 10 plates. Cloth. $750. Philadelphia, 1845. Frontispiece of Santa Anna. Wraps. $450.

HOVEY, Richard. *Poems*. Washington, 1880. Author's first book. Cloth. $1,000. Wraps. $750.

HOW the Buffalo Lost His Crown. (New York, 1894.) (By John H. Beacom.) Illustrated by Charles M. Russell. 44 pages, oblong, brown cloth. $3,500.

HOW to Win in Wall Street. New York, 1881. By a Successful Operator. (Joaquin Miller.) $450.

HOW, George E., and HOWE, Jane P. *English and Scottish Silver Spoons* . . . London, 1952–57. 3 vols. Photographs. One of 550 copies. In dustwrappers. $1,000. Without dustwrapper. $750. One of 50 specially bound copies. Issued without dustwrapper. $1,500.

HOWARD, Benjamin C. *A Report of the Decisions of the Supreme Court* . . . *in the Case of Dred Scott vs. John F. A. Sandford*. New York, 1857. (The Dred Scott Decision.) Brown paper wraps. $4,500.

HOWARD, Brian. *God Save the King.* Paris: Hours Press (1930). One of 150 copies. $350.

HOWARD, H. R. See *The Life and Adventures of Joseph T. Hare.*

HOWARD, H. R. (editor). *The History of Virgil A. Stewart, and His Adventures in Capturing and Exposing the "Great Western Land Pirate" (John A. Murrell) and His Gang.* New York, 1836. Howard's first book. $500.

HOWARD, (Jas.) H. W. *Bond and Free.* Harrisburg, 1886. Author's first book. First issue, with portrait frontispiece. $1,000. Portrait omitted in later editions.

HOWARD, John. *An Account of the Principal Lazarettos in Europe* . . . Warrington, 1789. 22 plates, large folding table. $1,500.

HOWARD, Joseph Jackson. *Baronets: The Wardour Press Series of Armorial Bookplates.* London, 1895. Limited to 200 copies signed by the compiler, Mitchell L. Hughes. $300.

HOWARD, McHenry. *Recollections of a Maryland Confederate Soldier.* Baltimore, 1914. 2 folding map and 24 plates. $375.

HOWARD, Oliver Otis. *Account of Gen. Howard's Mission to the Apaches and Navajos.* No place, no date. 12 pages, wraps. $300.

HOWARD, Oliver Otis. *My Life and Experiences Among Our Hostile Indians.* Hartford (1907). $500.

HOWARD, Oliver Otis. *Nez Percé Joseph.* Boston, 1881. 2 portraits and 2 maps. $500.

HOWARD, Robert E. *Always Comes Evening.* Sauk City, Wisc., 1957. $500.

HOWARD, Robert E. *The Coming of Conan.* New York (1953). $300.

HOWARD, Robert E. *Conan the Barbarian.* New York (1954). $350.

HOWARD, Robert E. *Conan the Conqueror.* New York (1950). $400.

HOWARD, Robert E. *The Dark Man and Others.* Sauk City, Wisc., 1963. $250.

HOWARD, Robert E. *Etchings in Ivory.* Pasadena, Tex., 1968. On laid paper, watermarked "Tweedweave." (268 copies.) Wraps. $250.

HOWARD, Robert E. *A Gent from Bear Creek.* London (1937). Author's first book. With "First printed . . . 1937" on copyright page. $7,500. West Kingston, R.I., 1965. First American edition. $125.

HOWARD, Robert E. *King Conan.* New York (1953). $350.

HOWARD, Robert E. *Skull-Face and Others.* Sauk City, Wisc., 1946. $850.

HOWARD, Robert E. *The Sword of Conan.* New York (1952). $300.

HOWBERT, Irving. *The Indians of the Pike's Peak Region.* New York, 1914. 4 plates. $125.

HOWE, E. D. *History of Mormonism*. Painesville, Ohio, 1840. Frontispiece. Second edition of *Mormonism Unvailed*. $1,500.

HOWE, E. D. *Mormonism Unveiled*. Painesville, 1834. Frontispiece. In original cloth. $10,000.

HOWE, E. W. *The Story of a Country Town*. Atchison, Kan., 1883. Author's first book. Illustrated by W. L. Wells. Green decorated cloth. First issue, with "D. Caldwell, Manufacturer, Atchison, Kan." rubber-stamped inside front cover and no lettering at foot of spine. $250. (Later in reddish-brown or blue cloth; or green cloth with paper label "McPike & Fox" on pastedown.)

HOWE, Henry. *Historical Collections of Ohio*. Cincinnati, 1847. Map, woodcuts. $300. Cincinnati, 1848. $200. Cincinnati, 1875. $150.

HOWE, Henry. *Historical Collections of the Great West*. Cincinnati, 1850. 2 vols. in 1. Cloth. $200. Cincinnati, 1852. $150.

HOWE, Henry. *Historical Collections of Virginia*. Charleston, S.C., 1845. Map, illustrations, engraved title page. $300.

HOWE, John. *A Journal Kept by Mr. John Howe, While He Was Employed as a British Spy, During the Revolutionary War*. Concord, N.H., 1827. 44 pages. $600.

HOWE, Julia Ward. See *Passion-Flowers*.

HOWE, Julia Ward. *Later Lyrics*. Boston, 1866. Green or purple cloth. (Contains first book appearance of "Battle Hymn of the Republic.") $350.

HOWE, Mark A. De Wolfe. *Rari Nantes: Being Verses and a Song*. Boston, 1893. Author's first book. Wraps. One of 80 copies. $350.

HOWE, Octavius T. *The Argonauts of '49*. Cambridge, Mass., 1923. Illustrated. Half cloth. In dustwrapper. $250.

HOWE, Octavius T., and MATTHEWS, Frederick C. *American Clipper Ships, 1833–58*. Salem, 1926–27. 2 vols. 114 plates. Vol. 1, marbled boards; vol. 2, cloth. In dustwrapper. $350. One of 97 copies. $500.

HOWELL, James. *Instructions for Forreine Travell*. London, 1642. $1,500.

HOWELLS, William Dean. See *Poems of Two Friends*.

HOWELLS, William Dean. *A Hazard of New Fortunes*. New York, 1890. Illustrated. Wraps. With the cloth edition of this title listed as "in-press" on inside of front wrapper. $600. With title listed at "$2.00." $300. 2 vols. Cloth. $250.

HOWELLS, William Dean. *My Mark Twain*. New York, 1910. Sage-colored cloth. $125.

HOWELLS, William Dean. *Niagara Revisited . . .* Chicago (1884). $1,000.

HOWELLS, William Dean. *The Rise of Silas Lapham*. Boston, 1885. Blue or brown cloth. With "Mr. Howells's Latest Works" (later "Novels"), ad facing title page and with unbroken type in the word "sojourner" at bottom of page 176. $250. Limited Editions Club, New York, 1961. Illustrated. Buckram. In slipcase. $75.

HOWELLS, William Dean. *Suburban Sketches.* Boston, 1871. Author's first book of fiction. Illustrated by A. Hoppin. $250. Boston, 1872. Revised and enlarged edition. $100.

HOWELLS, William Dean, and HAYES, J. L. *Lives and Speeches of Abraham Lincoln and Hannibal Hamlin.* Columbus, Ohio, 1860. 96 pages, printed buff wraps. First issue, with pages 95–96 blank. $600. Second issue, engraving of Republican Wigwam, Chicago, on page 96. $400.

HOWELLS, William Dean, TWAIN, Mark, et al. *The Niagara Book.* Buffalo, 1893. Cloth, or printed wraps. With no ads at end, page 226 blank, and copyright notice in 3 lines. $400.

HOWISON, John. *Sketches of Upper Canada . . .* Edinburgh, 1821. $500.

HOWITT, Samuel. *The British Sportsman.* London, 1812. (A reprint.) Frontispiece, 71 colored plates. $3,500.

HOWLAND, S. A. *Steamboat Disasters and Railroad Accidents in the United States . . .* Worcester, Mass., 1840. Calf. $400.

HOWLEY, James P. *The Beothucks or Red Indians of Newfoundland.* Cambridge, Mass., 1915. Plates. $450.

HOYEM, Andrew. *The Wake.* San Francisco, 1963. Author's first book. 35 deluxe copies. $200. Wraps. One of 750 copies. $40.

HOYNINGEN-HUENE, George. *African Mirage.* New York; 1938. Author's first book. $250.

HRDLICKA, Ales. *The Anthropology of Florida.* DeLand, 1922. Issued without dustwrapper. $200.

HUBBARD, Elbert. *A Message to Garcia.* East Aurora, N.Y., 1899. Suede. One of 450 copies. $450.

HUBBARD, Gurdon Saltonstall. *Incidents in the Life of Gurdon Saltonstall Hubbard.* (Chicago), 1888. Edited by Henry E. Hamilton. Frontispiece. $500.

HUBBARD, John Niles. *Sketches of Border Adventures, in the Life and Times of Maj. Moses Van Campen.* Dansville, N.Y., 1841. Leather. $300.

HUBBARD, L. Ron. *Buckskin Brigades.* New York, 1937. Author's first book. $3,500.

HUBBARD, L. Ron. *Dianetics.* New York (1950). $750.

HUBBARD, L. Ron. *Final Blackout.* Providence (1948). $500.

HUBBARD, L. Ron. *Slaves of Sleep.* Chicago, 1948. $500.

HUBBARD, L. Ron. *Typewriter in the Sky . . .* New York (1951). $300.

HUBBARD, Robert. *Historical Sketches of Roswell Franklin and Family.* Dansville, N.Y., 1839. In original half leather. $1,000.

HUBBARD, William. *The Present State of New-England.* London, 1677. $55,000. The Boston edition published the same year precedes this and is extremely rare and has not shown at auction in twenty years.

HUBLEY, Bernard. *The History of the American Revolution* . . . Northumberland, Pa., 1805. Errata leaf inserted. Vol. I. All published. $1,250.

HUDSON, Derek. *Arthur Rackham: His Life and Work.* London, 1960. Color plates. $250. New York (1960). $200.

HUDSON, Jeffrey. *A Case of Need.* New York (1968). (By Michael Crichton.) First novel. $750. London (1968). $250.

HUDSON River Portfolio. See Wall, W. G.

HUDSON, Stephen. *Celeste and Other Sketches.* (London) 1930. (By Sydney Schiff.) Wood engravings. Decorated cloth. One of 50 copies on Japan vellum, signed, with an extra set of engravings. In slipcase. $750. One of 700 copies. $100.

HUDSON, W. H. See Harford, Henry; Sclater, P. L., and Hudson, W. H. See also *A Crystal Age.*

HUDSON, W. H. *Birds in a Village.* London, 1893. Chocolate-colored buckram. $200.

HUDSON, W. H. *Birds of La Plata.* London, 1920. One of 200 copies with extra set of plates. $750. Trade. $250. New York, 1920. 2 vols. $350.

HUDSON, W. H. *British Birds.* London, 1895. With 8 plain and 8 color plates. Green cloth. $400.

HUDSON, W. H. *Far Away and Long Ago.* London, 1918. In dustwrapper. $350. London, 1931. Illustrated. Vellum. One of 110 copies. $500. Limited Editions Club, New York, 1943. Illustrated. Half leather. In slipcase. $200.

HUDSON, W. H. *Green Mansions.* London, 1904. Light-green cloth. First binding, without publisher's design on back cover. $350. Second issue. $150. London, 1926. Illustrated. One of 165 copies. $300. Limited Editions Club, New York, 1935. In slipcase. $100.

HUDSON, W. H. *Idle Days in Patagonia.* London, 1893. Crimson buckram. With 2 ad leaves at end and publisher's device on back cover. One of 1,750 copies. $250. Variants without ads or device. $150. New York, 1893. $200.

HUDSON, W. H. *The Purple Land That England Lost.* London, 1885. 2 vols. Author's first book. Light-blue cloth. First issue, with October ads in second volume. $2,000. Later issue in purple cloth. $1,000.

HUEFFER, Ford Madox. See Conrad, Joseph, and Hueffer, Ford Madox. See also Ford, Ford Madox (for books published after 1919, when he changed his name).

HUEFFER, Ford Madox. *Between St. Dennis and St. George.* London, 1915. (By Ford Madox Ford.) $500.

HUEFFER, Ford Madox. *The Brown Owl.* London, 1892 (actually 1891). (By Ford Madox Ford.) Author's first book. $750.

HUEFFER, Ford Madox. *The Feather.* London, 1892. (By Ford Madox Ford.) $400.

HUEFFER, Ford Madox. *The Fifth Queen.* London, 1906. (By Ford Madox Ford.) $450.

HUEFFER, Ford Madox. *The Queen Who Flew.* London, 1894. (By Ford Madox Ford.) Illustrated. Vellum. One of 25 signed copies. $2,500. Trade issue in decorated cloth. $500.

HUGHES, Dorothy B. *The So Blue Marble.* New York (1940). Author's first book. $1,000.

HUGHES, John T. *California: Its History, Population, Climate, Soil, Productions, and Harbors.* Cincinnati, 1848. 105 pages, printed wraps. $1,250.

HUGHES, John T. *Doniphan's Expedition: Containing an Account of the Conquest of New Mexico.* Cincinnati, 1847. 144 pages. Wraps. First issue does not state "Cheap Edition" on front wrap. $3,500. "Cheap Edition." $1,500. Cincinnati, 1848. Wraps. $750. Cloth. With portrait of Doniphan and map. $600. Second issue adding portrait of Price and list of illustrations. $500.

HUGHES, Langston. *Dear Lovely Death.* Amenia, N.Y., 1931. One of 100 signed copies. $2,500.

HUGHES, Langston. *Dream Keeper and Other Poems.* New York, 1932. $1,750.

HUGHES, Langston. *Fine Clothes to the Jew.* New York, 1927. $1,750.

HUGHES, Langston. *Scottsboro Limited: Four Poems and a Play in Verse.* New York, 1932. One of 30 copies signed by Hughes and Prentiss Taylor, the illustrator. $2,500. Trade. Wraps. $750.

HUGHES, Langston. *Shakespeare in Harlem.* New York, 1942. $850.

HUGHES, Langston. *The Weary Blues.* New York, 1926. Author's first book. First issue dust-wrapper without blurb for *Fine Clothes to the Jew.* $7,500. Second issue. In dustwrapper. $2,500.

HUGHES, Richard. *Gipsy-Night and Other Poems.* London: Golden Cockerel Press (1922). Author's first book. Portrait. One of 200 copies. $200. Chicago, 1922. Portrait. Boards and cloth. One of 63 signed copies, with a special proof of portrait. $400.

HUGHES, Richard. *A High Wind in Jamaica.* London, 1929. First complete English edition. One of 150 signed copies. $350. Trade edition. $250. (The first edition was published in New York as *The Innocent Voyage.*)

HUGHES, Richard. *The Innocent Voyage.* New York, 1929. Decorated blue boards and blue linen. $250. Limited Editions Club, New York, 1944. Leather. In slipcase. $150. (Published in England as *A High Wind in Jamaica.*)

HUGHES, Richard. *The Sisters' Tragedy.* Oxford, 1922. Wraps. $150.

HUGHES, Rupert. *The Lakerim Athletic Club.* New York, 1898. Author's first book. $450.

HUGHES, Sukey. *Washi, The World of Japanese Paper.* Tokyo (1978). One of 1,000 copies. 102 actual specimens of paper. In dustwrapper. $400.

HUGHES, Ted. *Animal Poems.* London (1967). Wraps. One of 100 signed copies. $600.

HUGHES, Ted. *Birthday Letters.* (London, 1998.) One of 300 signed copies. $750. Trade. $75.

HUGHES, Ted. *The Burning of the Brothel.* (London): Turret Books (1966). Woodcuts in color. Printed wraps. One of 300 copies. $150. One of 75 copies signed by Hughes. $450.

HUGHES, Ted. *Crow.* London, 1970. $100. London (1973). 12 drawings by Leonard Baskin. One of 400 signed copies. In slipcase. $1,500.

HUGHES, Ted. *Eat Crow.* London, 1971. Illustrated by Leonard Baskin. Black leather. One of 150 signed copies. In slipcase. $500.

HUGHES, Ted. *Eclipse.* Knotting, 1976. Wraps. One of 50 signed copies. $300.

HUGHES, Ted. *Four Tales Told by an Idiot.* The Sceptre Press, 1979. Stapled wrappers. 1 of 100 copies signed by Hughes. $250.

HUGHES, Ted. *The Hawk in the Rain.* London (1957). Author's first book. $450. New York (1957). $250.

HUGHES, Ted. *Mokomaki.* Leeds (Ma.), 1985. One of 50 copies. Full vellum. Each etching signed by Leonard Baskin. New in custom box. $3,000. One of 4 with extra suite. $6,000.

HUGHES, Ted. *Prometheus on His Crag.* London, 1973. Illustrated. Purple morocco. One of 160 signed copies, with a signed Leonard Baskin drawing. In slipcase. $750.

HUGHES, Ted. *Remains of Elmet.* (London), 1979. One of 70 copies signed by author and photographer Fay Godwin. Full tree-calf. In slipcase. $750. One of 110 signed copies. $500.

HUGHES, Ted. *Roosting Hawk.* (Northampton, Mass., circa 1950s.) Printed wrappers. Single poem bound in gray wrappers and issued for the private use of the poet, no copies for sale. Edition probably no more than 25 copies or less. $600.

HUGHES, Ted. *Spring Summer Autumn Winter.* London, 1973. One of 140 signed copies. In glassine jacket. In slipcase. $450.

HUGHES, Thomas. See *Tom Brown at Oxford; Tom Brown's School Days.*

HUGHES, William. *The American Physician* . . . London, 1672. $7,500.

HUGO, Richard F. *Poems.* (Portland, 1959.) Author's first book. Wraps. $450.

HUGO, Richard F. *A Run of Jacks.* Minnesota (1961). $500.

HUGO, Victor. *Hans of Iceland.* London, 1825. Author's first book. $1,000.

HUGO, Victor. *The History of a Crime.* London, 1877–78. 4 vols. Brown cloth. $1,500.

HUGO, Victor. The Hunchback of Notre Dame. London, 1833, 3 vols. $3,000. Philadelphia, 1834. 2 vols. $2,500.

HUGO, Victor. *Les Misérables.* London, 1862. 3 vols. Cloth. First edition in English. $3,500. New York, 1862. 5 vols. $2,500.

HUGO, Victor. *Toilers of the Sea.* London, 1866. 3 vols. Pebbled green cloth. First edition in English. $1,000. Limited Editions Club, New York, 1960. In slipcase. $200.

HUIE, William Bradford. *The Revolt of Mamie Stover.* New York (1951). $100.

HULL, Edward. *A Treatise on the Building and Ornamental Stones of Great Britain* . . . London, 1872. Two tipped-in photos of the Forum Romantum and Piazza of St. Mark. $400.

HULME, F. Edward. *Familiar Wild Flowers.* London [circa 1875]. 5 vols. $500. London, 1902. 7 vols. $350.

HULME, F. Edward. *Plants, Their Natural Growth and Ornamental Treatment.* London, 1874. $500.

HULME, F. Edward. *Suggestions in Floral Design.* London, no date [1878–79]. 52 plates. $2,000.

HULME, T. E. *An Introduction to Metaphysics.* New York (1912). Translation and introduction by Hulme (his first book) of Henri Bergson's work. $300. London, 1913. $250.

HULME, Wyndham E., et al. *Leather for Libraries.* London, 1905. $250.

HULTON, Paul, and QUINN, David Beers. *The American Drawings of John White, 1577–1590.* London, 1964. 2 vols. Frontispiece, 160 plates, 76 in color. Folio, red buckram. One of 600 copies. $1,250.

HUMANITAS (pseudonym). *Hints for the Consideration of the Friends of Slavery.* Lexington, Ky., 1805. 32 pages. $3,000.

HUMASON, W. L. *From the Atlantic Surf to the Golden Gate.* Hartford, 1869. $350.

HUME, Cyril. *Wife of the Centaur.* New York (1923). Author's first book. $175.

HUME, David. See *A Treatise of Human Nature.*

HUME, David. *An Enquiry Concerning the Principles of Morals.* London, 1751. Leaf L3 uncanceled. $4,000. L3 canceled. $2,500.

HUME, David. *Four Dissertations* . . . London, 1757. $1,500.

HUME, David. *The History of England.* London, 1754–62. 6 vols. Quarto. First collected edition. $3,000.

HUME, David. *Political Discourses.* Edinburgh, 1752. $6,000.

HUME, Fergus. *The Mystery of the Hansom Cab.* Melbourne, 1886. Author's first book. (4 known copies.) $3,000 or more. London, 1887. Wraps. $1,500. Early printings. $500.

HUME, Hamilton. *A Brief Statement of Facts in Connection with an Overland Expedition from Lake George to Port Phillip in 1824.* Sydney, 1855. Wraps. $20,000.

HUMOURIST (The). London, 1819–20. (By George Cruikshank.) 4 vols. 40 colored etchings, including vignette title pages by George Cruikshank. First issue, without "Vol. 1" on title page and with all plates dated 1819. $2,500. Second issue, dated 1819–22: 4 vols. $2,000. London, 1892. 4 vols. Half morocco. One of 70 copies on large paper. $1,500. One of 260. $500.

HUMPHREY, William. *The Last Husband and Other Stories.* New York, 1953. Author's first book. $250. London, 1953. $150.

HUMPHREYS, Arthur L. *Old Decorative Maps and Charts.* London, 1926. One of 1,500 copies. In dustwrapper. $500. Half vellum. Deluxe edition. One of 100 copies with separate mounted plates. $1,250.

HUMPHREYS, David. *An Historical Account of the Incorporated Society for the Propagation of the Gospel in Foreign Parts.* London, 1730. Two folding maps. $3,500.

HUMPHREYS, Henry Noel. *A History of the Art of Printing from Its Invention to . . .* London, 1867. One of 300 copies. $500. London, 1868. Second issue with the section on references at the end of the book in the first issue suppressed because of errors. 100 facsimiles in photolithography. $400.

HUMPHREYS, Henry Noel. *The Illuminated Books of the Middle Ages.* London, 1844–49. 39 colored plates, one plain plate. Folio, half calf. $2,250. Small-paper edition. $1,000.

HUMPHREYS, Henry Noel. *Masterpieces of the Early Printers and Engravers . . .* London, 1870. 81 full-page illustrations. $400.

HUMPHREYS, Henry Noel. *The Origin and Progress of the Art of Writing . . .* London, 1855. Second edition. First was 1852. $500.

HUMPHRIES, Sydney. *Oriental Carpets, Runners and Rugs.* London, 1910. Illustrated. Folio, cloth. $500.

HUMPHREYS, Henry Noel. *British Butterflies and Their Transformations.* London, 1841. Hand-colored title and 42 hand-colored plates. $1,500.

HUNEKER, James. *Mezzotints in Modern Music.* New York, 1899. Author's first book. $150.

HUNEKER, James. *Painted Veils.* New York (1920). Blue boards, vellum spine. First edition, on watermarked paper. One of 1,200 signed copies. $250. New York, 1929. 12 color plates by Majeska. One of 1,250 copies. $150.

HUNT, J.H.L. *Juvenilia; or, A Collection of Poems.* London, 1801. Leigh Hunt's first book. Frontispiece. $1,000.

HUNT, James H. *A History of the Mormon War.* St. Louis, 1844. $5,000.

HUNT, James H. *Mormonism: Embracing the Origin, Rise and Progress of the Sect.* St. Louis, 1844. Expanded edition of the foregoing title. With errata leaf. $5,000.

HUNT, John. *Gazetteer of the Border and Southern States.* Pittsburgh, 1863. Folding map in color. $500.

HUNT, Leigh. See Hunt, J.H.L. See also *Christianism; The Feast of the Poets; Sir Ralph Esher.*

HUNT, Leigh. *Amyntas, A Tale of the Woods.* From the Italian of Torquato Tasso. London, 1820. $600.

HUNT, Leigh. *The Autobiography of Leigh Hunt.* London, 1850. 3 vols. Portraits. $750.

HUNT, Leigh. *The Correspondence of Leigh Hunt.* London, 1862. 2 vols. Edited by His Eldest Son. Portrait. Tan cloth. $750.

HUNT, Leigh. *A Jar of Honey from Mount Hybla.* London, 1848. Engraved title page. First binding in glazed boards. $600. Later issue is plain cloth. $250.

HUNT, Leigh. *Men, Women and Books.* London, 1847. 2 vols. Portrait. Orange cloth. $350. New York, 1847. 2 vols. $250.

HUNT, Leigh. *The Old Court Suburb—Memorials of Kensington, Regal, Critical and Anecdotal.* London, 1902. 2 vols. One of 150 copies. $450.

HUNT, Leigh. *The Palfrey.* London, 1842. 6 woodcuts. $600.

HUNT, Leigh. *Stories from the Italian Poets . . .* London, 1846. 2 vols. Dark-blue cloth. With December ads (VAB). $350.

HUNT, Lynn Bogue. *An Artist's Game Bag.* New York: Derrydale Press, 1936. 4 color plates, other illustrations. Full leatherette. One of 1,250 copies. $450. Trade issue in cloth. $250.

HUNT, Richard S., and RANDEL, Jesse F. *Guide to the Republic of Texas.* New York, 1839. Folding map. 63 pages, in original cloth. $2,500.

HUNT, Richard S., and RANDEL, Jesse F. *A New Guide to Texas.* New York, 1845. Folding map, 62 pages, cloth. Second edition of preceding title. $4,000. New York, 1846 [*sic*]. With map dated 1848. $2,000.

HUNT, T. Dwight. *The Past and Present of the Sandwich Islands.* San Francisco, 1853. $1,000.

HUNT, Thomas Frederick. *Designs for Parsonage Houses . . .* London, 1827. $750.

HUNT, Violet. *The Maiden's Progress.* London, 1894. Author's first book. $300. New York, 1894. $250.

HUNTER, Alexander. *Johnny Reb and Billy Yank.* New York, 1905. Illustrated. $450.

HUNTER, Dard. *Before Life Began, 1883–1923.* Cleveland: Rowfant Club, 1941. In slipcase. One of 219 copies signed by Bruce Rogers. $750.

HUNTER, Dard. *The Literature of Papermaking, 1390–1800.* (Chillicothe, 1925.) Signatures loosely inserted in a three-quarter cloth portfolio with cloth ties. One of 190 signed copies. $3,500.

HUNTER, Dard. *Massachusetts Institute of Technology: Dard Hunter Paper Museum.* (Cambridge, Mass., 1939.) Frontispiece photograph. Printed wraps with woodcut on front. $200.

HUNTER, Dard. *My Life with Paper.* New York, 1958. Two specimens of paper tipped in. $200.

HUNTER, Dard. *Old Papermaking.* Chillicothe, 1923. Author's first book on papermaking. One of 200 signed copies. Nine leaves mounted with paper samples. $4,500.

HUNTER, Dard. *Papermaking: The History and Technique of an Ancient Craft.* New York, 1943. $300. New York, 1947. Second edition, revised and enlarged. Foldout map. $200.

HUNTER, Dard. *Papermaking by Hand in America.* Chillicothe, 1950. One of 210 copies signed by both Hunter and Dard Hunter, Jr. Hand-colored frontispiece. 96 facsimiles tipped in,

27 reproductions of watermarks, and 42 full-size reproductions of old paper labels. In dropleaf slipcase. 10,000.

HUNTER, Dard. *Papermaking by Hand in India.* New York, 1939. One of 370 copies signed by Hunter and Elmer Adler. 27 paper specimens. Boxed. $3,500.

HUNTER, Dard. *Papermaking in Indo-China.* (Chillicothe), 1947. One of 182 signed copies. In slipcase with leather tips on openings. Many reproductions and two actual specimens tipped in. $5,500.

HUNTER, Dard. *Papermaking in Pioneer America.* Philadelphia, 1952. $200.

HUNTER, Dard. *Paper-Making in the Classroom.* Peoria (1931). $250.

HUNTER, Dard. *A Papermaking Pilgrimage to Japan, Korea and China.* New York, 1936. One of 370 copies signed by Hunter and Elmer Adler. 50 tipped-in paper specimens. 68 photogravure illustrations. In slipcase. $4,500.

HUNTER, Dard. *Papermaking Through Eighteen Centuries.* New York, 1930. In dustwrapper. $350.

HUNTER, Dard. *Primitive Papermaking.* Chillicothe, 1927. Signatures loosely inserted in portfolio with cloth ties, in slipcase. One of 200 signed copies. $7,500.

HUNTER, Evan. *Find the Feathered Serpent.* Philadelphia (1952). Author's first book. $250.

HUNTER, George. *Reminiscences of an Old Timer . . .* San Francisco, 1887. 16 plates. Pictorial cloth. $350.

HUNTER, J. Marvin (compiler). *The Trail Drivers of Texas . . .* (San Antonio, 1920–23.) 2 vols., with an additional revised vol. 1. Illustrated. The set of three (usually sold this way). $3,000. Nashville, 1925. 2 vols. in 1. One of 100 copies. $1,500. Trade. $300. New York, 1963. 2 vols. $150. One of 97 copies. $350.

HUNTER, J. Marvin, and ROSE, Noah H. *The Album of Gun-Fighters.* (Banders, Tex., 1951.) Pictorial cloth. $250. One of 300 copies with signed slip. $450.

HUNTER, Capt. John. *An Historical Journal of the Transactions at Port Jackson and Norfolk Island . . .* London, 1793. With engraved title, portrait, 10 plates, and 5 folding maps. $6,000.

HUNTER, John. *A Treatise on the Blood, Inflammation, and Gun-Shot Wounds . . .* London, 1794. 9 engraved plates by William Skelton. $3,500.

HUNTER, John D. *Manners and Customs of Several Indian Tribes Located West of the Mississippi.* Philadelphia, 1823. $1,500.

HUNTER, John D. *Memoirs of a Captivity Among the Indians of North America.* London, 1823. $750.

HUNTER, Robert. *The Links.* New York, 1926. $1,250.

HUNTER, Stephen. *The Master Sniper.* New York, 1980. Author's first book. $600.

HUNTER, William S., Jr. *Hunter's Ottawa Scenery.* Ottawa, 1855. Engraved title page, folding map, and 13 plates. Folio, cloth. $3,500.

HUNTER, William S., Jr. *Panoramic Guide from Niagara Falls to Quebec.* Montreal/Boston, 1857. Engraved title, folding panoramic chart. Pictorial cloth. $350.

HUNTINGTON, D. B. *Vocabulary of the Utah and Sho-Sho-Ne, or Snake Dialect, with Indian Legends and Traditions.* Salt Lake City, 1872. 32 pages, stitched. Third edition. $10,000 at auction in 1999.

HUNTLEY, Lydia. *Moral Pieces . . .* Hartford, 1815. (By Lydia Huntley Sigourney.) Author's first book. $600.

HUNTON, Addie, and JOHNSON, Kathern M. *Two Colored Women with the American Expeditionary Forces.* Brooklyn, 1920. $450.

HURSTON, Zora Neale. *Jonah's Gourd Vine.* Philadelphia, 1934. Author's first book. $7,500. London, 1934. $2,500.

HURSTON, Zora Neale. *Mules and Men.* Philadelphia, 1935. $2,000. London, 1936. $1,000.

HURSTON, Zora Neale. *Seraph on the Suwanee.* New York, 1948. $1,000.

HURSTON, Zora Neale. *Tell My Horse.* Philadelphia (1938). $1,250.

HURSTON, Zora Neale. *Their Eyes Were Watching God.* Philadelphia (1937). $3,500. London, 1938. $2,500.

HUSTON, John. *Frankie and Johnny.* New York, 1930. Illustrated by Miguel Covarrubias. $350.

HUTCHINGS, James M. *Scenes of Wonder and Curiosity in California.* San Francisco (1860). Cloth. $500. Sheep. $750. San Francisco, 1861. Second edition (or issue). $450.

HUTCHINS, Thomas. *An Historical Narrative and Topographical Description of Louisiana and West Florida . . .* Philadelphia, 1784. $7,500.

HUTCHINS, Thomas. *A Topographical Description of Virginia, Pennsylvania . . .* London, 1778. $37,000 at auction in 1999. Boston, 1787. $12,500.

HUTCHINSON, Francis. *An Historical Essay Concerning Witchcraft.* London, 1718. $1,000.

HUTCHINSON, Horace. *British Golf Links.* 1897. One of 250 large-paper copies. Wraps. $4,000. Trade. $2,000.

HUTCHINSON, Horace. *50 Years of Golf.* London (1919). $500.

HUTCHINSON, Horace. *Golf: Badminton Library.* 1890. One of 250 copies in half leather. Large-paper copies. $2,500. Trade in cloth. $750.

HUTCHINSON, Horace. *A Golfing Pilgrim on Many Links.* London, 1898. $750. New York, 1898. $600.

HUTCHINSON, Horace (editor), with LANG, Andrew et al. *Famous Golf Links.* London, 1891. $1,500.

HUTTON, William. *The Life of William Hutton . . .* London, 1817. Second edition, with additions. $350.

HUXLEY, Aldous. See *Jonah*.

HUXLEY, Aldous. *After Many a Summer.* London, 1939. $450. New York, 1939. $300.

HUXLEY, Aldous. *Along the Road.* London, 1925. Top edge green. $250. New York (1925). Boards. One of 250 signed copies. In dustwrapper. In slipcase. $300.

HUXLEY, Aldous. *Antic Hay.* London, 1923. Top edge yellow. $500.

HUXLEY, Aldous. *Apennine.* Gaylordsville, N.Y., 1930. Boards and cloth, paper label. One of 91 signed copies. Issued without dustwrapper. In slipcase. $750.

HUXLEY, Aldous. *Arabia Infelix and Other Poems.* New York: Fountain Press, 1929. Boards and cloth. One of 692 signed copies. $250.

HUXLEY, Aldous. *Brave New World.* London, 1932. Buckram, leather label. One of 324 signed copies. In acetate dustwrapper. $5,000. Trade. $6,000. Garden City, 1932. First American edition. One of 250 signed copies. $3,500. Trade. $750. Limited Editions Club, New York, 1974. In slipcase. $125.

HUXLEY, Aldous. *Brief Candles.* New York: Fountain Press, 1930. First American edition. One of 842 signed copies. $250. Trade. $200. London, 1930. Red cloth. $200.

HUXLEY, Aldous. *The Burning Wheel.* Oxford, 1916. Author's first book. Woodcut decorations. Yellow wraps, paper label. $1,250.

HUXLEY, Aldous. *Crome Yellow.* London, 1921. Yellow cloth, top stained green. In dustwrapper. $500. New York (1922). $300.

HUXLEY, Aldous. *The Defeat of Youth and Other Poems.* (Oxford, 1918.) Without title page. Decorated stiff wraps. $400.

HUXLEY, Aldous. *Do What You Will.* London, 1929. One of 260 signed copies. In glassine jacket without slipcase. $300. Trade. $200.

HUXLEY, Aldous. *Essays New and Old.* London: Florence Press, 1926. One of 650 signed copies. In dustwrapper. (No trade edition.) $300.

HUXLEY, Aldous. *Eyeless in Gaza.* London, 1936. Decorated boards and brown buckram. One of 200 signed copies. Issued without dustwrapper or slipcase. $600. Trade. $400.

HUXLEY, Aldous. *Holy Face and Other Essays.* London, 1929. Colored illustrations. Buckram. One of 300 copies. Issued without dustwrapper in slipcase. $300.

HUXLEY, Aldous. *Leda.* London, 1920. One of 160 signed copies. $350. Trade edition in dustwrapper. $350. Garden City, 1929. One of 361 signed copies. Issued without dustwrapper in slipcase. $250.

HUXLEY, Aldous. *Music at Night and Other Essays.* New York: Fountain Press, 1931. One of 842 signed copies. Issued without dustwrapper in slipcase. $250. Trade edition. $125. London, 1931. $175.

HUXLEY, Aldous. *On the Margin.* London, 1923. Green cloth, top stained blue. First edition, with page "vi" numbered "v" in error (Cutler and Stiles), "vii" (Casanova). $200. Second issue corrected and top green edge. $150. New York, 1923. $150.

HUXLEY, Aldous. *Point Counter Point.* London, 1928. One of 256 signed copies. $600. Trade edition in orange cloth. $500. Garden City, 1928. $250.

HUXLEY, Aldous. *Vulgarity in Literature.* London, 1930. One of 260 signed copies. $250. (A few copies were bound in leather [VAB].) Trade in decorated boards. $150. Garden City, 1933. $125.

HUXLEY, Aldous. *Words and Their Meanings.* Los Angeles (1940). One of 100 signed copies. In dustwrapper. $450.

HUXLEY, Elspeth. *Murder at Government House.* London, 1937. Author's first book. $250. New York, 1937. $250.

HUXLEY, T. H. *Evidence as to Man's Place in Nature.* London, 1863. $750.

HYDE, George E. *The Early Blackfeet and Their Neighbors.* Denver, 1933. 45 pages, wraps. One of 75 copies. $350.

HYDE, George E. *The Pawnee Indians.* Denver, 1934. 2 vols. Printed wraps. One of 100 copies. $500. Denver, 1951. $125.

HYDE, George E. *Rangers and Regulars.* Denver, 1933. 47 pages, wraps. One of 50 copies. $300.

HYDE, S. C. *Historical Sketch of Lyon County, Iowa.* Le Mars, Iowa, 1872. Map. 40 pages, wraps. $300.

HYNE, C. J. Cutliffe. *The Lost Continent.* London, 1900. $200.

HYPERION: A Romance. New York, 1839. By the author of "Outre-Mer." (Henry Wadsworth Longfellow.) 2 vols. $750. London, 1865. With 24 mounted photos by Francis Firth. $1,000. Boston, 1868. First photo illustrations in an American novel. 24 mounted photos. $850.

I

IBSEN, Henrik. *A Doll's House.* London, 1889. One of 150 large-paper copies signed by the publisher. $2,500. New York, 1889. $250. (Published in Copenhagen in English under the title *Nora* in 1880.)

IBSEN, Henrik. *Peer Gynt: A Dramatic Poem.* London (1936). Illustrated in color by Arthur Rackham. Full white vellum. One of 460 copies signed by Rackham. In slipcase. $2,000. Trade edition. $350. Philadelphia (1936). $250. Limited Editions Club, New York, 1955. Illustrated. Pictorial boards. In slipcase. $75.

IDAHO: A Guide in Word and Picture. Caldwell, 1937. Illustrated. Pictorial cloth. (Edited by Vardis Fisher.) $750. First W.P.A. State Guide.

IDE, Simeon. *The Conquest of California: A Biography of William B. Ide.* Oakland: Grabhorn Press, 1944. Illustrations, map. Boards and cloth. One of 500 copies. $150.

IDE, William Brown. *A Biographical Sketch of the Life of William B. Ide . . . And . . . Account of the Virtual Conquest of California . . .* (Claremont, N.H., 1880.) (By Simeon Ide.) Half leather and cloth. One of 80 copies. $2,000. Another edition in printed wraps. (Claremont, 1885?) $600.

IDE, William Brown. *Who Conquered California?* Claremont, N.H. [1880?]. (By Simeon Ide.) Printed boards and cloth. $1,750.

IDEAL Husband (An). London, 1899. By the Author of *Lady Windermere's Fan.* (Oscar Wilde.) Lavender cloth. Large-paper issue. One of 100 signed copies. $6,000. One of 12 signed copies on vellum. $15,000. Trade issue. One of 1,000 copies. Light-brownish red linen. $1,250.

IDES, Evert Ysbrant. *Three Years Travel from Moscow Over-land to China.* London, 1706. Engraved title, 30 plates, folding engraved map. First edition in English. $3,000.

IGNATOW, David. *Poems.* Prairie City (1948). Author's first book. $350.

I KUNSTITUSHUN i Micha i nan vlhpisa Chickasha, Okla i nan apesa yvt apesa tokmak oke. ("Chickasaw People, Their Constitution and Their Law 1857–59. 1867–68. 1870–72.") Translated from English to Chickasaw by Allen Wright. Chickasha, Okla., 1872. $750.

ILES, Francis. *As for the Woman.* London (1939). (By Anthony Berkeley Cox.) $1,250.

I'LL Take My Stand . . . By Twelve Southerners. New York, 1930. (By Robert Penn Warren, et al.) $1,750.

ILLUSTRATED Atlas and History of Yolo County, California (The). San Francisco, 1879. 50 plates, map in color. Atlas folio, cloth. $1,750.

ILLUSTRATED History of Los Angeles County (An). Chicago, 1889. Illustrated. Full morocco. $750.

ILLUSTRATED History of San Joaquin County (An). Chicago, 1890. Full leather. $600.

IMAGINARY Conversations of Literary Men and Statesmen. London, 1824. (By Walter Savage Landor.) 2 vols. $200. (Note: Three other volumes of the *Conversations* subsequently appeared.) Limited Editions Club, New York, 1936. In slipcase. Signed by Mardersteig. $200.

IMAGIST Anthology (The). New York (1930). Edited by Ford Madox Ford and Glenn Hughes. One of 1,000. $400. London, 1930. Yellow cloth. First English edition. $350.

IMBERDIS, J. *Papyrus; Or, the Craft of Paper.* Bird & Bull Press. (North Hills), 1961. One of 113 copies. $400.

IMPARTIAL Appeal (An) to the Reason, Interest, and Patriotism of the People of Illinois, on the Injurious Effects of Slave Labour. [Philadelphia?], 1824. (By Morris Birkbeck.) 16 pages, unbound. $3,000. (Note: Only 4 copies known.)

IMPORTANCE of Being Earnest (The). London, 1899. By the Author of *Lady Windermere's Fan.* (Oscar Wilde.) Reddish-brown linen. One of 1,000 copies. $1,250. One of 100 copies on large paper, signed. $15,000. Vellum. One of 12 copies on Japan paper, signed. $25,000. New York, 1956. 2 vols. Decorated boards. One of 500 copies. In slipcase. $350.

IMPRINT (The). London, 1913. Complete set of 9 vols., all published. Stiff paper wraps. $400.

INCIDENTAL Numbers. London, 1912. (By Elinor Wylie.) Author's first book. Boards. One of 65 copies. $5,000.

INDIAN Council in the Valley of the Walla-Walla, 1855 (The). San Francisco, 1855. (By Lawrence Kipp.) 2 pages, pale-blue printed wraps. $1,000. Eugene, Ore., 1897. $125.

INDIAN Missions (The), in the United States of America, etc. Philadelphia, 1841. 34 pages, plain blue wraps. (This Jesuit report includes two letters of Pierre Jean De Smet.) $9,500 at auction in 1996.

INDIAN Treaties Printed by Benjamin Franklin, 1736–1762. Philadelphia, 1938. Folio, with leather spine label. Top stained red. In slipcase. One of 500 copies. $750.

INEZ: A Tale of the Alamo. New York, 1855. (By Augusta Jane Evans Wilson.) Author's first book. $400.

INFIDEL (The); or The Fall of Mexico. Philadelphia, 1835. (By Robert Montgomery Bird.) 2 vols. $400.

INGE, William. *Bus Stop.* New York (1955). $300.

INGE, William. *Come Back, Little Sheba.* New York (1950). Author's first book. First edition not stated. $500.

INGE, William. *Picnic.* New York (1953). $250.

INGELOW, Jean. *Poems.* London, 1867. $250.

INGERSOLL, Luther A. *Century Annals of San Bernardino County.* (1769 to 1904.) Los Angeles, 1904. Portraits and views. Full morocco. $250.

INGERSOLL, Robert G. *An Oration Delivered . . . at Rouse's Hall, Peoria, Ill., at the Unveiling of a Statue of Humboldt, September 14th, 1869.* Peoria, 1869. Author's first published work. Wraps. $200.

INGOLDSBY, Thomas. *The Ingoldsby Legends, or Mirth and Marvels.* London, 1840–42–47. (By Richard Harris Barham.) Etchings by George Cruikshank and John Leech. 3 vols. With misprint "topot" on page 350 of vol. 3 and blank page 236 in vol. 1 (VAB). $750. London, 1898. Illustrated by Arthur Rackham. Green cloth. $600. London, 1907. Illustrated by Rackham. White vellum. One of 560 copies signed by Rackham. $2,000. Ordinary issue, cloth. $450.

INGRAHAM, Joseph Holt. See *The South-West.*

INGRAHAM, Joseph Holt. *Pierce Tenning, or, The Lugger's Chase.* Boston, 1846. Illustrated. 95 pages, stitched. Wraps. $350.

IN MEMORIAM. London, 1850. (By Alfred, Lord Tennyson.) Dark-purple cloth. First (and perhaps second) printing, with "baseness" for "bareness" in line 3, page 198. $750. London: Nonesuch Press, 1933. One of 125 copies in vellum. $500. Boards. One of 1,875 copies. $175.

INMAN, Col. Henry. *The Old Santa Fe Trail.* New York, 1897. Frontispiece, 8 plates by Frederic Remington, folding map. $225.

INMAN, Col. Henry. *Stories of the Old Santa Fe Trail.* Kansas City, 1881. Author's first book. Pictorial cloth. $400.

INMAN, Col. Henry (editor). *Buffalo Jones' 40 Years of Adventure.* Topeka, 1899. 43 plates. Pictorial cloth. $350.

INMAN, Col. Henry, and CODY, William F. *The Great Salt Lake Trail.* New York, 1898. Map, 8 plates. Pictorial buckram. First binding, blue (later brown). $300.

INNES, Michael. *Death at the President's Lodging.* London, 1936. Author's first book. $1,500.

INNES, Michael. *Seven Suspects.* (New title for first book.) New York, 1936. $750.

INSTRUCTION for Heavy Artillery . . . for the Use of the Army of the United States. Charleston, 1861. 39 plates, tables, charts. $1,750.

INSUBORDINATION . . . New York, 1841. (By T. S. Arthur.) Author's first book. $350.

INVINCIBLE, Ned. *The Rose That Bloometh in My Heart.* [Louisville?] (1908.) (By Edward Smyth Jones.) Author's first book. $450.

IRELAND, Samuel. *Picturesque Views on the River Thames . . .* London, 1792. 2 vols. Colored frontispiece, 2 engraved maps, and 52 color plates. $1,250.

IRISH, William. *Phantom Lady.* Philadelphia, 1942. (By Cornell Woolrich.) $1,250.

IRON, Ralph. *The Story of an African Farm.* London, 1883. (By Olive Schreiner.) 2 vols. Author's first book. $1,250. Limited Editions Club, Uganda (New York), 1961. Illustrated by Paul Hogarth. In slipcase. $175.

IRVING, John. *The Hotel New Hampshire.* New York (1981). One of 550 signed copies. Full leather. In slipcase. $400. Trade. $40. London (1981). $50.

IRVING, John. *Setting Free the Bears.* New York (1968). Author's first book. $1,500.

IRVING, John. *The Water-Method Man.* New York (1972). $500. London, 1980. Wraps (assumed). $75.

IRVING, John Treat, Jr. *The Hawk Chief: A Tale of the Indian Country.* Philadelphia, 1837. 2 vols. $600.

IRVING, John Treat, Jr. *The Hunters of the Prairie, or the Hawk Chief.* London, 1837. 2 vols. In original boards and cloth. First English edition of *The Hawk Chief.* $350.

IRVING, John Treat, Jr. *Indian Sketches, Taken During an Expedition to the Pawnee Tribes.* Philadelphia, 1835. 2 vols. In original cloth. $500. London, 1835. 2 vols. First English edition. In original cloth. $500.

IRVING, Washington. See Crayon, Geoffrey; Depons, François; Knickerbocker, Diedrich; Langstaff, Launcelot; Oldstyle, Jonathan. See also *Abbotsford; Legends of the Conquest of Spain; A Tour on the Prairies.*

IRVING, Washington. *Astoria.* Philadelphia, 1836. 2 vols. In original cloth. First state: copyright on verso of Vol. I title page; footnote on page 239 of Vol. II reads "*Bra6.db ury. P. 6 / *Breckenridge"; first page of terminal ads has "Books Published"; terminal ads not boxed. $750. Second state. Vol. I title page verso blank. Page 239 footnote not present. Ads have "New Works." $500. London, 1836. 3 vols. $750.

IRVING, Washington. *Chronicles of Wolfert's Roost.* Edinburgh (London), 1855. Tan cloth or wraps. First issue, with *Constable's Miscellany* listed as "In the Press . . . Volume V" (later reading, "Volume VII"). $200.

IRVING, Washington. *A History of the Life and Voyages of Christopher Columbus.* London, 1828. 4 vols. 2 folding maps. $850. New York, 1828. 3 vols. First American edition. Folding map. $650.

IRVING, Washington. *The Legend of Sleepy Hollow.* New York (1897). Designs by Will Bradley. Pictorial boards. $300. London (1928). Cloth. Illustrated by Arthur Rackham. $600. One of 250 copies signed by Rackham. $2,500. Philadelphia (1928). $500. One of 125 copies signed by Rackham. $2,250.

IRVING, Washington. *The Life of George Washington.* New York, 1855–59. 5 vols., cloth. With dates as follows: vols. 1 and 2, 1855; 3, 1856; 4, 1857; and 5, 1859. $750. Large-paper edition (vol. 2 dated 1856). One of 110 copies. $1,000.

IRVING, Washington. *The Rocky Mountains.* Philadelphia, 1837. "Digested from the Journal of Captain B. L. E. Bonneville . . . by Washington Irving." 2 folding maps. 2 vols. in original blue cloth, printed labels. First issue, with no ads and 2 blank fly leaves at each end. $750.

IRVING, Washington. *Voyages and Discoveries of the Companions of Columbus.* London, 1831. $350. Philadelphia, 1831. $250.

IRWIN, Margaret. *Madame Fears the Dark . . .* London, 1935. $200.

ISELIN, Isaac. *Journal of a Trading Voyage Around the World, 1805–1808.* (New York, about 1897.) (100 copies printed.) $1,000.

ISHERWOOD, Christopher. See Auden, W. H., and Isherwood, Christopher; Baudelaire, Charles.

ISHERWOOD, Christopher. *All the Conspirators.* London, 1928. Author's first novel. $4,500.

ISHERWOOD, Christopher. *The Berlin Stories: The Last of Mr. Norris, Goodbye to Berlin.* (Norfolk, Conn.): New Directions, 1945. $250.

ISHERWOOD, Christopher. *Christopher and His Kind.* New York (1976). One of 100 signed copies. In slipcase. $500.

ISHERWOOD, Christopher. *Goodbye to Berlin.* London: Hogarth Press, 1939. $2,500. New York, 1939. $750.

ISHERWOOD, Christopher. *The Last of Mr. Norris.* New York, 1935. $1,000.

ISHERWOOD, Christopher. *Lions and Shadows: An Education in the Twenties.* London, 1938. Portrait frontispiece. Blue cloth lettered in black. $750. Later (most) lettered in gilt. $600. Norfolk: New Directions (1947). $250.

ISHERWOOD, Christopher. *The Memorial: Portrait of a Family.* London: Hogarth Press, 1932. First binding in pale pink, lettered in blue. $750. Later binding in blue or ocher. $500. Norfolk: New Directions [about 1946]. $200.

ISHERWOOD, Christopher. *Mr. Norris Changes Trains.* London: Hogarth Press, 1935. $2,500.

ISHERWOOD, Christopher. *Prater Violet*. New York (1945). Gray cloth. $200. London (1946). $150.

ISHERWOOD, Christopher. *Sally Bowles*. London: Hogarth Press, 1937. $1,250.

ISHIGURO, Kazuo. *A Pale View of the Hills*. (London, 1982.) Author's first book. $1,250. New York (1982). $250.

ISHIGURO, Kazuo. *The Remains of the Day*. London (1989). $300. New York, 1989. $150.

ISHIKAWA, T., and DRAEGER, D. F. *Judo Training Methods: A Sourcebook*. Tokyo, 1962. First edition stated. $150.

IVANHOE: A Romance. Edinburgh, 1820. (By Sir Walter Scott.) 3 vols. $1,500. Limited Editions Club, New York, 1951. 2 vols. Illustrated. Pictorial cloth. In slipcase. $150.

IVES, Charles. *Essays Before a Sonata*. New York, 1920. Author's first book. Issued without dustwrapper? $1,250.

IVES, Joseph C. *Report Upon the Colorado River of the West*. Washington, 1861. 2 folding maps, 8 folding panoramic views, 25 plates. House of Representatives Doc. 90. $1,750. Senate issue. 3 maps and 31 plates. $1,500.

IVINS, Virginia W. *Pen Pictures of Early Western Days*. (Keokuk, Iowa), 1905. Plates. $350. Second edition. (Keokuk), 1908. $300.

J

JACKSON, A. P., and COLE, E. C. *Oklahoma! Politically and Topographically Described*. Kansas City (1885). Map (not in all copies). Pictorial wraps in color. $600.

JACKSON, A. W. *Barbariana: or Scenery, Climate, Soils and Social Conditions of Santa Barbara City and County*. San Francisco, 1889. 48 pages, printed wraps. $300.

JACKSON, Andrew. *Message from the President of the United States, in Compliance with a Resolution of the Senate Concerning the Fur Trade and Inland Trade to Mexico*. (Washington, 1832.) 86 pages, unbound. Senate Doc. 90. $350.

JACKSON, Benjamin Daydon. *Guide to the Literature of Botany*. London, 1881. $300.

JACKSON, Benjamin Daydon. *Vegetable Technology: A Contribution Towards a Bibliography . . .* London, 1882. This is the vol. XI of the Publications of the Index Society. $150.

JACKSON, Charles. *The Lost Weekend*. New York (1944). Author's first book. $450.

JACKSON, Charles James. *An Illustrated History of English Plate . . .* London, 1911. 2 vols. Colored frontispiece. 76 photogravure plates. Half morocco. $650.

JACKSON, Mrs. F. Nevill. *Toys of Other Days*. London, 1908. 9 color plates, 273 plain illustrations. Full vellum. One of 50 copies. $600. Morocco. One of 150 copies. $500. Ordinary issue in cloth. $250.

JACKSON, George. *Sixty Years in Texas.* (Dallas, 1908.) First issue: 322 pages. Plates. Cloth. $250.

JACKSON, Helen Hunt. See H.H.

JACKSON, Helen Hunt. *Glimpses of Three Coasts.* Boston, 1886. $100.

JACKSON, Helen Hunt. *The Procession of Flowers in Colorado.* Boston, 1886. One of 100 copies. Illustrated by Alice A. Stewart. $750.

JACKSON, Helen (Hunt). *Ramona.* Boston, 1884. Decorated cloth. $1,000. Limited Editions Club, Los Angeles, 1959. Introduction by J. Frank Dobie. Cloth. In slipcase. $150.

JACKSON, Holbrook. *The Anatomy of Bibliomania.* London, 1930. 2 vols. One of 1,000 copies. $275. Morocco. One of 48 signed copies. $750. New York, 1931. 2 vols. $250.

JACKSON, Holbrook. *The Fear of Books.* London, 1932. Full black morocco. One of 48 signed copies. $600. Trade edition in buckram (2,008 copies). $125.

JACKSON, J. Hughlings. *Selected Writings of John Hughlings Jackson.* New York (1958). 2 vols. $300.

JACKSON, John. *The Practical Fly-Fisher.* London, 1854. 10 hand-colored plates. $750. London, 1880. $500.

JACKSON, Jon. *The Blind Pig.* New York (1978). $175.

JACKSON, Jon. *The Diehard.* New York (1977). Author's first book. $300.

JACKSON, Shirley. *The Bird's Nest.* New York (1954). $150.

JACKSON, Shirley. *Hangsaman.* New York (1951). $300.

JACKSON, Shirley. *The Haunting of Hill House.* New York, 1959. $1,000.

JACKSON, Shirley. *The Lottery.* New York, 1949. With publisher's initials on copyright page. Dustwrapper price: "$2.75." $1,500.

JACKSON, Shirley. *The Road Through the Wall.* New York (1948). Author's first book. $850.

JACKSON, William A. *An Annotated List of the Publications of the Rev. Thomas Frognall Dibdin . . .* Cambridge, 1965. One of 500 copies. $150.

JACOB, J. G. *The Life and Times of Patrick Gass.* Wellsburg, Va., 1859. Portrait and 3 plates. Cloth. $1,500.

JACOBS, Thomas Jefferson. *Scenes, Incidents and Adventures in the Pacific Ocean . . .* New York, 1844. Folding plate, numerous other illustrations. $750.

JACOBS, W. W. *Many Cargoes.* London, 1896. Author's first book. 52 pages of ads dated Autumn, 1896. With portrait and 6 hand-colored plates. $200.

JACOBSEN, Josephine. *Let Each Man Remember.* Dallas (1940). $250.

JAEGER, Benedict. *The Life of North American Insects.* Providence, 1854. With portrait and 6 hand-colored plates. $750.

JAEGER, Doris U. *Faculty of the College of Physicians & Surgeons.* New York, 1919. (By Doris Ullman.) Author's first book. $500.

JAKES, John. *The Texans Ride North* . . . Philadelphia (1952). $300.

JAMES, Edwin (editor). *Account of an Expedition from Pittsburgh to the Rocky Mountains.* Philadelphia, 1822–23. Folding profile. Folding map. 8 plates. 3 vols. (including atlas). $12,500. London, 1823. 3 vols. First English edition. Folding map, chart and 8 plates. $4,500.

JAMES, Edwin (editor). *A Narrative of the Captivity and Adventures of John Tanner.* New York, 1830. Frontispiece portrait. $1,250.

JAMES, F. L. *The Wild Tribes of the Soudan.* New York, (1883). Frontispiece, 3 color maps, and 39 plates. $800.

JAMES, Fred. *The Klondike Goldfields and How to Get There.* London, 1897. Map. 68 pages, tan wraps. $750.

JAMES, George Wharton. *California, Romantic and Beautiful.* Boston, 1914. Folding map, 72 plates (8 in color). $200.

JAMES, Henry. *The Ambassadors.* London, 1903. Crimson cloth. (Second printing in blue cloth.) $600. New York, 1903. Blue boards. "Published November, 1903" on copyright page. In blue linen dustwrapper. $750. Without dustwrapper. $300. Limited Editions Club, New York, 1963. In slipcase. $100.

JAMES, Henry. *The American.* Boston, 1877. With Osgood imprint on spine. Without period after "Co" on title page. $750. With period. $600. With Houghton on spine. $450. London (1877). Pictorial boards. $750.

JAMES, Henry. *The American Scene.* London, 1907. Maroon buckram. $200. New York, 1907. $175.

JAMES, Henry. *The Aspern Papers: Louisa Pallant: The Modern Warning.* London, 1888. 2 vols. Blue cloth. $1,500. London/New York, 1888. First American edition. $350.

JAMES, Henry. *The Awkward Age.* New York 1899. Brown cloth. The vol. bulking 1⅝ inches thick (1⅜ inches later—Edel & Laurence, although BAL doesn't agree). $300. London, 1899. Light-blue cloth. (Issued simultaneously.) $250.

JAMES, Henry. *The Beast in the Jungle.* Kentfield, Calif.: Allen Press, 1963. Illustrated. Boards. One of 130 copies. $500.

JAMES, Henry. *The Better Sort.* New York, 1903. Rose-colored cloth. With "Published, February, 1903" on copyright page. $200. London, 1903. Red cloth. First English edition (simultaneous). $200.

JAMES, Henry. *The Bostonians.* London, 1886. 3 vols. Blue cloth. $7,500. (Martin copy brought $12,000 in 1990.) London, 1886. First 1-vol. edition. $500. New York, 1886. Orange cloth with maroon spine. Probable first binding. $500. Blue-black cloth. $300.

JAMES, Henry. *A Bundle of Letters.* Boston (1880). Stiff printed wraps. First edition, Blanck's state A (no priority) is considered primary by Edel & Laurence, with comma after "Jr." on front cover and name in wide-serif letters. $400. State B has comma after "Jr." lacking. $200. State C has name in small-serif letters. $150.

JAMES, Henry. *Confidence.* London, 1880. 2 vols. $6,000. Boston, 1880. 1 vol. First issue, with Houghton, Osgood imprint on spine. $600. Second issue with Houghton, Mifflin. $250.

JAMES, Henry. *Daisy Miller: A Comedy.* (London) 1882. Wraps. (18 privately printed copies.) $3,500. Boston, 1883. First published edition with Osgood on spine. $1,000. With Ticknor monogram on spine. $500. With Houghton Mifflin on spine. $400.

JAMES, Henry. *Daisy Miller: A Study.* New York, 1879. Printed tan or gray wraps, or green cloth. First issue with 79 titles in Harper's Half Hour Series at front. Wraps. $7,500. Cloth. $3,500. Limited Editions Club, New York, 1969. In slipcase. $125.

JAMES, Henry. *Daisy Miller and An International Episode.* New York, 1892. Vellum. One of 250 copies. $300. Trade edition in cloth. $125.

JAMES, Henry. *Embarrassments.* London, 1896. Blue cloth. With 4 irises on front of binding and ads at back. $350. Second had 9 irises, no ads at back. $200. New York, 1896. $300.

JAMES, Henry. *English Hours.* London, 1905. Illustrated by Joseph Pennell. Gray cloth. $150. Second binding, with dark-green buckram spine and green boards. $125. Boston, 1905. Cloth, or half morocco. First American trade edition. $125. Boards. One of 421 ("400 copies printed") on large paper. $300.

JAMES, Henry. *The Europeans: A Sketch.* London, 1878. 2 vols. (3 printings of 250 copies each. See bibliography.) $2,000. Boston, 1879. First American edition in 1 vol. $750. London, 1879. 1 vol. $600.

JAMES, Henry. *The Golden Bowl.* New York, 1904. 2 vols. $450. London (1905). Catalogue dated February 1905. $400. Dated March. $350.

JAMES, Henry. *Hawthorne.* London, 1879. With this title as "In Preparation" in ads at back. $400. With "Now Published." $250. New York, 1880. $250.

JAMES, Henry. *An International Episode.* New York, 1879. Gray wraps, or flexible green cloth. First state, with last line on page 44 repeated as the first line of page 45. Wraps. $850. Cloth. $750. Second state, corrected. $250.

JAMES, Henry. *Letters of Henry James to Walter Berry.* Paris: Black Sun Press, 1928. Printed vellum wraps. One of 16 copies on Japan vellum, each with an original letter. $6,000. One of 100 copies on Van Gelder paper. $1,000.

JAMES, Henry. *A Little Tour in France.* Boston, 1885 (actually 1884). Light-brown cloth. First binding with James R. Osgood imprint. $350. Second issue had Houghton Mifflin. $200. London, 1900. One of 150 copies in vellum. $500.

JAMES, Henry. *The Madonna of the Future and Other Tales.* London, 1879. 2 vols. Blue cloth. $7,500.

JAMES, Henry. *The Novels and Tales of Henry James.* New York, 1907–18. One of 156 copies on Ruisdael handmade paper. Adds new prefaces to each novel and each volume of tales. 24 vols. $17,500. 26 vols. (Last two issued in 1918.) $20,000. Trade issue in half Levant on sheets watermarked "H.J." 24 vols. $12,500. 26 vols. $15,000. In plum cloth. 24 vols. $10,000. 26 vols. $12,500. (Also mixed issues and other bindings.)

JAMES, Henry. *The Other House.* London, 1896. 2 vols. Blue cloth. $1,500. (Note: Second edition so stated, but first 1-vol. in 1897 states "First edition, 2 vols., October, 1896." $350.) New York, 1896. First American edition in 1 vol. $200.

JAMES, Henry. *A Passionate Pilgrim, and Other Tales.* Boston, 1875. Author's first book. First binding, with "J. R. Osgood & Co." on spine. $3,000. Second issue, "Houghton Osgood & Co." $1,250. Third issue, "Houghton, Mifflin & Co." $500.

JAMES, Henry. *The Portrait of a Lady.* London, 1881. 3 vols. Blue or dark-green cloth. With or without ads. (Edel and Laurence believe December 1881 ads are first, but only 750 copies in total.) $8,500. London, 1882. Second impression. 3 vols. $3,500. Boston, 1882. 1 vol. in light-tan or forest-green cloth with period after "Copyright, 1881." $750. Limited Editions Club, New York, 1967. In slipcase. $100.

JAMES, Henry. *The Princess Casamassima.* London, 1886. 3 vols. Blue cloth. $8,500. London, 1886. In 1 vol. $350.

JAMES, Henry. *The Reverberator.* London, 1888. 2 vols. Blue or green cloth. $1,500. London/New York, 1888. 1 vol. First American edition. Blue cloth. $300.

JAMES, Henry. *Roderick Hudson.* Boston, 1876. Author's first novel. First binding, with J. R. Osgood imprint on spine. $1,000. Later binding, Houghton Mifflin imprint on spine. $600.

JAMES, Henry. *The Siege of London.* Boston, 1883. Cloth. First issue, with Osgood imprint on spine. $300. Second issue, with Houghton Mifflin. $150.

JAMES, Henry. *The Spoils of Poynton.* London, 1897. Blue cloth. With 4 irises on front. $450. With nine tulips on front. $350. Boston, 1897. (May have been simultaneous.) $250.

JAMES, Henry. *Stories Revived.* London, 1885. 3 vols. Primary binding, blue cloth with brown endpapers. $4,000. Variant binding in blue-green cloth with blue on white patterned endpapers. $3,000. London, 1885. 2 vols. Blue cloth. $500. Cream cloth. $400.

JAMES, Henry. *The Tragic Muse.* London, 1890. 3 vols. $3,500. Boston, 1890. 2 vols. 1,000 copies. $1,000. London, 1891. 1 vol. $350.

JAMES, Henry. *Transatlantic Sketches.* Boston, 1875. First binding, with Osgood imprint on spine. $750. Later binding, with Houghton Mifflin. $600.

JAMES, Henry. *Washington Square.* New York, 1881. Dark olive-green cloth. $850. Limited Editions Club, New York, 1971. In slipcase. $75.

JAMES, Henry. *Washington Square:The Pension Beaurepas:A Bundle of Letters.* London, 1881. 2 vols. With last page numbered "371" and "H. James Jr." on spine. $6,000. Second printing. 2 vols. (only 250 copies), with last page "271" and "Henry/James Jr." on spine. $2,500. London, 1881. 1 vol. Frontispiece and illustrations by George Du Maurier. $750.

JAMES, Henry. *Watch and Ward.* Boston, 1878. With blank leaf after page 219. $1,250. Later printings without last leaf. $350.

JAMES, Henry. *What Maisie Knew.* London, 1898. (Actually published a month earlier than U.S. edition.) Blue cloth with tulips instead of irises on front cover. (Approximately 125 review copies.) $1,000. Regular edition with irises on front cover. $250. Chicago and New York, 1897. Probable first issue, with "Stone & Kimball" watermark. Decorated gray cloth. $350. Possible second issue, with "H.S. Stone/Chap Book" watermark. $250.

JAMES, Jason W. *Memorable Events in the Life of Capt. Jason W. James.* No place [about 1911]. Frontispiece. $1,250.

JAMES, Jason W. *Memories and Viewpoints.* Roswell, N.M., 1928. Issued without dustwrapper. $750.

JAMES, Jesse, Jr. *Jesse James, My Father.* Kansas City, Mo. 1899. (Ghostwritten by A. B. Macdonald?) 4 portraits. White printed wraps. $250.

JAMES, M. R. *Ghost Stories of an Antiquary.* London, 1904. Author's first book. $2,500.

JAMES, M. R. *Wailing Well.* Stanford Dingley, 1928. One of 150 copies. Issued without dustwrapper. $1,250.

JAMES, Norah C. *Sleeveless Errand.* Paris, 1929. First Continental edition of the author's first book. First book published by J. Kahane. One of 50 signed copies. $400. One of 450 unsigned copies. $125.

JAMES, P. D. *Cover Her Face.* London (1962). Author's first book. $3,000. New York (1966). $500.

JAMES, P. D. *A Mind to Murder.* London, 1963. $1,000. New York, 1967. $500.

JAMES, P. D. *Unnatural Causes.* London (1967). $750. New York (1967). $300.

JAMES, Philip. *Children's Books of Yesterday.* London, 1933. Edited by G. Geoffrey Holme. Cloth. $200.

JAMES, Thomas. *Three Years Among the Indians and Mexicans.* Waterloo, Ill., 1846. 130 pages, plain wraps. $60,000 at auction in 1999. St. Louis, 1916. 12 plates. Half cloth. Second edition. One of 365 copies. $400.

JAMES, Will. *All in the Day's Riding.* New York, 1933. $350.

JAMES, Will. *Cow Country.* New York, 1927. $450.

JAMES, Will. *Cowboys North and South.* New York, 1924. Author's first book. $750.

JAMES, Will. *Drifting Cowboy.* New York, 1925. $1,000.

JAMES, Will. *Lone Cowboy: My Life Story.* New York, 1930. One of 250 copies. $750. Trade. $300.

JAMES, Will. *Smoky the Cowhorse.* New York, 1926. $750. New York, 1929. $600.

JAMES, Will. *Young Cowboy.* New York, 1935. $750.

JAMES, William. *A Full and Correct Account of the Military . . . War Between Great Britain and the United States . . .* London, 1817. $750. London, 1818. 2 vols. 4 folding maps. $1,250.

JAMES, William. *The Principles of Psychology.* New York, 1890. 2 vols. Author's first book. First issue with "PSY-CHOLOGY" hyphenated in the ads opposite the title pages in both volumes. $2,000. Second issue. $1,500. London (1890). First English edition. $1,000.

JAMES, William. *The Varieties of Religious Experience.* New York, 1902. First edition stated. $500.

JAMESON, Anna Brownell. *The Beauties of the Court of King Charles II.* London, 1833. 21 hand-colored engraved portraits on India paper. $750.

JANE, Fred T. *The Torpedo in Peace and War.* London, 1898. 37 plates. $500.

JANSON, Charles William. *The Stranger in America.* London, 1807. Engraved title page, plan of Philadelphia, 9 (sometimes 10) aquatint plates. $2,500. Philadelphia, 1807. $1,500.

JANVIER, Thomas A. *The Aztec Treasure-House.* New York, 1890. Illustrated by Frederic Remington. Decorated cloth. $150.

JANVIER, Thomas A. *Color Studies.* New York, 1885. Author's first book. One of 1,000 copies. $250.

JARRELL, Randall. See *Five Young American Poets.*

JARRELL, Randall. *Blood for a Stranger.* New York (1942). Author's first book. $450.

JARRELL, Randall. *Little Friend, Little Friend.* New York, 1945. First edition not stated. $250.

JARRELL, Randall. *Losses.* New York (1948). First edition stated. $250.

JARRELL, Randall. *Pictures from an Institution.* New York, 1954. $125. London (1954). $100.

JARRELL, Randall. *The Seven-League Crutches.* New York (1951). $200.

JARVES, James. *History of Hawaiian or Sandwich Islands.* Boston, 1843. Folding map. $1,000.

JEFFRIES, John. *A Narrative of the Two Aerial Voyages of Doctor Jeffries . . .* London, 1786. Portrait and plate. $1,500. (More if original wraps are bound in.)

JEFFERIES, Richard. See *The Gamekeeper at Home.*

JEFFERIES, Richard. *Bevis: The Story of a Boy.* London, 1882. 3 vols. Brown cloth with catalogue at end. $1,500. Green cloth. $1,000.

JEFFERIES, Richard. *Greene Ferne Farm.* London, 1880. $300.

JEFFERIES, Richard. *Hodge and His Masters.* London, 1880. 2 vols. $500.

JEFFRIES, Richard. *Jack Brass, Emperor of England.* London, 1873. 12 pages, tan wraps. $750.

JEFFERIES, Richard. *The Open Air.* London, 1885. Printed cloth. $300. San Francisco, 1935. One of 500 copies. $300.

JEFFERIES, Richard. *Restless Human Hearts.* London, 1875. 3 vols. $1,250.

JEFFERIES, Richard. *The Toilers of the Field*. London, 1892. One of 105 large-paper, numbered copies. $500. Trade. $150.

JEFFERIES, Richard. *Wood Magic: A Fable*. London, 1881. 2 vols. $650.

JEFFERS, Robinson. See Powell, Lawrence Clark.

JEFFERS, Robinson. *An Artist*. Frontispiece. (Austin, 1928.) 16 pages, wraps. One of 96 copies. (Alberts states records show 200 copies) (Printed by John S. Mayfield.) $1,000.

JEFFERS, Robinson. *Be Angry at the Sun*. New York (1941). Marbled boards and cloth. One of 100 signed copies. In glassine dustwrapper. In slipcase. $1,000. Trade edition. $175.

JEFFERS, Robinson. *Californians*. New York, 1916. Blue cloth. In dustwrapper. $1,000. Lacking dustwrapper. $450. "Advance Copy, For Review Only" (perforation on title page). $1,250. Lacking dustwrapper. $450. Author's first commercially published book. No place, 1971. Boards and cloth. Introduction by William Everson. One of 50 copies (of an edition of 500) signed by Everson. Issued without dustwrapper. $350. Ordinary copies. $150.

JEFFERS, Robinson. *Cawdor and Other Poems*. New York, 1928. Buckram. One of 375 copies on large paper, signed. In dustwrapper. In slipcase. $450. Trade edition. $250. London: Hogarth Press, 1929. Boards. Issued without dustwrapper. $450. (Covelo, 1983.) One of 225 signed (illustrator and author of afterword) copies. $400.

JEFFERS, Robinson. *Dear Judas and Other Poems*. New York, 1929. Boards and cloth. First edition (preceding the limited edition). $250. Also, one of 350 signed copies. In glassine dustwrapper. In slipcase. $450. Also, one of 25 lettered copies. $2,000. London: Hogarth Press, 1930. Boards. Issued without dustwrapper. $450.

JEFFERS, Robinson. *Descent to the Dead*. New York (1931). Boards and vellum. One of 500 signed copies. Issued without dustwrapper. In unmarked slipcase. $600. (No trade editions issued.) Also 50 copies marked "Review" signed. In slipcase. $750.

JEFFERS, Robinson. *Flagons and Apples*. Los Angeles, 1912. (By John Robinson Jeffers.) Author's first book. $1,500.

JEFFERS, Robinson. *Give Your Heart to the Hawks*. New York, 1933. One of 200 signed copies. 1–185 for sale. In slipcase. $550. Trade. $250.

JEFFERS, Robinson. *The Loving Shepherdess*. New York, 1956. One of 115 copies signed by Robinson and Jean Kellogg. Boxed. $1,750. (Some with extra suite of plates may be priced higher.)

JEFFERS, Robinson. *Medea*. New York (1946). First issue with pages 99–100 integral, word "least" lacking at page 99, line 21. $200. Word "least" present page 99, line 21. $125. First English issue with labels on title page and dustwrapper flap. $250.

JEFFERS, Robinson. *Poems*. San Francisco, 1928. One of about 10 signed copies. Specially bound in half (red) morocco in slipcase. $3,000. One of 310 signed copies. Issued in unmarked slipcase. $1,500. (Note: copies also signed by Ansel Adams would be priced higher.)

JEFFERS, Robinson. *Return: An Unpublished Poem*. San Francisco, 1934. One of 3 copies on vellum specially bound in morocco. $4,000. One of 250 copies. Issued in flexible wraps. $350.

JEFFERS, Robinson. *Roan Stallion, Tamar, and Other Poems.* New York, 1925. $1,250. (Note: dustwrappers of later printings are marked with the number of printing.) One of 12 signed copies in blue or red binding. $2,500. London, 1928. $1,000. Covelo, 1990. One of 60 deluxe copies. $1,000. One of 75 copies. $750.

JEFFERS, Robinson. *Solstice and Other Poems.* New York, 1935. One of 320 signed copies. In unprinted gray dustwrapper. $500. Trade. $250.

JEFFERS, Robinson. *Stars.* (Pasadena), 1930. 72 copies. Reportedly all but 6 were destroyed. Black boards without dustwrapper. $2,500. Second edition in blue wraps. One of 110 copies. $1,000.

JEFFERS, Robinson. *Such Counsels You Gave to Me.* New York (1937). One of 300 signed copies. In slipcase. $500. Trade. $200.

JEFFERS, Robinson. *Tamar and Other Poems.* New York: Peter Boyle (1924). One of 500 copies. Gray unmarked dustwrapper. $1,000.

JEFFERS, Robinson. *Thurso's Landing and Other Poems.* New York (1932). One of 200 signed copies. 1–185 for sale. There were also 6 out-of-series copies. Issued in cellophane dustwrapper and slipcase. $500. Trade. $250.

JEFFERS, Una. *Visits to Ireland: Travel Diaries of Una Jeffers.* Los Angeles: Ward Ritchie Press, 1954. Foreword by Robinson Jeffers. Boards and cloth. One of 300 copies. In slipcase. $250.

JEFFERSON, Thomas. See *A Native . . .*

JEFFERSON, Thomas. *An Appendix to the Notes on Virginia Relative to the Murder of Logan's Family.* Philadelphia, 1800. 58 pages, sewn. $3,500.

JEFFERSON, Thomas. *A Manual of Parliamentary Practice for the Use of the Senate of the United States.* Washington, 1801. $3,000.

JEFFERSON, Thomas. *Memoir, Correspondence, and Miscellanies, from the Papers of Thomas Jefferson.* Charlottesville, 1829. 4 vols. $1,250.

JEFFERSON, Thomas. *Message from the President of the United States, Communicating Discoveries Made in Exploring the Missouri, Red River, and Washita by Capts. Lewis and Clark, Dr. Sibley, and Mr. Dunbar . . .* Washington, 1806. 2 folding tables, map (in some copies). 171 pages, unbound. "Printed by Order of the Senate." With map. $25,000. Without map. $5,000.

JEFFERSON, Thomas. *Notes on . . . Virginia.* (Paris) 1782. (Printed 1785.) Folding table. Pages 51–54, 167–68, 181–82, and 183–84 in uncanceled state. One of 200 copies printed and given away. $250,000. For first published edition: see next entry. London, 1787. Map. Table. $30,000. Philadelphia, 1788. Folding chart of Indian tribes. $5,000.

JEFFERSON, Thomas. *Observations sur la Virginie.* Paris, 1786. Two errata lists (Howes: one on ¼ page, the other 2½ pages.) Folding map. The first published edition of his famous work on his native state, issued the year after the private issue for presentation. $30,000. Lacking map. $5,000.

JEFFERYS, Thomas. *The American Atlas . . .* London, 1776. 23 maps on 30 folding or double-page sheets, some partially colored. $60,000.

JEFFERYS, Thomas. *The Natural and Civil History of the French Dominions in North America* . . . London, 1760. 2 vols. in 1. 18 large folding engraved maps and plans. $12,500.

JEFFREY, J. K. See *The Territory of Wyoming.*

JEKYLL, Gertrude. *Some English Gardens.* London, 1904. Folio with 50 color plates. $750.

JEKYLL, Gertrude, and HUSSEY, Christopher. *Garden Ornament.* London, 1918. Color frontispiece. Large folio. $1,000.

JENKINS, C. Francis. *Vision by Radio, Radio Photographs, Radio Photograms.* Washington (1925). Original cloth. $500.

JENKINS, John. *The Art of Writing, Reduced to a Plain and Easy System* . . . Cambridge (1813). Book I (all published). Engraved title, portrait and 10 unnumbered engraved plates. $450.

JENKINS, John H. *Cracker Barrel Chronicles: A Bibliography of Texas Town and Country Histories.* Austin, 1965. $150. One of 15 signed copies. Full tan leather. $750.

JENKS, Ira C. *Trial of David F. Mayberry, for the Murder of Andrew Alger.* (Cover title.) Janesville, Wis., 1855. 48 pages, wraps. $450.

JENNINGS, N. A. *A Texas Ranger.* New York, 1899. Tan pictorial cloth. $600.

JENNINGS, Oscar. *Early Woodcut Initials* . . . London (1908). $250.

JEREMIAH. See *The Lamentations of Jeremiah.*

JEROME, Chauncey. *History of the American Clock Business for the Past 60 Years.* New Haven, 1860. $450.

JEROME, Jerome K. *The Idle Thoughts of an Idle Fellow.* London, 1886. $250.

JEROME, Jerome K. *On the Stage and Off.* London, 1885. Author's first book. $300.

JEROME, Jerome K. *Three Men in a Boat.* Bristol, England, 1889. With ". . . Arrowsmith, Quay Street . . ." address. $500. New York, 1890. $200.

JEROME, Jerome K. *Told After Supper.* New York, 1890. $100. London, 1891. Illustrated. Pictorial red cloth. $150.

JERROLD, Douglas. *A Man Made of Money.* London, 1849. 12 plates by John Leech. 6 parts, pictorial wraps, and cloth. In parts. $850. Cloth. $400.

JERROLD, Douglas M. *Men of Character.* London, 1838. Author's first book. $450.

JEWETT, Sarah Orne. *Betty Leicester.* Boston, 1890. Decorated cloth. With this title last in ad for 10 titles opposite title page (11 titles later). $175.

JEWETT, Sarah Orne. *Betty Leicester's English Christmas.* Baltimore, 1894. White cloth. $600.

JEWETT, Sarah Orne. *A Country Doctor.* Boston, 1884. $300.

JEWETT, Sarah Orne. *The Country of the Pointed Firs.* Boston, 1896. Without blank leaf following ads at end. $600. Second printing with extra leaf. $200.

JEWETT, Sarah Orne. *Deephaven.* Boston, 1877. Author's first book. Cloth. With the reading "was" versus "so" in line 16, page 65. $750. Later printing with "so." $250. Cambridge, 1894. One of 250 large-paper copies. $250.

JEWETT, Sarah Orne. *Old Friends and New.* Boston, 1879. $400.

JEWITT, John R. *A Journal, Kept at Nootka Sound.* Boston, 1807. 48 pages. $6,000.

JEWITT, John R. *Narrative of the Adventures and Sufferings of John R. Jewitt.* Middletown, 1815. Edited by Richard Alsop. 2 plates. First issue, with Loomis & Richards imprint. $1,000. Second issue, Seth Richards imprint. $750. New York (about 1815). $750.

JHABVALA, R. Prawer. *Amrita.* New York, 1956. (New title.) First American edition of first book. $150.

JHABVALA, R. Prawer. *To Whom She Will.* London (1955). Author's first book. $300.

JOAQUIN *(The Claude Duval of California); or The Marauder of the Mines.* New York (1865 [actually later, in the 1870s]). (By Henry L. Williams.) 160 pages, pictorial wraps. $300. New York, 1888. Decorated cloth. Second edition. $150.

JOCKNICK, Sidney. *Early Days on the Western Slope of Colorado.* Denver, 1913. 25 plates. $300.

JOHANNSEN, Albert. *The House of Beadle and Adams and Its Dime and Nickel Novels.* Norman, Okla. (1950). 2 vols. and *Volume III: Supplement* . . . 1962. $200.

JOHN *Cheney and His Descendants, Printers in Banbury Since 1767.* Banbury, 1936. 70 full-page plates, 2 large foldout plates. $250.

JOHN *Halifax, Gentleman.* London, 1856. (By Dinah M. Craik.) 3 vols. Brown cloth. First issue with 3 pages of ads at end of vol. 1, 1 page at end of vol. 2, and 2 pages at end of vol. 3 (VAB). $1,000.

JOHN *Marr* . . . New York, 1888. (By Herman Melville.) 103 pages, printed yellow wraps. One of 25 copies. $16,000 (Martin copy at auction in 1990). Princeton, 1922. Half cloth. One of 175 copies. $300. Trade. $150.

JOHN, W. D. *Swansea Porcelain.* Newport, 1958. 20 color illustrations, others in black-and-white. Buckram. Issued without dustwrapper. $300.

JOHN *Woodvil: A Tragedy.* London, 1802. (By Charles Lamb.) $750.

JOHNS, W. E. *Biggles in Africa.* London, 1936. $1,500.

JOHNS, W. E. *Biggles in Spain.* London, 1939. $1,500.

JOHNSON, A. F. *Decorative Initial Letters.* London, 1931. One of 500 copies. 122 plates of examples. $300.

JOHNSON, B. S. *Traveling People.* London (1963). $200.

JOHNSON, Ben. See LeGrand, Mr.

JOHNSON, Benj. F. (of Boone). *"The Old Swimmin'-Hole" and 'Leven More Poems.* Indianapolis, 1883. (By James Whitcomb Riley.) Author's first book. Wraps. $1,250. (Note: There exists a 1909 facsimile, which lacks the "W" in "William" on page 41. Value: about $100.)

JOHNSON, Charles R. *Black Humor.* Chicago, 1970. Author's first book. Wraps. $150.

JOHNSON, Charles R. *Faith and the Good Thing.* New York (1974). First novel. $250.

JOHNSON, Charles R. *Middle Passage.* New York, 1990. $300.

JOHNSON, Crisfield (compiler). *The History of Cuyahoga County, Ohio.* Cleveland, 1879. Double-column pages. Half morocco. $250.

JOHNSON, Denis. *The Man Among the Seals.* Iowa City (1969). One of 260 copies. Issued without dustwrapper. $750.

JOHNSON, Don Carlos. *A Brief History of Springville, Utah.* Springville, 1900. First edition, with errata slip. Illustrated. Wraps. $300.

JOHNSON, Dorothy. *Hanging Tree.* New York, 1957. $250.

JOHNSON, Dorothy. *Beulah Bunny Tells All.* New York, 1942. Author's first book. $200.

JOHNSON, Dorothy M. *Miss Bunny Intervenes.* London, 1948. $200.

JOHNSON, E. Pauline. *The White Wampum.* London, 1895. $600. Boston/Toronto, 1895. $500.

JOHNSON, Edmund C. *Tangible Typography: Or, How the Blind Read.* London, 1853. 10 plates of raised letters. $450.

JOHNSON, Edward A. *History of the Negro Soldiers in the Spanish American War.* Raleigh, 1899. $850.

JOHNSON, Edwin F. *Railroad to the Pacific, Northern Route.* New York, 1854. Second (actually first book) edition. 2 maps, 8 plates in Howes (but also noted with 3 and 4 maps?). Boards and calf. $1,500.

JOHNSON, Frank M. *Forest, Lake and River . . .* Boston, 1902. 2 vols. Portrait and colored frontispiece. Bound in suede. One of 350 copies. $600.

JOHNSON, Frank W. *A History of Texas and Texans.* Chicago and New York, 1914. 5 vols. Green buckram with gilt. $400. Chicago, 1916. 5 vols. $350.

JOHNSON, Georgia Douglas. *Bronze.* Boston, 1922. $2,000.

JOHNSON, Harrison. *Johnson's History of Nebraska.* Omaha, 1880. Frontispiece, other illustrations; folding map in color. Blue cloth. $200.

JOHNSON, Henry L. *Gutenberg and the Book . . .* New York, 1932. One of 750 copies. With facsimile page from the Gutenberg Bible. In folding case. $250.

JOHNSON, Henry L. *An Introduction to Logography* . . . London, 1783. $1,750.

JOHNSON, Jack. *Jack Johnson in the Ring and Out.* Chicago, 1927. First edition stated. $350.

JOHNSON, James Weldon. See *The Autobiography of an Ex-Colored Man.*

JOHNSON, James Weldon. *Along This Way.* New York, 1933. $750.

JOHNSON, James Weldon. *Black Manhattan.* New York, 1930. $1,250.

JOHNSON, James Weldon. *Fifty Years and Other Poems.* Boston (1917). Half cloth. One of 110 copies on Japan vellum, signed. $2,500. Trade. $750.

JOHNSON, James Weldon. *God's Trombones.* New York, 1927. $750.

JOHNSON, James Weldon. *Negro Americans, What Now?* New York, 1934. $600.

JOHNSON, James Weldon. *Saint Peter Relates an Incident of the Resurrection Day.* New York, 1935. $400. One of 200 signed copies. In slipcase. $1,000.

JOHNSON, James Weldon (editor). *The Second Book of Negro Spirituals.* New York, 1926. $600.

JOHNSON, John. *Typographia, or the Printer's Instructor* . . . London, 1824. 2 vols. Duodecimo. $450.

JOHNSON, Lieut. Col. John. *A Journey from India to England* . . . London, 1799. Folding map and 4 plates. $1,000. London, 1818. 13 plates (5 colored). $1,500.

JOHNSON, Lionel. *The Art of Thomas Hardy.* London, 1894. Portrait. Boards. One of 150 copies. $650. Trade edition in cloth. $200.

JOHNSON, Lionel. *Poems.* London, 1895. One of 750 copies. $750. One of 25 signed copies. $6,000.

JOHNSON, Lionel. *Sir Walter Raleigh in the Tower.* (Chester), 1885. Author's first book. Wraps. $6,000.

JOHNSON, Lionel. *Twenty One Poems.* Dundrum, Ireland: Dun Emer Press, 1904. Selected by William Butler-Yeats. Boards and linen. One of 220 copies. $1,000.

JOHNSON, Martin. *Through the South Seas.* New York, 1913. Author's first book. $450.

JOHNSON, Merle. *American First Editions, Revised and Enlarged by Jacob Blanck.* New York (1942). Fourth and best edition. $150.

JOHNSON, Merle. *A Bibliography of Mark Twain.* New York, 1910. Author's first book. (500 copies.) $350. New York, 1935. Second edition, revised and enlarged. $350.

JOHNSON, Merle. *High Spots of American Literature.* New York, 1929. One of 50 signed copies. Full leather. $250. One of 700 copies in three-quarter leather (numbered 51 to 750). $175.

JOHNSON, Osa. *I Married Adventure: The Lives and Adventures of Martin and Osa Johnson.* Philadelphia (1940). One of 520 copies of the deluxe issue (with 16 photographs not in the trade edition). $500. Trade edition. $100.

JOHNSON, Overton, and WINTER, William H. *Route Across the Rocky Mountains . . .* Lafayette, Ind., 1846. Cloth-backed boards. $20,000.

JOHNSON, Pamela Hansford. *Symphony for Full Orchestra.* London, 1934. Author's first book. Cloth. $250. Wraps. $125.

JOHNSON, Ronald. *A Line of Poetry, A Row of Trees.* Highlands, 1964. Author's first book. One of 50 signed copies. $600. Stiff wraps. One of 500 copies. $150.

JOHNSON, Samuel. *An Account of the Life of Mr. Richard Savage.* London, 1744. $5,000.

JOHNSON, Samuel. *A Diary of a Journey into North Wales.* London, 1816. Edited by R. Duppa. Plates. $750.

JOHNSON, Samuel. *A Dictionary of the English Language . . .* London, 1755. 2 vols. Title pages printed in red and black. $15,000. London, 1756. Octavo. First abridged edition. 2 vols. $2,500. London, 1765. 2 vols. $3,000. Philadelphia, 1818. 4 vols. First American edition. $4,500.

JOHNSON, Samuel. *A Journey to the Western Islands of Scotland.* London, 1775. First edition has 12-line errata list following page 384. $1,500. Second contains only a 6-line errata list. $750. Baltimore, 1810. First American edition. $500.

JOHNSON, Samuel. *London: A Poem, and the Vanity of Human Wishes.* London, 1930. Introduction by T. S. Eliot. One of 150 copies signed by Eliot. $1,500.

JOHNSON, Samuel. *The Plan of the English Language . . .* London, 1747. First issue, with Lord Chesterfield's name on A1 recto. $12,500. London, 1747. Second issue, without Chesterfield's name on A1 recto. $10,000.

JOHNSON, Samuel. *The Prince of Abissinia.* London, 1759. 2 vols. $4,000.

JOHNSON, Sid S. *Some Biographies of Old Settlers.* (Only vol. I published.) Tyler, Tex., 1900. $300.

JOHNSON, Sidney S. *Texans Who Wore the Gray.* Tyler, no date [about 1907]. Illustrated. $600.

JOHNSON, Mrs. Susannah. *A Narrative of the Captivity of Mrs. Johnson.* Windsor, Vt., 1807. Second edition. $400.

JOHNSON, Theodore T. *Sights in the Gold Region, and Scenes by the Way.* New York, 1849. $750. New York, 1850. Second edition. Folding map, 7 plates (2 colored). $450.

JOHNSTON, Charles. *A Narrative of the Incidents Attending the Capture, Detention, and Ransom of . . .* New York, 1827. $600.

JOHNSTON, H. H. *Livingstone and the Exploration of Central Africa.* London, 1891. One of 250 large-paper copies. Maps, plates, gilt-lettered vellum and boards. Untrimmed. $500.

JOHNSTON, Lieut. Col. J. E., et al. *Reports of the Secretary of War, with Reconnaissances of Routes from San Antonio to El Paso . . .* Washington, 1850. 2 folding maps, 72 plates. $1,750.

JOHNSTON, Theodore. *Sights in the Gold Region and Scenes by the Way.* New York, 1849. $750.

JOHNSTON, William G. *Experiences of a Forty-niner.* Pittsburgh, 1892. Portrait and 13 plates. (With later, separately issued, folding blueprint map and an extra portrait.) $1,250.

JOHNSTONE, Sir Harry. *George Grenfell and the Congo*. London, 1908. 2 vols. 6 maps (2 folding). $1,000.

JOHONNOT, Jackson. *The Remarkable Adventures of Jackson Johonnot*. Boston, 1793. $5,000 at auction in 1999. Many reprints in Howes, which includes *Providence,* which brought $12,000 at auction in 1999. (First appeared in Beer's almanac, Hartford [1792].)

JOINVILLE, John, Lord of. *The History of Saint Louis, King Louis of France*. Newtown, Wales: Gregynog Press, 1937. Illustrated. Dark-maroon morocco. One of 200 copies. In slipcase. $3,000. One of 15 specially bound copies. $9,500.

JOKL, Ernst, M.D. *The Medical Aspect of Boxing*. Pretoria, 1941. $200.

JOLAS, Eugene. See *Transition Stories.*

JOLAS, Eugene. *Cinema: Poems*. New York, 1926. $350.

JOLAS, Eugene. *Secession in Astropolis*. Paris: Black Sun Press, 1929. Wraps. One of 100 signed copies. In slipcase. $350.

JONAH: Christmas, 1917. Oxford: Holywell Press, 1917. Wraps. (By Aldous Huxley.) One of 50 copies. $3,500.

JONES, A. D. *Illinois and the West*. Boston, 1838. Folding map. $750.

JONES, Anson B. *Memoranda and Official Correspondence Relating to the Republic of Texas, Its History and Annexation*. New York, 1859. Portrait. $750. Chicago (1966). Map, facsimile letter. Leather. One of 150 copies. In slipcase. $150.

JONES, Charles C., Jr. *Antiquities of the Southern Indians*. New York, 1873. 30 plates. $600.

JONES, Charles C., Jr. *The Dead Towns of Georgia*. Savannah, 1878. Maps. $250.

JONES, Charles C., Jr. *Historical Sketch of the Chatham Artillery*. Albany, Ga., 1867. 3 maps. $350.

JONES, Charles C., Jr. *The History of Georgia*. Boston, 1883. 2 vols. 19 maps and plates. Cloth. $350.

JONES, Charles C., Jr. *The History of Savannah, Georgia*. Syracuse, 1890. 21 portraits. Half leather. $350.

JONES, Charles C., Jr. *The Siege of Savannah in December, 1864*. Albany, 1874. 184 pages, wraps. $300. One of 10 copies on large paper. $600.

JONES, Charles C., Jr. (editor). *The Siege of Savannah in 1779*. Albany, 1874. Map, index (not in all copies). Wraps. One of 100 copies. With the index. $500. Without index. $250.

JONES, Charles Colcock. *Religious Instruction of the Negroes in the United States*. Savannah, 1842. $1,000.

JONES, Charles Jess (Buffalo). See Inman, Col. Henry.

JONES, D. W. *Forty Years Among the Indians*. Salt Lake City, 1890. With portrait (not in all copies). $300.

JONES, David. *A Journal of Two Visits Made to Some Nations of Indians on the West Side of the River Ohio, in the Years 1772 and 1773.* Burlington, N.J., 1774. $37,500 at auction in 1999. New York, 1865. Wraps. Second edition. One of 200 copies. $400. One of 50 copies on large paper. $750.

JONES, David. *The Anathemata.* London (1952). $300.

JONES, David. *In Parenthesis.* London, 1937. Author's first book. Illustrated by the author. 1,000. London (1961). Introduction by T. S. Eliot. Blue cloth. One of 70 copies signed by Jones and Eliot. In plastic dustwrapper. $2,500. New York (1962). Tan cloth. First American edition. With Eliot introduction not listed on Contents page. $150. With introduction listed. $100.

JONES, David. *The Tribune's Visitation.* (London, 1969.) One of 150 signed copies. $450. Trade edition. $75.

JONES, E. Alfred. *The Old Silver of American Churches.* Letchworth, England, 1913. 145 plates. Folio, buckram. One of 500 copies. $850. One of 6 copies on handmade paper. $1,750.

JONES, Edith Newbold. *Verses.* Newport, R.I., 1878. (By Edith Wharton.) Author's first book. Wraps. $75,000.

JONES, Edward Smyth. See *Invincible Ned.*

JONES, Edward Smyth. *Souvenir Poem.* (Louisville?, 1908.) 300.

JONES, Gwyn. *The Green Island.* London: Golden Cockerel Press, 1946. Woodcuts by John Petts. Green and gray morocco. One of 100 copies. $450. Trade edition. One of 400 copies. $150.

JONES, Herschel V. *Adventures in Americana.* New York, 1928. 2 vols. 300 plates. Black cloth. One of 200 copies. $250. With third vol. of collection by W. Eames Publisher. New York, 1938. $500. New York, 1964. 3 vols. $300.

JONES, J. Wesley. *Amusing and Thrilling Adventures of a California Artist, while Daguerreotyping a Continent . . .* Boston, 1854. (By George Spencer Phillips.) (Written by John Ross Dix.) Illustrated, including 4 woodcuts in text. 92 pages, pictorial wraps. $4,500.

JONES, James. *From Here to Eternity.* New York, 1951. Author's first book. Presentation edition, with signed, numbered tipped-in page (no total limitation, but about 1,500 copies). $850. Without signed page. $600.

JONES, James. *The Thin Red Line.* New York (1962). $150.

JONES, James Athearn. See Murgatroyd, Matthew.

JONES, Jonathan H. *A Condensed History of the Apache and Comanche Indian Tribes.* San Antonio, 1899. Illustrated. (Note: Better known by its cover title, *Indianology*.) $2,500.

JONES, LeRoi. *Cuba Libre.* (Cover title.) New York (1961). Wraps. $450.

JONES, Leroi. *Spring and So Forth.* New Haven, 1960. Author's first book. $500.

JONES, Mother. *The Autobiography of Mother Jones.* Chicago, 1925. (By Mary Harris Jones.) $500.

JONES, Owen. *Examples of Chinese Ornament . . .* London, 1867. 100 plates. $2,500.

JONES, Owen. *The Grammar of Ornament.* London, 1856. 100 colored lithographs, engraved title page (illuminated), woodcuts. Large folio. $4,000.

JONES, Owen (illustrator). *Scenes from the Winter's Tale.* London (1866). $500.

JONES, Owen, and GOURY, Jules. *Plans, Elevations, Sections, and Details of the Alhambra . . .* London, 1842–45. 2 vols. Large folio. 104 plates (69 colored), including titles. $17,500.

JONES, Robert Tyre, Jr., and KEELER, O. B. *Down the Fairway.* New York, 1927. One of 300 signed copies. In slipcase. $10,000. Trade. $1,500. London, 1927. $1,000.

JONES, Thomas A. *J. Wilkes Booth . . .* Chicago, 1893. Illustrated. Cloth. $250.

JONES, William Carey. *Land Titles in California.* San Francisco, 1852. 55 pages, wraps. $1,000.

JONSON, Ben. *A Croppe of Kisses: Selected Lyrics.* London: Golden Cockerel Press, 1937. Edited by John Wallis. Folio, morocco, and buckram. One of 200 copies. $350. One of 50 copies specially bound in morocco. $1,000.

JONSON, Ben. *Every Man Out of His Humour.* London, 1600. Author's first book. $10,000.

JONSON, Ben. *The Masque of Queenes.* London, 1930. Illustrated by Inigo Jones. Folio, red vellum. One of 350 copies. In slipcase. $350.

JONSON, Ben. *Volpone: or The Foxe.* New York, 1898. Illustrated by Aubrey Beardsley. One of 100 copies on vellum. $2,750. Decorated cloth. One of 1,000 copies. $750. Limited Editions Club, New York, 1952. In slipcase. $150.

JONSON, Ben. *The Workes . . .* London, 1616–40. 3 vols. $12,500.

JORDAN, Neil. *Night in Tunisia.* Dublin (1976). Author's first book. Wraps. $300. London, 1979. $150. New York, 1989. $75.

JORDAN, Thomas, and PRYOR, J. P. *The Campaigns of Lieut. Gen. N. B. Forrest.* New Orleans, 1868. 6 maps, 6 plates. $650.

JORROCK'S Jaunts and Jollities. London, 1838. (By Robert Smith Surtees.) 12 illustrations by Phiz. $450. Philadelphia, 1838. 2 vols. First American edition. $350. London, 1843. 15 color plates by Henry Aiken. Green cloth. Second edition, first state, with 8 pages of ads and printer's imprint at end. $1,250. Second edition, late state, with ads announcing a new edition of *The Life of John Mytton.* $750. London, 1869. 16 colored Aiken plates. Third edition. $500. Limited Editions Club, New York, 1932. In slipcase. $150.

JOSEPHSON, Matthew. *Galimathias.* New York (1923). Author's first book. Stiff wraps. One of 250 copies. $200.

JOSSELYN, John. *An Account of Two Voyages to New-England.* London, 1674. Printer's dragon device on the recto of the preliminary license leaf. Errata. List of printer's advertisements. $12,500.

JOSSELYN, John. *New-Englands Rarities Discovered: In Birds, Beasts, Fishes, Serpents . . .* London, 1672. Folding plate woodcut and 11 text woodcuts. $9,500. Boston, 1865. One of 250 copies. $250. One of 75 large-paper copies. $400.

JOURNAL of a Few Months' Residence in Portugal . . . London, 1847. (By Dorothy Wordsworth Quillinan.) 2 vols. Author's first book. $750.

JOURNAL of the Convention to Form a Constitution for the State of Wisconsin: Begun and Held at Madison on the 5th Day of October, 1846. Madison, 1847. Boards and calf. $350.

JOURNAL of Sentimental Travels in the Southern Provinces of France. London, 1821. (By William Combe.) 18 colored plates by Thomas Rowlandson. $1,250.

JOURNAL of a Tour Around Hawaii, the Largest of the Sandwich Islands. Boston, 1825. (By William Ellis.) 5 plates, folding map. $1,250. London, 1826. $1,000.

JOURNAL of the First Session of the Senate of the United States . . . *March 4th, 1789* . . . New York, 1789. (Contains the Bill of Rights as originally proposed.) $15,000.

JOURNAL of the Hartford Union Mining and Trading Company. On board the *Henry Lee,* 1849. 88 pages, wraps. (By George G. Webster, or John Linville Hall, who printed it?) $6,000. Second edition (with title revised to *Around the Horn in '49: Journal* . . .): (Wethersfield, Conn., or Hartford, 1898.) $300. San Francisco: Book Club of California, 1928. Half cloth. One of 250 copies printed by the Grabhorns. $175.

JOURNAL of the March of a Detachment of Dragoons Under the Command of Col. Henry Dodge to the Rocky Mountains During the Summer of 1835. (Washington, 1836.) (By Lt. G. P. Kingsbury.) 2 folding maps. $1,000.

JOURNEY to California with Observations About the Country . . . San Francisco, 1937. (By John Bidwell.) (First of a series of three works republished by John Henry Nash.) $175.

JOYCE, James. See Gorman, Herbert; Skeffington, F.J.C., and Joyce, James A. See also *Des Imagistes.*

JOYCE, James. *Anna Livia Plurabelle.* New York, 1928. Edited by Padraic Colum. One of 800 signed copies. $4,500. One of 50 copies on green paper not signed. 6 were numbered. $4,500. 44 not numbered. $3,500. London (1930). Cloth in tissue dustwrapper. $300. Wraps. $150.

JOYCE, James. *Chamber Music.* London, 1907. First issue (16.2 by 11 cm) with thick laid endpapers, horizontal chain lines and poems, and signature "c" well centered. $7,500. Second issue (15.8 by 11 cm) with thick-wove endpapers and signature "c" poorly centered. $4,000. Third variant (15.9 by 10.9 cm) with thin-wove transparent endpapers. $3,000. (No priority on last two variants.)

JOYCE, James. *Collected Poems.* New York: Black Sun Press, 1936. Frontispiece portrait. Decorated boards. One of 750 copies. In glassine dustwrapper. $1,000. One of 50 copies on vellum, signed. In tissue dustwrapper. In slipcase. $7,500. One of 3 signed, lettered copies, $15,000. New York, 1937. First trade edition. In dustwrapper. $1,000.

JOYCE, James. *Dubliners.* London (1914). In dustwrapper. $50,000. Lacking dustwrapper. $4,500. New York, 1916. Cloth. First American issue (from the English sheets). In dustwrapper. $15,000. Lacking dustwrapper. $3,500. New York, 1917. First edition from American sheets. Second printing stated. In dustwrapper. $3,000. Lacking dustwrapper. $750.

JOYCE, James. *Exiles.* London, 1918. Green boards and cloth. $1,000. New York, 1918. Boards and buckram. $600. New York, 1951. Half cloth. One of 1,975 copies. In dustwrapper. $250.

JOYCE, James. *Finnegans Wake*. London, 1939. Buckram. One of 425 copies on large paper, signed. In slipcase. $10,000. One of 26 signed copies. $15,000. London (1939). $3,500. New York, 1939. $1,000.

JOYCE, James. *Haveth Childers Everywhere: Fragment from Work in Progress*. Paris/New York, 1930. Stiff printed wraps. One of 500 copies on Vidalon paper. In glassine dustwrapper. In slipcase. $1,500. Also 75 "Writer's Copies." $2,500. One of 100 copies on Japanese vellum, signed. In slipcase. $7,500. One of 10 copies on vellum, signed. In glassine dustwrapper. In slipcase. $10,000. London, 1931. Cloth. In tissue dustwrapper. $300. Wraps in dustwrapper. $200.

JOYCE, James. *The Holy Office*. (Pola, Austria-Hungary, 1904 or 1905?) The author's first separately published work. Preceded by *Two Essays*.) Broadside. (Fewer than 100 printed.) $12,500.

JOYCE, James. *Ibsen's New Drama*. London (1930). Foolscap, boards, paper label. One of 40 copies. Issued without dustwrapper. $7,500. Also noted in slipcase with *James Clarence Mangan*.

JOYCE, James. *James Clarence Mangan*. London (1930). Foolscap, boards, paper label. One of 40 copies. $7,500. Also noted in slipcase with *Ibsen's New Drama*.

JOYCE, James. *The Mime of Mick, Nick, and the Maggies*. The Hague, Netherlands, 1934. Designs in color by Lucia Joyce. Stiff white wraps. In slipcase. One of 1,000 copies. $1,250. One of 29 copies signed by Joyce and his daughter. $12,500.

JOYCE, James. *Pomes Penyeach*. Paris, 1927. With errata slip. $600. One of 13 copies on handmade paper. $6,000. Cleveland, 1931. One of 103 copies. $2,500. Paris and London, 1932. Oblong folio sheets on Japan paper, illuminated by Lucia Joyce. Green silk folder. One of 25 signed copies. $30,000. London: Faber & Faber (1933). Wraps. First edition printed in England. Wraps. $300.

JOYCE, James. *A Portrait of the Artist as a Young Man*. New York, 1916. Blue cloth in dustwrapper. $50,000. Lacking dustwrapper. $4,500. London (1917). First English issue (from American sheets). Green cloth. In dustwrapper. $42,000 at auction in 2000. Lacking dustwrapper. $4,000. London, 1924. Revised edition. $1,250. Limited Editions Club, New York, 1968. In slipcase. $175.

JOYCE, James. *Stephen Hero*. London, 1944. $500. New York (1944). $300.

JOYCE, James. *Storiella as She Is Syung*. (London): Corvinus Press (1937). Flexible orange vellum. One of 150 copies. In slipcase. $3,500. One of 25 copies (of the 176) signed by Joyce. In slipcase. $15,000.

JOYCE, James. *Tales Told of Shem and Shaun: Three Fragments from Work in Progress*. Paris: Black Sun Press, 1929. Portrait by Brancusi. Wraps. One of 500 copies on Van Gelder paper. In glassine dustwrapper. In slipcase. $1,500. One of 100 copies on vellum, signed. $8,500. Not signed. $2,500. London (1932). First English edition (retitled *Two Tales of Shem and Shaun*). In dustwrapper. Boards. $600.

JOYCE, James. *Two Essays*. See Skeffington, F.J.C.

JOYCE, James. *Ulysses*. Paris, 1922. Printed blue wraps. One of 100 copies on Dutch handmade paper, signed. $75,000. One of 150 copies on Verge d'Arches paper. $50,000. One of 740 copies on handmade paper. $35,000. (Various later printings of the Paris edition appeared through the 1920s.) London: Egoist Press, 1922. Second printing, first English edition (printed in France), with errata slip and 4-page leaflet of press notices. Blue wraps. One of 2,000 copies. $5,000. London, 1923. Second English edition (printed in France). Most confiscated by British customs agents. $7,500. Paris, 1928. Eighth printing, type entirely reset. $1,250. Hamburg: Odyssey Press (1932). 2 vols. Printed wraps. First Odyssey Press edition. One of 35 signed copies. $15,000. Trade. $750. (New York, 1934.) First authorized American edition. In dust-wrapper. $2,500. Limited Editions Club, New York, 1935. Illustrated by Henri Matisse. Pictorial buckram. One of 250 copies signed by Joyce and Matisse. $20,000. One of 1,250 copies signed only by Matisse. $6,000. (There were also 6 signed proofs of the Matisse etchings for this book issued in an edition of 150 in canvas portfolios.) London, 1936. Green buckram. First English edition to be printed in England. One of 900 copies. In dustwrapper. $2,000. Vellum. One of 100 signed copies. In slipcase. $30,000.

JOYCE, Col. John A. *A Checkered Life*. Chicago, 1883. $200.

JUDAH, Samuel B. H. *The Mountain Torrent* . . . New York, 1820. Author's first book. $450.

JUDD, A. N. *Campaigning Against the Sioux*. (Watsonville, Calif., 1906.) Plate, other illustrations. 45 pages, pictorial wraps. $1,750. Watsonville, 1909. Second edition. Wraps. $750.

JUDD, Silas. *A Sketch of the Life and Voyages of Capt. Alvah Judd Dewey* . . . Chittenango, N.Y., 1838. $1,000.

JUGAKU, Bunsho. *Paper-Making by Hand in Japan*. Tokyo, 1959. 24 specimens of handmade paper. $500.

JUSTICE, Donald. *The Old Bachelor* . . . Miami, 1951. Author's first book. Wraps. One of 240 copies. $600.

JUSTICE, Donald. *The Summer Anniversaries*. Middleton, Conn. (1960). Cloth. $150. Wraps. $35.

JUSTICE and Expediency; or Slavery Considered with a View to Its Rightful and Effectual Remedy, Abolition. Haverhill, Mass. 1833. Stitched without covers, as issued. (By John Greenleaf Whittier.) $1,000.

K

K., R.A. *Signa Severa*. Eton College, 1906. (By Ronald Knox.) Author's first book. Wraps. $350.

KABOTIE, Fred. *Designs from the Ancient Mimbrenos, with Hopi Interpretation*. San Francisco: Grabhorn Press, 1949. Half cloth. One of 250 copies. $500. Flagstaff, 1982. One of 100 signed copies. In slipcase. $350.

KAEMPFER, Englebert. *The History of Japan* . . . London, 1727. 2 vols. 45 copperplate engravings, many double-page or folding. $12,500. Glasgow, 1906. 3 vols. One of 100 copies. $1,500.

KAFKA, Franz. *Amerika*. London (1938). Translated by Edwin and Willa Muir. Cloth. $2,500. Norfolk, 1940. $1,000.

KAFKA, Franz. *The Castle*. London, 1930. Author's first book to be translated into English. $1,500. New York, 1930. $1,000.

KAFKA, Franz. *The Great Wall of China and Other Pieces.* London, 1933. Translated by Edwin and Willa Muir. $500.

KAFKA, Franz. *Metamorphosis.* London, 1937. Issued in acetate dustwrapper. $1,250. New York, 1946. $750.

KAFKA, Franz. *The Trial.* London, 1936. $1,250. New York, 1937. $750.

KAHANE, Jack. *Two Plays.* Manchester, 1912. Wraps. Author's first book. $450.

KAHN, Roger. *Inside Big League Baseball.* New York, 1962. Author's first separate book. Issued without dustwrapper. $250.

KAIN, Saul. *The Daffodil Murderer.* (London), 1913. (By Siegfried Sassoon.) Yellow (orange) wraps printed in red. $600.

KALM, Peter. *Travels into North America . . .* London, 1770–71. 3 vols. First English edition. 6 plates. Large folding map. $6,000. London, 1772. 2 vols. 6 plates. Folding map. $2,000.

KALTENBORN, H. V. *Kaltenborn Edits the News.* New York (1937). His columns ghostwritten or edited by Mary McCarthy, her first book. Cloth. $350. Wraps in dustwrapper. $150.

KAMINSKY, Stuart M. *Bullet for a Star.* New York, 1977. Author's first hardcover book. $200.

KANDINSKY, Wassily. *The Art of Spiritual Harmony.* London, 1914. $400.

KANE, Elisha Kent. *Arctic Explorations.* Philadelphia, 1856. 22 plates and 3 maps (2 folding). 2 vols. Pictorial cloth. $350.

KANE, Elisha Kent. *The U.S. Grinnell Expedition in Search . . .* New York, 1854. $300.

KANE, Paul. *Wanderings of an Artist Among the Indians of North America.* London, 1859. Folding map, 8 colored plates, woodcuts. $3,000.

KANE, Thomas Leiper. *The Mormons.* Philadelphia, 1850. 84 pages. Printed wraps. $750.

KANO, Jigoro. *Judo.* Tokyo, 1937. Wraps. $125.

KANO, Jigoro. *Ju Jutsu and Judo: What Are They?* Tokyo, no date. Wraps. $150.

KANT, Immanuel. *Critick of Pure Reason.* London, 1838. In original green cloth and paper label. First edition in English. $1,500.

KANTOR, MacKinlay. *Andersonville.* Cleveland (1955). $100. One of 1,000 signed copies. In slipcase. $350. Trade edition. $200.

KANTOR, MacKinlay. *Diversey.* New York, 1928. Author's first book. (Also first book published by Coward-McCann.) In dustwrapper without reviews. $150.

KAPPLER, Charles J. [comp. and ed.]. *Indian Affairs: Laws and Treaties.* Washington, 1904. 2 vols. $750.

KARAMZIN, Nicolai. *Travels from Moscow.* London, 1803. 3 vols. 2 portraits, colored folding map, and 2 other plates. $7,500.

KARPINSKI, Louis C. *Bibliography of Mathematical Works Printed in America Through 1850*. Ann Arbor, 1940. $450.

KATHERINE Walton; or, The Rebel of Dorchester. Philadelphia, 1851. (By William Gilmore Simms.) $500.

KAUFFER, E. McKnight. *The Art of the Poster* . . . New York, 1925. $600.

KAUFMAN, George. *Dulcy*. New York (1921). Author's first book (with Marc Connelly). $750.

KAUFMAN, George S., and HART, Moss. *The Man Who Came to Dinner*. New York, 1929. $600.

KAVAN, Anna. See Ferguson, Helen.

KAVAN, Anna. *Ice: A Novel*. London (1967). (By Helen Ferguson.) $200.

KAVANAGH, Dan. *Duffy*. London (1980). (By Julian Barnes.) First mystery. $200.

KAVANAGH, Patrick. *Collected Poems*. New York (1964). One of 100 signed copies. In slipcase. $750.

KAVANAGH, Patrick. *D'Olier Music Co's Famous Songs*. Dublin, 1930. Author's first book. Wraps. $1,250.

KAVANAGH, Patrick. *The Great Hunger*. Dublin: Cuala Press, 1942. Boards and linen. One of 250 copies. In dustwrapper. $600.

KAVANAGH, Patrick. *Ploughman* . . . London, 1936. Wraps. $1,000.

KAYE-SMITH, Sheila. *The Tramping Methodist*. London, 1908. Author's first book. $150.

KAZANTZAKIS, Nikos. *Christopher Columbus*. Kentfield, Calif.: Allen Press, 1972. 22 folded sheets in gold wraps. One of 140 copies. In slipcase. $500.

KAZANTZAKIS, Nikos. *Zorba the Greek*. London (1952). Author's first book. (First English translation.) $350. New York, 1953. $250.

KEATE, George. *An Account of the Pelew Islands* . . . London, 1788. Frontis, 14 plates, folding chart and folding views. $2,500.

KEATING, William H. (compiler). *Narrative of an Expedition to the Source of St. Peter's River, Lake Winnepeek* . . . Philadelphia, 1824. 2 vols. Folding map, 15 plates. $2,500. London, 1825. 2 vols. First English edition. Maps, 15 plates, tables. $1,250.

KEATS, John. *Endymion: A Poetic Romance*. London, 1818. First state, with one line of errata (not 5) was presumed to be first but as both errata sheets were printed at the same time, it is hard to know; and 2 (not 5) ad leaves at end. $8,500. Second state, with 5-line errata. $6,500. New York: Elston Press, 1902. Blue cloth. $450. London: Golden Cockerel Press (1947). Wood engravings. Buckram and vellum. One of 400 copies. $1,000. Vellum. One of 100 specially bound copies. $2,500.

KEATS, John. *The Eve of St. Agnes*. (River Forest, Ill.): Auvergne Press, 1896. Title page design by Frank Lloyd Wright. Cloth. One of 65 copies. $5,000. London: Essex House, 1900. Boards. One of 125 copies on vellum. $1,250.

KEATS, John. *Lamia, Isabella, The Eve of St. Agnes, and Other Poems.* London, 1820. With half title and 8 pages of ads at end. $8,500. Waltham Saint Lawrence, England: Golden Cockerel Press, 1928. Woodcuts by Robert Gibbings. Sharkskin and cloth. One of 485 copies. $1,000. One of 15 copies on vellum. In sharkskin binding by Sangorski & Sutcliffe. $7,500.

KEATS, John. *Letters of John Keats to Fanny Brawne, Written in the Years 1819 and 1820.* London, 1878. Edited by Harry Buxton Forman. Etched frontispiece and facsimile. One of 50 copies. $750. Trade edition. $200.

KEATS, John. *Life, Letters, and Literary Remains of John Keats.* London, 1848. 2 vols. Edited by Richard Monckton Milnes. Engraved portrait and facsimile. Cloth. $1,000. New York, 1848. $500.

KEATS, John. *Poems.* London, 1817. Woodcut vignette of Spenser on title page. In original boards, paper label on spine. $30,000. Rebound. $15,000. London: Doves Press, 1914. One of 200 copies. $1,500. One of 12 copies on vellum. $30,000.

KEEFE, Charles S. (editor). *The American House.* New York, 1924. $350.

KEEN HAND, A. See Farnie, H. B.

KEENE, Carolyn. *The Hidden Staircase.* New York (1930). First has dustwrapper advertising first three Nancy Drews and first eight Hardy Boys. $2,500. Second advertises 3 and 11 respectively. $1,000.

KEENE, Carolyn. *The Secret of the Old Clock.* New York, 1930. (By Mildred Benson.) First Nancy Drew. First has dustwrapper with Nancy Drews 1 through 3 advertised; book has ad for first 8 Hardy Boys books. $3,000. Second printing dustwrapper advertises first 4 Nancy Drews and book advertises 9 Hardy Boys. $1,500.

KEEP Cool. Baltimore, 1817. (By John Neal.) 2 vols. Author's first book. $750.

KEES, Weldon. *Collected Poems.* Iowa City: Stone Wall Press, 1960. Boards and leather. One of 200 copies. $1,250.

KEES, Weldon. *The Last Man.* San Francisco, 1943. Author's first book. One of 300 copies. (Issued without dustwrapper.) $750.

KEITH, G. M. *A Voyage to South America and the Cape of Good Hope.* London 1810. First issue, printed by Phillips. $3,500. London, 1819. Revised edition, printed by Vogel. With list of subscribers. $2,500.

KELEHER, William A. *The Fabulous Frontier.* Santa Fe (1945). 11 plates. Cloth. One of 500 copies. In dustwrapper. $175.

KELEHER, William A. *The Maxwell Land Grant.* Santa Fe (1942). Illustrated. Pictorial cloth. In dustwrapper. $400.

KELL, Joseph. *Inside Mr. Enderby.* London (1963). (By Anthony Burgess.) $500.

KELL, Joseph. *One Hand Clapping.* London (1961). (By Anthony Burgess.) $500.

KELLER, David H. *The Lady Decides.* Philadelphia, 1950. One of 400 signed copies. Issued without dustwrapper. In slipcase. $100.

KELLER, David H. *The Sign of the Burning Hart.* No place, 1938. One of 100 copies. $350. No place (1948). First American edition. One of 250 signed copies. In dustwrapper. $125.

KELLER, George. *A Trip Across the Plains.* (Masillon, Ohio 1851.) 58 pages, printed wraps. $5,000. Oakland (1955). One of 500. $125.

KELLET, Susanna, et al. *A Complete Collection of Cookery Receipts.* Newcastle, 1780. $3,000.

KELLEY, Edith Summers. *Weeds.* New York (1923). Author's first book. $750. London, 1924. $350.

KELLEY, Hall J. *General Circular to All Persons of Good Character Who Wish to Emigrate to the Oregon Territory.* Charlestown, Mass., 1831. 28 pages, original wraps with "To All Ministers of the Gospel" leaf and leaf listing those who bought shares. $10,000.

KELLEY, Hall J. *History of Colonization of the Oregon Territory.* Worcester, Mass., 1850. 12 pages, sewn. $6,000.

KELLEY, Hall J. *A History of the Settlement of Oregon and the Interior of Upper California.* Springfield, Mass., 1868. 128 pages, printed wraps. $6,000.

KELLEY, Hall J. *A Narrative of Events and Difficulties in the Colonization of Oregon and the Settlement of California.* Boston, 1852. 92 pages, printed wraps. $6,000.

KELLEY, William Melvin. *A Different Drummer.* Garden City, 1962. Author's first book. $200.

KELLOGG, Jay C. *The Broncho Buster Busted and Other Messages.* (Tacoma, 1932.) Wraps. $175.

KELLY, Charles. *Old Greenwood: The Story of Caleb Greenwood, Trapper, Pathfinder and Early Pioneer of the West.* Salt Lake City, 1936. One of 350 copies. In dustwrapper. $350.

KELLY, Charles. *The Outlaw Trail: A History of Butch Cassidy and His Wild Bunch.* Salt Lake City, 1938. Illustrated. Pictorial cloth (leatherette). One of 1,000 copies. In dustwrapper. $600.

KELLY, Charles. *Salt Desert Trails.* Salt Lake City, 1930. Illustrated. Cloth (leatherette). $350.

KELLY, Charles (editor). See Lee, John D.

KELLY, Charles, and HOWE, Maurice L. *Miles Goodyear, First Citizen of Utah.* Salt Lake City, 1937. One of 350 copies. $400.

KELLY, Emma D. *Four Girls at Cottage City.* Boston, 1898. $1,500.

KELLY, Emma Dunham. See Forget-Me-Not.

KELLY, L. V. *The Range Men: The Story of the Ranchers and Indians of Alberta.* Toronto, 1913. Illustrated. Pictorial cloth. $850.

KELLY, Robert. *Armed Descent.* (New York): Hawk's Well Press (1961). Author's first book. Wraps. $100.

KELLY, Robert. *Her Body Against Time.* Mexico City, 1963. Cloth. One of about 50 copies. $250. Wraps. $100.

KELLY, William. *An Excursion to California over the Prairie, Rocky Mountains, and Great Sierra Nevada.* London, 1851. 2 vols. $3,000.

KELTON, Elmer. *Buffalo Wagon.* New York, 1957. $450.

KELTON, Elmer. *The Day the Cowboys Quit.* New York, 1978. $400.

KELTY, Mary Ann. See *The Favourite of Nature.*

KEMBLE, Frances Anne. *Journal. By Frances Anne Butler.* London, 1835. 2 vols. $600. Philadelphia, 1835. 2 vols. First American edition. Original purple cloth. $500.

KEMBLE, Frances Anne. *The Views of Judge Woodward and Bishop Hopkins on Negro Slavery at the South . . .* (Phila.), 1863. Pictorial wraps. $1,000.

KEMPTON-Wace Letters (The). New York, 1903. Green decorated cloth. (By Jack London and Anna Strunsky.) $750. Second printing has authors' names on title page. $150.

KENDAL and Windermere Railway: Two Letters Reprinted from the Morning Post. Kendal: R. Branthwaite [1845]. (By William Wordsworth.) Wraps. $750. London: Whittaker (1845 or later). $200.

KENDALL, George W., and NEBEL, Carl. *The War Between the United States and Mexico . . .* New York/Philadelphia. 1851. Map and 12 hand-finished colored plates (which are susceptible to foxing, affecting price). Large folio laid in a folding cloth portfolio. $12,500.

KENDALL, Geo. Wilkins. *Narrative of the Texan Santa Fe Expedition . . .* New York, 1844. 5 plates, folding map. 2 vols. In original cloth. $1,500. London, 1844. 2 vols. First English edition. Map, 5 plates. $1,000. New York, 1856. 2 vols. Seventh edition, with two extra chapters and part of Falconer's diary. $2,500.

KENDALL, Henry Edward, Jr. *Designs for Schools and Schools Houses, Parochial and National.* London, 1847. $1,500.

KENDERDINE, T. S. *A California Tramp and Later Footprints.* Newtown, Pa., 1888. 39 views. Pictorial cloth. $350.

KENEALLY, Thomas. *The Place at Whitton.* London (1964). Author's first book. $500. New York, 1965. $350.

KENEALLY, Thomas. *Schindler's Ark.* London (1982). $400.

KENEALLY, Thomas. *Schindler's List.* New York (1982). $250.

KENILWORTH. Edinburgh, 1821. 3 vols. (By Sir Walter Scott.) $450.

KENNEDY, Edward G. *The Etched Work of Whistler . . .* New York: Grolier Club, 1910. 4 vols. (Text vol. and 3 portfolios.) One of 402 copies. $3,500. New York, 1910. 7 vols. $2,500.

KENNEDY, Jacqueline. *One Special Summer.* New York (1974). One of 500 signed copies. Issued without dustwrapper. In slipcase. $3,000.

KENNEDY, John F. *Inaugural Address.* Los Angeles, 1965. Portrait. Vellum. One of 1,000 copies. $750.

KENNEDY, John F. *Profiles in Courage*. New York (1956). $750. New York, 1961. "Inaugural Edition." $200.

KENNEDY, John F. *Why England Slept*. New York, 1940. Author's first book. $1,000. London (1940). Red cloth. With ads dated 1940. $300.

KENNEDY, John F. (editor). *As We Remember Joe*. (Cambridge, Mass., 1945.) Portrait frontispiece, photographs. Red cloth. Title page with red letters. $2,500. Reprinted with title page in black only. $300.

KENNEDY, John P., and BLISS, Alexander (editors). *Autograph Leaves of Our Country's Authors*. Baltimore, 1864. $200.

KENNEDY, John Pendleton. See Secondthoughts, Solomon. See also *Horse-Shoe Robinson; Rob of the Bowl; Swallow Barn*.

KENNEDY, John Pendleton. *Memoirs of the Life of William Wirt*. Philadelphia, 1849. 2 vols. Portrait and folding facsimile. Black cloth. $1,000.

KENNEDY, William. *Billy Phelan's Greatest Game*. New York (1978). $175.

KENNEDY, William. *The Ink Truck*. New York, 1969. Author's first book. $650. London (1970). $250.

KENNEDY, William. *Legs*. New York (1975). $250. London (1976). $125.

KENNEDY, William. *Texas: Its Geography, Natural History, and Topography*. New York, 1844. 118 pages, wraps. (Reprint in part of *Texas: The Rise, Progress* . . .) $2,000. Rebound. $750.

KENNEDY, William. *Texas: The Rise, Progress and Prospects of the Republic of Texas*. London, 1841. 2 vols. Maps, charts. $20,000. 2 vols. in 1. Cloth. $7,500. Second edition, same date. 1 vols. $5,000.

KENNER, Hugh. *Paradox in Chesterton*. New York, 1947. $125. London, 1948. Author's first book. $100.

KENT, Henry W. (compiler). *Bibliographical Notes on One Hundred Books Famous in English Literature*. New York: Grolier Club, 1903. Half vellum. One of 305 copies. $300. (Issued as a supplement to the Grolier Club title of 1902, *One Hundred Books Famous in English Literature*, which was also limited to 305 copies.) $200. Together, the two books. $500.

KENT, Rockwell. See Robinson, Selma. See also *Architec-tonics*.

KENT, Rockwell. *A Birthday Book*. New York, 1931. Illustrated by the author. Pictorial cloth (silk). One of 1,850 signed copies. Issued without dustwrapper. $300.

KENT, Rockwell. *The Bookplates and Marks of Rockwell Kent*. New York, 1929. 85 plates. Decorated cloth. One of 1,250 signed copies. In dustwrapper. $750.

KENT, Rockwell. *Forty Drawings . . . to Illustrate the Works of William Shakespeare*. (Garden City, 1936.) Portfolio of drawings. One of 1,000 copies. In slipcase. $750. With two prints signed by Kent. $3,000.

KENT, Rockwell. *Greenland Journal*. New York (1962). With a set of 6 lithographs, one signed. In slipcase. $500.

KENT, Rockwell. *Later Bookplates & Marks of Rockwell Kent.* New York, 1937. Illustrated. One of 1,250 signed copies. Issued in dustwrapper. $350.

KENT, Rockwell. *N. by E.* New York, 1930. Illustrated. Pictorial silvered blue buckram. One of 900 signed copies. $400. Linen, with an extra page, for presentation. One of 100 signed copies. In slipcase. $1,250. Trade edition. $175.

KENT, Rockwell. *The Seven Ages of Man.* New York, 1918. First collection of his illustrations. $350.

KENT, Rockwell. *Shakespeare, The Complete Works of . . .* Garden City, 1936. 2 vols. One of 750 signed copies. In slipcase. $750.

KENT, Rockwell. *Shakespeare, Venus & Adonis.* Rochester, 1931. One of 75 copies on hand-made paper. Typography by Will Ransom. $750. One of 1,175 copies. $300.

KENT, Rockwell. *Voyaging Southward from the Strait of Magellan.* New York, 1924. Tan buckram. In dustwrapper. $600. Blue boards. One of 110 signed copies, with an extra signed woodcut. $1,500. One of 10 signed copies in half vellum. $2,500.

KENT, Rockwell. *Wilderness: A Journal of Quiet Adventure in Alaska.* New York, 1920. Author's first book. 69 illustrations. First binding. Gray linen. In dustwrapper. $750. Second binding, tan pictorial boards. In dustwrapper. $600. Los Angeles (1970). One of 1,500 copies. In slipcase. $250.

KENTUCKIAN in New-York (The). By a Virginian. New York, 1834. 2 vols. (By W. A. Caruthers.) $750.

KENYON, Frederic G. *Ancient Books and Modern Discoveries.* Chicago, 1927. One of 350 copies. 20 plates. In dustwrapper. In slipcase. $450.

KENYON, William Asbury. *Miscellaneous Poems.* Chicago, 1845. $350.

KER, Henry. *Travels Through the Western Interior of the United States.* Elizabethtown, N.J., 1816. $1,000.

KERCHEVAL, Samuel. *A History of the Valley of Virginia.* Winchester, Va., 1833. $750.

KEROUAC, Jack. *Big Sur.* New York (1962). $350. (London, 1963.) Bound in blue or black cloth. $200.

KEROUAC, Jack. *The Dharma Bums.* New York, 1958. $600. (London, 1959.) First printing incorrectly states "First Published 1950." Red, blue, or black binding, priority unknown. $250.

KEROUAC, Jack. *Doctor Sax.* New York (1959). One of 4 signed copies. Numbered 1–4. $6,000. One of 26 signed, lettered copies. $4,500. Trade in dustwrapper. $2,000. Wraps. $150.

KEROUAC, Jack. *Excerpts from Visions of Cody.* (New York, 1959.) One of 750 signed copies. (There are an additional 55 out-of-series copies.) $2,000.

KEROUAC, Jack. *Mexico City Blues.* New York (1959). One of 4 signed copies. $6,000. One of 26 signed copies. $4,500. Trade in dustwrapper. $2,000. Wraps. Evergreen Original E-184. $125.

KEROUAC, Jack. *On the Road.* New York, 1957. Review copies issued with additional white dustwrapper with printed blurb, "This is a copy of the first edition." $5,000. Trade. $3,500. (London, 1958.) $1,000.

KEROUAC, Jack. *Pull My Daisy*. New York (1961). Wraps. $750.

KEROUAC, Jack. *The Subterraneans*. New York (1958). One of 100 copies bound in half cloth without dustwrapper. $1,500. Trade in dustwrapper. $2,000. Wraps. Printed in white on cover. $150.

KEROUAC, John. *The Town and the City*. New York (1950). (By Jack Kerouac.) Author's first book. $1,250. London (1951). $750.

KERR, Hugh. *A Poetical Description of Texas, etc.* New York, 1838. In original cloth. $2,500.

KERR, John. *The Golf Book of East Lothian*. Edinburgh, 1896. One of 500 small paper copies. $1,500. One of 250 large-paper copies. $3,500.

KERR, Philip. *March Violets*. (London, 1989.) $300. New York (1989). $150.

KERSH, Gerald. *Jews Without Jehovah*. London, 1934. Author's first book. $350.

KESEY, Ken. *One Flew Over the Cuckoo's Nest*. New York (1962). Author's first book. $7,500. London (1962 actually 1963). Some revisions. $600.

KESEY, Ken. *Sometimes a Great Notion*. New York (1964). First issue has publisher's logo (Viking ship) on half title (before title page). $600. On half title after title page (scarcer). $500. London, 1966. $250.

KESSELRING, Joseph. *Arsenic and Old Lace*. New York (1941). $750.

KETTELL, Samuel. *Specimens of American Poetry, with Critical and Biographical Notices*. Boston, 1829. 3 vols. $750.

KEYES, Daniel. *Flowers for Algernon*. New York (1966). $1,250.

KEYNES, Geoffrey. *A Bibliography of Dr. Robert Hooke*. Oxford, 1960. $150.

KEYNES, Geoffrey. *Bibliotheca Bibliographici: A Catalogue of the Library Formed by Geoffrey Keynes*. London, 1964. 45 plates. One of 500 copies. $350.

KEYNES, Geoffrey. *Blake Studies: Notes on His Life and Works in Seventeen Chapters*. London, 1949. 48 full-page plates. $150.

KEYNES, Geoffrey. *Engravings by William Blake; The Separate Plates, A Catalogue Raisonée*. Dublin, 1956. 45 plates. One of 500 copies. $400.

KEYNES, Geoffrey. *A Study of the Illuminated Books of William Blake, Poet, Printer, Prophet*. London (1964). 32 color plates. One of 525 copies. $400.

KEYNES, Geoffrey, and WOLF, Edwin 2nd. *William Blake's Illuminated Books, A Census*. New York, 1953. One of 400 copies. $300.

KEYNES, John Maynard. *The Economic Consequences of the Peace*. London, 1919. In dustwrapper. 1,000. Without dustwrapper. $250.

KEYNES, John Maynard. *The General Theory of Employment, Interest, and Money*. London, 1936. $2,000. New York, 1936. $600.

KEYNES, John Maynard. *Indian Currency and Finance.* London, 1913. Author's first book. $1,750.

KEYNES, John Maynard. *A Tract on Monetary Reform.* London, 1923. $750.

KEYNES, John Maynard. *A Treatise on Money.* London, 1930. 2 vols. Green cloth. $1,250. New York (1930). 2 vols. English sheets. $750.

KHERDIAN, David. *Homage to Adana.* Mt. Horeb, Wis. (1970). One of 120 copies. $125.

KHERDIAN, David. *On the Death of My Father and Other Poems.* Fresno (1970). Introduction by William Saroyan. One of 26 copies signed by the poet and Saroyan. $350.

KIDD, J. H. *Personal Recollections of a Cavalryman with Custer's Michigan Cavalry Brigade in the Civil War.* Ionia, Mich., 1908. $450.

KIDDER, Tracy. *The Road to Yuba City.* Garden City, 1974. $175.

KIDGELL, John. *Original Fables.* London, 1763. $5,000.

KIJEWSKI, Karen. *Katwalk.* New York, 1989. Author's first book. $300.

KIKI'S Memoirs. Paris, 1930. Translated by Samuel Putnam. Introduction by Ernest Hemingway. Illustrated. Wraps. With glassine wrapper and red printed band around book. In plain white cardboard slipcase. $750. [For separate printing of the introduction, see Hemingway.]

KILBOURN, John. *Columbian Geography.* Chillicothe, Ohio, 1815. $3,000.

KILBOURN, John. *The Ohio Gazeteer, or Topographical Dictionary.* Columbus, 1816. $4,000.

KILBOURNE, E. W. *Strictures on Dr. I. Garland's Pamphlet, Entitled "Villainy Esposed," with Some Account of His Transactions in Lands of the Sac and Fox Reservation, etc., in Lee County, Iowa.* Fort Madison, Iowa, 1850. 24 pages, sewn. $750.

KILGOUR Collection of Russian Literature, 1750–1920 . . . Cambridge, 1959. $250.

KILMER, Joyce. *Summer of Love.* New York, 1911. Gilt top. First issue, with the Baker & Taylor imprint at foot of spine (later Doubleday, Page & Co.). Author's first book. $500.

KILMER, Joyce. *Trees and Other Poems.* New York (1914). First few printings were in tan-gray boards, with top edge gilt, and without "Printed in U.S.A." on copyright page. $250.

KIMBALL, Fiske. *The Domestic Architecture of the American Colonies and of the Early Republic.* New York, 1922. In dustwrapper. $350.

KIMBALL, Fiske. *Mr. Samuel McIntire, Carver, the Architect of Salem.* Portland, Me., 1940. Illustrated. One of 675 copies. In slipcase. $600.

KIMBALL, Fiske. *Thomas Jefferson, Architect.* Boston, 1916. Illustrated. Cloth. One of 350 copies. $600.

KIMBALL, Heber C. *The Journal of Heber C. Kimball.* Nauvoo, Ill., 1840. Edited by R. B. Thompson. 60 pages, printed wraps. $1,750.

KINCAID, Jamaica. *At the Bottom of the River.* New York (1983). Author's first book. $175.

KINDER, Louis H. *Formulas for Bookbinders.* East Aurora, 1905. One of 490 signed copies. 2 full-page plates. $650.

KING, Alexander. *Gospel of the Goat.* Chicago, 1928. 30 plates. Folio, boards, and morocco. One of 100 copies. Issued without dustwrapper. $300.

KING and Queen of Hearts (The). London, 1805. (By Charles Lamb.) Engraved title dated 1805, but earliest cover dated 1806. Approximately 5¼ by 4 inches, with 15 plain or colored illustrations. Wraps bound. $4,500. Cover dated 1809. Bound. $1,500.

KING, C. W. *Antique Gems and Rings.* London, 1872. 2 vols. Illustrated. Leather. $1,000. Cloth. $600.

KING, C. W. *The Natural History of Gems or Decorative Stones.* London, 1867. $500.

KING, General Charles. *A Daughter of the Sioux.* New York, 1903. Illustrated by Frederic Remington and Edwin Deming. $200.

KING, Charles. *The Fifth Cavalry in the Sioux War to 1876: Campaigning with Crook.* Milwaukee, 1880. 134 pages, printed wraps. $2,500. Second edition, 1890. $250.

KING, Frank M. *Longhorn Trail Drivers.* (Los Angeles, 1940.) Illustrated. One of 400 signed copies. Issued without dustwrapper. $200.

KING, Frank M. *Wranglin' the Past.* (Los Angeles, 1935.) Portrait. Leatherette. One of 300 signed copies. Issued without dustwrapper. $250.

KING, Jeff, and CAMPBELL, Joseph. *Where the Two Came to Their Father: A Navaho War Ceremonial.* New York (1943). 2 vols. 18 silk-screen prints. Folio, loose in large cloth portfolio. $2,000. Princeton, 1969. $750.

KING, Jesse. *How Cinderella Was Able to Go to the Ball.* London, 1924. $1,000.

KING, John. *Lectures Upon Ionas.* Oxford, 1597. Author's first book. $750.

KING, Laurie R. *The Beekeeper's Apprentice.* New York, 1994. $400.

KING, Laurie. *A Grave Talent.* New York (1993). (By Laurie R. King.) Author's first book. With dedication printed upside down. $650. Printed correctly. $500. London, 1995. $100.

KING, Martin Luther, Jr. *Stride Toward Freedom.* New York, 1958. Author's first book. $350.

KING, Richard. *Narrative of a Journey to the Shores of the Arctic Ocean . . .* London, 1836. $5,000.

KING, Richard, and HOPPE, E. O. *The Book of Fair Women.* London, 1922. One of 560 copies. Text by King, photographs by Hoppe. In dustwrapper. $850.

KING, Stephen. *Carrie.* Garden City, 1974. $1,250. (London, 1974.) $1,000.

KING, Stephen. *Cujo.* Viking, New York (1981). $60. New York: Mysterious Press (1981). One of 26 signed copies "Not For Sale" in acetate dustwrapper and slipcase. $1,750. One of 750 signed copies without dustwrapper in slipcase. $600. London (1982). $75.

KING, Stephen. *The Dark Tower: The Gunslinger.* West Kingston, R.I. (1982). One of 26 signed copies. Issued in dustwrapper and slipcase. $3,000. One of 500 signed copies in dustwrapper and slipcase. $1,500. Trade. Dustwrapper also lists limited edition price. $750. Second printing indicated. Dustwrapper does not list limited edition. $250.

KING, Stephen. *The Dark Tower II: The Drawing of The Three.* (West Kingston, 1987.) One of 850 signed copies in dustwrapper and slipcase. $600. Trade. $150.

KING, Stephen. *Firestarter.* Huntington Woods, 1980. One of 725 signed copies. $750. One of 26 signed copies. Issued without dustwrapper or slipcase. $7,500. Trade. $125. London (1980). $175.

KING, Stephen. *Night Shift.* Garden City, 1978. Dustwrapper price: $8.95. $1,000. (London, 1978.) $500.

KING, Stephen. *Salem's Lot.* Garden City, 1975. First issue dustwrapper priced at $8.95, refers to "Father Cody" in dustwrapper write-up. $3,000. Second issue, dustwrapper price-clipped and $7.95 added. "Father Cody" in dustwrapper write-up. $1,750. Third issue priced at $7.95 and "Cody" changed to "Callahan" in dustwrapper write-up. $600. (London, 1976.) $500.

KING, Stephen. *The Stand.* Garden City, 1978. Dustwrapper price $12.95. $450. (London, 1979.) $350.

KING, Stephen. *The Stand: The Complete and Uncut Edition.* (New York, 1990.) One of 52 signed copies. $2,500. One of 1,250 copies signed by King and Bernie Wrightson. In ebony box. $1,250. Trade. $50. (London, 1990.) $75.

KING, Thomas H. *The Study-Book of Mediaeval Architecture and Art . . .* London, 1868. 4 vols. Folio. $1,000.

KING, W. Ross. *The Sportsman and Naturalist in Canada.* London, 1866. 6 color plates, other illustrations. $450.

KING, William. *Chelsea Porcelain . . .* London, 1922. 171 illustrations (7 colored). Buckram. $200. Pigskin. One of 75 signed copies. $300. One of 13 copies on vellum. Issued without dustwrapper. $750.

KINGLAKE, A. W. *Eothen, or Traces of Travel Brought Home from the East.* London, 1844. Frontispiece in color, colored plate. $350. London, 1913. One of 100 copies in half vellum. $600.

KINGMAN, John. *Letters, Written by John Kingman, While on a Tour to Illinois and Wisconsin, in the Summer of 1838.* Hingham, Mass., 1842. 48 pages, printed wraps. $1,500.

KINGSLEY, Charles. *At Last: A Christmas in the West Indies.* London, 1871. 2 vols. Cloth. $500. New York, 1871. 1 vol. $300.

KINGSLEY, Charles. *The Heroes; or, Greek Fairy Tales for My Children.* Cambridge, 1856. 8 illustrations by the author. Pink decorated cloth. $1,000. London, 1912. Riccardi Press. Illustrated by W. Russell Flint. Vellum. One of 500 copies. $750. One of 12 copies on vellum, with a duplicate set of plates. $4,500.

KINGSLEY, Charles. *The Saint's Tragedy . . .* London, 1848. Author's first book. $750.

KINGSLEY, Charles. *The Water-Babies.* London, 1863. First issue, with "L'Envoi" leaf. $2,000. Without the leaf. $1,250. London, 1909. 42 colored plates by Warwick Goble. Vellum. One of 250 copies. $1,750. New York (1916). Illustrated by Jessie Willcox Smith. $900.

KINGSLEY, Charles. *Westward Ho!* Cambridge, 1855. 3 vols. Blue cloth. With 16 pages of ads at end of vol. 3 dated February 1855. $1,500. Boston, 1855. $600. Limited Editions Club, New York, 1947. 2 vols. Illustrated. Boards. In slipcase. $100.

KINGSLEY, Henry. *The Recollections of Geoffrey Hamlyn.* Cambridge, 1859. 3 vols. Author's first book. Blue cloth. $750.

KINGSOLVER, Barbara. *The Bean Trees.* New York (1988). $300.

KINGSOLVER, Barbara. *Homeland and Other Stories.* New York (1989). $125.

KINNELL, Galway. *What a Kingdom It Was.* Boston, 1960. Author's first book. Boards. $175.

KINNELL, Galway (translator). *Bitter Victory.* By René Hardy. Garden City, 1956. Kinnell's first book appearance. $250.

KINSELLA, Thomas. *Nightwalker.* Dublin, 1967. Wraps. $125.

KINSELLA, Thomas. *The Starlit Eye.* Dublin, 1952. One of 175 copies. $1,250.

KINSELLA, W. P. *Dance Me Outside.* (Ottawa), 1977. Author's first book. Cloth. $1,250. Wraps. $100.

KINSELLA, W. P. *Scars: Stories.* (Ottawa), 1978. Cloth. $450. Wraps. $75.

KINSELLA, W. P. *Shoeless Joe.* Boston, 1982. $300. London, 1982. $150.

KINSELLA, W. P. *Shoeless Joe Jackson Comes to Iowa.* (Canada, 1980.) Hardcover, in dustwrapper. $750. Wraps. $125.

KINZIE, Mrs. Juliette A. See *Narrative of the Massacre at Chicago.*

KINZIE, Mrs. Juliette A. *Wau-Bun, the "Early Day" in the North-West.* New York, 1856. 6 plates. Pictorial cloth. $500. London, 1856. First English edition. $400.

KIP, Lawrence. See *The Indian Council in the Valley of the Walla Walla.*

KIP, Lawrence. *Army Life on the Pacific.* New York, 1859. $650.

KIPLING, Rudyard. See *Echoes; Quartette.*

KIPLING, Rudyard. *An Almanac of Twelve Sports . . .* London, 1898. 12 color plates by William Nicholson. Pictorial boards. $750.

KIPLING, Rudyard. *Barrack-Room Ballads and Other Verses.* London, 1892. $400. One of 225 copies on large paper. $750. Half vellum and buckram. One of 30 copies on vellum. $6,000. (For first American edition, see Kipling, *Departmental Ditties.*)

KIPLING, Rudyard. *"Captains Courageous": A Story of the Grand Banks.* London, 1897. 22 illustrations. Blue cloth, gilt edges. $750. New York, 1897. $300.

KIPLING, Rudyard. *The City of Dreadful Night and Other Places.* Allahabad, 1891. Gray-green pictorial wraps. No. 14 of Wheeler's Indian Railway Library. First published (and second Indian) edition. $2,000. (Only 3 known of first in brown wraps.) Allahabad and London (1891). Wraps. First English edition. $1,250. New York: Grosset & Co., 1899. $450.

KIPLING, Rudyard. *Collected Verse.* New York, 1907. Red cloth. Without index. $200. With index, 21-line copyright notice. $125. New York, 1910. Color illustrations. Half vellum. First illustrated edition (Heath Robinson). One of 125 signed copies. $1,750. London, 1912. Limp vellum. One of 100 signed copies. $1,750. One of 500 copies. $500.

KIPLING, Rudyard. *Departmental Ditties and Other Verses.* Lahore, India, 1886. Pictorial tan wraps. (Issued in the form of a government envelope with flap tied with red tape.) $3,000. Calcutta, India, 1886. Second edition. Printed boards. $1,500. New York (1890) with "Lovell" on spine. $500. London, 1897. Illustrated. Vellum and cloth. First English (and first illustrated) edition. One of 150 copies on large paper. $1,000.

KIPLING, Rudyard. *The Five Nations.* New York, 1903. $125. London, 1903. Limp vellum. One of 30 copies on vellum. $2,000. Boards. One of 200 large-paper copies. $750. Trade edition. With "David" for "Saul" on page 56. $150.

KIPLING, Rudyard. *In Black and White.* Allahabad (India, 1888). Cream-colored pictorial wraps. No. 3 of the Indian Railway Library. $1,250. Allahabad and London (1890). First English edition. Gray-green wraps. $750. New York, 1890. $500.

KIPLING, Rudyard. *The Jungle Book.* London, 1894. Blue pictorial boards. $1,500. New York, 1894. $450. Limited Editions Club, New York, 1968. (*The Jungle Books.*) In slipcase. $125.

KIPLING, Rudyard. *Just So Stories for Little Children.* London, 1902. Illustrated by the author. Decorated red cloth. $1,250. New York, 1902. $600.

KIPLING, Rudyard. *Kim.* New York, 1901. Green cloth. First issue, without chapter headings except chapters 8 and 13. $350. London, 1901. $450. Limited Editions Club, New York, 1962. Cloth. In slipcase. $100.

KIPLING, Rudyard. *Land and Sea Tales for Scouts and Guides.* London, 1923. Red pictorial cloth. $500.

KIPLING, Rudyard. *Life's Handicap.* London, 1891. $250.

KIPLING, Rudyard. *The Light That Failed.* New York: U.S. Book Company (1890). Wraps with December 5, 1890 on front and last number is 22 on back. $600. London, 1891. Blue cloth. $400.

KIPLING, Rudyard. *Limits & Renewals.* New York, 1932. One of 204 signed copies. $1,000.

KIPLING, Rudyard. *Out of India.* New York, 1895. $300.

KIPLING, Rudyard. *The Phantom 'Rickshaw and Other Tales.* Allahabad (India 1889). Gray-green pictorial wraps. No. 5 of the Indian Railway Library. First binding, without periods after "A H" in "A H Wheeler" and with "Mufid I am Press" below design on front cover. $2,000. Second issue, with periods and "Mayo School of Art..." below design. $1,500. London (1890). First English edition. Wraps. $1,000. New York, 1890. Wraps. $750.

KIPLING, Rudyard. *Plain Tales from the Hills.* Calcutta, 1888. $750.

KIPLING, Rudyard. *Poems, 1886–1929.* London, 1929. 3 vols. Red morocco. One of 525 signed copies. In dustwrapper. $2,500. Garden City, 1930. 3 vols. Vellum boards. One of 525 signed copies. $2,000. (Also 12 for presentation.)

KIPLING, Rudyard. *Puck of Pook's Hill.* London, 1906. $500. New York, 1906. 4 color plates by Arthur Rackham. Pictorial cloth. First illustrated edition. $300.

KIPLING, Rudyard. *Schoolboy Lyrics.* Lahore (India), 1881. Author's first book. Brown printed or plain white wraps. Plain white wraps presumed to precede. $25,000.

KIPLING, Rudyard. *Sea and Sussex from Rudyard Kipling's Verse.* London, 1926. 24 color plates by Donald Maxwell. Boards and vellum. One of 500 signed copies. In dustwrapper. In slipcase. $1,000. Garden City, 1926. One of 150 signed large-paper copies. $1,500.

KIPLING, Rudyard. *The Second Jungle Book.* London, 1895. $600. New York, 1895. $250.

KIPLING, Rudyard. *Soldier Tales.* London, 1896. Illustrated. Blue cloth. $400.

KIPLING, Rudyard. *Soldiers Three.* Allahabad (India), 1888. Pictorial wraps. First state, without cross-hatching on barrack doors on the cover. $1,500. Second issue, with the cross-hatching and without period after "No" in "No 1." $1,000. London, 1890. $750. New York (1890). "Authorized Edition." $500.

KIPLING, Rudyard. *Songs of the Sea.* London, 1927. Vellum and boards. One of 500 large-paper copies, signed. In dustwrapper. $750.

KIPLING, Rudyard. *The Story of the Gadsbys.* Allahabad (India, 1888). Gray-green pictorial wraps. No. 2 of the Indian Railway Library. With no date on front cover. $1,750. Second printing has "1889" on front cover. $600.

KIPLING, Rudyard. *Under the Deodars.* Allahabad (India, 1888). Wraps. No. 4 of the Indian Railway Library. First state of wraps, without shading around "No. 4" and "One Rupee." $1,500. Later, with shading on wraps. $750. London (1890). First English edition. Wraps. $600. New York (1890). Wraps. $600.

KIPLING, Rudyard. *Wee Willie Winkle and Other Child Stories.* Allahabad (India, 1888). Gray-green pictorial wraps. No. 6 of the Indian Railway Library. First issue, with periods after "A" and "H" on cover. $2,500. Second issue. $1,500. (Livingston notes the covers were retouched or reengraved at least five times.) Allahabad, 1889. Second edition. Wraps. $1,000. London (1890). Wraps. $1,000.

KIPLING, Rudyard. *The White Man's Burden.* London, 1899. First English edition (a Thomas J. Wise forgery). Lilac-colored printed wraps. $1,000. (Note: There also exists a true first edition, for copyright, issued in 10 copies, gray wraps, in New York in 1899. $2,000.)

KIPLING, Rudyard. *With the Night Mail.* New York, 1909. Color plates. $300.

KIRKALDY, Andrew. *Fifty Years of Golf: My Memories.* London, 1921. $300. New York, 1921. $250. (Note: Second edition leaves out "My" in title.)

KIRMSE, Marguerite. *Dogs.* New York, 1930. Folio. One of 750 copies with original etching signed by Kirmse as the frontispiece, plus 75 plates. $1,250.

KITCHIN, C.H.B. *Curtains.* Oxford, 1919. Author's first book. Wraps. $400.

KITTREDGE, William. *The Van Gogh Field+.* Columbia, Missouri, 1978. Issued without dustwrapper. $500

KIZER, Carolyn. *Poems.* (Portland, 1959). Author's first book. Wraps. $300.

KIZER, Carolyn. *The Ungrateful Garden.* Bloomington (1961). Cloth. $125. Wraps. $30.

KJELGAARD, Jim. *Forest Patrol.* New York, 1941. Author's first book. $150.

KLEIN, William. *Life Is Good* . . . Milan (1956). Author's first book. Including small guide-book attached with ribbon. $2,500. London (1956). With guidebook. $1,250.

KLEIN, William. *Tokyo.* New York (1964). $1,000.

KLINE, Otis Adelbert. *Maza of the Moon.* Chicago, 1930. First edition not stated. $600.

KLINE, Otis Adelbert. *The Planet of Peril.* Chicago, 1929. Author's first book. $600.

KLONDYKE Mines and the Golden Valley of the Yukon (The). No place, 1897. 24 pages, self-wraps. $250.

KLOSTERHEIM: or the Masque. By the English Opium Eater. Edinburgh, 1832. (By Thomas De Quincey.) $500.

KNEEDLER, H. S. *The Coast Country of Texas.* Cincinnati, 1896. 76 pages, wraps. $350.

KNEEDLER, H. S. *Through Storyland to Sunset Seas.* Cincinnati, 1896. Wraps. $200.

KNEELAND, Samuel. *The Wonders of the Yosemite Valley and California.* Boston, 1871. With 10 mounted albumen photographs by John Soule. $1,250. Boston, 1872. With 2 maps and 10 photos. $850.

KNIBBS, Henry Hubert. *Overland Red.* Boston, 1914. $100.

KNIBBS, Henry Hubert. *Sundown Slim.* Boston, 1915. $100.

KNICKERBOCKER, Diedrich. *A History of New York, from the Beginning of the World to the End of the Dutch Dynasty.* New York, 1809. (By Washington Irving.) Author's first book. 2 vols. En-graved plate. First state, with 268 pages in vol. 1. $1,500. New York, 1812. 2 vols. $350. Lon-don, 1839. Illustrated by George Cruikshank. $500. New York, 1867. 2 vols. Full morocco. Author's revised edition. $600. New York, 1900. Illustrated by Maxfield Parrish. $600.

KNIGHT, Clifford. *The Affair of the Scarlet Club.* New York, 1937. Author's first mystery. $600.

KNIGHT, Dr. (John), and SLOVER, John. *Indian Atrocities.* Nashville, 1843. 96 pages, plain yellow boards, cloth spine. $14,000 at auction in 1999. Cincinnati, 1867. Printed wraps. One of 500 copies. $200.

KNIGHT, Eric. *Lassie Come Home.* Philadelphia (1940). $750. London (1941). $600.

KNIGHT, J. H. *Notes on Motor Carriages.* London, 1896. $1,500.

KNISH, Anne. See Morgan, Emanuel.

KNOBLOCK, Byron W. *Bannerstones of the North American Indian.* La Grange, Ill., 1939. Fron-tispiece in color, 270 plates. Half leather. One of 50 signed copies. $350.

KNOWLES, John. *A Separate Peace.* London (1959). Author's first book. $1,250. New York, 1960. In pictorial dustwrapper. $750. In printed dustwrapper. $150.

KNOX, Dudley W. *Naval Sketches of the War in California.* New York, 1939. Introduction by Franklin D. Roosevelt. 28 colored plates by William H. Meyers. Grabhorn printing. One of 1,000 copies. $350.

KNOX, Ronald A. See K., R.A.

KOCH, Christopher J. *Across the Sea Wall.* London, 1965. $350.

KOCH, Christopher J. *The Boys in the Island.* London, 1958. $600.

KOCH, Frederick H. (editor). *Carolina Folk-Plays, Second Series.* New York, 1924. (Contains "The Return of Buck Gavin," Thomas Wolfe's first appearance in a book.) $350.

KOCH, Kenneth. *Poems.* (With Nell Blaine *prints.*) New York, 1953. Author's first book. Stiff wraps. $1,000.

KODOKAN, The. *Illustrated Kodokan Judo.* Tokyo, 1955. First edition stated. $150.

KOESTLER, Arthur. See Costler, Dr. A.

KOESTLER, Arthur. *Darkness at Noon.* London, 1940. $4,500. New York, 1941. $100.

KOESTLER, Arthur. *Spanish Testament.* London, 1937. Cloth. $450. Wraps. (Left Book Club.) $100.

KOHL, J. G. *Kitchi-Gami: Wanderings Round Lake Superior.* London, 1860. First edition in English. Illustrated. $1,250.

KOLDEWEY, Captain. *The German Arctic Expedition of 1869–70.* London, 1874. Includes 4 chromolithograph plates, 2 portraits and 2 colored maps. $1,000.

KONINGSMARKE, the Long Finne: A Story of the New World. New York, 1823. (By James Kirke Paulding.) 2 vols. $600.

KOONTZ, Dean. See Axton, David; Coffey, Brian; Dwyer, K. R.; North, Anthony.

KOONTZ, Dean. *Night Chills.* New York, 1976. $300.

KOOP, Albert J. *Early Chinese Bronzes.* London, 1924. 110 plates (3 colored). $450. Calf. One of 40 on China paper, signed. $1,000. New York, 1924. $450.

KOOPS, Matthias. *Historical Account of the Substances Which Have Been Used to Describe Events . . . from the Earliest Date to the Invention of Paper.* London, 1800. Printed on paper made of straw alone. $2,000. London, 1801. $1,500.

(KORAN). *The Alcoran of Mahomet.* London, 1649. $1,250.

KORNBLUTH, C. M. *Not This August.* Garden City, 1955. $175.

KOSEWITZ, W. F. von. *Eccentric Tales, from the German.* London, 1827. 20 hand-colored etched plates by George Cruikshank from sketches by Alfred Crowquill. $1,250.

KOSINSKI, Jerzy. See Novak, Joseph.

KOSINSKI, Jerzy. *The Painted Bird.* Boston (1965). First book under his name. Extraneous line top of page 270. $500.

KOTZEBUE, August Friedrich Ferdinand von. *The Constant Lover.* London, 1799. 2 vols. $450.

KOTZEBUE, Otto von. *A New Voyage Round the World, 1823–26.* London, 1830. 2 vols. 2 frontises, 2 folding maps, and folding plan. First edition in English. $3,500.

KOTZEBUE, Otto von. *A Voyage of Discovery, Into the South Sea and Beering's Straits.* London, 1821. 3 vols. First edition in English. 7 maps or charts and 9 plates (8 colored). $7,500.

KOTZWINKLE, William. *The Fireman.* New York, 1969. Author's first book. $400.

KOZLOFF, Max. *Jasper Johns.* New York [1966]. Oblong. $1,000.

KRAKEL, Dean F. *The Saga of Tom Horn.* (Laramie, 1954.) First edition (suppressed). In dustwrapper. $600. Second edition, with text on pages 13 and 54 revised. $400.

KRAMER, Sidney. *A History of Stone & Kimball and Herter S. Stone & Co. with a Bibliography . . .* Chicago, 1940. One of 500 copies. $200. One of 1,000 copies. $150.

KRASHENINNIKOV, Stepan. *The History of Kamtschatka...* Gloucester, 1764. 2 folding maps, 7 plates on 5 sheets. $3,000.

KREYMBORG, Alfred. *Love, Life, and Other Studies.* New York (1908). One of 500 copies. $150.

KREYMBORG, Alfred (editor). *Others for 1919: An Anthology of the New Verse.* New York, 1917. Boards. $150.

KROEBER, Alfred L. *Handbook of the Indians of California.* Washington, 1925. Folding map, 10 other maps, 73 plates on 38 sheets. Cloth. Issued without dustwrapper. $300.

KROMER, Tom. *Waiting for Nothing.* New York, 1935. Author's first book. $250.

KRUSENSTERN, A. J. von. *Voyage Round the World in the Years 1803, 1804, 1805, and 1806.* London, 1813. 2 vols. First edition in English. 2 color plates, folding map. $8,500.

KRUTCH, Joseph Wood. *Comedy and Conscience . . .* New York, 1924. Author's first book. Wraps. $300.

KRUTCH, Joseph Wood. *Edgar Allan Poe: A Study in Genius.* New York, 1926. One of 140 signed copies. $250.

KUNDERA, Milan. *The Joke.* London, 1969. Author's first book. $250. New York: Coward-McCann, 1969. "First American edition 1969" on copyright page. $150.

KUNITZ, Stanley J. *Intellectual Things.* Garden City, 1930. Author's first book. $200.

KUNZ, George Frederick. *The Book of the Pearl.* New York, 1908. Illustrated, including color plates. Pale-blue cloth. $1,250. London, 1908. First English edition. White buckram. $1,000.

KUNZ, George Frederick. *The Curious Lore of Precious Stones.* Philadelphia (1913). 86 illustrations (6 in color). Pictorial cloth. $750.

KUNZ, George Frederick. *Gems and Precious Stones of North America* . . . New York, 1890. 24 plates (8 colored), other illustrations. With errata slip. $1,000.

KUNZ, George Frederick. *Ivory and the Elephant in Art, in Archaeology, and in Science.* Garden City, 1916. Illustrated. $1,250.

KUNZ, George Frederick. *Rings for the Finger.* Philadelphia, 1917. $600.

KUTTNER, Henry. See Garth, Will; Padgett, Lewis.

KUTTNER, Henry, and MOORE, C. L. *No Boundaries.* New York (1955). $450.

KUWASHIMA, T. S., and WELCH, A. R. *Judo: Forty-one Lessons in the Modern Science of Jiu Jitsu.* New York, 1938. $125.

KUYKENDALL, Ivan Lee. *Ghost Riders of the Mogollon.* San Antonio (1954). Boards. In dust-wrapper. (Suppressed.) $1,250.

KUYKENDALL, Judge W. L. *Frontier Days.* (Denver) 1917. Portrait. $300.

KYNE, Peter B. *Long Chance.* New York, 1914. $200.

L

L., E. V. *Sparks from a Flint: Odd Rhymes for Odd Times.* London, 1890. (By E. V. Lucas.) Author's first book. $150.

L., W. (Walter Lowenfels.) *Episodes and Epistles.* New York, 1925. $300.

LA BREE, Ben (editor). *The Confederate Soldier in the Civil War, 1861–1865.* Louisville, 1895. Illustrated. Folio, cloth. $400.

LACKINGTON, James. *Memoirs of the First Forty-five Years of the Life of James Lackington* . . . London (1791.) $500.

LACROIX, Paul. *Science and Literature in the Middle Ages* . . . New York, 1878. First English translation. $300.

LA CUISINE Creole. New York: Coleman (1885). (By Lafcadio Hearn.) Olive-green cloth. With introduction on two pages. $3,000. New Orleans [1922]. Second edition. Red pictorial cloth. $400.

LADA-MOCARSKI, Valerian. *Bibliography of Books on Alaska Published Before 1868.* New Haven, 1969. $400.

LADIES Almanack . . . *Written and Illustrated by a Lady of Fashion.* Paris, 1928. (By Djuna Barnes.) Pictorial wraps. One of 1,000 copies. $500. Vellum. One of 40 copies with hand-colored plates. $4,500.

LADY of Philadelphia. See *Seventy Five Receipts* . . .

LA FARGE, Oliver. *Laughing Boy.* Boston, 1929. Author's first book. (Previous collaboration.) $750.

LAFEVER, Minard. *The Modern Builder's Guide.* New York, 1833. $1,500.

LAFITTE: The Pirate of the Gulf. New York, 1836. (By Joseph Holt Ingraham.) 2 vols. $750.

LA FONTAINE, Jean de. *The Fables of Jean de la Fontaine.* London, 1931. 2 vols. Translated into English verse by Edward Marsh. 26 engravings on copper by Stephen Gooden. Vellum. One of 525 copies signed by the translator and artist. $750.

LA FRENTZ, F. W. *Cowboy Stuff.* New York, 1927. Illustrated by Henry Ziegler. Boards. Issued without dustwrapper. First issue, with 49 plates. One of 500 signed copies. $750. One of 12 signed copies on handmade paper. $7,500.

LAHONTAN, Louis Armand, Baron de. *New Voyages to North-America . . .* London, 1703. 2 vols. 4 maps and 20 plates. Without the frontispiece in vol. 2 (which is not usually present). $4,500.

LAKESIDE Classics. Chicago, 1903–90. 87 vols. Complete set. $1,750. Individual volumes range from $20 to $100 or so.

LAMANTIA, Philip. *Erotic Poems.* (Berkeley), 1946. Author's first book. Issued without dustwrapper. $500.

LAMAR, Mirabeau B. *Verse Memorials.* New York, 1857. Author's first book. $2,000.

LAMB, Lady Caroline. See *Glenarvon.*

LAMB, Charles. See *The Adventures of Ulysses; The King and Queen of Hearts; The New Year's Feast on His Coming of Age; Poetry for Children.*

LAMB, Charles. *Album Verses, with a Few Others.* London, 1830. $750.

LAMB, Charles. *John Woodvil, a Tragedy . . .* London, 1802. $1,500.

LAMB, Charles. *The Letters of Charles Lamb, to Which Are Added Those of His Sister Mary Lamb.* (London, 1935.) 3 vols. Edited by E. V. Lucas. In original cloth. $500.

LAMB, Charles. *A Masque of Days.* London, 1901. Illustrated by Walter Crane. Half cloth. $250.

LAMB. Charles. *Specimens of English Dramatic Poets, Who Lived About the Time of Shakespeare: with Notes.* London, 1808. $600.

LAMB, Charles. *A Tale of Rosamund Gray . . .* Birmingham, 1798. (Two known copies with Birmingham on title page.) $7,500. London, 1798. First separate book. $2,500.

LAMB, Charles. *Tales from Shakespeare.* London, 1807. 2 vols. 20 plates by William Mulready. Earliest issue is thought to have no imprint on back of page 235. $6,500. With imprint on back of page 235. $5,000. London, 1909. Arthur Rackham color plates. Buckram with ties. One of 750 large-paper copies, signed by Rackham. $1,750. Trade edition in cloth. $500. (Note: Mary Lamb collaborated in writing this book.)

LAMB, Charles. *The Works of Charles Lamb.* London, 1818. 2 vols. With ads at end dated "June, 1818." $1,250. London, 1903. Edited by William Macdonald. 12 vols. In half vellum. $1,000. In morocco. $2,000.

LAMB, Harold. *Marching Sands*. New York, 1920. $300.

LAMB, M. C. *Leather Dressing Including Dyeing, Staining & Finishing*. London, 1925. Third edition and completely rewritten. $300.

LAMB, Patrick. *Royal Cookery; or, the Complete Court-Cook*. London, 1710. Engraved plates (some folding). $2,500.

LAMBERT, Aylmer Bouke. *A Description of the Genus Pinus*. London, 1803–7. 47 engraved plates, all but 3 colored by hand (Nissen 1123 states that 25 colored copies in all, with coloring by William Hooker). $50,000. London, 1832. 2 vols. Engraved portrait and 75 engraved or lithographed plates colored by hand. (The publisher was erratic in terms of how many plates were included but usually had at least 72.) $6,000.

LAMBERT, Gavin. *The Slide Area*. London, 1959. $350. New, 1959. $200.

LAMBETH, William Alexander, and MANNING, Warren H. *Thomas Jefferson as an Architect and a Designer of Landscapes*. Boston, 1913. 500 numbered copies. $400.

LAMBOURNE, Alfred. *An Old Sketch-Book Dedicated to the Memory of My Father*. Boston (1892). 18 plates. 53 pages, plates. 78 pages, atlas folio, half morocco and tan cloth. $500.

LAMBOURNE, Alfred. *Scenic Utah: Pen and Pencil*. New York, 1891. 20 plates. "Edition Deluxe" on printed label. In morocco. Numbered and signed. $850. Regular editions. $400.

LAMENTATIONS of Jeremiah (The). Newtown, Wales: Gregynog Press, 1933. Folio, morocco. Issued without dustwrapper or slipcase. One of 250 copies. $2,500. One of 15 copies specially bound. $6,000.

LAMON, Ward H. *The Life of Abraham Lincoln*. Boston, 1872. Plates and facsimiles. Green, or rust-colored cloth. $400.

L'AMOUR, Louis. See Burns, Tex.

L'AMOUR, Louis. *Burning Hills*. New York, 1956. $1,750.

L'AMOUR, Louis. *Guns of the Timberlands*. New York, 1955. $2,000.

L'AMOUR, Louis. *Silver Canyon*. New York, 1956. $1,500.

L'AMOUR, Louis. *Sitka*. New York, 1957. $1,000.

L'AMOUR, Louis. *Smoke from This Altar*. Oklahoma City (1939). Author's first book. Orange cloth. $1,000. Green cloth. $750.

LAMPLIGHTER (The). Boston, 1854. (By Maria S. Cummins.) Author's first book. (Noted in black [BAL], green, or blue cloth.) $1,000.

LAMPMAN, Archibald. *Among the Millet . . .* Ottawa, 1888. Author's first book. First issue, double rule above and below title on spine. In rose-colored cloth. $300.

LAMSON, David R. *Two Years' Experience Among the Shakers*. West Boylston, Mass., 1848. Illustrated. $250.

LANDAUER, Bella C. *Early American Trade Cards from the Collection of Bella C. Landauer.* New York, 1927. 44 plates. One of 500 copies. In dustwrapper. $250. One of 60 copies. $400.

LANDE, Lawrence. *The Lawrence Lande Collection of Canadiana in the Redpath Library* . . . Montreal, 1965. 113 pages of plates. With *Rare and Unusual Canadiana; First Supplement to the Lande Bibliography.* First volume is one of 950 copies. Second volume is one of 500 copies. Both signed. $600.

LANDOR, A. Henry Savage. *Across Coveted Lands.* London, 1902. 2 vols. Folding map. $650.

LANDOR, A. Henry Savage. *Across Unknown South America.* (London, 1913.) 2 vols. 2 maps, 1 folding. $650.

LANDOR, A. Henry Savage. *Across Widest Africa.* London, 1907. 2 vols. Folding map. $750.

LANDOR, Walter Savage. See *Imaginary Conversations; Pericles and Aspasia; Popery, British and Foreign.*

LANDOR, Walter Savage. *Gebir: A Poem.* London, 1798. Author's first book. In original wraps. $6,000. Rebound. $2,500.

LANDOR, Walter Savage. *Gebir, Count Julian and Other Poems.* London, 1831. $400.

LANDOR, Walter Savage. *The Last Fruit Off an Old Tree.* London, 1853. Purple cloth. First edition, with 8 pages of ads. $450.

LANE, Grant (Steve Fisher). *Spend the Night.* New York, 1935. $750.

LANE, Walter P. *Adventures and Recollections of Gen. Walter P. Lane.* Marshall, Tex., 1887. Portrait. 114 pages, wraps. $1,000.

LANG, Andrew. *Ballads and Lyrics of Old France, with Other Poems.* London, 1872. Author's first book. White cloth. $250.

LANG, Andrew. *The Blue Fairy Book.* London, 1889. Illustrated. Boards. One of 113 copies. $4,500. Trade edition. $4,000.

LANG, Andrew. *The Brown Fairy Book.* London, 1904. $750.

LANG, Andrew. *The Crimson Fairy Book.* London, 1903. $750.

LANG, Andrew. *The Green Fairy Book.* London, 1892. One of 150 copies. $1,000. Trade edition. Green cloth. $600.

LANG, Andrew. *The Grey Fairy Book.* London, 1900. $600.

LANG, Andrew. *The Olive Fairy Book.* London, 1907. $750.

LANG, Andrew. *The Orange Fairy Book.* London, 1906. $600.

LANG, Andrew. *Prince Charles Edward.* London, 1900. Illustrated. Half morocco. One of 350 copies. $400. One of 1,500 copies in wraps. $300.

LANG, Andrew. *The Princess Nobody.* London (1884). Illustrated. Half cloth. $450.

LANG, Andrew. *The Red Fairy Book*. London, 1890. Illustrated. Gray-and-white boards. One of 113 copies on large paper. $2,000. Trade edition. $1,500.

LANG, Andrew. *The Violet Fairy Book*. London, 1901. $750.

LANG, Andrew. *The Yellow Fairy Book*. London and New York, 1894. $750. One of 140 copies, $1,000.

LANG, Andrew (translator). *The Miracles of Madame Saint Katherine of Fierbois*. Chicago: Way & Williams, 1897. First American edition. Red vellum. One of 50 copies on vellum. $250.

LANG, Andrew, et al. *Batch of Golfing Papers*. London, 1892. $150. New York, 1897. $250.

LANGE, Dorothea. *An American Exodus . . .* New York, 1939. Written with Paul S. Taylor. Author's first book. $750.

LANGE, John. *Odds On*. New York, 1966. (By Michael Crichton.) Author's first book. Wraps. $300.

LANGE, John. *The Venom Business*. New York and Cleveland (1969). (By Michael Crichton.) $350.

LANGFORD, Nathaniel Pitt. *Vigilante Days and Ways*. Boston, 1890. 2 vols. 15 plates. Pictorial cloth. $650. New York, 1893. $450.

LANGLEY, Batty. *The City and Country Builder's and Workman's Treasury of Designs . . .* London, 1745. Second edition. Adds 14 plates in the appendix not in first edition. $3,750.

LANGLEY, Batty. *Practical Geometry Applied to the Useful Arts of Building, Surveying, Gardening, and Mensuration*. London, 1726. $4,500.

LANGLEY, Henry G. *The San Francisco Directory for the Year 1858*. San Francisco, 1858. $1,000.

LANGSDORFF, Georg H. von. *Narrative of the Rezanov Voyage to Nueva California, 1806*. San Francisco, 1927. Map, plates. Half cloth. In dustwrapper. One of 260 copies. $600.

LANGSDORFF, Georg H. von. *Voyages and Travels in Various Parts of the World During 1803–7*. London, 1813–14. 2 vols. First English edition. Folding map and 20 plates. $15,000. Carlisle, Pa., 1817. 2 vols. in 1. First American edition (abridged). Folding plate. $2,500.

LANGSTAFF, Launcelot, and others. *Salmagundi; or, The Whim-Whams and Opinions of Launcelot Langstaff, Esq., and Others*. New York, 1807–8. 2 vols. $750. (By Washington Irving, William Irving, and James Kirke Paulding.) Difficult to identify; see BAL.

LANGSTON, Mrs. George. *History of Eastland County, Texas*. Dallas, 1904. $300.

LANGTON, Jane. *The Transcendental Murder*. New York, 1964. Author's first mystery. $350.

LANGWORTHY, Franklin. *Scenery of the Plains, Mountains and Mines*. Ogdensburgh, N.Y., 1855. $1,250.

LANGWORTHY, Lucius H. *Dubuque: Its History, Mines, Indian Legends*. Dubuque, Iowa (1855). 82 pages, printed green wraps. $500.

LANHAM, Edwin. *Sailors Don't Care.* Paris, 1929. Author's first book. One of 10 signed copies. $1,000. Wraps. $750. New York, 1930. $300.

LANIER, Sidney. *The Boy's Mabinogion.* New York, 1881. Illustrated by Alfred Fredericks. Decorated cloth. $350.

LANIER, Sidney. *Florida: Its Scenery, Climate, and History.* Philadelphia, 1876. Illustrated. $500.

LANIER, Sidney. *Tiger-Lilies.* New York, 1867. Author's first book. First state, with title page on a stub. $500.

LANIER, Virginia. *Death in Bloodhound Red.* Sarasota, 1995. Author's first book. $400.

LANMAN, Charles. *Adventures in the Wilds of the United States and British American Provinces.* Philadelphia, 1856. 2 vols. First American edition. Illustrated. $1,250.

LANMAN, Charles. *Adventures of an Angler in Canada . . .* London, 1848. Frontispiece. Half leather. $750.

LANMAN, Charles. *A Summer in the Wilderness.* New York, 1847. $600.

LANMAN, Charles. *A Tour to the River Saguenay . . .* Philadelphia, 1848. $600.

LANMAN, James H. *History of Michigan.* New York, 1839. Folding map. $450.

LANTHORNE Book (The). New York (1898). (By Stephen Crane and others.) Half brown leather and green cloth. One of 125 copies signed by Crane and the other contributors. $7,500. Some not signed by Crane. $1,500.

LAPHAM, I. A. *A Geographical and Topographical Description of Wisconsin.* Milwaukee, 1844. Folding map (with 1844 copyright). (First bound book printed in Wisconsin.) $2,000.

LAPHAM, I. A. *A Wisconsin . . .* Milwaukee, 1846. Colored map (dated 1845). Second edition (of *A Geographical and Topographical Description of Wisconsin*). $750.

LaPLACE, P. S. *Mecanique Celeste.* Boston, 1829–39. (By the Marquis de la Place...). 4 vols. First edition in English. (250 copies.) $4,500.

LARCOM, Lucy. *Similitudes.* Boston, 1854. Author's first book. $200.

LARDNER, Ring W. *Bib Ballads.* Chicago (1915). Illustrated by Fontaine Fox. Decorated brown cloth. (500 printed.) First edition not stated. Issued without dustwrapper in box. $850. Without box. $350.

LARDNER, Ring W. *The Big Town.* Indianapolis (1921). Illustrated. In dustwrapper. $1,500. Without dustwrapper. $200.

LARDNER, Ring W. *Gullible's Travels.* Indianapolis (1917). First edition, not stated. In dustwrapper. $1,250. Without dustwrapper. $150.

LARDNER, Ring W. *How to Write Short Stories (with Samples).* New York, 1924. $600.

LARDNER, Ring. *Lose with a Smile.* New York, 1933. $500.

LARDNER, Ring W. *The Love Nest and Other Stories.* New York, 1926. $350.

LARDNER, Ring W. *March 6th the Homecoming.* (Chicago, 1914). First edition not stated. Issued without dustwrapper. $5,000.

LARDNER, Ring W. *My Four Weeks in France.* Indianapolis (1918). First edition not stated. In dustwrapper. $500. Without dustwrapper. $150.

LARDNER, Ring W. *Own Your Own Home.* Indianapolis (1919). (Apparently not issued in dustwrapper.) $350.

LARDNER, Ring W. *Stop Me If You've Heard This One.* New York, 1929. Boards. Issued without dustwrapper as a promotional item. First edition not stated. $350.

LARDNER, Ring W. *Symptoms of Being 35.* Indianapolis (1921). Issued in dustwrapper. $300.

LARDNER, Ring W. *You Know Me Al.* New York (1916). No Doran colophon. In dustwrapper. $2,000. Without dustwrapper. $450.

LARDNER, Ring W. *Zanzibar.* Niles, Michigan (1903). Author's first book. Wraps. $6,000.

LARDNER, Ring W., Jr. *The Young Immigrunts.* Indianapolis (1920). (With a preface by the father. Assume "Jr." is the pseudonym of "Sr.," as son is four now.) Portraits by Gaar Williams. Pictorial boards. First edition not stated. In dustwrapper. $300.

LARDNER, Ring W., Jr., and KAUFMAN, George S. *June Moon.* New York, 1930. (Junior is now fourteen years old.) Mauve cloth. With "A" on copyright page. $300.

LARIMER, Mrs. Sarah L. *The Capture and Escape; or, Life Among the Sioux.* Philadelphia, 1870. 5 plates. $1,250.

LARIMER, William. *Reminiscences of Gen. William Larimer and of His Son William H. H. Larimer.* Lancaster, Pa., 1918. Plates, portraits, folding chart. Morocco. $1,250.

LARKIN, Philip. *Aubade.* (Salem, 1980.) One of 250 copies initialed by author and printer. Wraps in silver-lined envelope. $450.

LARKIN, Philip. *The Fantasy Poets—Number Twenty One.* Swinford, Eynsham, 1954. One of 300 copies. Stapled wraps. $850.

LARKIN, Philip. *A Girl in Winter.* London (1947). $2,500.

LARKIN, Philip. *Jill.* London (1946). $2,000.

LARKIN, Philip. *The Less Deceived.* (Hessle, 1955.) With flat spine. Dustwrapper priced "6s," and rear printed in black only. $1,250. Second issue with rounded spine, and with "Second Edition, January 1956" on copyright page. Some copies of the dustwrapper are priced "7s. 6d." $600. Wraps with dustwrapper glued on as cover and priced "6s." $200.

LARKIN, Philip. *The North Ship.* London (1945). Author's first book. Black cloth. $3,500. London (1965). Dark-red cloth. $250. London: Faber (1966). $125.

LARKIN, Philip. *XX Poems.* Belfast, 1951. One of 100. $2,000.

LAROQUE, François A. *Journal of François A. Laroque from the Assiniboine to the Yellowstone, 1805.* Ottawa, 1910. 82 pages, printed wraps. $450.

LARPENTEUR, Charles. *Forty Years a Fur Trader of the Upper Mississippi.* New York, 1898. 2 vols. 18 maps and plans. Blue cloth. One of 950 copies. $750.

LARSEN, Nella. *Passing.* New York, 1929. $2,500.

LA SALLE, Charles E. *Colonel Crocket, the Texas Trailer.* New York, no date [1871]. 84 pages, pictorial wraps. $200.

LA SALLE, René Robert . . . *Relation of the Discoveries and Voyages* . . . Caxton Club. Chicago, 1901. English and French texts. Half vellum. One of 227 copies. $450.

LASCELLES, Arthur A. W. *A Treatise on the Nature and Cultivation of Coffee.* London, 1865. Brown cloth. 67 pages, plus ads. $600.

LAST Days of Pompeii (The). London, 1834. (By Edward Bulwer-Lytton.) 3 vols. In original cloth with errata slips in each vol. $750. New York, 1834. 2 vols. First American edition. $450. Limited Editions Club, New York, 1956. Illustrated. In slipcase. $125.

LAST Man (The). London, 1826. (By Mary Wollstonecraft Shelley.) 3 vols. With ad leaf at end of vol. 1. $3,500. Philadelphia, 1833. $1,500.

LAST of the Mohicans (The). Philadelphia, 1826. By the Author of "The Pioneers" (James Fenimore Cooper.) 2 vols. In original tan boards, paper labels. BAL notes various differences, but no clear priorities. $12,500 (although $28,000 at auction in 1993). Rebound. $3,500. London, 1826, 3 vols. First English edition. In original boards. $4,500. Rebound. $2,500. Limited Editions Club, New York, 1932. Illustrated. Quarter leather. In slipcase. $125.

LATHAM, H. *Trans-Missouri Stock Raising* . . . Omaha, 1871. Map. 88 pages, wraps. $6,000. Denver, 1962. Illustrated. Pictorial cloth. One of 999 copies. In dustwrapper. $75.

LATHEN, Emma. *Banking on Death.* New York, 1961. (By Mary Jane Latsis and Martha Heinissart.) Authors' first book. $400. London, 1961. $200.

LATHROP, Dr. David. *The History of Fifty-Ninth Regiment* . . . Indianapolis, 1865. 24 lithographed portraits. Original cloth. 3 plates. $400.

LATIMER, Jonathan. See Coffin, Peter.

LATIMER, Jonathan. *Headed for a Hearse.* New York, 1935. $1,250.

LATIMER, Jonathan. *Murder in the Madhouse.* Garden City, 1935. Author's first book. $750.

LATIMER, Jonathan. *Red Gardenias.* New York, 1939. $500.

LATIMER, Jonathan. *Solomon's Vineyard.* London, 1941. $600.

LATIMORE, Sarah Briggs, and HASKELL, Grace Clark. *Arthur Rackham: A Bibliography.* Los Angeles, 1936. One of 550 copies. In slipcase. $500.

LATOUR, A. Lacarriere. *Historical Memoir of the War in West Florida and Louisiana in 1814–15.* Philadelphia, 1816. 2 vols. With an atlas. $3,750.

LATROBE, Rev. C. I. *Journal of a Visit to South Africa*. London, 1818. Large folding map, 16 plates (12 colored). $2,500.

LATROBE, Charles Joseph. *The Rambler in Mexico*. London, 1836. Folding map. $350.

LATROBE, Charles Joseph. *The Rambler in North America*. London, 1835. Two vols. $1,250.

LATTER Struggles in the Journey of Life . . . Edinburgh, 1833. (By George Miller.) $400. New York, 1836. $350.

LAUD, William. *The History of the Troubles and Tryal* . . . London, 1695. Illustrated with an engraved frontispiece portrait. $600.

LAUD, William. *A Relation of the Conference Betweene William Laud* . . . London, 1639. $300.

LAUFER, Berthold. *Paper and Printing in Ancient China*. Chicago, 1931. One of 250 copies. $350.

LAUGHLIN, Clarence John. *New Orleans and Its Living Past*. Boston, 1941. Text by David L. Cohen. 1,030 signed copies (in glassine dustwrapper) in slipcase. $1,000.

LAUGHTON, L. G. Carr. *Old Ship Figure-Heads and Sterns*. London, 1925. 8 colored plates, 48 in monochrome. With 2 portfolios of plates. Three-quarter pigskin. One of 100 copies. $750. One of 1,500 copies. In dustwrapper. $500.

LAURENCE, Margaret. *A Tree for Poverty*. Nairobi, 1954. (Somali anthology edited by Laurence.) Author's first book. $1,500.

LAURENCE, Margaret. *This Side of Jordan*. Toronto, 1960. $500. Wraps. $100. New York, 1960. $150. London (1960). $100.

LAUTERBACH, Ann. *Book One*. New York, 1975. Oblong mimeographed stapled sheets in green wraps. One of 100 signed numbered copies. $350.

LA VALLIERE, Chevalier de. *The Art of War*. Philadelphia, 1776. $2,500.

LAVATER, Johann Caspar. *Essays on Phsysiognomy* . . . London, 1789–98. 3 vols in 5. $2,500. Boston (1794). $500.

LAVIN, Mary. *Tales from Bective Bridge*. Boston, 1942. Author's first book. One of 999 copies. $350. London (1943). $250.

LAW of Descent and Distribution Governing Lands of the Creek Nation, as Held by C. W. Raymond, Judge of the U.S. Court for the Indian Territory. No place: Democrat Printing Co., 1903. 14 pages, printed wraps. $500.

LAWRENCE, Ada, and GELDER, Stuart. *Young Lorenzo: Early Life of D.H. Lawrence*. Florence (1932). Illustrated. Vellum. One of 740 copies (or 750). In dustwrapper. $400.

LAWRENCE, D. H. See Davison, Lawrence H.; Grazzini, A. F.; Verga, Giovanni.

LAWRENCE, D. H. *Collected Poems*. London, 1928. 2 vols. Boards, parchment spines. One of 100 signed copies. $3,000. Trade edition. 2 vols. Brown cloth. $350. New York, 1929. 2 vols. First American edition. Brown cloth. $300.

LAWRENCE, D. H. *The Escaped Cock*. Paris: Black Sun Press, 1929. Color frontispiece by Lawrence. White wraps. One of 450 copies on Van Gelder paper. In glassine dustwrapper. In slipcase. $600. One of 50 copies on vellum, signed. $2,000. (Published later in England as *The Man Who Died*.)

LAWRENCE, D. H. *Fantasia of the Unconscious*. New York, 1922. Blue ribbed cloth. $500. London, 1923. $400.

LAWRENCE, D. H. *Kangaroo*. London (1923). $500. New York, 1923. $400.

LAWRENCE, D. H. *Lady Chatterley's Lover*. (Florence, Italy), 1928. Mulberry-colored boards, paper spine label. One of 1,000 signed copies. In plain dustwrapper. $15,000. London (1932). Expurgated. $1,250. New York, 1932. $1,000.

LAWRENCE, D. H. *Last Poems*. Florence, 1932. Edited by Richard Aldington and G. Orioli. Frontispiece in color. Boards, paper label. One of 750 copies. In dustwrapper. In slipcase. $650. (There were also 2 copies printed on blue paper.) London, 1933. $250. New York, 1933. $200.

LAWRENCE, D. H. *The Lost Girl*. London (1920). Brown cloth. First issue, with page 256, line 15 reading ". . . she was taken to her room . . ." and with page 268 reading "whether she noticed anything in the bedrooms, in the beds." In dustwrapper. $1,500. Second issue, page 256, reads ". . . she let be." and 268 deletes the last six words of first issue. Both pages are tipped in. In dustwrapper. $1,250. (There is also a third issue, changed on integral pages.) New York, 1921. $750.

LAWRENCE, D. H. *The Man Who Died*. London, 1931. (First English edition of *The Escaped Cock*.) Buckram. $300. New York, 1931. $250.

LAWRENCE, D. H. *Mornings in Mexico*. London, 1927. $500. New York, 1927. $450.

LAWRENCE, D. H. *The Paintings of D. H. Lawrence*. London: Mandrake Press (1929). 26 colored plates. Folio, half morocco and green cloth. One of 500 copies. In slipcase. $1,500. One of 10 copies on Japan vellum. Signed. $8,500.

LAWRENCE, D. H. *Pansies*. London: Martin Secker (1929). $250. One of 250 signed copies. In dustwrapper. $1,250. Another (later) edition, "Privately Printed." White wraps. Portrait frontispiece. One of 500 signed copies. In glassine dustwrapper and slipcase. $850. Limp leather. One of 50 copies. $3,500. Pink wraps. $250. New York, 1929. First American edition. In dustwrapper. $300.

LAWRENCE, D. H. *The Prussian Officer and Other Stories*. London (1914). Blue cloth stamped in gold with 20 pages of ads at back. $750. Second issue, in light-blue cloth stamped in dark blue and with 16 pages of ads. $500. New York, 1914. $350.

LAWRENCE, D. H. *The Rainbow*. London (1915). Blue-green cloth. $1,750. Variant issue. In red or brown cloth or wraps. $750. New York, 1916. Censored. $500.

LAWRENCE, D. H. *Rawdon's Roof*. London, 1928. Decorated boards. One of 530 signed copies. $750.

LAWRENCE, D. H. *St. Mawr*. (With "The Princess.") London (1925). Brown cloth with "Contents" showing text beginning on page 9. $450. Second issue corrected to show page 7. $300. New York, 1925. First separate edition (without "The Princess"). $300.

LAWRENCE. D. H. *Sea and Sardinia.* New York, 1921. 8 colored plates. Boards and cloth. $750. London, 1923. $1,000.

LAWRENCE, D. H. *Sons and Lovers.* London (1913). Dark-blue cloth. Presumed first state(s), without date on title page (Schwartz) or with dated title page tipped in (Roberts). $1,750. Dated page integral (agreed to be later). $600. New York, 1913. $600.

LAWRENCE, D. H. *Studies in Classic American Literature.* New York, 1923. $600. London (1924). $600.

LAWRENCE, D. H. *Sun.* London, 1926. One of 100.Wraps. $1,250. Black Sun Press. Paris, 1927 [actually published in 1928]. First unexpurgated edition. One of 15 on vellum, signed. In glassine dustwrapper and gold folder and in slipcase. $6,500. One of 150 tied in a gold folder. $2,000. No place: Privately printed, 1929. U.S. piracy. Assume no dustwrapper. $200.

LAWRENCE, D. H. *Tortoises.* New York, 1921. Pictorial boards. In glassine dustwrapper. $600.

LAWRENCE, D. H. *Touch and Go.* London, 1920. Flexible orange boards, paper labels. In dustwrapper. $400. New York, 1920. Orange boards. First American edition. In dustwrapper. $350.

LAWRENCE, D. H. *The Trespasser.* London, 1912. Presumed first issue in dark-blue cloth. $1,500. Colonial (or perhaps trial, but doubtful) issue in green cloth. $750. New York, 1912. $600.

LAWRENCE, D. H. *Twilight in Italy.* London (1916). Dark-blue cloth. $500. Variant noted in light-blue cloth. $400. New York, 1916. $400.

LAWRENCE, D. H. *The Virgin and the Gipsy.* Florence, 1930. White boards, paper label. One of 810. In dustwrapper and slipcase. $750. London (1930). $350. New York, 1930. $300.

LAWRENCE, D. H. *The White Peacock.* New York, 1911. Blue cloth. Author's first book. First issue, with integral title page and 1910 copyright date. $6,000. Second issue, with a tipped-in title page and 1911 copyright date. $2,000. London, 1911. Dark blue-green cloth. First issue, with publisher's windmill device on back cover and with pages 227–30 tipped in. $750. With leaves integral. $500.

LAWRENCE, D. H. *Women in Love.* New York, 1920. Dark-blue cloth. One of about 16 or 18 copies signed and numbered by Lawrence. Without dustwrapper. $6,500. Unsigned copies. $1,250. New York, 1920 [actually 1922]. Brown boards. First English edition put together by Martin Secker using the U.S. sheets. One of 50 signed. Without dustwrapper. $5,000. London (1921). First English published edition in brown boards. In dustwrapper. $2,500. New York, 1922. $1,000.

LAWRENCE, D. H. (translator). *The Story of Dr. Manente.* Florence (1929). By A. F. Grazzini. Frontispiece, 2 plates. Parchment boards. One of 200 signed by Lawrence. In tissue jacket. $850. One of 1,000 copies. In dustwrapper. $175. One of 1,200 unnumbered copies. $100.

LAWRENCE, Frieda. *"Not I, But the Wind."* Santa Fe, N.M., 1934. One of 1,000 signed. $450. New York, 1934. $150. London, 1935. $150.

LAWRENCE, John. *The History and Delineation of the Horse in all his Varieties* . . . London, 1809. 12 full-page plates. $600.

LAWRENCE, Richard. *Interest of Ireland in its Trade and Wealth.* Dublin, 1682. $2,000.

LAWRENCE, Richard Hoe (compiler). *History of the Society of Iconophiles of the City of New York.* New York, 1930. Reproductions of 119 plates. Boards and morocco issued without dustwrapper. One of 186. $300.

LAWRENCE, T. E. See Homer. See also *The Seven Pillars of Wisdom.*

LAWRENCE, T. E. *Carchemish.* London, 1914. Author's first book with C. L. Woolley. $1,500.

LAWRENCE, T. E. *Crusader Castles.* Golden Cockerel Press. London, 1936. 2 vols. Portraits and facsimiles, 2 maps in envelope. Half red morocco. One of 1,000 issued without dustwrapper or slipcase. $1,750.

LAWRENCE, T. E. *The Diary of T. E. Lawrence.* Corvinus Press. London, 1937. Illustrated. Boards and morocco. One of 203. $4,500. Morocco. One of 30 on Canute paper. In slipcase. $7,500. Another, limp vellum. One of 40 on Medway paper. In slipcase. $6,000.

LAWRENCE, T. E. *An Essay on Flecker.* Corvinus Press. London, 1937. Buckram. One of 26. In slipcase. $6,500. One of 4. Vellum. $10,000. One of 2. Leather. $12,500. New York, 1937. Printed wraps. First American edition. One of about 56 for copyright purposes (4 leaves stapled). $2,500.

LAWRENCE, T. E. *Letters.* London, 1938. Edited by David Garnett. Maps and plates. Buckram. Page 182, line 9: "Baltic." $200. Page 182, line 9: "Balkan" $150. Garden City, 1939. $150.

LAWRENCE, T. E. *Men in Print.* Golden Cockerel Press. (London, 1940.) Half morocco. One of 470. $600. Morocco. One of 30 specially bound with extra facsimile. In slipcase. $3,000.

LAWRENCE, T. E. *Minorities.* London (1971). Edited by J. M. Wilson. Preface by C. Day-Lewis. Frontispiece portrait. Half calf, leather label. One of 125 signed by Day-Lewis. In glassine dustwrapper. $500. Trade. $100. Garden City, 1972. $100.

LAWRENCE, T. E. *The Mint.* Garden City, 1936. One of 50 in half vellum for copyright purposes. $6,000.

LAWRENCE, T. E. *The Mint: A Day-book of the R.A.F. Depot Between August and December, 1922.* London (1955). Leather and blue cloth. First published edition. One of 2,000 issued without dustwrapper in slipcase. $350. Garden City, 1955. One of 1,000 issued without dustwrapper in slipcase. $300.

LAWRENCE, T. E. *Revolt in the Desert.* London, 1927. Frontispiece, map, and portraits. Buckram. In dustwrapper. $750. Half morocco. One of 315 on large paper. In dustwrapper. $2,500. New York, 1927. $600. Buckram. One of 250. $2,000.

LAWRENCE, T. E. *Secret Dispatches from Arabia.* Golden Cockerel Press. London (1939). Portrait frontispiece. Morocco and cloth. One of 970. $1,000. White pigskin. One of 30 with part of the manuscript of *The Seven Pillars of Wisdom.* $3,000.

LAWRENCE, T. E. *Seven Pillars of Wisdom (The).* (London), 1926. 66 plates, other illustrations, 4 folding maps. Full leather. Inscribed "Complete" and signed "T.E.S." (for T. E. Shaw, Lawrence's adopted name). $50,000. 32 copies initialed "T. E. S." and marked "Incomplete."

$35,000. (For first American copyright edition, with no author named, see title entry.) London (1935). Buckram and leather. First published edition. One of 750. In dustwrapper and slipcase. $3,500. Trade edition in buckram. In dustwrapper. $750. Garden City, 1935. Buckram and leather. First published American edition. One of 750 in dustwrapper and slipcase. $2,500. Trade. $450.

LAWRENCE, T. E. *Shaw-Ede:T. E. Lawrence's Letters to H. S. Ede.* Golden Cockerel Press. London, 1942. 7 pages of facsimiles. Morocco. One of 470. Issued without dustwrapper or slipcase. $650. One of 30 specially bound. $2,500.

LAWRENCE, T. E. *The Wilderness of Zin.* (London), 1914. (Written with C. L. Woolley.) Period after date on spine. $1,000.

LAWRENCE, W. J. *The Elizabethan Playhouse and Other Studies.* Shakespeare Head Press. Stratford-on-Avon, England, 1912–13. 2 vols. 30 plates. Boards and cloth. One of 760 copies. $150.

LAWS and Decrees of the State of Coahuila and Texas, in Spanish and English. Houston, 1839. In original calf. $1,000.

LAWS and Regulations of Union District, Clear Creek County, C. T. Central, C.T. (Colorado Territory), 1864. 19 pages, printed wraps. $1,500.

LAWS for the Better Government of California. San Francisco, 1848. 68 pages. Only 2 copies known of this first English book printed in California. $5,000 or more.

LAWS of the Cherokee Nation. Tahlequah, Indian Territory, 1852. Half leather. English language edition. $1,750.

LAWS of the Choctaw Nation, Made and Enacted by the General Council from 1886 to 1890. (In English and Choctaw.) Atoka, Indian Territory, 1890. One of 250. $500.

LAWS of Gregory District, February 18 & 20, 1860. (Cover title.) Denver, 1860. 12 pages, printed wraps. $2,000 or more.

LAWS of Jamaica, Passed by the Assembly . . . 1684 . . . London, 1684. Folding map. (First collected laws of the island.) $2,000.

LAWS of the Territory of Louisiana (The). St. Louis, 1808 (actually 1809). $12,500.

LAWS of the Territory of New Mexico. Santa Fe, N.M., 1862. 71 pages, wraps. $1,000.

LAWS of the Town of San Francisco (The). San Francisco, 1847. 8 pages, wraps. $3,000 or more.

LAWSON, Henry. *Short Stories in Verse and Prose.* Sydney, 1894. Wraps. Author's first book. $1,500.

LAWYERS and Legislators, or Notes on the American Mining Companies. London, 1825. (By Benjamin Disraeli.) $450.

LAY, William, and HUSSEY, Cyrus M. *A Narrative of the Mutiny on Board the Ship Globe of Nantucket.* New London, Conn., 1828. $2,000.

LAYARD, Austin. *Discoveries in the Ruins of Nineveh and Babylon.* London, 1853. 2 vols. 5 maps and plans, 11 plates. $2,000.

LAYARD, Georges. *George Cruikshank's Portraits of Himself.* London, 1897. Illustrated. Vellum and cloth. One of 250 large-paper copies signed by Layard. $500.

LAYNE, J. Gregg. *Annals of Los Angeles.* San Francisco, 1935. Plates. One of 200. $125.

LAYTON, Irving. *Here and Now.* Montreal, 1945. Author's first book. Wraps. $2,000.

LAYTON, Irving. *The Long Pea-Shooter.* Montreal (1954). In plain beige card covers with dust-wrapper (may be trial, advance, or remainder binding). $450. Montreal (1954). Cloth. $400.

LAYTON Court Mystery (The). London, 1925. By "?" (Anthony Berkeley, pseudonym of A.B. Cox.) Author's first book. $5,000.

LAZARUS, Emma. *Poems and Translations.* New York, 1867. Author's first book. $300.

LAZARUS, Emma. *Songs of a Semite.* New York, 1882. $200.

LEA, Albert M. *Notes on the Wisconsin Territory.* Philadelphia, 1836. Folding map. 53 pages, in original printed boards. $1,500.

LEA, Pryor. *An Outline of the Central Transit, in a Series of Six Letters to Hon. John Hemphill.* Galveston, 1859. 32 pages printed wraps. $250.

LEA, Tom. *Calendar of the Twelve Travelers Through the Pass of the North.* El Paso, Tex., 1946. Illustrated. Folio, cloth. Carl Hertzog printing. One of 365 signed. In dustwrapper. $1,000.

LEA, Tom. *Hands of Cantu.* Boston, 1964. $75. Specially signed on tipped-in sheet. $150. Also, one of 100 signed, full morocco in slipcase. $3,000.

LEA, Tom. *The King Ranch.* Boston, (1957). Illustrated by the author. 2 vols. Buckram. Issued without dustwrapper. In slipcase. $300. Kingville: King Ranch, 1957. 2 vols. Limited "Private Edition" printed on paper watermarked with running "W" brand. Decorated linen. One of 3,000 copies. In slipcase. $3,000.

LEA, Tom. *Peleliu Landing.* El Paso, 1945. Illustrated. Green cloth. Carl Hertzog printing. One of 500 signed. In glassine dustwrapper. $1,500.

LEA, Tom. *Randado.* (El Paso, 1941.) Carl Hertzog printing. Stiff wraps. One of 100 signed. $3,500. Cloth (bound later). $2,250.

LEACH, A. J. *Early Day Stories: The Overland Trail, etc.* (Norfolk, Neb., 1916.) 7 plates. $125.

LEACOCK, Stephen. *Canada: The Foundations of Its Future.* Montreal, 1941. 31 full-page illustrations. Issued without dustwrapper in slipcase. $75. Also issued in morocco. $350.

LEACOCK, Stephen. *Elements of Political Science.* Boston, 1906. Author's first book. $200.

LEACOCK, Stephen. *Literary Lapses: A Book of Sketches.* Montreal, 1910. Author's first book of humor. $200.

LEACOCK, Stephen. *Nonsense Novels.* London, 1911. $300. New York, 1911. $200. Montreal, 1911. Green cloth. First Canadian edition. $250. London, 1921. Illustrated by John Kettlewell, including 8 color plates. First illustrated edition. In dustwrapper. $350.

LEADBEATER, Mary. *Cottage Dialogues Among the Irish Peasantry.* London, 1811, and Dublin, 1813. Edited by Maria Edgeworth. Illustrated. 2 vols. $1,000.

LEADVILLE Chronicle Annual. Leadville, Colo., 1881. 40 pages, wraps. $350.

LEADVILLE, Colorado: The Most Wonderful Mining Camp in the World. Colorado Springs, 1879. 44 pages, printed wraps. (By John L. Loomis.) $450.

LEAF, Munro. *The Story of Ferdinand.* New York, 1936. Illustrated by Robert Lawson. Pink decorated boards, cloth spine. In dustwrapper. $2,000. London (1937). First stated. $750.

LEAF, Munro. *Wee Gillis.* New York, 1938. Illustrated by Robert Lawson. Burlap, paper labels. One of 525 signed. In slipcase. $750. Trade edition. Boards. In dustwrapper. $350.

LEAR, Edward. See *Derry, Derry Down.*

LEAR, Edward. *A Book of Nonsense.* London, 1855. Illustrated. Oblong, stiff wraps with 72 plates. Second (and enlarged) edition. $15,000. (For first edition see Derry Down Derry.)

LEAR, Edward. *Illustrated Excursions in Italy.* London, 1846. 2 vols. Map, 30 plates. Folio. Cloth. $7,500. Rebound. $4,000.

LEAR, Edward. *Illustrations of the Family Psittacidae, or Parrots.* London, 1830–32. 42 hand-colored plates. In original wraps. $150,000 or more. Rebound. $75,000. London, 1978. One of 530. $1,000.

LEAR, Edward. *Journal of a Landscape Painter in Corsica . . .* London, 1870. Frontispiece and 39 plates. $1,500.

LEAR, Edward. *Journals of a Landscape Painter in Albania.* London, 1851. Map and 20 plates. $3,000.

LEAR, Edward. *Journals of a Landscape Painter in Southern Calabria.* London, 1852. 2 maps and 20 plates. $2,000.

LEAR, Edward. *Laughable Lyrics.* London, 1877. $2,500.

LEAR, Edward. *Nonsense Songs, Stories, Botany, and Alphabets.* London, 1871. $1,250. Boston, 1871. $1,000.

LEAR, Edward. *Views in Rome and Its Environs.* London, 1841. Engraved title and 25 plates. Folio, half morocco. Author's first book. $6,500.

LEAR, Edward. *Views in the Seven Ionian Islands.* London, 1863. Illustrated. Folio. $8,500.

LEATHER Stocking and Silk. New York, 1854. (By John Esten Cooke.) Author's first book. $450.

LEAVES of Grass. Brooklyn, 1855. (By Walt Whitman.) [See also listing under author's name.] Portrait frontispiece on plain paper. Dark olive-green cloth, gilt and blindstamped, marbled endpapers. There are 2 issues of the first state. First issue, first state: copyright page is blank. Portrait of Whitman printed directly on the paper. Binding A (200 copies bound in June and 137 in July 1855): the triple-rule frame is gilt-stamped on front and back. Marbled endpapers, coated on one side. With and without flyleaves. All edges gilt. $75,000. First issue, second state: copyright information on copyright page. Portrait tipped onto leaf with frame. Binding B (169 copies bound in December 1855 and 169 January 1856): triple-rule frame on front and rear cover blindstamped; flyleaves; and white or pale-yellow endpapers. $60,000. Binding C: Light yellowish-green or pink wraps. (150 copies bound at same time as binding B). $50,000. [Above bibliographic information was from the new definitive bibliography by Joel Myerson. In regards ads, Myerson states that ads and reviews inserted in the front of some copies of binding B and C and could not locate any copies with ads at rear, while Wells and Goldsmith only mention that ads were inserted in front or back in the second issue.] London (1855). Label pasted above Brooklyn imprint reading "London: Wm. Horsell, 492, Oxford-street." Second state U.S. sheets in binding A, no flyleaves. $40,000. Brooklyn, 1856. Second edition, with 20 additional poems. $20,000. Boston, "Year '85 of the States (1860–61)." Third edition, first issue, with "George C. Rand & Avery" on copyright page, portrait on tinted paper, orange-colored (or brick-red) cloth. $850. Later issues without "Rand & Avery" same date. Portrait has three states (priority unknown). $500. New York, 1867. First issue has 338+72+24+36 pages. $2,500. Presumed second issue has 338+36 pages. $1,750. Presumed third issue has 338 pages. $1,000. Washington, 1871. Wraps. Title poem only. $1,500. Camden, 1876. Issued in 2 bindings. A: half light-brown leather and cloth. B: half cream leather and marbled boards. "Author's edition," signed on title page. $3,000. Unsigned. $500. Washington, D.C., 1872. Noted in various cloths. $400. Boston, 1881–82. First state has "1881–2" on title page. $1,000. Second state has "1881–82" on cancel-title page. Orange-yellow or medium olive-brown cloth. $450. London, 1881. "Trübner" (cancel) or "Osgood" or "Bogue" (cancel) imprint on title page. $450. Camden, 1882. Dark-green cloth. "Author's Edition," signed. $7,500. Philadelphia, 1882. Yellow cloth. "First Philadelphia edition," published by Rees, Welsh and Company. $450. Philadelphia, 1889. Limp black morocco. One of 300 signed. 70th Birthday Edition. $7,500. Philadelphia, 1891–92. "Death-bed edition." First issue, brown wraps with yellow paper label on backstrip. $2,500. Later issue: Dark-green cloth or gray wraps. $850. New York, 1930. Grabhorn printing. 37 woodcuts. Leather-backed mahogany boards. One of 400. $2,500. Limited Editions Club, New York, 1929. In slipcase. $350. New York, 1942. Edward Weston photographs. 2 vols. Boards. In slipcase. $1,500.

LEAVES of Grass Imprints: American and European Criticisms of "Leaves of Grass." Boston, 1860. 64 pages, printed brown wraps. $2,500.

LE BLANC, Maurice. *Memoirs of Arsene Lupin.* New York (1925). $350.

LE CARRÉ, John. *Call for the Dead.* London, 1961. Author's first book. $12,500. New York (1962). In white dustwrapper. $2,500.

LE CARRÉ, John. *A Murder of Quality.* London (1962). $6,000. New York, 1963. $2,500.

LE CARRÉ, John. *A Small Town in Germany.* London (1968). $150. New York (1968). 500 signed copies. In tissue dustwrapper. $400. Trade. $100.

LE CARRÉ, John. *The Spy Who Came in from the Cold.* London, 1963. $1,500. New York (1964). In dustwrapper priced $4.50 and no "W" on copyright page. $300.

LECHFORD, Thomas. *Plain Dealing: or, Newes from New England.* London, 1642. $10,000.

LE CONTE, Joseph. *A Journal of Ramblings Through the High Sierras of California.* San Francisco, 1875. 9 mounted photos. Blue cloth. $10,000. San Francisco, 1930. One of 500. $175.

LEDERER, William J., and BURDICK, Eugene. *The Ugly American.* First issue dustwrapper has blurb by John T. [sic] Marquand." $200.

LE DUC, W. G. *Minnesota Year Book and Traveller's Guide for 1851.* St. Paul (1851). Folding map. Boards, leather spine. First year of issue. $1,500.

LEDYARD, John. *A Journal of Captain Cook's Last Voyage to the Pacific Ocean* . . . Hartford, 1783. Without the rare map (which Howes states is "usually missing"). $10,000.

LEE, Andrew. *The Indifferent Children.* New York (1947). (By Louis Auchincloss.) Author's first book. $400.

LEE, Daniel and FROST, Joseph H. *Ten Years in Oregon.* New York, 1844. Folding frontispiece map. $500.

LEE, Dennis. *The Kingdom of Absence.* Toronto (1967). Author's first book. One of 300 copies. Wraps. $125.

LEE, George W. *Beale Street: Where the Blues Began.* New York, 1934. Author's first book. Author's first book. $500.

LEE, Harper. *Romance and High Adventure.* Birmingham, 1993. Wraps. One of 100. $1,000.

LEE, Harper. *To Kill a Mockingbird.* Philadelphia (1960). Author's first book. With author's dustwrapper photo by Truman Capote. First edition stated. $33,000 at auction in 2001. London (1960). $1,000. (New York) 1995. States "35th Anniversary edition published 1995" and has string of numbers on copyright page beginning with "95" and ending in "1." $150.

LEE, Maj. Henry, Jr. *The Campaign of 1781 in the Carolinas.* Philadelphia, 1824. $750.

LEE, James P. *Golf in America.* New York, 1895. First golf book published in U.S. $2,500.

LEE, John D. *The Journals of John D. Lee, 1846–47 and 1859.* Salt Lake City, 1938. Edited by Charles Kelly. One of 250. In dustwrapper. $600.

LEE, L. P. (editor). *History of the Spirit Lake Massacre!* (Cover title.) New Britain, Conn., Illustrated. 48 pages, pictorial wraps. 1857. $750.

LEE, Manfred Bennington. See Queen, Ellery.

LEE, Nelson. *Three Years Among the Comanches.* Albany, N.Y., 1859. 2 plates (including portrait title page). Wraps, or cloth. $3,000.

LEE, Richard H. *Memoir of the Life of Richard Henry Lee* . . . Philadelphia, 1825. 2 vols. $600.

LEE, William. *Junkie* (and) HELBRANT, Maurice. *Narcotic Agent.* New York (1953). Back-to-back in pictorial wraps. Ace Books. (*Junkie* is by William Burroughs, his first book.) $1,500.

LEECH, John. *Follies of the Year.* (London, 1866.) 21 hand-colored plates. Oblong, leather-backed cloth. First collected edition. $600.

LEECH, John. *Hunting: Incidents of the Noble Science.* London, 1865. 13 color plates. Oblong, half cloth portfolio. $2,000.

LEECH, John. *Portraits of Children of the Nobility.* London, 1841. Frontispiece and 7 plates. $750.

LEEPER, David Rohrer. *The Argonauts of 'Forty-nine.* South Bend, 1894. Illustrated. Cloth. $300.

LEESE, Jacob P. *Historical Outline of Lower California.* New York, 1865. 46 pages, printed wraps. $350.

LEE Trial (The)! An Exposé of the Mountain Meadows Massacre. Salt Lake City, 1875. 64 pages, printed wraps. $1,500.

LE FANU, Joseph Sheridan. See *The Fortunes of Colonel Torlogh O'Brien.*

LE FANU, Joseph Sheridan. *All in the Dark.* London, 1866. 2 vols. In claret cloth. $2,500. In white (presentation) cloth. $3,500.

LE FANU, Joseph Sheridan. *Checkmate.* London, 1871. 3 vols. $6,000. Philadelphia, 1871. $1,000.

LE FANU, Joseph Sheridan. *Chronicles of Golden Friars.* London, 1871. 3 vols., in violet cloth. $6,000.

LE FANU, Joseph Sheridan. *The Cock and the Anchor.* Dublin, 1845. Author's first book. 3 vols. In dark-green linen. $2,500.

LE FANU, Joseph Sheridan. *The Evil Guest.* London (1895). Illustrated. Dark-green cloth with March ads. $3,000.

LE FANU, Joseph Sheridan. *Ghost Stories and Tales of Mystery.* Dublin, 1851. Illustrated by "Phiz." Red pictorial cloth. $7,500. Violet cloth blocked in gold on front and spine. $3,500. Red cloth blocked on spine only. $2,500.

LE FANU, Joseph Sheridan. *Green Tea and Other Ghost Stories.* Sauk City, Wis., 1945. $350.

LE FANU, Joseph Sheridan. *The House by the Churchyard.* London, 1863. 3 vols., royal-blue cloth. $8,500. 3 vols., grass-green cloth. $6,000. New York, 1866. $2,500.

LE FANU, Joseph Sheridan. *In a Glass Darkly.* London, 1872. 3 vols. $7,500. London, 1929. Illustrated by Edward Ardizzone, his first book of illustrations. $400.

LE FANU, Joseph Sheridan. *Madame Crowl's Ghost and Other Tales of Mystery.* London, 1923. $750.

LE FANU, Joseph Sheridan. *The Rose and the Key.* London, 1871. 3 vols., brown cloth. $6,000.

LE FANU, Joseph Sheridan. *The Wyvern Mystery.* London, 1869. 3 vols., dark maroon cloth. $6,000.

LE GALLIENNE, Richard. *My Ladies' Sonnets.* (Liverpool), 1887. Author's first regularly published book. Boards. One of 50 signed. $500. Trade. $250.

LE GALLIENNE, Richard. *Robert Louis Stevenson: An Elegy and Other Poems, Mostly Personal.* London, 1895. One of 500. $250. One of 75 on large paper. $400. Boston, 1895. One of 500. $200.

LE GALLIENNE, Richard. *The Romance of Perfume.* New York and Paris, 1928. Illustrated by Georges Barbier. Boards. Issued without dustwrapper. With illustrated booklet in pocket at back. $400.

LE GALLIENNE, Richard. *Volumes in Folio.* London, 1889. 50 large-paper copies. $350. 250 regular copies. $250. (Also first book published by Elkin Mathews.)

LEGENDS of the Conquest of Spain. Philadelphia, 1835. By the Author of "The Sketch-Book" (Washington Irving). $750.

LEGION Book (The). London, 1929. Edited by H. Cotton Minchin. Stephen Gooden copperplate of "Mounted Soldier" (self-portrait) on title page, numerous other illustrations, including 9 color plates. Full white pigskin, gilt and blindstamped. One of 100 signed by authors and artists, by Edward, Prince of Wales, and by 5 prime ministers. (Gift book published for the Prince of Wales.) $5,000.

LEGMAN, Gershon. *Love & Death.* (New York, 1949.) Cloth. $250. Wraps. $75.

LEGMAN, Gershon. *Oragenitalism.* New York, 1940. $600.

LE GRAND, Mr. *A Voyage to Abyssinia by Father Jerome Lobo.* London, 1735. (Translated by Samuel Johnson, his first book.) $1,750.

LEGROS, Lucient Alphonse and GRANT, John Cameron. *Typographical Printing-Surfaces* . . . London, 1916. $450.

LE GUIN, Ursula. *The Dispossessed.* New York (1974). $350.

LE GUIN, Ursula. *The Farthest Shore.* New York, 1972. $200.

LE GUIN, Ursula. *From Elfland to Poughkeepsie.* Portland, 1973. Wraps. One of 100 signed. $125. One of 26 hardbound copies signed, issued without dustwrapper. $400. Also, one of 100 signed copies in wraps. $100. Trade edition in wraps. One of 650 copies. $40.

LE GUIN, Ursula. *The Lathe of Heaven.* New York (1971). $300.

LE GUIN, Ursula. *The Left Hand of Darkness.* Ace. New York (1969). Wraps. First edition not stated and no mention of Hugo and Nebula awards. $75. Walker, New York (1969). "Published in . . . 1969 . . ." First hardcover. $350. London, 1969. $200.

LE GUIN, Ursula. *A Wizard of Earthsea.* Berkeley (1968). No statement of edition. With vertical line or smudge "Published in . . . 1969 . . ." on title page in either library or trade bindings which are embossed on covers. Dustwrapper priced $3.95. $1,250. (Later printings have no smudge, covers printed without embossment [stamping] and dustwrapper unpriced.)

LEHMANN, John. *A Garden Revisited and Other Poems.* Hogarth Press. London, 1931. $200.

LEHMUSTO, Heikki. *Painin Historia.* (History of wrestling.) Helsinki, 1939. $350.

LEIBER, Fritz, Jr. *Night's Black Agents.* Sauk City, Wisc. 1947. Arkham House. Author's first book. $300. London, 1975. $100.

LEIDERMAN, E. E. *The Science of Wrestling and the Art of Jiu Jitsu.* New York, 1923. Issued without dustwrapper. $125.

LEIGH, William R. *The Western Pony.* New York (1933). 6 color plates. Cloth. (100 copies.) In dustwrapper. $750. With an extra signed plate laid in. $1,250.

LEIGHLY, John. *California as an Island.* San Francisco, 1972. Folio, quarter morocco gilt. One of 450 copies. $1,250.

LEIGHTON, John. *Suggestions in Design* . . . London, no date (circa 1880). 101 plates. $500.

LEINSTER, Murray. *Sidewise in Time.* Chicago, 1950. (By Will F. Jenkins.) $200.

LELAND, Charles Godfrey. *Meister Karl's Sketch-Book.* Philadelphia, 1855. Author's first book. $300.

LELAND, Charles Godfrey. *The Union Pacific Railway.* Philadelphia, 1867. 95 pages, printed wraps. $750.

LEMAY, Alan. *Gunsight Trail.* New York, 1931. $450.

LEMAY, Alan. *Painted Ponies.* New York (1927). Author's first book. $500.

LEMAY, Alan. *The Searchers.* New York, 1954. One of 835 signed. $600. Trade. $350.

LEMAY, Alan. *The Unforgiven.* New York, 1957. $200.

LEMOINE, Henry. *Typographical Antiquities.* London, 1797. $600.

LENGEL, Frances. *The Carnal Days of Helen Seferis.* Paris, 1954. (By Alexander Trocchi, his first book.) Wraps. $250.

LENZ, Hans. *Mexican Indian Paper.* Mexico City (1961). 11 original tipped-in paper samples, 313 color and black-and-white illustrations and 4 maps. In dustwrapper and slipcase. $750.

LEONARD, Elmore. *The Bounty Hunters.* Author's first book. Houghton-Mifflin. Boston, 1954. $3,500. Ballantine, New York, 1954. Wraps. $250. London, 1956. $1,500.

LEONARD, Elmore. *Escape from Five Shadows.* Boston, 1956. $2,500. London, 1957. $1,000.

LEONARD, Elmore. *Glitz.* New York (1965). One of 26 signed and lettered copies. Issued without dustwrapper in slipcase. $450. One of 500 signed copies. Issued without dustwrapper in slipcase. $75. Trade. $35.

LEONARD, Elmore. *The Law at Randado.* Boston, 1955. $3,000. London, 1957. $1,250.

LEONARD, Elmore. *Moonshine War.* Garden City, 1969. $850. London, 1970. $300.

LEONARD, Elmore. *Unknown Man: No. 89.* New York, 1977. $600. London (1977). $150.

LEONARD, H.L.W. *Oregon Territory.* Cleveland, 1846. 88 pages, printed blue or buff wraps. $5,000.

LEONARD, Hugh E. *Handbook of Wrestling.* New York, 1897. One of 300. $300.

LEONARD, William Ellery. *Byron and Byronism in America.* Boston, 1905. Author's first book. Wraps. $100.

LEONARD, William Ellery. *A Son of Earth: Collected Poems.* New York, 1928. Portrait frontispiece. Cream boards, paper label. One of 35 lettered copies, signed. $150.

LEONARD, William Ellery. *Two Lives.* New York, 1925. Cloth. First published edition. One of 150 signed. $125.

LEONARD, William Ellery (translator). *The Tale of Beowulf.* New York, 1932. Illustrated by Rockwell Kent. Folio. One of 950. Issued without dustwrapper. $400.

LEONARD, Zenas. *Narrative of the Adventures of Zenas Leonard.* Clearfield, Pa., 1839. 87 pages. $50,000. Cleveland, 1904. Illustrated. One of 520. $750.

LEOPOLD, Aldo. *Game Survey of the North Central States.* Madison, 1931. Author's first book. Issued without dustwrapper. $750.

LEOPOLD, Aldo. *A Sand County Almanac.* New York, 1949. $750.

LERMONTOFF, Michael. *A Hero of Our Days.* London, 1854. Translated by Theresa Pulasky. $450.

LERNER, Alan Jay. *Brigadoon.* New York (1947). $750.

LERNER, Alan Jay. *Paint Your Wagon.* New York (1952). $300.

LERNER, Alan Jay, and LOEWE, Frederick. *Camelot.* New York (1961). $200.

LEROUX, Gaston. *The Mystery of the Yellow Room.* London, 1908 $250. New York, 1908. $150.

LEROUX, Gaston. *The Perfume of the Lady in Black.* New York, 1908. $200.

LEROUX, Gaston. *The Phantom of the Opera.* Indianapolis, 1911. Illustrated in color. $1,000. New York (1925). Photoplay edition. $600.

LEROUX DE LINCY, A. J. V. *Researches Concerning Jean Grolier, His Life and His Library.* Grolier Club. New York, 1907. Color plates. Full leather. One of 300. $850.

LESLIE, Eliza. See *Seventy-five Receipts, for Pastrie, Cakes, and Sweetmeats.*

LESLIE, Eliza. *Miss Leslie's New Cookery Book.* Philadelphia (1857). $1,250.

LESLIE, Miss. *The House Book; or, A Manual of Domestic Economy.* Philadelphia, 1840. $350.

LESLIE, Shane. *The Cantab.* London, 1925. (Suppressed.) Cloth. $250.

LESLIE, Shane. *Songs of Oriel.* Dublin, 1908. Author's first book. $125.

LESSING, Doris. *African Stories.* London (1964). $150.

LESSING, Doris. *The Golden Notebook.* London (1962). $750. New York, 1962. $250.

LESSING, Doris. *The Grass is Singing.* London (1950). Author's first book. $600. New York, 1950. $200.

LESSING, Doris. *The Habit of Loving.* London, 1957. Cloth. $250.

LESSING, Doris. *Martha Quest.* London (1952). $350.

LESSING, Julius. *Ancient Oriental Carpet Patterns* . . . London, 1879. 30 plates. $1,750.

LESTER, C. Edwards. *Sam Houston and His Republic.* New York, 1846. Portrait (not in all copies) and 10 plates. $600.

LESTER, John C., and WILSON, D. L. *Ku Klux Klan: Its Origin, Growth and Disbandment.* Nashville, 1884. 117 pages, wraps. $1,250.

LESTER, Julius. *To Be a Slave.* New York (1989). $150.

LETTER of Amerigo Vespucci (The), Describing His Four Voyages to the New World. Grabhorn Press. San Francisco, 1926. Hand-colored map and illustrations by Valenti Angelo. Vellum. One of 250. In slipcase. $350. Few bound in orange morocco. $1,250.

LETTERS from An American Farmer. (By Michael Crevecoeur.) London, 1782. Author's first book. Two folding maps. $4,000. Dublin, 1782. Wraps. Two folding maps. $2,500. Philadelphia, 1793. $750.

LETTERS of Runnymede (The). London, 1836. (By Benjamin Disraeli.) In original cloth. $450.

LETTS, J. M. See *California Illustrated; A Pictorial View of California.*

LEVER, Charles. See Lorrequer, Harry. See also *The Confessions of Harry Lorrequer.*

LEVER, Charles. *Davenport Dunn.* London, 1857–59. Illustrated by H. K. Browne ("Phiz"). 22 parts in 21. $750.

LEVER, Charles. *The Knight of Gwynne: A Tale of the Time of the Union.* London, 1846–47. Frontispiece, title page, and 38 plates by "Phiz." 20 parts in 19, wraps. $1,000.

LEVER, Charles. *Luttrell of Aran.* London, 1863–65. Illustrated. 16 parts in 15, pictorial wraps. $750.

LEVER, Charles. *The O'Donoghue: A Tale of Ireland.* Dublin, 1845. 13 parts in 11, wraps. Dublin, 1845. $1,000. First binding in red cloth. $400.

LEVER, Charles. *Roland Cashel.* London, 1848–49. 20 parts in 19, wraps. $750. London, 1850. First book edition. $200.

LEVERTOFF (LEVERTOV), Denise. *The Double Image.* Cresset Press. London, 1946. Author's first book. $300.

LEVERTOV, Denise. *The Cold Spring and Other Poems.* New Directions. (New York), 1968. One of 100 signed. Chocolate-brown fibered paper over boards, tan label on spine printed in red up spine. $750. Variant in tan paper over boards, printed in black and red across front cover. $600.

LEVERTOV, Denise. *In the Night: A Story.* Albondocani Press. New York, 1968. Wraps. One of 150 signed. $150.

LEVERTOV, Denise. *Three Poems.* Perishable Press. Mt. Horeb, Wis., 1968. Stiff wraps. One of 250. In dustwrapper. $125.

LEVI, Peter. *Earthly Paradise.* (Privately printed, 1958.) Author's first book. $200.

LEVI, Primo. *If This Is a Man.* New York, 1959. (First English translation.) $250.

LEVIN, Ira. *A Kiss Before Dying.* New York, 1953. Author's first book. Issued without endpapers. $450.

LEVIN, Ira. *Rosemary's Baby.* New York, 1967. $250.

LEVIN, Ira. *The Stepford Wives.* New York (1972). $125.

LEVINE, Norman. *Myssium.* Toronto, 1948. Author's first book. $300.

LEVINE, Philip. *The Names of the Lost: Poems.* (Iowa City) 1976. One of 200 signed. Issued without dustwrapper. $400.

LEVINE, Philip. *On the Edge.* Stone Wall Press. Iowa City (1963). Author's first book. One of 220 signed copies. Issued without dustwrapper. $1,000.

LEVY, Esther. *Jewish Cookery Book* . . . Philadelphia, 1871. With errata slip preceding title. $2,500.

LEVY, Julien. *Surrealism.* Black Sun Press. New York, 1936. 64 illustrations. Pictorial boards. In dustwrapper. $750.

LEWIS, Alfred Henry. *Black Lion Inn.* New York, 1903. $200.

LEWIS, Alfred Henry. *Confessions of a Detective.* New York, 1906. $250.

LEWIS, Alfred Henry. *Wolfville.* New York (1897). First issue, with "Moore" in perfect type on page 19, line 18. Author's first book. $250.

LEWIS, Alfred Henry. *Wolfville Days.* New York (1902). Red cloth. $150.

LEWIS, Alfred Henry. *Wolfville Folks.* New York, 1908. $300.

LEWIS, C. S. See Clerk, N. W., and Hamilton, Clive.

LEWIS, C. S. *Christian Behaviour.* London, 1943. Orange cloth. $300.

LEWIS, C. S. *That Hideous Strength.* London, 1945. Black cloth. $600.

LEWIS, C. S. *The Horse and His Boy.* London (1954). $9,500 at auction in 2001. New York, 1954. $1,500.

LEWIS, C. S. *The Last Battle.* London, 1956. $2,000. New York, 1956. $600.

LEWIS, C. S. *The Lion, the Witch and the Wardrobe.* London, 1950. $20,000 at auction in 2001. New York, 1950. $3,500.

LEWIS, C. S. *The Magician's Nephew.* London, 1955. $2,000. New York, 1955. $750.

LEWIS, C. S. *Prince Caspian. The Return to Narnia.* London (1951). $3,500. New York, 1951. $1,250.

LEWIS, C. S. *The Screwtape Letters.* London, 1942. $1,500. New York, 1943. $750.

LEWIS, C. S. *The Voyage of the Dawn Treader.* London, 1952. $3,000. New York, 1952. $1,250.

LEWIS, Cecil Day. See Day-Lewis, Cecil.

LEWIS, C. T. *George Baxter (Colour Printer)* . . . London, 1908. $150.

LEWIS, C. T. Courtney. *George Baxter, the Picture Printer of the Nineteenth Century.* London, 1911. 21 illustrations in full color. $300.

LEWIS, C. T. Courtney. *The Story of Picture Printing in England During the Nineteenth Century.* London (1928). 61 plates. $350.

LEWIS, Elisha J. *The American Sportsman.* Philadelphia, 1855. Illustrated. $400.

LEWIS, Elisha J. *Hints to Sportsmen.* Philadelphia, 1851. Cloth. $350.

LEWIS, J. O. *The Aboriginal Port Folio.* Philadelphia, 1836 (actually 1835). 72 colored portraits. (Sometimes more, but frequently fewer, which would affect the price.) 3 advertisement leaves (constituting, with title leaf, all the text). 10 parts, wraps. $35,000. Bound set: Philadelphia, 1835–36. 72 plates. Folio. Cloth. $25,000.

LEWIS, Janet. *The Friendly Adventures of Ollie Ostrich.* Garden City, 1923. $750.

LEWIS, Janet. *The Indian in the Woods.* (Bonn, Germany, 1922.) Author's first book. Wraps. $350.

LEWIS, Janet. *The Wife of Martin Guerre.* San Francisco, 1941. One of 300 hand-colored by Angelo and signed by both $300.

LEWIS, John Frederick. *Illustrations of Constantinople* . . . London (1838). Folio. Litho title, dedication, and 25 plates. $15,000.

LEWIS, John Frederick. *Sketches of Spain and Spanish Character.* London (1836). Lithograph title page and 25 tinted plates. Folio, in original half morocco. $5,000.

LEWIS, Matthew Gregory. See *Tales of Terror.*

LEWIS, Matthew Gregory. *Journal of a West India Proprietor in the Island of Jamaica.* London, 1834. $750.

LEWIS, Matthew Gregory. *The Life and Correspondence of Matthew Gregory Lewis.* London, 1839. Illustrated. 2 vols. $750.

LEWIS, Matthew Gregory. *The Monk.* London, 1796. Author's first book. $3,500. Dublin, 1796. $2,750. London, 1798. 3 vols. Revised. $750.

LEWIS, Matthew Gregory. *Poems.* London, 1812. $1,000.

LEWIS, Matthew Gregory. *Romantic Tales.* London, 1808. 4 vols. $2,000.

LEWIS, Matthew Gregory. *Tales of Wonder.* London, 1801. 2 vols. $1,000. 2 vols. on large paper. $1,250. Dublin, 1801. 2 vols. $600.

LEWIS, Meriwether, and CLARK, William. *History of the Expedition Under the Command of Captains Lewis and Clark* . . . Philadelphia, 1814. Prepared for the press by Paul Allen (actually by Nicholas Biddle). 2 vols. Folding map and 5 charts. $100,000. New York, 1842. 2 vols. Folding map. Calf. Abridged edition. $3,500. New York, 1893. 4 vols. Edited by E. Coues. Map. Boards and cloth. $2,000. New York, 1902. 3 vols. One of 210 facsimile copies. $1,250. Chicago, 1903. 3 vols. Edited by James K. Hosmer. One of 210 copies. $1,500. Trade edition. 2 vols. $400.

LEWIS, Meriwether, and CLARK, William. *The Journal of Lewis and Clark.* Dayton, 1840. Illustrated with 14 woodcuts, including portraits of Lewis and Clark. $1,000.

LEWIS, Meriwether, and CLARK, William. *Journals of the Lewis and Clark Expedition.* Limited Editions Club, Hartford, 1962. 2 vols. In slipcase. $450.

LEWIS, Meriwether, and CLARK, William. *Original Journals of the Lewis and Clark Expedition, 1804–1806.* New York, 1904–5. Edited by Reuben Gold Thwaites. 8 vols. Cloth, including atlas of maps and plates. One of 790. $5,000. 7 vols. in 14, plus atlas, boards. One of 50 sets on Japan vellum. $22,500. One of 200 sets on Van Gelder paper. $12,500. New York, 1959–60. 8 vols. Facsimile of 1904–5 edition. Cloth. $1,000.

LEWIS, Meriwether, and CLARK, William. *Travels of Capts. Lewis and Clark, from St. Louis, By Way of the Missouri and Columbia Rivers . . .* 1804, 1805 and 1806 . . . London, 1809. Folding map. $3,000.

LEWIS, Meriwether, and CLARK, William. *Travels to the Source of the Missouri River and Across the American Continent to the Pacific Ocean.* London, 1814. Edited by Thomas Rees. Folding map and 5 maps on 3 plates. First English edition of *History of the Expedition* . . . $12,500. London, 1815. 3 vols. Folding map and 6 full-page maps. $7,500. London, 1817. 3 vols. $5,000.

LEWIS, Oscar. *Hearn and His Biographers.* Westgate Press (Grabhorn printing). San Francisco, 1930. Facsimiles. Boards and cloth in portfolio. One of 350 copies. $300.

LEWIS, Oscar. *The Origin of the Celebrated Jumping Frog of Calaveras County.* Grabhorn Press. San Francisco, 1931. Decorated by Valenti Angelo. Boards. One of 250. $250.

LEWIS, Sinclair. See Graham, Tom.

LEWIS, Sinclair. *Arrowsmith.* New York (1925). Blue boards and buckram. One of 500 signed. In glassine dustwrapper and slipcase. $3,000. First trade edition, with "second printing" on copyright page. $3,500.

LEWIS, Sinclair. *Babbitt.* New York (1922). Blue cloth. First state, with "Purdy" for "Lyte" in line 4, page 49. $3,500. Second state. $2,500.

LEWIS, Sinclair. *Cheap and Contented Labor.* (New York) 1929. Illustrated. 32 pages, pictorial blue wraps. First state, without quotation marks in front of "Dodsworth" on title page. $750. Later, error corrected. $250.

LEWIS, Sinclair. *Dodsworth.* New York (1929). With "Published, March, 1929" on copyright page. Special edition. Issued without dustwrapper. $1,000. First trade edition. "Published, March, 1929." In dustwrapper without reviews at bottom of front flap. $2,000. London, 1929. $500.

LEWIS, Sinclair. *Elmer Gantry.* New York (1927). Blue cloth. First binding with "G" on spine resembling "C" (reading "Elmer Cantry"). $2,000. Later binding, corrected. $1,250.

LEWIS, Sinclair. *Free Air.* New York, 1919. Decorated blue cloth. In dustwrapper. $3,000. Without dustwrapper. $300.

LEWIS, Sinclair. *The Innocents.* New York (1917). With "Published October, 1917/F-R" on copyright page. In dustwrapper. $2,500. Without dustwrapper. $200.

LEWIS, Sinclair. *The Job.* New York (1917). Green cloth. With "Published February, 1917/B-R" on copyright page. In dustwrapper. $2,500. Without dustwrapper. $350. (Remaindered copies have tipped-in leaf advertising *Main Street* and others.)

LEWIS, Sinclair. *Keep Out of the Kitchen.* (New York, 1929.) Printed boards. First edition not stated. (Advertising promotion piece for the story in *Cosmopolitan* magazine.) $750.

LEWIS, Sinclair. *Kingsblood Royal.* New York (1947). One of 1,050 signed. $450. Trade. $100.

LEWIS, Sinclair. *Main Street.* New York, 1920. Dark-blue cloth. First issue, with perfect folio on page 54. In dustwrapper without review of this book on front flap. $25,000. With review. $15,000. Without dustwrapper. $600. Limited Editions Club, New York, 1937. Grant Wood illustrations. In slipcase. $750.

LEWIS, Sinclair. *Our Mr. Wrenn.* New York, 1914. With "M-N" on copyright page. Author's second book and the first under his own name. (For first book, see entry under Graham, Tom.) $350.

LEWIS, W. S., and PHILLIPS, P. C. (editors). *The Journal of John Work.* Cleveland, 1923. Map. Illustrations. Issued without dustwrapper. $300.

LEWIS, Wyndham. *The Apes of God.* London (1931). Illustrated by the author. Light-tan cloth. One of 750 signed. In dustwrapper. $600. Trade. $250. New York, 1932. $250.

LEWIS, Wyndham. *The Art of Being Ruled.* London, 1926. $600.

LEWIS, Wyndham. *Blasting and Bombardiering: Autobiography 1914–1926.* London, 1937. $300.

LEWIS, Wyndham. *The Caliph's Design.* London, 1919. The Egoist, Ltd. Boards. No statement of edition. Issued without dustwrapper. $500.

LEWIS, Wyndham. *The Childermass: Section I.* (All published.) London, 1928. Yellow buckram. One of 225 signed. In dustwrapper. $750. Trade edition. $350. New York, 1928. $250.

LEWIS, Wyndham. *Count Your Dead: They Are Alive!* London (1937). Yellow cloth. First edition stated. $750.

LEWIS, Wyndham. *The Diabolical Principle and the Dithyrambic Spectator.* London, 1931. First binding in gold-stamped cloth. $300.

LEWIS, Wyndham. *Doom of Youth.* London, 1932. First English edition (withdrawn). $1,000. New York, 1932. $600.

LEWIS, Wyndham. *Hitler.* London, 1931. $750.

LEWIS, Wyndham. *The Ideal Giant.* London (1917). Boards and cloth. (About 200.) Author's first written work, a collection of stories. $1,500.

LEWIS, Wyndham. *One-Way Song.* London (1933). On of 40 signed, in full vellum. $2,500. Trade. $300.

LEWIS, Wyndham. *Tarr.* New York, 1918. Red cloth. $500. Blue cloth. $300. London, 1918. $400. New York, 1926. $350.

LEWIS, Wyndham. *Thirty Personalities and a Self-Portrait.* London (1932). 31 plates, loose in buckram-and-board portfolio. One of 200 signed. $1,250.

LEWIS, Wyndham. *Timon/Athens/Timon/Shakespeare/Timon* (upside down). (Cover title.) (London, 1913.) 16 illustrations for Shakespeare's *Timon of Athens,* without a title page. Limited edition, 16 plates laid loose in a folder. Author's first "book." $6,000.

LEWIS, Wyndham. *The Wild Body: A Soldier of Humour and Other Stories.* London, 1927. Decorated boards, cloth spine. One of 79 signed (of 85 total). In dustwrapper. $1,250. Trade edition. Orange or red cloth. In cream-colored dustwrapper. $400.

LHOMOND, M. *Elements of French Grammar.* Portland (Brunswick), Me., 1830. (Translated anonymously by Henry Wadsworth Longfellow, his first book.) $300.

LHOMOND, M. *French Exercises.* Portland (Brunswick), Me., 1830. (Translated anonymously by Henry Wadsworth Longfellow.) $300. This book and Lhomond's *Elements of French Grammar* were bound as one volume later in 1830, and this combined book edition was "the first book to bear Longfellow's name on the title page." $400.

LIBER Amoris: or, The New Pygmalion. London, 1823. (By William Hazlitt.) $750. London, 1894. Illustrated. Buckram. One of 500. $200.

LIBER Scriptorum: The First Book of the Authors Club. New York, 1893. Full morocco. One of 251 signed by contributors. $4,500. *The Second Book . . . Liber Scriptorum.* New York, 1921. Simulated morocco. One of 251 signed. $750.

LICHTENSTEIN, Roy. *Roy Lichtenstein: Drawings and Prints.* (New York, 1970.) One of 100. $1,250.

LIEBLING, A. J. *Back Where I Came From.* New York (1938). Orange-tan cloth. $600.

LIEBLING, A. J. *Chicago: The Second City.* New York, 1952. Illustrated by Steinberg. Pictorial boards. $150.

LIEBLING, A. J. *Mink and Red Herring.* Garden City, 1949. $250.

LIEBLING, A. J. *The Telephone Booth Indian.* Garden City, 1942. $350.

LIEBLING, A. J. *They All Sang . . .* New York, 1934. Author's first book. $400.

LIFE and Adventures of Broncho John: His Second Trip Up the Trail, by Himself. (Valparaiso, Ind., 1908.) (Cover title.) Illustrated. 32 pages, pictorial wraps. (By John H. Sullivan.) $400.

LIFE and Adventures of Calamity Jane. By Herself. Livingston, Mont. (1896). Portrait. 8 pages, wraps. $350.

LIFE and Adventures of Joseph T. Hare, the Bold Robber and Highwayman (The). New York, 1847. 16 engravings. Pictorial wraps. (By H. R. Howard.) $600.

LIFE and Adventures of Robert Voorhis, the Hermit of Massachusetts. Providence, 1829. Portrait. Wraps. First edition, first issue, with "Voorhis" in the title. $200. Later: *Life and Adventures of Robert.* $200.

LIFE and Strange Surprizing Adventures of Robinson Crusoe (The). London, 1719–1720. (By Daniel Defoe.) 3 vols. (check points on these). Vol. II: *The Farther Adventures . . .* [and] Vol III:

Serious Reflections . . . $130,000 at auction in 1999. London, 1831. 2 vols. Adds a Biographical Sketch of Defoe. $1,500.

LIFE and Travels of Josiah Mooso (The). Winfield, Kan., 1888. Portrait. $1,250.

LIFE and Writings of Maj. Jack Downing of Downingville (The): Away Down East in the State of Maine. Boston, 1833. (By Seba Smith.) In original boards. $500.

LIFE in California During a Residence of Several Years . . . By an American (Alfred Robinson). New York, 1846. 9 plates. $1,250. San Francisco, 1925. One of 250. In dustwrapper. $300.

LIFE of Col. Edwards. No place or date [1842]. 8 engravings. 31 pages, folded sheets, uncut and unsewn. First edition (?). $2,000.

LIFE of Friedrich Schiller (The). London, 1825. (By Thomas Carlyle.) Author's first book. $500.

LIFE of Joaquin Murieta the Brigand Chief of California (The). San Francisco, 1859. (By John R. Ridge.) 7 full-page plates, pictorial wraps (dated 1861). Second ("spurious") edition. $2,500. (See also *Yellow Bird.*)

LIFE of MA-KA-TAI-ME-SHE-KIA-KIAK or Black Hawk. Cincinnati, 1833. Tan boards and cloth. (J. B. Patterson, editor.) $1,250. Boston, 1834. In original pale-green boards. $250.

LIFE of Stonewall Jackson (The). By a Virginian. Richmond, 1863. Printed wraps. (By John Esten Cooke.) First edition, with Ayres & Wade imprint. $3,500. (See also Cooke, John Esten.)

LILLIBRIDGE, Will. *Ben Blair.* Chicago, 1905. $100.

LIMÓN, Graciela. *María de Belén: The Autobiography of an Indian Woman.* New York (1990). $125.

LIN, Frank. *What Dreams May Come.* Chicago (1888). Author's first book. (By Gertrude Atherton.) (For first English edition, see author listing.) Wraps. $750. Cloth. $400. London, 1889. $300.

LINCOLN, Abraham. *The Life and Public Services of General Zachary Taylor.* Boston, 1922. Marbled boards. One of 435. In slipcase. $125.

LINCOLN, Abraham, President. ["House Divided" speech.] *Speech of Hon. Abram* [sic] *Lincoln, Before the Republican State Convention, June 16, 1858.* Sycamore [Illinois], 1858. 16 pages, uncut and unbound. $34,500 at auction in 1996.

LINCOLN, Abraham, and DOUGLAS, Stephen A. *Political Debates.* Columbus, Ohio, 1860. Brown rippled, or tan, cloth. First issue, with no ads, no rule on copyright page, and with a "2" at foot of page 17. $3,000. Rebound. $1,500.

LINCOLN, Abraham, and EVERETT, Edward. *The Gettysburg Solemnities: Dedication of the National Cemetery at Gettysburg, Pennsylvania, November 19, 1863* . . . (Cover title.) Washington (1863). 16-page printed pamphlet. First known printing in pamphlet form of the Gettysburg Address. $25,000 or more. See also Everett, Edward.

LINCOLN, Mrs. D. A. *Frozen Dainties.* Nashua, N.H., 1889. 32 pages, wraps. $500.

LINCOLN, Mrs. D. A. *Mrs. Lincoln's Boston Cook Book.* Boston, 1884. Marbled boards, cloth spine and corners. With 6 ads on page 4. $2,500. With 16 ads on page 7. $1,000.

LINCOLN, Joe. *Cape Cod Ballads and Other Verse.* Trenton, N.J., 1902. (By Joseph C. Lincoln.) Drawings by E. W. Kemble. Decorated yellow cloth. Author's first book. $200.

LINDBERGH, Charles A. *The Spirit of St. Louis.* New York, 1953. Limited and signed "Presentation Edition." In clear dustwrapper. $1,250. Trade edition. $300.

LINDBERGH, Charles A. *"We":The Famous Flier's Own Story of His Life and His Trans-Atlantic Flight.* New York, 1927. Illustrated. Half vellum. One of 100 signed copies. $6,000. One of 1,000 signed copies. In publisher's numbered box. $4,000. Trade in red buckram with top edge gilt. In first issue dustwrapper with "They called me 'Lucky' . . ." on front flap. $600. Blue cloth. $300. (Priority assumed. Dummy in red.)

LINDERMAN, Frank Bird. *Beyond the Law.* New York, 1933. $500.

LINDERMAN, Frank Bird. *Lige Mountains: Free Trapper.* New York, 1922. $750.

LINDLEY, John. *Pomologia Britannica; or Figures and Descriptions of the Most Important Varieties of Fruit Cultivated in Great Britain.* London, 1841. 3 vols. 152 colored plates. Half brown morocco. $15,000.

LINDSAY, David. *Devil's Tor.* London (1932). $1,500.

LINDSAY, David. *Journal of the Elder Scientific Exploring Expedition 1891–92.* Adelaide, 1893. Wraps, with a folder of maps. $2,000.

LINDSAY, David. *A Voyage to Arcturus.* London (1920). Author's first book. (Red cloth, 8-page catalogue at rear.) In dustwrapper. $2,500. Later binding in dustwrapper. $2,000.

LINDSAY, Jack. *Fauns and Ladies.* Sydney, 1923. Author's first book. One of 210 signed copies. With first woodcut signed in full, next 2 initialed. $2,000. Trade edition. $750.

LINDSAY, Jack. *Storm at Sea.* London, 1935. Illustrated. Half morocco. One of 250 signed. $350.

LINDSAY, Joan. *Picnic at Hanging Rock.* London, 1967. $125.

LINDSAY, Norman. *The Etchings of Norman Lindsay.* London, 1927. Cloth folio. One of 129. $2,000. Buckram, vellum spine. One of 31 signed copies with a signed etching by Lindsay. $3,500.

LINDSAY, Norman. *A Homage to Sappho.* Fanfrolico Press. London, 1928. Illustrated by Jack Lindsay. Vellum. One of 70 signed. $6,000.

LINDSAY, Norman. *Norman Lindsay's Book Number One.* Sydney, 1912. Wraps. $300. With *Norman Lindsay's Book Number 2.* Sydney, 1915. $600. Author's first books preceded by illustrated book.

LINDSAY, Norman. *Redheap.* London (1930). $350.

LINDSAY, Norman. *Selected Pen Drawings.* Sydney, 1968. $350.

LINDSAY, Vachel. *Collected Poems.* New York, 1923. Half cloth. One of 400 signed. $300. Trade edition. $150. New York, 1925. Illustrated by Lindsay. Pictorial boards. First illustrated edition. One of 350 signed. In slipcase. $250. Trade edition. $75.

LINDSAY, Vachel. *General William Booth Enters into Heaven and Other Poems.* New York, 1913. Red cloth. Author's first book. $150.

LINDSAY, Vachel. *A Handy Guide for Beggars.* New York, 1916. $400.

LINDSAY, Vachel. *A Memorial of Lincoln Called the Heroes of Time.* (Springfield, Ill., 1908/1909.) 12 pages, stitched wraps. $1,250.

LINDSAY, Vachel. *Rhymes to Be Traded for Bread.* (Springfield, 1912.) 12 pages, self-wraps. $600.

LINDSAY, Vachel. *The Tramp's Excuse and Other Poems.* (Cover title.) (Springfield, Ill., 1909.) Decorations by the author. Printed wraps with cord tie. $1,500.

LINDSAY, Vachel. *The Tree of Laughing Bells.* (New York, 1905.) Author's first book. Wraps. $2,500.

LINDSAY, William S. *History of Merchant Shipping and Ancient Commerce.* London, 1874–76. 4 vols. 3 maps, 3 plates, numerous other illustrations. Cloth. $750.

LINDSEY, Charles. *The Prairies of the Western States.* Toronto, 1860. 100 pages, wraps. $500.

LINDSLEY, John Berrien. *The Military Annals of Tennessee.* Nashville, 1886. 2 plates. $750.

LINES on Leaving the Bedford St. Schoolhouse. (Boston, 1880.) (By George Santayana.) 4 pages, plain wraps. Author's first published work. $750.

LINFORTH, James (editor). *Route from Liverpool to Great Salt Valley.* Liverpool, July 1854 to September 1855. Folding map and 30 full-page plates. 120 pages, plus "Notice to Subscribers." 15 paperbound parts (bound). $10,000. Liverpool, 1855. Boards. First book edition with a map partly colored by hand. $7,500.

LINGUAL Exercises for Advanced Vocabularians. By the Author of *Recreations* (Siegfried Sassoon*).* Cambridge, 1925. One of 99 in plain slipcase. $2,000.

LINN, John J. *Reminiscences of Fifty Years in Texas.* New York, 1883. Illustrated. With errata slip. $350.

LINSLEY, Daniel C. *Morgan Horses.* New York, 1857. Illustrated. $600.

LINTON, William James. *The History of Wood-Engraving in America.* Boston, 1882. 1,000 signed copies. 20 full-page plates. $225. One of 500. $300.

LINTON, William James. *The Masters of Wood-Engraving.* London, 1889. 196 plates (165 mounted), colored frontispiece. One of 600 signed. $500. One of 100 large-paper copies. $1,000.

LIPSCOMB, George. *The History and Antiquities of the County of Buckingham.* London, 1831–47. 4 vols. Numerous maps, plates and woodcuts. $1,250. London, 1847. 4 vols. $1,250.

LISLE, Edward. *Observations in Husbandry.* London, 1757. Illustrated with an engraved frontispiece portrait of the author. $1,000. 2 vols. Second edition. $750.

LIST of Catalogues of English Book Sales, 1676–1900 Now in the British Museum. (London), 1915. $350.

LITERARY Antiquary (A), Memoir of William Oldys, Esq. London, 1862. $350.

LITTELL, William. *Festoons of Fancy.* Louisville, Ky., 1814. $6,000.

LITTLE, James A. *From Kirtland to Salt Lake City.* Salt Lake City, 1890. $350.

LITTLE, James A. *Jacob Hamblin, A Narrative of His Personal Experience . . .* Salt Lake City, 1881. $200.

LITTLE, James A. *What I Saw on the Old Santa Fe Trail.* Plainfield, Ind. (1904). Frontispiece. 127 pages, printed wraps. $350.

LITTLEFIELD, George Emery. *The Early Massachusetts Press, 1638–1711.* Boston, 1907. 2 vols. One of 175. $250.

LIVESAY, Dorothy. *Green Pitcher.* Toronto, 1928. (200 copies.) Author's first book. $1,250.

LIVING Issue (A). Washington, 1882. (By Richard Irving Dodge.) 37 pages, wraps. (Suppressed portion of Dodge's *Our Wild Indians.*) $300.

LIVINGSTON, Luther S. *Auction Prices of Books . . .* New York, 1905. Four volumes. Limited to 750 sets. $200.

LIVINGSTON, Luther S. *Franklin and His Press at Passy.* Grolier Club. New York, 1914. Illustrated. Boards and cloth. One of 300. $400.

LIVINGSTONE, David. *Missionary Travels and Researches in South Africa.* London, 1857. 24 engraved plates, 2 hand-colored folding maps (one in pocket), elevation chart of South Central Africa, and folding frontispiece view of Victoria Falls. First issue with plates 1 and 8 wood-engraved. $1,000. Second issue no plates wood-engraved. $600.

LIZARS, John. *A System of Anatomical Plates of the Body, with Descriptions and Observations.* Edinburgh (1822-26). Text volume, plus folio atlas of 101 colored plates (sometimes 103). $3,500.

LLEWELLYN, Richard. *How Green Was My Valley.* London (1939). Yellow buckram, leather label. Author's first book. One of 200 signed copies. In slipcase. $750. Trade edition. In dustwrapper. $200. New York, 1940. $175.

LLEWELLYN, Richard. *None But the Lonely Heart.* London, 1943. One of 250 signed. $125. Trade edition. $60.

LLOYD, Harold. *An American Comedy.* New York, 1928. $600.

LLOYD, John Uri. *Etidorpha or the End of the Earth.* Cincinnati, 1895. Limited author's edition. $600.

LOBO, Father Jerome. See Le Grand, Mr.

LOCKE, Alan (editor). *The New Negro.* New York, 1925. $750.

LOCKE, David Ross. See Nasby, Petroleum V.

LOCKE, John. See *Essay Concerning Humane Understanding, An.*

LOCKE, John. *Directions Concerning Education . . .* London, 1933. $2,000.

LOCKE, John. *Some Thoughts Concerning Education.* London, 1693. First issue? with the reading "patronnge" on verso of leaf A3, line 19. $6,000.

LOCKER, Frederick. *London Lyrics.* London, 1857. Author's first book. $400.

LOCKRIDGE, Richard. *Mr. and Mrs. North.* New York, 1936. Author's first book. $400.

LOCKRIDGE, Richard and Frances. *The Norths Meet Murder.* New York, 1940. $750.

LOCKRIDGE, Ross, Jr. *Raintree County.* Boston, 1948. Author's first (and only) book. $250. London (1949). $125.

LOCKWOOD, Frank C. *Arizona Characters.* Los Angeles, 1928. Illustrated. Pictorial cloth. $200.

LOCKWOOD, Frank C. *Pioneer Days in Arizona.* New York, 1932. Illustrated. $150.

LOCKWOOD, James D. *Life and Adventures of a Drummer Boy.* New York, 1893. $600.

LOCKWOOD, Luke Vincent. *The Pendleton Collection.* Providence, 1904. 102 full-page plates. Morocco. One of 150 on Japan vellum, signed. $3,000.

LOCKYER, Joseph N., and RUTHERFORD, W. *Rules of Golf.* London, 1896. $1,000. New York, 1896. $750.

LODGE, David. *The Picturegoers.* London, 1960. Author's first book. $400.

LODGE, Henry Cabot. *Theodore Roosevelt: A Memorial.* Boston and New York, 1919. One of 500 signed copies. $500.

LOFTING, Hugh. *Doctor Dolittle's Post Office.* New York (1923). $600.

LOFTING, Hugh. *The Story of Doctor Dolittle.* New York, 1920. Illustrated by the author. In dustwrapper. $1,250.

LOFTING, Hugh. *The Voyages of Doctor Dolittle.* New York, 1922. $500.

LOGAN, James, and McIAN, R. R. *The Clans of the Scottish Highlands.* London, 1845–47. 2 vols. Folio, 2 colored armorial frontispieces, 72 colored plates. Original black morocco-backed cloth gilt, exhibiting the Arms of Scotland, backs fully gilt. $8,500.

LOGUE, Christopher. *The Girls.* London, 1969. Half leather. One of 26, signed. $250.

LOGUE, Christopher. *Wand and Quadrant.* Paris, 1953. Author's first book. Wraps. One of 300 copies. $250. 300 unnumbered copies. $125.

LOMAX, John A., and LOMAX, Alan. *American Ballads and Folksongs.* New York, 1934. One of 500 copies signed by the authors. $750.

LOMAX, John A. *Cowboy Songs.* New York, 1910. Pictorial cloth. $350.

LONDON, Charmian. *The Book of Jack London.* New York, 1921. 2 vols. First American edition. In dustwrappers. $1,000.

LONDON, Jack. See *The Kempton-Wace Letters.*

LONDON, Jack. *The Abysmal Brute.* New York, 1913. "Published May, 1913" on copyright page. Smooth olive-green cloth stamped in black. $450. Variant binding in rough green cloth stamped in black and green. $350.

LONDON, Jack. *The Acorn Planter.* New York, 1916. "Published February, 1916" on copyright page. Three forms of binding, no known priority. $1,750. London (1916). $500.

LONDON, Jack. *Adventure.* London/Edinburgh . . . (1911). "First published in 1911" on copyright page (actually published in February). $750. New York, 1911. "Published March 1911." Blue cloth stamped in white and blue. $400.

LONDON, Jack. *Burning Daylight.* New York, 1910. First printing: "Published October 1910" on copyright page. One blank leaf follows page (374). At foot of spine "Macmillan" or "The | Macmillan | Company"—no clear priority. $450. Second printing, as above but 3 blank leaves follow page (374). $150. London, 1911. $75. (Chicago, 1911.) Wraps. $100.

LONDON, Jack. *The Call of the Wild.* New York/London, 1903. "Set Up, Electrotyped and Published July 1903" on copyright page. $1,500. London, 1903. $750. Limited Editions Club, New York, 1960. In slipcase. $125.

LONDON, Jack. *Children of the Frost.* New York/London, 1902. "Set Up and Electrotyped September, 1902" on copyright page. $750. London, 1902. $350.

LONDON, Jack. *The Cruise of the Dazzler.* New York, 1902. "Published October, 1902" on copyright page. $2,500. London, 1906. $1,500.

LONDON, Jack. *A Daughter of the Snows.* Philadelphia, 1902. "Published October, 1902" on copyright page. $600. (Note: second editions are exactly the same except "Second Edition" added on first half title.) London, 1904. $300.

LONDON, Jack. *Dutch Courage and Other Stories.* New York, 1922. "Published September 1922" on copyright page. $3,000. London (1923). $600.

LONDON, Jack. *The God of His Fathers and Other Stories.* New York, 1901. $1,250. London, 1902. $450.

LONDON, Jack. *Hearts of Three.* London, (no-date). Published 1918. (Note: in later printings *"Island Tales"* is listed under "Books by Jack London" on page [iv].) $750. New York, 1920. "Published, September, 1920" on copyright page. In dustwrapper. $2,500. Without dustwrapper. $500.

LONDON, Jack. *The Human Drift.* New York, 1917. "Published, February, 1917" on copyright page. $750. London (1919). $250.

LONDON, Jack. *The Iron Heel.* New York, 1908. "Published February, 1908" on copyright page. $500. London, 1908. $250.

LONDON, Jack. *The Jacket.* London (1915). "Published 1915." (First U.K. edition of *The Star Rover.*) With color frontis. $450.

LONDON, Jack. *The Little Lady of the Big House.* New York, 1916. "Published April, 1916" on copyright page. (Variant: Copyright notices read "Copyright 1915 | by Jack London | copyright, 1916 | by Jack London." BAL also notes a "variant" with 1915 on title page. This would seem to us to be an advance copy and would be worth considerably more than the 1916.) $350. London (1916). $125.

LONDON, Jack. *Lost Face.* New York, 1910. "Published March, 1910" on copyright page. $500. London, [no-date] [1915]. $150.

LONDON, Jack. *Love of Life.* New York/London, 1907. "Published September, 1907" on copyright page. $500. London, 1908. $200.

LONDON, Jack. *Martin Eden.* Chicago: Donohue, 1908. $600. New York, 1909 "Published September 1909" on copyright page. $450. London, 1910. $150.

LONDON, Jack. *Michael, Brother of Jerry.* New York, 1917. "Published, November, 1917" on copyright page. $300.

LONDON, Jack. *The Mutiny of the Elsinore.* New York, 1914. "Published September 1914" on copyright page. $750. London: Mills & Boon (1915). $200.

LONDON, Jack. *On the Makaloa Mat.* New York, 1919. "Published, September 1919" on copyright page. In dustwrapper. $2,500. Without dustwrapper. $400. London (1920). $150.

LONDON, Jack. *The People of the Abyss.* New York, 1903. "Published October, 1903" on copyright page. Gray-blue cloth. $850. Dark-blue cloth. $500. London, 1903. $250.

LONDON, Jack. *Revolution.* Chicago (1909). Wraps. Ads on page (32) headed: "A Socialist Success." Publisher's address: 118 Kinzie Street. Terminal ads. $350. Ads on page (32) headed: "Pocket Library of Socialism." Publisher's address in terminal ads: 118 W. Kinzie Street. $300. Ads on page (32) headed "Socialist Periodicals." Address is "118 West Kinzie." $250. Ads on page (32) headed: "Study Socialism." $175. Ads on page 32 headed: "Socialist Literature." $125.

LONDON, Jack. *Revolution and Other Essays.* New York, 1910. "Published March, 1910" on copyright page. Maroon stamped in gold and blindstamped, on spine "The Macmillan Company." Terminal ads (priority listed as probable in BAL). $1,000. Variant: brown cloth, stamped in black, on spine: "Macmillan." No ads. $500. London, 1920. $200.

LONDON, Jack. *The Road.* New York, 1907. "Published November, 1907" on copyright page. Gray cloth stamped in gold and black. $750. Variant binding (possible remainder), cream cloth, stamped in black only, top edges not gilt. $400. London, 1914. $200.

LONDON, Jack. *The Scarlet Plague.* New York, 1915. "Published May 1915" on copyright page. $750. London, 1915. $200.

LONDON, Jack. *Scorn of Women.* New York/London, 1906. "Published November, 1906" on copyright page. Top edges gilt. On spine "The Macmillan Company." $2,500. Variant binding with top edges not gilt. "Macmillan" on spine. $2,000. London, 1907. $750.

LONDON, Jack. *The Sea-Wolf.* New York, 1904. Title page not a cancel. Copyright notices dated 1904 only. $6,500 at auction in 1993. Title page is a cancel. Copyright notices dated 1903 and 1904. "Published October, 1904." Some copies stamped in gold on spine (not white) but no known priority. $750. London, 1904. $300. Limited Editions Club, Hartford, 1961. $125.

LONDON, Jack. *The Son of the Sun.* Garden City, 1912. $600. London, 1913. $200.

LONDON, Jack. *The Son of the Wolf.* Boston/New York, 1900. Author's first book. Three trial bindings (no priority). Rough grass-green V cloth, stamped in silver; greenish-black V cloth, stamped in silver; white buckram stamped in red only. $4,000. First printing, gray cloth stamped in silver. Pagination (i–viii); no blank leaf following page (252); collation: (4), 2–22(6). $1,750. Second printing, gray cloth stamped in silver. Pagination: (i–vi) blank leaf following page (252). $1,000. Third printing, same as second except collation differs: 1–21(6), 22(4). $450. London: A. A. Watt, 1900. Cancel-title page of first printing. $1,500. London: Isbister, 1902. Copyright page blank. Red cloth stamped in gold on front and spine, spine imprint "Pitman," gold-stamped design on spine, blindstamp design on front. Collation: (i–viii), (1)–251, (251–253). Ads including *God of His Father* and Gorky's *Three Men*. $750.

LONDON, Jack. *The Star Rover*. New York, 1915. "Published October, 1915." $750. (For first U.K. edition, see *The Jacket* above.)

LONDON, Jack. *White Fang*. New York, 1906. "Published October, 1906" on copyright page. Presumed earliest state with title leaf integral. $500. Presumed later state with title leaf tipped in. $250. London, 1907. $200. Limited Editions Club, Lutenburg, Vt., 1973. $125.

LONG, Frank Belknap. *The Hounds of Tindalos*. Sauk City, Wisc. 1946. Black cloth. $250.

LONG, Frank Belknap. *A Man from Genoa and Other Poems*. Athol, Mass., 1926. Author's first book. $750.

LONG, Haniel. *Poems*. New York, 1920. Author's first book. $300.

LONG, Huey P. *My First Days in the White House*. Harrisburg, 1935. Illustrated. Boards. $250.

LONG, John. *Voyages and Travels of an Indian Interpreter and Trader* . . . London, 1791. Large folding map. $2,750.

LONG, Stephen H. *Voyage in a Six-Oared Skiff to the Falls of St. Anthony in 1817*. Philadelphia, 1860. Wraps. $300.

LONGFELLOW, Henry Wadsworth. See M. Lhomond's *Elements of French Grammar* (Longfellow's first book) and *French Exercises*. See also *Hyperion; Outre-Mer*.

LONGFELLOW, Henry Wadsworth. *The Belfry of Bruges* . . . Cambridge, 1846. Wraps. $1,500.

LONGFELLOW, Henry Wadsworth. *The Courtship of Miles Standish*. London, 1858. 135 pages, drab printed wraps, imprinted "Author's Protected' Edition." $1,250. Cloth. Second printing. $350. Boston, 1858. Brown or blue-green cloth. 4 printings in 1858, all examined (BAL) had "treacherous" for "ruddy" in third line of page 124, so ads may determine. "October 1858" earliest. $500. Also, purple-blue, or salmon cloths with extra gilt. $750.

LONGFELLOW, Henry Wadsworth. *Evangeline: A Tale of Acadie*. Boston, 1847. Brown or yellow boards, paper label. With line 1, page 61, reading "Long . . ." (for "Lo . . ."). $3,000. Reading "Lo." $600.

LONGFELLOW, Henry Wadsworth. *The Golden Legend*. Boston, 1851. Brown cloth, gilt. $500.

LONGFELLOW, Henry Wadsworth. *Poems on Slavery*. Cambridge, 1842. 31 pages, printed yellow wraps. $2,000.

LONGFELLOW, Henry Wadsworth. *The Song of Hiawatha.* London, 1855. With March ads. Wraps. $1,250. Second printing. Cloth. $750. (Both have November ads.) Boston, 1855. Brown cloth with panels blindstamped. First printing, with October or November ads and "dove" for "dived" in line 7 of page 96. $600. Gray-green, or red with panel stamped in gilt. $1,000. Boston, 1891. Illustrated by Frederic Remington. Vellum. One of 250. $600. Cloth or half leather. $750.

LONGFELLOW, Henry Wadsworth. *Tales of a Wayside Inn.* Boston, 1863. $450.

LONGFELLOW, Henry Wadsworth. *Voices of the Night.* Cambridge, 1839. In original tan or drab boards with paper label. First state, with line 10 on page 78 reading "His, Hector's arm" instead of "The arm of Hector." $1,000. Second state. $500. Author's first book of poetry. (There are other points worth checking, as BAL states "no copy examined had all the original readings.")

LONGLEY, Michael. *Ten Poems.* Belfast (1965). White printed wraps. $400. Second issue in green wraps. $150.

LONGMAN, W. *Tokens of the Eighteenth Century Connected with Booksellers . . .* London, 1916. Three plates. $300.

LONGSHORE, J. S., M.D. *The Principles and Practice of Nursing . . .* Philadelphia, 1842. $1,000.

LONGSTREET, Augustus Baldwin. See *Georgia Scenes . . .*

LONGSTREET, Augustus Baldwin. *An Oration . . .* (Augusta, 1831.) Wraps. $3,500. Rebound. $2,000.

LONGSTREET, James. *From Manassas to Appomattox.* Philadelphia, 1896. 44 maps and plates, 2 leaves of facsimiles. Cloth. $750.

LOOMIS, Augustus. *Scenes in the Indian Country.* Philadelphia (1859). $350.

LOOMIS, Chester A. *A Journey on Horseback Through the Great West, in 1825.* Bath, N.Y. (1820s). 27 pages. $500.

LOOS, Anita. *Breaking Into the Movies.* New York (1921). (With John J. Emerson.) $450.

LOOS, Anita. *"Gentlemen Prefer Blondes."* New York, 1925. Illustrated. First issue, with "Divine" for "Devine" on contents page. $1,000.

LOOS, Anita. *How to Write Photoplays.* New York, 1920. Author's first book (with W. J. Emerson). $500.

LOPEZ, Barry. *Desert Notes.* Kansas City (1976). Author's first book. $300.

LOPEZ, Barry Holstun. *Of Wolves and Men.* New York (1978). $250.

LORIMER, George Horace. *Letters from a Self-Made Merchant to His Son.* Philadelphia, 1901. 36 pages, wraps. $200. Boston, 1902. Cloth. First (complete) edition. $150.

LORING, Rosamond B. *Decorated Book Papers . . .* Cambridge, 1942. One of 250 copies. $850.

LORREQUER, Harry. *Charles O'Malley, the Irish Dragoon.* Dublin, 1841. (By Charles Lever.) Illustrated by H. K. Browne ("Phiz"). 22 parts in 21, printed pink pictorial wraps. $1,250. Dublin, 1841. 2 vols., boards. First edition in book form. $600. London, 1897. 16 plates by Arthur Rackham. $750.

LOSKIEL, George Henry. *History of the Mission of the United Brethren Among the Indians in North America.* In three parts. London, 1794. Folding frontispiece map. $750.

LOSSING, Benson J. *A Memorial of Alexander Anderson, M.D., the First Engraver on Wood in America.* New York, 1872. 38 plates. $250.

LOTHROP, Harriet M.S. See Sidney, Margaret.

LOUDON, Archibald. *A Selection of Some of the Most Interesting Narratives, of Outrages, Committed by the Indians, in Their Wars, with the White People.* Carlisle, Pa., 1808–11. 2 vols. $5,000 or more.

LOUDON, J. C. *The Suburban Gardener and Villa Companion . . .* London, 1838. In original cloth. $1,000.

LOUDON, Mrs. Jane. *British Wild Flowers.* London, 1846. 60 hand-colored plates. Cloth. $2,500. London (1849). Second edition. $2,250. Later editions—1855, 1859, etc. $1,500.

LOUGHBOROUGH, John. *The Pacific Telegraph and Railway . . .* St. Louis, 1849. Two folding maps. $3,500.

LOUGHEED, Victor. *Vehicles of the Air.* Chicago (1909). $250.

LOVE Epistles of Aristaenetus (The). London, 1771. (Translated by Richard Sheridan, his first book.) $1,500.

LOVE, Robertus. *The Rise and Fall of Jesse James.* New York, 1926. Frontispiece. Issued without dustwrapper. $200.

LOVECRAFT, H. P. *At the Mountains of Madness and Other Novels.* Sauk City, Wis., 1964. $250.

LOVECRAFT, H. P. *Beyond the Wall of Sleep.* Sauk City, Wis. 1943. $2,000.

LOVECRAFT, H. P. *The Cats of Ulthar.* (Cassia, Fla.), 1935. 16 pages, wraps. One of 40 on ordinary paper. $2,500. Also 2 copies on red lion text. $3,500.

LOVECRAFT, H. P. *The Haunter of the Dark.* London, 1951. Introduction by August Derleth. Cloth. $250.

LOVECRAFT, H. P. *Looking Backward . . .* (Cover title). Haverhill, Mass. [1920]. Wraps. 40 copies. Author's first book. $3,500.

LOVECRAFT, H. P. *Marginalia.* Sauk City, Wis. 1944. $400.

LOVECRAFT, H. P. *The Outsider and Others.* Sauk City, Wis., 1939. (First book published by August Derleth's Arkham House.) $3,000.

LOVECRAFT, H. P. *The Shadow Over Innsmouth.* Everett, Pa., 1936. Illustrated. In dustwrapper. $8,500. Author's first published book. (Earliest copies—about 10—were issued without errata sheet. The dustwrappers [two types: one printed in yellow and one with an illustration in green] were a later addition, according to Currey.)

LOVECRAFT, H. P. *The Shunned House.* Athol, Mass., 1928. Author's first book, other than four pamphlets/offprints. About 8 copies. Bound by Paul Cook. $10,000. Unbound, folded. signatures sold by Derleth (about 50). $3,000. Various bindings 1928–63. $3,000. Arkham House. Sauk City, Wis. 1963. 100 copies in plain brown dustwrapper. $5,000.

LOVECRAFT, H. P. *Something About Cats and Other Pieces.* Sauk City, Wis., 1949. Edited by August Derleth. Cloth. $250.

LOVECRAFT, H. P., and DERLETH, August. *The Lurker at the Threshold.* Sauk City, 1945. $175.

LOVELL, Robert. See Bion and Moschus; Southey, Robert.

LOVER, Samuel. *Handy Andy: A Tale of Irish Life.* London, January–December, 1842. Illustrated by the author. 12 parts, printed wraps. $600. London, 1842. Green cloth. First edition in book form. $300.

LOVESEY, Peter. *Wobble to Death.* (London, 1970.) Author's first book. $350. New York (1970). $125.

LOVING, James C. *Loving Brand Book.* Austin, 1965. One of 119 copies with original page of manuscript from Loving's book of brands. In slipcase. $850.

LOW, John L. F. G. Tait: A Record. London, 1900. $400.

LOWE, Percival. *Five Years a Dragoon '49 to '54.* Kansas City, 1906. $300.

LOWELL, Amy. See *Dream Drops.*

LOWELL, Amy. *A Dome of Many-Colored Glass.* Boston, 1912. Boards, cloth spine, paper labels. Author's first book aside from *Dream Drops.* $400.

LOWELL, Amy. *The Madonna of Carthagena.* No place, 1927. Wraps. One of 50. $300.

LOWELL, Amy. *What's O'Clock.* Boston, 1925. Gray-blue boards and cloth. $200.

LOWELL, James Russell. See Wilbur, Homer. See also *Class Poem.*

LOWELL, James Russell. *Ode Recited at the Commemoration of the Living and Dead Soldiers of Harvard University, July 21, 1865.* Cambridge, 1865. Gray boards, paper label. One of 50. $4,500.

LOWELL, James Russell. *Poems.* Boston, 1849. 2 vols. Boards or cloth. $350.

LOWELL, James Russell. *A Year's Life.* Boston, 1841. Boards, paper label. First edition, with or without errata slip. Author's first book (preceded by *Class Poem* pamphlet). $300.

LOWELL, Maria. *The Poems of Maria Lowell.* Cambridge, Mass., 1855. 68 pages, half leather. $450. Boston, 1907. One of 300. $200.

LOWELL, Robert. *4 by Robert Lowell.* (Cambridge, Mass., 1969.) Illustrated by Robert Scott. Decorated wraps, stitched. One of 100 copies, signed by Lowell. (4 broadsides, 1 for each poem.) $600. One of 26. $750.

LOWELL, Robert. *Land of Unlikeness.* Cummington, Mass., 1944. Author's first book. Printed boards. One of 224 copies. In tissue jacket. $2,000. One of 26 signed copies. $7,500.

LOWELL, Robert. *Life Studies.* London (1959). $350. New York, 1959. $200.

LOWELL, Robert. *Lord Weary's Castle.* New York (1946). $750.

LOWELL, Robert. *The Mills of the Kavanaughs.* New York (1951). $250.

LOWELL, Robert. *Poems, 1938–1949.* London (1950). $350.

LOWELL, Robert. *The Voyage and Other Versions of Poems by Baudelaire.* London (1968). One of 200 (out of 210) signed. In slipcase. $400.

LOWES, John Livingston. *The Road to Xanadu.* Boston, 1927. One of 300. In slipcase. $300.

LOWMAN, Al. *Printing Arts in Texas.* (Austin, Tex, 1975.) One of 395. $250.

LOWMAN, Al (compiler). *This Bitterly Beautiful Land: A Texas Commonplace Book.* (Austin, 1972.) Woodcuts. Folio, cloth. One of 275 signed. $1,250.

LOWNDES, Mrs. Belloc. *The Lodger.* London (1913). $600.

LOWNDES, William Thomas. *The Bibliographer's Manual of English Literature.* London, 1834. 4 vols. $500. London, 1864. Best edition. $400. London, 1890. 6 vols. $350.

LOWRY, Malcolm. *Lunar Caustic.* London (1968). First edition in English. Cloth. $150. Wraps, in dustwrapper. $50. (Published in Paris, in French, in 1963.)

LOWRY, Malcolm. *Ultramarine.* London (1933). Author's first book. $7,500. Philadelphia, 1962. First American edition revised. $200. Toronto (1963) or London (1963). $125.

LOWRY, Malcolm. *Under the Volcano.* New York (1947). Gray cloth. First edition not stated. $4,500. London (1947). $1,000.

LOWRY, Robert. *Hutton Street.* Cincinnati, 1940. Illustrated. Pictorial wraps. $125.

LOWRY, Robert. *Murder Pie.* Cincinnati, 1939. Wraps. $250.

LOWRY, Robert. *Trip to Bloomin' Moon.* Cincinnati, 1939. Wraps. $150.

LOWTHER, George. *The Adventures of Superman.* New York, 1942. $1,500.

LOY, Mina. *Lunar Baedeker.* (Paris, 1923.) Printed wraps. $2,000.

LOY, Mina. *Lunar Baedeker & Time Tables.* Highlands, N.C., 1958. Cloth. Jargon 23. Wraps. $400. One of 50 signed "author's copies." In acetate dustwrapper. (Contains an introduction by William Carlos Williams and others.) $1,500.

LOY, Mina. *Songs to Joannes.* New York, 1917. Author's first book. (April issue of *Others* magazine.) Wraps. $350.

LUBBOCK, Basil. *Adventures by Sea from the Art of Old Time.* London, 1925. 115 plates, including 22 in color. Buckram. One of 1,750. $750.

LUBBOCK, Basil. *The Last of the Windjammers.* Boston, 1927–29. Illustrated. 2 vols., cloth. $750.

LUBBOCK, Basil, and SPURLING, John. *Sail: The Romance of the Clipper Ship.* London, 1927–30–36. 78 full-page color plates. 3 vols. One of 1,000. In dustwrapper. $1,250.

LUCAS, E. V. See L., E.V.

LUCAS, E. V. *Edwin Austin Abbey Royal Academician:The Record of His Life and Work.* New York, 1921. 2 vols. Without dustwrappers. $200. One of 50 with original drawing by Abbey. 2 vols. $1,500.

LUCAS, E. V. *Playtime and Company.* London (1925). Illustrated by Ernest H. Shepard. Vellum. One of 15 on vellum, signed by author and artist. $1,750. Boards and cloth. One of 100 signed. In dustwrapper. $1,000.

LUCAS, Thomas J. *Camp Life and Sport in South Africa.* London, 1878. Frontispiece and 3 plates. $750.

LUCAS, Thomas J. *Pen and Pencil Reminiscences of a Campaign in South Africa.* London (1861). 21 colored plates. $2,000.

LUCAS, Victoria. *The Bell Jar.* London (1963.) (By Sylvia Plath.) $5,000. New York, 1971. $200.

LUCE, Edward S. *Keogh, Comanche and Custer.* (St. Louis), 1939. Illustrated. Cloth. Limited, signed edition. In dustwrapper. $750.

LUDLOW, Fitz-Hugh. See *The Hasheesh Eater.*

LUDLOW, N. M. *Dramatic Life as I Found It.* St. Louis, 1880. $175.

LUDLUM, Robert. *The Osterman Weekend.* New York (1972). Printed acetate dustwrapper. Priced $6.95 with "A 3918" on bottom right corner of back (dustwrapper) panel. Also noted: "First Printing" copies with "7452" where price should be and same number (A 3918) on back; and "First Printing" copies with no price and "7452" at bottom right corner of back dustwrapper panel. The latter two editions do not have Book-of-the-Month dots, but the covers (book) are smoother and lighter blue than the true first. $250. London, 1972. $125.

LUDLUM, Robert. *The Scarlatti Inheritance.* New York (1971). Author's first book. In printed acetate dustwrapper (Note: there is also a Book-of-the-Month Club edition that states "First . . ." It does have a blindstamp on the bottom right corner of the back cover, but this is easy to overlook.) $300. London (1971). $150.

LUHAN, Mabel Dodge. *Lorenzo in Taos.* New York, 1932. Illustrated. Author's first book. $300. London, 1933. $150.

LUHAN, Mabel Dodge. *Taos and Its Artists.* New York, 1947. Illustrated. Red cloth. $300.

LUMPKIN, Wilson. *The Removal of the Cherokee Indians from Georgia.* Wormsloe, Ga., 1907. 2 vols. 2 portraits. Cloth. $1,250.

LURIE, Alison. *V. R. Lang.* Munich (1959). Author's first book. (300 copies.) Wraps. (Edward Gorey cover.) $350.

LUTTIG, John C. *Journal of a Fur-Trading Expedition on the Upper Missouri.* St. Louis, 1920. Folding map, 4 plates. Boards and cloth. One of 365. Issued without dustwrapper. $350.

LYDEKKER, Richard. *The Game Animals of Africa.* (London, 1908.) $500.

LYDEKKER, Richard. *The Great and Small Game of India . . .* London, 1900. One of 250. $3,000.

LYELL, Charles. *Principles of Geology.* London, 1830–32–33. 3 vols. Maps and plates. Leather. $600. Philadelphia, 1837. 2 vols. $1,000.

LYELL, Charles. *Travels in North America.* London, 1845. Map, 6 plates. 2 vols. $750. New York, 1845. 2 vols. $600.

LYELL, James P. R. *Early Book Illustration in Spain.* London, 1926. Colored frontispiece, 247 other illustrations. One of 500. Issued without dustwrapper. $300.

LYMAN, Albert. *Journal of a Voyage to California, and Life in the Gold Diggings.* Hartford, 1852. Illustrated. Wraps. $2,500. Cloth. $2,000.

LYMAN, George D. *John Marsh, Pioneer.* New York, 1930. One of 150 signed. Issued without dustwrapper. $300.

LYMINGTON, Lord. *Spring Song of Iscariot.* Black Sun Press. Paris, 1929. Wraps. One of 125 on Van Gelder paper. $400. One of 25 on Japan paper. $850.

LYNCH, Bohun. *The Prize Ring.* London, 1925. One of 1,000. Issued without dustwrapper. $350. Trade. $75.

LYNCH, Thomas. *The Printer's Manual: A Practical Guide for Compositors and Pressmen.* Cincinnati, 1872. Second edition. First appeared in 1859. $200.

LYON, Danny. *The Bikeriders.* New York, 1968. Author's first book. Stiff wraps. $450.

LYON, G.F. *A Brief Narrative of an Unsuccessful Attempt to Reach Repulse Bay . . .* London, 1825. Folding map and 7 plates. $600.

LYON, G. F. *A Narrative of Travels in Northern Africa, in the Years 1818 . . .* London, 1821. 17 hand-colored plates. Folding map. $2,500.

LYON, G. F. *The Private Journal of Capt. G. F. Lyon, of H.M. Hecla.* London, 1824. With frontispiece, folding map, and 6 plates. $850. Boston, 1824. $650.

LYON, Harris Merton. *Sardonics: Sixteen Sketches.* New York, 1909. Author's first book. $150.

LYON, John. *The Harp of Zion, A Collection of Poems.* Liverpool, 1853. Errata slip. $250.

LYONS, Arthur. *All God's Children.* New York, 1975. $350.

LYONS, Arthur. *The Dead Are Discreet.* New York (1974). $350.

LYONS, Arthur. *The Second Coming: Satanism in America.* New York (1970). Author's first book. $200.

LYONS, Danny. *The Bikeriders.* New York (1968). Wraps. $600.

LYRICAL Ballads with a Few Other Poems. Bristol, 1798. (By William Wordsworth and Samuel Taylor Coleridge.) $25,000. London, 1798. $7,500. London, 1800. *"With Other Poems."* 2 vols. Second edition (so designated on the first vol. alone). $7,500. London, 1802. 2 vols., boards. Third edition. $2,000. Philadelphia, 1802. 2 vols. $1,500.

LYTLE, Andrew. *At the Moon's Inn.* Indianapolis/New York (1941). First edition stated. $350.

LYTLE, Andrew. *Bedford Forrest and His Critter Company.* New York: Minton, Balch, 1931. Author's first book. $750. New York: Putnam (1931). $300.

LYTLE, Andrew. *The Long Night.* Indianapolis (1936). $350.

LYTLE, Andrew. *A Name for Evil.* Indianapolis (1947). $250.

LYTTON, Lord (Edward Bulwer). See Bulwer-Lytton, Edward.

LYTTON, Edward Robert. See *Clytemnestra.*

M

MACARIA: or, Altars of Sacrifice. Richmond, 1864. 183 pages, wraps. (By Augusta Jane Evans Wilson.) $750.

MacARTHUR, Charles, and HECHT, Ben. *The Front Page.* New York, 1928. $1,250.

MacARTHUR, Douglas. *Military Demolitions.* (Fort Leavenworth, Kan., 1909.) Printed wraps. $600.

MacARTHUR, Douglas. *Reminiscences.* New York, 1964. One of 1,750 signed copies. In slipcase. $850.

MacARTHUR, James. *New South Wales: Its Present State and Future Prospects.* London, 1837. Colored map. (Written by Edward Edwards from MacArthur's notes.) $1,000.

MACARTNEY, Mervyn E. *The Practical Exemplar of Architecture.* London, 1907–1928. 7 vols. $1,000.

MACAULAY, Catharine. *The History of England from the Revolution to the Present Time.* Bath, 1768. $750.

MACAULAY, Rose. *Abbots Verney.* London, 1906. Author's first book. $150.

MACAULAY, Rose. *Catchwords and Claptrap.* Hogarth Press. London, 1926. Printed boards. Issued without dustwrapper. $350.

MACAULAY, Thomas Babington. *Evening: A Poem.* (Cambridge, 1821.) $350.

MACAULAY, Thomas Babington. *Lays of Ancient Rome.* London, 1842. Brown cloth. $600.

MACAULAY, Thomas Babington. *Pompeii.* (Cambridge, 1819.) Author's first book. $450.

MacBETH, George. *A Form of Words.* Oxford, 1954. Author's first book. One of 150 copies. $300.

MacCABE, Julius P. Bolivar. *Directory of Cities of Cleveland and of Ohio City for the Years 1837–1838.* Cleveland, 1837. In original printed boards. $3,000.

MacCABE, Julius P. Bolivar. *Directory of the City of Detroit.* Detroit, 1837. $1,250.

MacCABE, Julius P. Bolivar. *Directory of the City of Milwaukee.* Milwaukee, 1847. Full leather. $850.

MacCARTHY, Desmond. *The Court Theatre 1904–1907.* London, 1907. Author's first book. $125.

MacDIARMID, Hugh. See Duval, K. D.; Grieve, C. M.

(Note: the following listings under MacDiarmid's name include books with title pages reading "M'Diarmid" and "McDiarmid.")

MacDIARMID, Hugh. *Direadh I, II, III.* Frenich, Foss, England, 1974. (By C. M. Grieve.) Boards and leather. One of 200 signed copies. In slipcase. $300.

MacDIARMID, Hugh. *A Drunk Man Looks at the Thistle.* Edinburgh, 1926. (By C. M. Grieve.) $350. Verona, 1969. One of 160. $1,500.

MacDIARMID, Hugh. *The Kind of Poetry I Want.* Edinburgh, 1961. (By C. M. Grieve.) Boards and vellum. One of 300 signed copies. In slipcase. $600. One of 500 copies. In slipcase. $150.

MacDIARMID, Hugh. *Penny Wheep.* (Edinburgh) 1926. (By C. M. Grieve.) Dark blue cloth stamped in gilt. $500. Second binding in light blue boards stamped in black. $300.

MacDIARMID, Hugh. *Sangschaw.* (Edinburgh) 1925. (By C. M. Grieve.) Poet's first book of verse. Dark blue cloth stamped in gilt. $350. The light blue boards are presumed to be a later issue. $350.

MacDIARMID, Hugh. *Stony Limits and Other Poems.* London, 1934. (By C. M. Grieve.) $300.

MacDONAGH, Donagh. *Twenty Poems.* Dublin, 1934. Author's first book (with Niall Sheridan). Wraps. $200.

MacDONAGH, Donagh. *Veterans and Other Poems.* Dublin, 1941. Cuala Press. Boards and linen. One of 270 copies. $250.

MacDONALD, George. *At the Back of the North Wind.* London, 1871. Illustrated by Arthur Hughes. In bright-blue pictorial (gold-stamped) cloth. $4,000. Second binding omits gold framing. $2,500. New York, 1871. $750. Philadelphia, 1919. Illustrated by J. W. Smith. $350.

MacDONALD, George. *Dealings with the Fairies.* London, 1867. Illustrated by Arthur Hughes. Blue cloth. $1,500. Green cloth. $1,000.

MacDONALD, George. *Malcolm.* London, 1875. 3 vols. $1,250.

MacDONALD, George. *Phantasies.* London, 1858. With 16 pages of ads at end dated September 1858 (Shaberman). $1,250.

MacDONALD, George. *Poems.* London, 1857. $600.

MacDONALD, George. *Within and Without: A Dramatic Poem.* London, 1855. Author's first book. $3,500. New York, 1872. $400.

MacDONALD, James. *Food from the Far West.* London, 1878. Decorated cloth. $500. New York (1878). Cloth. First American edition. $300.

MacDONALD, James, and SINCLAIR, James. *History of Hereford Cattle.* London, 1886. Illustrated. $500.

MacDONALD, John D. *The Brass Cupcake.* New York, 1950. Author's first book. Wraps. $250. London, 1974. First Hardback. $350. London (1955). $25.

MacDONALD, John D. *Darker Than Amber.* Greenwich (1966). Wraps. $75. London (1968). $450. Philadelphia, 1970. $1,000.

MacDONALD, John D. *The Deep Blue Goodbye.* Greenwich (1964). Wraps. $200. London (1965). Cloth. $750. New York (1975). Cloth. $500.

MacDONALD, John D. *The Executioners.* New York, 1958. $1,000.

MacDONALD, John D. *Nightmare in Pink.* Greenwich (1964). Wraps. $125. London (1966). $500. New York (1976). $400.

MacDONALD, John D. *Wine of the Dreamer.* New York (1951). Author's first hardback book. $350.

MACDONALD, John Ross. *The Drowning Pool.* New York, 1950. (By Kenneth Millar.) $1,750.

MACDONALD, John Ross. *The Way Some People Die.* New York, 1951. $1,500.

MacDONALD, Marianne. *Death's Autograph.* London (1996). $500. New York (1997). $100.

MacDONALD, Philip. See Fleming, Oliver.

MacDONALD, Philip. *List of Adrian Messenger.* Garden City, 1959. $250. London, 1960. $200.

MacDONALD, Philip. *Persons Unknown.* Garden City, 1931. $500.

MACDONALD, Ross. See Millar, Kenneth.

MACDONALD, Ross. *The Chill.* New York, 1964. (By Kenneth Millar.) In dustwrapper. $250.

MACDONALD, Ross. *The Galton Case.* New York, 1959. (By Kenneth Millar.) $750.

MACDONALD, Ross. *Lew Archer: Private Investigator.* New York, 1977. (By Kenneth Millar.) One of 250 signed copies. In slipcase. $250.

MACDONALD, Ross. *The Zebra-Striped Hearse.* New York, 1962. $300.

MacDONALD, William Colt. *Law of the Forty Fives.* New York (1933). $200.

MacDONALD, William Colt. *Restless Guns.* New York, 1929. Author's first book. $400.

MacDOUGALL, William. *The Red River Rebellion*. Toronto, 1870. 68 pages, wraps. $250.

MacEWAN, Gwendolyn. *Selah*. Toronto, 1961. $1,200.

MacFALL, Haldane. *Aubrey Beardsley: The Clown, the Harlequin, the Pierrot of His Age*. New York, 1927. In dustwrapper. $200.

MacFALL, Haldane. *Aubrey Beardsley: The Man and His Work*. London, 1928. Portrait and 10 plates. Half cloth. In dustwrapper. $300. Cloth. One of 100 copies on handmade paper, with 6 extra illustrations. $500.

MacFALL, Haldane. *The Book of Lovat*. London, 1923. Half cloth. One of 150 signed copies. In dustwrapper. $400. Trade in dustwrapper. $250.

MacFALL, Haldane. *The Wooings of Jezebel Pettyfer*. London, 1898. Pictorial cloth. Author's first book. First issue, with portrait of Jezebel on front cover. (Most copies reportedly destroyed by fire.) $300.

MACHEN, Arthur. See Siluriensis, Leolinus.

MACHEN, Arthur. *Bridles and Spurs*. Cleveland, 1951. Green boards and cloth. Grabhorn printing for the Rowfant Club. One of 178 copies. In slipcase. $350.

MACHEN, Arthur. *The Canning Wonder*. London, 1925. Boards and vellum. One of 130 signed copies. In dustwrapper. $300. Trade edition. $125.

MACHEN, Arthur. *Dog and Duck*. London, 1924. Illustrated. Batik boards and cloth. One of 150 (of an edition of 900) signed copies. In dustwrapper. $300. Trade edition. $175.

MACHEN, Arthur. *Eleusinia*. Hereford, 1881. Author's first book. Wraps. (2 known copies). $15,000.

MACHEN, Arthur. *The Glorious Mystery*. Chicago, 1924. $200.

MACHEN, Arthur. *The Green Round*. London (1933). $200. Sauk City, Wis., 1968. $100.

MACHEN, Arthur. *The Hill of Dreams*. London, 1907. Frontispiece. Dark-red buckram. First edition, with "E. Grant Richards" at bottom of spine. $200. London (1922). One of 150 signed copies. In dustwrapper. $350.

MACHEN, Arthur. *The Shining Pyramid*. Chicago, 1923. Edited by Vincent Starrett. Illustrated. Black cloth. One of 875 copies. In dustwrapper. $250. London, 1925. Blue cloth. First English edition. One of 250 signed copies. In dustwrapper. $300. Trade edition. $125.

MACHEN, Arthur. *Strange Roads—With the Gods In Spring*. London, 1923. With sketches by Joseph Simpson. $200.

MACHEN, Arthur. *The Three Impostors*. London, 1895. Blue cloth. $400.

MACHIAVELLI, Niccolò. *The Art of War*. (By Nicholas Machiavel.) Albany, 1815. First American edition. 7 folding plans. $500.

MACHIAVELLI, Niccolò. *The Prince*. London, 1640. $20,000.

MacINNES, Colin. *To the Victor the Spoils.* London (1950). Author's first book. $175.

MACK, Doctor Ebenezer. *The Cat-Fight; A Mock Heroic Poem.* New York, 1824. $750.

MACK, Solomon. *A Narraitive [sic] of the Life of Solomon Mack.* Windsor, Vt. (1811?). 48 pages. $1,250.

MACKAIL, J. W. *The Life of William Morris.* London, 1899. 2 vols. 22 illustrations. $350.

MACKAIL, J. W. *William Morris: An Address.* London, 1901. One of 300 signed copies. $350.

MACKAY, Charles. *Memoirs of Extraordinary Popular Delusions and the Madness of Crowds.* London, 1841. 3 vols. 5 portraits. $1,500.

MACKAY, Charles. *The Mormons: Their Progress and Present Condition.* London (1851). 10 parts, wraps. $750. London (1851). First book edition. Cloth. $300.

MACKAY, Malcolm S. *Cow-Range and Hunting Trail.* New York, 1925. 38 illustrations. $600.

MACKAY, Sheena. *Toddler on the Run . . .* London, 1964. $175.

MACKAYE, Percy. *Johnny Crimson.* Boston, 1895. Author's first book. Wraps. 50 copies. $500. Trade edition. $250.

MACKAYE, Percy. *The Mystery of Hamlet, King of Denmark.* New York, 1950. Folio, cloth. One of 357 signed copies. Issued without dustwrapper. $350.

MACKENNA, F. Severne. *Worcester Porcelain.* Leigh-on-Sea, 1950. Frontispiece in color, 80 plates. Buckram. One of 500 signed copies. In dustwrapper. $450.

MACKENZIE, Alexander. *Voyages from Montreal, on the River St. Lawrence, Through the Continent of North America.* London, 1801. Frontispiece, 3 folding maps. $6,000. London, 1802. 2 vols. Second edition. $2,500. New York, 1802. Folding map. $1,000. Philadelphia, 1802. 2 vols. $1,000.

MACKENZIE, Alister. *Golf Architecture.* Kent [1920]. In dustwrapper. $2,500. Worcester, 1993. Limited to 700 copies. $250.

MACKENZIE, Alister. *Golf Architecture: Economy in Course Construction.* London, 1920. $1,500.

MACKENZIE, Compton. *Extraordinary Women.* London, 1928. One of 100 signed copies. $300.

MACKENZIE, Compton. *Greek Memories.* London, 1932. (Reportedly withdrawn.) $400.

MACKENZIE, Compton. *Poems.* Oxford, 1907. Author's first book. Gray wraps. $200.

MACKENZIE, Henry. *The Man of Feeling.* London, 1771. $2,500.

MACKENZIE, Henry. *The Man of the World.* London, 1773. 2 vols. $1,000.

MACKENZIE, Seaforth. *The Young Desire It.* London, 1937. $1,250.

MACKERN, Louie (Mrs.), and BOYS, M. *Our Lady of the Green.* London, 1899. $1,500.

MACKLEY, George. *Engraved In the Wood: A Collection of Wood Engravings.* London, 1889. One of 600 copies signed by Mackley. Stiff wraps. $2,000. London, 1968. One of 300 copies. 68 plates on loose sheets. Wraps. $1,000.

MacLAREN, Ross J. *The Stuff to Give the Troops.* London, 1944. $150.

MacLAVERTY, Bernard. *Secrets and Other Stories.* Belfast, 1977. Author's first book. $200.

MacLEAN, Norman. *A River Runs Through It.* Chicago (1976). First edition not stated. $1,500. Chicago, 1983. One of 500 signed copies. $1,000. West Hatfield (1989). One of 200 signed copies. Issued without dustwrapper. $1,000.

MacLEISH, Archibald. *American Letters for Gerald Murphy.* Arroyo Grande, 1935. Half leather and cloth. One of 150 copies. Issued without dustwrapper. $250.

MacLEISH, Archibald. *CLASS Poem. 1915.* (New Haven), 1915. 4 pages. Author's first separately published work. $3,000

MacLEISH, Archibald. *Einstein.* Black Sun Press. Paris, 1929. Printed wraps. One of 100 copies on Van Gelder paper. In slipcase. $750. One of 50 copies on vellum, signed. In slipcase. $2,000.

MacLEISH, Archibald. *The Happy Marriage and Other Poems.* Boston, 1924. Boards, paper label. $150.

MacLEISH, Archibald. *Land of the Free.* New York (1938). Numerous plates by Dorothea Lange, Ben Shahn, and other WPA photographers. $350.

MacLEISH, Archibald. *New Found Land.* Black Sun Press. Paris, 1930. Wraps. One of 100 copies. In slipcase. $250. One of 25 copies on vellum, signed. In slipcase. $1,250. One of 10 of the vellum copies initialed by Harry Crosby. $1,750. Boston, 1930. (Printed in Paris.) One of 500 copies. Blue boards. In slipcase. $125.

MacLEISH, Archibald. *Nobodaddy.* Cambridge, Mass., 1926. One of 700 copies. Black cloth. Issued without dustwrapper. $100. One of 50 large-paper copies. $150.

MacLEISH, Archibald. *The Pot of Earth.* Cambridge, 1925. One of 100 copies on handmade paper. Gold decorated boards. In dustwrapper and slipcase. $250. Boston, 1925. $150.

MacLEISH, Archibald. *Songs for a Summer Day.* (New Haven), 1913. Author's first regularly published book. Wraps. $500.

MacLEISH, Archibald. *Tower of Ivory.* New Haven, 1917. $200.

MacLENNAN, Hugh. *Oxyrhynehus: An Economic & Social Study.* Princeton University Press. Princeton, 1935. First book under this name. $750.

MacLEOD, Charlotte. *Mystery of the White Knight.* New York (1964). $500.

MacLEOD, Charlotte. *Rest You Merry.* Bath, New Brunswick, 1978. $350. Garden City, 1978. $150.

MacLEOD, Fiona. *Pharais.* Derby, 1894. One of 75 signed copies. Author's first book. $250.

MacLEOD, George H. B. *Notes on the Surgery of the War . . .* Richmond, 1862. $2,000.

MacMICHAEL, H. A. *A History of the Arabs in the Sudan.* Cambridge University Press, 1922. 2 vols. Folding map in pocket at the rear of volume 2. $1,500.

MacNEICE, Louis. *Blind Fireworks.* London, 1929. Author's first book. Light-gray cloth. $750.

MacNEICE, Louis. *The Earth Compels.* London, 1939. $150.

MacNEICE, Louis. *The Last Ditch.* Dublin, 1940. Cuala Press. One of 450 copies. Boards, linen spine, paper label. In tissue dustwrapper. $300. One of 25 signed copies. $750.

MacNEICE, Louis. *Meet the U.S. Army.* London, 1943. Wraps. $250.

MacNEICE, Louis. *Poems.* London, 1935. $450.

MacNEICE, Louis. *Poems.* New York (1937). (Same title as the 1935 book but not the same content.) $300.

MACOMB, David B. *Answer to Enquiries Relative to Middle Florida.* Tallahassee, 1827. 5 unnumbered leaves. $2,000.

MacPHERSON, Jay. *Nineteen Poems.* Mallorca, 1952. Author's first book. Wraps. $650.

MacQUOID, Percy. *The History of English Furniture.* London, 1904–8. 4 vols. Illustrated, including color plates. Buckram. $1,000.

MacQUOID, Percy, and EDWARDS, Ralph. *The Dictionary of English Furniture.* London, 1924–27. 3 vols., with 52 color plates. In dustwrappers. $1,250.

MADAN, Falconer. *The Early Oxford Press: A Bibliography of Printing and Publishing at Oxford.* Oxford, 1895. One of 700 copies issued with the 3 actual specimen leaves. $250.

MADARIAGA, Salvador de. *Don Quixote: An Introductory Essay in Psychology.* Gregynog Press. Newtown, Wales, 1934. One of 250 copies. Boards and linen. $400. One of 15 specially bound copies. $1,500.

MADDEN, Frederic W. *Coins of the Jews.* London, 1881. Illustrated. Folio, half leather. $600.

MADDEN, R. R. *The Island of Cuba.* London, 1849. $750.

MADERSTEIG, Hans. *The Officina Bodoni: The Operation of a Hand-Press During the First Six Years of Its Work.* Paris/New York, 1929. Illustrations, tipped-in specimen sheets, cloth binding with gold stamping on spine and front cover. $850.

MADISON, James. *Message from the President of the United States, Recommending an Immediate Declaration of War Against Great Britain.* Washington, 1812. 12 pages. $300.

MAGEE, David. *The Hundredth Book: A Bibliography of . . . the Book Club of California.* San Francisco, 1958. One of 400 copies. 18 reproductions, many in color. Folio, half cloth. Grabhorn printing. In dustwrapper. $450.

MAGEE, Dorothy, and MAGEE, David. *Bibliography of the Grabhorn Press, 1940–1956.* San Francisco, 1957. One of 225 copies. Illustrated. Folio, half morocco. $850. (See Heller entry for related work.)

MAGOFFIN, Susan Shelby. *Down the Santa Fe Trail and into Mexico.* New Haven, 1926. Edited by Stella M. Drumm. Map, plates. In dustwrapper. $300.

MAGOUN, F. Alexander. *The Frigate Constitution and Other Historic Ships.* Salem, 1928. One of 97 large-paper copies. Illustrated, including 16 folding plates. Buckram. Issued without dustwrapper. $1,000. Trade edition. Issued without dustwrapper. $250.

MAGRA, James (attributed). *A Journal of a Voyage Round the World in His Majesty's Ship . . .* London, 1771. First state with dedication leaf. $35,000. Without dedication. $20,000. Author remains unknown, though the sailor James Magra is the likeliest candidate.

MAGRUDER, Allan B. *Political, Commercial and Moral Reflections, on the Late Cession of Louisiana, to the United States.* Lexington, Ky., 1803. $5,000.

MAGUIRE, H. N. *The Coming Empire: A Complete and Reliable Treatise on the Black Hills, Yellowstone and Big Horn Regions.* Sioux City, Iowa, 1878. 7 plates, folding map. $700.

MAGUIRE, H. N. *The Lakeside Library: The People's Edition of the Black Hills and American Wonderland.* (Caption title.) Chicago, 1877. Illustrations and map. 36 pages, stitched. $750.

MAHAN, A. T. *The Influence of Sea Power upon History.* Boston, 1890. $750.

MAHAN, A. T. *The Navy in the Civil War.* New York, 1883. Author's first book. $350.

MAHON, Derek. *Twelve Poems.* Belfast, no date [1965]. Wraps. Author's first book. $600.

MAID Marian. London, 1822. (By Thomas Love Peacock.) $750.

MAILER, Norman. *Barbary Shore.* New York (1951). Black boards with white lettering. 2 dustwrappers on first edition apparently issued simultaneously: red and black; green and black. $350. Proof copies with both variants of dustwrapper also noted. London (1952). $150.

MAILER, Norman. *Deaths for the Ladies and Other Disasters.* New York (1962). Black-and-white cloth, with white lettering, in black-and-white dustwrapper. $300. Simultaneously published in wraps. $75. (London, 1962.) Wraps. $50.

MAILER, Norman. *Gargoyle, Guignol, False Closet.* Dublin, 1964. 2 pages. One of 100 copies. $400.

MAILER, Norman. *Marilyn.* Grosset & Dunlap (New York, 1973.) Limited signed edition in clamshell case. $300. Trade, tan cloth. $75. (London, 1973.) $75.

MAILER, Norman. *The Naked and the Dead.* New York (1948). First regularly published book. $2,000. London, 1949. 253 copies, 240 numbered. In full leather. $2,000. Trade. $300. Franklin Library, 1979. Signed by Mailer. $150.

MAILER, Norman. *Of a Small and Modest Malignancy Wicked and Bristling with Dots.* Northridge, 1980. 100 signed copies. In leather without dustwrapper in slipcase. $250. 300 signed copies. Cloth in slipcase. $125.

MAILLARD, N. Doran. *The History of the Republic of Texas, from the Discovery of the Country to the Present Time.* London, 1842. Folding map. Dark-blue cloth. $4,000.

MAINWARING, Daniel. (Geoffrey Homes.) *One Against the Earth.* New York, 1933. $750.

MAITLAND, Barry. *The Marx Sisters.* London, 1994. $650.

MAITLAND, Margaret. *Passages in the Life of . . .* London, 1849. 3 vols. Author's first book. $450.

MAJOR, Clarence. *All-Night Visitors.* New York (1969). $200.

MAJOR, Clarence. *The Fires That Burn in Heaven.* [Chicago, circa 1954.] Wraps. 2 copies known. $2,500.

MAJORS, Alexander. *Seventy Years on the Frontier.* Chicago, 1893. Frontispiece and plates. (Without illustrations.) Blue pictorial cloth or wraps. $250.

MALAMUD, Bernard. *The Assistant.* New York, 1957. Reviews of *The Natural* on back panel of dustwrapper. $500. Reviews of this title on back panel. $250. London, 1959. $150.

MALAMUD, Bernard. *The Natural.* New York (1952). Author's first book. Red, blue, or gray cloth (priority unknown but author's copy was blue). $4,500. London, 1963. Glossary added. $750.

MALCOM, (Sir John). *The History of Persia.* London, 1815. 2 vols. Large folding map of Persia and 22 plates. $3,500.

MALCOLM, John. *A Back Room in Somers Town.* London (1984). $400.

MALCOLM X. *The Autobiography of Malcolm X.* New York (1965). Author's first book. Written with Alex Haley. $1,000.

MALET, Capt. H. E. *Annals of the Road.* London, 1876. 10 colored plates, woodcuts. $400.

MALKIN, B. H. *A Father's Memoirs of His Child.* London, 1806. Folding map, 3 plates. $750.

MALONE, Michael. *The Delectable Mountains.* New York, 1976. $250.

MALORY, Sir Thomas. *Le Morte D'Arthur.* London (1893-94). Illustrated by Aubrey Beardsley. 12 parts printed wraps. One of 300 copies on Dutch handmade paper. $12,500. 3 vols. One of 300 copies. Pictorial cloth. $6,500. 2 vols. One of 1,500 copies. Cloth. $3,000. London. 1909. Cloth. Second Beardsley edition. $1,750. London, 1910–11. 4 vols. One of 500 copies. Riccardi Press. Illustrated in color by W. Russell Flint. Limp vellum or boards. In dustwrappers and slipcases. $2,500. Also, one of 12 copies on vellum in a Riviere binding. $15,000. London: Ashendene Press, 1913. One of 145 copies. $5,000. One of 8 copies on vellum. $60,000. London, 1917. Illustrated by Arthur Rackham. One of 500 copies signed by Rackham. Vellum. $3,000. New York, 1917. One of 250 copies. American Rackham edition. Full leather. In slipcase. $3,000. London or New York, 1917. Clothbound Rackham trade issues. $1,000. London, 1927. One of 1,600 copies. Illustrated by Beardsley. In dustwrapper. $3,000. One of 3 copies on vellum. $20,000. London, 1933. Shakespeare Head Press. 2 vols. One of 370 copies. Illustrated. Morocco. $2,000. Limited Editions Club, New York, 1936. 3 vols. Illustrated by Robert Gibbings. Boards. In slipcase. $450.

MALOUF, David. *Bicycle and Other Poems.* St. Lucia (1970). Author's first book. Wraps. $450.

MALOUF, David. *The Neighbors in the Thicket.* St. Lucia, 1974. $300.

MALRAUX, André. *The Conquerors.* London, 1929. Author's first book. (First English translation.) $300.

MALRAUX, André. *The Metamorphosis of the Gods.* Garden City, 1960. First American edition. One of 50 signed copies. Illustrated. Red morocco. In slipcase. $750. Trade edition. $125.

MALRAUX, André. *The Psychology of Art.* (New York, 1949–50.) 3 vols. Illustrated. Cloth. In dustwrapper and slipcase. $300.

MALRAUX, André. *The Voices of Silence.* Garden City, 1953. First American edition. Illustrated. Cloth. In dustwrapper and slipcase. $150. One of 160 signed copies. Full leather. In slipcase. $600.

MALTHUS, Thomas Robert. *Definitions in Political Economy . . .* London, 1827. $2,500.

MALTHUS, Thomas Robert. *An Essay on the Principle of Population . . .* [Note: see listing under the title for the anonymous first edition.] London, 1803. Second edition. $4,500. London, 1806. 2 vols. Third edition. $2,500. London, 1807. 2 vols. Fourth edition. $1,750. Washington City, 1809. 2 vols. First American edition. $1,750. (Some copies with George Town as place.)

MALTHUS, Thomas Robert. *Principles of Political Economy . . .* London, 1820. $4,000. Boston, 1821. First American edition. $2,000.

MALTZ, Albert. *Black Pit.* New York (1935). Author's first book. $150.

MAMET, David. *American Buffalo.* New York: Samuel French (1977). Author's first book. Wraps. $250. New York: Grove Press (1977). Wraps. $300. Cloth. $750. San Francisco: Arion Press, 1992. One of 400 signed copies. $650.

MAN, Henry. *Mr. Bentley, The Rural Philosopher.* London, 1775. Author's first book. $2,000.

MAN Without a Country (The). Boston, 1865. (By Edward Everett Hale.) 23 pages, terra-cotta wraps. First issue, without the publisher's printed yellow "Announcement" slip tipped in. $1,500. Second issue, with the "Announcement" slip tipped in. $1,250. New York, 1902. One of 80 signed copies. $600. Limited Editions Club, New York, 1936. In slipcase. $150.

MANDEL, Eli Fuseli. *Poems.* Toronto (1960). Author's first book. One of 250 copies. Wraps. $300.

MANDEVILLE, John. *The Voiage and Travaile.* New York, 1928. Illustrated by Valenti Angelo. One of 150 copies signed by Angelo. $1,750.

MANFRED, Frederick. *Lord Grizzly.* New York, 1954. $250.

MANGAM, William D. *The Clarks of Montana.* (New York: Silver Bow Press), 1939. Illustrated, including folding facsimile. Stiff brown wraps. $350. Second edition (rewritten and retitled *The Clarks: An American Phenomenon*). New York, 1941. Blue cloth. $300.

MANLY, William Lewis. *Death Valley in '49.* San Jose, 1894. 4 plates. $500.

MANN, E. B. *Blue-Eyed Kid.* New York, 1932. $250.

MANN, E. B. *Gamblin' Man.* New York, 1934. $200.

MANN, E. B. *The Man from Texas.* New York, 1931. Author's first book. $250.

MANN, Horace. *Lectures on Education.* Boston, 1845. Author's first book preceded by a number of pamphlets. $250.

MANN, Thomas. *The Beloved Returns.* New York, 1940. First American edition. One of 395 signed copies. In dustwrapper and slipcase. $850. Trade. $125.

MANN, Thomas. *The Black Swan.* New York, 1954. $125. Limited Editions Club, New York, 1990. One of 375. $1,250.

MANN, Thomas. *Buddenbrooks.* London, 1924. 2 vols. Author's first book. Translated by H. T. Lowe-Porter. First edition in English. $2,500. New York, 1924. 2 vols. $2,000.

MANN, Thomas. *Death in Venice and Other Stories.* New York, 1925. $1,000.

MANN, Thomas. *Doctor Faustus.* New York, 1948. First edition in English. $150.

MANN, Thomas. *The Magic Mountain.* London, 1927. 2 vols. $1,500. New York, 1927. 2 vols. One of 200 signed copies. Half vellum. $2,500. Trade. 2 vols. Tissue dustwrapper and slipcase. $1,250. Limited Editions Club, New York, 1962. Illustrated. Half cloth. In slipcase. $250.

MANN, Thomas. *Nocturnes.* New York, 1934. One of 1,000 signed copies. Lithographs by Lynd Ward. Pictorial cloth. In slipcase. $750.

MANN, Thomas. *Royal Highness.* New York, 1916. First English translation of author's first book. $300. New York, 1926. $300.

MANN, Thomas. *Sleep, Sweet Sleep.* (New York), 1934. One of 60 copies. Boards. In glassine dustwrapper. $250.

MANNING, Frederick. See *The Middle Parts of Fortune.*

MANSFIELD, Edward D. *Exposition of the Natural Position of Mackinaw City, and the Climate, Soil, and Commercial Elements of the Surrounding Country.* Cincinnati, 1857. 2 maps. 47 pages, printed wraps. $750.

MANSFIELD, Katherine. *The Aloe.* London, 1930. One of 750 copies. Buckram. $600. New York, 1930. First American edition. One of 975 copies. In dustwrapper and slipcase. $400.

MANSFIELD, Katherine. *Bliss and Other Stories.* London (1920). Brick-red cloth. With page 13 numbered 3. In white dustwrapper with author's portrait. $1,250. New York, 1921. First American edition. Cloth, paper label. In dustwrapper. $1,000.

MANSFIELD, Katherine. *The Doves' Nest and Other Stories.* London (1923). One of 25 copies. First issue, with verso of title page blank. Blue-gray cloth, blue spine lettering. $2,000. Second issue, with "First published June, 1923" on verso of title page. $750.

MANSFIELD, Katherine. *The Garden Party and Other Stories.* London (1922). One of 25 copies. With "sposition" for "position" in last line on page 103. Light-blue cloth, lettered in blue. In strawberry-colored dustwrapper with blue lettering. In dustwrapper. $2,500. Without dustwrapper. $750. Later binding state, orange (ocher) lettering. $1,500. New York, 1922. One of 50 copies "for booksellers." $750. Trade. $750. London: Verona Press, 1939 [1947]. One of 1,170. 16 color lithographs by Marie Laurencin. Decorated cloth. In dustwrapper and slipcase. $3,000. One of 30 copies. Full morocco. In slipcase. $7,500.

MANSFIELD, Katherine. *In a German Pension.* London (1911). Author's first book. Green cloth. In orange (ocher) dustwrapper. $5,000. Without dustwrapper. $2,000.

MANSFIELD, Katherine. *Prelude.* Hogarth Press. Richmond, England (1918). Blue pictorial wraps. With design on front cover by J. D. Fergusson. $1,750. Without design. $1,500. (Also noted with design on both covers sold for $2,000 at auction in 1990.)

MANSFIELD, Katherine. *Something Childish and Other Stories.* London (1924). First issue, without "First published 1924" on verso of title page. Gray buckram. $1,500. Second issue. $600.

MANSFIELD Park: A Novel. London, 1814. By the Author of *Sense and Sensibility and Pride and Prejudice* (Jane Austen.) 3 vols. First edition, with vols. I and III bearing Sidney imprint on back of half titles (Schwartz) and vol. II the Roworth imprint. $15,000. Keynes has the reverse (I and III by Roworth and II by Sidney). But at least they both agree that Sidney wasn't involved in the Second edition. London, 1816. 3 vols. $5,000.

MANTAGUE, William K. *Golf of Our Fathers.* Duluth, MN, 1952. Limited edition (no limitation cited). $250.

MANUAL of Military Surgery. Prepared for the Use of the Confederate States Army . . . Richmond, 1861. (By John J. Chisholm.) 30 lithographic plates. $6,000. Richmond, 1862. $4,500. Richmond, 1863. Wraps. $3,500.

MARCH, William. *Company K.* New York, 1933. Author's first book. Issued in clear dustwrapper with printed paper flaps. $450.

MARCH of the First (The). (First Regiment of Colorado Volunteers.) Denver, 1863. 36 pages, stitched, plus 4 pages of ads. $4,000 or more. (See Hollister, Ovando J.)

MARCLIFFE, Theophilus. *The Looking Glass: A True History of the Early Years of an Artist.* London, 1805. (By William Godwin.) $750.

MARCY, Randolph B. *Exploration of the Red River of Louisiana . . .* (Senate Exec. Doc. 54.) Washington, 1853. 2 vols. 65 plates. 2 maps. Brown cloth and green cloth (atlas case). $750. Washington, 1854. Second edition, printed by Tucker. $600. Washington, 1854. House version, printed by Nicholson. $600.

MARCY, Randolph B. *The Prairie Traveler: A Hand-Book for Overland Expeditions.* New York, 1859. Map, frontispiece. 30 plates. $1,250.

MARDERSTEIG, Hans. *Pastonchi: A Specimen of a New Letter for Use on the "Monotype."* (London, 1928.) One of 200 copies on Fabriano paper, printed by Mardersteig. Illustrated with plates and booklet inserts. Marbled boards and vellum. $450. Trade edition. $125.

MARGARET Percival In America. Boston, 1850. (By Edward Everett Hale.) His first book. $200.

MARK Twain's Sketches. See Twain, Mark.

MARKET Harborough; or, How Mr. Sawyer Went to the Shires. London, 1861. (By George John Whyte-Melville.) $450.

MARKHAM, Albert Hastings. *The Great Frozen Sea . . .* London, 1878. $600.

MARKHAM, Beryl. *West with the Night.* Boston, 1942. Author's first book. $750. London (1943). $450.

MARKHAM, Edwin. *The Man with the Hoe*. San Francisco, 1899. First book edition. 4 pages, printed wraps. $250. (Earlier, Jan. 15, 1899, as special supplement to San Francisco *Sunday Examiner*, containing first separate printing of the poem. $400.) New York: Doubleday, 1899. Second edition, first issue, with "fruitless" for "milkless" in line 5, page 35. Green cloth. $125. New York: Doxey's (1899). $100.

MARKHAM, Edwin. *New Poems: Eighty Songs at Eighty*. Garden City, 1932. One of 100 signed copies. Portrait. Boards and leather. In slipcase. $250. Trade edition. $75.

MARLOWE, Christopher. *Edward the Second*. London: Aquila Press, 1929. One of 40 copies. Hand-colored illustrations. Folio, vellum. $500. One of 500 copies. $250.

MARQUAND, John P. See Clark, Charles E.

MARQUAND, John P. *Last Laugh, Mr. Moto*. Boston, 1942. $750.

MARQUAND, John P. *The Late George Apley*. Boston, 1937. First issue, with "Pretty Pearl" in first line of page 19. $1,250.

MARQUAND, John P. *Ming Yellow*. Boston, 1935. $2,000.

MARQUAND, John P. *Mr. Moto Is So Sorry*. Boston, 1941. $1,000.

MARQUAND, John P. *No Hero*. Boston, 1935. $2,000.

MARQUAND, John P. *Thank You, Mr. Moto*. Boston, 1936. $1,250.

MARQUAND, John P. *The Unspeakable Gentleman*. New York, 1922. Author's first novel. Scribner seal on copyright page. $350. Limited, signed, for booksellers. Boards and cloth with ABA label on front. Issued without dustwrapper. $175.

MÁRQUEZ, Gabriel García. See García Márquez, Gabriel.

MARQUIS, Don. *Archy and Mehitabel*. Garden City, 1927. $300.

MARQUIS, Don. *Danny's Own Story*. Garden City, 1912. Author's first book. Illustrated by E. W. Kemble. Green cloth. $75.

MARQUIS, Don. *How Hank Signed the Pledge in a Cistern*. New York (about 1912). Wraps. $250.

MARQUIS, Thomas B. *A Warrior Who Fought Custer*. Minneapolis, 1931. First binding, with "Midwest" on spine. $400. With "Caxton." $300.

MARRA, John (Captain James Cook). *Journal of the Resolution's Voyage in 1772, 1773, 1774, and 1775*. London, 1775. Folding engraved map and five engraved plates. $7,500. Dublin, 1776. $3,500.

MARRIAGE: A Novel. Edinburgh, 1818. 3 vols. (By Susan Edmonstone Ferrier, her first book.) $450.

MARROT, H. V. *William Bulmer—Thomas Bensley: A Study in Transition*. London, 1930. One of 300 copies. $250. One of 25 copies. $500.

MARRYAT, Frank. *Mountains and Molehills* . . . London, 1855. (By Francis S. Marryat.) 18 woodcuts, 8 color plates. Salmon-colored cloth. $1,250. New York, 1855. Frontispiece. Pictorial cloth. $1,000.

MARRYAT, (Frederick) Captain, R. N. *The Phantom Ship.* London, 1839. 3 vols. $500.

MARRYAT, Frederick. See *Mr. Midshipman Easy; Olla Podrida; Percival Keene; Snarleyyow.*

MARRYAT, Frederick. *A Code of Signals for Use of Vessels* . . . London, 1818. Author's first book. $350.

MARRYAT, Frederick. *A Diary of America* . . . London, 1839. 6 vols. (Parts I and II, each 3 vols.), in original boards. $850. Philadelphia, 1839–40. 3 vols. First American edition. In original half cloth (2 vols., 1839, and 2d series, 1 vol., 1840). $500.

MARRYAT, Frederick. *Masterman Ready.* London, 1841–42–43. 3 vols. Illustrated. Cloth. $600.

MARRYAT, Frederick. *The Mission.* London, 1845. 2 vols. First edition, with 32 pages of ads in vol. 1. Map, frontispiece. Cloth. $500.

MARRYAT, Frederick. *Narrative of the Travels and Adventures of Monsieur Violet, in California, Sonora and Western Texas.* London, 1843. 3 vols. Map. $1,250. Second edition. London, 1843. 3 vols. With map. Retitled: *The Travels and Romantic Adventures of Monsieur Violet, etc.* Cloth. $1,000.

MARSH, James B. *Four Years in the Rockies.* New Castle, Pa., 1884. Portrait. Red pictorial cloth. $1,000.

MARSH, Ngaio. *A Man Lay Dead.* London, 1934. Author's first book. $2,000.

MARSH, Ngaio. *The Nursing Home Murder.* London, 1935. $1,250.

MARSH, Richard. *The Beetle.* London, 1897. $1,000.

MARSH, W. Lockwood. *Aeronautical Prints and Drawings.* London, 1924. One of 1,000 copies. Illustrated, including color plates. In dustwrapper. $600. Pigskin. One of 100 copies. $1,000.

MARSHALL, Alfred. *Principles of Economics* . . . London, 1890. Vol. I (all published). In original cloth. $3,500.

MARSHALL, George. *Marshall's Practical Marine Gunnery.* Norfolk, 1822. Folding table. $2,000.

MARSHALL, Humphrey. *Arbustrum Americanum.* Philadelphia, 1785. $3,000.

MARSHALL, Humphrey. *The History of Kentucky.* Frankfort, 1812. $1,500. Frankfort, 1824. 2 vols. Second edition. $1,000.

MARSHALL, John. *The Life of George Washington* . . . Philadelphia, 1804–07. 5 volumes plus atlas containing 10 maps. $2,000. Without atlas. $1,500.

MARSHALL, John. *Opinion of the Supreme Court, etc. in the Case of Samuel Worcester Versus the State of Georgia.* Washington, 1832. 39 pages. $250. Second edition, same date. 20 pages. $125.

MARSHALL, L. G. *The Arabian Art of Taming and Training Wild and Vicious Horses.* (Circleville, Ohio), 1857. 36 pages, wraps. $450.

MARSHALL, Paule. *Brown Girl, Brownstones.* New York, 1959. Author's first book. $750. London, 1960. $300.

MARSHALL, Paule. *Soul Clap Hands and Sing.* New York, 1961. $300. London, 1962. $125.

MARSHALL, William I. *Acquisition of Oregon, and the Long Suppressed Evidence About Marcus Whitman.* (Seattle), 1911. 2 vols. Portrait. Green cloth. $350.

MARSTON, Philip. *Song-Tide* . . . London, 1871. Author's first book. $250.

MARTIAL Achievements of Great Britain and Her Allies from 1799 to 1815 (The). London (1814–15). 53 colored plates (including frontis and dedication). $6,000. London (about 1835). $4,500.

MARTIN, Aaron. *An Attempt to Show the Inconsistency of Slave-Holding, with the Religion of the Gospel.* Lexington, Ky., 1807. 16 pages. $2,500.

MARTIN, H. B. *Fifty Years of American Golf.* New York, 1936. Signed limited edition. $1,750. Trade. $450.

MARTIN, H. B. *Garden City Golf Club 1899–1949.* Garden City, 1949. Limited to 600 copies. $450.

MARTIN, H. B., and HALLIDAY, A. B. *St. Andrews* [New York] *Golf Club 1888–1938.* Hastings on Hudson, 1938. One of 500 copies. $600.

MARTIN Faber, the Story of a Criminal. New York, 1838. 2 vols. (By William Gilmore Simms.) $600.

MARTIN, J. Wallis. *A Likeness in Stone.* (London, 1977.) $500.

MARTIN, John Stuart. *The Curious History of the Golf Ball.* New York, 1968. One of 500 copies. $600. Trade. $250.

MARTIN, Thomas. *The Circle of the Mechanical Arts* . . . London, 1813. $1,500.

MARTINEAU, Harriet. *The English Lakes.* Windermere, 1858. With folding map and plates. $750.

MARTINEAU, Harriet. *Retrospect of Western Travel.* London, 1838. 3 vols. Cloth. $450. New York, 1838. 2 vols. $350.

MARTINEAU, Harriet. *Society in America.* London, 1837. 3 vols. $600. New York, 1837. 2 vols. $400.

MARTYR, Peter. *The Decades of the Newe Worlde* . . . London, 1555. First edition in English. Third issue. $42,000 at auction in 1991.

MARTYR, Peter. *The History of Travayle in the West and East Indies* . . . London, 1577. Expanded version of the foregoing. $35,000.

MARVEL, Ik. *Fresh Gleanings.* New York, 1847. (By Donald G. Mitchell.) 2 vols., printed wraps. $150. 1 vol. Cloth. $75.

MARVELL, Andrew. *Miscellaneous Poems.* London, 1681. $3,500.

MARVIN, Frederic R. *Yukon Overland: The Gold-Digger's Handbook.* Cincinnati, 1898. Folding map, 18 plates. Printed orange wraps. $450.

MARX, Groucho. *Beds.* New York, 1930. With publisher's colophon on copyright page. $750.

MARX, Karl. *Capital.* New York: Humboldt Publishing Co. (1886). First edition in English. $5,000. London, 1887. 2 vols., red (maroon) cloth. $5,000. 1 vol. $2,500. New York, 1889. Mustard yellow cloth. $1,250. (Note: auction records have always given priority to the Humboldt. The U.S. and U.K. translations are the same.) Chicago, 1906. 3 vols. First complete edition. $1,250.

MARY BARTON; A Tale of Manchester Life. London, 1848. (By Elizabeth C. Gaskell.) 2 vols., mulberry cloth. Author's first book. $6,000.

MASEFIELD, John. *Ballads.* London, 1903. Printed wraps. No. 13 of "The Vigo Cabinet Series." $300.

MASEFIELD, John. *John M. Synge: A Few Personal Recollections.* Cuala Press. Dundrum, Ireland, 1915. One of 350 copies. Boards and linen. $250. New York, 1915. One of 500 (of 650) copies. $150.

MASEFIELD, John. *Salt Water Ballads.* London, 1902. Author's first book. Blue buckram. First issue, with Grant Richards imprint on title page. $600. Second issue with "Elkin Mathews" (much less common). $350.

MASEFIELD, John. *Some Memories of W. B. Yeats.* Cuala Press. Dublin, 1940. One of 370 copies. Boards and linen. In tissue dustwrapper. $250.

MASON, Bobbie Ann. *The Girl Sleuth.* (Old Westbury), 1975. Wraps. $200.

MASON, Bobbie Ann. *Nabokov's Garden.* Ann Arbor (1974). Author's first book (precedes *The Girl Sleuth*). Cloth. $250. Wraps. $75.

MASON, George Henry. *The Costume of China.* London (1800). Folio with 60 hand-colored plates. $3,000. London (1804). $2,500. London, 1806. $2,000. (Actual dates of publication can be found on watermarks on plates.)

MASON, John. *More Papers Hand Made by John Mason.* Leicester, 1967. Numbered and signed. $750.

MASON, Otis T. *Aboriginal American Basketry . . .* Washington, 1902. 2 vols. 248 plates, $400. Washington, 1904. 3 vols. $400.

MASON, Otis T. *Indian Basketry.* New York, 1904. 2 vols. Illustrated, including color plates. Pictorial buckram. $1,000.

MASON, Richard. *The Gentleman's New Pocket Companion . . .* Petersburg, 1811. Frontis and 4 plates. $4,500. Richmond, 1828. $3,000.

MASON, Richard Lee. *Narrative of Richard Lee Mason in the Pioneer West.* New York (1915). One of 160 copies. Half leather. $100. One of 10 copies on vellum. $200.

MASON, Van Wyck. See Coff, Geoffrey.

MASON, Van Wyck. *Seeds of Murder.* New York, 1930. Author's first book. $500.

MASON, Van Wyck. *The Vesper Service Murders.* New York, 1931. $500.

MASON, Z. H. *A General Description of Orange County, Florida.* Orlando (1881). Map. 56 pages, wraps. $500.

MASQUE of Poets (A). Boston, 1878. Black or red cloth. In "No Name Series" with Emily Dickinson's poem "Success," her only book appearance in her lifetime. $1,250.

MASSEY, T. Gerald. *Voice of Freedom and Lyrics of Love.* London, 1851. Author's first book. $250.

MASSEY, W. *The Origin and Progress of Letters.* London, 1763. Five foldout plates in first section and one foldout plate at the end of the second section. $500.

MASSIE, James William. *America: The Origin of Her Present Conflict . . . During a Tour in the Summer of 1863 . . .* London, 1864. Large hand-colored folding map in rear pocket. $600.

MASSON, L.F.R. *Les Bourgeois de la Compagnie du Nord-Ouest.* Quebec, 1889–90. 2 vols. Folding map. Green-and-orange wraps. $1,000. New York, 1960. 2 vols. $150.

MASTERS, Edgar Lee. See Ford, Webster.

MASTERS, Edgar Lee. *A Book of Verses.* Chicago, 1898. Author's first book. Gray boards. $1,000.

MASTERS, Edgar Lee. *Gettysburg, Manila, Acoma.* New York, 1930. One of 375 signed copies. In acetate and slipcase. $400.

MASTERS, Edgar Lee. *Lee: A Dramatic Poem.* New York, 1926. One of 250 signed copies. Issued without dustwrapper. $200. Trade edition in dustwrapper. $75.

MASTERS, Edgar Lee. *Lincoln: The Man.* New York, 1931. One of 150 signed copies. Illustrated. Half vellum and cloth. In glassine dustwrapper. $350.

MASTERS, Edgar Lee. *Spoon River Anthology.* New York, 1915. Blue cloth. First issue, book measuring exactly ⅞ inch across top. $750. Limited Editions Club, New York, 1942. Illustrated. Buckram. In slipcase. $250.

MASTERS, John. *The Compleat Indian Angler.* London, 1938. Author's first book. $450.

MATHER, Cotton. *The Christian Philosopher . . .* London, 1721. $3,000.

MATHER, Cotton. *Marginalia Christi Americana . . .* London, 1702. Folio. Engraved folding map. $7,500.

MATHER, Cotton. *Psalterium Americanum.* Boston, 1718. Woodcut headpieces and initial ornaments. $3,000.

MATHER, E. Powys. *Procreant Hymn.* Golden Cockerel Press. Waltham St. Lawrence, England, 1916. One of 175 copies. Engravings by Eric Gill. Buckram. $1,500.

MATHER, Increase. *A Disquisition Concerning Ecclesiastical Councils* . . . Boston, 1716. $4,000.

MATHER, Increase. *The Mystery of Israel's Salvation.* (London), 1669. Author's first book. $7,500.

MATHER, Samuel. *The Life of the Very Reverend and Learned Cotton Mather* . . . Boston, 1729. $650.

MATHERS, John, and A Solid Gentleman. *The History of Mr. John Decastro* . . . London, 1815. (By George Colman, the Younger.) 4 vols. $450.

MATHESON, Richard. *Born of Man and Woman.* Philadelphia, 1954. Author's first hardback book. $500.

MATHESON, Richard. *Hell House.* New York (1971). $300.

MATHESON, Richard. *I Am Legend.* New York, 1970. $450.

MATHESON, Richard. *The Shrinking Man.* London, 1973. $500.

MATHESON, Richard. *Someone Is Bleeding.* New York (1953). Author's first book. Pictorial wrappers. $250.

MATHESON, Richard. *A Stir of Echoes.* Philadelphia (1958). $300.

MATHEWS, A. E. *Canyon City, Colorado, and Its Surroundings.* New York, 1870. Map. 5 plates. $5,000.

MATHEWS, A. E. *Pencil Sketches of Colorado.* (New York), 1866. 23 plates in color. $45,000. Facsimile reprint. (Denver, 1961.) Oblong folio, cloth. $400.

MATHEWS, A. E. *Pencil Sketches of Montana.* New York, 1868. 31 plates (4 folding). $17,500.

MATHEWS, Alfred E. *Gems of Rocky Mountain Scenery.* New York, 1869. 20 plates. $5,000.

MATHEWS, Alfred E. *Interesting Narrative; Being a Journal of the Flight of Alfred E. Mathews, of Stark Co., Ohio, from the State of Texas, etc.* (New Philadelphia, Ohio), 1861. 34 pages, sewn. $17,500.

MATHEWS, Edward J. *Crossing the Plains . . . in '59.* No-place, 1930. Issued without dust-wrapper. $600.

MATHEWS, J. Howard. *Firearms Identification.* Madison, WI, 1962. 2 vols. $750.

MATHEWS, Mrs. M. M. *Ten Years in Nevada.* Buffalo, N.Y., 1880. Illustrated. Leather, or cloth. $600.

MATHISON, Thomas. *The Goff: A Heroi-Comical Poem in Three Cantos.* Edinburgh, 1743. $24,000 at auction in 1986. London, 1763. £10,000 at auction in 1984. Edinburgh, 1793. $70,000 at auction in 1998.

MATISSE, Henri. *Jazz.* (Paris, 1947.) Facsimile text and cover from artist's handwritten original, 270 copies of which 20 were hors de commerce. 20 color plates. Signed in pencil below colophon. $268,000 at auction in 1999 in original wraps. Also $125,000 that year with wraps bound in. New York, 1983. Folio, in dustwrapper and slipcase. $500.

MATSELL, George W. *Vocabulum; or, the Rogue's Lexicon.* New York (1857). Cloth. $350.

MATSON, N. *French and Indians of the Illinois River.* Princeton, Ill., 1874. Frontispiece (an original signed photograph). Green cloth. $450.

MATSON, N. *Memories of Shaubena.* Chicago, 1878. Illustrated. $350.

MATTHEWS, John A. *A Voyage to the River Sierra-Leone, on the Coast of Africa . . .* London, 1788. Folding chart and folding view. $2,750.

MATTHEWS, Sallie Reynolds. *Interwoven: a Pioneer Chronicle . . .* Houston, 1936. Portrait. Orange suede. First binding. $750. El Paso, 1958. One of 1,500 copies. $300.

MATTHEWS, William. *Modern Bookbinding Practically Considered . . .* New York, 1889. 8 full-page plates. One of 300 copies. $300.

MATTHIESSEN, Peter. *At Play in the Fields of the Lord.* New York (1965). $450.

MATTHIESSEN, Peter. *In the Spirit of Crazy Horse.* New York (1983). (This book was recalled by the publisher.) $200.

MATTHIESSEN, Peter. *Men's Lives.* No place, (1986). 2 vols. One of 500 signed copies. In full-cloth clamshell box stamped in silver. $1,000. 2 vols. Unnumbered and unsigned, issued in slipcase. $450.

MATTHIESSEN, Peter. *Race Rock.* New York (1954). Author's first book. $600. London, 1954. $200.

MATTHIESSEN, Peter. *Seal Pool.* Garden City, 1972. $350.

MATTHIESSEN, Peter. *The Shorebirds of North America.* New York, (1967). 2 vols. One of 350 signed copies. In slipcase. $1,250. Trade (one volume). $350.

MATTHIESSEN, Peter. *Wildlife in America.* New York, 1959. $200.

MATURIN, Charles Robert. See *Melmoth the Wanderer.*

MATURIN, Charles Robert. *Women; Or, Pour et Contre: A Tale.* Edinburgh, 1818. 3 vols. $750.

MAUGHAM, Robin. *The 1946 Ms.* London, 1943. Author's first book. $150.

MAUGHAM, W. Somerset. *Ah King: Six Stories.* London (1933). Blue cloth. $200. One of 175 signed copies. Buckram. In slipcase. $500. Garden City, 1933. $150.

MAUGHAM, W. Somerset. *Ashenden, or The British Agent.* London, 1928. Blue-gray cloth. $4,500. Garden City, 1928. $1,500.

MAUGHAM, W. Somerset. *Cakes and Ale.* London (1930). Blue cloth. Presumed first state with "won" instead of "won't" in line 14 of page 147. $500. Second issue, corrected. $400. Garden City, 1930. $200. London (1954). One of 1,000 signed copies. Decorations by Graham Sutherland. Boards and leather. In slipcase. $600.

MAUGHAM, W. S. *The Casuarina Tree.* London, 1926. $2,000.

MAUGHAM, W. Somerset. *The Explorer.* London, 1908 ("Copyright 1907"). $600. New York, 1909. $400.

MAUGHAM, W. Somerset. *The Gentleman in the Parlour.* London (1930). Black cloth. $400. New York, 1930. $250.

MAUGHAM, W. Somerset. *The Hero.* London, 1901. With evil eye symbol on front cover upside down. $1,000. Printed correctly. $600.

MAUGHAM, W. Somerset. *The Land of the Blessed Virgin.* London, 1905. Blue boards and parchment spine, with "The Land" 3.3cm. $600.

MAUGHAM, W. Somerset. *Liza of Lambeth.* London, 1897. Author's first book. With brackets around "All Rights Reserved" on copyright page. Decorated green cloth. $3,000. Without brackets. $2,000. London, 1947. Jubilee edition. One of 1,000 signed copies. Vellum and boards. In dustwrapper. $750.

MAUGHAM, W. Somerset. *The Magician.* London, 1908. Blue cloth. $450. New York, 1909. $350.

MAUGHAM, W. Somerset. *The Making of a Saint.* Boston, 1898. First issue, with "In Press" under this title in ads and in pictorial cloth with spine lettering in gold. $500. Second issue without "In Press" and spine in gold and black or black only. $300.

MAUGHAM, W. Somerset. *A Man of Honour.* London, 1903. Printed wraps. Chapman & Hall. $750. (London: Fortnightly Review, 1903.) Issued as supplement. $600.

MAUGHAM, W. Somerset. *Mrs. Craddock.* London, 1902. $600. New York (1920). Dustwrapper priced "$1.90." $500. Dustwrapper priced "$2.00." $400.

MAUGHAM, W. Somerset. *The Moon and Sixpence.* London (1919). No statement of edition, first issue, with 4 pages of ads, including a list of 6 (not 7) novels by Eden Phillpotts. Sagegreen cloth. In dustwrapper. $3,000. Without dustwrapper. $600. New York (1919). Green cloth with "Maughan" on cover. In dustwrapper. $2,000. Without dustwrapper. $400. Second has "Maugham." Also brown cloth with both spelling variants. All somewhat less.

MAUGHAM, W. Somerset. *My South Sea Island.* Chicago, 1936. Wraps. First issue, with "Sommerset" on title page. $1,250. Second issue, error corrected. $1,000. (50 copies in total.)

MAUGHAM, W. Somerset. *Of Human Bondage.* Doran, New York (1915). Green cloth. First issue, without Doran monogram on copyright page, weighing 33½ ounces and misprint in line 4 of page 257. $1,500. Second issue corrects page 257 and weighs 30 ounces. $600. London (1915). Blue cloth. First English edition. $2,000. Garden City, 1936. Illustrated by Schwabs. Buckram. First illustrated edition. One of 751 signed copies. In dustwrapper and slipcase. $1,000. Limited Editions Club, New York, 1938. Edited by Theodore Dreiser. Illustrated by John Sloan. 2 vols. In slipcase. $750.

MAUGHAM, W. Somerset. *Of Human Bondage; With a Digression on the Art of Fiction.* (Washington), 1946. One of 500 signed copies. Printed boards. Issued without dustwrapper. $400. One of 300 unsigned copies. Wraps. $125.

MAUGHAM, W. Somerset. *The Painted Veil.* New York (1925). $1,000. Boards. One of 250 signed copies. In dustwrapper. $2,000. London (1925). Blue cloth. First English edition, first issue, 8 books listed on verso of half title. $1,500. With 26 titles listed on verso of half title. $1,000.

MAUGHAM, W. Somerset. *The Razor's Edge*. Garden City, 1944. One of 750 signed copies. Buckram. Issued without dustwrapper. In slipcase. $1,500. Trade edition. $1,000. London (1944). $1,250.

MAUGHAM, W. Somerset. *The Summing Up*. London (1938). $300. Garden City, 1938. $150. New York, 1954. One of 391 signed copies. Buckram. In slipcase. $450.

MAUGHAM, W. Somerset. *A Writer's Notebook*. London (1949). One of 1,000 signed copies. Blue buckram, vellum spine. In slipcase. $650. Trade edition. In first issue dustwrapper not listing "Maughamiana" on back flap. $125. Garden City, 1949. One of 1,000 signed copies. In slipcase. $600. Trade. $75.

MAULDIN, Bill. *Mud, Mules and Mountains*. (Italy), 1944. Introduction by Ernie Pyle. 48 pages, wraps. $150.

MAULDIN, William Henry (Bill). *Star Spangled Banter*. San Antonio, 1941. The cartoonist's first book. Pictorial wraps. $200.

MAUND, Benjamin. *The Botanic Garden*. 1825 (–1850). Vols. I–XIII plus supplements. 312 hand-colored plates. $12,000.

MAURELLE, Don Antonio. *Abstract of a Narrative of an Interesting Voyage from Manilla to San Blas* . . . Boston, 1801. $750.

MAUROIS, Andre. *Ariel: A Shelley Romance*. (London) 1935. Penguin Books. Wraps. First edition of the first Penguin paperback. In dustwrapper. $250.

MAUROIS, André. *The Silence of Colonel Bramble*. London, 1919. Author's first English publication. In dustwrapper. $250. New York, 1920. $200.

MAURY, M. F. *The Physical Geography of the Sea*. New York, 1855. 8 folding plates. $600.

MAVOR, William. *The English Spelling-Book*. London, 1885. Illustrated by Kate Greenaway. Pictorial boards. First Greenaway edition. $250.

MAW, George. *A Monograph of the Genus Crocus* . . . London, 1886. Cloth, with a colored double-page map, 2 double-page tables, and 81 hand-colored plates. $6,000.

MAW, Henry Lister. *Journal of a Passage from the Pacific to the Atlantic* . . . London, 1829. Folding map. $750.

MAWE, John. *Travels in the Interior of Brazil*. London, 1812. Map, 8 plates. $2,500. Philadelphia, 1816. Illustrated. $2,000. London, 1821. Map, 5 color plates. Second edition. $1,250.

MAWSON, Sir Douglas. *The Home of the Blizzard*. London [1915]. 2 vols. 2 photo frontises, 3 folding maps, 18 color and 202 black-and-white plates, 14 text maps, and 23 text illustrations. $2,000.

MAXIM, Sir Hiram. *Artificial and Natural Flight*. New York and London, 1908. 95 photo illustrations and diagrams. $400.

MAXIMILIAN, Prince of Wied. *Travels in Brazil* . . . London, 1820. First English edition. Portrait, folding map, and 9 plates. $2,500.

MAXIMILIAN, Prince of Wied. *Travels in the Interior of North America*. London, 1843–44. 2 vols. (text plus atlas folio volume). Translated by H. E. Lloyd. Folding map, 81 colored vignettes and plates. $195,000 at auction in 1988.

MAXWELL, James Clerk. *An Elementary Treatise on Electricity and Magnetism*. Oxford, 1873. 20 plates. $6,000. Oxford, 1881. Second edition. $600.

MAXWELL, William. *Bright Center of Heaven*. New York, 1934. Author's first book. $1,250. Toronto, 1934. $500. London, 1937. $450.

MAXWELL, William. *They Came Like Swallows*. New York, 1937. First edition stated. "1186" bottom back panel of dustwrapper. $750. Toronto, 1937. $350. London, 1937. $350.

MAXWELL, William Henry. *Life and Times of the Right Honourable William Henry Smith, M.P.* . . . Edinburgh/London, 1893. 2 vols. 25 illustrations. $250.

MAY, Robert L. *Rudolph the Red-Nosed Reindeer*. (Chicago) 1939. One of 200 copies. Illustrated in color by Denver Gillen. In pictorial boards. $1,500. Pictorial orange wraps. (Christmas giveaway for Montgomery Ward.) $400.

MAYDMAN, Henry. *Naval Speculations, and Maritime Politicks* . . . London, 1691. $1,250.

MAYER, Alfred M. (editor). *Sport with Gun and Rod* . . . *in American Woods and Waters*. Edinburgh, 1884. 2 vols. Illustrated. Half leather. $500.

MAYER, Luigi. *Views in the Ottoman Dominions* . . . London, 1810. 71 colored plates. 2 or 3 vols., folio. $7,500.

MAYHEW, Augustus. *Paved with Gold, or The Romance and Reality of London Streets*. London (1857–58). Illustrated by Hablot K. Browne. 13 parts, wraps. $750. London, 1858. First book edition. Frontis, engraved title, and 25 plates. Cloth. $250.

MAYHEW, Experience. *Indian Narratives*. Boston (1829). First American edition. Frontispiece. Half leather and boards. $1250.

MAYHEW, Henry. *London Labour and the London Poor with Those That Will Not Work*. London, 1861–62. 4 vols. $2,500.

MAYNARD, Charles J. *An Atlas of Plates from the Directory to the Birds of Eastern North America*. West Newton, Mass., 1906–[10]. 10 parts in wraps. $7,500.

MAYNARD, Charles J. *The Butterflies of New England*. Boston, 1886. 10 hand-colored lithographs. $350.

MAYO, Robert. *Political Sketches of Eight Years in Washington*. Baltimore, 1839. Part I (all published). Cloth. $350.

McADAM, R. W. *Chickasaws and Choctaws*. Comprising the Treaties of 1855 and 1866. Ardmore, Okla., 1891. 67 pages, wraps. $500.

McAFEE, Robert B. See *History of the Late War in the Western Country*.

M'CALL, Captain Hugh. *The History of Georgia* . . . Savannah, 1811–16. 2 vols. $2,000.

McALMON, Robert. *Being Geniuses Together.* London (1938). Blue cloth. First edition not stated. $3,000.

McALMON, Robert. *A Companion Volume.* Contact Editions. (Paris, 1923.) Gray wraps. $600.

McALMON, Robert. *Distinguished Air (Grim Fairy Tales).* Contact Editions. Paris, 1925. One of 100 copies on Arches paper. Half leather. $1,000. One of 12 copies on vellum. $4,500.

McALMON, Robert. *Explorations.* Egoist Press. London, 1921. Author's first book. Issued without dustwrapper. $750.

McALMON, Robert. *A Hasty Bunch.* Contact Editions. (Paris, 1923.) Wraps. $750.

McALMON, Robert. *Not Alone Lost.* New Directions. Norfolk, Conn. (1937). $500.

McALMON, Robert. *Post-Adolescence.* Contact Editions. (Paris, 1923.) Wraps. First edition not stated. In glassine dustwrapper. $750.

McALMON, Robert. *The Portrait of a Generation.* Contact Editions. Paris (1926). One of 200 copies. Stiff wraps. $1,500. Vellum. One of 10 signed copies. $4,500.

McCAFFREY, Anne. *Restoree.* New York (1967). Author's first book. "First Printing: September 1967." Wraps. $60. London (1968). First hardcover. $750.

McCAIN, Charles W. *History of the S.S. "Beaver."* Vancouver, 1894. Illustrated. Blue cloth. $300.

McCALL, Ansel J. *Pick and Pan: Trip to the Diggins in 1849.* Bath, N.Y., 1889. Printed wraps. $1,000.

McCALL, Captain Hugh. *The History of Georgia* . . . Savannah, 1811–1816. 2 vols. $2,000.

McCALL, George A. *Letters from the Frontiers.* Philadelphia, 1868. $750.

McCALLA, William L. *Adventures in Texas.* Philadelphia, 1841. Black cloth. $3,000.

McCAMMON, Robert R. *Baal.* New York (1978). Author's first book. Wraps. $75. New York, 1979. $500. Bath, 1985. $400.

McCAMMON, Robert R. *Swan Song.* Arlington Heights, 1989. $100. Illinois, 1989. One of 52 signed copies. Slipcase. $650. One of 650 copies. $250.

McCARTER, Margaret H. *Price of the Prairie.* Chicago, 1910. $125.

McCARTER, Margaret H. *Winning the Wilderness.* New York, 1914. $100.

McCARTHY, Cormac. *All the Pretty Horses.* New York, 1992. $300.

McCARTHY, Cormac. *Orchard Keeper.* New York (1965). Author's first book. $3,500.

McCARTHY, Cormac. *Outer Dark.* New York (1968). $1,500.

McCARTHY, Cormac. *Suttree.* New York (1979). $1,500.

McCARTHY, Mary. See Kaltenborn, H. V.

McCARTHY, Mary. *The Company She Keeps.* (New York), 1942. Author's first book under her own name. $125.

McCARTHY, Mary. *The Group.* New York (1963). $100.

McCAULEY, J. E. *A Stove-Up Cowboy's Story.* Dallas, 1943. One of 700 copies. $350.

McCLELLAN, Henry B. *The Life and Campaigns of Maj. Gen. J.E.B. Stuart.* Boston, 1885. Portrait and 7 folding maps. $500.

McCLELLAND, Nancy. *Duncan Phyfe . . .* New York (1939). One of 350 signed copies. In slipcase. $600. One of 1,000 copies. $350.

McCLELLAND, Nancy. *Historic Wallpapers . . .* Philadelphia, 1924. One of 350 copies. Illustrated, including color plates. Half cloth. $750. Trade edition. $450.

McCLINTOCK, John S. *Pioneer Days in the Black Hills.* Deadwood (1939). Edited by Edward Senn. Illustrated. Cloth. Issued without dustwrapper. $250.

McCLINTOCK, Walter. *Old Indian Trails.* Boston, 1923. 28 plates, including 4 in color. Pictorial cloth. $150.

McCLINTOCK, Walter. *The Old North Trail.* London, 1910. Folding map, 9 color plates. $200.

McCLURE, James. *The Steam Pig.* London, 1971. Author's first book. $300. New York (1971). $100.

McCLURE, Michael. *The Cherub.* Black Sparrow Press. Los Angeles, 1970. One of 26 signed copies, with a drawing by the author. $250. Boards. One of 250 signed copies. $75.

McCLURE, Michael. *Hail Thee Who Play.* Black Sparrow Press. Los Angeles, 1968. One of 75 signed, with a drawing by the author. Printed yellow boards and cloth. $200. One of 250 signed copies. Printed wraps. $75.

McCLURE, Michael. *Passage.* Big Sur, Calif., 1956. Author's first book. Jargon 20. One of 200 copies. Stiff wraps. $600.

McCLURE, Michael. *The Sermons of Jean Harlow & The Curses of Billy the Kid.* San Francisco, 1968. Wraps. $40. Later, boards. One of 50 signed copies. $200.

McCLURE, S. S. *My Autobiography.* New York (1914). (Ghostwritten by Willa Cather.) First issue, with "Sept, 1914" on copyright page and an extraneous line 13 on page 239. "H.H. Rogers . . ." $750. Second issue corrects page 239 with cancel page. $350. (Second printing had "May 1914" on copyright page.) London, 1914. $50.

McCOLLUM, William. *California As I Saw It.* Buffalo, 1850. 72 pages, wraps. $7,500. Los Gatos, 1960. One of 750 copies. $75.

McCONKEY, Mrs. Harriet E. (Bishop). *Dakota War Whoop; or, Indian Massacres and War in Minnesota.* St. Paul, 1863. 6 portraits. Cloth. $500.

McCONNELL, H. H. *Five Years a Cavalryman.* Jacksboro, 1889. Text on pink paper. $500.

McCONNELL, Joseph Carroll. *The West Texas Frontier.* Jacksboro, 1933. $500.

McCOOK, Henry C. *American Spiders and Their Spinningwork.* Philadelphia, 1889–93. 3 vols. "Author's Edition." One of 250 copies. Portrait, 35 hand-colored plates. $2,000.

McCORKLE, Jill. *The Cheer Leader.* (Chapel Hill, 1984.) Author's first book. Published simultaneously with *July 7th.* $150.

McCORKLE, Jill. *July 7th.* Chapel Hill, 1984. Published simultaneously with *The Cheer Leader.* $150.

McCORKLE, John, and BARTON, O. S. *Three Years with Quantrell.* Armstrong, Mo. (1914). 11 plates. Stiff maroon wraps. $1,500.

McCORMICK, Richard C. *Arizona: Its Resources and Prospects.* New York, 1865. Folding map. 22 pages, buff printed wraps. $350.

McCORMICK, S. J. *Almanac for the Year 1864; Containing Useful Information Relative to the Population, Progress and Resources of Oregon, Washington and Idaho.* Portland (1866). 56 pages, wraps. $1,250.

McCOURT, Frank. *Angela's Ashes.* New York (1996). $500.

McCOY, Horace. *They Shoot Horses, Don't They?* New York, 1935. Author's first book. $750. London, 1935. $300.

McCOY, Isaac. *History of Baptist Indian Missions* . . . Washington, 1840. $600.

McCOY, Isaac. *Remarks on the Practicability of Indian Reform.* Boston, 1827. 47 pages, wraps. $1,000. Rebound. $500. New York, 1829. Second edition. $300.

McCOY, Isaac. *Remove Indians Westward.* (Caption title.) (Washington), 1829. 48 pages. $750.

McCOY, James C. *Jesuit Relations of Canada, 1632–1673, A Bibliography.* Paris, 1937. One of 350 copies. $350.

McCOY, Joseph G. *Historic Sketches of the Cattle Trade of the West and Southwest.* Kansas City, 1874. Portraits and plates. Pictorial cloth. $3,000. Glendale, 1940. $250. Columbus, 1951. $200.

McCRACKEN, Harold. *The American Cowboy.* Garden City, 1973. One of 300 signed copies. Illustrated, including color plates. Cloth. In slipcase. $250. Trade. $100.

McCRACKEN, Harold. *The Charles M. Russell Book.* Garden City, 1957. One of 250 signed copies. Illustrated, including color plates. Leather. $750. Trade edition in buckram. $175.

McCRACKEN, Harold. *The Frank Tenney Johnson Book.* Garden City, 1974. Illustrated, including color plates, by Johnson. One of 350 signed copies, with an extra color plate. In slipcase. $400. Trade or "Limited" edition (4,000 copies). $150.

McCRACKEN, Harold. *The Frederic Remington Book.* Garden City, 1966. One of 500 signed copies. Illustrated. Leather. In slipcase. $500.

McCRACKEN, Harold. *Frederic Remington's Own West.* New York, 1960. One of 167 signed copies. Illustrated. Calf. In slipcase. $350. Trade. $75.

McCRACKEN, Harold. *George Catlin and the Old Frontier.* New York, 1959. Illustrated, including colored plates. One of 250 copies, with extra color plate tipped in at front. Decorated leather. In slipcase. $400. Trade edition. $100.

McCREERY, John. *The Press, A Poem*. Liverpool, 1803–27. 2 vols. $500.

McCULLERS, Carson. *The Ballad of the Sad Café*. Boston, 1951. $250.

McCULLERS, Carson. *The Heart Is a Lonely Hunter*. Boston, 1940. Author's first book. $3,000. London, 1943. $450.

McCULLERS, Carson. *The Member of the Wedding*. Boston, 1946. Cloth. $350.

McCULLERS, Carson. *Reflections in a Golden Eye*. (Boston), 1941. First issue with clear cellophane window on front panel of dustwrapper. $1,250. Second issue, printed dustwrapper. $250.

McCULLEY, Johnson. *John Standon of Texas*. New York, 1924. $250.

McCULLEY, Johnson. *Mark of Zorro*. New York, 1924. $500.

McCULLOUGH, Colleen. *The Thorn Birds*. New York (1977). $100.

McCULLOUGH, Colleen. *Tim*. New York (1974). Author's first book. $125.

McCUTCHEON, George Barr. See Greaves, Richard.

McCUTCHEON, George Barr. *A Fool and His Money*. New York, 1913. One of 50 signed copies. In plain green dustwrapper and unpainted green slipcase. $250.

McCUTCHEON, George Barr. *Graustark*. Chicago, 1901. Pictorial cloth. Author's first book. First issue, with "Noble" instead of "Lorry" in line 6 of page 150. $100.

McCUTCHEON, George Barr. *The Prince of Graustark*. New York, 1914. One of 40 signed copies. Color illustrations by A. I. Keller. In plain brown dustwrapper and unprinted brown slipcase. $250. Trade edition. $75.

McCUTCHEON, John T. *Bird Center*. Chicago, 1904. Illustrated. Pictorial boards and cloth. $200.

McDANIELD, H. F., and TAYLOR, N. A. *The Coming Empire: or, 2,000 Miles in Texas on Horseback*. New York (1877). $200.

McDERMOTT, Alice. *A Bigamist's Daughter*. New York (1982). $200.

McDONALD, Charles B. *Scotland's Gift, Golf: Reminicenses*. New York, 1928. Limited signed edition in slipcase. $2,000. Trade. $500.

McDONALD, John. *Biographical Sketches of Gen. Nathaniel Massie, Gen. Duncan McArthur, Capt. William Wells, and Gen. Simon Kenton*. Cincinnati, 1838. In original calf. $1,000.

McELROY, Joseph. *Ship Rock. A Place*. Concord, N.H. (1980). 13 copies specially bound for presentation. Quarter leather and boards. $250. 26 signed and lettered copies. $150. 200 signed copies. $100.

McELROY, Joseph. *A Smuggler's Bible*. New York (1966). Author's first book. $250. London (1968). $150.

McEWAN, Ian. *First Love, Last Rites*. London, 1975. Author's first book. $450. New York (1975). $150.

McFALL, Frances Elizabeth. See Grand, Sarah.

McFEE, William. See Shay, Frank.

McFEE, William. *Casuals of the Sea*. London, 1916. Frontispiece in color. $150.

McFEE, William. *The Harbourmaster.* Garden City, 1931. One of 377 signed copies. Boards and cloth. In slipcase. $175. Garden City, 1932. $100.

McFEE, William. *Iron Men and Wooden Ships*. New York, 1924. One of 200 signed copies. Woodcuts by Edward A. Wilson. Folio, boards. In slipcase. $350.

McFEE, William. *Letters from an Ocean Tramp.* London, 1908. Author's first book. Colored frontispiece. Blue cloth. First state, with "Cassell & Co." at foot of spine. $200.

McGAHERN, John. *The Barracks*. London, 1963. Author's first book. $500. New York, 1964. $100.

McGAW, James F. *Philip Seymour, or, Pioneer Life in Richland County, Ohio*. Mansfield, Ohio, 1858. 2 plates. $750.

McGEE, I. and Maria. *The Mormon Endowment: A Secret Drama, or Conspiracy in the Nauvoo Temple in 1846*. Syracuse, 1847. Illustrated. 24 pages, pictorial wraps. (2 known copies.) $5,000 or more.

McGEE, Joseph H. *Story of the Grand River Country, 1821–1905*. (Gallatin, Mo., 1909.) Portrait. Brown printed wraps. $300.

McGINLEY, Phyllis. *On the Contrary*. Garden City, 1934. Author's first book. $200.

McGLASHAN, C. F. *History of the Donner Party: A Tragedy of the Sierras*. Truckee, Calif. (1879). Cloth. $1,500. San Francisco, 1880. Illustrated. Second edition. $600.

McGOVAN, James. *Brought to Bay*. Edinburgh, 1878. (By William C. Honeyman.) Author's first book. $250.

McGOWAN, Edward. *Narrative of Edward McGowan*. San Francisco, 1857. Illustrated. Pictorial wraps. $1,250. San Francisco, 1917. One of 200 copies. $350.

McGREEVY, Thomas. *Introduction to . . . Da Vinci*. London, 1929. Author's first book, One of 875 copies. (McGreevy's translation of Valéry's work.) $100.

McGUANE, Thomas. *The Bushwhacked Piano*. New York (1971). $300.

McGUANE, Thomas. *In the Crazies*. Seattle, 1984. 185 signed copies with large portfolio of 10 various-sized plates signed and numbered by artist Russell Chatham. Book signed by both McGuane and Chatham. $2,000.

McGUANE, Thomas. *The Sporting Club*. New York (1968). Author's first book. $350.

McHARRY, Samuel. *The Practical Distiller . . .* Harrisburg, 1809. $2,000.

McILVAINE, William Jr. *Sketches of Scenery and Notes of Personal Adventure, in California and Mexico*. Philadelphia, 1850. 16 plates, including engraved title page. Purplish cloth. $6,500. San Francisco, 1951. Grabhorn printing. Folio, half cloth. One of 400 copies. $300.

McINTIRE, Jim. *Early Days in Texas: A Trip to Hell and Heaven.* Kansas City, Mo. (1902). 16 plates, pictorial cloth. $1,000.

McKAY, Claude. *Banjo.* New York, 1929. $1,000.

McKAY, Claude. *Gingertown.* New York, 1932. $1,000.

McKAY, Claude. *Harlem Shadows: The Poems of Claude McKay.* New York (1922). Boards and cloth, paper label. $1,750.

McKAY, Claude. *A Long Way from Home.* New York (1937). Rust-colored cloth with labels. $850. Green cloth printed in yellow. $750.

McKAY, Claude. *Songs of Jamaica.* Kingston, 1912. Wraps over boards. Author's first book. $2,000.

McKAY, Claude. *Spring in New Hampshire and Other Poems.* London, 1920. Wraps. $1,500.

McKAY, George L. *American Book Auction Catalogues 1713–1934: A Union List.* New York, 1937. $250.

McKAY, George L. *A Stevenson Library Catalogue . . . Volumes One and Two.* New Haven, 1951–64. 6 vols. One of 500 copies. $600.

McKAY, William, and ROBERTS, W. *John Hoppner, R.A.* London, 1909. $350. London, 1909–14. 2 vols. Buckram (including supplement). $500.

McKEE, James Cooper. *Narrative of the Surrender of a Command of U.S. Forces at Fort Fillmore, N.M., in July A.D. 1861.* (Cover title.) New York, 1881. 30 pages, printed self-wraps. Second edition. $750. (The rare first edition appeared in Prescott, Arizona Territory, in 1878. Estimated value, $5,000 or more.)

McKEE, Dr. W. H. *The Territory of New Mexico and Its Resources.* New York, 1866. Map. 12 pages, printed wraps. $1,500.

McKENNEY, Thomas L. *Sketches of a Tour to the Lakes.* Baltimore, 1827. 29 full-page engravings, some in color. $2,000.

McKENNEY, Thomas L., and HALL, James. *History of the Indian Tribes of North America.* Biddle, Philadelphia, 1836–38–44. 3 vols. Map, 120 colored plates and list of subscribers. Folio. Cloth or half leather. $150,000. Philadelphia, 1848–49–50. 3 vols. First octavo edition. $25,000. Many early editions are still prized for the quality of the Indian portraits and prices have ranged in recent years from $10,000 to $30,000. Edinburgh, 1933–34. 3 vols., blue cloth. In dustwrappers. Slipcase. $1,500.

McKIM, Randolph H. *A Soldier's Recollections: Leaves from the Diary of a Young Confederate.* New York, 1911. $300.

McKINNON, Ian. *Garroot: Adventures of a Clydeside Apprentice.* London, 1933. $1,350 at auction in 1996.

McKNIGHT, George S. *California 49er: Travels from Perrysburg to California.* (Cover title.) Perrysburg, Ohio, 1903. 27 pages, printed red wraps. $500.

McKUEN, Rod. *And Autumn Came.* New York (1954). Author's first book. $200.

McLEOD, Donald. *A Brief Review of the Settlement of Upper Canada.* Cleveland, 1841. Cloth, paper label. $1,250.

McLEOD, Donald. *History of Wiskonsan, from Its First Discovery to the Present Period.* Buffalo, 1846. 4 plates, folding map. $1,750. (Howes notes some copies have plates and no map and others map and no plates.) Without map. $600.

McLOUGHLIN, Maurice E. *Tennis As I Play It.* New York, 1915. (Ghostwritten by Sinclair Lewis.) $750.

McLUHAN, Herbert Marshall. *The Mechanical Bride.* New York (1951). Author's first book. $250. Reprinted in "Ltd. Edition" (dustwrapper flap) [1973]. Priced at $12.50 versus $4.50 for original. White endpapers and white lettering on cover versus yellow endpaper and gold lettering on reprint. Copyright pages the same.

M'CLUNG, John A. *Sketches of Western Adventure.* Maysville, Ky., 1832. In original boards, linen spine. $2,500. Philadelphia, 1832. Second edition. $600.

McMASTER, S. W. *Sixty Years on the Upper Mississippi . . .* Rock Island, Ill., 1893 (printer's foreword dated Galena, Ill., 1895). 300 pages, flexible wraps. $750.

McMILLAN, Terry. *Mama.* Boston, 1987. Author's first book. $400. London, 1987. $125.

McMURTRIE, Douglas C. *The Disabled Soldier.* New York, 1919. Author's first book. $200.

McMURTRIE, Douglas C. *Early Printing in New Orleans, 1764–1810.* New Orleans, 1929. Illustrated. Half cloth. One of 410 copies. Issued without dustwrapper. $250.

McMURTRIE, Douglas C. *The Golden Book.* Chicago, 1927. Illustrated. Half morocco. One of 220 signed copies. $250. Trade edition. Cloth. In dustwrapper. $75.

McMURTRY, Larry. See Ray, Ophelia.

McMURTRY, Larry. *Horseman, Pass By.* New York (1961). Author's first book. $2,500.

McMURTRY, Larry. *In a Narrow Grave.* Austin, 1968. First edition not stated. First printing with "skycrapers" vs "skyscrapers" on page 105, line 12, and many other errors. All but 15 reportedly destroyed but seems more common. $3,500. 250 signed copies. Slipcase. $3,500. Second printing (edition not stated). $750. Third printing with "B" on copyright page. $350.

McMURTRY, Larry. *It's Always We Rambled: An Essay on Rodeo.* New York, 1974. 300 signed copies. Issued without dustwrapper. $750.

McMURTRY, Larry. *The Last Picture Show.* New York, 1966. $750.

McMURTRY, Larry. *Leaving Cheyenne.* New York (1963). $2,000. London, 1972. Wraps. $150.

McMURTRY, Larry. *Lonesome Dove.* New York (1985). $300.

McNEIL, Samuel. *McNeils [sic] Travels in 1849, to, Through and from the Gold Regions.* Columbus, Ohio, 1850. 40 pages, plain wraps. $12,500.

McPHEE, John. *Alaska—Images of the Country.* San Francisco (1981). One of 500 signed. Issued without dustwrapper in slipcase. $250. Trade. $75.

McPHEE, John. *The Headmaster.* New York (1966). $175.

McPHEE, John. *The Pine Barrens.* New York (1968). $200.

McPHEE, John. *A Sense of Where You Are.* New York (1965). Author's first book. $1,500.

McPHERSON, James A. *Hue and Cry.* Boston (1969). Author's first book. $350. (London, 1969.) $150.

McSHEEHY, H. J. *A Hunt' in the Rockies.* Logansport, Ind., 1893. Frontispiece and photographs. 135 pages, printed red wraps. $750.

McWILLIAMS, John. *Recollections . . .* Princeton [1919]. Portrait. Cloth. $300.

M'DONELL, Alexander. *A Narrative of Transactions in the Red River Country.* London, 1819. Folding map. $1,500.

MEAD, Margaret. *Coming of Age in Samoa.* London, 1929. Author's first book. $250. London (1929). $200.

MEAD, Peter B. *An Elementary Treatise on American Grape Culture and Wine Making.* (New York) 1867. $400.

MEADE, L. T. *The Medicine Lady.* London, 1892. Author's first book. $250.

MEADE, William. *An Enquiry into the Chymical Character . . .* Boston, 1808. $2,000.

MEANS, James. *Manflight.* Boston, 1891. 29 pages, printed wraps. $250.

MEANS, James. *The Problem of Manflight.* Boston, 1894. Diagrams. 20 pages, pictorial wraps. $500.

MEARES, John. *Voyages Made in the Years 1788 and 1789, from China . . .* London, 1790. 10 charts and 17 plates, and frontispiece portrait of Meares. $6,000.

MEEKER, Ezra. *Washington Territory West of the Cascade Mountains.* Olympia, Wash., 1870. 52 pages, printed wraps. $1,500.

MEIGS, John. *The Cowboy in American Prints.* Chicago (1972). One of 300 signed by the editor, Meigs, and with original lithograph by Peter Hurd, signed by him in pencil. Slipcase. $500.

MEIKLE, James. *Famous Clyde Yachts, 1880–87.* Glasgow, 1888. 31 colored aquatints, mounted as drawings, with tissue guards. Atlas folio, cloth. $5,500.

MELANTER. *Poems.* London, 1854. (By R. D. Blackmore, his first book.) $1,000.

MELINCOURT. London, 1817. By the Author of *Headlong Hall.* (Thomas Love Peacock.) 3 vols. $600.

MELINE, James F. *Two Thousand Miles on Horseback.* New York, 1867. Map. $250.

MELISH, John. *A Geographical Description of the United States . . .* Philadelphia, 1815. 3 maps. $1,250. Philadelphia, 1816. 5 maps. Second edition. $1,000. Philadelphia, 1818. 4 maps. Third edition. $750. Philadelphia, 1822. 12 maps. $1,000.

MELISH, John. *A Military and Topographical Atlas of the United States.* Philadelphia, 1813. 8 maps and plans, 5 folding. $11,000 at auction in 1999. Philadelphia, 1815. 12 maps and plans, 9 folding and colored in outline. Half leather. $3,000.

MELLICHAMPE: A Legend of the Santee. New York, 1836. (By William Gilmore Simms.) 2 vols., in original cloth, paper labels. $750.

MELLON, James. *African Hunter.* New York (1975). 382 photos. $450.

MELMOTH the Wanderer. Edinburgh, 1820. (By Charles Robert Maturin.) 4 vols. $3,000. London, 1821. 4 vols. $1,000.

MELTZER, David. *Round the Poem Box.* Los Angeles, 1969. Leather. One of 26 signed copies, with an original illustration by the author. $150. One of 125 signed copies. Issued without dustwrapper. $400.

MELTZER, David, and SCHENKER, Donald. *Poems.* (San Francisco, 1957.) First book for both poets. One of 470 copies. Glazed white wraps, taped spine (as issued). $125. Hardbound. One of 25 signed copies. $250. 5 copies signed in blood. $350.

MELVILLE, Herman. See *John Marr and Other Sailors.*

MELVILLE, Herman. *The Apple Tree and Other Sketches.* Princeton, 1922. Boards. One of 175 copies on handmade paper. In slipcase. $350. Trade edition. Without dustwrapper. $150.

MELVILLE, Herman. *Battle-Pieces and Aspects of the War.* New York, 1866. $2,000. (There was no English edition.)

MELVILLE, Herman. *Billy Budd [and] Benito Cereno.* Limited Editions Club, New York, 1965. Illustrated. White sailcloth. In slipcase. $100.

MELVILLE, Herman. *Clarel: A Poem and Pilgrimage in the Holy Land.* New York, 1876. 2 vols. $12,500.

MELVILLE, Herman. *The Confidence-Man.* New York, 1857. With Miller and Holman on copyright page. $6,000. London, 1857. Orange cloth. First English edition, first issue, without "Roberts" in publisher's name below ads on recto of front free endpaper (VAB—not in BAL). $6,000.

MELVILLE, Herman. *Israel Potter.* New York, 1855. Purple-brown or green cloth, yellow endpapers. With spine initials F.Y. & E ornamented with pendants and heading on page 141 "Chapter XVI." (Corrected to "XIV" in second printing.) $2,500. London, 1855. $1,500.

MELVILLE, Herman. *Mardi: and A Voyage Thither.* London, 1849. 3 vols., pale-green cloth, white endpapers with blue designs. $7,500. New York, 1849. 2 vols. First American edition. Blindstamped purple cloth. $5,000.

MELVILLE, Herman. *Moby-Dick; or, The Whale.* New York, 1851. First American edition, with publisher's circular device blindstamped at center of sides. (For first edition, see *The Whale.*) Black, blue, gray, green, drab purple-brown, red, or slate cloth, orange or marbled endpapers. $35,000. Second-state binding without publisher's circular device on the sides. $25,000. New York, 1855. Second printing. $5,000. New York, 1863. Third printing. Brown cloth. $3,500. Chicago, 1930. Lakeside Press. Illustrated by Rockwell Kent, 3 vols., silver-decorated cloth. One of 1,000 copies. In aluminum slipcase. In acetate dustwrapper with plain paper flaps.

$4,500. Without dustwrapper. $2,500. In full black morocco (a few). $15,000. Trade edition. 1 vol. in dustwrapper. $750. Limited Editions Club, New York, 1943. Illustrated by Boardman Robinson. 2 vols., full morocco. In slipcase. $750. Mount Vernon, 1975. One of 2,500 copies signed by Leroy Neiman and Jacques Cousteau. In slipcase. $2,500. San Francisco, 1979. Illustrated by Barry Moser. Full morocco. One of 250 copies. In slipcase. $5,000.

MELVILLE, Herman. *Narrative of a Four Months' Residence Among the Natives of a Valley of the Marquesas Islands; or, A Peep at Polynesian Life.* London, 1846. Author's first book. Map. 2 parts, wraps, or cloth (2 parts bound as one). (Published later that year in New York as *Typee*), first issue, with the reading "Pomarea" on page 19, line 1. Wraps. $15,000. Red cloth. First book edition. $4,000. Second issue: "Pomare." $2,500. London, 1847. Cloth. $1,500.

MELVILLE, Herman. *Omoo: A Narrative of Adventures in the South Seas.* London, 1847. Map. 2 parts printed gray or brown wraps, or cloth (in 1 vol.). Wraps. $12,500. Red cloth. First book edition. $4,500. New York, 1847. Frontispiece map, 1 illustration. 2 parts, cream–white wraps, or pictorial cloth (1 vol.). First American edition. Wraps. $7,500. Cloth. $3,500. Limited Editions Club, New York, 1961. Illustrated. White linen. In slipcase. $150.

MELVILLE, Herman. *The Piazza Tales.* New York, 1856. Pale-blue cloth. (Schwartz noted that the first copies off the press had yellow endpapers, not mentioned in BAL.) $5,000. London, 1856. First English edition. American sheets with tipped-in title page. $3,500.

MELVILLE, Herman. *Pierre; or, The Ambiguities.* New York, 1852. Cloth. $3,500. Wraps. $4,000. London, 1852. Blue embossed cloth, yellow endpapers. American sheets with tipped-in title page. $2,500.

MELVILLE, Herman. *Redburn: His First Voyage.* London, 1849. 2 vols., dark-blue cloth, white endpapers with the blue pattern (Schwartz). Yellow or white no priority (BAL). $12,500. New York, 1849. With ads ending on page 10 (BAL). Cloth. $3,500. Wraps. $5,000. (Schwartz had 14-page catalogue dated October 1849 as first issue, BAL would seem to call this the second printing.) London, 1853. 2 vols. bound as one. Red cloth. Sheets from the 1849 edition with cancel title pages for each volume, with the new date. $1,500.

MELVILLE, Herman. *Typee: A Peep at Polynesian Life.* New York, 1846. 2 vols. First American edition of the author's first book (*Narrative of a Four Months' Residence Among the Natives of a Valley of the Marquesas*). Map frontispiece. First volume identified as "Nos XIII & XIV" (later "No. XIII"). Thick fawn-colored printed wraps. $10,000. Various cloth colors. 1 vol. First American book edition. $4,500. New York, 1846. Cloth or 2 volumes in wraps. Revised edition, with 8 pages of ads (but see BAL). $2,500. Limited Editions Club, New York, 1935. Illustrated. In slipcase. $300.

MELVILLE, Herman. *The Whale.* London, 1851. 3 vols., bright-blue cloth with off-white cloth spine, cream-colored endpapers. (Published later that year in New York as *Moby-Dick*.) $150,000. (Remainder binding in purple [BAL].)

MELVILLE, Herman. *White-Jacket: or, the World in a Man-of-War.* London, 1850. 2 vols., light-blue cloth. $6,500. New York, 1850. 2 parts, yellow wraps. $24,000 at auction in 1995. Cloth with "Harper and Brothers" in ornate frame on sides, 6 pages of ads at end and signature mark "T" not on page 433. 1 vol. $2,000. London, 1853. 2 vols. in one using first edition sheets. $1,500. First English 1-vol. edition. $1,000.

Memoirs of a Coxcomb. London, 1751. (By John Cleland.) $1,500.

MEMOIRS of a Fox-Hunting Man. London (1928). (By Siegfried Sassoon.) Blue cloth. First issue, with rough-trimmed fore edges. $500. One of 260 signed copies. $1,500. London (1929).

Illustrated by William Nicholson. $300. Vellum. One of 300 signed copies. In dustwrapper and slipcase. $1,250. Limited Editions Club. (London) 1977. In slipcase. $125.

MEMOIRS of the Life of the Late John Mytton, Esq. London, 1835. (By C. J. Apperley.) 12 plates in color by John Alken. $2,250. London, 1837. 18 plates. In original cloth. Second edition. $1,750. London, 1851. 18 plates. Third edition. $1,250.

MEMOIRS of William Burke, A Soldier of the Revolution, Reformed from Intemperance . . . Hartford, 1837. (By William Burke.) $350.

MEMORANDA: Democratic Vistas. Washington, 1871. (By Walt Whitman.) Light-green wraps. $1,500. (For later printing, see Whitman entry under this title.)

MEMORIAL and Biographical History of Johnson and Hill Counties, Texas. Chicago, 1892. Illustrated. Leather. $450.

MEMORIAL and Biographical History of McLennan, Falls, Bell and Coryell Counties, Texas. Chicago, 1893. Half leather. $750.

MEMORIAL to the President and Congress for the Admission of Wyoming Territory to the Union. Cheyenne, 1889. 75 pages, wraps. $300.

MENCKEN, H. L. See Hatteras, Owen; Hirshberg, Dr. L. K.

MENCKEN, H. L. The American Language. New York, 1919. One of 1,500 copies. Black cloth. In dustwrapper. $2,500. Without dustwrapper. $750. One of 25 signed copies. In dustwrapper shorter than book. $5,000.

MENCKEN, H. L. The Artist. Boston, 1912. Pictorial boards. $350. (Facsimile in 1923 in plain boards [almost cardboard] and dustwrapper, no indication of later printing $100.)

MENCKEN H. L. Damn! A Book of Calumny. New York, 1918. In dustwrapper. $2,500. Without dustwrapper. $600.

MENCKEN, H. L. George Bernard Shaw: His Plays. Boston, 1905. $400.

MENCKEN, H. L. In Defense of Women. New York, 1918. Philip Goodman on title page. No statement of edition, first issue, with publisher's name misspelled "Ppilip." In dustwrapper. $1,750. Without dustwrapper. $450. Later printings, with name corrected. In dustwrapper. $1,000.

MENCKEN, H. L. A Little Book in C Major. New York, 1916. $600.

MENCKEN, H. L. Notes on Democracy. New York (1926). $300. One of 200 signed copies. $1,000. Vellum. One of 35 copies on vellum, signed. $4,000.

MENCKEN, H. L. The Philosophy of Friedrich Nietzsche. Boston, 1908. Red cloth. With "Friedrich" omitted on spine. $500. London, 1908. $350.

MENCKEN, H. L. Prejudices: First Series. New York (1919). All edges cut. In dustwrapper. $1,250. Without dustwrapper. $250. One of few signed, with all edges uncut. $2,000.

MENCKEN H. L. Prejudices: Second Series. New York (1920). All edges cut. In dustwrapper. $1,000. Without dustwrapper. $200. One of a few large-paper copies, signed. All edges uncut. $1,500.

MENCKEN, H. L. *Prejudices: Third Series.* New York (1922). $750. A few with all edges uncut, signed. $1,000.

MENCKEN, H. L. *Prejudices: Fourth Series.* New York (1924). $600. One of 100 signed copies. In slipcase. $750. One of 10 lettered, signed copies. $2,000.

MENCKEN, H. L. *Prejudices: Fifth Series.* New York (1926). $500. One of 192 signed copies In slipcase. $750. One of 8 lettered copies. $2,000.

MENCKEN, H. L. *Prejudices: Sixth Series.* New York (1927). $350. One of 50 copies on vellum, signed. $1,250. One of 140 copies on rag paper, signed. $750.

MENCKEN, H. L. *Ventures into Verse.* Baltimore, 1903. Author's first book. Illustrated. Boards, paper label, or brown wraps. Wraps. $6,000. Boards. $10,000. (About 100 copies believed printed in all; 15 in boards, and the rest in wraps.) Baltimore (1960). Second edition (facsimile of the first edition). One of 250 copies. $75.

MENCKEN, H. L.; NATHAN, George Jean; and WRIGHT, Willard Huntington. *Europe After 8:15.* New York, 1914. 7 plates by Thomas Hart Benton. First binding, decorated yellow cloth with blue stamping. $450. Second binding, stamped in gold. $300. It does show up in dustwrapper, more often than others of this era, in the $1,000 range.

MENDOZA, Daniel. *The Art of Boxing.* London, 1789. $2,500.

MENGER, Carl. *Principles of Economics.* Glen, Illinois, 1950. $500.

MERA, H. P. *The Rain Bird: A Study in Pueblo Design.* Santa Fe, 1937. Illustrated by Tom Lea. Wraps. In dustwrapper. $400.

MERCEDES of Castile: Or, the Voyage to Cathay. Philadelphia, 1840. By the Author of *The Bravo.* 2 vols., in original cloth, paper labels. (By James Fenimore Cooper.) $500.

MERCER, A. S. *The Banditti of the Plains.* (Cheyenne, 1894.) Illustrated. Map. Cloth. $4,500. Grabhorn Press. San Francisco, 1935. Illustrated. Half cloth. One of 1,000 copies. $150.

MERCER, A. S. *Washington Territory: The Great North-West.* Utica, 1865. 38 pages, printed wraps. $1,500.

MEREDITH, George. *Diana of the Crossways.* London, 1885. 3 vols. First complete book edition. $750.

MEREDITH, George. *The Egoist.* London, 1879. 3 vols. $750.

MEREDITH, George. *Farina.* London, 1857. $400.

MEREDITH, George. *Modern Love and Poems of the English Roadside.* London, 1862. Green cloth. $500. Portland, Me., 1891. Heavy printed wraps. First American edition. $200.

MEREDITH, George. *The Ordeal of Richard Feverel.* London, 1859. 3 vols., brown cloth. $1,250.

MEREDITH, George. *Poems.* London (1851). Author's first book. With half title and with errata slip at end. Purple cloth. $1,500. Green cloth. $1,000.

MEREDITH, George. *The Shaving of Shagpat*. London, 1856. $450. Limited Editions Club, New York, 1955. Illustrated. Boards and leather. In slipcase. $100.

MEREDITH, William. *Love Letter from an Impossible Land*. New Haven, 1944. Author's first book. Boards. $200.

MERRICK, George B. *Old Times on the Upper Mississippi*. Cleveland, 1909. Illustrated. Blue cloth. $175.

MERRILL, James. *The Black Swan and Other Poems*. Athens, 1946. Wraps. One of 100 copies. $4,500.

MERRILL, James. *Bronze*. New York (1984). One of 26 signed copies. In paper folding box. $600. One of 150 signed copies. $175.

MERRILL, James. *First Poems*. New York, 1951. Author's first commercially published book. One of 990 copies. $350.

MERRILL, James. *Jim's Book: A Collection of Poems and Short Stories*. New York, 1942. Maroon buckram and gray boards. In glassine dustwrapper. $7,500.

MERRILL, James. *Short Stories*. Pawlet (1954). Wraps. One of 210 copies. $1,000.

MERRILL, James. *Yannina*. New York, 1973. One of 26 signed copies. Decorated wrappers with labels. $750. One of 100 copies. $300.

MERRIMAN, Henry Seton. *From One Generation to Another*. London, 1892. (By Hugh Stowell Scott.) 2 vols., pea-green cloth. $500.

MERRITT, Abraham. *Dwellers in the Mirage*. New York (1932). $1,750.

MERRITT, Abraham. *The Face in the Abyss*. New York (1931). $1,250.

MERRITT, Abraham. *The Moon Pool*. New York, 1919. Author's first book. First printing, without ad on page (434). Sheets bulk 3.2 cm. Spine imprint "Putnam" in upper- and lower-case. In dustwrapper on brown paper matching book cover. $2,500. In pictorial dustwrapper. $1250. Without dustwrapper. $200.

MERRITT, Abraham. *The Ship of Ishtar*. New York, 1926. $1,000.

MERRY-MOUNT; a Romance of the Massachusetts Colony. Boston, 1849. 2 vols. (By John Lathrop Motley.) $300.

MERTON, Thomas. *Elected Silence*. (London, 1949.) First U.K. edition of *The Seven Storey Mountain*. $300.

MERTON, Thomas. *Encounter—Thomas Merton & D. T. Suzuki*. (Monterey, KY), 1988. One of 60 copies. Issued without dustwrapper. $200. Trade in dustwrapper. $75.

MERTON, Thomas. *Hagia Sophia*. Lexington, 1962. One of 69 copies. Number of copies signed undetermined. Signed. $1,500. Unsigned. $500.

MERTON, Thomas. *Original Child Bomb*. New Directions. (New York, 1961.) One of 500 signed copies. Issued in plain cellophane wrapper. $750. Trade. Issued without dustwrapper. $100.

MERTON, Thomas. *Seeds of Contemplation.* (Mount Vernon, N.Y., 1949) One of 100 signed copies. Issued in brown slipcase. $2,000. Trade. $300.

MERTON, Thomas. *The Seven Storey Mountain.* New York (1948). Off-white cloth with black lettering in first-state dustwrapper with caption on one of the pictures on back "Author second from the left." $1,500. Assumed second issue in black cloth. $1,000. In second-issue dustwrapper with caption "Author on the left." $750. Both issues state "First Edition." See *Elected Silence* for first U.K. edition.

MERTON, Thomas. *Thirty Poems.* Norfolk (1944). Author's first book. Boards in dustwrapper. $500. Wraps in dustwrapper. $200.

MERTON, Thomas. *The Tower of Babel.* (Jubilee, New York, no date, 1955?) An offprint. 16 pages in pictorial cover, priced 25 cents on back. $300. (New Directions, Norfolk, 1957.) One of 250 signed copies. In slipcase. $1,500.

MERWIN, W. S. *The Dancing Bears.* New Haven, 1954. $450.

MERWIN, W. S. *A Mask for Janus.* New Haven, 1952. Foreword by W. H. Auden. Author's first book. Blue boards. $500.

MERYMAN, Richard. *Andrew Wyeth.* Boston, 1968. Color plates. $450. One of 300 signed copies. $2,000.

MESSAGE from the President to Both Houses of Congress . . . First Session of the 18th Congress. Giles & Seaton, Washington, 1823. (By James Monroe.) 8 leaves. $1,000. Washington, National Intelligencer . . . , December 2, 1823. Broadside. $17,000 at auction in 1998. Senate issue (simultaneous with House issue). $1,000. (The Monroe Doctrine.)

METALIOUS, Grace. *Peyton Place.* New York (1946). $300.

METCALF, Samuel L. *A Collection of Some of the Most Interesting Narratives of Indian Warfare in the West.* Lexington, 1821. Portrait. $5,000.

METCALFE, John. *The Feasting Dead.* Sauk City, Wis., 1954. $200.

METCALFE, John. *The Smoking Leg.* London, 1925. Author's first book. $350.

METZDORF, Robert F. *The Tinker Library, A Bibliographical . . .* New Haven (1959). One of 500 copies. $300.

MEW, Charlotte. *The Farmer's Bride.* London, 1916. Author's first book. Wraps. $200. London, 1921. $75.

MEXICO in 1842 . . . to Which Is Added, an Account of Texas and Yucatán, and of the Santa Fe Expedition. New York, 1842. (By George F. Folsom.) Folding colored map. $3,800 at auction in 1999.

MEYER, George. *Autobiography of George Meyer: Across the Plains with an Ox Team in 1849.* Shenandoah, Iowa, 1908. 2 portraits. Printed tan wraps. $350.

MEYERS, John C. *Wrestling from Antiquity to Date.* St. Louis, 1931. Gilt wrestler on cover. Issued without dustwrapper issued. $175.

MEYERS, William H. *Journal of a Cruise to California and the Sandwich Islands.* Grabhorn Press. San Francisco, 1955. Frontispiece, 10 color plates. Folio, half leather. One of 400 for the Book Club of California. In dustwrapper. $400.

MEYERS, William H. *Sketches of California and Hawaii.* (San Francisco), 1970. Folio, cloth, paper label. One of 450 copies. Issued without dustwrapper. $300.

MEYNELL, Alice. See Thompson, A. C.

MEYNELL, Alice. *Poems.* London, 1893. Brown cloth. First edition (under this title). One of 50 signed copies. $250. (For first edition, see Thompson, A. C., *Preludes.*) London, 1913. Portrait. Blue boards and cloth. One of 250 signed copies. $150. Trade edition. Blue buckram. $50.

MEYNELL, Alice. *Ten Poems, 1913–1915.* Westminister (London), 1915. Limp vellum. One of 50 copies. $250.

MEYNELL, Francis. *Typography.* Pelican Press. London, 1923. Illustrated, including color. Buckram. Issued without dustwrapper. $300.

MEYRICK, Samuel R. *A Critical Inquiry into Antient Armour . . .* London, 1824. 3 vols. 80 plates (some hand-colored). Folio. $2,500.

MEYRICK, Samuel R., and SKELTON, J. *Engraved Illustrations of Antient Arms and Armour, from the Collection of Llewelyn Meyrick.* London, 1830. 2 vols. 2 frontispieces, 2 engraved titles, 2 vignettes, and 151 engraved plates. $1,250.

MEYRINK, Gustav. *The Golem.* Boston (1928). Dustwrapper designed by E. McKnight Kauffer. $300.

MICHAELS, Anne. *The Weight of Oranges.* Toronto, 1985. Wraps. $450.

MICHAELS, Barbara. *The Master of Black Tower.* New York, 1966. First mystery. $250. London, 1967. $150.

MICHAUX, Francois-André. *The North America Sylva.* Paris, 1819. 3 vols. First English edition. 156 plates printed in colors and finished by hand. $4,500.

MICHAUX, F. A. *Travels to the Westward of the Alleghany Mountains.* London, 1805. Translated by B. Lambert. (Printed by Mawman.) First English edition. Folding map. $1,000. London, 1805. (Printed by Crosby.) Boards. Second English edition. $600. London, 1805. (Printed by Phillips.) Another translation. Third English edition. $500.

MICHEAUX, Oscar. See *The Conquest.*

MICHEAUX, Oscar. *The Story of Dorothy Stanfield.* New York, 1946. $200.

MICHENER, James. *The Bridges of Toko-Ri.* New York (1953). First not stated. Blue endpapers are presumed to be the first. $400. With white endpapers. $350.

MICHENER, James. *The Fires of Spring.* New York (1949). $750.

MICHENER, James. *The Floating World.* New York (1954). $300.

MICHENER, James. *Hawaii.* New York (1959). $300. One of 400 signed copies. Issued without dustwrapper. In slipcase. $750.

MICHENER, James. *Japanese Prints.* Rutland, Vt., 1959. First edition stated. In dustwrapper and slipcase. $500.

MICHENER, James. *The Modern Japanese Print.* Rutland (1962). One of 500 signed copies with 10 original prints signed by artist. In wooden case. $4,000.

MICHENER, James. *Return to Paradise.* New York (1951). $350.

MICHENER, James. *Tales of the South Pacific.* New York, 1947. $3,000. New York, 1950. One of 1,500 signed copies. Special ABA edition without dustwrapper. $500. London, 1951. $750.

MICHENER, James. *The Unit in the Social Studies.* Cambridge (1940). Author's first book with Harold M. Long. Wraps. $1,000.

MIDDLE Parts of Fortune (The). (By Frederic Manning.) (London) 1929. 2 vols. One of 520 copies. In slipcase. $600.

MIDDLETON, Christopher. *Poems.* London (1944). Author's first book. $100.

MILBURN, William. *Oriental Commerce . . .* London, 1813. 2 vols. Frontispiece and 19 maps. $3,000.

MILES, Henry D. *Pugilistica: Being One Hundred and Forty-four Years in the History of British Boxing.* London, 1880. 3 vols. Stated first. $1,500.

MILES, Gen. Nelson A. *Personal Recollections and Observations . . .* Chicago, 1896. Illustrated by Frederic Remington and others. Pictorial cloth, leather, or half leather. First issue, with caption under frontispiece reading "General Miles." $600. Second issue, with rank under portrait as "Maj. Gen." $400.

MILES, William. *Journal of the Sufferings and Hardships of Capt. Parker H. French's Overland Expedition to California.* Chambersburg, Pa., 1851. 24 pages, printed wraps. $5,000.

MILL, John Stuart. *Autobiography.* London, 1873. Green cloth. First issue, without errata. $350. With errata. $300.

MILL, John Stuart. *Considerations on Representative Government.* London, 1861. $1,250.

MILL, John Stuart. *On Liberty.* London, 1859. $2,500.

MILL, John Stuart. *Principles of Political Economy.* London, 1848. 2 vols. $4,500. London, 1849. 2 vols., cloth. Second edition. $850.

MILL, John Stuart. *The Subjection of Women.* London, 1869. $1,750. New York, 1869. $1,000.

MILLAIS, John Guille. *A Breath from the Veldt.* London, 1899. Green cloth. $750.

MILLAR, Kenneth. See Macdonald, John Ross, and Macdonald, Ross (pseudonyms).

MILLAR, Kenneth. *Blue City.* New York, 1947. $1,000.

MILLAR, Kenneth. *The Dark Tunnel.* New York, 1944. Author's first book. $5,000.

MILLAR, Kenneth. *Trouble Follows Me.* New York, 1946. $3,500.

MILLAR, Margaret. *The Invisible Worm.* Garden City, 1941. Author's first book. $350.

MILLAY, Edna St. Vincent. See Boyd, Nancy; Earle, Ferdinand.

MILLAY, Edna St. Vincent. *The Ballad of the Harp-Weaver.* New York, 1922. One of 500 copies. Illustrated. Pictorial wraps. First edition stated, and code K-X. $200. One of 5 copies on Japan vellum. $3,500.

MILLAY, Edna St. Vincent. *The Buck in the Snow and Other Poems.* New York, 1928. $150. One of 479 signed copies. In glassine dustwrapper and slipcase. $300. Boards and vellum. One of 36 copies on Japan vellum. In glassine dustwrapper and slipcase. $1,250. London, 1928. $125.

MILLAY, Edna St. Vincent. *The Harp-Weaver and Other Poems.* New York, 1923. $250.

MILLAY, Edna St. Vincent. *Huntsman, What Quarry?* New York, 1939. One of 551 signed copies. In slipcase. $300. Trade. $100.

MILLAY, Edna St. Vincent. *The King's Henchman.* New York, 1927. Boards and cloth. $100. One of 158 signed copies. In glassine dustwrapper and slipcase. $350. One of 31 copies on Japan vellum, signed. $1,250. "Artist's Edition." One of 500 signed copies. $350.

MILLAY, Edna St. Vincent. *Poems.* London, 1923. $350.

MILLAY, Edna St. Vincent. *Renascence and Other Poems.* New York, 1917. Author's first book. Black cloth. First issue, on Glaslan watermarked paper. 2 blank leaves precede half title. In dustwrapper. $1,500. Without dustwrapper. $300. White vellum paper boards. One of 15 (actually 17) on Japan vellum, signed. $7,500.

MILLER, Arthur. *All My Sons.* New York (1947). $750.

MILLER, Arthur. *The Crucible.* New York, 1953. $750.

MILLER, Arthur. *Death of a Salesman.* New York, 1949. Pictorial orange cloth. $2,500. London, 1949. $350.

MILLER, Arthur. *Situation Normal.* New York (1944). Author's first book. $350.

MILLER, Benjamin S. *Ranch Life in Southern Kansas and the Indian Territory.* New York, 1896. Frontispiece. 163 pages, printed wraps. $2,000.

MILLER, Cincinnatus H. *Joaquin, et al.* Portland, Ore., 1869. (By Joaquin Miller.) $1,250.

MILLER, Francis Trevelyan. *The Photographic History of the Civil War.* New York 1911–12. 10 vols. Original cloth. $1,250.

MILLER, Francis Trevelyan. *The World in the Air.* New York, 1930. 1,200 illustrations, 2 vols. $600. One of 500 signed copies. $1,500.

MILLER, Henry. *Account of a Tour of the California Missions, 1856.* Grabhorn Press. San Francisco, 1952. Pencil drawings by Miller. One of 375 copies. 59 pages, boards. In slipcase. $250.

MILLER, Henry. *The Air-Conditioned Nightmare.* New Directions. (New York, 1945.) Tan cloth with photos tipped in. $300. (Second printing, 1948, in gray cloth with photos printed.)

MILLER, Henry. *Aller Retour New York.* Paris (1935). One of 150 signed copies. Wraps. $2,000. (New York), 1945. One of 500 copies. Cloth. Issued without dustwrapper. $125.

MILLER, Henry. *Black Spring.* Obelisk Press. Paris (1936). Pictorial wraps. $2,000. Paris (1938). Wraps. Second edition. $300. New York (1963). $75. (Somewhat more with yellow paper censorship band, "Cannot be bought in England and U.S.A.")

MILLER, Henry. *The Books in My Life.* (Norfolk, Conn., 1952.) (Printed in Ireland.) First issue with four tipped in photographs. $250.

MILLER, Henry. *The Colossus of Maroussi.* Colt Press. San Francisco (1941). Boards and cloth. One of 100 signed copies. Issued without dustwrapper. $1,500. In dustwrapper. $600. London, 1942. $250.

MILLER, Henry. *The Cosmological Eye.* New Directions. Norfolk (1939). His first U.S. publication. Tan cloth, with brown lettering and photograph of an eye inset on front cover. In first-state dustwrapper, spine lettered in white. Priced at $2.50. $500. (Second was in 1944, without eye and priced at $3.00.) London (1945). $200.

MILLER, Henry. *Insomnia or the Devil at Large.* Albuquerque (1970). Limited edition, signed and dated by Miller. In large folio panel box with pictorial onlay. $1,000. There was also a signed issue with 12 prints and a 13th illustration (signed original). $3,000. One of 26 signed copies inscribed to buyer, as above, but lacking original illustration. $2,000. One of 12 copies signed but not inscribed. $1,750 and 6 other issues. See Shifreen & Jackson.

MILLER, Henry. *Into the Night Life.* (Berkeley, 1947.) Illustrated by Bezalel Schatz. Folio, cloth. One of 800 copies signed by the author and the artist. Without dustwrapper in slipcase. $1,250. (300 reportedly destroyed.) One of 14 signed, numbered copies without illustrations. $1,750.

MILLER, Henry. *Maurizius Forever.* Colt Press. San Francisco, 1946. Colored drawings by Miller. Green boards. One of 500 copies. Printed at the Grabhorn Press. In plain brown dustwrapper. $300.

MILLER, Henry. *Max and the White Phagocytes.* Paris (1938). Wraps. $1,000.

MILLER, Henry. *Money and How It Gets That Way.* Paris (1938). Wraps. Booster Broadside No. 1. With copyright notice written in by Miller. $1,250. The other copies. $450. Berkeley, 1946. Wraps. $150.

MILLER, Henry. *Quiet Days in Clichy.* Olympia Press. Paris, 1956. Photographs by Brassai. Printed wraps. $1,500.

MILLER, Henry. *Scenario (A Film with Sound).* Paris, 1937. Double-page frontispiece by Abraham Rattner. Wraps, unbound. One of 200 signed copies. $1,750.

MILLER, Henry. *The Smile at the Foot of the Ladder.* New York (1948). Pictorial boards and cloth. $350.

MILLER, Henry. *Tropic of Cancer.* Obelisk Press. Paris (1934). Preface by Anaïs Nin. Author's first book. Pictorial wraps. With "First published September 1934" on copyright page and with wraparound band. $12,500. New York, 1940. First (pirated) American edition. Issued without dustwrapper. $450. Also, wraps. $250. New York (1961). Grove Press. Introduction by Karl Shapiro. Preface by Anaïs Nin. Patterned boards and cloth. One of 100 signed copies. First authorized American edition. (Issued without dustwrapper.) $2,500. Trade edition. Boards. In dustwrapper. $150.

MILLER, Henry. *Tropic of Capricorn*. Obelisk Press. Paris (1939). Decorated wraps. "First published Feb., 1939" with price on spine and with errata slip. $2,250.

MILLER, Henry. *Watercolors, Drawings and His Essay "The Angel Is My Watermark!"* London, 1962. Illustrated. Small folio, cloth. With each of the 12 reproductions signed by Miller. $1,500. New York (1962). In acetate dustwrapper. $250.

MILLER, Henry. *What Are You Going to Do About Alf?* Paris (1935). Printed wraps. $2,500. Paris (1938). Wraps. Second edition with two-page foreword not in first edition. $350. Berkeley (1944). Printed self-wraps. $125. (London, 1971.) First English edition. One of 100 signed copies. In dustwrapper. $350. Unsigned copies (250). $100.

MILLER, Henry. *The World of Sex*. (Chicago, 1940.) One of 250 copies. In dustwrapper. $600. Later edition in blue cloth. (New York, no date.) "One of 1,000." Issued without dustwrapper. $150. Paris (1957). 125 pages in wraps. Revised edition. $150.

MILLER, Henry; HILER, Hilaire; and SAROYAN, William. *Why Abstract?* New Directions. (New York, 1945.) $200. Falcon Press. London (1948). First English edition. $150.

MILLER, Joaquin. See Miller, Cincinnatus H. See also *How to Win in Wall Street—Specimens.*

MILLER, Joaquin. *First Fam'lies in the Sierras.* London, 1875. $350.

MILLER, Joaquin. *'49, The Gold-Seeker of the Sierras.* New York, 1884. Printed wraps. $750. Also issued in cloth, and in boards and cloth. $500.

MILLER, Joaquin. *An Illustrated History of Montana.* Chicago, 1894. 2 vols., morocco. $750.

MILLER, Joaquin. *Life Amongst the Modocs: Unwritten History.* London, 1873. $750.

MILLER, Joaquin. *Pacific Poems.* London, 1871. Green cloth, gilt. $1,500.

MILLER, Joaquin. *Songs of the Mexican Seas.* Boston, 1877. $300.

MILLER, Joaquin. *Songs of the Sierras.* London, 1871. $250. Boston, 1871. Probable first binding, with "R.B." at foot of spine and "Thoughts about Art" on page (i) not (iv). $300.

MILLER, Joaquin. *Unwritten History: Life Among the Modocs.* Hartford, 1874. First American edition (of *Life Amongst the Modocs*). $750.

MILLER, Lewis B. *A Crooked Trail.* Pittsburgh (1908). Wraps, cloth spine. $500.

MILLER, Lewis. B. *Saddles and Lariats.* Boston, 1912. Illustrated. Pictorial cloth. $150.

MILLER, Patrick. *The Green Ship.* Golden Cockerel Press. London, 1936. 8 wood engravings by Eric Gill, with an extra set of the plates on Japan vellum. Full morocco. One of 62 copies. $1,250. Half morocco and boards. One of 134 copies. $600. One of 4 copies on vellum. $7,500.

MILLER, Patrick. *The Natural Man*. London, 1924. Author's first book. $150. New York, 1924. $75.

MILLER, Patrick. *Woman in Detail*. Golden Cockerel Press. London, 1947. 5 illustrations by Mark Severin, with a duplicate set of the 5 plates and with 3 additional ones in a pocket at the end. Half morocco and boards. One of 100 signed copies. $450. One of 430 copies. $150.

MILLER, T. L. *History of Hereford Cattle*. Chillicothe, Mo., 1902. Illustrated. Pictorial cloth. $150.

MILLER, Thomas. *Common Wayside Flowers*. London, 1860. Illustrated by Birket Foster. Decorated brown cloth. $400.

MILLER, Walter M., Jr. *A Canticle for Leibowitz*. Philadelphia/New York, 1960. $1,000. London (1960). $350.

MILLHAUSER, Steven. *Edwin Mullhouse*. New York, 1972. $350. London (1979). $75.

MILLS, Anson. *Big Horn Expedition*. No place or date (1874?). Folding map. 15 pages, tan printed wraps. $750.

MILLS, Robert. *Atlas of the State of South Carolina*. Baltimore, (about 1826). 29 double-page maps, colored by hand. Folio, half leather. (Issued to accompany *Mills' Statistics;* see item following.) $12,500.

MILLS, Robert. *Statistics of South Carolina*. Charleston, 1826. Map (not in all copies). $750. Without map. $350.

MILLS, Samuel J., and SMITH, Daniel. *Report of a Missionary Tour . . . West of the Alleghany Mountains*. Andover, 1815. $400.

MILLS, William W. *Forty Years at El Paso, 1858–1898*. (Chicago, 1901.) Frontispiece. Cloth. (Printed at El Paso, Tex.) $350. El Paso, 1962. Mesquite Edition. $200.

MILLSPAUGH, Charles F. *American Medicinal Plants . . .* New York and Philadelphia, 1882. 2 vols. 180 colored plates. $2,000.

MILMINE, Georgine. *The Life of Mary Baker G. Eddy and the History of Christian Science*. New York, 1909. Edited by Willa S. Cather. (Largely written by Cather.) $1,000. London, 1909. $750.

MILNE, A. A. *The Christopher Robin Story Book*. London (1929). Illustrated by Ernest H. Shepard. Pictorial cloth. $750. New York (1929). One of 350 signed copies. Pictorial boards and cloth. In box. $3,000. Trade. $600.

MILNE, A. A. *The House at Pooh Corner*. London (1928). Decorations by Ernest H. Shepard. One of 350 signed copies. Boards and buckram. In dustwrapper. $6,000. Vellum. One of 20 signed copies on Japan vellum. $10,000. Trade edition in pink cloth. $2,000. Deluxe edition in full leather. In box. $2,500. New York (1928). Illustrated. Cloth. First American edition. One of 250 signed copies. $3,000. Trade. $500.

MILNE, A. A. *Lovers in London*. London, 1905. Author's first book. $600.

MILNE, A. A. *Now We Are Six*. London (1927). Illustrated by Ernest H. Shepard. Boards and cloth. In dustwrapper and original publisher's paper box. One of 200 signed copies. In dustwrapper. $6,000. Vellum. One of 20 signed copies on Japan vellum. $10,000. Trade edition.

Pictorial maroon cloth. $2,000. Deluxe edition in crimson leather. In box. $2,500. New York (1927). One of 200 signed copies. In dustwrapper. $3,000. Trade. $500.

MILNE, A. A. *The Red House Mystery.* London (1922). $1,500.

MILNE, A. A. *Songs from "Now We Are Six."* London (1927). Limited to 100 copies, signed by Milne, Fraser-Simson, and E. H. Shepard. $1,750.

MILNE, A. A. *Toad of Toad Hall: A Play from Kenneth Grahame's Book "The Wind in the Willows."* London (1929). Boards and buckram. One of 200 copies signed by Milne and Grahame. In dustwrapper. $3,500. Trade edition. $500. New York (1929). $300.

MILNE, A. A. *When We Were Very Young.* London (1924). Illustrated by Ernest H. Shepard. Boards and cloth. One of 100 signed copies. In dustwrapper. $20,000. Trade edition, first issue; pictorial blue cloth, plain endpapers. Although the bibliography does not differentiate, it has been assumed, and was stated in Bradley's guides, that the first issue had page "ix" unnumbered. We presume this is because the limited edition had page ix unnumbered and the same plates were used for both editions. Of course, the limited was such a relatively elaborate production, one could also argue that it was actually produced after the trade and thus the trade with page ix numbered could have been first. So, either issue in dustwrapper. $7,500. New York (1924). Pictorial boards and cloth. First American edition. One of 100 signed deluxe copies. In dustwrapper. $7,500. One of 400. $2,000.

MILNE, A. A. *When We Were Very Young; Winnie-the-Pooh; Now We Are Six; The House at Pooh Corner.* London, 1924–28. With decorations by Ernest H. Shepard. First trade editions of all four of the Pooh books, in dustwrappers. $17,500.

MILNE, A. A. *Winnie-the-Pooh.* London (1926). Illustrated by Ernest H. Shepard. Boards and buckram. One of 350 signed copies. In dustwrapper and box. $15,000. Vellum. One of 20 signed copies on vellum. $25,000. Trade edition. Pictorial green cloth. $6,000. Deluxe edition in blue leather. In box. $3,500. New York (1926). Pictorial boards and cloth. First American edition. One of 200 signed copies. In dustwrapper. $7,500. Trade edition. $1,500.

MILNER, Henry Ernest. *The Art and Practice of Landscape Gardening.* London, 1890. $600.

MILNS, William. *The Penman's Repository* . . . Clerkenwell, 1787. First edition title page states that 20 alphabets are included. $1,500.

MILOSZ, Czeslaw. *The Captive Mind.* London, 1953. $200. New York, 1953. $150. New York, Limited Editions Club, 1983. One of 1500 signed copies. $200.

MILTON, John. *Four Poems: L'Allegro, Il Penseroso, Arcades, Lycidas.* Gregynog Press. Newtown, 1933. Wood engravings by Blair Hughes-Stanton. Red morocco. One of 250 copies on Japan vellum. $1,000.

MILTON, John. *Paradise Lost* [and] *Paradise Regained.* Doves Press. London, 1902-5. 2 vols. Printed in red and black. Vellum. One of 300 copies. $3,000. 2 vols. One of 25 copies on vellum. $20,000. London, 1931. Illustrated by D. Galanis. 2 vols., folio, pigskin. One of 195 copies. In slipcase. $1,250. 2 vols. Sharkskin. One of 10 copies on vellum. In slipcase. $15,000. Golden Cockerel Press. London, 1937. Woodcuts by Mary Groom. Half pigskin. One of 200 copies. $1,750. One of 4 copies on vellum. $20,000.

MILTON, John. *Paradise Lost: A Poem in Twelve Books,* with *Paradise Regain'd, A Poem in Four Books.* To which is added Samson Agonistes, and Poems Upon Several Occasions. 2 vols. London, 1758. $1,500.

MILTON, John. *Paradise Regain'd: A Poem. In IV Books.* London, 1671. First issue with misprint "loah" on page 67, 2 parts in one, separate title pages and pagination but continuous quiring, license leaf before general title, errata leaf page 4 at end. $5,000.

MILTON, John. *Poems.* London, 1645. 2 parts in one volume. First issue omitting the "S" before "Pauls" in imprint, and with Milton's first published portrait, engraved by William Marshall. $15,000.

MILTON, John. *Poems in English.* Nonesuch Press. London, 1926. 53 plates by William Blake. 2 vols., half vellum and brown boards. One of 1,450 copies on Van Gelder paper. $1,000. 2 vols. in one, vellum. One of 90 copies on India paper. $1,750.

MILTON, John. *The Reason of Church-Governement Urg'd Against Prelaty . . . in Two Books.* London, 1641. $3,000.

MILTON, John. *Three Poems of John Milton.* Ashendene Press. London, 1896. One of 50 copies. $2,500.

MINER, Dorothy (editor). *Studies in Art and Literature for Belle Da Costa Greene.* Princeton, 1954. $350.

MINER, Harriet Stewart. *Orchids: The Royal Family of Plants.* Boston, 1885. Small folio. 24 chromolithographic plates. $1,250.

MIRIAM Coffin, or, The Whale Fisherman: A Tale. New York/Philadelphia, 1834. (By Joseph C. Hart.) 2 vols. $500. London, 1834. 3 vols. $1,000.

MIRÓ, Joan. *The Indelible Miró.* New York, 1972. Contains 2 original lithographs done for this book, plus the front cover. In dustwrapper. $300.

MIRÓ, Joan. *Joan Miró Lithographs.* New York (1972). 4 vols. In dustwrappers. $2,500.

MIRÓ, Joan. *Sculptures.* (Paris, 1970.) Plates, including 2 color lithographs by Miró. Pictorial wrappers, slipcase. One of 150 copies signed by Miró. $2,500.

MIRRLEES, Hope. *Paris: A Poem.* Hogarth Press. Richmond, England, 1919. Wraps, paper label. $1,000.

MIRROR of Olden Time Border Life. Abingdon, Va., 1849. (By Joseph Pritts.) 13 plates (17 in some). Leather. $400.

MISFORTUNES of Elphin (The). London, 1829. (By Thomas Love Peacock.) $850. Newtown, Wales, 1928. Gregynog Press. Woodcuts. Buckram-backed cloth. One of 250 copies. $400. Morocco. One of 25 copies bound by George Fisher. $2,500.

MR. DOOLEY in Peace and in War. Boston, 1898. (By Finley Peter Dunne.) Author's first book. Green cloth. $250.

MR. FACEY Romford's Hounds. London, 1864–65. (By Robert Smith Surtees.) 24 color plates by John Leech and "Phiz" (H. K. Browne). 12 parts, pictorial wraps. First edition, with first state wraps of Part I reading "Mr. Facey Romford's Hounds" (second state and all subsequent parts read "Mr. Romford's Hounds"). $2,000. London, 1865. Pictorial cloth. First book edition. $350.

MR. MIDSHIPMAN Easy. London, 1836. (By Frederick Marryat.) 3 vols., in original boards. $450.

MR. SPONGE'S Sporting Tour. London, 1852–53. (By Robert Smith Surtees.) 13 color plates and 84 woodcuts by John Leech. 13 parts in 12, pictorial wraps. First edition, first issue, with the dedication to Lord Elcho (second issue reading "Earl Elcho"). $1,750. Second issue. $1,000. London, 1853. First book edition in pictorial cloth. $500.

MITCHEL, Martin. *History of the County of Fond du Lac Wisconsin.* Fond du Lac, 1854. 96 pages, printed yellow wraps. $450.

MITCHELL, Dewey. *Skilled Defense.* Cleveland, 1936. $250.

MITCHELL, Donald G. See Marvel, Ik.

MITCHELL, Donald G. *The Dignity of Learning: A Valedictory Oration.* New Haven, 1841. Printed wraps. $350.

MITCHELL, Gladys. *Speed Death.* New York, 1929. Author's first book. $750.

MITCHELL, Isaac. *The Asylum; or, Alonzo and Melissa.* Poughkeepsie, 1811. 2 vols. Frontispiece. Author's first (and only) book. (Note: Many later editions appeared with Daniel Jackson, Jr., as the author.) $750

MITCHELL, Joseph. *The Missionary Pioneer.* New York, 1827. $2,000.

MITCHELL, Joseph. *McSorley's Wonderful Saloon.* New York (1943). $1,500.

MITCHELL, Joseph. *My Ears Are Bent.* New York (1938). Author's first book. $600.

MITCHELL, Margaret. *Gone with the Wind.* New York, 1936. Gray cloth. First printing, with "Published May, 1936" on copyright page and no note of other printings. In first issue dustwrapper, with *Gone with the Wind* listed in the second column of Macmillan book list on back panel. $10,000. In second-issue jacket, with the novel listed at top of list in first column. $3,500. Without jacket. $1,250.

MITCHELL, S. Augustus (publisher). *Description of Oregon and California, Embracing An Account of the Gold Regions.* Philadelphia, 1849. Folding map in color. Gold-stamped cloth. $8,500.

MITCHELL, S. Augustus (publisher). *A New Map of Texas . . . and An Accompaniment to Mitchell's New Map of Texas, Oregon and California, with the Regions Adjoining.* Philadelphia, 1846. Cloth and 46 pages, text and large colored map, folding into leather covers. $10,000.

MITCHELL, S. Augustus. *Traveller's Guide Through the United States.* Philadelphia (1836). Folding map. 74 pages. First edition under this title. $1,750. Philadelphia, 1838. $1,250.

MITCHELL, S. Weir. See S., E.W. and M., S.W. See also *The Wonderful Stories of Fuz-Buz the Fly.*

MITCHELL, S. Weir. *Hugh Wynne, Free Quaker.* New York, 1897. Illustrated by Howard Pyle. 2 vols. First issue, in tan cloth with tipped-in title page and with last word on page 54, vol. 1, being "in" (later "her") and line 16 on page 260, vol. 2, reading "between" (later "lines of in-"). $500. Later issue, text corrected. 2 vols., gray boards, white cloth spines, paper labels. $200.

One of 60 signed large-paper copies with separate plates by Howard Pyle laid in. $1,000. (Note: A few copies of the first issue exist with an 1896 title page, as publication was delayed).

MITCHELL, S. Weir. *Researches upon the Venom of the Rattlesnake.* Washington, 1861. Folio, wraps. $2,500.

MITCHELL, S. Weir, et al. *Gunshot Wounds and Other Injuries of Nerves.* Philadelphia, 1864. Wraps. $5,000.

MITCHELL, W. H. *Geographical and Statistical Sketch of the Past and Present of Goodhue County.* Minneapolis, 1869. 191 pages, wraps. $200.

MITCHELL, W. O. *Who Has Seen the Wind.* Toronto, 1947. Author's first book. $600. Boston, 1947. $300.

MITCHELL, Wesley C. *Gold, Prices, and Wages Under the Greenback Standard.* University of California, 1908. Wraps. $350.

MITFORD, John. *The Adventures of Johnny Newcome in the Navy.* London, 1819. Color plates. Second edition. $500. London, 1823. Third edition with 20 colored plates. $600. (See Alfred Burton entry for first edition.)

MITFORD, Mary Russell. *Our Village.* London, 1824–32. 5 vols. $850. London, 1893. Illustrated by Hugh Thompson. Cloth. One of 470 copies. $500. London, 1910. Thompson illustrations. Half leather. $300.

MITFORD, Mary Russell. *Poems.* London, 1810. Author's first book. With leaf of "Alterations." $1,500.

MITFORD, Nancy. *Highland Fling.* London, 1931. Author's first book. $250.

MIVART, St. George. *Dogs, Jackals, Wolves, and Foxes . . .* London, 1890. With 45 color plates. $3,000.

MIVART, St. George. *A Monograph of the Lories, or Brush-Tongued Parrots.* London, 1896. 61 colored plates and 4 colored maps. First binding with "R. H. Porter" (publisher) on spine. $9,000. Second with "Quaritch" on spine. $7,500.

MIYAKE, T., and TANI, Y. *The Game of Ju Jitsu.* London, 1906. $250.

M'MAHON, Bernard. *The American Gardener's Calendar.* Philadelphia, 1806. Folding table. $600.

MO, Timothy. *The Monkey King.* (London, 1978.) Author's first book. $300. New York: Doubleday, 1980. $100.

MODERN Griselda (The). London, 1805. (By Maria Edgeworth.) $750.

MODERN Painters . . . London, 1843. (By John Ruskin.) $2,000.

MOELLHAUSEN, Balduin. *Diary of a Journey from the Mississippi to the Coasts of the Pacific with a United States Government Expedition.* London, 1858. 2 vols. First edition in English. 19 plates (some colored). Folding map. $2,500.

MOFFETT, Cleveland (Langston). *Through the Wall.* New York, 1909. $500.

MOFFETTE, Joseph F. *The Territories of Kansas and Nebraska.* New York, 1855. 2 folding maps. $3,000. New York, 1856. Second edition. $1,000.

MOKLER, A. J. *History of Natrona County, Wyoming.* Chicago, 1923. Illustrated. Buckram. $400.

MOLL Pitcher: A Poem. Boston, 1832. (By John Greenleaf Whittier.) In original wraps. $7,500. Philadelphia, 1840. *(Moll Pitcher, and the Minstrel Girl: Poems.)* Wraps. $600.

MOMADAY, N. Scott. *House Made of Dawn.* New York (1968). $350.

MOMADAY, N. Scott. *The Journey of Tai-Me.* Santa Barbara (1968). (100 copies.) Slipcase. $2,500.

MONASTERY (The). Edinburgh, 1820. (By Sir Walter Scott.) 3 vols. $400.

MONETTE, John W. *History of the Discovery and Settlement of the Valley of the Mississippi.* New York, 1846. 3 maps, 4 plans, 2 plates. $750.

MONIKINS (The): A Tale. By the Author of *"The Spy."* London, 1835. (By James Fenimore Cooper.) 3 vols. $1,000. Philadelphia, 1835. 2 vols. First American edition. $750.

MONK, Maria. *Awful Disclosures.* New York, 1836. Author's first book. $400.

MONKS, William. *History of Southern Missouri and Northern Arkansas.* West Plains, Mo., 1907. $250.

MONROE, Harriet. *Valeria and Other Poems.* Chicago, 1891. Author's first book. Vellum and cloth. Subscriber's edition, 300 copies. $200. Chicago, 1892. Cloth. First published edition. $75.

MONROE, James. *The Memoir of James Monroe, Esq., Relating to His Unsettled Claims Upon the People and Government of the U.S.* Charlottesville, Va., 1828. 60 pages, sewn. $750.

MONROE Doctrine (The). See *Message of the President . . .* (1823).

MONT Saint Michel and Chartres. Washington, 1904. (By Henry Adams.) Blue cloth, leather label on spine. Privately printed. $5,000. Washington, 1912. Second (first revised and enlarged) edition. (500 copies.) $1,000. Boston, 1913. Half brown cloth and tan boards. First published edition. $150. Limited Editions Club, New York, 1957. Cloth and leather. In slipcase. $150.

MONTAGU, Charles. See *The Hind and the Panther . . .*

MONTAGUE, C. E. *A Hind Let Loose.* London (1910). Author's first book. One of 150 copies. $350. Regular edition. $150.

MONTAIGNE, Michel Eyquem de. *The Essayes or Morall, Politike and Millitarie Discourses.* London, 1603. Translated by John Florio. 3 parts in 1 folio. $7,500. As *Essays.* Boston, 1902-3-4. 3 vols., folio, half cloth. One of 265 copies designed by Bruce Rogers. In folding cases. $1,250. London, 1931. Nonesuch Press. 2 vols., full morocco. One of 1,375 copies. In slipcase. $350. Limited Editions Club, New York, 1946. 4 vols. In slipcase. $200. Garden City, 1947. One of 1,000 copies signed by Dali. $1,250.

MONTANA, Its Climate, Industries and Resources. Helena, Mont., 1884. Illustrated. 74 pages, wraps. $450.

MONTANA Territory, History and Business Directory 1879. Helena (1879). (By F. W. Warner.) Map. 5 plates. Printed boards and leather. $1,500.

MONTESSORI, Maria. *The Montessori Method.* London, 1912. First English translation of author's first book. $350. New York, 1912. $200.

MONTGOMERY, Field Marshall. *A History of Warfare.* London, 1969. (By Bernard Law Montgomery.) One of 265 signed copies in full morocco. In slipcase. $750.

MONTGOMERY, L. M. *Anne of Green Gables.* Boston, 1908. Author's first book. $20,000.

MONTULE, Eduard. *A Voyage to North America, and the West Indies, in 1817.* London, 1821. 6 folding and full-page plates. First edition in English. $750.

MOODIE, Susanna. *Roughing It in the Bush; Or, Life in Canada.* New York, 1852. 2 vols. Wraps. $1,000.

MOODY, Rick. *Garden State.* Wainscott (1992). $200.

MOODY, William Vaughn. *The Masque of Judgment.* Boston, 1900. Author's first book. $60. Boards. One of 150 copies. $125.

MOODY, William Vaughn. *Poems.* Boston, 1901. Boards. One of 150 copies on large paper. $125.

MOORCOCK, Michael. See Reid, Desmond.

MOORCOCK, Michael. *The Stealer of Souls.* London, 1963. In orange boards. $200. Later binding in green. $150.

MOORCOCK, Michael. *Stormbringer.* London (1965). $250.

MOORE, Sir Alan Hilary. *Sailing Ships of War, 1800–1860.* London, 1926. 90 full-page plates, 12 in color. One of 1,500 copies. Issued without dustwrapper. $400. Half leather. One of 100 copies. Issued without dustwrapper. $1,000.

MOORE, Brian. *Judith Hearne.* (London, 1955.) (First hardback.) $1,000.

MOORE, Brian. *The Lonely Passion of Judith Hearn.* Boston (1955). $300.

MOORE, Brian. *Wreath for a Redhead.* Toronto, 1951. Author's first book. Wraps. $750.

MOORE, C. L. *Doomsday Morning.* Garden City, 1957. $150.

MOORE, C. L. *Shambleau and Others.* New York (1953). $300.

MOORE, Catherine Lucile. See Padgett, Lewis.

MOORE, Clement C. See *A New Translation; The New York Book of Poetry; Observations upon Certain Passages in Mr. Jefferson's "Notes on Virginia."*

MOORE, Clement C. *Account of a Visit from St. Nicholas.* Philadelphia, 1825. $26,000 at auction in 1995.

MOORE, Clement C. *The Night Before Christmas.* New York, 1902. Color plates by W. W. Denslow. Pictorial boards. First state of binding. $2,000. Second binding in pictorial cloth. $1,000. London, 1903. "Denslow's *Night* . . ." $1,500. Philadelphia (1931). 4 color plates and text drawings by Arthur Rackham. One of 275 signed copies. $3,000. Trade in dustwrapper. $1,000. London (1931). One of 550 signed copies in vellum. In slipcase. $2,000. Trade in dustwrapper. $750.

MOORE, Clement C. *Poems.* New York, 1844. Brown boards. $1,500.

MOORE, Edward. *We Moderns: Enigmas and Guesses.* London (1918). (By Edwin Muir, his first book.) Blue pebble-grained cloth, with spine label lettered in red. In dustwrapper. $750. Without dustwrapper. $200.

MOORE, Edward A. *The Story of a Cannoneer Under Stonewall Jackson.* New York, 1907. $450.

MOORE, Francis. *A Voyage to Georgia* . . . London, 1744. $7,500.

MOORE, George. *Flowers of Passion.* London, 1878. Black cloth. Author's first book. With 1877 copyright and errata slip. $750.

MOORE, George. *Literature at Nurse, or, Circulating Morals.* London, 1885. Self-wraps, sewn. $1,000.

MOORE, George. *A Modern Lover.* London, 1883. 3 vols., blue cloth. $3,000.

MOORE, George. *Peronnik the Fool.* New York, 1926. Boards. Issued without dustwrapper. Bruce Rogers printing. $300. Chapelle-Reanville, France, 1928. Hours Press. Revised edition. One of 200 signed copies. Issued without dustwrapper. $600. London, 1933. Engravings by Stephen Gooden. Full vellum. Issued without dustwrapper. One of 525 copies signed by author and artist. $300.

MOORE, H. Judge. *Scott's Campaign in Mexico.* Charleston, 1849. $1,000.

MOORE, Henry. *Heads, Figures and Ideas.* London, 1958. $300. One of 150 copies with a signed Moore lithograph in color. $2,500.

MOORE, Marianne. *The Absentee: A Comedy in Four Acts.* New York, 1962. Blue cloth. One of 326 signed copies. In tissue dustwrapper. $250.

MOORE, Marianne. *Complete Poems.* New York (1967). Half buckram. First printing, with "flowrrs" on page 65, line 34. $150.

MOORE, Marianne. *Eight Poems.* New York (1962). 10 hand-colored drawings. Half cloth. One of 195 signed copies. In slipcase. $1,000.

MOORE, Marianne. *Observations.* New York, 1924. $2,500.

MOORE, Marianne. *The Pangolin and Other Verse.* (London), 1936. Drawings by George Plank. Decorated boards, paper label. One of 120 copies. $1,250.

MOORE, Marianne. *Poems.* Egoist Press. London, 1921. Author's first book. Decorated wraps, paper label. $1,000.

MOORE, Marianne (translator). *The Fables of La Fontaine.* New York, 1954. One of 400 signed copies. In glassine jacket and slipcase. $350. Trade. $125. New York (1965). Revised edition. $75.

MOORE, Marinda B. (Mrs. M. B.) *The Geographical Reader for the Dixie Children.* Raleigh, 1863. 48 pages, boards. $1,500.

MOORE, Robin. *The Green Berets.* New York (1965). $200.

MOORE, Robin. *The French Connection.* Boston (1969). $200.

MOORE, S. S., and JONES, T. W. *The Traveller's Directory.* Philadelphia, 1802. 38 maps on 22 leaves. 52 pages. $4,000. Philadelphia, 1804. $2,000.

MOORE, Thomas. *The Epicurean: A Tale.* London, 1827. $250.

MOORE, Thomas. *Lyrics and Satires.* Cuala Press. Dublin, 1929. Selected by Sean O'Faolain. 5 designs by Hilda Roberts. Boards and cloth. One of 130 copies. In dustwrapper. $750.

MOORE, Thomas. *Paradise and the Peri.* (London, 1860.) Illuminated borders. Folio, leather, or cloth. $500.

MOORE, Thomas. *Tom Crib's Memorial to Congress.* London, 1819. $600.

MOORE, Thomas (translator). *The Odes of Anacreon.* London, 1800. Author's first book. $400.

MOORE, T. Sturge. *A Brief Account of the Origin of the Eragny Press.* London, 1903. Eragny Press. Illustrated. Boards. One of 235 copies. $1,750. One of 6 copies on vellum. $7,500.

MOORE, T. Sturge. *The Little School: A Posy of Rhymes.* Eragny Press. London, 1905. Woodcuts. Boards. One of 185 copies. In dustwrapper. $1,250. Morocco. One of 10 copies on vellum. $5,000.

MOORE, T. Sturge. *Two Poems.* London, 1893. Author's first book. $250.

MOORE, T. Sturge. *The Vinedresser and Other Poems.* Unicorn Press. London, 1899. Cloth. $200.

MORE, Hannah. See *Hints Towards Forming the Character of a Young Princess.*

MORE, Hannah. *Sacred Dramas, Chiefly Intended for Young Persons.* London, 1782. $750.

MORE, Hannah. *Slavery: A Poem.* London, 1788. $1,000.

MORE, Hannah. *Strictures on the Modern System of Female Education.* London, 1799. 2 vols. $1,250. Philadelphia, 1800. $350.

MORE, Sir Thomas. *Utopia.* [The first edition published in Louvain (1516) sold at auction in May 1996 for $210,000.] Kelmscott Press. London, 1893. Woodcut borders and initials, printed in black and red. Vellum with ties. $2,500. One of 6 copies on vellum. $12,500. Golden Cockerel Press. Waltham Saint Lawrence, England, 1929. Decorations by Eric Gill. Buckram. One of 500 copies. $750. Limited Editions Club, New York, 1934. Woodcuts by Bruce Rogers. Vellum and boards. In slipcase. $250.

MORECAMP, Arthur. *The Live Boys; or, Charlie and Nasho in Texas.* Boston (1878). (By Thomas Pilgrim, his first book.) Pictorial cloth. $1,000.

MORES, Edward Rowe. *A Dissertation Upon English Typographical Founders and Founderies . . .* New York, 1924. Limited to 250 copies. $250.

MORFI, Juan Agustín. *History of Texas, 1673–1779.* Albuquerque, 1935. Map, 4 plates. 2 vols., boards and cloth. One of 500 copies. $650. New York, 1967. Facsimile edition. $150.

MORGAN, Charles. *The Gunroom.* London, 1919. Author's first novel. $250.

MORGAN, Claire. *The Price of Salt.* New York: Coward McCann (1952). (By Patricia Highsmith.) $2,000.

MORGAN, Dale L. See Ashley, William H.

MORGAN, Dale L. *Jedediah Smith and the Opening of the West.* Indianapolis (1953). 20 plates. Cloth. In dustwrapper. $200.

MORGAN, Dale L., and WHEAT, Carl I. *Jedediah Smith and His Maps of the American West.* San Francisco, 1954. 7 folding maps. One of 530 copies. Issued without dustwrapper. $1,000.

MORGAN, Dick T. *Morgan's Manual of the U.S. Homestead and Townsite Laws.* Gutfirie, Okla., 1893. Buff printed wraps. $500.

MORGAN, Emanuel. *Pins for Wings.* (New York, 1920.) (By Witter Bynner.) Illustrated by William Sophier. Boards. Issued without dustwrapper. $350.

MORGAN, Emanuel, and KNISH, Anne. *Spectra: A Book of Poetic Experiments.* New York, 1916. (By Witter Bynner [Morgan] and Arthur Davison Ficke [Knish].) (Issued without dustwrapper.) $300.

MORGAN, Jane. *Tales for Fifteen.* New York, 1823. (By James Fenimore Cooper.) $3,000.

MORGAN, John Hill, and FIELDING, Mantle. *The Life Portraits of Washington and Their Replicas.* Philadelphia (1931). Illustrated. Folio, cloth. One of 1,000 copies. $350. Full morocco. Limited, signed by the authors. In dustwrapper and slipcase. $750.

MORGAN, Lewis H. *The American Beaver and His Works.* Philadelphia, 1868. Map, 23 plates. $600.

MORGAN, Lewis H. *The League of the Ho-De'-No-Sau-Nee, or Iroquois.* Rochester, N.Y., 1851. 21 plates, map, table. $600. Maps and plates colored by hand. $1,000.

MORGAN, Martha M. (editor). *A Trip Across the Plains in the Year 1849.* San Francisco, 1864. 31 pages, printed wraps. $7,500.

MORGAN, Thomas Hunt. *The Development of the Frog's Egg.* New York, 1897. Author's first book. $500.

MORGAN, Thomas J. *A Glance at Texas.* Columbus, 1844. 16 pages, three-quarter morocco. $1,500.

MORGANSTERN, S. See Goldman, William.

MORIER, James. See *Ayesha.*

MORIER, James. *A Journey Through Persia, Armenia, and Asia Minor* . . . London, 1812. Illustrated with 3 folding maps and 26 plates. $2,500.

MORING, Thomas. *50 Book Plates Engraved on Copper.* London, 1901. 50 full-page plates. $200.

MORISON, Samuel Eliot. *Admiral of the Ocean Sea.* Boston, 1942. 2 vols. $400. 1 vol. $150. London (1942). $200.

MORISON, Samuel Eliot. *Harrison Gray Otis.* Boston, 1913. 2 vols. Author's first book. $250.

MORISON, Samuel Eliot (translator). *Journals* . . . *Life and Voyages of Christopher Columbus.* New York, 1963. In slipcase. $150.

MORISON, Stanley. *The Art of the Printer.* London, 1925. $250. New York, 1926. $125.

MORISON, Stanley. *The English Newspaper.* Cambridge, 1932. Illustrated. Folio, cloth. In dustwrapper. $500.

MORISON, Stanley. *Four Centuries of Fine Printing.* London (1924). One of 390 copies. Issued without dustwrapper. $500. Morocco. One of 13 signed copies. $1,000. London (1949). 272 facsimile title pages. Calf. Second edition, revised. One of 200 copies. $300.

MORISON, Stanley. *John Bell, 1745–1831, Bookseller, Printer, Publisher, Typefounder* . . . Cambridge, 1930. One of 300 copies. In dustwrapper. $500.

MORISON, Stanley. *John Fell, The University Press and the "Fell" Types* . . . Oxford, 1967. One of 1,000 copies. In dustwrapper. $500.

MORISON, Stanley. *Modern Fine Printing.* London, 1925. Facsimiles. Folio, cloth. One of 650 copies in English. In dustwrapper. $500.

MORISON, Stanley. *On Type Faces, Examples of the Use of Type for the Printing of Books.* London, 1923. One of 750 copies. $250.

MORISON, Stanley. *Splendour of Ornament* . . . London, 1968. One of 400 copies. $200.

MORISON, Stanley. *The Typographic Book 1450–1935.* Chicago, 1963. $250.

MORISON, Stanley. *Typographic Design in Relation to Photographic Composition.* San Francisco, 1959. One of 400 copies. $200.

MORIYAMA, Daido. *Japan: A Photo Theatre.* Tokyo, 1968. The photographer's first book. Unpaginated black-and-white photos. Stiff wraps. In slipcase. $3,250.

MORLEY, C. D. *The Eighth Sin.* Oxford, 1912. (By Christopher Morley.) Author's first book. One of 250 copies. Printed pale blue-gray wraps. $1,500.

MORLEY, Christopher. *The Haunted Bookshop.* New York, 1919. First edition not stated. The first-state points have been disputed for years. Both Johnson and Casanova state: "First state has number 76 at bottom of proper page, type above it, "Burroughs" is unbroken; page 100, line 1, reads "Sty" vs. "Styx." Lee (no.5) remained uncertain. In dustwrapper. $1,500. Without dustwrapper. $200.

MORLEY, Christopher. *Parnassus on Wheels*. Garden City, 1917. First edition not stated. With space between the "Y" and "e" in "Years" on page 4, line 8, and missing an "L" from "goldenrod" on page 169, line 11. In first-state dustwrapper with "vibrating" instead of "beating" on front cover. $1,250. Without dustwrapper. $200.

MORLEY, Christopher. *Songs for a Little House*. New York (1917). Boards. First edition without publisher's monogram, first state has quotation from Southwell facing title page. In dustwrapper. $750. Without dustwrapper. $150.

MORLEY, Christopher. *Where the Blue Begins*. Garden City, 1922. Pictorial cream-and-blue boards, blue cloth spine. $200. London (1925). Illustrated by Arthur Rackham, including 4 color plates. Half black cloth and white boards. First Deluxe illustrated edition. One of 175 copies signed by Rackham. In slipcase. $1,750. London and New York (1925). Rackham illustrations. Half black cloth and green-and-blue boards. First American Deluxe edition. One of 100 copies signed by Morley and Rackham. In tissue dustwrapper and slipcase. $1,500. London (1925). Rackham illustrations. Blue cloth. First Rackham trade edition. In dustwrapper. $350.

MORPHIS, J. M. *History of Texas*. New York, 1874. Plates, folding map in color. $750.

MORRELL, Benjamin. *Narrative of Four Voyages to the South Seas, North and South Pacific Ocean*. New York, 1832. Portrait. $750.

MORRELL, Z. N. *Flowers and Fruits in the Wilderness; or 36 Years in Texas*. Boston, 1872. $500.

MORRIS, Beverley R. *British Game Birds and Wildfowl*. London, 1855. 60 hand-colored engraved plates. $4,500. London, 1864. 60 hand-colored engraved plates. $4,000. London, 1891. Third edition. 60 hand-colored engraved plates. $4,000.

MORRIS, Eastin. *The Tennessee Gazetteer*. Nashville, 1834. In original printed boards, leather spine. $1,500.

MORRIS, Rev. F. O. *A History of British Birds* . . . London, 1851–57. 6 vols. 358 hand-colored plates. $2,500. London, 1870. Second edtion with 365 plates. $2,750.

MORRIS, Henry, *Guilford & Green*. (North Hills, 1970.) With pocket containing a specimen of the paper that was to be used for the cover of the book. One of 210 copies. $500.

MORRIS, Henry. *Japonica* . . . North Hills, 1981. One of 250 copies in half morocco. $600.

MORRIS, Henry. *No. V-109, The Bibliography of a Printing Press*. No place, 1978. Miniature book (6.1 by 4.7 cm). One of 150 copies. $200.

MORRIS, Henry. *Omnibus, Instructions for Amateur Papermakers* . . . (North Hills), 1967. One of 500 copies. $350.

MORRIS, Henry. *The Paper Maker, A Survey of Lesser-Known Hand Paper Mills in Europe and North America* . . . North Hills, 1974. One of 175 copies. $1,000.

MORRIS, Henry. *Pepperpot: Ingredients* . . . North Hills, 1977. "Approximately 250 copies." $300.

MORRIS, Henry. *Roller-Printed Paste Papers for Bookbinding*. North Hills, 1975. One of 215 copies. $400.

MORRIS, Joseph. *The "Spirit Prevails:" Containing the Revelations, Articles and Letters Written by* . . . San Francisco, 1886. $2,000.

MORRIS, Maurice O. *Rambles in the Rocky Mountains.* London, 1864. $600.

MORRIS, William. *Child Christopher and Goldilind the Fair.* Kelmscott Press. London, 1895. 2 vols. Woodcuts. Decorated boards and cloth. One of 600 copies. $1,000. One of 12 copies on vellum. $4,000.

MORRIS, William. *The Defence of Guenevere, and Other Poems.* Kelmscott Press. London, 1858. Author's first book. $750. Kelmscott Press. London, 1892. Printed in black and red. Woodcut borders. Vellum with ties. One of 300 copies. $1,500. One of 10 copies on vellum. $10,000.

MORRIS, William. *A Dream of John Ball and a King's Lesson.* Kelmscott Press. London, 1892. Woodcut borders and designs by Morris and E. Burne-Jones. Vellum with ties. One of 300 copies. $2,500. Another issue, one of 11 copies on vellum. $10,000.

MORRIS, William. *The Earthly Paradise.* Kelmscott Press. London, 1896-97. 8 vols. Woodcut title. Vellum with ties. One of 225 copies. $6,000. One of 6 copies on vellum. $15,000.

MORRIS, William. *News from Nowhere.* Kelmscott Press. London, 1892. Woodcut frontispiece, borders, and initials. Vellum with ties. One of 300 copies. $2,500. One of 10 copies on vellum. $10,000.

MORRIS, William. *Poems by the Way.* Kelmscott Press. London, 1891. Vellum. One of 300 copies on paper. $1,750. One of 13 copies on vellum. $10,000.

MORRIS, William. *Printing: An Essay.* Park Ridge, Ill., 1903. Boards. $400.

MORRIS, William. *The Story of the Glittering Plain.* Kelmscott Press. London, 1891. Woodcut title and borders. Illustrations by Walter Crane. Vellum with ties. One of 200 copies. In slipcase. $4,000. London, 1894. Vellum. One of 250 copies. In slipcase. $3,000. One of 7 copies on vellum. $12,500.

MORRIS, William. *The Water of the Wondrous Isles.* Kelmscott Press. London, 1897. Woodcut borders and initials. Vellum with ties. One of 250 copies. $4,000. One of 6 copies on vellum. $12,500.

MORRIS, William. *The Wood Beyond the World.* Kelmscott Press. London, 1894. Woodcut frontispiece, other illustrations. Vellum with ties. One of 350 copies. $2,500. One of 8 copies on vellum. $12,500. Boston, 1895. Trade edition. Limited to 500 copies. $300.

MORRIS, Wright. *The Cat's Meow.* Los Angeles, 1975. With original photograph of a cat mounted on frontispiece; silver print, 4¼ x 6½ inches. One of 125 signed copies. $350.

MORRIS, Wright. *The Home Place.* New York, 1948. Illustrated. $300.

MORRIS, Wright. *The Inhabitants.* New York, 1946. Illustrated with author's photographs. $250.

MORRIS, Wright. *The Man Who Was There.* New York, 1945. $250.

MORRIS, Wright. *My Uncle Dudley.* New York (1942). Author's first book. $1,250.

MORRISON, Arthur. *Chronicles of Martin Hewitt.* London, 1895. $500. New York, 1896. $250.

MORRISON, Arthur. *The Dorrington Deed-Box.* London (1896). Illustrated. Red cloth. $750.

MORRISON, Arthur. *Martin Hewitt, Investigator.* London, 1894. $1,000.

MORRISON, Arthur. *The Painters of Japan.* London, 1911. 2 vols. $600.

MORRISON, Arthur. *The Shadows Around Us . . .* London, 1891. Author's first book. $350.

MORRISON, Arthur. *Tales of Mean Streets.* London, 1894. Green cloth. With October ads (VAB). $350.

MORRISON, James. *The Journal of Boatswain's Mate of the Bounty.* Golden Cockerel Press. (London), 1935. Buckram. One of 325 copies. $1,500.

MORRISON, James. *The American Prayer.* No place, 1970. Boards. $1,500.

MORRISON, James Douglas. *The Lords.* [Los Angeles], 1969. Author's first book. (100 copies.) Large string-tied portfolio. $2,500.

MORRISON, James Douglas. *The Lords and the New Creatures.* New York (1970). $200.

MORRISON, James Douglas. *The New Creatures.* Los Angeles, 1969. (100 copies.) $1,000.

MORRISON, Toni. *The Bluest Eye.* New York (1970). Author's first book. $3,500. London, 1979. $450.

MORRISON, Toni. *Song of Solomon.* New York, 1977. $450.

MORRISON, Toni. *Sula.* New York, 1974. $1,500. London, 1974. $300.

MORROW, William C. *Blood-Money.* San Francisco, 1882. Cloth. $400.

MORSE, A. Reynolds. *Salvador Dali: A Study of His Life and Work.* Greenwich, Conn. (1958). Illustrated. Oblong folio, cloth. First American edition. In acetate dustwrapper. $750.

MORSE, Jedidiah. *A Report to the Secretary of War . . . on Indian Affairs.* New Haven, 1822. Folding colored map. With errata leaf. $650.

MORSE, John F., and COLVILLE, Samuel. *Illustrated Historical Sketches of California.* Sacramento, 1854. No. 1 (all published). Frontispiece. Pictorial wraps. $25,000 at auction in 1985.

MORSE, Samuel French. *Time of Year.* (Cummington), 1943. One of 275 copies. $150.

MORSE, Samuel French. *Two Poems.* Hanover, 1934. One of 35 signed. Wraps. $350.

MORSE, Samuel French. *The Yellow Lilies.* Hanover, 1935. One of 85 signed copies. $250.

MORSE, Willard S., and BRINCKLE, Gertrude. *Howard Pyle: A Record of His Illustrations and Writings.* Wilmington, 1921. One of 500 copies. $250.

MORTENSEN, William. *Monsters & Madonnas.* San Francisco, 1936. Spiral bound. $650. Hollywood, 1967. Revised. $175.

MORTIMER, John. *Charade.* London (1947). Author's first book. $300.

MORTIMER, Ruth. *French 16th Century Books.* Cambridge, 1964. 2 vols. $500.

MORTIMER, Ruth. *Italian 16th Century Books.* Cambridge, 1974. 2 vols. In slipcase. $500.

MORTIMER, W. Golden. *Peru: History of Coca* . . . New York, 1901. Original cloth, with gilt vignettes on the spine and front cover. Frontispiece, 178 illustrations. $500.

MORTON, Sarah Wentworth. *Quabi: Or the Virtues of Nature.* Boston, 1790. Author's first book. $500.

MORTON, Thomas. *A Catholike Appeale for Protestants* . . . London, 1610. $750.

MORTON of Morton's Hope . . . London, 1839. (By John Lothrop Motley.) 3 vols. Author's first book. In original cloth. $450.

MORTON'S Hope . . . New York, 1839. (By John Lothrop Motley). 2 vols. $250.

MOSELEY, William. *The New Token for Children.* New Haven, 1806. First American from the second London edition. $500.

MOSES, Grandma. *My Life's History.* New York (1952). One of 275 signed copies. In slipcase. $750.

MOSES, Henry. *A Series of Twenty-nine Designs of Modern Costume.* London, 1823. 29 plates. $850.

MOSKOWITZ, Sam. *The Immortal Storm: A History of Science-Fiction Fandom.* Atlanta, 1951. Spiral-bound wraps. One of 150 copies. $200.

MOSLEY, Walter. *Devil in a Blue Dress.* New York, 1990. $175.

MOSS, Howard. *The Wound and the Weather.* New York (1946). Author's first book. $125.

MOTLEY, John Lothrop. See *Morton* . . . and *Morton's Hope.*

MOTLEY, John Lothrop. *The Rise of the Dutch Republic.* London, 1856. 3 vols. $500. New York, 1856. 3 vols. Three-quarter tan calf and cloth. $500. Cloth. $400.

MOTLEY, Willard. *Knock on Any Door.* New York (1947). Gray cloth. Author's first book. $200.

MOTT, Mrs. Mentor. *The Stones of Palestine.* London, 1865. 12 mounted photographs by Francis Bedford. $750.

MOULTRIE, William. *Memoirs of the American Revolution.* New York, 1802. 2 vols. $3,500.

MOUNSEER Nontongpaw: A New Version. (By Mary W. Shelley.) London, 1808. Author's first book. Wraps. $10,000. Rebound. $2,500.

MOUNTFORD, Charles. *Nomads of the Australian Desert. Adelaide, 1976. $500.*

MOWAT, Farley. People of the Deer. Boston, 1952. Author's first book. $150.

MOWRY, Sylvester. *Memoir of the Proposed Territory of Arizona.* Washington, 1857. Map (not in all copies). 30 pages, printed wraps. $3,000.

MOXON, Joseph. *Mechanick Exercise on the Whole Art of Printing (1683–4)*. London, 1962. 2 foldout plates. Second edition. Contains a bibliography of Moxon's work. $250.

MOXON, Joseph. *Moxon's Mechanick Exercises or the Doctrine of Handy Works Applied to the Art of Printing.* New York, 1896. 2 vols. One of 450 copies. $600. A reprint of the first edition of 1683 (which has sold for over $60,000 at auction).

MUDD, Harvey. *The Plain of Smokes.* Santa Barbara, 1981. Folio, plus 20 looseleaf original serigraph prints after illustrations by Price. One of 150 copies signed by the poet and the illustrator, and with 2 prints numbered and signed by Price. Folding box and slipcase. $1,750.

MUELLER, Hans Alexander. *Woodcuts & Wood Engravings: How I Make Them.* New York, 1939. Loose signatures inserted in a clamshell box. One of 250 copies. $450.

MUIR, Edwin. See Moore, Edward.

MUIR, Edwin. *Chorus of the Newly Dead.* Hogarth Press. Richmond, England, 1926. Wraps, paper label. $300.

MUIR, Edwin. *First Poems.* Hogarth Press. London, 1925. Boards, printed label. Issued without dustwrapper. $350.

MUIR, Edwin. *Latitudes.* New York, 1924. $200. London, 1926. $150.

MUIR, Edwin. *We Moderns.* New York, 1920. Author's first book. Includes Mencken introduction. $200.

MUIR, John. *The Cruise of the Corwin.* Boston, 1917. With 26 plates, including some by Edward Curtis. $300. One of 550 large-paper copies. In half cloth. $450.

MUIR, John. *The Mountains of California.* New York, 1894. Illustrated. Tan cloth. Author's first book. First edition, first issue, with folio 1 on first text page. $750. Without folio 1. $600. London, 1894. $500.

MUIR, John. *My First Summer in the Sierra.* Boston, 1911. $450. (Covelo, 1988.) One of 15 signed copies by McCurdy with an extra suite of signed illustrations. In white pine box with cowhide label. $3,500. One of 125 copies. $1,500.

MUIR, John. *Our National Parks.* Boston, 1901. $350.

MUIR, John. *Travels in Alaska.* Boston, 1915. One of 450 copies. In slipcase. $850. Trade. $350.

MUIR, John (editor). *Picturesque California.* San Francisco (1887–88). 2 vols., folio, calf. $1,750.

MUIR, Percy. *Catnachery.* San Francisco, 1955. Five foldout plates. One of 325 copies. $125.

MUIR, Percy H. *English Children's Books, 1600–1900.* London, 1954. Illustrated, including color plates. $125. New York, 1954. Illustrated. Blue cloth. First American edition. $125.

MUIR, Percy H. *Points, Second Series, 1866–1934.* London, 1934. One of 750 copies. Issued without dustwrapper. $150.

MUIR, Percy H. *Points, 1874–1930: Being Extracts from a Bibliographer's Note-Book.* London, 1931. One of 500 copies. Issued without dustwrapper. $175.

MUIR, Percy H. (editor). *A. F. Johnson: Selected Essays on Books and Printing.* Amsterdam, 1970. Two folding maps. $125.

MUJUMDAR, D. C. *Encyclopedia of Indian Physical Culture.* Baroda (India), 1950. First edition stated. $150.

MUJUMDAR, S. *Strongmen Over the Years.* Lucknow, (India) 1942. $200.

MULDOON, Paul. *Knowing My Place.* (Belfast, 1971). $400.

MULFORD, Clarence E. *Bar-20.* New York, 1907. First issue with "Blazing star" in list of illustrations. Author's first book. $450. Second issue. $300.

MULFORD, Clarence E. *Bar-20 Days.* Chicago, 1911. $300.

MULFORD, Clarence E. *Buck Peters Ranchman.* Chicago, 1912. $300.

MULFORD, Clarence E. *Hopalong Cassidy.* Chicago, 1910. $500.

MULLAN, John. *Miners' and Travelers' Guide to Oregon . . .* New York, 1865. Folding colored map. $1,750.

MULLAN, John. *Report on the Construction of a Military Road from Fort WallaWalla to Fort Benton.* Washington, 1863. 4 folding maps, 10 plates. $750.

MULLER, Marcia. *Ask the Cards a Question.* New York, 1982. $350.

MULLER, Marcia. *The Cheshire Cat's Eye.* New York, 1983. $350.

MULOCK, Dinah Maria (Mrs. Craik). See *The Adventures of a Brownie; John Halifax, Gentleman; The Ogilvies.*

MUMEY, Nolie. *Calamity Jane.* Denver, 1950. Folding map, illustrations, 2 pamphlets in envelope at end. Boards, pictorial label. One of 200 signed copies. $500.

MUMEY, Nolie. *John Williams Gunnison.* Denver, 1955. Colored portrait, plates, folding map. Boards. One of 500 signed copies. Issued without dustwrapper. $200.

MUMEY, Nolie. *The Life of Jim Baker.* Denver, 1931. Frontispieces, other illustrations, map. Boards. One of 250 signed copies. Issued without dustwrapper. $400. New York, 1972. One of 125 copies. $150.

MUMEY, Nolie. *March of the First Dragoons to the Rocky Mountains in 1835.* Denver, 1957. Errata slip, plates, folding map. Boards. One of 350 signed copies. $200.

MUMEY, Nolie. *A Study of Rare Books.* Denver, 1930. One of 1,000 signed copies. Author's first book. Issued without dustwrapper. $200.

MUMFORD, Lewis. *The Story of Utopias.* New York (1922). Author's first book. $400.

MUMMY! A Tale of the Twenty-second Century (The). Henry Colburn, 1827. (By Jane Webb.) 3 vols. $4,000.

MUNBY, A.M.L. *Phillipps Studies.* Cambridge, 1951–1960. 5 vols. (complete set). $600.

MUNDY, Talbot. *The Ivory Trail.* Indianapolis (1919). Cloth. In dustwrapper. $400. Without dustwrapper. $100.

MUNDY, Talbot. *Jimgrim.* New York (1931). (By William Lancaster Gribbon.) $350.

MUNDY, Talbot. *King of the Kyber Rifles.* Indianapolis (1916). (By William Lancaster Gribbon.) In dustwrapper. $2,500. Without dustwrapper. $350.

MUNDY, Talbot. *Queen Cleopatra.* Indianapolis (1929). One of 265 signed copies. $350.

MUNDY, Talbot. *Rung Ho!* New York, 1914. Author's first book. $200.

MUNDY, Talbot. *Tros of Samothrace.* New York, 1934. $500.

MUNRO, Alice. *Dance of the Happy Shades.* (Toronto, 1968.) Author's first book. $600. (New York, 1973.) $150.

MUNRO, H. H. See Saki.

MUNRO, H. H. *The Rise of the Russian Empire.* London, 1900. Author's first book. $350.

MUNRO, Robert. *A Description of the Genessee Country, in the State of New-York.* New York, 1804. (By Charles Williamson.) Map, 16 pages. $750.

MUNSELL, Charles. *Collection of Songs of the American Press* . . . Albany, 1868. $350.

MUNSELL, J. *A Chronology of Paper and Paper-Making.* Albany, 1857. Second edition, revised and enlarged. Wraps. $400.

MUNSON, Gorham. *Waldo Frank: A Study.* New York (1923). Original photographic frontispiece portrait by Alfred Stieglitz not silvered on edges. Boards. One of 500 copies. $750.

MUNSON, Laura Gordon. *Flowers from My Garden.* New York, 1864. Frontispiece and 17 hand-colored reproductions. $2,000.

MURDOCH, Iris. *The Flight from the Enchanter.* London, 1956. $600.

MURDOCH, Iris. *Sartre: Romantic Rationalist.* Cambridge, 1953. Author's first book. $300. New York, 1953. $150.

MURDOCH, Iris. *Under the Net.* London, 1954. $600.

MURDOCK, Joseph S.F. *The Library of Golf 1743–1966.* Detroit, 1968. In slipcase. $600.

MURGATROYD, Captain Matthew. *The Refugee.* New York, 1825. (By James Athearn Jones, his first book.) 2 vols. In original boards. $2,000. Rebound. $400.

MURRAY, A. W. *Forty Years' Mission Work in Polynesia* . . . New York, 1876. Frontispiece, 2 folding maps. $300.

MURRAY, Charles A. *Travels in North America.* London, 1839. 2 vols. 2 plates. In original cloth. $650. New York, 1839. 2 vols., in original cloth. First American edition. $500.

MURRAY, Hugh. *Historical Account of Discoveries and Travels In North America* . . . London, 1829. 2 vols. bound in 1, plus folding map. $750.

MURRAY, John. *Practical Remarks on Modern Paper.* North Hills, PA, 1981. One of 300 copies printed on "Hahnemuhle Ingre-Butten papier." $250.

MURRAY, Lois L. *Incidents of Frontier Life.* Goshen, Ind., 1880. 2 portraits. $350.

MURRAY, Pauli. *Proud Shoes.* New York (1956). $200

MURRELL, William. *A History of American Graphic Humor.* New York, 1933–38. 2 vols. $300.

MUSIL, Robert. *The Man Without Qualities.* London, 1953–54–60. 3 vols. Translated by Eithne Wilkins and Ernst Kaiser. First edition in English. $750.

MYERS, J. C. *Sketches on a Tour Through the Northern and Eastern States.* Harrisonburg, Va., 1849. Leather. $300.

MYRICK, Herbert. *Cache la Poudre: The Romance of a Tenderfoot in the Days of Custer.* New York, 1905. $150. One of 500 signed copies. Buckskin. $750.

MYSTERIES and Miseries of San Francisco (The). New York (1853). By a Californian (Edward Judson). $2,500.

MYSTERIES of Mormonism (The): A Full Exposure of Its Secret Practices and Hidden Crimes. By an apostle's wife. New York (1882). Wraps. $250.

MYSTERIOUS Marksman (The): or The Outlaws of New York. Cincinnati (about 1855). (By Emerson Bennett.) Wraps. $600.

N

NABOKOFF, Vladimir. *Laughter in the Dark.* Indianapolis (1938). (By Vladimir Nabokov.) Author's first book to be issued in the United States. (Published in England as *Camera Obscura.*) First issue in green cloth. $3,500. Variant cloth colors. $3,000. London (1961). $500.

NABOKOFF-SIRIN, Vladimir. *Camera Obscura.* London (1936). Translated by Winifred Roy. (By Vladimir Nabokov.) First novel by the author to be published in English. (See *Laughter in the Dark,* above.) $25,000. Without dustwrapper. $3,500.

NABOKOFF-SIRIN, Vladimir. *Despair.* London (1937). (By Vladimir Nabokov.) $20,000. Without dustwrapper. $3,000.

NABOKOV, Vladimir. *Bend Sinister.* New York (1947). $300. London (1960). $200.

NABOKOV, Vladimir. *Conclusive Evidence: A Memoir.* New York (1951). First stated. Also has "A-A" on copyright page. $400.

NABOKOV, Vladimir. *Invitation to a Beheading.* New York (1959). $300. London (1960). $125.

NABOKOV, Vladimir. *Lolita.* Olympia Press. Paris (1955). 2 vols. Printed price "Francs: 900" on back cover. $6,500. New York (1958). 1 vol. (Note: book-club copies have "Book Club Edition" on the corner of front flap [without dustwrapper cannot be distinguished from the trade edition].) $300. London (1959). $250.

NABOKOV, Vladimir. *Nikolai Gogol.* Norfolk, Conn. (1944). Tan cloth with brown lettering, 5 titles listed on verso of half title. Dustwrapper priced "$1.50." $350. Tan cloth with blue stamping and 14 titles listed on verso of half title. Dustwrapper price "$2.00" and 14 titles listed on back flap. $200. London (1947). $200.

NABOKOV, Vladimir. *Nine Stories.* (New York, 1947.) Published as *Direction Two* in wraps. This issue was devoted entirely to Nabokov. $350. (Probably a few copies in cloth, perhaps black, would be worth quite a bit more.)

NABOKOV, Vladimir. *Pale Fire.* New York (1962). Red endpapers. $250. London (1962). $300.

NABOKOV, Vladimir. *Poems.* Garden City, 1959. The Library of Congress deposit copy has "A25" on lower-right corner of page 44. $250. "A26" on lower-right corner of page 44. (Priority unknown; but we assume this might be a later issue.) $150. London (1961). $150.

NABOKOV, Vladimir. *The Real Life of Sebastian Knight.* Norfolk, Conn. (1941). First-issue binding: woven red burlap. $850. Bound in smooth red cloth. There were two variant dustwrappers with author's name spelled "Nabokov" or "Nabokoff" but priority unknown, however latter probably printed first and set aside and used later. London (1945). $400.

NABOKOV, Vladimir. *Speak, Memory.* London, 1951. First issue in blue-green cloth with black stamping, in dustwrapper without Daily Mail device on spine and at bottom of front flap. $450. Second issue in blue cloth and gilt stamping in dustwrapper with Daily Mail device on spine and at bottom of front flap. $300. New York (1966). "Revised edition." $125.

NABOKOV, Vladimir (translator). *Three Russian Poets: Selections from Pushkin, Lermontov, and Tyutchev.* Norfolk (1944). Stiff wraps. Variant A: Plain gray paper boards. Dustwrapper gray with brown lettering and "$1.00" upper corner of front flap. $300. Variant B: Tan stapled pamphlet. Dustwrapper bluish-gray with brown lettering and $0.50 in lower right corner of front flap. $175.

NAIPAUL, Shiva. *Fireflies.* London, 1970. Cloth. Author's first book. $200. Wraps. $50. New York, 1971. $75.

NAIPAUL, V. S. *A House for Mr. Biswas.* (London, 1961.) $1,000. New York (1961). $500.

NAIPAUL, V. S. *The Middle Passage.* (London, 1962.) $600. New York, 1963. $200.

NAIPAUL, V. S. *Miguel Street.* London, 1959. $600. New York (1960). $200.

NAIPAUL, V. S. *The Mystic Masseur.* (London, 1957.) Author's first book. $850. New York (1959). $250.

NAIPAUL, V. S. *The Suffrage of Elvira.* (London, 1958.) $1,000.

NANSEN, Fridtjof. *Farthest North.* London, 1897. 2 vols. 127 maps and 16 colored plates. Pictorial cloth. $500. New York, 1897. 2 vols. $450.

NANSEN, Fridtjof. *In Northern Mists.* New York, 1911. 2 vols. Over 150 illustrations. Blue cloth with gilt titles. $850. London, 1911. 2 vols. Tipped-in color frontispiece in each volume. $500.

NAPTON, William B. *Over the Santa Fe Trail, 1857.* Kansas City, 1905. Illustrated. 99 pages, pictorial wraps. $350.

NARAHARA, Ikko. *Where Time Has Stopped.* (Tokyo, 1967.) Issued without dustwrapper. In slipcase. $1,750.

NARES, Sir G. S. *Narrative of a Voyage to the Polar Sea* . . . London, 1878. 2 vols. $2,500. Second edition. $1,500. Third edition. $1,000.

NARRATIVE and Report of the Causes and Circumstances of the Deplorable Conflagration at Richmond. (Richmond, Va.?), 1812. $500.

NARRATIVE of Arthur Gordon Pym (The). New York, 1838. (By Edgar Allan Poe.) In original blue or gray cloth, paper label on spine. $5,000. London, 1838. Cloth. First English edition. $3,000. Limited Editions Club, New York, 1930. Boards. In slipcase. $200.

NARRATIVE of Captivity Among the Indians of North America . . . Chicago (1912). 2 vols. Stiff paper wraps. $250.

NARRATIVE of Dr. Livingston's Discoveries in Central Africa, from 1849 to 1856. London, 1857. Folding woodcut map. Illustrated boards. With David Livingstone's name spelled "Livingston." $1,000.

NARRATIVE of Occurences (A), in the Indian Countries of North America. London, 1807. (By Samuel Hull Wilcocke?) $1,750.

NARRATIVE of the Adventures and Sufferings of Capt. Daniel D. Heustis (A). Boston, 1847. Frontispiece, 168 pages, printed wraps. $2,500.

NARRATIVE of the Captivity and Providential Escape of Mrs. Jane Lewis. (Cover title.) (New York), 1833. (By William P. Edwards?) Woodcut plate. 24 pages. $750.

NARRATIVE of the Captivity and Sufferings of Ebenezer Fletcher of New-Ipswich (A). Windsor, Vt., 1813. (By Ebenezer Fletcher.) Second edition. $1,250. New-Ipswich, N.H., 1827. Fourth edition (so stated; it is actually the third edition). $750. New-Ipswich (about 1828). $300. (Note: There are only 3 known copies of the first edition, published in Amherst in 1798.)

NARRATIVE of the Captivity and Sufferings of Mrs. Hannah Lewis. Boston, 1811. (By William P. Edwards.) 24 pages, including folding woodcut plate. $750. Second edition, same date. $500.

NARRATIVE of the Capture and Burning of Fort Massachusetts. Albany, 1870. (By the Reverend John Norton.) Boards. One of 100 copies. $350. (Note: The first edition, Boston, 1748, is very rare.)

NARRATIVE of the Capture and Providential Escape of Misses Frances and Almira Hall, etc. (St. Louis?), 1832. (By William P. Edwards?) Plate. 24 pages. $650. Later, 26 pages (1833). Second edition. $400.

NARRATIVE of the Extraordinary Life of John Conrad Shafford. New York, 1840. Frontispiece, 25 pages, wraps. $500. New York, 1841. $250.

NARRATIVE of the Facts and Circumstances Relating to the Kidnapping and Presumed Murder of William Morgan (A). Batavia, N.Y., 1827. 36 pages. $250.

NARRATIVE of the Massacre at Chicago, August 15, 1812, and of Some Preceding Events. Chicago, 1844. (By Mrs. Juliette A. Kinzie.) Frontispiece map. 34 pages, printed wraps. $10,000.

NARRATIVE of the Sufferings and Adventures of Capt. Charles H. Barnard (A). New York, 1829. Folding map, 6 plates. $1,250.

NARRATIVE of the Sufferings of Massy Harbison. Pittsburgh, 1825. 66 pages. $750. Pittsburgh, 1828. 98 pages. Second edition. $500. Beaver, Pa., 1836. Fourth edition. $250.

NARRATIVE of the Suppression by Col. Burr (A), of the "History of the Administration of John Adams." New York, 1802. (By James Cheetham.) $250.

NARRATIVE of the Tragical Death of Mr. Darius Barber and His Seven Children (A). Boston (about 1818). Frontispiece. 24 pages. $18,000 in original wraps at auction in 1999.

NASBY, Petroleum V. The Nasby Papers. Indianapolis, 1864. (By David Ross Locke.) Author's first book. 64 pages, printed wraps. First binding, with "Indianapolic" on front cover. $350. Second binding, spelled correctly. $250.

NASH, Ogden. The Cricket of Carador. Garden City, 1925. Author's first book. Written with J. Alger. $750.

NASH, Ogden. Free Wheeling. New York, 1931. $250.

NASH, Ogden. Happy Days. New York, 1933. $200.

NASH, Ogden. Hard Lines. New York, 1931. Illustrated by O. Soglow. Tan cloth. $300.

NATHAN, George Jean. See Hatteras, Owen; Mencken, H. L., and Nathan, George Jean.

NATHAN, Robert. Autumn. New York, 1921. $750.

NATHAN, Robert. Peter Kindred. New York, 1919. Author's first book. In dustwrapper. $750. Without dustwrapper. $150.

NATIVE (A). (By Thomas Jefferson.) A Summary View of the Rights of British America . . . Williamsburg (1774). Author's first book. $300,000. Philadelphia, 1774. $40,000. London, 1774. $30,000.

NATURAL History and Antiquities of Selborne . . . (The). London, 1789. (By Gilbert White.) Folding frontispiece and 7 engraved plates. $4,000. London, 1813. 2 vols. $600. Limited Editions Club, Ipswich, 1972. In slipcase. $200.

NATURE. Boston, 1836. (By Ralph Waldo Emerson.) Emerson's first published book. First state, with page 94 misnumbered 92. In original cloth. $3,500. Rebound. $1,500. Correctly numbered. $2,500. Rebound. $750.

NAVAL Achievements of Great Britain and Her Allies from 1793 to 1817 (The). London (1817). Engraved title, 2 portraits and 55 hand-colored plates [Abbey Life]. $10,000. (Almost as much with plates watermarked in the 1820s.)

NAVAL Monument (The) . . . Boston, 1816. (By Abel Bowen.) 26 plates. $400.

NAVIGATOR (The). Pittsburgh, 1804. (By Zadok Cramer.) Fourth edition (of The Ohio and Mississippi Navigator, which see) and first edition with this title. $10,000. Pittsburgh, 1806. 14 charts. 94 pages. Fifth edition. $7,500. Also, Pittsburgh, 1808. $2,500. Pittsburgh, 1811. $2,500. Pittsburgh, 1814. $1,500.

NAYLOR, Gloria. The Women of Brewster Place. New York, 1982. Author's first book. $600.

NEAGOE, Peter (editor). Americans Abroad. The Hague, Netherlands, 1932. Illustrated. First binding in gray cloth. $450. Second binding in yellow cloth, tan cloth spine. $350. (Contains Henry Miller's first book appearance, as well as new material by William Carlos Williams and others.)

NEAGOE, Peter. *Storm.* New Review. Paris, 1932. Author's first book (preceded by Obelisk edition). Wraps. $250. (One copy noted in cloth.)

NEAL, Daniel. *The History of New-England* . . . London, 1720. 2 vols. With folding map. $2,500.

NEAL, John. See Adams, Will. See also *Brother Jonathan; Keep Cool; Seventy-Six.*

NEAL, John. *The Moose-Hunter; or, Life in the Maine Woods.* New York (1864). Wraps. First issue, with no. 73 announced on the inside of the front cover. $750.

NEAL, John. *Rachel Dyer: A North American Story.* Portland, Me., 1828. $750.

NEELY, Barbara. *Blanche on the Lam.* New York, 1992. Author's first book. $300.

NEESE, George M. *Three Years in the Confederate Horse Artillery.* New York, 1911. $500.

NEFF, Wallace. *Architecture of Southern Calif.* . . . Chicago, 1964. $250.

NEGRO Pioneer, A. See *The Conquest.*

NEIHARDT, John G. *Black Elk Speaks.* New York, 1932. Illustrated, including color plates. Decorated cloth. $300.

NEIHARDT, John G. *A Bundle of Myrrh.* (New York, 1903.) Limp leather. One of 5 copies. $1,000. New York, 1907. Boards and cloth. Revised edition. $150.

NEIHARDT, John G. *Collected Poems.* New York, 1926. 2 vols. One of 250 signed copies. $250.

NEIHARDT, John G. *The Divine Enchantment: A Mystical Poem.* New York, 1900. Author's first book. $750.

NEIHARDT, John G. *The Song of the Indian Wars.* New York, 1925. One of 500 signed copies. $250. Trade edition. $150.

NEIL, John B. *Biennial Message of the Governor of Idaho to the 11th Session of the Legislature of Idaho Territory.* Boise City, Idaho, 1880. 19 pages, wraps. $250.

NEILSON, Shaw. *Heart of Spring.* Sydney, 1919. $250.

NEMEROV, Howard. *The Image and the Law.* (New York, 1947.) Author's first book. $150.

NEMEROV, Howard. *The Painter Dreaming in the Scholar's House.* New York, 1968. Oblong, stiff wraps. One of 100 signed copies. In dustwrapper. $100. One of 26 signed copies. $200.

NEPHITE Records (The). (Independence, Mo.), 1899. (First printing of *The Book of Mormon* under this title.) $500.

NERUDA, Pablo. *Bestiary/Bestiario.* New York (1965). Woodcuts by Antonio Frasconi. Folio, boards, and cloth. One of 300 signed copies, with a signed frontispiece woodcut. In slipcase. $400.

NERUDA, Pablo. *Heights of Macchu Picchu.* London (1966). First English edition. $300.

NERUDA, Pablo. *We Are Many.* London (1967). Translated by Alastair Reid. Boards. First edition in English. One of 100 signed copies. In dustwrapper. $450.

NESBIT, Edith. *Ballads and Lyrics of Socialism, 1883–1908.* London, 1908. $150.

NESBIT, Edith. *Lays and Legends.* London, 1886. Author's first book. $250.

NESBIT, Edith. *The Railway Children.* London (1906). 20 plates. $750.

NEVILL, Ralph. *British Military Prints.* London, 1909. Plates, including color. $250.

NEVILL, Ralph. *Old English Sporting Books.* London, 1924. Plates, including color. Buckram. One of 1,500 copies. Issued in dustwrapper. $350.

NEVILL, Ralph. *Old English Sporting Prints and Their History.* London, 1923. 103 full-page plates, 47 in color. Buckram. One of 1,500 copies. Issued without dustwrapper. $350.

NEW Bath Guide, or, Memoirs . . . (The). (By Christopher Anstey.) London, 1766. Author's first book. $300.

NEW-ENGLANDS Plantation. London, 1630. 11 leaves. First issue without the author's name (Francis Higginson) on title. $12,500.

NEW ENGLAND Primer Improved . . . Paisley, 1776. $4,000.

NEW SPAIN and the Anglo-American West: Historical Contributions Presented to Herbert E. Bolton. (Los Angeles, 1932.) 2 vols. in cloth. Portrait. One of 500 copies. Slipcase. $400.

NEW TESTAMENT of Our Lord and Saviour Jesus Christ. New York, 1848. Translated into the Choctaw Language. Leather. $1,000. New York, 1854. Second edition. $500.

NEW Texas Spelling Book (The). Houston, 1863. (By E. H. Cushing.) Pictorial boards. $1,250.

NEW Topographical Atlas of St. Lawrence County, New York. Philadelphia, 1865. Colored maps and plans. $300.

NEW Translation with Notes (A), of the Third Satire of Juvenal. New York, 1806. (By Clement C. Moore and John Duer.) With "Additional Errata" leaf. Moore's first book appearance. $750.

NEW Year's Feast on His Coming of Age (The). London, 1824. (By Charles Lamb.) Hand-colored woodcuts. $600.

NEW YORK Book of Poetry (The). New York, 1837. (Edited anonymously by Charles Fenno Hoffman.) Engraved half title. In original cloth. (Contains first book appearance of Clement C. Moore's "A Visit from St. Nicholas.") $750.

NEW ZEALAND, Graphic and Descriptive. London, 1877. Edited by W.T.L. Travers and C. D. Barraud. Colored title, 6 plain and 24 colored plates. Map. Woodcuts in text. Folio, half cloth. $2,500.

NEWBERRY, J. S. *Report on the Properties of the Ramshorn Consolidated Silver Mining Company at Bay Horse, Idaho.* New York (1881). 16 pages, wraps. $250.

NEWBOLT, Sir Henry. See *A Fair Death.*

NEWCASTLE, William Cavendish, Duke of. *A General System of Horsemanship in All It's Branches.* London, 1743. 2 vols. Folio. Double-page engraved title and 62 plates (44 double-page). $12,500.

NEWELL, Rev. Chester. *History of the Revolution in Texas.* New York, 1838. Folding map. In original cloth. $4,500.

NEWELL, Peter. See *Topsys & Turveys.*

NEWELL, Peter. *The Hole Book.* New York (1908). Illustrated in color by the author. Stapled blue cloth, pictorial cover label. With "Published October 1908" below copyright notice. $450.

NEWELL, Peter. *The Rocket Book.* New York, 1912. $400.

NEWELL, Peter. *A Shadow Show.* New York, 1896. 36 color plates. Pictorial boards. $600.

NEWELL, Peter. *The Slant Book.* New York, 1910. $400.

NEWHALL, J. B. *The British Emigrants' "Hand Book."* (Cover title.) London, 1844. 99 pages, printed yellow wraps. $1,500.

NEWHALL, John B. *Sketches of Iowa.* New York, 1841. Map in color. Cloth. $2,000.

NEWHOUSE, Edward. *You Can't Sleep Here.* New York (1934.) Author's first book. $500.

NEWLOVE, John. *Grave Sirs.* Vancouver, 1962. Author's first book. Stiff, smooth black wraps. $750. Grainy black wraps. $350.

NEWMAN, Frances. *The Hard-Boiled Virgin.* New York, 1926. $600.

NEWMAN, John Henry, Cardinal. See *The Dream of Gerontius; Verses on Various Occasions.*

NEWMAN, John Henry, Cardinal. *Apologia Pro Vita Sua.* London, 1864. 8 parts, printed wraps. $2,000. London, 1864. First book edition. $750.

NEWMAN, John Henry, Cardinal, et al. (editors). *Lyra Apostolics.* Derby, England, 1836. Purple cloth. $1,250.

NEWMARK, Harris. *Sixty Years in Southern California. 1853–1913.* New York, 1916. 33 plates. $200. Boston, 1930. Edited by M. H. and M. R. Newmark. 43 plates. Cloth. $200.

NEWTON, A. Edward. *The Amenities of Book Collecting and Kindred Affections.* Boston, 1918. Author's first book. First issue, without index and page 268, line 3, "piccadilly." In first-state dustwrapper with no printing on the covers except for the spine. $500. With index. Second-state dustwrapper with printing on the front panel. $300.

NEWTON, A. Edward. *The Greatest Book in the World and Other Papers.* Boston (1925). One of 450 copies. In slipcase. $175. Trade. First issue with "The Autograph of Cruikshank" in list of illustations on page 341 vs. page 334. Slipcase. $75.

NEWTON, A. Edward. *A Magnificent Farce and Other Diversions of a Book Collector.* Boston (1921). One of 265 signed copies. In slipcase. $200. Trade edition. $75.

NEWTON, A. Edward. *Mr. Strahan's Dinner Party.* San Francisco, 1930. One of 350 signed copies. $250.

NEWTON, A. Edward. *On Books and Business.* (New York), 1930. Boards. One of 325 signed copies. $75.

NEWTON, A. Edward. *Rare Books, etc.* (Auction catalogue.) New York, 1941. Illustrated. 3 vols. Printed gray boards. In dustwrappers. $175.

NEWTON, Sir Isaac. *The Mathematical Principles of Natural Philosophy.* London, 1729. 2 vols. 2 folding tables, 47 folding plates, and 2 engraved allegorical frontises and vignettes. $20,000. London, 1803. 3 vols. Second edition in English, the first to include earlier version of "The System of the World." 54 folding plates, 2 folding tables, a frontispiece portrait, and Life of Newton. $2,000.

NEWTON, Sir Isaac. *Opticks . . .* London, 1718. Second edition with 12 folding plates. $5,000. [See *Opticks . . .* for first-edition (published anonymously).] London, 1721. Third edition with 12 folding plates. $3,500.

NEWTON, Sir Isaac. *Universal Arithmetick.* London, 1720. 8 fold-out plates of geometric diagrams. $4,000.

NEWTON, J. H. (editor). *History of the Pan-handle . . . West Virginia.* Wheeling, W. Va., 1879. Maps and plates. $300.

NEWTON, J. H. (editor). *History of . . . Venango County, Pennsylvania.* Columbus, Ohio, 1879. 47 plates. Half leather. $750.

NEWTON, James. *A Complete Herbal.* London, 1752. With portrait and 175 plates numbered 2 to 176. $1,000.

NICHOLS, Beach. *Atlas of Schuyler County, New York.* Philadelphia, 1874. Folio, 21 maps in color, 31 leaves. $500.

NICHOLS, Beverly. *Prelude.* London, 1929. Author's first book. $300.

NICHOLS, John. *The Milagro Beanfield War.* New York, 1974. $400.

NICHOLS, John. *The Sterile Cuckoo.* New York (1965). Author's first book. $200. London (1965). $100.

NICHOLSON, James B. *A Manual of the Art of Bookbinding . . .* Philadelphia, 1856. 12 plates of bindings and 7 samples of marbled paper. $1,500.

NICHOLSON, Peter. *The Carpenter's New Guide.* Philadelphia, 1867. $500.

NICHOLSON, Peter. *The New Practical Builder . . .* London, 1823–25. 2 parts in 1 vol. $750.

NICHOLSON, William. *An Alphabet.* London, 1898. 14 leaves. $2,000.

NICK of the Woods, or The Jibbenainosay. Philadelphia, 1837. (By Robert Montgomery Bird.) 2 vols. $1,250.

NICOLLETT, Joseph Nicolas. *Report Intended to Illustrate a Map of the Hydrographical Basin of the Upper Missouri River.* Senate Doc. 237, 26th Congress, 2d session. Washington, 1843. Folding map, 170 pages, wraps. or cloth. $650. Washington, 1845. House Doc. 52. Smaller map. Sewn. $350.

NICOLSON, Harold. *Paul Verlaine.* London (1921 on spine). Author's first book. $350. Boston, 1921. $200.

NICOLSON, Harold. *Sweet Waters.* London, 1921. $350. Boston, 1921. $200.

NIEDECKER, Lorine. *New Goose.* Prairie City (1946). Author's first book. $1,500.

NIEDIECK, Paul. *With Rifle in Five Continents.* London, 1908. Original gilt-stamped cloth, zebra endpapers. $600.

NIELSEN, Kay (illustrator). *East of the Sun and West of the Moon.* London: Hodder and Stoughton (1914). (By Peter Christen Asbjornsen and Jorgen I. Moe.) 25 color plates. Cloth. $4,500. Vellum. One of 500 signed copies. $12,500. New York (1914). $1,750.

NIETZSCHE, Friedrich. *Thus Spake Zarathustra.* New York, 1896. First English translation. Volume eight in the first authorized edition of the Collected Works. $1,250. Limited Editions Club, New York, 1964. In slipcase. $125.

NIGGER of the "Narcissus" (The). Preface. (Caption title only.) (Hythe, England, 1902.) (By Joseph Conrad.) Wire-stitched sheets. One of 100 copies. Privately printed for Conrad, who had suppressed this preface in the first edition of his 1898 novel. (About 40 copies were accidentally destroyed.) $3,000.

NIGHTINGALE, Florence. *Notes on Nursing.* London (1859). Flexible cloth. $750. Later ads dated 1860 with translation-rights notice below imprint. $600. London, 1860. $350. New York, 1860. $500. Boston, 1860. $350.

NIGHTMARE Abbey. London, 1818. (By Thomas Love Peacock.) $1,750.

NILE Notes of a Howadji. New York, 1851. (By George William Curtis.) Author's first book. Tan wraps. $350. Cloth. $200.

NIMMO, Joseph, Jr. *Range and Ranch Cattle Traffic.* (Caption title.) (Washington, 1884.) 4 folding maps, 200 pages, wraps. $3,000. Washington, 1885. $1,500.

NIMROD. *The Life of a Sportsman.* London, 1842. (By C. J. Apperley.) 36 colored plates by Alken. First issue, in blue cloth. $3,500. Second issue, red cloth. $2,500. London, 1901. 2 vols., boards, folio. One of 60 large-paper copies. $1,000. Trade edition. $350.

NIMROD'S Hunting Tours . . . London, 1903. (By C. J. Apperley.) 18 hand-colored plates. One of 500 copies. $600. One of 50 copies. $1,000.

NIN, Anaïs. *Children of the Albatross.* New York, 1947. $200.

NIN, Anaïs. *D. H. Lawrence: An Unprofessional Study.* Paris, 1932. Facsimiles. Black cloth. Author's first book. One of 550 copies. $600. London, 1961. $100.

NIN, Anaïs. *The House of Incest.* Paris (1936). Wraps. One of 249 signed copies. $650. (New York, 1947.) Gemor Press. Illustrated by Ian Hugo. Pictorial orange cloth. $350. One of 50 signed copies. $750.

NIN, Anaïs. *Ladders to Fire.* New York, 1946. $200.

NIN, Anaïs. *This Hunger.* Gemor Press. (New York, 1945.) 5 hand-colored woodcuts by Ian Hugo. Decorated boards. One of 50 signed copies. Issued without dustwrapper. $1,000. Trade edition. One of 1,000 copies. Issued without dustwrapper. $200.

NIN, Anaïs. *Under a Glass Bell and Other Stories.* New York (1944). (300 copies.) In dustwrapper. $500.

NIN, Anaïs. *Winter of Artifice.* Obelisk Press. Paris (1939). Wraps. $750. (New York, 1942.) Copper engravings by Ian Hugo. Pictorial boards. Issued without dustwrapper. (500 printed.) $400.

NINA Balatka. Edinburgh, 1867. (By Anthony Trollope.) 2 vols. First issue, with ad leaf inset in vol. 1. $11,000 at auction in 1990.

NINETY-FIRST Psalm (The). Golden Cockerel Press. (London, 1944.) 4 leaves. Wood engravings. One of 350 copies. In slipcase. $450. One of 50 specially bound copies. $1,250.

NISHIYAMA, H., and BROWN, Richard. *Karate, the Art of "Empty Hand" Fighting.* Tokyo, 1960. Stated first. $100.

NIVEN, Larry. *World of Ptavvs.* New York (1966). Author's first book. $35. (London, 1968.) $250.

NIXON, Howard M. *Sixteenth-Century Gold-Tooled Bookbindings in the Pierpont Morgan Library.* New York, 1971. $350.

NIXON, Richard. *The Challenges We Face.* New York (1960). Author's first book. $250.

NOAH, Mordecai Manuel. See *The Fortress.*

NOBLE Fragment (A), Being a Leaf of the Gutenberg Bible 1450–1455 . . . New York, 1921. Title page, 4-page introduction by Newton and original leaf from the Gutenberg Bible. Slipcase. $30,000.

NOBLE Heritage (A), Two Conjugate Leaves from the First Edition of the Bishops' Bible . . . No place (1973). Stiff wraps, slipcase. One of 220 copies. $350.

NOGUCHI, Isamu. *A Sculptor's World.* New York, 1968. 13 color plates and 255 black-and-white plates. $450.

NOGUCHI, Yone. *Hiroshige.* New York, 1921. Wraps. One of 750 with color frontispiece and 19 collotype plates. $400. London/New York/Tokyo, 1934. One of 1,000 copies. $400.

NOGUCHI, Yone. *Seen & Unseen.* San Francisco, 1896. Author's first book. $350.

NONESUCH Century (The): An Appraisal, a Personal Note and a Bibliography of the First Hundred Books Issued by the Press, 1923–1934. London, 1936. Illustrated. Buckram. One of 750 copies. In dustwrapper. $750.

NORDAN, Lewis. *The All-Girl Football Team.* Baton Rouge, 1986. Author's second book. $1,000.

NORDAN, Lewis. *Welcome to the Arrow Catcher Fair.* Baton Rouge, 1983. Author's first book. $1,000. Wraps. $50.

NORDEN, Charles. *Panic Spring.* New York (1937). (By Lawrence Durrell.) $3,000.

NORDHOFF, Charles. *California for Health, Pleasure and Residence...* New York, 1873. Illustrated, map. Leather. $250. Cloth. $200.

NORDHOFF, Charles B. See Hall, James Norman (for *The Lafayette Flying Corps*).

NORDHOFF, Charles B., and HALL, James Norman. *Men Against the Sea.* Boston, 1934. Dustwrapper priced at $2.00 and no printing on spine. $1,000.

NORDHOFF, Charles B., and HALL, James Norman. *Mutiny on the Bounty.* Boston, 1932. First issue, with plain endpapers. $750. (Note: second printing dustwrapper has reviews on back flap.) With pictorial endpapers. $350. London, 1933. $600. Limited Editions Club, New York, 1947. In slipcase. $300.

NORMAN, Don Cleveland. *The 500th Anniversary, Pictorial Census of the Gutenberg Bible.* Chicago, 1961. Illustrated. Full leatherette. One of 985 copies. In slipcase. $850.

NORMYX. *Unprofessional Tales.* London, 1901. (By Norman Douglas and Elsa Fitzgibbon.) Pictorial white cloth. One of 750 copies. Norman Douglas's first hardbound book, written in collaboration with his wife. $750.

NORRIS, Frank. *McTeague: A Story of San Francisco.* New York, 1899. Red cloth. With "moment" as last word on page 106. $1,000. New York (1923). Photoplay edition. $350. San Francisco, 1941. Colt Press. Illustrated. Buckram and boards. One of 500 copies. Issued without dustwrapper. $200.

NORRIS, Frank. *Moran of the Lady Letty.* New York, 1898. Green cloth. $250.

NORRIS, Frank. *The Octopus.* New York, 1901. Red cloth. With "J. J. Little" device on copyright page. Page 287, line 14 "consider small"; later "consider serious." (Later printings have "Manhattan Press.") $400.

NORRIS, Frank. *The Responsibilities of the Novelist and Other Literary Essays.* New York, 1903. In green cloth stamped in gold. (Also, a variant stamped in white with spine label.) $250.

NORRIS, Frank. *Yvernelle: A Legend of Feudal France.* Philadelphia, 1892 (actually 1891). Author's first book. Illustrations, some in color. Cloth. $2,000. Leather. $1,500.

NORRIS, George W. *The Early History of Medicine in Philadelphia.* Philadelphia, 1886. One of 125 copies. $750.

NORRIS, J. W. *A Business Advertiser and General Directory of the City of Chicago for the Year 1845–6.* Chicago, 1845. Folding plate. 156 pages, wraps. $3,000.

NORRIS, J. W. *General Directory and Business Advertiser of the City of Chicago for the Year 1844.* Chicago, 1844. 116 pages, printed wraps. First printing. $3,500. Cloth, with binder's slip bound in. $2,500. (Note: This is the first Chicago city directory.)

NORRIS, Kathleen. *Mother: A Story.* New York, 1911. Author's first book. $100.

NORTH-American and the West-Indian Gazetteer. London, 1776. Two folding maps. $2,500.

NORTH and South. London, 1855. 2 vols. (By Elizabeth C. Gaskell.) $4,000.

NORTH, Andrew. *Plague Ship.* New York (1956). (By Alice Mary Norton, whose main pseudonym is André Norton.) Probable first issue in tan boards. (Tan and red cloth believed later). $350.

NORTH, Anthony. *Strike Deep.* New York, 1974. (By Dean Koontz.) $600.

NORTH, Joseph. *Men in the Ranks: The Story of 12 Americans in Spain.* New York, 1939. Foreword by Ernest Hemingway. Wraps. $250.

NORTH, Thomas. *Five Years in Texas; or, What You Did Not Hear During the War.* Cincinnati, 1870. $600.

NORTHANGER Abbey; and Persuasion. London, 1818. By the Author of *Pride and Prejudice* . . . (By Jane Austen.) 4 vols. $10,000. See also Austen, Jane, *Persuasion.*

NORTHERN Route to Idaho (The). St. Paul (1864). (By D.D. Merrill.) Large folding map, 8 pages of text. $9,000.

NORTON, André. See North, Andrew.

NORTON, André. *The Beast Master.* New York (1959). (By Alice Mary Norton.) $300.

NORTON, André. *The Prince Commands* . . . New York, 1934. (By Alice Mary Norton, her first book.) $1,500.

NORTON, André. *Shadow Hawk.* New York (1960). (By Alice Mary Norton.) $150.

NORTON, André. *Star Man's Son, 2250 A.D.* New York (1952). (By Alice Mary Norton, her first science fiction novel.) $1,000.

NORTON, Charles. See *Considerations* . . .

NORTON, F. J. *A Descriptive Catalogue of Printing in Spain and Portugal, 1501–1520.* Cambridge (1978). $250.

NORTON, Mary. *The Magic Bed-knob* . . . New York, 1943. Author's first book. $300.

NOSTRADAMUS, Michel de. *The True Prophecies or Prognostications.* London, 1672. First edition in English. $4,500.

NOTES on California and the Placers. New York, 1850. (By James Delavan.) 2 plates (not in all copies). 128 pages, printed wraps. $6,000.

NOTORIOUS Outlaw (The), Jesse James. New York (1883?). 13 pages, pictorial wraps. First (?) edition. $750.

NOTT, Kathleen. *Mile End.* Hogarth Press. London, 1938. Author's first book. $150.

NOTT, Stanley Charles. *A Catalogue of Rare Chinese Jade Carvings.* Palm Beach, 1940. $250.

NOTT, Stanley Charles. *Chinese Jade Carvings of the XVIth to XIXth Century in the Collection of Mrs. Georg Vetlesen.* London, 1939–40. 3 vols. Folio. $3,500.

NOTT, Stanley Charles. *Chinese Jade Throughout the Ages.* London, 1936. 39 color illustrations, 182 in black-and-white. In dustwrapper. $350. New York, 1937. $300.

NOVAK, Joseph. *The Future Is Ours, Comrade.* Garden City, 1960. (By Jerzy Kosinski.) His first book. $300.

NOWLIN, William. *The Bark Covered House.* Detroit, 1876. 6 plates. $2,000.

NOYES, Alva J. *In the Land of Chinook: or, The Story of Blaine County.* Helena, Mont. (1917). 24 plates. $450.

NOYES, Alva J. *The Story of Ajax: Life in the Big Horn Basin.* Helena, Mont. 1914. Frontispiece, 12 plates. $750.

NOYES, John H. *The Berean* . . . Putney, 1847. Author's first book. $750.

NOYES, John Humphrey. *History of American Socialisms.* Philadelphia, 1870. $350.

NUTT, Charles. See Beaumont, Charles.

NUTT, Frederic. *The Complete Confectioner.* New York, 1807. Frontispiece. First American edition. $600.

NUTTALL, Thomas. *The Genera of North American Plants.* Philadelphia, 1818. 2 vols. $1,000.

NUTTALL, Thomas. *Journal of Travels into the Arkansa Territory, During the Year 1819* . . . Philadelphia, 1821. Folding map and 5 aquatints. $5,000. Cleveland, 1905. $300.

NUTTING, Wallace. *The Clock Book.* Framingham, Mass., 1924. In dustwrapper. $175.

NYE, Edgar Wilson. *A Howl in Rome.* Chicago (1880). Wraps. Author's first book. $200.

NYE, Nelson C. *Pistols for Hire.* New York, 1941. $150.

NYE, Nelson C. *Two-Fisted Cowboy.* New York, 1936. Author's first book. $250.

NYE-STARR, Kate. *A Self-Sustaining Woman; or, The Experience of Seventy-two Years.* Chicago, 1888. Portrait. Red cloth. $4,000.

O

OAK Openings (The); or, The Bee-Hunter. New York, 1848. By the Author of *The Pioneers,* James Fenimore Cooper. 2 vols., printed tan wraps. First American edition. $750.

OAKES, William. *Scenery of the White Mountains.* Cambridge, 1848. 16 colored plates $2,750. Tinted plates. $750.

OATES, Joyce Carol. *By the North Gate.* New York (1963). Author's first book. $450.

OATES, Joyce Carol. *Expensive People.* New York (1968). $150.

OATES, Joyce Carol. *Them.* New York (1969). $250.

OATES, Joyce Carol. *Upon the Sweeping Flood and Other Stories.* New York (1966). $200.

OATES, Joyce Carol. *With Shuddering Fall.* New York (1964). $200.

OATES, Joyce Carol. *Women in Love and Other Poems.* New York, 1968. Decorated wraps. One of 150 signed copies. $250.

O'BETJEMAN, Deirdre. *Some Immortal Hours: A Rhapsody of the Celtic Twilight.* London, 1962. (By John Betjeman.) One of 12 copies. 7 leaves, folio. A facsimile printing of the author's holograph manuscript, hand-colored and signed by Betjeman. $2,000.

O'BRIAN, Patrick. See also Russ, Richard Patrick.

O'BRIAN, Patrick. *The Catalans.* New York (1953). Precedes the English edition published as *The Frozen Flame.* $1,250.

O'BRIAN, Patrick. *The Frozen Flame.* London, 1953. $750.

O'BRIAN, Patrick. *The Golden Ocean.* London, 1956. $1,000. New York (1957). $750.

O'BRIAN, Patrick. *The Last Pool.* London, 1950. Author's first book. $1,500.

O'BRIAN, Patrick. *Master and Commander.* Philadelphia/New York (1969). $1,000. London, 1970. $1,250.

O'BRIAN, Patrick. *Post Captain.* London, 1972. $850. Philadelphia (1972). $750.

O'BRIAN, Patrick. *The Road to Samarcand.* London, 1954. $750.

O'BRIAN, Patrick. *Testimonies.* New York (1952). First U.S. edition of *Three Bear Witness.* $500.

O'BRIAN, Patrick. *Three Bear Witness.* London, 1952. Front flap of dustwrapper has code "W434." Noted in cream-colored boards lettered in red as well as in green boards lettered in silver. Priority, if any, unknown. $1,000.

O'BRIEN, Fitz-James. *A Gentleman from Ireland.* New York, no date [1858]. Author's first book. Wraps. $250.

O'BRIEN, Fitz-James. *Poems and Stories.* Boston, 1881. $300.

O'BRIEN, Fitz-James. *What Was It?* New York, 1974. Drawings by Leonard Baskin. Wraps. One of 200 copies signed by Baskin. $150.

O'BRIEN, Flann. *At Swim-Two-Birds.* London (1939). Black cloth. Author's first book. $5,000. Gray-green cloth. Issued in 1941 or 1942. $4,000. New York (1951). "First published 1939" stated. $350.

O'BRIEN, Flann. *The Hard Life.* London, 1961. Red cloth, in price-clipped dustwrapper. $200. New York, 1962. Red cloth-backed blue boards, dustwrapper. $100.

O'BRIEN, Flann. *The Poor Mouth (An Beal Bocht).* London (1973). One of 130 copies signed by the illustrator Ralph Steadman. $1,000. Trade. $150.

O'BRIEN, John. *Leaving Las Vegas.* Wichita, 1990. Author's first book. $200.

O'BRIEN, Kate. *Distinguished Villa.* London, 1926. Author's first book. $350.

O'BRIEN, Tim. *If I Die in a Combat Zone.* New York (1973). Author's first book. $2,000. London (1973). $350.

O'BRIEN, Tim. *Northern Lights.* (New York, 1975.) $1,250. London (1976). $350.

O'BRYAN, William. *A Narrative of Travels in the United States . . . and Advice to Emigrants and Travellers Going to That Interesting Country.* London, 1836. Portrait. Dark-blue cloth. $350.

OBSERVATIONS on the Wisconsin Territory. Philadelphia, 1835. (By William Rudolph Smith.) Folding map. $1,000.

OBSERVATIONS upon Certain Passages in Mr. Jefferson's "Notes on Virginia." New York, 1804. 32 pages, plain blue-gray wraps, bound in. (Attributed to Clement C. Moore, his first, if he wrote it.) $750.

O'CASEY, Sean. See O'Cathasaigh, P.

O'CASEY, Sean. *The Plough and the Stars.* London, 1926. Portrait. Boards and cloth. $300. New York, 1926. $250.

O'CATHASAIGH, P. *The Story of the Irish Citizen Army.* Dublin, 1919. (By Sean O'Casey, his first book.) Gray wraps. $350. Second issue in tan wraps. $175.

O'CONNOR, Flannery. *The Artificial Nigger and Other Tales.* London (1957). The first U.K. edition of *A Good Man Is Hard to Find.* $500.

O'CONNOR, Flannery. *A Good Man Is Hard to Find.* New York (1955). First-issue dustwrapper has *Wise Blood* on rear panel. (Dustwrapper spine is usually faded. The estimated price would be for unfaded one.) $1,000. In second-issue dustwrapper, this book on rear. $500.

O'CONNOR, Flannery. *The Violent Bear It Away.* New York (1960). $600. London (1960). $450.

O'CONNOR, Flannery. *Wise Blood.* New York (1952). Author's first book. $5,000. London, (1955). $750.

O'CONNOR, Frank. *Guests of the Nation.* London, 1931. Author's first book. $750.

O'CONNOR, Frank. *A Lament for Art O'Leary.* Cuala Press. Dublin, 1940. Boards. One of 130 copies. In dustwrapper. $500.

O'CONNOR, Frank. *A Picture Book.* Cuala Press. Dublin, 1943. Illustrated by Elizabeth Rivers. Boards, linen spine. One of 480 copies. In dustwrapper. $350.

O'CONNOR, Frank. *The Saint and Mary Kate.* London, 1932. $300.

O'CONNOR, Frank. *Three Tales.* Cuala Press. Dublin, 1941. Boards, linen spine. One of 250 copies. In dustwrapper. $350.

O'CONNOR, Frank. *The Wild Bird's Nest.* Cuala Press. Dublin, 1932. Boards and cloth. One of 250 copies. $250.

O'CONNOR, Jack. *Boom Town.* New York, 1938. $250.

O'CONNOR, Jack. *Conquest.* New York, 1930. Author's first book. $250.

OCULUS. *The Home of the Badgers.* Milwaukee, 1845. (By Josiah B. Grinnell.) 36 pages, tan printed wraps. $2,500. (For second edition, see *Sketches of the West.*)

O'DAY, Nell. *A Catalogue of Books Printed By John Henry Nash . . .* San Francisco, 1937. One of 500 copies. $150.

ODE *Performed in the Senate-House, Cambridge, on the Sixth of July, MDCCCXLVII at the First Commencement After the Installation of His Royal Highness the Prince Albert, Chancellor of the University.* Cambridge, 1847. (By William Wordsworth.) 8 pages, printed wraps. $1,250.

ODE *to Napoleon Buonaparte.* London, 1814. (By George Gordon Noel, Lord Byron.) 16 pages, wraps bound in. $3,000.

ODES. (London, 1868.) (By Coventry Patmore.) Gray wraps. $750.

ODETS, Clifford. *Golden Boy.* New York (1937). $200.

ODETS, Clifford. *Three Plays.* New York: Covici-Friede (1935). Author's first book. $300. New York: Random House (1935). $150.

O'DONOVAN, Edmond. *The Merv Oasis* . . . New York, 1883. 2 vols. Portrait, maps, folding map in rear. $500.

OE, Kenzaburo. *A Personal Matter.* New York (1968). First English translation of author's first book. $200. London (1969). $125.

OEHLER, Andrew. *The Life, Adventures, and Unparalleled Sufferings of Andrew Oehler.* (Trenton, N.J.), 1811. $750.

O'FAOLAIN, Sean. *Midsummer Night Madness & Other Stories.* London (1932). Preface by Edward Garnett. Author's first book. $300. New York, 1932. $175.

O'FAOLAIN, Sean. *A Nest of Simple Folk.* London (1933). $250.

OFFICIAL *Historical Atlas of Alameda County.* Oakland, 1878. Folding maps, full-page views. Atlas folio, half leather. $1,500.

OFFICIAL *State Brand Book of Colorado (The).* Denver, 1894. Illustrated. $1,000.

OFFICINA *Bodoni (The), The Operation of A Hand-Press During the First Six Years of Its Work.* Paris/New York, 1929. One of 500 copies. $1,500.

O'FLAHERTY, Liam. *The Assassin.* London (1928). One of 150 signed copies. Issued without dustwrapper. $400. Trade. In dustwrapper. $250.

O'FLAHERTY, Liam. *The Black Soul.* London (1924). $250.

O'FLAHERTY, Liam. *The Child of God.* London, 1926. Wraps. One of 100 signed copies. $250. One of 25 signed copies. $500.

O'FLAHERTY, Liam. *Civil War.* London, 1925. Wraps. One of 100 signed copies. $250.

O'FLAHERTY, Liam. *The Hollywood Cemetery.* London, 1935. $600.

O'FLAHERTY, Liam. *The Informer.* London (1925). $1,000.

O'FLAHERTY, Liam. *Return of the Brute.* London, 1929. $300. New York, 1930. $200.

O'FLAHERTY, Liam. *Thy Neighbor's Wife.* London (1923). Black cloth. Author's first book. $300.

OGDEN, George W. *Letters from the West.* New Bedford, Mass., 1823. $2,500.

OGDEN, James. *Ogden on Fly Tying.* Cheltenham, 1879. 2 mounted photographs. Bookplate. Original cloth. $450.

OGILBY, John. *America: Being the Latest, and Most Accurate Description of the New World . . .* London, 1671. Folio. Engraved frontispiece, 6 portraits, 19 double-page maps and 30 double-page plates. $25,000.

OGILVIES (The). London, 1849. (By Dinah Maria Mulock.) 3 vols. Author's first novel. Cloth. $500.

O'HARA, Frank. *A City Winter and Other Poems.* New York, 1951. Illustrated by Larry Rivers. Decorated wraps. One of 130 copies. $2,000. Boards and cloth. One of 20 copies with an original drawing by Rivers. $15,000.

O'HARA, Frank. *The Collected Poems of Frank O'Hara.* New York, 1971. In suppressed dustwrapper with a photograph of Larry Rivers' drawing of a nude O'Hara. $250. In later jacket. $75.

O'HARA, Frank. *In Memory of My Feelings.* New York (1967). Illustrated. Folio, printed sheets in folder and slipcase. One of 2,500 copies. $300.

O'HARA, John. *And Other Stories.* New York (1968). One of 300 signed copies. In slipcase. $150.

O'HARA, John. *Appointment in Samarra.* New York (1934). Author's first book. Black cloth. Errata slip laid in. In dustwrapper with "Recent Fiction" on back panel. $3,500. London (1935). $1,000.

O'HARA, John. *Butterfield 8.* New York (1935). $1,750.

O'HARA, John. *The Doctor's Son.* New York (1935). $2,500.

O'HARA, John. *Files on Parade.* New York (1939). With author's foreword tipped in. $600.

O'HARA, John. *Hope of Heaven.* New York (1938). $500.

O'HARA, John. *Pal Joey.* New York (1940). $500.

O'HARA, John. *A Rage to Live.* New York (1949). $150. One of 750 copies stamped "Presentation Edition," in acetate dustwrapper. $125.

OHARA, Ken. *One Tokyo, 1970.* Stiff wraps. In dustwrapper. $750.

O'HARA, Mary. *Green Grass of Wyoming.* Philadelphia (1946). $150.

OHASHI, M. *Scientific Jiu-Jitsu.* New York, 1912. Wraps. $100.

Okavango River . . . (The). See Andersson, Charles.

O'KEEFFE, *Georgia O'Keeffe.* New York (1976). Folio, in cloth folding case with additional portfolio of reproductions. One of 200 (175 for sale) signed copies. $4,000. Folio. Linen. Dustwrapper. $300.

OKRI, Ben. *Flowers and Shadows.* London (1980). Wraps. $250.

OLD, R. O. *Colorado: United States, of America. Its History, Geography, and Mining.* London, 1869. 64 pages, printed tan wraps. $2,000.

OLDER, (Mr. and Mrs.) Fremont. *The Life of George Hearst, California Pioneer.* San Francisco, 1933. Illustrated. Vellum. John Henry Nash printing. $600.

OLDHAM, J. Basil. *Blind Panels of English Binders.* Cambridge, 1958. 67 plates. $250.

OLDHAM, J. Basil. *English Blind-Stamped Bindings.* Cambridge, 1952. 61 plates. One of 750 copies. $300.

OLDHAM, J. Basil. *Shrewsbury School Library Binding, Catalogue Raisonné.* Oxford, 1943. Frontispiece and 62 plates. One of 200 copies. $1,000.

OLDHAM, Williamson S., and WHITE, George W. *Digest of the General Statute Laws of the State of Texas.* Austin, 1859. $1,750.

OLDSTYLE, Jonathan. *Letters of Jonathan Oldstyle, Gent.* New York, 1824. By the Author of *The Sketch-Book,* Washington Irving. $450.

OLIPHANT, Laurence. *Minnesota and the Far West.* Edinburgh, 1855. Folding map and 7 plates. Half leather. $500.

OLIPHANT, Margaret. See Maitland, Margaret.

OLIVER, Chad. *Mists of Dawn.* Philadelphia (1952). $250. London, 1954. $150.

OLIVER, Chad. *Shadows in the Sun.* New York: Ballantine (1954). Second book, first science fiction. $450. Wraps. $35.

OLIVER, John W. (publisher). *Guide to the New Gold Region of Western Kansas and Nebraska.* New York, 1859. Folding map. 32 pages, printed wraps. $7,500.

OLIVER, Mary. *No Voyage . . .* London (1963). Author's first book. $750. Boston, 1965. (Enlarged edition.) $300. Wraps. $100.

OLLA Podrida. London, 1840. (By Frederick Marryat.) 3 vols., in original boards and cloth, or cloth. $350.

OLLIVANT, Alfred. *Bob: Son of Battle.* New York, 1898. Author's first book. Green decorated cloth. Stamped in gilt. $200.

OLMAN, Morton and John. *The Encyclopedia of Golf Collectibles.* Florence, Ala. (1985). Limited edition. $250.

OLMSTED, Frederick Law. See *Walks and Talks of an American Farmer . . .*

OLMSTED, Frederick Law. *A Journey Through Texas . . .* New York, 1857. Frontispiece and folding map. $600.

OLSEN, Tillie. *Tell Me a Riddle.* Philadelphia, 1961. Author's first book. Cloth. $400. Wraps. $50. London (1964). First English edition. $200. New York, 1978. One of 100 signed copies. Issued without dustwrapper. In slipcase. $250.

OLSON, Charles. See *Spanish Speaking* . . .

OLSON, Charles. *Apollonius of Tyana.* Black Mountain, N.C., 1951. One of 20 signed and dated hardbound copies. $4,000. One of 30 copies. Wraps. $2,500.

OLSON, Charles. *Call Me Ishmael.* New York (1947). Author's first book. First edition not stated. $450. New York (1958). One of 100 copies. Issued without dustwrapper. $250. Wraps. $25.

OLSON, Charles. *Human Universe and Other Essays.* San Francisco, 1965. Edited by Donald Allen. Woodcut by Robert LaVigne, photography by Kenneth Irby. Decorated boards, vellum spine. One of 250 copies. In plain dustwrapper. $350.

OLSON, Charles. *Letter for Melville 1951.* (Black Mountain, N.C., 1951.) Wraps. One of about 40 copies. $1,000. One of 10 copies with watercolor design by Charles Oscar. $2,500.

OLSON, Charles. *The Maximus Poems.* Stuttgart, 1953–56. *Jargon* 7 & 9. 2 vols. Volume I. One of 50 signed copies. Volume II. One of 25 signed copies. $5,000. New York, 1960. Boards. First complete edition. One of 26 lettered and signed copies. $1,000. One of 75 signed copies. $750. (Issued without dustwrapper.) Trade edition. Wraps. (First printing has $1.95 on back cover.) $100.

OLSON, Charles. *Mayan Letters.* Mallorca, 1953. Illustrated self-wraps. $300.

OLSON, Charles. *Y & X.* Black Sun Press. (Washington), 1948. Illustrated by Corrado Cagli. Printed gray wraps. First edition not stated. One of at least 118 copies in slipcase. $1,250. White wraps. One of 400 copies in envelope. $400. (There was also an offset reprint in 1950 without date on title page.)

OMAR Khayyam. See *Rubaiyat of Omar Khayyam.*

ON English Prose Fiction as Rational Amusement. (Caption title.) (London, 1869?) (By Anthony Trollope.) 44 pages. $2,400 at auction in 1986 "unbound as issued."

ON the Plains; or, The Race for Life. New York (1863). 62 pages, pictorial yellow wraps. (By Edward S. Ellis.) $500.

ON the "White Pass" Pay-Roll. Chicago, 1908. By the President of the White Pass & Yukon Route (S. H. Graves). 15 plates. Dark-blue cloth. $450.

O'NAN, Stewart. *In the Walled City.* Pittsburgh (1993). $200.

ONDAATJE, Michael. *The Dainty Monsters.* Toronto, 1967. Author's first book. One of 500 copies. $2,000.

ONDAATJE, Michael. *The English Patient.* London, 1992. $250. Toronto, 1992. $250. New York, 1992. $200.

ONDAATJE, Michael. *Running in the Family.* Toronto (1982). $250.

ONDERDONK, James L. *Idaho: Facts and Statistics.* San Francisco, 1885. Wraps. $750.

ONE and Twenty: Duke Narrative and Verse, 1924–1945. (Contains two short stories by William Styron, his first book appearance.) $200.

ONE Hundred and Seventy-six Historic and Artistic Book-Bindings Dating from the Fifteenth Century to the Present Time. New York, 1895. 2 vols. One of 200 copies on Imperial Japanese Paper. $2,000.

ONE Hundred Books Famous in English Literature. See Kent, Henry W.

ONE Hundred Influential American Books Printed Before 1900. New York, 1947. One of 600 copies. $350.

O'NEILL, Eugene. *Ah, Wilderness!* New York, 1933. $150. One of 325 signed copies. Blue calf. In slipcase. $500. Limited Editions Club, New York, 1972. In slipcase. $125.

O'NEILL, Eugene. *All God's Chillun Got Wings, and Welded.* New York (1924). Buff boards and cloth. $350.

O'NEILL, Eugene. *Anna Christie.* London (1923). First separate edition. Yellow boards. In dustwrapper. $400. Wraps. $300. New York, 1930. 12 illustrations by Alexander King. Purple and red boards, black cloth spine. First illustrated (and first American) edition. One of 775 copies. In dustwrapper and slipcase. $500. One of 12 copies in morocco, signed and with an original lithograph. $2,000.

O'NEILL, Eugene. *Before Breakfast.* New York, 1916. First separate edition. Light blue-green wraps. $600.

O'NEILL, Eugene. *Beyond the Horizon.* New York (1920). Brown boards and cloth. Probable first state, with small letters on front cover ¼ inch high. In dustwrapper. $600. Second state with letters ⅛ inch high. (Atkinson considers them variants.) $500.

O'NEILL, Eugene. *Desire Under the Elms.* New York, 1925. First separate edition. Pictorial black cloth. $750.

O'NEILL, Eugene. *Dynamo.* New York, 1929. $250. Purple vellum. One of 775 signed copies. In slipcase. $400.

O'NEILL, Eugene. *The Emperor Jones; Diff'rent; The Straw.* New York (1921). Buff boards and cloth. First issue (VAB) with plain (not mottled) boards. In dustwrapper. $750. (Atkinson identifies 2 variants, both in tan boards. One has "Eugene G. O'Neill" and the other lacks the "G.") Cincinnati (1921). White wraps. $350. New York, 1928. 8 illustrations in color by Alexander King. Boards and cloth. One of 775 signed copies. In dustwrapper and slipcase. $500.

O'NEILL, Eugene. *Gold.* New York, with 1920 copyright but published in (1921). Blue-green boards and cloth. In dustwrapper. $600.

O'NEILL, Eugene. *The Great God Brown; The Fountain; The Moon of the Caribbees and Other Plays.* New York, 1926. Green cloth. $400. London (1926). *(The Great God Brown.)* First English edition. Bright-blue cloth. $250.

O'NEILL, Eugene. *The Hairy Ape.* New York (1929). 9 illustrations in color by Alexander King. Boards. First separate and illustrated edition. One of 775 signed copies. In dustwrapper and slipcase. $500.

O'NEILL, Eugene. *The Hairy Ape; Anna Christie; The First Man.* New York (1922). Buff boards and cloth. In dustwrapper. $600. London (1923). *(The Hairy Ape and Other Plays.)* First English edition. Bright-blue cloth. In dustwrapper. $400. [Also see next entry.]

O'NEILL, Eugene. *The Iceman Cometh.* New York (1946). Blue cloth. In dustwrapper. $300. Limited Editions Club, New York, 1982. Illustrated and signed by Leonard Baskin. In slipcase. $250.

O'NEILL, Eugene. *Lazarus Laughed.* New York, 1927. $200. One of 775 signed copies. In slipcase. $450.

O'NEILL, Eugene. *Long Day's Journey into Night.* New Haven, 1956. Black-and-gray cloth. First edition stated. $300.

O'NEILL, Eugene. *Marco Millions.* New York, 1927. $350. Vellum and boards. One of 450 signed copies. In slipcase. $500.

O'NEILL, Eugene. *The Moon of the Caribbees and Six Other Plays of the Sea.* New York, 1919. Brown boards and cloth. First state, ⅞ inch thick, including covers (Johnson). In dustwrapper. $750. Second state, 1³⁄₁₆ inches thick. In dustwrapper. $650. (Atkinson calls these variants, not states.)

O'NEILL, Eugene. *Mourning Becomes Electra.* New York, 1931. Cloth. $350. Japan vellum. One of 550 signed copies. In slipcase. $500. One of 50 signed presentation copies. $1,000.

O'NEILL, Eugene. *Strange Interlude.* New York, 1928. $500. Another (later) issue: vellum. One of 775 signed copies. In slipcase. $750.

O'NEILL, Eugene. *Thirst and Other One Act Plays.* Boston (1914). Author's first book. Dark-gray boards, tan cloth spine, paper labels. In dustwrapper. $2,000. Without dustwrapper. $400.

ONIONS, Oliver. *The Compleat Bachelor.* London, 1900. Author's first book. $100.

ONKEN, Otto. See Wells, William.

OPPEN, George. *Discreet Series.* New York, 1934. Preface by Ezra Pound. Author's first book. $1,000.

OPPENHEIM, E. Phillips. *Expiation.* London, 1887. Author's first book. $300.

OPPENHEIMER, Joel. *The Dancer.* Highlands, N.C. 1952. (*Jargon 2.*) Graphic by Robert Rauschenberg. $2,500.

OPPENHEIMER, Joel. *Four Poems to Spring.* (Black Mountain, 1951.) Author's first book. Wraps. $1,500.

OPTIC, Oliver. See Ashton, Warren T.

OPTIC, Oliver. *The Boat Club; or, The Bunkers of Rippleton.* Boston, 1855. (By William Taylor Adams.) First Oliver Optic book. Frontispiece, 3 plates. Slate-purple pictorial cloth. $350. Pictorial presentation binding. $500.

OPTICKS: Or, a Treatise of the Reflections . . . London, 1704. (By Isaac Newton.) First issue with 19 copper-engraved folding plates. Published anonymously, with only the initials "I. N." at the end of the Advertisement. $40,000. [See entry under Newton for second issue.]

ORCUTT, William Dana. *The Book in Italy.* New York, 1928. Plates, including color. Folio, boards. One of 750 copies. In dustwrapper. $200. London, 1928. One of 12 lettered copies (reserved for the author). $450.

ORCUTT, William Dana. *In Quest of the Perfect Book.* Boston, 1926. Plates, including color. Half vellum. One of 365 copies. In slipcase. $250. Trade edition. $75.

ORCZY, Baroness. *The Emperor's Candlesticks.* London, 1899. Author's first book. $600.

ORCZY, Baroness. *The Scarlet Pimpernel.* London, 1905. Blue cloth. $1,500.

OREGON: Agricultural, Stock Raising, Mineral Resources, Climate, etc. (Published by U.P.R.R.) Council Bluffs, Iowa, 1888. 68 pages, wraps. $350.

ORIGO, Iris. See *Gianni June 23rd . . .*

O'REILLY, Bernard. *Greenland, the Adjacent Seas, and the North-West Passage . . .* London, 1818. 3 folding charts, 18 plates. $1,250.

O'REILLY, Harrington. *Fifty Years on the Trail.* London, 1889. Illustrated by Paul Frenzeny. Pictorial cloth. $200. London, 1890. Wraps. Second edition. $100. New York, 1889. First American edition. $100.

ORIGINAL Leaf from Francisco Paolou's Life of the Venerable Father Junipero Serro, 1787 . . . (San Francisco), 1958. One of 177 copies. Contains an original leaf. Stiff paper wraps. $250.

ORIGINAL Leaf from the Polycronicon Printed by William Caxton at Westminster in the Year 1482 . . . with an Appreciation . . . By Edwin Grabhorn. San Francisco, 1938. 297 copies with an original leaf from the *Polycronicon* mounted. $1,250.

ORIGO, Iris. *Allegra.* Hogarth Press. London, 1935. In dustwrapper with wraparound band. $200.

ORIOLI, G. *Adventures of a Bookseller.* Florence, Italy [1937]. Stiff paper wraps. One of 300 signed copies. $250.

ORME, Edward. *Collection of British Field Sports . . .* London, 1807–8. Colored title page and 20 colored plates after Howitt. Oblong folio. $65,000. Guildford, England, 1955. 29 color plates. Facsimile. Folio, full crimson morocco. One of 20 copies with an original plate included. $2,500. Trade edition in half morocco. $750.

ORR, George. *The Possession of Louisiana by the French.* London, 1803. 44 pages. $600.

ORR, N. M. (compiler). *The City of Stockton.* Stockton, Calif., 1874. 64 pages, printed wraps. $400.

ORR and RUGGLES. *San Joaquin County.* Stockton, 1887. Map, plates. 130 pages, wraps. $350.

ORTEGA Y GASSETT, Jose. *The Revolt of the Masses.* London (1932). Author's first book. $350. New York (1932). $250.

ORTON, Richard H. *Records of California Men in the War of the Rebellion, 1861–1867.* Sacramento, 1890. $350.

ORVIS, Charles F., and CHENEY, A. Nelson (compilers). *Fishing with the Fly . . .* Manchester, Vt., 1883. Frontispiece map and 15 color plates. $600.

ORWELL, George. *Animal Farm: A Fairy Story.* London, 1945. $3,500. New York (1946). Black cloth. First edition stated. $450.

ORWELL, George. *Burmese Days.* New York, 1934. $1,500. London, 1935. $4,500.

ORWELL, George. *A Clergyman's Daughter.* London, 1935. $2,500. New York, 1936. $1,500.

ORWELL, George. *Coming Up for Air.* London, 1939. $10,000.

ORWELL, George. *Down and Out in Paris and London.* London, 1933. First printing. $4,000. Second printing. $750. Third printing. $350. New York, 1933. $2,000.

ORWELL, George. *Homage to Catalonia.* London, 1938. $3,500. New York (1952). $125.

ORWELL, George. *Inside the Whale.* London, 1940. $1,750.

ORWELL, George. *Keep the Aspidistra Flying.* London, 1936. $3,500. New York (1956). $125.

ORWELL, George. *Nineteen Eighty-four.* London, 1949. Red dustwrapper seems to be preferred (priority uncertain), both noted in Book Society wraparound bands. $4,500. Green dustwrapper. $3,500. New York (1949). Red dustwrapper also preferred on U.S. edition. $1,000. Blue dustwrapper. $750.

ORWELL, George. *The Road to Wigan Pier.* London, 1937. Cloth. In dustwrapper. $2,500. Left Book Club edition. Limp oilcloth covers. $150. First half of text as supplementary offering for May 1937. 32 plates, chapters 1 to 7 only. Limp oilcloth covers. $750. New York (1958). $150.

OSBORNE, Eric. *Victorian Detective Fiction.* London, 1966. Introduction by John Carter. One of 475 copies signed by Carter, Dorothy Glover, and Graham Greene, whose collection is catalogued in the book. In dustwrapper. $600. One of 25 copies for presentation. $1,500.

OSBORNE, John. *Look Back in Anger.* London: Evans Brothers, 1957. His first published play. Wraps. $250. London: Faber, 1957. Cloth. $150. New York, 1957. $100.

OSBORNE, John, and CREIGHTON, Anthony. *Epitaph for George Dillon.* London (1958). $200.

OSCEOLA; or, Fact and Fiction: A Tale of the Seminole War. New York, 1838. By a Southerner (James Birchett Ransom). $750.

OSGOOD, Ernest Staples. *The Day of the Cattleman.* Minneapolis, 1929. 14 plates and maps. In dustwrapper. $300.

OSGOOD, Frances S. *The Floral Offering . . . of Poetry.* Philadelphia, 1847. With 10 hand-colored plates. $1,000.

O'SHAUGHNESSY, Arthur W. E. *An Epic of Women and Other Poems.* London, 1870. Author's first book. Pictorial title page, 2 plates, precedes title page. Purple cloth. $250.

O'SHAUGHNESSY, Arthur W. E. *Songs of a Worker.* London, 1881. $175.

OSLER, Sir William. *An Alabama Student and Other Biographical Essays.* Oxford, England, 1908. $350. New York, 1908. $250.

OSLER, Sir William (editor). *Bibliotheca Osleriana: A Catalogue of Books Illustrating the History of Medicine and Science.* Oxford, 1929. $750.

OSLER, Sir William. *The Cerebral Palsies of Children.* Philadelphia, 1889. $1,750.

OSLER, Sir William. *The Evolution of Modern Medicine.* New Haven, 1921. $300.

OSLER, Sir William. *Incunabula Medica: A Study of the Earliest Printed Medical Books, 1467–1480.* Oxford, 1923. Illustrated. Boards and cloth. Issued without dustwrapper. $750.

OSLER, Sir William. *The Principles and Practice of Medicine.* New York, 1892. With "Georgias" on leaf preceding table of contents, and last set of ads dated November 1891. In sheep or half-morocco. $5,000. Cloth. $4,000. New York, 1892. Second issue with "Gorgias" correctly spelled on verso of the third leaf. $1,000. Edinburgh/London, 1892. First issue. With same issue points as New York first issue. $2,000. Second issue. With same points as New York second issue. $1,500.

OSLER, Sir William. *Science and Immortality.* Boston, 1904. $200.

O'SULLIVAN, Seamus. *The Twilight People.* Dublin, 1905. (By James Sullivan Starkie.) Author's first book. Wraps. $200.

O'SULLIVAN, Vincent. *A Book of Bargains.* London, 1896. Red cloth. $600.

OTIS, James. *Toby Tyler or Ten Weeks with a Circus.* New York, 1881. (By James Otis Kaler.) Illustrated by W. A. Rogers. Light-brown, green, or orange cloth. Spine title and illustration centered. $400.

OTTLEY, William Young. *An Inquiry Concerning the Invention of Printing . . .* London, 1862. 37 full-page plates. $450.

OUIDA. *Syrlin.* London, 1880. (By Marie Louise de la Ramee.) 3 vols., cloth. $500.

OUIDA. *Under Two Flags.* London, 1867. (By Marie Louise de la Ramee.) 3 vols. $600.

OUIMET, Francis. *A Game of Golf: A Book of Reminiscenses.* Boston, 1932. One of 550 signed copies. In slipcase. $1,000.

OUR Exagmination Round his Factification for Incamination of Work in Progress. See Beckett, Samuel.

OUR NIG; Or, Sketches from the Life of a Free Black . . . Boston, 1859. (By Harriet E. Wilson.) Author's first book. $7,500.

OURSLER, Fulton. See Abbot, Anthony.

OUTCROPPINGS: Being Selections of California Verse. San Francisco, 1866. (Edited anonymously by Bret Harte.) Probable first issue, with "Staining" spelled "Sraining" on page 70 and with no ornament on page 102. Publisher's imprint not on spine. Edges plain. $400.

OUTERBRIDGE, Paul. *Photographing in Color.* New York (1940). $600.

OUTRE-MER: A Pilgrimage Beyond the Sea. Nos. I and II. Boston, 1833 and 1834. (By Henry Wadsworth Longfellow.) In original marbled wraps and blue wraps or boards. $3,000. (See BAL.) Also issued clothbound as 2 vols. in one. $750. New York, 1935. 2 vols. $750.

OVID. The Amores of P. Ovidius Naso. Golden Cockerel Press. Waltham Saint Lawrence, England, 1932. Translated by E. Powys Mathers. 5 engravings on copper by T. E. Laboureur. Half morocco issued without dustwrapper. One of 350 copies. $400.

OWEN, James. *The Bronxville Portfolio* . . . Bronxville, New York, 1927. Ribbon-tied cloth-backed portfolio, tips rubbed, containing 60 loose halftone plates, 10 x 13 inches, with title and single-leaf text. Each plate captioned. $300.

OWEN, John Pickard. *The Fair Haven.* London, 1873. By the Late John Pickard Owen. Edited by William Bickersteth Owen. (By Samuel Butler, of *Erewhon.*) $200.

OWEN, Mary Alicia, editor. *Voodoo Tales as Told Among the Negroes* . . . New York, 1893. Author's first book. $750.

OWEN, Richard E., and COX, E. T. *Report on the Mines of New Mexico.* (Cover title.) Washington, 1865. 59 pages, printed wraps. $1,000.

OWEN, Robert. See Campbell, Alexander.

OWEN, Robert. *A New View of Society.* London, 1813–14. 4 parts in one. $40,000. London, 1816. Second edition. $2,500.

OWEN, Robert Dale. *Hints on Public Architecture.* New York, 1849. 15 plates. $1,000.

OWEN, Wilfred. *Poems.* London, 1920. Author's first book. Cloth, paper label. In dustwrapper. $3,500. New York (1921). In dustwrapper. $2,000. London, 1931. First complete edition. $500.

OWEN, Wilfred. *Thirteen Poems.* Gehenna Press. Northampton, Mass., 1956. Drawings by Ben Shahn and Leonard Baskin. Folio, half morocco. One of 400 copies signed by Baskin. Issued without dustwrapper. $500. One of 35 copies specially bound and with a proof of portrait signed by both artists. $1,500.

OWL Creek Letters (The). (By William C. Prime.) New York, 1848. Author's first book. $250.

OXENHAM, Elsie J. *Goblin Island.* London, 1907. Author's first book. $450.

OXLEY, John. *Journals of Two Expeditions into the Interior of New South Wales.* London, 1820. 5 folding maps, plates and charts, 1 folding etching and 5 aquatints (2 of them hand-colored). $6,000.

OZICK, Cynthia. *Trust.* New York (1966). Author's first book. $500. (London, 1966.) $200.

P

P., E. *Hugh Selwyn Mauberley.* Ovid Press. (London), 1920. (By Ezra Pound.) One of 165 copies from an edition of 200. $7,500. Cloth. One of 20 signed copies. $10,000. Parchment boards. One of 15 copies on vellum. $12,500.

PACKARD, Wellman, and LARISON, G. *Early Emigration to California 1845–1850.* Bloomington, Ill., 1928. 2 portraits, 23 pages, printed wraps. One of 30 copies. $600.

PADGETT, Lewis. *The Brass Ring.* New York (1946). (By H. Kuttner and C. L. Moore.) Author's first book. First edition stated. $350.

PADGETT, Lewis. *A Gnome There Was and Other Tales of Science Fiction and Fantasy.* New York, 1950. (By H. Kuttner and C. L. Moore.) First edition not stated. $250.

PAGAN Anthology (A). New York (1918). Orange cloth spine and blue boards, paper label. (Contains 2 poems by Hart Crane, constituting his first book appearance.) $450.

PAGE, Stanton. *The Chevalier of Pensieri-Vani.* Boston (1890). (By Henry Blake Fuller, his first book.) Wraps. $400. Cloth. $200.

PAGE, Thomas Nelson. *In Old Virginia.* New York, 1887. Pictorial cloth. Author's first book. First issue, with advertisement headed "Popular Books . . . Old Creole Days . . ." $175.

PAGE, Thomas Nelson. *Two Little Confederates.* New York, 1888. Illustrated. Blue cloth. With 10 ad pages at back. (Second had 8 pages.) $250.

PAIN, William. *The Carpenter's and Joiner's Repository.* London, 1792. Third edition. 2 frontis plates, 67 engraved plates. $3,750.

PAGES, Pierre Marie. *Travels Round the World in the Years 1767 . . .* London, 1791. 3 vols. Folding frontispiece plate in vol. 1. Folding frontispiece table in vol. 3. [First English edition, after the first, in French, in 1782.] $2,500.

PAINE, Albert Bigelow. See White, William Allen, and Paine, Albert Bigelow.

PAINE, Albert Bigelow. *Captain Bill McDonald, Texas Ranger.* New York, 1909. Illustrated. $500. Morocco. $600.

PAINE, Albert Bigelow. *Gabriel a Poem.* (Fort Scott, Kan. 1889). Author's first book. Wraps. $300.

PAINE, Albert Bigelow. *Thomas Nast: His Period and His Pictures.* New York, 1904. Illustrated. $200.

PAINE, Thomas. See *Common Sense.*

PALEY, Grace. *The Little Disturbances of Man.* Garden City, 1959. Author's first book. $350. London, 1960. $150.

PALGRAVE, Francis Turner. *The Golden Treasury of the Best Songs and Lyrical Poems of the English Language.* Cambridge, 1861. 1,000 copies issued in four states. First state: half title printed in roman type with four notes only on page 323 (later six notes) and price gilt-stamped at foot of spine. $500. New York, 1911. Illustrated by Maxfield Parrish. $250.

PALGRAVE, William Gifford. *Narrative of a Year's Journey Through Central and Eastern Arabia (1862–1863).* London, 1865. 2 vols. 4 extending plans and a colored folding map. $1,500.

PALINURUS. *The Unquiet Grave: A Word Cycle.* London, 1944. (By Cyril Connolly.) Curwen Press. Frontispiece and 3 collotype plates. Cloth. In dustwrapper. One of 1,000 copies. $500. Wraps. $200.

PALLADINO, Lawrence B. *Indian and White in the Northwest.* Baltimore, 1894. Illustrated. Cloth, or half leather. $600.

PALLAS, P. S. *Travels Through the Southern Provinces of the Russian Empire* . . . London, 1802–3. 4 folding maps and 51 plates (42 folding). 2 vols. First English edition. $6,000. (The more hand-colored plates the better.) London, 1812. $1,750.

PALLISER, John. *Exploration—British North America.* London, 1859–65. Four parts bound in 1. 16 maps. $12,500.

PALMER, H. E. *The Powder River Indian Expedition, 1865.* Omaha, 1887. 59 pages, printed gray wraps. $500.

PALMER, Harry. *Base Ball:The National Game of the Americans.* Chicago, 1888. 69 pages, wraps. $1,500.

PALMER, Joel. *Journal of Travels over the Rocky Mountains, to the Mouth of the Columbia River, etc.* Cincinnati, 1847. Brown printed wraps. First issue, with date 1847 on paper cover not over-printed or changed, and with errata slip tipped in. $6,000. Cincinnati, 1852. Half leather. Second edition. $2,000.

PALMER, S. *The General History of Printing, from Its First Invention in the City of Mentz* . . . London, 1732. $850.

PALMER, Samuel. *The Life and Letters.* London, 1892. Frontispiece, an original etching, and 22 illustrations. Blue cloth. $750.

PALMER, Stuart. *The Ace of Jades.* New York, 1931. Author's first book. $750.

PALMER, Stuart. *The Penguin Pool Murders.* New York, 1931. $600.

PALMER, William J. *Report of Surveys Across the Continent.* Philadelphia, 1869. 3 maps and profile, 20 photographic plates. Wraps. $1,500. Later issue, cloth. $1,250.

PALTSITS, Victor Hugo. *Washington's Farewell Address, in Facsimile* . . . New York, 1935. One of 100 copies. In calf. $350. One of 400 copies. In cloth. $200.

PAPWORTH, John B. *Hints on Ornamental Gardening.* London, 1823. 28 hand-colored plates, sepia plate, woodcut plans. $2,500.

PAPWORTH, John B. *Rural Residences* . . . London, 1818. 27 full-page hand-colored aquatint plates. Boards. $2,500.

PAPWORTH, John B. *Select Views of London.* London, 1816. First book edition. 76 colored aquatint plates, 5 folding. $6,000.

PARETSKY, Sara. *Deadlock.* Garden City, 1984. $500. London, 1984. $350

PARETSKY, Sara. *Indemnity Only.* New York (1982) Author's first book. $1,250. London, 1982. $300.

PARETSKY, Sara. *Killing Orders.* New York (1985). $200. London, 1986. $100.

PARGETER, Edith. See Peters, Ellis.

PARGETER, Edith. *Hortensius* . . . London, 1936. One of 125 signed copies. Author's first book. $1,250. Trade. $600. New York, 1937. $350.

PARK, James Allen. *A System of the Law of Marine Insurances* . . . Philadelphia, 1789. Octavo. First work on insurance to appear in America. $1,500.

PARK, Mungo. *Travels in the Interior Districts of Africa.* London, 1799. With 3 folding maps, 6 plates and 2 leaves of music. $1,750.

PARK, Ruth. *The Harp In the South,* London, 1948. $300. New York, 1948. $75.

PARK, William J. *Art of Putting.* Edinburgh, 1920. $1,500.

PARK, William, Jr. *Game of Golf.* London, 1896. $1,500.

PARKER, A. A. *A Trip to the West and Texas.* Concord, N.H., 1835. 2 plates. Map. $2,500. Concord/Boston, 1836. Colored folding map, frontis, and 2 plates. Second edition. $1,500. (Note: Howes states not all copies of the second edition included the map; in such cases the value would be less.)

PARKER, Aaron. *Forgotten Tragedies of Indian Warfare in Idaho.* Grangeville, Idaho, 1925. 10 pages, double column, wraps. $250.

PARKER, Dorothy. *After Such Pleasures.* New York, 1933. One of 250 signed copies. In slipcase. $750. Trade edition. $200.

PARKER, Dorothy. *Death and Taxes.* New York, 1931. One of 250 signed copies. In slipcase. $750. Trade edition, "First Printing" on front panel of dustwrapper. No statement of "First Edition" $350. (FPAA states that copyright page has "Second printing before publication," which would be the second printing.)

PARKER, Dorothy. *Enough Rope.* New York, 1926. $750.

PARKER, Dorothy. *High Society.* New York (1920). Author's first book, written with W. George Chappell and Frank Crowninshield. $1,000.

PARKER, Dorothy. *Men I'm Not Married To.* Garden City, 1922. First edition stated. Author's first separate book, preceded by some collaborations. (Bound dos-à-dos with *Women I'm Not Married To,* by Franklin P. Adams.) In dustwrapper. $600.

PARKER, Dorothy. *Not So Deep as a Well.* New York, 1936. One of 485 signed copies. Slipcase. $600. Trade. $300.

PARKER, Dorothy. *Sunset Gun.* New York, 1928. Boards and cloth. One of 275 signed copies. In slipcase. $750. Trade edition. $450.

PARKER, Frank J. (editor). *Washington Territory! The Present and Prospective Future of the Upper Columbia Country.* Walla Walla, Wash., 1881. 17 pages, printed wraps. $2,000.

PARKER, J. M. *An Aged Wanderer: A Life Sketch of* . . . *A Cowboy, on the Western Plains in Early Days.* San Angelo, Tex., no date. 32 pages, wraps. $1,000.

PARKER, James. *The Old Army: Memories, 1872–1918.* Philadelphia, 1929. $300.

PARKER, John R. *The United States Telegraph Vocabulary.* Boston, 1832. 3 plates, one in color. $750.

PARKER, Mary Ann. *A Voyage Round the World, in the Gorgon Man of War.* London, 1795. $6,000.

PARKER, Robert B. *The Godwulf Manuscript*. Boston, 1974. Author's first Spenser mystery. $400. (London, 1974.) $150.

PARKER, Robert B. *God Save the Child*. Boston, 1974. $400. (London, 1975.) $200.

PARKER, Robert B. *Mortal Stakes*. Boston, 1975. $300. (London, 1976.) Issued without front endpaper. $125.

PARKER, Samuel. *Journal of an Exploring Tour Beyond the Rocky Mountains*. Ithaca, N.Y. 1838. Folding map, plate. In original cloth. $750.

PARKER, Solomon. *Parker's American Citizen's Sure Guide*. Sag Harbor, N.Y., 1808. $250.

PARKER, Theodore. *The Previous Question* . . . Boston, 1840. Wraps. Author's first book. $200.

PARKER, W. B. *Notes Taken During the Expedition Commanded by Capt. R. B. Marcy* . . . Philadelphia, 1856. $750.

PARKER & HUYETT. *The Illustrated Miners' Hand-Book and Guide to Pike's Peak*. St. Louis, 1859. (By Nathan H. Parker and D. H. Huyett.) 6 plates, 2 folding maps. Cloth. $14,000 at auction in 1999 (Streeter copy).

PARKINSON, C. Northcote. *Edward Pellew* . . . London (1934). Author's first book. $250.

PARKINSON, John. *Paradisi in Sole Paradisus Terrestris. Or, a choice Garden for all Sorts of Pleasant Flowers* . . . London, 1629. Folio. 110 full-page woodcuts of flowers etc. and frontispiece portrait of Parkinson. $6,000.

PARKINSON, Sydney. *A Journal of a Voyage to the South Seas* . . . London, 1773. Frontis portrait. 27 copperplates, including a map. $9,500.

PARKMAN, Francis. *The California and Oregon Trail*. New York, 1849. 2 vols. Printed wraps. $30,000 or more (only one complete set known). Or clothbound in 1 vol. with frontispiece and engraved title page, and terminal catalogue inserted, not integral. $4,500. Second printing with integral catalogue paged 1–6. $2,500. Third printing. The same but "See page 260" added to frontispiece. $1,500.

PARKMAN, Francis. *History of the Conspiracy of Pontiac and the War of the North American Tribes* . . . Boston, 1851. 4 maps. $600.

PARKMAN, Francis. *The Oregon Trail*. Boston, 1892. Illustrated by Frederic Remington. Leather. $750. Pictorial tan cloth. $500. Boston, 1925. Illustrated by Remington and N. C. Wyeth. Half cloth. One of 975 copies. $1,250. New York, 1943. Limited Editions Club. In slipcase. $350. Garden City, 1945. One of 1,000 copies signed by illustrator Thomas Hart Benton. $750.

PARKS, Gordon. *Flash Photography*. Grosset & Dunlap. New York (1947). Wraps. Author's first book. $200.

PARLEY, Peter. *Peter Parley's Universal History, on the Basis of Geography*. Boston, 1837. (By Nathaniel Hawthorne and his sister Elizabeth.) 2 vols., in original cloth. $7,500.

PARLEY, Peter. *The Tales of Peter Parley About America*. Boston, 1827. (By Samuel G. Goodrich.) Author's first book. 32 (30?) engravings. In original blue boards, red leather spine. $20,000. Rebound. $5,000.

PARMLY, Levi Spear. *A Practical Guide to the Management of the Teeth.* Philadelphia, 1819. $1,000.

PARNELL, Thomas. *Poems.* Cuala Press. Dublin, 1927. Selected by Lennox Robinson. Boards and linen. One of 200 copies. In dustwrapper. $250.

PARRISH, Anne. *A Pocketful of Poses.* New York (1923). Author's first book. $200.

PARRISH, Maxfield. See Baum, L. Frank.

PARRISH, M. L. *Charles Kingsley and Thomas Hughes, First Editions* . . . London, 1936. One of 150 copies. In dustwrapper. $450.

PARRISH, M. L. *Victorian Lady Novelists* . . . London, 1933. One of 150 copies. In dustwrapper. $750.

PARRISH, M. L. *Wilkie Collins and Charles Reade* . . . London, 1940. One of 150 copies. $500.

PARRY, William Edward. *Journal of a Second Voyage for the Discovery of a North-West Passage* . . . London, 1824–25. 2 vols. 39 plates, maps and charts. $2,500.

PARRY, William Edward. *Journal of a Voyage for the Discovery of a North-West Passage* . . . *in the Years, 1819–20.* London, 1821. 20 plates and maps. $2,000. Philadelphia, 1821. $1,250.

PARSONS, Edward Alexander. *The Wonder and the Glory* . . . New York, 1962. $150.

PARSONS, Samuel B. *The Rose: Its History, Poetry, Culture and Classification.* New York, 1847. 2 hand-colored plates, 3 lithographed plates. In original cloth. $600.

PARTINGTON, C. F. *The Printer's Complete Guide.* London, 1825. $350.

PARTISAN (The): A Tale of the Revolution. New York, 1835. (By William Gilmore Simms.) 2 vols. $750.

PARTRIDGE, C.S. *Stereotyping, The Papier Mache Process.* Chicago, 1892. $250.

PASADENA As It Is Today from a Business Standpoint. (Cover title.) (Pasadena, 1886.) 32 pages, printed wraps. $450.

PASADENA, California, Illustrated. Pasadena, 1886. Plates. 45 pages, pictorial wraps. $300.

PASADENA, Los Angeles County, Southern California. Los Angeles, 1898. 36 pages, wraps. $250.

PASCAL, Blaise. *Monsieur Pascal's Thoughts, Meditations and Prayers* . . . London, 1688. $3,500.

PASKO, W. W. *American Dictionary of Printing and Bookmaking* . . . New York, 1894. Illustrated, leather spine label. $350.

PASSAGES from the Diary of a Late Physician. (By Samuel Warren.) New York, 1831. Author's first book. (Pirated.) $350. London, 1832. 2 vols. $250.

PASSION-Flowers. Boston, 1854. (By Julia Ward Howe.) Author's first book. $600.

PASTERNAK, Boris. *Doctor Zhivago.* London, 1958. First edition in English. $350. New York, 1958. $250.

PASTERNAK, Boris. *Selected Poems.* London, 1946. $350.

PATCHEN, Kenneth. *Before the Brave.* New York (1936). Red cloth. Author's first book. $350.

PATCHEN, Kenneth. *The Dark Kingdom.* New York (1942). Wraps, painted by the author. One of 75 signed copies. In slipcase with an original watercolor on cover. $850. Trade edition. $250. (New York, 1948.) $75.

PATCHEN, Kenneth. *The Famous Boating Party.* (New York, 1954.) Cloth (per Morgan A22) but noted in boards (as well or error?). One of 50 signed copies with covers handpainted by Patchen. $1,000. Trade edition in dustwrapper. $250.

PATCHEN, Kenneth. *First Will and Testament.* New Directions. Norfolk (1939). Red buckram. One of 800 copies. $450. Padell. New York (1948). Second edition. With poem added. $100.

PATCHEN, Kenneth. *Hurrah for Anything.* Highlands, N.C., 1957. Illustrated. Gray self-wraps. One of 100 copies "Prepared and painted by . . ." $1,500. Trade edition. $100.

PATCHEN, Kenneth. *The Journal of Albion Moonlight.* (Mount Vernon, N.Y., 1941.) Three-quarter leather and buckram. One of 50 signed copies. In slipcase. $1,750. Second issue: One of 295 signed copies. In dustwrapper. $600. First trade edition, United Book Guild. New York, 1944. $250. (Reprinted later by both Padell and New Directions.)

PATCHEN, Kenneth. *Orchards, Thrones and Caravans.* San Francisco (1952). Boards. "Vellum edition." One of 120 signed copies. $750. Boards. One of 90 copies. "Engraver's edition," with cover engraving by David Ruff, signed by Patchen and Ruff. $1,000.

PATCHEN, Kenneth. *Panels for the Walls of Heaven.* (Berkeley), 1946. Boards and dustwrapper. $300. Also, 150 copies with cover painted by Patchen and numbered and signed on back, in acetate dustwrapper. $1,250.

PATCHEN, Kenneth. *Sleepers Awake.* New York (1946.) Red cloth. First (black paper) edition. One of 148 signed copies. In dustwrapper. $500. White cloth, with original decoration on cover by the author. One of 75 signed copies. $850. Trade edition. $200.

PATCHEN, Kenneth. *When We Were Here Together.* Norfolk (1957). One of 75 copies with covers handpainted by author and with limitation notice in Patchen's hand, signed. $1,000.

PATER, Walter. *An Imaginary Portrait.* Daniel Press. Oxford, 1894. Wraps. One of 250 copies. $650.

PATER, Walter. *Imaginary Portraits.* London, 1887. $200.

PATER, Walter. *Plato and Platonism: A Series of Lectures.* New York, 1893. One of 100 copies. $200.

PATER, Walter. *Sebastian Van Storck.* London, 1927. 8 colored plates. One of 1,050 copies. With one plate signed by the artist Alastair. First English edition. $450.

PATER, Walter. *Studies in the History of the Renaissance.* London, 1873. Dark-green cloth. Author's first book. $300.

PATHFINDER (The); or, The Inland Sea. By the author of *The Pioneers.* London, 1840. (By James Fenimore Cooper.) 3 vols., in original boards and cloth, paper labels. $2,500. Rebound.

$750. Philadelphia, 1840. 2 vols., green or purple cloth, paper labels. First American edition, first issue, without copyright notice in vol. I and with printer's imprint at about center of page 2. $1,500. Limited Editions Club, New York, 1965. Buckram. In slipcase. $125.

PATMORE, Coventry. See *The Angel in the House; Odes.*

PATMORE, Coventry. *Faithful for Ever.* London, 1860. $400.

PATMORE, Coventry. *Poems.* London, 1844. Author's first book. $850.

PATMORE, Henry John. *Poems.* Daniel Press. Oxford, 1884. Vellum. One of 125 copies. $600.

PATON, Alan. *Cry, the Beloved Country.* London, 1948. $1,000. New York, 1948. $500.

PATON, Alan. *Meditation for a Young Boy Confirmed.* London, 1944. Author's first book. Wraps. $1,250.

PATON, Lucy Allen. *Selected Bindings from the Gennadius Library.* Cambridge, 1924. One of 300 copies. 38 plates in color. $750.

PATON, Walter. *Paton's Flowers of Penmanship.* London, 1840. 2 engraved title pages and 12 engraved plates. $250.

PATRICK, Q. *Cottage Sinister.* London, 1931. (By Richard Wilson Webb et al.) Author's first book. $750.

PATTERSON, A. W. *History of the Backwoods; or, The Region of the Ohio.* Pittsburgh, 1843. Folding map. $1,250.

PATTERSON, Harry. *Sad Wind from the Sea.* London, 1959. $200.

PATTERSON, James. *The Thomas Berryman Number.* Boston, 1976. $600. London (1977). $150.

PATTERSON, Lawson B. *Twelve Years in the Mines of California.* Cambridge, Mass., 1862. $600.

PATTERSON, Mark. *The Estiennes, A Biographical Essay . . .* San Francisco, 1949. One of 390 copies. Contains leaves printed by Henri Estienne in 1510, Robert Estienne in 1544 and Henri II in 1592. $500.

PATTERSON, Richard North. *The Lasko Tangent.* New York, 1979. $500.

PATTERSON, Samuel. *Narrative of the Adventures and Sufferings of Samuel Patterson.* Rhode Island, 1817. $3,000. Palmer, Mass., 1817. Second issue (Howes). $1,250. (Ghostwritten by Ezekiel Terry.)

PATTIE, James O. *The Personal Narrative of James O. Pattie, of Kentucky . . .* Cincinnati, 1831. Edited by Timothy Flint. 5 plates. Mottled calf. Published by John H. Wood. $20,000. Cincinnati, 1833. Second issue (reissue of the 1831 sheets with new title page). $5,000.

PATTON, George S., Jr. See *Saber Exercises.*

PATTON, The Reverend W. W., and Isham, R. N. *U.S. Sanitary Commission, No. 38: Report on the Condition of Camps and Hospitals at Cairo . . . Paducah and St. Louis.* Chicago, 1861. 12 pages, stitched. $350.

PAUL, Elliot. *Imperturbe: A Novel of Peace Without Victory.* New York, 1924. "Published, April 1924" on copyright page. $500.

PAUL, Elliot. *Impromptu: A Novel in Four Movements.* New York, 1923. "Published, March 1923." on copyright page. $500.

PAUL, Elliot. *Indelible, A Story of Love* . . . Boston, 1922. Author's first book. $600.

PAUL, Elliot, and ALLEN, Jay. *All the Brave.* New York (1939). Illustrated by Luis Quintanilla. Preface by Ernest Hemingway. Pictorial wraps. $150. One of 440 calf in half calf. $350.

PAUL, William. *The Rose Garden.* London, 1848. 15 color plates. $1,250.

PAULDING, Hiram. *Journal of a Cruise of the United States Schooner Dolphin.* New York, 1831. Folding map. $1,500.

PAULDING, James Kirke. See Langstaff, Launcelot. See also *Chronicles of the City of Gotham; Koningsmarke; A Sketch of Old England; Westward Ho!*

PAULDING, James Kirke. *The Backwoodsman: A Poem.* Philadelphia, 1818. With pages (177–80) present. $450. Second state with pages (177–80) excised. $300.

PAULDING, James Kirke. *Slavery in the United States.* New York, 1836. In original cloth. $500.

PAULINE: A Fragment of a Confession. London, 1833. (By Robert Browning.) Author's first book. Gray or brown boards, paper label. $50,000. London, 1886. Edited by Thomas J. Wise. Boards. One of 400 copies. $300. One of 25 copies on large paper. $600.

PAULISON, C. M. K. *Arizona: The Wonderful Country* . . . Tucson, 1881. 31 pages, printed wraps. $5,000.

Pause! London, 1910. (By Arthur Henry Sarfield Ward, a.k.a. Sax Rohmer). $1,000.

PAXTON, Elisha F. *Memoir and Memorials: Elisha Franklin Paxton, Brigadier-General, C.S.A* . . . [New York] 1905. $500.

PAYNE, John Howard. *Clari; or, The Main of Milan; An Opera, in Three Acts.* London, 1823. (Contains the first printing of "Home! Sweet Home!") $1,000.

PAYNE, John Howard. *Indian Justice: A Cherokee Murder Trial at Tahlequah in 1840.* Oklahoma City, 1934. Edited by Grant Foreman. Illustrated. $150.

PAYNE, John Howard, and BISHOP, Henry R. *Home! Sweet Home! Sung by Miss M. Tree, in Clari.* London (1823). 4 pages, folio, sheet music. First separate edition. $2,000.

PAZ, Octavio. *Three Poems.* New York, 1987. One of 750 copies signed by Paz and Robert Motherwell (the illustrator). $3,500.

PEABODY, Elizabeth Palmer. See *First Lessons* . . .

PEACOCK, Francis. *Sketches Relative to the History and Theory, but More Especially to the Practice of Dancing.* Aberdeen, Scotland, 1805. $750.

PEACOCK, Thomas Love. See *Crotchet Castle; Headlong Hall; Maid Marian; Melincourt; The Misfortunes of Elphin; Nightmare Abbey; Rhododaphne.*

PEACOCK, Thomas Love. *The Genius of the Thames.* London, 1810. $1,250.

PEACOCK, Thomas Love. *Palmyra and Other Poems.* London, 1806. Frontispiece. $2,000.

PEAKE, Mervyn. *Captain Slaughterboard Drops Anchor.* (London, 1939.) Author's first book. Reportedly most destroyed. In dustwrapper. $6,000. London, 1945. Color illustrations. Second edition. $500.

PEAKE, Mervyn. *Gormenghast.* London, 1950. $500.

PEAKE, Mervyn. *Letter from a Lost Uncle.* London, 1948. $350.

PEAKE, Mervyn. *Mr. Pye.* London, 1953. $300.

PEAKE, Mervyn. *Shapes and Sounds.* London, 1941. $350.

PEAKE, Mervyn. *Titus Alone.* London, 1959. $600.

PEAKE, Mervyn. *Titus Groan.* (London), 1946. $450.

PEALE, Rembrandt. *Graphics; A Manual of Drawing and Writing . . .* New York, 1835. Errata slip. $500.

PEARSE, James. *A Narrative of the Life of James Pearse.* Rutland, Vt., 1825. $350.

PEARSON, Edwin. *Banbury Chap Books and Nursery Toy Book Literature . . .* London, 1890. One of 550 copies. $250.

PEARY, Robert E. *Nearest the Pole . . .* London, 1907. With color frontispiece, 2 folding maps, and 95 photogravures. $300.

PEARY, Robert E. *The North Pole.* London, 1910. $350. London/New York, 1910. One of 500 signed copies. $1,500. New York, 1910. $250.

PEARY, Robert E. *Northward Over the "Great Ice."* New York, 1898. 2 vols. Maps, diagrams and nearly 800 illustrations. Cloth. $450. London, 1898. 2 vols. $600.

PEATTIE, Donald Culross. *An Almanac for Moderns.* New York (1935). Lynd Ward illustrations. $150. Limited Editions Club, New York, 1938. In slipcase. $150.

PEATTIE, Donald Culross. *Audubon's America.* Boston, 1940. Color plates and other illustrations. $125. Limited edition, with an extra set of color plates. $350.

PEATTIE, Donald Culross. *Blown Leaves.* (Chicago), 1916. Author's first book. Wraps. $1,000.

PECK, George. *Adventures of One Terrence McGrant . . .* New York, 1871. Author's first book. $350.

PECK, George. *Peck's Bad Boy and His Pa.* Chicago, 1883. First issue, with the text ending on page 196, the last word in perfect type, and with the printer's rules on the copyright page ⅞ inch apart (later either spaced differently or rules lacking). Wraps. $750. Cloth. $300.

PECK, John M. *A Gazetteer of Illinois.* Jacksonville, Ill., 1834. $1,000. Philadelphia, 1837. Second edition. $750.

PECK, John M. *A Guide for Emigrants, Containing Sketches of Illinois, Missouri, and the Adjacent Parts.* Boston, 1831. Map in color. $1,250. Enlarged edition. Boston, 1836. (Retitled *A New Guide for Emigrants to the West.*) $400.

PEEK, Peter V. *Inklings of Adventure in the Campaigns of the Florida Indian War.* (Cover title.) Schenectady, N.Y. 1846. 72 pages, double columns, printed yellow wraps. $7,500. Schenectady, 1860. Pictorial wraps. $500.

PEESLAKE, Gaffer. *Bromo Bombastes: A Fragment from a Laconic Drama.* Caduceus Press. London, 1933. (By Lawrence Durrell.) Black boards, paper label. One of 100 copies. $5,000.

PEIRCE, A. C. *A Man from Corpus Christi.* New York, 1894. $300.

PELAYO: A Story of the Goth. New York, 1838. (By William Gilmore Simms.) 2 vols. $750.

PELECANOS, George P. *A Firing Offense.* New York, 1992. $200.

PELECANOS, George P. *Nick's Trip.* New York (1993). $850.

PEMBERTON, Sir Max. *Diary of a Scoundrel.* London, 1891. Author's first book. $600.

PEMBERTON, Sir Max. *Jewel Mysteries I Have Known . . .* London, 1894. $450.

PEN Knife Sketches; Or, Chips off the Old Block. Sacramento, 1853. (By Alonzo Delano.) 24 full-page illustrations. Wraps. $1,500. Second edition, same year. $1,000.

PEN Owen. Edinburgh, 1822. (By James Hook.) 3 vols. Author's first book. $300.

PENDENNIS, Arthur (editor). *The Newcomes.* London, 1853–55. (By William Makepeace Thackeray.) Illustrated by Richard Doyle. 24 parts in 23. Yellow wraps. $1,750. London, 1854–55. 2 vols., cloth. First book edition. $1,000.

PENDLETON, Nathaniel Green. *Military Posts-Council Bluffs to the Pacific Ocean.* (Caption title.) (Washington, 1843.) Folding map. Sewn. $750.

PENN, Irving. *Moments Preserved.* New York (1960). Profusely illustrated with photographs. Beige cloth, spine stamped in black. Dustwrapper (spine half chipped away). In the photo-illustrated slipcase. $650.

PENNANT, Thomas. *Arctic Zoology.* London 1784–87. 3 vols. Includes supplement. $3,500. London, 1792. Second and best edition. 3 vols. $4,500.

PENNELL, Elizabeth R., and PENNELL, Joseph. *The Glory of New York.* New York, 1926. 24 color reproductions. Folio, cloth. One of 350 copies. In dustwrapper and slipcase. $350.

PENNELL, E. R., and PENNELL, Joseph. *The Life of James McNeil Whistler.* London, 1908. 2 vols. One of 150 copies on Japan vellum, signed by Joseph Pennell and the publisher. In cloth slipcase. $500.

PENNELL, Elizabeth R., and PENNELL, Joseph. *Our Philadelphia.* Philadelphia, 1914. Boards. One of 289 signed copies. With 10 extra lithographs. $200. Trade edition. $100.

PENNELL, Joseph. *The Adventures of an Illustrator . . .* Boston, 1925. Half leather. Signed limited edition with 14 extra plates including a signed etching. Issued without dustwrapper. $450. Trade edition. Cloth. In dustwrapper. $175.

PENTLAND Rising (The). Edinburgh, 1866. (By Robert Louis Stevenson.) His first book. Green wraps. $5,000.

PEPPER, George W. *Personal Recollections of Sherman's Campaigns in Georgia and the Carolinas.* Zanesville, 1866. In original cloth. $750.

PEPYS, Samuel. *Memoirs of Samuel Pepys . . . Comprising His Diary from 1659 to 1669.* London, 1825. 2 vols. Edited by Richard, Lord Braybrooke. Portraits, views, and facsimiles. $3,500. London, 1828. 5 vols. Second (and first octavo) edition. Boards. $1,250. Limited Editions Club, New York, 1942. 10 vols. Illustrated. Pictorial boards and buckram. $350.

PERCIVAL Keene. London, 1842. (By Frederick Marryat.) 3 vols. $450.

PERCY, Stephen. *Robin Hood and His Merry Foresters.* New York, 1855. (By Joseph Cundall.) 8 full-page hand-colored illustrations. $1,250.

PERCY, Walker. *Bourbon.* Winston-Salem (1979). One of 50 signed (roman numerals) copies. Marbled wraps and dustwrapper. $350. One of 200 signed copies. $250. (Reissued in 1981. Adds Percy's favorite drink.)

PERCY, Walker. *The Last Gentleman.* New York (1966). $350. London (1967). $200.

PERCY, Walker. *The Moviegoer.* New York, 1961. Author's first book, preceded by a number of offprints. $3,500. London, 1963. $600.

PERCY, Walker. *Questions They Never Asked Me.* Northridge, 1979. One of 50 signed copies. Bound in full blue leather. $450. One of 300 signed copies in patterned paper-covered boards and cloth spine. $200.

PERCY, Walker. *Symbol as Need.* (New York) 1954. Author's first work. Offprint from *Thought.* Stapled printed wraps with title page as cover. $850.

PERELMAN, S. J. *Dawn Ginsbergh's Revenge.* New York (1929). Author's first book. Apple green "plush" binding. $2,500. Second silver binding. $1,500.

PERELMAN, S. J. *Look Who's Talking!* New York (1940). $500.

PEREZ DE LUXAN, Diego. *Expedition into New Mexico Made by Antonio de Espejo, 1582–1583 . . .* Los Angeles, 1929. Translated by George Peter Hammond and Agapito Rey. Half vellum in dustwrapper. One of 500 copies. $400.

PERICLES and Aspasia. London, 1836. (By Walter Savage Landor.) 2 vols. In original drab boards, blue-green cloth, paper labels. $500. Philadelphia, 1839. 2 vols. First American edition. $300.

PERKINS, Charles Elliott. *The Pinto Horse.* Santa Barbara, 1927. Illustrated by Edward Borein. Pictorial boards. In dustwrapper. $500.

PERKINS, Charlotte. *In This Our World . . .* London, 1893. Author's first book. $5,000. San Francisco, 1895. Wraps. $2,000. San Francisco, 1895. Second edition in blue cloth. Adds 46 poems. $500.

PERLES, Alfred. *Reunion in Big Sur.* London, 1959. Wraps. One of 25 signed copies. $125. Trade. $60.

PERRAULT, Charles. *Cinderella* . . . London, 1808. Original wraps. $8,500. Rebound. $3,000. [See also Evans, C. S.]

PERRY, Anne. *Callander Square.* London, 1980. $2,000. New York (1980). $1,500.

PERRY, Anne. *The Cater Street Hangman.* London (1979). Author's first book. $3,500. New York (1979). $2,500.

PERRY, Matthew C. *Narrative of the Expedition of an American Squadron to the China Seas* . . . Washington, 1856. 3 vols. Quarto. 21 colored plates, 22 maps and charts, 91 plates, 3 colored reproductions of portraits, and 352 full-page woodcut illustrations. Including "Public Bath at Simoda." Preferred with plate of nude bathing scene. $4,000.

PERRY, Oliver Hazard. *Hunting Expeditions of Oliver Hazard Perry.* Cleveland, 1899. 3 plates. Cloth. One of 100 copies. $1,250.

PERRY, T. *An Easy Grammar of Writing; Or, Penmanship Analysed.* London, 1817. Third edition. First issued in 1810. $250.

PERRY, Thomas. *The Butcher's Boy.* New York, 1982. Author's first book. $1,000.

PERSE, St. John. *Anabasis.* London, 1930. (By Alexis St. Leger Leger.) French and English texts. Translated by T. S. Eliot. First edition in English. Blue-green cloth, top page edge green. In white dustwrapper. $350. One of 350 copies signed by Eliot. In cellophane dustwrapper and slipcase. $750. Second trade issue. London, 1930 (actually 1937). Green cloth. In green dustwrapper. $200. New York (1938). Black cloth. First American edition (second edition, revised). $200.

PERSHING, John. *My Experiences in the World War.* New York, 1931. 2 vols. Author's Autograph Edition. $450.

PETER Pilgrim; or a Rambler's Recollections. Philadelphia, 1838. (By Robert Montgomery Bird.) 2 vols. In original green or purple muslin, paper labels. $600.

PETERKIN, Julia. *Black April.* Indianapolis (1927). First edition not stated. First issue with "wood ducks quacked" on page 17, lines 32–33, and dustwrapper without Crawford blurb on front. $450. Second issue with "ducks piped" and Crawford blurb. $250.

PETERKIN, Julia. *Green Thursday.* New York, 1924. Author's first book. One of 2,000 copies. $250.

PETERKIN, Julia. *Roll, Jordon, Roll.* New York, 1933. One of 375 copies signed by Peterkin and the photographer, Doris Ullman. In slipcase. $17,500. Trade in dustwrapper. $1,250. London (1934). $1,000.

PETERKIN, Julia. *Sister Scarlet Mary.* Indianapolis (1928). Signed by author on tipped-in sheet, which is numbered "755." With publisher's scarce wraparound band proclaiming it a "Pulitzer Prize Novel." $1,250. Unsigned. $750.

PETERS, DeWitt C. *Kit Carson's Life* . . . Hartford, 1873. Illustrated. $300. Hartford, 1875. $150. London (about 1875). $150. (Note: this is an enlarged version of the following entry.)

PETERS, DeWitt C. *The Life and Adventures of Kit Carson, the Nestor of the Rocky-Mountains.* New York, 1858. 10 plates. $450.

PETERS, Ellis. See Pargeter, Edith.

PETERS, Ellis. *Death Mask*. London, 1959. Author's first book under this name. $600. Garden City, 1960. $350.

PETERS, Ellis. *Monk's Hood*. London, 1980. $750. New York, 1981. $125.

PETERS, Ellis. *A Morbid Taste for Bones*. London, 1977. First Brother Cadfael novel. $2,500. New York, 1978. $750.

PETERS, Ellis. *One Corpse Too Many*. London, 1979. $1,000. New York, 1980. $350.

PETERS, Fred J. *Railroad, Indian and Pioneer Prints by N. Currier and Currier and Ives*. New York, 1930. Illustrated. One of 750 copies. In dustwrapper and slipcase. $300.

PETERS, Fred J. *Sporting Prints By N. Currier* . . . New York, 1930. One of 750 copies. In dustwrapper and slipcase. $300.

PETERS, Harry T. *America on Stone: A Chronicle of American Lithography*. Garden City, 1931. 154 plates, 18 in color. One of 751 copies. In dustwrapper and slipcase. $650.

PETERS, Harry T. *California on Stone*. Garden City, 1935. 112 plates. One of 501 copies. In dustwrapper and slipcase. $750.

PETERS, Harry T. *Currier and Ives, Printmakers to the American People*. Garden City, 1929–31. 2 vols. 300 reproductions (including color). One of 501 copies. In dustwrapper. $750. Garden City, 1942. Cloth. Special edition in 1 vol. In dustwrapper. $150.

PETERS, J. G. *A Treatise on Equitation*. London, 1835. $400.

PETERSEN, Carl. *Each in Its Ordered Place: A Faulkner Collector's Notebook*. Ann Arbor (1975). First printing in green morocco-grained cloth. (1,000 copies.) In dustwrapper (VAB). $175. Second printing (identified on copyright page as "first printing"). Orange cloth. (400 printed.) Issued without dustwrapper. $125.

PETERSON, Roger Tory and Virginia Marie. *Audubon's Birds of America*. New York (1981). the Audubon Society Baby Elephant Folio. Deluxe edition. One of 2,500 signed copies. $400.

PETRY, Ann. *Country Place*. Boston, 1947. $250.

PETRY, Ann. *The Drugstore Cat*. New York (1949). $350.

PETRY, Ann. *The Street*. Boston, 1946. Author's first book. $400.

PETTER, Rodolphe. *English-Cheyenne Dictionary*. Kettle Falls, Wash., 1913–15. Folio, full black calf. One of 100 copies. $500.

PFEIFFER, Ida. *A Lady's Second Journey Around the World: From London to* . . . New York, 1856. $600.

PHAIR, Charles. *Atlantic Salmon Fishing*. Derrydale Press. New York (1937). Edited by Richard C. Hunt. Illustrated. Folio, cloth. One of 950 copies. In dustwrapper. $1,000. 2 vols., half morocco. One of 40 signed copies, with portfolio of mounted flies. $7,500.

PHELPS and Ensign's Traveller's Guide Through the United States. New York, 1838. (By Humphrey Phelps.) Folding map. $2,000. New York, 1849. $1,500.

PHILBY, H. St. J.B. *The Heart of Arabia.* London, 1922. 2 vols. 48 plates, 2 folding maps and a plan. $1,250.

PHILBY, H. St. J.B. *A Pilgrim in Arabia.* Golden Cockerel Press. London, 1943. Portrait. Buckram, leather spine. One of 350 copies. $850. One of 30 signed copies with cellotype supplement. $1,500.

PHILIP Dru, Administrator. New York, 1912. (By Col. E. M. House.) $250.

PHILLIP, Gov. Arthur. *The Voyage of Governor Phillip to Botany Bay . . .* London, 1789. With engraved frontis and title, 2 portraits, 7 maps, 31 hand-colored and 13 plain plates. Includes the "wulpine opossum" plate. $6,000.

PHILLIPS, Catherine Coffin. *Jessie Benton Fremont, A Woman Who Made History.* San Francisco, 1935. Signed by Phillips. Dustwrapper. $300.

PHILLIPS, D. L. *Letters from California.* Springfield, Ill., 1877. $450.

PHILLIPS, Jayne Anne. *Sweethearts.* Carrboro, 1976. Author's first book, preceded by two related broadsides. 10 copies handbound in boards and signed. $750. (400 copies.) Wraps. $200. St. Paul, 1978. (600 copies.) Wraps. $75.

PHILLIPS, John C. *A Bibliography of American Sporting Books.* Boston (1930). $350.

PHILLIPS, John C. *A Natural History of the Ducks.* Boston, 1922–26. 4 vols. 102 plates (72 in color). In dustwrappers. In slipcases. $2,500.

PHILLIPS, Philip A. S. *Paul de Lamerie, Citizen and Goldsmith of London.* London, 1935. Illustrated. Folio, cloth. In dustwrapper. One of 250 copies. $1,500.

PHILLIPS, Philip Lee. *A List of Geographical Atlases in the Library of Congress with Bibliographical Notes.* Washington, 1909, 1909, 1914, 1920. 4 vols. $750.

PHILLIPS, Sir Richard. *Modern London . . .* London, 1804. Folding frontispiece, folding map, 31 colored plates. $6,000. London, 1805. With engraved frontispiece, folding map and 52 plates (31 hand-colored). $4,000.

PHILLPOTTS, Eden. See *The Ghost in the Bank of England.*

PHILLPOTTS, Eden. *Adventure in the Flying Scotsman.* London, 1888. Rainbow-colored cloth. $1,500. Wraps. $1,750.

PHILLPOTTS, Eden. *A Dish of Apples.* London (1921). Illustrations, including color, by Arthur Rackham. White cloth. One of 500 signed copies. $1,000. One of 55 copies on Batchelor's Kelmscott paper. $2,500. Trade edition. Cloth. In dustwrapper. $250.

PHILLPOTTS, Eden. *The Girl and the Faun.* London, 1916. Illustrated by Frank Brangwyn. Half vellum. One of 350 signed copies. $750. Trade edition. $150.

PHILOBIBLION (The), A Monthly Bibliographical Journal. New York, 1861–63. 2 vols. Complete in XXIV numbers. Complete set of this periodical. $250.

PHIPPS, Constantine John. *A Voyage Towards the North Pole* . . . London, 1774. 11 folding tables; 14 plates, including 3 maps. $2,000.

PHOTOGRAPHIC Sketch Book of the War. Washington (1865–66). (By Alexander Gardner.) 2 vols. 100 gold-toned albumen prints, with leaf of text for each. Oblong folio, morocco. $75,000 at auction in 1999.

PIAGET, Jean. *Rational Psychology* . . . Auburn, 1849. $600.

PIATT, John J. See *Poems of Two Friends.*

PICASSO, Pablo. *Linoleum Cuts* . . . New York, (1962). 45 color plates. Illustrated beige linen stamped in black. Color illustrated slipcase. $750.

PICASSO, Pablo. *Picasso's Posters.* New York, 1971. Thick folio. The complete posters. $350.

PICHON, Baron Jerome. *The Life of Charles Henry Count Hoym* . . . New York, 1899. (Binding executed by The Club Bindery of New York.) Limited to 303 copies. $250.

PICHON, Leon. *The New Book-Illustration in France.* London, 1924. Translated by Herbert B. Grimsditch. $150.

PICKETT, Albert James. *History of Alabama, and Incidentally of Georgia and Mississippi.* Charleston, 1851. 2 vols. Map, 3 plans, 8 plates. $1,500. Second edition, same place and date. $1,000.

PICKETT, Albert James. *Invasion of the Territory of Alabama, by 1,000 Spaniards, Under Ferdinand de Soto, in 1540.* Montgomery, 1849. 41 pages, wraps. $500.

PICTORIAL View of California (A). By a Returned Californian. New York, 1853. (By J. M. Letts.) 48 plates. Later edition of *California Illustrated.* $750.

PIDGIN, Charles Felton. *The Further Adventures of Quincy Adams Sawyer.* Boston, 1909. $150.

PIEROTTI, Ernete. *Jerusalem Explored.* London, 1864. 2 vols. Text and 63 full-page plates (some tinted, some folding). Folio. $1,750.

PIGMAN, Walter Griffith. *Journal.* Mexico, Mo., 1942. Edited by Ulla Staley Fawkes. Boards. $100.

PIGS Is Pigs. Chicago, 1905. Railways Appliances Company. (By Ellis Parker Butler.) Decorated oyster white wraps. (Note: author's name appears only in decoration on first text page.) $500.

PIKE, Albert. *Prose Sketches and Poems, Written in the Western Country.* Boston, 1834. Author's first book. Brown cloth, leather label. $4,000.

PIKE, Corp. (James). *The Scout and Ranger.* Cincinnati, 1865. Portrait, 24 plates. Black cloth. First issue, with errata leaf and hair parted on left in portrait. $1,000. Second issue, without errata leaf and hair parted on right. $750.

PIKE, Zebulon M. *An Account of Expeditions to the Sources of the Mississippi* . . . Philadelphia, 1810. 2 vols. Portrait, 4 maps, 2 charts, 3 tables. $10,000.

PIKE, Zebulon M. *An Account of a Voyage up the Mississippi River.* (Washington, 1807.) Map. 68 pages. $12,500.

PIKE, Zebulon M. *Exploratory Travels Through the Western Territories of North America.* London, 1811. 2 maps (one folding). First English edition (of *An Account of Expeditions to the Sources of the Mississippi*). $3,500.

PIKE County Puzzle, Vol. 1. No. 1. (Burlesque of country newspaper.) Camp Interlaken, Pa., 1894. (By Stephen Crane.) 4 pages. $3,500.

PILCHER, Joshua. *Report on the Fur Trade and Inland Trade to Mexico.* Washington, 1832. $350.

PILGRIM, Thomas. See Morecamp, Arthur.

PILOT (The): A Tale of the Sea. New York, 1823. By the author of *The Pioneers,* James Fenimore Cooper. 2 vols. $750. London, 1824. 3 vols. First English edition. $600. Limited Editions Club, New York, 1968. In slipcase. $100.

PIM, Herbert Moore. *The Pessimist.* Dublin, 1914. Author's first book. $125.

PINCKNEY, Josephine. *Sea-Drinking Cities.* New York, 1927. Author's first book. One of 225 signed copies. $350. Trade. $250.

PINEL, Phillipe. *A Treatise on Insanity . . .* Sheffield, 1806. 2 copperplates and folding chart. $2,000.

PINKERTON, A. F. *Jim Cummins: or, The Great Adams Express Robbery.* Chicago, 1887. Illustrated. Pictorial cloth. $250.

PINKERTON, Allan. *The Expressman and the Detective.* Chicago, 1874. $350.

PINKERTON, Allan. *Tests on Passenger Conductors.* Chicago, 1867. Author's first book. 35 pages, wraps. $350.

PINKERTON, Allan. *Thirty Years a Detective.* Hartford, 1884. Illustrated. $350.

PINTER, Harold. *The Birthday Party: A Play in Three Acts.* London: Encore Publishers (1959). Author's first book. Pictorial wraps. $350.

PINTER, Harold. *The Birthday Party and Other Plays.* London (1960). $250.

PINTER, Harold. *The Birthday Party and the Room.* New York (1961). Hardback. $250. Wraps. $50.

PINTER, Harold. *The Caretaker.* London: Encore (1960). Wraps. $200. London: Methuen (1960). $200.

PINTER, Harold. *Monologue.* (London, 1973.) Full leather. One of 100 signed copies. In slipcase. $250. Trade, in boards with oversize dustwrapper. $50.

PINTER, Harold. *Old Times.* London, 1971. One of 150 signed copies. In acetate jacket. $175.

PIONEERS, The; or The Sources of the Susquehanna; A Descriptive Tale. (London, 1823.) (By James Fenimore Cooper.) 3 vols. $1,000.

PIPER, H. Beam. *Murder in the Gunroom.* New York, 1953. Author's first book. $300.

PIPER, Watty. *The Little Engine That Could As Told to* . . . New York: Platt & Munk (1930). Illustrated in color by Lois Lenski. 28 pages including color pictorial endpaper. Red cloth. Pictorial label on front. In dustwrapper. $2,000.

PIRSIG, Robert M. *Zen and the Art of Motocycle Maintenance.* New York (1974). Author's first book. $250. London (1974). $125. New York, 1984. One of 1,000 signed copies. $250.

PITMAN, Benn (reporter). *The Assassination of President Lincoln and the Trial of the Conspirators.* Cincinnati, 1865. Illustrated. $750.

PITTER, Ruth. *First Poems.* London, 1920. Stiff wraps. Author's first book. $175.

"PLAIN or Ringlets?" London, 1859–60. (By Robert Smith Surtees.) 13 colored plates. Other illustrations by John Leech. 13 parts in 12, wraps. $1,500. London, 1860. Pictorial cloth. First book edition. $450. Wraps. $750.

PLAIN Speaker (The): Opinions on Books, Men, and Things. London, 1826. (By William Hazlitt.) 2 vols. First collected edition. $350.

PLANTE, David. *The Ghost of Henry James.* London (1970). Author's first book. No errata slip. $150. Errata slip tipped in correcting errors on pages 8, 113, or 133. $125. Boston, 1970. $75.

PLATH, Sylvia. See Lucas, Victoria. See also *A Winter Ship.*

PLATH, Sylvia. *Ariel.* London (1965). $500. New York (1966). $200.

PLATH, Sylvia. *The Colossus.* London (1960). Author's first regularly published book. $1,500. New York, 1962. $400.

PLATH, Sylvia. *Lyonnesse.* Rainbow Press. London, 1971. Vellum, leather, or half leather. One of 300 copies. Issued without dustwrapper. In slipcase. $250. One of 100 copies with special manuscript reproductions on endpapers. In slipcase. $750. One of 10 copies in full vellum. $1,250.

PLATH, Sylvia. *Pursuit.* Rainbow Press. (London), 1973. Drawings and an etching by Leonard Baskin. Morocco. One of 100 copies with signed frontispiece by Baskin. In slipcase. $1,250.

PLATO. *The Phaedo of Plato.* Golden Cockerel Press. Waltham Saint Lawrence, England, 1930. Translated by William Jowett. Title and initials in red buckram. With letter laid in calling attention to error of translator's name as William instead of Benjamin. $300.

PLATO. *The Works of Plato* . . . London, 1804. 5 vols. The first complete edition in English. $3,500.

PLATT, P. L., and SLATER, N. *The Travelers' Guide Across the Plains, upon the Overland Route to California.* Chicago, 1852. Folding map. 64 pages, printed yellow wraps. $7,500 or more. San Francisco, 1963. Edited by Dale Morgan. Illustrated. Black boards, orange cloth spine. Second edition. One of 475 copies. In acetate dustwrapper. $300.

PLAW, John. *Rural Architecture* . . . London (1794). 61 aquatint plates. $1,500.

PLEASANTS, J. Hall, and SILL, Howard. *Maryland Silversmiths, 1715–1830.* Baltimore, 1930. Illustrated. Half cloth. One of 300 copies. Issued without dustwrapper. $500. New York, 1972. One of 1,000 copies. In dustwrapper. $150.

PLEASANTS, W. J. *Twice Across the Plains, 1849–1856.* San Francisco, 1906. 10 plates, 2 portraits. Pictorial green cloth. $1,500.

PLIMPTON, George. *Letters in Training.* No place, 1946. Author's first book. $750.

PLIMPTON, George. *The Rabbit's Umbrella.* New York, 1955. $200.

PLOMER, Henry R. *English Printers' Ornaments.* London, 1924. One of 500 copies. $300. One of 75 signed copies. With 4 additional plates. $750.

PLOMER, Henry R. *Wynkyn De Worde & His Contemporaries from the Death of Caxton to 1535.* London, 1925. $200.

PLOMER, William. *Address Given at the Memorial Service for Ian Fleming.* (London, 1964.) One of 350 copies. $600.

PLOMER, William. *The Case Is Altered.* Hogarth Press. London, 1932. $250.

PLOMER, William. *Notes for Poems.* Hogarth Press. London, 1927 (actually 1928). Cloth. In tissue jacket. $200.

PLOMER, William. *Sado.* London, 1931. $350.

PLOMER, William. *Turbott Wolfe.* London, 1925. Author's first book. $600.

PLOT, Robert. *Natural History of Stafford-Shire.* Oxford, 1686. Folding map, 38 plates. $3,500.

PLUMBE, John, Jr. *Sketches of Iowa and Wisconsin . . .* St. Louis, 1839. Folding map on thin paper. 103 pages in original printed wraps. $5,000.

PLUNKETT, Joseph Mary. *The Circle and the Sword.* Dublin, 1911. Author's first book. Wraps. $250.

PLUTARCH. *The Philosophie, Commonlie Called, the Morals . . .* London, 1603. $4,500.

POE, Edgar Allan. See *The Narrative of Arthur Gordon Pym; Tamerlane and Other Poems.*

POE, Edgar Allan. *Al Aaraaf, Tamerlane, and Minor Poems.* Baltimore, 1829. In original blue or reddish-tan boards, ivory paper spine. (Some copies misdated 1820 on title page; a few also stitched, without covers.) $100,000. Rebound. $20,000.

POE, Edgar Allan. *The Bells and Other Poems.* London [1912]. 28 color plates by Edmund Dulac. One of 750 copies signed by Dulac. $2,500. London, 1913. $500.

POE, Edgar Allan. *The Conchologist's First Book.* Philadelphia, 1839. Illustrated. In original printed pictorial boards and leather spine. First state, with snail plates in color. $3,000. Plates uncolored. $1,750. Philadelphia, 1840. Boards. Second edition. $750.

POE, Edgar Allan. *Eureka: A Prose Poem.* New York, 1848. Black cloth. With 12 or 16 pages of ads at end. $4,000. (New York [circa 1928].) Facsimile edition of a copy with Poe's own handwritten revisions. One of 50 copies. $750. San Francisco, 1991. One of 250 copies. $500.

POE, Edgar Allan. *The Fall of the House of Usher.* Black Sun Press. Paris, 1928. Illustrated by Alastair. Printed wraps. One of 300 copies. $1,750. Limited Edition Club, New York, 1985.

Signed by the illustrator, Alice Neel. $1,000. Signed by Raphael Soyer (Neel died before publication). $650.

POE, Edgar Allan. *Mesmerism: "In Articulo Mortis . . ."* London, 1846. 16 pages, stitched, without covers. $3,500.

POE, Edgar Allan. *Murders in the Rue Morgue.* Philadelphia (1895). Facsimile of Drexel Institute manuscript. 2 watercolors. Folio, half morocco. $300. Allen Press. Antibes (1958). Boards. One of 150 copies. $500.

POE, Edgar Allan. *Poems.* New York, 1831. In original pale-green cloth. Second edition (so identified on title page, but actually the first edition). $35,000. London, 1900. Illustrated by W. Heath Robinson. $750. Limited Editions Club, New York, 1943. In slipcase. $200.

POE, Edgar Allan. *The Prose Romances of Edgar A. Poe, etc. Uniform Serial Edition . . . No. 1. Containing the Murders in the Rue Morgue, and The Man That Was Used Up.* Philadelphia, 1843. 40 pages. Rebound copy at auction in 1990 for $60,000. See also Poe, *Murders in the Rue Morgue.*

POE, Edgar Allan. *The Raven and Other Poems.* New York, 1845. Printed wraps, $75,000. Rebound. $10,000. London, 1846. First English edition with new title page tipped in over sheets of the American first. $15,000.

POE, Edgar Allan. *The Raven and Other Poems. (&) Tales.* New York, 1845. 2 vols. in one, dark-blue cloth. First edition of each work in the 1-vol. format; first issue of *The Raven* (see preceding entry) and third issue of *Tales* (see entry following), without stereotyper's slug. $17,500. (Easthampton, 1980.) Title poem only. Illustrated by Alan James Robinson, his first book. Folio, one of 100 signed copies in box. $1,250. One of 25 deluxe copies with an extra set of signed plates. $2,500.

POE, Edgar Allan. *The Tales.* New York, 1845. First state, with T. B. Smith and H. Ludwig slugs on copyright page, 12 pages of ads at back. Printed buff wraps. $50,000 at auction in 1990. Cloth. $25,000. Rebound. $7,500. London, 1845. U.S. sheets with cancel-title page. $7,500.

POE, Edgar Allan. *Tales of the Grotesque and Arabesque.* Philadelphia, 1840. 2 vols., in original purplish cloth, paper labels. First state, with page 213 in vol. 2 wrongly numbered 231. $25,000. Second state, page 213 correctly numbered. $17,500. 2 vols. in one. Page 213 correctly numbered, 4 pages of ads bound in at end. $12,500. (Only 750 copies in total, and the sheets were issued up to 1849 with new title pages per Robertson.) Chicago, 1930. Lakeside Press. Full morocco. One of 1,000 copies. $450.

POE, Edgar Allan. *Tales of Mystery and Imagination.* London, 1919. Illustrated by Harry Clarke. Pictorial vellum. One of 170 copies signed by Clarke. $6,000. Trade. $750. New York, 1933. $750. London (1935). Illustrated by Arthur Rackham. Full pictorial vellum. One of 460 copies signed by Rackham. $4,000. One of 10 copies with original drawing. $20,000. First trade edition. Cloth. In dustwrapper. $750. Limited Editions Club, New York, 1941. In slipcase. $250.

POE, Edgar Allan. *The Works of Edgar Allan Poe.* New York, 1850–56. 4 vols. $1,500.

POEM on The Rising Glory of America. (By Hugh Henry Brackenridge and Philip Freneau, both author's first book.) Philadelphia, 1772. $3,500.

POEMS. Chiswick Press. (London, 1906.) (By Siegfried Sassoon.) Author's first book. Wraps. $5,000. London (1911). Wraps. One of 35 signed copies. $2,000.

POEMS. London, 1773. (By Anna Laetitia Alkin.) Author's first book. $300.

POEMS by Two Brothers. London (1827). (By Alfred, Charles, and Frederick Tennyson.) Alfred Tennyson's first book. Large-paper copies. In original boards. $8,500. Rebound. $3,500. Small-paper copies. Wraps. $4,000. Rebound. $1,500.

POEMS of Two Friends. Columbus, Ohio, 1860. (By William Dean Howells and John J. Piatt.) Brown cloth. Howells's first book. $750.

POET at the Breakfast-Table (The). Boston, 1872. (By Oliver Wendell Holmes.) First state, with "Talle" for "Table" in the running head on page 9. $150.

POETRY for Children, Entirely Original. London, 1809. (By Charles and Mary Lamb.) Illustrated. 2 vols. $2,000. Boston, 1812. $1,000.

POGANY, Willy. See *The Wimp and the Woodle and Other Stories.*

POHL, Frederik. *Alternating Currents.* New York, 1956. Author's first separate book. Cloth. $500. Wraps. $35.

POIKILOGRAPHIA, Or Various Specimens of Ornamental Penmanship . . . London [circa 1830s]. 23 engraved plates. $750.

POLK, James K. *The Diary of James K. Polk.* Chicago, 1910. 4 vols. One of 500 copies. $600.

POLLARD, Alfred W. *An Essay on Colophons . . .* Chicago, 1905. One of 252 copies. $500.

POLLARD, Alfred W. *Shakespeare Folios and Quartos.* London, 1909. Illustrated. Boards. $600.

POLLARD, Edward A. *The First Year of the War.* Richmond, 1862. 374 pages, printed wraps. $400.

POLLARD, Edward A. *Observations in the North.* Richmond, 1865. 142 pages, wraps. $1,250.

POLLARD, Edward A. *The Seven Days' Battles in Front of Richmond.* Richmond, 1862. 45 pages, printed wraps. $1,250.

POLLARD, Edward A. *The Southern Spy.* Richmond, 1861. 103 pages, wraps. $1,000.

POLLARD, Hugh B. C. *A History of Firearms.* London, 1926. Illustrated. Cloth. Issued without dustwrapper. $300. London, 1930. $200.

POLLARD, Hugh B.C., and BARCLAY-SMITH, Phyllis. *British and American Game-Birds.* Derrydale Press. New York, 1939. Illustrated. Half leather. One of 125 copies. $1,500. London, 1945. Half leather. Issued without dustwrapper. $600. One of 10 copies with original watercolor by Philip Rickman. $7,500.

POLLEY, J. B. *Hood's Texas Brigade.* New York, 1910. 25 plates. $1,250.

POLLEY, J. B. *A Soldier's Letters to Charming Nellie.* New York, 1908. 16 plates. $600.

POLLOCK, J. M. *The Unvarnished West: Ranching as I Found It.* London (1911). Illustrated. Pictorial cloth. $500.

POLONIUS: A Collection of Wise Saws and Modern Instances. London, 1852. (By Edward Fitz Gerald.) Green cloth. $350.

POOLE, Ernest. *Katharine Breshovsky: For Russia's Freedom.* Chicago, 1905. Author's first book. Pictorial wraps. $300.

POOR, M. C. *Denver, South Park and Pacific.* Denver, 1949. Illustrated, with map in pocket. Cloth. One of 1,000 signed copies. In dustwrapper. $500. One of 15 unnumbered copies. Bound in red fabrikoid. In dustwrapper. $1,000.

POOR Sarah. (Park Hill, Indian Territory, Oklahoma), 1843. Park Hill Mission Press. 18 pages, sewn. $3,750 at auction in 1999. (Note: originally this story of "a pious Indian woman" was a publication of the American Tract Society of New York.)

POORE, Ben Perley. *A Descriptive Catalogue of the Government Publications of the United States . . .* Washington, 1885. Cloth. $250. New York, 1962. 2 vols., cloth. $200.

POORTENAAR, Jan. *The Art of the Book and Its Illustration.* London (1935). $300.

POPE, Alexander. *The Rape of the Lock.* London, 1714. First separate edition with frontispiece and 5 plates. $10,000 in original wraps at auction in 1990. Rebound. $3,000. London, 1896. Illustrated by Aubrey Beardsley. $750. One of 25 copies on Japon vellum. $7,500.

POPERY, British and Foreign. London, 1851. (By Walter Savage Landor.) Printed wraps. $750.

PORCHER, Francis P. *Resources of the Southern Fields and Forests, Medical, Economical, and Agricultural, Being Also a Medical Botany of the Confederate States.* Charleston, 1863. Half leather. $5,000.

PORTALIS, Baron Roger (editor). *Researches Concerning Jean Grolier, His Life and His Library.* New York, 1907. One of 300 copies. 13 chromolithographed plates. $600.

PORTEAUX, A. *Practical Guide for the Manufacture of Paper and Boards.* Philadelphia, 1866. Translated from the French by Horatio Paine. $300.

PORTER, Cole. *Red Hot & Blue.* New York, 1936. One of 300 signed copies. $4,000.

PORTER, Capt. David. *Journal of a Cruise Made to the Pacific Ocean.* Philadelphia, 1815. $2,500.

PORTER, Edwin H. *The Fall River Tragedy . . .* Fall River, Mass., 1893. Plates. $1,500.

PORTER, Eleanor H. *Pollyanna.* Boston, 1913. Illustrated. Pink silk cloth. $750. London, 1913. Blue cloth, pictorial cover label. First English edition. $500.

PORTER, Gene Stratton. See *The Strike at Shane's.*

PORTER, Gene Stratton. *Friends in Feathers.* Garden City, 1917. Pictorial cloth. $300.

PORTER, Gene Stratton. *The Keeper of the Bees.* Garden City, 1925. Pictorial cloth. $250.

PORTER, Gene Stratton. *Laddie: A True-Blue Story.* New York, 1913. $200.

PORTER, Gene Stratton. *The Song of the Cardinal.* Indianapolis (1903). Illustrated by the author's camera studies. Buckram. Author's first book. $150.

PORTER, Hal. *The Hexagon*. Sydney, 1956. $500.

PORTER, Jane. *Duke Christian of Luneburg*. London, 1824. 3 vols. $750.

PORTER, Jane. *The Scottish Chiefs: A Romance*. London, 1810. 5 vols. With errata leaf at end of vol. 1. $1,250.

PORTER, Jonathan. *All Under Heaven: The Chinese World*. New York (1983). One of 250 signed copies with an original color photograph laid in, which is also signed by Porter. Slipcase. $600.

PORTER, Katherine Anne. See F., M. T.

PORTER, Katherine Anne. *A Christmas Story*. New York (1967). Illustrated by Ben Shahn. Oblong cloth. One of 500 copies signed by both author and artist. In slipcase. $250.

PORTER, Katherine Anne. *Flowering Judas*. New York (1930). Boards and cloth. One of 600 copies. With publisher slip laid on front cover under glassine dustwrapper. $350. New York (1935). Cloth. First augmented edition. $250.

PORTER, Katherine Anne. *French Song Book*. (Paris), 1933. Blue boards and cloth. One of 595 signed copies. In dustwrapper. $350. One of 15 copies on Spanish paper specially bound, signed. $2,500.

PORTER, Katherine Anne. *Hacienda*. (New York, 1934.) One of 895 copies. With errata slip and page 52 uncorrected. In slipcase. $350. With page 52 corrected and tipped in. $200.

PORTER, Katherine Anne. *The Leaning Tower and Other Stories*. New York (1944). $150.

PORTER, Katherine Anne. *Noon Wine*. Detroit, 1937. Decorated boards, paper label. One of 250 signed copies. In slipcase. $400.

PORTER, Katherine Anne. *Outline of Mexican Popular Arts and Crafts*. (Los Angeles), 1922. Pictorial wraps. $2,500.

PORTER, Katherine Anne. *Pale Horse, Pale Rider*. New York (1939). $350.

PORTER, Katherine Anne. *Ship of Fools*. Boston (1962). $200.

PORTER, Robert Ker. *Traveling Sketches in Russia and Sweden During the Years 1805, 1806, 1807 & 1808*. London, 1809. 2 vols. 41 aquatint plates of views and costumes. $2,500.

PORTER, William Sidney (or, later, Sydney). See Henry, O.

PORTFOLIO Honoring Harold Hugo for His Contribution to Scholarly Printing (A). No place, 1978. 38 separate folders loosely inserted in a cloth case. $250.

PORTLOCK, Capt. Nathaniel. *A Voyage Round the World . . .* London, 1789. Contains title page, dedication with list of plates on verso, and contents. Engraved portrait frontispiece, 6 folding engraved maps, and 13 engraved plates. $6,000.

PORTRAIT and Biographical Record of Denver and Vicinity. Chicago, 1898. Leather. $350.

POSNER, David. *And Touch Cleaned Earth*. Trenton, 1940. Author's first book. Wraps. $200.

POSNER, David. *Love as Image*. London, 1952. Wraps. One of 150 copies. $150.

POSNER, David. *A Rake's Progress*. London (1967). 17 plates. Black cloth with black plastic spine. Issued without dustwrapper. With errata leaf. $600.

POSNER, David. *S'un Casto Amor*. Oxford, 1953. Wraps. One of 30 copies. $450.

POST, Melville Davisson. *The Corrector of Destinies*. New York (1908). $250.

POST, Melville Davisson. *The Strange Schemes of Randolph Mason*. New York, 1896. Author's first book. Wraps. $1,500. Cloth. $1,250.

POST, Melville Davisson. *Uncle Abner . . .* New York, 1918. Blue cloth. $300.

POSTGATE, Raymond. *Verdict of Twelve*. London (1940). Author's first book. $300. New York, 1940. $200.

POSTON, Charles D. *Apache-Land*. San Francisco, 1878. Portrait and views. $350.

POSTON, Charles D. *Speech of the Hon. Charles D. Poston, of Arizona, on Indian Affairs*. New York, 1865. 20 pages, printed wraps. $1,750. Also issued without wraps. $1,350.

POTOK, Chaim. *The Chosen*. New York (1967). Author's first book. $250.

POTT, J. S. *A Plain Statement of Fact . . .* (Claims of Florida inhabitants against British forces.) London, 1838. 16 pages, half morocco. $750.

POTTER, Ambrose George. *A Bibliography of the Rubaiyat of Omar Khayyam . . .* London, 1929. One of 300 copies. In dustwrapper. $600.

POTTER, Beatrix. *Ginger and Pickles*. London, 1909. Illustrated by the author. Pictorial boards. $1,000. New York, 1909. $750.

POTTER, Beatrix. *The Pie and the Patty-Pan*. London, 1905. Illustrated in color by the author. Pictorial cloth. $1,000. New York, 1905. $600.

POTTER, Beatrix. *The Roly-Poly Pudding*. London, 1908. Illustrated in color by the author. With "All rights reserved" at bottom of title page. $1,000. New York (1908). First with "All Rights Reserved . . ." on title page. $600.

POTTER, Beatrix. *The Story of a Fierce Bad Rabbit*. London, 1906. Illustrated by the author. Panoramic wallet-style cloth binding. $1,750.

POTTER, Beatrix. *The Story of Miss Moppet*. London, 1906. Illustrated in color by the author. Original cloth wallet-style binding. $1,750.

POTTER, Beatrix. *The Tailor of Gloucester*. (London, December 1902). One of 500 copies. $7,500. London, 1903. $2,500.

POTTER, Beatrix. *The Tale of Benjamin Bunny*. London, 1904. Illustrated in color by Potter. $1,250.

POTTER, Beatrix. *The Tale of Jemima Puddle-Duck*. London, 1908. Illustrated in color by Potter. Deluxe edition in brown cloth. $3,500. Green boards with color pictorial paper label on front. $1,250.

POTTER, Beatrix. *The Tale of Mr. Jeremy Fisher.* London, 1906. Illustrated in color by Potter. Original boards. $1,500.

POTTER, Beatrix. *The Tale of Mrs. Tiggy-Winkle.* London, 1905. Frontispiece and 26 colored illustrations by the author. $1,000.

POTTER, Beatrix. *The Tale of Mrs. Tittlemouse.* London, 1910. Color plates. Boards. $750.

POTTER, Beatrix. *The Tale of Peter Rabbit.* London (1901). Colored frontispiece, 41 illustrations in black-and-white by the author. Boards, flat spine. December, 1901 (privately printed). One of 250 copies. $100,000. Second issue, February 1902 (also privately printed). One of 200 copies. $25,000. London, 1902. First published edition (trade edition) with Holly Lear endpapers; and "wept" for "shed" on page 51. $4,000. New York, 1995. One of 250 copies signed by Sendak. $1,250.

POTTER, Beatrix. *The Tale of the Flopsy Bunnies.* London, 1909. Illustrated in color by Potter. Original brown boards with color pictorial paper label on cover. $1,000.

POTTER, Beatrix. *The Tale of Timmy Tiptoes.* London, 1911. Illus. in color by Potter. $850.

POTTER, Beatrix. *Wag-by-Wall.* London/New York (1944). Illustrated. Cloth. One of 100 copies. In dustwrapper. $1,750.

POTTER, Jack. *Lead Steer and Other Tales.* Clayton, N.M., 1939. Illustrated. Pictorial wraps. $600.

POTTLE, Frederick A. *The Literary Career of James Boswell.* Oxford, 1929. $300.

POTTLE, Frederick A. *Shelley and Browning.* Chicago, 1923. One of 125 copies. Author's first book. $250.

POUND, Ezra. See P., E.; Bosschere, Jean de; De Gourmont, Remy; Fenollosa, Ernest. See also *The Book of the Poets' Club; The Catholic Anthology; Des Imagistes.*

POUND, Ezra. *A Lume Spento.* (Venice), 1908. Green wraps. Author's first book. About 15 or 20 copies trimmed to 13.5 x 19.5 cm. $75,000. The balance are untrimmed. $60,000. Milan (1958). Stiff gray wraps. One of 2,000 copies. In dustwrapper. $300. (New York, 1965.) First American edition. In acetate dustwrapper. $100. London (1966). $100.

POUND, Ezra. *ABC of Reading.* London, 1934. Red cloth. $600. New Haven, 1934. $450.

POUND, Ezra. *Antheil and the Treatise on Harmony.* Paris, 1924. Three Mountains Press. Red wraps. One of 40 copies on Arches paper. $1,500. Trade edition. One of 300. $1,000. Unsold copies later issued with buff label pasted on title page "Contact Editions . . ." $750. Chicago, 1927. Brown cloth. First American edition. $400.

POUND, Ezra. *Canto CX.* (Cambridge, 1965.) Frontispiece drawing of Pound. Wraps. One of 80 copies signed by the artist, Laurence Scott. $350. One of 26 signed copies. $750. Also 12 "hors serie" unsigned. $200.

POUND, Ezra. *Cantos LII–LXXI.* London (1940). $300. Norfolk (1940). First American edition. One of 500 copies with envelope, containing pamphlet, pasted at rear, *Notes on Ezra Pound's Cantos, Structure and Rhetoric.* $350. One of 500 copies without the envelope. $250.

POUND, Ezra. *Canzoni.* London, 1911. First binding in gray cloth with Pound's name on cover. $750. Second binding in brown boards without author's name. $500.

POUND, Ezra. *Cathay.* London, 1915. (Translated by Pound.) Printed wraps. $750. Limited Editions Club, New York (1992). One of 300 copies signed by Francesco Clemente in box. $3,500.

POUND, Ezra. *Diptych Rome-London.* New Directions. (Norfolk, 1958.) Folio, boards. One of 125 signed copies. In slipcase. $2,000. (London): Faber & Faber (1958). One of 50 signed copies. In slipcase. $2,250. Milan (1958). One of 25 signed copies. In slipcase. $2,500. (These books were issued simultaneously as part of a total edition of 200 produced at the Officina Bodoni in Verona, Italy.)

POUND, Ezra. *A Draft of the Cantos 17–27.* London, 1928. Initials by Gladys Hynes. Folio, red vellum boards. Issued without dustwrapper. One of 70 copies on Roma paper. $2,000. (Also 4 copies on vellum signed by the author and the artist. $12,500. 5 copies on Japan paper, signed by Pound. $7,500. 15 copies on Whatman paper. $3,500.)

POUND, Ezra. *A Draft of XXX Cantos.* Paris, 1930. Hours Press. Beige linen. One of 200 copies. $2,000. Red-orange leather. One of 10 signed copies on Texas Mountain paper. $20,000. (Note: There were also 2 copies on vellum for Pound. $25,000.) New York (1933). First American edition with "shit" 11 lines up on page 62. $1,750. With "sh-t". $350. London (1933). Black cloth. First English edition. In dustwrapper. $350.

POUND, Ezra. *Drafts and Fragments of Cantos CX–CXVII.* New Directions. (New York, 1969.) $75. New Directions & The Stone Wall Press (New York/Iowa City, 1969). One of 310 signed copies (in total for the three publishers. 200 for U.S. numbered "1 to 200"). Folio, red cloth, paper labels. With errata slip. In slipcase. $750. Faber & Faber. London (1970). One of 100 signed copies (numbered 201 to 300). $850. (Numbers 301 to 310 were for Stone Wall Press.) First U.K. trade edition. $75.

POUND, Ezra. *Exultations.* London, 1909. Dark-red boards. Presumed first issue with "Exultations/of/Ezra Pound" on front cover. $850. Second deletes "of." $750.

POUND, Ezra. *Gaudier-Brzeska: A Memoir.* London, 1916. Illustrated. Gray-green cloth with design on front. $1,000. Without design. $400. American issue: Olive-green cloth. $750. London (1939). Green cloth. In dustwrapper. $600. New Directions. New York (1961). ". . . this edition first published 1960." $250.

POUND, Ezra. *Imaginary Letters.* Black Sun Press. Paris, 1930. Stiff printed white wraps. One of 300 copies. In glassine dustwrapper and slipcase. $650. One of 50 signed copies on vellum. In slipcase. $3,500. 25 unnumbered copies not for sale. $1,000.

POUND, Ezra. *Indiscretions; or Une Revue de Deux Mondes.* Three Mountains Press. Paris, 1923. Gray boards and yellow cloth. Issued without dustwrapper. $1,500. Unbound. $750.

POUND, Ezra. *Instigations.* New York (1920). In dustwrapper. $1,500. Without dustwrapper. $300.

POUND, Ezra. *Pavannes and Divisions.* New York, 1918. Frontispiece. First state binding in blue cloth stamped in gold. Top edge blue. $350. Later bindings, blue or gray cloth, or gray boards stamped in green. $250.

POUND, Ezra. *Personae.* London, 1909. Drab-brown boards. $1,250. Light-brown boards. $750. Also with 2 pages of ads following page (60). $600. New York, 1926. $1,250. New York (1949). $250.

POUND, Ezra. *The Pisan Cantos.* (New York, 1948.) Black cloth. No statement of edition. $600. London (1949). Black cloth. First English edition with a number of omissions and expurgations. $450.

POUND, Ezra. *Poems 1918–1921, Including Three Portraits and Four Cantos.* New York (1921). Boards and vellum. In dustwrapper. $750.

POUND, Ezra. *Provenca: Poems Selected from "Personae" "Exultations" and "Canzoniere."* Boston (1910). With tan boards stamped in dark brown measuring 1.5 cm across the top. $1,000. Later (1917?) in tan boards stamped in green measuring 1.4 cm across. $200.

POUND, Ezra. *Quia Pauper Amavi.* London (1919). Egoist, Ltd. Boards and cloth, paper label. One of 110 signed copies on handmade paper. Issued without dustwrapper. $3,000. One of 10 numbered copies for presentation (roman numerals). $10,000. First trade edition issued without dustwrapper. $600.

POUND, Ezra. *A Quinzaine for This Yule.* (London, 1908.) Wrapper. First issue, with "Weston St. Llewmy" for "Weston St. Llewmys" in line 6 on page 21. $35,000. Second issue, corrected. $25,000.

POUND, Ezra. *Selected Poems.* London (1928). Introduction by T. S. Eliot. Gray boards. One of 100 signed copies. Issued without dustwrapper. $3,500. Trade edition. Green cloth. In dustwrapper. $500.

POUND, Ezra. *The Sonnets and Ballate of Guido Cavalcanti.* Boston (1912). (Translated by Pound.) Boards, vellum paper spine. $600. London, 1912. Gray cloth. First English edition, with ads at back. $750. (Most destroyed by fire.)

POUND, Ezra. *Umbra.* London, 1920. Gray boards and cloth. In dustwrapper. $1,000. Boards, parchment. One of 100 signed copies. $4,000. Also, at least 4 "out of series" copies lettered and signed. $15,000.

POWELL, Anthony. *The Acceptance World.* London, 1955. $750.

POWELL, Anthony. *Afternoon Men.* London, 1931. Author's first novel. $6,000. New York (1932). $2,000.

POWELL, Anthony. *Agents and Patients.* London, 1936. $5,000.

POWELL, Anthony. *Barnard Letters.* London, 1928. Author's first book. (Edited and introduction.) $2,000.

POWELL, Anthony. *Caledonia: A Fragment.* London (1934). About 100 copies in boards. Without dustwrapper. $4,500.

POWELL, Anthony. *From a View to a Death.* London, 1933. $5,000.

POWELL, Anthony. *A Question of Upbringing.* London (1951). $1,500. New York, 1951. $500.

POWELL, Anthony. *Venusberg.* London, 1932. $6,000. New York: Periscope, 1952. As *Venusberg/Agents and Patients.* $150. Boston: Little Brown [about 1964]. $50.

POWELL, C. Frank. *Life of Major Gen. Zachary Taylor . . .* New York, 1846. 96 pages, wraps. $400.

POWELL, Dawn. *The Golden Spur.* New York (1962). $300.

POWELL, Frank. *The Wolf-Men.* London, 1906. Pictorial green cloth. 8-page publisher's catalogue inserted at rear. $600.

POWELL, H.M.T. *The Santa Fe Trail to California, 1849–1852.* Grabhorn Press. San Francisco (1931). Edited by Douglas S. Watson. Folio. Plates, folding map, folding frontis. Half morocco. One of 300 copies. $2,500.

POWELL, J. W. *Canyons of the Colorado.* Meadville, Pa., 1895. Illustrated, including 10 folding plates. Cloth. $5,000.

POWELL, J. W. *Exploration of the Colorado River of the West . . .* Washington, 1875. 80 views on 68 sheets and 2 maps on 1 sheet (Howes) (2 charts in pocket in the rear. Copy at auction). $2,000.

POWELL, Lawrence Clark. *Heart of the Southwest . . .* Los Angeles, 1955. $250.

POWELL, Lawrence Clark. *An Introduction to Robinson Jeffers.* (Dijon, France, 1932.) Author's first book. 225 copies, 85 for presentation. $500.

POWELL, Lawrence Clark. *Robinson Jeffers, the Man and His Work.* Los Angeles, 1934. Foreword by Robinson Jeffers. Decorations by Rockwell Kent. One of 750 copies. $250.

POWELL, Lawrence Clark. *A Southwestern Century . . .* Van Nuys (1958). One of 500 copies. In dustwrapper. $200.

POWELL, W. *Wanderings in a Wild Country . . .* London, 1884. Folding frontispiece map, 4 full-page maps. $500.

POWELL, Willis J. *Tachyhippodamia, or, Art of Quieting Wild Horses in a Few Hours.* New Orleans, 1838. $2,000.

POWER of Sympathy . . . (The). Boston, 1789. (By William Hill Brown. Originally attributed to Sara Wentworth Morton.) 2 vols. $10,000.

POWER, Tyrone. *Impressions of America.* London, 1836. 2 plates. 2 vols. $500. Philadelphia, 1836. 2 vols. $300.

POWERS, J. F. *Prince of Darkness and Other Stories.* Garden City, 1947. Author's first book. $150.

POWERS, Richard. *Three Farmers on Their Way to a Dance.* New York (1985). Author's first book. $300. London (1988). $100.

POWERS, Stephen. *Afoot and Alone: A Walk from Sea to Sea by the Southern Route.* Hartford, 1872. 12 plates. Cloth. $300.

POW-KEY, Sohn. *Early Korean Typography.* No place, 1982. Revised edition. $400.

POWYS, John Cowper. *Corinth.* (Oxford, 1891). Author's first book. Wraps. Cover states "English Verse." Powys's name appears at the end of text. $1,000.

POWYS, John Cowper. *A Glastonbury Romance.* New York, 1932. One of 204 signed copies. Issued without dustwrapper. $600.

POWYS, John Cowper. *In Defense of Sensuality.* New York, 1930. $200. London, 1930. First English edition. $150.

POWYS, John Cowper. *Lucifer, a Poem.* London, 1956. Half morocco. Issued without dust-wrapper. One of 560 signed copies. $250.

POWYS, John Cowper. *Odes and Other Poems.* London, 1896. $750.

POWYS, John Cowper. *The Owl, the Duck and—Miss Rowe! Miss Rowe!* Black Archer Press. Chicago, 1930. Boards. One of 250 signed copies. In slipcase. $400.

POWYS, John Cowper. *Poems.* London, 1899. Boards. $350.

POWYS, John Cowper. *Rodmoor: A Romance.* New York, 1916. $200.

POWYS, John Cowper, and POWYS, Llewellyn. *Confessions of Two Brothers.* Rochester, 1916. In dustwrapper. $450. Without dustwrapper. $100.

POWYS, Llewellyn. *The Book of Days.* Golden Cockerel Press. London, 1937. 12 etchings. Half green morocco. One of 55 signed copies, with an extra set of plates. $750. Ordinary copies (245 of 300): $500.

POWYS, Llewellyn. *Glory of Life.* Golden Cockerel Press. (London, 1934.) Woodcuts by Robert Gibbings. Vellum and cloth. One of 275 copies. $1,000. One of 2 copies on vellum. $7,500.

POWYS, Llewellyn. *The Twelve Months.* Oxford, 1936. Illustrated by Robert Gibbings. Morocco. Issued without dustwrapper. One of 100 signed copies. $600.

POWYS, T. F. *An Interpretation of Genesis.* London, 1907. $600. London, 1929. One of 490 signed copies. In slipcase. $250. New York, 1929. White boards. First American edition. One of 260 signed copies. In glassine dustwrapper and slipcase. $250.

POWYS, T. F. *The Key of the Field.* London, 1930. Woodcut frontispiece. Buckram. One of 550 signed copies. In dustwrapper. $250.

POWYS, T. F. *Mr. Weston's Good Wine.* London, 1927. Illustrated. One of 650 signed copies. $250.

POWYS, T. F. *Soliloquies of a Hermit.* London, 1918. First English edition (of *The Soliloquy of a Hermit*). Light-blue boards. In dustwrapper. $300. Without dustwrapper. $75. Dark-blue boards, a little less.

POWYS, T. F. *The Soliloquy of a Hermit.* New York, 1916. Author's first book. In dustwrapper. $400. Without dustwrapper. $150.

POWYS, T. F. *Two Stories.* Hastings, England, 1967. Illustrated with wood engravings. Half leather. One of 25 copies signed by the illustrator Reynolds Stone. In slipcase. $1,250. One of 525 copies. $400.

POWYS, T. F. *Uncle Dottery.* Bristol, England, 1930. Illustrated by Eric Gill. Half vellum and green linen. One of 300 signed copies. In dustwrapper. $250. One of 50 signed copies, with an extra set of engravings. $750. (Note: of the 50, 26 were lettered "A" to "Z" and marked "for presentation" by the publisher.)

POWYS, T. F. *When Thou Wast Naked.* Golden Cockerel Press. London, 1931. One of 500 signed copies. $250.

PRACTICAL Guide for Emigrants to North America (A). London, 1850. (By George Nettle.) Folding map in color. 57 pages, printed wraps. $600.

PRAIRIE (The): A Tale, By the Author of *The Spy.* London, 1827. (By James Fenimore Cooper.) 3 vols. $600. Philadelphia, 1827. 2 vols. First American edition, with copyright notices corrected by slip pasted in. $750. Limited Editions Club, New York, 1940. In slipcase. $200.

PRAIRIEDOM: Rambles and Scrambles in Texas. New York, 1845. By A. Suthron, (Frederick Benjamin Page.) Map. $2,500. New York, 1846. Second edition. $1,000.

PRATCHETT, Terry. *The Carpet People.* London, 1971. $850.

PRATCHETT, Terry. *The Dark Side of the Sun.* London, 1976. $750.

PRATT, E. J. See *Rachel . . .*

PRATT, Orson. *A Series of Pamphlets . . . to Which Is Appended a Discussion Held in Bolton . . . Also a Discussion Held in France . . .* Liverpool, 1851. Folding plate. Primary variant of this omnibus issue with "R. James" listed as the publisher on the general title. $1,000. Variant (later) printing of the general title leaf, with Richards listed as the publisher. $750.

PRATT, Orson. *A Series of Pamphlets on the Doctrines of the Gospel . . .* Salt Lake City, 1884. First American edition. $125.

PRATT, Parley Parker. *History of the Late Persecution Inflicted by the State of Missouri Upon the Mormons . . .* Detroit, 1839. Three known copies. Only one has all the original pages. The other two have a few facsimile pages. An imperfect copy. $10,000.

PRATT, Parley Parker. *Key to the Science of Theology . . .* Liverpool/London, 1855. $2,500.

PRATT, Parley Parker. *A Voice of Warning and Instruction to All People . . .* New York, 1837. In original cloth. $5,000.

PRECAUTION: A Novel. New York, 1820. (By James Fenimore Cooper, his first book.) 2 vols. First issue, with errata leaf in. In original boards. $5,000. Rebound. $1,500. London, 1821. 3 vols. $1,500.

PRESCOTT, George Bartlett. *The Speaking Telephone . . .* New York, 1878. Illustrated. $750.

PRESCOTT, William H. *The History of the Conquest of Mexico.* London, 1843. 3 vols. First two volumes each have 2-page maps. Vol. 3 issued without half title. $850. New York, 1843. 3 vols., with "tract" on page 5, sixth line up. (Second printing had "Tracy.") $750.

PRESCOTT, William H. *The History of the Conquest of Peru.* London, 1847. Illustrated. 2 vols., cloth. $600. New York, 1847. 2 vols. First issue, with no period after "integrity," line 20, page 467, in vol. II (VAB), not mentioned by BAL. $500. Mexico City, 1957. Limited Editions Club. Leather. In slipcase. $150.

PRICE, Reynolds. *Late Warning.* New York, 1968. Wraps. One of 26 signed and lettered copies. $350. One of 150 signed copies. Wraps. $150.

PRICE, Reynolds. *A Long and Happy Life.* New York, 1962. Author's first book preceded by an offprint. First-state dustwrapper: rear panel prints names in pale green. $175. Second-state dustwrapper: names in dark green. $125 London, 1962. $100.

PRICE, Reynolds. *The Names and Faces of Heroes.* New York, 1963. $125. London, 1963. $100.

PRICE, Richard. *Observations on the Nature of Civil Liberty . . .* London, 1776. $4,500. Philadelphia, 1776. $3,500.

PRICHARD, James C. *A Treatise on Diseases of the Nervous System.* Part I (all published.) London, 1822. $1,500.

PRICHARD, James C. *A Treatise on Insanity . . .* London, 1835. $1,250. Philadelphia, 1837. $750.

PRIDE and Prejudice. London, 1813. By the Author of *Sense and Sensibility* (Jane Austen). 3 vols. With November ads (VAB). $35,000. Rebound. $20,000. "Second Edition" so stated. Rebound. $6,000. London, 1817. "Third Edition." Rebound. $2,000. London, 1894. One of 275 copies illustrated by Hugh Thomson. $1,500. Limited Editions Club, New York, 1940. In slipcase. $250.

PRIDEAUX, Sara T. *Bookbinders and Their Craft.* New York, 1903. One of 500 copies. $350.

PRIDEAUX, S. T. *An Historical Sketch of Bookbinding.* London, 1893. $300.

PRIEST, Josiah. *Stories of the Revolution . . .* Albany, 1836. Folding plate. 32 pages, in original wraps. $1,000.

PRIEST, Josiah. *A True Narrative of the Capture of David Ogden.* (Cover title.) Lansingburgh, 1840. Woodcut. Self-wraps. $500.

PRIESTLEY, J. B. *Angel Pavement.* London, 1930. One of 1,025 signed copies. In slipcase. $250.

PRIESTLEY, J. B. *Brief Diversions.* Cambridge, 1922. $350.

PRIESTLEY, J. B. *The Chapman of Rhymes.* London, 1918. Wraps. Author's first book. $750.

PRIESTLEY, J. B. *The Town Major of Miraucourt.* London, 1930. Vellum. Issued without dustwrapper. One of 525 signed copies. $400.

PRIESTLEY, Raymond E. *Antarctic Adventure . . .* London (1914). 3 folding maps. $1,000.

PRIME, William Cowper. See *The Owl Creek Letters . . .*

PRIMULA . . . (By Richard Garnett, his first book.) London, 1858. $350.

PRINCE, William Robert, and PRINCE, William. *A Treatise on the Vine.* New York, 1830. $1,000.

PRINTED Pages from English Literature. New York (1925). Clamshell box with title page and 20 folders, each containing a leaf from a book important in the history of English literature. One of 200 copies. $1,500.

PRINTED Pages from European Literature. New York, 1925. Drop-back box containing explanatory leaf and 20 folders, each containing a leaf from a book famous in European literature. One of 200 copies. $1,000.

PRITCHETT, R. T. *Smokiana, Ye Pipes of All Nations.* London, 1890. $1,000.

PRITCHETT, V. S. *Marching Spain.* London (1928). Author's first book. Cloth. $400. Wraps. (Left Book Club.) $100.

PRITTS, Joseph. *Mirror of Olden Time Border Life.* Abingdon, Va., 1849. 13 plates (17 in a few copies). $350.

PROCEEDINGS *of Congress, in 1796, on the Admission of Tennessee as a State, into the Union.* Detroit, 1835. 15 pages. $750.

PROCEEDINGS *of a Convention to Consider the Opening of the Indian Territory, Held at Kansas City, Mo., Feb, 8, 1888.* Kansas City, 1888. 80 pages, wraps. $600.

PROCEEDINGS *of the First Annual Session of the Territorial Grange of Montana.* Diamond City, 1875. $500.

PROCEEDINGS *of a General Meeting Held at Chester Courthouse, July 5th, 1831.* Columbia, S.C., 1832. 16 pages. $400.

PROCEEDINGS *of the Harbor and River Convention. Held in Chicago, July 5th, 1847.* Chicago, 1847. 79 pages, wraps. (With Abraham Lincoln listed as delegate.) $750.

PROCEEDINGS *of a Meeting, and Report of a Committee of Citizens in Relation to Steamboat Disasters in the Western Lakes.* Cleveland, 1850. 22 pages, sewn. $450.

PROCEEDINGS *of the National Ship Canal Convention.* Chicago, 1863. Wraps. $250.

PROCEEDINGS *of the Republican National Convention, Held at Chicago, May 16, 17 and 18, 1860.* Albany, 1860. 153 pages, wraps. $1,000. Chicago, 1860. 44 pages, sewn. $750.

PROCEEDINGS *of the St. Louis Chamber of Commerce, in Relation to the Improvement of the Navigation of the Mississippi River.* St. Louis, 1842. 44 pages, sewn. $600.

PROCEEDINGS *of Sundry Citizens of Baltimore, Convened for the Purpose of Devising the Most Efficient Means of Improving the Intercourse Between That City and the Western States.* Baltimore, 1827. 38 pages, sewn. $1,000.

PROCEEDINGS *of the Virginia Assembly, on the Answers of Sundry States to Their Resolutions . . . December, 1798.* Philadelphia, 1800. $1,500.

PROCTER, Adelaide Anne. *The Victoria Regia.* London, 1861. Blue cloth. $600.

PROCTOR, Robert. *The Printing of Greek in the Fifteenth Century.* Oxford, 1900. $400.

PROGRESSIVE *Men of Southern Idaho.* Chicago, 1904. Frontispiece by Charles M. Russell, other illustrations. Leather. $450.

Progressive Men of the State of Montana. Chicago (1902). Full blindstamped leather, gilt lettering. $600.

PROKOSCH, Frederic. *Age of Thunder.* New York (1945). One of 30 signed copies. Sheet of original manuscript bound in. Issued without dustwrapper. In slipcase. $300. Trade edition. $75.

PROKOSCH, Frederic. *Death at Sea: Poems.* New York, 1940. Cloth. One of 55 signed copies. Sheet of original manuscript bound in. Issued without dustwrapper. In slipcase. $250.

PROKOSCH, Frederic. *Three Mysteries.* New Haven, 1932. Wraps. $250.

PROMETHEUS Bound. London, 1833. Translated from the Greek of Aeschylus. And *Miscellaneous Poems by the Translator.* (By Elizabeth Barrett Browning.) In original dark-blue cloth, paper label on spine. $8,500. New York, 1851. $1,500.

PROPERT, W. A. *The Russian Ballet in Western Europe, 1909–1920 . . .* London or New York, 1921. Illustrated, including color plates. Issued without dustwrapper. One of 500 copies. $850.

PROSCH, T. W. *McCarver and Tacoma.* Seattle (1906). 2 plates. $150.

PROSE and Poetry of the Live Stock Industry of the United States. Vol. 1. (All published.) Denver and Kansas City (1905). Leather. (Edited by James W. Freeman.) One of 550 copies. $15,000. New York, 1959. Half leather. In slipcase. $600.

PROSPECTUS of the Leadville & Ten Mile Narrow Gauge Railway Company of Leadville, Col. (Cover title.) Leadville, 1880. 20 pages, printed wraps. $500.

PROSPERO and Caliban. *The Weird of the Wanderer.* London, 1912. (By Baron Corvo [Frederick William Rolfe] and Charles Harry Pirie-Gordon.) $1,000.

PROTEUS. *Sonnets and Songs.* London, 1875. (By Wilfrid Scawen Blunt.) Author's first book. $200.

PROUD, Robert. *The History of Pennsylvania, in North America . . .* Philadelphia, 1797–98. 2 vols. Folding map. Frontispiece portrait. $750.

PROULX, E. Annie. *The Complete Dairy Foods Cookbook.* Emmaus, Penna. (1982). Written with Lew Nichols. Pictorial boards. Perhaps issued both with dustwrapper. $200. Without. $150.

PROULX, E. Annie. *Heart Song . . .* New York, 1988. $500. London, 1989. Wraps. $75.

PROULX, E. Annie. *Postcards.* New York (1992). $500.

PROUST, Marcel. *47 Unpublished Letters from Marcel Proust to Walter Berry.* Paris, 1930. Black Sun Press. White wraps. One of 200 copies on Arches paper. In slipcase. $450. Also an issue of 15 copies, including an original autograph letter. $2,500.

PROUST, Marcel. *Swann's Way.* Limited Editions Club, New York, 1954. In slipcase. $250.

PROVOST (The). Edinburgh, 1822. (By John Galt.) $200.

PROWELL, Sandra West. *By Evil Means.* New York (1993). $400.

PSALMAU Dafydd. Gregynog Press. (Newtown, Wales, 1929.) Decorated paper covers, morocco spine. One of 200 copies. $500. (Note: *The Psalms of David* in Welsh.) Also, one of 25 copies bound in morocco. $7,500.

PUBLIC Libraries in the United States . . . Washington, 1876. $200.

PUGET SOUND Business Directory and Guide to Washington Territory, 1872. Olympia (1872). 3 colored plates of ads. Boards and leather. $1,000.

PUGET SOUND Directory, 1887. No place, 1887. (By R. L. Polk.) Illustrated. Boards. $600.

PUGIN, A. *Gothic Furniture*. London (1828). Hand-colored aquatint title and 26 hand-colored aquatint plates. $2,250.

PUIG, Manuel. *Betrayed by Rita Hayworth*. New York, 1971. First English translation of Author's first book. $175.

PULLEIN, Samuel, Rev. *The Culture of Silk*. London, 1758. $1,250.

PURDY, Al. *The Enchanted Echo*. Vancouver, 1944. Author's first book. $600.

PURDY, James. *Don't Call Me by My Right Name and Other Stories*. New York, 1956. Author's first book. Blue-gray or white (variant) printed wraps. $250.

PURDY, James. *An Oyster Is a Wealthy Beast*. (San Francisco, 1967.) Oblong boards. One of 50 signed copies, with an original drawing. $300. Also, 200 signed copies in wraps. $150.

PURDY, James. *63: Dream Palace*. New York, 1956. Printed wraps. $175.

PUSHKIN, Alexander. *The Tale of the Golden Cockerel*. Waltham, 1936. One of 100 copies. $400. Limited Editions Club, New York (1949). As *The Golden Cockerel*. Illustrated and signed by Edmund Dulac. Cloth. In slipcase. $300.

PUSS in Boots. New York (1880s). Illustrated in color. 10 pages, pictorial boards. McLaughlin book with overlays on center spread. $750.

PUTNAM, Samuel. *Evaporation . . .* Winchester, 1923. (Author's first book, with Mark Turbyfill.) $150.

PUZO, Mario. *The Dark Arena*. New York (1955). Author's first book. $150.

PUZO, Mario. *The Godfather*. New York (1969). $1,500.

PYLE, Howard. *Howard Pyle's Book of the American Spirit*. New York, 1923. Edited by Merle Johnson and Francis J. O'Dowd. With "First Edition B-X" on copyright page. In dustwrapper. $400. One of 50 copies signed by the editors. In dustwrapper. $2,000. Also, one of 6 signed copies, with an original Pyle drawing for the book. $4,500.

PYLE, Howard. *Howard Pyle's Book of Pirates*. New York, 1921. Compiled by Merle Johnson. Illustrated including color plates, by Pyle. Boards and cloth. With "D-V" on copyright page. In dustwrapper. $500. One of 50 copies on Japan vellum, signed by Johnson. In dustwrapper and slipcase. $2,500.

PYLE, Howard. *The Merry Adventures of Robin Hood*. New York, 1883. Illustrated by Pyle. Full leather. $2,000. Cloth. $1,000. London, 1883. $1,500.

PYLE, Howard. *Otto of the Silver Hand*. New York, 1888. Illustrated by the author. Half calf. $600.

PYLE, Howard. *Pepper and Salt*. New York, 1886. Illustrated by the author. Pictorial buckram. $400.

PYLE, Howard. *The Ruby of Kishmoor*. New York, 1908. Illustrated by the author. $250.

PYLE, Howard. *The Story of the Champions of the Round Table.* New York. 1905. $500.

PYLE, Howard. *The Story of the Grail and the Passing of Arthur.* New York, 1910. Illustrated by the author. $350.

PYLE, Howard. *The Story of King Arthur and His Knights.* New York, 1903. Illustrated by author. Cloth. $500.

PYLE, Howard. *The Wonder Clock.* New York, 1888. Illustrated by author. Half leather. $450.

PYLE, Howard. *Yankee Doodle.* New York, 1881. Pictorial boards. First book illustrated by Pyle. $750.

PYM, Barbara. *Some Tame Gazelle.* London, 1950. Author's first book. $350.

PYNCHON, Thomas. *The Crying of Lot 49.* Philadelphia (1966). $750. London (1967). $350.

PYNCHON, Thomas. *Gravity's Rainbow.* New York (1973). $2,500. Wraps. Simultaneous paperback issue. $150. London (1973). $750.

PYNCHON, Thomas. *V.* Philadelphia (1963). Author's first book. In first issue/printing dustwrapper without reviews on back. $2,500. Second issue/printing dustwrapper with reviews. $1,000. London, 1963. $750.

PYNE, W. H. *The Costume of Great Britain.* London, 1804 or 1808. Engraved title and 60 hand-colored plates some of which are watermarked later, up to 1823 in some cases. $2,500.

PYNE, W. H. *The History of the Royal Residences of Windsor Castle, St. James's Palace, Carlton House, Kensington Palace, Hampton Court, Buckingham House, and Frogmore.* London, 1819. 3 vols. 100 hand-colored plates. $12,500. Large-paper edition. $15,000. Plates not colored. $4,000.

Q

QUARTETTE. By Four Anglo-Indian Writers. Lahore, India, 1885. (By Rudyard Kipling and his sister, mother, and father.) Wraps. $2,500.

QUARTO-Millenary, The First 250 Publications and First 25 years . . . Limited Editions Club . . . New York, 1959. One of 2,250 copies. In slipcase. $300.

QUAYLE, Eric. *The Collector's Book of Detective Fiction.* London, 1972. $150.

QUEEN, Ellery. *The Chinese Orange Mystery.* New York, 1934. (By Frederic Dannay and Manfred B. Lee.) $1,250.

QUEEN, Ellery. *The Dutch Shoe Mystery.* New York, 1931. (By Frederic Dannay and Manfred B. Lee.) $3,000.

QUEEN, Ellery. *The Egyptian Cross Mystery.* New York, 1932. (By Frederic Dannay and Manfred B. Lee.) $2,500.

QUEEN, Ellery. *The Four of Hearts.* New York, 1938. $500.

QUEEN, Ellery. *The French Powder Mystery.* New York, 1930. (By Frederic Dannay and Manfred B. Lee.) $3,500.

QUEEN, Ellery. *Roman Hat Mystery.* New York, 1929. (By Frederic Dannay and Manfred B. Lee, author's first book.) $6,000. New York (1974). One of 250 signed copies. $200.

QUEEN, Ellery. *The Spanish Cape Mystery.* New York, 1935. (By Frederic Dannay and Manfred B. Lee.) $2,000.

QUEEN, Ellery (editor). *The Misadventures of Sherlock Holmes.* Boston, 1944. Frontispiece by F D. Steele. (Edited by Frederic Dannay and Manfred B. Lee.) $500. One of 125 copies. $1,750.

QUEENY, Edgar M. *Cheechako.* New York, 1941. Illustrated. One of 1,200 copies. $150.

QUEENY, Edgar M. *Prairie Wings: Pen and Camera Flight Studies.* New York, 1946. Illustrated. $400. Morocco. One of 225 signed copies. $1,750. Philadelphia, 1947. Cloth. Second edition. $250.

QUENNELL, Peter. *Masques and Poems.* Waltham Saint Lawrence (1922). Author's first book. One of 550 copies (375 copies for England, 175 for USA). $450.

QUILLER-COUCH, Sir Arthur. See also Rackham, Arthur.

QUILLER-COUCH, Sir Arthur. *In Powder and Crinoline.* London (1913). Illustrated by Kay Nielsen (her first book), including 26 color plates. Boards, buckram spine. $1,500. Vellum. One of 500 signed copies. $6,000.

QUILLER-COUCH, Sir Arthur. *The Sleeping Beauty and Other Fairy Tales.* London [1910]. 30 colored plates by Edmund Dulac. $750. Morocco. One of 1,000 copies. $1,750.

QUILLER-COUCH, Sir Arthur. *The Twelve Dancing Princesses and Other Fairy Tales.* New York (about 1920). Illustrated by Kay Nielsen. Pictorial cloth. In dustwrapper. $750.

QUILLINAN, Dorothy Wordsworth. See *Journal of a Few Month's Residence in Portugal . . .*

QUIN, Edward Richard Windham. *Notes on Irish Architecture.* London, 1875. 2 vols. 125 mounted plates (including 5 double-page); and 13 plans. $6,000.

QUINBY, Jane. *Beatrix Potter: A Bibliographical Check List.* New York, 1954. Cloth with stiff paper wraps bound in. Limited to 250 copies. $350.

QUINN, Seabury. *Roads.* (New York, 1938.) Wraps. Reprinted from "Weird Tales." $2,500. Sauk City, Wis., 1948. $300.

QUINTANILLA, Luis. *All the Brave.* New York (1939). Preface by Ernest Hemingway. One of 440 copies signed by Quintanilla. Vellum and blue cloth. $500. Trade. In wraps. $200.

R

R., C.G. *Verses.* London, 1847. (By Christina G. Rossetti.) Unlettered blue cloth wraps or lettered cloth boards. $7,500. Also see under author's name for other printings.

R., E. (W.W.E. Ross.) *Laconics.* Ottawa, 1930. Author's first book. $2,500.

R., J. *Poems.* (London), 1850. (By John Ruskin.) $8,500 at auction in 1990.

RACHEL: A Sea-Story of Newfoundland. (By E. J. Pratt). New York, 1917. Author's first book. Wraps. $3,000.

RACKHAM, Arthur. See Aesop; Barrie, James M.; Browning, Robert; Dickens, Charles; Evans, C. S.; Grahame, Kenneth; Grimm, Jacob L. K. and W. K.; Irving, Washington; Poe, Edgar Allan; Quiller-Couch, Sir Arthur; Rossetti, Christina; Shakespeare, William; Wagner, Richard; and Walton, Izaac. See also *Some British Ballads;* and *English Fairy Tales.*

RACKHAM, Arthur. *The Arthur Rackham Fairy Book.* London (1933). 10 (of 460) special copies with an original signed watercolor drawing. Full vellum. $15,000. One of 460 signed copies. In slipcase. $3,500.

RACKHAM, Arthur. *Arthur Rackham's Book of Pictures.* London, 1913. Edited by Sir Arthur Quiller-Couch. Illustrated, including color. $1,000. One of 1,030 copies signed by Rackham. $2,000. One of 30 copies, inscribed and with an original drawing. $7,500. New York (1914). $500. London (1927). In dustwrapper. $500.

RACKHAM, Arthur. *Mother Goose . . .* London (1913). One of 1,130 copies signed by the illustrator. 13 mounted color plates. White pictorial cloth. $2,000.

RACKHAM, Arthur. *Romance of King Arthur and His Knights of the Round Table.* London, 1917. (Abridged from Malory's *Morte d'Arthur.*) Vellum. One of 500 signed copies. 16 full-page mounted illustrations. $2,500. Trade. $300.

RACKHAM, Bernard. *The Ancient Glass of Canterbury Cathedral.* London, 1949. 21 plates in color and 80 in monochrome. Buckram. Issued without dustwrapper. $300.

RACKHAM, Bernard, and READ, Herbert. *English Pottery . . .* London, 1924. $300. Pigskin. One of 75 signed copies. $1,000. New York, 1924. $300.

RADCLIFFE, Ann. See *The Romance of the Forest.*

RADCLIFFE, Ann. *The Italian.* London, 1797. 3 vols. $2,500.

RADCLIFFE, Ann. *The Mysteries of Udolpho.* London, 1794. 4 vols. $2,500.

RADCLIFFE, James. *The British Youth's Instructor.* With *New British Penman.* With *Beauties of Writing.* London, no date (circa 1794). 3 vols.: 12 plates, 12 plates, 23 plates, respectively. $750.

RADER, Jesse L. *South of Forty . . .* Norman, Okla., 1947. $200.

RADIGUET, Raymond. *The Count's Ball.* New York (1929). First edition in English. $300.

RADIGUET, Raymond. *The Devil in the Flesh.* New York, 1932. First American edition. $300.

RAE, John. *Narrative of an Expedition to the Shores of the Arctic Sea in 1846 and 1847.* London, 1850. Green cloth. $10,000.

RAFINESQUE, C. S. *Medical Flora; Or, Manual of the Medical Botany . . .* Philadelphia, 1828–30. 2 vols. 100 plates printed in colored ink. $6,000.

RAFINESQUE-SCHMALTZ, C. S. *The American Nations* . . . Philadelphia, 1836. $3,000.

RAINE, Kathleen. *Six Dreams and Other Poems*. London, 1968. One of 100 signed copies. $250.

RAINE, Kathleen. *Stone and Flower.* London (1943). Illustrated. Author's first book. $300.

RAINE, William MacLeod. *Brand Blotters*. New York (1912). $125.

RAINE, William MacLeod. *Cattle Brands: A Sketch of Bygone Days in the Cow-Country*. Boston (1920). 8 pages, wraps. $350.

RAINE, William MacLeod. *A Daughter of Raasay.* New York (1902). Author's first book. $150.

RAINE, William MacLeod. *Texas Ranger.* New York (1911). $250.

RAINE, William MacLeod. *Wyoming.* New York (1908). $200.

RAINES, C. W. *A Bibliography of Texas.* Austin, Tex., 1896. $200. Facsimile reprint; Houston, 1955. One of 500 copies. In slipcase. $75.

RAITT, W. *The Digestion of Grasses and Bamboo for Paper-Making.* London, 1931. 20 plates and a tipped-in specimen of paper produced from bamboo. $250.

RAKOSI, Carl. *Two Poems.* New York (1932). Pictorial wraps. $500.

RALFE, J. *The Naval Chronology of Great Britain.* London, 1820. 3 vols. 60 colored plates. $6,000.

RALPH, Julian. *On Canada's Frontier.* New York, 1892. Illustrated. By Frederic Remington. $300.

RAMAL, Walter. *Songs of Childhood.* London, 1902. Frontispiece. Decorated blue cloth and vellum. (By Walter De La Mare, his first book.) $850. London, 1923. One of 310 copies. In dustwrapper. $350.

RAMPLING, Anne. *Exit to Eden.* New York (1985). (By Anne Rice.) $125.

RAMSAY, David. *The History of South Carolina.* Charleston, 1809. 2 vols. 2 folding maps. $3,000.

RAMSAY, David. *Military Memoirs of Great Britain* . . . Edinburgh, 1779. 12 portraits. $1,000.

RAMSAYE, Terry. *A Million and One Nights.* New York, 1926. 2 vols. One of 327 copies signed by Ramsay and Thomas Edison. Leather spine. In slipcase. $4,500. Bound in blue cloth. $3,500.

RAMSEY, J.G.M. *The Annals of Tennessee.* Charleston, 1853. Folding map and plan. Leather, or cloth. $600. Philadelphia, 1853. Second edition. $400.

RAND, Ayn. *Atlas Shrugged.* New York (1957). "10/57" bottom of front dustwrapper flap and publisher's name and address bottom of back flap. $3,000. New York (1967). One of 2,000 signed copies. Acetate dustwrapper. In slipcase. $3,500.

RAND, Ayn. *The Fountainhead.* Indianapolis (1943). First edition stated. Red cloth, dustwrapper priced at $3.00 with Bobbs Merrill titles on back. $6,000. Green cloth. First edition stated.

Dustwrapper priced at $3.00 with photograph of author on back with three reviews. $3,500. London, 1947. $2,000.

RAND, Ayn. *The Night of January 16th.* New York (1936). Issued in blue wraps with several different addresses. Priority of addresses unknown, but First Edition stated. $1,000. New York/Cleveland (1968). "First Printing 1968." $150.

RAND, Ayn. *We the Living.* New York, 1936. Author's first book. "Published April, 1936." $5,000. London (1936). $3,000. New York, 1959. (Revised.) $350.

RANKIN, Ian. *The Flood.* Edinburgh, 1986. (200 copies.) $1,500.

RANKIN, Ian. *Hide & Seek.* New York (1990). $100. London, 1991. $750.

RANKIN, Ian. *Knots and Crosses.* London, 1987. $2,500. Garden City, 1987. $1,500.

RANKIN, Melinda. *Texas in 1850.* Boston, 1850. $500.

RANSOM, John Crowe. See *Armageddon* . . .

RANSOM, John Crowe. *Chills and Fever.* New York, 1924. $750.

RANSOM, John Crowe. *Grace After Meat.* London, 1924. Boards, paper label. Issued without dustwrapper. $600.

RANSOM, John Crowe. *Poems About God.* New York, 1919. Author's first book. Brown boards, paper label. $600.

RANSOM, John Crowe. *Two Gentlemen in Bonds.* New York, 1927. $750.

RANSOM, Will. *Private Presses and Their Books.* New York, 1929 One of 1,200 copies. $250.

RANSOM, Will. *Selective Check Lists of Press Books* . . . New York, 1945–50. 12 parts bound in 1. Original paper wrappers bound in. $250.

RANSOME, Arthur. *Oscar Wilde: A Critical Study.* London, 1912. $400.

RANSOME, Arthur. *The Souls of the Street* . . . London, 1904. Author's first book. $600.

RAPHAELSON, Samson. *The Jazz Singer.* New York, 1925. Author's first book. $1,250.

RAREY, J. S. *The Modern Art of Taming Wild Horses.* Columbus, Ohio, 1856. Wraps. $750. Austin, 1856. 62 pages, wraps. Third edition, revised and corrected. $450.

RATHBONE, Frederick. *Old Wedgwood.* London, 1898. Illustrated, including color plates. 8 parts in 1 vol. Folio. Half morocco. One of 200 copies. $2,500.

RATHBORNE, Aaron. *The Surveyor in Foure Bookes* . . . London, 1616. Engraved title and two portraits. $5,000.

RATTIGAN, Terrence (Mervyn). *French Without Tears.* London, 1937, Author's first book. Cloth. $200. Wraps. $75. New York, 1938. $150.

RAUCHER, Herman. *Summer of '42.* New York (1971). $125.

RAUSCHENBERG, Robert. *Photos In + Out City Limits Boston.* (New York, 1981). Bound in full white leather with silver stamping. One of 68 signed copies. In unprinted tissue dust-jacket. $600.

RAVEN, Simon. *The Feathers of Death.* London, 1959. Author's first book. $200.

RAVENSCROFT, Edward James. *The Pinetum Britannicum.* Edinburgh/London, [1863–] 1884. 3 vols. 48 hand-colored plates, 4 mounted albumen prints, 1 engraved plate of maps. $10,000.

RAVENSNEST: or, The Redskins. London, 1846. (By James Fenimore Cooper.) 3 vols., in original boards, green or blue cloth spine. First English edition of *The Redskins.* $1,000.

RAWLINGS, Marjorie Kinna. *Cross Creek.* New York, 1942. Scribner's "A" on copyright page. $300. London (1942). $200.

RAWLINGS, Marjorie Kinnan. *Cross Creek Cookery.* New York, 1942. First printing in pictorial cloth and endpapers. Dustwrapper priced $2.50. $200. Later printings in pictorial or tan cloth with white endpapers, the Scribner's "A" was on the first 5 printings. $75.

RAWLINGS, Marjorie Kinnan. *Golden Apples.* New York, 1935. $600. London [1939]. $300.

RAWLINGS, Marjorie Kinnan. *The Marjorie Rawlings Cookbook.* London (1960). First British edition of *Cross Creek Cookery.* $125.

RAWLINGS, Marjorie Kinnan. *The Secret River.* New York, 1955. With Scribners "A" on copyright page. $400.

RAWLINGS, Marjorie Kinnan. *South Moon Under.* New York, 1933. Author's first book. With Scribners "A" on copyright page. $1,250. London (1933). $750.

RAWLINGS, Marjorie Kinnan. *When the Whippoorwill.* New York, 1940. With Scribners "A" and seal on copyright page. $450. London (1940). $200.

RAWLINGS, Marjorie Kinnan. *The Yearling.* New York, 1938. Decorations by Edward Shenton. $600. London [1938]. $250. New York, 1939. Illustrated. One of 770 copies signed by author and illustrator, N. C. Wyeth. In slipcase. $2,500.

RAWLINGS, Thomas. *The Confederation of the British North American Provinces . . .* London, 1865. Folding map. full-page plates. $750.

RAWSON, Clayton. *Death from a Top Hat.* New York, 1938. Author's first book. $1,000.

RAWSTORNE, Lawrence. *Gamonia: or the Art of Preserving Game.* London, 1837. 15 hand-colored plates. In original green morocco. With errata slip at end (VAB). $3,500.

RAY, Gordon N. *The Art of the French Illustrated Book, 1700–1914.* New York (1982). 2 vols. $350.

RAY, Isaac. *Mental Hygiene.* Boston, 1863. $500.

RAY, Isaac. *A Treatise on the Medical Jurisprudence of Insanity.* Boston, 1838. $4,000.

RAY, Man. *Photographs 1920–1934.* Paris (1934). Spiral-bound. $2,500.

RAY, Ophelia. *Daughter of the Tejas.* New York (1965). (By Larry McMurtry, as ghostwriter.) In gray dustwrapper. $250. In white jacket. $150.

REACH, Angus B. *Clement Lorimer* . . . London (1849). Author's first book. $750.

READ, C. Rudston. *What I Heard, Saw and Did at the Australian Gold Fields.* London, 1853. Large folding map and 4 tinted lithograph plates. $1,000.

READ, Herbert. See Rackham, Bernard.

READ, Herbert. *English Stained Glass.* London (1926). Colored frontispiece, 70 full-page plates. Issued without dustwrapper. $300.

READ, Herbert. *The Green Child.* London (1935). $600.

READ, Herbert. *In Retreat.* 1925. Hogarth Press. Wraps. $150.

READ, Herbert. *Mutations of the Phoenix.* Hogarth Press. London, 1923. Issued without dustwrapper. $350.

READ, Herbert. *Naked Warriors.* London, 1919. (First commercial book.) $200.

READ, Herbert. *Songs of Chaos.* London (1915). Author's first book. $450.

READ, Herbert, et al. *Surrealism.* London, 1936. Plates. Cloth. $350.

READ, Thomas Buchanan. *Paul Redding* . . . Boston, 1845. Author's first book. $500.

READE, Charles. *The Cloister and the Hearth.* London, 1861. 4 vols. First issue, without ads and with words transposed on page 372 of vol. 2. $2,000. New York, 1861. $300. Limited Editions Club, New York, 1932. In slipcase. $150.

READE, Charles. *A Good Fight, and Other Stories.* New York, 1859. Green cloth. 14 plates. $350.

READE, Charles. *"It Is Never Too Late to Mend."* London, 1856. 3 vols. Duodecimo. $600. Second edition. Octavo. $250.

READE, Charles. *Peg Woffington.* London, 1853. Author's first book. $350. London, 1899. One of 200 copies illustrated by Hugh Thomson. $300.

READING and Collecting, A Monthly Review of Rare and Recent Books. Chicago, 1936–38. Complete run (vol. 1, no. 1, to vol. 2, no. 3). Bound in 2 vols. $300.

REAGAN, John H. *Memoirs, with Special Reference to Secession and the Civil War.* New York, 1906. 4 plates. $300.

REANEY, James. *The Red Heart.* Toronto, 1949. Author's first book. $300.

REAVEY, George. *Faust's Metamorphoses* . . . Seine (1932). Author's first book. One of 100 copies. Wraps. $1,250.

REDDING, J(ay). Saunders. *No Day of Triumph.* New York (1942). $300.

REDDING, J(ay) Saunders. *To Make a Poet Black.* Chapel Hill, 1939. Author's first book. $350.

REDGAUNTLET. Edinburgh, 1824. (By Sir Walter Scott.) 3 vols. 4 pages of ads at rear of volume 3. $450.

REDPATH, James, and HINTON, Richard J. *Hand-book to Kansas Territory and the Rocky Mountains' Gold Region.* New York, 1859. 3 maps in color on 2 large folding sheets. $10,000.

REDSKINS (The). New York, 1846. By the author of *The Pathfinder* (James Fenimore Cooper). 2 vols., in original printed brown wraps. $1,500. (For first English edition, see *Ravensnest.*)

REED, Andrew, and MATHESON, James. *A Narrative of the Visit to the Americas Churches by the Deputation from the Congregational Union of England and Wales.* London, 1835. 2 vols. 4 plates, folding map. In original leather. $400.

REED, Ishmael. *The Free-Lance Pallbearers.* Garden City, 1967. Author's first book. $175.

REED, J. W. *Map of and Guide to the Kansas Gold Region.* New York, 1859. Map. 24 pages, printed wraps. $7,500.

REED, John. *The Day in Bohemia.* New York, 1913. Stiff printed wraps. One of 500 copies. In slipcase. $350.

REED, John. *Sangar: To Lincoln Steffens.* Boards. Riverside, Conn., 1913. Stiff wraps. 500 copies. In slipcase. $400.

REED, John. *Ten Days That Shook the World.* Illustrated. New York, 1919. In dustwrapper. $2,500. Without dustwrapper. $500.

REED, John Silas. *Diana's Debut.* Harvard (Cambridge, 1910). Lyrics by Reed. Author's first book. Wraps. $1,500.

REED, Nathaniel. *The Life of Texas Jack.* (Tulsa, 1936.) Illustrated. Pictorial wraps. $1,000.

REED, Ronald. *The Nature and Making of Parchment.* (Leeds, 1975.) One of 450 copies. $300. One of 25 copies in full vellum. $500.

REED, S. G. *A History of the Texas Railroads.* Houston (1941). Blue cloth. Limited, signed edition. Issued without dustwrapper. $350.

REED, Silas. *Report of . . . Surveyor General of Wyoming Territory, for the Year 1871.* Washington, 1871. Tables. 46 pages, wraps. $600.

REED, Talbot Baines. *A History of the Old English Letter Foundries . . .* London, 1887. Half leather. $450. London, 1952. Revised and enlarged. $200.

REES, William. *Description of the City of Keokuk.* Keokuk, Iowa, 1854. 24 pages, printed self-wraps. $1,250. Keokuk, 1855. 22 pages, with wrapper title. Second edition. $750.

REES, William. *The Mississippi Bridge Cities: Davenport, Rock Island and Moline.* (Rock Island, Ill.), 1854. Woodcut frontispiece. 32 pages, sewn. $450.

REESE, Lizette Woodworth. *A Branch of May: Poems.* Baltimore, 1887. Author's first book. Gray cloth. $450.

REEVE, Arthur B. *The Black Hand.* London, 1912. $500.

REEVE, Arthur B. *The Silent Bullet.* New York, 1912. Author's first book. $600. London, 1916. $250.

REGESTER, Seeley. *The Dead Letter.* New York, 1867. $5,000.

REID, Desmond. (Michael Moorcock and Jim Cawthorn.) *Caribbean Crisis.* London (1962). Author's first book. Wraps. $100.

REID, Forrest. *Apostate.* London (1926). One of 50 signed copies. $400.

REID, Forrest. *Illustrators of the Sixties.* London (1928). $150.

REID, Forrest. *The Kingdom of Twilight.* London, 1904. Author's first book. $350.

REID, John. *The American Atlas.* New York, 1798. 5 vols. 24 plates in text volumes, 21 maps, including map of (future) Washington City. $30,000.

REID, John C. *Reid's Tramp, or A Journal of the Incidents of Ten Months' Travel Through Texas, New Mexico, Arizona, Sonora, and California.* Selma, Ala., 1858. $15,000.

REID, Mayne. *The Headless Horseman.* London (1866). (By Thomas M. Reid.) 2 vols. 20 plates. $1,000.

REID, Mayne. *No Quarter!* London, 1888. (By Thomas M. Reid.) 3 vols. Cloth. $750.

REID, Mayne. *Osceola the Seminole.* New York, 1858. $350.

REID, Mayne. *The Quadroon; or, A Lover's Adventures in Louisiana.* London, 1856. (By Thomas M. Reid.) 3 vols. Orange or gray cloth. $600.

REID, Mayne. *The White Chief: A Legend of Northern Mexico.* London, 1855. (By Thomas M. Reid.) 3 vols. Author's first book. $1,000.

REID, Mayne. *The Wood-Rangers.* London, 1860. 3 vols. (Translated by Thomas M. Reid.) $750.

REID, Samuel C., Jr. *The Scouting Expeditions of McCulloch's Texas Rangers.* Philadelphia, 1847. 12 plates and double-page map. $1,000. Philadelphia, 1848. $600.

REID, Thomas. *Essays on the Intellectual Powers of Man.* Edinburgh, 1785. $1,250.

REID, Thomas M. See Reid, Mayne.

REIGN of Terror in Kanzas (The). Boston, 1856. (By Charles W. Briggs.) 34 pages, wraps. $1,250.

REIK, Theodore. *Ritual Psycho-Analytic Studies.* London, 1931. Preface by Sigmund Freud. $600.

REISER, Anton. *Albert Einstein: A Biographical Portrait.* New York, 1931. Author's first book (translated anonymously by Louis Zukofsky). $750. London (1931). $500.

RELIEF Business Directory, Names and New Locations in San Francisco, Oakland, Berkeley and Alameda of 4,000 San Francisco Firms and Business Men. Berkeley, May 1906. 64 pages, wraps. (Issued after the great earthquake and fire of 1906.) $500.

RELIGIO Bibliopolae, in Imitation of Dr. Browns Religio Medici . . . London, 1691. (John Dunton.) $750.

REMARQUE, Erich Maria. *All Quiet on the Western Front.* London (1929). First edition in English. Buckram. $1,000. Boston, 1929. Gray cloth. $350. Limited Editions Club, New York, 1969. In slipcase. $125.

REMARQUE, Erich Maria. *The Road Back.* London (1931). First edition in English with misprints in line 8, page 243, and line 1, page 250. $450. Boston, 1931. $200.

REMBRANDT. *Drawings of Rembrandt.* London, 1954–57. 6 vols. $1,250. London, 1973. $750.

REMINGTON, Frederic. *Crooked Trails.* New York, 1898. 49 plates. Pictorial tan cloth. $350. Suede. $1,000.

REMINGTON, Frederic. *Done in the Open.* New York, 1902. Introduction by Owen Wister. Illustrations by Remington. 90 pages, folio, cream-colored pictorial boards. First issue, with Russell imprint and with "Frederick." $750. With "Frederic" on front cover. $500. Suede leather. One of 250 signed copies. $2,000.

REMINGTON, Frederic. *Drawings.* New York, 1897. 61 plates. Oblong folio, pictorial boards and cloth. $1,000. Suede leather. One of 250 signed copies. $3,000. New York, 1898. $750.

REMINGTON, Frederic. *Frontier Sketches.* Chicago (1898). Illustrated by the author. Oblong, pictorial boards. $1,000.

REMINGTON, Frederic. *John Ermine of the Yellowstone.* New York, 1902. Illustrated by the author. Brown cloth. $250. (First editions and reprints misspell "Reminigton" on spine.)

REMINGTON, Frederic. *Men with the Bark On.* New York, 1900. Illustrated by the author. Pictorial orange-tan cloth. First issue, ⅞ inch thick. $300. Second issue, 1⅛ inches. $200.

REMINGTON, Frederic. *Pony Tracks.* New York, 1895. Author's first book. Illustrated by the author. Brown decorated cloth. $500. Suede. $1,000.

REMINGTON, Frederic. *A Rogers Ranger in the French and Indian War.* (New York), 1897. Printed wraps. $500.

REMINGTON, Frederic. *Sundown Leflare.* New York, 1899. Illustrated by the author. Brown pictorial cloth. $250.

REMINGTON, Frederic. *Way of an Indian.* New York, 1906. With page 9 numbered. $500. With page 9 unnumbered. $250.

REMINISCENCES of a Campaign in Mexico. Nashville, 1849. (By John B. Robertson.) Map, frontispiece. $1,500.

REMSBURG, John E., and REMSBURG, George J. *Charley Reynolds, Soldier, Hunter, Scout and Guide.* Kansas City, 1931. First book edition. Portrait. One of 175 copies. $300.

REMY, Jules, and BRENCHLEY, Julius L. *A Journey to Great Salt Lake City*. London, 1861. 2 vols. First edition in English. Map, 10 plates. Cloth. $2,000.

RENAULT, Mary. *Purposes of Love*. London, 1939. Author's first book. $350.

RENAULT, Mary. *Promise of Love*. New York, 1940. (New title.) $250.

RENDELL, Ruth. *The Fallen Curtain and Other Stories*. London (1976). $350. Garden City, 1976. $250.

RENDELL, Ruth. *From Doon with Death*. London (1964). Author's first book. $4,000. Garden City, 1965. $1,000.

RENDELL, Ruth. *A New Lease of Death*. London, 1967. $750. New York, 1967. $250.

RENDELL, Ruth. *To Fear a Painted Devil*. London, 1965. $1,000. New York, 1965. $400.

RENDELL, Ruth. *Wolf to the Slaughter*. London (1967). $3,000. Garden City, 1967. $250.

RENNER, Frederic G. *Charles M. Russell: Paintings, Drawings, and Sculpture in the Amon G. Carter Collection. A Descriptive Catalogue*. Austin (1966). Illustrated, including color. Decorated cloth. One of 250 copies signed, and with an extra color plate and a portfolio of color plates laid in. Slipcase. $450. Trade. $150.

REPLY to the Essay on Population, by the Rev. T. R. Malthus (A). London, 1807. (By William Hazlitt.) $2,000.

REPORT from a Select Committee of the House of Representatives, on the Overland Emigration Route from Minnesota to British Oregon. St. Paul, Minn., 1858. Printed wraps, marbled spine. $3,000.

REPORT from the Select Committee on the Hudson's Bay Company. (London, 1857.) 3 elephant-folio colored folding maps by Arrowsmith. Half morocco. $2,500. There was also an advance issue in wraps, 2 parts; same date would be same value.

REPORT of the Proceedings Connected with the Disputes Between the Earl of Selkirk and the North-West Company. London, 1819. (Samuel Hull Wilcocke, editor.) $3,000.

REPORT on the Governor's Message Relating to the "Political Situation" "Polygamy," and "Governmental Action." Salt Lake, 1882. 13 pages, wraps. $300.

REPORT on the Typography of the Cambridge University Press . . . (No place), 1950. One of 500 copies as one of the Cambridge Christmas books. $200.

REPORTS of the Committee of Investigation Sent in 1873, by the Mexican Government, to the Frontier of Texas. New York, 1875. 3 folding maps. Boards and leather. $1,250.

REPPLIER, Agnes. *Books and Men*. Boston, 1882. Author's first book. $100.

REPTON, Humphry. *The Landscape Gardening . . .* London, 1840. $1,000. With hand-colored plates would be more.

REPTON, Humphry. *Observations on the Theory and Practice of Landscape Gardening*. London, 1803. Portrait frontispiece and 27 plates, 10 in full color. $10,000. London, 1805. $8,500.

REUBEN. (Robert Stephen Hawker.) *Tendrils*. London, 1821. $3,500.

REVELL, Alexander H. *Pro and Con of Golf.* Chicago (1915). $250.

REVERE, Joseph W. *A Tour of Duty in California.* New York, 1849. 6 plates, folding map. $1,250.

REXROTH, Kenneth. *The Art of Worldly Wisdom.* Decker Press. Prairie City, Ill., 1949. $500. Sausalito, Calif. (1953). Second edition. In dustwrapper. $200.

REXROTH, Kenneth. *In What Hour.* New York, 1940. Author's first book. $300.

REXROTH, Kenneth. *The Phoenix and the Tortoise.* New York, 1944. $300.

REXROTH, Kenneth. *The Signature of All Things.* (New York, 1950.) $200.

REYNARDSON, C.T.S. Birch. *'Down the Road' or Reminiscences of a Gentleman Coachman.* London, 1875. Colored lithographs. $500. Second edition, same date. $350.

REYNOLDS, J. N. *Voyage of the United States Frigate Potomac.* New York, 1835. Map and 9 plates. $600.

REYNOLDS, John. *My Own Times.* (Belleville), 1855. Portrait. $1,500.

REYNOLDS, John. *The Pioneer History of Illinois.* Belleville, 1852. $850.

REYNOLDS, John. *Sketches of the Country on the Northern Route from Belleville, Ill., to the City of New York, and Back by the Ohio Valley.* Belleville, 1854. $2,500.

REZNIKOFF, Charles. *Five Groups of Verse.* New York (1927). One of 375 copies. In dustwrapper. $450.

REZNIKOFF, Charles. *Going To and Fro and Walking Up and Down.* New York (1941). $300.

REZNIKOFF, Charles. *Jerusalem the Golden.* New York (1934). $400.

REZNIKOFF, Charles. *Nine Plays.* New York (1927). One of 400 copies. In dustwrapper. $250.

REZNIKOFF, Charles. *Rhythms.* Brooklyn (1918). Author's first book. Wraps. $2,000.

RHEES, William J. *Manual of Public Libraries* . . . Philadelphia, 1859. $350.

RHODE, John (Major Cecil John Charles Street.), A.S.F. *The Story of a Great Conspiracy.* London (1924). Author's first book. $1,500. Also see next entry.

RHODE, John. *The White Menace.* New York (1926). New title for author's first book. $1,000.

RHODES, Eugene Manlove. *Bransford in Arcadia.* New York, 1914. First page of ads dated "xi '13." $200.

RHODES, Eugene Manlove. *The Desire of the Moth.* New York, 1916. Ads dated "3 '16." $150.

RHODES, Eugene Manlove. *Good Men and True.* New York, 1910. Author's first book. $500.

RHODES, Eugene Manlove. *Once in the Saddle and Paso por Aquí.* Boston, 1927. $500.

RHODES, Eugene Manlove. *The Proud Sheriff.* Boston, 1935. $350.

RHODES, Eugene Manlove. *Stepsons of Light.* Boston (1921). $600.

RHODES, Eugene Manlove. *West Is West.* New York, 1917. $150.

RHODES, W. H. *Caxton's Book.* San Francisco, 1876. Author's first book. $250.

RHODODAPHNE: or The Thessalian Spell: A Poem. London, 1818. (By Thomas Love Peacock.) $500.

RHYS, Jean. *After Leaving Mr. MacKenzie.* London, 1931. $1,000. New York, 1931. $600.

RHYS, Jean. *Good Morning, Midnight.* London, 1939. $600.

RHYS, Jean. *Left Bank . . .* New York (1927). Author's first book. $1,000. London (1927). $750.

RHYS, Jean. *Voyage in the Dark.* London (1937). $750. (New York, 1935.) $650.

RICARDO, David. *On the Principles of Political Economy, and Taxation.* London, 1817. First issue with "differently" on last line of page 589. $20,000. Second issue. $17,500. London, 1819. Second edition. $2,500.

RICE, Anne. See Rampling, Anne; and Roquelaure, A. N.

RICE, Anne. *The Feast of All Saints.* New York (1979). $200.

RICE, Anne. *Interview with the Vampire.* New York, 1976. Author's first book. $750. London, 1976. $350.

RICE, Craig. *8 Faces at 3.* New York, 1939. Author's first book. $350.

RICH, Adrienne Cecile. *Ariadne: A Play in Three Acts and Poems.* (Baltimore), 1939. (The poet's first published work.) 59 pages, blue wraps. In tissue dustwrapper. $3,000.

RICH, Adrienne Cecile. *A Change of World.* New Haven, 1951. Foreword by W. H. Auden. Author's first book as an adult. $1,000.

RICH, Adrienne Cecile. *Not I, But Death.* Baltimore, 1941. Wraps. $1,500. Green boards. $2,000.

RICH, Adrienne Cecile. *(Poems.)* Swinford: Fantasy Poets (1952). $750.

RICH, Barbara. *No Decency Left.* London (1932). (By Laura Riding and Robert Graves.) $3,000.

RICHARD Hurdis; or, the Avenger of Blood. Philadelphia, 1838. (By William Gilmore Simms.) 2 vols. $450.

RICHARDS, David Adams. *Coming of Winter.* Ottawa, 1974. Author's first novel. Cloth. $350. Wraps. $40.

RICHARDS, David Adams. *Small Heroics.* Fredericton (1972) Author's first book. Stapled card covers. $250.

RICHARDS, Frank. *Old Soldiers Never Die*. London (1933). (Published under Richards's name but actually rewritten by Robert Graves.) $1,500.

RICHARDS, Franklin D. (editor). *A Compendium of the Faith and Doctrines of the Church of Jesus Christ of the Latter-Day Saints* . . . Liverpool, 1857. $400. Salt Lake City, 1882. Second edition, expanded. Errata slip. $250.

RICHARDS, Laura E. *Five Mice in a Mouse-Trap*. Boston, 1880. $300.

RICHARDS, Thomas Addison. *American Scenery Illustrated*. New York (1854). Morocco. $400.

RICHARDS, Thomas Addison. *Georgia Illustrated*. Penfield, Ga., 1842. Plates. 44 pages, leather. $1,000.

RICHARDS, Thomas Addison. *The Romance of American Landscape*. New York (1854). 16 engravings. Morocco. $350.

RICHARDSON, Dorothy. *Dawn's Left Hand*. London (1931). $200.

RICHARDSON, Dorothy. *Gleanings from the Work of George Fox*. London, 1914. $250.

RICHARDSON, Dorothy. *Interim*. London (1919). In dustwrapper. $500.

RICHARDSON, Dorothy. *Pointed Roofs*. London, 1915. $200. New York, 1916. $150.

RICHARDSON, Dorothy. *The Quakers Past and Present*. London, 1914. Author's first book. $300.

RICHARDSON, Rupert N. *The Comanche Barrier to South Plains Settlement*. Glendale, Calif., 1933. Cloth. Issued without dustwrapper. $500.

RICHARDSON, Samuel. *Clarissa* . . . London, 1748. 7 vols. $3,500.

RICHARDSON, William H. *The Journal of William H. Richardson: A Private Soldier in Col. Doniphan's Command*. Baltimore, 1847. 84 pages, wraps. $6,000. Baltimore, 1848. Illustrated. Half leather. Second edition. $2,000. New York, 1848. Third edition. $1,250.

RICHLER, Mordecai. *The Acrobats*. (London, 1954.) Author's first book. $450. New York, 1954. $250.

RICHLER, Mordecai. *The Apprenticeship of Duddy Kravitz*. London, 1959. $250.

RICHMOND, C. W., and VALLETTE, H. F. *A History of Du Page County, Illinois*. Chicago, 1857. $450.

RICHMOND During the War: Four Years of Personal Observation. New York, 1867. (By Sally A. Brock.) $300.

RICHTER, Conrad. *Brothers of No Kin and Other Stories*. New York (about 1924). Author's first book. Red cloth. In white (first) dustwrapper. $750. In later (orange) jacket. $500.

RICHTER, Conrad. *Human Vibrations, The Mechanics of Life and Mind*. Harrisburg (1925). First edition not stated. $750.

RICHTER, Conrad. *Sea of Grass.* New York, 1937. One of 250 signed copies. $250. Trade. $150.

RICHTER, Conrad. *Tracy Cromwell.* New York, 1942. $150.

RICHTER, Conrad. *The Trees.* New York, 1940. One of 255 copies. In slipcase. $200. Trade. $150.

RICHTHOFEN, Walter, Baron von. *Cattle-Raising on the Plains of North America.* New York, 1885. $600.

RICKETTS, W. P. *50 Years in the Saddle.* Sheridan, WY, 1942. Frontispiece, portrait, map and 3 illustrations. $1,250.

RIDDELL, Robert. *The Carpenter and Joiner, Stair Builder and Hand-Railer.* Edinburgh (circa 1870). Folio. 57 plates. Plates 54–57 are in duplicate and mounted on cardboard so that the plans could be cut and folded into three-dimensional models. $1,250.

RIDGE, John R. See Yellow Bird.

RIDGE, John R. *Poems.* San Francisco, 1868. Original photograph as frontispiece. $350.

RIDGE, Lola. *Firehead.* New York, 1929. Half morocco. One of 30 signed copies. $250. Trade edition. $100.

RIDGE, Lola. *The Ghetto . . .* New York, 1918. Author's first book. In dustwrapper. $250. Without dustwrapper. $75.

RIDING, Laura. See Gottschalk, Laura Riding; Rich, Barbara.

RIDING, Laura. *Collected Poems.* London (1938). Green cloth over boards, buff dustwrapper printed in black and orange. $300. New York (1938). Royal-blue cloth over boards, buff dust-wrapper printed in dark blue and black. $350.

RIDING, Laura. *Four Unposted Letters to Catherine.* Paris (1930). One of 200 signed copies. Issued in tissue dustwrapper. $500.

RIDING, Laura. *Laura and Francesca.* Deya, Majorca, 1931. One of 200 signed copies. Issued in tissue dustwrapper. $400.

RIDING, Laura. *The Life of the Dead.* London (1933). One of 200 signed copies. Wraps. Signed by both Riding and the illustrator, John Aldridge. $500.

RIDING, Laura. *Lives of Wives.* London (1939). Green cloth, buff dustwrapper, printed in black and sienna. $350. New York (1939). Brown cloth, buff dustwrapper printed in black and yellow. $250.

RIDING, Laura. *Love as Love, Death as Death.* London, 1928. One of 175 signed copies. Beige cloth over boards. Issued in tissue dustwrapper. $500.

RIDING, Laura. *A Trojan Ending.* Majorca/London (1937). Folding map in rear. $350. New York (1937). Gray cloth over boards. $250. Variant binding in red cloth, front design in black, spine omits design. $200.

RIDING, Laura. *Twenty Poems Less.* Paris, 1930. One of 200 signed copies. Issued in tissue dustwrapper. $450.

RIDINGS, Sam P. *The Chisholm Trail.* Guthrie, Okla. (1936). Folding map, frontispiece, and text illustrations. $400.

RIDLER, Anne. See Bradby, Anne.

RIDLER, Anne. *Poems.* London, 1939. Author's first book. (Most destroyed in the Blitz.) $125.

RILEY, James Whitcomb. See Johnson, Benj. F. (of Boone).

RILEY, James Whitcomb. *The Flying Islands of the Night.* Indianapolis, 1892. Cloth. In vellum dustwrapper. $350. Another issue (actually 1891): white flexible boards. In dustwrapper. $450.

RILKE, Rainer Maria. *Poems.* New York, 1918. The author's first English translation. $300.

RIMBAUD, Arthur. *A Season in Hell.* Norfolk (1939). (Translated by Delmore Schwartz.) One of 750 copies. $350. One of 30 signed copies. $1,000. New York, The Limited Editions Club, 1986. One of 1,000 copies signed by Paul Schmidt (translator) and Robert Mapplethorpe (photographer). $2,000.

RINEHART, Mary Roberts. *The Circular Staircase.* Indianapolis (1908). $150.

RINEHART, Mary Roberts. *The Man in Lower Ten.* Indianapolis (1909). Illustrated by Howard Chandler Christy. $200.

RINGAN Gilhaize or The Coveenanters. Edinburgh, 1823. (By John Galt.) 3 vols. $300.

RINGWALT, John Luther (editor). *American Encyclopedia of Printing.* Philadelphia, 1871. 20 plates including a full-color frontispiece. $400.

RINK, Henry. *Tales and Traditions of the Eskimo.* Edinburgh and London, 1875. Original cloth. 6 plates. $750.

RIPLEY, R. S. *The War with Mexico.* New York, 1849. 2 vols. $750. London, 1850. $600.

RISTER, Carl Coke. *The Southwestern Frontier, 1865–1881.* Cleveland, 1928. Maps. $300.

RITCHIE, Ward. *Job Printing in California.* Los Angeles, 1955. One of 200 copies. $200.

RIVERA, Tomás. . . . *Y No Se Lo Tragó la Tierra / . . . And the Earth Did Not Part.* (Berkeley) 1971. $150.

RIVERS, Elizabeth. *Stranger in Aran.* Dublin: Cuala Press, 1946. Illustrations (4 in color) by author. Boards, linen spine. One of 280 copies. In dustwrapper. $350.

RIVES, Reginald. *The Coaching Club, Its History, Records, and Activities.* Derrydale Press. New York, 1935. Illustrated. One of 300 copies. $1,000. One of 30 copies. $3,500.

ROB of the Bowl. Philadelphia, 1838. 2 vols., in original cloth, paper labels on spines. (By John Pendleton Kennedy.) $1,250.

ROBBE-GRILLET, Alain. *The Voyeur.* New York (1958). Cloth and boards. One of 26 specially bound copies signed by the author. $500. Trade. $150.

ROBBINS, Aurelia. *A True and Authentic Account of the Indian War, etc.* New York, 1836. 28 pages. $500.

ROBBINS, Tom. *Another Roadside Attraction.* Garden City, 1971. $750. London, 1973. $350.

ROBBINS, Tom. *Even Cowgirls Get the Blues.* Boston, 1976. $600.

ROBERTS, B. H. *The Life of John Taylor.* Salt Lake, 1892. Author's first book. $200.

ROBERTS, David. *The Holy Land.* London, 1842–43–49. 6 vols. 241 plates, 2 maps, portrait, and 6 litho tinted titles. $60,000. London 1855–56. 6 quarto vols. $12,500.

ROBERTS, Elizabeth Madox. *In the Great Steep's Garden.* (Cover title.) (Colorado Springs, 1915.) Wraps. Author's first book. $5,000.

ROBERTS, Elizabeth Madox. *Under the Tree.* New York, 1922. $600.

ROBERTS, Keith. *The Furies.* (London, 1966.) $600.

ROBERTS, Kenneth. *Europe's Morning After.* New York (about 1921). First issue, with "B-V" on copyright page. Author's first book. $1,250.

ROBERTS, Kenneth. *Lydia Bailey.* Garden City, 1947. Gray buckram. One of 1,050 signed copies, with a page of the typescript, with corrections in Roberts's hand, laid in. In glassine dustwrapper and slipcase. $300. Trade edition. $100.

ROBERTS, Kenneth. *Northwest Passage.* Garden City, 1937. $200. 2 vols., cloth. One of 1,050 signed copies. In dustwrappers and slipcase. $600.

ROBERTS, Kenneth. *Rabble in Arms.* Garden City, 1933. $250.

ROBERTS, Kenneth. *Sun Hunting.* Indianapolis (1922). Gilt stamping. $500. Black stamping. $400.

ROBERTS, Kenneth. *Trending into Maine.* Boston, 1938. Illustrated by N. C. Wyeth. $250. One of 1,075 copies signed by Roberts and Wyeth. In slipcase. $1,500. With an extra set of the Wyeth plates in envelope. $2,000.

ROBERTS, Kenneth. *Why Europe Leaves Home.* (Indianapolis, 1922.) $1,250.

ROBERTS, Morley. *The Western Avernus* . . . London, 1887. Author's first book. $1,000.

ROBERTS, Oran M. *A Description of Texas.* St. Louis, 1881. 8 colored plates, 5 double-page maps. $1,000.

ROBERTS, Robert. *The House Servant's Directory* . . . Boston/New York, 1827. Author's first book. $7,500. New York, 1828. Second edition. $3,500.

ROBERTS, W. Adolphe. *The Haunting Hand.* New York, 1926. Author's first book. First black detective novel. $1,500.

ROBERTS, W. H. *Northwestern Washington.* Port Townsend, Wash., 1880. Folding map. 52 pages, wraps. $750.

ROBERTSON, Ben. *Travelers' Rest.* Clemson, South Carolina (1938). Author's first book. $500.

ROBERTSON, E. *Conversations with Trotsky.* London, 1936. (By Earle Birney.) Author's first book. $3,000.

ROBERTSON, John W. *Francis Drake and Other Early Explorers Along the Pacific Coast.* 28 maps. Grabhorn Press. San Francisco, 1927. Illustrations by Valenti Angelo. Vellum and boards. One of 1,000 copies. $350.

ROBERTSON, William. *The History of America . . .* London, 1777. 2 vols. Four folding maps and 1 plate. $1,500.

ROBERTSON, Wyndham, Jr. *Oregon, Our Right and Title . . .* Washington, 1846. Folding map. Boards and cloth, or printed wraps. $5,000.

ROBESON, Paul. *Here I Stand.* New York (1958). Author's first book. Cloth. $350. Wraps. $100. London (1958). $150.

ROBIDOUX, Mrs. Orral M. *Memorial to the Robidoux Brothers.* Kansas City, 1924. Map. 16 plates. Cloth. Issued without dustwrapper. $450.

(ROBINSON, Alfred.) *Life in California . . .* New York, 1846. 9 plates. The first book in English on California written by a resident. $1,000.

ROBINSON, Charles. *The Home Beautiful . . .* London (1904). Decorated printed box. $750.

ROBINSON, Charles. N. *Old Naval Prints, Their Artists and Engravers.* London, 1924. Illustrated, including 24 plates in color. One of 1,500 copies. $500.

ROBINSON, Edwin Arlington. *Cavender's House.* New York, 1929. One of 500 signed copies. In slipcase. $125. Trade edition. $75.

ROBINSON, Edwin Arlington. *The Children of the Night.* Muslin. Boston, 1897. One of 50 copies on Japan vellum. $2,500. Cloth. One of 450 copies on Batchworth laid paper. $600.

ROBINSON, Edwin Arlington. *The Glory of the Nightingales.* New York, 1930. One of 500 signed copies. In slipcase. $125. Trade edition. $75.

ROBINSON, Edwin Arlington. *King Jasper.* New York, 1935. Introduction by Robert Frost. One of 250 large-paper copies. $250. Trade edition. $125.

ROBINSON, Edwin Arlington. *The Man Who Died Twice.* New York, 1924. One of 250 signed copies. In slipcase. $200. Trade edition. $100.

ROBINSON, Edwin Arlington. *The Torrent and the Night Before.* (Gardiner, Maine), 1896. Blue wraps. Author's first book. $2,500. New York, 1928. One of 110 signed copies. $400.

ROBINSON, J. C. *The Treasury of Ornamental Art.* London (1858). Folio. 71 colored plates. $600.

ROBINSON, Jacob. *Sketches of the Great West.* Portsmouth, N.H., 1848. 71 pages, wraps. $7,500.

ROBINSON, John, and DOW, George F. *The Sailing Ships of New England, 1607–1907.* Salem, 1922–24–28. 3 vols., cloth. Series I, II, and III. $450.

ROBINSON, Lennox (editor). *A Little Anthology of Modern Irish Verse.* Dublin: Cuala Press, 1928. Blue boards, linen back, paper label. One of 300 copies. In plain dustwrapper. $250.

ROBINSON, Peter. *Gallows View.* Markham (Canada), 1987. $125. New York, 1990. $40.

ROBINSON, Peter. *With Equal Eye.* Toronto, 1979. Author's first book. Wraps. $250.

ROBINSON, Rowland Evans. See *Awahsoose the Bear.*

ROBINSON, Selma. *City Child.* New York (1931). One of 300 copies signed by Robinson and with illustrator Rockwell Kent's mark, a heart-shaped thumbprint. In dustwrapper and slipcase. $350. New York, 1931. Trade. $150.

ROBINSON, W. Heath. *Bill the Minder.* London, 1912. Illustrated by the author, including 16 color plates. Vellum. One of 380 signed copies. $3,000.

ROBINSON, William. *The Parks, Promenades & Gardens of Paris . . .* London, 1869. 376 text illustrations, 48 plates and 3 maps. $450.

ROBINSON, William Davis. *Memoirs of the Mexican Revolution.* Philadelphia, 1820. $750. London, 1821. 2 vols. With portrait and folding map. $1,250.

ROCHESTER, John Wilmot, Earl of. *Collected Works.* Nonesuch Press. London, 1926. Edited by John Hayward. Boards and buckram. One of 900 copies. $150. Boards and vellum. One of 75 copies. $400.

ROCK, Marion Tuttle. *Illustrated History of Oklahoma.* Topeka, 1890. 90 plates. $850.

ROCKY Mountain Directory and Colorado Gazettier for 1871. Denver (1870). Illustrated. $1,250.

RODD, Rennell. *Songs to the South.* London, 1881. Author's first book. (Previously 1880 Newdigate prize poem.) $1,000. Philadelphia, 1882. $350.

RODENBOUGH, Theodore F. *From Everglade to Canon with the Second Dragoons.* New York, 1875. 2 folding maps. $2,500.

RODGERS, Richard, and HAMMERSTEIN, Oscar. *Oklahoma!* New York, 1943. $850.

RODITI, Edouard. *Poems for F.* Paris (1935). Author's first book. Wraps. $250.

RODITI, Edouard. *Prison Within Prison.* Prairie City, Ill. (1941). Wraps. $250.

RODITI, Edouard. *The Temptations of a Saint.* (Rancho Sante Fe), 1980. One of 90 signed copies. $350. One of 15 signed copies. In vellum. 2 original etchings by José Hernández. $750.

RODKER, John. *Poems.* London (1914). Wraps. Author's first book. One of 50 signed copies. $1,000. Trade. $400.

ROETHKE, Theodore. *The Lost Son and Other Poems.* Garden City, 1948. First edition stated. $350. London (1948). $125.

ROETHKE, Theodore. *Open House.* New York, 1941. Author's first book. One of 1,000 copies. $750.

ROETHKE, Theodore. *Praise to the End!* Garden City, 1951. $350.

ROETHKE, Theodore. *Sequence, Sometimes Metaphysical.* Iowa City (1963). Illustrated. Boards. One of 270 copies. In slipcase. $450. One of 60 signed copies. In slipcase. $2,000.

ROETHKE, Theodore. *The Waking: Poems 1933–1953.* Garden City, 1953. First edition stated. $150.

ROETHKE, Theodore. *Words for the Wind.* London, 1957. $150. Garden City, 1958. $150.

ROGERS, A. N. *Communication Relative to the Location of the U.P.R.R. Across the Rocky Mountains Through Colorado Territory.* Central City, Colo., 1867. Wraps. $750.

ROGERS, Bruce. *Paragraphs on Printing . . .* New York, 1943. $150. One of 199 large-paper copies. $500.

ROGERS, Robert. *A Concise Account of North America . . .* London, 1765. $1,750.

ROGERS, Robert. *Journals of Maj. Robert Rogers.* London, 1765. $2,000.

ROGERS, Will. *The Illiterate Digest.* New York, 1924. One of 250 signed copies. In dust-wrapper. $1,000. Trade. $350.

ROGERS, Will. *Letters of a Self-Made Diplomat to His President.* New York, 1926. $250.

ROGET, Peter Mark. *Thesaurus of English Words.* Boston, 1854. First American edition. $250.

ROHMER, Sax. *The Book of Fu-Manchu.* New York, 1929. $1,250.

ROHMER, Sax. *Daughter of Fu-Manchu.* Garden City, 1931. $1,000.

ROHMER, Sax. *Dr. Fu-Manchu.* London (1913). $1,000.

ROHMER, Sax. *The Insidious Dr. Fu-Manchu.* New York, 1913. $750.

ROHMER, Sax. *The Island of Fu Manchu.* London, 1941. $1,500. New York, 1941. $750.

ROHMER, Sax. *Mystery of Dr. Fu-Manchu.* London (1913). $1,250.

ROHMER, Sax. *Pause!* London, 1910. Author's first book. $750.

ROHMER, Sax. *President Fu Manchu.* New York, 1936. $1,000.

ROHMER, Sax. *She Who Sleeps.* Garden City, 1928. $750.

ROHMER, Sax. *Tales of East and West.* New York, 1933. $750.

ROLFE, Frederick William. See Corvo, Baron; *Prospero and Caliban; The Weird of the Wanderer . . .*

ROLFE, Fr. *Don Tarquinio.* London, 1905. First binding in violet cloth. $1,500. Later, red cloth. $750.

ROLFE, Fr. *Hadrian the Seventh.* London, 1904. First issue purple cloth; title and drawing stamped in white. $2,000. Second issue, title and drawing blindstamped. $1,250.

ROLLESTON, T. W. *Parsifal or the Legend of the Holy Grail.* London (1912). One of 525 copies, signed by the illustrator, Willy Pogany. Sixteen mounted color plates, plus text illustrations. Full vellum, gilt. $1,250.

ROLLINSON, John K. *History of the Migration of Oregon-Raised Herds to Mid-Western Markets: Wyoming Cattle Trails.* Caldwell, Idaho, 1948. Plates, maps, colored frontispiece by Frederic Remington. One of 1,000 signed copies. Issued without dustwrapper. $250.

ROLVAAG, O. E. *Giants in the Earth.* New York, 1927. $300.

ROMAN, Alfred. *The Military Operations of General Beauregard in the War Between the States 1861–1865 . . .* New York, 1884. 2 vols. $350.

Romance of the Forest (The). London, 1791. (By Ann Radcliffe.) 3 vols. $2,500.

ROMBAUER, Irma S. *The Joy of Cooking.* (St. Louis, 1931.) $3,000. Indianapolis (1936). $1,000.

RONALDS, Alfred. *The Fly-Fisher's Entomology . . .* London, 1836. 19 hand-colored plates. $1,250.

ROQUELAURE, A. N. *Beauty's Punishment.* New York (1984). (By Anne Rice.) Cloth. $250. Wraps. $60.

ROQUELAURE, A. N. *Beauty's Release.* New York (1985). (By Anne Rice.) Cloth. $250. Wraps. $60.

ROQUELAURE, A. N. *The Claiming of Sleeping Beauty.* New York (1983). (By Anne Rice.) Cloth. $300. Wraps. $100.

ROOSEVELT, Eleanor. *On My Own.* New York (1958). Signed on tipped in leaf for ". . . friends of the author and publisher." $750. Trade. $100.

ROOSEVELT, Eleanor. *This I Remember.* New York (1949). Frontispiece and plates. Buckram. One of 1,000 signed copies. In slipcase. $750. Trade. $100.

ROOSEVELT, Eleanor. *This Is My Story.* New York, 1937. One of 258 signed copies. $1,000. Trade. $100.

ROOSEVELT, Mrs. Franklin D. *It's Up to the Women.* New York, 1933. Author's first book. One of 250 signed copies. $1,000. Trade. $300.

ROOSEVELT, Franklin D. *The Democratic Book, 1936.* (Philadelphia), 1936. One of 898 signed copies. $2,000.

ROOSEVELT, Franklin D. *The Happy Warrior: Alfred E. Smith.* Boston, 1928. $750.

ROOSEVELT, Franklin D. *Whither Bound?* Boston, 1926. Author's first book. $1,000.

ROOSEVELT, Theodore. *African Game Trails.* New York, 1910. 2-vol. deluxe edition. One of 500 signed copies. Bound in three-quarter pigskin. In publisher's box. $3,000. Trade in olive-green cloth. $450.

ROOSEVELT, Theodore. *Big Game Hunting in the Rockies and on the Great Plains.* New York, 1899. 55 etchings. Full tan buckram. One of 1,000 signed copies. $3,500.

ROOSEVELT, Theodore. *Hunting Trips of a Ranchman.* New York, 1885. 20 plates. Buckram. Limited Medora Edition of 500 copies. $1,750. Various deluxe publisher bindings. $2,000. New York 1886. $500. London, 1886. Illustrated. First English (and second) edition. $350.

ROOSEVELT, Theodore. *Naval War of 1812.* New York, 1882. Author's first separate book. $1,250.

ROOSEVELT, Theodore. *Outdoor Pastimes of an American Hunter.* New York, 1905. 49 plates. Half calf and boards. One of 260 signed copies. $3,500. Trade edition. $400.

ROOSEVELT, Theodore. *Ranch Life and the Hunting Trail.* New York (1888). Illustrated by Frederic Remington. All edges gilt, light-colored, coarse weave, tan buckram, cover design in green and gold. $1,000.

ROOSEVELT, Theodore. *The Rough Riders.* New York, 1899. $850.

ROOSEVELT, Theodore. *Some American Game.* New York, 1897. $1,250.

ROOSEVELT, Theodore. *The Summer Birds of the Adirondacks.* (Salem, 1877.) Author's first book with H. D. Minot. Wraps. $3,000.

ROOSEVELT, Theodore. *The Wilderness Hunter.* New York (1893). Tan or brown cloth. First edition, with chapter headings in brown (VAB). $1,000. Buckram. One of 200 signed copies. $3,500.

ROOSEVELT, Theodore. *The Winning of the West.* New York, 1889–96. 4 vols. First issue, with "diame-" as last word on page 160 and "ter" as first word on page 161. $1,500. Second issue, with "diameter" changed to "circumference." $1,000. New York, 1900. 4 vols. $600. Half morocco. One of 200 copies with a page of manuscript. $4,500.

ROOT, Frank A., and CONNELLEY, William E. *The Overland Stage to California.* Topeka, 1901. Map. Pictorial cloth. $500.

ROOT, Riley. *Journal of Travels from St. Josephs . . . to Oregon . . .* Galesburg, Ill., 1850. 143 pages, printed wraps. $10,000.

ROS, Amanda. *Irene Iddesleigh.* Belfast, 1897. Author's first book. With slip of "Printer's Errors." (A novel often called the foremost example in the English language of bad writing— VAB.) $200.

ROSCOE, Thomas. *Wanderings and Excursions in North Wales.* London, 1836. Engraved title, 96 plates and 4 maps. $750.

ROSCOE, Thomas. *Wanderings and Excursions in South Wales.* London, no date (circa 1837). Illustrated with steel engravings. $750.

ROSE, Barbara. *Frankenthaler.* New York (1970). 205 illustrations, 54 color plates. Cloth. Dustwrapper. $400.

ROSE, Victor M. *Ross' Texas Brigade.* Louisville, 1881. Illustrated. $3,500.

ROSEN, Peter. *Pa-Ha-Sa-Pah, or The Black Hills of South Dakota*. St. Louis, 1895. 27 plates. Pictorial cloth. $750.

ROSEN, R. D. *Strike Three You're Dead*. New York, 1984. Author's first book. With red stamped text on page 128. $250. Without red stamped text. $150.

ROSENBACH, A.S.W. *A Book Hunter's Holiday, Adventures with Books and Manuscripts*. Boston, 1936. One of 760 signed copies. In slipcase. $250.

ROSENBACH, A.S.W. *Books and Bidders: The Adventures of a Bibliophile*. Boston, 1927. One of 785 signed copies. $250. One of 25 signed (reserved) copies. $350. Trade. $150.

ROSENBACH, A.S.W. *Early American Children's Books*. Portland, Me., 1933. One of 585 signed copies. In slipcase. $500. One of 88 signed copies. In pigskin. $2,000. Trade. $200.

ROSENBACH, A.S.W. *Samuel Johnson's Prologue* . . . New York, 1902. Author's first book. One of 90 copies. $500. One of 30 copies. Japan vellum. $1,250.

ROSENBERG, Harold. *De Kooning*. New York, 1974. Quarter-bound cloth on paper. 265 illustrations (65 full-color plates). $1,250.

ROSENBERG, Isaac. *Night and Day*. (London, 1912.) Author's first book. Wraps. $7,500.

ROSENBERG, Isaac. *Poems*. London, 1922. Portrait. $500.

ROSENBERG, Isaac. *Youth*. London, 1915. Wraps. $1,250.

ROSENTHAL, Leonard. *The Kingdom of the Pearl*. London (1920). Illustrated in color by Edmund Dulac. Boards and vellum. One of 100 copies signed by Dulac. In dustwrapper. $2,000. New York [1920]. One of 675 copies. Boards and cloth. In dustwrapper. $1,000.

ROSENWALD, Lessing. *Recollections of a Collector*. Jenkintown, 1976. One of 250 copies. Slipcase. $600.

ROSIS, Angelo. *A New Book of Ornaments* . . . London, 1753. 23 plates. $6,000. (Originally published in 1747.)

ROSS, Alexander. *Adventures of the First Settlers on the Oregon or Columbia River*. London, 1849. Frontispiece (in some copies), folding map. $2,500.

ROSS, Alexander. *The Fur Hunters of the Far West*. London, 1855. 2 vols. Folding map, frontis, view and portrait. $1,500.

ROSS, Alexander. *The Red River Settlement*. London, 1856. Frontispiece. $850.

ROSS, Captain Sir James. *A Voyage of Discovery and Research in the Southern and Antarctic Regions . . . 1839–43*. London, 1847. 15 hand-colored plates, 3 folding maps, tables. $5,750.

ROSS, James, and GARY, George. *From Wisconsin to California, and Return* . . . Madison, 1869. Wraps. $1,500.

ROSS, John. *Narrative of a Second Voyage in Search of a North-West Passage* . . . London, 1835. 6 charts or maps (1 folding), 25 plates (9 in color). $2,000. Also issued in 2 vols. With 52 plates (20 hand-colored), 4 maps and large colored folding chart. $3,000.

ROSS, John. *A Voyage of Discovery . . . for the Purpose of Exploring Baffin's Bay* . . . London, 1819. 7 maps and charts (5 folding) and 25 plates. $5,000.

ROSS, Mrs. William P. *The Life and Times of Honorable William P. Ross*. Fort Smith, 1893. Portrait. $200.

ROSS, W.W.E. See R., E.

ROSSETTI, Christina. See R., C.G.

ROSSETTI, Christina. *Goblin Market*. London, 1862. With 16-page catalogue at rear. $1,500. London, 1893. One of 160 copies. Illustrated by Laurence Housman. $1,500. London (1933). Illustrated by Arthur Rackham, including 4 color plates. Pictorial wraps. First Rackham edition. In dustwrapper. $350. First deluxe Rackham edition. Limp vellum. One of 400 copies signed by Rackham. In slipcase. $1,250. One of 10 copies with drawing. $12,500. Philadelphia (1933). First American edition. In dustwrapper. $250.

ROSSETTI, Christina. *Poems*. Gregynog Press. Newtown, Wales, 1930. Chosen by Walter de la Mare. Wood-engraving portrait by R. A. Maynard. Printed on Japanese vellum. Red morocco, by the Gregynog bindery. One of 25 copies specially bound. In slipcase. $4,500. Boards and calf. One of 300 copies. $500.

ROSSETTI, Christina. *Speaking Likenesses*. London, 1874. Blue cloth. First binding. $750.

ROSSETTI, Christina. *Verses*. Hammersmith (London): Eragny Press, 1906. One of 175 copies on paper. $1,250. One of 10 copies on vellum. $3,500. For first edition see R., C.G.

ROSSETTI, Dante Gabriel. *Ballads and Narrative Poems*. Kelmscott Press. London, 1893. Woodcut title and initials. Limp vellum with ties. One of 310 copies. $2,000. One of 6 copies on vellum. $7,500.

ROSSETTI, Dante Gabriel. *Hand and Soul*. London (1869). Wraps. First separate edition. $1,500. Kelmscott Press (for Way & Williams, Chicago). London, 1895. Woodcut title and borders. Vellum. One of 525 copies (300 for America and 225 for England). $1,250. One of 21 copies on vellum (10 for England and 11 for America). $4,000. London, 1899. Vale Press. One of 210 copies. Morocco. In dustwrapper. $600.

ROSSETTI, Dante Gabriel. *Poems*. (London, 1869.) Printed wraps. First edition privately printed. $2,500. London, 1870. Cloth. First published edition. $500. Boston, 1870. $200.

ROSSETTI, Dante Gabriel. *Sir Hugo the Heron*. London, 1843. Author's first book. $2,500.

ROSSETTI, Dante Gabriel. *Sonnets and Lyrical Poems*. Kelmscott Press. London, 1894. Woodcut title and borders by William Morris. Printed in black and red. Vellum with ties. One of 310 copies. $1,500. One of 6 copies on vellum. $5,000.

ROSSETTI, William Michael. *The Comedy of Dante Alighieri*. London, 1865. Translated by Rossetti, his first book. $450.

ROSSETTI, William Michael. *Swinburne's Poems and Ballads*. London, 1866. $300.

ROSSI, Mario M. *Pilgrimage in the West*. Dublin: Cuala Press, 1933. Boards and linen. One of 300 copies. $200.

ROSSNER, Judith. *What Kind of Feet Does a Bear Have?* Indianapolis, 1963. Author's first book. $250.

ROTH, Henry. *Call It Sleep.* New York, 1934. Author's first book. $5,000. Paterson, N.J., 1960. $250. London, 1963. $250. San Francisco, 1995. One of 300 signed copies. $750.

ROTH, Henry Ling. *The Natives of Sarawak and British North Borneo* . . . London, 1896. 2 vols. One of 700 copies. Illustrated, 1 folding plate, folding map. $1,750.

ROTH, Philip. *Goodbye, Columbus.* Boston, 1959. Black cloth. Author's first book. $1,500. London, 1959. (Title story only.) $400.

ROTH, Philip. *Portnoy's Complaint.* New York (1969). One of 600 signed copies. In slipcase. $500.

ROUSSEAU, Jean-Jacques. *The Confessions of J.J. Rousseau* . . . [with] *The Reveries of the Solitary Walker.* London, 1783. 2 vols. Translated from the French. $3,000. London, 1938. 2 vols. One of 800 copies. $500.

ROWLANDSON, Mary. *A True History of the Captivity & Restoration of Mrs. Mary Rowlandson* . . . London, 1682. $15,000.

ROWLING, J. K. *Harry Potter and the Chamber of Secrets.* London, 1998. $3,000. London, 1999. Collector's edition in blue cloth. $300. New York, 1999. Green cloth, without "2" on spine of book or dustwrapper. Number series with a "1." Dustwrapper priced $17.95 (later editions $19.95). $300.

ROWLING, J. K. *Harry Potter and the Goblet of Fire.* London, 2000. $150. London, 2000. Collector's edition in purple cloth. $150. New York, 2000. One of 25 special copies with original drawing of Harry Potter by illustrator Mary GrandPre, with certificate of authenticity. $4,000. Trade. $100.

ROWLING, J. K. *Harry Potter and the Philosopher's Stone.* London, 1997. Author's first book and the first of the Harry Potter books. Proof in white wraps. $6,000. Pictorial boards. Issued without dustwrapper. $15,000. New York, 1998. Priced $16.95 with bar code on back with "51695." Stated first with "1" in number series on copyright page. In purple boards with diamond design and dark endpapers. $4,000. (The Book Club states "First" with the "1" in the number series but is in black boards with white endpapers.) London, 1999. Collector's edition in red cloth. $600.

ROWLING, J. K. *Harry Potter and the Prisoner of Azkaban.* London, 1999. With number series including a "1" and "Joanne Rowling" instead of "J. K. Rowling" on copyright page. $4,000. With "J. K. Rowling" on copyright page. $1,000. London, 1999. Collector's edition in green cloth. $1,500 (published at same time as trade). New York, 1999. $150.

ROYALL, Anne. See *Sketches of History, Life, and Manners, in the United States.*

ROYCE, Josiah. *The Religious Aspect of Philosphy.* Boston, 1885. Author's first book. $125.

RUARK, Robert C. *Horn of the Hunter.* Garden City, 1953. $600.

RUBAIYAT of Omar Khayyam, The Astronomer-Poet of Persia. London, 1859. Translated into English verse. Brown wraps. (Translated by Edward FitzGerald.) First edition (250 copies printed). $20,000. London, 1868. Wraps. Second English edition. $4,000. London, 1872. Half leather and dark-red cloth. Third English edition. $1,500. London, 1879. Fourth English edition. Quarter dark-brown roan and purple cloth. $600. London, 1896. Ashendene Press. Gray wraps. One of 50 copies. $3,500. Boston, 1898. First American edition. $1,000. London, 1909. Illustrated by Edmund Dulac. Vellum. One of 750 copies signed by Dulac. In slipcase. $2,500. London, 1913. Riccardi Press. One of 12 copies on vellum. $1,500. One of 250 copies. $600. London, 1938. Golden Cockerel Press. Illustrated. Vellum. One of 270 copies. $600. Morocco. One of 30 copies with extra engravings. $3,500. Limited Editions Club (Westport), 1935. In slipcase. $250. New York, 1940. Heritage Press. Color plates by Arthur Szyk. Pictorial padded calf and marbled boards. $200. Note: There are hundreds of editions. It would be wise to check further.

RUBIN, William S. *Dada and Surrealist Art.* London (1969). Profusely illustrated (including 60 color mounted plates). $500.

RUDO Ensayo. See Smith, Buckingham.

RUKEYSER, Muriel. *Elegies.* No place (1949). Boards. One of 300 signed copies. In slipcase. $200.

RUKEYSER, Muriel. *Theory of Flight.* New Haven, 1935. Author's first book. $300.

RULE, Jane. *The Desert of the Heart.* Toronto, 1964. $300. London, 1964. $100. New York, 1964. $200.

RULES and Orders of the House of Representatives of the Territory of Washington, 1864–5. Olympia, Washington Territory, 1864. 32 pages. $500.

RULES and Regulations of the Utah and Northern Railway, for the Government of Employees. Salt Lake City, 1879. Calf. $300.

RULES, Regulations, and By-Laws of the Board of Commissioners to Manage the Yosemite Valley and Mariposa Big Tree Grove. Sacramento, 1885. 23 pages, wraps. $500.

RUNYON, Damon. *Guys and Dolls.* New York, 1931. $7,500.

RUNYON, Damon. *Take It Easy.* New York, 1938. $750.

RUNYON, Damon. *The Tents of Trouble.* New York [1911]. Flexible cloth. Author's first book. $300.

RUPPANEER, Antoine. *Hypodermic Injections in the Treatment of Neuralgia, Rheumatism, Gout, and Other Diseases.* Boston, 1865. $1,500.

RUSCHA, Edward. *Babycakes and Weights.* New York, 1970. Wraps. $750.

RUSCHA, Edward. *Dutch Details.* Netherlands, 1971. Wraps. $2,000.

RUSH, Benjamin. *Medical Inquiries and Observations Upon the Diseases of the Mind.* Philadelphia, 1812. $7,500. Second issue with gathering "H" reset. $1,000.

RUSHDIE, Salman. *Grimus.* London, 1975. Author's first book. $500. New York (1979). $150.

RUSHDIE, Salman. *Midnight's Children.* New York, 1981. $1,000. London, 1981. Using U.S. sheets. $1,250.

RUSHDIE, Salman. *The Satanic Verses.* (London, 1988.) In blue binding. (Also variant in green library binding?) $250. One of 12 signed and numbered (Roman numerals) copies. $5,000. One of 100 signed copies. $1,250. (New York, 1989). $100.

RUSKIN, John. See R., J. See also *Modern Painters*.

RUSKIN, John. *The Harbours of England*. London, 1856. 12 mezzotint plates by J. M. W. Turner. Folio, decorated blue cloth. $750.

RUSKIN, John. *The King of the Golden River*. London, 1851. Illustrated by Richard Doyle. $1,500. New York, 1930. Illustrated. Black calf. One of 50 copies, each with a holograph letter, signed by Ruskin, tipped in. In slipcase. $1,250. London (1932). Illustrated by Arthur Rackham. Vellum. One of 570 copies signed by Rackham. In slipcase. $1,250. One of 9 copies with original drawing. $10,000. Trade. In dustwrapper. $500.

RUSKIN, John. *Lectures on Landscape*. Orpington, 1897. One of 150 copies. 25 plates. Folio, cloth. $500.

RUSKIN, John. *The Nature of Gothic: A Chapter of the Stones of Venice*. Kelmscott Press. London, 1892. Preface by William Morris. Illustrated. Vellum with ties. One of 500 copies. $1,750.

RUSKIN, John. *Praeterita: Outlines of Scenes and Thoughts Perhaps Worthy of Memory in My Life Past*. Sunnyside, Orpington, Kent, 1885-1889. 28 original parts, printed wraps. $1,750. One of 600 large-paper copies with an extra plate. $750.

RUSKIN, John. *Salsette and Elephanta . . .* Oxford, 1839. Author's first book. Wraps. $2,000.

RUSKIN, John. *The Seven Lamps of Architecture*. London, 1849. 14 plates. $750.

RUSKIN, John. *The Stones of Venice*. London, 1851–53. Illustrated, 3 vols. $2,000. New York, 1851. $600.

RUSS, R. P. *Hussien*. London, 1938. (Birth name of Patrick O'Brian.) $3,000.

RUSS, Richard Patrick. See also O'Brian, Patrick.

RUSS, Richard Patrick. *Ceasar: The Life Story of a Panda Leopard*. London/New York (1930). (Birth name of Patrick O'Brian. His first book.) $3,000.

RUSSELL, Alex J. *The Red River Country, Hudson's Bay and Northwest Territories, etc.* Ottawa, 1869. Folding map. Wraps. $450. Montreal, 1879. Third edition. Folding map, 8 folding plates. Wraps. $500.

RUSSELL, Bertrand. See Whitehead, Alfred North.

RUSSELL, Bertrand. *German Social Democracy*. London, 1896. Author's first book. $1,750.

RUSSELL, Bertrand. *The Principles of Mathematics*. Cambridge, 1903. Vol. 1 (all published). $2,000.

RUSSELL, Charles M. (illustrator). See *How the Buffalo Lost His Crown*.

RUSSELL, Charles M. *Back-trailing on the Old Frontiers*. Great Falls, Mont., 1922. 16 full-page drawings by the author. 56 pages, pictorial wraps. $1,000.

RUSSELL, Charles M. *Good Medicine*. Garden City, 1929. One of 134 copies. Blue buckram with vellum sides. 2 plates (including 1 separate extra). In dustwrapper. $3,500. Garden City, 1930. Trade edition. (With title page dated 1929.) Brown buckram with the extra plate used as endpapers. $450. From the same issue: Blue buckram with vellum sides. One of 59 copies for presentation. $6,000.

RUSSELL, Charles M. *More Rawhides.* Great Falls, 1925. Illustrated by the author. 60 pages, green or tan pictorial wraps. $400.

RUSSELL, Charles M. *Pen and Ink Drawings.* Pasadena (1946). 2 vols. Oblong boards and cloth. $750.

RUSSELL, Charles M. *Pen Sketches.* (Great Falls, 1899.) 12 plates. Oblong, in cloth. No title page. Title and author are on front cover "Indian head" plate. $1,500. Second, in black morocco with titles printed on each plate and "skull" on front cover. $1,250. Third lacks titles on plates. $1,000. Fourth has "Published by W. T. Ridgley Printing Company . . ." stamped in lower left-hand corner. $1,000. Others in portfolios, bound in blue boards, etc. $1,000.

RUSSELL, Charles M. *Rawhide Rawlins Stories.* Great Falls, 1921. Author's first book. Illustrated by the author. Pictorial wraps. $500. Cloth. $400. Full limp leather. Presentation copy. $1,000.

RUSSELL, Charles M. *Studies of Western Life.* Copyright New York (1890). $6,000. New York, 1890. First issue, no text on "War" plate. $2,500. Second issue, text on "War" plate on verso of title page. $2,000.

RUSSELL, Charles M. *Trails Plowed Under.* New York, 1927. $400.

RUSSELL, Eric Frank. *Sinister Barrier.* Surrey (1943). Author's first book. $500. Reading, 1948. One of 500 signed copies. $200. Trade edition. $100.

RUSSELL, George W. See E., A.

RUSSELL, Osborne. *Journal of a Trapper, or Nine Years in the Rocky Mountains . . .* (Boise, 1914.) Blue cloth. (100 copies printed.) $2,500. Boise (1921). Second edition. (100 copies.) $400.

RUSSELL, W. Clark. See *The Wreck of the "Grosvenor."*

RUSSELL, W. Clark. *Fra Angelo.* London, 1865. Author's first book. Wraps. $2,500.

RUSSELL, W. Clark. *The Hunchback's Charge.* London, 1867. 3 vols. $2,500.

RUSSELL, W. Clark. *The Tale of the Ten.* London, 1896. 3 vols. $750.

RUSSELL, William. See Waters.

RUST, Margaret. *The Queen of the Fishes.* Eragny Press. Epping, England, 1894. 16 woodcuts, 4 colored, by Lucien Pissarro. One of 130 copies on vellum. (The first book produced by this press.) $5,000.

RUTHERFORD, Ernest. *Radio-Activity.* Cambridge, 1904. $1,250.

RUXTON, George F. *Life in the Far West.* Edinburgh, 1849. $500. New York, 1849. $350.

RUZICKA, Rudolph. *Studies in Type Design: Alphabets with Random Quotations.* Hanover (1968). Slipcase containing 11 folders and 10 plates. $125.

RYAN, Abram Joseph. *Father Ryan's Poems.* Mobile, 1879. Portrait and one illustration. Author's first book. $450. Baltimore, 1880. Large-paper edition. (Retitled *Poems: Patriotic, Religious, Miscellaneous.*) $250.

RYAN, William R. *Personal Adventures in Upper and Lower California in 1848–49.* London, 1850. 2 vols. In original cloth. 23 plates. $4,500. Rebound. $2,500.

RYGA, George. *Songs of My Hands . . .* Edmonton, Alberta, 1956. Author's first book. Wraps. $300.

S

S., E.W., and M., S.W. *The Children's Hour.* Philadelphia, 1864. (By Elizabeth W. Stevenson and S. Weir Mitchell.) $750. Philadelphia, 1866. (May be same sheets.) $400.

S., I. *Doctor Transit.* New York, 1925. (By Isidor Schneider, his first book.) $250.

S., P. B. *Zastrozzi: A Romance.* London, 1810. (By Percy Bysshe Shelley.) $15,000. Golden Cockerel Press. London, 1955. Plates. Morocco. One of 60 copies on vellum with duplicate set of 8 plates. In slipcase. $600. Boards. One of 200 copies. In slipcase. $200.

S., S. *Vigils.* (Bristol), 1934. Frontispiece by Stephen Gooden. Full morocco. (By Siegfried Sassoon.) One of 23 copies signed by the author and the artist. $3,000. One of 272 copies signed by Sassoon. $750. One of 8 copies on vellum. $3,500.

S., S. H. *Nine Experiments.* Hempstead, England, 1928. (By Stephen Spender.) Author's first book. Green wraps. One of about 18 copies issued. $15,000.

SABATINI, Rafael. *Scaramouche.* Boston, 1921. $600.

SABATINI, Rafael. *The Tavern Knight.* London, 1904. Author's first book. $250.

SABATO, Ernesto. *The Outsider.* New York, 1950. $300.

Saber Exercises. Washington, D.C.: GPO, 1914. Wraps. (By George S. Patton, Jr.—p. 3 "Prepared by Second Lieutenant . . ."). $600.

SABIN, Edwin L. *Building the Pacific Railway.* Philadelphia, 1919. $100.

SABIN, Edwin L. *Kit Carson Days (1809–1868).* Chicago, 1914. Maps, plates. Brown cloth. $300. New York, 1935. 2 vols. Cloth. Revised edition. One of 1,000 copies. In slipcase. $400. One of 200 signed. $450.

SABIN, Edwin L. *Magic Mashie and Other Golf Stories.* New York, 1902. Decorative cloth. $600.

SACK and Destruction of the City of Columbia, S.C. Columbia, 1865. Wraps. (By William Gilmore Simms.) $5,000.

SACKS, Oliver. *Awakenings.* London, 1973. $200. Garden City, 1974. $75.

SACKVILLE-WEST, Edward. *Piano Quintet*. London, 1925. Author's first book. $250. New York, 1925. (English sheets.) $150.

SACKVILLE-WEST, Victoria. *All Passion Spent*. London, 1931. $500. New York, 1931. $250.

SACKVILLE-WEST, Victoria. *Chatterton*. Seven Oaks, 1909. Author's first book. Printed wraps. $6,000. Sevenoaks, 1909. Dark-blue boards with gilt lettering (2 known copies). No known dustwrapper. $7,500.

SACKVILLE-WEST, Victoria. *Constantinople*. London, 1915. Wraps. $750.

SACKVILLE-WEST, Victoria. *The Edwardians*. (London), 1930. One of 125 signed copies. Issued without dustwrapper. $600. Trade. With dustwrapper. $350. Garden City, 1930. $200.

SACKVILLE-WEST, Victoria. *The Garden*. London, 1946. One of 750 signed copies. Issued in plain paper dustwrapper. $600. Trade. Red boards with silver lettering on spine in decorated red dustwrapper lettered in black. $150. New York, 1946. Light-green boards printed in dark green. In yellow and green dustwrapper lettered in green and white. $100.

SACKVILLE-WEST, Victoria. *Heritage*. London (1919). Red cloth blindstamped on front. Spine printed in black. Dustwrapper gray printed in red. $750. New York (1919). Light-brown cloth printed on front and spine or with just a paper label on front. (Priority unknown.) In dustwrapper. $450.

SACKVILLE-WEST, Victoria. *Knole and the Sackvilles*. London, 1922. White boards and light-tan dustwrapper, both illustrated by William Nicholson. $750. New York, no date (1924?). Verso states "Printed in England." Tipped-in title page. Doran imprint at foot of spine. No colophon on copyright page. $500.

SACKVILLE-WEST, Victoria. *The Land*. London, 1926. One of 125 signed copies. In slip-case. $1,250. Trade edition. $400. New York, 1927. In printed dustwrapper. $300.

SACKVILLE-WEST, Victoria. *Nursery Rhymes*. London, 1947. One of 25 signed and numbered copies. Orange-red cloth with vellum parchment corners and spine. In white dustwrapper with gilt decoration (as on book), lettered in black on spine. $1,500. One of 525 copies. $300. London (1950). Trade. Yellow boards lettered in red. In white dustwrapper lettered and decorated in blue, red, and black. $150.

SACKVILLE-WEST, Victoria. *Orchard and Vineyard*. London, 1921. "To–" on verso of title. Light-blue boards with paper labels and cloth spine. Light-blue dustwrapper lettered in black. $400.

SACKVILLE-WEST, Victoria. *Sissinghurst*. London, 1931. One of 500 signed copies. Issued without dustwrapper. $750. Warlingham [1933]. One of 500 signed copies. "Second Edition." Flexible beige cloth without dustwrapper. $400. London, 1964. Wraps. $60.

SACKVILLE-WEST, Victoria. *Twelve Days*. London, 1928. $750. New York, 1928. $400.

SADLEIR, Michael. *The Evolution of Publishers' Binding Styles, 1770–1900*. London, 1930. One of 500 copies. $350.

SADLEIR, Michael. *Fanny by Gaslight*. London (1940). $150.

SADLEIR, Michael. *XIX Century Fiction: A Bibliographical Record*. London (1951). 2 vols. Illustrated. Cloth. One of 1,025 copies. $500. New York, 1969. Reprint. $350.

SAGE, Rufus B. *Scenes in the Rocky Mountains* . . . Philadelphia, 1847. Second edition. $1,500. (For first edition, see title entry.)

SAGE, Rufus B. *Wild Scenes in Kansas and Nebraska, the Rocky Mountains* . . . Philadelphia, 1855. Half leather. Third ("revised") edition (of *Scenes in the Rocky Mountains,* which see under title entry). $1,000.

SAINT-AUBIN DE TERAN, Lisa. *Keepers of the House.* London (1982). $200.

SAINT-AUBIN DE TERAN, Lisa. *The Streak.* London, 1980. Author's first book. One of 50 signed copies. Wraps. $350.

SAINT Bride Foundation Catalogue of the Technical Reference Library of Works on Printing . . . London, 1919. $500.

ST. CLAIR, Maj. Gen. (Arthur). *A Narrative of the Manner in Which the Campaign Against the Indians, in the Year 1791, Was Conducted.* Philadelphia, 1812. First edition, with errata. $1,250.

SAINT-EXUPÉRY, Antoine de. *Flight to Arras.* New York (1942). Illustrated by Bernard Lamotte. First American edition. $250. Also one of 500 copies signed by both. In slipcase. $1,250.

SAINT-EXUPÉRY, Antoine de. *Le Petit Prince.* New York (1943). One of 260 signed copies. Text in French. $8,500.

SAINT-EXUPÉRY, Antoine de. *The Little Prince.* London, 1943. $2,500. New York: Reynal & Hitchcock (1943). Translated from the French by Katherine Woods. Illustrated in color by the author. One of 525 signed copies. In dustwrapper. $5,000. Trade edition. In dustwrapper priced $2.00 with publisher's address as "386 Fourth Ave" on front flap. $1,750.

SAINT-EXUPÉRY, Antoine de. *Night-Flight.* Paris, 1932. Translated by Stuart Gilbert. Wraps. In cellophane dustwrapper. $500. London (1932). $600. New York (1932). $500.

SAINT-EXUPÉRY, Antoine de. *Wind, Sand and Stars.* New York (1939). Translated by Lewis Galentiere. First American edition. One of 500 signed copies. In slipcase. $1,250. Trade. $250.

ST. IRVYNE; or, The Rosicrucian: A Romance. London, 1811. By a Gentleman of the University of Oxford. (Percy Bysshe Shelley.) $10,000.

ST. RONAN'S Well. (By Sir Walter Scott.) Edinburgh, 1824. 3 vols. In original boards. $500.

SAISSY, Jean-Antoine. *An Essay on the Diseases of the Internal Ear.* Baltimore, 1829. Frontispiece sheep. First American edition. $500.

SAKI. See Munro, H. H.

SAKI. *Beasts and Super-Beasts.* London, 1914. (By H. H. Munro.) $200.

SAKI. *Reginald.* London (1904). (By H. H. Munro.) Red cloth. $250.

SAKI. *The Westminster Alice.* London, 1902. (By H. H. Munro.) Pale-green wraps. $400. Dark matte green wraps. $350. Pictorial cloth. $300.

SALAMAN and Absal: An Allegory. London, 1856. Translated from the Persian of Jami by Edward FitzGerald. Frontispiece. Blue cloth. $300.

SALAMANCA, J. R. *The Lost Country.* New York, 1958. $150.

SALE, Edith Tunis. *Manors of Virginia in Colonial Times.* Philadelphia, 1909. 49 plates. $300.

SALINGER, J. D. *The Catcher in the Rye.* Boston, 1951. Author's first book. First edition so stated. Bixby states the first-issue dustwrapper has a photograph of Salinger on the back panel, which was dropped on later printings, but we have seen later printings with the photo in a priced dustwrapper that was slightly taller than the first printing. Presumed earliest form of dustwrapper omits Book-of-the-Month Club slug, but we have never seen a copy without slug at the bottom of rear flap. $33,000 at auction in 2001. London (1951). $1,000.

SALINGER, J. D. *For Esmé—With Love and Squalor . . .* London (1953). $500. First U.K. edition of *Nine Stories.*

SALINGER, J. D. *Nine Stories.* Boston (1953). $2,000.

SALINGER, J. D. *Raise High the Roof Beam, Carpenters, and Seymour: An Introduction.* Boston (1963). Copyright dates are 1955 and 1959 but published in 1963. First issue contains no dedication page. $2,000. Second issue has dedication page before half title (in front of title page). $400. Third issue has dedication tipped in (or later bound in) after title page. $150. London (1963). $100.

SALLIS, James. *A Few Last Words.* New York (1970). $200.

SALMON, Richard. *Trout Flies.* New York, 1975. Fly-tying material tipped in. Full maroon leather. First edition, deluxe issue. One of 29 signed copies, with an original drawing by the author. In dustwrapper and slipcase. $2,000. Green cloth. One of 560 signed copies. In slipcase. $650.

SALPOINTE, John B. *A Brief Sketch of the Mission of San Xavier del Bac with a Description of Its Church.* San Francisco, 1880. 20 pages, wraps. $350.

SALPOINTE, John B. *Soldiers of the Cross.* Banning, Calif., 1898. Portrait. 45 plates. $250.

SALT, Henry. *A Voyage to Abyssinia . . .* London, 1814. Engraved vignette head and tailpieces, 27 engraved illustrations, 2 folding engraved maps (1 hand-colored), and 6 charts. $2,500.

SALT Lake City Directory and Business Guide (The). Salt Lake City, 1869. Folding map, folding view. 53–219 pages, as issued, boards. (By Edward L. Sloan.) $2,000.

SALTEN, Felix. *Bambi: A Life in the Woods.* New York, 1928. First edition in English. Illustrated by Kurt Wiese. Pictorial boards. In dustwrapper. In slipcase. $1,000.

SALTER, James. *The Hunters.* New York (1956). Author's first novel. $750.

SALTUS, Edgar. *Balzac.* Boston, 1884. Author's first book. $100.

SALZMANN, C. G. *Gymnastics for Youth.* London, 1800. Frontis and 9 plates. First English edition. [Translation attributed to Mary Wollstonecraft.] $1,500. Philadelphia, 1802. $1,250.

Samples. A Collection of Stories . . . New York (1927). Includes F. Scott Fitzgerald, et al. $600.

SAMPSON, Henry. *A History of Advertising from the Earliest Times.* London, 1874. $300.

SAN BERNARDINO County, California, Illustrated Description of. San Bernardino, 1881. 34 pages, printed wraps. $600.

SAN FRANCISCO Bay and California in 1776. Providence, 1911. Maps and facsimiles. 7 pages, boards. (By Pedro Font.) One of 125 copies. $750.

SAN FRANCISCO Board of Engineers: Report upon the City Grades. San Francisco, 1854. 27 pages, wraps. $400.

SAN FRANCISCO Directory for the Year 1852–53. San Francisco, 1852. Frontispiece, double-page map. Half leather. $6,000.

SANBORN, Franklin Benjamin. *Emancipation in the West Indies.* Concord, 1862. Author's first book. Wraps. $600.

SÁNCHEZ, Ricardo. *Hechizo Spells.* Los Angeles (1976). Issued without dustwrapper. $75. Wraps. $35.

SANDBURG, Carl. See Sandburg, Charles A.

SANDBURG, Carl. *Abraham Lincoln: The Prairie Years.* New York (1926). 2 vols., blue cloth. In dustwrapper. In slipcase. $400. 2 vols. Large-paper issue. One of 260 signed copies. Boards and cloth. First state, with line 9 on page 175 of vol. I reading "ears" instead of "eyes." (Estimated at 12 copies by Merle Johnson.) In dustwrapper. $1,500. Second state. $1,000.

SANDBURG, Carl. *Abraham Lincoln: The War Years.* New York (1939–41). 4 vols. Blue cloth. In plain white dustwrappers. In slipcase. $350. Large-paper issue: Brown buckram. One of 525 sets on all rag paper, signed. In dustwrapper. In slipcase. $1,500.

SANDBURG, Carl. *The American Songbag.* New York (1927). Red cloth. $350.

SANDBURG, Carl. *Chicago Poems.* New York, 1916. With ads at back dated "3'16." In dust-wrapper. $1,000. Without dustwrapper. $300.

SANDBURG, Carl. *The Chicago Race Riots.* New York, 1919. Printed wraps. $300. Cloth. $350.

SANDBURG, Carl. *Cornhuskers.* New York, 1918. First state with page 3 so numbered at foot of page. In dustwrapper. $750. Without dustwrapper. $250.

SANDBURG, Carl. *Early Moon.* New York (1930). $250.

SANDBURG, Carl. *Good Morning, America.* New York, 1928. $125. Limited issue. One of 811 signed copies. Issued without dustwrapper. $250.

SANDBURG, Carl. *Incidentals.* Galesburg (1907). The poet's first book, aside from the pamphlet *In Reckless Ecstasy.* Wraps. $4,500.

SANDBURG, Carl. *A Lincoln and Whitman Miscellany.* Chicago, 1938. One of 250 copies. $300.

SANDBURG, Carl. *Mary Lincoln, Wife and Widow.* New York (1932). $200. Large-paper issue. One of 260 signed copies. Issued without dustwrapper. $1,250.

SANDBURG, Carl. *Potato Face.* New York (1930). $250.

SANDBURG, Carl. *Remembrance Rock.* New York (1948). $125. 2 vols. Buckram. One of 1,000 signed copies. In glassine dustwrapper. In slipcase. $300.

SANDBURG, Carl. *Rootabaga Pigeons.* New York (1923). Illustrated. Pictorial cloth. $500.

SANDBURG, Carl. *Rootabaga Stories.* New York (1922). Illustrated by Maud and Miska Petersham. Pictorial cloth. $450.

SANDBURG, Carl. *Smoke and Steel.* New York, 1920. Green boards. In dustwrapper. $500. Without dustwrapper. $75.

SANDBURG, Carl. *Steichen the Photographer.* New York (1929). One of 925 copies signed by author and artist. Issued without dustwrapper. $2,500.

SANDBURG, Charles A. *In Reckless Ecstasy.* Galesburg, Ill., 1904. (By Carl Sandburg.) Author's first book. Wraps. $8,500.

SANDER, August. *Men Without Masks.* Greenwich (1973). $450.

SANDERS, Daniel C. *A History of the Indian Wars with the First Settlers of the United States.* Montpelier, Vt., 1812. $2,250.

SANDERS, Capt. John. *Memoir on the Military Resources of the Valley of the Ohio.* Pittsburgh, 1845. 19 pages, unbound. $350. Washington, 1845. 24 pages, unbound. $200.

SANDERSON, J. *An Ocean Cruise and Deep Water Regatta of the Pacific Yacht Club, July, 1884.* San Francisco, 1884. 8 inserted colored plates. $2,000.

SANDOZ, Mari. *The Beaver Men.* New York (1964). Illustrated. Half leather. One of 185 signed copies. $600. Trade edition. $100.

SANDOZ, Mari. *The Cattlemen.* New York (1958). $75. Advance presentation copy, signed. $175. Half cloth. One of 199 signed copies. In slipcase. $300.

SANDOZ, Mari. *Crazy Horse.* New York, 1942. $350.

SANDOZ, Mari. *Old Jules.* Boston, 1935. Author's first book. $125.

SANDOZ, Mari. *Old Jules Country.* New York, 1965. Folding map. Illustrated by Bryan Forsyth. Half leather. One of 250 signed and specially bound copies. $350. Trade edition. $100.

SANDOZ, Maurice. *On the Verge.* Garden City (1950). Illustrated in color by Salvador Dali. $125.

SANDS, Frank. *A Pastoral Prince: The History and Reminiscences of Joseph Wright Cooper.* Santa Barbara, 1893. Illustrated. Pictorial cloth. $850.

SANFORD, John. See Shapiro, Julian L.

SANFORD, John. *The Old Man's Place.* New York, 1935. 25 signed (later) and numbered copies. $200. Unsigned. $100.

SANSOM, Joseph. *Sketches of Lower Canada, Historical and Descriptive.* New York, 1817. Frontispiece view of Quebec. $400.

SANSOM, William. See *Fire Over London.*

SANSOM, William. *Fireman Flower.* London, 1944. $200.

SANTAYANA, George. See *Lines on Leaving the Bedford St. Schoolhouse.*

SANTAYANA, George. *Poems.* London (1922). One of 100 signed copies. $500.

SANTAYANA, George. *Sonnets and Other Verses.* Cambridge, Mass., 1894. One of 450 copies. $250. Limp vellum. One of 60 large-paper copies on vellum. $750.

SANTEE, Ross. *Babbling Springs.* New York, 1949. $200.

SANTEE, Ross. *Cowboy.* New York, 1928. $200.

SANTEE, Ross. *Hardrock & Silver Stage.* New York, 1949. $150.

SANTEE, Ross. *Men and Horses.* New York (1926). Author's first book. $250.

SANTLEBEN, August. *A Texas Pioneer.* New York, 1910. $500.

SAPPINGTON, John. *The Theory and Treatment of Fevers.* Arrow Rock, Mo., 1844. $450.

SARGENT, Charles Sprague. *The Silva of North America.* Boston, 1890–1902. 14 vols. Printed boards. $4,000.

SARGENT, George B. *Notes on Iowa.* Map. New York, 1848. 74 pages. $1,500.

SARGENT, John Singer. *John Singer Sargent.* New York, 1970. 152 plates. $150.

SAROYAN, William. See Hirschfeld, Al.

SAROYAN, William. *A Christmas Psalm.* Grabhorn Press. San Francisco (1935). In brown boards. (Also variant in rose boards, white cloth spine.) With greeting card and envelope, as issued, laid in. One of 200 signed copies. $500.

SAROYAN, William. *The Daring Young Man on The Flying Trapeze.* New York, 1934. Author's first book. $550. London (1935). First English edition. $250. (Covelo, 1984.) One of 220 copies. In slipcase. $300.

SAROYAN, William. *The Fiscal Hoboes.* New York, 1949. One of 250 signed copies. In green boards. Issued without dustwrapper. $350. Wraps. Also 250 copies, but assume not signed. $125.

SAROYAN, William. *Fragment.* (San Francisco, 1938.) Folio, wraps. One of 150 signed copies. $350.

SAROYAN, William. *Little Children.* New York (1937). $250.

SAROYAN, William. *My Name Is Aram.* New York (1940). "First" stated. $400.

SAROYAN, William. *A Native American.* San Francisco, 1938. One of 450 signed copies. Issued without dustwrapper. $250.

SAROYAN, William. *The Time of Your Life.* New York, 1939. $350.

SAROYAN, William. *Those Who Write Them and Those Who Collect Them.* Black Archer Press. Chicago, 1936. In pale-green calendered wraps with portrait of author on front. One of 50 copies. $450. Later reissued with same limitation statement, but in rough rose-colored wraps. $100.

SAROYAN, William. *Three Times Three.* Los Angeles (1936). One of 250 signed copies. $350.

SARRE, F. *Islamic Bookbindings.* London (no date) (circa 1923). One of 550 copies. 36 color plates. $1,250.

SARTON, George. *Introduction to the History of Science.* (Washington), 1927. 3 vols. In 5 parts. $750.

SARTON, May. *Encounter in April.* Boston, 1937. Author's first book. $500.

SARTON, May. *Inner Landscape.* Boston, 1939. $350. London, 1939. $200.

SARTOR Resartus. (London) 1834. (By Thomas Carlyle.) (Reprinted from *Fraser's Magazine.*) Wraps. $3,000. One of 58 copies privately printed for the author's friends. In full morocco, $5,000. London, 1838. In original boards and calf. First published English edition. $2,000. Doves Press. London, 1907. Vellum. One of 300 copies. $1,000. One of 15 copies on vellum. $5,000.

SARTRE, Jean-Paul. *No Exit & The Time Flies.* London, 1946. Author's first book. First English translation. $250. New York, 1947. $150.

SASSOON, Siegfried. See Kain, Saul; S., S. See also *Lingual Exercises for Advanced Vocabularians;* and *Poems.*

SASSOON, Siegfried. *Counter-Attack and Other Poems.* London, 1918. Wraps. $350. Cloth. $600. New York (1918). First American edition. $100.

SASSOON, Siegfried. *Emblems of Experience.* Cambridge, 1951. Wraps. One of 75 signed copies. $300.

SASSOON, Siegfried. *The Heart's Journey.* New York/London, 1927. Boards and parchment. One of 590 signed copies. $600. One of 9 copies on green paper. $1,500. London, 1928. Trade edition. $150. New York, 1929. First edition not stated. $125.

SASSOON, Siegfried. *MEMOIRS of an Infantry Officer.* London (1930). (By Siegfried Sassoon.) Blue cloth. First issue, with untrimmed edges. In dustwrapper. $350. Blue cloth. One of 750 signed copies. Issued without dustwrapper. $750. New York, 1930. $250. London, 1931. Illustrated by Barnett Freedman. Parchment (or vellum) boards. One of 320 signed copies. In dustwrapper. In slipcase. $1,000. One of 12 signed copies. $3,000. Trade edition. $200.

SASSOON, Siegfried. *The Old Huntsman and Other Poems.* London, 1917. With errata slip. In dustwrapper. $750. Without dustwrapper. $150. New York (1917). English sheets in dustwrapper. $600. Without dustwrapper. $150. New York (1918). In dustwrapper. $400. Without dustwrapper. $75.

SASSOON, Siegfried. *Picture Show.* (Cambridge) 1919. Boards. One of 200 copies. In plain dustwrapper. $750. Without dustwrapper. $600. New York (1920). $450.

SASSOON, Siegfried. *The Redeemer.* Cambridge, 1916. One of about 250 copies. Unnumbered leaves, an offprint from *Cambridge* magazine. $450.

SASSOON, Siegfried. *Satirical Poems.* London, 1926. $500. New York, 1926. $250.

SASSOON, Siegfried. *Sherston's Progress.* London, 1936. Buckram. One of 300 signed copies. $500. Trade. $150.

SASSOON, Siegfried. *To the Red Rose.* London, 1931. One of 400 signed copies. In green boards. Issued without dustwrapper. $250. Wraps. $75.

SASSOON, Siegfried. *War Poems.* London, 1919. In dustwrapper. $600.

SATANSTOE; or, The Littlepage Manuscripts. By the Author of *Miles Wallingford.* New York, 1845. (By James Fenimore Cooper.) 2 vols. Printed yellow wraps. First American edition. $1,500. London, 1845. 3 vols. Boards, paper label. $1,000. (Cooper's name appeared on the title page of this edition.)

SATTERLEE, M. P. *Massacre at the Redwood Indian Agency.* Minneapolis, 1916. Wraps. $400.

SATTERTHWAIT, Walter. *Miss Lizzie.* New York, 1989. $500.

SATTERTHWAIT, Walter. *Wall of Glass.* New York, 1987. First hardback book. $750.

SAUER, Martin. *An Account of a Geographical and Astronomical Expedition to the Northern Parts of Russia . . .* London, 1802. Folding map, 14 plates. $2,500.

SAUNDERS, Frederic. *The Author's Printing and Publishing Assistant . . .* New York, 1839. $300.

SAUNDERS, James E. *Early Settlers of Alabama.* Part 1. (All published.) New Orleans, 1899. $200.

SAUNDERS, Louise. *The Knave of Hearts.* New York, 1925. Illustrated in color by Maxfield Parrish. Pictorial cloth with pictorial plate mounted on cover. In plain buff dustwrapper. $2,500. Spiral-bound. $1,000.

SAUNDERS, Marshall. *Beautiful Joe: An Autobiography.* Philadelphia, 1894. (By Margaret Marsh Saunders.) Mottled olive cloth. First issue, with American Baptist Publication Society imprint. $450.

SAUVAN, Jean-Baptiste-Balthazar. *Picturesque Tour of the Seine, from Paris to the Sea.* London, 1821. Map, colored vignette title and tailpiece, 24 colored aquatint plates. $6,500. One of 50 copies on large paper. $10,000.

SAVAGE, Timothy. *The Amazonian Republic, Recently Discovered in the Interior of Peru.* New York, 1842. $400.

SAVAGE, William. *A Dictionary of the Art of Printing.* London, 1841. $400.

SAVAGE, William. *Practical Hints on Decorative Printing.* London, 1822. 60 plates and engravings. $8,500.

SAVAGE-LANDOR, A. Henry. *China and the Allies.* New York, 1901. Maps, numerous photographic illus. Cloth. $600.

SAVOY (The): An Illustrated Quarterly. London, 1896. Illustrations by Aubrey Beardsley. 8 parts. (All published.) Decorated boards and wraps. $3,500.

SAWYER, Charles J., and DARTON, F. J. Harvey. *English Books, 1475–1900: A Signpost for Collectors.* Westminister, 1927. 2 vols. One of 2,000 copies. $250.

SAWYER, Lorenzo. *Way Sketches* . . . New York, 1926. One of 385 copies. $350. Large-paper issue. Boards, parchment spine. One of 35 copies. In glassine dustwrapper. $500.

SAXTON, Charles. *The Oregonian; or History of the Oregon Territory.* Oregon City, 1846. No. 1 (all published). 48 pages, printed wraps. $2,500.

SAY, Jean-Baptiste. *A Treatise on Political Economy.* London, 1821. 2 vols. $1,750.

SAY, Thomas. *American Entomology.* Philadelphia, 1824–25, 1828. 3 vols. 18 hand-colored engraved plates. $4,500.

SAYERS, Dorothy L. *Catholic Tales and Christian Songs.* (Oxford, 1918.) Stiff wraps and dustwrapper. $350.

SAYERS, Dorothy L. *Clouds of Witness.* London (1926). $3,000. New York, 1927. $2,000.

SAYERS, Dorothy L. *Gaudy Night.* London, 1935. $1,250. New York (1936). $600.

SAYERS, Dorothy L. *Lord Peter Views the Body.* London, 1928. $2,500. New York (1929). $1,500.

SAYERS, Dorothy L. *In the Teeth of the Evidence.* London, 1939. $1,000. New York (1939). $600.

SAYERS, Dorothy L. *The Nine Tailors.* London, 1934. $1,750. New York (1934). $1,250.

SAYERS, Dorothy L. *Op. 1.* Oxford, 1916. Wraps. Author's first book. $1,000.

SAYERS, Dorothy L. *Unnatural Death.* London, 1927. $3,000. New York, 1928. $2,000.

SAYERS, Dorothy L. *The Unpleasantness at the Bellona Club.* London, 1928. $4,000. New York, 1928. $2,000.

SAYERS, Dorothy L. *Whose Body?* New York (1923). First issue, without "Inc." after Boni & Liveright on title. $5,000. London (1923). $3,500.

SAYERS, Dorothy L., and Byrne, M. St. Clare. *Busman's Honeymoon: A Detective Comedy.* London, 1937. $1,000. New York (1937). $750.

SAYERS, E. *A Treatise on the Culture of the Dahlia and Cactus.* Boston, 1839. $1,000.

SAYLES, John. *Pride of the Bimbos.* Boston, 1975. Author's first book. $300.

SAYLOR, Steven. *Roman Blood.* New York (1991). $1,250.

SCALE, Bernard. *An Hibernian Atlas.* London, 1776. 37 hand-colored maps. $2,500.

SCAMMON, Charles M. *The Marine Mammals of the North-Western Coast of North America* . . . San Francisco, 1874. 27 plates. $2,500.

SCARBOROUGH, Dorothy. See *The Wind.*

SCENES in the Rocky Mountains, Oregon, California, New Mexico, Texas and Grand Prairies. Philadelphia, 1846. By a New Englander (Rufus B. Sage). Folding map. Printed wraps. $10,000 at auction in 1999. Cloth. $5,000 for a worn copy at auction in 1999. (For later editions, see author.)

SCHAEFER, Jack. *Big Range.* Boston, 1953. $750.

SCHAEFER, Jack. *The Canyon.* Boston, 1953. $600.

SCHAEFER, Jack. *Monte Walsh.* Boston, 1963. $500. London, 1965. $250.

SCHAEFER, Jack. *Shane.* Boston, 1949. Author's first book. $6,000. Boston, 1954. First illustrated edition. $1,000. London, 1954. $750. London, 1963. With other stories. $100.

SCHAEFFER, L. M. *Sketches of Travels in South America, Mexico and California.* New York, 1860. $250.

SCHALDACH, William J. *Carl Rungius, Big Game Painter.* West Hartford (1945). Illustrated. One of 160 copies. $7,500. One of 1,275 copies. $1,500.

SCHALDACH, William J. (artist). *Fish by Schaldach.* Philadelphia, 1937. One of 157 signed copies. 60 full-page plates, 8 in color. Pictorial parchment. $1,250. One of 1,500 copies. Issued without dustwrapper. $300.

SCHARF, John Thomas. *History of the Confederate States Navy . . .* New York, 1887. 42 plates. $500. Albany, 1894. Second edition. $250.

SCHARF, John Thomas. *History of Delaware.* Philadelphia, 1888. 2 vols. Half morocco. $750.

SCHARF, John Thomas. *History of Maryland . . .* Baltimore, 1879. 3 vols. Folding charts and maps. Illustrated. Half leather. $600.

SCHARF, John Thomas. *History of Westchester County, New York.* Philadelphia, 1886. 2 vols. Illustrated. $450.

SCHARF, John Thomas. *History of Western Maryland.* Philadelphia, 1882. 2 vols. Map, 109 plates, table. Cloth. $500.

SCHARMAN, H(erman). B. *Scharman's Overland Journey to California.* [New York, 1918.] First edition in English. In original cloth. $750.

SCHARMANN, H. B. *Overland Journey to California . . .* New York, 1918. Portrait. First edition in English. One of 50 copies. $750.

SCHATZ, A. H. *Opening a Cow Country.* Ann Arbor, 1939. Plates, maps. Wraps. $250.

SCHLEY, Frank. *American Partridge and Pheasant Shooting.* Frederick, Md., 1877. $350.

SCHLOSSER, Leonard B., and MORRIS, Henry. *A Pair on Paper, Two Essays on Paper History and Related Matters.* North Hills, 1976. One of 220 copies. $300.

SCHNEIDER, Isidor. See S., I.

SCHOBERL, Frederick. *Picturesque Tour from Geneva to Milan by Way of the Simplon.* London, 1820. Plan and 36 color plates. $4,000.

SCHOEPF, Johann David. *Travels in the Confederation*. Philadelphia, 1911. 2 vols. Translated and edited by Alfred J. Morrison. Portrait, 2 facsimiles. First edition in English. $250.

SCHOMBURGK, Robert H. *The History of Barbados* . . . London, 1848. Map, 8 plates. Half calf. $1,750.

SCHOOLCRAFT, Henry R. *Algic Researches*. New York, 1839. 2 vols. In original cloth. $1,000.

SCHOOLCRAFT, Henry R. *Historical and Statistical Information Respecting the . . . Indian Tribes* . . . Philadelphia, 1851–57. 6 vols. Numerous maps, plates, and tables. Cloth. $10,000. (For reprint, see Schoolcraft, *Information Respecting the History, etc.*)

SCHOOLCRAFT, Henry R. *The Indian Tribes of the United States*. Philadelphia, 1884. 2 vols. Edited by Francis S. Drake. 100 plates. Buckram. $2,000. London, 1885. 2 vols. Cloth. $1,500. (A condensation from Schoolcraft.)

SCHOOLCRAFT, Henry R. *Information Respecting the History, Condition, and Prospects of the Indian Tribes of the United States*. Philadelphia, 1853–57. 6 vols. Illustrated. Cloth. Reprint of *Historical and Statistical Information* in a smaller format. $12,500.

SCHOOLCRAFT, Henry R. *Inquiries Respecting the History . . . of the Indian Tribes of the United States*. (Caption title.) (Washington, 1847.) Printed wraps. $1,500.

SCHOOLCRAFT, Henry R. *Journal of a Tour into the Interior of Missouri and Arkansaw*. London, 1821. Folding map. $750.

SCHOOLCRAFT, Henry R. *The Myth of Hiawatha, and Other Oral Legends*. Philadelphia, 1856. $400.

SCHOOLCRAFT, Henry R. *Narrative of an Expedition Through the Upper Mississippi to Itasca Lake* . . . New York, 1834. 5 maps (2 folding). $750.

SCHOOLCRAFT, Henry R. *Narrative Journal of Travels Through the Northwestern Regions of the U.S.* . . . Albany, 1821. Engraved title page, folding map, 7 plates. $850.

SCHOOLCRAFT, Henry R. *Notes on the Iroquois*. New York, 1846. $500. Albany, 1847. Enlarged edition. $450.

SCHOOLCRAFT, Henry R. *Personal Memoirs of a Residence of 30 Years with the Indian Tribes*. Philadelphia, 1851. Portrait (not in all copies). $1,000.

SCHOOLCRAFT, Henry R. *Travels in the Central Portions of the Mississippi Valley*. New York, 1825. 5 maps and plates. $1,000.

SCHOOLCRAFT, Henry R. *A View of the Lead Mines of Missouri*. New York, 1819. Author's first book. 3 plates. $1,500.

SCHOOLCRAFT, Henry R., and ALLEN, James. *Expedition to North-West Indians*. (Caption title.) (Washington, 1834.) Map. 68 pages. $500.

SCHREINER, Olive. See Iron, Ralph.

SCHREYVOGEL, Charles. *My Bunkie and Other Pictures of Western Frontier Life*. New York, 1909. 36 plates. Oblong pictorial boards. $1,500.

SCHULBERG, Budd. *What Makes Sammy Run?* New York (1941). Author's first book. $1,000.

SCHULTZ, Christian. *Travels on an Inland Voyage* . . . New York, 1810. 2 vols. bound in 1. Portrait, 2 plates, and 5 folding maps. $1,250.

SCHULTZ, James Willard. *Red Crow's Brother.* Boston, 1927. $450.

SCHULTZ, James Willard. *Sinopah the Indian Boy.* Boston, 1913. $150.

SCHULTZ, James Willard. *Skull Head the Terrible.* Boston, 1929. $350.

SCHUYLER, Eugene. *Turkistan.* New York, 1876. 2 vols. 3 maps (2 folding, 1 extending). $750.

SCHUYLER, James. *Salute.* New York (1960). Original silk-screen prints by Grace Hartigan. Folio, boards. One of 200 signed copies. In glassine dustwrapper. $1,500.

SCHUYLER, James (Marcus). *Alfred and Guinevere.* New York, 1953. $250.

SCHWARTZ, Delmore. *Genesis: Book One.* New Directions. (New York, 1943.) First edition not stated. $600.

SCHWARTZ, Delmore. *In Dreams Begin Responsibilities.* Norfolk, Conn. (1938). Author's first book. $750.

SCHWARTZ, Delmore. *Shenandoah.* Norfolk (1941). Boards. $350. Wraps. $200.

SCHWARTZ, Delmore. *The World Is a Wedding.* (Norfolk, 1948.) $175.

SCHWARTZ, Delmore (translator). *A Season in Hell.* Norfolk, Conn.: New Directions, 1939. Translation of the work of Arthur Rimbaud. One of 30 copies on Worthy Signature paper. Signed by the translator. In slipcase. $750. One of 750 copies. In slipcase. $150.

SCHWARZ, George. *Almost Forgotten Germany.* Majorca/London (1936). Translated by Robert Graves and Laura Riding. $1,250.

SCHWATKA, Frederick. *Report of a Military Reconnaissance in Alaska Made in 1883.* Washington, 1885. With 20 large folding maps. $350.

SCHWATKA, Frederick. *A Summer in Alaska.* St. Louis, 1893. $300.

SCHWERDT, C.F.G.R. *Hunting, Hawking, Shooting* . . . London, 1928–37. 4 vols. 382 plates, including many in color. Folio, in original full or half morocco. One of 300 signed copies. $6,000.

SCLATER, P. L., and HUDSON, W. H. *Argentine Ornithology.* London, 1888–89. 2 vols. 20 hand-colored plates. Blue-gray boards. One of 200 signed copies. $4,000. Trade edition. $2,500.

SCORESBY, William, Jr. *Journal of a Voyage to the Northern Whale-Fishery.* Edinburgh, 1823. 2 folding maps and 6 plates. $1,000.

SCOT, Reginald. *The Discoverie of Witchcraft.* London, 1584. $22,500 at auction in 2000. London, 1651. $10,000. London, 1665. $7,500. London, 1886. One of 250 copies. $1,500.

(London), 1930. Edited by Montague Summers. Cloth, or morocco and buckram. One of 1,275 copies. In dustwrapper. $750.

SCOTT, Anthony (David Dresser.) *Mardi Gras Madness.* New York, 1934. $500.

SCOTT, Duncan Campbell. *In the Village of Viger.* Boston, 1896. $350.

SCOTT, Evelyn. *On William Faulkner's "The Sound and the Fury."* (New York, 1929.) Wraps. $300.

SCOTT, Evelyn. *Precipitations.* New York, 1920. Author's first book. First issue, blue-green cloth with labels. $300. Second issue, red cloth (priority assumed). $250.

SCOTT, J. E. *A Bibliography of the Works of Sir Henry Rider Haggard.* Bishop's Stortford, 1947. One of 500 copies. $250.

SCOTT, James L. *A Journal of a Missionary Tour Through Pennsylvania . . .* Providence, 1843. $1,000.

SCOTT, John. See *Four Elegies.*

SCOTT, Major John. *Partisan Life With Col. John S. Mosby.* New York, 1867. Illustrations, folding map. $500.

SCOTT, Joseph. *The United States Gazetteer.* Philadelphia, 1785. Engraved title page and 19 engraved folding maps, errata leaf. $6,000.

SCOTT, Michael. See *Tom Cringle's Log.*

SCOTT, Paul. *"I Gerontius."* London [1941]. Author's first book. Wraps. $1,000.

SCOTT, Paul. *Johnnie Sahib.* London, 1952. $300.

SCOTT, Peter. *Morning Flight.* London, 1935. 16 color plates. One of 750 signed copies. In dustwrapper. $500.

SCOTT, Peter. *Wild Chorus.* London (1938). Illustrated by the author, including mounted color plates. Blue cloth. One of 1,250 signed copies. In dustwrapper. In slipcase. $600.

SCOTT, R. F. *Scott's Last Expedition.* London, 1913. 2 vols. 2 photo frontises, 6 sketches. Illustrated, including 18 folding maps and color plates. $850. New York, 1913. 2 vols. $600.

SCOTT, Captain Robert F. *The Voyage of the 'Discovery.'* London and New York, 1905. 2 vols. Photogravure frontispieces, 12 color plates, maps (2 folding). $1,250.

SCOTT, Sir Walter. See Clutterbuck, Captain. See also *Harold the Dauntless; Ivanhoe; Kenilworth; The Monastery; Redgauntlet; St. Ronan's Well;* and *Waverley.*

SCOTT, Sir Walter. *The Lady of the Lake.* London, 1810. Portrait. $600. Large-paper issue. $1,000.

SCOTT, William. *An Essay of Drapery or the Complete Citizen.* London, 1635. Engraved frontispiece. 12,500.

SCOTT, William Henry. *British Field Sports . . .* London, 1818. 34 steel engraved plates, including frontispiece, with wood engravings in text. $850.

SCOTT, Winfield Toynley. *Elegy for Robinson.* New York (1936). Author's first book. Wraps. $250.

SCOTT, Winfield. *Memoirs of Lieut. Gen. Scott.* New York, 1864. 2 vols. Portraits. $250.

SCRIPPS, J. L. *The Undeveloped Northern Portion of the American Continent.* Chicago, 1856. 20 pages, printed wraps. $500.

SCROPE, William. *The Art of Deer-Stalking.* London, 1838. 12 plates. In original wraps. $1,000.

SCROPE, William, *Days and Nights of Salmon Fishing in the Tweed.* London, 1843. 13 plates. Wraps. $1,000.

SEABURY, Samuel. *The Congress Canvassed.* (New York), 1774. $2,500.

SEALSFIELD, Charles. *The Cabin Book; or, Sketches of Life in Texas.* New York, 1844. (By Karl Posti.) 3 parts, printed wraps. First American edition. $1,500. London, 1852. First English edition. $450.

SEALSFIELD, Charles. *Life in the New World.* New York, 1844. $500.

SEARLE, Ronald. *Co-Operation in a University Town.* London (1939). (By W. Henry Brown.) Searle's first book illustrations. $500.

SEARLE, Ronald. *Forty Drawings.* Cambridge, 1946. $750.

SEARLE, Ronald. *Slightly Foxed—But Still Desirable.* London, 1989. One of 150 signed copies. $750. Trade edition. $75.

SEAVER, James E. *A Narrative of the Life of Mrs. Mary Jemison, Who Was Taken by the Indians in the Year 1755* . . . Canandaigua, N.Y., 1824. $3,500. Howden, 1826. First U.K. edition. $2,500.

SECONDTHOUGHTS, Solomon. *Quodlibet.* Philadelphia, 1840. (By John Pendleton Kennedy.) $450.

SEDGWICK, Catharine M. *The Linwoods; or "Sixty Years Since" in America.* New York, 1835. 2 vols. $250.

SEDGWICK, John. *Correspondence of John Sedgwick.* (New York), 1902–3. 2 vols. One of 300 copies. $450.

SEEBOHM, Henry. *A History of British Birds.* London, 1883–85. 4 vols. $1,000. London, 1896. 4 vols. Extended to 7. $1,000.

SEGARD, Sir W., and TESTARD, Francois Martin. *Picturesque Views of Public Edifices in Paris* . . . London, 1814. 40 pages, 20 plates. $850.

SELF-CONTROL. (Mary Brunton.) London, 1810. Author's first book. 3 volumes. $750.

SELKIRK (Thomas Douglas), Earl of. *A Narrative of Occurrences in the Indian Countries* . . . London, 1817. $1,500.

SELKIRK (Thomas Douglas), Earl of. *A Sketch of the British Fur Trade in North America.* London, 1816. $2,500.

SELTZER, Charles Alden. *The Range Rider.* New York, 1911. $250.

SELTZER, Charles Alden. *The Two-Gun Man.* New York, 1911. $250.

SENDAK, Maurice. *Atomics for the Millions.* New York (1947). By Edinoff & Ruchlis. (First book illustrated by Sendak.) (Statement on paper quality on copyright page omitted in later printings.) In dustwrapper priced $3.50 (on both flaps). $1,000.

SENDAK, Maurice. *The Happy Rain.* New York (1956). First edition not stated. Dustwrapper priced $2.50. With blurb on book on front flap. Back flap has illustrated blurb for the book followed by "60/80/Harper & Brothers." $750.

SENDAK, Maurice. *Kenny's Window.* (New York, 1956.) Author's first book. First edition not stated. Dustwrapper priced $2.00. $1,000.

SENDAK, Maurice. *The Sign on Rosie's Door.* New York (1960). First edition not stated. Pictorial cloth. Front dustwrapper flap priced $2.50, has blurb on this book, and "No. 9759A/50-80" at the bottom. Back flap has 4 paragraph write-up on Sendak with "No. 9760A" at bottom. $600.

SENDAK, Maurice. *Very Far Away.* New York (1957). First edition not stated. In dustwrapper priced 2.00 with blurb on book on front flap and ". . . 40-80/No. 7316A" at bottom; and 4 reviews of *Kenny's Window* on back flap with "No. 7317A" at bottom. $750.

SENDAK, Maurice. *Where the Wild Things Are.* (New York) 1963. First edition not stated. Dustwrapper priced $3.50 with 3-paragraph blurb on the book, "40-80/1163" at the bottom, and no mention of Caldecott award. $20,000 at auction in 2001. New York (1988). One of 220 signed copies. 25th Anniversary edition. Original ink sketch signed by Sendak laid in. In clamshell box. $2,500.

SENIOR Tabula. Oak Park, Ill., June, 1917. (Includes "Class Prophecy," by Ernest Hemingway.) Printed wraps. $1,500.

SENSE and Sensibility. London, 1811. By a Lady (Jane Austen). 3 vols. $40,000. London, 1813. Second edition. 3 vols. $8,500. London, 1833. Third edition. First 1-vol. edition. $5,000. Philadelphia, 1833. 2 vols. (Note: The ruled lines on the half title in vol. 1 are ⅕ inch in first and ⅖ inch in second edition, and ⅕ inch vs. ¹³⁄₁₀ inch in vol. 3 per Schwartz, in case someone switches them.) $2,500.

SERVICE, Robert W. *Rhymes of a Red Cross Man.* Toronto, 1916. $250. New York, 1916. Pictorial red cloth. $150.

SERVICE, Robert W. *Roughneck.* New York, 1913. $250.

SERVICE, Robert W. *Songs of a Sourdough.* Toronto, 1907. "Author's Edition" on title page. (Only 100 copies per author.) $3,000. Trade edition. Without "Author's Edition." $350.

SERVISS, Garrett P. *A Columbus of Space.* Illustrated. New York, 1911. $250.

SERVISS, Garrett P. *The Moon Metal.* New York, 1900. $200.

SETH, Vikram. *From Heaven Lake: Travels Through Sinkiang and Tibet.* London (1983). $250.

SETH, Vikram. *Mappings.* (Saratoga, California, 1980.) Author's first book. One of 150 signed copies. Wraps. $600.

SETH-SMITH, David. *Parrakeets.* London, 1903. 20 hand-colored plates. $1,750. London, 1926. 18 hand-colored and 2 color plates. $1,000.

SETON, Anya. *Dragonwyck.* Boston, 1944. $200.

SETON, Ernest Thompson. *Animal Heroes.* New York, 1905. $200.

SETON THOMPSON, Ernest. *The Birch-Bark Roll of the Woodcraft Indians.* New York, 1906. Illustrated. 71 pages, birchbark wraps. First separate edition (part of *How to Play Indian*). $600.

SETON THOMPSON, Ernest. *Boy Scouts of America: A Handbook of Woodcraft, Scouting, and Life-craft.* New York, 1910. Pictorial wraps. "Probable earlier state," with printer's slug on copyright page (VAB). $500. Cloth. $400.

SETON, Ernest Thompson. *How to Play Indian.* Philadelphia, 1903. $600. This book was reissued under many titles and eventually became *Boy Scouts of America* . . .

SETON, Ernest Thompson. *Life Histories of Northern Animals.* New York, 1909. 2 vols. $600. London, 1910. 2 vols. $500.

SETON, Ernest Thompson. *A List of the Mammals of Manitoba.* Toronto (1886). Author's first book. Wraps. $3,000.

SETON, Ernest Thompson. *Studies in the Art Anatomy of Animals.* London, 1896. $850.

SETON, Ernest Thompson. *Wild Animals I Have Known.* New York, 1898. 20 drawings by author. Pictorial cloth. First issue, without the words "The Angel whispered don't go" in the last paragraph on page 265. $350. London (1898). First English edition. $300.

SETTLE, Mary Lee. *The Kiss of Kin.* London (1955). $300. New York (1955). Code on copyright page "G-E." First edition not stated. $250.

SETTLE, Mary Lee. *The Love Eaters.* London (1954). Author's first book. $350. New York (1954). (First edition not stated.) $250.

SEUSS, Dr. *And to Think That I Saw It on Mulberry Street.* New York, 1937. (By Theodore Geisel.) Author's first book for children. First edition not stated. Illustrated in color by the author. Pictorial boards. $3,500.

SEUSS, Dr. *The Cat in the Hat.* New York, 1957. (By Theodore Geisel.) "200/200" price on front inner flap of dustwrapper. First edition not stated. In unglazed boards. $7,500.

SEUSS, Dr. *The 500 Hats of Bartholomew Cubbins.* New York, 1938. (By Theodore Geisel.) Illustrated by the author. First edition not stated. 1.50 on front inner flap of dustwrapper. Other points not available. $2,000.

SEUSS, Dr. *Green Eggs and Ham.* New York, 1960. (By Theodore Geisel.) First edition not stated. $1,250.

SEUSS, Dr. *Horton Hatches the Egg.* New York, 1940. (By Theodore Geisel.) First edition stated. Dustwrapper priced 250/250 and Horton's Ear is complete on back interfering with blurbs. $1,000.

SEUSS, Dr. *How the Grinch Stole Christmas!* New York (1957). (By Theodore Geisel.) Pictorial boards. 250/250 on front inner flap of dustwrapper and 14 titles listed on back flap. First edition not stated. $2,500.

SEUSS, Dr. *The King's Stilts.* New York, 1939. (By Theodore Geisel.) First edition not stated. Other points not available. $1,500.

SEUSS, Dr. *The Seven Lady Godivas.* New York (1939). (By Theodore Geisel.) First edition stated. Color illustrations. Pictorial cloth. $1,000. New York (1987). One of 300 signed copies. In slipcase. $1,000.

SEVEN Pillars of Wisdom (The). George H. Doran. New York, 1926. (By T. E. Lawrence.) Specimen sheets. In half red buckram. First American (copyright) edition, with author's name accidentally omitted from title page. One of 24 copies (stated 22), signed by the publisher, of which 10 were offered for sale. $30,000. (For first edition, see Lawrence.)

1796–1896, One Hundred Years, MacKellar, Smiths and Jordan Foundry. Philadelphia (1896). $300.

SEVENTY-FIVE Receipts, for Pastrie, Cakes and Sweetmeats. New York/Boston, 1828. By a Lady of Philadelphia [Eliza Leslie]. January copyright date. $4,000.

SEVENTY-SIX . . . (A Novel). Baltimore, 1823. 2 vols. (By John Neal.) $450.

SEVERN, Walter. *The Golden Calendar . . .* London (1865). Paper overlays on cloth cover. $600.

SEWARD, W. H. *Communication upon the Subject of an Intercontinental Telegraph, etc.* Washington, 1864. Folding map. 52 pages, wraps. $2,000.

SEWELL, Anna. *Black Beauty.* London (1877). Blue, red, or green pictorial cloth. With horse's head looking right, but see Carter's *More Binding Variants* for more details. $7,500. Boston (1890). First American edition. Orange printed wraps or buff boards. $1,000. London, 1915. Illustrated in color by Lucy Kemp-Welch. Cloth. One of 450 signed copies. $750. Trade. $100.

SEXAGENARIAN (The); Or, The Recollections of a Literary Life. London, 1817. 2 vols. $275.

SEXTON, Anne. *All My Pretty Ones.* Boston, 1962. $250.

SEXTON, Anne. *To Bedlam and Part Way Back.* Boston, 1960. Author's first book. $400.

SEYD, Ernest. *California and Its Resources . . .* London, 1858. 18 plates (some tinted), 2 folding maps. $1,500.

SEYMOUR, E. S. *Emigrant's Guide to the Gold Mines of Upper California.* Chicago, 1849. Folding map. 104 pages. Wraps. $5,000.

SEYMOUR, E. S. *Sketches of Minnesota.* New York, 1850. Printed wraps. $400. Cloth. $350.

SEYMOUR, Silas. *A Reminiscence of the Union Pacific Railroad.* Quebec, 1873. Plates. Printed wraps. $600.

SEYMOUR, W. D. *The Isthmian Routes.* New York, 1863. 27 pages, sewn. $250.

SEYMOUR. William N. *Madison Directory and Business Advertiser.* Madison, Wis., 1855. Map. Leather. $500.

SHAARA, Michael. *The Killer Angels.* New York, 1974. $3,000.

SHACKLEFORD, Otis M. *Lillian Simmons.* Kansas City (1915). Pictorial boards. $1,000.

SHACKLETON, E. H. *The Heart of the Antarctic.* London, 1909. 2 vols. Illustrated, including color plates and folding maps. $1,000. Limited issue. 3 vols. Signed by all in the Shore party. One of 300 copies. $10,000. Philadelphia, 1909. 2 vols. $850.

SHAFFER, Ellen. *The Garden of Health* . . . Book Club of California. (San Francisco, 1957.) Folio, boards and linen. One of 300 copies, with a leaf from the 1499 *Hortus Sanitates.* In dust-wrapper. $350.

SHAFFER, Ellen. *The Nuremberg Chronicle* . . . *A Monograph.* Plantin Press. Los Angeles, 1950. Illustrated. 61 pages, pictorial cloth. One of 300 copies with an original leaf from *The Chronicle* (1497). $600.

SHAHN, Ben. See Berry, Wendell.

SHAHN, Ben (illustrator). *The Alphabet of Creation* . . . New York (1954). Signed frontispiece, other illustrations. One of 50 signed copies with an original drawing. In slipcase. $2,500. One of 500 signed copies. In slipcase. Trade. $75.

SHAHN, Ben. *Haggadah for Passover.* London, 1966. One of 292 copies with signed color lithograph, color collotype illustrations, and calligraphy by Shahn. $3,000. Paris, 1966. Folio, unsewn sheets, wrappers, enclosed in a parchment-covered box with metal clasp. One of 228 copies, frontispiece signed by Shahn. $3,000. New York (1970). Large oblong folio. 26 lettered copies (of 240). $1,500. One of 214 copies. $750.

SHAHN, Ben. *Hallelujah.* New York (1970). 24 original color lithographs, all of which are double-page. One of 240 copies (of 250). In publisher's folding box. $1,250.

SHAHN, Ben. *Love and Joy About Letters.* New York, 1963. Slipcase. $200.

SHAHN, Bernarda Bryson. *Ben Shahn.* New York (1972). Oblong folio. Red linen. In color dustjacket. $400.

SHAKESPEARE, William. *Comedies, Histories and Tragedies.* [See specific bibliographies for all points on first four folios.] London, 1623. First folio. $400,000. London, 1632. Second folio. $150,000. London, 1664. Third folio. $150,000. London, 1685. Fourth folio. First state of imprint without Chiswell's name. $75,000. Oxford, 1901 (1902). Introduction by Sidney Lee. Facsimile from the first folio edition. Folio, cloth. One of 1,000 signed copies. $750. Limited Editions Club, New York, 1939–40. 37 vols. $2,250.

SHAKESPEARE, William. *Julius Caesar.* London, 1913. Doves Press. Vellum. One of 200 copies. $2,000. One of 15 copies on vellum. $7,500. Grabhorn Press. San Francisco, 1954. Illustrated by Mary Grabhorn. Folio, half leather. One of 180 copies. $300.

SHAKESPEARE, William. *Macbeth.* Grabhorn Press. (San Francisco, 1952.) Illustrations in color by Mary Grabhorn. Boards, leather spine. One of 180 copies. In slipcase. $400.

SHAKESPEARE, William. *The Merry Wives of Windsor.* London, 1910. Illustrated by Hugh Thomson. Pictorial vellum, silk ties. One of 350 copies signed by the artist. $750. Trade. $250.

SHAKESPEARE, William. *A Midsummer Night's Dream.* London, 1908. Illustrated by Arthur Rackham. Full white vellum with ties. One of 1,000 copies signed by Rackham. $4,000.

Trade. Gold-stamped cloth. $750. London, 1914. One of 250 copies signed by W. Heath Robinson. $1,750. Trade. $500. Grabhorn Pre San Francisco, 1955. Illustrated in color by Mary Grabhorn. Parchment. One of 180 copies. In slipcase. $750.

SHAKESPEARE. William. *Othello.* Grabhorn Press. San Francisco, 1956. Portraits in color by Mary Grabhorn. Boards, leather spine. One of 185 copies. $400.

SHAKESPEARE, William. *Poems and Sonnets.* Golden Cockerel Press. London, 1960. Morocco. One of 100 copies. $750. Buckram. One of 470 copies. $350. Limited Editions Club, New York, 1941. 2 vols. In slipcase. $300.

SHAKESPEARE, William. *The Poems of William Shakespeare.* Boston, 1807. $2,000. Kelmscott Press. London, 1893. Edited by F. S. Ellis. Limp vellum with ties. One of 500 copies. $2,000. One of 10 copies on vellum. $12,500.

SHAKESPEARE, William. *Sonnets.* London, 1909. Doves Press. Vellum. One of 250 copies. $1,500. One of 15 copies on vellum. $8,500.

SHAKESPEARE, William. *The Tempest.* London, 1908. 40 color plates by Edmund Dulac. Vellum with ties. One of 500 copies signed by Dulac. $2,000. Cloth. $350. Montagnola, Italy, 1923 (actually 1924). Green vellum. One of 230 copies. $1,500. London (1926). Vellum. 21 color plates by Rackham. One of 520 copies signed by Rackham. In dustwrapper. $2,000. Trade edition. Cloth. In dustwrapper. $750. San Francisco, 1951. Grabhorn Press. Illustrated by Mary Grabhorn. Half cloth. One of 160 copies. $300.

SHAKESPEARE, William. *The Tempest and Two Gentleman of Verona.* London, 1623. A complete extract of the first two plays from the First Folio. First appearance in print of each play. $25,000.

SHAKESPEARE, William. *Venus and Adonis.* Doves Press. London, 1912. Vellum. One of 200 copies. $1,500. One of 15 copies on vellum. $7,500.

SHAKESPEARE, William. *The Works of Shakespear.* London [1723]–1725. 6 vols. plus supplemental vol. First quarto edition, edited by Alexander Pope. 750 sets. $6,000.

SHANGE, Ntozake. *For Colored Girls Who Have Considered Suicide . . .* (San Lorenzo, 1975.) Author's first book. Wraps. First issue, name spelled Ntosake; $.95 cover price. $250. New York (1977). $100.

SHAPIRO, Julian L. *The Water Wheel.* Ithaca (1933). Author's first book. $2,000.

SHAPIRO, Karl. *Poems.* Baltimore, 1935. Cloth. Author's first book. One of 200 signed copies. $500.

SHAPIRO, Karl. *Trial of a Poet.* New York (1947). One of 250 signed copies. In tissue dustwrapper. In slipcase. $250. Trade edition. $75.

SHAPIRO, Karl. *V-letter and Other Poems.* New York (1944). $150.

SHARP, William. See MacLeod, Fiona.

SHARP, William. *The Human Inheritance, The New Hope, Motherhood.* London, 1882. Author's first book. $250.

SHARPE, Tom. *Riotus Assembly.* London (1971). Author's first book. $250. New York, 1973. $100.

SHAW, Edward. *The Modern Architect.* Boston, 1855. 65 plates. $750.

SHAW, Fred G. *The Complete Science of Fly Fishing and Spinning.* New York, 1914. 152 illustrations. $150. London, 1920. $75.

SHAW, George Bernard. See *This Is the Preachment on Going to Church.*

SHAW, George Bernard. *Androcles and the Lion.* London, 1913. Printed wraps. First edition, with title page reading: "Rough Proof—Unpublished." One of 50 privately printed copies. $750. London, 1916. Cloth. (With *Overruled and Pygmalion* added to title.) $100.

SHAW, George Bernard. *Back to Methuselah: A Metabiological Pentateuch.* London, 1921. Light gray-green cloth. $400. Limited Editions Club, New York, 1939. In slipcase. $125.

SHAW, George Bernard. *Cashel Byron's Profession.* (London), 1886. Printed blue wraps 24.8 x 15.4 cm. $2,000. 22.9 x 14 cm to 23.6 x 14.9 cm. $1,500. New York (1886). Seaside Library. Wraps. (Unauthorized.) $600. Chicago, 1901. Pictorial cloth. First American edition. $200.

SHAW, George Bernard. *How to Settle the Irish Question.* Dublin (1917). Blue printed wraps. $200. Second issue. Green wraps. $125.

SHAW, George Bernard. *The Intelligent Woman's Guide to Socialism and Capitalism.* London, 1928. Green cloth. With "were" for "was" page 442 line 5. $400. New York, 1928. $250.

SHAW, George Bernard. *Love Among the Artists.* Chicago, 1900. Green cloth. First authorized edition. $350.

SHAW, George Bernard. *Man and Superman.* Westminster (London), 1903. $400. Limited Editions Club, New York, 1962. 2 vols. Pictorial cloth and wraps. In slipcase. $125.

SHAW, George Bernard. *Nine Answers.* No place (1923). Green boards. One of 62 copies privately printed by Jerome Kern. $750. One of 150 copies. $300.

SHAW, George Bernard. *Plays: Pleasant and Unpleasant.* London, 1898. 2 vols. Portrait. Green cloth. $350. Chicago, 1898. 2 vols. First American edition. $250.

SHAW, George Bernard. *Pygmalion: A Romance in Five Acts.* London, 1912. Printed wraps. First issue, with title page reading: "Rough Proof, Unpublished." $1,250. Three other "proofs" in 1913 and 1914. $750. New York (1914). Extract from *Everybody's Magazine.* In cloth. $350.

SHAW, George Bernard. *Saint Joan: A Chronicle Play.* London, 1924. First published edition. $350. London (1924). Illustrated by Charles Ricketts. Folio, boards and cloth. First illustrated edition. One of 750 copies. In dustwrapper. $1,000.

SHAW, George Bernard. *Shaw Gives Himself Away: An Autobiographical Miscellany.* Gregynog Press. Newtown, Wales, 1939. Frontispiece woodcut portrait. Dark-green morocco, inlaid with red leather. With original crayon caricature of Shaw by Paul Nash. One of 250 copies. $1,250. One of 25 specially bound copies. $2,500.

SHAW, George Bernard. *An Unsocial Socialist.* London, 1887. Scarlet cloth. First edition, first state, with title of Shaw's first novel incorrectly given on title page as "The Confessions of Byrn Cashel's . . ." and with publisher's name spelled wrong on spine. $2,000. Second state, with novel's title corrected and with publisher's name on spine stamped over. $1,500.

SHAW, George Bernard. *War Issues for Irishmen: An Open Letter to Col. Arthur Lynch from Bernard Shaw.* Dublin, 1918. Gray wraps. (Supressed.) $1,500.

SHAW, George Bernard. *Widowers' House.* London, 1893. $1,250.

SHAW, Henry. *The Decorative Arts, Ecclesiastical and Civil, of the Middle Ages.* London, 1851. 41 engravings, 18 in color. Half leather. $750.

SHAW, Henry. *Dresses and Decorations of the Middle Ages.* London, 1843. 2 vols. Hand-colored plates and other illustrations. Folio, boards. $2,000.

SHAW, Henry. *Examples of Ornamental Metal Work.* London, 1836. 50 plates. $1,000.

SHAW, H(enry). *The History and Antiquities of the Chapel . . .* London 1829. Author's first book. 19 plates. $1,000.

SHAW, Henry. *Illuminated Ornaments Selected from Manuscripts and Early Printed Books from the Sixth to the Seventh Centuries . . .* London, 1833. Small folio. Chromolithographic title page. Large-paper copy. $2,000.

SHAW, Irwin. *Bury the Dead.* New York (1936). Author's first book. $300.

SHAW, Irwin. *The Gentle People.* New York (1939). $300.

SHAW, Irwin. *Sailor Off the Bremen.* New York, 1939. $400.

SHAW, Irwin. *The Young Lions.* New York (1948). $350. Also special numbered copies for booksellers issued in acetate dustwrapper. $300.

SHAW, R. C. *Across the Plains in Forty-nine.* Farmland, Ind., 1896. $450.

SHAW, Richard Norman. *Architectural Sketches from the Continent.* London [1858]. $750. London, 1872. $650.

SHAW, Robert. *Visits to High Tartary . . .* London, 1871. 2 folding maps, 7 tinted plates. $1,250.

SHAW, T. E. (adopted name). See Homer; Lawrence, T. E.

SHAW, Thomas George. *Wine, the Vine, and the Cellar.* London, 1863. Folding frontispiece. $485.

SHAY, Frank (editor). *Iron Men and Wooden Ships.* Garden City, 1924. Introduction by William McFee. Illustrated by Edward A. Wilson. One of 200 copies with a lithograph signed by Wilson. $300.

SHEA, John Gilmary. *Discovery and Exploration of the Mississippi Valley . . .* Clinton Hall, 1852. Folding map. $300.

SHEA, John Gilmary. *Early Voyages Up and Down the Mississippi . . .* Albany, N.Y., 1861. $125. One of 100 copies. Boards or wraps. $300.

SHEA, John Gilmary. *A History of the Catholic Church Within . . . the United States.* New York, 1886–92. 4 vols. Illustrated. $300.

SHEARMAN, Montague. *Athletics and Football.* London, 1887. One of 250 copies. $350.

SHELLEY, Donald A. *The Fraktur Writings of Illuminated Manuscripts of the Pennsylvania Germans.* (Allentown, 1961.) $125.

SHELLEY, G. E. *A Handbook to the Birds of Egypt.* London, 1872. Large octavo. 14 hand-colored plates. One of 125 copies signed by Valenti Angelo (artist). $1,000.

SHELLEY, Mary W. See *Falkner; The Fortunes of Perkin Warbeck; Frankenstein; History of a Six Weeks Tour . . . ; The Last Man; Mounseer Nontongpaw . . . ; Valperga.*

SHELLEY, Percy Bysshe. See S., P.B. See also *Epipsychidion; History of a Six Weeks' Tour, etc . . . ; St. Irvyne.*

SHELLEY, Percy Bysshe. *Adonais: An Elegy on the Death of John Keats.* Pisa, Italy, 1821. 25 pages, in original blue ornamental wraps. $50,000. Rebound copies. $5,000. Cambridge (London), 1829. In original green wraps. Second (first English) edition. $2,500.

SHELLEY, Percy Bysshe. *Alastor: or, The Spirit of Solitude: and Other Poems.* London, 1816. $3,500.

SHELLEY, Percy Bysshe. *The Cenci.* (Leghorn) Italy, 1819. (250 copies.) $6,000. London, 1821. First English edition. $1,250.

SHELLEY, Percy Bysshe. *The Complete Works of Percy Bysshe Shelley.* London, 1926–27. 10 vols. Cloth, vellum spines. One of 780 copies. In slipcase. $2,000.

SHELLEY, Percy Bysshe. *Hellas: A Lyrical Drama.* London, 1822. $3,500.

SHELLEY, Percy Bysshe. *Laon and Cythna.* London, 1818. First issue, with 4-line quotation from Pindar on half title. $8,500. Second issue, same date, without Pindar lines. $6,500.

SHELLEY, Percy Bysshe. *Letters of Percy Bysshe Shelley.* London, 1852. With an Introductory Essay by Robert Browning. Dark-red cloth. (Suppressed as forgeries.) $1,000.

SHELLEY, Percy Bysshe. *The Masque of Anarchy: A Poem.* London, 1832. Preface by Leigh Hunt. In original gray-blue boards. With white spine label lettered vertically "Shelley's Masque." $2,000.

SHELLEY, Percy Bysshe. *Poems. (Poetical Works.)* Kelmscott Press. (Hammersmith, 1894–95). 3 vols. Vellum. (250 copies.) $3,000. One of 6 copies on vellum. $10,000. (London, 1901–2.) Vale Press. 3 vols. (310 copies.) Decorations by Charles Ricketts. White buckram. $1,000. London, 1914. Doves Press. Limp vellum. One of 200 copies. $1,500. One of 12 copies on vellum. $7,500. Limited Editions Club, New York, 1971. In slipcase. $125.

SHELLEY, Percy Bysshe. *Posthumous Poems.* London (1824). First issue, without errata leaf. $2,500.

SHELLEY, Percy Bysshe. *Prometheus Unbound.* London, 1820. First issue, with "Miscellaneous" misprinted "Misellaneous" in table of contents. $2,750. Second issue, with misprint corrected. $2,000. Essex House Press, London, 1904. Morocco. One of 20 copies on vellum. $3,000. Limp vellum. One of 200 copies on paper. $750.

SHELLEY, Percy Bysshe. *Queen Mab: A Philosophical Poem.* London, 1813. First (privately printed) edition. Shelley removed the title, dedication, and imprint from many copies. Unmutilated copy. $17,500. Mutilated copy. $2,500. London, 1821. Second (first published) edition. $1,250.

SHELLEY, Percy Bysshe. *Rosalind and Helen.* London, 1819. With 2 ad leaves at end. $6,000.

SHEPARD, Sam. *Five Plays.* Indianapolis (1967). $250. Wraps. $50. London (1969). $150.

SHEPARD, Sam. *Hawk Moon.* Los Angeles, 1973. 26 signed and lettered copies. $650. One of 200 copies. $350.

SHEPERD, Mr. Thomas. *Metropolitan Improvements.* London, 1829. 2 vols. $2,500.

SHEPPARD, Elizabeth Sara. See *Charles Auchester.*

SHEPPARD Lee. New York, 1836. Written by Himself. (By Robert Montgomery Bird.) 2 vols. $750.

SHERATON, Thomas. *The Cabinet Dictionary . . .* London, 1803. 87 plates. $2,500.

SHERATON, Thomas. *The Cabinet Maker and Upholsterer's Drawing Book.* London, 1793. $6,000.

SHERIDAN, Philip H. *Outline Descriptions of the Posts in the Military Division of the Missouri, etc.* Chicago, 1872. Maps, including a folding map. $3,000.

SHERIDAN, Philip H. *Record of Engagements with Hostile Indians Within the Military Division . . .* Chicago, 1882. $750.

SHERIDAN, Richard Brinsley. See *The Love Epistles . . .*

SHERIDAN, Richard Brinsley. *The Critic . . .* London, 1781. (Half title indicates second through sixth editions.) $1,000.

SHERIDAN, Richard Brinsley. *Pizarro.* London, 1799. $300.

SHERRINGTON, Charles. *The Integrative Action of the Nervous System.* London, 1906. $2,500. New York, 1906. $2,250.

SHERWOOD, J. Ely. *California: Her Wealth and Resources . . .* New York, 1848. 40 pages, wraps. $8,500.

SHERWOOD, Robert E(mmet). *Barnum Was Right.* Cambridge, 1920. Author's first book. Stiff wraps. $300.

SHERWOOD, Robert. *The Petrified Forest.* New York, 1935. $500.

SHIEL, M. P. *Children of the Wind.* London, 1923. $1,000.

SHIEL, M. P. *The Dragon.* London (1913). $300.

SHIEL, M. P. *The Last Miracle.* London, 1906. Pictorial black cloth. $150.

SHIEL, M. P. *Prince Zaleski.* London, 1895. Author's first book. Decorated purple cloth. First edition with 2 ad catalogues (16 pages) at back. $1,250. Boston, 1895. $300.

SHIEL, M. P. *The Purple Cloud.* London, 1929. One of 105 signed copies. Issued without dust-wrapper. $600.

SHIEL, M. P. *Shapes in the Fire*. London, 1896. $600. Boston, 1896. $500.

SHIELDS, Carol. *Others*. Ottawa, 1972. Author's first book. $350.

SHIELDS, Carol. *Small Ceremonies*. Toronto, 1976. (First edition.) $350.

SHIELDS, G. O. *The Battle of the Big Hole*. Chicago/New York, 1889. 8 plates. $600.

SHIELDS, G. O. *Cruising in the Cascades*. Chicago/New York, 1889. $300.

SHILLIBEER, Lieut. J. *A Narrative of the Briton's Voyage to Pitcairn's Island* . . . Taunton, 1817. 12 plates. With errata leaf and instructions to the binder. $3,500. London, 1817. 11 plates. Second edition. $1,750. London, 1818. 12 plates. Half calf. Third edition. $1,000.

SHINN, Charles Howard. *Graphic Description of Pacific Coast Outlaws*. (Caption title.) (San Francisco, about 1890–95.) Portrait. 32 pages, wraps. $1,000.

SHINN, Charles Howard. *Mining Camps*. New York, 1885. $600.

SHINN, Charles Howard. *Pacific Rural Handbook*. San Francisco, 1879. $350.

SHINTON, William Edward. *Lectures on an Improved System of Teaching the Art of Writing*. London, 1823. 13 engraved plates. $350.

SHIPLEY, Conway. *Sketches in the Pacific*. London, 1851. Litho title and 25 tinted plates. Folio, cloth. $11,000 at auction in 1996.

SHIPMAN, Mrs. O. L. *Taming the Big Bend*. (Marfa, Tex., 1926.) Folding map, 4 plates. $500.

SHOLOKHOV, Mikhair. *And Quiet Flows the Don*. London (1934). Author's first book. (First English translation.) $250.

SHONE, Patric. *The House in the Valley*. London (1951). (By James Hanley.) $500.

SHORT, Luke. *Ambush*. Boston, 1950. (Pseudonym of Frederick D. Glidden). $150.

SHORT, Luke. *Hard Money*. New York, 1940. (Pseudonym of Frederick D. Glidden). $200.

SHORT, Luke. *Raiders of the Rimrock*. New York, 1939. (Pseudonym of Frederick D. Gliddon.) $250.

SHORT Account of the Life and Work of Wynkyn de Worde . . . *(A)*. San Francisco, 1949. One of 375 copies. Includes an original leaf from the Golden Legend. $600.

SHORTER, Alfred H. *Paper Mills and Paper Makers in England, 1495–1800*. Hilversum, 1957. One of 600 copies. $750.

SHORTHOUSE, J. Henry. *John Inglesant*. Birmingham (England). 1880. Author's first book. 3 vols. $750. Also 1 vol. $350. London, 1881. 2 vols. $350. London, 1881. 2 vols. $150.

SHULMAN, Neil. *Finally* . . . *I'm A Doctor*. New York (1976). Author's first book. Ghostwritten by Carl Hiaasen. $200.

SHUTE, Henry A. *The Real Diary of a Real Boy*. Boston, 1902. $150.

SHUTE, Nevil. *Marazan.* London, 1926. Author's first book. $2,000.

SHUTE, Nevil. *On the Beach.* London (1957). $500. New York (1957). $300.

SIDNEY Lawton Smith, Designer, Etcher, Engraver . . . Boston, 1931. One of 200 copies. $400.

SIDNEY, Margaret. *Five Little Peppers and How They Grew.* (By Harriet M. S. Lathrop, her first book.) Boston (1880). Green, blue, or brown pictorial cloth. First state, with 1880 copyright and with caption on page 231 reading ". . . said Polly." $750.

SIDNEY, Philip. *A Woorke Concerning the Trewnesse of the Christian Religion* . . . London, 1587. Author's first book. Translation of Philippe de Mornay. $1,250.

SIEBERT, Wilbur Henry. *Loyalists in East Florida.* DeLand, Fla., 1929. 2 vols. 6 maps and plates. Buckram. Issued without dustwrapper. One of 355 copies. $400.

SIEGE of Corinth (The). (By George Gordon Noel, Lord Byron.) London, 1816. $400.

SIGOURNEY, Lydia Huntley. See Lydia Huntley.

SILKIN, Jon. *The Portrait* . . . Ilfracombe (1950). Author's first book. Wraps. $200.

SILKO, Leslie Marmon. *Ceremony.* New York (1977). First issue without reviews of this book on dustwrapper. $450. Second issue with review. $200.

SILKO, Leslie Marmon. *Laguna Woman.* Greenfield Center. New York (1974). Author's first book. Wraps. $1,750.

SILKO, Leslie Marmon. *Storyteller.* New York (1981). $250.

SILL, Edward Rowland. *The Hermitage* . . . New York or San Francisco, 1868. $125.

SILLIMAN, Benjamin. *A Description of the Recently Discovered Petroleum Region in California.* (Cover title.) New York, 1864. Printed wraps. $750.

SILLIMAN, Benjamin. *Report upon the Oil Property of the Philadelphia and California Petroleum Co.* Philadelphia, 1865. 2 maps. 36 pages, wraps. $1,000.

SILLITOE, Alan. *The Loneliness of the Long Distance Runner.* London (1959). $300.

SILLITOE, Alan. *Without Beer or Bread.* Dulwich Village, 1957. Author's first book other than a translation. Wraps. $400.

SILURIENSIS, Leolinus. *The Anatomy of Tobacco.* (By Arthur Machen.) London (1884). White parchment boards. Author's first book (aside from the anonymous privately printed pamphlet *Eleusinia*). $750.

SILVER Mines of Virginia and Austin, Nevada. Boston, 1865. 19 pages, wraps. $750.

SIMAK, Clifford D. *All Flesh Is Grass.* Garden City, 1965. $175.

SIMAK, Clifford D. *City.* (New York, 1952.) $650.

SIMAK, Clifford D. *The Creator.* (Los Angeles, 1946.) Wraps. No statement of edition. Author's first book. $100.

SIMAK, Clifford D. *Time and Again.* New York, 1951. $125.

SIMAK, Clifford D. *Way Station.* Garden City, 1963. $1,750.

SIMENON, Georges. *The Crime of Inspector Maigret.* New York, 1932. $1,500.

SIMENON, Georges. *The Death of Monsieur Gallet.* New York, 1932. (First English translation.) Author's first book. $2,000.

SIMMONS, Albert Dixon. *Wing Shots: A Series of Camera Studies of . . . Birds . . . on the Wing.* Derrydale Press, New York (1936). $250.

SIMMONS, Dan. *Hyperion.* New York (1989). Cloth. $250. Wraps. $35.

SIMMONS, Dan. *Song of Kali.* (New York, 1985.) Author's first book. $250.

SIMMS, Jeptha R. *The American Spy, or Freedom's Early Sacrifice.* Albany, 1846. 63 pages, wraps. $250.

SIMMS, Jeptha R. *Trappers of New York.* Albany, 1850. 4 plates. $400. Albany, 1860. $250.

SIMMS, William Gilmore. See *Beauchampe; Border Beagles; Grouped Thoughts and Scattered Fancies; Guy Rivers; Martin Faber; Mellichampe; The Partisan; Pelayo; Richard Hurdis; Sack and Destruction of Columbia, S.C.; The Wigwam and the Cabin; The Yemassee.*

SIMMS, William Gilmore. *Areytos; or, Songs of the South.* Charleston, 1846. Wraps. $750.

SIMMS, William Gilmore. *The Cassique of Accabee.* Charleston, 1849. Wraps. $600.

SIMMS, William Gilmore. *The Forayers; or, The Raid of the Dog-Days.* New York, 1855. $350.

SIMMS, William Gilmore. *Helen Halsey; or, The Swamp State of Conelachita.* New York, 1845. Wraps. $750.

SIMMS, William Gilmore. *Lyrical and Other Poems.* Charleston, 1827. Author's first book. $1,250.

SIMMS, William Gilmore. *Poems: Descriptive, Dramatic, Legendary and Contemplative.* New York, 1853. 2 vols. $600. Charleston, 1853. 2 vols. $400.

SIMMS, William Gilmore. *Southward Ho! A Spell of Sunshine.* New York, 1854. $400.

SIMON, Andre L. *Bibliotheca Vinaria . . .* (London, 1979). One of 600 copies. Facsimile reprint of the 1913 edition. $150.

SIMON, Neil. *Barefoot in the Park.* New York (1964). $600.

SIMON, Neil. *Come Blow Your Horn.* New York, 1963. First printing not stated. $750.

SIMON, Neil. *Heidi.* New York, 1959. Author's first book with William Friedberg. Wraps. $350.

SIMON, Neil. *The Odd Couple.* New York (1966). $400.

SIMON, Oliver (editor). *The Curwen Press Miscellany.* London, 1931. One of 275 copies. Slipcase. $950.

SIMPSON, George. *Narrative of a Journey Round the World, During the Years 1841 and 1842.* London, 1847. 2 vols. Portrait, folding map. $1,000. Philadelphia, 1847. 2 vols. in 1. First American edition. $650.

SIMPSON, Harriette. See Arnow, Harriette.

SIMPSON, Harriette. *Mountain Path.* New York (1936). $1,000.

SIMPSON, Henry I. *The Emigrant's Guide to the Gold Mines.* New York, 1848. Folding map. 30 pages, wraps. $10,000. Without map. $2,500. Haverford: Bird & Bull Press, 1978. One of 250 copies. $175.

SIMPSON, James H. *Journal of a Military Reconnaissance from Santa Fe, N.M., to the Navajo Country.* Philadelphia, 1852. Folding map, 72 plates, including color. First separate printing. $1,750.

SIMPSON, Capt. James H. *Report of Explorations Across the Great Basin of the Territory of Utah . . .* Washington, 1876. Folding map, plates, errata leaf. $750.

SIMPSON, James H. *Report from the Secretary, of War . . . and Map of the Route from Fort Smith, Ark., to Santa Fe, N.M.* (Caption title.) (Washington, 1850.) 4 folding maps. Stitched. Senate issue. $1,000. House issue. 1 folding map. 2 plates. $600.

SIMPSON, James H. *Report of the Secretary of War . . . and Map of Wagon Roads in Utah.* (Caption title.) (Washington, 1859.) Large folding map. $750.

SIMPSON, James H. *Report of . . . on the Union Pacific Railroad and Branches . . .* Washington, 1866. 4 folding maps. Wraps. $1,000.

SIMPSON, Louis. *The Arrivistes: Poems, 1940–1949.* New York (1949). Wraps. Author's first book. $250. Paris (1950). $200.

SIMPSON, Thomas. *Narrative of the Discoveries on the Northwest Coast of America.* London, 1843. 2 maps in front pocket. $1,250.

SIMPSON, Walter G. *Art of Golf.* Edinburgh, 1887. $750. New York, 1892. $2,000.

SINCLAIR, Upton. See Fitch, Ensign Clarke.

SINCLAIR, Upton. *The Jungle.* Jungle Publishing Co. New York, 1906. First state, with unbroken type on copyright page and with "Sustainers' Edition" label on front pastedown. $1,000. New York, 1906. Green cloth. First issue, with Doubleday imprint and with the "I" in date on copyright page in perfect type. $600. Limited Editions Club, Baltimore, 1965. In slipcase. $200.

SINCLAIR, Upton. *King Midas.* New York, 1901. $400.

SINCLAIR, Upton. *Springtime and Harvest.* New York (1901). $500.

SINGER, I. J. *The Brothers Ashkenazi.* New York, 1936. One of 550 copies signed on extra colophon leaf tipped in before the title page. $400.

SINGER, Isaac Bashevis. *The Family Moskat.* New York, 1950. Author's first English publication. $350. London, 1966. $150.

SINGER, Isaac Bashevis. *Gimpel the Fool . . .* New York, 1957. $400. London, 1958. $300.

SINGER, Isaac Bashevis. *The Golem.* New York (1982). One of 450 copies signed by Singer and illustrator, Uri Shulevitz. $300. Trade. $50.

SINGER, Isaac Bashevis. *A Little Boy in Search of God.* New York, 1976. One of 150 copies signed by Singer and Moscowitz, with an original etching signed by Moscowitz laid in. $350.

SINGER, Isaac Bashevis. *Lost in America.* Garden City, 1981. One of 500 signed copies. Original print signed by artist, Rafael Soyer, laid in. $300.

SINGER, Isaac Bashevis. *Magician of Lublin.* New York, 1960. $250. London, 1961. $250. Limited Editions Club, New York, 1984. In slipcase. $400.

SINGER, Isaac Bashevis. *Satan in Goray.* New York, 1955. $300. London, 1958. $250. New York (1981). One of 50 signed copies. In box. $1,250. One of 75 signed copies. In slipcase. $1,000. One of 350 signed copies. In slipcase. $450.

SINGER, Isaac Bashevis. *A Young Man in Search of Love.* New York, 1978. One of 300 copies signed by Singer and artist, Rafael Soyer. Color print signed by Soyer laid in. $250. Trade. $50.

SINGLETON, Arthur. *Letters from the South and West.* Boston, 1824. (By Henry Cogswell Knight.) $250.

SINISTRARI, Ludovico. *Demoniality.* London, 1927. Translated into English by Montague Summers. Vellum. Issued without dustwrapper. One of 90 copies on handmade paper, signed by Summers. $750. One of 1,200 copies. $175.

SINJOHN, John. *From the Four Winds.* London, 1897. (By John Galsworthy, his first book.) Olive-green cloth. One of 500 copies. $750.

SINJOHN, John. *Jocelyn.* London, 1898. (By John Galsworthy.) First issue, with "you" for "my" on page 257, third line from bottom (VAB. Not mentioned in Fabes or Marrot). $600.

SINJOHN, John. *A Man of Devon.* Edinburgh and London, 1901. (By John Galsworthy.) Blue cloth. With ads dated 4/01. $500.

SINJOHN, John. *Villa Rubein.* London, 1900. (By John Galsworthy.) Cherry red cloth. $600.

SIR John Chiverton. London, 1826. (By William H. Ainsworth and John P. Aston.) Ainsworth's first book. $450.

SIREN, Osvald. *Gardens of China.* New York (1949). Small folio, color frontispiece, 208 plates from photographs and paintings. In slipcase. $650.

SIRINGO, Charles A. *A Cowboy Detective.* Chicago, 1912. Pictorial cloth. First issue, published by Conkey. $450. Another binding: Special first-issue presentation copies, in pebble-grained leather (unrecorded in bibliographies—VAB), inscribed by Siringo. $750. 2 vols. Second issue, same date. Wraps. $350. New York, 1912. Pictorial wraps. $250.

SIRINGO, Charles A. *History of "Billy the Kid."* (Santa Fe, 1920.) 142 pages, stiff pictorial wraps. $1,000.

SIRINGO, Charles A. *A Lone Star Cowboy.* Santa Fe, 1919. Pictorial cloth. $300.

SIRINGO, Charles A. *Riata and Spurs . . .* Boston, 1927. 16 plates. Pictorial cloth. $750. Boston (1927). Pictorial cloth. Second printing, with many changes. $200.

SIRINGO, Charles A. *The Song Companion of a Lone Star Cowboy.* Santa Fe (1919). Pictorial wraps. $2,500.

SIRINGO, Charles A. *A Texas Cowboy, or, Fifteen Years on the Hurricane Deck of a Spanish Pony.* Chicago, 1885. Illustrated, including chromolithographic frontispiece in color. Wraps. $15,000. Black pictorial cloth. $15,000. Chicago, 1886. Siringo & Dobson. 8 plates, 347 pages. Second edition. $1,000. Another issue, same collation, same place and date. Rand McNally, wraps. $1,250. New York (1886). Wraps. $300. New York (1950). Illustrated by Tom Lea. Cloth. $125.

SIR Ralph Esher; or, Adventures of a Gentleman of the Court of Charles II. London, 1832. 3 vols. (By Leigh Hunt.) $600.

SISKIND, Aaron. *Photographs.* New York, 1959. Author's first book. $250.

SISTER Years (The); Being the Carrier's Address, to the Patrons of the Salem Gazette, for the First of January, 1839. (Cover title.) Salem, Mass., 1839. 8 pages, in original printed self-wraps. (By Nathaniel Hawthorne.) $2,500.

SITGREAVES, Lorenzo. *Report of an Expedition down the Zuni and Colorado Rivers.* Washington, 1853. 79 plates, some tinted; folding map. $1,250. Washington, 1854. $1,000.

SITWELL, Edith. See Sitwell, Osbert.

SITWELL, Edith. *Alexander Pope.* London (1930). Illustrated. Yellow buckram. One of 220 signed copies. In dustwrapper and slipcase. $500.

SITWELL, Edith. *Collected Poems.* London, 1930. One of 320 signed copies. In dustwrapper. $350. Trade. $100.

SITWELL, Edith. *Facade.* London, 1922. Colored frontispiece. One of 150 signed copies. Issued without dustwrapper. $600.

SITWELL, Edith. *Five Poems.* London, 1928. One of 275 signed copies. $250.

SITWELL, Edith. *The Mother and Other Poems.* Oxford, 1915. Author's first book. (500 copies, 200 pulped.) Wraps. $750.

SITWELL, Edith. *The Pleasures of Poetry.* First, second, and third series. London, 1930–31–32. 3 vols. $300.

SITWELL, Edith. *The Wooden Pegasus.* Oxford, 1920. In dustwrapper. $350.

SITWELL, Osbert. *At the House of Mrs. Kinfoot.* London, 1921. Wraps. One of 101 signed copies. Issued without dustwrapper. $350.

SITWELL, Osbert. *The Collected Satires and Poems of Osbert Sitwell.* (London), 1931. Portrait frontispiece. Cloth. In dustwrapper. One of 110 signed copies. $300. Trade. $75.

SITWELL, Osbert. *England Reclaimed.* London, 1927. One of 165 signed copies. In dustwrapper. $200. Trade. $75.

SITWELL, Osbert. *Twentieth Century Harlequinade . . .* Oxford, 1916. (Author's first book with Edith Sitwell). (500 copies.) Wraps. $400.

SITWELL, Osbert. *Who Killed Cock-Robin?* London, 1921. In yellow paper wrapper pasted to spine (8⅕ inches high [Fifoot bibliography]). $200. Later with wrapper pasted to boards. (7⅜ inches high.) $150.

SITWELL, Osbert. *The Winstonburg Line: 3 Satires.* London, 1919. Pictorial wraps. Author's first separate book. $300.

SITWELL, Sacheverell. *The Cyder Feast and Other Poems.* (London), 1927. Yellow buckram. One of 165 signed copies. In pale-pink dustwrapper. $250.

SITWELL, Sacheverell. *The People's Palace.* Oxford, 1918. Author's first book. Frontispiece. Wraps. (400 copies.) $200.

SITWELL, Sacheverell. *Two Poems, Ten Songs.* London, 1929. Decorated boards. One of 275 signed copies. $250.

SITWELL, Sacheverell; BLUNT, Wilfred; and SYNGE, Patrick M. *Great Flower Books, 1700–1900.* London, 1956. 36 plates, 20 in color. Folio, half morocco. One of 295 copies signed by the authors. In slipcase. $1,250. Half cloth. One of 1,750 copies. In dustwrapper. $650.

SITWELL, Sacheverell; BUCHANAN, Handasyde; and FISHER, James. *Fine Bird Books, 1700–1900.* London, 1953. 38 plates in color, 36 in black-and-white. Folio, half morocco. One of 295 copies signed by the three authors. $1,500. Buckram and boards. One of 2,000 copies. In dustwrapper. $650.

SITWELL, Sacheverell, and LAMBERT, Constant. *The Rio Grande.* London, 1929. One of 75 signed copies. $350. Unsigned (but numbered). $200.

SIX to One; A Nantucket Idyl. New York, 1878. Tan or gray cloth. (By Edward Bellamy, his first book). Cloth. $500. Later state, printed wraps. $350.

SIXTY Years of the Life of Jeremy Levis. New York, 1831. 2 vols. (By Laughton Osborn.) $150.

SKEEN, William. *Early Typography.* Colombo, 1872. Revised edition. $650.

SKEFFINGTON, F.J.C., and JOYCE, James A. *Two Essays.* Dublin (1901). 4 leaves, pink printed wraps. Joyce's first published book, containing his essay "The Day of the Rabblement." $10,000.

SKETCH of the Geographical Rout [sic] of a Great Railway . . . Between the Atlantic States and the Great Valley of the Mississippi. New York, 1829. (By William C. Redfield.) Folding map. 16 pages. $1,000. New York, 1830. Second edition. $500.

SKETCH of Old England (A). New York, 1822. By a New England Man. 2 vols. (By James Kirke Paulding.) $600.

SKETCH of St. Anthony and Minneapolis. St. Anthony, 1857. Frontispiece, 4 plates, map. 32 pages, wraps. With errata slip. $500.

SKETCH of the Seminole War, and Sketches During the Campaign. Charleston, 1836. (By W. W. Smith.) $17,000 at auction in 1999.

SKETCHES by "Boz." London, 1836–37. Illustrated by George Cruikshank. 3 vols. (First series, 1836, 2 vols., dark-green cloth; second series, 1837, pink cloth.) (By Charles Dickens, his first book.) $15,000. Rebound. $5,000. London, 1837–39. 20 parts, pictorial pink wraps. (Complete sets with all ads and wraps in the first state are rare.) $35,000.

SKETCHES of History, Life and Manners in the United States. New Haven, 1826. (By a Traveller, Anne Royall, her first book.) Woodcut frontispiece view. $850.

SKETCHES of the West, or the Home of the Badgers. Milwaukee, 1847. Folding map. 48 pages, wraps. (By Josiah B. Grinnell.) Second edition (of The Home of the Badgers, which see under Grinnell's pseudonym, Oculus.) $2,000.

SKINNER, B. F. The Behavior of Organisms. New York, 1938. $750.

SKINNER, J. S. The Dog and the Sportsman. New York, 1845. Illustrated, including engraved title page. $500.

SLAUGHTER, Mrs. Linda W. The New Northwest. Bismarck, 1874. 24 pages, wraps. $1,750.

SLAVE (The); or, The Memoirs of Archy Moore. (By Richard Hildreth, his first book.) Boston, 1836. 2 vols. $1,000.

SLEEPING Beauty. London, no date [1910]. One of 1,000 copies signed by illustrator Edmund Dulac. 30 mounted color plates. Issued in cardboard slipcase. $2,500.

SLICK, Jonathan. High Life in New York. (New York, 1843.) (By Ann Sophia Stephens.) Author's first separate book. Wraps. $1,000.

SLOAN, Edward L. See Salt Lake City . . .

SLOAN, Sir Hans. A Voyage to the Islands Madera. London, 1707–25. 2 vols. Folio, with 240 plates. $12,500.

SLOAN, John. Morse, Peter. John Sloan's Prints . . . New Haven and London, 1969. $350. One of 150 copies. With a proof etching by Sloan signed by Mrs. Sloan in pencil. $750.

SLOAN, Robert. W. Utah Gazetteer and Directory of Logan, Ogden, Provo and Salt Lake Cities. Salt Lake City, 1884. $750.

SLOAN, Samuel. City and Suburban Architecture . . . Philadelphia, 1859. 136 plates. $2,000.

SLOAN, Samuel. The Modern Architect . . . Philadelphia (1852). 2 vols. Author's first book. $2,000. New edition. Philadelphia, 1860. 2 vols. $1,250.

SLOAN, Samuel. Sloan's Constructive Architecture . . . Philadelphia, 1859. 66 plates. In original cloth binding. $1,000.

SLOCUM, John J., and CAHOON, Herbert. A Bibliography of James Joyce, 1882–1941. London, 1953. $200.

SLOCUM, Joshua. Sailing Alone Around the World. New York, 1900. $500.

SLOCUM, Joshua. Voyage of the Liberdale from New York to Brazil. Boston, 1894. 47 pages. $500.

SMART, Stephen F. Leadville, Ten Mile . . . and All Other Noted Colorado Mining Camps. Kansas City, 1879. 2 folding maps, 56 pages, printed wraps. $1,750.

SMEDLEY, Frank E. See *Frank Fairleigh*.

SMEDLEY, William. *Across the Plains in '62*. (Denver, 1916.) Map and portrait. 56 pages, boards. $500.

SMILEY, Jane. *At Paradise Gate*. New York (1981). $350.

SMILEY, Jane. *Barn Blind*. New York (1980). Author's first book. $600.

SMILEY, Jane. *Duplicate Keys*. New York, 1984. $175.

SMITH, A. J. M. *Poetry of Robert Bridges*. Montreal, no date on title page and not known. (Early 1930s.) Author's first book. Wraps. $1,500.

SMITH, Adam. *An Inquiry into the Nature and Causes of the Wealth of Nations*. London, 1776. 2 vols. Publisher's ads on verso of 3F2. $100,000. London, 1778. 2 vols. Second edition. $15,000. London, 1784. Third edition. 3 vols. $5,000. Philadelphia, 1789. 3 vols. First American edition. $5,000.

SMITH, Adam. *The Theory of Moral Sentiments*. London, 1759. Author's first book. $15,000. London and Edinburgh, 1761. Second edition. $6,000. London, 1804. 2 vols. $2,000. Philadelphia, 1819. 2 vols. $1,250.

SMITH, Alexander. *Dreamthorp*. London, 1863. $150. Boston, 1864. $150.

SMITH, Alexander. *Poems*. London, 1853. Author's first book. With inserted ads dated November 1852. $125.

SMITH, Alice R. H., and SMITH, D. E. H. *The Dwelling Houses of Charleston*. Philadelphia, 1917. $450.

SMITH, Captain Allan C. U.S.A. *The Secrets of JuJitsu: A Complete Course in Self Defense*. Columbus, 1920. 7 vols. Wraps. $200.

SMITH, Ashbel. *Reminiscences of the Texas Republic*. Galveston, 1876. Wraps. One of 100 copies. $1,500.

SMITH, Buckingham (translator). *The Discovery of Florida*. Grabhorn printing for the Book Club of California. (San Francisco, 1946.) Decorations by Mallette Dean. Folio, gold boards and cloth. One of 280 copies. $500. (For an earlier printing, see next entry.)

SMITH, Buckingham (translator). *Narratives of the Career of Hernando de Soto in the Conquest of Florida*. New York, 1866. Folding map. Boards. One of 75 copies. $1,000.

SMITH, Buckingham (translator). *Rudo Ensayo, Tentativa de una Provencional Descripción Geográfica de la Provincia de Sonora*. San Agustin (St. Augustine, Fla., actually Albany, N.Y.). 1863. (By Juan Nentuig?) 208 pages, printed gray wraps. One of 10 large-paper copies. $1,750. Regular issue. One of 160 copies. $1,000.

SMITH, Charles Hamilton. *Selections of the Ancient Costume of Great Britain & Ireland . . .* London, 1814. 60 full-page color plates. $1,500. London, 1815. $1,250.

SMITH, Clark Ashton. *The Abominations of Yondo*. Sauk City, Wis., 1960. $200.

SMITH, Clark Ashton. *The Dark Chateau and Other Poems*. Sauk City, Wis., 1951. $1,000.

SMITH, Clark Ashton. *Genius Loci and Other Tales.* Sauk City, Wis., 1948. $350.

SMITH, Clark Ashton. *Lost Worlds.* Sauk City, Wis., 1944. $450.

SMITH, Clark Ashton. *Odes and Sonnets.* San Francisco, 1918. Blue boards, tan cloth spine, paper label. One of 300 copies. Issued without dustwrapper. $500.

SMITH, Clark Ashton. *Out of Space and Time.* Sauk City, Wis., 1942. $1,000.

SMITH, Clark Ashton. *Spells and Philtres.* Sauk City, Wis., 1958. $750.

SMITH, Clark Ashton. *The Star-Treader and Other Poems.* San Francisco, 1912. Author's first collection of verse. Buff pictorial boards. In dustwrapper. $500. Without dustwrapper. $150.

SMITH, Dave. *Bull Island.* Poquoson, Virginia (1970). Author's first book. Wraps. $600.

SMITH, David Eugene. *Rara Arithmetica* . . . Boston, 1908. $400.

SMITH, Dodie (Dorothy Gladys). *The Hundred and One Dalmations.* London, 1956. (By Dorothy Gladys Smith.) Author's first book for children. $450. New York, 1957. $300.

SMITH, Edward E. *The Skylark of Space.* (Buffalo Book Co. Providence, 1946.) (Author's first book with Mrs. Lee Hawkins Garby.) $400. Hadley Co. Providence (1947). $75.

SMITH, Edward E. *The Spacehounds of IPC* . . . Reading, 1947. First edition stated. In dustwrapper listing 4 titles on rear panel. $150. One of 300 signed copies. $350. In second issue dustwrapper with 11 titles on back. $75. (The first Fantasy Press book.)

SMITH, Edward E. *Triplanetary.* Reading, Pa., 1948. $200. One of 500 signed copies. $350.

SMITH, Emma (editor). *A Collection of Sacred Hymns for the Church of the Latter Day Saints.* Kirtland, Ohio, 1835. In original marbled boards and cloth. $7,500 or more.

SMITH, F. Hopkinson. *American Illustrators.* New York, 1892. Folio, 5 parts, printed wraps in printed board folder. One of 1,000 copies. $850.

SMITH, F. Hopkinson. *Colonel Carter of Cartersville.* Boston, 1891. Olive-green cloth. With apostrophe in "Carter'sville" on spine, and vignette of staircase on page (i). $200. Later, without apostrophe, in blue-gray cloth and vignette moved to page 3. $100.

SMITH, F. Hopkinson. *Old Lines in New Black.* Boston, 1885. Author's first book. $200.

SMITH, F. Hopkinson. *Venice of Today.* New York, 1896. 21 colored plates, 12 plain plates. Half morocco. $500. One of 118 copies on handmade paper. $850. New York, 1902. Half morocco. $350.

SMITH, Frank Meriweather (editor). *San Francisco Vigilance Committee of '56.* San Francisco, 1883. 83 pages, wraps. $300.

SMITH, Garden C. *The World of Golf.* London, 1898. $600.

SMITH, Harry B. *A Sentimental Library* . . . (No place) 1914. issued in dustwrapper and slipcase. $500.

SMITH, J. Calvin. *A New Guide for Travelers Through the United States.* New York, 1846. Folding map in color. Cloth, or leather. $1,250.

SMITH, J. Calvin. *The Western Tourist and Emigrant's Guide . . .* New York, 1839. Colored folding map. $2,500. New York, 1840. $1,000. New York, 1845. $750.

SMITH, James. *The Carpenter's Companion . . .* London, 1733. 41 plates. $3,500.

SMITH, James E. *A Famous Battery and Its Campaigns, 1861–64.* Washington, 1892. $200.

SMITH, James Edward. *Exotic Botany.* London, 1804. 119 engraved plates, including frontispiece and 6 folding plates. $2,500.

SMITH, James F. *The Cherokee Land Lottery . . .* New York, 1838. $1,500.

SMITH, John. *The True Travels, Adventures and Observations of Captaine John Smith in Europe . . .* Richmond, 1819. 2 engraved frontispieces, 2 folding maps, one folding engraved plate. $650.

SMITH, John Thomas. *Antiquities of Westminster.* London, 1807–(09). 2 vols. Illustrated, including color plates. $850.

SMITH, John Thomas. *Cries of London, Exhibiting Several of the Itinerant Traders of Ancient and Modern Times.* London, 1839. Portrait and 30 hand-colored etchings. In original half leather and cloth. $850. Large-paper edition. $1,000.

SMITH, Johnston. *Maggie: A Girl of the Streets.* (New York, 1893.) (By Stephen Crane, his first book.) Yellow printed wraps. (For the second edition, see the entry under Crane, Stephen.) $17,500.

SMITH, Joseph, Jr. See *A Book of Commandments.*

SMITH, Joseph, Jr. *The Book of Mormon.* Palmyra, N.Y., 1830. Author's first book. First edition, first issue, with 2 page preface and testimonial leaf at end and without index. In original leather. $100,000. Rebound. $60,000. Second issue, without testimonials, etc. $35,000. Kirtland, Ohio, 1837. Second edition. $30,000. Nauvoo, Ill. (actually Cincinnati), 1840. Third edition. Original sheep. $12,500. Liverpool, 1841. Leather. First English edition. $3,500. Edinburgh, 1841. $2,500. Nauvoo, Ill., 1842. Fourth edition. $3,500.

SMITH, Joseph, Jr., et al. (editors). *Doctrine and Covenants of the Church of the Latter Day Saints.* Kirtland, 1835. In original leather. $20,000 or more.

SMITH, Julie. *Death Turns a Trick.* New York (1982). Author's first book. $250.

SMITH, Kate Douglas. *The Story of Patsy. A Reminiscence.* San Francisco, 1883. (By Kate Douglas Wiggin, her first separate publication.) 27 pages, wraps. $1,250.

SMITH, Lee. *The Last Day the Dogbushes Bloomed.* New York (1968). Author's first book. $450.

SMITH, Lee. *Something in the Wind.* New York (1971). $250.

SMITH, Lillian. *There Are Things to Do.* Clayton, Ga. 1943. Author's first book. Wraps. (16-page offprint, stapled). $75.

SMITH, Lillian. *Strange Fruit.* New York, 1944. $150.

SMITH, Logan Pearsall. *Trivia.* London, 1902. One of 300 copies. $300. Garden City, 1917. Half leather. One of 100 copies. $250.

SMITH, Logan Pearsall. *The Youth of Parnassus and Other Stories.* London, 1895. Author's first book. Blue or red cloth (priority unknown). $250.

SMITH, Lucy. *Biographical Sketches of Joseph Smith The Prophet, and His Progenitors for Many Generations.* Liverpool, 1853. $1,000.

SMITH, Martin (Cruz). *Gypsy In Amber.* New York (1971). $250.

SMITH, Martin (Cruz). *The Indians Won.* New York (1970). Author's first book. Wraps. $200. (London, 1982.) $200.

SMITH, Michael. *A Geographical View, of the Province of Upper Canada, and Promiscuous Remarks upon the Government* . . . Hartford, 1813. 107 pages. $750. New York, 1813. Second edition. $600. Baltimore, 1814. Revised. $500.

SMITH, Moses. *History of the Adventures and Sufferings of Moses Smith* . . . Brooklyn, N.Y., 1812. 2 plates. $500.

SMITH, Nathan. *A Practical Essay on Typhous Fever.* New York, 1824. $600.

SMITH, Nathan R. *Surgical Anatomy of the Arteries.* Baltimore, 1830. 18 hand-colored lithographs. $750.

SMITH, Robert W. *Chinese Boxing: Masters and Methods.* Tokyo, 1974. Stated first. $125.

SMITH, Robert W. (editor). *A Complete Guide to Judo: Its Story and Practice.* Tokyo, 1958. Stated first. $125.

SMITH, Mrs. Sarah. *A Journal Kept by Mrs. Sarah Foote Smith While Journeying with Her People from Wellington, Ohio, to Footeville, Town of Nepeuskun, Winnebago County, Wis., April 15 to May 10, 1846.* (Kilbourn, Ohio, 1905.) Boards, paper label. $300.

SMITH, Mrs. Seba. *The Western Captive.* (New York, 1842.) Folio, original wrappers. 48 double-column pages uncut. $750.

SMITH, Sidney Lawton. See *Sidney Lawton Smith* . . .

SMITH, Stevie. *Novel on Yellow Paper.* London (1936). Author's first book. $750. New York, 1937. Patterned cloth. Dustwrapper price clipped, stamped $2.00. $250. Blue cloth. Dustwrapper priced $2.50. $150. (We had assumed $2.50 was first, but copy of a proof in wraps price-clipped with $2.00 stamped on flap and publication date and $2.00 price noted was reported to us, which would indicate $2.00 and patterned cloth is first. The "bibliography," and there is one, almost 200 pages long, gives absolutely no information on the books other than title, publication and date.)

SMITH, T. Dudley. *Into the Happy Glade.* London, 1943. $250.

SMITH, T. Dudley. *Over the Wall.* London, 1943. (A.K.A. Elleston Trevor.) $300.

SMITH, Thorne. *Biltmore Oswald: The Diary of a Hapless Recruit*. New York (1918). Author's first book. Pictorial boards. In dustwrapper. $350. Without dustwrapper. $100.

SMITH, Thorne. *Skin and Bones*. Garden City, 1933. $400. London, 1936. $300.

SMITH, Thorne. *Stray Lamb*. New York, 1929. $600. London, 1930. $400.

SMITH, Thorne. *Topper: An Improbable Adventure*. New York, 1926. $2,000. London, 1926. $1,250.

SMITH, Thorne. *Topper Takes a Trip*. Garden City, 1932. $450. London, 1935. $300.

SMITH, Wallace. *Garden of the Sun: A History of the San Joaquin Valley, 1772–1939*. Los Angeles (1939). $300.

SMITH, Wilbur. *When the Lion Feeds*. London (1964). Author's first book. $250. New York (1964). $200.

SMITH, William H. *History of Canada*. Quebec, 1815. Folding table. 2 vols. $2,000. Later edition. (Quebec 1827.) 2 vols. $1,000.

SMITH, William H. *Smith's Canadian Gazetteer* . . . Toronto, 1846. Large folding map. $300.

SMITH, William Jay. *Poems*. New York, 1947. Author's first book. One of 500 copies. Issued without dustwrapper. $125.

SMITHWICK, Noah. *The Evolution of a State* . . . Austin (1900). $850. One of 10 signed copies. $2,000.

SMOLLETT, Tobias. See *The Adventures of Peregrine Pickle; The Adventures of Roderick Random;* and *The Expedition of Humphrey Clinker.*

SMYTH, C. Piazzi. *Life and Work at the Great Pyramid* . . . Edinburgh, 1867. 3 vols. $1,250.

SMYTH, C. Piazzi. *Teneriffe, An Astronomer's Experiment* . . . London, 1858. Illustrated with 20 mounted photostereographs and a map. Original purple cloth, gilt-stamped. $2,000.

SMYTHE, F. S. *The Valley of Flowers*. London, 1938. 16 colored, mounted plates and 1 extending map, and packet of seeds. One of 250 signed copies. $1,000.

SMYTHE, Henry. *Historical Sketch of Parker County and Weatherford, Texas*. St. Louis, 1877. $1,750.

SMYTHE, Henry de Wolf. *Atomic Energy for Military Purposes (The)*. Princeton, 1945. First commercial edition, possibly preceding GPO edition. First three printings are indistinguishable. Cloth in dustwrapper. $300. Wraps. $100.

SMYTHE, Henry de Wolf. *A General Account of the Development of Methods of Using Energy for Military Purposes* . . . (Washington, 1945.) 193 pages in stapled wraps. Text printed by lithoprint. Issued with broadside headed: "FUTURE RELEASE . . ." laid in. $2,000. One of 4 (?) copies in spiral binding with name of recipient printed on front wrapper. $3,250. Superintendent of Documents, Washington, 1945. Stiff printed wraps. 182 pages with "1945" at foot of last page. First public edition, printed by GPO. $500.

SNARLEYYOW, or The Dog Fiend. London, 1837. 3 vols. (By Frederick Marryat.) $450. Philadelphia, 1837. 2 vols. First American edition. (Published with byline "F. Marryat.") $350.

SNELLING, William J. See Bell, Solomon. See also *Tales of the Northwest.*

SNELLING, William J. *The Polar Regions of the Western Continent Explored.* Boston, 1831. $1,000.

SNODGRASS, W. D. *Heart's Needle.* New York, 1959. Author's first book. $300. Hessle (England), 1960. First English edition. Adds an addendum. $200.

SNOW, C. P. *Death Under Sail.* London (1932). Author's first book. $750. Garden City (1932). $350.

SNOW, C. P. *Strangers and Brothers.* London, 1940. $600.

SNOW, Charles Wilbert. *Songs of the Neukluk.* Council, Alaska, 1912. Written with Ewen MacLennan. $1,000.

SNYDER, Gary. *The Back Country.* London (1967). One of 100 signed copies. In dustwrapper. $650. Trade. $300.

SNYDER, Gary. *The Blue Sky.* New York, 1969. Oblong, wraps. One of 126 signed copies. $450. One of 26 copies. $750.

SNYDER, Gary. *Myths and Texts.* New York (1960). Illustrated. Decorated wraps. $250.

SNYDER, Gary. *Riprap.* Origin Press. (Ashland, Mass.), 1959. Author's first book. Japanese-style blue-and-white wraps. $750.

SNYDER, Gary. *Six Sections from Mountains and Rivers Without End.* (San Francisco), 1965. Wraps. $75. Fulcrum Press. London (1967). Green cloth. First English edition. One of 100 signed copies. In dustwrapper. $500. Trade edition. $100.

SNYDER, Gary (translator). *The Wooden Fish: Basic Sutras & Gathas of Rinzai Zen.* (Kyoto, Japan), 1961. Prepared by Kanetsuki Gutesu and Gary Snyder. Wraps. First edition, with errata slip laid in. $1,500.

SOBY, James Thrall. *Ben Shahn, His Graphic Art.* New York, 1957. One of 250 copies signed by Shahn and Soby, and with an original hand-colored lithograph mounted as the frontispiece, signed by Shahn. Slipcase. $600.

SOLZHENITSYN, Alexander. *August 1914 . . .* New York (1989). $60. One of 200 signed copies. In slipcase. $600.

SOLZHENITSYN, Alexander. *One Day in the Life Of Ivan Denisovich.* New York: Praeger (1963). Author's first book. (First English translation.) $250. New York: Dutton, 1963. Cloth. $150. Wraps. $40. Pall Mall, London, 1963. (Never seen.) $200. Gollancz, London, 1963. $250.

SOLZHENITSYN, Alexander. *"We Never Make Mistakes."* Columbia, SC, 1963. $250.

SOMBRERO (The). Quarter-Centennial Number. Yearbook of the Class of 1895. University of Nebraska. Lincoln, Neb. (1894). White and red cloth. $1,500. (Contains Willa Cather and Dorothy Canfield's prize story "The Fear That Walks by Noonday.")

SOME Antiquarian Notes. Naples, 1907. 56 pages, red wraps. (By Norman Douglas.) One of 250 copies. $300.

SOME British Ballads. London (1919). One of 575 copies signed by the illustrator, Arthur Rackham. $1,250.

SOME Papers Hand Made by John Mason. One of 100 copies signed by John Mason. In cardboard box. $500.

SOMEBODY Had to Do Something. Los Angeles, 1939. Wraps. (Contains tributes to James P. Lardner, killed in the Spanish Civil War, including material by Ernest Hemingway and Ring Lardner, Jr.) $750.

SONDHEIM, Stephen. *A Funny Thing Happened on the Way to the Forum.* New York (1962). Music and lyrics by Sondheim. From the book by Burt Shevelove and Larry Gelbart. $250.

SONN, Albert H. *Early American Wrought Iron.* New York, 1928. 3 vols. In dustwrappers. $750.

SOTHEBY, Samuel Leigh. *Principia Typographica.* London, 1858. 3 vols. 128 plates. One of 215 copies. $750.

SOTO, Gary. *Elements of San Joaquin.* (Pittsburgh, 1976.) One of 50 signed copies. In tissue dustwrapper. $450. Trade. $75.

SOULE, Frank, GIHON, Frank, and NISBET, James. *The Annals of San Francisco.* New York, 1855. 6 plates, 2 maps. Leather. $750.

SOUSTER (Holmes) Raymond. *When We Were Young.* Montreal, 1946. Author's first book. Wraps. $1,250.

SOUTAR, Daniel C. *Australian Golfer.* Sydney, 1906. $750.

SOUTH Carolina Jockey Club (The). Charleston, 1857. (By John B. Irving.) $600.

SOUTHARD, Charles Zibeon. *Trout Fly-Fishing in America.* New York, 1914. One of 100 copies. 20 color plates. $950. Trade. $250. New York, 1928. One of 100 copies. 20 color plates. $850. Trade. $175.

SOUTHERN, Terry. *Flash & Filigree.* (London, 1958.) Author's first book. $250. New York (1958). In full cloth with dustwrapper price of $3.50 and no mention of Dr. Strangelove in blurbs. $100.

SOUTHERN, Terry, and HOFFENBERG, Mason. *Candy.* New York (1964). First hardcover edition. $200.

SOUTHEY, Robert. See Bion and Moschos.

SOUTHEY, Robert. *All for Love; and The Pilgrim to Compostella.* London, 1829. $750.

SOUTHEY, Robert. *History of Brazil . . .* London, 1810–19. 3 vols. Folding map. $3,500.

SOUTHEY, Robert. *Poems . . .* Bath, 1795. (With Robert Lovell.) $3,500. Boston, 1799. $1,000.

SOUTHEY, Robert. *Specimens of the Later English Poets.* London 1807. 3 vols. $1,250.

SOUTHSPRING Ranch (The). Colorado Springs (1902?). Illustrated. 28 pages, wraps. $250.

SOUTHWARD, John. *Artistic Printing.* London, 1892. Four plates (3 in color). $500.

SOUTHWARD, John. *The Principles and Progress of Printing Machinery.* London, no date (circa 1889). $150.

SOUTHWARD, John. *Progress in Printing and the Graphic Arts During the Victorian Era.* London, 1897. Stiff paperwraps. $250.

SOUTH-WEST (The). By a Yankee. New York, 1835. (By Joseph Holt Ingraham, his first book.) 2 vols. $400.

SOWELL, A. J. *Early Settlers and Indian Fighters of Southwest Texas.* Austin, 1900. 12 plates. $1,250.

SOWELL, A. J. *Rangers and Pioneers of Texas.* San Antonio, 1884. Illustrated. Pictorial cloth. $3,000.

SPALDING, C. C. *Annals of the City of Kansas.* Kansas City, 1858. 7 plates. $7,500.

Spanish Speaking Americans In The War. (Charles Olson.) Washington (D.C.) (1944). Author's first book. Wraps. $2,000.

SPARAGO, John. *Anthony Haswell: Printer, Patriot, Balladist.* Rutland, Vt., 1925. One of 300 signed copies. 35 facsimiles. $200.

SPARAGO, John. *The Potters and Potteries of Bennington.* Boston, 1926. Boards. Issued without dustwrapper. One of 800 copies. $250.

SPARK, Muriel. See Camberg, Muriel.

SPARK, Muriel. *Child of Light.* Essex (1951). $250.

SPARK, Muriel. *The Comforters.* London, 1957. $500.

SPARK, Muriel. *The Fanfarlo . . .* Kent, 1952. Wraps. First issue, wraps printed in red. $150.

SPARK, Muriel. *Not to Disturb.* London, 1971. Illustrated. Boards and cloth. One of 500 signed copies, with an original etching by Michael Ayrton. In glassine dustwrapper. $250.

SPARK, Muriel. *The Prime of Miss Jean Brodie.* London, 1961. $400.

SPARK, Muriel. *Robinson.* London, 1958. $300.

SPARKS, Timothy. *Sunday Under Three Heads.* London, 1836. (By Charles Dickens.) In original drab wraps. With the title at the beginning of chapter III on page 35 and "hair" spelled correctly in line 15 on page 7. $3,500.

SPARLING, H. Halliday. *The Kelmscott Press and William Morris, Master Craftsman.* London, 1924. 16 plates and portrait frontispiece of Morris. $200.

SPARRMAN, Andrew. *A Voyage to the Cape of Good Hope . . .* London, 1785. 2 vols. Vol. 1: frontispiece, folding map, 2 plates. Vol. 2: pages 353/354 numbered 349/350, 7 plates. $6,000.

SPARROW, Walter Shaw. *A Book of Sporting Painters.* London (1931). 138 illustrations, some in color. Buckram. $250. One of 125 copies with 2 extra plates. $350.

SPARROW, Walter Shaw. *British Sporting Artists, from Barlow to Herring.* London (1922). 27 color plates, other illustrations. $300. One of 95 signed copies. $600.

SPAULDING, Thomas M., and KARPINSKY, Louis C. *Early Military Books in the University of Michigan Libraries.* Ann Arbor, 1941. $300.

SPEARMAN, Frank. *Nan of Music Mountain.* New York, 1916. $150.

SPEARMAN, Frank. *Whispering Smith.* New York, 1906. $300.

SPEARS, John R. *Illustrated Sketches of Death Valley and Other Borax Deserts of the Pacific Coast.* Chicago, 1892. Printed wraps. $450.

"SPEC." *Line Etchings.* St. Louis, 1875. (Pseudonym of Beverly R. Keim and William Weston.) $750.

SPECIMENS. (Canyon City, Ore., 1868.) 54 pages, pink wraps, stitched. (By Joaquin Miller—preface signed "C. H. Miller.") Author's first book, suppressed by him. $5,000.

SPECIMENS of Woodcuts and Engravings: A Portfolio of Original Leaves . . . (New York, 1926.) 15 folders each containing a leaf, enclosed in case. One of 120 copies. $550.

SPEER, Emory. *The Banks County Ku-Klux.* Atlanta, 1883. 60 pages, wraps. $300.

SPEKE, John Hanning. *What Led to the Discovery of the Source of the Nile.* Edinburgh, 1864. Engraved frontispiece, folding map, and a double-page map. $1,250.

SPENCER, Elizabeth. *Fire in the Morning.* New York, 1948. Author's first novel. $600.

SPENCER, Elizabeth. *This Crooked Way.* New York (1952). $200. London, 1953. $125.

SPENCER, Mrs. George E. *Calamity Jane: A Story of the Black Hills.* New York (about 1887). (By William L. Spencer.) Frontispiece. Wraps. $500.

SPENCER, Herbert. *Education: Intellectual, Moral, and Physical.* New York, 1861. $350.

SPENCER, Herbert. *The Principles of Biology.* 2 vols. London, 1864–67. $450.

SPENCER, Herbert. *The Proper Sphere of Government.* London, 1843. Author's first book. $350.

SPENCER, Herbert. *Social Statistics.* London, 1851. $300.

SPENCER, J. W. *Reminiscences of Pioneer Life in the Mississippi Valley.* Davenport, Iowa, 1872. Portrait. $500.

SPENCER, O. M. *Indian Captivity: A True Narrative of the Capture of* . . . New York, 1835. Wraps. $11,000 at auction in 1999. (Washington, Penna., 1835 edition may precede.) New York, 1836. Third edition. $1,000.

SPENDER, Stephen. See S., S.H.

SPENDER, Stephen. *Poems.* London (1933). $250. New York, 1934. $175.

SPENDER, Stephen. *Returning to Vienna 1947.* Banyan Press. (London, 1947.) Wraps. One of 500 signed copies. $250.

SPENDER, Stephen. *Twenty Poems.* Oxford (1930). Wraps. Signed copies (75 of 135 copies). $1,000. Unsigned. $750.

SPENDER, Stephen. *Vienna.* London, 1934. $250.

SPENSER, Edmund. *Minor Poems.* Ashendene Press. London, 1925. One of 200 copies on paper. $1,500.

SPENSER, Edmund. *The Faerie Queene.* London, 1590–96. 2 vols. $30,000. London: Ashendene Press, 1923. One of 180 copies. $3,000. One of 12 copies on vellum. $15,000. Limited Editions Club, Oxford, 1953. 2 vols. In slipcase. $300.

SPENSER, Edmund. *The Shepheardes Calender.* London, 1579. $65,000 at auction in 1990. (A copy with the final signature N in an earlier uncorrected state and woodcut vignette of a woman's head flaked by cornucopias above the colophon was auctioned at $105,000 in 1980.) London (1581). $60,000. London, 1586. $25,000. London, 1591. $7,500. Kelmscott Press. London, 1896. 12 woodcuts. Boards and linen. One of 225 copies. $3,000. One of 6 copies on vellum, specially bound. $20,000. Cresset Press. London, 1930. Boards, vellum spine. One of 350 copies. In dustwrapper and slipcase. $750.

SPEYER, Leonora. *Holy Night: A Yuletide Masque.* New York, 1919. Designs by Eric Gill. Stiff blue decorated wraps. Author's first book. One of 500 copies. $200.

SPICER, Jack. *After Lorca.* (San Francisco, 1957.) Wraps. Author's first separate book. One of 26 signed copies. $2,500. One of 474 copies. $1,250.

SPICER, Jack. *Correlation Methods of Comparing Idolects . . .* Author's first book with David W. Reed. (Offprint of "Language" 1952.) Wraps. (Fewer than 100 copies.) $1,250.

SPICER, Jack. *Lament for the Makers.* (Oakland, 1962.) Wraps. One of 100 copies. $300.

SPIELBERG, Steven. *Close Encounters of the Third Kind.* New York, 1977. $125.

SPIELMANN, M. H., and JERROLD, Walter. *Hugh Thomson, His Art, His Letters, His Humour and His Charm.* London, 1931. 13 plates in color. $175.

SPIELMANN, M. H., and LAYARD, G. S. *Kate Greenaway.* London, 1905. 53 colored plates, other illustrations. White cloth. One of 500 copies with an original pencil sketch by Kate Greenaway inserted. $2,000. Trade. Purple cloth. $400.

SPILLANE, Mickey. (Frank Morrison Spillane.) *I, the Jury.* New York, 1947. Author's first book. $3,000.

SPILLANE, Mickey. *Kiss Me Deadly.* New York, 1952. $750.

SPILLANE, Mickey. *The Long Wait.* New York, 1951. $2,500.

SPILLANE, Mickey. *My Gun Is Quick.* New York, 1950. $1,500.

SPILLER, Robert E. *The Philobiblon Club of Philadelphia; The First Eighty Years, 1893–1973.* (North Hills), 1973. One of 275 copies. $200.

SPILLER, Robert E., and BLACKBURN, Philip C. *A Descriptive Bibliography of the Writings of James Fenimore Cooper.* New York, 1934. One of 500 copies. $125.

SPIRIT of the Age (The). London, 1825. (By William Hazlitt.) $500.

SPORTSMAN'S Portfolio of American Field Sports (The). Boston, 1855. 20 full-page wood engravings, title-page vignette, illustration at end. Oblong wraps. $3,500.

SPOTTS, David L. *Campaigning with Custer . . .* Los Angeles, 1928. Map, 13 plates. One of 800 copies (All but about 300 burned—Howes). $750.

SPRAGUE, John T. *The Treachery in Texas.* New York, 1862. 35 pages, wraps. $175.

SPRING, Agnes Wright. *The Cheyenne and Black Hills Stage and Express Routes.* Glendale, Calif., 1949. Map, 17 plates. Cloth. $250.

SPRINGARN, J. E. *A History of Literary Criticism in the Renaissance . . .* New York, 1899. Author's first book. $250.

SPRINGS, Elliot White. *Nocturne Militaire.* New York (1927). Author's first book. $350.

SPRINGS, Elliot White. *War Birds . . .* New York, 1926. Edited by Springs. His first publication. One of 210 signed copies. $500. Trade. $350.

SPURRIER, John. *The Practical Farmer.* Wilmington, Del., 1793. $1,000.

SPY (The): A Tale of the Neutral Ground. New York, 1821. By the Author of *Precaution* (James Fenimore Cooper). 2 vols. $10,000. Limited Editions Club, New York, 1963. Cloth. In slipcase. $75.

SPYRI, Johanna. *Heidi.* Boston, 1885. 2 vols in 1. Translated by Louise Brooks. First American edition. $5,000. Philadelphia, 1922. Illustrated by Jessie Wilcox. In dustwrapper. $450.

SQUARE, A. (By Edward Abbott Abott.) *Flatland . . .* London, 1884. Author's first book. $1,250. Boston, 1885. $450.

SQUIER, E. G. *Travels In Central America . . .* (New York, 1853). 2 vols. 21 tinted lithographed plates, 8 black-and-white plates, 4 maps. $1,000.

SQUIER, E. G., and DAVIS, E. H. *Ancient Monuments of the Mississippi Valley.* Washington, 1848. Map, 48 plates. Folio, cloth. $1,000. New York, 1848. Second issue. $750.

SQUIRE, Ephraim G. See *Waikna.*

SQUIRE, J. C. *Socialism and Art.* London (1907). Author's first book. $150.

STACTON, David. *An Unfamiliar Country.* (Swinsford, 1953.) Author's first book. Wraps. $400.

STAFFORD, Jean. *Boston Adventure.* New York (1944). Author's first book. $150.

STAFFORD, William E. *Down in My Heart.* Elgin, Ill. (1947). Author's first book. Green cloth. $1,500.

STAFFORD, William E. *Traveling Through the Dark.* New York (1962). $300.

STAFFORD, William E. *Weather.* Mt. Horeb, Wis. (1969). Wraps. One of 207 copies. In dust-wrapper. $300.

STAFFORD, William E. *West of Your City.* Los Gatos, 1960. $1,000. Wraps. $350. (Both issued in plain white dustwrapper with price seen on both front and rear flaps.)

STAGG, A. Alonzo, and WILLIAMS, Henry L. *A Scientific and Practical Treatise on American Football for Schools and Colleges.* Hartford, 1893. $600.

STANFORD, Ann. *In Narrow Bound.* Gunnison (1943). Author's first book. Wraps. $125.

STANFORD, Don. *New England Earth . . .* San Francisco (1941). Author's first book. One of 300 copies. Boards. Issued without dustwrapper. $75.

STANLEY, David S. *Diary of a March from Fort Smith, Ark., to San Diego, Calif., Made in 1853.* No place or date. 37 pages, multigraphed. In cloth case. $350.

STANLEY, F. *The Grant That Maxwell Bought.* (Denver, 1952.) (By Father Stanley Crocchiola. His first book.) Map, 15 plates. Cloth. One of 250 signed copies. $600.

STANLEY, Henry M. *The Congo and the Founding of Its Free State.* New York, 1885. 2 vols. Numerous illustrations. $750.

STANLEY, Henry M. *In Darkest Africa.* London, 1890. 2 vols. 3 folding maps. $750. One of 250 signed copies. $6,000. New York, 1890. 2 vols. 43 plates. 3 folding maps. $650. One of 250 signed copies. $5,000.

STANLEY, Henry M. *Through the Dark Continent.* London, 1878. 2 vols. 3 folding maps (2 in pockets). $750. New York, 1878. 2 vols. Folding map and 13 plates. $600.

STANSBERY, Lon R. *The Passing of 3D Ranch.* (Tulsa, 1930.) $500.

STANSBURY, Howard. *An Expedition to the Valley of the Great Salt Lake of Utah . . .* Philadelphia, 1852. 57 plates (some folding). 3 folding maps, 2 maps bound in separate portfolio. $850. Another issue: *Exploration . . . of the Valley . . .* Philadelphia, 1852. $1,000.

STANSBURY, P. *A Pedestrian Tour of 2,300 Miles, in North America . . .* New York, 1822. 9 plates. $500.

STANTON, Schuyler. *Daughters of Destiny.* Chicago (1906). Red cloth. (By L. Frank Baum.) $1,000.

STAPLEDON, Olaf. *Darkness and the Light.* London (1942). $200.

STAPLEDON, Olaf. *Last and First Men . . .* London (1930). $1,000.

STAPLEDON, Olaf. *Latter-Day Psalms.* Liverpool, 1914. Author's first book. $200.

STAPLEDON, Olaf. *Star Maker.* London (1937). Blue cloth stamped in red. Dustwrapper priced 8s.6d.net. $3,000.

STAPLEDON, Olaf. *Walking World*. London (1934). $350.

STAPP, William P. *The Prisoners of Perote*. Philadelphia, 1845. Wraps. $1,750. Cloth. $1,250.

STAR City of the West (The): Pueblo and Its Advantages. Pueblo, Colo., 1889. 24 pages, folded. $250.

STARBUCK, Alexander. *History of the American Whale Fishery* . . . Waltham, Mass., 1878. 6 plates. $600. New York, 1964. 2 vols. Half leather. In slipcase. One of 50 copies. $450. Trade edition. 2 vols. In slipcase. $200.

STARK, Freya. *Baghdad Sketches*. Baghdad, 1932. Author's first book. $750. New York (1938). Includes photos, drawings and text not in the London edition. $500.

STARKEY, James. *Reminiscences of Indian Depredations*. St. Paul, 1891. 25 pages, wraps. $300.

STARR, Emmet. *History of the Cherokee Indians and Their Legends and Folk Lore*. Oklahoma City, 1921. $750.

STARR, Frederick. *Indians of Southern Mexico*. Chicago, 1899. One of 560 signed copies. In original cloth. $1,750.

STARR, Julian. *The Disagreeable Woman*. New York, 1895. (By Horatio Alger, Jr.) $2,500.

STARRETT, Vincent. *All About Mother Goose*. (Glen Rock, Pa.), 1930. One of 275 copies. In glassine jacket. $300.

STARRETT, Vincent. *Arthur Machen: A Novelist of Ecstasy and Sin*. Chicago, 1918. Author's first book. Boards and cloth. One of 250 copies. $250.

STARRETT, Vincent. *The Private Life of Sherlock Holmes*. New York, 1933. $350.

STARRETT, Vincent (editor). *221B: Studies in Sherlock Holmes*. New York, 1940. $300.

STARRETT, Vincent. *The Unique Hamlet*. Chicago, 1920. Boards. One of 250 copies. Issued without dustwrapper. $1,500.

STARRETT, Vincent (editor). *In Praise of Stevenson*. Chicago, 1919. One of 300 copies. $250.

STATE of Indiana Delineated (The). New York, 1838. Boards, leather spine. (Published by J. H. Colton to accompany his separately published map, which is inserted in some copies.) With the map. $1,250. Without the map. $350.

STATEMENT Respecting the Earl of Selkirk's Settlement of Kildonan, upon the Red River, in North America. (By John Halkett.) London [1816]. Folding map. 125 pages. $3,000. London, 1817. Second (enlarged) edition. 194 pages, boards. With title altered to *Statement Respecting the Earl of Selkirk's Settlement upon the Red River, in North America*. $750.

STATIONERS Catalogue, Tags and Specialties. South Framingham, 1910. $250.

STATIONERS' Hand-Book; and Guide to the Paper Trade. London, 1870. Fifth edition, revised and enlarged. $150.

STATTON, Vargo. *Creature from the Black Lagoon*. (Pseudonym of John Russell Fearn.) (London, 1954.) Pictorial wraps. $400.

STEAD, Christina. *The Man Who Loved Children.* New York, 1940. With "800" crossed out on front and back flaps of dustwrapper and corrected to read "530." $1,250. With "800" eliminated altogether. $500.

STEAD, Christina. *The Salzburg Tales.* London (1934). Author's first book. $400. New York, 1934. $250.

STEAD, Christina. *Seven Poor Men of Sydney.* London, 1934. $500. New York, 1935. $350.

STEADMAN, Ralph. *Jelly Book.* London, 1967. Author's first book. Orange boards. In dustwrapper. $500. New York, 1970. $150.

STEADMAN, Ralph. *Little Red Computer.* London, 1969. Red boards. $750. Blue boards. $500.

STEADMAN, Ralph. *Still Life With Raspberry . . .* London, 1969. In pink dustwrapper with self portrait. $1,000. In white dustwrapper with raspberry. About 500 signed copies. $750. About 1,500 unsigned copies. $500. We know of two copies that appear to be signed and numbered by Steadman as among fifty such copies. Steadman does not remember an edition of fifty.

STEAM-BOAT (The). Edinburgh, 1822. (By John Galt.) $300.

STEARNS, Samuel. *The American Herbal or Materia Medica.* Walpole, N.H., 1801. $3,000.

STEARNS, Samuel. *The American Oracle.* London, 1791. $750.

STEDMAN, Charles. *The History of the Origin, Progress, and Termination of the American War . . .* London, 1794. 2 vols. 15 maps and plans (11 folding). $6,000.

STEDMAN, Edmund C. *Poems, Lyrical and Idyllic.* New York, 1860. Author's first book. $100.

STEDMAN, John G. *Narrative of a Five Years' Expedition Against the Revolted Negroes of Surinam in Guiana on the Wild Coast of America.* London, 1796. 2 vols. $3,500. London, 1813. 2 vols. Third edition. 80 full-page colored engravings, 3 maps, and 1 folding plate. $4,000.

STEEDMAN, Charles J. *Bucking the Sagebrush.* New York, 1904. 3 portraits, folding map, 9 Charles M. Russell plates. Pictorial cloth. $600.

STEEL, Flora A. (editor). *English Fairy Tales.* London, 1918. 16 color plates by Arthur Rackham. Vellum. One of 500 copies signed by Rackham. $2,000. Trade. Cloth. $300. New York, 1918. 250 copies. 16 mounted plates. $1,500. Trade. Half cloth. $250.

STEELE, James W. *The Klondike.* Chicago, 1897. Illustrated, 2 maps. 80 pages, pictorial gray wraps. $350.

STEELE, John. *Across the Plains in 1850.* Caxton Club. Chicago, 1930. One of 350 copies. 7 plates. Issued without dustwrapper. In slipcase. $300.

STEELE, John. *In Camp and Cabin: Mining Life and Adventure, in California . . .* Lodi, Wis., 1901. 81 pages, printed wraps. $1,000.

STEELE, R. J., and others (compilers). *Directory of the County of Placer.* San Francisco, 1861. Boards and calf. $1,250.

STEELE, Robert. *The Revival of Printing . . .* (London, 1912.) One of 350 copies. $200. One of 12 copies on vellum. $3,000.

STEELE, Zadock. *The Indian Captive.* Montpelier, Vt., 1818. $850. Springfield, 1908. One of 526 copies. $100.

STEFANSSON, Vilhjalmur. *My Life with the Eskimo.* New York, 1913. Author's first book. $250. London, 1913. (U.S. sheets.) $200.

STEFANSSON, Vilhjalmur. *Ultima Thule: Further Mysteries of the Arctic.* New York, 1940. Maps, illustrated. One of 100 signed copies. Issued without dustwrapper. $500.

STEFFENS, Lincoln. *John Reed Under the Kremlin.* Chicago, 1922. Introduction by Clarence Darrow. Wraps. One of 235 copies. $600.

STEFFENS, Lincoln. *The Shame of the Cities.* New York, 1904. Author's first book. $200.

STEGNER, Wallace. *Angle of Repose.* Garden City, 1971. $300.

STEGNER, Wallace. *Beyond the Hundredth Meridian: John Wesley Powell and the Second Opening of the West.* Boston, 1954. Folding map. $400.

STEGNER, Wallace. *The Big Rock Candy Mountain.* New York, 1943. $1,500.

STEGNER, Wallace. *Clarence Edward Dutton: An Appraisal.* Salt Lake City (1935?). Author's first book. Wraps. $7,500.

STEGNER, Wallace. *On a Darkling Plain.* New York (1940). $2,500.

STEGNER, Wallace. *The Potter's House.* Muscatine, Iowa, 1938. Issued in glassine dustwrapper. $3,500.

STEGNER, Wallace. *Remembering Laughter.* Boston, 1937. $500.

STEGNER, Wallace. *Two Rivers.* Covelo (1989). 50 roman-numbered signed copies. $1,000. Wraps. (150 copies.) $500.

STEIN, Aaron Marc. *Spirals.* New York, 1930. $300.

STEIN, Gertrude. See Toklas, Alice B.

STEIN, Gertrude. *An Acquaintance with Description.* Seizin Press. London, 1929. Oyster white linen. One of 225 signed copies. In glassine dustwrapper. $1,250.

STEIN, Gertrude. *Before the Flowers of Friendship Faded Friendship Faded.* Paris (1931). Wraps. One of 118 signed copies (of an edition of 120). In glassine dustwrapper. $2,000.

STEIN, Gertrude. *Blood on the Dining Room Floor.* Banyan Press. (Pawlet, Vt., 1948.) Half buckram and boards. One of 26 copies. In glassine dustwrapper and slipcase. $1,000. One of 600 copies in glassine dustwrapper and slipcase. $350.

STEIN, Gertrude. *A Book Concluding with As a Wife Has a Cow: A Love Story.* Paris (1926). 4 lithographs (one in color) by Juan Gris. Wraps. One of 102 signed copies. In glassine dustwrapper. $3,500. One of 10 copies on Japan vellum, signed. $15,000.

STEIN, Gertrude. *Composition as Explanation.* Hogarth Press. London, 1926. Green boards. Issued without dustwrapper. $250.

STEIN, Gertrude. *Dix Portraits.* Paris (1930). Translated by G. Hugnet and Virgil Thomson. Illustrated by Picasso and others. Decorated wraps. One of 10 copies on Japan vellum, signed, and with an autograph page of text by Stein. In glassine jacket. $5,000. One of 25 copies on Holland paper, signed by author and translators. In glassine dustwrapper. $2,000. One of 65 copies on Velin d'Arches paper, signed. In dustwrapper. $1,750. Trade edition. One of 402 copies on Alfa paper without illustrations. In printed dustwrapper plus glassine jacket. $450.

STEIN, Gertrude. *An Elucidation.* (Cover title.) (Paris), 1927. Wraps. (Issued as a supplement to *Transition* magazine after having been printed there with errors.) $250.

STEIN, Gertrude. *The Geographical History of America or The Relation of Human Nature to the Human Mind.* (New York, 1936.) Black and white cloth. $1,250.

STEIN, Gertrude. *Geography and Plays.* Boston (1922). Foreword by Sherwood Anderson. First binding, with lettering on front cover. $750. Second binding, cover unlettered. $600.

STEIN, Gertrude. *Have They Attacked Mary. He Giggled.* (Westchester, Pa., 1917.) Woodcut. Printed red wraps. One of 200 copies. $1,000.

STEIN, Gertrude. *How to Write.* Paris (1931). Boards, paper labels on spine. One of 1,000 copies. (Issued without dustwrapper.) $350.

STEIN, Gertrude. *Lectures in America.* New York, 1935. Beige cloth, top edge gray, frontispiece. $400. Brown cloth. Without frontis and top edge unstained. $150.

STEIN, Gertrude. *Lucy Church Amiably.* Paris, 1930. Boards. In plain brown paper dustwrapper. $750.

STEIN, Gertrude. *The Making of Americans.* (Dijon, 1925.) Wraps. One of 400 copies (of 500) but only a portion released. $2,500. One of 5 copies on vellum, with a letter by Stein inserted. $10,000. New York, 1926. First American issue. 100 copies bound up from French sheets. Issued without dustwrapper. $2,000.

STEIN, Gertrude. *Matisse Picasso and Gertrude Stein, with Two Shorter Stories.* Paris (1933). Wraps. In glassine dustwrapper and slipcase. $450.

STEIN, Gertrude. *Narration: Four Lectures.* Chicago (1935). Introduction by Thornton Wilder. Blue, black, and gilt cloth. One of 120 copies signed by Stein and Wilder. In slipcase. $1,000. Trade (unsigned). Orange cloth. $300. Chicago (1969). In slipcase. $75.

STEIN, Gertrude. *Operas and Plays.* Paris (1932). Wraps. In slipcase. $600.

STEIN, Gertrude. *Picasso.* Paris, 1938. Illustrated. Pictorial wraps. $350. London (1938). Rose-colored cloth. First English edition. $250. (New York), 1939. $200.

STEIN, Gertrude. *Portrait of Mabel Dodge at the Villa Curonia.* (Florence, 1912.) Stitched wraps. With imprint at foot of last page. One of 300 copies. $2,000.

STEIN, Gertrude. *Portraits and Prayers.* New York (1934). Pictorial cloth. In cellophane dustwrapper. $600.

STEIN, Gertrude. *Tender Buttons. Objects. Food. Rooms.* New York, 1914. Boards, paper label. (Issued without dustwrapper.) $1,250.

STEIN, Gertrude. *Things as They Are*. Pawlet, Vt. 1950. One of 26 lettered copies. $600. One of 490 copies. $350.

STEIN, Gertrude. *Three Lives*. New York, 1909. Author's first book. Blue cloth. (1,000 printed; issued without dustwrapper.) $1,750. New York and London, 1915. First English issue (300 from American sheets, with new title page). $1,500. London, 1920. First English trade edition. In dustwrapper. $750.

STEIN, Gertrude. *Useful Knowledge*. New York (1928). $450. London (1928). First English edition. $350.

STEIN, Gertrude. *A Village Are You Ready Yet Not Yet*. Paris (1928). Illustrated by Elie Lascaux. Wraps. One of 90 signed copies. In glassine dustwrapper. $1,750. One of 10 (numbered I–X) signed copies. $2,000. (Also 2 [numbered 0 and 00] for depot legal.) One of 10 copies on vellum, signed. $4,000.

STEIN, Gertrude. *What Are Masterpieces?* (Los Angeles, 1940.) Portrait frontispiece. Blue cloth. $250. One of 50 signed copies. $1,250.

STEIN, Gertrude. *The World Is Round*. New York (1939). Illustrated by Clement Hurd. Boards. One of 350 signed copies. In slipcase. $1,000. Trade. $300. London (1939). First English edition. $250.

STEIN, M. Aurel. *Ruins of Desert Cathay*. London, 1912. Two vols. $1,750.

STEINBECK, John. See *El Gabilan*.

STEINBECK, John. *Bombs Away*. New York, 1942. $400. (Note: "Second Printing" on bottom of rear panel of dustwrapper of that later printing.)

STEINBECK, John. *Cannery Row*. New York, 1945. Light-buff cloth. $1,000. Second issue in yellow cloth. $400. London/Toronto (1945). Strong orange-yellow cloth (variants: brilliant orange-yellow and deep orange cloth). $200.

STEINBECK, John. *Cup of Gold: A Life of Henry Morgan, Buccaneer*. McBride. New York, 1929. Author's first book. First issue, top edges stained blue and "First Published August, 1929" on copyright page. $25,000. Second issue, New York: Covici-Friede (1936). Maroon cloth, spine stamped in gilt. Using McBride sheets. $1,500. Second printing, New York: Covici-Friede (1936). Blue cloth. $450. London/Toronto (1937). Blue cloth, spine stamped in gilt. $2,000.

STEINBECK, John. *East of Eden*. New York, 1952. 1,500 signed copies (750 for private distribution). Issued in glassine dustwrapper and slipcase. $2,500. Trade. $1,250. London (1952). $250.

STEINBECK, John. *The First Watch*. (Los Angeles), 1947. One of 60 copies. Buff wraps with hand ties in envelope. $6,000.

STEINBECK, John. *Foreword to "Between Pacific Tides."* (Stanford), 1948. Wraps. (Estimated at 10 copies in Harvard Library Catalogue and at 25 copies by Cohn in a letter to Hersholt.) $10,000.

STEINBECK, John. *The Grapes of Wrath*. New York (1939). Dustwrapper states "First Edition" on lower right corner of front flap. $7,500. London/Toronto (1939). $750. Limited Editions Club, New York, 1940. 2 vols. 1,146 copies signed by the illustrator, Thomas Hart Benton. Issued in glassine dustwrapper in slipcase. $1,000.

STEINBECK, John. *How Edith McGillicuddy Met RLS.* Cleveland, 1943. One of 152 copies. Issued in plain green dustwrapper. $3,500. Without dustwrapper. $3,000.

STEINBECK, John. *In Dubious Battle.* New York (1936). One of 99 signed copies. In tissue dustwrapper and black slipcase with orange paper label printed in black. $7,500. Lettered copies. $10,000. Trade. Top edges stained red. $2,500. London/Toronto (1936). $1,000.

STEINBECK, John. *The Log from the Sea of Cortez.* New York, 1951. New title of *Sea of Cortez* with narrative portion only "About Ed Ricketts" by Steinbeck. Various cloth colors with maroon being the preferred. $500. London (1958). $250.

STEINBECK, John. *The Long Valley.* New York, 1938. $1,500. London/Toronto (1939). $450.

STEINBECK, John. *The Moon Is Down.* New York, 1942. Large period between "talk" and "this" on page 112, line 11. $400. Period deleted. $100. London/Toronto (1942). Terra-cotta cloth. $150.

STEINBECK, John. *Of Mice and Men.* New York (1937). First issue/printing. Page 88 has bullet between the 8s. "and only moved because the heavy hands were pendula" on page 9, line 20–21. $3,500. Second issue/printing, with line 21 reading "loosely." on page 9 and bullet on page 88 deleted. In priced dustwrapper. $300. London/Toronto (1937). Blue cloth, spine stamped in gilt, top edges stained blue, blue dustwrapper printed in black. (Some copies with wraparound band) (Also a variant with pink top edge and dustwrapper printed in black.) $1,000. Limited Editions Club, New York, 1970. 1,500 copies signed by the illustrator, Fletcher Martin. Issued in slipcase. $250.

STEINBECK, John. *Of Mice and Men: A Play.* New York (1937). Beige cloth, top edges stained blue. First-issue dustwrapper (reportedly) without reviews on back panel, although also noted with reviews of play (no book) on back of review copy. $2,000.

STEINBECK, John. *The Pastures of Heaven.* Brewer, Warren & Putnam, New York, 1932. Green cloth, front cover stamped in gilt, top edges stained black. $10,000. Robert O. Ballou imprint on cloth spine and title page, dustwrapper still has Brewer imprint. $5,000. Ballou on title page, book spine, and dustwrapper. $3,500. London (1933). Green cloth, spine printed in black. $2,000. Covici-Friede. New York, no date (circa 1935). $1,250.

STEINBECK, John. *The Red Pony.* New York, 1937. One of 699 signed copies. Flexible beige cloth, clear cellophane dustwrapper, in tan slipcase with limitation number on spine. $3,500. 52 (?) lettered copies (have seen "H" and "QQ" catalogued). $10,000. New York, 1945. Printed by Kipe Offset Process Company. Issued without dustwrapper in blue-gray slipcase. $200. London (1949). Stiff wraps. States "First Published in *The Long Valley* 1939. Reprinted 1949." $200.

STEINBECK, John. *Saint Katy the Virgin.* (New York, 1936.) One of 199 signed copies. Issued in decorated boards, gilt cloth spine printed in red. In glassine dustwrapper. $2,500.

STEINBECK, John. *Tortilla Flat.* New York (1935). Tan cloth printed in blue, top edges stained blue. $5,000. London (1935). Blue cloth stamped in gilt. $1,750.

STEINBECK, John. *The Wayward Bus.* New York, 1947. Dark reddish-orange cloth with blindstamped bus showing up lighter than rest of binding. $300. Variants. $200. (600,000 copies with Book-of-the-Month Club dot on back.) London/Toronto (1947). Coarse red cloth. $150.

STEINBECK, John, and Ricketts, Edward F. *Sea of Cortez*. New York, 1941. Green cloth, top edges stained orange. $1,250.

STEPHENS, Mrs. Ann S. *Malaeska: The Indian Wife of the White Hunter*. New York (1860). Printed orange wraps. First issue, with covers 6⅝ inches by 4½ inches, and without woodcut on cover. $3,000.

STEPHENS, Ann Sophia. See Slick, Jonathan.

STEPHENS, Ann Sophia (editor). *The Portland Sketch Book*. Portland, Me., 1836. Author's first book appearance. In original cloth. $150.

STEPHENS, James. See Esse, James.

STEPHENS, James. *Collected Poems*. London, 1926. Boards and vellum. One of 500 signed, large-paper copies. $200.

STEPHENS, James. *The Crock of Gold*. London, 1912. Green cloth. $250. London, 1926. Illustrated. Half vellum. One of 525 signed copies. In dustwrapper. $600. Limited Editions Club, New York, 1942. In slipcase. $175.

STEPHENS, James. *Green Branches*. Dublin, 1916. Wraps. One of 500 copies. $125. New York, 1916. First American edition. Half vellum. One of 500 copies. $125.

STEPHENS, James. *The Insurrection in Dublin*. London, 1916. $300.

STEPHENS, James. *Insurrections*. Dublin, 1909. Author's first book. In dustwrapper priced 1/-net and single imprint of Maunsel. $600. In dustwrapper, without price and with both Maunsel and MacMillan on front (second printing). $350. Without dustwrapper. $100.

STEPHENS, James. *Irish Fairy Tales*. London, 1920. Illustrated by Arthur Rackham. Vellum and boards. One of 520 copies signed by Rackham. $2,500. Trade issue. $600. Without dustwrapper. $300.

STEPHENS, John L. *Incidents of Travel in Central America, Chiapas and Yucatan*. New York, 1841. 2 vols. Folding map, other maps and plans, plates, other illustrations. Cloth. $1,500.

STEPHENS, Lorenzo Dow. *Life Sketches of a Jayhawker of '49*. (San Jose), 1916. 6 plates. 68 pages, printed wraps. $350.

STEPHENS, W. P. *American Yachting*. New York, 1904. Frontispiece halftone illustration on Japan vellum. Dark olive-green morocco over marbled boards. $750.

STEPHENSON, Neal. *The Big U.* New York (1984). Wraps. $500.

STERLING, George. *Ode on the Opening of the Panama-Pacific International Exposition . . .* San Francisco, 1915. Boards and cloth. One of 525 copies. $175.

STERLING, George. *The Testimony of the Suns and Other Poems*. San Francisco, 1903. Author's first book. Black cloth. $125. San Francisco, 1927. John Henry Nash printing. Folio, boards. One of 300 copies. (Facsimile of title poem with comments by Ambrose Bierce.) $250.

STERLING, George; TAGGARD, Genevieve; and RORTY, James. *Continent's End: An Anthology of Contemporary California Poets.* Book Club of California. San Francisco, 1925. Boards, pigskin spine. One of 600 copies. $200.

STERLING *Library (The): A Catalogue of the Printed Books* . . . No place (1954). $350.

STERN, Gerald. *The Naming of Beasts* . . . Omaha, 1973. Author's first book. (100 copies.) $1,500.

STERN, James. *The Heartless Land.* London, 1932. Author's first book. (First regular publication.) $250.

STERNE, Laurence. *A Sentimental Journey Through France and Italy.* London, 1768. 2 vols. $2,000. Waltham Saint Lawrence, 1928. One of 500 copies. $250. Black Sun Press. Paris, 1929. Illustrated by Polia Chentoff. Wraps. One of 333 copies on Arches paper. In tissue jacket and slipcase. $600. One of 15 copies on Japan vellum. In slipcase. $3,500. Limited Editions Club, Wycombe, 1936. In slipcase. $300.

STERNE, Laurence. *The Life and Opinions of Tristram Shandy.* London, 1760–67. 9 vols. $7,500. Philadelphia, 1774. 2 vols. $5,000. Golden Cockerel Press. Waltham St. Lawrence, 1929–30. 3 vols. Illustrated. Cloth. One of 500 copies. $350. Limited Editions Club, New York, 1935. 2 vols. In slipcase. $125.

STETSON, Charlotte Perkins. *In this Our World.* London, 1893. $5,000. San Francisco, 1895. Wraps. $2,000. San Francisco, 1895. Second edition in blue cloth. Adds 46 poems. $450.

STETSON, Charlotte Perkins. *Women and Economics.* Boston, 1898. $2,500.

STETSON, Charlotte Perkins. *The Yellow Wall Paper.* Boston, 1899. $2,000. Boston, 1901. $1,000.

STEUBEN, Baron Frederick William von. *Regulations for the Order and Discipline of the Troops of the United States. Part 1.* (All published.) (Philadelphia, 1779.) 8 folding plates. $6,000.

STEVENS, C. A. *Berdan's United States Sharpshooters in the Army of the Potomac.* St. Paul, 1892. Illustrated. $450.

STEVENS, Henry. *American Books with Tails To 'Em* . . . London, 1873. $125.

STEVENS, Henry. *Recollections of Mr. James Lenox of New York and the Formation of His Library.* London, 1886. Large-paper copy on Whatman paper. Three portraits done in proof on India paper. $250.

STEVENS, Henry. *Who Spoils Our New English Books.* London, 1884. $150.

STEVENS, Isaac I. *Campaigns of the Rio Grande and of Mexico.* New York, 1851. 108 pages, wraps. $1,000.

STEVENS, Isaac I. *A Circular Letter to Emigrants Desirous of Locating in Washington Territory.* Washington, 1858. 21 pages, sewn. $600.

STEVENS, Wallace. See *Harvard Lyrics; Verses from the Harvard Advocate.*

STEVENS, Wallace. *The Auroras of Autumn.* New York, 1950. $350.

STEVENS, Wallace. *The Collected Poems of Wallace Stevens.* New York, 1954. First collected edition. One of 2,500 copies. $600.

STEVENS, Wallace. *Esthétique du Mal*. Cummington Press. (Cummington, Mass.), 1945. Illustrated by Wightman Williams. Half leather. One of 40 copies signed by author and artist. In glassine dustwrapper. $10,000. One of 300 copies (unsigned). in glassine dustwrapper. Rose boards. $3,500. Green boards. $1,500.

STEVENS, Wallace. *Harmonium*. New York, 1923. Author's first book. First binding in checkered boards. $15,000. Second binding in striped boards. $12,500. Third binding. Blue cloth. $7,500. New York, 1931. Gray boards. $1,000. Other bindings. $750.

STEVENS, Wallace. *Ideas of Order*. New York (Alcestis Press), 1935. One of 135 signed copies. In glassine dustwrapper and slipcase. $5,000. One of 20 signed copies (I–XX). $7,500. 10 copies signed for review. $2,500. New York: Knopf, 1936. First edition stated. First binding in striped cloth. $1,500. In rose-colored boards. $1,000. In yellow boards. $750.

STEVENS, Wallace. *The Man with the Blue Guitar & Other Poems*. New York, 1937. First issue dustwrapper, with "conjunctioning" on front flap. $1,500. Second issue with "conjunctions." $750.

STEVENS, Wallace. *The Necessary Angel*. New York, 1951. $350.

STEVENS, Wallace. *Notes Toward a Supreme Fiction*. Cummington, Mass., 1942. One of 190 copies. In acetate dustwrapper. $1,000. One of 80 signed copies. $5,000. Cummington (1943). Boards. Second edition. One of 330 copies. In plain paper jacket. $400.

STEVENS, Wallace. *Owl's Clover*. New York (1936). Wraps. One of 85 signed copies. $5,000. One of 20 (i–xx) signed copies. $7,500.

STEVENS, Wallace. *Parts of a World*. New York, 1942. $1,000.

STEVENS, Wallace. *A Primitive Like an Orb*. New York, 1948. Illustrated by Kurt Seligmann. Olive-green wraps. One of 500 copies. $300.

STEVENS, Wallace. *Raoul Dufy: A Note*. (New York, 1953.) 4 pages, wraps. One of 200 copies. $1,250.

STEVENS, Wallace. *Three Academic Pieces*. Cummington, MA, 1947. One of 102 copies. $2,500. One of 92 copies (i–xcii). $2,500. One of 52 signed copies (I–LII). Light-tan hand-colored boards. In slipcase. $6,000. (All three issues in plain white dustwrappers.)

STEVENS, Wallace. *Transport to Summer*. New York, 1947. $500.

STEVENS, William. *A System for the Discipline of the Artillery . . .* New York, 1797. Vol. I (all published). $1,250.

STEVENSON, Elizabeth Ware. See S., E. W., and M., S. W.

STEVENSON, R. Randolph, M.D. *The Southern Side: or, Andersonville Prison*. Baltimore, 1876. $350.

STEVENSON, Robert Louis. See *The Pentland Rising*.

STEVENSON, Robert Louis. *Across the Plains*. London, 1892. Cream-colored cloth. One of 100 large-paper copies. $750. Trade. $200. (Hillsborough, Calif., 1950.) Allen Press. Illustrated. Boards. One of 200 copies. $300.

STEVENSON, Robert Louis. *The Black Arrow.* London, 1888. Wraps. $750. Cloth. $500. New York, 1916. Illustrated by N. C. Wyeth. $300.

STEVENSON, Robert Louis. *Catriona: A Sequel to "Kidnapped."* London, 1893. $350.

STEVENSON, Robert Louis. *A Child's Garden of Verses.* London, 1885. Blue cloth. $4,500. New York, 1885. $1,000. London, 1896. Illustrated by Charles Robinson. First illustrated edition. One of 150 large-paper copies. $1,250. Trade. $350. Limited Editions Club, New York, 1944. In slipcase. $200.

STEVENSON, Robert Louis. *Father Damien.* Sydney, Australia, 1890. Wraps, stapled. One of 25 copies. $3,000. Edinburgh, 1890. Unbound sheets in board portfolio. One of 30 copies on vellum. $2,000. London, 1890. Wraps. First published edition. $500. San Francisco, 1930. John Henry Nash printing. 2 vols., half vellum. $250.

STEVENSON, Robert Louis. *The Graver & the Pen, or Scenes from Nature with Appropriate Verses.* Edinburgh (1882). Woodcuts. Gray wraps. $1,000.

STEVENSON, Robert Louis. *An Inland Voyage.* London, 1878. Frontispiece by Walter Crane. Blue cloth. Author's first novel. $1,250. Boston, 1883. $350.

STEVENSON, Robert Louis. *Island Nights' Entertainments.* New York, 1893. $300. London, 1893. First English edition, first issue, with price correction in ink in list of Stevenson's works. $300.

STEVENSON, Robert Louis. *Kidnapped.* (London), 1886. Folding frontispiece map. Issued in various colors of cloth. First issue with the reading "business" in line 11 of page 40 and ads dated "5.G. 4.86" and "5.B. 4.86." $2,500. Second printing with the reading "pleasure" on line 11 of page 40. $750. New York, 1886. Decorated red smooth cloth. 8 pages of advertisements. Folding frontispiece map. $1,000. Wraps. No advertisements. $750. New York, 1913. Illustrated by N. C. Wyeth. $300. Limited Editions Club, New York, 1938. In slipcase. $125.

STEVENSON, Robert Louis. *The Master of Ballantrae.* London, 1889. Red cloth. $500. Limited Editions Club (New York), 1965. In slipcase. $125.

STEVENSON, Robert Louis. *The Merry Men and Other Tales and Fables.* London, 1887. Decorated blue cloth. With 32 pages of ads at end dated September 1886. $500.

STEVENSON, Robert Louis. *New Arabian Nights.* London, 1882. 2 vols., green cloth. First issue, with yellow endpapers in vol. 1. and ads in vol. 2 dated May 1882. $1,500.

STEVENSON, Robert Louis. *The Silverado Squatters.* London, 1883. Decorated green cloth. First issue, with "his" lacking in penultimate line on page 140 and 32-page catalogue dated October 1883 at back. $750. Grabhorn Press. San Francisco, 1952. Boards and cloth. One of 900 copies. In original plain wrapper. $200.

STEVENSON, Robert Louis. *The Strange Case of Dr. Jekyll and Mr. Hyde.* New York, 1886. Wraps. $4,500. Cloth. $3,000. London, 1886. First issue, in wraps, with the date on front cover altered in ink from 1885 to 1886. $6,000. Cloth. $3,500. Limited Editions Club, New York, 1952. Marbled boards. In slipcase. $150.

STEVENSON, Robert Louis. *Ticonderoga.* Edinburgh, 1887. Vellum boards. One of 50 copies. $1,250. (A Thomas J. Wise forgery.)

STEVENSON, Robert Louis. *Travels with a Donkey in the Cevennes.* London, 1879. Frontispiece by Walter Crane. Green cloth. $1,250. Limited Editions Club, New York, 1957. In slipcase. $100.

STEVENSON, Robert Louis. *Treasure Island.* London, 1883. Green, gray, blue, or rust-colored cloth. First issue, with "rain" for "vain" in last line of page 40, "dead man's chest" on page 2, line 7, not capitalized; "7" dropped from page number on page 127; period dropped from line 20 on page 178 (after "opportunity"); "worse" for "worst" in line 3 on page 197; frontispiece map in three colors; and ads dated "5R-1083" at end, and with this title listed incorrectly as having 304 pages. $10,000. Boston, 1884. Frontispiece map, illustrated. Pictorial cloth. First American (and first illustrated) edition. $3,000. London, 1885. Illustrated. Red cloth. First English illustrated edition. $1,000. London, 1911. One of 250 copies. Vellum. 12 tipped-in plates by John Cameron. $1,250. London, 1927. Illustrated by Edmund Dulac. Vellum. One of 50 signed copies. $2,000. Trade edition. Cloth. $500. New York (1927). Dulac illustrations. First American trade edition. $450. Philadelphia, 1930. Illustrated by Lyle Justis. Tan cloth. In dustwrapper and slipcase. $450. Limited Editions Club, New York, 1941. In slipcase. $250. Extra lithograph bound in. $350. London, 1949. Illustrated by Mervyn Peake. In dustwrapper. $400.

STEVENSON, Robert Louis, and OSBOURNE, Lloyd. *The Wrecker.* London, 1892. $250.

STEVENSON, Robert Louis, and VAN DE GRIFT, Fanny. *More New Arabian Nights. The Dynamiter.* London, 1885. Cloth. $750. Green pictorial wraps. $950.

STEWART, George R. *Earth Abides.* New York, 1949. $300.

STEWART, James. *Plocacosmos: or The Whole Art of Hairdressing . . .* London, 1782. 10 engraved plates. $2,500.

STEWART, James Lindsey (editor). *Golfiania Miscellanea.* London, 1887. $1,500.

STEWART, Mary. *Madam, Will You Talk?* London, 1955. Author's first book. $250. New York (1956). $100.

STEWART, Sir William Drummond. See *Altowan.*

STICKLEY, Gustav. *Craftsman Homes.* New York (1909). Small quarto. Rough linen. $500.

STIEGLITZ, Alfred. See *Camera Work.*

STIFF, Edward. *The Texan Emigrant.* Cincinnati, 1840. Folding map in color. Cloth. $5,000.

STILL, James. *Hounds on the Mountain.* New York, 1937. Author's first book. One of 700 copies. $1500. One of 50 copies not for sale. $350.

STILL, James. *River of Earth.* New York, 1940. $125.

STILL, William. *The Underground Rail Road.* Philadelphia (1872). $750.

STILLMAN, Jacob D.B.B. *The Horse in Motion, as Shown by Instantaneous Photography.* Boston, 1882. 107 plates, 9 in color, by Eadweard Muybridge. $2,000. London, 1882. $1,750.

STILLWELL, Margaret Bingham. *Gutenberg and the Catholicon of 1460.* New York, 1936. Folio, cloth. With an original leaf of the *Catholicon* printed by Gutenberg in 1460. In slipcase. $5,000.

STIPP, G. W. (compiler). *The Western Miscellany.* Xenia, Ohio, 1827. $3,500.

STIRLING, James. *Letters from the Slave States.* London, 1857. Map. $500.

STIVENS, DAL. *Jimmy Brockett.* London, 1951. Author's first book. $350.

STOCKTON, Frank R. *The Floating Prince and Other Fairy Tales.* New York, 1881. $350.

STOCKTON, Frank R. *The Great War Syndicate.* Collier. New York, 1889. Printed wraps. $250.

STOCKTON, Frank R. *The Lady, or the Tiger? and Other Stories.* New York, 1884. Pictorial gray and brown cloth. $400.

STOCKTON, Frank R. *Tales Out of School.* New York, 1876. Illustrated. Pictorial cloth. $150.

STOCKTON, Frank R. *Ting-a-Ling.* New York, 1870. Illustrated. Pictorial purple cloth. Author's first book. $300.

STODDARD, Maj. Amos. *Sketches, Historical and Descriptive of Louisiana.* Philadelphia, 1812. $1,000.

STODDARD, Herbert L. *The Bob-White Quail . . .* New York, 1931. One of 260 signed copies, and with an original drawing signed by Frank W. Benson. $1,000.

STODDARD, Richard Henry. *Footprints.* New York, 1849. Author's first book. Wraps. $1,500.

STOKER, Bram. *Dracula.* Westminster (London), 1897. Yellow cloth. First issue, without ads. $20,000. Second issue, with ad for *The Shoulder of Shasta* on page (392). $12,500. Second or third printing with multiple pages of ads. $7,500. (Fourth impression is stated.) New York, 1899. Pictorial cloth. First American edition. $3,000. Grosset & Dunlap. New York, 1931. Photoplay edition. $2,000. Limited Editions Club, New York, 1965. In slipcase. $250.

STOKER, Bram. *Dracula's Guest . . .* London, 1914. $1,250.

STOKER, Bram. *The Lady of the Shroud.* London, 1909. $750.

STOKER, Bram. *The Lair of the White Worm.* London (1911). Page 325 with ad for *Cheiro's Memoirs* as "Ready shortly." $750.

STOKER, Bram. *The Shoulder of Shasta.* Westminster, 1895. Decorated red cloth. $1,000. London/New York, 1895. Dark-green cloth. $600.

STOKER, Bram. *Under the Sunset.* London, 1882. $600.

STOKES, I.N. Phelps. *The Iconography of Manhattan Island.* 6 vols. New York, 1915–28. Many plates, some in color. One of 360 copies. In dustwrappers and slipcase. $7,500. One of 42 copies on Japan vellum. $10,000. New York, 1967. 6 vols. Facsimile edition. $2,500.

STOKES, I.N. Phelps, and HASKELL, Daniel C. *American Historical Prints: Early Views of American Cities.* New York, 1932. $600. New York, 1933. $500.

STONE, Henry A. *Wrestling Intercollegiate and Olympic.* New York, 1939. $100.

STONE, Herbert Stuart. *First Editions of American Authors.* Cambridge, 1893. $150.

STONE, Irving. *Pageant of Youth*. New York, 1933. Author's first book. $300.

STONE, Reynolds. *The Old Rectory.* London, 1976. 17 engravings. One of 150 copies. Matted title page and imprint page. 17 wood engravings. Small booklet enclosed (also limited to 150 copies). In solander case. $5,500. Trade. $25.

STONE, Robert. *Dog Soldiers.* Boston, 1974. $250. (London, 1975). $150.

STONE, Robert. *A Hall of Mirrors.* Boston, 1967. Author's first book. $600. London (1968). $300.

STONE, Wilbur Macey. *The Gigantick Histories of Thomas Boreman.* Portland, 1933. One of 250 signed copies. In glassine wrap. $175.

STOPPARD, Tom. *Lord Malquist and Mr. Moon.* London (1966). Author's first book. $350. New York, 1968. First printing stated. $150.

STOPPARD, Tom. *Rosencrantz and Guildenstern Are Dead.* London (1967). $750. New York (1967). First edition stated. $500. Wraps. $50.

STOREY, David. *This Sporting Life.* (London, 1960.) Author's first book. $450. New York, 1960. $150.

STORY, Joseph. *The Power of Solitude.* Boston (1800). Author's first book. $500.

STOUT, Rex. *Fer-de-Lance.* New York, 1934. (First of the Nero Wolfe detective novels.) $10,000. London, 1935. $2,500.

STOUT, Rex. *How Like a God.* New York, 1929. Author's first book. $1,750. London, 1931. $750.

STOUT, Rex. *The League of Frightened Men.* New York (1935). $6,000. London, 1935. $1,500.

STOUT, Rex. *Over My Dead Body.* New York (1940). $2,000. London, 1940. $300.

STOUT, Rex. *Some Buried Caesar.* New York (1939). $3,500. London, 1939. $1,000.

STOUT, Rex. *The Rubber Band.* New York (1936). $4,500. London, 1938. $1,250.

STOUT, Rex. *Too Many Cooks.* New York (1938). $3,000. London, 1938. $1,000. Also: Same title *American Magazine* (no place) 1938. Consisting of a box shaped like a book, in dustwrapper. Box contains title page and cards laid in as follows: "Important" note from Nero Wolfe, "menu," and 34 menu cards. The dustwrapper is attached to the back of the box. $2,000.

STOW, Randolph. *A Haunted Land.* London, 1956. Author's first book. $500.

STOW, Randolph. *Outrider.* London, 1962. $350.

STOWE, Harriet Beecher. See Beecher, Harriet Elizabeth.

STOWE, Harriet Beecher. *Dred: A Tale of the Great Dismal Swamp.* London, 1856. 2 vols. $600. Boston, 1856. 2 vols. $400.

STOWE, Harriet Beecher. *A Key to Uncle Tom's Cabin.* Boston, 1853. Wraps. $400. Cloth. $250.

STOWE, Harriet Beecher. *Uncle Sam's Emancipation.* Philadelphia, 1853. $600.

STOWE, Harriet Beecher. *Uncle Tom's Cabin.* Boston, 1852. 2 vols. Title vignette, 6 plates. First issue, pictorial wraps, with slug of Hobart and Robbins on copyright page. (Later "George C. Rand.") $15,000. First printing, second issue (cloth) binding, $12,500. Also, "Gift" binding of gilt-decorated brown cloth. $20,000. London: Cassell, 1852. Illustrated by George Cruikshank. 13 parts, pictorial wraps. $3,000. Cloth. $1,500. Normally cited as the first English edition. However, BAL states the Clarke and Co edition actually was advertised for April while the Cassell was October. So we also estimate the Clarke and Co. at $1,500. Cambridge, 1892. 2 vols. One of 250 copies signed by Stowe. Suede binding. In slipcase. $5,000. Limited Editions Club, New York, 1938. Marbled boards and leather. In slipcase. $750.

STOWER, Caleb. *The Printer's Grammer . . .* London, 1808. $1,250.

STRACHEY, Lytton. *Books and Characters.* London, 1922. $200.

STRACHEY, G. L(ytton). *Landmarks in French Literature.* London (1912). Author's first book. First issue: top edge stained green. 8 pages ads. $250.

STRACHEY, Mrs. Richard. *Nursery Lyrics.* London, 1893. Author's first book. $450. Reissued with new title page and binding—"Lady Strachey." $150.

STRAHORN, Mrs. Carrie A. *15,000 Miles by Stage . . .* New York, 1911. Numerous illustrations, including 4 in color by Charles M. Russell. $750. New York, 1915. Second edition. $350.

STRAHORN, Robert E. *The Hand-book of Wyoming, and Guide to the Black Hills and Big Horn Regions.* Cheyenne, 1877. 14 plates. 272 pages, printed wraps. $1,000. Cloth. $600.

STRAHORN, Robert E. *Montana and Yellowstone National Park.* Kansas City, 1881. 191 pages, flexible cloth wraps, plus 14 pages ads. $1,000.

STRAHORN, Robert E. *The Resources of Montana Territory.* Helena, 1879. Map. Wraps. $1,000.

STRAHORN, Robert E. *To the Rockies and Beyond . . .* Omaha, 1878. Folding map. Wraps. $1,250. Cloth. $1,000. Omaha, 1879. Cloth. Second edition. $750.

STRAND, Mark. *Sleeping with One Eye Open.* Stone Wall Press. Iowa City, 1963. Author's first book. One of 225 copies. In acetate dustwrapper. $1,500.

STRAND, Paul. *The Mexican Portfolio.* New York, 1967. One of 1,000 signed copies. $3,000.

STRAND, Paul. *Paul Strand: A Retrospective Monograph . . . 1915–45* and *A Retrospective Monograph . . . 1950–68.* New York, 1972. 2 vols. One of 100 copies signed by the photographer. In slipcase. $1,200.

STRANG, William. *Death and the Ploughman's Wife.* London, 1894. One of 110 copies with each of the original etchings and mezzotints signed in pencil by Strang. $1,500.

STRANG, William. *The Earth Fiend.* London, 1892. Etchings by the author. Buckram. One of 150 signed copies. $750.

STRANGE, Edward F. *The Colour-Prints of Hiroshige . . .* London, 1925. 16 colored, 36 plain plates. Buckram. In dustwrapper. $350. Vellum. One of 250 copies. $600.

STRANGER in Lowell (The). Boston, 1845. (By John Greenleaf Whittier.) Wraps. $450.

STRATTON, R. B. *Captivity of the Oatman Girls* . . . San Francisco, 1857. Woodcut portrait and map. 231 pages, printed wraps. Second edition of *Life Among the Indians* (entry following). $2,500. Chicago, 1857. (Reprint.) $1,000. New York, 1858. 3 plates. Third edition, enlarged. $600.

STRATTON, R. B. *Life Among the Indians.* San Francisco, 1857. Illustrated. 183 pages, wraps. $16,000 at auction in 1999. Grabhorn Press. San Francisco, 1935. Plates, half cloth. One of 550 copies. $200. (See preceding entry.)

STRAUB, Peter. *Ishmael.* (London, 1972.) Author's first book. Wraps. One of 100 signed copies. In dustwrapper. $200.

STRAUS, Ralph. *The Unspeakable Curll, Being Some Account of Edmund Curll, Bookseller* . . . New York/London, 1928. One of 525 copies. $250.

STRAUSS, David Friedrich. *The Life of Jesus.* London, 1846. 3 vols. Translated by George Eliot (Mary Ann Evans). First edition in English. George Eliot's first book. Blue-green cloth. $5,000. Rebound. $1,500.

STREET, Cecil John Charles. See Rhode, John.

STREET, George Edmund. *Brick and Marble in the Middle Ages.* London, 1855. Author's first book. $300.

STREETER, Floyd Benjamin. *Prairie Trails and Cow Towns.* Boston (1936). 12 plates. $750.

STREETER, Thomas W. See *Americana-Beginnings.*

STREETER, Thomas W. *Bibliography of Texas.* Cambridge, Mass., 1955–56–60. 5 vols. Part I, 2 vols.; part II, 1 vol.; part III, 2 vols. One of 600 copies. In dustwrapper. $1,500.

STREETER, Thomas W. (sale). *The Celebrated Collection of Americana Formed by the Late Thomas Winthrop Streeter.* New York, 1966–69. 8 vols. (including index). $750.

STRIBLING, T. S. *The Cruise of the Dry Dock.* Chicago (1917). Author's first book. 4 color illustrations. $150.

STRICKLAND, William. *Reports on Canals, Railways, Roads, and Other Subjects* . . . Philadelphia, 1826. Plates. $2,000.

STRICTURES *on a Voyage to South America, as Indicated by the "Secretary of the (Late) Mission" to La Plata* . . . Baltimore, 1819. By a Friend of Truth and Sound Policy. (By H. M. Brackenridge.) $500.

Strike At Shanes, The. Boston: American Humane Education (1893). (By Gene Stratton Porter but questionable.) Author's first book. $500. Chicago: A. Flanaghan (1896).Wraps. $200.

STRONG, L.A.G. *Dallington Rhymes.* Author's first book. 200 copies privately printed 1919. $400.

STRONG, Gen. W. E. *A Trip to the Yellowstone National Park in July, August, and September, 1875.* Washington, 1876. 2 folding maps, 7 signed photos, 7 plates. Half morocco. $3,500.

STRUTT, Joseph. *A Biographical Dictionary.* London, 1785, 1786. 2 vols. $500.

STUART, Granville. *Forty Years on the Frontier.* Cleveland, 1925. 2 vols. 15 plates. $1,000.

STUART, H. *We Have Kept the Faith.* Dublin, 1923. Author's first book. $350.

STUART, Jesse. *Beyond Dark Hills.* New York, 1938. $350. New York (1972). Pictorial cloth. One of 950 signed copies. In slipcase. $250.

STUART, Jesse. *Harvest of Youth.* Howe, Okla. (1930). 80 pages. Author's first book. Possibly as few as 20 copies, according to Stuart. $3,500.

STUART, Jesse. *Head O'W-Hollow.* (New York) 1936. $400.

STUART, Jesse. *Man with a Bull-Tongue Plow.* New York, 1934. $600.

STUART, Jesse. *Men of the Mountains.* New York, 1941. $600.

STUART, Jesse. *Taps for Private Tussie.* New York, 1943. First edition stated. $150.

STUART, Joseph A. *My Roving Life.* Auburn, Calif., 1895. 2 vols. $2,000.

STUART, Robert. *The Discovery of the Oregon Trail.* New York, 1935. Edited by Philip Ashton Rollins. $250.

STUDER, Jacob H. *The Birds of North America.* New York, 1888. 119 color plates. Folio, morocco. $1,250. New York, 1903. Half leather. $750.

STUDER, Jacob H. *Studer's Popular Ornithology: The Birds of North America.* New York and Columbus (1874–78). 2 vols. $1,750.

STURGEON, Theodore. *More Than Human.* New York (1953). $450. Wraps. $100.

STURGEON, Theodore. *Without Sorcery.* Philadelphia (1948). Author's first book. $300. Red buckram. One of 80 (or 88) signed copies. In slipcase. $1,750.

STURGIS, Thomas. *Common Sense of the Sioux War.* Cheyenne, 1877. 52 pages, wraps. $1,000.

STYRON, William. *The Confessions of Nat Turner.* New York (1967). One of 500 signed copies. In slipcase. $300. Trade edition with extra leaf signed. $250. Trade. $100. London (1968). $125. Franklin Press, 1976. "Limited" edition (not signed). $75. Franklin Library, 1979. Signed limited edition. $100.

STYRON, William. *Lie Down in Darkness.* Indianapolis (1951). Author's first book. First edition stated. $600. London (1952). $200. Franklin Library. Signed "limited" edition. $100.

STYRON, William. *Sophie's Choice.* New York, 1979. One of 500 signed copies. In slipcase. $300. Trade edition with extra leaf "Advance Presentation Edition" bound in. Light-blue cloth in tissue dustwrapper. $125. Trade. $75. London, 1979. $75.

SUCKLING, George. *An Historical Account of the Virgin Islands.* London, 1780. $1,000.

SUE, Eugene. *The Wandering Jew.* London, 1844. 3 vols. $500. New York, 1845. $300.

SUGDEN, Alan V. *A History, of English Wallpaper, 1509–1914.* New York or London (1925). 70 color plates and 190 halftone illustrations. Folio, blue buckram. In dustwrapper and slipcase. $1,000.

SULLIVAN, James. *The History of the District of Maine.* Boston, 1795. Folding frontispiece map. $2,000.

SULLIVAN, Louis H. *A System of Architectural Ornament.* New York, 1924. Illustrated. Folio, half cloth. One of 1,000 copies. $1,250.

SULLIVAN, Maurice S. *The Travels of Jedediah Smith* . . . Santa Ana, Calif., 1934. With 2 plates and folding map. Pictorial cloth. Issued without dustwrapper. $750.

SULLIVAN, W. John L. *Twelve Years in the Saddle for Law and Order on the Frontiers of Texas.* Austin, 1909. 13 plates. $2,500.

SULZBERGER, Cyrus. *The Resistentialists.* New York (1962). (Suppressed because of the author's unauthorized use of three Ernest Hemingway letters.) $600.

SUMMERS, Montague. See Scot, Reginald; Sinistrari, Ludovico.

SUMMERS, Montague. *Antinous* . . . London [1907]. Author's first book. $450.

SUMNER, Charles. *'Cross the Plains.* (San Francisco, 1869.) Folding map. Wraps. $450.

SUMNER, James. *The Mysterious Marbler.* North Hills, 1976. One of 250 copies. With 11 original marbled samples. $450.

SUNDERLAND, LaRoy. *Mormonism Exposed and Refuted.* New York, 1838. 54 pages, printed wraps. $2,500.

SUPERNATURALISM of New England (The). New York, 1847. (By John Greenleaf Whittier—his name on cover but not on title page.) Printed wraps. $1,250.

SURTEES, Robert Smith. See *The Analysis of the Hunting Field; "Ask Mama"; Handley Cross; Hawbuck Grange; Jorrocks' Jaunts and Jollities; Mr. Facey Romford's Hounds; Mr. Sponge's Sporting Tour; "Plain or Ringlets?"*

SUTHERLAND, Thomas A. *Howard's Campaign Against the Nez Percé Indians.* Portland, Ore., 1878. 48 pages, wraps. $1,250.

SUTPHEN, William. *Golfer's Alphabet.* New York, 1898. (Sketches by A. B. Frost.) $750.

SUTPHEN, William. *Golficide and Other Tales of the Fair Green.* New York, 1898. $600.

SUTPHEN, William. *19th Hole.* New York, 1901. $250.

SUTRO, Adolph. *The Mineral Resources of the United States.* Baltimore, 1868. Folding map, plates. $600.

SUTRO, Adolph. *The Sutro Tunnel and Railway to the Comstock Lode in Nevada.* London, 1873. 2 folding maps. 37 pages, printed wraps. $750.

SUTTER, Johann August. *Diary of Johann August Sutter.* Grabhorn Press. San Francisco, 1932. Edited by Douglas S. Watson. 3 colored plates, 3 facsimiles. Boards. One of 500 copies. $150.

SUTTER, Johann August. *New Helvetia Diary.* Grabhorn Press. San Francisco, 1939. 2 color plates, facsimile, map. Half cloth. One of 950 copies. $175.

SWALLOW Barn, or A Sojourn in the Old Dominion. Philadelphia, 1832. (By John Pendleton Kennedy, his first book.) 2 vols., in original half cloth and boards, paper labels. $1,200.

SWAN, Abraham. *The British Architect* . . . London (1745). Folio. 60 engraved plates. $2,000.

SWAN, James G. *The Northwest Coast* . . . New York, 1857. Folding map, plates. $600.

SWASEY, William F. *The Early Days and Men of California.* Oakland (1891). Portrait, 2 plates. Calf. $850.

SWAYZE, J. C. H. *P. Hill & Co's Confederate States Rail-Road Guide.* Griffin, Ga., 1862. $3,000.

SWIGERT, J. *The Kentucky Justice.* Frankford, 1823. $1,750.

SWIFT, Graham. *The Sweet Shop Owner.* London, 1980. Author's first book. $500. New York (1985). Wraps. $75.

SWIFT, Jonathan. See *Travels into Several Remote Nations of the World.*

SWIFT, Jonathan. *Gulliver's Travels.* London, 1909. 13 color plates by Arthur Rackham. Cloth. One of 750 copies signed by Rackham. With extra color plate. $2,000. Trade. $400. Waltham Saint Lawrence in Berkshire: Golden Cockerel Press, 1925. One of 450 copies. 2 vols. $2,000. One of 30 deluxe copies signed by the artist David Jones. White buckram. $6,000. New York, 1929. Limited Editions Club. $350 (The first Limited Edition Club book). $400. London, 1930. Cresset Press. Colored engravings by Rex Whistler. 2 vols. Morocco and boards. One of 195 copies. In slipcase. $12,500. (For true 1726 first edition, see *Travels into Several Remote Nations of the World.*)

SWIFT, J(onathan). *The Lady's Dressing Room.* London, 1732. $6,000.

SWIFT, Jonathan. *A Tale of a Tub* . . . London, 1704. $3,000.

SWINBURNE, Algernon Charles. *Atalanta in Calydon: A Tragedy.* London, 1865. White cloth. With only 111 pages of text. (Second printing had 130 pages.) $2,500. Kelmscott Press. London, 1894. Woodcut title, initials, etc. Vellum, silk ties. One of 250 copies. $2,000. One of 8 copies on vellum. $7,500.

SWINBURNE, Algernon Charles. *Chastelard: A Tragedy.* Moxon. London, 1865. $1,250.

SWINBURNE, Algernon Charles. *Erechtheus: A Tragedy.* London, 1876. $125.

SWINBURNE, Algernon Charles. *Laus Veneris.* Golden Cockerel Press. London, 1948. One of 650 copies. $250. One of 100 specially bound copies. $1,750.

SWINBURNE, Algernon Charles. *Lucretia Borgia.* Golden Cockerel Press. (London), 1942. Illustrated. Full leather. One of 30 specially bound copies with manuscript facsimile. $1,000. One of 320 copies. $300.

SWINBURNE, Algernon Charles. *Poems and Ballads.* E. Moxon. London, 1866. $1,250. London: J. C. Hotten, 1866. Second issue. $450. London, 1908–10. 3 vols. $400.

SWINBURNE, Algernon Charles. *The Queen-Mother. Rosamond. Two Plays.* London, 1860. Author's first book. Slate-gray cloth, white spine label. First issue, with "A. G. Swinburne" on spine label. $2,500. Second issue: Pickering imprint and the label is corrected to "A. C." $2,000. Third issue with a Hotten imprint on title page. $350.

SWINBURNE, Algernon Charles. *A Song of Italy.* London, 1867. $250.

SWINBURNE, Algernon Charles. *Songs Before Sunrise.* London, 1871. Blue-green cloth. $200. Large-paper issue in morocco. One of 25 copies. $1,250. Florence Press. London, 1909. Levant morocco extra. One of 12 copies on vellum. $2,250. One of 600 copies on paper. $400.

SWINBURNE, Algernon Charles. *The Springtide of Life: Poems of Childhood*. London, 1918. 9 color plates, numerous text illustrations by Arthur Rackham. Half vellum. One of 765 copies (100 of which sent to U.S.) signed by Rackham. With extra color plate. $1,500. Trade. $250. Philadelphia, 1918. One of 100 (of 765) signed copies. $1,500.

SWINBURNE, Algernon Charles. *Under the Microscope*. London, 1872. Wraps. With suppressed leaf laid in. $1,500.

SWISS Family Robinson (The). New York, 1832. 2 vols., in original cloth. (By Johann David Wyss.) First American edition. $2,000. Limited Editions Club, New York, 1963. In slipcase. $150. See also *The Family Robinson Crusoe*.

SYM, John. *Lifes Preservative Against Selfkilling* . . . London, 1637. $5,000.

SYMONDS, John Addington. *The Escorial: A Prize Poem*. Oxford, 1860. Wraps. Author's first book. $400.

SYMONDS, John Addington. *In the Key of Blue and Other Prose Essays*. London, 1893. Light-blue or cream cloth. First edition, with 16 pages of ads at end. $400. Vellum. One of 50 large-paper copies. $750.

SYMONDS, John Addington. *The Life of Michael Angelo Buonarotti* . . . London, 1893. 2 vols. $300.

SYMONDS, John Addington. *The Renaissance*. Oxford, 1863. Wraps. $250.

SYMONDS, John Addington. *Walt Whitman: A Study*. London, 1893. 5 plates. $200.

SYMONDS, Mary, and PREECE, Louisa. *Needlework Through the Ages*. London, 1928. 8 color plates, 96 other plates. Half vellum. $600.

SYMONS, A.J.A. *Desmond Flower, Francis Meynell. The Nonesuch Century; An Appraisal* . . . London, 1936. One of 750 copies. $750.

SYMONS, A.J.A. *The Quest for Corvo*. London (1934). $200. New York, 1934. $150.

SYMONS, Arthur. *Aubrey Beardsley*. London, 1898. Half cloth. $500. London, 1905. Half vellum. Second edition. One of 150 large-paper copies. $500. Trade. Boards. $250.

SYMONS, Arthur. *Days and Nights*. London, 1889. $250.

SYMONS, Arthur. *An Introduction to the Study of Browning*. London, 1886. Green cloth (later decorated brown cloth). Author's first book. With ads dated January 1887. $200.

SYMONS, Arthur. *A Study of Thomas Hardy*. London, 1927. Photogravures of Hardy by Alvin Langdon Coburn. One of 100 signed copies by Symons and Coburn. $600.

SYMONS, Julian. *Confusions About X*. London (1939). Author's first book. $200.

SYNGE, John M. *The Aran Islands*. Dublin, 1907. Illustrated by Jack B. Yeats. $1,500. One of 150 large-paper copies signed by Synge and Yeats. $4,500.

SYNGE, John M. *Deirdre of the Sorrows: A Play*. Cuala Press. Dundrum, Ireland, 1910. Preface by W. B. Yeats. Boards, linen spine. One of 250 copies. $600. New York, 1910. Boards and cloth. One of 50 copies. $4,500. (All except 5 on vellum and 5 on handmade paper were reported destroyed by the publisher, John Quinn.)

SYNGE, John M. *In the Shadow of the Glen*. New York, 1904. Author's first book. Pale-gray printed wraps. One of 50 copies published for copyright purposes. $2,500. (For first English edition, see *The Shadow of the Glen*.)

SYNGE, John M. *The Playboy of the Western World*. Dublin, 1907. Portrait. $2,000. White linen. One of 25 copies on handmade paper. $7,500.

SYNGE, John M. *Poems and Translations*. Cuala Press. Dundrum, 1909. Blue boards, tan linen spine, paper label. One of 250 copies. $750. New York, 1909. Boards and cloth. One of 50 copies. $1,250.

SYNGE, John M. *The Shadow of the Glen, Riders to the Sea*. London, 1905. Synge's first commercially published book. Printed green wraps. $600. (For first edition, see *In the Shadow of the Glen*.) Boston, 1911. Half vellum. $150.

SYNGE, John M. *The Tinker's Wedding*. Dublin, 1907. Rust-colored cloth, beige spine. $300.

SYNGE, John M. *The Well of the Saints*. London, 1905. Wraps. First issue. $600. London, 1905. Boards and cloth. Second issue, with introduction by William Butler Yeats. $500. New York, 1905. First American edition. One of 50 copies. $1,000.

SYNGE, John M. *The Works of John Millington Synge*. Dublin, 1910. Portraits. 4 vols. $600. Boston, 1912. 4 vols. $300.

SYNTAX, Doctor. *The Life of Napoleon: A Hudibrastic Poem in 15 Cantos*. London, 1815. (By William Combe.) 30 color plates by George Cruikshank. $1,250.

SYNTAX, Doctor. *The Tours* . . . (1st, 2nd, and 3rd.) (By William Combe.) *The Tour of Doctor Syntax in Search of the Picturesque*. London, 1812. Frontispiece, title page, and 29 colored plates by Thomas Rowlandson. *The Tour of Doctor Syntax in Search of Consolation*. London, 1820. 24 colored plates by Rowlandson. *The Tour of Doctor Syntax in Search of a Wife*. London, 1821. 24 colored plates by Rowlandson. $1,500.

SZYK, Arthur (artist). *Ink and Blood: A Book of Drawings*. New York, 1946. Text by Struthers Burt. 74 plates. Morocco. One of 1,000 copies signed by Szyk. In slipcase. $1,250.

SZYK, Arthur. *The New Order*. New York (1941). $250.

T

TABB, John Banister. *Poems*. (Baltimore, 1882.) Author's first book. $400.

TACITUS, C. Cornelius. *De Vita et Moribus Julii Agricolae Liber*. Doves Press. London, 1900. Vellum. One of 225 copies. $750. One of 5 copies on vellum. In special morocco binding by the Doves Bindery. $6,000. First book printed at the Doves Press.

TAFT, Robert. *Artists and Illustrators of the Old West*. New York, 1953. $125.

TAFT, Robert. *Photography and the American Scene: A Social History, 1839–89*. New York, 1938. $200. New York, 1942. $150.

TAGGARD, Genevieve. *For Eager Lovers*. New York, 1922. Boards, paper labels. $100.

TAGGARD, Genevieve. *The Life and Mind of Emily Dickinson*. New York, 1930. One of 200 large-paper copies, signed. $250. Trade. $75.

TAGGARD, Genevieve. *What Others Have Said . . .* Berkeley (1919). Author's first book. Wraps. $150.

TAGORE, Rabindranath. *The Post Office: A Play*. Cuala Press. Dundrum, Ireland, 1914. Preface by William Butler Yeats. Boards and cloth. One of 400 copies. $150. New York, 1914. $100.

TAINE, John. *The Purple Sapphire*. New York (1924). Author's first book. $250.

TALBOT, Clare Ryan. *Historic California in Bookplates*. Los Angeles, 1936. One of 30 copies illustrated with extra bookplates. $600. Trade. $150.

TALBOT, William Henry Fox. *The Pencil in Nature*. London, 1844–46. Author's first book. In 6 installments in printed wraps. (First illustrated published book to use photographic illustrations.) $250,000. New York, 1969. $250.

TALES of a Tub. London, 1704. (By Jonathan Swift.) Initial advertisement leaf. $3,000.

TALES of the Northwest; or, Sketches of Indian Life and Character. By a Resident from Beyond the Frontier. Boston, 1830. (By William J. Snelling.) Author's first book. $350.

TALES of Terror; with an Introductory Dialogue. London, 1801. Engraved half title. (Falsely attributed to Matthew G. Lewis.) $750.

TALES of Travels West of the Mississippi . . . Boston, 1830. Map. (By William J. Snelling.) With double-page map. $750.

TALLACK, William. *Friendly Sketches in America*. London, 1861. $300.

TALLAHASSEE Girl (A). Boston, 1882. (By Maurice Thompson.) $150.

TALLENT, Annie D. *The Black Hills; or The Last Hunting Grounds of the Dakotahs*. St. Louis, 1899. 50 plates. Cloth, or half leather. Either binding: $450.

TAMERLANE and Other Poems. Boston, 1827. By a Bostonian. (By Edgar Allan Poe, his first book.) Printed wraps. $300,000. London, 1884. Vellum. One of 100 copies. $2,500. San Francisco, 1923. 2 vols. Boards (folio plus a smaller facsimile volume). One of 150 copies. $600.

TAN, Amy. *The Joy Luck Club*. New York (1989). Author's first book. Price of $26.50 Canadian and publication blurb in box at bottom of rear flap on first. Changed to $24.95 (Canadian) and ad at bottom of front flap on later printings. $250. London (1989). $100.

TANNER, Henry S. *A New American Atlas . . .* Philadelphia, 1823. Engraved title. 16 double-page and 2 large folding maps. $29,225 at auction in 1998.

TANNER, J. M. *A Biographical Sketch of James Jensen*. Salt Lake City, 1911. $750.

TANSELLE, G. Thomas. *Guide to the Study of United States Imprints.* Cambridge, 1971. 2 vols. $150.

TAPLEY, Harriet Silvester. *Salem Imprints 1768–1825.* Salem, 1927. $125.

TAPPLEY, William G. *Death at Charity's Point.* New York (1984). Author's first book. $150.

TAPPLEY, William G. *The Dutch Blue Error.* New York (1984). $300.

TARASCON, Louis A., et al. *Petition . . . Praying the Opening of a Wagon Road from the River Missouri, North of the River Kansas, to the River Columbia.* Washington, 1824. 12 pages. $300.

TARBELL, Ida M. *The History of the Standard Oil Company.* New York, 1904. 2 vols. $500.

TARCISSUS: The Boy Martyr of Rome, in the Diocletian Persecution, A.D. CCCIII. (By Baron Corvo [Frederick William Rolfe].) (Essex, England, 1880—actually 1881.) Author's first book. 4 leaves, printed gray wraps. $4,000.

TARG, William (editor). *Bibliophile in the Nursery.* Cleveland, 1957. $100.

TARG, William (editor). *Carrousel for Bibliophiles.* New York, 1947. $100.

TARKINGTON, Booth. *The Gentleman from Indiana.* New York, 1899. Author's first published book. First issue: "eye" as last word in line 12, page 245; line 16 reading "so pretty." Pictorial green cloth, top stained green. $150. Second issue: page 245:12 as in first issue; page 245:16 reads "her heart." Corn pointing down. $100. Third issue: page 245:12 last word "glance." $75.

TARKINGTON, Booth. *Penrod.* Garden City, 1914. Illustrated by Gordon Grant. In blue mesh cloth. First state, with page viii so numbered and with "sence" for "sense" in third line from bottom of page 19. $250.

TARKINGTON, Booth. *Penrod and Sam.* Garden City, 1916. Illustrated by Worth Brehm. First state in pictorial light-green cloth, with imprint at foot of spine stamped in black. $175. Foot of spine stamped in white. $200.

TARKINGTON, Booth. *Penrod Jashber.* Garden City, 1929. $250.

TARKINGTON, Booth. *Seventeen.* New York (1916). With letters "B-Q" on copyright page. $150.

TATE, Allen. *The Golden Mean . . .* (Nashville, 1923.) Author's first book with R. Wills. One of 200 copies. $2,500.

TATE, Allen. *The Hovering Fly and Other Essays.* (Cummington, Mass.), 1949. Illustrated. Boards. One of 245 copies. $750.

TATE, Allen. *Jefferson Davis, His Rise and Fall.* New York, 1929. $600.

TATE, Allen. *The Mediterranean and Other Poems.* New York, 1936. Green wraps. One of 165 signed copies on Strathmore all-rag paper. In tissue jacket and slipcase. $1,000. One of 30 copies for review. $1,000. One of 12 (I–XII) signed copies. $2,000. Signed but not numbered (bound up later by Gotham). $300.

TATE, Allen. *Mr. Pope and Other Poems.* New York, 1928. $1,000.

TATE, Allen. *Poems, 1928–1931.* New York, 1932. In glassine jacket. $600.

TATE, Allen. *Stonewall Jackson, the Good Soldier: A Narrative.* New York (1928). Author's first separate book. $600.

TATE, Allen. *Two Conceits for the Eye to Sing, If Possible.* (Cummington, Mass.) 1950. Wraps, paper label. One of 300 copies. $250.

TATE, Allen. *The Winter Sea: A Book of Poems.* (Cummington, Mass.) 1944. Decorated cloth. One of 300 copies. In plain paper dustwrapper. $400.

TATE, James. *Cages.* Iowa City, 1966. Wraps. Author's first book. One of 45 copies. $3,000.

TATE, James. *The Lost Pilot.* New Haven, 1967. $300.

TATTERSALL, C.E.C. *A History of British Carpets.* London (1934). 116 plates (55 in color). Buckram. Issued without dustwrapper. $350.

TATTERSALL, George. *The Pictorial Gallery of English Race Horses.* London, 1844. 90 plates. Cloth. $1,250. London, 1850. Frontis and 72 plates. $750.

TATTERSALL, George. *Sporting Architecture.* London, 1841. $1,250.

TAUBERT, Sigfred. *Bibliopola: Pictures and Texts About the Book Trade.* Hamburg (1966). In slipcase. $250.

TAUNTON, Thomas Henry. *Portraits of Celebrated Racehorses . . .* London, 1887–88. 4 vols. 463 plates. Half morocco. $3,000.

TAUT, Bruno. *Modern Architecture.* London, 1929. $300.

TAYLOR, Arthur V. *Origines Golfianae.* Woodstock, 1912. One of 500 copies. In slipcase. $1,250.

TAYLOR, Bayard. *Eldorado, or, Adventures in the Path of Empire . . .* New York, 1850. 2 vols. 8 lithograph views. First edition with list of illustrations in Vol. 2 giving Mazatlán at page 8 instead of page 80. $1,500. Second edition, with Mazatlán reference corrected. $850. London, 1850. 2 vols. First English edition. $750.

TAYLOR, Bayard. *Ximena and Other Poems.* Philadelphia, 1844. Author's first book. $1,750.

TAYLOR, Deems. *Walt Disney's Fantasia.* New York, 1940. Color and black-and-white illustrations including 15 hand-tipped color plates. Pictorial dustjacket. $3,000.

TAYLOR, Derek. *Fifty Years Adrift.* (Guilford, Surrey, England, 1984.) Illustrated. Double column text. Ltd. to 2,000 copies signed by Taylor, and with foreword signed by the editor, George Harrison. In publisher's slipcase. $750.

TAYLOR, Elizabeth. *At Mrs. Lippincote's.* London, 1945. Author's first book. $250. New York (1946). $100.

TAYLOR, F. W. *The Principles of Scientific Management.* New York, 1911. 118 pages, green cloth. $3,000. Later, enlarged issue, 144 pages. Red cloth. $500.

TAYLOR, James W. *Northwest British America and Its Relations to the State of Minnesota.* St. Paul, 1860. Map. $5,000.

TAYLOR, James W. *The Sioux War.* St. Paul, 1862. Wraps. $1,500. St. Paul, 1863. Second edition. $1,000.

TAYLOR, Jane and Ann. *Little Ann and Other Poems.* (London, 1883.) Illustrated in color by Kate Greenaway. Pictorial boards and cloth. $400.

TAYLOR, John Henry. *Golf: My Life's Work.* London, 1943. $350.

TAYLOR, John Henry. *Taylor on Golf.* London, 1902. $750. New York, 1902. $600.

TAYLOR, John W. *Iowa, the "Great Hunting Ground" of the Indian; and the "Beautiful Land" of the White Man.* Dubuque, 1860. 16 pages, printed wraps. $750.

TAYLOR, Joseph Henry. *Beavers—Their Ways and Other Sketches.* Washburn, N.D., 1904. 20 plates. $850.

TAYLOR, Joseph Henry. *Sketches of Frontier and Indian Life . . .* Pottstown, Pa., 1889. 12 plates. Half leather and boards. $1,000.

TAYLOR, Joseph Henry. *Twenty Years on the Trap Line.* Bismarck, N.D., 1891. 8 plates. 154 pages, boards and calf. $1,250. Second edition, same place and date. 173 pages, maroon cloth. $750.

TAYLOR, Oliver I. *Directory of Wheeling and Ohio County.* Wheeling, W. Va., 1851. 2 plates, including tinted frontispiece. Half leather. $350.

TAYLOR, Peter. *A Long Fourth and Other Stories.* New York (1948). Author's first book. $600. London (1949). $200.

TAYLOR, Peter. *A Woman of Means.* New York (1950). $400. London, 1950. $300.

TAYLOR, Philip Meadows. *Confessions of a Thug.* London, 1839. 3 vols. Author's first book. In original boards or half cloth and boards. $1,000.

TAYLOR, Phoebe Atwood. *The Cape Cod Mystery.* Indianapolis (1931). Author's first book. $1,000.

TAYLOR, Thomas U. *The Chisholm Trail and Other Routes.* San Antonio, 1936. $200.

TEASDALE, Sara. *Love Songs.* New York, 1917. In dustwrapper. $600. Without dustwrapper. $150.

TEASDALE, Sara. *Sonnets to Duse and Other Poems.* Boston, 1907. Author's first book. Boards, paper labels. $1,000.

TEASDALE, Sara. *Stars To-Night.* New York, 1930. Illustrated by Dorothy P. Lathrop. One of 150 copies signed by author and artist. In dustwrapper. $300.

TEERINK, H. *A Bibliography of the Writings of Jonathan Swift.* Philadelphia (1963). Second edition, revised and corrected. $250.

TEN Thousand a Year. Philadelphia, 1840–41. (By Samuel Warren.) 6 vols. Boards, paper labels. First issue, without vol. number on title page of vol. 1 (VAB). $1,250. Second issue, with vol.

number on title page of first vol. $1,000. Edinburgh and London, 1841. 3 vols. First English edition. Dark-brown or plum-colored cloth. $600.

TENNANT, Emma. See Aydy, Catherine.

TENNANT, Emma. *The Time of the Crack.* London, 1973. Author's first book under her own name. $100.

TENNYSON, Alfred, Lord. See *In Memoriam; Poems by Two Brothers.*

TENNYSON, Alfred, Lord. *Enoch Arden.* London, 1864. Green cloth. First edition, first issue, with ads dated August 1864 (VAB). $350. Boston, 1864. Brown cloth. First American edition. $200.

TENNYSON, Alfred, Lord. *Idylls of the King.* London, 1859. Green cloth. First issue, with verso of title page blank. $1,250. Boston, 1859. July 1859 ads. $500. London, 1868. Illustrations after Gustave Doré. Folio, cloth. $1,000. London, 1875. 20 mounted photographs by Julia Margaret Cameron. Half leather. $22,500. London (1911). One of 350 copies illustrated by Eleanor Fortescue Brickdale. Vellum. 21 colored plates. $850. Limited Editions Club, New York, 1953. Illustrated by Lynd Ward. In slipcase. $150.

TENNYSON, Alfred, Lord. *Maud, and Other Poems.* London, 1855. Green cloth. First edition, with yellow endpapers and 8 pages of ads dated July 1855 and a last leaf advertising Tennyson's books (VAB). $600. (Note: Contains first printing of "The Charge of the Light Brigade.") London, 1905. Essex House. One of 125 copies on vellum. $1,500.

TENNYSON, Alfred, Lord. *Poems.* London, 1833. In original boards, white spine label. $1,250. London, 1842. 2 vols. Boards. $600.

TENNYSON, Alfred, Lord. *Poems, Chiefly Lyrical.* London, 1830. In original drab or pink boards, white spine label. First issue, with page 91 misnumbered 19. Author's first separate, regularly published, book. $2,500. Rebound. $1,500. Second issue, correctly numbered. $1,750. Rebound. $1,000.

TENNYSON, Alfred, Lord. *Poems MDCCCXXX. MDCCCXXXIII.* Toronto (London), 1862. Printed wraps. Pirated edition. $500.

TENNYSON, Alfred, Lord. *Seven Poems and Two Translations.* Doves Press. London, 1902. Vellum. One of 325 copies. $1,250. One of 25 copies on vellum. In slipcase. $4,500.

TENNYSON, Alfred, Lord. *Timbuctoo.* (Cambridge Prize poem, 1829.) Wraps. $3,000. Rebound. $2,000.

TENNYSON, Alfred, Lord. *Tiresias and Other Poems.* London, 1885. $250. Gehenna Press. Northampton, Mass. (1970). Engraved title page. 5 signed etchings 1 in color, by Leonard Baskin. One of 50 signed copies. In slipcase. $1,500.

TENNYSON, Charles. *Sonnets and Fugitive Pieces.* $400.

TENNYSON, Frederick. *Days and Hours.* London, 1854. Author's first book. $200.

TENTH MUSE, Lately Sprung Up in America (The). (By Anne Bradstreet.) London, 1650. Author's first book. $12,500. Boston, 1678. $35,000.

TERHUNE, Albert Payson. *Lad of Sunnybank*. New York, 1929. $1,000.

TERHUNE, Albert Payson. *My Friend the Dog*. New York, 1926. Illustrated by Marguerite Kirmse. One of 200 signed copies with an original signed etching by Kirmse. In slipcase. $750.

TERHUNE, Albert Payson. *Syria from the Saddle*. New York, 1896. Author's first book. $250.

TERHUNE, Mary Hawes. See Harland, Marion.

TERKEL, Studs. *Giants of Jazz*. New York (1957). Author's first book. $150.

TERRITORY of Wyoming (The); Its History, Soil, Climate, Resources . . . Laramie City, Wyoming Territory, 1874. (By J. K. Jeffrey.) 84 pages, printed wraps. $4,500.

TEVIS, Walter. *The Hustler*. (New York, 1959.) Author's first book. $750. London (1960). $300.

TEXAS Almanac (The). Galveston, 1857. (First of this series.) Wraps. $350. Other issues: 1859, $300; 1860, $300; 1861, $300; 1867, $200; 1868, $200; 1870, $175.

TEXAS in 1840, or The Emigrant's Guide to the New Republic. New York, 1840. Colored frontispiece. Cloth. (By A. B. Lawrence and C. J. Stille.) $4,500 in original cloth at auction in 1999.

TEXAS, The Home for the Emigrant from Everywhere. Houston, 1875. (By J. B. Robertson.) Folding map, wraps. $1,250. St. Louis, 1876. $500.

TEY, Josephine. See Daviot, Gordon.

THACHER, J. B. *Christopher Columbus*. New York, 1903–4. 3 vols. Plates. Half vellum. $450. 3 vols. in 6, plus portfolio of facsimiles of published accounts of the voyages of Columbus. One of 100 copies. $850.

THACHER, J. B. *The Continent of America*. New York, 1896. One of 250 copies. $600.

THACHER, James. *The American Orchardist*. Boston, 1822. $450.

THACHER, James. *Observations on Hydrophobia* . . . Plymouth, Mass., 1812. Hand-colored plate. $600.

THACKERAY, William Makepeace. See Pendennis, Arthur; Titmarsh, M. A.; Wagstaff, Theophile. See also *The History of Henry Esmond*.

THACKERAY, William Makepeace. *The Adventures of Philip on His Way Through the World*. London, 1862. 3 vols. Brown cloth. $750.

THACKERAY, William Makepeace. *The English Humourists of the Eighteenth Century*. London, 1853. $250. New York, 1853. First American edition. $100.

THACKERAY, William Makepeace. *The Four Georges* . . . New York, 1860. $250. London, 1861. First English edition, first issue, with title page reading "Sketches of Manners, Morals, Court, and Town Life." $350.

THACKERAY, William Makepeace. *The Great Hoggarty Diamond*. New York (1848). Vignette on title page. Buff wraps. (Harper's Library . . . No. 122). First issue, with "82 Cliff Street" on title page (later "306 Pearl Street"—VAB). $2,500.

THACKERAY, William Makepeace. *The History of Samuel Titmarsh and the Great Hoggarty Diamond*. London, 1849. Pictorial glazed white wraps. First English edition. $1,500.

THACKERAY, William Makepeace. *The Newcomes* . . . London, 1854–55. 2 vols. 43 wood-engraved vignettes and 76 wood-engraved initials. $1,000.

THACKERAY, William Makepeace. *The Orphan of Pimlico, and Other Sketches*. London, 1876. Illustrated by Thackeray. Boards. $450.

THACKERAY, William Makepeace. *Vanity Fair: A Novel Without a Hero*. London, 1847–48. Illustrated by the author. 20 parts in 19, yellow pictorial wraps. $7,500. London, 1848. First issue with engraved title page date of 1849 and made up from the parts with the heading in rustic type on page 1, woodcut of the Marquis of Steyne on page 336 (later omitted), and the reading "Mr. Pitt" on page 453. $4,500. With "Sir Pitt" on page 453. $2,000. New York, 1848. $1,000. Limited Editions Club, New York, 1931. 2 vols. In slipcase. $175.

THACKERAY, William Makepeace. *The Virginians: A Tale of the Last Century*. London, 1857–59. 24 parts. Printed yellow wraps. $1,250. London, 1858–59. 2 vols. First book edition. $600.

THACKERAY, William Makepeace. *The Yellow Plush Correspondence*. Philadelphia, 1838. In original brown boards and brown cloth spine. $2,000. Green cloth wraps. $2,500.

THAXTER, Celia. *An Island Garden*. Boston, 1894. Illustrated by Childe Hassam. White cloth (no priority but difficult to find in nice shape). $2,000. Green cloth. $1,500. London, 1894. First English edition. $500. Boston, 1895. $600.

THAXTER, Celia. *Poems*. New York, 1872. Author's first book. $450.

THAYER, Ernest L. *Casey at the Bat*. Amsterdam Book Co., New York (1901). Author's first book. Printed in green pictorial wraps. Printed on in green and red on recto only (except copy on verso of title, marginal illus in sepia). $6,000. Chicago, 1912. First hardbound. $1,500.

THERION, The Master. *The Book of Thoth*. (London), 1944. (By Aleister Crowley.) 8 color plates. 78 other illustrations. Half morocco. One of 200 signed copies. $3,500.

THEROUX, Alexander. *Three Wogs*. Boston, 1972. Author's first book. First issue dustwrapper with sepia-toned author photo on rear flap that mentions "Trappist Monastery in Kentucky." $250. (London, 1973.) $150.

THEROUX, Paul. *Fong and the Indians*. Boston, 1968. $200. London (1976). $100.

THEROUX, Paul. *Girls at Play*. Boston, 1969. $175. London (1969). $250.

THEROUX, Paul. *Murder in Mount Holly*. (London, 1969.) $1,500.

THEROUX, Paul. *V. S. Naipaul* . . . (London, 1972.) $1,000.

THEROUX, Paul. *Waldo*. Boston, 1967. Author's first book. (Indeterminate number of dust-wrappers printed in red vs. white, priority unknown.) $250. London (1968). $200.

THIS Is the Preachment on Going to Church. Roycroft. East Aurora, N.Y., 1896. (By George Bernard Shaw.) One of 26 copies on Japan vellum. $1,750. Half cloth. $150.

THISSELL, G. W. *Crossing the Plains in '49* . . . Oakland, 1903. 11 plates. $400.

THOBURN, Joseph B. *A Standard History of Oklahoma* . . . Chicago, 1916. $500.

THOM, Adam. *The Claims to the Oregon Territory Considered.* London, 1844. $250.

THOMAS, D. M. *Personal and Possessive.* London, 1964. Author's first book. $500.

THOMAS, D. M. *Two Voices.* London, 1968. Cloth. One of 50 signed copies. In glassine jacket. $250. Trade. Wraps in glassine dustwrapper. $75.

THOMAS, D. M. *The White Hotel.* London, 1981. $150. New York (1981). $75.

THOMAS, David. *Travels Through the Western Country in the Summer of 1816.* Auburn, N.Y., 1819. Folding map. Errata slip. $1,250.

THOMAS, Dylan. *A Child's Christmas in Wales.* Norfolk (1955 but copyright 1954). $200. London (1968). Wraps. $60. New York, 1969. One of 100 copies signed by the illustrator, Fritz Eichenberg with portfolio of signed prints. $1,500. Trade. $50.

THOMAS, Dylan. *Collected Poems 1934–1952.* London (1952). One of 65 signed copies. Issued in full dark-blue morocco and plain cellophane dustwrapper. $4,000. Trade. $250. (New York, 1953.) The word "daughter" misspelled on page 199 (corrected in later printings). $200.

THOMAS, Dylan. *Conversation About Christmas.* (New York), 1954. Stapled wraps. Christmas greeting. In mailing envlope. $200.

THOMAS, Dylan. *Deaths and Entrances.* London (1946). $750. Gregynog, 1984. One of 250 copies. In slipcase. $600. One of 28 (Roman numerals) copies. In slipcase. $1,500.

THOMAS, Dylan. *18 Poems.* Sunday Referee & Parton Bookshop. London (1934). Author's first book. Black cloth, flat spine, lacks ad leaf between half-title and title pages, front edge roughly trimmed. $3,000. London (1936). Rounded spine, has ad leaf between half-title and title pages, front edge cut evenly. $750. London: Fortune Press (circa 1942). Verso of title page still states "First Published in 1934 . . . ;" red buckram, lettered in gold. First issue printer is "Knole Park Press." With "nor" page 12, line 8, and "world" page 23, line 7. Second issue printer is "Poole J. Looker." $300. Third issue with Knole Park Press again but page 12 line 8 has "no" for "nor"; page 23, line 7, has "word" for "world." $250.

THOMAS, Dylan. *In Country Sleep and Other Poems.* (New York, 1952.) One of 100 signed copies. Issued in dark-brown slipcase. $4,000. Trade. $300.

THOMAS, Dylan. *The Map of Love: Verse and Prose.* London (1939). First issue in fine-grained mauve cloth, an almost silky texture. Title blocked in gold on front cover. Title and author's name in gold on spine. "Dent" blindstamped at foot of spine. Top edge stained dark purple. $750. Second issue bound in coarser and plum-colored cloth, same as above. $400. Third issue bound in purple cloth intermediate between fine- and coarse-grained. Blocked in blue (including "Dent" at foot of spine). Top edge stained purple. $250. Fourth issue bound as third issue but top edge unstained. $150.

THOMAS, Dylan. *New Poems.* Norfolk (1943). Paper boards. In dustwrapper. $400. Wraps. In dustwrapper. Issued simultaneously. $150.

THOMAS, Dylan. *Portrait of the Artist as a Young Dog.* London (1940). $600. Norfolk (1940). "Printed for New Directions . . . September 1940." $400.

THOMAS, Dylan. *Selected Writings of Dylan Thomas.* (New York, 1946.) Rolph notes that reprints are identifiable only by the dustwrapper, which has printing number stated on front flap. But we think Jeff Towns is correct in believing the first has a 2-page title page and copyright is 1946. Later printings have a 1-page title page and copyright of 1939 and 1946. $250.

THOMAS, Dylan. *Twenty-five Poems.* London (1936). $1,000.

THOMAS, Dylan. *Twenty-six Poems.* (Norfolk: New Directions, 1950.) One of 8 signed copies on Japanese vellum (numbered III–X). Issued in slipcase. $12,500. One of 87 signed copies on handmade paper (numbered 61–147). Issued in slipcase. $3,500. Dent. London (1950). One of 2 signed copies on Japanese vellum (numbered I–II). In slipcase. $12,500. One of 50 signed copies (numbered 11–60). Issued in slipcase. $4,000.

THOMAS, Dylan. *Under Milk Wood.* London (1954). $350. (New York, 1954.) $150.

THOMAS, Dylan. *The World I Breathe.* Norfolk (1939). With one star on either side of author's name on title page and spine (VAB, not in Rolph or Maud). $1,000. Five stars on either side of author's name on title page and spine. $750.

THOMAS, Edward. *Poems.* London, 1917. One of 525 copies. Drab paper boards. In dustwrapper. $1,500.

THOMAS, Edward. *Selected Poems.* Gregynog Press. Newtown, Wales, 1927. Buckram. One of 275 copies on vellum. $350. One of 25 specially bound copies. $1,500.

THOMAS, Edward. *Horae Solitaiae.* London, 1902. $400. New York: Dutton, no date. $250.

THOMAS, Edward. *Woodland Life.* London, 1897. Author's first book. Red cloth. $750. Blue-green buckram. $600. Smooth green cloth. $500.

THOMAS, George C., Jr. *Golf Architecture in America.* Los Angeles, 1927. $650

THOMAS, Henry. *Early Spanish Bookbindings XI–XV Centuries.* London, 1939. 99 plates. $250.

THOMAS, Isaiah. *The History of Printing in America.* Worcester, 1810. 2 vols. 2 folding plates, 3 facsimiles. $2,000. Albany, 1874. 2 vols. Second edition. Cloth. $350.

THOMAS, Jerry. *The Bar-Tender's Guide.* New York, 1862. $450.

THOMAS, Joseph B. *Hounds and Hunting Through the Ages.* Derrydale Press. New York, 1928. One of 750 copies. $400. One of 50 copies. Signed frontis. $1,000.

THOMAS, Lowell. *The First World Flight.* Boston, 1925. Illustrated. Half vellum. One of 575 copies signed by Thomas and the aviators. $750.

THOMAS, P. J. *Founding of the Missions.* San Francisco, 1877. Map, plates. $350.

THOMAS, Pascoe. *A True and Impartial . . .* London, 1745. $3,000.

THOMAS, R. S. *The Stones of the Field.* Carmarthen, 1946. Author's first book. $500.

THOMAS, Robert Bailey. *The Farmer's Almanac for . . . 1793.* Boston [1792]. $5,000.

THOMAS, Ross. *The Cold War Swap.* New York, 1965. Author's first book. $1,250.

THOMAS, Ross. *The Seersucker Whipsaw.* New York, 1967. $500. London, 1968. $250.

THOMAS, Ross. *The Singapore Wink.* New York, 1969. $300. London, 1969. $150.

THOMAS, Ross. *Spy in the Vodka.* (London, 1967.) U.K. edition of *The Cold War Swap.* Author's first book. $350.

THOMASON, John W. *Fix Bayonets.* New York, 1926. Author's first book. $250.

THOMASON, John W. *Gone to Texas.* New York, 1937. $150.

THOMASON, John W. *Lone Star Preacher.* New York, 1937. $150.

THOMES, William Henry. See *The Gold-Hunter's . . .*

THOMPSON, A. C. *Preludes.* London, 1875. (By Alice Meynell, her first book.) First issue, with brown endpapers. (Republished later under the name Alice Meynell as *Poems.*) $600.

THOMPSON, Daniel Pierce. See *The Adventures of Timothy Peacock, Esquire; The Green Mountain Boys.*

THOMPSON, Daniel Pierce (editor). *The Laws of Vermont, 1824–34, Inclusive.* Montpelier, 1835. In original calf. Author's first book under his name. $200.

THOMPSON, David. *David Thompson's Narrative of His Explorations in Western America: 1784–1812.* Toronto, 1916. 23 maps and plates (including 4 large folding maps laid into rear pocket). One of 550 copies. $2,000.

THOMPSON, David. *History of the Late War, Between Great Britain and the U.S.A.* Niagara, U.C. (Upper Canada), 1832. $350.

THOMPSON, Dorothy. *The Depths of Prosperity.* New York (1925). Author's first book with P. Bottome. $200.

THOMPSON, Edwin P. *History of the First Kentucky Brigade.* Cincinnati, 1868. 6 plates. Morocco and boards. $1,000. Cloth. $750.

THOMPSON, Francis. *The Life and Labours of Blessed John Baptist . . .* London (1891). Author's first book. Green wraps. $2,000.

THOMPSON, Francis. *New Poems.* Westminster (London), 1897. $150. Boston, 1897. One of 500 copies. $100.

THOMPSON, Francis. *Poems.* London, 1893. Decorated boards. With ads dated October. One of 500 copies. $400. Vellum. One of 12 signed copies. $4,500.

THOMPSON, Francis. *Sister-Songs: An Offering to Two Sisters.* London, 1895. Green, gray, or brown cloth. With ads at back dated 1895. (First published edition of *Songs Wing-to-Wing.*) $250.

THOMPSON, Francis. *Songs Wing-to-Wing: An Offering to Two Sisters.* (Cover title.) London (1895). Wraps. First edition (of *Sister-Songs*), with no title page and no dedication leaf. $600.

THOMPSON, Hunter S. *Fear and Loathing in Las Vegas.* New York (1971). $650.

THOMPSON, Hunter S. *Hell's Angels.* New York (1967). Author's first book. $1,000.

THOMPSON, James Westfall. *The Frankfort Book Fair; The Francofordiense Emporium of Henri Estienne.* Chicago, 1911. One of 300 copies. $250.

THOMPSON, Jim. *Heed the Thunder.* New York, 1946. $2,500.

THOMPSON, Jim. *The Killer Inside Me.* New York, 1952. Wraps. $1,250.

THOMPSON, Jim. *Now and on Earth.* New York, 1942. Author's first book. $5,000.

THOMPSON, John. *The Life of John Thompson . . .* Worcester, 1856. $650.

THOMPSON, Kay. *Eloise.* New York, 1955. Drawings by Hilary Knight. $750.

THOMPSON, Kay. *Eloise at Christmastime.* Random House (1958). $750.

THOMPSON, Maurice. See *A Tallahassee Girl.*

THOMPSON, Maurice. *Hoosier Mosaics.* New York, 1875. Author's first book. $150.

THOMPSON, Maurice. *The Witchery of Archery.* New York, 1878. $300.

THOMPSON, Peter G. *A Bibliography of the State of Ohio.* Cincinnati, 1880. $200.

THOMPSON, R. A. *Central Sonoma: A Brief Description of the Township and Town of Santa Rosa, Sonoma County, California.* Santa Rosa, Calif., 1884. Printed wraps. $350.

THOMPSON, R. A. *Conquest of California.* Santa Rosa, 1896. Portrait, 3 plates. 33 pages, wraps. $300.

THOMPSON, R. A. *Historical and Descriptive Sketch of Sonoma County, California.* Philadelphia, 1877. Map. Printed wraps. $450.

THOMPSON, R. A. *The Russian Settlement in California Known as Fort Ross . . .* Santa Rosa, 1896. 2 plates, other illustrations. 34 pages, wraps. One of 700 copies. $300.

THOMPSON, Ruth Plumly. *The Gnome King of Oz.* Chicago (1927). Illustrated. Green cloth. $1,250.

THOMPSON, Ruth Plumly. *Handy Mandy in Oz.* Chicago (1937). First with 16-page signatures (later 32). $750.

THOMPSON, Ruth Plumly. *Pirates in Oz.* Chicago (1931). $750.

THOMPSON, Ruth Plumly. *The Princess of Cozy Town.* Chicago, 1922. Issued in box. $750.

THOMPSON, Ruth Plumly. *The Royal Book of Oz.* Chicago (1912). (Author's first Oz book.) Light-gray cloth. 12 color plates coated on one side only. $750.

THOMPSON, Ruth Plumly. *The Wishing Horse of Oz.* Chicago (1935). $750.

THOMPSON, William. *Appeal of One Half of the Human Race, Women . . .* London, 1825. $6,000.

THOMPSON, Winfield M., and LAWSON, Thomas W. *The Lawson History of America's Cup.* Boston, 1902. One of 3,000 copies. $1,000.

THOMSON, James. *The City of Dreadful Night and Other Poems.* London, 1880. One of 40 large-paper copies. $1,000. Trade. $300.

THOMSON, Virgil. *The State of Music.* New York, 1939. Author's first book. $125.

THOMSON, William, Lord Kelvin. *Notes of Lectures on Molecular Dynamics and the Wave Theory of Light . . .* Baltimore, 1884. $4,000.

THOREAU, Henry David. *Autumn: From the Journal of Henry D. Thoreau.* Boston, 1892. $450.

THOREAU, Henry David. *Cape Cod.* Boston, 1865. Purple, green, or brown cloth. Brown-coated endpapers. $1,750. Boston, 1896. 2 vols. Colored illustrations by Amelia M. Watson. Decorated cloth. $250.

THOREAU, Henry David. *Early Spring in Massachusetts: From the Journal of Henry D. Thoreau.* Boston, 1881. $750.

THOREAU, Henry David. *Excursions.* Boston, 1863. Engraved portrait. Green cloth. $1,250.

THOREAU, Henry David. *Letters to Various Persons.* Boston, 1865. Cloth, various colors. With "Tickner & Co." on spine. $1,250. With "James R. Osgood & Co." on spine. $750.

THOREAU, Henry David. *The Maine Woods.* Boston, 1864. Green cloth. First issue, with 1 leaf ad of *Atlantic Monthly* at end reading "The Thirteenth Volume" (Johnson), although Borst notes ads dated April 1864 in some copies. There was another 1864 printing, which may be the same as the first. $1,750.

THOREAU, Henry David. *Summer: From the Journal of Henry D. Thoreau.* Boston, 1884. Double-page frontispiece map. Green cloth. $500.

THOREAU, Henry David. *Walden or, Life in the Woods.* Boston, 1854. Brown cloth. Yellow endpapers. Lithographed map of Walden Pond facing p. 307. (Tipped-in ads range from April to October; April ads presumably are earliest.) With April ads. $17,500. With later ads. $15,000. London, 1886. Red or dark-blue cloth. $1,500. Boston, 1897. 2 vols. $350. Boston, 1909. 2 vols. One of 483 copies. $1,250. London, 1927. One of 100 copies signed by artist Eric Fitch Daglish. $750. Trade. $200. Boston, 1927. One of 520 copies. $350. Chicago, 1930. Lakeside Press. Illustrated. Half buckram. One of 1,000 copies. $250. Limited Editions Club, New York, 1936. Illustrated (photos) and signed by Edward Steichen. In slipcase. $1,500.

THOREAU, Henry David. *A Week on the Concord and Merrimack Rivers.* Boston, 1849. Author's first book. Light-brown, brown or black cloth, yellow endpapers. With 3 lines dropped at bottom of page 396, written in with pencil by Thoreau. $15,000. Not written in. $10,000. Boston, 1862. $3,000. Boston, 1868. $500.

THOREAU, Henry David. *Winter: From the Journal of Henry D. Thoreau.* Boston, 1888 [1887]. $500.

THOREAU, Henry David. *A Yankee in Canada, with Anti-Slavery and Reform Papers.* Boston, 1866. (Contains "Civil Disobedience.") Green or purple cloth with brown-coated endpapers. $1,500.

THORNTON, Alfred. See *The Adventures of a Post Captain*.

THORNTON, J. Quinn. *Oregon and California in 1848* . . . New York, 1849. 2 vols. Folding map. $1,500. New York, 1855. 2 vols. 12 plates. $1,000.

THORNTON, Robert John. *The Temple of Flora* . . . London, 1810. 25 portraits, 31 hand-colored plates. $40,000. London, 1951. In dustwrapper. $750. One of 250 copies in half morocco. $1,000.

THORP, N. Howard (Jack). *Songs of the Cowboys*. Estancia, N.M. (1908). Pictorial wraps. $1,500.

THORPE, T(homas) B(angs). *The Mysteries of the Backwoods* . . . Philadelphia, 1846. Author's first book. $600.

THORPE, T. B. *Our Army on the Rio Grande* . . . *From Corpus Christi to the Surrender of Matamoros*. Phila., 1846. Carey and Hart. $750.

THOUGHTS on the Cloister and the Crowd. (Sir Arthur Helps.) London, 1835. Author's first book. In original cloth. $250.

THOUGHTS on the Proposed Annexation of Texas to the United States. New York, 1844. (By Theodore Sedgwick.) 55 pages, wraps. $250.

THOUSAND Miles in a Canoe from Denver to Leavenworth (A). Bushnell, Neb., 1880. Wraps. (By W. A. Spencer.) $500.

THRASHER, Halsey. *The Hunter and Trapper*. New York (1868). 6 full-page wood engravings. $175.

THREE Monographs. Naples, Italy, 1906. (By Norman Douglas.) 56 pages, light-brown printed wraps. One of 250 copies. $400.

THUCYDIDES. *The Historye* . . . *of the Warre, whiche was betwene the Peloponesians and the Athenyans*. London, 1550. First edition in English. Translated by Thomas Nicolls. $5,000. London, 1930. One of 260 copies. $2,500.

THUDICHUM, J. L.W., and DUPRE, Andre. *A Treatise on the Origin* . . . *of Wine*. London, 1872. $1,500.

THURBER, James. *The Last Flower: A Parable in Pictures*. New York, 1939. Oblong, boards. $350.

THURBER, James. *Let Your Mind Alone*. New York, 1937. Presumed first state has drawing on front cover with extra lines. Clear line around dots in motorman's cheek, and extra line curving from top of head toward ear. $500. Presumed second state lacks both lines. $400.

THURBER, James. *The Middle-Aged Man on the Flying Trapeze*. New York, 1935. $500.

THURBER, James. *My Life and Hard Times*. New York, 1933. $500.

THURBER, James. *The Owl in the Attic and Other Perplexities*. New York, 1931. Introduction by E. B. White. $1,250.

THURBER, James. *The Seal in the Bedroom.* New York, 1932. $1,500.

THURBER, James. *The 13 Clocks.* New York (1950). Illustrated in color by Marc Simont. Boards and cloth. First edition not stated. $200. (The illustrator's first name, Marc, is misspelled "Mark" on all copies.)

THURBER, James, and WHITE, E. B. *Is Sex Necessary? Or Why You Feel the Way You Do.* New York, 1929. Thurber's first book. In dustwrapper with 6-line author statement and green background. $2,500. With Brown and Patterson quotes and orange background. $1,500. London (1930). $750.

THURMAN, Wallace. *The Blacker the Berry: A Novel of Negro Life.* New York, 1929. $2,000.

THURMAN, Wallace. *Infants of the Spring.* New York (1932). $1,500.

THURMAN, Wallace. *Negro Life in New York's Harlem.* Little Blue Book #494. Girard, Kans. No date of publication and not certain, but believe it would have preceded *The Blacker the Berry;* if so, author's first book. Wraps. $600.

THURMAN, Wallace, and FURMAN, A. L. *The Interne.* New York (1932). $2,000.

THWAITES, Reuben Gold. *Historic Waterways: Six Hundred Miles of Canoeing Down the Rock, Fox, and Wisconsin Rivers.* Chicago, 1888. Author's first book. $200.

TIERNEY, Luke. *History of the Gold Discoveries on the South Platte River.* Pacific City, Iowa, 1859. 27 pages, wraps. $15,000 or more.

TIETJENS, Eunice. *Profiles from China.* Chicago, 1917. Author's first book. $200.

TIFFANY, Louis Comfort. *The Art Work of Louis Comfort Tiffany.* Garden City, 1914. One of 492 copies on Japan vellum. $3,000.

TILLINGHAST, Arthur W. *Cobble Valley Golf Yarns & Other Sketches.* Philadelphia (1915). $1,750. Far Hills, no date. 2 vols. Facsimile. One of 1,500 copies. Issued without dustwrapper. In slipcase. $100.

TILLSON, Christina Holmes. *Reminiscences of Early Life in Illinois by Our Mother.* (Amherst, Mass., 1872.) 4 plates. $2,500.

TIMLIN, William M. *The Ship That Sailed to Mars.* London (1923). 48 mounted color plates. Boards. In dustwrapper. $3,500. New York (1923). $3,000.

TIMOTHY Crump's Ward; or, The New Year's Loan and What Came of It. Loring Publishing. Boston (1866). (By Horatio Alger, Jr.) Purple cloth, or wraps. Either binding: $4,000.

TIMPERLEY, C. H. *A Dictionary of Printers and Printing . . .* London, 1839. With *Manual Containing Instructions to Learners.* London, 1838. The two. $600.

TINDALE, Thomas Keith, and TINDALE, Harriett Ramsey. *Handmade Papers of Japan.* Rutland, Vt., and Tokyo, 1952. Four booklets bound in Japanese fashion with hand-stenciled wraps enclosed in a protective slipcase. One of 150 copies. $7,000.

TINGRY, P(ierre) F(rancis). *The Painter and Varnisher's Guide.* London, 1804. 5 plates, 1 folding chart. $1,200.

TITMARSH, M. A. *Doctor Birch and His Young Friends*. London, 1849. (By William Makepeace Thackeray.) 16 color plates by the author. Wraps. $500.

TITMARSH, M. A. *The Irish Sketch-Book*. London, 1843. (By William Makepeace Thackeray.) 2 vols. Wood engravings. Dark-green cloth. $2,000.

TITMARSH, M. A. *Jeames's Diary; or, Sudden Riches*. New York, 1846. (By William Makepeace Thackeray.) Woodcuts. Wraps. $3,500.

TITMARSH, M. A. *"Our Street."* London, 1848. (By William Makepeace Thackeray.) 16 color plates. Wraps. $1,250.

TITMARSH, M. A. *The Second Funeral of Napoleon: In Three Letters to Miss Smith, of London, and the Chronicle of the Drum*. London, 1841. (By William Makepeace Thackeray.) Frontispiece, 3 plates, picture of Napoleon on front cover. Wraps. With six lines of shading on the cheek of Napoleon on front cover and inscription on plate opposite title page and page 120. Line 13 has five stars (not four). $1,000.

TITTSWORTH, W. G. *Outskirt Episodes*. (Avoca, Iowa, 1927.) Portrait (tipped to title page). Red cloth. In dustwrapper. $750.

TOCQUEVILLE, Alexis de. *Democracy in America*. London, 1835. Translated by Henry Reeve. 2 parts in 4 vols. In original cloth. Folding map. $25,000. Rebound. $5,000. New York, 1838. First American edition. In original cloth. $3,500. Rebound. $1,500.

TODD, Frederick P. *Soldiers of the American Army, 1775–1941*. New York, 1941. Frontispiece and 24 hand-colored plates by Fritz Kredel. One of 500 copies. $300.

TODD, Mabel. *Footprints*. Amherst, 1883. Author's first book. Wraps. $750.

TODD, The Rev. John. *The Lost Sister of Wyoming*. Northampton, Mass., 1842. Frontispiece. $450.

TODD, Ruthven. *Laughing Mulatto . . .* London (1939 or 1940?). $350.

TODD, Ruthven. *Over the Mountain*. London (1939). $450. New York, 1939. $200.

TOKLAS, Alice B. *The Autobiography of Alice B. Toklas*. Harcourt Brace. New York (1933). (By Gertrude Stein.) $600. (The Literary Guild also states "First edition," but is not.)

TOLKIEN, J.R.R. *The Adventures of Tom Bombadil*. London (1962). $200. Boston, 1963. $125.

TOLKIEN, J.R.R. *The Devil's Coach-Horses*. London (circa 1925). Wraps. $2,000.

TOLKIEN, J.R.R. *The Father Christmas Letters*. London (1976). "First published in 1976" on page (48). Issued without dustwrapper. $100.

TOLKIEN, J.R.R. *Farmer Giles of Ham*. London, 1949. Illustrated, including 2 color plates. Boards. $400. Boston, 1950. $250.

TOLKIEN, J.R.R. *The Fellowship of the Ring*. London, 1954. (First vol. in the *Lord of the Rings* trilogy.) $7,500. Boston, 1954. $2,500.

TOLKIEN, J.R.R. *The Hobbit*. London (1937). Frontispiece illustrated by the author. Green cloth. $75,000. Boston, 1938. Bowing Hobbit decoration on title page. $10,000. Publisher's flute-player device on title page. $7,500.

TOLKIEN, J.R.R. *The Lord of the Rings.* 3 vols. Cloth. *The Fellowship of the Ring,* London, 1954; *The Two Towers,* London, 1954; *The Return of the King,* London, 1955.) $50,000. Boston editions. Same dates. 3 vols. $5,000. London, 1966. 3 vols. Second edition revised. $1,500. Boston, 1967. 3 vols. With a new foreword by the author. First American revised edition. $600.

TOLKIEN, J.R.R. *A Middle English Vocabulary.* Oxford, 1922. Wraps. First issue: ads dated October 1921. 186 ornaments in cover design. $1,000. Second issue: ads undated; "Printed in England" at bottom of title page. 184 ornaments. $500.

TOLKIEN, J.R.R. *The Return of the King.* London, 1955. (Third vol. in the *Lord of the Rings* trilogy.) $2,500. Boston, 1955. $1,000.

TOLKIEN, J.R.R. *The Silmarillion.* London (1977). With "William Clowes" imprint on copyright page. In blue simulated leather. $750. London (1977) First issue/printing in cloth, without price on dustwrapper. $100. With price. $75. Boston, 1977. First American edition, probable first issue, with perfect text on lines 27–32 of page 229. $50.

TOLKIEN, J.R.R. *The Two Towers.* London, 1954. (Second vol. in the *Lord of the Rings* trilogy.) $5,000. Boston, 1954. $1,500.

TOLLER, Ernest. *Masses and Men.* London, 1923. Author's first English translation. Issued without dustwrapper. $100.

TOLSTOY, Leo. *Anna Karenina.* New York (1886). First edition in English. Wraps. $1,750. Limited Editions Club, New York, 1933. 2 vols. In slipcase. $200. Another issue, 1951. 2 vols. In slipcase. $250.

TOLSTOY, Leo. *Childhood and Youth.* London, 1862. Author's first English translation. $750. New York (1886). $200.

TOLSTOY, Leo. *Ivan Ilyitch and Other Stories.* New York, 1887. $500.

TOLSTOY, Leo. *Resurrection.* New York, 1900. First edition in English. $350.

TOLSTOY, Leo. *War and Peace.* New York, 1886. Translated from the French by Clara Bell. 6 vols. Decorated brown cloth. First edition in English. $10,000. Limited Editions Club, New York, 1938. 6 vols. $450.

TOLSTOY, Leo. *Where God Is Love Is.* Ashendene Press. London, 1924. Blue wraps. One of about 200 copies issued as a Christmas token from St. John and Cicely Hornby. $750.

TOM Brown at Oxford. Cambridge, 1861. 3 vols. Blue cloth. (By Thomas Hughes.) $850.

TOM Brown's School Days. Cambridge, 1857. By an Old Boy, Thomas Hughes. Blue cloth. With "nottable" for "notable" in line 15 on page 24. Author's first book. $1,000.

TOM Cringle's Log. London, 1833. 2 vols., in original cloth. (By Michael Scott, his first book.) $600. Boston, 1833. 2 vols. $300.

TOMATSU, Shomei. *11:02 Nagasaki.* (Tokyo), 1966. Author's first book. In cardboard slipcase. $1,250.

TOMKINSON, G. S. *A Select Bibliography of the Principal Modern Presses . . . in Great Britain and Ireland.* London, 1928. Illustrated. Boards and cloth. $250.

TOMLINSON, H. M. *The Sea and the Jungle.* London (1912). Author's first book. Frontispiece. Green cloth. $250. New York, 1913. $125. London, or New York, 1930. Illustrated by Clare Leighton. One of 515 signed copies. $300. Trade. $100.

TOMLINSON, H. M. *Thomas Hardy.* New York, 1929. Frontispiece by Zhenya Gay, signed. One of 761 copies signed by the author. $175.

TOMPKINS, Thomas. *Beauties of Writing . . .* London, 1777. Engraved title page, dedication (numbered 2), 37 plates (numbered 3–39). $450.

TOOLE, John Kennedy. *A Confederacy of Dunces.* Baton Rouge, 1980. Author's first book. (2,500 copies.) $3,500. (London, 1981.) (1,500 copies.) $1,000.

TOOMER, Jean. *Cane.* New York, 1923. Author's first book. $12,500. Without dustwrapper. $2,500.

TOOMER, Jean. *Essentials.* Chicago, 1931. One of 1,000 signed copies. $2,000. Out-of-series copies without signature or number. $1,000.

TOOMER, Jean. *The Flavor of Man.* Philadelphia (1949). Wraps. $650.

TOPOGRAPHICAL *Description of the State of Ohio, Indian Territory, and Louisiana (A).* Boston, 1812. (By Jervis Cutler.) 5 woodcut plates, errata slip. $3,000.

TOPONCE, Alexander. *Reminiscences of Alexander Toponce, Pioneer, 1839–1923.* (Ogden, Utah, 1923.) 14 plates. $200.

TOPPING, E. S. *The Chronicles of the Yellowstone.* St. Paul, 1883. Folding map. $1,000.

TOPSYS & Turveys. New York, 1893. (By Peter Newell, his first book.) 31 leaves with colored illustrations. Oblong folio, pictorial boards. $750.

TORY, Geoffroy. *Champfleury.* Grolier Club. New York, 1927. Translated by George B. Ives. Vellum and boards. Printed by Bruce Rogers. One of 7 copies on larger paper (of an edition of 397). $3,000. Trade. One of 390 copies. In dustwrapper and slipcase. $1,000.

TOUR *Through Part of Virginia in the Summer of 1808 (A).* New York, 1809. (By John E. Caldwell.) 31 pages. $600.

TOUR *on the Prairies (A).* London, 1835. By the author of *The Sketch-Book* (Washington Irving). $500. Philadelphia, 1835. Without catalogue with sheets bulking ⁹⁄₁₆ inch and last line on page 247 reading "Binger of dawn." $400. Second state. Printing is ¹¹⁄₁₆ inch and page 247 reads "Harbinger of dawn." $300.

TOURGEE, Albion W. See Churton, Henry, See also *A Fool's Errand.*

TOURGEE, Albion. *Book of Forms.* (Raleigh, 1868.) Author's first book. Wraps. $350.

TOURTEL, Mary. *A Horse Book.* London, 1901. Author's first book. $350.

TOWNSEND, George Alfred. *The Real Life of Abraham Lincoln.* New York, 1867. Frontispiece. 15 pages, printed wraps. $400.

TOWNSEND, John K. *Narrative of a Journey Across the Rocky Mountains . . .* Philadelphia, 1839. $750.

TOWNSEND, John K. *Ornithology of the United States* . . . Philadelphia, 1839. Vol. 1 (all published). Wraps. 4 hand-colored plates. $35,000.

TOWNSEND, John K. *Sporting Excursions in the Rocky Mountains* . . . London, 1840. 2 vols. Engraved frontispieces. In original full leather. First English edition of the preceding item, with the author's name spelled "Townshend" instead of "Townsend." $1,000.

TOYNBEE, Paget. *Journal of the Printing-Office at Strawberry Hill* . . . London, 1923. One of 650 copies. $200.

TRACY, J. L. *Guide to the Great West.* St. Louis, 1870. 2 maps. $750.

TRAGEDY of Count Alarcos (The). London, 1839. (By Benjamin Disraeli.) In original wraps. $650.

TRAITS of American Indian Life and Character. London, 1853. (Attributed to Peter Skene Ogden.) $2,750. San Francisco, 1933. One of 500 copies. $125.

TRANSITION Stories. New York, 1929. Edited by Eugene Jolas and R. Sage. Pictorial boards and cloth. One of 100 copies. In dustwrapper. $750.

TRAUBEL, Horace L. (editor). *Camden's Compliment to Walt Whitman* . . . Philadelphia, 1889. Frontispiece. Red cloth. $350.

TRAUBEL, Horace L. (editor). *The Graveside of Walt Whitman.* (Philadelphia), 1892. 37 pages, printed gray wraps. One of 750 copies. $350.

TRAVELLER'S Pocket Directory and Stranger's Guide. Schenectady, 1831. 3 folding plates. 32 pages advertisements. $600.

TRAVELS in Louisiana and the Floridas, in the Year, 1802. New York, 1806. (By Berquin-Duvallon.) Translated from the French by John Davis. First edition in English. $6,000.

TRAVELS into Several Remote Nations of the World. By Lemuel Gulliver (Jonathan Swift). London, 1726. 2 vols. [See the Swift bibliography by Herman Teerink for the various points in the editions.] Teerink's state "A" has among the other points, a frontispiece portrait with inscription *"Captain Lemuel Gulliver . . ."* on tablet under oval and 6 plates. $40,000. Later states. $20,000. London, 1727. 2 vols. Second edition. Includes "Verses," which is compressed into 20 pages and inserted after the title and before the text. Earliest copies contain the portrait frontispiece. $3,500. With spurious vol. III. $7,500.

TRAVELS of Capts. Lewis and Clarke (The). Philadelphia, 1809. Folding map and 5 portraits of Indians. (Unauthorized edition. For authentic first edition see entry under Lewis's name.) $2,500.

TRAVEN, B. *The Bridge in the Jungle.* New York, 1938. First American edition. $500. London (1940). $250.

TRAVEN, B. *The Death Ship: The Story of an American Sailor.* London, 1934. Author's first book. First edition in English. Translated by Eric Sutton. $2,500. New York, 1934. First American edition, revised and written in English by Traven. $1,250.

TRAVEN, B. *The General from the Jungle.* London (1954). First edition in English. $200. New York, 1972. $75.

TRAVEN, B. *Government.* London, 1935. $2,500.

TRAVEN, B. *The Rebellion of the Hanged.* London (1952). First edition in English. $300. New York, 1952. First American edition. $200.

TRAVEN, B. *The Treasure of the Sierra Madre.* London, 1934. First edition in English. $7,500. New York, 1935. First American edition. $4,500.

TRAVER, Robert. *Anatomy of a Fisherman.* New York (1964). (By John Donaldson Voelker.) $200.

TRAVER, Robert. *Anatomy of a Murder.* New York (1958). $400.

TRAVER, Robert. *Trouble-shooter.* New York, 1943. (By John Donaldson Voelker, his first book.) $250.

TRAVERS, Jerome David, and CROWELL, James. *The Fifth Estates: 30 Years of Golf.* New York, 1926. $450.

TRAVERS, P. L. *Mary Poppins.* (London, 1934.) Author's first book. Illustrated by Mary Shepard. $1,000. New York (1934). $750.

TRAVERS, P. L. *Mary Poppins Comes Back.* London, 1935. $500.

TRAVIS, Walter. *Practical Golf.* New York, 1901. $350. New York, 1903. $250.

TREATISE of Human Nature (A). (By David Hume.) London, 1739–40. Author's first book. 3 vols. $35,000.

TREATISE on Tennis (A). London, 1822. By a Member of the Tennis Club (Robert Lukin). Folding engraved diagram of court. $4,000.

TREATY Between the United States and the Chasta and Other Tribes of Indians. (Washington, 1855.) (By Joel Palmer.) Wraps. $500.

TREATY Between the United States and the Comanche and Kiowa Tribes of Indians . . . Proclaimed May 26, 1866. (Washington, 1866.) 8 pages, folio. $500.

TREATY Between the United States and the Confederated Tribes of Sacs and Foxes of the Mississippi. (Washington, 1860.) Printed wraps. $300.

TREATY Between the United States and the Creek and Seminole Tribes of Indians . . . Ratified March 6, 1845. (Washington, 1845.) 6 pages, folio. $500.

TREATY Between the United States and the Klamath and Moadoc Tribes and Yahooskin Band of Snake Indians . . . Proclaimed Feb. 17, 1870. (Washington, 1870.) 8 pages, folio. $500.

TREATY Between the United States and the Nez Percé Tribe of Indians . . . Proclaimed April 20, 1867. (Washington, 1867.) 10 pages, folio. $500.

TREATY Between the United States and the Senecas . . . Washington, 1868. Folio, 20 pages, sewn. $400.

TREE, Iris. *Poems.* Nassau, 1917. Author's first book. Wraps. $400.

TRELAWNY, Edward John. See *The Adventures of a Younger Son.*

TREVOR, Elleston. See Smith, T. Dudley.

TREVOR, Glen. *Murder at School.* London, 1933. (By James Hilton). $2,500.

TREVOR, Glen. *Was It Murder?* New York, 1933. (By James Hilton). $1,500.

TREVOR, William. *The Boarding House.* London (1965). (By William Trevor Cox.) $300. New York, 1965. $150.

TREVOR, William. *The Day We Got Drunk on Cake and Other Stories.* London (1967). (By William Trevor Cox.) $750. New York (1967). $200.

TREVOR, William. *The Love Department.* London (1966). (By William Trevor Cox.) $300. New York (1966). $150.

TREVOR, William. *Marrying Damian.* (London) 1995. (By William Trevor Cox.) One of 26 signed copies. Cloth. $350. One of 175 signed copies. In card covers. $75.

TREVOR, William. *The Old Boys.* London (1964). (By William Trevor Cox.) $350. New York, 1964. $200.

TREVOR, William. *A Standard of Behaviour.* London, 1958. (By William Trevor Cox.) Author's first book. $1,000.

TRIALS of A. Arbuthnot and R. C. Ambrister (The), Charged with Exciting the Seminole Indians to War Against the United States of America. London, 1819. 80 pages. $600.

TRIBUNE Book of Open Air Sports (The). New York, 1887. Edited by Henry Hall. Illustrated. Pictorial cloth. (Note: This is the first book composed by linotype.) $250.

TRIBUNE Tracts No. 6, Life of Abraham Lincoln. Horace Greeley. (New York), 1860. 32 pages, sewn. (By John Locke Scripps.) $500. (See also Ward H. Lamon.) Detroit, 1900. Leather, with Lincoln photograph on heavy porcelain bound in. $400.

TRIBUTES to Brooke Crutchley on His Retirement as University Printer. Cambridge, 1975. One of 650 copies. $100.

TRIGGS, H. Inigo. *The Art of Garden Design in Italy.* London, 1906. Folio, with 66 text illustrations and 128 plates (73 collotypes, 28 halftones, and 27 plans and drawings). $1,000.

TRIGGS, H. Inigo. *Formal Gardens in England and Scotland.* London, 1902. Folio. 122 plates on heavy paper. $600.

TRIGGS, J. H. *History and Directory of Laramie City, Wyoming Territory.* Laramie City, 1875. 91 pages, printed wraps. $4,000.

TRIGGS, J. H. *History of Cheyenne and Northern Wyoming, etc.* Omaha, 1876. Folding map. 144 pages, printed wraps. $4,500.

TRIPLETT, Frank. *The Life, Times and Treacherous Death of Jesse James.* Chicago, 1882. Plates. Pictorial cloth. $500.

TRIPP, C. E. *Ace High: The Frisco Detective.* Grabhorn Press. San Francisco, 1948. Introduction by David Magee. Illustrated. Boards and cloth. One of 500 copies. $125.

TRISTRAM, W. Outram. *Coaching Days and Coaching Ways.* London, 1888. Pictorial cloth. Large-paper issue. $600. Trade. $250. London, 1893. One of 250 copies. $750. London, 1924. Illustrated. Leather. $600.

TROCCHI, Alexander. See Lengel, Frances.

TROLLOPE, Anthony. See *Nina Balatka; On English Prose Fiction as a Rational Amusement.*

TROLLOPE, Anthony. *The American Senator.* London, 1877. 3 vols. First binding in pinkish ocher cloth. $2,500. In blue, red-brown, or green cloth. $1,750.

TROLLOPE, Anthony. *Australia and New Zealand.* London, 1873. 2 vols. 8 colored maps. First issue, with dark-green endpapers. $1,500. With yellow endpapers. $1,000.

TROLLOPE Anthony. *An Autobiography.* Edinburgh, 1883. 2 vols. Portrait. First issue, with smooth red cloth covers and green endpapers. $1,250. Second issue in ribbed red cloth with green or brown endpapers. $600.

TROLLOPE, Anthony. *Ayala's Angel.* London, 1881. 3 vols. Orange cloth. $3,500.

TROLLOPE, Anthony. *Barchester Towers.* London, 1857. 3 vols. First issue with pale-brown cloth with brick red endpapers. Some with ads dated December 1857. $12,500. Second issue with dark brown (liver-colored) endpapers. With 24 pages of ads dated October 1860. $7,500. Limited Editions Club, New York, 1958. In slipcase. $100.

TROLLOPE, Anthony. *Castle Richmond.* London, 1860. 3 vols. Dark purple-gray cloth. First binding, without line under the author's name on spine, 16-page catalogue dated February 1860 and "W. Clowes & Sons" on verso of title page. $4,000. Second issue, with line under author's name on spine, 32-page catalogue dated May 1860, and "William Clowes & Sons." $2,000.

TROLLOPE, Anthony. *Doctor Thorne.* London, 1858. 3 vols., gray-purple cloth with "mamma" on page 18, line 15. $12,500. Rebound. $4,500. Second edition same date with "mammon." $1,000. New York, 1858. $400.

TROLLOPE, Anthony. *Dr. Wortle's School.* London, 1881. 2 vols. Original gray silk-grained cloth. $2,500.

TROLLOPE, Anthony. *The Eustace Diamonds.* New York, 1872. Printed wraps. $1,500. Cloth. $1,000. London, 1873. 3 vols., brown cloth, spine title in gold. (Later all lettering in black). First English edition. $1,500.

TROLLOPE, Anthony. *The Fixed Period.* Edinburgh, 1882. 2 vols., red cloth. $3,000.

TROLLOPE, Anthony. *Framley Parsonage.* London, 1861. 3 vols. Millais illustrations. Gray-purple cloth. With April ads at end of vol. 3. $2,000.

TROLLOPE, Anthony. *He Knew He Was Right.* London, 1868–69. Illustrated by Marcus Stone. 32 parts, gray-green wraps. $6,500. London, 1869. 2 vols. Illustrated. Green cloth. First English book edition. $3,000.

TROLLOPE, Anthony. *How the "Mastiffs" Went to Iceland.* London, 1878. Illustrated. Blue cloth. $2,000.

TROLLOPE, Anthony. *Hunting Sketches.* London, 1865. With May ads. $1,000.

TROLLOPE, Anthony. *John Caldigate.* London, 1879. 3 vols. First binding, lilac-gray cloth. $2,500. In dark-green cloth. $1,750.

TROLLOPE, Anthony. *The Kellys and the O'Kellys.* London, 1848. 3 vols. Boards. $5,000. New York, 1860. First American edition. $750.

TROLLOPE, Anthony. *Lady Anna.* London, 1874. 2 vols. Bright red-brown cloth. $3,500.

TROLLOPE, Anthony. *The Landleaguers.* London, 1883. 3 vols. Green cloth. $1,750.

TROLLOPE, Anthony. *The Last Chronicle of Barset.* London, 1866–67. Illustrated. 32 parts, pictorial wraps. $5,000. London, 1867. 2 vols. 32 plates. Blue cloth. First book edition. $2,500. (Note: Both the parts and book issues are complicated books. See Sadleir.)

TROLLOPE, Anthony. *The Macdermots of Ballycloran.* London, 1847. 3 vols. Author's first book. Dark-brown cloth. $25,000. London, 1848. Second printing (with 1848 title page). $1,500.

TROLLOPE, Anthony. *Miss Mackenzie.* London, 1865. 2 vols. Dark-green cloth. $3,000.

TROLLOPE, Anthony. *North America.* London, 1862. 2 vols. Pinkish-maroon patterned cloth. With October ads. $2,000. New York, 1862. Gray cloth. First American (pirated Harper) edition. $350. Lippincott. New York, 1862. 2 vols. First authorized American edition. $450.

TROLLOPE, Anthony. *Orley Farm.* London, 1861–62. Illustrated by J. E. Millais. 20 parts, buff wraps. $10,000. London, 1862. 2 vols. Purple-brown cloth. (First book edition is a complex book, see Sadleir's bibliography.) $6,000.

TROLLOPE, Anthony. *Phineas Finn, The Irish Member.* London, 1869. 2 vols. Original grained cloth. $1,250. New York, 1868. Original pebble-grain cloth. $350.

TROLLOPE, Anthony. *The Prime Minister.* London, 1876. 8 parts. Gray wraps or brown cloth. $6,000. London, 1876. 4 vols. Red-brown cloth. First book edition. $1,750.

TROLLOPE, Anthony. *Rachel Ray.* London, 1863. 2 vols. Pinkish-red cloth. With volume numbers on spines in roman capitals with serifs (not block) type. $2,000.

TROLLOPE, Anthony. *Ralph the Heir.* London, 1871. 3 vols. $3,500.

TROLLOPE, Anthony. *Sir Harry Hotspur of Humblethwaite.* London, 1871. Scarlet-orange cloth. With "th" in "the" on page 40 line 1 in perfect type and with a period after "iv" at head of page 43 (many others). $2,000. New York, 1871. Cherry-red or green cloth. First American edition. $600.

TROLLOPE, Anthony. *The Struggles of Brown, Jones, and Robinson.* New York, 1862. Wraps. $2,500. London, 1870. Illustrated. Brown cloth. First English and first illustrated edition. $1,000.

TROLLOPE, Anthony. *Tales of All Countries.* London, 1861 and 1863. (First and second series.) 2 vols. Blue cloth. $2,500.

TROLLOPE, Anthony. *Thackeray.* London, 1879. In smooth cream cloth, paper label with Church's *Spenser* in ads as "in the press." $750.

TROLLOPE, Anthony. *The Three Clerks.* London, 1858. 3 vols. Boards, blue cloth spine, labels. $4,000. Also, variant issue. Full cloth. $3,000.

TROLLOPE, Anthony. *Travelling Sketches.* London, 1866. $750.

TROLLOPE, Anthony. *The Vicar of Bulhampton.* London, 1869–70. Illustrated. 11 parts, decorated gray-blue wraps. $4,000. London, 1870. Brown cloth. First book edition. $2,000.

TROLLOPE, Anthony. *The Warden.* London, 1855. Pale-brown cloth. With 24 pages of ads dated September, 1854. $3,000. With catalogue dated March 1856 or no catalogue. $2,000. With October 1859 catalogue. $1,500.

TROLLOPE, Frances. See *Domestic Manners of the Americans.*

TROLLOPE, Frances. *The Vicar of Wrexhill.* London, 1837. 3 vols. $750.

TROLLOPE, T. Adolphus. *A Summer in Brittany.* London, 1840. Author's first book. Edited by Frances Trollope. 2 vols. 14 plates, 2 in color. Purple cloth. $450.

TROTSKY, Lev Davydovich. *From the Workers Movement . . .* Geneva, 1900. Author's first book. $1,250.

TROTTER, Thomas. *An Essay, Medical, Philosophical, and Chemical on Drunkenness . . .* London, 1804. $1,250.

TROWBRIDGE, John Townsend. See Creyton, Paul.

TROWBRIDGE, John Townsend. *Cudjo's Cave.* Boston, 1864. Pictorial half title. Cloth. Listing "L'Envoy" as beginning on page 503 in table of contents (later, page 501). $400.

TROWBRIDGE, John Townsend. *The Old Battleground.* New York, 1860. Author's first book under his name. $350.

TROWBRIDGE, John Townsend. *The South: A Tour of Its Battlefields and Ruined Cities.* Hartford, 1866. $300.

TRUE Copies of the Letters Between . . . John Bishop . . . and D. Cole . . . (The). (Bishop John Jewel.) (London), 1560. $4,500.

TRUMAN, Maj. Ben. C. *Life, Adventures and Capture of Tiburcio Vasquez, the Great California Bandit and Murderer.* Los Angeles, 1874. Frontispiece map. 44 pages, pictorial wraps. $1,000. Los Angeles, 1941. Cloth and leather. One of 100 copies. $250.

TRUMAN, Harry S. *Mr. Citizen.* (New York, 1960.) One of 1,000 signed copies. In slipcase. $750. Trade. $100.

TRUMBO, Dalton. *Eclipse.* London (1935). Author's first book. $3,000.

TRUMBO, Dalton. *Johnny Got His Gun.* Philadelphia (1939). $1,000.

TRUMBO, Dalton. *Washington Jitters.* New York, 1936. $200. Noted in both blue and yellow cloth. Priority unknown.

TRUTH, Sojourner. *Narrative of Sojourner Truth, A Northern Slave . . .* Boston, 1850. $2,000.

TRYPHE. Cinq Petits Dialogues Grecs. (By Natalie C. Barney.) Paris, 1902. Wraps. $400.

TSA TOKE, Monroe. *The Peyote Ritual.* Grabhorn Press. San Francisco, 1957. 15 color plates. Boards and cloth. One of 325 copies. $500.

TUCHMAN, Barbara. See Wertheim, Barbara.

TUCKER, Beverley. *The Partisan Leader.* Richmond, 1862. Printed wraps. Reprint of the anonymous 1836 novel forecasting the Civil War. $1,250.

TUCKER, George. *The Life of Thomas Jefferson . . .* Philadelphia, 1837. 2 vols. Frontispiece portrait. $750.

TUCKER, Dr. Joseph C. *To the Golden Goal, and Other Sketches.* San Francisco, 1895. One of 50 copies. $350.

TUCKER, St. George. *A Dissertation on Slavery . . .* Philadelphia, 1796. $2,500.

TUCKEY, J. K. *Narrative of an Expedition to Explore the River Zaire . . .* London, 1818. Folding map and 13 plates (one hand-colored). $1,500.

TUER, Andrew W. *History of the Horn-Book.* London, 1896. 2 vols. with 7 facsimile hornbooks in pockets (3 in first vol. and 4 in second vol.). $1,500.

TUER, Andrew W. *Pages and Pictures from Forgotten Children's Books.* London, 1898–99. $125. One of 112 large-paper copies. $350.

TUFTS, James. *A Tract Descriptive of Montana Territory.* New York, 1865. Map. 15 pages, unbound folded sheets. $1,750.

TUFTS, Richard S. *The Principles Behind the Rules of Golf.* Pinehurst, 1960. $300.

TULLIDGE, Edward W. *The History of Salt Lake City and Its Founders.* Salt Lake City, 1886. Third edition, revised and enlarged. $450.

TULLIDGE, Edward W. *Tullidge's Histories, (Volume II). Containing the History of all the Northern, Eastern and Western Counties of Utah . . .* Salt Lake City, 1889. The only vol. published. (Covers the rest of Utah, not in the previous entry.) $450.

TULLOCH, W. W. *Life of Tom Morris.* London [1908?]. With 27 photographic plates. $1,750.

TULLY, Jim. *Emmett Lawler.* New York (1922). Author's first book. $400.

TUNNEY, Gene. *A Man Must Fight.* Boston, 1932. One of 500 signed copies. $750.

TUPPER, James Perchard. *An Essay on the Probability of Sensation in Vegetables . . .* London, 1811. $1,000.

TURBYFILL, Mark. *The Living Frieze.* Evanston (1921). Author's first book. One of 350 copies. $125.

TURGENEV, Ivan. *Father and Sons.* New York, 1867. $500.

TURGENEV, Ivan. *Russian Life In the Interior . . .* Edinburgh, 1855. Author's first book. First English translation. $1,000.

TURNBULL, Robert J. See Brutus.

TURNER, A. A. *Light and Shadows of New York Picture Galleries.* New York, 1864. Contains 40 mounted albumen photos of the painted works of art. Gilt morocco, all edges gilt. $750.

TURNER, Frederick Jackson. *The Character and Influence of the Fur Trade* . . . (Madison, 1889.) Author's first book. Wraps. $400.

TURNER, Frederick Jackson. *The Significance of the Frontier in American History.* Madison, Wis., 1894. 34 pages. $2,500.

TURNER, Mary Honeyman Ten Eyck. *These High Plains.* Amarillo, 1941. Portrait and plates. Cloth pictorial label. Issued without dustwrapper. One of 150 copies. $150.

TURNER, Orsamus. *History of the Pioneer Settlement of Phelps and Gorham's Purchase* . . . Rochester, 1851. Boards and leather. $250.

TURNER, Samuel. *An Account of an Embassy to the Court* . . . London, 1800. Folding map and 13 plates (one folding). $3,500.

TURNER, T. G. *Gazetteer of the St. Joseph Valley.* Chicago, 1867. Frontispiece and plate. $750.

TURNER, T. G. *Turner's Guide from the Lakes to the Rocky Mountains.* Chicago, 1868. $1,000.

TURNLEY, Parmenas T. *Reminiscences of Parmenas T. Turnley, from the Cradle to Three-Score and Ten.* Chicago (1892). 6 plates. $750.

TUROW, Scott. *One L.* New York, 1977. Author's first book. $300.

TURPIN, Waters Edward. *These Low Grounds.* New York, 1937. Author's first book. $125.

TURRILL, H. B. *Historical Reminiscences of the City of Des Moines.* Des Moines, 1857. Double-page frontispiece plate and 7 other plates. 144 pages, printed dark-blue wraps. $500.

TUTHILL, Louisa C. *History of Architecture* . . . Philadelphia, 1848. $600.

TUTTLE, J. H. *Wam-dus-ky: A Descriptive Record of a Hunting Trip to North Dakota.* Minneapolis, 1893. Illustrated. $1,500.

TWAIN, Mark. See Harte, Bret, and Twain, Mark. See also *Date 1601; What Is Man?*

TWAIN, Mark. *Adventures of Huckleberry Finn.* London, 1884. Red cloth. Publisher's catalogue dated October 1884 inserted at back. $2,000. New York, 1885. Issued in blue and in green cloth. Earliest state: title page with copyright notice on verso (1884) tipped in. page (13); "Him and another man" listed incorrectly at page 88; page 57, line 11 up: ". . . with the was . . ."; page 155: Johnson has final 5 in page number same font in various "off-balance" position; page 283: fly outline of trousers a pronounced curve; leaf bound in (seen only in prospectuses and leather-bound copies). Portrait frontispiece: cloth under bust visible. "Heliotype" imprint. Although the current thinking is that only pages (13) and 57 are important because the others were put in at random before publication, which seems to us to say that different states don't matter because they all occur before publication. Blue cloth. $10,000. Green cloth. $7,500. Mixed state copies would bring less. See Blank, Johnson, McBride, or the *Author Price Guides* for further details. Limited Editions Club, New York, 1933. In slipcase. $200. Limited Editions Club, New York, 1942. One of 1,500 copies signed by the illustrator, Thomas Hart Benton.

In slipcase. $750. Pennyroyal Press. West Hatfield, 1985. One of 25 signed copies with extra suite of wood engravings signed by the artist, Barry Moser. In slipcase. $5,000. One of 350 signed copies with separate suite of plates. In slipcase. $1,750.

TWAIN, Mark. *The Adventures of Tom Sawyer.* London, 1876. $12,000. Toronto, 1876. $2,500. American Publishing Co. Hartford/Chicago/Cincinnati. A. Roman & Co. San Francisco. 1876. First printing is on wove paper. Front matter paged (I)–xvi, fly title, Page(I). Pages(II–III) blank. Frontispiece, page (iv). Collation: (I)–xvi (17)–(275); blank, page (276); 4 pages ads. (Verso of half title and preface blank.) Half morocco (200 copies). $40,000. Calf (1,500 copies). $25,000. Blue cloth, edges gilt. $20,000. Blue cloth, edges plain. $15,000. Limited Editions Club, Cambridge, 1939. One of 1,500 copies signed by illustrator, Thomas Hart Benton. In slipcase. $750.

TWAIN, Mark. *The American Claimant.* New York, 1892. Gray-green or olive-green cloth. $450. London, 1892. $300.

TWAIN, Mark. *The Celebrated Jumping Frog of Calaveras County, And Other Sketches.* New York, 1867. Author's first book. First issue/printing has single leaf of ads on cream-yellow paper before title page; page 66: last line "life" unbroken; page 198: last line "this" unbroken. In various cloth colors. Usually with frog in left corner of front cover, variant has frog in middle. Favored color is plum. $20,000. Second issue/printing: lacks ads and type broken or worn. $4,500. London, 1867. Wraps. $6,000.

TWAIN, Mark. *A Connecticut Yankee in King Arthur's Court.* New York, 1889. With "s" like ornament between "The" and "King" on page 59. $2,500. Toronto, 1889. Printed from U.S. edition with "s" like ornament between "The" and "King" on page 59. $750.

TWAIN, Mark. *A Curious Dream.* London (1872). Pictorial yellow boards. Earliest printing: endpapers blank; leaf L4 blank; "Bradbury, Evans" imprint on pages (2) and/or page 150. $1,500.

TWAIN, Mark. *A Double-Barrelled Detective Story.* New York, 1902. Red or maroon cloth. $250. London, 1902. $150.

TWAIN, Mark. *Facts for Mark Twain's Memory Builder.* (Cover title.) New York, 1891. Wraps. Designed to accompany "Mark Twain's Memory Builder," a board game (includes board and small box with facts . . . and pins). $1,000.

TWAIN, Mark. *Following the Equator.* Hartford, 1897. Blue cloth. $600. One of 250 signed copies. $7,500.

TWAIN, Mark. *Life on the Mississippi.* London, 1883. Red cloth. Ads dated March 1883. $1,000. Boston, 1883. First state: page 441: present is a tailpiece depicting an urn, flames, and the head of Twain; page 443: the caption reads "The St. Louis Hotel." $2,500. Mixed states. $1,000. Second state: no urn and "St. Charles Hotel." $750. Limited Editions Club, New York, 1944. One of 1,200 copies signed by Thomas Hart Benton. $750.

TWAIN, Mark. *The Man That Corrupted Hadleyburg and Other Stories and Essays.* New York, 1900. Earliest state: sheets bulk about 1 1/16 inches; the plate opposite page 2 has, in addition to the caption, the line: "[Page 2." $350. London, 1900. Ads dated June 1900. $200.

TWAIN, Mark. *Mark Twain's (Burlesque) Autobiography and First Romance.* New York (1871). First issue lacks ads for Ball, Black & Co. on copyright page. Wraps. $750. Cloth (green, terracotta or purple cloth). $600. Second issue. $500. John Camden Hotten. London, no date. Unauthorized. Cloth. $600. Pictorial wraps. $400. George Routledge & Sons. London, no date. Wraps. English edition following Hotten's unauthorized edition published two weeks earlier. $250.

TWAIN, Mark. *The £1,000,000 Bank-Note and Other New Stories.* New York, 1893. $450. London, 1893. Ads dated March or April 1893. $350.

TWAIN, Mark. *Personal Recollections of Joan of Arc.* New York, 1896. Earliest state: page (463): "Some books for the Library The Abbey Shakespeare . . ." The fourth entry is for "Memoirs of Barras" described as in 4 vols. with vols. I–II offered at $3.75 each; vols. III–IV as "just ready." Twain's name on binding but not title page. $400. Second state: "Some books for the Library George Washington and Memoirs . . . 4 vols. At $15." $250. London, 1896. Ads dated March 1896. $200.

TWAIN, Mark. *The Prince and the Pauper.* London, 1881. Red cloth. Publisher's catalogue dated November 1881 inserted at back. $1,250. Montreal, 1881. Gray-blue wraps. $5,000. Title page is a cancel with "Author's Canadian Edition . . ." added. Tan cloth stamped in gold and black. $1,250. Boston, 1882. 6–8 copies printed on China paper, bound in white linen, stamped in gold, inner hinges of blue linen. $30,000. Trade. First state: at front true binder's endpapers of white, or toned white, paper. At back: leaf (26)8 used as pastedown. Leaf (26)7 present as a blank uppermost. Rosette on spine ⅛ inch below fillet. Franklin Press imprint on copyright page. Cloth. $2,000. Second state: leaf (26)7–8 blanks, rosette ⅙ inch below fillet. $850. Limited Editions Club. (New York), 1964. One of 1,500 copies signed by illustrator, Clarke Hutton. Slipcase. $150.

TWAIN, Mark. *Pudd'nhead Wilson: A Tale.* London, 1894. Ads dated September 1894. $500. Limited Editions Club, Avon, 1974. 2 vols. (including the calendar). $125.

TWAIN, Mark. *Roughing It.* Hartford, et al, 1872. Probable earliest issue with "premises—said he/was occupying his/" on page 242, lines 20–21. $2,000. Later state or words lacking. $850.

TWAIN, Mark. *The Stolen White Elephant.* London, 1882. Presumed first state: list of books on verso of half titles does not list *The White Elephant;* title page has imprint on verso; foot of page 285 has 1-line imprint. Publisher's catalogue dated May 1882. $500. Second state: lists title, no imprints on the two pages. $300. Boston, 1882. Tan cloth. $350.

TWAIN, Mark. *Tom Sawyer Abroad, Tom Sawyer Detective . . .* New York, 1896. $2,500.

TWAIN, Mark. *Tom Sawyer, Detective as Told by Huck Finn . . .* London, 1897. Publisher's catalogue dated November 1896 inserted at back. First U.K. edition of *Tom Sawyer Abroad, Tom Sawyer Detective . . .* $1,000.

TWAIN, Mark. *The Tragedy of Pudd'nhead Wilson.* Hartford, 1894. Earliest state: sheets bulk about 1⅛ inches. The title leaf is clearly joined to the next leaf. $1,000. Second state sheets bulk 1¼ inches. Title leaf is an insert on slightly different paper. $450. (For English first edition see *Pudd'nhead Wilson.*)

TWAIN, Mark. *A Tramp Abroad.* Hartford/London, 1880. First state: frontispiece captioned "Moses." Priority of other points in BAL not established. Cloth. $1,250. Second state with "Titian's Moses." $500.

TWAIN, Mark. *A Yankee at the Court of King Arthur.* London, 1889. $750. (For U.S. edition see *A Connecticut Yankee . . .*)

TWEEDIE, William. *The Arabian Horse: His Country and People.* Edinburgh, 1894. 10 plates, 25 text illustrations, maps and tables. Green decorated cloth. $2,000. Large-paper issue. Half morocco. One of 100 copies. Folding map at rear. $6,000.

TWENTIETH Century History of Southwest Texas (A). Chicago, 1907. 2 vols. Illustrated. Quarto, morocco. $750.

TWENTY Letters to Joseph Conrad. London, 1926. 12 pamphlets, wraps. One of 220 sets. In cloth folder. $750.

TWIN Cities Directory and Business Mirror for the Year 1860, Including the Cities of Davenport, Iowa, Rock Island, Ill., and Moline, Ill. Davenport, 1859. Vol. 1. (E. Coy & Co., publisher.) $400.

TWINING, Elizabeth. *Illustrations of the Natural Order of Plants, Arranged in Groups.* London, 1849–55. 2 vols. 160 colored lithograph plates. Tall folio, half morocco. $60,000.

TWISS, Richard. *Travels Through Portugal and Spain in 1772 and 1773.* London, 1775. 2 extending and 1 folding maps. $2,500.

TWISS, Travers. *The Oregon Question, In Respect to Facts and the Law of Nations.* London, 1846. 2 large folding maps and ads. $750.

TWITCHELL, Ralph Emerson. *The Leading Facts of New Mexican History.* Cedar Rapids, Iowa, 1911–17. 5 vols. Folding maps, color frontispiece, other illustrations. $1,750.

TWITCHELL, Ralph Emerson. *Old Santa Fe . . .* (Santa Fe., 1925.) Illustrated. Cloth. One of 1,000 copies. $150.

TWITCHELL, Ralph Emerson. *The Spanish Archives of New Mexico . . .* Cedar Rapids, 1914. 2 large octavo vols., illustrations and photographs. $600.

TWO Admirals (The): A Tale. Philadelphia, 1842. By the Author of *The Pilot* (James Fenimore Cooper). 2 vols. First American edition. Purple muslin, paper labels. $750. London, 1842. 3 vols. Boards and cloth, paper labels. (Issued under Cooper's name.) $600.

Two Gentlemen of Philadelphia. See *Epistles and Gospels for All Sundays . . .*

TWO Philosophers (The). Boston (1892). (By John Jay Chapman, his first book.) Wraps. $200.

TWO Years Before the Mast. A Personal Narrative of Life at Sea. New York, 1840. (By Richard Henry Dana, Jr., his first book.) (Harpers' Family Library No. CVI.) Tan, black, or gray cloth. First issue, with perfect "i" in the word "in," first line of copyright notice. Ads in back list 1–105. $6,000. Second issue: with "i" undotted. Ads for 1–121. $3,000. Third issue: ads 1–129. $2,000. Boston, 1869. With new preface and added chapter. $750. London (1904). Illustrated by Arthur Rackham. $350. Chicago, 1930. Lakeside Press. Illustrated by Edward A. Wilson. Pictorial linen. One of 1,000 copies. In slipcase. $250. New York, 1936. Grabhorn printing. Illustrated. Boards. One of 1,000 copies. In dustwrapper. $350. Limited Editions Club, New York, 1947. In slipcase. $150.

TYLER, Anne. *The Clock Winder.* New York, 1972. $2,000. London, 1973. $750.

TYLER, Anne. *If Morning Ever Comes.* New York, 1964. Author's first book. $2,500. London, 1965. "that" for "than" in quote on front dustwrapper flap (all copies?). $750.

TYLER, Anne. *Slipping Down Life.* New York, 1970. $750.

TYLER, Anne. *The Tin Can Tree.* New York, 1965. $1,500. London, 1966. $450.

TYLER, Daniel. *A Concise History of the Mormon Battalion in the Mexican War.* Salt Lake City, 1881. Full leather. $1,250.

TYLER, Parker. See Ford, Charles.

TYLER, Parker. *The Metaphor in the Jungle and Other Poems.* Prairie City, Ill., 1940. Portrait by Tchelitchew. Cloth. Issued without dustwrapper. $500.

TYLER, Parker (editor). *Modern Things.* New York (1934). Purple and white cloth. $250.

TYNAN, Katherine. *Twenty One Poems.* Dun Emer Press. Dundrum, Ireland, 1907. Selected by W. B. Yeats. Blue boards and linen. One of 200 copies. $400.

TYNAN, Kenneth. *He That Plays the King.* London, 1950. Half leather. Author's first book. One of 50 copies. $200.

TYNDALL, John. *Essays on the Floating-Matter of the Air in Relation to Putrefaction and Infection.* London, 1881. $450. New York, 1882. $250.

TYPES and Bookmaking Containing Notes on the Books Printed at the Southworth-Anthoensen Press. Portland, 1943. One of 500 copies. $175.

TYPES of Successful Men in Texas. Austin, Tex., 1890. Red leather. $250.

TYSON, James L., M.D. *Diary of a Physician in California.* New York, 1850. 92 pages, printed wraps. $1,000. Oakland, 1955. One of 500 copies. $60.

TYSON, Philip T. *Geology and Industrial Resources of California.* Baltimore, 1851. 3 large folding maps. 9 folding plates. Second edition, following the government document edition of the previous year. $750.

TYSON, Robert A. *History of East St. Louis.* East St. Louis, 1875. Folding map and folding view of stockyards. 152 pages, wraps. $600.

U

UDELL, John. *Incidents of Travel to California, Across the Great Plains.* Jefferson, Ohio, 1856. Portrait, errata leaf. One of 26 copies. $1,250.

UDELL, John. *Journal of John Udell, Kept During a Trip Across the Plains.* Jefferson, Ohio, 1868. Vignette portrait. 47 pages, wraps. Second edition. $2,000. Los Angeles, 1946. Edited by Lyle H. Wright. Half morocco. One of 35 copies signed by Wright. $450. One of 750 copies. $150. (Note: The first edition of Udell's *Journal,* 45 pages, printed wraps, including cover title, appeared in Suisun City, Calif., in 1859 and is known in only 1 surviving copy). (New Haven, 1952.) Printed wraps. One of 200 copies. $125.

ULLMAN, Doris. See Jaeger, Doris U., and Peterkin, Julia.

UNDER the Greenwood Tree. London, 1872. (By Thomas Hardy.) 2 vols. Green cloth. $3,000. Sheets were bound in one volume in 1874. In various cloth colors. $1,500. New York, 1873. $500.

UNIFORM and Dress of the Army of the Confederate States. Richmond, 1861. 15 plates by Ernest Crehen. 5 pages, boards, paper label. First edition, first issue, with black-and-white plates. $500. Second issue, same date, with 9 of the 15 plates in color, plus errata slip and tipped-in colored strip illustrating field caps. $3,500.

UNITED States "History" as the Yankee Makes and Takes It. By a Confederate Soldier. Glen Allen, 1900. (By John Cussons.) 99 pages, yellow wraps. $100.

UNSWORTH, Barry. *The Hide.* London, 1970. $200.

UNSWORTH, Barry. *The Partnership.* London (1966). Author's first book. $500.

UPDIKE, D. B. (Printer). *Vexilla Regis Quotioe.* Boston, 1893. Author's first book. 100 copies. $350.

UPDIKE, John. *The Angels.* Pensacola, 1968. One of 150 copies. Sewn wraps in mailing envelope. $1,250.

UPDIKE, John. *Assorted Prose.* New York, 1965. With tipped-in leaf signed by Updike. $300. Without signed leaf. $200. (London, 1965.) $150.

UPDIKE, John. *Bath After Sailing.* Stevenson, Conn. (1968). 125 signed copies in stiff wraps. $750.

UPDIKE, John. *The Carpentered Hen and Other Tame Creatures.* New York (1958.) Author's first book. In first state dustwrapper, with "two children" in biographical information. $850.

UPDIKE, John. *The Dance of the Solids.* (New York, 1969.) Was to be used as a Season's greeting (along with W. H. Auden's *A New Year Greeting,* both in cardboard sleeve). $1,500.

UPDIKE, John. *Hoping for a Hoopoe.* London, 1959. First U.K. edition of *The Carpentered Hen.* $200.

UPDIKE, John. *The Magic Flute.* New York (1962). Edition not stated. Cloth in dustwrapper. $1,000. Pictorial cloth. Without dustwrapper. $600.

UPDIKE, John. *Midpoint and Other Poems.* New York, 1969. One of 350 signed copies. In dustwrapper. In slipcase. (Dustwrapper differs from trade edition.) $250. Trade. $125. (London, 1969.) $100.

UPDIKE, John. *The Music School.* New York, 1966. Page 46, line 15 starts "the state . . ." $400. Page 46, line 15 states "The King . . ." on tipped-in leaf. $200. Page 46, line 15, starts "The King . . ." on integral leaf. $100. (London, 1967.) $100.

UPDIKE, John. *On Meeting Authors.* Newburyport, 1968. One of 250 copies. Wraps. $850.

UPDIKE, John. *Pigeon Feathers.* New York, 1962. $250. (London, 1962.) $150.

UPDIKE, John. *The Poorhouse Fair.* New York, 1959. (Note: the second printing dustwrapper has a biographical note as second paragraph on back flap which is not on first printing dustwrapper.) $600. London, 1959. $300.

UPDIKE, John. *Rabbit Is Rich.* New York, 1981. One of 350 signed copies. In dustwrapper (which differs from trade edition) and slipcase. $350. Trade. $75. (London, 1982.) $75. Franklin Library, 1984. $100.

UPDIKE, John. *Rabbit Redux*. New York, 1971. One of 350 signed copies. In acetate dustwrapper. In slipcase. $450. Trade. $125. (London, 1972.) $100. Franklin Library, 1979. Signed limited edition. $125.

UPDIKE, John. *Rabbit, Run*. New York, 1960. Dustwrapper with 16-line blurb on front flap. $1,250. (London, 1961.) $350. Franklin Library, 1977. Limited signed edition. $175.

UPDIKE, John. *The Same Door*. New York, 1959. Dustwrapper has "Also by John Updike *The Poorhouse Fair*." $500. (London, 1962.) $175.

UPFIELD, Arthur W. *The House of Cain*. London (1928). Author's first book. $6,000. New York, 1928. $3,500.

UPHAM, Samuel C. *Notes of a Voyage to California Via Cape Horn* . . . Philadelphia, 1878. $850.

UPHAM, Samuel C. *Notes from Sunland, on the Manatee River, Gulf Coast of South Florida*. Braidentown, Fla., 1881. Frontispiece. 83 pages, printed wraps. $400. Second edition (so stated), same date. $200.

UPHAM, Thomas C. *Elements of Intellectual Philosophy* . . . Portland, 1827. $450.

UPHAM, Thomas C. *Mental Philosophy* . . . Portland (Maine), 1827. $500.

UPTON, Florence K. *The Golliwogg at the Sea-Side*. London, 1898. $600.

UPWARD, Edward. *Journey to the Border*. Hogarth Press. London, 1938. Author's first book. $400.

URIS, Leon. *The Angry Hills*. New York (1955). $350. London, 1956. $150.

URIS, Leon. *Battle Cry*. New York (1953). Author's first book. $750. London, 1953. $250.

URQUART, Jane. *False Shuffles*. Victoria, 1982. Wraps. $200.

UTTLEY, Alsion (Alice Jane.) *The Squirrel, The Hare and the Little Grey Rabbit*. London, 1929. Author's first book. $450.

UZANNE, Octave. *The French Bookbinders of the Eighteenth Century*. Chicago, 1904. One of 252 copies. $500.

V

VAIL, Alfred. *Description of the American Electro-Magnetic Telegraph* . . . Philadelphia, 1845. $1,000.

VAIL, Isaac Newton. *Alaska: Land of the Nugget. Why?* Pasadena, 1897. 68 pages, wraps. $250.

VALENTIA, George, Viscount. *Voyages and Travels to India, Ceylon, the Red Sea, Abyssinia, and Egypt, 1802–6*. London, 1809. 3 vols. 69 engraved views and folding maps. $4,000. London, 1811. 4 vols. (including atlas). $3,000.

VALENTINO, Rudolph. *Day Dreams*. New York, 1923. Author's first book. Assumed issued without dustwrapper. $400. London, 1923. $350.

VALÉRY, Paul. See McGreevy, Thomas.

VALIN, Jonathan. *The Lime Pit.* New York (1980). Author's first book. $175.

VALPERGA: Or, The Life and Adventures of Castruccio, Prince of Lucca. London, 1823. (By Mary Wollstonecraft Shelley.) 3 vols. $3,000.

VALUABLE Secrets Concerning Arts and Trades. London, 1775. Written anonymously. Contains earliest reference to use of steel plates for engraving. $1,500.

VAN ALLSBURG, Chris. *Jumanji.* Boston, 1981. $750.

VAN ALLSBURG, Chris. *The Polar Express.* Boston, 1985. $750.

VAN BUREN, A. D. *Jottings of a Year's Sojourn in the South.* Battle Creek, 1859. $450.

VANCE, Jack. *The Dying Earth.* New York (1950). Author's first book. Wraps. $350. San Francisco/Columbia, Penna., 1976. One of 11 signed lettered copies. First hardback. $1,250. One of 111 copies signed by Vance and artist, George Barr. $750. 1,000 unnumbered copies. $200.

VANCE, Jack. *Emphyrio.* Garden City, 1969. $500.

VANCE, Jack. *The Language of Pao.* New York (1958). $350.

VANCE, Jack. *To Live Forever.* New York (1956). $600.

VANCE, Jack. *Vandals of the Void.* Philadelphia (1953). $300.

VANCOUVER, George, Capt. *A Voyage of Discovery to the North Pacific Ocean, and Round the World . . .* London, 1798. 4 vols. (including atlas). 34 plates and charts. $25,000. Without atlas. $12,500. London, 1801. 6 vols. 2 folding maps and 17 folding plates. $6,000.

VANDERBILT, Harold S. *On the Wind's Highway.* New York, 1939. Issued without dustwrapper. In slipcase. $450.

VANDERBILT, William K. *Taking One's Own Ship Around the World.* New York, 1929. 19 color plates. 112 photographs. Half (or full) morocco. One of 200 copies. In slipcase. $1,250.

VANDERBILT, William K. *To Galápagos on the Ara, 1926.* (New York, 1927.) Boards and leather. One of 900 copies. $750. New York, 1927. One of 500 copies. $1,000.

VANDERBILT, William K. *West Made East with the Loss of a Day.* New York, 1933. 7 color plates, 13 charts. Cloth. Issued without dustwrapper. In slipcase. One of 800 copies. $450. Half morocco. One of 200 copies on Rives paper. $750.

VAN DER ZEE, James (photographer). *The Harlem Book of the Dead.* Dobbs Ferry (1978). $400. Stiff wraps. $200.

VAN DINE, S. S. *The Benson Murder Case.* New York, 1926. (By Willard Huntington Wright, his first book under this name.) $4,500. Without dustwrapper. $500.

VAN DINE, S. S. *The Canary Murder Case.* New York, 1927. $750.

VAN DINE, S. S. *The Gracie Allen Murder Case.* New York, 1938. $500.

VAN DINE, S. S. *The Scarab Murder Case.* New York, 1930. $600.

VANDIVEER, Clarence A. *The Fur Trade and Early Western Exploration.* Cleveland, 1929. $300.

VAN DOREN, Carl. *The Life of Thomas Love Peacock.* New York, 1911. Author's first book. $125. London, 1911. $100.

VAN DOREN, Mark. *Henry David Thoreau.* Boston, 1916. Author's first book. $100.

VAN EVERY, Edward. *Muldoon the Solid Man of Sport.* New York, 1929. Stated first. $150.

VAN GIESON, Judith. *North of the Border.* New York (1988). Author's first book. $450. London, 1990. Wraps. $75.

VAN GULIK, Robert. *The Chinese Gold Murders.* London (1959). $459.

VAN GULIK, Robert. *The Chinese Maze Murders.* The Hague, 1956. $500. London, 1957. $450.

VAN GULIK, Robert. *Dee Goong An.* Tokyo, 1949. One of 1,200 signed copies. Plain white dustwrapper. $1,500.

VAN GULIK, Robert. *The Lacquer Screen.* (Kuala Lumpur) 1962. $1,000.

VAN GULIK, Robert. *The Lore of Chines Lute . . .* Tokyo, 1940. Author's first book. Wraps. $750.

VAN GULIK, Robert. *New Year's Eve in Lan-Fang.* Beirut, 1958. Sewn wraps. 200 copies. $1,250.

VAN MOE, Emile A. *The Decorated Letter . . .* Paris, 1950. Parchment covers. In dustwrapper. $125.

VAN TRAMP, John C. *Prairie and Rocky Mountain Adventures.* Columbus, Ohio, 1858. 61 plates. $200.

VAN VECHTEN, Carl. *Music After the Great War.* New York, 1915. Purple cloth, paper labels. Author's first book aside from a musical score and a promotional pamphlet. $100.

VAN VECHTEN, Carl. *Nigger Heaven.* New York, 1926. Decorated cloth, printed spine label. One of 205 signed copies. In slipcase. $1,000. Trade. $750.

VAN VECHTEN, Carl. *Spider Boy: A Scenario for a Moving Picture.* New York, 1928. Half cloth. One of 220 copies. In slipcase. $250. Red vellum. One of 75 copies on vellum. In slipcase. $750. Trade. $200.

VAN VECHTEN, Carl. *The Tattooed Countess.* New York, 1924. Boards and cloth. One of 150 signed copies. In slipcase. $350. Trade. $150.

VAN VECHTEN, Carl. *The Tiger in the House.* New York, 1920. Half cloth. In dustwrapper. $350.

VAN VOGT, A. E. *Slan: A Story of the Future.* Sauk City, Wis., 1946. Author's first regularly published book. $300.

VAN VOGT, A. E. *Tomorrow on the March*. (Los Angeles, 1946). 14-page stapled, self-wraps. Author's first book. $200.

VAN VOGT, A. E. *The Weapon Makers*. Hadley. Providence (1947). $250.

VAN WINKLE, C. S. *The Printers' Guide* . . . New York, 1818. Foldout frontispiece table, 32-page section entitled "A Specimen of Printing Types . . ." and 22-page section entitled *"A Specimen of Printing Types Cast . . ."* $7,500.

VAN ZANDT, Nicholas Biddle. *A Full Description of the Soil, Water, Timber, and Prairies of Each Lot, or Quarter Section of the Military Lands Between the Mississippi and Illinois Rivers*. Washington City, 1818. 127 pages, plus separately issued folding map. $4,500. Much less without map.

VARDON, Harry. *My Golfing Life*. London (1933). $1,250. London (1985). One of 200 copies. $250.

VARDY, John. *Some Designs of Mr. Inigo Jones and Mr. Wm. Kent*. (London), 1744. 53 plates. $5,000.

VARGAS LLOSA, Mario. *Conversation in the Cathedral*. New York (1975). $300.

VARGAS LLOSA, Mario. *The Time of the Hero*. New York, 1966. First English translation. $200. London (1967). $100.

VAUGHN, Robert. *Then and Now, or 36 Years in the Rockies* . . . Minneapolis, 1900. Illustrated. Pictorial cloth. $350.

VEBLEN, Thorstein. *The Theory of the Leisure Class*. London, 1899. Author's first book. $3,500. New York, 1899. $2,500.

VEDDER, Elihu. *Miscellaneous Moods in Verve*. Boston, 1914. One of 100 copies. $450.

VEGA CARPIO, Lope Felix de (attributed to). *The Star of Seville*. Gregynog Press. Newtown, Wales, 1935. Translated by Henry Thomas. Half morocco. One of 175 copies. $1,250.

VELASCO, José Francisco. *Sonora: Its Extent, Population, Natural Productions, Indian Tribes, Mines, Mineral Lands* . . . San Francisco, 1861. Translated by William F. Nye. First American edition. $1,000.

VELIKOVSKY, Immanuel. *Worlds in Collision*. New York, 1950. $250.

VENABLES, Robert. *The Experienc'd Angler*. London, 1662. $1,750.

VENEGAS, Miguel. *A Natural and Civil History of California*. London, 1759. 2 vols. Folding map and 2 plates in vol. 1. Second vol. has 2 plates. $2,000.

VERGA, Giovanni. *Mastro-Don Gesualdo*. New York, 1923. Translated by D. H. Lawrence. $350. London, 1925. $250.

VERNE, Jules. *Adrift in the Pacific*. London, 1889. 2 parts in one. $750. London/New York, 1889. First American edition. $750.

VERNE, Jules. *An Antarctic Mystery*. London, 1898. $1,000. Philadelphia, 1899. $350.

VERNE, Jules. *Around the World in Eighty Days.* London, 1873. $1,500. Boston, 1873. $1,000. London, 1874. Publisher's catalogue dated October, 1872. $1,000. Boston, 1874. $750. See also *The Tour of the World in Eighty Days.*

VERNE, Jules. *Five Weeks in a Balloon.* New York, 1869. Green cloth. First edition in English. $3,000. London, 1870. Different translation. $1,500. Boston, 1873. First fully illustrated edition. $1,000. Boston, 1874. $350.

VERNE, Jules. *From the Earth to the Moon.* Newark: Newark Printing and Publishing (1869). Wraps. Double columns (one known copy). $4,000. London, 1873. $1,000. New York, 1874. $750.

VERNE, Jules. *The Fur Country; or, Seventy Degrees North Latitude.* London, 1874. 100 full-page illustrations. Pictorial red cloth. First edition in English. $600. Boston, 1874. $450.

VERNE, Jules. *Journey to the Center of the Earth.* London, 1872. $2,000. New York: Scribner, 1874. Pictorial cloth with no ads in book or address under publisher's imprint. $1,500. New York: Scribner (1874). Plain cloth. $300.

VERNE, Jules. *Mistress Branican.* New York (1891). First is 15 by 20 cm. (Later 13 by 18 cm.) Illustrated. First edition in English. $750. London, 1892. $350.

VERNE, Jules. *The Mysterious Island, Wrecked in the Air.* New York, 1875. First edition in English. $1,250. Wraps with 1874 on front cover. (Both were actually published in 1874.) $1,250. Boston, 1875. $350. (There are 8 other titles in this series in 1875 and 1876. See bibliography.)

VERNE, Jules. *The Tour of the World in Eighty Days.* Boston, 1873. $1,500. Boston, 1873. Later issue/printing with the added note on the title page "Translated By George M. Towle." $300. Reprinted in 1874 and 1875, same collation and size. See also *Around the World in Eighty Days.*

VERNE, Jules. *Twenty Thousand Leagues Under the Sea.* London, 1873. Various colors with publisher's catalogue dated 1872–1873. $1,250. Boston: Osgood, 1873. About 15 copies known. $10,000. Boston: George Smith, 1873. With "The end" on page 303. $2,500. Later without "The end." $1,000.

VERSES. (Edith Wharton.) Newport, Rhode Island, 1878. Wraps. $60,000.

VERSES by Two Undergraduates. (Cambridge, Mass.) 1905. Wraps. (By Van Wyck Brooks and John Hall Wheelock.) First book for both authors. $600.

VERSES from the Harvard Advocate. Cambridge, 1906. (Contains 5 poems by Wallace Stevens.) $350.

VERSES on Various Occasions. London, 1868. (By John Henry, Cardinal Newman.) With text ending on page 340. $350.

VERVE. *Numbers 1–4.* Paris, 1937–39. Together, 4 vols. Original wrappers, slipcase. $1,750.

VERVLIET, Hendrick D.L. (editor). *The Book Through Five Thousand Years.* London/New York (1972). $400.

VERY, Jones. *Essays and Poems.* Boston, 1839. Author's first book. $500.

VESEY, Paul. *El Fenbein Zahne.* (Ivory Tusks.) Heidelberg (1956). (By Samuel Allen, his first book.) English/German text. $400.

VESPUCCI, Amerigo. *Letters of Amerigo Vespucci Describing His Four Voyages to the New World.* San Francisco, 1926. Map in color, illustrations by Valenti Angelo. Vellum. One of 250 copies. In slipcase. $750.

VESTAL, Stanley. *Fandango.* Boston, 1927. (By Walter S. Campbell, his first book.) $300.

VICENTIO, Ludovico. *The Calligraphic Models of Ludovico degli Arrighi, Surnamed Vicentio.* Montagnola (Paris), 1926. Edited by Stanley Morrison. 64 pages, facsimile. One of 300 copies. $1,750.

VIDAL, Gore. See Box, Edgar.

VIDAL, Gore. *The City and the Pillar.* New York (1948). $750.

VIDAL, Gore. *Dark Green, Bright Red.* New York, 1950. $400.

VIDAL, Gore. *In a Yellow Wood.* New York, 1947. $450.

VIDAL, Gore. *A Search for the King.* New York, 1950. $300.

VIDAL, Gore. *The Season of Comfort.* New York, 1949. $250.

VIDAL, Gore. *Williwaw.* New York, 1946. Author's first book. $1,250.

VIDOCQ, François Eugene. *Memoirs of Vidocq* . . . London, 1829. (Also noted as 1828–30.) Author's first book. 4 vols. $1,500.

VIERECK, Georg Sylvester. *Gedichte.* New York, 1904. Author's first book. Wraps. One of 300 copies. $300.

VIERTEL, Peter. *White Hunter, Black Heart.* Garden City, 1953. $200.

VIGNOLES, Charles. *Observations Upon the Floridas.* New York, 1823. $3,000.

VILLARREAL, José Antonio. *Pocho.* Garden City, 1959. $150.

VILLASEÑOR, Victor. *Jury: the Trial of Juan Corona.* Boston (1977). $100.

VIRGINIA Illustrated . . . New York, 1857. (By David Hunter Strother.) $300.

VISCHER, Edward. *Missions of Upper California.* San Francisco, 1872. 15 plates. Wraps. $750.

VISCHER, Edward. *Sketches of the Washoe Mining Region.* San Francisco, 1862. Cloth portfolio with 26 mounted plates (Howes) and 24 pages of text, wraps. $5,000 or more.

VISCHER, Edward. *VISCHER'S Pictorial of California.* San Francisco, 1870. 2 vols. With 169 (or so) mounted plates. $15,000. (Howes calls for 100 or 120 plates. Auction records show copies with 110, 114, 167, 169, and 209 plates.)

VISIAK, E. H. *Medusa. A Story of Mystery, Ecstasy, and A Strange Horror.* London, 1929. $400.

VISIT to Texas (A). New York, 1834. In original cloth with folding map in color, 4 plates. $6,000. New York, 1836. Second edition, with plates omitted. $1,250.

VISSCHER, William Lightfoot. *"Black Mammy": A Song of the Sunny South.* Cheyenne, 1885. Author's first book. $450.

VIVIAN, A. Pendarves. *Wanderings in the Western Land.* London, 1879. Frontispiece, plates, two folding. $300.

VIVIAN, George. *Scenery of Portugal and Spain.* London, 1839. With litho title and 35 views on 31 sheets. In original half morocco. $10,000.

VIVIAN, George. *Spanish Scenery.* London, 1838. With litho title and 31 views on 27 plates. In original half morocco. $10,000.

VIVIAN Grey. London, 1826–27. 5 vols. (By Benjamin Disraeli.) Author's first novel. $750.

VIZETELLY, Henry. *A History of Champagne . . .* London, 1882. $750.

VLIET, Russ. *A Manual of Woodslore Survival.* (Cimarron, 1949.) Author's first book. $400.

VOLLMANN, William T. *You Bright and Risen Angels.* (London, 1987.) Author's first book. $150. New York, 1987. $125.

VOLNEY, C. F. *A View of the Soil and Climate of the United States . . .* Philadelphia, 1804. 2 folding plates, 2 folding maps. First American edition. $500.

VOLTAIRE, Jean Francois Marie Arouet de. *Candide.* London, 1759. $7,500. New York, 1928. Translated by Richard Aldington. Illustrated by Rockwell Kent and colored by hand. Cloth, leather spine. One of 95 signed copies. In slipcase. $2,500. Ordinary issue (not handcolored). Buckram. One of 1,470 copies signed by Kent. $350. (First book published by Random House.)

VOLTAIRE, F. M. A. *Letters Concerning the English Nation.* London, 1733. $850.

VOLTAIRE, F. M. A. *The Philosophical Dictionary for the Pocket.* London, 1765. $1,000.

VOLTAIRE, F. M. A. *Zadig; or, The Book of Fate.* London, 1749. $2,000. London, 1775. Second edition. $350.

VON HAGEN, Victor W. *The Aztec and Maya Papermakers.* New York, 1943. Illustrated, including paper samples. One of 220 signed copies. Issued without dustwrapper. $750. Trade. 39 full-page plates at end and a tipped-in sample on Huun-Paper as the frontispiece. $200.

VON WINNING, Hasso. *Pre-Columbian Art of Mexico and Central America.* New York (1968). One of 100 signed copies. In slipcase. $600. One of 1800 copies. 595 illustrations, including 175 mounted plates. In dustwrapper. $350. One of 15 lettered dedication copies. $750.

VONNEGUT, Kurt, Jr. *Canary in a Cat House.* Greenwich, Conn. (1961). Wraps. $250.

VONNEGUT, Kurt, Jr. *Cat's Cradle.* New York (1963). $1,000. London, 1963. $400.

VONNEGUT, Kurt, Jr. *Happy Birthday, Wanda June.* New York, 1971. Black cloth and orange endpapers. In dustwrapper with price at top on front flap. (Book Club edition in black boards also states "First Printing.") $1,500 Wraps. $150. London (1973). $350.

VONNEGUT, Kurt, Jr. *Mother Night.* Greenwich, Conn. (1962). Wraps. $200. New York (1966). $350. London (1968). $150.

VONNEGUT, Kurt, Jr. *Player Piano.* New York, 1952. Author's first book. Publisher's seal and "A" on copyright page. (There is a Book Club edition which has an "A," but no seal.) $1,250. London, 1953. $500.

VONNEGUT, Kurt, Jr. *The Sirens of Titan.* (New York, 1959.) Wraps. $250. Boston, 1961. Cloth. $2,500.

VONNEGUT, Kurt, Jr. *Slapstick.* New York (1976). Trade. $50. One of 250 signed copies. Issued without dustwrapper in slipcase. $350. Franklin Library. Limited edition. $150. London (1976). $75.

VONNEGUT, Kurt, Jr. *Slaughterhouse-Five.* (New York, 1969.) $1,500. London (1970). $350. Franklin Library, 1978. Signed limited edition. $250.

VONNEGUT, Kurt, Jr. *Welcome to the Monkey House.* (New York, 1968.) $750. London (1969). $250.

VOORHEES, Luke. *Personal Recollections of Pioneer Life on the Mountains and Plains of the Great West.* (Cheyenne, 1920.) Portrait. 75 pages, cloth. $750.

VOORN, Henk. *Old Ream Wrappers.* North Hills, 1969. 2 copper plate prints of nineteenth-century Dutch ream wrappers. One of 375 copies. $400.

VOSBURGH, W. S. *Cherished Portraits of Thoroughbred Horses from the Collection of William Woodward.* New York, 1929. Derrydale Press. 70 plates. Full morocco. One of 200 copies. $2,500. One of 21 copies with hand-colored plates in Sangorski binding for $40,000 at auction in 2000.

VOYAGE to Mexico and Havanna (A); Including Some General Observations on the United States. New York, 1841. By an Italian (Charles Barinetti). Half calf. $1,000.

W

W., E.B. *The Lady Is Cold: Poems by E. B. W.* New York, 1929. (By E. B. White.) Author's first book. First issue with Plaza Hotel statue on cover, spine lettered in gold. $500. Second issue with city skyline on cover, spine lettered in green. $400.

WADDINGTON, Miriam. *Green World.* Montreal, 1945. Author's first book. Stiff wraps. In dustwrapper. $300.

WADE, Allan. *A Bibliography of the Writings of W. B. Yeats.* (London), 1958. Second edition, revised. $200.

WADE, Henry. *The Verdict of You All.* London, 1926. (By Henry Lancelot Aubrey-Fletcher, his first book.) $1,500.

WAFER, Lionel. *A New Voyage and Description of the Isthmus of America* . . . London, 1699. Folding frontispiece map and 2 folding plates. $2,000.

WAGNER, Lieut. Col. A. L., and KELLEY, Comdr. J. D. *The United States Army and Navy: Their Histories* . . . Akron, Ohio 1899. 43 colored plates. Oblong folio, leatherette. $1,000.

WAGNER, Henry R. *Bullion to Books, Fifty Years of Business and Pleasure.* Los Angeles, 1962. $150.

WAGNER, Henry R. *The Cartography of the Northwest Coast of America to the Year 1800.* Berkeley, 1937. 2 vols. Folio. In dustwrapper and slipcase. $1,000.

WAGNER, Henry R. *The Plains and the Rockies.* San Francisco, 1920. Boards and cloth. First edition (suppressed). With 6-page pamphlet of corrections. $1,500. San Francisco, 1921. Cloth and boards. One of 350 copies. First published edition. $300. One of 50 copies on Japan vellum. $750. Grabhorn Press. San Francisco, 1937. Revised by C. L. Camp. Second edition. One of 600 copies. $200. Columbus, Ohio, 1953. Third edition. $250. Boards, deluxe edition. One of 75 copies. In slipcase. $600. San Francisco, 1982. Fourth edition. Revised by Charles L. Camp and then by Robert H. Becker. $200.

WAGNER, Henry R. *Sir Francis Drake's Voyage Around the World* . . . San Francisco, 1926. Maps, plates. $450. Morocco and cloth, extra illustrated. One of 100 signed copies. $650.

WAGNER, Henry R. *Spanish Explorations in the Strait of Juan de Fuca.* Santa Ana, Calif., 1933. Maps, illustrations. One of 425 copies. $750. Vellum. One of 25 signed and extra illustrated copies. $1,000.

WAGNER, Henry R. *The Spanish Southwest. 1542–1794.* Berkeley, 1924. Half morocco. One of 100 copies. $2,000. Vellum. One of 20 signed and extra-illustrated copies. $2,500. Albuquerque, 1937. 2 vols. Half vellum. One of 401 copies. $600. New York, 1967. $450.

WAGNER, Henry R. *The Spanish Voyages to the Northwest Coast of America* . . . San Francisco, 1929. Maps, plates. One of 400 copies. $600. Vellum. One of 25 signed and extra-illustrated copies. $1,250.

WAGNER, Richard. *The Flying Dutchman.* Corvinus Press. London, 1938. Vellum. One of 130 copies. In slipcase. $300.

WAGNER, Richard. *The Rhinegold & The Valkyrie.* London, 1910. Translated by Margaret Armour. 34 color plates by Arthur Rackham. Vellum. One of 1,150 copies signed by the artist. $1,000. Cloth. Trade edition. $500. New York, 1910. Vellum. One of 1,150 signed copies. $1,000. New York, 1910. American trade edition. $350.

WAGSTAFF, Theophile. *Flore et Zephyr: Ballet Mythologique.* London, 1836. (By William Makepeace Thackeray, his first separate publication.) 9 tinted plates (including cover title) by the author. Wraps. $3,500.

WAIKNA . . . (Ephraim G. Squier.) New York, 1855. Author's first book. $400.

WAIN, John. *Mixed Feelings! Nineteen Poems.* Reading, England, 1951. Wraps. Author's first book. One of 120 copies. $400.

WAITE, A. E. *A Lyric of the Fairy Land* . . . London, 1879. Author's first book. $750.

WAKEFIELD, H. R. *Gallimaufry.* London (1928). Author's first book. $500.

WAKEFIELD, H. R. *They Return at Evening.* New York, 1928. $400.

WAKEFIELD, John A. *History of the War Between the United States and the Sac and Fox Nations of Indians* . . . Jacksonville, Ill., 1834. $1,750.

WAKEFIELD, Priscilla. *Excursions in North America* . . . London, 1806. With the fold-out 16 x 15-inch map of the travels, with the route outlined in red. $650.

WAKEMAN, Geoffrey. *Aspects of Victorian Lithography, Anastatic Printing and Photozincography.* Wymondham, 1970. One of 250 copies. 3 mounted examples inserted. $350.

WAKEMAN, Geoffrey. *English Hand Made Papers Suitable for Bookwork.* (Loughborough), 1972. One of 75 copies. Contains 41 specimens of paper. $750.

WAKEMAN, Geoffrey. *English Marbled Papers, A Documentary History.* (Loughborough), no date [1978]. 16 specimens of marbled papers. Limited to 112 copies. $600.

WAKEMAN, Geoffrey. *Twentieth Century English Vat Paper Mills.* (Loughborough), 1980. Small pocket at rear containing 5 paper samples. One of 102 copies. $500.

WAKOSKI, Diane. *Coins and Coffins.* (New York, 1962.) Author's first regular book. Printed wraps. $150.

WAKOSKI, Diane. *The Diamond Merchant.* Cambridge, Mass. (1968). Gray cloth, paper label. One of 99 signed copies. In dustwrapper. $125.

WAKOSKI, Diane. *Justice Is Reason Enough.* (Berkeley, private printing) 1959. Author's first book. (50 mimeographed copies.) $500.

WAKOSKI, Diane. *Thanking My Mother for Piano Lessons.* Mt. Horeb, Wis., 1969. Wraps. One of 250 copies. $150.

WALCOTT, Derek. *In a Green Night.* London, 1962. Author's fourth book. (First outside Caribbean.) $350.

WALCOTT, Derek. *Selected Poems.* New York (1964). $175.

WALCOTT, Mary Vaux. *North American Wild Flowers.* Washington, 1925–29. 5 vols. 400 color plates (loose) in cloth portfolios. $1,000. Washington, 1950. 5 vols. $400.

WALDBERG, Patrick. *Marino Marini. Complete Works.* New York (1970). 1,000 reproductions (80 in color). Natural linen stamped in red. In dustwrapper and slipcase. $500.

WALDROP, Keith. *Songs from the Decline of the West.* Mt. Horeb (1970). Calf. One of 120 copies. $250.

WALEY, Arthur. See *Chinese Poems.*

WALGAMOTT, Charles S. *Reminiscences of Early Days.* (Twin Falls, Idaho, 1926–27.) 2 vols. Plates. Cloth. $350.

WALKER, Alice. *The Color Purple.* New York (1982). Cloth. $750. Wraps. (Issued simultaneously.) $60. (London, 1983.) Wraps. $50. (London, 1986.) "This hardcover edition published 1986." $75.

WALKER, Alice. *Once.* New York (1968). Author's first book. $1,000.

WALKER, Alice. *Revolutionary Petunias.* New York (1973). $600. Wraps. $60.

WALKER, Alice. *The Third Life of Grange Copeland.* New York (1970). $450.

WALKER, Charles D. *Biographical Sketches of the Graduates and Eleves of the Virginia Military Institute Who Fell During the War Between the States.* Philadelphia, 1875. $150.

WALKER, Judson E. *Campaigns of General Custer in the North-West, and the Final Surrender of Sitting Bull.* New York, 1881. Illustrated. Wraps. $1,000.

WALKER, Margaret. *Come Down from Yonder Mountain.* (Toronto, 1962.) $300.

WALKER, Margaret. *For My People.* New York, 1942. Author's first book. $750. New York, 1992. Limited Editions Club. 200 copies signed by Walker and Elizabeth Catlett. Large folio. $2,500.

WALKER, Mary Willis. *Zero at the Bone.* New York, 1991. Author's first book. $1,000.

WALKS and Talks of an American Farmer in England. New York, 1852. (By Frederick Law Olmsted.) Author's first book. $250.

WALL, Oscar G. *Recollections of the Sioux Massacre.* Lake City, Minn., 1909. $250.

WALL, W. G. *Wall's Hudson River Portfolio.* New York (about 1826). 21 color plates. Oblong atlas folio. Last complete set about $80,000 at auction in 1983.

WALLACE, Alfred Russel. *Palm Trees of the Amazon.* London, 1953. Author's first book. (250 copies.) $1,750.

WALLACE, David Foster. *The Broom of the System.* New York (1987.) Author's first book. Cloth (1,300 copies.) $1,000. Wraps. $100.

WALLACE, Ed. R. *Parson Hanks: 14 Years in the West.* Arlington, Tex. (1906?). Wraps. $450.

WALLACE, Edgar. *The Four Just Men.* London, 1905. Frontispiece. Yellow cloth. First issue, with folding frontispiece plate and "Solution" leaf at end. $250.

WALLACE, Edgar. *The Mission That Failed! A Tale of the Raid and Other Poems.* (Cape Town, 1898.) Author's first book. Wraps. $750.

WALLACE, Edgar. *Writ in Barracks.* London, 1900. $350.

WALLACE, Edgar, and COOPER, Merian C. *King Kong.* New York: Grosset & Dunlap (1932). $3,000.

WALLACE, Lew. *Ben-Hur: A Tale of the Christ.* New York, 1880. With six-word dedication (which was in first few printings). $500. London, 1880. $400. Limited Editions Club, New York, 1960. In slipcase. $75.

WALLACE, Lew. *The Fair God.* Boston, 1873. Author's first book. First issue: sheets bulk 1-inch scant, signature mark "k" on page 161. $300. Second issue: sheets bulk 15/16 inch, signature mark "k" on page 161 usually lacking. $200.

WALLANT, Edward Lewis. *The Pawn Broker.* New York (1961). $125.

WALLER, Robert James. *The Bridges of Madison County.* New York, 1992. $200.

WALLER, Robert. *Love in Black and White.* London, 1992. First U.K. of *The Bridges of Madison County.* $75.

WALLIS, James. *An Historical Account of the Colony of New South Wales and Its Dependent Settlements.* London, 1821. Folio. 12 plates (6 double-page) and map. $12,500.

WALLIS, N. *The Complete Modern Joiner, or a Collection of Original Designs in the Present Taste . . .* London, no date [1772]. 36 engraved plates. $4,500.

WALPOLD, Horace. See *The Castle of Otranto, A Story.*

WALROND, Eric. *Tropic Death.* New York, 1926. Author's first book. $600.

WALSH, Ernest. *Poems and Sonnets.* New York (1934.) Author's first book. $175.

WALTERS, L. D. O. (compiler). *The Year's at the Spring: An Anthology of Recent Poetry.* London or New York, 1920. Illustrated by Harry Clarke. Vellum. One of 250 copies signed by Clarke. $2,000. Trade. In dustwrapper. $400.

WALTERS, Lorenzo D. *Tombstone's Yesterday.* Tucson, 1928. Illustrated. $250.

WALTERS, Minette. *The Ice House.* London (1992). Author's first book. Trial/proof dust-wrapper with two heads under ice. Supposedly only 6 copies printed. $2,500. With one head under ice. $1,000. Third issue (later?) with image of country lane. $300. New York (1992.) $600.

WALTERS, Minette. *The Scold's Bridle.* Bristol (1994). One of 15 signed copies. $750. One of 75 signed copies. $200. London, 1994. $125. New York (1994). $50.

WALTERS, Minette. *The Sculptress.* London (1993). $175. New York (1993). $100.

WALTON, Izaak (or Isaac), and COTTON, Charles. *The Compleat [or Complete] Angler.* London, 1653. $60,000. London, 1655. $15,000. London, 1661. Adds "The Laws of Angling." $7,500. London, 1668. Corrected and enlarged. $6,000. London, Edinburgh and Philadelphia, 1837. 2 vols. $2,500. New York, 1847. Edited by George W. Bethune. 2 portraits, 2 plates, other illustrations. 2 parts bound in one vol. "First American edition." One of 50 copies. Large-paper issue, with proof impressions of plates. $2,500. Trade. $1,000. London, 1888. "Lea & Dove Edition." Edited by R. B. Marston. 2 vols. Illustrated, including 54 photogravures. Full morocco (large-paper issue of 250 copies). $3,500. Half morocco (trade issue of 500 copies). $2,000. (The photos are on India paper in the large-paper version.) London, 1893. 2 vols. "Tercentenary Edition." Illustrated. Half vellum and green cloth. One of 350 copies. $1,250. Chicago, 1893. 2 vols. One of 500 copies. $1,000. London, 1902. 2 vols. "Winchester Edition." Illustrated with etchings by William Strang and D. Y. Cameron. Full vellum. One of 150 large-paper copies signed by the artists. $1,500. Cheswick, 1905. One of 350 copies. $1,000. One of 14 copies on vellum. $4,500. London (1927). 16 wood engravings by Eric Fitch Daglish. Half vellum. One of 100 copies with an extra signed engraving. In slipcase. $1,500. Trade. $750. London (1931). Illustrated by Arthur Rackham. Vellum. One of 775 copies signed by Rackham. $1,500. One of 10 copies with signed watercolor. $6,000. Trade. $600. Philadelphia, 1931. $500. Limited Editions Club, New York, 1948. In slipcase. $250.

WALTON, W. M. *Life and Adventures of Ben Thompson, the Famous Texan.* Austin, 1884. 15 plates, 229 pages, pictorial wraps. $5,000.

WANDREI, Donald. *Dark Odyssey.* St. Paul (1931). One of 400 copies. $400.

WANDREI, Donald. *Ecstasy.* Athol, 1928. Author's first book. Issued in tissue dustwrapper. $400.

WANDREI, Donald. *Poems for Midnight.* Sauk City, 1964. One of 742 copies. $300.

WAR in Florida (The). Baltimore, 1836. By a Late Staff Officer (Woodburn Potter). 3 maps/plans. In original green cloth. $750.

WAR in Texas (The). Philadelphia, 1836. By a Citizen of the United States (Benjamin Lundy). 57 pages, in original printed wraps. First edition under this title (but second, enlarged, edition of an earlier Philadelphia pamphlet of the same date, *The Origin and True Causes of the Texas Insurrection*). $1,250.

WARD, D. B. *Across the Plains in 1853.* (Cover title.) (Seattle, 1911.) Portrait. 55 pages, printed wraps. $750.

WARD, Harry Parker. *Some American College Bookplates.* Columbus, 1915. One of 500 signed. $125.

WARD, Henry George. *Mexico in 1827.* London, 1828. 2 vols. 2 folding maps, 13 plates, some folding, one colored. $850. London, 1829. 2 vols. Enlarged. $1,000.

WARD, Mrs. Humphrey. *Robert Elsmere.* London, 1888. 3 vols. Blue-green cloth. $750.

WARD, Lynd. *God's Man: A Novel in Woodcuts.* New York (1929). Author's first book. 143 plates, no text. Pictorial boards and cloth. $300. One of 409 signed copies. In slipcase. $1,000.

WARD, Lynd. *Madman's Drum: A Novel in Woodcuts.* New York (1930). 309 signed copies. In slipcase. $750. Trade. In dustwrapper. $450.

WARD, Lynd. *Prelude to a Million Years: A Book of Wood Engravings.* New York, 1933. One of 920 signed copies. Issued without dustwrapper. $600.

WARD, Lynd. *Song Without Words: A Book of Engravings on Wood.* (New York, 1936.) One of 1,250 signed copies. $500.

WARD, Lynd. *Vertigo: A Novel in Woodcuts.* New York, 1937. Pictorial cloth. In dustwrapper. $350.

WARD, Nathaniel B. *On the Growth of Plants in Closely Glazed Cases.* London, 1842. $450.

WARDER, T. B., and Catlett, J. M. *Battle of Young's Branch, or, Manassas Plain.* Richmond, 1862. 2 folding maps. Wraps or half leather. $3,500.

WARDROP, Major A. E., et al. *Modern Pig-Sticking.* (London, 1914.) Numerous illustrations in black-and-white. $175.

WARDROP, James. *The Script of Humanism, Some Aspects of Humanistic Script, 1460–1560.* Oxford, 1963. $150.

WARE, Eugene. *The Indian War of 1864* . . . Topeka, 1911. Frontispiece. $300.

WARE, Isaac. *A Complete Body of Architecture*. London, 1756. Frontis and 115 engraved plates (some folding). $3,750.

WARE, Joseph E. *The Emigrants' Guide to California*. St. Louis (1849). Folding map. 56 pages, cloth. $10,000 (with map).

WARHOL, Andy. *Andy Warhol's Index Book*. New York, 1967. One of 365 signed copies. (Issued in 1970.) In half cloth. $3,500. Trade. $1,250.

WARHOL, Andy. *A Gold Book*. (New York, 1957). 19 printed illustrations, including 13 on gold paper, and 6 on white paper, 5 hand-colored. Folio. One of 100 signed copies. $3,500.

WARHOL, Andy. *Holy Cats by Andy Warhol's Mother*. No place [New York] or date [c.1950]. Illustrated with lithographs by Warhol. Unbound, as issued, in printed wrappers. $1,750.

WARHOL, Andy. *Love Is a Pink Cake by Corkie & Andy*. No place [New York] or date [1953]. Author's first book. 23 leaves in folder. $1,000.

WARNER, Charles Dudley. *Backlog Studies*. Cambridge, Mass., 1899. Illustrated. Boards. One of 250 signed copies. $150.

WARNER, Charles Dudley. *The Book of Eloquence*. Cazenovia, New York 1852. Author's first book. $150.

WARNER, Charles Dudley. *My Summer in a Garden*. Boston, 1871. $100.

WARNER, Susan B. See Wetherell, Elizabeth.

WARNER, Sylvia Townsend. *Elinor Barley*. London, 1930. One of 350 signed copies. In slipcase. $250. One of 30 copies. $1,250.

WARNER, Sylvia Townsend. *The Espalier*. London, 1925. Author's first book. $300. New York, 1925. $200.

WARRE, Henry J. *Sketches in North America and the Oregon Territory*. (London, 1848.) Map, 20 colored views (on 16 sheets). Large folio, boards. $110,000 at auction in 1999. Barre, 1970. One of 950 copies. In slipcase. $100.

WARREN, Arthur. *The Charles Whittinghams Printers*. New York, 1896. One of 388 copies. $350.

WARREN, Edward. *An Epitome of Practical Surgery for Field and Hospital*. Richmond, 1863. Boards and cloth. $1,500.

WARREN, G. K. *Explorations in the Dacota Country, in the Year 1855*. Washington, 1856. 3 folding maps. $750.

WARREN, John C. *Anatomical Descriptions of the Arteries of the Human Body*. No place, 1813. 15 engraved plates, five of which are folding. $3,000.

WARREN, John C. *Etherization: With Surgical Remarks*. Boston, 1848. $2,000.

WARREN, Mercy. *Poems, Dramatic and Miscellaneous.* Boston, 1790. $750.

WARREN, Robert Penn. See *I'll Take My Stand.*

WARREN, Robert Penn. *All the King's Men.* New York (1946). Dark-red (maroon) cloth, spine lettered in gilt. Dustwrapper panel has "What Sinclair Lewis says . . ." $6,000. (Later printing dustwrappers moved Lewis's statement to the flap and had 2 other reviews on back panel.) London (1948). Revised. Dustwrapper in blue and white. $400. Dustwrapper in red with English reviews. $300. Franklin Library, 1977. Signed limited edition. $150. Limited Editions Club. (New York, 1989.) One of 600 copies signed by Warren and the photographer, Hark O'Neal. Slipcase. $1,250.

WARREN, Robert Penn. *Blackberry Winter.* (Cummington, Mass.), 1946. One of 50 copies signed by Warren and the illustrator, Wightman Williams. Numbered in small roman numerals 1–50. In clear wax-paper and plain white (unprinted) dustwrapper. $3,000. One of 280 copies. Numbered 1–280. Issued in clear wax-paper dustwrapper and plain white paper dustwrapper (unprinted). $1,500.

WARREN, Robert Penn. *Chief Joseph of the Nez Percé.* (No place, 1982.) A *Georgia Review* offprint in printed white wraps. $200. (Winston-Salem, 1982.) One of 5 signed and lettered copies. Issued in red quarter leather. $2,000. One of 7 signed copies. In quarter leather. $1,000. New York (1983). One of 250 signed copies. Issued without dustwrapper in slipcase. $300. Trade. $60. London (1983). $50.

WARREN, Robert Penn, et al. *For Aaron Copeland.* (Winston-Salem, 1978.) One of 28 signed copies (numbered I–XXVIII). Reserved for authors. Broadsides by Warren, James Dickey, and Reynolds Price. Laid-in quarter cloth folio. $750. One of 50 signed copies. $450.

WARREN, Robert Penn. *John Brown: The Making of a Martyr.* New York, 1929. Author's first book. $1,750.

WARREN, Robert Penn. *Meet Me in the Green Glen.* New York (1971). One of 300 signed copies. Issued in acetate dustwrapper and slipcase. $250. Trade. $75. London (1972). $50.

WARREN, Robert Penn. *Night Rider.* Boston, 1939. Gray cloth with maroon lettering on front and spine. $1,000. London (1940). $300.

WARREN, Robert Penn. *Selected Poems: New and Old, 1923–1966.* New York (1966). One of 250 signed copies. Issued in dustwrapper and slipcase. $350. Trade. $100.

WARREN, Robert Penn. *Thirty-six Poems.* New York, 1935. Wraps. One of 135 copies. Printed on Strathmore permanent all-rag paper. Clear wax-paper dustwrapper. $2,500. There were also 10 "out-of-series" copies for review and 20 signed copies [numbers I–XX] on Duca Di Dudena Paper with clear wax-paper dustwrapper. $3,000.

WARREN, Robert Penn. *To a Little Girl . . .* No place (1956). Issued without dustwrapper. $2,500.

WARREN, Samuel. See *Ten Thousand a Year; Passages from the Diary.*

WASHBURNE, The Reverend Cephas. *Reminiscences of the Indians.* Richmond (1869). $450.

WASHINGTON, Booker T. *Black Belt Diamonds.* New York, 1898. $1,500.

WASHINGTON, Booker T. *Daily Resolves.* London/New York, 1896. Author's first book. "Booker T. Washington" on title page. $3,500.

WASHINGTON, Booker T. *The Future of the American Negro.* Boston, 1899. $750.

WASHINGTON, Booker T. *Up from Slavery: An Autobiography.* New York, 1901. $350. Limited Editions Club, New York, 1970. In slipcase. $150.

WASHINGTON, George. *The Diaries of George Washington 1748–1799.* Boston, 1925. 4 vols. $300.

WASHINGTON, George. *The Journal of Major George Washington* . . . Williamsburg, 1754. Without map. $150,000. London, 1754. Folding map. $75,000.

WASHINGTON'S Farewell Address to the People of the United States. San Francisco, 1922. One of 125 copies. $450. One of 50 copies. $750.

WASSON, R. Gordon. *The Hall Carbine Affair.* Danbury, Conn., 1971. Illustrated. Half morocco. One of 250 copies. In slipcase. $250.

WASSON, R. Gordon. *Soma: Divine Mushroom of Immortality.* New York, 1968. Illustrated, including color plates. Half morocco. One of 680 copies. In slipcase. $750.

WASSON, Valentina Pavlona, and WASSON, R. Gordon. *Mushrooms, Russia and History.* New York (1957). 2 vols. Color plates, folding maps, and plates. Folio, buckram. One of 510 copies. In slipcase. $2,500.

WATER Witch (The), or The Skimmer of the Seas. Dresden, 1830. By the Author of *The Pilot* (James Fenimore Cooper). 3 vols. In original boards. $7,500. Rebound. $3,500. London, 1830. 3 vols. First English edition. $850. Philadelphia, 1831. First American edition. 2 vols. $750.

WATERS. *Recollections of a Detective Police Officer.* New York, 1856. (By William Russell Waters.) $750.

WATERS. *Recollections of a Policeman.* New York, 1852. (By William Russell Waters, his first book.) $750.

WATERS, Frank. *The Colorado.* New York (1946). $300.

WATERS, Frank. *Fever Pitch.* New York (1930). Author's first book. $1,250.

WATERS, Frank. *Leon Gaspard.* Flagstaff, Ariz., 1964. Illustrated, including color, by Gaspard. One of 500 signed copies. In slipcase. $450. Trade. First edition not stated. In dustwrapper. $125. Flagstaff (1981). One of 150 signed copies. Issued without dustwrapper. In slipcase. $250. Trade. In dustwrapper. $125.

WATERS, Frank. *Midas of the Rockies.* New York (1937). $300.

WATERS, Frank. *The Wild Earth's Nobility.* New York, 1935. $400.

WATERTON, Charles. *Wanderings in South America* . . . London, 1825. $750.

WATHEN, James. *Journal of a Voyage in 1811 and 1812 to Madras and China.* London, 1814. 24 colored aquatints. $5,000.

WATKINS, C. L. *Photographic Views of the Falls and Valley of Yosemite*. San Francisco, 1863. Map and 53(?) mounted phtographs. Folio, morocco. $60,000 or more depending on condition of the prints.

WATKINS, C. L. *Photographs of the Columbia River and Oregon*. San Francisco (about 1873). 51 mounted albumen prints. Elephant folio, morocco with redwood inlay. $100,000 or more depending on conditions of prints.

WATKINS, C. L. *Photographs of the Pacific Coast*. San Francisco (about 1873). 49 mounted albumen prints. Elephant folio, morocco with redwood inlay. $100,000 or more, depending on condition of prints.

WATKINS, C. L. *Watkins' New Series Columbia River Scenery, Oregon*. No place (about 1880). 40 plates. Oblong, leather. $40,000 or more depending on condition of prints.

WATKINS, Paul. *Night Over Day Over Night*. London, 1988. $200. New York, 1988. $50.

WATSON, Colin. *Coffin Scarcely Used*. London, 1958. Author's first book. $250. New York, 1967. $100.

WATSON, Douglas S. *West Wind: The Life Story of Joseph Reddeford Walker . . .* Los Angeles, 1934. Plates, folding map. Boards. One of 100 copies. $1,000. Trade. $350.

WATSON, Douglas S. (editor). *California in the Fifties*. San Francisco, 1936. 50 views. Oblong folio, cloth. One of 850 copies. In dustwrapper. $500. One of 50 copies. $850.

WATSON, Douglas S. (editor). *The Spanish Occupation of California*. Grabhorn Press. San Francisco, 1934. Illustrated. Boards and cloth. One of 550 copies. $450.

WATSON, Frederick. *Hunting Pie*. Derrydale Press. New York (1938). Illustrated. Boards. One of 750 copies. $500.

WATSON, Lawrence. *In a Dark Time*. New York (1980). $350.

WATSON, Sheila. *The Double Hook*. Toronto, 1959. Author's first book. $400.

WATSON, William. *The Father of the Forest and Other Poems*. London, 1895. Frontispiece portrait. One of 75 copies. $500.

WATSON, William. *Odes and Other Poems*. London, 1894. One of 75 copies. $200.

WATTS, Alan W. *An Outline of Zen Buddhism*. London (1932). Author's first book. Wraps. $250.

WATTS, W. J. *Cherokee Citizenship and a Brief History of Internal Affairs in the Cherokee Nation*. (Cover title.) Muldrow, Indian Territory (Okla.), 1895. Portrait. Wraps. $1,250.

WATTS, W. W. *Old English Silver*. New York, 1924. 307 plates. $250. London, 1924. First English edition. $200. One of 40 copies in leather binding. $400.

WATTS, W. W. *Works of Art in Silver and Other Metals . . .* (London) 1936. 100 photographic illustrations. One of 150 copies signed by Watts. $600.

WAUGH, Alec. *The Loom of Youth*. London, 1917. Author's first book. $250. New York, no date [1917]. $150.

WAUGH, Evelyn. See Merton, Thomas (*Elected Silence*).

WAUGH, Evelyn. *Basil Seal Rides Again*. London, 1963. One of 750 signed copies. Issued in glassine dustwrapper. $750. Boston (1963). One of 1,000 signed copies. Issued in blue buckram and acetate dustwrapper. $500.

WAUGH, Evelyn. *Black Mischief.* London (1932). One of 250 signed copies. Issued in dustwrapper. $3,000. Black cloth with variant noted in gray blue cloth. (Some copies with Book Society wraparound band.) $1,500. New York (1934). $500.

WAUGH, Evelyn. *Brideshead Revisited*. London, 1945. Wraps. (50 copies.) $10,000. Trade with catalogue number on verso of title page. $3,000. Boston, 1945. One of 600 copies. "Published September 1945" on copyright page. $1,250. Boston, 1946. "First edition after . . . 600 copies"—"Published January 1946." Blue cloth. $750. (The Book-of-the-Month Club edition is dated 1945 but does not have statement on edition on verso. The BOMC dustwrapper has "Printed in U.S.A." on bottom of rear flap and is not priced.)

WAUGH, Evelyn. *Decline and Fall*. London, 1928. "Originally publ . . . September 1928" on copyright page. Pages 168 and 169 have "Martin Gaythorn-Brodie" and "Kevin Saunderson," respectively. $15,000. Second issue, pages 168 and 169 with "The Hon. Miles Malpractice" and "Lord Parakeet," respectively. $12,500. Garden City: Doubleday, 1929. $2,500. New York: Farrar & Rinehart, 1929. Doubleday remainder sheets with Farrar title page tipped in. $1,250.

WAUGH, Evelyn. *A Handful of Dust*. London, 1934. Noted in Book Society wraparound band. $3,500. New York (1934). $750.

WAUGH, Evelyn. *The Holy Places*. London, 1952. One of 50 copies signed by Waugh and the illustrator, Reynolds Stone. Issued in red niger morocco and dustwrapper. $2,000. One of 900 copies. Bound in red buckram and numbered 51–950. Issued in pictorial gray dustwrapper printed in black and blue. $300. London/New York, 1953. One of 50 signed copies. $2,000. One of 950 copies. $300.

WAUGH, Evelyn. *Labels: A Mediterranean Journal*. (London) 1930. One of 110 signed copies. With a page of author's holograph manuscript tipped in. $3,500. London, 1930. $1,000.

WAUGH, Evelyn. *Love Among the Ruins*. London, 1953. One of 350 signed copies. Issued in glassine dustwrapper with printed paper flaps. $1,000. Trade. $250.

WAUGH, Evelyn. *The Loved One*. Boston, 1948. Also states "Published June 1948." $200. (London, 1948.) One of 250 copies signed by Waugh and the illustrator, Stuart Boyle. In glassine dustwrapper. $2,000. Trade. $350.

WAUGH, Evelyn. *P.R.B.: An Essay on the PreRaphaelite Brotherhood*. London, 1926. Half cloth. $6,000. (Kent, 1982.) One of 475 copies. In acetate dustwrapper. $200.

WAUGH, Evelyn. *Remote People*. London, 1931. $2,000.

WAUGH, Evelyn. *Rossetti: His Life and Works.* London, 1928. $2,500. New York, 1928. $1,500.

WAUGH, Evelyn. *Scoop.* London (1938). First issue with "s" in "as" in last line of page 88 and "Daily Beast" logo in black letters on front cover of dustwrapper. $2,500. Without "s" in "as" on page 88 and without "Daily Beast" on dustwrapper. $1,250. Boston, 1938. First edition stated and "Publ . . . July 1938." $500.

WAUGH, Evelyn. *They Were Still Dancing.* New York: Cape & Smith (1932). The U.S. edition of *Remote People.* $750. New York: Farrar & Rinehart (1932). Noted with bottom edge trimmed and untrimmed. $400.

WAUGH, Evelyn. *The World to Come.* (Privately printed), 1916. Author's first book. $12,500.

WAUGH, Frederic J. *The Clan of Munes.* New York, 1916. Author's first book. $750.

WAVERLEY; or, 'Tis Sixty Years Since. Edinburgh, 1814. (By Sir Walter Scott.) 3 vols. First issue, with "our" instead of "your" in first line on page 136 in vol. 2. $4,000. New York, 1815. $1,250.

WAYLAND, John W. *History of Rockingham County.* Dayton, Va., 1912. Plates. Buckram. $125.

WEALE, W. H. James. *Bookbindings and Rubbings of Bindings in the National Art Library, South Kensington Museum.* London, 1898. 2 vols. bound in 1. $350.

WEARY, Ogdred. *The Beastly Baby.* (New York, 1962.) (By Edward Gorey.) Wraps. One of 500 copies. $750.

WEATHERLY, Frederick Edward. *A Happy Pair.* London, no date [1890]. 6 colored illustrations by Beatrix Potter, her first book illustrations. $60,000.

WEATHERLY, Frederick Edward. *Magic Pictures: A Book of Changing Scenes.* London (about 1890). 16 pages with pull slides to change pictures (a movable book). Pictorial cloth. $750.

WEATHERLY, Frederick Edward. *Pretty Polly: A Novel Book for Children.* London (about 1895). 4 double-page three-dimensional color plates. Half cloth. $500.

WEATHERLY, Frederick Edward. *Punch and Judy and Some of Their Friends.* London (1885). Illustrated by Patty Townsend. Half cloth. $350.

WEBB, Charles. *The Graduate.* New York (1963). $750.

WEBB, Jane. See *The Mummy! A Tale of the Twenty-second Century.*

WEBB, Mary. *The Chinese Lion.* London, 1937. Decorated boards, red cloth spine, red label on front cover. One of 350 copies. In slipcase. $100.

WEBB, Mary. *The Golden Arrow.* London, 1916. Author's first book. $250.

WEBB, Mary. *Gone to Earth.* London (1917). Dark-red cloth. $150.

WEBB, Mary. *Precious Bane.* London (1924). $500.

WEBB, Walter Prescott. *The Great Plains.* Boston (1931). Illustrated. With error in heading of chapter 2. $250.

WEBB, Walter Prescott. *The Texas Rangers . . .* Boston, 1935. $200. Half leather. One of 200 signed copies. In slipcase. $750.

WEBBER, C. W. *The Hunter-Naturalist; Romance of Sporting, or Wild Scenes and Wild Hunters.* Philadelphia (1851). Vol. 1 (all published). Engraved title page and 9 colored lithographs, other illustrations. Cloth, leather spine and corners. $1,000. Philadelphia, 1852. Engraved title. 9 chromolithograph plates. $600.

WEBBER, C. W. *Old Hicks the Guide* . . . New York, 1848. $450.

WEBBER, C. W. *Wild Scenes and Song Birds.* New York, 1854. 20 colored plates. Morocco. $750. New York, 1855. $500.

WEBER, Bruce. *Bruce Weber.* Los Angeles, 1983. $500.

WEBER, Carl J. *Fore-Edge Painting, A Historical Survey of a Curious Art in Book Decoration.* Irvington-on-Hudson, New York 1966. Originally appeared as *A Thousand and One Fore-Edge Paintings.* $450.

WEBER, Carl J. *A Thousand and One Fore-Edge Paintings.* Waterville, Me., 1949. Illustrated. Half cloth. One of 1,000 copies. In dustwrapper. $750.

WEBER, Max. *Cubist Poems.* London, 1914. Author's first book. One of 100 copies. $500. Blue pictorial cloth. $350. Wraps. $300.

WEBSTER, John. *The Displaying of Supposed Witchcraft* . . . London, 1677. Folio. $4,500.

WEBSTER, John. *Metallographia: or, an History of Metals.* London, 1671. $1,500.

WEBSTER, John White. *A Description of the Island of St. Michael.* Boston, 1821. Author's first book. First issue with "par't" on page 117. Folding chart. 2 views and 2 folding maps. $500. With "part" on page 117. $450.

WEBSTER, Noah. See Ford, Paul Leicester (for *Webster Genealogy*).

WEBSTER, Noah. *An American Dictionary of the English Language.* New York, 1828. Portrait. 2 vols. $12,500.

WEBSTER, Noah. *A Compendious Dictionary of the English Language.* Hartford, 1806. $1,500.

WEBSTER, Noah, Jr. *A Grammatical Institute, of the English Language* . . . Part II Hartford, 1784. [Part I was published in 1783 but no copy has been auctioned in 20 years.] This volume frequently reprinted as *A Plain and Comprehensive Grammer of the English Language* . . . $3,500 or more.

WEEDOM, J. *Round Text Copies, with a Set of Roman Ciphers for Marking Goods.* London, 1794. 15 engraved plates. $750.

WEEDON, Howard. *Shadows on the Wall.* New York, 1898. Author's first book. $350.

WEEGEE. See Harris, Mel.

WEEGEE. *Naked City.* New York (1945). (By Arthur Fellig, his first book.) Gray-green buckram. $850. Smooth tan cloth. $600.

WEEGEE. *Weegee's People.* New York (1946). $300.

WEEKS, Andrew Gray, Jr. *Illustrations of Diurnal Lepidoptera (Butterflies) with Description.* Boston, 1905 and 1911. 2 vols. 2 portraits and 66 full-page color lithographic plates from watercolor sketches. $300.

WEIBEL, A. C. *2,000 Years of Textiles* . . . New York, 1952. Folio, 256 plates. $250.

WEIDENMANN, J. *Beautifying Country Homes.* New York, 1870. 24 chromolithograph plates of landscape design. $1,750.

WEIDMAN, Jerome. *I Can Get It for You Wholesale.* New York, 1937. Author's first book. $350.

WEINBAUM, Stanley G. *Dawn of Flame and Other Stories.* (Jamaica, New York, 1936.) Author's first book. One of 5 copies with introduction by Palmer. $2,500. With introduction by Keating. (250 copies.) $1,500.

WEIR, Hich C. *Miss Madelyn Mack, Detective.* Boston, 1914. $250.

WEIRD of the Wanderer, Being the Papyrus Records of Some Incidents in One of the Previous Lives of Mr. Nicholas Crabbe (The). London, 1912. (By Frederick William Rolfe and Pirie-Gordon, Charles Henry. 16-page publisher's catalogue at rear. Dark-blue cloth. $1,000.

WEITENKAMPF, Frank. *The Etching of Contemporary Life.* Marlborough-on-Hudson, 1916. One of 250 copies (although 270 actually produced) with signed and dated original etching. $1,250.

WEITENKAMPF, Frank. *The Illustrated Book.* Cambridge, 1938. One of 210 copies. In slip-case. $200.

WEIZMANN, Chaim. *Trial and Error.* New York (1949). 2 vols. One of 500 signed copies. $1,250. Trade. $350.

WELBY, Adlard. *A Visit to North America* . . . London, 1821. 14 plates. $2,500.

WELCH, Charles A. *History of the Big Horn Basin With Stories of Early Days* . . . (Salt Lake City), 1940. $350.

WELCH, Denton. *Maiden Voyage.* London, 1943. Frontispiece portrait. Author's first book. $500. New York. $150.

WELCH, James. *Riding the Earthboy 40.* World. New York/Cleveland (1971). Author's first book. Reportedly not distributed. $200. Harper. New York (1976). Revised. $125.

WELD, Isaac, Jr. *Travels Through the States of North America, and the Provinces of Upper and Lower Canada, During the Years 1795, 1796 and 1797.* London, 1799. 8 pages of ads, 16 maps (1 folding) and plates. $2,500.

WELDON, Fay. *The Fat Woman's Joke.* London, 1967. Author's first book. $300.

WELLER, George. *Not to Eat Not for Love.* New York, 1933. Author's first book. $150.

WELLES, Orson. *Everybody's Shakespeare: Three Plays.* (Written with Roger Hill.) Woodstock, Illinois (1934). Author's first book. $300.

WELLMAN, Paul. *Broncho Apache.* New York, 1936. $600.

WELLMAN, Paul. *The Callaghan Yesterday and Today.* Encinal (about 1945). Illustrated, map. Stiff pictorial wraps. $400.

WELLMAN, Paul. *The Iron Mistress.* New York, 1951. $150.

WELLS, Carolyn. *Murder in the Bookshop*. Philadelphia, 1936. $350.

WELLS, Carolyn. (Mrs. Hadwin Houghton.) *The Story of Betty.* New York, 1899. Author's first book. $200.

WELLS, H. G. *The Adventures of Tommy.* London (1929). $400.

WELLS, H. G. *The Country of the Blind*. London (1911). First edition not stated. Dark-blue cloth. $300. New York, 1915. $300. Golden Cockerel Press. London, 1939. Wood engravings. Orange vellum. One of 30 signed copies. $1,750. Trade. One of 280 copies. $600.

WELLS, H. G. *The Door in the Wall*. New York, 1911. Illustrated with Alvin Langdon Coburn photogravures. Boards. One of 300 copies. With plates in photogravure. $3,500. One of 300 copies with aquatone illustrations. $850. London (1915). One of 60 copies signed by both Wells and Coburn. $4,500.

WELLS, H. G. *The First Men in the Moon*. Indianapolis (1901). $2,500. London, 1901. Illustrated by Claude Shepperson. First issue dark-blue cloth, gilt lettering on cover, and black endpapers. $1,000. Second issue the same but with white endpapers. $750. Third issue in light-blue cloth with black or dark-blue lettering. $500. Fourth issue in blue-green cloth stamped in black. $300.

WELLS, H. G. *The Invisible Man*. London, 1897. $2,500. New York, 1897. First American edition. With 4-page epilogue at end. $1,250. Limited Editions Club, New York, 1967. In slipcase. $100.

WELLS, H. G. *The Island of Doctor Moreau*. London, 1896. First issue with publisher's monogram blindstamped on back cover. (No priority established on ads.) $1,000. Second issue lacking monogram. $500. New York, 1896. Black cloth stamped in gold. $500. Blue and green cloths were later issues. $150.

WELLS, H. G. *The Sea Lady*. London, 1902. First issue in red cloth with catalogue dated in 1902. $650. Second binding in green cloth (1907). $300. Third binding in red but catalogue dated 1910. $200. New York, 1908. Green cloth. First American edition. $100.

WELLS, H. G. *Select Conversations with an Uncle (Now Extinct) and Two Other Reminiscences.* London, 1895. Wells's first literary work. $750. New York, 1895. $450.

WELLS, H. G. *Tales of Space and Time*. London: Harper, 1900 (actually 1899). Light-brown cloth. $1,250. New York: Doubleday, 1899. First American edition. With errata slip at page 109. Maroon cloth. $600. Green cloth. $450. (Currey considers the English edition as the first.)

WELLS, H. G. *Text Book of Biology*. London (1893). 2 vols. Author's first book preceded by a doctoral thesis. First binding dark-green cloth. $1,250. Later in brown cloth. $750.

WELLS, H. G. *Thirty Strange Stories*. New York, 1897. Green cloth stamped in black, green, and gold. Top edge gilt. White endpapers. $1,500.

WELLS, H. G. *The Time Machine*. New York, 1895. In tan cloth with Wells's name on title page as "H. S. Wells" and 6 pages of ads. $1,250. London, 1895. First issue in gray cloth stamped in purple and 16 pages of undated ads. $3,500. Second printing in red cloth. $1,500. London, 1895. Light blue-gray wraps printed in dark blue, no catalogue. $2,500. Whitish-gray cloth lettered in purple with 16-page catalogue headed "The Manxman." $2,000. With 32-page catalogue, which includes a review of "The War of the Worlds." $1,000. Note: one copy of

English edition with "H. S. Wells" on front cover catalogued in 2000 for $35,000 (not noted elsewhere).

WELLS, H. G. *Tono Bungay.* London, 1909. With 8-pages of ads dated "1.09." $300. With ads dated "2.09." $200. New York, 1908 (which may precede English). $150. Limited Editions Club, New York, 1960. $100.

WELLS, H. G. *Twelve Stories and a Dream.* London, 1903. $1,250. New York, 1905. $600.

WELLS, H. G. *The War in the Air.* London, 1908. 16 plates. First issue in pictorial blue cloth. With all lettering and decorations in gilt and "George Bell & Son" at base of spine. $750. Second issue in blue cloth. Title stamped in blind. $500. New York, 1908. Illustrated by Eric Pape. $350.

WELLS, H. G. *The War of the Worlds.* London, 1898. Gray cloth. With 16 pages of ads dated "Autumn mdcccxcviii" at end. $2,000. With 32-page catalogue. $1,000. New York, 1898. $500.

WELLS, H. G. *When the Sleeper Wakes.* London, 1899. Red cloth. 3 plates. $750. New York, 1899. Green cloth. $500.

WELLS, H. G. *The Wonderful Visit.* London, 1895. Red cloth. Probable first with front cover blank. $750. Red cloth with front cover stamped in gold (angel). $600. New York, 1895. $350.

WELLS, H. G. *The World of William Clissold.* London, 1926. 3 vols. One of 218 (20 for presentation) signed copies. $600. 3 vols. Trade. Top edges brown. $300. 3 vols. Top edges plain. $250.

WELLS, Oliver. See *An Anthology of the Younger Poets.*

WELLS, William, and ONKEN, Otto. *Western Scenery: or, Land and River, Hill and Dale, in the Mississippi Valley.* Cincinnati, 1851. Pictorial title page, 19 full-page lithographic views, 52 pages of text. Boards and calf. $7,500.

WELLS, William Charles. *An Essay on Dew . . .* London, 1814. $500. Philadelphia, 1838. First American edition. $350.

WELSH, Charles. *A Bookseller of the Last Century . . .* London, 1885. $200.

WELSH, Irvine. *Trainspotting.* London (1993). Hardbound with attached dustwrapper. $2,000. Wraps. $500.

WELTY, Eudora. *The Bride of the Innisfallen.* New York (1955). Copyright notice of first issue contains only one date: "copyright . . . 1955, by Eudora Welty." Issued in blue and green mottled boards, green cloth spine, silver stamping. $750. Second issue copyright contains 5 dates: "copyright . . . 1949, 1951, 1952, 1954, 1955 . . ." Copyright page tipped in. Binding as in first issue. $300. Third issue and second binding: copyright notice with 5 dates, but issued in light grayish-brown cloth, blue and gold stamping. $200. London (1955). $150.

WELTY, Eudora. *A Curtain of Green.* Garden City, 1941. Author's first book. Preceded by a pre-publicity pamphlet. $2,500. London (1943). $450.

WELTY, Eudora. *Delta Wedding.* New York (1946). $600. London (1947). $250.

WELTY, Eudora. *Eudora Welty: A Note on the Author and Her Work.* (Garden City, 1941). Wraps. A pre-publicity pamphlet for *A Curtain of Green* written by Katherine Anne Porter and containing Welty's short story "The Key." Considered to be Welty's first book. $2,750.

WELTY, Eudora. *The Golden Apples.* New York (1949). $400. London (1950). Issued without endpapers. $200.

WELTY, Eudora. *Losing Battles.* New York (1970). One of 300 signed copies. Issued in acetate dustwrapper and slipcase. $400. Trade. $100.

WELTY, Eudora. *Music from Spain.* Greenville, Miss., 1948. One of 750 signed copies. Issued in glassine dustwrapper. $850.

WELTY, Eudora. *The Optimist's Daughter.* New York (1972). One of 225 signed copies. Approximately 75 copies were destroyed of projected edition of 300 because of defective bindings. Issued without dustwrapper in slipcase. $600. Trade. $250. (London, 1953.) $150. Franklin Library, 1978. Limited edition. $100. Franklin Library, 1980. Signed limited edition. $200.

WELTY, Eudora. *Place in Fiction.* No place or date [circa 1956]. Printed wraps. About 50 copies. An offprint from the *South Atlantic Quarterly.* $1,000. New York, 1957. One of 26 signed copies. Issued in glassine dustwrapper. $750. One of 300 signed copies. Issued in glassine dustwrapper. Part of the edition was destroyed. $850.

WELTY, Eudora. *The Ponder Heart.* New York (1954). $400. London (1954). $150.

WELTY, Eudora. *The Robber Bridegroom.* Garden City, 1942. $1,000. London (1944). $300. West Hatfield, 1987. One of 150 copies signed by Welty and the illustrator, Barry Moser. In full red leather without slipcase. $1,000. Trade (illustrated by Moser). $75.

WELTY, Eudora. *The Shoe Bird.* New York (1964). $300.

WELTY, Eudora. *A Sweet Devouring.* New York, 1969. Wraps. One of 26 signed copies. $750. One of 150 signed copies. Wraps. $450.

WELTY, Eudora. *Twenty Photographs.* (Winston-Salem, 1980.) One of 20 signed copies (roman numerals). Photographs mounted on heavy rag board in clamshell folio box. Errata slip laid in. 5 of these copies were for the author's use. $4,000. One of 75 signed copies. Issued in clamshell box. Errata slip laid in. $2,500.

WELTY, Eudora. *The Wide Net and Other Stories.* New York (1943). $1,000. London (1945). On reverse of Welty dustwrapper is dustwrapper for F. E. Mills Young's *Unlucky Farm.* $750.

WENDEHACK, Clifford Charles. *Golf and Country Clubs.* New York, 1929. $600.

WENTWORTH, Lady Judith Anne. *The Authentic Arabian Horse and His Descendants.* London (1945). 26 color plates, numerous other illustrations. Blue cloth. In dustwrapper. $1,250. New York, 1963. $300.

WENTWORTH, Lady Judith Anne. *Thoroughbred Racing Stock and Its Ancestors.* London, 1938. 21 color plates. Red buckram. In dustwrapper. $1,250. London (1960). Second edition. In dustwrapper and slipcase. $450.

WENTWORTH, Lady Judith Anne. *Toy Dogs and Their Ancestors.* London, 1911. $850.

WENTWORTH, Patricia. *The Astonishing Adventure of Jane Smith.* London, 1923. $750. Boston, 1923. $600.

WENTWORTH, Patricia. *Down Under.* London, 1937. $500.

WEPT of Wish Ton Wish (The): A Tale. Florence, 1829. By the Author of *The Pioneers.* (By James Fenimore Cooper.) $6,000. Philadelphia, 1829. 2 vols. First American edition. $750.

WERTH, John J. *A Dissertation on the Resources and Policy of California.* Benicia, 1851. 87 pages. $1,500.

WERTHAM, Fredric. *Seduction of the Innocent.* New York (1954). Page 399 usually has biographical note excised. $400. With page 399. $750.

WERTHEIM, Barbara. *The Lost British Policy.* London, 1938. (Maiden name of Barbara Tuchman, her first book.) Stiff wraps. $450.

WERTHER'S Younger Brother . . . New York/Paris (1931). (By Michael Fraenkel.) Author's first book. Stiff wraps. $200.

WESCOTT, Glenway. *The Babe's Bed.* Paris, 1930. One of 375 signed copies. $350. One of 18 copies on parchment. $600.

WESCOTT, Glenway. *The Bitterns: A Book of Twelve Poems.* Evanston, Ill. (1920). Author's first book. Black wraps with printed silver design. One of 200 copies. $750.

WESCOTT, Glenway. *A Calendar of Saints for Unbelievers.* Paris, 1932. Illustrated by Pavel Tchelitchew. Half morocco. One of 40 signed copies. In slipcase with copperplate of one of the illustrations. $1,500. Cloth. One of 695 copies. In glassine dustwrapper and slipcase. $350.

WESCOTT, Glenway. *Goodbye, Wisconsin.* New York, 1928. One of 250 signed copies. In slipcase. $200. Trade. $75.

WESCOTT, Glenway. *The Grandmothers.* New York, 1927. Cloth-backed boards. One of 250 signed copies. In slipcase. $200. Trade. $75.

WESCOTT, Glenway. *Natives of Rock, XX Poems: 1921–1922.* New York, 1925. One of 25 copies on vellum. In slipcase. $500. One of 550 plain copies. In glassine dustwrapper and slipcase. $125.

WEST, Anthony. *Gloucestershire.* London, 1939. Author's first book. $150.

WEST, Dorothy. *Living Is Easy.* Boston, 1948. Author's first book. $1,250.

WEST, John C. *A Texan in Search of a Fight.* Waco, 1901. 189 pages. Wraps. $500. Also in cloth. $350.

WEST, Mae. *Babe Gordon.* New York, 1930. Author's first book. $350.

WEST, Mae. *She Done Him Wrong.* New York, 1932. $300.

WEST, Nathanael. *A Cool Million.* New York (1934). First binding in light-tan cloth. $2,500. Also variants in green and rust cloths. $2,000. London (1954). First English edition. $500.

WEST, Nathanael. *The Day of the Locust.* New York (1939). $1,750.

WEST, Nathanael. *The Dream Life of Balso Snell.* Paris: Contact Editions (1931). Author's first book. Printed stiff wraps. One of 485 copies. In tissue dustwrapper. $2,500. One of 15 signed and bound in cloth. $7,500.

WEST, Nathanael. *Miss Lonelyhearts.* New York: Liveright (1933). $7,500. Harcourt, Brace, New York (1933). $1,500. New York: Greenberg (1933). (Remainder imprint.) $1,000.

WEST, Rebecca. *The Judge.* London (1922). $250.

WEST, Samuel. *Essays on Liberty and Necessity* . . . Boston, 1793. $600. Boston, 1795. Part Second. $300.

WESTCOTT, Edward Noyes. *David Harum.* New York, 1898. Author's first book. First state, with perfect "J" in "Julius" in penultimate line on page 40. Yellow cloth. $75.

WESTLAKE, Donald. *The Mercenaries.* New York (1960). Author's first book. $750.

WESTMACOTT, Charles Molloy. *The English Spy* . . . London, 1825–26. 2 vols. Frontis in panels and 71 colored plates. $3,500.

WESTON, Charis W. *Edward Weston: Nudes.* No place (New York): Aperture, 1977. Cloth. In slipcase. One of 350 copies signed by Charis Wilson Weston. With platinum print signed by Cole Weston. $2,000.

WESTON, Edward (photographer). *Edward Weston.* New York, 1932. 40 plates. Half vellum. One of 550 signed copies. $3,000.

WESTON, Edward (photographer). *Fifty Photographs.* New York (1947). (By Weston and others.) Half cloth. One of 1,500 copies initialed by Weston. $1,500.

WESTON, Edward (photographer). *My Camera on Point Lobos.* Yosemite National Park and Boston, 1950. Illustrated. Folio, spiral binding. In dustwrapper. $500.

WESTON, Patrick. *Desert Dreamers.* London (1914). Author's first book. One of 250 copies. $250.

WESTON, Silas. *Four Months in the Mines of California; or, Life in the Mountains.* Providence, 1854. 24 pages, printed wraps. Second edition (of *Life in the Mountains.*) $1,000.

WESTON, Silas. *Life in the Mountains: or Four Months in the Mines of California.* Providence, 1854. 36 pages, printed wraps. $1,500.

WESTROP, M. S. Dudley. *Irish Glass.* London (about 1920). 40 plates. Buckram. Issued without dustwrapper. $400. Philadelphia, 1921. Issued without dustwrapper. $300.

WESTWARD Ho! New York, 1832. (By James Kirke Paulding.) 2 vols. In original cloth. $450.

WESTWOOD, T. *Bibliotheca Piscatoria.* London, 1883. Half leather. Large-paper copy. $1,250. Trade. $200.

WESTWOOD, T. *A New Bibliotheca Piscatoria.* London, 1861. $300.

WETHERBEE, J., Jr. *A Brief Sketch of Colorado Territory and the Gold Mines of That Region.* Boston, 1863. 24 pages, printed wraps. $2,500.

WETHERED, H. N., and SIMPSON, T. *The Architectural Side of Golf.* London, 1929. One of 50 large-paper copies. $13,000 at auction in 1997. Trade. $3,000.

WETHERELL, Elizabeth. *The Wide, Wide World.* New York, 1851. (By Susan B. Warner.) 2 vols. Author's first book. "Edward O. Jenkins" imprint on copyright page of both volumes. $1,250. London: Nisbet . . . , 1852. 2 vols. With preface by Anna Warner. Red cloth. $1,000. (BAL indicates there was an English adaptation that may precede.)

WETMORE, Alphonso (compiler). *Gazetteer of the State of Missouri* . . . St. Louis, 1837. Frontispiece and folding map. In original cloth. $1,000.

WETMORE, Helen Cody. *Last of the Great Scouts:The Life Story of Col.William F. Cody, "Buffalo Bill."* (Duluth, 1899.) First edition, with 267 pages. $450. 296 pages. One of 500 copies signed by Cody. $1,000. Trade. $200.

WEYMAN, Stanley J. *The House of the Wolf.* London, 1890. Decorated gray cloth. Author's first book. $125.

WHALON, Philip. *Three Satires.* (Portland, Oregon, 1951.) Author's first book. Wraps. $450.

WHARTON, Edith Newbold Jones. See *Verses.*

WHARTON, Edith. See Jones, Edith Newbold.

WHARTON, Edith. *The Age of Innocence.* New York, 1920. First issue of dustwrapper without mention of the Columbia (Pulitzer) Prize. $7,500. Limited Editions Club, Avon, 1973. In slipcase. $125.

WHARTON, Edith. *Artemis to Actaeon.* New York, 1909. $500.

WHARTON, Edith. *The Decoration of Houses.* (With O. Codman.) New York, 1897. $2,000. London, 1898. $1,250.

WHARTON, Edith. *Ethan Frome.* New York, 1911. Cloth. Top edges gilt on early copies. First issue, with perfect type in last line of page 135. $2,000. New York, 1922. With new introduction. One of 2,000 copies. $500. Limited Editions Club (New York), 1939. Cloth. In slipcase. $250.

WHARTON, Edith. *The Greater Inclination.* New York, 1899. $500.

WHARTON, Edith. *Here and Beyond.* New York (1926). $600.

WHARTON, Edith. *Italian Villas and Their Gardens.* New York, 1904. Illustrated by Maxfield Parrish and others. Pictorial cloth. $3,000. London, 1904. Full cloth. $1,500. Cloth and boards. $1,250.

WHARTON, Edith. *A Motor-Flight Through France.* New York, 1908. $400.

WHARTON, Edith. *Twelve Poems.* Medici Society. London, 1926. Buckram and boards. One of 130 signed copies. In dustwrapper. $5,000.

WHARTON, Edith. *The Valley of Decision.* New York, 1902. 2 vols. Maroon cloth. Top page edges gilt. $350.

WHARTON, Edith (editor). *The Book of the Homeless.* New York, 1916. One of 125 copies on Van Gelder paper. $1,500. One of 50 copies with portfolio of plates and facsimiles. $2,500. Trade. $350.

WHARTON, J. E. *History of the City of Denver.* Denver, 1866. Printed pink wraps. $4,500.

WHAT Is Man? New York, 1906. (By Samuel Langhorne Clemens.) Gray-blue boards, green-black leather label on spine. First issue, with "thinks about" as last line of page 131. One of 250 copies. $2,500. Second issue with "thinks about it." $1,500. London, 1910. Identifies Twain as author. $350.

WHEAT, Carl I. *Books of the California Gold Rush.* San Francisco, 1949. Pictorial boards and cloth. In dustwrapper. One of 500 copies. $350.

WHEAT, Carl I. *Mapping the Transmississippi West.* Grabhorn Press. San Francisco, 1957–63. 5 vols. in 6. Illustrated. Folio, buckram, leatherette spine. In plain dustwrapper. One of 1,000 copies. $4,500.

WHEAT, Carl I. *The Maps of the California Gold Region 1848–57.* Grabhorn Press. San Francisco, 1942. 26 maps. Folio. Cloth. One of 300 copies. $2,000. Three-quarter calf. One of 22 copies with map by Gibbs added. $2,500.

WHEAT, Carl I. *The Pioneer Press of California.* Oakland, 1948. One of 450 copies. $250.

WHEAT, Marvin T. See Cincinnatus.

WHEATLEY, Dennis. *The Forbidden Territory.* London (1933). Author's first book. $350. New York (1933). $250.

WHEATLEY, Phillis. *Poems on Various Subjects, Religious and Moral.* London, 1773. Author's first book. $20,000. Philadelphia, 1786. $7,500.

WHEELER, Alfred. *Land Titles in San Francisco, and the Laws Affecting the Same . . .* San Francisco, 1852. Map. $2,000.

WHEELER, Ella. *Drops of Water: Poems.* New York, 1872. (By Ella Wheeler Wilcox.) Author's first book. $125.

WHEELER, Ella. *Poems of Pleasure.* London, 1907. One of 500 copies. Vellum. $450.

WHEELOCK, John Hall. See *Verses by Two Undergraduates.*

WHEELOCK, John Hall. *The Human Fantasy.* Boston, 1911. $125.

WHEELWRIGHT, John Brooks. *North Atlantic Passage.* (Florence, Italy 1924.) Author's first book. $1,000.

WHIGHAM, Henry James. *How to Play Golf.* Chicago, 1897. $450.

WHILLDIN, M. A. *Description of Western Texas . . .* Galveston, 1876. 28 plates, folding map, 120 pages, pictorial wraps. $3,000.

WHISTLER, James McNeill. *The Gentle Art of Making Enemies.* Paris, 1890. Edited by Sheridan Ford. Gray-green wraps. $1,250. New York: Stokes, 1890. (Paris sheets.) Wraps. $1,000. London, 1890. (Whistler's own version.) $350. One of 150 large-paper copies. $1,000. New York: Lovell, 1890. $300. One of 100 large-paper copies. $1,000.

WHISTLER, James Abbott McNeill. *Whistler v. Ruskin.* Chelsea, 1878. Author's first book. Wraps. First edition. Duodecimo. $600. Second edition. Quarto. $300.

WHITE, Antonia. *Frost in May.* London (1933). Author's first book. $600.

WHITE, Diana. *The Descent of Ishtar.* London: Eragny Press, 1903. Frontispiece. Boards, paper label. One of 226 copies. In dustwrapper. $600. One of 10 copies on vellum. $3,500.

WHITE, E. B. See W., E.B., Finny, Sterling. See also Thurber, James.

WHITE, E. B. *Charlotte's Web.* New York (1952). Illustrated by Garth Williams. Pictorial cloth. $1,500. London (1952). $750.

WHITE, E. B. *Quo Vadimus? or The Case for the Bicycle.* New York, 1939. $750.

WHITE, E. B. *The Second Tree from the Corner.* New York (1954). 500 copies initialed by White. $350. Trade. $100. London (1954). $125.

WHITE, E. B. *Stuart Little.* New York (1945). Illustrated by Garth Williams. Pictorial cloth. $1,000. London (1946). $750.

WHITE, E. L. *A Popular Essay on the Disorder . . . A Cold.* London, 1807. $1,250. Philadelphia, 1808. $750.

WHITE, Edmund. *Forgetting Elena.* New York (1973). Author's first book. $125.

WHITE, Edward Lucas. *Lukundoo and Other Stories . . .* New York (1927). Decorated blue cloth. $350.

WHITE, The Reverend George. *Statistics of the State of Georgia.* Savannah, 1849. Large hand-colored map. With errata leaf. $400.

WHITE, Gilbert. See *The Natural History and Antiquities of Selborne.*

WHITE, Gilbert. *The Writings of Gilbert White of Selborne.* Nonesuch Press. London, 1938. 2 vols. Wood engravings by Eric Ravilious. Gray buckram. One of 850 copies. In slipcase. $1,500.

WHITE, Grace Miller. *A Child of the Slums.* New York, 1904. Author's first book. Wraps. $300.

WHITE, Jean Claude. *Sikhim and Bhutan.* London, 1909. 1 extending map at rear. $1,000.

WHITE, John. *Journal of a Voyage to New South Wales.* London, 1790. 65 hand-colored plates, engraved title page with a view of Port Jackson, list of subscribers, 2 leaves of ads at the rear. $10,000.

WHITE, John. *Rural Architecture . . .* Glasgow, 1852. 90 plates. $1,250. (Originally published in 1845.)

WHITE, Minor. *Mirrors Messages Manifestation.* New York (1969). $600.

WHITE, Owen P. *The Autobiography of a Durable Sinner.* New York (1942). Cloth. First issue, with pages 239–44 intact as part of original binding. $275. Second issue, with pages 239–44 reset and tipped in. $75.

WHITE, Owen P. *Just Me . . .* El Paso, 1924. Author's first book. Stiff wraps. (Carl Hertzog's first typography.) One of 275 copies. $350.

WHITE, Owen P. *Out of the Desert.* El Paso, 1923. Illustrated. $150.

WHITE, Patrick. *The Aunt's Story.* London, 1948. $1,250. New York, 1948. $350.

WHITE, Patrick. *Happy Valley.* London, 1939. $4,000. New York, 1940. $2,000.

WHITE, Patrick. *The Living and the Dead.* London, 1941. $1,500. New York, 1941. $1,000.

WHITE, Patrick. *The Ploughman . . .* Sydney, 1935. Author's first book. One of 300 copies. $7,500.

WHITE, Randy Wayne. *Sanibel Flats.* New York, 1990. $850.

WHITE, Stewart Edward. *Arizona Nights.* New York, 1907. $400.

WHITE, Stewart Edward. *The Birds of Mackinac Island.* New York, 1893. Author's first book. Wraps. $1,000.

WHITE, Stewart Edward. *The Claim Jumpers.* New York, 1901. Pictorial cloth. $200. Printed wraps. $200. Marbled boards with leather spine. $250.

WHITE, Stewart Edward. *The Forest.* New York, 1903. Illustrated by Thomas Fogarty. Paper label. One of 80 large-paper copies signed by the author. $400. Trade. $150.

WHITE, Stewart Edward. *Gold.* New York, 1913. Yellow cloth. $200.

WHITE, Stewart Edward. *The Gray Dawn.* New York, 1915. $150.

WHITE, Stewart Edward. *The Long Rifle.* New York, 1932. $300.

WHITE, Stewart Edward. *Rules of the Game.* New York, 1910. $250.

WHITE, T. H. See Aston, James.

WHITE, T. H. *England Have My Bones.* London, 1936. $350. New York, 1936. $125.

WHITE, T. H. *Farewell Victoria.* London, 1933. $450. New York, 1934. First binding in orange cloth, paper labels. $300.

WHITE, T. H. *The Green Bay Tree.* (Cambridge, England, 1929.) Author's first book. Wraps. $350.

WHITE, T. H. *Loved Helen and Other Poems.* London (1929). $400.

WHITE, T. H. *The Once and Future King.* London, 1958. $500. New York, 1958. $250.

WHITE, T. H. *The Sword in the Stone.* London, 1938. $750. New York, 1939. $250.

WHITE, T. H. *The Witch in the Wood.* New York, 1939. $600. London (1940). First English edition. $750.

WHITE, Walter F. *The Fire In the Flint.* New York, 1924. Author's first book. $1,500.

WHITE, William Allen. *The Court of Boyville.* New York, 1899. Illustrated by Orson Lowell and Gustav Verbeek. Pictorial buckram. $100.

WHITE, William Allen, and PAINE, Albert Bigelow. *Rhymes by Two Friends.* First book for each author. Illustrated. Blue cloth. Fort Scott, Kan. (1893). $175.

WHITEHEAD, Alfred North, and Russell, Bertrand. *Principia Mathematica.* Cambridge, 1910–12–13. 3 vols. $30,000. Second edition. 1925–27. 3 vols. $2,500.

WHITEHEAD, Charles E. *Wild Sports in the South.* New York, 1860. $350.

WHITEHEAD, Henry S. *Jumbee and Other Uncanny Tales.* (Sauk City, Wis.), 1944. Author's first book. $350.

WHITEHEAD, John. *The Exploration of Mount Kina Balu, North Borneo.* London, 1893. 32 plates, some hand-colored. $2,600.

WHITELY, Ike. *Rural Life in Texas.* Atlanta, 1891. 82 pages, pictorial wraps. $500.

WHITMAN, Albrey A. *The Rape of Florida.* St. Louis, 1884. $750.

WHITMAN, Paul. *Jazz.* New York, 1926. $1,250.

WHITMAN, Walt. See *Leaves of Grass; Leaves of Grass Imprints.*

WHITMAN, Walt. *After All, Not to Create Only.* (Washington, 1871.) 11 folio numbered sheets, printed on 1 side only, stitched. First edition, first (proof) issue. $2,500. Boston, 1871. Green, maroon, or brown cloth. First book edition. $1,000. Limp cloth wraps. $600.

WHITMAN, Walt. *As a Strong Bird on Pinions Free, And Other Poems.* Washington, 1872. Green cloth. (Note: Although "Leaves of Grass" appears in small letters at top of title page, this is not one of the later editions of the book of the same title.) $850. Same but London imprint stamped on title page. $750.

WHITMAN, Walt. *Calamus: A Series of Letters, Written During the Years 1868–80 . . . to a Young Friend (Peter Doyle).* Boston: Laurens Maynard, 1897. $450. One of 35 copies on large paper. $1,000. Boston: Small, Maynard & Co., 1897. $250. London: Putnam, 1897. $250.

WHITMAN, Walt. *Complete Poems and Prose . . . 1855–1888.* (Philadelphia, 1888–1889.) Portrait title page, one plate. One of 600 signed copies. 3 bindings but price would be the same. $6,000.

WHITMAN, Walt. *Democratic Vistas.* See entry under the title *Memoranda: Democratic Vistas.*

WHITMAN, Walt. *Drum-Taps.* New York, 1865. First issue. Grayish-red or deep yellowish-brown cloth. (500 copies.) 72 pages. $2,500. Washington, 1865–6. *Sequel to Drum Taps.* "When Lilacs Last in the Door-Yard Bloom'd" on title page. (1,000 copies.) $1,750.

WHITMAN, Walt. *Franklin Evans; or The Inebriate.* New York, 1842. Whitman's first separately published work, priced at 12½ cents. 31 pages. Pamphlet without covers. Issued as a supplement to the *New World.* $25,000. Priced at 6½ cents. $20,000. Rebound. $4,500. New York, 1929. One of 700 copies. $200.

WHITMAN, Walt. *Goodbye, My Fancy. 2nd Annex to Leaves of Grass.* Philadelphia, 1891. Phototype portrait. Red cloth presumed to precede green. $600.

WHITMAN, Walt. *The Half Breed and Other Stories.* New York, 1927. Edited by T. O. Mabbott. Illustrated. Half cloth. One of 155 copies. $200. One of 30 copies with illustrations signed in proof by the artist, Allen Lewis. $600.

WHITMAN, Walt. *Leaves of Grass.* [Originally published without author's name, see also listing under title.] Camden, 1876. Author's edition. Signed in ink on title page. 2 portraits of author inserted (Hollyer's after page 28 and Linton's on page 284). $10,000. Camden, 1882. Author's edition. Signed. Probably fewer than 100 copies done. $7,500. New York, 1930. Folio. One of 400 copies. Half red morocco over wooden boards. Inscribed by Valenti Angelo on verso of title page. $2,500. Limited Editions Club, Mt. Vernon, 1929. In slipcase. $200. New York, 1942. Signed by photographer, Edward Weston. In slipcase. $1,500.

WHITMAN, Walt. *Leaves of Grass. With Sands at Seventy and A Backward Glance o'er Travel'd Roads.* Philadelphia, 1889. One of 300 signed copies. Bound in "Pocket-book" flexible roan with wraparound flap. $6,000

WHITMAN, Walt. *Memoranda: Democratic Vistas.* Washington, 1871. Light-green wraps. First edition, later printing (the first did not have Whitman's name on title page but only in copyright notice). $1,000. (For first printing, see the title entry.)

WHITMAN, Walt. *Memoranda During the War.* Camden, N.J., 1875–76. 2 portraits. Red-brown cloth, green endpapers. First printed page beginning "Remembrance Copy" and with space below for autograph (signed). $10,000. Another issue, without the portraits and the leaf headed "Remembrance Copy." (Signed.) $8,500.

WHITMAN, Walt. *Notes & Fragments.* (London, Ont., Canada), 1899. Edited by Richard Maurice Bucke. Blue pebbled cloth. One of 225 copies signed by Bucke. $500.

WHITMAN, Walt. *November Boughs.* Philadelphia, 1888. Frontispiece portrait. Maroon cloth. $600. (Green cloth later.)

WHITMAN, Walt. *Pictures: An Unpublished Poem.* New York, 1927. Boards, paper label. One of 700 copies. $350.

WHITMAN, Walt. *Poems . . .* London, 1868. Edited by William Michael Rossetti. Frontispiece portrait. Ad leaf pasted in. Cloth, gilt panel on cover. First issue, without price on spine (VAB). BAL states no sequence established (4 bindings). $750.

WHITMAN, Walt. *Rivulets of Prose.* New York, 1928. Edited by Carolyn Wells and Alfred F. Goldsmith. One of 499 copies. $250.

WHITMAN, Walt. *Specimen Days & Collect.* Philadelphia, 1882–83. First issue, with Rees Welsh & Co. imprint. Light-blue wraps. $750. Yellow cloth. $500. Philadelphia, 1883. David McKay imprint. Second issue. $350.

WHITMAN, Walt. *Two Rivulets.* Camden, 1876. Portrait frontispiece, signed "Walt Whitman." Half calf. $10,000.

WHITMAN, Walt. *Walt Whitman's Diary in Canada.* Boston, 1904. Edited by W. S. Kennedy. Gray boards and vellum. One of 500 copies. $350.

WHITMAN, Walt. *When Lilacs Last in the Dooryard Bloomed.* Essex House Press. London, 1900. Vellum. One of 125 copies. $1,250.

WHITNEY, Asa. *Memorial of A. Whitney, Praying a Grant of Public Land to Enable Him to Construct a Railroad . . .* (Washington, 1846.) Folding map. $250.

WHITNEY, J. D. *The Yosemite Book.* New York, 1868. 28 photographic plates, 2 maps. Half leather. (250 printed.) $10,000. Second edition. Cambridge, 1869. (Retitled *The Yosemite Guide Book.*) $2,500.

WHITTIER, John Greenleaf. See *Justice and Expediency; Moll Pitcher; The Stranger in Lowell; The Supernaturalism of New England.*

WHITTIER, John Greenleaf. *At Sundown.* Cambridge, 1890. Pea-green cloth. One of 250 copies with facsimile autograph presentation slip. $300. Boston, 1892. Final plate listed at page 64 in "List of illustrations, page 46, lines 11 and 12 about the same length. $200.

WHITTIER, John Greenleaf. *The Captain's Well.* Supplement to *New York Ledger,* January 11, 1890. Illustrated by Howard Pyle. 4 pages, in imitation alligator leather. $750.

WHITTIER, John Greenleaf. *Legends of New England.* Hartford, 1831. Author's first book. First state, with last line on page 98 reading "the go" for "they go." $450.

WHITTIER, John Greenleaf. *Mogg Megone: A Poem.* Boston, 1836. In original slate-colored cloth. $600.

WHITTIER, John Greenleaf. *The Panorama, and Other Poems.* Boston, 1856. $150.

WHITTIER, John Greenleaf. *Poems.* Philadelphia, 1838. In original leather. $400. Cloth. $300. Limited Editions Club, New York, 1945. In slipcase. $100.

WHITTIER, John Greenleaf. *Poems Written During the Progress of the Abolition Question in the United States.* Boston, 1837. Frontispiece. In original cloth. First issue, 96 pages. $350. Second issue, 103 pages. $200.

WHITTIER, John Greenleaf. *Snow-Bound.* Boston, 1866. Green, blue, or terra-cotta cloth. With last page of text numbered "52." $500. With last page unnumbered. $400. Limited Editions Club, New York, 1930. Boards and cloth. In slipcase. $125. Also, one of 50 large-paper copies (issued later in the year). $500.

WHITTIER, John Greenleaf. *The Supernaturalism of New England.* New York, 1847. Wraps. $1,250. London, 1847. $500.

WHITTOCK, Nathaniel. *The Art of Drawing and Colouring . . . Birds, Beasts . . .* London, 1830. 24 (12 hand-colored) plates. $1,500.

WHITTOCK, Nathaniel. *The Decorative Painters' and Glazeers' Guide.* London, 1827. Plates, many colored. $1,500. London, 1828. Second edition. $750.

WHYTE-MELVILLE, George John. See *Market Harborough.*

WHYTE-MELVILLE, George John. *Digby Grand: An Autobiography.* London, 1853. 2 vols. Author's first novel. Cloth. $500.

WHYTE-MELVILLE, George John. *The Queen's Maries: A Romance of Holyrood.* London, 1862. 2 vols. $250.

WICKERSHAM, James. *A Bibliography of Alaskan Literature, 1724–1924.* Cordova, 1927. Vol. 1 of the Miscellaneous Publications. $250.

WIDEMAN, John Edgar. *A Glance Away.* New York (1967). Author's first book. $300.

WIELAND; or, The Transformation . . . New York, 1798. (By Charles Brockden Brown.) $2,000.

WIENER, Norbert. *Cybernetics.* New York (1948). Author's first book. $500.

WIENERS, John. *Ace of Pentacles.* New York, 1964. Boards. One of 75 signed copies, with manuscript portion tipped in. In glassine dustwrapper. $150. Leather. One of 12 signed copies with a poem tipped in. $250. Trade. Wraps. $60.

WIERZBICKI, F. P. *California as It Is and as It May Be.* San Francisco, 1849. 60 pages, glazed lavender wraps. First edition, with errata leaf. (The first book written and published in California.) $60,000. San Francisco, 1849. 76 pages, errata, saffron wraps. Second edition. $30,000 or more. Grabhorn Press. San Francisco, 1933. Boards and cloth. One of 500 copies. In dustwrapper. $175.

WIESEL, Elie. *Night.* Paris, 1958. Author's first book. $300. New York (1960). $200.

WIGGIN, Kate Douglas. See Smith, Kate Douglas.

WIGGIN, Kate Douglas. *Kindergarten Chimes.* Boston, 1885. $250.

WIGGIN, Kate Douglas. *Rebecca of Sunnybrook Farm.* Boston, 1903. Green pictorial cloth. First issue: publisher's imprint on spine in type $\frac{1}{16}$ inch high, and page 327, line 13 "bricks glowing in the sun of . . ." $400. Second issue: spine same, page 327, line 13 now reads "bricks glowing in the October Sun . . ." $250. Third issue: spine type $\frac{1}{8}$ inch high, page 327, line 13 reading same as second issue. $200. London, 1903. $350.

WIGWAM and the Cabin (The). First series. New York, 1845. (By William Gilmore Simms.) In original wraps. $2,000. Later with the Second Series. 2 vols. in one, in original cloth. New York, 1845. $500.

WIJDEVELD, H. T. *The Life-Work of the American Architect Frank Lloyd Wright.* Santpoort, 1925. Square folio. $1,250.

WILBARGER, J. W. *Indian Depredations in Texas.* Austin, 1889. 38 plates (37 listed). Pictorial cloth. $850. Austin, 1890. Second edition. $450.

WILBUR, Homer (editor). *Meliboeus Hipponax. The Biglow Papers.* Cambridge, Mass., 1848. (By James Russell Lowell.) Cloth, or glazed boards. First issue. With George Nichols only as publisher. $350. Later, Putnam's name added to imprint. $250.

WILBUR, Richard. *The Beautiful Changes and Other Poems.* New York (1947). Author's first book. $400.

WILBUR, Richard (compiler). *A Bestiary.* New York (1955). One of 750 signed copies. Illustrated by Alexander Calder. Pictorial buckram. In slipcase. $600. Folio, half morocco. One of 50 copies signed by author and artist and with a signed pen and ink drawing by Calder. $5,000.

WILBUR, Richard. *Ceremony and Other Poems.* New York (1950). $300.

WILBUR, Richard. *Seed Leaves: Homage to R. F.* Boston (1974). Illustrated by Charles E. Wadsworth. Wraps, paper label. One of 160 copies signed by poet and artist. In portfolio wraps. $500.

WILBUR, Richard. *Things of This World.* New York (1956). $300.

WILCOX, Ella Wheeler. See Wheeler, Ella.

WILDE, Oscar. See C.3.3. See also *An Ideal Husband; The Importance of Being Earnest.*

WILDE, Oscar. *The Ballad of Reading Gaol.* [For first edition see C.3.3.] London, 1898. Third edition. One of 99 signed copies. $8,500.

WILDE, Oscar. *The Birthday of the Infants.* Black Sun Press. Paris, 1928. One of 100 copies. Illustrated by Alastair. Wraps. $2,500. Also, one of 9 copies on vellum with an original drawing. $4,500. New York, 1929. Illustrated by Pamela Bianco. Boards. One of 500 copies signed by the artist. In slipcase. $1,000.

WILDE, Oscar. *Children in Prison and Other Cruelties of Prison Life.* London, 1898. Wraps. $1,750.

WILDE, Oscar. *De Profundis.* London (1905). Blue buckram. With ads dated February. $300. Later, ads dated March. $250. Large-paper issues: White cloth. One of 200 copies on hand-made paper. $750. One of 50 copies on Japan vellum. $2,500.

WILDE, Oscar. *The Happy Prince and Other Tales.* London, 1888. Illustrated by Walter Crane and Jacomb Hood. Vellum boards. $2,500. One of 75 signed copies. $10,000. Boston, 1888. Original gray cloth stamped in red, gilt spine. $750. London, 1913. Vellum. Illustrated by Charles Robinson. One of 260 copies. $3,000. Stamford, 1936. 250 copies. Wood engravings in color by Rudolph Ruzika. $750. One of 20 copies with extra signed suite of woodcuts. $4,500.

WILDE, Oscar. *A House of Pomegranates.* London, 1891. 4 plates. White cloth, green cloth spine. $2,000. London, 1915. Color plates by Jessie M. King. Decorated cloth. $1,750.

WILDE, Oscar. *Intentions.* London, 1891. Moss-green cloth. $850.

WILDE, Oscar. *Lady Windermere's Fan: A Play About a Good Woman.* London, 1893. Reddish-brown linen. $2,000. Large-paper issue. One of 50 copies. $5,000. Limited Editions Club, New York, 1973. In slipcase. $125.

WILDE, Oscar. *Lord Arthur Savile's Crime & Other Stories.* London, 1891. Salmon-colored boards. $1,000. (London, 1904.) One of 300 copies. Wraps. $300.

WILDE, Oscar. *Oscariana. Epigrams.* (London), 1895. Printed wraps. $500.

WILDE, Oscar. *The Picture of Dorian Gray.* Philadelphia (1890). Wraps. A piracy. $2,000. London (1891). Rough gray beveled boards, vellum spine. 10 small butterflies on cover. First edition, with letter "a" missing from "and" on page 208 in line 8 from bottom. $3,000. One of 250 signed copies. (Error corrected.) $20,000. Limited Editions Club, New York, 1957. In slipcase. $150.

WILDE, Oscar. *Poems.* London, 1881. White parchment boards. First edition, first issue, with the word "may" in line 3, stanza 2, page 136. One of 250 copies. $3,000. Boston, 1881. $600. London, 1892. Violet cloth. One of 220 signed copies. $10,000.

WILDE, Oscar. *Ravenna.* Recited in the Theatre. Oxford, June 26, 1878. Oxford, 1878. Author's first book with exception of a collaboration. 16 pages, printed wraps. With Oxford University seal on title page and cover. (The Newdigate Prize Poem.) $2,000.

WILDE, Oscar. *Salome: Drame en Un Acte.* Paris, 1893. Purple wraps. One of 50 on Van Gelder paper. $4,000. London, 1894. First English edition. Illustrated by Aubrey Beardsley. Decorated cloth. One of 500 copies. $2,500. Large-paper issue. One of 100 copies with illustration on vellum. $4,000. Grabhorn Press. San Francisco, 1927. Illustrated. Boards. One of 195 copies. In slipcase. $1,250. Limited Editions Club, New York, 1938. 2 vols. One of 1,500 copies signed by the illustrator, Andre Derain. In slipcase. $750. London, 1907. Translated by Wilde, with 16 drawings by Aubrey Beardsley. First edition has the hermaphrodite illustration on the title page. $1,000.

WILDE, Oscar. *The Sphinx.* London, 1894. Decorations by Charles Ricketts. Vellum. One of 250 copies (50 for America). $6,500. One of 25 large-paper copies. $10,000. London, 1920. Illustrated by Alastair. One of 1,000 copies. $1,250.

WILDE, Oscar. *A Woman of No Importance.* London, 1894. One of 500 copies. $1,750. Deluxe edition. One of 50 large-paper copies. $4,000.

WILDE, Oscar. *The Writings of Oscar Wilde.* New York, 1925. 12 vols. One of 575 large-paper copies. $2,500.

WILDENSTEIN, Daniel. *Claude Monet . . .* Paris (1974–85). 4 vols. In dustwrappers. $2,500.

WILDER, Amos N(iven). *Battle-Retrospect and Other Poems.* New York, 1923. Author's first book. $250.

WILDER, Laura Ingalls. *Farmer Boy.* New York, 1933. Illustrated by Helen Sewell. Pictorial cloth. $600.

WILDER, Laura Ingalls. *Little House on the Prairie.* New York, 1935. Illustrated by Helen Sewell. Pictorial cloth. $750.

WILDER, Thornton. *The Angel That Troubled the Waters.* New York, 1928. Blue boards and cloth. One of 775 signed copies. $400. Trade. (2,000 copies.) $150. London, 1928. Blue cloth. First English edition. One of 260 signed copies. $250.

WILDER, Thornton. *The Bridge of San Luis Rey.* London, 1927. First edition (preceding American edition by a few days). $1,500. New York, 1927. First American edition, "preliminary issue" (actually preceding U.K. by a day) with title page printed only in black. $4,000. Regular trade issue, title page printed in green and black. $2,500. New York, 1929. Illustrated by Rockwell Kent. Pictorial cloth, leather label. One of 1,000 copies signed by Wilder and Kent. In slipcase. $500. One of 100 deluxe copies. $750.

WILDER, Thornton. *The Cabala.* New York, 1926. Author's first book. First issue, with "conversation" for "conversion" in line 13, page 196 and "explaininn" for "explaining" line 12, page 202. Blue figured cloth or tan figured cloth. Blue supposedly scarcer than tan. $400. New York, 1926. $200.

WILDER, Thornton. *The Ides of March.* New York (1948). One of 750 signed copies. In dustwrapper. $250. Trade. $75.

WILDER, Thornton. *James Joyce, 1882–1941.* (Aurora, N. Y., 1941.) Wraps. One of 150 copies. $750.

WILDER, Thornton. *The Merchant of Yonkers.* New York, 1939. $600.

WILDER, Thornton. *Our Town.* New York (1938). $1,000.

WILDER, Thornton. *The Woman of Andros.* New York, 1930. $200. London, 1930. First English edition. One of 260 signed copies. $450. Trade. $150.

WILKES, Charles. *Narrative of the United States Exploring Expedition, During the Years 1838–42* . . . Philadelphia, 1844. $50,000. Philadelphia, 1845. 6 vols., including atlas vol. Illustrated. Cloth. First unofficial edition (after the 1844 set printed for Congress). $6,000.

WILKES, Charles. *Western America, Including California and Oregon* . . . Philadelphia, 1849. 3 folding maps. Printed tan wraps. $2,500.

WILKES, George. *The History of Oregon, Geographical and Political.* New York, 1845. Folding map. 127 pages, printed wraps. $5,000.

WILKESON, Frank. *Recollections of a Private Soldier in the Army of the Potomac.* New York: G. P. Putnam's Sons, 1887. 8 vols. $200.

WILKESON, Samuel. *Wilkeson's Notes on Puget Sound.* (New York, 1870?) 47 pages. Wraps. $450. Second edition, 44 pages. $500. Abridged edition, 32 pages. $200.

WILKINS, Mary E. *Decorative Plaques.* Boston (1883). Author's first book (written with George F. Barnes). $2,000.

WILKINSON, Gen. James. *Memoirs of My Own Times.* Philadelphia, 1816. 4 vols. Including atlas of 19 maps and plans. 9 folding tables, 3 folding facsimiles. $2,500.

WILKINSON, Sir J. Gardner. *Dalmatia and Montenegro.* London, 1848. 2 vols. 7 tinted lithographed plates (two folding), 7 wood-engraved plates, folding engraved map, 2 folding tables. $1,250.

WILLCOX, Joseph. *Ivy Mills, 1729–1866* . . . Baltimore, 1910. $200.

WILLCOX, R. N. *Reminiscences of California Life.* (Avery, Ohio), 1897. $850.

WILLEFORD, Charles. *The Burnt Orange Heresy.* New York, 1971. $250.

WILLEFORD, Charles. *Honey Gal.* New York, 1958. Wraps. $500.

WILLEFORD, Charles. *Miami Blues.* New York, 1984. $450. London, 1984. $350.

WILLEFORD, Charles. *Poontang and Other Poems.* (Crescent City, 1967.) Wraps. $1,250.

WILLEFORD, Charles. *Proletarian Laughter.* Yonkers, 1948. Author's first book. Wraps. (1,000 copies.) $250.

WILLETT, Ralph. *A Description of the Library at Merly* . . . London, 1785. 26 plates (6 folding). $4,500.

WILLETT, William M. (editor). *A Narrative of the Military Actions of Col. Marinus Willet.* New York, 1831. Portrait, plan, facsimile letter. $1,250.

WILLEY, S. H. *An Historical Paper Relating to Santa Cruz, California.* San Francisco, 1876. 37 pages, printed wraps. $350.

WILLIAMS, Alpheus F. *The Genesis of the Diamond.* London, 1932. 2 vols. 221 plates, 30 colored. Buckram. Issued without dustwrapper. $750.

WILLIAMS, Ben Ames. *All the Brothers Were Valiant.* New York, 1919. Author's first book. In N. C. Wyeth dustwrapper. $600.

WILLIAMS, Charles. *Poems of Conformity.* London, 1917. $200.

WILLIAMS, Charles. *The Silver Stair.* London, 1912. Author's first book. $450.

WILLIAMS, Charles. *War in Heaven.* London, 1930. $300. New York, 1949. $100.

WILLIAMS, C(harles) K(enneth). *A Day for Anne Frank.* Philadelphia (1968). Wraps. $500.

WILLIAMS, C(harles) K(enneth). *Lies.* Boston, 1969. $250.

WILLIAMS, G. T. *Receipts and Shipments of Livestock at Union Stock Yards for 1890.* Chicago, 1891. 40 pages. Wraps. $500.

WILLIAMS, Gardiner. *The Diamond Mines of South America.* New York, 1902. 2 vols. $600. One of 100 copies. $1,000. New York, 1905. 2 vols. One of 1,000 copies. $750.

WILLIAMS, Mrs. H. Dwight. *A Year in China: and A Narrative of Capture and Imprisonment . . .* New York, 1864. $300.

WILLIAMS, Iola A. *Points in Eighteenth-Century Verse: A Bibliographer's and Collector's Scrapbook.* London, 1934. One of 500 copies. Vol. 7 of the 10-vol. Bibliographia Series edited by Michael Sadleir. $150.

WILLIAMS, Jesse. *A Description of the United States Lands of Iowa.* New York, 1840. Folding map in color. Green cloth. $1,500.

WILLIAMS, John. *Farther Observations on the Discovery of America . . .* London, 1792. $1,250.

WILLIAMS, John A. *Africa: Her History, Lands and People.* New York, 1962. First edition stated. $250.

WILLIAMS, John A. *The Angry Ones.* New York (1960). Author's first book. Pictorial wraps. Ace paperback. $150.

WILLIAMS, John A. *Nightsong.* New York (1961). $200.

WILLIAMS, John Camp. *An Oneida County Printer, William Williams . . .* New York, 1906. One of 165 copies. 29 plates. $200.

WILLIAMS, John Lee. *The Territory of Florida.* New York, 1837. Folding map, portrait, 2 plates. $3,000. New York, 1839. $750.

WILLIAMS, John Lee. *A View of West Florida.* Philadelphia, 1827. Folding map. $6,000.

WILLIAMS, Jonathan (Chamberlain). *Painting & Graphics.* Highlands, 1950. Author's first book. (Exhibition folder.) Previous pamphlet may exist. $500.

WILLIAMS, Joseph. *Insanity, Its Causes Prevention, and Cure . . .* London, 1845. $600. 1852. Revised and enlarged edition. $500.

WILLIAMS, Joseph. *Narrative of a Tour from the State of Indiana to the Oregon Territory.* Cincinnati, 1843. 48 pages, plain blue wraps. $20,000 or more. New York, 1921. Cloth. One of 250 copies. $200.

WILLIAMS, Margery. *The Velveteen Rabbit or How Toys Become Real.* London, 1922. Illustrated by William Nicholson. Pictorial boards. In dustwrapper. $20,000. New York (1922). $15,000.

WILLIAMS, Samuel. *The Natural and Civil History of Vermont.* Walpole, 1794. Folding frontispiece map. $1,000.

WILLIAMS, Tennessee. *American Blues.* (New York, 1948.) Printed wraps. Only the first printing had misspelling of "Tennessee" as "Tennesse." Other first-issue points exist but are not necessary to list as this error appears on the front cover/wrapper. $450.

WILLIAMS, Tennessee. *Baby Doll.* (New York, 1956.) First edition not stated. $300. London, 1957. First English edition. $200.

WILLIAMS, Tennessee. *Battle of Angels.* (Murray, Utah, 1945.) Author's first book. Printed wraps (comprising double number, nos. 1 and 2, of *Pharos,* Spring, 1945). $750.

WILLIAMS, Tennessee. *Cat on a Hot Tin Roof.* (Norfolk, Conn., 1955.) Tan cloth. First edition not stated. First printing has no credit on the verso of the title leaf to the *New York Times* for a previous appearance of the foreword. No credit appears at page xii to Jo Mielziner and Lucinda Ballard for scene and costume design, as these were inadvertently left off and added to subsequent printings. (Later printings also noted at the bottom of the front dustwrapper flap.) $500.

WILLIAMS, Tennessee. *The Glass Menagerie.* New York, 1945. Rust or blue cloth. $1,500.

WILLIAMS, Tennessee. *Grand: A Short Story.* New York, 1964. One of 300 signed copies. In glassine dustwrapper. $450. One of 26 lettered copies, signed. $1,000.

WILLIAMS, Tennessee. *Hard Candy.* (New York, 1954.) Patterned boards, cloth spine. Limited edition. In slipcase. $250. (New York, 1959.) Black cloth boards lettered down the spine in bronze and silver. "New trade edition" on verso of title leaf. (Later printings are noted on copyright page.) $100.

WILLIAMS, Tennessee. *In the Winter of Cities: Poems.* (Norfolk, 1956.) White parchment boards, gilt. One of 100 signed copies. In slipcase. $2,000. Trade. Patterned boards and cloth. First edition not stated. $300.

WILLIAMS, Tennessee. *I Rise in Flame, Cried the Phoenix.* Norfolk (1952). One of 300 signed copies. In slipcase. $1,250. One of 10 signed copies on Umbria paper. In slipcase. $3,000.

WILLIAMS, Tennessee. *The Kingdom of Earth, with Hard Candy.* No place [New York]: New Directions (1954). One of 100 signed copies, plus 20 for "presentation." $2,500.

WILLIAMS, Tennessee. *The Milk Train Doesn't Stop Here Anymore.* Norfolk, 1964. First issue with pages 19–22 integral and Scene Two beginning on page 22. $300. Second issue with pages 19–22 tipped in and Scene Two starting on page 21. $125. Third issue, pages 19–22 are bound in. $50.

WILLIAMS, Tennessee. *One Arm and Other Stories.* (Norfolk, 1949.) Boards, vellum spine. One of 50 signed copies. In slipcase. $3,000. (Norfolk, 1949.) Trade edition. (1,500 copies.) Boards and cloth in dustwrapper. First edition not stated. Most of the first edition copies bear a tipped-in title leaf with the copyright in Williams's name. $200. About 20 copies with an integral title leaf with an incorrect copyright credit by New Directions. $1,250. (New York, 1954.) $150.

WILLIAMS, Tennessee. *The Roman Spring of Mrs. Stone*. (Norfolk, 1950.) Marbled boards, vellum spine. One of 500 signed copies. In slipcase. $500. Trade. First edition not stated. $150.

WILLIAMS, Tennessee. *The Rose Tattoo*. (New York or Norfolk, 1951.) First edition stated. First binding in rose cloth. $600. Second binding in tan cloth. $250.

WILLIAMS, Tennessee. *A Streetcar Named Desire*. (Norfolk, 1947.) First edition not stated, but in lavender decorated boards not on later printings. (Extremely vulnerable to fading and edge wear.) Author's name on spine of book in gold or white. Gold scarcer. $5,000. London (1949). $300. Limited Editions Club, New York, 1982. $300.

WILLIAMS, Tennessee. *Summer and Smoke*. (Norfolk, 1948.) First edition stated. Light-blue cloth boards. First issue dustwrapper lists three Williams plays on inside back flap. $350.

WILLIAMS, Tennessee. *27 Wagons Full of Cotton and Other One Act Plays*. (Norfolk, 1946.) Bound in beige cloth boards. Dustwrapper in brown. $350. Second issue is in yellow boards with black cloth spine; and adds the essay "Something Wild." Dustwrapper in black. $200. (Norfolk), 1953. Third issue. Yellow cloth boards lettered in green down the spine. Dustwrapper in black. (First appearance of two plays, *Something Unspoken and Talk to Me Like the Rain*.). $100. London (1949). $150.

WILLIAMS, Tennessee. *The Two Character Play*. (New York, 1969.) One of 350 signed copies. In slipcase. $450.

WILLIAMS, Tennessee, and WINDHAM, Donald. *You Touched Me! A Romantic Comedy*. New York (1947). 506 hardcover copies in white pictorial dustwrapper printed in dark-green ink. $450. Gray wraps printed in black with 85-cent cover price. $200. (All subsequent wraps editions in bright orange.)

WILLIAMS, Terry Tempest. *The Secret Language of Snow*. New York: Sierra Club (1984). Written with Ted Major. $500.

WILLIAMS, Thomas J.C. *A History of Washington County* (Maryland). (Chambersburg, Pa.), 1906. 2 vols. (Hagerstown in Howes.) $750.

WILLIAMS, William Carlos. See Ginsberg, Allen; Loy, Mina.

WILLIAMS, William Carlos. *Adam & Eve & The City*. Peru, Vt. 1936. 20 signed copies numbered I–XX. Olive-green wraps. In green slipcase. $5,000. 135 signed copies numbered 1–135. Wraps and slipcase as above. $4,000.

WILLIAMS, William Carlos. *Al Que Quiere! A Book of Poems*. Boston, 1917. Yellow-orange boards printed in black. $750. Also variant with tan paper boards and author's name misspelled "Willams" on spine. Assume later. $600.

WILLIAMS, William Carlos. *The Broken Span*. Norfolk (1941). First binding: gray paper boards printed in black and fuchsia, front flap of dustwrapper has comments about book, rear flap lists 12 *Poet of the Month* pamphlets. $350. Second binding: blank stiff white paper covers, dustwrapper as above. $200. Yellow paper wraps. $200.

WILLIAMS, William Carlos. *The Clouds* . . . (No place, 1948.) 60 signed copies numbered I–LX on English handmade paper. Slate cloth boards. In slipcase. $3,000. 250 copies numbered 61–310 on rag paper. In similar binding but issued without slipcase. $600.

WILLIAMS, William Carlos. *The Cod Head.* San Francisco, 1932. Wraps. One of 125 signed copies. $600. One of 100 copies on a single sheet folded to make 4 pages. For friends of Milton Abernathy. No date. $200.

WILLIAMS, William Carlos. *The Collected Later Poems.* (Norfolk, 1950.) "The Rose" section loosely inserted. One of 100 signed copies. Issued without dustwrapper in slipcase. $1,500. Trade. "The Rose" section loosely inserted. $175. Later binding with "The Rose" correctly bound in. $125. (Norfolk, 1950 [actually 1956].) 52 copies of which 50 are signed and numbered copies in red. Facing title page "Horace Mann School Editions." Gray slipcase ("The Rose" section bound in). $1,250. Trade. In plain brown dustwrapper with circular cut out to reveal H. Mann School seal. "The Rose" section loosely inserted. $150. London, 1965. $75.

WILLIAMS, William Carlos. *Collected Poems, 1921–1931.* New York, 1934. $850.

WILLIAMS, William Carlos. *The Desert Music and Other Poems.* New York (1954). 111 copies of which 100 were signed. Issued in glassine dustwrapper and slipcase. $1,250. Trade. $150.

WILLIAMS, William Carlos. *An Early Martyr.* New York, 1935. Wraps. One of 135 signed copies. $2,000. One of 20 signed copies. $3,000.

WILLIAMS, William Carlos. *The Great American Novel.* Paris, 1923. One of 300 copies. Some copies have a rectangular slip covering name of the press (on the title page) upon which is printed "Contact Editions, 29 Quai d'Anjou, Paris"—priority unknown. $600.

WILLIAMS, William Carlos. *In the American Grain.* New York, 1925. Original price $3.00, but raised to $3.50 right after publication. $1,000. Norfolk (1939). Yellow cloth boards, lettered in red. Yellow dustwrapper printed in green and red. $150. (London, 1967.) $50.

WILLIAMS, William Carlos. *In the Money / White Mule.* Part II. Norfolk (1940). $350. (London, 1965.) $75.

WILLIAMS, William Carlos. *Kora in Hell: Improvisations.* Boston, 1920. Issued in orange dustwrapper printed in black. (Some copies had glassine dustrappers.) $750. San Francisco (1957). Wraps. $40.

WILLIAMS, William Carlos. *Paterson (Book One).* (Norfolk, 1946.) One of 1,000 copies. $400.

WILLIAMS, William Carlos. *Paterson (Book Two).* (Norfolk, 1948.) One of 1,000 copies. $300.

WILLIAMS, William Carlos. *Paterson (Book Three).* (Norfolk, 1949.) One of 1,000 copies. $250.

WILLIAMS, William Carlos. *Paterson (Book Four).* (Norfolk, 1951.) One of 1,000 copies. $200.

WILLIAMS, William Carlos. *Paterson (Book Five).* (Norfolk, 1958.) No limitation but 3,000 copies printed. $200.

WILLIAMS, William Carlos. *Paterson . . .* The 5 vols. (listed above) together. $2,000.

WILLIAMS, William Carlos. *Poems.* (Rutherford, N.J.) 1909. Author's first book. 22 pages, printed brown wraps. First state, with "of youth himself, all rose-y-clad," in line 5 of first poem. (100 copies printed, of which two are known.) $35,000. Second state, with "of youth himself all roseyclad." $20,000. London, 1913. *The Poems.* $2,000.

WILLIAMS, William Carlos. *Selected Poems*. (Hove, Sussex, 1981.) Illustrated by Geoffrey Treneman. Folio, quarter red morocco, boards. One of 25 copies. Designed and illustrated by Treneman. $500.

WILLIAMS, William Carlos. *Sour Grapes*. Boston, 1921. Author's name on spine label only. $1,000.

WILLIAMS, William Carlos. *The Tempers*. London, 1913. In glassine dustwrapper. $1,250.

WILLIAMS, William Carlos. *White Mule*. Norfolk, 1937. White cloth boards printed in black, or gray cloth printed in crimson on spine. Priority unknown. $600. (London, 1965.) $75.

WILLIAMSON, George C. *The History of Portrait Miniatures*. London, 1904. 2 vols. 107 plates. Folio. White cloth. One of 520 copies. $750. One of 50 copies with hand-colored plates. $5,500 at auction in 1991. London, 1910. $250.

WILLIAMSON, Henry. *The Beautiful Years*. London (1921). Author's first book. (750 copies.) $850. New York, 1929. $150.

WILLIAMSON, Henry. *The Lone Swallows*. London (1922). One of 500 copies. $500.

WILLIAMSON, Henry. *The Patriot's Progress*. London (1930). Wood engravings by William Kermode. Half vellum. One of 350 signed copies. In slipcase. $350.

WILLIAMSON, Henry. *Salar the Salmon*. (Privately published by the author. September, 1935.) One of 13 numbered copies corrected and signed by the author. Half morocco. $2,500. London: Faber (1935). $175.

WILLIAMSON, Henry. *The Star Born*. London, 1933. Vellum. One of 70 copies signed by author and C. F. Tunnicliffe (illustrator). Issued without dustwrapper. $500.

WILLIAMSON, Henry. *Tarka the Otter . . .* (London) 1927. Vellum. One of 100 signed copies. $1,000. Trade edition. Buckram. Issued without dustwrapper. $450. Another issue/printing later in the year. Cloth in dustwrapper. $350.

WILLIAMSON, Henry. *The Wet Flanders Plain*. London, 1929. Half vellum. Issued without dustwrapper. One of 80 copies. $750. One of 240 copies. Issued without dustwrapper. $300.

WILLIAMSON, Hugh. *The History of North Carolina*. Philadelphia, 1812. 2 vols. Folding frontispiece map. $1,250.

WILLIAMSON, Jack. *The Legion of Space*. Reading, 1947. One of 500 signed copies. $300. Trade edition. $175.

WILLIAMSON, James J. *Mosby's Rangers*. New York, 1896. $600.

WILLIAMSON, John. *Fern Etchings*. Louisville, 1879. 65 engraved plates. $750.

WILLIAMSON, Joseph. *A Bibliography of the State of Maine from the Earliest Period to 1891*. Portland, 1896. 2 vols. $250.

WILLINGHAM, Calder. *End as A Man*. New York (1947). Author's first book. First issue, dustwrapper with back panel blank. $200. Dustwrapper with text on back. $125.

WILLINGTON, John (translator). *Memoirs of a Protestant.* London, 1758. (By Oliver Goldsmith.) Author's first book, a translation of the memoirs of Jean Marteilhe. $3,000.

WILLIS, Nathaniel Parker. *American Scenery.* London, 1840. 2 vols. 117 views by W. H. Bartlett. Leather. $2,000. Cloth. $1,250.

WILLIS, Nathaniel Parker. *Canadian Scenery.* London, 1842. 2 vols. Illustrated by W. H. Bartlett. With engraved titles, portrait, map, and 117 plates. $1,750.

WILLIS, Nathaniel Parker. *Pencillings by the Way.* London, 1835. 3 vols. $300.

WILLIS, Nathaniel Parker. *Sketches.* Boston, 1827. Author's first book. $200.

WILLIS, William L. *History of Sacramento County.* Los Angeles, 1913. Illustrated. Three-quarter leather. $300.

WILLMOTT, Ellen Ann. *The Genus Rosa.* London (1910)-14. Colored and plain plates. 25 parts, gray wraps. $5,000. London, 1914. 2 vols. $4,000.

WILLOUGHBY, Edwin Elliott. *The Making of the King James Bible.* Los Angeles, 1956. With a leaf from the "She" Bible of 1611 inserted in a specially made folder. One of 290 copies. $750.

WILLUGHBY, Francis. *The Ornithology of Francis Willughby* . . . London, 1678. First edition in English. 3 parts in 1. Folio. 80 copper-engraved plates of birds. 2 tables. $3,500. London, 1972. One of 400 copies. $250.

WILLYAMS, Cooper. *A Voyage up the Mediterranean in HMS "Swiftsure."* London, 1802. Engraved dedication, double-page chart and 41 hand-colored plates. $3,500.

WILSON, Adrian. *Printing for the Theatre.* San Francisco, 1957. Author's first book. (250 copies.) $1,250.

WILSON, Alexander. *American Ornithology* . . . Philadelphia, 1808–14. 9 vols. With 76 hand-colored plates. $25,000. New York/Philadelphia, 1828–29. 4 vols., including atlas. Also, with 76 hand-colored plates. $17,500. Large-paper copy. $20,000. London, 1832. 3 vols. Wilson and Charles Bonaparte portrait and 97 hand-colored plates. $2,000.

WILSON, A(ndrew) N(orman). *The Sweets of Pimlico.* London (1977). Author's first book. $450.

WILSON, Angus. *The Wrong Set and Other Stories.* London, 1949. Author's first book. $150.

WILSON, Augusta Jane Evans. See *Inez* . . .

WILSON, Carroll A. *Thirteen Author Collections of the Nineteenth Century and Five Centuries of Familiar Quotations.* New York, 1950. 2 vols. One of 375 copies. In slipcase. $250.

WILSON, Colin. *The Outsider.* London, 1956. Author's first book. $250. Boston, 1956. According to the publisher, the first printing has the date on the title page. $150. There are at least 3 variants that state "First American Edition" but do not have a date on the title page. We assume these are later printings or book club editions.

WILSON, Colin. *Tree by Tolkien.* (London, 1973.) One of 100 signed copies. $250. Trade in olive cloth. $100. Santa Barbara, 1974. One of 200 copies. Issued without dustwrapper. $125. Wraps. $30.

WILSON, Colin. *Voyage to a Beginning.* New York (1969). Blue cloth with black letters. Precedes U.K. edition. $60. London, 1969. One of 200 signed copies. $200. Trade. Red cloth. $75.

WILSON, Derek. *The Triarchs.* London (1944). $250.

WILSON, Edmund. *Axel's Castle.* New York, 1931. $750.

WILSON, Edmund. *The Boys in the Back Room.* San Francisco, 1941. One of 100 signed copies. Issued in acetate dustwrapper. $1,000. Trade. $300.

WILSON, Edmund. *Discordant Encounters.* New York, 1926. $1,250.

WILSON, Edmund. *I Thought of Daisy.* New York, 1929. $450.

WILSON, Edmund, *Memoirs of Hecate County.* Garden City, 1946. $250. London (1952). $100.

WILSON, Edmund. *Note Books of Night.* San Francisco, 1942. Reportedly 100 signed copies were to be sold but only 10 or so were ever issued. These were in decorated floral boards with cloth spine. $2,500. 21 signed copies in later binding, blue paper boards with a black leather spine stamped in gold. $1,500. Trade. Inner tissue and outer dustwrappers. $300. London, 1945. $100.

WILSON, Edmund. *Poets, Farewell!* New York, 1929. $600.

WILSON, Edmund. *This Room & This Gin & These Sandwiches.* New York, 1937. One of 100 signed copies. Issued in acetate dustwrapper. $1,250. Trade. Wraps. $350.

WILSON, Edmund. *To the Finland Station.* New York, 1940. $350. London, 1940. $200.

WILSON, Edmund. *The Triple Thinkers.* New York, 1938. Noted in dark-green cloth, gold lettering and top edge yellow; and medium brown, white lettering and top edge unstained. Priority unknown but latter seems cheaper and may have been a remainder binding. $300. London, 1939. $200.

WILSON, Edmund, and BISHOP, John Peale. *The Undertaker's Garland.* New York, 1922. Wilson's first book. One of 50 copies for "Bookseller Friends." Issued without dustwrapper. $250. Trade. In dustwrapper. $500.

WILSON, Elijah N. *Among the Shoshones.* Salt Lake City (1910). Rigidly suppressed. 222 pages. 8 plates. Pictorial cloth. $1,000. Second edition, same place and date, 247 pages. (Howes W520: "The 247-page reprint omits account of how he lost his Mormon fiancée [given on pages 194 to 200 of original edition]." $250.

WILSON, Fred. J. F. *Typographic Printing Machines and Machine Printing . . .* London (1879). $600.

WILSON, Fred. J. F., and GREY, Douglas. *A Practical Treatise Upon Modern Printing Machinery and Letterpress Printing.* London, 1888. $350.

WILSON, Harry Leon. *Merton of the Movies.* Garden City, 1922. $400.

WILSON, Harry Leon. *Ruggles of Red Gap.* Garden City, 1915. In dustwrapper. $600. Without dustwrapper. $100.

WILSON, Harry Leon. *Zigzag Tales from the East to the West.* New York, 1894. Author's first book. Illustrated by C. Jay Taylor. Decorated wraps. $200. Cloth. $150.

WILSON, James. *A Missionary Voyage to the Southern Pacific Ocean*. London, 1799. Boards. 7 maps and plans, 6 plates (some copies with 7 plates). $1,500.

WILSON, John Albert. *History of Los Angeles County, California*. Oakland, 1880. Illustrated. Leather and cloth. $2,000. Berkeley, 1959. $150.

WILSON, Sir John. *The Royal Philatelic Collection* . . . London, 1952. Edited by Clarence Winchester. 12 color facsimiles, 48 monochrome plates, other illustrations. Full red morocco. $600.

WILSON, Mona. *The Life of William Blake*. London, 1927. One of 1,480 copies. Vellum, black marbled boards, 24 plates. $350.

WILSON, Richard L. *Short Ravelings from a Long Yarn, or Camp and March Sketches of the Santa Fe Trail*. Chicago, 1847. Edited by Benjamin F. Taylor. Illustrated. Printed boards. $6,000. Santa Ana, Calif., 1936. $350.

WILSON, Robert. *The Travels of Robert Wilson: Being a Relation of Facts*. London, 1807. Portrait, plates. $750.

WILSON, S. A. Kinnier. *Neurology*. London (1904). 2 vols. $400.

WILSON, William Rae. *Travels in Russia*. London, 1828. 2 vols. $750.

WILSON, Woodrow. *Congressional Government*. Boston, 1885. Author's first book. First issue, with publisher's monogram on spine. $350.

WILSON, Woodrow. *George Washington*. New York, 1897. $200.

WILSON, Woodrow. *A History of the American People*. New York, 1902. 5 vols. Alumni edition. One of 350 copies. $600. New York (1918). 10 vols. One of 400 signed copies. $2,500.

WILTSEE, Ernest A. *Gold Rush Steamers (of the Pacific)*. Grabhorn Press. San Francisco, 1938. Illustrated. Cloth. One of 500 copies. Issued without dustwrapper. $350.

WIMP and the Woodle and Other Stories, The. Los Angeles, 1935. (Illustrated by Willy Pogany.) 7 color plates. $300.

Wind (The). New York, 1925. (By Dorothy Scarborough.) $450.

WIND, Herbert Warren. *Story of American Golf*. New York, 1948. $300.

WINDELER, B. C. *Elimus*. Three Mountains Press. Paris, 1923. 12 designs by Dorothy Shakespear. One of 300 copies. Gray boards. Issued without dustwrapper. $350.

WINDELER, Bernard. *Sailing Ships and Barges of the Western Mediterranean and the Adriatic Seas*. London, 1926. Map, engraved title and 17 hand-colored copperplate engravings by Edward Wadsworth. One of 450 copies. In slipcase. $750.

WINDHAM, Donald. See also Williams, Tennessee.

WINDHAM, Donald. *The Hitchhiker*. (Florence, 1950.) Printed wraps. One of 250 signed copies. $125.

WING and Wing (The). Philadelphia, 1842. By the Author of *The Pilot* (James Fenimore Cooper). 2 vols. First American edition (of the novel issued first in London as *The Jack*

O'Lantern under Cooper's name). Printed terra-cotta wraps. $1,500. Later issue, wraps dated 1843. $750.

WINGFIELD, R. D. *A Touch of Frost.* London, 1990. Author's first book. $2,500.

WINKLER, A. V. *The Confederate Capital and Hood's Texas Brigade.* Austin, 1894. $650.

WINOGRAND, Garry. *Women Are Beautiful.* New York: Light Gallery, 1975. Wraps. $400. New York: Farrar, 1975. $250.

WINSHIP, George Parker. *William Caxton.* London, 1909. One of 300 copies on paper. $600. One of 15 copies on vellum. $3,500.

WINSLOW, Don. *A Cool Breeze on the Underground.* New York (1991). $350.

WINSOR, Justin. *A History of the Town of Duxbury* . . . Boston, 1849. Author's first book. $300.

WINSOR, Justin (Editor). *The Memorial History of Boston, Including Suffolk County, Massachusetts, 1630–1880.* Boston (1880). 4 vols. $400.

WINSOR, Kathleen. *Forever Amber.* New York, 1944. Author's first book. $350. London, 1944. $150.

WINTER in the West (A). New York, 1835. By a New Yorker (Charles Fenno Hoffman, his first book). 2 vols. In original cloth. $850.

WINTER Ship (A). Edinburgh, 1960. (By Sylvia Plath.) Leaflet. $2,000.

WINTER, William. *Poems.* Boston, 1855. Author's first book. $200.

WINTERS, Yvor. *Before Disaster.* Tryon, N.C., 1934. Printed green wraps. $250.

WINTERS, Yvor. *Diadems and Fagots.* Santa Fe (1920). Author's first book. (Translated by Winters.) (50 copies.) $750.

WINTERS, Yvor. *The Immobile Wind.* Evanston (1921). Author's first book other than the translation. Wraps. $750.

WINTERS, Yvor. *The Magpie's Shadow.* Chicago, 1922. Printed blue wraps. $400.

WINTERS, Yvor. *The Proof.* New York, 1930. $250.

WINTERSON, Jeanette. *Boating for Beginners.* (London, 1985.) Cloth. $600. Wraps. $150.

WINTERSON, Jeanette. *Fit for the Future.* London (1986). Cloth. $350. Wraps. $75.

WINTERSON, Jeanette. *Oranges Are Not the Only Fruit.* London (1985). Author's first book. Wraps. $450. New York (1987). Wraps with $6.95 price. States "First American Edition, September, 1987." $150.

WIRT, Mrs. E. W. *Flora's Dictionary.* Baltimore (after 1837). 2 color titles and 56 hand-colored plates. In original morocco. $6,000. Baltimore (1855). $4,500.

WISE, George. *Campaigns and Battles of the Army of Northern Virginia.* New York, 1916. 2 portraits. $400.

WISE, John. *A System of Aeronautics* . . . Philadelphia, 1850. Portrait and 12 plates. Cloth or half leather. $1,750.

WISE, Kelly. *Lotte Jacobi.* Danbury, N.H. (1978). Profusely illustrated with photos, mostly portraits. One of 125 signed copies with an original photograph, signed by Jacobi, laid in. Beige linen stamped in brown. Housed in a folding cloth box with brown leather label. $650. Trade. $150.

WISE, Thomas J. *The Ashley Library* . . . London, 1922–36. 11 vols. One of 200 copies. $1,250. One of 50 copies. $2,500.

WISLIZENUS, Frederick A. *A Journey to the Rocky Mountains in the Year 1839.* St. Louis, 1912. Folding map. First edition in English. One of 500 copies. $300.

WISLIZENUS, Frederick A. *Memoir of a Tour to Northern Mexico* . . . Washington, 1848. 2 folding maps and a folding profile. Boards. $750.

WISTAR, Caspar. *A System of Anatomy for the Use of Students of Medicine.* Philadelphia, 1811–14. 2 vols. Large folding table. $750.

WISTAR, Isaac Jones. *Autobiography of Isaac Jones Wistar, 1827–1905.* Philadelphia, 1914. 2 vols. Folding map, portrait, plates. Boards and cloth, leather spine labels. One of 250 copies. $600.

WISTER, Owen. *The Lady of the Lake.* (Cambridge) 1881. Author's first book. (Chorus book.) $400.

WISTER, Owen. *Members of the Family.* New York, 1911. $250.

WISTER, Owen. *The New Swiss Family Robinson.* (Cambridge, 1882.) $1,000.

WISTER, Owen. *The Virginian.* New York, 1902. Yellow pictorial cloth. $600. New York, 1911. Illustrated by Frederick Remington and Charles M. Russell. Boards. One of 100 signed copies. $3,000. Limited Editions Club, Los Angeles, 1951. In slipcase. $100.

WITHER, George. *A Collection of Emblemes, Ancient and Moderne* . . . London, 1635–34. 4 parts in 1 vol. Engraved frontispiece portrait, and 200 emblematic illustrations. $2,500.

WITHERING, William. *An Account of the Foxglove, And Some of Its Medical Uses* . . . Birmingham, 1785. Folding hand-colored plate. $7,500. London, 1949. One of 250 copies. $300.

WITHERS, Alexander S. *Chronicles of Border Warfare* . . . Clarksburg, Va., 1831. $750.

WITTMAN, William. *Travels in Turkey, Asia-Minor, Syria* . . . London, 1803. Folding frontis, folding map, folding plate of Firman and 21 plates (16 hand-colored). $3,500.

WODEHOUSE, P. G. *Big Money.* Garden City, 1931. $600. London (1931). Orange cloth, black letters. $1,000.

WODEHOUSE, P. G. *Carry On, Jeeves!* London, 1925. 13 titles on half-title verso ending with *The Coming of Bill.* $1,250. New York (1927) $1,000.

WODEHOUSE, P. G. *A Gentleman of Leisure.* London, 1910. Royal-blue cloth lettered in gold. (First U.K. edition of *Intrusion of Jimmy.*) $1,500.

WODEHOUSE, P. G. *The Globe By the Way Book.* London (1908). Vermilion pictorial wraps. $10,000.

WODEHOUSE, P. G. *The Intrusion of Jimmy.* New York (1910). "Published May" on copyright page. Bound in black, lettered in gold with circular color portrait pasted on. $750. For U.K. edition, see *A Gentleman of Leisure* above.

WODEHOUSE, P. G. *The Little Nugget.* London (1913). Bound in red cloth. 2 sets of advertisements dated May and Autumn 1913. $1,500. New York (1914). "Published January" beneath copyright notice. $750.

WODEHOUSE, P. G. *Love Among the Chickens.* London (1906). Tan pictorial cloth with frontis and 3 illustrations by H. M. Brock. $6,000. Later ads. "August 1905" on copyright page. $2,000. New York, 1909. Some copies have paged tipped in after half title "This Advance Copy No. –," which seems more common than the regular issue (7 copies of this catalogued in recent years vs. one of other). $1,000. London, 1921. List on half-title verso ends with *Indiscretions of Archie.* "Entirely rewritten . . ." on title page. In dustwrapper. $2,000. Without dustwrapper. $600.

WODEHOUSE, P. G. *The Man with Two Left Feet.* London (1917). $2,500. New York: A. L. Burt Co., 1933. Burt is normally a reprint house but this is the first U.S. edition. "First edition" on copyright page. $1,750.

WODEHOUSE, P. G. *Mike.* London, 1909. Olive-green cloth, frontispiece and 11 illustrations by T. M. R. Whitwell. $4,000.

WODEHOUSE, P. G. *Not George Washington.* London, 1907. Written with H. Westbrook. Eight small circles under title on cover and "Cassell & Company" on spine and "9–1907" between pages 96–97. $4,500. Publisher's name on spine reads "Cassell" only. No number on pages 96–97. Seven small circles on cover. $3,000. New York (1980). $100.

WODEHOUSE, P. G. *The Pothunters.* London, 1902. Author's first book. No ads. Royal-blue cloth, silver lettering on spine with silver loving cup on front cover and spine. $4,000. Gray-blue pictorial cloth (runners) and 8 pages ads ending with *Mike.* $1,000. Later early printings. $300.

WODEHOUSE, P. G. *A Prefect's Uncle.* London, 1903. Red cloth lettered and decorated in gold, black, lavender, and pink. No advertisements. $3,000.

WODEHOUSE, P. G. *Psmith in the City.* London, 1910. Blue cloth. Frontispiece and 11 illustrations by Whitwell. $2,000.

WODEHOUSE, P. G. *The Swoop.* London, 1909. Wraps. $5,000.

WODEHOUSE, P. G. *Ukridge.* London, 1924. 13 titles on half-title verso beginning with *A Damsel in Distress* and ending with *Leave It to Psmith.* $3,500.

WODEHOUSE, P. G. *Uncle Fred in the Springtime.* Garden City, 1939. $500. London (1939). Dark-red cloth (reissued in orange cloth). $1,000.

WODEHOUSE, P. G. *William Tell Told Again.* London, 1904. Off-white cloth lettered in gilt on spine and front cover, top edge gilt, publisher's monogram on title page. 2 pages of ads. $1,500. Second issue: with 12 pages of ads, including *The White Feather.* $750. Third issue: tan or light brown pictorial cloth, gilt on spine only; 2 pages of ads; and gilt on cover. $650. Variant state in buff boards with black lettering without date on title page and publisher's address on title page. $400.

WODEHOUSE, P. G. *Wodehouse on Golf.* New York, 1940. First edition stated. $450.

WOLF, Edwin, II, and FLEMING, John. *Rosenbach:A Biography.* Cleveland (1960). One of 250 signed copies. In slipcase. $300. Trade. $100.

WOLF, Joseph. *Zoological Sketches . . . Made for the Zoological Society of London . . .* London, 1861, 1867. 2 vols. 2 pictorial titles and 100 mounted colored plates. $22,500.

WOLFE, Humbert. *Cursory Rhymes.* London, 1927. Illustrated by Albert Rutherston. One of 500 signed copies. $125.

WOLFE, Humbert. *The Old Man of Koenigsberg . . .* Holy Well, 1907. Author's first book. $300.

WOLFE, Humbert. *The Uncelestial City.* London, 1930. One of 400 signed copies. $100.

WOLFE, Richard J. *Jacob Bigelow's American Medical Botany, 1817–1821.* (North Hills, 1979.) One of 300. 2 plates (one hand-colored, the other uncolored). $350.

WOLFE, Susan. *The Last Billable Hour.* New York, 1989. Author's first book. $250.

WOLFE, Thomas. See Koch, Frederick H.

WOLFE, Thomas. *America.* (San Mateo, Calif., 1942.) Wraps. Published by the Greenwood Press. First separate edition. One of 150 copies. $350.

WOLFE, Thomas. *The Crisis in Industry.* Chapel Hill, N.C., 1919. 14 pages, printed wraps. Author's first book. $7,500. Hillsborough, 1978. One of 50 copies. $100. One of 250 copies. $50.

WOLFE, Thomas. *The Face of a Nation.* New York, 1939. Johnston states the Scribner dummy had an "A" on copyright page and the first edition had "CL," therefore this title did not follow Scribners' normal method of identifying the first with an "A." $300.

WOLFE, Thomas. *From Death to Morning.* New York, 1935. $450. London (1936). $250.

WOLFE, Thomas. *Gentlemen of the Press.* Chicago (1942). Cloth, paper label. One of 350 copies. Issued without dustwrapper. $300.

WOLFE, Thomas. *The Hills Beyond.* New York (1941). $350.

WOLFE, Thomas. *Look Homeward, Angel.* New York, 1929. Author's first novel. Blue cloth, gilt. In first-state dustwrapper with Wolfe's picture on back. $8,500. Without picture. $2,000. London (1930). First English edition with a few textual changes. $750.

WOLFE, Thomas. *Mannerhouse:A Play in a Prologue and Three Acts.* New York, 1948. One of 500 copies. In dustwrapper and slipcase. $300. Trade. $125.

WOLFE, Thomas. *A Note on Experts: Dexter Vespasian Joyner.* New York, 1939. One of 300 copies. In glassine dustwrapper. $350.

WOLFE, Thomas. *Of Time and the River.* New York, 1935. $600.

WOLFE, Thomas. *The Story of a Novel*. New York, 1936. $300.

WOLFE, Thomas. *To Rupert Brooke*. (Paris), 1948. 4 leaves, printed wraps. One of 100 copies used as a Christmas greeting. $500.

WOLFE, Thomas. *The Web and the Rock*. New York, 1939. $350.

WOLFE, Thomas. *You Can't Go Home Again*. New York (1940). $350. London (1947). First English edition. $150.

WOLFE, Tom. *The Bonfire of the Vanities*. Franklin Center, 1987. $250. New York (1987). One of 250 signed copies. In slipcase. $450. Trade. $60. London, 1988. $100.

WOLFE, Tom. *The Electric Kool-Aid Acid Test*. New York (1968). $600.

WOLFE, Tom. *The Kandy Kolored . . .* New York (1965). Author's first book. $450.

WOLFF, Tobias. *Ugly Rumours*. London, 1975. Author's first book. $1,250.

WOLFF, Tobias. *In the Garden . . .* New York (1981). With dustwrapper priced $14.95. $750. Price clipped with publisher's $10.95 sticker. $200. With dustwrapper priced $10.95. $100. Wraps. $35.

WOLLSTONECRAFT, Mary. *A Vindication of the Rights of Woman*. London, 1792. Octavo. Last page of text has a vol. 1 notation but 1 vol. is all that was published. $8,500. Philadelphia, 1794. $3,000.

WOMAN'S Daring; As Shown by the Testimony of the Rock. Recorded by an Exultant Woman and a Hughmillerated Man. (Annisquam, Mass., 1872.) 24 pages, wraps. (Note: Contains a contribution by Thomas A. Janvier, his first book appearance.) $450.

WONDERFUL Stories of Fuz-Buz the Fly and Mother Grabem the Spider (The). Philadelphia, 1867. (By S. Weir Mitchell.) 9 engraved plates. Half morocco. One of 170 large-paper copies. $850. Trade. Cloth. $250.

WOOD, Arnold. *A Bibliography of "The Complete Angler" of Izaak Walton and Charles Cotton . . .* New York, 1900. One of 120 copies. $500.

WOOD, Charles Erskine Scott. *Imperialism Versus Democracy*. New York, 1899. An offprint from *Pacific Monthly*. Wraps. Author's first book. $150.

WOOD, Harry B. *Golfing Curios and "The Like."* London, 1910. $1,250. One of 150 large-paper copies. $4,000. (Note: auction shows LPC as 1910. Donovan shows 1911. Also there appears to have been an offprint from *Pacific Monthly* in wraps.)

WOOD, Mrs. Henry (Ellen). *East Lynne*. London, 1861. 3 vols. Violet cloth. (presentation binding). One of 12 copies. $6,000. Trade binding in maroon cloth. $3,500. London, 1862. 3 vols. Second edition in violet cloth. $1,750.

WOOD, James H. *The War, Stonewall Jackson, His Campaigns and Battles, The Regiment, as I Saw Them*. Cumberland, Md. (about 1910). $500.

WOOD, John. *Journal of John Wood*. Chillicothe, Ohio, 1852. 76 pages, printed wraps. $7,500 or more. Columbus, Ohio, 1871. 112 pages, printed wraps. Second edition. $3,000.

WOOD, Nicholas. *A Practical Treatise on Rail-Roads* . . . London, 1825. 6 folding plates. $1,250. Philadelphia, 1832. 9 folding plates. $1,000. London, 1838. 13 folding plates. $1,000.

WOOD, R. E. *Life and Confessions of James Gilbert Jenkins: The Murderer of 18 Men.* Napa City, Calif. 1864. Illustrated. 56 pages, wraps. $750.

WOOD, Silas. *A Sketch of the First Settlement of the Several Towns on Long Island.* Brooklyn, 1824. One of 250 copies. $600. Brooklyn, 1826. One of 100 copies. $600. Brooklyn, 1828. One of 100 copies. $500. Brooklyn, 1865. With additions. One of 200 copies. $300. One of 50 copies. $450.

WOOD, Ted. *Dead in the Water.* Toronto, 1983. Author's first book. $250. New York, 1983. $75.

WOOD, William. *Zoography, or the Beauties of Nature Displayed.* London, 1807. 3 vols. Aquatint plates by William Daniell. $1,250.

WOOD and the Graver (The). The Work of Fritz Eichenberg. New York, 1977. One of 500 signed copies. Signed woodcut in pocket mounted on the back inside cover. $300.

WOODBERRY, George Edward. *History of Wood Engraving.* New York, 1883. $125.

WOODBERRY, George Edward. *The Relations of Pallas Athene to Athens.* Private printing, 1877? Author's first book. Wraps. $300.

WOODMAN, David, Jr. *Guide to Texas Emigrants.* Boston, 1835. Map, plate. $32,000 at auction in 1999.

WOODRUFF, W. E. *With the Light Guns in '61–'65.* Little Rock, 1903. $600.

WOODS, Daniel B. *Sixteen Months at the Gold Diggings.* New York, 1851. $750. London, no date [1851]. 8 pages ads. $450.

WOODS, John. *Two Years' Residence . . . on the English Prairie, in the Illinois Country.* London, 1822. 2 maps and plan. $1,500.

WOODS, Stuart. *Chiefs.* New York, 1981. Author's first book. $300.

WOODTHORPE, R. C. *Death in a Little Town.* New York, 1935. $350.

WOODWORTH, Samuel. *The Champions of Freedom* . . . New York: Charles N. Baldwin, 1816. 2 vols. $1,250.

WOOLF, Leonard. See Bunin, I. A.

WOOLF, Leonard. *Stories of the East.* Hogarth Press. Richmond, England, 1921. Buff wraps. $600.

WOOLF, Leonard. *The Village in the Jungle.* London, 1913. Author's first book. Blue cloth. $500. London, 1931. First Hogarth Press edition. $250.

WOOLF, Virginia. See Cameron, Julia M.

WOOLF, Virginia. *Beau Brummell.* New York, 1930. Boards and cloth. One of 550 signed copies. In glassine dustwrapper and slipcase. $1,500.

WOOLF, Virginia. *Between the Acts.* Hogarth Press. London, 1941. $600. New York (1941). $300.

WOOLF, Virginia. *The Common Reader.* Hogarth Press. London, 1925. White boards with gray cloth spine. $1,750. With gray cloth boards. $1,250. New York (1925). $750. London, 1932. *The Common Reader: Second Series.* $600. New York (1932). *The Second Common Reader.* $250. New York, 1948. First and second series in 1 vol. First American edition thus. Blue cloth. $200.

WOOLF, Virginia. *Flush: A Biography.* Hogarth Press. London, 1933. Illustrated by Vanessa Bell. Buff cloth. "Large-paper Edition" on dustwrapper. $500.

WOOLF, Virginia. *Hours in a Library.* New York (1958). Frontispiece. Boards and cloth. $150.

WOOLF, Virginia. *Jacob's Room.* Hogarth Press. Richmond, 1922. Yellow cloth. $7,500. One of about 40 signed copies, with subscriber's list. $12,500. New York (1923). $3,000.

WOOLF, Virginia. *Kew Gardens.* Hogarth Press. Richmond, 1919. Woodcut by Vanessa Bell. Wraps. $7,500. "Second edition," $2,500. London (1927). Hogarth Press. Boards. One of 500 copies. In cellophane dustwrapper. $1,750. Some signed by Woof and Bell. $2,500.

WOOLF, Virginia. *The Mark on the Wall.* (Cover title, no title page.) Richmond, 1919. White wraps. "Second edition" (actually first separate edition, having previously appeared in *Two Stories,* published jointly with her husband, Leonard Woolf). $2,250.

WOOLF, Virginia. *Mr. Bennett and Mrs. Brown.* Hogarth Press. London, 1924. White wraps. $350.

WOOLF, Virginia. *Mrs. Dalloway.* London, 1925. $15,000. New York, 1925. $3,500.

WOOLF, Virginia. *Monday or Tuesday.* Hogarth Press. Richmond, 1921. Woodcuts by Vanessa Bell. Decorated boards and cloth. (Issued without dustwrapper.) $2,500. New York, 1921. Cloth spine and boards. $1,500. Full cloth. (Catalogued as first issue. However, Kirkpatrick says it is a variant.) $1,750.

WOOLF, Virginia. *Night and Day.* London, 1919. $1,500. In dustwrapper. $6,000. New York, 1920. In dustwrapper. $2,500.

WOOLF, Virginia. *On Being Ill.* Hogarth Press. (London), 1930. Vellum and cloth. One of 250 signed copies (with a rule through "125" and "250" above). In dustwrapper. $3,500. With "250" printed. $3,000.

WOOLF, Virginia. *Orlando: A Biography.* New York, 1928. One of 861 signed copies. Issued without dustwrapper. $2,500. Half morocco. One of 11 copies on green paper. In slipcase. $7,500. Hogarth Press. London, 1928. First English edition, presumed first issue (possibly advance), brown cloth. $1,000. Orange cloth. $600. New York (1928). $350.

WOOLF, Virginia. *A Room of One's Own.* Fountain Press. New York and Hogarth Press London, 1929. One of 492 signed copies. Of this edition, 100 were reserved for Great Britain and issued in pink dustwrapper. $10,000. Without dustwrapper. $7,500. Trade. London, 1929. $2,500.

WOOLF, Virginia. *Street Haunting.* Grabhorn Press. San Francisco, 1930. Boards and blue or green morocco. One of 500 signed copies. In slipcase. $4,000. (Also purple, but possibly a trial binding.)

WOOLF, Virginia. *Three Guineas.* London, 1938. 5 plates. Yellow cloth. $750. New York (1938). $400.

WOOLF, Virginia. *To the Lighthouse.* Hogarth Press. London, 1927. $20,000. New York (1927). $4,000.

WOOLF, Virginia. *The Voyage Out.* London, 1915. Author's first book. Green cloth. $2,000. Red cloth (trial binding?). $2,500. New York, 1920. First American edition with text revised by Woolf. In dustwrapper. $2,500. London (1920). $2,500. New York: Harcourt (1926). $750. London, 1929. $400.

WOOLF, Virginia. *The Waves.* Hogarth Press. London, 1931. $2,500. New York (1931). $750.

WOOLF, Virginia. *The Years.* Hogarth Press. London, 1937. $1,750. New York (1937). $450.

WOOLF, Virginia, and WOOLF, L. S. *Two Stories.* Hogarth Press. Richmond, 1917. Wraps or paper-backed cloth. First book of the Hogarth Press. $12,500.

WOOLLCOTT, Alexander. *While Rome Burns.* New York, 1934. One of 500 signed copies. In glassine dustwrapper. $350.

WOOLMAN, John. *The Works of John Woolman in Two Parts.* Philadelphia, 1774. $750.

WOOLNER, Thomas. *My Beautiful Lady.* London, 1863. Author's first book. $450.

WOOLNOUGH, C. W. *The Whole Art of Marbling as Applied to Paper, Book-Edges, Etc.* London, 1881. Contains 54 examples of marbled paper. $2,250.

WOOLRICH, Cornell. See Irish, William.

WOOLRICH, Cornell. *After Dinner Story.* New York (1944). $1,250.

WOOLRICH, Cornell. *The Black Angel.* Garden City, 1943. $1,750.

WOOLRICH, Cornell. *The Black Curtain.* New York, 1941. $2,500.

WOOLRICH, Cornell. *The Bride Wore Black.* New York, 1940. $2,500.

WOOLRICH, Cornell. *Cover Charge.* New York, 1926. Author's first book. $3,000.

WOOLRICH, Cornell. *Dead Man Blues.* Philadelphia, 1948. $750.

WOOLRICH, Cornell. *Manhattan Love Song.* New York, 1932. $1,250.

WOOLWORTH, James M. *Nebraska in 1857.* Omaha, 1857. Colored folding map. Printed cloth. $3,000.

WOOTEN, Dudley G. (editor). *A Comprehensive History of Texas, 1865 to 1897.* Dallas, 1898. 2 vols. 23 plates. Leather. $1,250.

WORDSWORTH, William. See *Kendal and Windermere Railway . . . ; Lyrical Ballads; Ode Performed in the Senate House.*

WORDSWORTH, William. *An Evening Walk.* London, 1793. Author's first book. $60,000.

WORDSWORTH, William. *The Excursion, Being a Portion of the Recluse, a Poem.* London, 1814. $8,500.

WORDSWORTH, William. *Memorials of a Tour on the Continent, 1820.* London, 1822. $1,000.

WORDSWORTH, William. *Ode on the Intimations of Immortality . . .* Essex House Press. London, 1903. Colored frontispiece by Walter Crane. One of 150 copies on vellum. $1,250.

WORDSWORTH, William. *Poems.* London, 1807. 2 vols. First edition, first issue, with period after "Sonnets" on page (103) of vol. 1 and "fnuction" on page 98 of vol. 2. $4,500. London (1902). Vale Press. 6 woodcuts. White buckram. One of 310 copies. $600.

WORDSWORTH, William. *The Prelude, or Growth of a Poet's Mind: An Autobiographical Poem.* London, 1850. Dark-red cloth. $600. London, 1915. Doves Press. Vellum. One of 155 copies. $1,500. One of 10 copies on vellum. $10,000.

WORDSWORTH, William. *The White Doe of Rylstone.* London, 1815. Frontispiece. $1,000.

WORDSWORTH, William. *Yarrow Revisited, and Other Poems.* London, 1835. In original drab boards, paper label on spine, or cloth. With inserted errata slip. $1,250.

WORK, John. See Lewis, W. S., and Phillips, P. C.

WORKMAN, Fanny Bullock, and HUNTER, William. *Peaks and Glaciers of Nun Kun.* London, 1909. Folding map and 91 plates. $2,500.

WOUK, Herman. *Aurora Dawn.* New York, 1947. First edition not stated. $250. (Note: large Book-of-the-Month Club printing with dot on back.) London, 1947. $125.

WOUK, Herman. *The Caine Mutiny.* Garden City, 1951. $2,000.

WOUK, Herman. *The Man in the Trench Coat.* New York (1941). Author's first book. Wraps. $1,500.

The Wreck of the "Grosvenor." London, 1877. (By W. Clark Russell.) 3 vols. $2,000.

WREN, P.C. *Beau Geste.* London (1927). One of 1,000 signed copies. $750.

WRIGHT, Andrew. *Court Hand Restored; Or, The Student's Assistant in Reading Old Deeds, Charters . . .* London, 1776. 20 engraved plates. $500.

WRIGHT, Austin Tappan. *Islandia.* New York (1942). Author's first and only book. Beige buckram. In dustwrapper. With Basil Davenport prospectus *An Introduction to Islandia,* in white boards without dustwrapper. The two: $450.

WRIGHT, Charles. *The Dream Animal.* Toronto, 1968. Author's first book. Issued without a dustwrapper. $250. Wraps. $50.

WRIGHT, E. W. (editor). *Lewis and Dryden's Marine History of the Pacific Northwest . . .* Portland, 1895. Plates. Morocco. $750. New York, 1961. $250.

WRIGHT, Frank Lloyd. See Gannet(t), William C.; and Wijdeveld, H. T.

WRIGHT, Frank Lloyd. *An Autobiography.* New York, 1932. In dustwrapper. $750. New York (1943). Oblong. Second edition. In dustwrapper. $500.

WRIGHT, Frank Lloyd. *Buildings, Plans and Designs.* New York (1963). 100 plates, loose in half-cloth portfolio. $1,750.

WRIGHT, Frank Lloyd. *The Disappearing City.* New York, 1932. Illustrated. Green cloth, with black map design. First edition, first binding. In dustwrapper. $600. Second binding in blue cloth, map label on cover. $500.

WRIGHT, Frank Lloyd. *Drawings for a Living Architecture.* New York, 1959. 200 drawings by the author (75 colored). Oblong folio, cloth. In dustwrapper. $1,250.

WRIGHT, Frank Lloyd. *The Early Work.* New York, 1968. 207 photos and plans. Folio. In slipcase. $200.

WRIGHT, Frank Lloyd. *The Future of Architecture.* New York, 1953. $300.

WRIGHT, Frank Lloyd. *Genius and the Mobocracy.* New York (1949). Illustrated by Louis H. Sullivan. In dustwrapper. $350.

WRIGHT, Frank Lloyd. *The Industrial Revolution Runs Away.* New York (1969). One of 1,250 copies. In slipcase. $350.

WRIGHT, Frank Lloyd. *The Japanese Print.* Chicago, 1912. Illustrated. Orange wraps. First edition (suppressed). $5,000. (All except about 50 burned by the publisher when Wright protested the binding.) First published edition. Printed boards. One of 35 copies on vellum. $4,000. Trade. $2,000. New York (1967). In slipcase. $300.

WRIGHT, Frank Lloyd. *The Life-Work of the American Architect . . .* Santpoort (Holland), 1925– (26). With contributions by Wright, an introduction by H. Th. Wijdeveld and many articles by famous European architects and American writers. 7 parts in one vol. The Wendingen Edition, with the sheets printed on one side. $1,750. Chicago, 1925. $1,750. New York, Horizon Press, 1965. Introductions by H. Th. Wijdeveld and Mrs. Frank Lloyd Wright. $500.

WRIGHT, Frank Lloyd. *The Living City.* New York, 1958. Folded map in front. $200.

WRIGHT, Frank Lloyd. *Modern Architecture.* Princeton, 1931. Spiral-bound stiff wraps. Issued without dustwrapper. $600.

WRIGHT, Frank Lloyd. *The Natural House.* New York, 1954. $400.

WRIGHT, Frank Lloyd. *Selected Drawings: Portfolio.* New York, 1977–82. 3 vols. $4,500.

WRIGHT, Frank Lloyd. *Studies and Executed Buildings.* (Berlin, 1910.) 2 vols. Oblong folio, cloth. $4,500.

WRIGHT, Harold Bell. *Mine with the Iron Door.* New York, 1923. $150.

WRIGHT, Harold Bell. *When a Man's a Man.* Chicago: Book Supply Co. (1916). $250.

WRIGHT, Harry. *Harry Wright's Pocket Base Ball Score Book, No. 1.* Boston, 1876. $1,500.

WRIGHT, Harry. *Short History of Golf in Mexico.* Privately printed, 1938. Signed limited edition. $400.

WRIGHT, James. *The History and Antiquities of the County of Rutland . . .* London, 1684. Double-page map. $1,250.

WRIGHT, James. *The Branch Will Not Break.* Middletown, Conn. (1963). $250. London, 1963. $200.

WRIGHT, James. *The Green Wall.* New Haven, 1957. Author's first book. Foreword by W. H. Auden. $750.

WRIGHT, Joseph (editor). *The English Dialect Dictionary.* London, 1898–1905. 6 vols. including supplement. $500. 7 vols. including supplement. One of 150 copies on handmade paper. $1,250. London, 1961. 6 vols. $400. New York, 1962. 6 vols. $300.

WRIGHT, Judith. *The Moving Image.* Melbourne (1946). Author's first book. $400.

WRIGHT, Richard. *Black Boy.* New York (1945). "First Edition M-T" stated. With designs on spine in blind. Dustwrapper priced $2.50. $350. (We believe the issue with four designs in gold on spine is a Book-of-the-Month Club edition.) London, 1945. $200.

WRIGHT, Richard. *How "Bigger" Was Born.* (New York, 1940.) Printed wraps. $400.

WRIGHT, Richard. *Native Son.* New York, 1940. First binding in dark-blue cloth, stamped in red. In yellow and green (first) dustwrapper. $2,500. Second binding, gray cloth. In grayish (second) dustwrapper with price. $200. (Book-of-the-Month Club issued this binding stating "First Edition" in unpriced dustwrapper.) New York (1941). (A play.) Written with Paul Green. Front dustwrapper flap with 3 blurbs. $500. Second issue with 7 blurbs. $400. London, 1940. $500.

WRIGHT, Richard. *The Outsider.* New York (1953). $250. London, 1954. $150.

WRIGHT, Richard. *12 Million Black Voices: A Folk History of the Negro in the United States.* New York, 1941. Photographs selected by Edwin Rosskam. $500.

WRIGHT, Richard. *Uncle Tom's Children: Four Novellas.* New York, 1938. Author's first book. $3,000. (See also next entry.) London, 1939. $1,000.

WRIGHT, Richard. *Uncle Tom's Children: Five Long Stories.* New York (1938). First edition not stated. "G-P" on copyright page. Enlarged edition of first book. $1,000.

WRIGHT, Richard B. *Andrew Tolliver.* Toronto, 1965. Author's first book. $150.

WRIGHT, Robert M. *Dodge City, the Cowboy Capital* . . . (Wichita, 1913.) Colored frontispiece, 40 plates. With 344 pages. $400. Second edition, same place and date, 342 pages, black-and-white portrait. $300.

WRIGHT, S. Fowler. *The Amphibians.* London (1925). Author's first book. $350.

WRIGHT, Sarah E. *Give Me a Child.* (Written with Lucy Smith.) Philadelphia (1955). Author's first book. Wraps. $250.

WRIGHT, Thomas. *A History of Domestic Manners* . . . London, 1862. $400.

WRIGHT, Willard Huntington. See Van Dine, S.S.

WRIGHT, Willard Huntington. *Songs of Youth.* New York, 1913. Author's first book. $500.

WRIGHT, William. See De Quille, Dan.

WRIGHT, William. *The Oil Regions of Pennsylvania.* New York, 1865. $400.

WROTH, Lawrence C. *The Colonial Printer.* New York, 1931. One of 300 copies. $250. Portland, 1938. One of 1,500 copies. Slipcase. $200.

WROTH, Lawrence C. *The Early Cartography of the Pacific.* New York, 1934. Folding facsimile maps. One of 100 copies. Issued without dustwrapper. $450.

WYANDOTTE; or The Hutted Knoll. London, 1843. 3 vols. (By James Fenimore Cooper.) In original boards. $2,000. Philadelphia, 1843. 2 vols. First American edition. Wraps. $1,000.

WYATT, M. D., and TYMMS, William Robert. *The Art of Illuminating.* London, 1860. Illustrated. Decorated brown cloth, or morocco. $450.

WYETH, Andrew. See Meryman, Richard.

WYETH, Andrew. *Four Seasons.* New York (1963). Preface by Lloyd Goodrich. 12 reproductions. Folio. Cloth. Boxed. $450. One of 500 copies. In portfolio. $2,000.

WYETH, John A. *Life of Gen. Nathan Bedford Forrest.* New York, 1899. (By Nathan B. Forrest.) 55 plates, maps. $450.

WYETH, John B. *Oregon; or A Short History of a Long Journey.* Cambridge, Mass., 1833. 87 pages. First issue, with half title. $8,500.

WYLIE, Elinor. See *Incidental Numbers.*

WYLIE, Elinor. *Angels and Earthly Creatures: A Sequence of Sonnets.* Henley on Thames, 1928. Decorated wraps. One of 51 copies. About half of this edition were signed, the rest left unsigned at the author's death. In dustwrapper, signed. $1,000. Unsigned. $350. New York, 1929. First American edition (and first commercially published). Portrait. Black cloth. One of 200 copies. In slipcase. $200. Trade. $125.

WYLIE, Elinor. *Mr. Hodge & Mr. Hazard.* New York, 1928. One of 145 signed copies. In slipcase. $250.

WYLIE, Elinor. *Nets to Catch the Wind.* New York, 1921. (First book under her name.) First issue, on unwatermarked paper. In dustwrapper. $250. London, 1928. $125.

WYLIE, Elinor. *The Orphan Angel.* New York, 1926. One of 160 signed copies on rag paper. In slipcase. $300. One of 30 signed copies on vellum. In slipcase. $600.

WYLIE, Philip. *Heavy Laden.* New York, 1928. Author's first book. $300.

WYNDHAM, John. See Beynon, John.

WYNDHAM, John. *The Day of the Triffids.* New York, 1951. (By John Beynon Harris.) $600. London (1951). First English edition containing revisions. $650.

WYSS, Johann David. See *The Family Robinson Crusoe; The Swiss Family Robinson.*

X

XENOS, Stefanos. *East and West: A Diplomatic History of the Annexation History of the Annexation of the Ionian Islands to the Kingdom of Greece*. London, 1865. $600.

Y

YABE, Yae K. *A Course of Instruction in Jiu-Jitsu*. London, 1904. $125.

YARRELL, William. *A History of British Birds*. London, 1843. 3 vols. Octavo. $600.

YATES, Edmund Hodgson. *My Haunts and Their Frequenters*. London, 1854. Author's first book. Illustrated. Wraps. $200.

YATES, Richard. *Eleven Kinds of Loneliness*. Boston (1962). $250.

YATES, Richard. *Revolutionary Road*. Boston (1961). Author's first book. $450. (London, 1962.) $125.

YATES, William Holt. *The Modern History & Condition of Egypt*. London, 1843. 2 vols. 2 folding maps. $750.

YE Minutes of Ye CLXXVIIth Meeting of Ye Sette of Odd Volumes. Ashendene Press. (London, 1896.) Transcribed by John Todhunter. Printed wraps. One of 154 copies. $750.

YEARY, Mamie. *Reminiscences of the Boys in Gray, 1861–1865*. Dallas, 1912. $1,000.

Note: All Dun Emer/Cuala Press books were issued in glassine, tissue, or unprinted plain paper dustwrappers. The prices below assume the copies do not have these. If present and in perfect condition, we would expect something could be added to the prices but do not think it would be much.

YEATS, John Butler. *Early Memories*. Dundrum, Ireland: Cuala Press, 1923. Preface by W.B. Yeats. Boards and linen. One of 500 copies. $350.

YEATS, John Butler. *Further Letters*. Dundrum: Cuala Press, 1920. Selected by Lennox Robinson. Boards and linen. One of 400 copies. $250.

YEATS, John Butler. *James Flaunty*. London (1901). Author's first book. Wraps. $400.

YEATS, John Butler. *La la Noo*. Dublin: Cuala Press, 1943. Boards and linen. One of 250 copies. $350.

YEATS, John Butler. *Passages from the Letters of John Butler Yeats*. Dundrum: Cuala Press, 1917. Selected by Ezra Pound. Boards and linen. One of 400 copies. $500.

YEATS, William Butler. See Allingham, William; Bax, Clifford; Dunsany, Lord; Ganconagh; Gogarty, Oliver St. John.

YEATS, William Butler. *The Bounty of Sweden.* Dublin: Cuala Press, 1925. Boards and linen. One of 400 copies. $300.

YEATS, William Butler. *The Cat and the Moon and Certain Poems.* Dublin: Cuala Press, 1924. Boards and linen. One of 500 copies. $400.

YEATS, William Butler. *Cathleen ni Houlihan.* London: Caradoc Press, 1902. One of 8 copies on Japan vellum. Silk ties. $7,500. First regular edition. Cream-colored boards, leather spine. (300 copies.) $1,000.

YEATS, William Butler. *The Celtic Twilight.* London, 1893. Olive-green cloth. First binding, with publisher's name on spine in capital letters. $1,000. Later binding, capitals and lower-case lettering. $350. New York, 1894. First American issue (English sheets). $500.

YEATS, William Butler. *The Countess Kathleen.* London, 1892. Frontispiece. Japan vellum boards. One of 30 copies signed by the publisher. $4,500. Dark-green boards, parchment spine. One of 500 copies. $750. Boston, 1892. $600. London, 1912. Wraps. Revised edition. $200.

YEATS, William Butler. *The Cutting of an Agate.* New York, 1912. $400. London, 1919. First English edition. Dark-blue cloth. In dustwrapper. $750.

YEATS, William Butler. *The Death of Synge . . .* Dublin: Cuala, 1928. Original printed boards, cloth backstrip, printed paper label. One of 400 copies. $400.

YEATS, William Butler. *Early Poems and Stories.* London, 1925. $350. New York, 1925. First American edition. One of 250 signed copies. In slipcase. $1,250. Trade. $300.

YEATS, William Butler. *Eight Poems.* London: Morland Press (1916). Folio, wraps. One of 8 copies on Dutch paper. $750. One of 70 copies on Japan vellum. $600. One of 122 copies on Italian paper. $500. Limitations are fictitious; numerous subvariants within each issue.

YEATS, William Butler. *Essays.* London, 1924. $450. New York, 1924. $300. Boards and cloth. One of 250 signed copies. $1,250.

YEATS, William Butler. *The Golden Helmet.* New York, 1908. Gray boards. One of 50 copies. $5,000.

YEATS, William Butler. *The Hour Glass.* London, 1903. (12 copies issued for copyright; without covers.) $7,500. New York, 1904. Adds other plays. Blue cloth. $400. Parchment. One of 100 copies on Japan vellum. $1,750. (Dublin): Cuala Press (1914). Gray wraps. (50 copies.) $3,000.

YEATS, William Butler. *Ideas of Good and Evil.* London, 1903. Green boards and cloth. $300. New York, 1903. English sheets. $200. Dublin, 1905. Sheets of second London edition. $150.

YEATS, William Butler. *In the Seven Woods.* Dundrum: Dun Emer Press, 1903. Printed in red and black. Linen. One of 325 copies. $1,000. (First book from the Dun Emer Press.) New York/London, 1903. $250.

YEATS, William Butler. *The King's Threshold.* New York, 1904. Gray boards. One of 100 copies. $1,500. (Many, but not all, signed. $2,500.) London, 1904. With other plays. $350.

YEATS, William Butler. *The Land of Heart's Desire.* London, 1894. Wraps. First edition, presumed first state without the two fleurons after the word "Desire" on front cover. $1,500.

Chicago, 1814 (actually 1894). First American edition. Boards. One of 450 copies. $500. Portland, Me., 1903. Revised. Boards. One of 100 copies on Japan paper. $750. One of 10 copies on vellum, signed by T. B. Mosher as publisher. $3,500.

YEATS, William Butler. *Michael Robartes and the Dancer.* Dundrum: Cuala Press, 1920. Printed in red and black. Boards and linen. One of 400 copies. $450.

YEATS, William Butler. *Modern Poetry.* London, 1936. Bright green wraps. One of 1,000 copies. $300.

YEATS, William Butler. *Mosada: A Dramatic Poem.* Dublin, 1886. Author's first book. Brown wraps. $85,000. Dublin: Cuala Press, 1943. Cream-colored parchment wraps. One of 50 copies. In dustwrapper. $2,500. (Note: This poem was first published in the *Dublin University Review,* June, 1886, vol. 2, no. 6, original decorated wraps. $1,500.)

YEATS, William Butler. *On the Boiler.* Dublin: Cuala Press (1939). Pictorial blue-green wraps. Second edition. (All but 4 copies of the first edition were destroyed.) $150.

YEATS, William Butler. *A Packet for Ezra Pound.* Dublin: Cuala Press, MCMXXVIV (but 1929). Boards and linen. Issued without dustwrapper. One of 425 copies. $750.

YEATS, William Butler. *The Player Queen.* London, 1922. Wraps. $200.

YEATS, William Butler. *Plays and Controversies.* London, 1923. $500. New York, 1924. Boards and cloth. Issued without dustwrapper. One of 250 signed copies. In slipcase. $850.

YEATS, William Butler. *Plays for an Irish Theatre.* London, 1911. First issue, with dark-brown (later white) endpapers. $400.

YEATS, William Butler. *Poems.* London, 1895. Light-brown cloth. One of 25 copies printed on Japan vellum, signed by Yeats. $10,000. Trade. 750 copies. $750. American issue with Boston imprint of Copeland & Day added to title page. $750. London, 1899. Dark-blue cloth. Second English edition. $500. London, 1901. Dark-blue cloth. Third English edition. $350. London, 1904. Fourth English edition. $200. London, 1949. 2 vols. Definitive edition. Olive-green cloth. One of 375 signed copies. In slipcase. $4,500.

YEATS, William Butler. *Poems.* Dublin: Cuala Press, 1935. Blue wraps. One of 30 copies with only 9 poems. Made up as a gift edition. $4,500.

YEATS, William Butler. *Poems Written in Discouragement, 1912–1913.* Dundrum: Cuala Press, 1913. Dark-gray wraps, stitched with red cord. One of 50 copies. $4,000.

YEATS, William Butler. *Responsibilities and Other Poems.* London, 1916. $300. New York, 1916. Gray boards and cloth. $250.

YEATS, William Butler. *Reveries over Childhood and Youth.* Dundrum: Cuala Press, 1915. 2 vols. including a blue board portfolio containing a colored plate and 2 portraits. Gray boards and linen. One of 425 copies. $750. New York, 1916. First American edition. $200. London, 1916. Dark-blue cloth. $300.

YEATS, William Butler. *The Secret Rose.* London, 1897. Illustrated by John Butler Yeats. Dark-blue cloth. First binding, with "Lawrence & Bullen" on spine. $600. New York, 1897. English sheets. $500. Dublin, 1905. English sheets with cancel title. $500.

YEATS, William Butler. *The Singing Head and the Lady.* (Bryn Mawr, Pa.), 1934. Decorated wraps. One of 2 or 3 copies signed by Yeats from an edition of 20 on different papers. $6,000. Unsigned. $2,500.

YEATS, William Butler. *Stories of Red Hanrahan.* Dundrum: Dun Emer Press, 1904. Blue boards and linen. One of 500 copies. $400.

YEATS, William Butler. *The Tables of the Law. The Adoration of the Magi.* (London), 1897. Portrait frontispiece. Buckram. One of 110 copies. $2,500. London, 1904. First unlimited edition. Blue-gray boards. $350. Green cloth. $250. Wraps. $200. Stratford-on-Avon: Shakespeare Head Press, 1914. Second limited edition. One of 510 copies. $150.

YEATS, William Butler. *The Tower.* London, 1928. Pictorial cloth. $2,000. New York, 1928. First American edition. Green cloth. $750.

YEATS, William Butler. *The Trembling of the Veil.* London, 1922. Portrait. Blue boards and parchment. One of 1,000 signed copies. In dustwrapper. $1,250.

YEATS, William Butler. *The Variorum Edition of the Poems of William Butler Yeats.* New York, 1957. Buckram. One of 825 signed copies. In slipcase. $2,000.

YEATS, William Butler. *A Vision.* London, 1925. Blue boards. One of 600 signed copies. In dustwrapper. $1,500. London, 1937. (Revised.) $250.

YEATS, William Butler. *The Wanderings of Oisin and Other Poems.* London, 1889. Author's first regularly published hardbound book. First binding in dark-blue cloth. With imprint "Kegan Paul Trench & Co." and blindstamped publisher's device on back cover. (500 copies.) $5,000. Second state of the binding, without the blindstamped device on the back cover, and the imprint at the toe of the spine: "Paul, Trench, Truber & Co." $3,000.

YEATS, William Butler. *The Wind Among the Reeds.* London, 1899. Dark-blue cloth. First issue, without correction slip. $1,000. Second issue, same date, with correction slip. $750. Deluxe binding (full gilt vellum). $7,500.

YEATS, William Butler. *The Winding Stair.* New York: Fountain Press, 1929. Dark-blue cloth. One of 642 signed copies. In dustwrapper. $1,500. (Another New York edition of 1929, unpublished, bears the imprint of Crosby Gaige with a limitation of 700 copies on handmade paper and 12 copies on green paper. Sheets of this printing have appeared in the market at various times, signed by Yeats. $3,500.) London, 1933. Olive-green cloth. First English edition (with *And Other Poems* added to title). $750. New York, 1933. First American trade edition. $450.

YEATS, William Butler. *Works.* Portraits. Stratford-on-Avon, 1908. 8 vols. Half vellum and cloth. $3,000. Remainder bound in cloth and boards. With frontispieces. $1,250. Without frontispieces. $1,000.

YEATS, William Butler (editor). *Fairy and Folk Tales of the Irish Peasantry.* London, 1888. With errata slip. $600. Deluxe binding in pictorial gilt cloth. $1,500. Later printings drop date from title page.

YEATS, William Butler (editor). *Irish Fairy Tales.* London, 1892. $600.

YEATS, William Butler, and JOHNSON, Lionel. *Poetry and Ireland: Essays.* Cuala Press. Dundrum, 1908. One of 250 copies. $1,000.

YELLOW BIRD. *The Life and Adventures of Joaquin Murieta.* San Francisco, 1854. 2 plates. 90 pages, wraps. (By John R. Ridge.) $60,000 at auction in 1994 in facsimile wraps. (For later editions, see *The Life of Joaquin Murieta.*)

YELLOW *Book (The): An Illustrated Quarterly.* London, 1894–97. 13 vols. In pictorial yellow cloth. $2,000.

YELLOWPLUSH *Correspondence (The).* Philadelphia 1838. (By William Makepeace Thackeray.) In original boards and cloth, paper label. With text starting at page 13. $3,000.

YEMASSEE *(The): A Romance of Carolina.* New York, 1835. (By William Gilmore Simms.) 2 vols. First issue, with copyright notice pasted in vol. 1. $500.

YEOMAN, R. S. *A Guide Book of United States Coins.* Racine, WI, 1946. Illustrated. Red cloth, gilt. $1,000.

YERBY, Frank (Garvin). *The Foxes of Harrow.* New York, 1946. Author's first book. $200. London, 1946. $175.

YOAKUM, Henderson K. *History of Texas.* New York, 1855. 2 vols. Folding document, 4 maps, 5 plates. Cloth. $2,000. New York, 1856. 2 vols. Second edition. $1,000. Austin, 1935. 2 vols. Facsimile edition. $150.

YOKOYAMA, S., and OSHIMA, E. *Judo.* Tokyo, 1915. $150.

YONGE, Charlotte M. See *The History of Sir Thomas Thumb.*

YORE, Clem. *Ranger Bill.* New York, 1931. $200.

YORE, Clem. *Raw Gold.* Garden City, 1926. $150.

YOUNG, Al. *Dancing.* New York (1969). Author's first book. Wraps. One of 50 copies. $100. Trade. $50.

YOUNG, Andrew W. *History of Chautauqua County, New York.* Buffalo, 1875. Half morocco. $200.

YOUNG, Andrew. *Song of Night.* London (1910). Author's first book. $200.

YOUNG, Ansel. *The Western Reserve Almanac for the Year 1844.* Cleveland (1843). 32 pages, wraps. $600.

YOUNG, Arthur. *Travels During the Years 1787, 1788 and 1789 . . .* Bury St. Edmunds, 1792. $1,000. Dublin, 1793. First Dublin edition. $750. London, 1794. $750.

YOUNG, Harry (Sam). *Hard Knocks: A Life Story of the Vanishing West.* Portland, 1915. 25 plates. Boards. $200. Chicago (1915). 18 plates. $175.

YOUNG, John R. *Memoirs.* Salt Lake City, 1920. 4 portraits. $200.

YOUNG *Lady, A.* See Agnes De Castro.

YOUNG, Stark. *The Blind Man at the Window . . .* New York, 1906. Author's first book. $200.

YOUNG, Thomas. *A Course of Lectures . . .* London, 1807. 2 vols. $4,000.

YOUNG, Thomas. *Outlines of Experiments and Inquiries Respecting Sound and Light.* (London), 1800. 5 folding plates. Offprint of Young's first important published work on sound and light. $5,000.

YOUNG, William. *Town and Country Mansions . . .* London, 1879. $500.

YOUNGBLOOD, Charles L. *Adventures of Chas. L. Youngblood During Ten Years on the Plains.* Boonville, Ind., 1882. Portrait. Cloth. $1,500.

YOUNGBLOOD, Charles L. *A Mighty Hunter.* Chicago, 1890. (Second edition of *Adventures . . .*) $200.

YOUNG Duke (The). By the author of *Vivian Grey.* London, 1831. (By Benjamin Disraeli.) 3 vols. $500.

Z

ZAENSDORF, Joseph W. *The Art of Bookbinding.* London, 1880. One of 50 copies. $1,000. Trade. $250.

ZACCARELLI, John. *Zaccarelli's Pictorial Souvenir Book of the Golden Northland.* Dawson (1908). Oblong, wraps. $750.

ZAMORANO 80 (The): A Selection of Distinguished California Books. Los Angeles, 1945. One of 500 copies. In dustwrapper. $400.

ZANGWILL, Israel. *The Bachelor's Club.* London, 1891. Author's first book. $200. New York, 1891. $100.

ZANGWILL, Israel. *The Big Bow Mystery.* London, 1892. Wraps. $1,250. Chicago (1895). $750.

ZANGWILL, Israel. *Children of the Ghetto.* London, 1892. 3 vols. Decorated cloth. $750. Philadelphia, 1892. $100.

ZAPF, Hermann. *Manuale Typographicum . . .* New York, 1968. One of 1,000 signed copies. $750.

ZAPF, Hermann. *Pen and Graver, Alphabets & Pages of Calligraphy.* New York (1952). One of 2,000 copies. $600.

ZAPF, Hermann. *Typographic Variations Designed by Hermann Zapf on Themes in Contemporary Book Design . . .* New York, 1964. One of 500 signed copies. $500.

ZATURENSKA, Marya. *Threshold and Hearth.* New York, 1934. Author's first book. $150.

ZEITLIN, Jake. *For Whispers and Chants.* San Francisco, 1927. Author's first book. (500 copies.) $100. One of 50 signed copies. In slipcase. $125.

ZEITLINGER, Heinrich, and SOTHERAN, Henry Cecil. *Bibliotheca Chemico-Mathematica . . .* London, 1921–1952. 6 vols. (2 vols. of original edition plus the first, second, and third supplements [all done]). $750.

ZELAZNY, Roger. *The Dream Master.* New York (1966). Wraps. $75. London, 1968. $600. Boston, 1976. Issued without dustwrapper. $250.

ZELAZNY, Roger. *Lord of Light.* Garden City, 1967. $1,250. London (1968). $250.

ZELAZNY, Roger. *This Immortal.* New York, 1966. Author's first book. Wraps. $100. London, 1967. First hardback. $600.

ZIMMER, John Todd. *Catalogue of the Edward E. Ayer Ornithological Library.* Chicago, 1926. 2 vols. $450.

ZOGBAUM, Rufus F. *Horse, Foot and Dragoons.* New York, 1888. $250.

ZOLA, Émile. *Assomoir: The Prelude to Nana.* London, 1884. $250.

ZOUCH, Thomas. *The Life of Isaac Walton.* London, 1823. $350.

ZUKOFSKY, Louis. See Reiser, Anton.

ZUKOFSKY, Louis. *"A" 1–12.* (Ashland, Mass.), 1959. With note by W. C. Williams. One of 200 copies. Errata slip laid in. In glassine dustwrapper. $500.

ZUKOFSKY, Louis. *"A"–14.* (London, 1967.) One of 250 signed copies. $175. One of 26 signed copies. $250.

ZUKOFSKY, Louis. *Barely and Widely.* New York, 1958. Oblong, wraps. One of 300 signed copies. $250.

ZUKOFSKY, Louis. *First Half of "A"–9.* New York (1940). Author's first book. Mimeographed. In manila envelope. "First Edition, Limited to 55 Autographed Copies." $2,000.

ZUKOFSKY, Louis. *It Was.* (Kyoto, Japan, 1961.) One of 50 signed copies. $500. One of 200 copies. $250.

ZUKOFSKY, Louis. *Le Style Apollinaire.* Paris, 1934. Author's first book. Wraps. $2,000.

ZUKOFSKY, Louis. *An Unearthing.* (Cambridge, 1965.) Wraps. One of 77 signed copies. $400.

ZUKOFSKY, Louis (editor). *An "Objectivists" Anthology.* (Dijon, France), 1932. Wraps. (Contributors include T. S. Eliot, William Carlos Williams.) $1,500.

APPENDIX A.
SELECTED BIBLIOGRAPHY
OF WORKS CONSULTED

The following is a listing of individual author bibliographies, general bibliographies that include several authors, and our own *Author Price Guides* (which are priced bibliographic checklists and are available from us at 1137 Sugarloaf Mountain Road, Dickerson, MD 20842, or through e-mail at firsts@qb.com). We have broken this section into two areas: "General Bibliographies Consulted" and "Individual Bibliographies Consulted."

The second section ("Individual Bibliographies Consulted") is self-explanatory, except that where the author, press, or subject was included in a general bibliography, we have noted where this information may be found (e.g., under the listing for Malcolm Cowley you will find "see FPAA #4" and know that this information is in volume 4 of *First Printings of American Authors*). The general bibliographies we refer to the most are APG (*Author Price Guides*), BAL (*Bibliography of American Literature*), Currey (*Science Fiction and Fantasy Authors* . . .), FPAA (*First Printings of American Authors*), and Johnson (*American First Editions*). Full bibliographic information for APG, BAL, etc. can be found in the "General Bibliographies Consulted" section.

GENERAL BIBLIOGRAPHIES CONSULTED

Abbey, J. R. *Travel* . . . (2 vols.) | *Scenery* . . . | *Life* . . . San Francisco: Alan Wofsy Fine Arts, 1991.

Adams, Ramon F. *The Rampaging Herd*. Cleveland: (Zubal, 1982).

Adams, Ramon F. *Six-Guns and Saddle Leather*. (Cleveland): Zubal (1982).

Ahearn, Allen and Patricia. *Author Price Guides*. Dickerson, Maryland: Quill & Brush, 1992–99. (APG)

Ahearn, Allen and Patricia. *Collected Books: The Guide to Values*. 1998 Edition. New York: G. P. Putnam's Sons (1998).

American Book Prices Current. New York: Bancroft-Parkman, 1975–98.

Blanck, Jacob. *Bibliography of American Literature*. New Haven: Yale University, 1953–73. (7 vols.). 1990–91 (vols. 8 & 9 edited and completed by Michael Winship). (BAL)

Blanck, Jacob. *Peter Parley to Penrod*. Waltham, Mass.: Mark Press, 1974.

Bleiler, E. F. *The Checklist of Science-Fiction and Supernatural Fiction*. Glen Rock, N.J.: Firebell Books (1978).

Bradley, Van Allen. *The Book Collector's Handbook of Values, 1982–83*. New York: G. P. Putnam's Sons, 1982 (VAB).

Bruccoli, Matthew J.; Clark, C. E. Frazer, Jr.; Layman, Richard; and Franklin, Benjamin V. (editors). *First Printings of American Authors*. 5 vols. Detroit: Gale Research, 1977–89 (FPAA).

CASANOVA Booksellers' Checklists of Twentieth Century Authors. Second Series, Milwaukee: 1933 (Richard Aldington, Martin Armstrong, Aldous Huxley, James Joyce, and Christopher Morley); Third Series, Milwaukee: 1935 (Erskine Caldwell, Frank Harris, Robert Nathan, A. Edward Newton, and Gertrude Stein).

Currey, L. W. *Science Fiction and Fantasy Authors: A Bibliography of First Printings . . .* Boston: G. K. Hall (1979).

Cutler, B. D., and Stiles, Villa. *Modern British Authors*. New York: Greenberg Publisher (1930).

Dykes, Jeff. *Western High Spots*. No place: Northland Press (1977).

Fabes, Gilbert H. *The First Editions of A. E. Coppard, A. P. Herbert and Charles Morgan*. London: Myers & Co. (1933).

Fabes, Gilbert H., and Foyle, William A. *Modern First Editions: Points and Values*. The first, second, and third series. London: W. & G. Foyle Limited, 1929, 1931, and 1932.

Ford, Hugh. *Published in Paris . . .* London: Garnstone Press (1975).

Franklin, Colin. *The Private Presses*. (Chester Springs): Dufour (Editions), (1969).

Gawsworth, John. *Ten Contemporaries: Notes Toward Their Definitive Bibliography*. London: Ernest Benn Ltd. (1932).

Howes, Wright. *U.S. Iana (1650–1950)*. New York: Bowker, 1962.

Hubin, Allen J. *Crime Fiction 1749–1980: A Comprehensive Bibliography*. New York: Garland Publishing, 1984.

Johnson, Merle. *American First Editions*. Revised and Enlarged by Jacob Blanck. Waltham, Mass.: Mark Press, 1969.

Kirkpatrick, D. L., ed. *Twentieth-Century Children's Writers*. 2d ed. New York: St. Martin's Press (1983).

Kirkpatrick, D. L., and Vinson, James, eds. *Contemporary Novelists*. 4th ed. New York: St. Martin's Press (1986).

Kunitz, Stanley J., ed. *Twentieth Century Authors First Supplement: A Biographical Dictionary of Modern Literature*. New York: The H. W. Wilson Co, 1945.

Kunitz, Stanley J., and Haycraft, Howard, eds. *Twentieth Century Authors: A Biographical Dictionary of Modern Literature*. New York: The H. W. Wilson Co., 1942.

Lepper, Gary M. *A Bibliographical Introduction to Seventy-five Modern American Authors*. Berkeley: Serendipity Books, 1976.

McGrath, Ann F., ed. *Bookman's Price Index*. (Vols. 47–51) Detroit: Gale Research (1993–1996).

Morrison, Shelley. *Texana Catalogue Prices: 1994/1995*. Austin: W. M. Morrison Books (1995/1996).

Morrison, Shelley. *Western Americana Catalogue Prices: 1994/1995*. Austin: W. M. Morrison Books (1995/1996).

Phillips, John C. *A Bibliography of American Sporting Books: Sport-Natural History-Hunting-Dogs-Trapping-Shooting-Early American . . .* New York: James Cummins Bookseller, 1991.

Ransom, Will. *Private Presses and Their Books*. New York: Bowker Co., 1929.

Rees, David. *Brian Moore, Alasdair Gray, John McGahern: A Bibliography of Their First Editions*. (London): Colophon Press (1991).

Rees, David. *Bruce Chatwin, Martin Amis, Julian Barnes: A Bibliography of Their First Editions*. (London): Colophon Press (1992).

Rees, David. *Muriel Spark, William Trevor, Ian McEwan: A Bibliography of Their First Editions*. (London): Colophon Press (1992).

Reilly, John M., ed. *Twentieth-Century Crime and Mystery Writers*. 2d ed. New York: St. Martin's Press (1985).

Sadleir, Michael. *XIX Century Fiction*. 2 vols. Cambridge: Maurizio Martino Publisher, no date [reprint of original 1951 edition].

Schwartz, Dr. Jacob. *1100 Obscure Points*. Bristol (England): Chatford House Press (1931).

Smith, Curtis C., ed. *Twentieth-Century Science-Fiction Writers.* New York: St. Martin's Press (1981).
Streeter, Thomas W. *Bibliography of Texas 1795–1845.* Cambridge: Harvard University Press, 1960.
Vinson, James, and Kirkpatrick, D. L., eds. *Contemporary Poets.* 4th ed. New York: St. Martin's Press (1985).
Wagner, Henry R., and Camp, Charles L. *The Plains & the Rockies.* San Francisco: John Howell-Books, 1982.
Work, Monroe N. *A Bibliography of the Negro in Africa and America.* Tuskegee Tuskegee Institute, no date.
Zemple, Edward N., and Linda A. *Book Prices: Used and Rare, 1996.* (Peoria): Spoon River Press (1996).
Zemple, Edward N., and Linda A. *First Editions: A Guide to Identification.* 2d ed. (Peoria): Spoon River Press (1989).

INDIVIDUAL BIBLIOGRAPHIES CONSULTED

(ABBEY) Maxwell,Spencer. *Collecting Abbey: A Checklist of the First Editions of Edward Abbey.* Santa Fe, New Mexico: Vinegar Tom Press (1991).
See also APG.
(ABBEY PRESS) See Ransom.
(ABERCROMBIE) Cooper, Jeffrey. *A Bibliography and Notes on the Works of Lascelles Abercrombie.* (London): Archon Books, 1969.
See also Gawsworth.
(ACE SCIENCE FICTION DOUBLES) Corrick, James A. Brooklyn: 1991.
(ACTON) Ritchie, Neil. *A Bibliography of Harold Acton.* Florence: no publisher, 1934.
(ADAMIC) Christian, Henry A. *Louis Adamic: A Checklist.* No place: Kent State University Press (1971).
(ADAMS, A.) See FPAA #4.
(ADAMS, H.) See BAL #1, and Johnson.
(ADAMS, J. T.) See BAL #4, and FPAA #4.
(ADAMS, L.) See FPAA #4.
(ADAMS, O. F.) See BAL #1.
(ADE) Russo, Dorothy Ritter. *A Bibliography of George Ade, 1866–1944.* Indianapolis: Indiana Historical Society, 1947.
See also FPAA #2, and Johnson.
(AFRICAN-AMERICAN) Saifer. *A Century of Fiction by American Negroes.* 1974.
(AGEE, J.) See APG, and FPAA #1.
(AIKEN) Bonnell, F. W. and F. C. *Conrad Aiken: A Bibliography (1902–1978).* San Marino: Huntington Library, 1982.
See also FPAA #4, and Johnson.
(ALBEE, E.) Green. *Edward Albee: A Bibliography,* 1980.
See also APG, and FPAA #3.
(ALCOTT, A. B.) See BAL #1.
(ALCOTT) Gulliver, Lucille. *Louisa May Alcott: A Bibliography.* Boston: Little Brown, 1932.
See also BAL #1, and Johnson.
(ALDERBRINK PRESS) See Ransom.
(ALDERGATE PRESS) See Ransom.
(ALDINGTON) Kershaw, Alister. *A Bibliography of the Works of Richard Aldington from 1915 to 1948.* London: The Quadrant Press, 1950.
See also Casanova.
(ALDISS, B.) Manson, Margaret. *Brian Aldiss: A Bibliography, 1954–62.* (Birmingham: Dryden Press, 1962.)
See also Currey.

(ALDRICH, T. B.) See BAL #1, and Johnson.
(ALGER) Bennett, Bob. *A Collector's Guide to the Published Works of Horatio Alger, Jr.* Newark: MAD Book Company, 1999.
Gardner, Ralph D. *Road to Success: A Bibliography of the Works of Horatio Alger.* Mendota, Ill.: Wayside Press, 1971.
See Also FPAA #5, and Lepper.
(ALGREN) Bruccoli, Matthew J. *Nelson Algren: A Descriptive Bibliography.* (Pittsburgh): University of Pittsburgh Press, 1985.
See Also APG, FPAA #1, and Lepper.
(ALLEN, E. A.) See BAL #1.
(ALLEN, H.) See Johnson.
(ALLEN, J. L.) See BAL #1, and Johnson.
(ALLEN, P.) See FPAA #4.
(ALLEN, W.) See APG.
(ALLSTON, W.) See BAL #1.
(ALSOP, R.) See FPAA #1.
(ALWIL PRESS) See Ransom.
(AMIS, K.) Gohn, Jack Benoit. *Kingsley Amis: A Checklist.* No place: Kent State University Press, (1976).
(AMIS, M.) See Rees.
(AMMONS, A. R.) See FPAA #1.
(ANDERSON, M.) See FPAA #1.
(ANDERSON, P.) See Currey.
(ANDERSON) Sheehy, Eugene P., and Lohf, Kenneth A. *Sherwood Anderson: A Bibliography.* Los Gatos: Talisman Press, 1960.
See also APG, FPAA #2, and Johnson.
(ANDREWS) Webber, William Hallam. *William Loring Andrews: A Study and Bibliography.* Rockville, Md.: (no publisher) 1980.
See also FPAA #2, and Johnson.
(ANGEL ALLEY PRESS) See Ransom.
(ANOUILH, J.) Kelly. *Jean Anouilh: A Bibliography,* 1973.
(ANTIN, M.) See FPAA #5.
(ANTONINUS, B.) See Everson.
(APPLEDORE PRESS) See Ransom.
(AQUILA PRESS) See Ransom.
(ARGONAUT PRESS) See Ransom.
(ARIES PRESS) See Ransom.
(ARMED SERVICES EDITIONS) Cole, John V. *Books in Action: The Armed Services Editions.* Washington, D.C.: Center for the Book, Library of Congress, 1984.
(ARMSTRONG) See *Casanova.*
(ARNOLD) Smart, Thomas Burnett. *The Bibliography of Matthew Arnold.* Reprinted. New York: Burt Franklin (1968).
(ARNOW, H. S.) See FPAA #2.
(ASHBERY) Kermani, David K. *John Ashbery: A Comprehensive Bibliography.* New York: Garland Publishing, 1976.
See Also FPAA #1 and Lepper.
(ASHENDENE PRESS) See Franklin, and Ransom.
(ASIMOV) Miller, Marjorie M. *Isaac Asimov: A Checklist of Works Published in the United States, March 1939—May 1972.* No place: Kent State University Press (1972).
See also Currey.
(ATHERTON, G.) McClure, Charlotte. *Gertrude Atherton.* Twayne, 1979.
See also Johnson.
(ATTAWAY, W.) See FPAA #2.
(ATWOOD) Horne, Alan J. *A Preliminary Checklist of Writings By and About Margaret Atwood.*

In the *Malahat Review* No. 41. Victoria, British Columbia, Canada: University of Victoria, 1977.
See also APG.
(AUCHINCLOSS, L.) Bryer, Jackson. *Louis Auchincloss and His Critics*, Hall, 1977.
See also FPAA #1, and Lepper.
(AUCHINLECK PRESS) See Ransom.
(AUDEN) Bloomfield, B. C., and Mendelson, Edward. *W. H. Auden: A Bibliography, 1924–1969*. Charlottesville: University of Virginia (1972).
(AUDUBON, J. J.) See FPAA #1, and Johnson.
(AUSTEN) Gilson, David. *A Bibliography of Jane Austen*. Winchester / New Castle: St. Paul's / Oak Knoll, 1997.
Keynes, Geoffrey. *Jane Austen: A Bibliography*. London: Nonesuch Press, 1929.
See also Schwartz.
(AUSTER, P.) See APG.
(AUSTIN, J. G.) See BAL #1, and Johnson.
(AUSTIN, M.) Fink, Augusta. *I, Mary: A Bibliography*. 1983.
See also Johnson.
(BACHELLER, I.) See Johnson.
(BACON, D. S.) See BAL #1.
(BAGBY, G. W.) See BAL #1.
(BAKER, D.) See FPAA #2.
(BAKER, E.) See FPAA #1.
(BALDWIN, J.) See APG, FPAA #5, and Lepper.
(BALDWIN, J. G.) See BAL #1.
(BALLANTINE BOOKS) Aronovitz, David. *Ballantine Books: the First Decade*. Rochester, Michigan: Bailiwick Books (1987).
(BALLANTYNE) Quayle, Eric. *R. M. Ballantyne: A Bibliography of First Editions*. London: Dawsons of Pall Mall, 1968.
(BALLARD, J. G.) See Currey.
(BANCROFT, G.) See BAL #1.
(BANDER-LOG PRESS) See Ransom.
(BANGS, J. K.) See BAL #1, and Johnson.
(BARING) Chaundy, Leslie. *A Bibliography of the First Editions of the Works of Maurice Baring*. London: Dulau & Co., 1925.
See also Cutler and Stiles.
(BARKER, J. N.) See BAL #1.
(BARLOWE, J.) See BAL #1.
(BARNES, D.) Messeri, Douglas. *Djuna Barnes: A Bibliography*. (New York): David Lewis, 1975.
See also FPAA #1.
(BARNES, J.) See APG, and Rees.
(BARRIE) Cutler, B. D. *Sir James M. Barrie: A Bibliography*. New York, 1931.
Garland, Herbert. *A Bibliography of the Writings of Sir James Matthew Barrie*. London: Bookman's Journal, 1928. (BARTH) Weixlmann, Joseph. *John Barth: A Descriptive . . . Bibliography*. New York: Garland, 1976.
See also APG, FPAA #2, and Lepper.
(BARTHELME) Klinkowitz, Jerome; Pieratt, Asa; and Davis, Robert Murray. *Donald Barthelme: A Comprehensive Bibliography*. (Hamden, Ct.): Archon Books, 1977.
See also APG, FPAA #2, and Lepper.
(BARTRAM, W.) See FPAA #4.
(BASKIN, L.) See Gehenna Press.
(BASSLER, T. J.) See Currey.
(BASSO, H.) See FPAA #2.
(BATES, H.) See Currey.

(BATES, H. E.) Eads, Peter. *A Bibliographical Study.* Winchester: St. Paul's Bibliographies, 1990.

(BAYLEY, B.) See Currey.

(BAUM) See Oz.

(BEAGLE, P. S.) See Currey, and FPAA #2.

(BEARDSLEY) Gallatin, A. E. *Aubrey Beardsley, Catalogue of Drawings and Bibliography.* Mamaroneck NY: Paul Appel (no date).

Lasner, Mark Samuels. *A Selective Checklist of the Published Work of Aubrey Beardsley.* Boston: Thomas G. Boss Fine Books, 1995.

(BEATTIE, A.) See APG.

(BEAUMONT PRESS) See Ransom.

(BECKETT) Lake, Carlton, et al. *No Symbols Where None Intended.* (Samuel Beckett.) Austin: Humanities Research Center, University of Texas (1984).

(BEEBE) Berra, Tim. *William Beebe: An Annotated Bibliography.* (Hamden, Ct.): Archon Books, 1977.

See also Johnson.

(BEER, T.) See FPAA #2.

(BEERBOHM) Gallatin, A. E., and Oliver, L. M. *A Bibliography of the Works of Max Beerbohm.* London: Rupert Hart-Davis, 1952.

See also Cutler and Stiles.

(BELDORNIE PRESS) See Ransom.

(BELKNAP, J.) See BAL #1.

(BELL, E. T.) See Currey.

(BELLAMY, E.) See BAL #1, and Johnson.

(BELLOC) Cahill, Patrick. *The English First Editions of Hilaire Belloc.* London: (Privately published), 1953.

(BELLOW, S.) Cronin, Gloria L., and Blaine H. Hall. *Saul Bellow: An Annotated Bibliography.* Second edition. New York: Garland Publishing, 1987.

Also see APG, and Lepper.

(BEMELMANS) Pomerance, Murray. *Ludwig Bemelmans: A Bibliography.* New York: James Heineman, 1993.

(BENET, S. V.) See Johnson.

(BENET, W. R.) See Johnson.

(BENFORD, G.) See Currey.

(BENJAMIN, P.) See BAL #1.

(BENNETT) Pound. *Arnold Bennett: A Bibliography.* 1953.

(BENNETT, E.) See BAL #1.

(BENNETT, G.) See Currey.

(BENSON, Mildred Wirt) See Drew.

(BERGER, T.) See APG, FPAA #2, and Lepper.

(BERRIGAN, D.) See Lepper.

(BERRIGAN, T.) See Lepper.

(BERRY, W) Freedman, Russell. G. *Wendell Berry: A Bibliography.* Lexington: University of Kentucky Libraries, 1998.

See also Lepper.

(BERRYMAN) Kelly. Stefanik, Ernest C., Jr. *John Berryman: A Descriptive Bibliography.* [Pittsburgh]: University of Pittsburgh, 1974.

See also FPAA #1, and Lepper.

(BESTER, A.) See Currey.

(BETJEMAN) Stapleton, Margaret L. *Sir John Betjeman: A Bibliography of Writings By and About Him.* Metuchen, N.J.: Scarecrow Press, 1974.

(BIANCHI, M. G.) See FPAA #2.

(BIERCE) Starrett, Vincent. *Ambrose Bierce: A Bibliography.* Philadelphia: The Centaur Book Shop, 1929.

See also BAL #1, Johnson, and Schwartz.

(BIGGERS) Pensler, Otto. *Earl Derr Biggers' Charlie Chan: A Descriptive Bibliography and Price Guide*. New York: Mysterious Bookshop (1999).

(BIGGLE, L.) See Currey.

(BILLINGS, J.) See BAL #1.

(BINDER, O. O.) See Currey.

(BIRD, R. M.) See BAL #1, and Johnson.

(BIRDS) See Sitwell.

(BISHOP) MacMahon, Candace. *Elizabeth Bishop: A Bibliography, 1927–1979*. Charlottesville: University of Virginia (1980).
See also FPAA #2.

(BISHOP, J. P.) See FPAA #1.

(BISHOP, M.) See Currey.

(BLACK, A. and C.) Inman, Colin. *Colour Books*. London: Werner Shaw Ltd., 1990.

(BLACK, M.) See FPAA #2.

(BLACKBURN, P.) See Lepper.

(BLACKMORE, R. D.) Sutton. *R. D. Blackmore: A Bibliography*. 1979.

(BLACK SPARROW PRESS) Minkoff, George Robert. *A Bibliography of the Black Sun Press*. Great Neck: G. R. Minkoff, 1970.
Morrow & Cooney. *A Bibliography 1966–78*. 1981.
See also Ransom.

(BLAINE, M.) Legman, G. *The Art of Mahlon Blaine*. No place: Peregrine Books, 1982.

(BLAKE, W.) Lindsay. *William Blake*. 1978.

(BLAKENEY PRESS) See Ransom.

(BLECHMAN, B.) See FPAA #2.

(BLEEKER, A. E.) See FPAA #4.

(BLISH, J. B.) See Currey.

(BLIXEN, K.) See Dinesen, Isak.

(BLOCH, R.) Larson, Randall D. *The Complete Robert Bloch*. Sunnyvale, Calif.: Fandom Unlimited, 1986.
See also Currey.

(BLOCK, L.) *Lawrence Block: Bibliography 1958–1993*. (A.S.A.P. Press, Mission Viejo, Calif.): 1993.

(BLUE SKY PRESS) See Ransom.

(BLUNDEN) Kirkpatrick, Brownlee. *A Bibliography of Edmund Blunden*. Oxford: Clarendon Press, 1979.

(BLY) Roberson, William H. *Robert Bly: A Primary and Secondary Bibliography*. Metuchen, N.J., and London: The Scarecrow Press, 1986.
See also Lepper.

(BODMAN, M.) See *FPAA* #4.

(BOGAN, L.) See FPAA #1.

(BOKER, G. H.) See BAL #1.

(BOND, N.) See Currey.

(BOOTH, P. E.) See FPAA #2.

(BORGES) Loewenstein, C. Jared. *A Description Catalogue of the Jorge Luis Borges Collection at the University of Virginia Library*. Charlottesville: University Press of Virginia (1993).

(BORROW) Collie, Michael, and Fraser, Angus. *George Borrow: A Bibliographical Study*. Hampshire: St. Paul's Bibliographies, 1984.

(BOURJAILY, V.) See FPAA #1.

(BOVA, B. W.) See Currey.

(BOWLES, J.) Dillion. See FPAA #5.

(BOWLES, P.) Miller, Jeffrey. *Paul Bowles: A Descriptive Bibliography*. Santa Barbara: Black Sparrow, 1986.
See also Lepper.

(BOWLING GREEN PRESS) See Ransom.

(BOX, E.) (Vidal) See FPAA #3.

(BOYD, J.) See Johnson.

(BOYESEN, H. H.) See BAL #1.

(BOYLE, K.) See FPAA #3.

(BRACE, G. W.) See FPAA #2.

(BRACKENRIDGE, H. H.) See BAL #1, and Johnson.

(BRACKETT, L.) See Currey.

(BRADBURY) Nolan, William F. *The Ray Bradbury Companion.* Detroit: Bruccoli Clark/Gale Research, 1975.
   See also APG, FPAA #1, Currey.

(BRADFORD, G.) See Johnson.

(BRADFORD, R.) See Johnson.

(BRADFORD, W.) See FPAA #3.

(BRADLEY, M. E.) See Currey.

(BRADSTREET, A.) See FPAA #3.

(BRAINARD, J. G.) See BAL #1.

(BRAND) Richardson, Darrell C. *Max Brand (Frederick Faust): The Man and His Work.* Los Angeles: Fantasy Publishing (1952).

(BRAUTIGAN) Barber, John F. *Richard Brautigan: An Annotated Bibliography.* Jefferson, North Carolina, and London: McFarland & Co. (1990).
   See also Lepper.

(BRENNAN, J. P.) See Currey.

(BRESLIN, J.) See FPAA #2.

(BRIGGS, C. F.) See BAL #1.

(BRODEUR, P.) See FPAA #1.

(BROMFIELD, L.) See FPAA #4, and Johnson.

(BRONK, W.) See FPAA #3.

(BRONTË) Wise, Thomas J. *A Bibliography of the Writings . . . of the Brontë Family.* London: Dawsons of Pall Mall (1917).

(BROOKE, R.) Keynes, Geoffrey. *A Bibliography of the Works of Rupert Brooke.* London: Rupert Hart-Davis, 1964.

(BROOKS, C. T.) See BAL #1.

(BROOKS, G.) Luff, J. N. *Gwendolyn Brooks: A Bibliography.*
   See also APG.

(BROOKS, M. G.) See BAL #1.

(BROOKS, V. W.) Nelson. *Van Wyck Brooks: A Writer's Life.*
   See also FPAA #5.

(BROOKS PRESS) See Ransom.

(BROSSARD, C.) See APG, and FPAA #2.

(BROWN, A.) See FPAA #3.

(BROWN, C. B.) See BAL #1, and Johnson.

(BROWN, F.) Baird, Newton. *A Key to Frederic Brown's Wonderland.* Georgetown, Calif.: Talisman Literary Research, 1981.
   See also APG, and Currey.

(BROWN, R. G.) See Currey.

(BROWN, W. H.) See BAL #1, and FPAA #1.

(BROWNE, C. F.) See BAL #1.

(BROWNELL, H. H.) See BAL #1.

(BROWNING, E. B.) Barnes, Warner. *A Bibliography of Elizabeth Barrett Browning.* (Austin): University of Texas . . . (1967).
   See also Schwartz.

(BROWNING, R.) Wise, Thomas J. *A Bibliography of the Writings . . . of Robert Browning.* London: Dawsons of Pall Mall, 1971.
   See also Schwartz.

(BROWNSON, O. A.) See FPAA #4.

(BRUNNER, J. K.) See Currey.

(BRYAN, C.D.B.) See FPAA #2.

(BRYANT, E.) See Currey.

(BRYANT, W. C.) Scribner. *William Cullen Bryant: A Bibliography*. 1971. See also BAL #1, and Johnson.

(BUCHAN, J.) Blanchard, Robert G. *The First Editions of John Buchan.* (Hamden, Conn.): Archon Books, 1981.

(BUCK, P.) See Johnson.

(BUDRYS, A. J.) See Currey.

(BUECHNER, F.) See FPAA #1.

(BUKOWSKI, C.) Dorbin, Sanford. *A Bibliography of Charles Bukowski*. Los Angeles: Black Sparrow, 1969.

Fogel, Al. *Charles Bukowski: A Comprehensive Price Guide & Checklist: 1944–1999*. (Miami: Sole Proprietor Press, 2000).

Fogel, Al. *Under the Influence: A Collection of Works by Charles Bukowski, Illustrated with Original Drawings by the Author*. (Sudbury, Mass.: Jeffrey H. Weinberg Books, 1984).

Krumhansl, Aaron. *A Descriptive Bibliography of the Primary Publications of Charles Bukowski*. Santa Rosa: Black Sparrow Press, 1999.

See also Lepper.

(BULFINCH, T.) See FPAA #4.

(BULMER, H. K.) See Currey.

(BULWER, L.) See Sadlier.

(BUNNER, H. C.) See BAL #1, and Johnson.

(BUNTING, B.) Guedalla, Roger. *Basil Bunting: A Bibliography of Works and Criticism*. Norwood, Pa.: Norwood Editions, 1973.

(BURDETTE, R. J.) See BAL #1.

(BURGESS, A.) Brewer, Jeutonne. *Anthony Burgess: A Bibliography*. Metuchen, N.J. & London: The Scarecrow Press, 1980.

(BURGESS, G.) See Johnson.

(BURGESS, T.) Dowhan, Michael W., Jr. *Thornton W. Burgess, Harrison Cady: A Book, Magazine and Newspaper Bibliography*. New York: Carlton Press (1990).

Wright, Wayne W. *Thornton W. Burgess: A Descriptive Book Bibliography*. Sandwich, Mass.: Burgess Society, 1979.

(BURKE, E.) Todd, William B. *A Bibliography of Edmund Burke*. (Surrey, England): St. Paul's Bibliographies, 1982.

(BURKE, J. L.) See APG.

(BURNETT, F. H.) See BAL #1.

(BURNS, R.) (Gibson, James). *The Bibliography of Robert Burns. . . .* Reprinted. New York: Kraus Reprint Co., 1969.

(BURROUGHS, E. R.) Heins, Henry Hardy. *A Golden Anniversary Bibliography of Edgar Rice Burroughs*. (Revised). West Kingston, R.I.: Donald Grant, 1964.

Zeuschner, Robert B. *Edgar Rice Burroughs: The Exhaustive Scholar's and Collector's Descriptive Bibliography*. Jefferson, North Carolina / London: McFarland and Company, Inc. (1996).

See also Currey.

(BURROUGHS, J.) See BAL #1, and Johnson.

(BURROUGHS, W.) Maynard, Joe, and Miles, Barry. *William S. Burroughs: A Bibliography, 1953–73*. Charlottesville: University of Virginia Press (1978).

See also APG, FPAA #5, and Lepper.

(BURTON, R.) Penzer, Norman M. *An Annotated Bibliography of Sir Richard Francis Burton*. New York: Burt Franklin (1970).

(BUSCH, F.) See FPAA #2.

(BUTLER, S.) Harkness, Stanley B. *The Career of Samuel Butler (1835–1902): A Bibliography*. London: The Bodley Head (1955).

Hoppe, A. J. *A Bibliography of the Writings of Samuel Butler.* New York: Burt Franklin (1968). See also Schwartz.

(BUTLER, W. A) See BAL #1.

(BUTLER, W. H.) See BAL #1.

(BYLES, M.) See FPAA #1.

(BYNNER, E. L.) See BAL #1.

(BYNNER, W.) See Johnson.

(BYRD, W.) See FPAA #4.

(BYRNE, D.) Wetherbee, Winthrop, Jr. *Donn Byrne: A Bibliography.* New York: New York Public Library, 1949.
See also BAL #1, and Johnson.

(BYRON, L.) Wise, Thomas J. *A Bibliography of the Writings in Verse and Prose of George Gordon Noel, Lord Byron.* 2 vols. London: Dawsons of Pall Mall, 1972.
See also Schwartz.

(CABELL, J. B.) Brussel I. R. *James Branch Cabell: A Revised Bibliography.* Philadelphia: Centaur Book Shop, 1932.
See also FPAA #2, and Johnson.

(CABLE, G. W.) See BAL #2, and Johnson.

(CAHAN, A.) See FPAA #2.

(CAIN, J. M.) See FPAA #1.

(CAIN, P.) See FPAA #4.

(CALDWELL, E.) See *Casanova,* FPAA #2, and Johnson.

(CALIFORNIA LITERATURE) Gaer. *Bibliography Pre Gold Rush.* 1970.

(CALISHER, H.) See FPAA #2, and Lepper.

(CALVERT, G. H.) See BAL #2.

(CAMUS, A.) Roeming. *Albert Camus: A Bibliography.* 1968.

(CANTWELL, R.) See FPAA #5.

(CAPOTE, T.) See APG, and Lepper.

(CARADOC PRESS) See Franklin.

(CARLETON, W.) See BAL #2.

(CARLYLE, T.) Dyer, Isaac Watson. *A Bibliography of Thomas Carlyle's Writings . . .* New York: Burt Franklin (1968).
Tarr, Rodger L. *Thomas Carlyle: A Descriptive Bibliography.* (Pittsburgh): University of Pittsburgh Press, 1989.

(CARMAN, B.) See BAL #2, Johnson.

(CARREFOUR PRESS) See Ford.

(CARROLL, L.) Williams, Sidney Herbert. *A Bibliography of the Writings of Lewis Carroll.* (Charles Lutwidge Dodgson.) London: *Bookman's Journal,* 1924.
See also Cutler and Stiles.

(CARROLL, P.) See FPAA #2.

(CARRUTH, H.) See FPAA #2.

(CARRYL, G. W.) See BAL #2.

(CARSON, R.) See FPAA #3.

(CARTER, H.) See FPAA #4.

(CARUTHERS, W. A.) See BAL #2.

(CARY, A.) See BAL #2.

(CARY, P.) See BAL #2.

(CASTLEMON) Blanck, Jacob. *Harry Castlemon Boy's Own Author.* Waltham, Mass.: Mark Press, 1969.

(CATHER, W.) Crane, Joan. *Willa Cather: A Bibliography.* Lincoln: University of Nebraska Press (1982).
See also APG, FPAA #4, and Johnson.

(CATHERWOOD, M.) See BAL #2.

(CATTLE INDUSTRY) See Adams.

(CAWEIN, M.) See BAL #2.

(CENTAUR PRESS) See Ransom.

(CERVANTES) Grismer, Raymond L. *Cervantes: A Bibliography.* Reprinted. New York: Kraus, 1970.

(CHANDLER, R.) Bruccoli, Matthew. *Raymond Chandler: A Descriptive Bibliography.* University of Pittsburgh Press, 1979.
See also APG, and FPAA #1.

(CHANNING, W. E.) See BAL #2, and FPAA #4.

(CHARTERIS, L.) See APG.

(CHATWIN, B.) See APG, and Rees.

(CHEEVER, J.) See APG, FPAA #5, Lepper.

(CHEKHOV) Meister, Charles W. *Chekhov Bibliography: Works in English By and About Anton Chekhov; American, British and Canadian Performances.* Jefferson, N.C., and London: McFarland & Co. (1985).

(CHESNUTT, C.) See APG, FPAA #3, and Johnson.

(CHESTERTON, G. K.) Sullivan, John. *G. K. Chesterton: A Bibliography.* Warwick Square, London: University of London Press (1958).

(CHILD, L. M.) See BAL #2.

(CHILDREN'S BOOKS) Blanck, Jacob. *Peter Parley to Penrod.* Waltham, Mass.: Mark Press, 1974.
Kirkpatrick, D. L., ed. *Twentieth-Century Children's Writer's.* 2nd ed. New York: St. Martin's Press (1983).

(CHIVERS, L. M.) See BAL #2, and Johnson.

(CHOPIN, K.) See BAL #2.

(CHRISTIE, A.) See APG.

(CHURCHILL, W.) Woods, Frederick. *A Bibliography of the Works of Sir Winston Churchill.* (London): St. Paul's Bibliographies (1975).
See also APG, and Johnson.

(CIARDI, J.) See FPAA #2.

(CITY LIGHTS) Cook, Ralph T. *The City Lights Pocket Poets Series: A Descriptive Bibliography.* La Jolla, Calif.: Laurence McGilvery/Atticus Books, 1982.

(CIVIL WAR) Menendez, Albert. *Civil War Novels: An Annotated Bibliography.* New York and London: Garland Publishing, 1986.

(CLANCY, T.) See APG.

(CLARK, E.) See FPAA #4.

(CLARK, J. F.) See FPAA #4.

(CLARK, M. H.) See APG.

(CLARK, T.) See Lepper.

(CLARK, W. G.) See BAL #2.

(CLARK, W. V.) See FPAA #5.

(CLARKE, J. F.) See FPAA #4.

(CLARKE, M.) See BAL #2.

(CLAVELL, J.) See APG.

(CLEMENS, S.) See BAL #2, and Johnson.

(CLERK'S PRESS) See Ransom.

(COATES, R. M.) See FPAA #4.

(COBB, E.) See Johnson.

(COBB, H.) See FPAA #3.

(COBB, I. S.) See Johnson.

(COKER, E.) See FPAA #4.

(COLERIDGE) Haney, John Louis. *A Bibliography of Samuel Taylor Coleridge.* Philadelphia: Privately printed, 1903.

(COLLINS, W.) Beetz, Kirk H. *Wilkie Collins: An Annotated Bibliography, 1889–1976.* Metuchen, N.J., and London: The Scarecrow Press, 1978.

(COLLINS CRIME CLUB) Foord, Peter, and Williams, Richard. *Collins Crime Club: A Checklist of the First Editions.* South Humberside (England): Dragonby Press, 1987.

(CONDON, R.) See FPAA #2.

(CONNELL, E.) See FPAA #2.

(CONNELLY, M.) See APG.

(CONRAD, J.) Cagle, William. *A Bibliography of Joseph Conrad.* (Unpublished).
  Wise, Thomas J. *A Bibliography of the Writings of Joseph Conrad, (1895–1921).* (London): Dawsons of Pall Mall, 1972.
  See also APG, Cutler and Stiles, and Schwartz.

(CONROY, J.) See FPAA #1.

(CONROY, P.) See APG.

(CONTACT EDITIONS) See Ford.

(COOKE, J. E.) See BAL #2, and Johnson.

(COOKE, R. T.) See BAL #2.

(COOPER, J. F.) Spiller, Robert E., and Blackburn, Philip C. *A Descriptive Bibliography of the Writings of James Fenimore Cooper.* New York: R. R. Bowker Company, 1934.
  See also BAL #2, and Johnson.

(COOPER, S. F.) See BAL #2.

(COOVER, R.) See FPAA #1, and Lepper.

(COPPARD, A. E.) Schwartz, Jacob. *The Writings of Alfred Edgar Coppard.* London: The Ulysses Bookshop, 1931.
  See also Fabes.

(CORMAN, C.) See Lepper.

(CORNFORD, F.) Anderson, Alan. *A Bibliography of the Writings of Frances Cornford.* Edinburgh: Tragara Press, 1975.

(CORNWELL, B.) See APG.

(CORNWELL, P.) See APG.

(CORSO, G.) Wilson, Robert. *A Bibliography of Works by Gregory Corso, 1954–1965.* New York: The Phoenix Book Shop, Inc., 1966.

(CORVO, F. R.) Woolf, Cecil. *A Bibliography of Frederick Rolfe Baron Corvo.* London: Rupert Hart-Davis, Soho Square, 1957.

(COTTON, J.) See FPAA #4.

(COWBOY) See Adams.

(COWLEY, A.) Perkin, M. R. *Abraham Cowley: A Bibliography.* (Kent, England): Dawson (1977).

(COWLEY, M.) See FPAA #4.

(COX, P.) Dickerson, Richard E. *A Brownie Bibliography: The Books of Palmer Cox 1840–1924.* (Pasadena): Golden Pippin Press, 1995. (Second edition.)

(COZZENS, F. S.) See BAL #2.

(COZZENS) Bruccoli, Matthew. *James Gould Cozzens: A Descriptive Bibliography.* (Pittsburgh): University of Pittsburgh Press, 1981.
  See also FPAA #1.

(CRANCH, C.) See BAL #2.

(CRANE, H.) Schwartz, Joseph, and Schweik, Robert C. *Hart Crane: A Descriptive Bibliography.* [Pittsburgh]: University of Pittsburgh Press (1972).
  See also FPAA #1.

(CRANE, S.) Stallman, R. W. *Stephen Crane: A Critical Bibliography.* Ames: Iowa State University Press, 1972.
  Williams, Ames W., and Starrett, Vincent. *Stephen Crane: A Bibliography.* Glendale, Calif.: John Valentine, Publisher, 1948.
  See also BAL #2, FPAA #1, and Johnson.

(CRAPSEY, A.) See BAL #2.

(CRAWFORD, F. M.) See BAL #2.

(CREASEY, J.) *John Creasey: Master of Mystery.* (London: Hodder & Stoughton, no date.)

John Creasey in Print. (New York, and London: Walker and Company, and Hodder & Stoughton, 1969).

(CREELEY, R.) Novik, Mary. *Robert Creeley: An Inventory, 1945–1970*. No place: Kent State University Press (1973).
See also FPAA #3, and Lepper.

(CRESSET PRESS) See Ransom.

(CREWS, H.) Hargraves, Michael. *Harry Crews: A Bibliography*. (Westport, Ct.): Meckler Publishing Corporation (1986).
See also APG, and FPAA #2.

(CROSBY, C.) See FPAA #4.

(CROSBY, H.) See FPAA #2.

(CROSBY GAIGE PRESS) See Ransom.

(CRUMB) Fine, Donald M. *R. Crumb Checklist of Works and Criticism* . . . Cambridge: Boatner Norton Press, 1981.

(CRUMLEY, J.) See APG.

(CUALA PRESS) See Ransom.

(CULLEN, C.) See APG.

(CUMMINGS, E. E.) Firmage, George J. *E. E. Cummings: A Bibliography*. (Middletown, Ct.): Wesleyan University Press (1960).
See also Johnson.

(CUMMINS, M.) See BAL #2.

(CUNNINGHAM, J. V.) Gullans, Charles. *A Bibliography of the Published Works of J. V. Cunningham*. Los Angeles: University of California Library, 1973.

(CURTIS, G. W.) See BAL #2, and Johnson.

(CUSHING, E. L.) See FPAA #5.

(D., H. [Hilda Doolittle]) Boughn, Michael. *H. D.: A Bibliography 1905–1990*. Charlottes ville/London: Bibliographical Society of the University of Virginia/University of Virginia Press (1993).

(DABBS, J. M.) See FPAA #4.

(DAHLBERG, E.) Billings, Harold. *A Bibliography of Edward Dahlberg*. Austin: University of Texas Press (1971).
See also FPAA #1.

(DANA, R. H., Sr.) See BAL #2, and Johnson.

(DANIEL PRESS) See Franklin, and Ransom.

(DARROW, C.) Hunsberger, Willard D. *Clarence Darrow: A Bibliography*. Metuchen, NJ: Scarecrow Press, 1981.

(DARWIN, C.) Freeman, R. B. *The Works of Charles Darwin: An Annotated Bibliographical Handlist*. (Hamden, Ct.): Dawson-Archon Books (1977).

(DAVENPORT, G.) Crane, Joan. *Guy Davenport: A Descriptive Bibliography*. Haverford: Greenshads, 1996.

(DAVIDSON, D.) Young, Thomas D., and Inge, Thomas. *Donald Davidson: An Essay and Bibliography*. Nashville: Vanderbilt University Press, 1965.

(DAVIDSON, J.) See Cutler and Stiles.

(DAVIES, Rhys) See Gawsworth.

(DAVIES, Robertson) Ryrie, John. *Robertson Davies: An Annotated Bibliography*. (Downsview, Ontario: Stong College, York University, 1981).
See also APG.

(DAVIES, W. H.) Harlow, Sylvia *W. H. Davies: A Bibliography*. Winchester, and New Castle, Delaware: St. Paul's Bibliographies, and Oak Knoll Books, 1993.

(DAVIS, C. A.) See BAL #2.

(DAVIS, R. H.) Quinby, Henry Cole, A. M. *Richard Harding Davis: A Bibliography*. New York: E. P. Dutton & Company (1924).
See also BAL #2, FPAA #5, and Johnson.

(DAWES, R.) See BAL #2.

(DAWSON, F.) See FPAA #5.

(DAY-LEWIS, C.) Handley-Taylor, Geoffrey, and Smith, Timothy d'Arch. *C. Day-Lewis the Poet Laureate: A Bibliography.* Chicago and London: St. James Press, 1968.

(DE CAMP, L. S.) Laughlin, Charlotte, and Levack, Daniel J. H. *An L. Sprague De Camp Bibliography.* San Francisco, Calif./Columbia, Pa.: Underwood/Miller, 1983.

(DE FOREST, J. W.) See BAL #2.

(DEIGHTON, L.) Milward-Oliver, Edward. *Len Deighton: An Annotated Bibliography, 1954–1985.* (Kent, England): The Sammler Press (1985).

(DELAND, M.) See Johnson.

(DeLILLO, D.) See APG, and FPAA #1.

(DELL, F.) See FPAA #3.

(DELL PAPERBACK) Lyles, William. *Putting Dell on the Map 1942–1962.* Two volumes.

(DENNIE, J.) See BAL #2.

(DERBY, G. H.) See BAL #2.

(DEREKSEN, D.) See Stacton.

(DERLETH, A.) *100 Books by August Derleth.* Sauk City: Arkham House, 1962.

Wilson, Alison M. *August Derleth: A Bibliography.* Metuchen, N.J., and London: Scarecrow Press, 1983.

(DERRYDALE PRESS) Frazier, Don, and Koch, Jo. *Derrydale Press Books.* Long Valley, N.J.: Calderwoods Books [circa 1984].

(DE VRIES, P.) Bowden, Edwin T. *Peter De Vries: A Bibliography, 1934–1977.* Austin: University of Texas (1978).

See also FPAA #4.

(DEWEY, J.) See FPAA #1.

(DEXTER, C.) See APG.

(DIBDIN, T. F.) O'Dwyer, E. J. *Thomas Frognall Dibdin: Bibliographer & Bibliomaniac Extraordinary 1776–1847.* Pinner (Middlesex, England): Private Libraries Association (1967).

Windle, John, and Karma Pippen. *Thomas Frognall Dibdin 1776–1847: A Bibliography.* New Castle: Oak Knoll Press, 1999.

(DICK, P. K.) Levack, Daniel J. H. *PKD: A Philip K. Dick Bibliography.* San Francisco, Calif./Columbia, Pa.: Underwood/Miller, 1981.

(DICKENS, C.) Carr, Sister Lucille. *A Catalog of the Vanderpoel Dickens Collection . . .* Austin: University of Texas (1968).

Eckel, John C. *The First Editions of the Writings of Charles Dickens and Their Values: A Bibliography.* London: Chapman & Hall, Ltd., 1913.

Podeschi, John B. *Dickens and Dickensiana: A Catalogue of the Richard Gimbel Collection . . .* New Haven: Yale University Library, 1980.

Smith, Walter E. *Charles Dickens in the Original Cloth: A Bibliographical Catalogue. Part I: The Novels with Sketches by Boz.* Los Angeles: Heritage Book Shop, 1982.

Smith, Walter E. *Charles Dickens in the Original Cloth: A Bibliographical Catalogue. Part II: The Christmas Book and Selected Secondary Novels.* Los Angeles: Heritage Book Shop, 1982.

See also Sadlier.

(DICKEY, J.) Bruccoli, Matthew J., and Baughman, Judith S. *James Dickey: A Descriptive Bibliography.* (Pittsburgh): University of Pittsburgh Press, 1990.

See also FPAA #1, Lepper.

(DICKINSON, E.) Myerson, Joel. *Emily Dickinson: A Descriptive Bibliography.* (Pittsburgh): University of Pittsburgh Press, 1984.

See also BAL #2, and Johnson.

(DIDION. J.) See APG, and FPAA #2.

(DINESEN, I.) Henriksen, Liselotte. *Isak Dinesen: A Bibliography.* (Viborg, Denmark): Gyldendal (1977).

(DiPRIMA, D.) See Lepper.

(DISCH, T. M.) Stephens, Christopher. *A Checklist of Thomas M. Disch.* (Hastings-on-Hudson, N.Y.): Ultramarine, 1991.

(DOBIE, J. F.) McVicker, Mary Louise. *The Writings of J. Frank Dobie: A Bibliography.* Lawton (Okla.): Museum of the Great Plains (1968).

(DOBSON) Dobson, Alban. *A Bibliography of the First Editions . . .* New York: Burt Franklin (1970). A reprint of the 1925 edition with a preface by Edmund Gosse.

(DOCTOROW, E. L.) See APG, and FPAA #1.

(DODGE, M. A.) See BAL #1.

(DODGE, M. M.) See BAL #2, and Johnson.

(DONLEAVY, J. P.) See FPAA #2.

(DONNELLY, I.) See BAL #2.

(Doolittle, Hilda.) See D., H.

(DORN, E.) Streeter, David. *A Bibliography of Ed Dorn.* New York: The Phoenix Bookshop, 1973.
See also FPAA #3, and Lepper.

(DOS PASSOS, J.) Sanders, Harvey. *John Dos Passos: A Comprehensive Bibliography.* New York and London: GarlandPublishing, Inc., 1987.
See also APG, FPAA #1, and Johnson.

(DOUGLAS, N.) McDonald, Edward D. *A Bibliography of the Writings of Norman Douglas.* Philadelphia: The Centaur Book Shop, 1927.
See also Schwartz.

(DOVES PRESS) See Franklin, and Ransom.

(DOWSON, E.) See Cutler and Stiles, and Schwartz.

(DOYLE, A. C.) Green, Richard Lancelyn, and Gibson, John Michael. *A Bibliography of A. Conan Doyle.* Oxford: Clarendon Press (1983).
See also APG.

(DRAKE, J. R.) See BAL #2, and Johnson.

(DREISER, T.) McDonald, Edward D. *A Bibliography of the Writings of Theodore Dreiser.* New York: Burt Franklin (1968).
See also APG, FPAA #4, Schwartz, and Johnson.

(DREW, N.) Farah, David. *Farah's Price Guide to Nancy Drew Books and Collectibles.* Seventh Printing. No place: Farah's Books (1990).

(DRIFTWIND PRESS) See Ransom.

(DRINKWATER, J.) See Cutler and Stiles.

(DUGAN, A.) See FPAA #2.

(DUGANNE, A.J.H.) See BAL #2.

(DUNBAR, P. L.) See BAL #2.

(DUNCAN, R.) Bertholf, Robert J. *Robert Duncan: A Descriptive Bibliography.* Santa Rosa, Calif.: Black Sparrow Press, 1986.
See also FPAA #3, and Lepper.

(DUNLAP, W.) See BAL #2.

(DUNNE, F. P.) See Johnson.

(DUNNING, J.) See APG.

(DUNSANY, L.) See Cutler and Stiles.

(DURRELL, L.) Fraser, G. S., and Thomas, Alan G. *Lawrence Durrell: A Study.* London: Faber and Faber (1968).

(DWIGHT, Theodore) See FPAA #1.

(DWIGHT, Timothy) See BAL #2.

(DYKE, H. V.) See FPAA #2.

(DYKEMAN, W.) See FPAA #4.

(E., A.) Denson, Alan. *Printed Writings by George W. Russell (A.E.): A Bibliography.* Evanston: Northwestern University Press, 1961.

(EASTLAKE, W.) See APG, and FPAA #2.

(EBERHART, R.) See FPAA #1.

(EDGERTON, G.) See Gawsworth.

(EDMONDS, W. D.) See Johnson.

(EGGLESTON, E.) See BAL #3, and Johnson.

(EIGNER, L.) Wyatt, Andrea. *A Bibliography of Works by Larry Eigner.* Berkeley: Oyez, 1970.

(ELIOT, G.) Lake, Brian, and Nassau, Janet. *George Eliot in Original Cloth: A Bibliographical Catalogue.* (Bloomsbury): Jarndyce Antiquarian Books (1988).
See also Sadlier.

(ELIOT, T. S.) Gallup, Donald. *T. S. Eliot: A Bibliography.* London: Faber & Faber (1970).
See also APG, and Schwartz.

(ELKIN, S.) See FPAA #1.

(ELLIOTT, G. P.) See FPAA #4, and Lepper.

(ELLIOTT, W.) See FPAA #1.

(ELLISON, R.) See FPAA #3.

(ELY, D.) See FPAA #2.

(EMERSON, R. W.) Myerson, Joel. *Ralph Waldo Emerson: A Descriptive Bibliography.* (Pittsburgh): University of Pittsburgh Press, 1982.
See also BAL #3, FPAA #2, Johnson, and Schwartz.

(ENGLISH, T. D.) See BAL #3.

(EPSTEIN, S.) See FPAA #1.

(ERAGNY PRESS) See Franklin, and Ransom.

(ESHLEMAN, C.) See FPAA #3, and Lepper.

(ESSEX HOUSE) See Franklin, and Ransom.

(EVANS, WALKER) Kingston, Rodger. *Walker Evans in Print.* (Belmont): R. P. Kingston, 1995.

(EVERSON, W.) Sipper, Ralph. *William Everson: A Collection of Books & Manuscripts.* Santa Barbara: Joseph the Provider (1987).
See also Lepper.

(EXLEY, F.) See FPAA #3.

(FAIRFIELD, S. L.) See BAL #3.

(FANFROLIC PRESS) See Ransom.

(FARRELL, J. T.) Branch, Edgar. *A Bibliography of James T. Farrell's Writings 1921–1957.* Philadelphia: University of Pennsylvania Press (1959).
See also FPAA #5, and Johnson.

(FAULKNER, W.) Brodsky, Louis Daniel, and Hamblin, Robert W. *Faulkner: A Comprehensive Guide to the Brodsky Collection.* Jackson: University Press of Mississippi (1982).
Massey, Linton R. *"Man Working," 1919–1962: William Faulkner.* Charlottesville, Va.: Bibliographical Society of the University of Virginia (1968).
Petersen, Carl. *Each in Its Ordered Place: A Faulkner Collector's Notebook.* Ann Arbor: Ardis (1975).
See also APG, FPAA #1, and Johnson.

(FAUST, I.) See FPAA #1.

(FAWCETT, E.) See BAL #3.

(FAY, T.) See BAL #3.

(FEARING, K.) See FPAA #1.

(FEIBLEMAN, P.) See APG.

(FERBER, E.) See Johnson.

(FERLINGETTI, L.) See Lepper.

(FERRINI, V.) See FPAA #3.

(FIELD, E.) See BAL #3, and Johnson.

(FIELDS, J. T.) See BAL #3.

(FIRBANK, R.) Benkovitz, Miriam J. *A Bibliography of Ronald Firbank.* London: Rupert Hart-Davis, 1963.
Benkovitz, Miriam J. *Supplement to a Bibliography of Ronald Firbank.* London: Enitharmon Press, 1980.
See also Cutler and Stiles.

(FISHER, V.) See Johnson.

(FISKE, J.) See BAL #3.

(FITCH, C.) See BAL #3.

(FITZGERALD, E.) Prideaux, Colonel W. F. *Notes for a Bibliography of Edward FitzGerald.* New York: Burt Franklin (1968).

(FITZGERALD, F. S.) Bruccoli, Matthew J. *F. Scott Fitzgerald: A Descriptive Bibliography.* (Pittsburgh): University of Pittsburgh Press, 1987.
See also APG, and FPAA #1.

(FITZGERALD, Z.) See FPAA #2.

(FLANNER, J.) See FPAA #4.

(FLEMING, I.) Campbell, Iain. *Ian Fleming: A Catalogue of a Collection.* Liverpool: Iain Campbell (1978).
See also APG.

(FLETCHER, J. G.) Morton, Bruce. *John Gould Fletcher: A Bibliography.* (Kent): Kent State University Press (1979).

(FLEURON PRESS) See Ransom.

(FLINT, T.) See BAL #3.

(FLORENCE PRESS) See Ransom.

(FLOWERS) See Sitwell.

(FOOTE, S.) See FPAA #2.

(FORD, F. M.) Harvey, David Dow. *Ford Madox Ford 1873–1939.* New York: Gordian Press, 1972.

(FORD, P. L.) See BAL #3, and Johnson.

(FORESTER, C. S.) See APG.

(FORESTER, F.) See Herbert, H. W.

(FORSTER, E. M.) Kirkpatrick, B. J. *A Bibliography of E. M. Forster.* Oxford: Clarendon Press, 1985.

(FORTUNE PRESS) See Ransom.

(FOSTER, H.) See BAL #3.

(FOWLES, J.) See APG.

(FOX, J., Jr.) See BAL #3, and Johnson.

(FOX, W. P.) See FPAA #1.

(FRANCIS, D.) See APG.

(FRANKLIN, B.) Ford, Paul Leicester. *A List of Books Written By, or Relating to Benjamin Franklin.* Reprinted. New York: Burt Franklin (1968).

(FRANKLIN PRESS) See Ransom.

(FREDERIC, H.) See BAL #3, and Johnson.

(FREEMAN, M.E.W.) See BAL #3, and Johnson.

(FRENEAU, P.) See BAL #3, and Johnson.

(FRIEDMAN, B. J.) See FPAA #4, and Lepper.

(FROST, R.) Crane, Joan St. C. *Robert Frost: A Descriptive Catalogue of Books and Manuscripts in the Clifton Waller Barrett Library.* Charlottesville: University Press of Virginia (1974).
See also APG, FPAA #1, Johnson, and Schwartz.

(FUCHS, D.) See FPAA #1.

(FULLER, H. B.) See BAL #3, and Johnson.

(FULLER, M.) Myerson, Joel. *Margaret Fuller: A Descriptive Bibliography.* (Pittsburgh): University of Pittsburgh Press, 1978.
See also BAL #3, and FPAA #1.

(FULLER, S. M.) See BAL #3, and FPAA #1.

(GADDIS, W.) See APG, and FPAA #1.

(GAINES, E.) See APG, and FPAA #1.

(GALLAGHER, W. D.) See BAL #3.

(GALSWORTHY, J.) Fabes, Gilbert H. *John Galsworthy His First Editions: Points and Values.* London: W. and G. Foyle (1932).
See also Cutler and Stiles, and Schwartz.

(GARCÍA MÁRQUEZ, G.) See APG.

(GARDNER, J.) Howell, John M. *John Gardner: A Bibliographical Profile.* Carbondale and Edwardsville: Southern Illinois University Press (1980). See also FPAA #3, and Lepper.

(GARLAND, H.) See Johnson.

(GARRETT, G.) Wright, Stuart. *George Garrett: A Bibliography, 1947–1988.* (Huntsville, Tx.): Texas Review Press, Sam Houston State University, 1989. See also FPAA #2.

(GASCOYNE, D.) Benford, Colin T. *David Gascoyne: A Bibliography of His Works (1929–1985).* Isle of Wight: Heritage Books (no date).

(GASKELL, Mrs.) See Sadlier.

(GASS, W. H.) See APG, FPAA #4, and Lepper.

(GEHENNA PRESS) Franklin, Colin; Baskin, Hosea; and Baskin, Leonard. *The Gehenna Press: The Work of Fifty Years, 1942–1992.* No place: The Birdwell Library, and The Gehenna Press (1992).

(GELLHORN, M.) See FPAA #4.

(GIBBINGS, R.) Kirkus, A. Mary. *Robert Gibbings: A Bibliography.* London: J. M. Dent (1962).

(GIBSON, Wilfrid) See Gawsworth.

(GIBSON, William) See FPAA #5.

(GILBRETH, F. B.) See FPAA #3.

(GILDER, R. W.) See BAL #3.

(GILL, B.) See FPAA #3.

(GILL, E.) Gill, Evan R. *Bibliography of Eric Gill.* (Revised by D. Steven Corey and Julia MacKenzie.) 2nd edition. St. Paul's Bibliographies. Wincester/Omnigraphics. Detroit: 1991.

(GINSBERG, A.) Dowden, George. *A Bibliography of Works by Allen Ginsberg.* (San Francisco): City Lights Books (1971).

(GISSING, G.) Collie, Michael. *George Gissing: A Bibliography.* (Toronto and Buffalo): Dawson (1975).

(GLASGOW, E.) Kelly, William W. *Ellen Glasgow: A Bibliography.* Charlottesville: The Bibliographical Society of the University of Virginia (1964). See also FPAA #2, and Johnson.

(GOLD, H.) See FPAA #1, and Lepper.

(GOLDEN COCKEREL PRESS) See Franklin.

(GOLF) Donovan, Richard E., and Murdoch, Joseph S. F. *The Game of Golf and the Printed Word 1566–1985: A Bibliography of Golf Literature in the English Language.* Endicott, N.Y.: Castalio Press, 1988.

(GOODMAN, P.) See Lepper.

(GORDIMER, N.) See APG.

(GORDON, C.) See FPAA #1.

(GORES, J.) See FPAA #3.

(GOREY, E.) Toledano, Henry. *Goreyography: A Divers Compendium of and Price Guide to the Works of Edward Gorey.* San Francisco: Word Play Publications (1996).

(GOVER, R.) See FPAA #2.

(GOYEN, W.) Wright, Stuart. *William Goyen: A Descriptive Bibliography, 1938–1985.* (Westport, Ct.): Meckler Publishing (1986). See also APG, FPAA #4, and Lepper.

(GRABHORN PRESS) See Ransom.

(GRAFTON, S.) See APG.

(GRAHAM, S.) See FPAA #3.

(GRAU, S.) See APG, FPAA #4, and Lepper.

(GRAVES, R.) Higginson, F. H., and Williams, William P. *Robert Graves: A Bibliography.* (Hampshire, England): St. Paul's Bibliographies, 1987. See also APG.

(GRAY, Alasdair) See Rees.

(GREEN, A. K.) See FPAA #4, and Johnson.

(GREEN, B. K.) Wilson, Robert A. *Ben K. Green: A Descriptive Bibliography of Writings By and About Him.* Flagstaff: Northland Press (1977).

(GREENAWAY, K.) Engen, Rodney. *Kate Greenaway: A Biography.* New York: Schocken Books, 1981.

Kiger, Robert, ed. *Kate Greenaway: Catalogue of an Exhibition of Original Artworks and Related Materials . . .* Pittsburgh: Hunt Institute for Botanical Documentation, Carnegie-Mellon University, 1980.

(GREENBERG, J.) See FPAA #2.

(GREENE, G.) Wobbe, R. A. *Graham Greene: A Bibliography and Guide to Research.* New York and London: Garland Publishing, Inc., 1979.

See also APG.

(GREGOR, A.) See FPAA #2.

(GREGYNOG PRESS) See Franklin, and Ransom.

(GREY, Z.) Myers, Edward and Judith. *A Bibliographical Check List of the Writings of Zane Grey.* Collinsville, Ct.: Country Lane Books, 1986.

See also APG, and FPAA #5.

(GRIMES, M.) See APG.

(GRISWOLD, R. W.) See BAL #3.

(GROSSMAN, A.) See FPAA #4.

(GRUBB, D.) See APG.

(GRUMBACH, D.) See APG.

(GUEST, B.) See FPAA #5.

(GUINEY, L.I.) See BAL #3, and Johnson.

(GUNN) Hagstrom, Jack W. C., and Bixby, George. *Thom Gunn: A Bibliography 1940–78.* London: Bertram Rota (1979).

(HAGGARD, H. R.) McKay, George L. *A Bibliography of the Writings of Sir Rider Haggard.* London: *The Bookman's Journal*, 1930.

Scott, J. E. *Sir Henry Rider Haggard 1856–1925.* Takeley (England): Elkin Mathews Ltd., 1947.

(HALE, N.) See FPAA #1.

(HALE, S. J.) See BAL #3.

(HALL, B. R.) See BAL #3.

(HALL, D.) Kelleher, Jack. *Donald Hall: A Bibliographical Checklist.* Easthampton: Warwick Press, 2000.

See also Lepper.

(HALL, J.) See BAL #3.

(HALL, J. N.) See FPAA #3.

(HALLECK, F.) See BAL #3, and Johnson.

(HALPINE, C. G.) See BAL #3.

(HAMMETT, D.) Layman, Richard. *Dashiell Hammett: A Descriptive Bibliography.* (Pittsburgh): University of Pittsburgh Press, 1979.

See also APG, and FPAA #1.

(HANLEY, J.) Gibbs, Linnea. *James Hanley: A Bibliography.* Vancouver: William Hoffer, 1980.

(HARDY, A. S.) See BAL #3.

(HARDY, J. E.) See FPAA #2.

(HARDY, T.) Purdy, Richard Little. *Thomas Hardy: A Bibliographical Study.* Reprinted. Oxford: Clarendon Press (1978).

Webb, A. P. *A Bibliography of the Works of Thomas Hardy 1865–1915.* New York: Burt Franklin (1968).

See also Cutler and Stiles, and Sadlier.

(HARLAND, H.) See BAL #3.

(HARRIS, F.) See *Casanova*.

(HARRIS, G. W.) See BAL #3.

(HARRIS, J. C.) See BAL #3, and Johnson.

(HARRIS, M.) See FPAA #1.

(HARRISON, C.) See BAL #3.

(HARRISON, J.). See APG.

(HARRISON OF PARIS) See Ford.

(HARTE, B.) See BAL #3, and Johnson.

(HASSLER, J.) Powers, Michael. *An Interview with Jon Hassler*. With a bibliography by Larry Dingman. Minneapolis: Dinkytown Antiquarian Bookstore, 1990.

(HAWKES, J.) See FPAA #1, Gawsworth, and Lepper.

(HAWTHORNE, N.) Clark, C. E. Frazer, Jr. *Nathaniel Hawthorne: A Descriptive Bibliography*. (Pittsburgh): University of Pittsburgh Press, 1978.
See also BAL #4, FPAA #1, Johnson, and Schwartz.

(HAY, J.) See BAL #4, and Johnson.

(HAYNE, P. H.) See BAL #4.

(HAZO, S.) See FPAA #2.

(HAZZARD, S.) See FPAA #4.

(HEARN, L.) Perkins, P. D. and Ione. *Lafcadio Hearn: A Bibliography of His Writings*. Boston and New York: Houghton Mifflin Company, 1934.
See also BAL #4, and Johnson.

(HEDGE, F. H.) See FPAA #3.

(HEINLEIN, R. A.) Owings, Mark. *Robert A. Heinlein: A Bibliography*. Baltimore: Croatan House (1973). See also APG.

(HELLER, J.) See APG, FPAA #2, and Lepper.

(HELLMAN, L.) See FPAA #2.

(HEMINGWAY, E.) Hanneman, Andre. *Ernest Hemingway: A Comprehensive Bibliography*. Princeton, N.J.: Princeton University Press, 1967.
Hanneman, Andre. *Supplement to Ernest Hemingway: A Comprehensive Bibliography*. Princeton, N.J.: Princeton University Press, 1975.
See also APG, FPAA #1, and Johnson.

(HENRY, O.) See Porter, BAL #7, and Johnson.

(HENTY, G. A.) Dartt, Robert L. *G. A. Henty: A Bibliography*. Cedar Grove (N.J.), and Altricham: Dar-Web, Inc., and John Sherratt (1971).

(HERBERT, A. P.) See Fabes.

(HERBERT, F.) Levack, Daniel J. H. *Dune Master: A Frank Herbert Bibliography*. (Westport, Ct.): Meckler (1988).

(HERBERT, H. W.) Van Winkle, William Mitchell. *Henry William Herbert [Frank Forester]: A Bibliography of His Writings 1832–1858*. Portland, Ore.: Southworth-Anthoesen Press, 1936.
See also BAL #4, and Johnson.

(HERBST, J.) See FPAA #1.

(HERFORD, O.) See Johnson.

(HERGESHEIMER, J.) Swire, H.L.R. *A Bibliography of the Works of Joseph Hergesheimer*. Philadelphia: Centaur Book Shop, 1922.
See also Johnson, and Schwartz.

(HERLIHY, J. L.) See FPAA #5.

(HEWLETT, M.) See Cutler and Stiles.

(HEYEN, W.) See FPAA #2.

(HEYWARD, D.) See FPAA #3, and Johnson.

(HIGGINS, G. V.) See FPAA #1.

(HIGGINSON, T. W.) See BAL #4.

(HILLERMAN, T.) *Collecting Tony Hillerman: A Checklist of the First Editions of Tony Hillerman*. Sante Fe, New Mexico: Vinegar Tom Press (1992).
Heib, Louis A. *Tony Hillerman: A Bibliography*. Tucson: Press of the Gigantic Hound, 1990.
See also APG.

(HILLHOUSE, J. A.) See BAL #4.

(HIMES, C.) See APG.

(HIRSHMAN, J.) See Lepper.

(HODGSON, R.) Sweetser, Wesley D. *Ralph Hodgson: A Bibliography*. New York and London: Garland Publishing, Inc., 1980.

(HOFFMAN, C. F.) See BAL #4, and Johnson.

(HOFFMAN, D.) See FPAA #2.

(HOGARTH PRESS) Woolmer, J. Howard. *A Checklist of the Hogarth Press 1917–1946*. Revere, Pennsylvania: Woolmer/Brotherson Ltd., 1986.

(HOLLAND, J. G.) See BAL #4.

(HOLLEY, M.) See FPAA #4.

(HOLMES, J.) See FPAA #5.

(HOLMES, J. C.) Ardinger, Richard K. *An Annotated Bibliography of Works by John Clellon Holmes*. Pocatello, Idaho: Idaho State University Press, 1979.
See also FPAA #2.

(HOLMES, M. J.) See BAL #4.

(HOLMES, O. W.) Currier, Thomas Franklin. *A Bibliography of Oliver Wendell Holmes*. Washington Square, N.Y., and London: New York University Press, and Oxford University Press, 1953.
See also BAL #4, Johnson, and Schwartz.

(HOOKER, T.) See FPAA #4.

(HOPKINS, G. M.) Dunne, Tom. *Gerard Manley Hopkins: A Comprehensive Bibliography*. Oxford: Clarendon Press (1978).

(HOPLEY, G.) See FPAA #3, and Woolrich.

(HORGAN, P.) Horgan, Paul. *Approaches to Writing*. Farrar, Straus and Giroux, New York (1973).

(HOSMER, W.H.C.) See BAL #4.

(HOUGH, E.) See BAL #4, and Johnson.

(HOUSMAN, A. E.) Carter, John, and Sparrow, John. *A. E. Housman: A Bibliography*. 2d ed. Revised by William White. (Suffolk): St. Paul's Bibliographies, 1982.
Ehrsam, Theodore G. *A Bibliography of Alfred Edward Housman*. Boston: F. W. Faxon Company, 1941.

(HOVEY, R.) See BAL #4, and Johnson.

(HOWARD, R. E.) Lord, Glenn. *The Last Celt: A Bio-Bibliography of Robert Ervin Howard*. West Kingston (R.I.): Donald M. Grant, 1976.

(HOWE, E. W.) See FPAA #2.

(HOWE, J. W.) See BAL #4.

(HOWELLS, W. D.) Gibson, William M., and Arms, George. *A Bibliography of William Dean Howells*. New York: New York Public Library (1971).
See also BAL #4, Johnson.

(HUDSON, S.) See Gawsworth.

(HUDSON) Payne, John R. *W. H. Hudson: A Bibliography*. (Hamden, Ct.): Archon Books (1977).
See also Schwartz, Cutler and Stiles.

(HUGHES, L.) Dickinson, Donald C. *A Bio-bibliography of Langston Hughes 1902–1967*. (Hamden, Ct.): Archon Books, 1972.
See also APG, and FPAA #3.

(HUGHES, T.) Sagar, Keith, and Tabor, Stephen. *Ted Hughes: A Bibliography 1946–1980*. (London): Mansell Publishing Limited (1983).

(HUMPHREY, W.) See FPAA #1.

(HUNEKER, J.) See BAL #4, and Johnson.

(HUNT, LEIGH) Brewer, Luther A. *My Leigh Hunt Library: The First Editions*. New York: Burt Franklin (1970). A reprint of the 1932 edition.

(HURSTON, Z. N.) See APG, and FPAA #1.

(HUXLEY, A.) Eschelbach, Claire John, and Shober, Joyce Lee. *Aldous Huxley: A Bibliography 1916–1959*. Berkeley: University of California Press, 1961.
See also Casanova, and Cutler and Stiles.

(INGE, W.) See FPAA #2.

(INGERSOLL, R. G.) Stein, Gordon. *Robert G. Ingersoll: A Checklist.* No place: Kent State University Press (1969).

(INGRAHAM, J. H.) See BAL #4.

(IRISH, W.) See Woolrich.

(IRVING, J.) See APG.

(IRVING, W.) Langfeld, William R. *Washington Irving: A Bibliography.* New York: New York Public Library, 1933.

Williams, Stanley T., and Edge, Mary Allen. *A Bibliography of the Writings of Washington Irving: A Check List.* Reprinted. New York: Burt Franklin (1970).

See also BAL #5, and Johnson.

(ISHERWOOD, C.) Westby, Selmer, and Brown, Clayton M. *Christopher Isherwood: A Bibliography.* Los Angeles: California State College at Los Angeles Foundation, 1968.

(ISHIGURO, K.) See APG.

(JACKSON, C.) See FPAA #3.

(JACKSON, H. H.) See BAL #5, and Johnson.

(JACKSON, J.) See APG.

(JACKSON, S.) See FPAA #2.

(JACOBS, W. W.) Lamerton, Chris. *W. W. Jacobs: A Bibliography.* (Margate, Kent): Greystone Press (1988).

(JAMES, HENRY) Edel, Leon, and Laurence, Dan H. *A Bibliography of Henry James.* Oxford: Clarendon Press, 1982.

Philips, LeRoy. *A Bibliography of the Writings of Henry James.* New York: Coward McCann, 1930.

See also APG, BAL #5, and Johnson.

(JAMES, P. D.) See APG.

(JAMES, W.) See Johnson.

(JANVIER, T. A.) See BAL #5, Johnson.

(JARRELL) Wright, Stuart. *Randall Jarrell: A Descriptive Bibliography 1929–1983.* Charlottesville: University Press of Virginia (1986).

See also FPAA #4.

(JEFFERIES, R.) See Sadlier.

(JEFFERS, R) Alberts, S. S. *A Bibliography of the Works of Robinson Jeffers.* Rye, N.Y.: Cultural History Research, 1961.

See also APG, FPAA #3, and Johnson.

(JEWETT, S. O.) See BAL #5, and Johnson.

(JOHNSON, J.) See FPAA #5.

(JOHNSON, O.) See FPAA #5.

(JOHNSON, S.) Courtney, William Prideaux, and Smith, David Nichol. *A Bibliography of Samuel Johnson.* With *Johnsonian Bibliography: A Supplement to Courtney* by R. W. Chapman and Allen Hazen. (New Castle, Del.): Oak Knoll Books and Gerald M. Goldberg, 1984.

See also FPAA #3.

(JOHNSTON, M.) See Johnson.

(JOHNSTON, R. M.) See BAL #5.

(JONES, J.) Hopkins, John R. *James Jones: A Checklist.* Detroit: Gale Research Co., 1974.

See also FPAA #1.

(JONES, J. B.) See BAL #6.

(JONES, L.) Dace, Letitia. *LeRoi Jones (Imamu Amiri Baraka): A Checklist of Works By and About Him.* London: Nether Press, 1971.

See also FPAA #1.

(JONES, M. P.) See FPAA #1.

(JONES, R. F.) See Currey.

(JONG, E.) See FPAA #1.

(JOSEPHSON, M.) See FPAA #1.

(JOYCE, J.) Slocum, John J., and Cahoon, Herbert. *A Bibliography of James Joyce.* Westport, Ct.: Greenwood Press (1953).
See also APG, and *Casanova.*
(JUDAH, S.B.H.) See BAL #5.
(JUDD, S.) See BAL #5.
(KAFKA, F.) Flores, Angel. *A Kafka Bibliography 1908–1976.* New York: Gordian Press, 1976.
(KAHN, R.) See FPAA #5.
(KEATS, J.) MacGillivray, J. R. *Keats A Bibliography and Reference Guide with an Essay on Keats' Reputation.* Canada: University of Toronto Press (1949).
See also Schwartz.
(KELLER, D. H.) See Currey.
(KELLEY, E. S.) See FPAA #1.
(KELLEY, R.) See Lepper.
(KELLEY, W. M.) See FPAA #2.
(KELLY, W.) See FPAA #4.
(KELMSCOTT PRESS) Peterson, William S. *A Bibliography of the Kelmscott Press.* Reprinted with corrections. Oxford: Clarendon Press, 1985.
See also Franklin, and Ransom.
(KENNEDY, J. P.) See BAL #5, and Johnson.
(KENNEDY, W.) See APG.
(KENNEDY, X.) See FPAA #1.
(KENNEDY, X. J.) See FPAA #2.
(KENT, R.) See Johnson.
(KEROUAC, J.) Charters, Ann. *A Bibliography of Works by Jack Kerouac.* New York: Phoenix Bookshop, 1975.
See also APG, and FPAA #1.
(KESEY, K.) See APG, and FPAA #1.
(KEY, F. S.) See BAL #5.
(KEYES, D.) See Currey.
(KILLENS, J. O.) See FPAA #2, and Lepper.
(KILMER, J.) See BAL #5, and Johnson.
(KING, S.) See APG, and Currey.
(KINNELL, G.) See FPAA #2.
(KIPLING) Livingston, Flora V. *Bibliography of the Works of Rudyard Kipling.* New York: Burt Franklin (1968).
Livingston, Flora V. *Supplement to a Bibliography of the Works of Rudyard Kipling.* New York: Burt Franklin (1968).
See also Cutler and Stiles.
(KIRKLAND, C. M.) See BAL #5.
(KIRKLAND, J.) See BAL #5.
(KLASS, P. J.) See Currey.
(KLINE, O. A.) See Currey.
(KNEALE, T. N.) See Currey.
(KNIGHT, D. F.) See Currey.
(KNOWLES, J.) See FPAA #3.
(KOCH, K.) See Lepper.
(KOESTLER, A.) Merrill, Reed, and Frazier, Thomas. *Arthur Koestler: An International Bibliography.* Ann Arbor: Ardis (1979).
(KOONTZ, D. R.) Stephens, Christopher P. *A Checklist of Dean R. Koontz.* Hastings-on-Hudson, N.Y.: Ultramarine Publishing Co., 1987.
(KORNBLUTH, K. M.) See Currey.
(KOSINSKI, J.) See FPAA #4.
(KUNITZ, S.) See FPAA #1.

(KUTTNER, H.) See Currey.

(LAFFERTY, R. A.) See Currey.

(LAMANTIA, P.) See Lepper.

(LAMB, C.) Livingston, Luther S.; Thomson, J. C.; and Roff, Renée (compiler). *A Bibliography of the Writings of Charles and Mary Lamb.* Bronxville, New York: Nicholas T. Smith (1979).

(LANDON, M. D.) See BAL #5.

(LANDOR, W. S.) Wise and Wheeler. *Walter Savage Landor: A Bibliography.* L: 1979.

(LANGE, J. F.) See Currey.

(LANIER, Sidney) See BAL #5, and Johnson.

(LANIER, Sterling) See Currey.

(LARCOM, L.) See BAL #5.

(LARDNER, R.) Bruccoli, Matthew J., and Richard Layman. *Ring W. Lardner: A Descriptive Bibliography.* (Pittsburgh): University of Pittsburgh Press (1976).
See also FPAA #1, and Johnson.

(LARKIN, P.) Bloomfield, B. C. *Philip Larkin: A Bibliography 1933–1976.* London/Boston: Faber and Faber (1979).

(LARNER, J.) See FPAA #2.

(LATHROP, G. P.) See BAL #5.

(LAUMER, J. K.) See Currey.

(LAWRENCE, D. H.) Roberts, Warren. *A Bibliography of D. H. Lawrence.* 2d ed. Cambridge: Cambridge University Press (1982).
See also APG, Cutler and Stiles, and Schwartz.

(LAWRENCE, T. E.) O'Brien, Philip M. *T. E. Lawrence: A Bibliography.* Boston: G. K. Hall (1988). **And** the second revised and expanded edition. New Castle: Oak Knoll Press, 2000.
See also APG.

(LAZARUS, E.) See BAL #5.

(LEACOCK, S.) Lomer, Gerhard R. *Stephen Leacock: A Check-list and Index of His Writings.* Ottawa: National Library of Canada, 1954.
Spadoni, Carl. *A Bibliography of Stephen Leacock.* (Toronto): ECW Press (1998).

(LEAVIS, F. R.) McKenzie, D. F., and Allum, M-P. *F. R. Leavis: A Check-list 1924–1964.* London: Chatto & Windus, 1966.

(LE CARRÉ, J.) See APG.

(LE GALLIENNE, R.) See Cutler and Stiles.

(LE GUIN, U.) Cogell, Elizabeth Cummins. *Ursula K. LeGuin: A Primary and Secondary Bibliography.* Boston: G. K. Hall (1983).
See also Currey.

(LEIBER, F.) Morgan, Chris. *Fritz Leiber: A Bibliography 1934–1979.* Selly Oak, Birmingham, England: Morgenstern, 1979.
See also Currey.

(LELAND, C. G.) See BAL #5.

(LEONARD, E.) Stephens, Christopher P. *A Checklist of Elmore Leonard.* (Hastings-on-the-Hudson, NY: Ultramarine 1991.)
See also APG.

(LESSING, D.) Brueck, Eric T. *Doris Lessing: A Bibliography of Her First Editions.* (London): Metropolis (Antiquarian Books) Ltd, 1984.

(LEVERTOV, D.) Wilson, Robert. *A Bibliography of Denise Levertov.* New York: Phoenix Bookshop, 1972.
See also FPAA #3, and Lepper.

(LEVIN, I.) See FPAA #2.

(LEWIS, A. H.) See BAL #5.

(LEWIS, C. S.) Christopher, Joe R., and Ostling, Joan K. *C. S. Lewis: An Annotated Checklist of Writings About Him and His Works.* (Rochester): Kent State University Press (no date).
See also Currey.

(LEWIS, J.) See FPAA #4.
(LEWIS, S.) Pastore, Stephen R. *Sinclair Lewis: A Descriptive Bibliography*. New Haven: Yale Books, 1997.
See also FPAA #3, and Johnson.
(LEWIS, W.) Morrow, Bradford, and Lafourcade, Bernard. *A Bibliography of the Writings of Wyndham Lewis*. Santa Barbara: Black Sparrow Press, 1978.
(LEY, R. A.) See Currey.
(LIMITED EDITIONS CLUB) See APG.
(LINCOLN, A.) Smith, William H., Jr. *A Priced Lincoln Bibliography*. New York: Privately published, 1906.
(LINDSAY, D.) See Currey.
(LINDSAY, V.) See Johnson.
(LINEBARGER, P.) See Currey.
(LIPPARD, G.) See BAL #5.
(LOCKE, D. R.) See BAL #5.
(LODGE, G. C.) See FPAA #1.
(LOEB, H.) See FPAA #1.
(LOEWINSOHN, R.) See Lepper.
(LONDON, J.) Sisson, James E., III, and Martens, Robert W. *Jack London First Editions*. Oakland: Star Rover House, 1979.
Walker, Dale L., and Sisson, James E., III. *The Fiction of Jack London: A Chronological Bibliography*. El Paso: Texas Western Press, 1972.
Woodbridge, Hensley C.; London, John; and Tweney, George H. *Jack London: A Bibliography*. Georgetown: Talisman Press, 1966.
See also APG, BAL #5, and Johnson.
(LONG, F. B.) See Currey.
(LONG, H.) See FPAA #5.
(LONGFELLOW) Livingston, Luther S. *A Bibliography of the First Editions . . . of Henry Wadsworth Longfellow*. New York: Burt Franklin (1968).
See also BAL #5, Johnson, and Schwartz.
(LONGFELLOW, S.) See FPAA #3.
(LONGSTREET, A. B.) See BAL #6, and FPAA #1.
(LOOS, A.) See FPAA #3.
(LOVECRAFT, H. P.) Owings, Mark, with Chalker, Jack L. *The Revised H. P. Lovecraft Bibliography*. Baltimore: Mirage Press, 1973.
See also Currey.
(LOWELL, A.) See BAL #6, and Johnson.
(LOWELL, J. R.) Chamberlain, Jacob Chester, and Livingston, Luther S. *A Bibliography of the First Editions in Book Form of the Writings of James Russell Lowell*. New York: Privately printed, 1914.
See also BAL #6, and Johnson.
(LOWELL, R.) See FPAA #1.
(LOWELL, R.T.S.) See BAL #6.
(LOWNDES, R. A.) See Currey.
(LOWRY, M.) Woolmer, J. Howard. *Malcolm Lowry: A Bibliography*. Revere, Mass.: Woolmer/Brotherson Ltd., 1983.
(LUDLUM, R.) See APG.
(LUMPKIN, G.) See FPAA #2.
(LUPOFF, R. A.) See Currey.
(LURIE, A.) See FPAA #5.
(LYON, H. M.) See FPAA #4.
(LYTLE, A.) Wright, Stuart. *Andrew Nelson Lytle: A Bibliography 1920–1982*. Sewanee (Tenn.): University of the South, 1982.
See also FPAA #1.

(MacDONALD, J. D.) Shine, Walter and Jean. *A MacDonald Potpourri—Being a Miscellany of Post-perusal Pleasures of the John D. MacDonald Books* . . . Gainesville, Fla.: University of Florida Libraries, 1988.
See also APG.

(MACDONALD, R.) Bruccoli, Matthew J. *Ross Macdonald / Kenneth Millar A Descriptive Bibliography.* (Pittsburgh): University of Pittsburgh Press, 1983.
See also APG, and FPAA #1 (Millar).

(MacGREGOR, J. M.) See Currey.

(MACHEN, A.) Danielson, Henry. *Arthur Machen: A Bibliography.* London: Henry Danielson, 1923.
Goldstone, Adrian, and Sweetser, Wesley. *A Bibliography of Arthur Machen.* New York: Haskell House, 1973.

(MacLEAN, K. A.) See Currey.

(MacLEISH, A.) Mullaly, Edward J. *Archibald MacLeish: A Checklist.* No place: Kent State University Press (1973).
See also Johnson.

(MacNEICE, L.) Brown, Terence, and Reid, Alec. *Time Was Away: The World of Louis MacNeice.* (Dublin): Dolmen Press (1974).

(MAILER, N.) Lennon, J. Michael, and Pedro, Donna. *Norman Mailer: Works and Days.* Shavertown, Penna.: Sligo Press, 2000. See also APG, FPAA #5, and Lepper.

(MAJOR, C.) See BAL #6.

(MALAMUD, B.) Kosofsky, Rita Nathalie. *Bernard Malamud: An Annotated Checklist.* No place: Kent State University Press (1969).
See APG, FPAA #5, and Lepper.

(MALZBERG, B. N.) See Currey.

(MANSFIELD, K.) Kirkpatrick, J. *A Bibliography of Katherine Mansfield.* Oxford: Clarendon Press, 1989.

(MARCH, W. E.) See FPAA #3.

(MARKFIELD, W.) See FPAA #1.

(MARKHAM, E.) See Johnson.

(MARKSON, D.) See APG.

(MARQUAIS, D.) See Johnson.

(MARQUAND, J. P.) Penzler, Otto. John P. Marquand's Mr. Moto. New York: Mysterious Bookshop (2000). See also FPAA #1.

(MARSH, N.) Gibbs, Rowan, and Williams, Richard. *Ngaio Marsh: A Bibliography of English Language Publications in Hardback and Paperback.* South Humberside, England: Dragonby Press, 1990.

(MARSHALL, P.) See APG.

(MARTIN, G.R.R.) See Currey.

(MARVEL, I.) See Johnson.

(MASEFIELD, J.) Handley-Taylor, Geoffrey. *John Masefield, O.M.: The Queen's Poet Laureate.* London: Cranbrook Tower Press (1960).
Simmons, Charles H. *A Bibliography of John Masefield.* New York: Columbia University Press, 1930.
See also Cutler and Stiles.

(MASON, D. R.) See Currey.

(MASSON, D. I.) See Currey.

(MASTERS, E. L.) See FPAA #2, and Johnson.

(MATHESON, R.) See APG, and Currey.

(MATHEWS, C.) See BAL #6.

(MATTHIESSEN, P.) Nicholas, D. *Peter Matthiessen: A Bibliography 1951–1979.* Canoga Press, Calif.: Orirana Press (1979).
See also FPAA #1.

(MAUGHAM, W. S.) Stott, Raymond Toole. *A Bibliography of the Works of W. Somerset Maugham*. Edmonton: University of Alberta Press, 1973.

(MAXWELL, W.) See APG.

(McALMON, R.) See FPAA #1.

(McCAFFREY, A. I.) See Currey.

(McCARTHY, Cormac.) See APG, and FPAA #1.

(McCARTHY, M.) Goldman, Sherli Evens. *Mary McCarthy: A Bibliography*. New York: Harcourt, Brace & World (1968).
See also FPAA #4.

(McCLURE, M.) Clements, Marshall. *A Catalog of Works by Michael McClure 1956–1965*. New York: Phoenix Bookshop (1965).
See also Lepper, and *Six Poets*.

(McCOY, H.) See FPAA #1.

(McCULLERS, C.) Shapiro, Adrian M., Bryer, Jackson R., and Field, Kathleen. *Carson McCullers: A Descriptive Listing and Annotated Bibliography of Criticism*. New York and London: Garland Publishing Inc., 1980.
See also FPAA #2.

(McCUTCHEON, G. B.) See BAL #6, and Johnson.

(McELROY, J.) See APG.

(McEWAN, I.) SEE REES.

(McFEE, W.) Babb, James T. *A Bibliography of the Writings of William McFee*. Garden City: Doubleday, Doran & Co., 1931.
See also Johnson.

(McGAHERN, J.) See Rees.

(McGUANE, T.) See APG, and FPAA #5.

(McHENRY, J.) See BAL #6.

(McILWAIN, D.) See Currey.

(McINTYRE, V.) See Currey.

(McLANAHAN) Bartholomew, W. E. *Ed McClanahan: A Descriptive Bibliography 1954–2000*. Tucson: Sylph Publications (1999).

(McMURTRIE, D. C.) Bruntjen, Scott, and Young, Melissa L. *Douglas C. McMurtrie: Bibliographer and Historian of Printing*. Metuchen, N.J., and London: Scarecrow Press, 1979.

(McMURTRY, L.) See APG, FPAA #4, and Lepper.

(McPHEE, J.) See APG.

(MELTZER, D.) Kherdian, David. *David Meltzer: A Sketch from Memory and Descriptive Checklist*. Berkeley: Oyez, 1965.
See also Lepper.

(MELVILLE, H.) See BAL #6, Johnson, and Sadlier.

(MENCKEN, H. L.) Adler, Betty, and Wilhelm, Jane. *H. L. M.: The Mencken Bibliography*. Baltimore: Enoch Pratt Free Library (1961).
Frey, Carroll. *A Bibliography of the Writings of H. L. Mencken*. Philadelphia: The Centaur Book Shop, 1924.
Schrader, Richard J. (with the assistance of Thompson, George H., and Sanders, Jack R.) *H. L. Mencken: A Descriptive Bibliography*. (Pittsburgh): University of Pittsburgh Press (1998).
See APG, Johnson, and Schwartz.

(MEREDITH, G.) Collie, Michael. *George Meredith: A Bibliography*. (Toronto and Buffalo): University of Toronto Press (1974).
Forman, Maurice Buxton. *A Bibliography of the Writings in Prose and Verse of George Meredith*. New York: Haskell House, 1971.
Forman, Maurice Buxton. *Meredithiana, Being a Supplement to the Bibliography of Meredith*. New York: Haskell House, 1971.

(MEREDITH, W.) See FPAA #2.

(MERRIL, J.) See Currey.

(MERRILL, J.) See FPAA #2.

(MERRITT, A.) See Currey.

(MERRYMOUNT PRESS) See Ransom.

(MERTON, T.) Breit, Marquita E. *Thomas Merton: A Comprehensive Bibliography*. New ed. New York and London: Garland Publishing, Inc., 1986.
See also APG.

(MERWIN, W. S.) See FPAA #1.

(METCALF, P.) See FPAA #3.

(MICHENER, J.) Groseclose, David A. *James A. Michener: A Bibliography*. Austin: State House Press, 1996.
See also APG.

(MILES, J.) See Lepper.

(MILL, JOHN STUART) MacNinn, Ney, et al. *Bibliography of the Published Writings of John Stuart Mill*. Evanston: North Wester University, 1945.

(MILLAR, K.) See FPAA #1.

(MILLAY) Yost, Karl. *A Bibliography of the Works of Edna St. Vincent Millay*. New York and London: Harper & Brothers. 1937.
See also FPAA #4, and Johnson.

(MILLER, A.) Jensen, George H. *Arthur Miller: A Bibliographical Checklist*. (Columbia, S.C.): J. Faust & Co. (1976).
See also APG, and FPAA #1.

(MILLER, H.) Moore, Thomas H. *Bibliography of Henry Miller*. (Minneapolis): Henry Miller Literary Society, 1961.
Porter, Bern. *Henry Miller: A Chronology and Bibliography*. (Baltimore: Waverly Press, 1945).
Shifreen, Lawrence J., and Jackson, Roger. *Henry Miller: A Bibliography of Primary Sources*. (Ann Arbor, Mich., and Glen Arm, Md.: Roger Jackson, and Lawrence J. Shifreen) 1993.

(MILLER, J.) See BAL #6, and Johnson.

(MILLER, Walter. M.) See Currey.

(MILLER, Warren.) See Lepper.

(MILNE, A. A.) See Cutler and Stiles.

(MITCHELL, D.) See BAL #6, and Johnson.

(MITCHELL, I.) See BAL #6.

(MITCHELL, J. A.) See BAL #6.

(MITCHELL, S. W.) See BAL #6, and Johnson.

(MOLLOY, R.) See FPAA #4.

(MOODY, W. V.) See BAL #6, and Johnson.

(MOORCOCK, M.) See Currey.

(MOORE, B.) See Rees.

(MOORE, C. C.) See BAL #6.

(MOORE, C. L.) See Currey.

(MOORE, G.) Gilcher, Edwin. *A Bibliography of George Moore*. Dekalb: Northern Illinois University Press (1970).
See also Cutler and Stiles.

(MOORE, JULIA) Greely, A. H. *The Sweet Singer of Michigan Bibliographically Considered*. New York: The Bibliographical Society of America, 1945.

(MOORE, M.) Abbott, Craig S. *Marianne Moore: A Descriptive Bibliography*. (Pittsburgh): University of Pittsburgh Press, 1977.
See also FPAA #1.

(MORGAN, C.) See Coppard.

(MORLEY, C.) Lee, Alfred P. *A Bibliography of Christopher Morley*. Garden City: Doubleday, Doran & Company, 1935.
Lyle, Guy R., and Brown, H. Tatnall, Jr. *A Bibliography of Christopher Morley*. Washington, D.C.: The Scarecrow Press, 1952.
See also *Casanova* and Johnson.

(MORMON) Flake, Chad J. *A Mormon Bibliography, 1830–1930.* Salt Lake City: University of Utah Press, 1978.

(MORRIS, G. P.) See BAL #6.

(MORRIS, W.) Pye, John William. *A Bibliography of the American Editions of William Morris Published by Roberts Brothers, Boston, 1867–1898.* Brockton, Mass.: John William Pye Rare Books, 1993.

See also FPAA #5, and Lepper.

(MORRISON, T.) See APG.

(MORTON, S. W.) See BAL #6, and FPAA #2.

(MOSKOWITZ, S.) See Currey.

(MOSS, H.) See FPAA #2.

(MOTLEY, J. L.) See BAL #6.

(MOTLEY, W.) See FPAA #2.

(MOULTON, E. L.) See BAL #6.

(MUIR, E.) Mellown, Elgin W. *Bibliography of the Writings of Edwin Muir.* University, Ala.: University of Alabama Press (1964).

(MUIR, J.) Kimes, William F. and Maymie B. *John Muir: A Reading Bibliography.* Fresno: Panorama West Books, 1986.

See also BAL #6, and Johnson.

(MUIR, P. H.) *P. H. Muir: A Check List of His Published Work.* (No author listed.) Blakeney (Norfolk, England): Elkin Mathews, 1983.

(MUMFORD, L.) Newman, Elmer S. Lewis. *Lewis Mumford: A Bibliography 1914–1970.* New York: Harcourt Brace Jovanovich, Inc. (1971).

(MUNDY, T.) Grant, Donald M. *Talbot Mundy: Messenger of Destiny.* West Kingston (R.I.): Donald M. Grant, 1983.

(MURDOCH, I.) Tominaga, Thomas T., and Schneidermeyer, Wilma. *Iris Murdoch and Muriel Spark: A Bibliography.* Metuchen, N.J.: Scarecrow Press, 1976.

(MURFREE, M. N.) See BAL #6.

(MURRY, JOHN. M.) Lilley, George P. *A Bibliography of John Middleton Murry 1889–1957.* Toronto/Buffalo: University of Toronto Press (1974).

See also Currey.

(MYERS, P. H.) See BAL #6.

(NABOKOV, V.) Juliar, Michael. *Vladimir Nabokov: A Descriptive Bibliography.* New York and London: Garland Publishing, Inc., 1986.

See also APG, and FPAA #5.

(NASH, JOHN HENRY PRESS) See Ransom.

(NASH, O.) See FPAA #3.

(NATHAN, G. J.) See Johnson.

(NATHAN, R.) Laurence, Dan H. *Robert Nathan: A Bibliography.* New Haven: Yale University Library, 1960.

See also *Casanova,* FPAA #2, and Johnson.

(NEAL, John) See BAL #6.

(NEAL, Joseph C.) See BAL #6.

(NEIHARDT, J. G.) See Johnson.

(NEMEROV, H.) See FPAA #2.

(NEUGEBOREN, J.) See FPAA #5.

(NEWELL, R. H.) See BAL #6.

(NEWHOUSE, E.) See FPAA #2.

(NEWMAN, F.) See FPAA #1.

(NEW REVIEW PRESS) See Ford.

(NEWTON, Edward.) (Fleck, Robert). *A. Edward Newton: A Collection of His Work.* (New Castle, Del.): Oak Knoll Books, 1986.

See also *Casanova* and Johnson.

(NEWTON, Sir Isaac.) Gray, George J. *A Bibliography of the Works of Sir Isaac Newton.* Second

Edition, Revised and Enlarged. Cambridge: Bowes and Bowes, 1907 (Facsimile edition. Mansfield Centre, CT: Martino Fine Books [1998]).

(NICHOLS, R.) See Gawsworth.

(NIMS, J. F.) See FPAA #4.

(NIN, A.) Franklin, Benjamin, V. *Anaïs Nin: A Bibliography.* No place: Kent State University Press (1973).
See also FPAA #1.

(NIVEN, L.) See Currey.

(NOAH, M. M.) See BAL #6.

(NONESUCH PRESS) See Ransom.

(NORDHOFF, C. B.) See FPAA #3.

(NORRIS, F.) Lohf, Kenneth A., and Sheehy, Eugene P. *Frank Norris: A Bibliography.* Los Gatos (Calif.): The Talisman Press, 1959.
See also BAL #6, and Johnson.

(NORTON, A.) See Currey.

(NOURSE, A. E.) See Currey.

(NYE, B.) See BAL #6.

(OATES, J. C.) Lercangee, Francine. *Joyce Carol Oates: An Annotated Bibliography.* New York and London: Garland Publishing, Inc., 1986.
See also FPAA #5, and Lepper.

(OBELISK PRESS) See Ford.

(O'BRIAN, P.) See APG.

(O'BRIEN, F.) See BAL #6.

(O'BRIEN, P.) See APG.

(O'CASEY, S.) Ayling, Ronald, and Durkan, Michael J. *Sean O'Casey: A Bibliography.* Seattle: University of Washington Press (1978).

(O'CONNOR, E.) See FPAA #5.

(O'CONNOR, Flannery) Farmer, David. *Flannery O'Connor: A Descriptive Bibliography.* New York and London: Garland Publishing, 1981.
See also APG, and FPAA #1.

(O'CONNOR, Frank) Sheehy, Maurice. *Michael/Frank: Studies on Frank O'Connor.* Dublin: Gill & Macmillan (1969).

(OFFICINA BODINI PRESS) See Ransom.

(O'FLAHERTY, L.) Doyle, Paul A. *Liam O'Flaherty: An Annotated Bibliography.* Troy, N.Y.: Whitston Publishing Co., 1972.

(O'HARA, F.) Smith, Alexander Jr. *Frank O'Hara: A Comprehensive Bibliography.* New York and London: Garland Publishing Inc., 1979.
See also FPAA #4, and Lepper.

(O'HARA, J.) Bruccoli, Matthew J. *John O'Hara: A Descriptive Bibliography.* (Pittsburgh): University of Pittsburgh Press, 1978.
See also FPAA #1.

(OLIVER, S. C.) See Currey.

(OLSON, C.) Butterick, George F., and Glover, Albert. *A Bibliography of Works by Charles Olson.* New York: Phoenix Bookshop, 1967.
See also FPAA #3.

(OLYMPIA PRESS) Kearney, Patrick J. *The Paris Olympia Press.* London: Black Spring Press (1987).

(O'NEILL, E.) Atkinson, Jennifer McCabe. *Eugene O'Neill: A Descriptive Bibliography.* (Pittsburgh): University of Pittsburgh Press, 1974.
See also FPAA #1, and Johnson.

(OPPENHEIMER, J.) See FPAA #3

(O'REILLY, J. B.) See BAL #6.

(ORWELL, G.) Fenwick, Gillian. *George Orwell: A Bibliography.* New Castle: Oak Knoll Press, 1998.
See also APG.

(OSGOOD, F. S.) See BAL #6.
(OSLER, W.) Golden, Richard L., M.D., and Roland, Charles G., M.D. *Sir William Osler: An Annotated Bibliography with Illustrations.* San Francisco: Norman Publishing, 1988.
(OZ) Martin, Dick; Haff, James E.; and Greene, David L. *Bibliographia Oziana: A Concise Bibliographical Checklist of the Oz Books by L. Frank Baum and His Successors.* No place: International Wizard of Oz Club (1976).
(OZICK, C.) See APG.
(PAGE, T. N.) See BAL #6, and Johnson.
(PAINE, A. B.) See FPAA #5.
(PALEY, G.) See FPAA #2.
(PALMER, H. P.) See Gawsworth.
(PANGHORN, E.) See Currey.
(PANSHIN, A.) See Currey.
(PARIS) See Ford.
(PARKER, D.) See FPAA #4, and Johnson.
(PARKER, R.) See APG.
(PARKER, T.) See FPAA #4.
(PARKMAN, F.) See BAL #6, and Johnson.
(PARRISH, A.) See FPAA #4.
(PARSONS, T. W.) See BAL #6.
(PASTERNAK, B.) Holtzman, Irwin T. *A Check List of Boris Leonidovich Pasternak (1890–1960): Books in English.* (Southfield, Mich.: Irwin T. Holtzman, 1990.)
(PATCHEN, K.) Morgan, Richard G. *Kenneth Patchen.* Mamaroneck, N.Y: Paul P. Appel (1978).
(PATER, W.) See Cutler and Stiles.
(PAUL, E.) See FPAA #5.
(PAULDING, J. K.) See BAL #7, and Johnson.
(PAYNE, J. H.) See BAL #7.
(PEABODY, E. P.) See FPAA #3.
(PEAKE, M.) See Currey.
(PEARSON, E. L.) Webber, Hallum. *Edmund Lester Pearson.* Not published.
(PEGASUS PRESS) See Ransom.
(PEGNANA PRESS) See Ransom.
(PERCIVAL, J. G.) See BAL #7.
(PERCY, W.) Hobson, Linda Whitney. *Walker Percy: A Comprehensive Descriptive Bibliography.* New Orleans: Faust Publishing Co., 1988.
  Wright, Stuart. *Walker Percy: A Bibliography: 1930–1984.* (Westport, Ct.): Meckler Publishing (1986).
  See also APG, and FPAA #2.
(PERCY, W. A.) See FPAA #2.
(PETERKIN, J.) See FPAA #1.
(PETERS, E.) See APG.
(PETRY, A.) See FPAA #1.
(PHILBRICK, C.) See FPAA #5.
(PHILLIPS, D. G.) See BAL #7.
(PIATT, J. J.) See BAL #7.
(PIKE, A.) See BAL #7.
(PINCKNEY, J.) See FPAA #2.
(PINKERTON, A.) See Johnson.
(PINKNEY, E. C.) See BAL #7.
(PIPER, H.) See Currey.
(PLAIN EDITIONS) See Ford.
(PLANTE, D.) See APG.
(PLATH, S.) See FPAA #2.

(POE, E. A.) Heartman, Charles F., and Canny, James R. *A Bibliography of First Printings of the Writings of Edgar Allan Poe*. Hattiesburg, Miss: The Book Farm, 1940.
Robertson, John W., M.D. *Bibliography of the Writings of Edgar A. Poe*. New York: Kraus Reprint Co., 1969.
See also BAL #7, Johnson, and Schwartz.
(POETRY BOOKSHOP) Woolmer, J. Howard. *The Poetry Bookshop 1912–1935: A Bibliography*. Revere, Penn., and Winchester (England): Woolmer/Brotherson Ltd., and St. Paul's Bibliographies, 1988.
(POHL, F.) See Currey.
(POLLINI, F.) See FPAA #2.
(POOL, M. L.) See FPAA #5.
(PORPOISE PRESS) See Ransom.
(PORTER, G. S.) MacLean, David G. *Gene Stratton-Porter*. Decatur: (Americana Books), 1987.
(PORTER, K. A.) Waldrip, Louise, and Bauer, Shirley Ann. *A Bibliography of the Works of Katherine Anne Porter* and *A Bibliography of the Criticism of the Works of Katherine Anne Porter*. Metuchen, N.J.: Scarecrow Press, 1969.
See also FPAA #2, Johnson, and Schwartz.
(PORTER, W. S.) Clarkson, Paul S. *A Bibliography of William Sydney Porter (O.Henry)*. Caldwell (Idaho): Caxton Printers, 1938.
See also BAL #7, and Johnson.
(PORTIS, C.) See FPAA #4.
(POTTER) Linder, Leslie. *A History of the Writings of Beatrix Potter*. London/New York: Frederick Warne (1971).
(POUND, E.) Gallup, Donald. *Ezra Pound: A Bibliography*. Charlottesville: University Press of Virginia (1983).
See also APG.
(POURNELLE, J.) See Currey.
(POWELL, A.) Lilley, George. *Anthony Powell: A Bibliography*. Winchester, and New Castle, Del.: St. Paul's Bibliographies, and Oak Knoll Books, 1993.
(POWELL, D.) See FPAA #5.
(POWERS, J. F.) See FPAA #5.
(POWYS, J. C.) Thomas, Dante. *A Bibliography of the Writings of John Cowper Powys: 1872–1963*. Mamaroneck, N.Y.: Paul P. Appel, 1975.
(POWYS, T. F.) Riley, Peter. *A Bibliography of T. F. Powys*. Hastings: R.A. Brimmell, 1967.
See also Cutler and Stiles.
(PRATT, F.) See Currey.
(PRESCOTT, W. H.) See BAL #7.
(PRICE, R.) Wright, Stuart, and West, James L. W., III. *Reynolds Price: A Bibliography 1949–1984*. Charlottesville: University Press of Virginia (1986).
See also APG, FPAA #1, and Lepper.
(PRIEST, C.) See Currey.
(PRINGLE, E. W.) See FPAA #2.
(PURDY, J.) See FPAA #2, and Lepper.
(PUTNAM, H. P.) See FPAA #2.
(PUZO, M.) See FPAA #5.
(PYLE, H.) See BAL #7, and Johnson.
(PYNCHON, T.) Mead, Clifford. *Thomas Pynchon: A Bibliography of Primary and Secondary Materials*. (Elmwood Park, Ill.): Dalkey Archive Press (1989).
See also APG, FPAA #1, and Walsh & Northouse.
(PYNSON PRESS) See Ransom.
(QUILLER-COUCH) Brittain, F. *Arthur Quiller-Couch: A Biographical Study of Q.* Cambridge and New York: University Press/Macmillan 1948.
(QUINN, S. G.) See Currey.

(RACKHAM, A.) Latimore, Sarah Briggs, and Haskell, Grace Clark. *Arthur Rackham: A Bibliography.* Jacksonville, Fla.: San Marco Bookstore (1936).

(RAND) Perinn, Vincent L. *Ayn Rand: First Descriptive Bibliography.* (Rockville, Md.): Q & B [Quill & Brush], 1990.
See *Author Price Guides.*

(RANDALL, M.) See Currey.

(RANDOM HOUSE) See Ransom.

(RANSOM, J. C.) Young, Thomas Daniel. *John Crowe Ransom: Critical Essays and a Bibliography.* Baton Rouge: Louisiana State University Press (1968).
See also FPAA #5.

(RANSOME) Hammond, Wayne G. *Arthur Ransome: A Bibliography.* Winchester/New Castle: St. Paul's/Oak Knoll, 2000.

(RAWLINGS, M. K.) See FPAA #2.

(READ, T. B.) See BAL #7.

(READE, C.) See Sadlier.

(RECHY, J.) See FPAA #3.

(REED, I.) See FPAA #2.

(REMINGTON, F.) See BAL #7, and Johnson.

(REPPLIER, A.) See Johnson.

(REYNOLDS, D. M.) See Currey.

(REXROTH, K.) Hartzell, James, and Zumwinkle, Richard. *Kenneth Rexroth: A Checklist of His Published Writings.* Los Angeles: Friends of the UCLA Library, 1967.

(RICCARDI PRESS) See Ransom.

(RICHTER, C.) See FPAA #1.

(RICKETTS, C.) Barclay, Michael Richard. *Catalogue of the Works of Charles Ricketts R.A. (from The Collection of Gordon Bottomley.)* Stroud Glos: Catalpa Press Ltd., 1985.

(RIDING, L.) Wexler, Joyce Piell. *Laura Riding: A Bibliography.* New York and London: Garland Publishing, Inc., 1981.
See also APG.

(RIIS, J. A.) Fried, Lewis, and Fierst, John. *Jacob A. Riis: A Reference Guide.* Boston: G. K. Hall & Co. (1977).

(RILEY, J. W.) Russo, Anthony J. and Dorothy R. *A Bibliography of James Whitcomb Riley.* Indianapolis: Indiana Historical Society, 1944.
See also BAL #7, and Johnson.

(RIPLEY, G.) See FPAA #3.

(ROBERTS, E. M.) See FPAA #2, and Johnson.

(ROBERTS, K. J.) See Currey.

(ROBERTS, K. L.) Murphy, P. *Kenneth Lewis Roberts: A Bibliography.* Privately printed (1975).
See also FPAA #2, and Johnson.

(ROBINSON, E. A.) Hogan, Charles Beecher. *A Bibliography of Edwin Arlington Robinson.* New Haven and London: Yale University Press and Oxford University Press, 1936.
See also FPAA #2, Johnson, and Schwartz.

(ROBINSON, F. M.) See Currey.

(ROBINSON, P.) See Currey.

(ROBINSON, R. E.) See BAL #7, and Johnson.

(ROE, E. P.) See BAL #7.

(ROETHKE, T.) McLeod, James Richard. *Theodore Roethke: A Bibliography.* No place: The Kent State University Press, 1973.
See also FPAA #1.

(ROGERS, B.) See Ransom.

(ROOSEVELT, T.) Wheelock, John Hall. *A Bibliography of Theodore Roosevelt.* New York: Charles Scribner's Sons, 1920.
See also Johnson.

(ROSS, Sir Ronald) See Gawsworth.

(ROTH, H.) See APG.

(ROTH, P.) See Lepper.

(ROTHENBERG, J.) See FPAA #4, and Lepper.

(ROVING EYE PRESS) See Ford.

(ROWSON, S. H.) See BAL #7, and Johnson.

(ROYALL, A. N.) See BAL #7.

(ROYCROFT PRESS) See Ransom.

(RUDGE, W. P.) See Ransom.

(RUMAKER, M.) See FPAA #3.

(RUSHDIE, S.) See APG.

(RUSKIN, J.) *The Bibliography . . . Arranged in Chronological Order of the Published Writings in Prose and Verse of John Ruskin, M.A. (From 1834 to 1881).* Paternoster Row, London: Eliot Stock, no date.

Wise, Thomas J., and Smart, James P. *A Complete Bibliography of the Writings in Prose and Verse of John Ruskin, LL.D.* Reprinted. 2 vols. Folkestone and London: Dawsons of Pall Mall, 1974.

(RUSS, J.) See Currey.

(RUSSELL, C. M.) Yost, Karl, and Renner, Frederic G. *A Bibliography of the Published Works of Charles M. Russell.* Lincoln: University of Nebraska Press (1971).

(RUSSELL, E. F.) See Currey.

(RUSSELL, G.W.) See A.E.

(RUSSELL, I.) See BAL #7.

(RYAN, A. J.) See BAL #7.

(SABERHAGEN, F. T.) See Currey.

(SACKVILLE-WEST,V.) Cross, Robert and Ann Ravenscroft-Hulme. *Vita Sackville-West: A Bibliography.* Winchester/New Castle: St. Paul's/Oak Knoll Press, 1999.

See also APG.

(SALINGER) Starosciak, Kenneth. *J. D. Salinger: A Thirty-Year Bibliography, 1938–1968.* (No place: no publisher, no date.)

See also APG, and FPAA #1.

(SALTUS, E. E.) See BAL #7, and Johnson.

(SANBORN, F. B.) See FPAA #4.

(SANDBURG, C.) See Johnson.

(SANDOZ, M.) See FPAA #2.

(SANDY, S.) See FPAA #5.

(SANTAYANA, G.) See Johnson.

(SARGENT, E.) See BAL #7.

(SAROYAN) Kherdian, David. *A Bibliography of William Saroyan 1934–64.* San Francisco: Roger Beacham (1965).

See also APG.

(SARTRE, J-P.) Belkind, Allen. *Jean-Paul Sartre: Sartre and Existentialism in English, A Bibliographical Guide.* No place: Kent State University Press (1970).

(SASSOON, S.) Farmer, David. *Siegfried Sassoon: A Memorial Exhibition.* Austin: Humanities Research Center, University of Texas, 1969.

(SAXE, J. G.) See BAL #7.

(SAYERS, D.) Gilbert, Colleen B. *A Bibliography of the Works of Dorothy L. Sayers.* Hamden, Ct.: Archon Books, 1978.

(SCHMITZ, J. H.) See Currey.

(SCHULBERG, B.) See FPAA #1.

(SCHWARTZ, D.) See FPAA #1.

(SCORTIA, T. N.) See Currey.

(SCOTT, E.) See APG, and FPAA #5.

(SCOTT, W. T.) See FPAA #5.

(SCOTT, Sir W.) Bodd, William B. and Bowden, Ann. *Sir Walter Scott: A Bibliographical History 1796–1832*. (New Castle): Oak Knoll Press (1998).
(SEDGWICK, C. M.) See BAL #7.
(SEEGER, A.) See BAL #7.
(SEIZEN PRESS) See Ford.
(SENDAK) Hanrahan, Joyce Y. *Works of Maurice Sendak 1947–1994*. Portsmouth, New Hampshire: Peter E. Randall Publisher, 1995.
(SERVIRE PRESS) See Ford.
(SERVISE, ROBERT) Mitham, Peter J. *Robert W. Service: A Bibliography*. (New Castle); Oak Knoll Press, 2000.
(SERVISS, G. P.) See Currey.
(SETON, E. T.) See Johnson.
(SETTLE, M.) See APG.
(SHAKESPEARE & CO.) See Ford.
(SHAKESPEARE HEAD) See Franklin.
(SHAKESPEARE HEAD PRESS) See Franklin.
(SHAPIRO, K.) See FPAA #1.
(SHAW, B.) See Currey.
(SHAW, G. B.) See Cutler and Stiles.
(SHAW, H. W.) See BAL #7.
(SHAW, I.) See FPAA #5.
(SHECKLEY, R. E.) See Currey.
(SHEED, W.) See FPAA #4.
(SHELDON, A.) See Currey.
(SHELLEY, M. & P.) See Schwartz.
(SHERMAN, F. D.) See BAL #7.
(SHIEL, M. P.) Morse A. Reynolds. *The Works of M. P. Shiel*. Los Angeles: Fantasy Publishing Co., Inc., 1948.
See also Gawsworth.
(SHILLABER, B. P.) See BAL #7.
(SHUTE) Giffuni, Cathy. *Nevil Shute: A Bibliography*. Adelaide: Auslip Press, 1988.
See also APG.
(SIGOURNEY, L. H.) See BAL #7.
(SILL, E. R.) See BAL #7.
(SILLITOE, A.) Gerard, David. *Alan Sillitoe: A Bibliography*. (London, England): Mansell Publishing Limited, 1988.
(SILVERBERG, R.) See Currey.
(SIMAK, C.) See Currey.
(SIMENON, G.) Foord, Peter; Williams, Richard; and Swan, Sally. *Georges Simenon: A Bibliography of the British First Editions . . . and of the Principal French and American Editions*. South Humberside, England: Dragonby Press, 1988.
(SIMMS, W.) See BAL #7, FPAA #1, and Johnson.
(SIMPSON, L.) See FPAA #2.
(SINCLAIR, U.) See FPAA #5.
(SINGER, I. B.) See APG.
(SITWELL, E., O. and S.) Fifoot, Richard. *A Bibliography of Edith, Osbert and Sacheverell Sitwell*. London: Rupert Hart-Davis, 1963.
See also Gawsworth.
(SLADEK, J. T.) See Currey.
(SLOANE, W. M.) See Currey.
(SMITH, B.) See FPAA #3.
(SMITH, C. A.) Sidney-Fryer, Donald, and Hands, Divers. *Emperor of Dreams: A Clark Ashton Smith Bibliography*. West Kingston, Rhode Island: Donald M. Grant, Publisher, 1978.
See also Currey.

(SMITH, E. E.) See Currey.

(SMITH, E. H.) See FPAA #1.

(SMITH, F. H.) See BAL #7, and Johnson.

(SMITH, G. O.) See Currey.

(SMITH, R. P.) See BAL #7.

(SMITH, S. F.) See BAL #7.

(SMITH, Seba) See BAL #7.

(SMITH, Stevie) Barbera, Jack, et al. *Stevie Smith: A Bibliography*. London: Mansell Publ. Ltd. (1987).

(SMITH, T.) See APG.

(SMITH, W. G.) See FPAA #2.

(SNELLING, W. J.) See BAL #7.

(SNODGRASS, W. D.) See FPAA #1.

(SNYDER, G.) Kherdian, David. *Gary Snyder: A Biographical Sketch and Descriptive Checklist*. Berkeley: Oyez, 1965.

McNeil, Katherine. *Gary Snyder: A Bibliography*. New York: The Phoenix Bookshop, 1983. See also Lepper.

(SOHL, G.) See Currey.

(SOLZHENITSYN, A.) Fiene, Donald M. *Alexander Solzhenitsyn: An International Bibliography of Writings By and About Him*. Ann Arbor: Ardis (1973).
See also APG.

(SONTAG, S.) See FPAA #1.

(SORRENTINO, G.) See FPAA #1.

(SPACKMAN, W. M.) See APG.

(SPARKS, M.) Tominaga, Thomas T., and Schneidermeyer, Wilma. *Iris Murdoch and Muriel Spark: A Bibliography*. Metuchen, N.J.: Scarecrow Press, 1976.

(SPEICHER, J.) See FPAA #2.

(SPENCER, E.) See APG.

(SPENDER, S.) Kulkarni, H. B. *Stephen Spender Works and Criticism: An Annotated Bibliography*. New York and London: Garland Publishing, 1976.

(SPICER, J.) See Lepper.

(SPINRAD, N. R.) See Currey.

(SPOFFORD, H. P.) See BAL #7.

(SPRINGS, E. W.) See FPAA #1.

(STABLEFORD, W. O.) See Currey.

(STACTON, D.) See FPAA #3.

(STANFORD, A.) See FPAA #2.

(STAPLETON, O.) See Currey.

(ST. CLAIR, M.) See Currey.

(STEADMAN, R.) Dinsmore, John, and Pilarz, John. *Ralph Steadman Bibliography*. Blue & Green Press.

(STEDMAN, E. C.) See BAL #7.

(STEGNER, W.) Colberg, Nancy. *Wallace Stegner: A Descriptive Bibliography*. Lewiston, Idaho: Confluence Press, Inc. (1990).

(STEIN, G.) Wilson, Robert A. *Gertrude Stein: A Bibliography*. Rockville, Md.: Quill & Brush, 1994.
See also *Casanova* and FPAA #1.

(STEINBECK, J.) Goldstone, Adrian H., and Payne, John R. *John Steinbeck: A Biographical Catalogue of the Adrian H. Goldstone Collection*. Austin: The University of Texas Press (1974).
See also APG, FPAA #1, and Johnson.

(STERLING, G.) See BAL #7, and Johnson.

(STEVENS, W.) Edelstein, J. M. *Wallace Stevens: A Descriptive Bibliography*. (Pittsburgh): University of Pittsburgh Press, 1973.
See also FPAA #1.

(STEVENSON, R. L.) Prideaux, Colonel W. F. *A Bibliography of the Works of Robert Louis Stevenson.* New York: Burt Franklin (1968).
   See also Cutler and Stiles.
(STEWART, D. O.) See FPAA #1.
(STOCKTON, F. R.) See BAL #7, and Johnson.
(STODDARD, C. W.) See BAL #8.
(STODDARD, E. D.) See BAL #8.
(STODDARD, R. H.) See BAL #8.
(STONE, R.) Lopez, Ken, and Chaney, Bev. *Robert Stone: A Bibliography, 1960–1992.* Hadley, Mass.: Numinous Press, 1992.
   See also APG.
(STORY, W. W.) See BAL #8.
(STOUT, R.) Townsend, Guy M. *Rex Stout: An Annotated Primary and Secondary Bibliography.* New York and London: Garland Publishing, Inc., 1980.
   See also APG.
(STOWE, H. B.) Hildreth, Margaret Holbrook. *Harriet Beecher Stowe: A Bibliography.* (Hamden, Ct.): Archon Books, 1976.
   See also BAL #8, and Johnson.
(STRATTON-PORTER, G.) See Porter.
(STRAWBERRY HILL PRESS) See Ransom.
(STRIBLING, T. S.) See FPAA #4, and Johnson.
(STUART, J.) See FPAA #4.
(STUBBS, H.C.) See Currey.
(STURGEON, T.) See Currey.
(STYRON, W.) See APG, FPAA #4, and Lepper.
(SUMMERS, H.) See FPAA #2.
(SUMMERS, M.) Smith, Timothy d'Arch. *Montague Summers: A Bibliography.* Wellingborough, Northamptonshire: The Aquarian Press (1983).
(SWADOS, H.) See Lepper.
(SWANN, T. B.) See Currey.
(SWIFT, J.) Teerink, H. *A Bibliography of the Writings of Jonathan Swift.* 2d ed., revised and corrected. Philadelphia: University of Pennsylvania Press (1963).
(SWINBURNE, A. C.) Wise, Thomas J. *A Bibliography of the Writings in Prose and Verse of Algernon Charles Swinburne.* Vols. 1 & 2. London: Dawsons of Pall Mall, 1966.
   See also Schwartz.
(SYMONDS, J. A.) Babington, Percy L. *Bibliography of the Writings of John Addington Symonds.* New York: Burt Franklin (1968).
   See also Cutler and Stiles.
(SYMONS, J.) Walsdorf, John J. *Julian Symons: A Bibliography.* New Castle/Winchester: Oak Knoll Press/St. Paul's Bibliographies, 1996.
(TABB, J. B.) See BAL #8, and Johnson.
(TAGGARD, G.) See FPAA #1.
(TARKINGTON, B.) Currie, Barton. *Booth Tarkington: A Bibliography.* Garden City, New York: Doubleday, Doran & Company, Inc., 1932.
   Russo, Dorothy Ritter, and Sullivan, Thelma L. *A Bibliography of Booth Tarkington, 1869–1946.* Indianapolis: Indiana Historical Society, 1949.
   See also FPAA #1, and Johnson.
(TATE, A.) Falwell, Marshall Jr. *Allen Tate: A Bibliography.* New York: David Lewis, 1969.
   See also FPAA #4.
(TATE, J.) See FPAA #2.
(TAYLOR, B.) See BAL #8.
(TAYLOR, E.) Gefvert, Constance J. *Edward Taylor: An Annotated Bibliography, 1668–1970.* No place: Kent State University Press (1971).
   See also FPAA #5.

(TAYLOR, P.) Wright, Stuart. *Peter Taylor: A Descriptive Bibliography, 1934–87*. Charlottesville: University Press of Virginia (1988).
See also APG, and FPAA #1.

(TEASDALE, S.) See Johnson.

(TENNYSON, A.) Shepherd, Richard Herne. *The Bibliography of Tennyson*. New York: Haskell House Publishers Ltd., 1970.
Tennyson, Charles, and Fall, Christine. *Alfred Tennyson: An Annotated Bibliography*. Athens: University of Georgia Press (1967).
See also Schwartz.

(TERHUNE) Rais, Kathleen. *Albert Payson Terhune: A Bibliography of Primary Works*. Phoenixville, Pennsylvania: Kathleen Rias, 1997.

(THACKERAY, W. M.) Van Duzer, Henry Sayre. *A Thackeray Library*. New York: Burt Franklin (1971). See also BAL #8.

(THAXTER, C.) See BAL #8.

(THEROUX, A.) See APG.

(THEROUX, P.) See APG.

(THOMAS, D.) Maud, Ralph. *Dylan Thomas in Print: A Bibliographical History*. London: J. M. Dent (1970).
Rolph, J. Alexander. *Dylan Thomas: A Bibliography*. New York: New Directions (1956).
See also APG.

(THOMAS, E.) Eckert, Robert P. *Edward Thomas: A Biography and a Bibliography*. London: Dent & Sons Ltd. (1937).

(THOMAS, F.) See BAL #8.

(THOMAS, R.) See APG.

(THOMPSON, D. P.) See BAL #8, and Johnson.

(THOMPSON, F.) See Cutler and Stiles.

(THOMPSON, H.) See APG.

(THOMPSON, Jim.) Stephens, Christopher P. *A Checklist of Jim Thompson*. (Hastings-on-Hudson, N.Y.): Ultramarine, 1991.

(THOMPSON, M.) See BAL #8, and Johnson.

(THOMPSON, S. E.) See Johnson.

(THOMPSON, W. T.) See BAL #8.

(THOMSON, James.) See Cutler and Stiles.

(THOMSON, M. N.) See BAL #8.

(THOREAU, H. D.) Borst, Raymond R. *Henry David Thoreau: A Descriptive Bibliography*. (Pittsburgh): University of Pittsburgh Press, 1982.
See also BAL #8, FPAA #3, Johnson, and Schwartz.

(THORPE, T. B.) See BAL #8.

(THREE MOUNTAINS PRESS) See Ransom, and Ford.

(THURBER, J.) Bowden, Edwin T. *James Thurber: A Bibliography*. Columbus: Ohio State University Press (1968).
See also FPAA #1.

(THURMAN, W.) See FPAA #4.

(TICKNOR & FIELDS.) Pye, John William. *The 100 Most Significant Books Published by Ticknor & Fields 1832–1871: A Guide Book for Collectors*. Brockton, Mass: John William Pye Rare Books, 1995.

(TIMROD, H.) See BAL #8, and FPAA #1.

(TOLKIEN, J.R.R.) Hammond, Wayne G., and Anderson, Douglas A. *J.R.R. Tolkien: A Descriptive Bibliography*. Winchester (England), and New Castle, Del.: St. Paul's Bibliographies, and Oak Knoll Books, 1993.
See also Currey, and Lewis.

(TORREY, B.) See FPAA #3.

(TOURGEE, A.) See BAL #8, and FPAA #1.

(TOYNBEE, A. J.) Morton, S. Fiona. *A Bibliography of Arnold J. Toynbee.* Oxford: Oxford University Press, 1980.

(TRAVEN, B.) See FPAA #1.

(TREVOR, W.) See Rees.

(TRILLING, L.) See FPAA #5.

(TROLLOPE, A.) Sadleir, Michael. *Trollope: A Bibliography.* (Kent, England): Dawson, 1977. See also Sadlier.

(TROWBRIDGE, J. T.) See BAL #8, and FPAA #4.

(TRUMBULL, J.) See BAL #8, and FPAA #4.

(TUBB, E. C.) See Currey.

(TUCKER, A. W.) See Currey.

(TUCKER, N. B.) See BAL #8.

(TUCKER, St. G.) See FPAA #4.

(TUCKERMAN, H. T.) See BAL #8.

(TUDOR) Hare, Wm. John, and Hare, Priscilla T. *Tasha Tudor: A Bio-Bibliography.* New Castle: Oak Knoll Press (1998).

(TWAIN, M.) Johnson, Merle. *A Bibliography of the Work of Mark Twain.* New York and London: Harper & Brothers Publishers, 1910.

McBride, William M. *Mark Twain: A Bibliography of the Collections of the Mark Twain Memorial and the Stowe-Day Foundation.* Hartford, Ct.: McBride/Publisher (1984).

See also APG, and Schwartz.

(TYLER, A.) See APG.

(TYLER, R.) See FPAA #4.

(UPDIKE, J.) See APG, FPAA #5, and Lepper.

(URIS, L.) See FPAA #4.

(VALE PRESS) See Franklin, and Ransom.

(VAN DINE) Pensler, Otto. *S. S. Van Dine: A Descriptive Bibliography and Price Guide.* New York: Mysterious Press (1999).

(VAN DYKE, H.) See FPAA #2.

(VAN LOON, H. W.) See Johnson.

(VAN VECHTEN) Kellner, Bruce. *A Bibliography of the Work of Carl Van Vechten.* Westport, Ct., and London, England: Greenwood Press (1980).

See also Schwartz.

(VAN VOGT, A. E.) See Currey.

(VARLEY, J.) See Currey.

(VERNE, J.) Gallagher, Edward J.; Mistichelli, Judith A.; and Van Eerde, John A. *Jules Verne: A Primary and Secondary Bibliography.* Boston: G. K. Hall & Co. (1980).

Myers, Edward and Judith. *Jules Verne: A Bibliography.* New Hartford, Ct.: Country Lane Books, 1989.

Taves, Brian; Michaluk, Stephen; Jr., et al. *The Jules Verne Encyclopedia.* Lanham/London: Scarecrow Press (1996).

(VERY, J.) See FPAA #3.

(VIDAL, G.) See FPAA #3.

(VLIET, R. G.) Freedman, Russell. *A Bibliography of the Writings of R. G. Vliet.* In *At Paisano,* by R. G. Vliet. Lanesborough, Mass.: Second Life Books, 1989.

(VOELKER, J. D.) See FPAA #3 (under Traver).

(VONNEGUT, K.) Pieratt, Asa B., Jr., Huffman-Klinkowitz, Julie, and Klinkowitz, Jerome. *Kurt Vonnegut: A Comprehensive Bibliography.* (Hamden, Ct.): Archon Books, 1987.

See also APG, FPAA #1, and Currey.

(WAKEFIELD, H. R.) See Currey.

(WAKOSKI, D.) See Lepper.

(WALKER, A.) See APG, and FPAA #2.

(WALKER, M.) See FPAA #2.

(WALLACE, E.) Kiddle, Charles. *A Guide to the First Editions of Edgar Wallace.* Motcombe, Dorset (England): The Ivory Head Press (1981).
Lofts, W.O.G., and Adley, Derek. *The British Bibliography of Edgar Wallace.* London: Howard Baker (1969).
(WALLACE, L.) See BAL #8, and Johnson.
(WALLANT, E. L.) See FPAA #1, and Lepper.
(WALPOLE, H.) Hazen, A. T. *A Bibliography of Horace Walpole.* Folkestone, England: Dawsons of Pall Mall, 1973.
(WALTON, E.) See Currey.
(WAMBAUGH, J.) See FPAA #5.
(WANDREI, D.) See Currey.
(WARD, E.S.P.) See BAL #8.
(WARNER, A. B.) See BAL #8.
(WARNER, C. D.) See BAL #8.
(WARNER, S. B.) See BAL #8.
(WARREN, R. P.) Grimshaw, James A., Jr. *Robert Penn Warren: A Descriptive Bibliography, 1922–79.* Charlottesville: University Press of Virginia (1981).
See also APG, and FPAA #1.
(WATERS, F.) Tanner, Terence A. *Frank Waters: A Bibliography.* Glenwood, Ill.: Meyerbooks (1983).
(WATSON, I.) See Currey.
(WAUGH, E.) Davis, Robert Murray; Doyle, Paul A.; Gallagher, Donat; Linck, Charles E.; and Bogaards, Winifred M. *A Bibliography of Evelyn Waugh.* Troy, N.Y.: The Whitston Publishing Company, 1986.
See also APG.
(WEAVER, J.V.A.) See FPAA #5.
(WEINBAUM, S. G.) See Currey.
(WELCH, L.) See Lepper.
(WELLMAN, M. W.) See Currey.
(WELLS, H. G.) Chappell, Fred A. *Bibliography of H. G. Wells.* Chicago: Covici-McGee Co., 1924.
Feir, Gordon D. *The Collector's Bibliography of the Works of H. G. Wells.* Houston/Vancouver: Southern Maple Publication (1992).
Wells, Geoffrey H. *A Bibliography of the Works of H. G. Wells 1893–1925 (With Some Notes and Comments).* Reprinted. New York: Burt Franklin (1968).
H. G. Wells Society (compilers). *H. G. Wells: A Comprehensive Bibliography.* 4th. edition, revised. London: H.G. Wells Society (1986).
See also Currey, and Cutler and Stiles.
(WELTY, E.) Polk, Noel. *Eudora Welty: A Bibliography of Her Work.* Jackson: University Press of Mississippi (1994).
See also APG, and FPAA #1.
(WESCOTT, G.) See Johnson.
(WEST, N.) White, William. *Nathanael West: A Comprehensive Bibliography.* No place: The Kent State University Press (1975).
See also FPAA #1.
(WESTCOTT, E. N.) See BAL #9, and Johnson.
(WHALEN, P.) See Lepper.
(WHARTON, E.) Davis, Lavinia. *A Bibliography of the Writings of Edith Wharton.* Portland, Maine: The Southworth Press, 1933.
Garrison, Stephen. *Edith Wharton: A Descriptive Bibliography.* (Pittsburgh): University of Pittsburgh Press, 1990.
Melish, Lawson McClung. *A Bibliography of the Collected Writings of Edith Wharton.* New York: The Brick Row Book Shop, Inc., 1927.
See also FPAA #3, and Johnson.
See also APG.

(WHEELER, M.) See Ford.

(WHEELWRIGHT, J. B.) See FPAA #5.

(WHIGHAM, P.) Sipper, Ralph B. *A Checklist of the Works of Peter Whigham: With a Memoir of the Poet.* Santa Barbara, Calif.: Joseph the Provider, no date.

(WHISTLER, J.A.M.) See BAL #9, and Johnson.

(WHITE, E. B.) Hall, Katherine Romans. *E. B. White: A Bibliographical Catalogue of Printed Materials in the Department of Rare Books, Cornell University Library.* New York and London: Garland Publishing, 1979.

(WHITE, J.) See Currey.

(WHITE, P.) Lawson, Alan. *Patrick White.* London and Melbourne: Oxford University Press (1974).

(WHITE, S. E.) See FPAA #5, and Johnson.

(WHITE, T. H.) Gallix, Francois. *T. H. White: An Annotated Bibliography.* New York and London: Garland Publishing, Inc., 1986.

(WHITE, Terence H.) See Currey.

(WHITE, Theodore E.) See Currey.

(WHITE, W. A.) See FPAA #2, and Johnson.

(WHITEHEAD, H. S.) See Currey.

(WHITEMAN, S. H.) See BAL #9, and FPAA #3.

(WHITMAN, S. H.) See BAL #9, and FPAA #3.

(WHITMAN, W.) Myerson, Joel. *Walt Whitman: A Descriptive Bibliography.* Pittsburgh: University of Pittsburgh, 1993.

   Shay, Frank. *The Bibliography of Walt Whitman.* New York: Friedmans', 1920.

   Wells, Carolyn, and Alfred F. Goldsmith. *A Concise Bibliography of the Works of Walt Whitman.* New York: Burt Franklin (1968).

   See also BAL #9, Johnson, and Schwartz.

(WHITTEMORE, R.) See FPAA #1.

(WHITTIER, J. G.) See BAL #9, and Johnson.

(WHYTE-MELVILLE, G. J.) See Sadlier.

(WIENERS, J.) See Lepper.

(WIGGIN, K. D.) See BAL #9.

(WILBUR, R.) See FPAA #2.

(WILDE, O.) Mason, Stuart. *Bibliography of Oscar Wilde.* London: T. Werner Laurie Ltd. (1914). See also Cutler and Stiles, and Schwartz.

(WILDER, A.) See FPAA #3.

(WILDER, T.) Edelstein, J. M. *A Bibliographical Checklist of the Writings of Thornton Wilder.* New Haven: Yale University Library, 1959.

   Goldstone, Richard H., and Gary Anderson. *Thornton Wilder: An Annotated Bibliography* . . . New York: AMS Press (1982).

   See also FPAA #3, and Johnson.

(WILHELM, K.) See Currey.

(WILLIAMS, C.) Glenn, Lois. *Charles W. S. Williams: A Checklist.* No place: The Kent State University Press (1975).

   See also Currey.

(WILLIAMS, J.) Jaffe, James S. *Jonathan Williams: A Bibliographical Checklist of His Writings, 1950–1988.* Haverford, Penn.: No publisher, 1989.

(WILLIAMS, John A.) See FPAA #2.

(WILLIAMS, T.) Gunn, Drewey Wayne. *Tennessee Williams: A Bibliography.* Metuchen, N.J., and London: The Scarecrow Press, Inc., 1980.

   Tennessee Williams: A Catalogue. New York: Gotham Book Mart, no date.

   See APG.

(WILLIAMS, W. C.) Wallace, Emily Mitchell. *A Bibliography of William Carlos Williams.* Middletown, Ct.: Wesleyan University Press (1968).

   See also APG, and FPAA #3.

(WILLIAMSON, J.) See Currey.
(WILLINGHAM, C.) See FPAA #1.
(WILLIS, N. P.) See BAL #9.
(WILSON, A. J.) See BAL #9.
(WILSON, C.) Stanley, Colin. *The Work of Colin Wilson: An Annotated Bibliography and Guide.* San Bernardino: The Borgo Press, 1989.
See also APG.
(WILSON, E.) See APG.
(WILSON, H. L.) See Johnson.
(WILSON, M.) See FPAA #5.
(WILSON, W.) See Johnson.
(WINTER, W.) See BAL #9.
(WINTERS, Y.) See FPAA #2.
(WINTHORP, T.) See BAL #9.
(WISE, J.) See FPAA #4.
(WISTER, O.) See FPAA #4, and Johnson.
(WODEHOUSE, P. G.) Jasen, David A. *A Bibliography and Reader's Guide to the First Editions of P. G. Wodehouse.* (London): Greenhill Books (1970).
McIlvaine, Eileen; Sherby, Louise S.; and Heineman, James H. *P. G. Wodehouse: A Comprehensive Bibliography and Checklist.* New York, and Detroit, Mich.: James H. Heineman, and Omnigraphics (1990).
See also APG.
(WOIWODE, L.) See FPAA #2.
(WOLFE, G.) See Currey.
(WOLFE, T.) Johnston, Carol. *Thomas Wolfe: A Descriptive Bibliography.* (Pittsburgh): University of Pittsburgh Press, 1989.
See also APG, FPAA #1, and Johnson.
(WOLLHEIM, D. A.) See Currey.
(WOLLSTONECRAFT, M.) Todd, Janet M. *Mary Wollstonecraft: An Annotated Bibliography.* New York and London: Garland Publishing, Inc., 1976.
Windle, J. R. *Mary Wollstonecraft (Godwin): A Bibliography of Her Writings.* Los Angeles: (John Windle) 1988.
(WOODBERRY, G. E.) See BAL #9.
(WOODWARD, W.) See Currey.
(WOODWORTH, S.) See BAL #9.
(WOOLF, L.) Luedeking, Leila, and Edmonds, Michael. *Leonard Woolf: A Bibliography.* Winchester (England), and New Castle, Del.: St. Paul's Bibliographies, and Oak Knoll Books, 1992.
(WOOLF, V.) Kirkpatrick, B. J. *A Bibliography of Virginia Woolf.* Oxford: Clarendon Press, 1980.
See also APG.
(WOOLRICH, C.) Penzler, Otto. *Cornell Woolrich: A Descriptive Bibliography and Price Guide.* New York: The Mysterious Bookshop, (1999).
See FPAA #3.
(WOOLRICH, CORNELL) Penzler, Otto. *Cornell Woolrich Part II (William Irish & George Hopley).* New York: Mysterious Bookshop, 2000.
(WOOLSON, C. F.) See BAL #9.
(WORDSWORTH, W.) Wise, Thomas J. *A Bibliography of the Writings in Prose and Verse of William Wordsworth.* London: Printed for Private Circulation, 1916.
(WOUK, H.) See FPAA #1.
(WRIGHT, A. T.) See Currey.
(WRIGHT, H. B.) See FPAA #2.
(WRIGHT, J.) See FPAA #1.
(WRIGHT, R.) See FPAA #1.
See also APG.

(WRIGHT, S. F.) See Currey.

(WURLITZER, R.) See FPAA #2.

(WYLIE, E.) See BAL #9, and Johnson.

(WYLIE, P.) See Currey.

(YEATS, W. B.) Wade, Allan. *A Bibliography of the Writings of W. B. Yeats.* London: Rupert Hart-Davis, 1958.

See also Cutler and Stiles, and Schwartz.

(YOUD, C.) See Currey.

(YOUNG, M.) See FPAA #2.

(YOUNG, R. F.) See Currey.

(ZUKOFSKY) Zukofsky, Celia. *A Bibliography of Louis Zukofsky.* Los Angeles: Black Sparrow Press, 1969.

APPENDIX B.
FIRST-EDITION IDENTIFICATION
BY PUBLISHER

In the case of titles published before 1900, the key to first-edition identification is often the date on the title page. The vast majority of first editions published before 1900 had the year of publication on the title page (this is true for fiction and nonfiction titles). The presence of a date on the title page alone may identify books published prior to the mid-1800s as first editions. A matching date on the copyright page (or the back of the title page) often identifies a book published in the mid- to late 1800s as a first edition. After 1900, a number of publishers did not or currently do not put the date on the title page of their first editions.

In the early 1900s, many publishers began to identify the first edition on the copyright page. A variety of statements have been used and continue to be used to denote a first edition, such as "First Edition," "First Printing," "First Impression," "First published (Year, or Month and Year)," or simply "Published (Year, or Month and Year)." A few publishers have placed or place their logo, colophon, or a code (generally "1" or "A") on the copyright page of the first edition. Publishers who did not or do not use a first-edition statement, in most cases, note subsequent printings on the copyright page. For these publishers, the absence of a later printing statement is the key to identifying the first edition.

Over the past few decades, the majority of publishers have used a number row on the copyright page to identify a book's printing and occasionally the date of publication. Sometimes the number row is accompanied by a first-edition statement (often it is not). It is important to note that regardless of the order of the numbers in the row, the lowest number indicates the printing. The presence of the number "1" (with few exceptions) indicates a first printing. Some examples follow:

"1 2 3 4 5 6 7 8 9 10"
"10 9 8 7 6 5 4 3 2 1"*and*
"1 3 5 7 9 10 8 6 4 2"
all indicate a first edition

"76 77 78 79 80 10 9 8 7 6 5 4 3 2"
indicates a second printing published in 1976

"3 4 5 6 7 8 9 10 90 89 88 87 86"
indicates a third printing published in 1986

"1 3 5 7 9 11 13 15 17 19 H/C 20 18 16 14 12 10 8 6 4 2"
*indicates a first printing, manufactured by "H" in a cloth binding
(used by Scribners)*

*Unfortunately, publishers sometimes fail to omit a first-edition statement from
subsequent printings:*

First Edition
3 4 5 6 7 8 9 10

and

First Printing
10 9 8 7 6 5 4 3 90 89 88 87 86 85 84

are both third printings.

The list below provides at-a-glance information for first-edition identification by publisher. For more detailed information on identifying first editions by a wide range of publishers, we recommend the 1995 edition of Edward N. Zempel and Linda A. Verkler's *First Editions: A Guide to Identification* (The Spoon River Press, 2319-C West Rohmann Avenue, Peoria, IL 61604). This superb reference provides publishers' verbatim statements, collected over nearly 70 years, on their practices for identifying first editions and later printings. In addition, we highly recommend the occasional series "A Collector's Guide to Publishers" featured in the monthly magazine for book collectors *Firsts* (4493 N. Camino Gacela, Tucson, AZ

85718. Telephone: 520-529-5847). This interesting and informative series provides a history, some notable writers and books published, and standard practices for first-edition identification (and, in some cases, notable exceptions), for the publishers profiled—over thirty major publishers to date. We used our experience over the past thirty years, our stock, and both of the above-mentioned references to compile the list below.

A final, important note: It is always prudent to consult a bibliography for conclusive first-edition identification (see Appendix E, Selected Bibliography of Works Consulted, for a comprehensive list of bibliographies).

D. APPLETON & CO. Used a numerical identification, in parentheses or brackets, at the foot of the last page: "(1)" = first printing, "(2)" = second printing, etc. (May have occasionally used a "first edition" statement instead of the numerical identification.)

D. APPLETON-CENTURY CO. Prior to the 1980s, used a numerical identification, in parentheses or brackets, at the foot of the last page: "(1)" = first printing, "(2)" = second printing, etc. (May have occasionally used a "first edition" statement instead of the numerical identification.) Since the 1980s, have used a number row to indicate year of publication and printing.

ARKHAM HOUSE / ARKHAM HOUSE PUBLISHERS, INC. With the exception of collected works of H. P. Lovecraft, did not reprint titles and, as late as the 1980s, always included a colophon at the back of each book (reprints would be noted there). According to the publisher, began using a first-edition statement and noting later printings on the copyright page sometime in the late 1970s to early 1980s.

ATHENEUM. States first edition on copyright page. Began using a number row in the mid-1980s.

ATLANTIC MONTHLY PRESS. Prior to 1925, did not use a first edition statement (or put the publication date on the title page of first editions as was the case for many publishers in the late 1800s to early 1900s) and did not consistently list later printings on the copyright page. See Little, Brown for books published after 1925 (Little, Brown began publishing the Atlantic Monthly Books in 1925 and using their methods for first-edition identification).

AVALON BOOKS. Does not normally reprint books, but according to the publisher, later printings would be noted.

BALLANTINE BOOKS. In general, hardcover editions stated "First edition (Month, Year)" or "First printing (Month, Year)"; paperback originals carried no statement on the copyright page for first printings; later printings were noted.

ROBERT A. BALLOU. No consistent practice.

A. S. BARNES. According to the publisher, have noted later printings on the copyright page since at least 1976. Prior to this, designation of later printings was erratic. (Does not use a first-edition statement.)

ERNEST BENN. States "First published in (Year)" on the copyright page of first editions; or sometimes omits the "first published" statement and puts the year of publication on the title page with their imprint to designate a first edition. In either case, subsequent printings are noted.

WILLIAM BLACKWOOD. No statement on first editions, but subsequent printings noted. (According to the publisher, in the early 1900s may have designated some first editions "second edition" as a marketing tool.)

BLAKISON. Reprint publisher.

BOBBS-MERRILL. Prior to the 1920s, sometimes used a bow-and-arrow design on the copyright page of their first editions; after 1920, generally stated "First edition" or "First printing" (but not consistent in either practice).

BODLEY HEAD. States "First published 19.." or "First published in Great Britain 19.."; subsequent printings would presumably be noted.

ALBERT & CHARLES BONI. No statement on first editions, but subsequent printings noted.

BONI & LIVERIGHT. May have occasionally stated first edition, but in general, the absence of a later printing statement indicates a first edition.

BOOK SUPPLY CO. Uses a first-edition statement; subsequent printings presumably noted.

BRENTANO'S. Prior to 1928, no statement on first editions; subsequent printings noted. In 1928, began stating "First printed 19.." on copyright page of first editions and continued noting subsequent printings.

EDGAR RICE BURROUGHS, INC. Published only the books of Edgar Rice Burroughs. No statement on books published prior to 1933; began using a first-edition statement sometime in 1933. (Although both were published in 1933, there is no statement on the first edition of *Apache Devil,* but *Tarzan and the City of Gold* states first edition on the copyright page.)

A. L. BURT. Primarily a reprint publisher, but published the first U.S. edition of P. G. Wodehouse's *Man with Two Left Feet* (states first edition on the copyright page). For those authors whose first editions have become very high-priced, A. L. Burt reprints in dust jackets closely matching the first editions are sometimes desirable.

CALDER & BOYARS. States "First published (Year)" or "First published in Great Britain (Year)"; subsequent printings would presumably be noted.

JONATHAN CAPE. States "First published (Year)" or "First published in Great Britain (Year)" on copyright page of first editions; subsequent printings noted.

JONATHAN CAPE & HARRISON SMITH. States "First published (Year)" or "First published in America (Year)"; subsequent printings would presumably be noted.

CASSELL & CO. Prior to the early 1920s, put the year of publication on the title page of the first edition and left the copyright page blank; subsequent printings would presumably be noted or carry a later date on the copyright page. In the early 1920s, began stating "First published (Year)" or "First published in Great Britain (Year)" on copyright page of first editions; subsequent printings noted.

CAXTON PRINTERS. No statement on first editions, but subsequent printings noted.

CENTURY CO. No consistent practice.

CHAPMAN & HALL. Either stated "First published (Year)" or made no statement on first editions; subsequent printings noted.

CHATTO & WINDUS. In general, no statement on first editions, although sometimes states "Published by Chatto & Windus" (without a date); subsequent printings noted. May have added a number row in the early 1990s.

CLARKE, IRWIN. No statement on the first edition; subsequent printings presumably noted.

COLLIER. In our limited experience with this publisher, no statement on the first edition; subsequent printings presumably noted.

COLLINS (U.K.). No statement on the first edition; presumably subsequent printings would be noted (with either a statement, or a date subsequent to the copyright date).

CONTACT EDITIONS. Limited editions included a colophon page. Did not generally use a first-edition statement on trade editions, but subsequent printings would presumably be noted.

PASCAL COVICI. May have occasionally stated first edition, but in general the absence of a later printing statement indicates a first edition.

COVICI-FRIEDE. No statement on first editions, but subsequent printings noted.

COVICI MCGEE. No statement on the first edition, but presumably later printings would be noted.

COWARD-MCCANN. Not consistent in their practices for identifying first editions, but in general subsequent printings noted. (Until mid-1930s, usually placed a colophon with a torch design on the copyright page of first editions and removed the torch portion of the colophon on subsequent printings. After 1935, stated "first American edition" on the copyright page of books first published outside the United States, but made no statement on books first published in the United States.)

COWARD, MCCANN AND GEOGHEHAN. No statement on first editions, but subsequent printings noted.

CREATIVE AGE. No statement on first editions, but subsequent printings noted.

CRIME CLUB (U.K.). See Collins.

CRIME CLUB (U.S.). See Doubleday, Doran & Co.

THOMAS Y. CROWELL. No statement on first editions, but subsequent printings noted. May have used a number row to indicate printings as early as the 1940s.

CROWN PUBLISHERS. Prior to the 1970s, no statement on first editions, but subsequent printings noted. Began using a number row and first-edition statement in the 1970s.

JOHN DAY CO. / JOHN DAY IN ASSOCIATION WITH REYNAL AND HITCH-COCK [1935–38] / JOHN DAY & CO. First few years (beginning in 1928) may have stated "First Published (Month, Year)" on first editions and noted later printings. In the 1930s, switched to designating only later printings (no statement on first editions). In the 1970s, began using a number row. (In the late 1970s, may have added a first-edition statement to the number row.)

DELACORTE PRESS / SEYMOUR LAWRENCE. Now uses a number row; previously stated "first printing" or "first American printing."

DEVIN-ADAIR. Although may have consistently stated "First Edition" in recent years, in general first editions can be identified by the absence of a later printing statement.

DIAL PRESS. Although occasionally stated "First Printing" prior to the mid-1960s, did not list subsequent printings. In general, first editions published prior to the mid-1960s can be identified by the presence of the same date on the title page and the copyright page (also true for books published before the mid-1930s with the imprint "Lincoln MacVeagh / The Dial Press"). In the late 1960s, began stating "First Printing (Year)" on first editions and noting subsequent printings. Currently uses a number row.

DILLINGHAM. In our limited experience with this publisher, no statement on the first edition; subsequent printings would presumably be noted.

DODD, MEAD. Prior to 1976, no statement on first editions, and often subsequent printings were not noted. In late 1976, added a number row to most titles (occasionally deleting the row from subsequent printings and replacing it with a later printing statement). Note: According to *Firsts* magazine, in the 1970s first-printing dustwrappers of some mystery titles were issued without a price on the flap, making them appear to be book-club editions.

GEORGE H. DORAN. Generally placed a colophon with the initials "GHD" on the copyright page of the first edition (but not consistently until the early 1920s). Occasionally, stated "first printing." Merged with Doubleday in 1927.

DOUBLEDAY & CO. States "first edition" on copyright page; no statement on later printings.

DOUBLEDAY, DORAN & CO. States "first edition" on copyright page; no statement on later printings.

DOUBLEDAY & McCLURE CO. In general, the date on the title page should match last date on the copyright page of a first edition.

DOUBLEDAY, PAGE & CO. Before the early 1920s, no statement on the first edition. In early 1920s, began stating "first edition," but may not have used any statement on books first published outside the U.S. (no statement on later printings).

DUELL, SLOAN AND PEARCE. In general, either stated "First Edition" or placed a Roman numeral "I" on the copyright page of first editions. Later printings were usually denoted similarly—e.g., "Second Printing" or "II."

E. P. DUTTON. Prior to 1929, the date on the title page should match the last date on the copyright page of a first edition. In the 1930s, began stating "First edition" or "First printing." In recent years, added a number row (they adjust the numbers for subsequent printings, but often fail to remove the first-edition statement).

EDITIONS POETRY. States "First published . . . (Year)" on the copyright page of the first edition; subsequent printings would presumably be noted.

EGOIST PRESS. Limited editions included a colophon page. Did not generally use a first-edition statement on trade editions, but subsequent printings would presumably be noted.

EYRE & SPOTTISWOODE. Either printed the year of publication under their name at the bottom of the title page of first editions, or stated "This book, first published 19.., is printed . . ." on the copyright page; subsequent printings were noted.

FABER & FABER, LTD. States "First Published (Month, Year)" on copyright page and notes subsequent printings. Prior to 1968, the year of publication was in roman numerals; beginning in 1968, switched to arabic numerals. Since World War II, the month has generally been omitted from the first-edition statement. Recently added a number row to most publications.

FABER & GWYER, LTD. Stated "First published by Faber & Gwyer in (Month, Year)" on copyright page of first editions; noted subsequent printings.

Fantasy Press. States "First Edition" on copyright page; may have occasionally left "First Edition" statement of original publisher on offset reprints with their imprint.

Farrar, Rinehart. Publisher's logo appears on the copyright page of first editions; no statement on subsequent printings. Very rarely stated "first edition" (in place of the logo).

Farrar, Straus. Publisher's stylized initials (FS) appear on the copyright page of first editions; no statement on subsequent printings.

Farrar, Straus & Cudahy. States either "First published (Year)" or "First printing" on the copyright page of first editions.

Farrar, Straus & Giroux. States either "First published (Year)," "First printing (Year)," or "First edition (Year)" on the copyright page of first editions.

Farrar, Straus & Young. Used either a first-edition statement or a colophon on the copyright page of first editions.

Fawcett. Uses a number row to designate printings.

Four Seas. In general, no statement on first editions, but subsequent printings noted.

Funk & Wagnalls. Used a Roman numeral I on the copyright page of first editions. According to the publisher's statements, beginning in 1929, stated "First published (Month, Year)" on first editions and noted subsequent printings (presumably no statement on first editions published prior to 1929). But the first edition of John Cheever's *The Enormous Radio*, published in 1953, has the Roman numeral I and does not have a first-edition statement.

Lee Furman. Made no attempt to identify first editions or subsequent printings.

Gambit, Inc. States "First printing" on the copyright page of first editions; subsequent printings are noted.

Bernard Geis. States "First printing" on the copyright page of first editions; presumably subsequent printings are noted.

Gnome Press. States "First Edition" on copyright page; may have occasionally left "First Edition" statement of original publisher on offset reprints with their imprint.

Victor Gollancz, Ltd. Prior to 1984, no statement on first editions, but subsequent printings noted [e.g., "First published (Year) | Second impression (Year)"]. In 1984, began stating "First published in . . ." on the copyright page of first editions.

Grosset & Dunlap. Primarily a reprint house, but some notable first editions have been published by Grosset & Dunlap: *King Kong* (photoplay); Nancy Drew and Hardy Boys series; Fran Striker's "Lone Ranger" series; and Zane Grey's *The Redheaded Outfield and Other Stories*. In addition,

Grosset & Dunlap's "photoplay" editions (illustrated with stills from motion pictures) are collectible. In our experience, there is no statement of edition or printing on Grossett & Dunlap publications. It is, however, possible to eliminate obvious later printings by checking the list of other books published in the series. A later printing would probably list titles that were published after the book in hand. (Note: For those authors whose first editions have become very high-priced, Grosset & Dunlap reprints in dust jackets closely matching the first edition's are sometimes desirable.)

GROVE PRESS. First editions and subsequent printings are always noted on the copyright page; currently uses a number row. Later-printing dust-wrappers are identifiable by small letter code on the rear panel (e.g., "ii" designates a second-printing dustwrapper).

ROBERT HALE. Prior to 1958, either no statement on first editions or stated "First published (Year)," but in both cases subsequent printings were noted. Beginning in 1958, stated "First published in Great Britain in (Year)" on first editions; continued to identify subsequent printings. According to the publisher, a number row was adopted in 1994 for nonfiction titles only.

HAMISH HAMILTON. States "First published (Year)" or "First published in Great Britain in (Year)" on copyright page; notes subsequent printings. Added a number row in 1988.

HARCOURT, BRACE & CO. (1921–1960.) From 1921 to 1931, did not state on first printings. In about 1931, it started putting "First Edition" or First American Edition" on the copyright page. In many instances, it did not state later printings but took the first-edition statement off after the first printing. Occasionally, through the 1940s, it would use a "1" on the first printing. The "1" was removed for later printings.

HARCOURT, BRACE & HOWE. (1919–1921.) Usually placed the number "1" on the copyright page of first printings, "2" on second printings, etc. May have occasionally stated "Published (Month) (Year)" on the copyright page of first printings and noted later printings.

HARCOURT, BRACE & WORLD. (1960–1970.) States "first edition" or "first American edition" on the copyright page. Succeeded by Harcourt Brace Jovanovich in 1970.

HARCOURT BRACE JOVANOVICH. (Established in 1970.) States "first edition" or "first American edition" on the copyright page, or, placed "First Edition/ABCDE" on the copyright page of first editions except during the years 1973 to 1983, when they did not use the "A" but used "First Edition/BCDE." In both cases, they dropped "First Edition" and the appropriate letter(s) on later printings.

HARPER & BROTHERS. Prior to 1912, the date on the title page should match the last date on the copyright page. Began stating "First Edition" on the copyright page in 1922. A letter code for the month and year the book was printed, which would actually be earlier than the official publication date, was introduced in 1912. In most cases for first editions published between 1912 and 1922, the letter code for the year on the copyright page should match (or precede) the date on the title page.

Months (the letter "J" was not used)

A = January	D = April	G = July	K = October
B = February	E = May	H = August	L = November
C = March	F = June	I = September	M = December

Years (the letter "J" was not used)

M = 1912	B = 1927	R = 1942	G = 1957
N = 1913	C = 1928	S = 1943	H = 1958
O = 1914	D = 1929	T = 1944	I = 1959
P = 1915	E = 1930	U = 1945	K = 1960
Q = 1916	F = 1931	V = 1946	L = 1961
R = 1917	G = 1932	W = 1947	M = 1962
S = 1918	H = 1933	X = 1948	N = 1963
T = 1919	I = 1934	Y = 1949	O = 1964
U = 1920	K = 1935	Z = 1950	P = 1965
V = 1921	L = 1936	A = 1951	Q = 1966
W = 1922	M = 1937	B = 1952	R = 1967
X = 1923	N = 1938	C = 1953	S = 1968
Y = 1924	O = 1939	D = 1954	
Z = 1925	P = 1940	E = 1955	
A = 1926	Q = 1941	F = 1956	

HARPER & ROW. States "First Edition" on the copyright page (also see month and date code above). In 1969, added a number row to the bottom of the last page (directly before the rear free endpaper) but often failed to remove the "First Edition" statement from later printings. By 1975, the number row was usually placed on the copyright page (still often failed to remove "First Edition" statement from later printings).

HARPERCOLLINS. [Harper & Row changed its name to HarperCollins in 1990]. States "First Edition" and uses a number row, which indicates the year of publication and printing (may sometimes fail to remove the "First Edition" statement from later printings).

RUPERT HART-DAVIS. Although usually stated "First published (Year)" on copyright page of first editions, sometimes placed the publication date on the title page of first editions (with no statement on the copyright page); in both cases, subsequent printings were noted.

HART-DAVIS, MACGIBBON LIMITED. States "Published . . . (Year)" on first editions; subsequent printings are noted.

HARVARD UNIVERSITY PRESS. Places the year of publication on the title page of first editions, removing it from subsequent printings and adding a notice to the copyright page. In addition, may have used a number row in the 1980s.

W. HEINEMANN, LTD. / WILLIAM HEINEMANN, LTD. / WILLIAM HEINEMANN. From 1890 to 1921, placed the year of publication on the title page of first editions, removing it from subsequent printings and adding a notice to the copyright page (very occasionally, books reprinted in the year of initial publication may not have a notice on the copyright page). In the 1920s, began stating "First published (Year)" or "First published in Great Britain (Year)" on copyright page of first editions; continued to note subsequent printings.

HERITAGE PRESS. Publishes reprints or "trade editions" of the Limited Editions Club.

HODDER & STOUGHTON LTD. Prior to the 1940s, had no consistent practice for identifying first editions or later printings. In the 1940s, may have begun to state "First Printed (Year)" on first editions and to note subsequent printings. By 1976, were consistent in stating "First published in (Year)" on first editions and noting subsequent printings.

HOGARTH PRESS. No statement on first editions; subsequent printings are identified on the title page and/or copyright page. Currently use a number row.

HENRY HOLT. Prior to 1945, first editions can generally be identified by the lack of a later printing statement on the copyright page. Beginning in 1945, usually placed a first-edition statement on the copyright page of books produced in the United States (no statement on books produced outside the United States). After 1985, began using a first-edition statement and number row.

HOLT, RINEHART & WINSTON. Prior to the 1970s, may have used a first-edition statement (with the exception of books produced outside the United States). Presumably in the 1970s began using a first-edition statement and number row.

HOUGHTON MIFFLIN. Almost invariably places the date, in arabic numerals, on the title page of first printings, removing it on subsequent printings. Additionally, in the late 1950s, began consistently placing a "first printing" statement on the copyright page. In the early 1970s, replaced the "first printing" statement with a number row, which includes a manufacturer code.

B. W. HUEBSCH. No statement on first editions; subsequent printings noted.

HURST. Reprint publisher.

HUTCHINSON & CO. States "First published (Year)" or "First published in Great Britain (Year)" on copyright page of first editions. (May be no statement on books published early in this century).

MICHAEL JOSEPH LTD. Since at least the mid-1930s, have stated "First published . . . (Month, Year)" on copyright page of first editions, and noted subsequent printings. In the late 1980s and early 1990s, a number row was added to the printing statement.

ALFRED A. KNOPF. Until 1933–34, sometimes stated "Published (Month or Year)" on the copyright page of first editions; later printings were noted. Since 1933–34 have consistently stated "First Edition" (with the possible exception of children's books). Books with "First and second printings before publication" on the copyright page are second printings (e.g., booksellers' demand warranted a second printing prior to the publication date).

JOHN LANE. Prior to 1925, no statement on first editions, but subsequent printings were noted. Since 1925, have stated "First Published in (Year, or Month and Year)" on first editions and continued to note subsequent printings.

LIMITED EDITIONS CLUB. Does not reprint titles (see Heritage Press for "trade" editions), and always includes a colophon at the back of each book. In general, limited to 1,500 copies; issued in fine bindings and slipcases or boxes. Nearly all the titles are signed by the illustrator, and occasionally by the author or others.

J. B. LIPPINCOTT. Until mid-1920s, the date on the title page should match the date on the copyright page, but in the case of "fall titles," the date on the title page may predate the one on the copyright page by one year. Beginning in roughly 1925, sometimes placed a first-edition statement on the copyright page but always indicated later printings (or "impressions"). In the mid-1970s, added a number row to the first-edition statement.

LIPPINCOTT AND CROWELL. States "First Edition" and uses a number row.

LITTLE, BROWN. Prior to the early 1930s, no statement on first editions, but subsequent printings noted. In the 1930s, stated "Published (Month) (Year)" on the copyright page of first editions; later printings were normally indicated. Since 1940, have stated "First Edition" or "First Printing," and added a number row in the late 1970s.

HORACE LIVERIGHT, INC. / LIVERIGHT PUBLISHING CORP. Prior to the 1970s, in general, no statement on first editions, but subsequent printings noted (may have occasionally used a first-edition statement). In recent years, may have used a number row in addition to stating "First Edition."

JOHN LONG. No statement on first editions, but subsequent printings noted.

LONGMANS, GREEN CO. (U.K.) Prior to the late 1920s, no statement on the first edition, but subsequent printings noted. Since the late 1920s, have stated "First Published (Year)" on the copyright page of first editions; subsequent printings are noted.

LONGMANS, GREEN CO. (U.S.) Prior to the late 1920s, no statement on the first edition; subsequent printings are presumably noted or carry a date on the copyright page later than the date on the title page. Since the late 1920s, have stated "First Edition" on the copyright page and noted subsequent printings.

THE MACAULAY CO. No statement on first editions; subsequent printings generally noted.

THE MACMILLAN CO. / MACMILLAN PUBLISHING CO., INC. (U.K.) Prior to the mid-1920s, no statement on the first edition, but subsequent printings noted. Since the mid-1920s, have stated "First Published (Year)" on the copyright page of first editions.

THE MACMILLAN CO. / MACMILLAN PUBLISHING CO., INC. (U.S.) Prior to the late 1800s, the date on the title page should match the last date on the copyright page for first editions (did not always designate later printings, but did change the date on the copyright page). Also, beginning sometime in the late 1800s, usually placed the statement "Set up and electrotyped. Published (Month, Year)" on first editions, and generally indicated subsequent printings. Midyear 1936, began stating "First printing" on the copyright page; added a number row in the 1970s.

MACMILLAN OF CANADA. Does not designate first editions.

ROBERT M. MCBRIDE. Stated "First Published (Month, Year)," "Published (Month, Year)," or more recently "First Edition" on the copyright page of first editions; subsequent printings were noted.

MCCLURE, PHILLIPS. Either no statement or "Published (Month, Year, occasionally followed by a letter code)" on the copyright page of the first edition; subsequent printings presumably noted with either a statement or a later date.

A. C. MCCLURG. Stated "Published in (Year)" on the first edition, but may have failed to change this notice on later printings.

MCDOWELL, OBOLENSKY. No statement on the first edition or sometimes stated "First printing"; subsequent printings would presumably be noted.

MCGRAW-HILL. Until 1956, may not have used a first-edition statement. Since 1956, have used a first-edition statement and noted subsequent printings.

METHUEN & CO. Since 1905, have stated "First published in (Year)" or "First published in Great Britain (Year)" on the copyright page of first editions, and noted subsequent printings. Prior to 1905, no statement on first editions, but subsequent printings noted (sometimes with a "thousands" statement on the title page such as "43rd Thousand").

METROPOLITAN BOOKS. No statement on the first edition; subsequent printings presumably noted.

MODERN LIBRARY. Reprint series published by Random House (prior to 1925 published by Boni & Liveright). Early titles in the series, especially in dust jacket, "Modern Library Giants," and titles with new forewords by the author or original publisher, are collectible. Since 1925, have stated "First Modern Library Edition" on the copyright page of the first edition (only haphazardly prior to 1925); occasionally left the first-edition statement on subsequent printings, but the presence of later-published titles within the book in hand will often identify it as a later edition. Note: later-issue dustwrappers are often found on the first editions.

WILLIAM MORROW. Prior to 1973, only sometimes placed "First Printing (Month, Year)" on the copyright page but always indicated later printings. Since 1973, have used a number row and sometimes a first-edition statement (occasionally fail to remove first-edition statement from later printings).

MUSEUM OF MODERN ART. No statement on first editions, but subsequent printings are noted.

MYCROFT & MORAN. See Arkham House.

NEW AMERICAN LIBRARY. Uses a first-edition statement and number row.

NEW DIRECTIONS. Not consistent in using a first-edition statement or identifying subsequent printings, and often bound up first-edition sheets later, so binding variations are important in first-edition identification.

NEW ENGLISH LIBRARY. States "First published by New English Library in (Year)" or "First published in Great Britain (Year)" on the copyright page of first editions. In general, the year in the "first published" notice should match the copyright year.

GEORGE NEWNES. No statement on first editions.

W. W. NORTON. In past years, usually used a first-edition statement but did not indicate later printings. Currently uses a first-edition statement and number row, but occasionally fails to remove the first-edition statement from subsequent printings.

PETER OWEN. States "First published by Peter Owen (Year)" on the copyright page of first editions and notes subsequent printings.

OXFORD UNIVERSITY PRESS. (NEW YORK AND U.K.) Until the late 1980s, no statement on first editions, but subsequent printings noted. Started using a number row in the late 1980s.

PANTHEON BOOKS, INC. Until 1964, no statement on first editions, but subsequent printings noted (may have occasionally stated "First Printing"). Since 1964, have stated "First Edition." May have begun using a number row, in addition to the first-edition statement, in the late 1980s.

PAYSON & CLARKE. No statement on first editions, but subsequent printings noted.

G. P. PUTNAM'S SONS. Prior to 1985, no statement on first editions, but subsequent printings noted. Since 1985, have used a number row.

RANDOM HOUSE. States "First Edition" on the first printing; does not indicate subsequent printings. In recent years, added a number row beginning with "2"—i.e., "First Edition/23456789"—to first editions, and removed the first edition statement from subsequent printings (e.g., "23456789" without a first-edition statement would indicate a second printing).

RAPP & WHITING. Generally stated "First published (Year)" on the copyright page of the first edition.

REYNAL & HITCHCOCK. Until 1947, no statement on first editions, but subsequent printings noted. For books published after 1947, see Harcourt, Brace & Co.

GRANT RICHARDS. No statement on the first edition.

RINEHART & CO. Placed an "R" in a circle on first editions and removed from subsequent printings (subsequent printings not otherwise noted).

ST. MARTIN'S PRESS. Until the early 1980s, no first-edition statement, but subsequent printings noted. Since the early 1980s, have used a number row and a first-edition statement.

SCRIBNERS. Until 1930, the Scribners seal and the date of publication (month and year) generally appeared on first editions, and subsequent printings were usually noted (although did not strictly adhere to either practice). Since 1930, have used an "A" on the copyright page to denote the first edition, sometimes with the Scribner seal, and sometimes with a code representing the month and year of publication and the book's manufacturer (later printings were either not noted, or indicated with a "B," etc.). In the 1970s, added a number row, which includes a letter code for the manufacturer and type of binding (at the center).

MARTIN SECKER, LTD. / SECKER & WARBURG. Prior to the 1940s, no statement on first editions or occasionally stated "First Published in . . . (Year)"; subsequent printings noted. In the 1940s, began stating "First published in . . . (Year)" on the copyright page of first editions; continued noting subsequent printings.

SIMON & SCHUSTER. Until 1952, no statement on first editions, but subsequent printings noted (possibly with symbols as, reportedly, a few titles in the 1930s carried a series of dots or asterisks on the copyright page to indicate additional printings). In 1952, began using a first-edition statement. In the early 1970s, began using a number row (occasionally with a first-edition statement).

WILLIAM SLOANE ASSOCIATES. States "First Printing" on the copyright page of first editions, and notes subsequent printings.

SMALL, MAYNARD. No statement on the first edition.

SMITH, ELDER. No statement on the first edition.

HARRISON SMITH & ROBERT HAAS. Not consistent in use of a first-edition statement, but subsequent printings noted.

STANTON & LEE. See Arkham House.

FREDERICK A. STOKES CO. No statement on first editions, but subsequent printings noted.

SUN DIAL. Reprint publisher.

ALAN SWALLOW. No statement on the first edition; subsequent printings presumably noted.

TIME INC. / TIME-LIFE BOOKS. Until 1976, used a small hourglass design on the last page to designate the printing (i.e., one hourglass for the first printing, two for the second, etc.); since 1976, have stated the printing on the copyright page.

TOWER BOOKS. See World Publishing Co.

TRIANGLE. Reprint publisher.

TRIDENT PRESS. In our limited experience with this publisher, no statement on the first edition; subsequent printings presumably noted.

UNITED BOOK. In our limited experience with this publisher, no statement on the first edition; subsequent printings presumably noted.

T. FISHER UNWIN. Prior to 1914, no statement on the first edition. Since 1914, states "First published in (Year)" on the copyright page of the first edition.

VANGUARD. No statement on first editions, and sometimes failed to note subsequent printings. In the 1970s, instituted a number row (but may have abandoned it in the mid-1980s).

VIKING PRESS. Until the late 1930s, no first edition statement, but subsequent printings noted. In 1937, began stating "First Published by Viking in (Year)" or "Published by Viking in (Year)" on first editions, and continued the practice of noting subsequent printings. In the 1980s, added a number row to later printings only.

VILLARD BOOKS. See Random House.

VINTAGE BOOKS. See Random House.

WALKER AND CO. States "First Published . . . (Year)" on first editions, and uses a number row to indicate subsequent printings.

WARD, LOCK. Prior to the 1930s, generally placed the year of publication on the title page of first editions and removed it from subsequent printings. Beginning in the mid–1930s, generally stated "First published in . . ." on the copyright page of first editions.

WEIDENFELD & NICOLSON. Either states "First published in . . ." or no statement on first editions, but subsequent printings are generally noted.

WESLEYAN UNIVERSITY. States "First Edition" or "First Printing" on first editions, and notes subsequent printings.

JOHN WILEY & SONS. Prior to 1969, no statement on first editions, but subsequent printings noted. Have used a number row since 1969.

JOHN C. WINSTON. Until the 1940s, no statement on either first editions or subsequent printings. Started stating the printing some time in the 1940s.

WORLD PUBLISHING CO. States "First Edition" or "First Printing" on the copyright page of the first edition. Note: World's "Tower Books" are reprints, with the exception of two Raymond Chandler first editions: *Red Wind* and *Spanish Blood* (both state "First Printing (Month, Year)."

CONDITION AND EDITION
ARE VERY IMPORTANT

Check the date on the title page carefully. If the entry herein does not have the date in parentheses, the date must be on the title page. Compare your book's condition with the conditions listed below. All prices in this volume are for books in the following condition:

Books published before 1800: Rebound in the nineteenth century unless otherwise stated. Copies in original bindings (even extensively repaired) or contemporary bindings would have a much higher value.

Books published from 1800 to 1839: Rebound at some early date after the date of publication unless otherwise stated. Binding is clean and intact. The original binding would greatly increase the value.

Books published from 1840 to 1919: In original leather, cloth (cloth-covered boards), boards (paper-covered boards), or wraps unless otherwise stated. Books published from 1840 to 1879 are in good to very good condition with only minor edge wear or loss and still tight and clean. Books published from 1880 to 1919 are clean and bright with no loss or tears on the edges. Copies in fine to very fine condition would bring much more.

Books published from 1920 to 1949: Must be in very good to fine condition with only minimal (if any) soiling. In original dust-wrapper (unless in wraps or in limited-edition slipcase) that is clean, with only minimal soiling or fading, and only a few *small* chips and closed tears. If the dustwrapper is missing, the value is greatly reduced (75 percent on fiction and 20 percent or more on nonfiction).

Books published after 1950: Those published from 1950 to 1975 must be in fine condition, in original dustwrapper that shows only very minor wear, fading, or soiling and that may or may not be price-clipped. Those published from 1975 until the present must, like their dustwrapper, look new, and the dustwrapper must not be price-clipped.